Practice and Procedure
in
The Church of Scotland

Practice and Procedure
IN
The Church of Scotland

EDITED BY

The late Rev. JAMES T. COX, D.D.

FORMERLY MINISTER AT DYCE AND
PRINCIPAL CLERK OF THE GENERAL ASSEMBLY

SIXTH EDITION

EDITED BY

Rev. D. F. M. MACDONALD, M.A., LL.B.

PRINCIPAL CLERK OF THE GENERAL ASSEMBLY

Published by
The Committee on General Administration
The Church of Scotland
1976

Sixth Edition 1976

ISBN 0 7152 0326 6

Printed in Great Britain by
William Blackwood and Sons Limited, Edinburgh.

PREFACE TO THE SIXTH EDITION

In the preparation of this edition I have followed, and to a large extent adopted, the text which first took form in 1934 under the editorship of the then Principal Clerk for whom the volume is named. This now is the fifth time that the volume has been brought up-to-date, each revision making its new contribution. It did occur to the Editorial Committee that there might be considerable advantage in an entirely new manual being written, condensing much of the present material and leaving out entirely many of the appendices which now are only of historical interest. However, because of the urgent need throughout the Church for this Sixth Edition, the last edition being three or more years out of print it was decided to leave this decision until the next occasion when revision again becomes due.

I am greatly indebted for editorial assistance and proof reading to my Editorial Committee, the Very Rev. Andrew Herron, M.A., B.D., LL.B., D.D., the Rev. Charles A. Smith, M.A., and the Rev. A. Gordon McGillivray, M.A., B.D., S.T.M.

Grateful acknowledgement is made of the co-operation and assistance of Mr J. R. Snowball of Messrs William Blackwood & Sons Ltd.

D. F. M. MACDONALD.

January 1976.

PREFACE TO THE FIRST EDITION

PRIOR to the Union of 1929 the Church of Scotland and the United Free Church of Scotland had each a useful guide to its practice and procedure, the late Dr William Mair's 'Digest' in the one case and the 'Manual of Practice and Procedure' in the other. There were divergences in the practice and procedure of the two Churches, necessitating for the reunited Church a considerable amount of new legislation and the preparation of a volume which should take their place. With the approval of the General Assembly of 1931, accordingly, the General Administration Committee remitted to a Sub-Committee to undertake this task; and the present work is the result.

With regard to its contents, what are termed "binding laws and constitutions" of the Church will be recognised where they occur. For the rest, the volume no more lays claim to plenary Church authority than did those which it now supersedes, but authorities are quoted as far as possible. It is offered in the hope that it may prove a reliable guide to Church Courts and Committees, Ministers, Elders, and other office-bearers.

The Editor has been assisted by the following contributors: the Rev. Louis C. Phillips, B.D. (who also acted as Secretary); the Rev. A. P. Sym, D.D.; the Very Rev. James Harvey, D.D., Joint Senior Clerk of the General Assembly; Sir William Chree, K.C., LL.D., Procurator for the Church; and Mr John Macgregor, K.C. Assistance has been given also by other members of the Sub-Committee, including the Junior Clerk of the General Assembly, the Rev. James G. Sutherland, D.D., and the Joint Law Agents, Messrs J. A. S. Millar, M.V.O., W.S., A. H. M'Lean, W.S., and E. J. M'Candlish, W.S.

Grateful acknowledgment is made of the kindness of Messrs William Blackwood & Sons Ltd., the owners of the copyright of Dr Mair's 'Digest,' in placing it at the disposal of the Sub-Committee.

THE EDITOR.

September 1934.

CONTENTS

APPENDICES

APPENDICES

ABBREVIATIONS

A. & S.	Assistant and Successor.
App.	Appendix.
A. S.	Act of Sederunt of the Court of Session.
C. F.	The Confession of Faith.
C. S.	The Court of Session.
C. & S.	Colleague and Successor.
C. of S.	The Church of Scotland.
Dir.	The Directory for the Public Worship of God, 1645, 10.
e.g.	*Exempli gratia*, for example.
Erskine.	Erskine's Principles of the Law of Scotland by Rankine, 1890.
F. C.	Free Church of Scotland.
F. P.	The Form of Process.
G. A.	The General Assembly.
H. L.	The House of Lords.
i.e.	*Id est*, that is.
K. S.	Kirk Session.
L. G.	Local Government.
Ld. J.-C.	Lord Justice-Clerk.
Ld. O.	Lord Ordinary.
Ld. P.	Lord President.
Mair.	Dr William Mair's Digest of Church Laws, Fourth Edition, with Supplement, 1923.
Palgrave.	The Chairman's Handbook, by Sir Reginald F. D. Palgrave, K.C.B., Clerk of the House of Commons, 1896.
P.	Parliament, or Act of Parliament.
Presb.	Presbytery.
q.o.	*Quoad omnia.*
q.s.	*Quoad sacra.*
Reg.	Regulation or Regulations.
Rep.	The annually published volume of Reports to the Assembly.
S. D. N.	These letters in the Latin subscription to the Queen's Commission in favour of the Lord High Commissioner stand for either *Supremae Dominae Nostrae* or *Serenissimae Dominae Nostrae*.
S. L. T.	Scots Law Times.
S. O.	Standing Orders in the Assembly.
Steuart.	Walter Steuart, of Pardovan (Advocate): "Collections and Observations Methodised concerning the Worship, Discipline, and Government of the Church of Scotland," 1709.
U. F. C.	The United Free Church of Scotland.
U. P. C.	The United Presbyterian Church.
2 B. Dis.	Second Book of Discipline, 1581; 1638.
1886, vii.	Assembly 1886, Act vii.—and so in like cases.
1886. 7.	Assembly 1886, session 7— ,, ,,
1886. ult.	Assembly 1886, last session— ,, ,,

ABBREVIATIONS

PRACTICE AND PROCEDURE
IN
THE CHURCH OF SCOTLAND

CHAPTER I.

Concerning the Constitution of the Church of Scotland.

The Church of Scotland entered on a new era of its long and chequered history when, on 2nd October 1929, its sundered sections became once more united under the old name ; but it was not a new Church that came into existence on that date. In like manner a new chapter, perhaps rather a new volume, of its chronicles was begun when in August 1560 there was accomplished the Reformation so greatly needed, so marvellously achieved by the blessing of God ; but then also it was not a new Church that suddenly sprang into being. That achievement was not its origin but its re-formation, while in great measure also its transformation, without loss of its identity. The Church of our fathers has a much longer lineage and a much greater heritage than is comprised in four centuries. It has been built up, stage by stage, " upon the foundation of the apostles and prophets, Jesus Christ Himself being the chief corner-stone." The Church of Scotland is a part of the One Holy and Catholic Church.

The fact that the Church of Scotland existed before the Reformation is of great importance in relation to its Constitution. In one sense, indeed, the Constitution cannot be written in precise terms, for the reason that the Church is not a mere society which came into being on a definite date, when its laws, articles, and regulations were carefully framed and promulgated. No doubt there was provided for the Reformed Church, by the genius of Knox, a 'Book of Discipline' which stated the principles, and guided the practice, of those who conformed to the Protestant faith ; yet even that important document proved but temporary, and after a score of years was supplanted in 1581 by another of still greater and more lasting value, styled 'The Second Book of Discipline,' due largely to the sagacity of Andrew Melville. As a matter of fact, however, some part of the Church's polity at the Reformation was dependent on principles which prevailed and practices that were current prior to that momentous event. It could hardly be otherwise, for a considerable number of the leaders of the Reformation, including John Knox himself, had been trained in the Romish system, and, while they aimed at a better and purer system, such as existed before the Popish hierarchy arose, they carried with them insensibly and inevitably some of the elements of ecclesiastical life in which they had been trained and to which no objection could be taken. The people, too, who formed the membership of the Reformed Church, could not wholly divest themselves of manners and customs to which they were habituated. What was, or seemed to be, savouring of superstition, idol-worship, and error had to be rejected ; but much that was sound and valuable, and not out of accord with Scripture, remained in force. The whole parochial system, for example, was not discarded, and responsibility for the spiritual provision and supervision of territorial areas was a feature of the newer régime, as it had been of that which was overthrown. Even to this day there are principles of ecclesiastical law and procedure which have their roots in canons that existed long before 1560. While certainly most of the polity of the Church of to-day may be traced to the Continent of Europe, and especially to Geneva, there are features indigenous to Scotland. Particularly with regard to the relations of Church and State there is much that is the evolution of events that preceded the Reformation, in which evolution may be clearly discerned the overruling of the only King and Head of the Church, who has settled it firmly in the affections of our nation. It is essentially theocratic and thoroughly democratic, the Church of God and the Church of the people, truly a National Zion.

Notwithstanding what has been said, the Constitution of the Church of Scotland is, if not wholly, at least to a large extent, set forth in certain documents to which it is bound within limits to adhere. Though as a Divine institution it must remain free to follow the guidance of the Spirit of God, as He interprets from one generation to another the Holy Scriptures, which form at once its royal charter and its supreme standard, from which there can be no deviation, yet as a human institution the Church requires a clear and authoritative statement of its principles and definite rules, according to which the affairs of the Church are to be transacted, that there may be neither injustice nor confusion. These principles and rules, framed as they have been in successive ages in accordance with the necessities of the time in the light of experience gained in the past, yet always liable to be modified by vision of future developments, may in their totality be said to form the Constitution of the Church of Scotland as we know it in our own day.

The Constitution may be said to have been set forth in certain important instruments drawn up in times quite recent, and therefore it is unnecessary for the purposes of this book to give a historical catena of the laws affecting the Church.

"Articles Declaratory of the Constitution of the Church of Scotland in Matters Spiritual" (1921).

(i) The first is a series of "Articles Declaratory of the Constitution of the Church of Scotland in Matters Spiritual." These articles, prepared by the Church of Scotland in anticipation of the union with the United Free Church of Scotland, were carefully considered by the Presbyteries, and, having been approved in 1919 by a very large majority, were ratified by the General Assembly through its Commission in December of that year, with a view to an approach to Parliament which the Constitution of the Church of Scotland as then existing rendered necessary. In the same year the Assembly of the United Free Church had by a large majority declared satisfaction with the Articles as a full and adequate statement of the rights and liberties of the Church in spiritual matters. On 28th July 1921 the Royal Assent was given to the Bill which, having gone through both Houses of Parliament, declared the Articles to be lawful for the Church of Scotland to hold; but at the same time the Act thus passed provided that it was not to come into force till the Articles, already provisionally approved, as has been stated, should be finally adopted by a majority of the Presbyteries of the Church of Scotland; and this measure was postponed until another Bill relating to the property of the Church had also become an Act. Accordingly, the Declaratory Articles, though commonly quoted as the Articles of 1921, really did not become effective till the General Assembly of 1926, being made operative by an Order in Council of date 28th June 1926. Reference to the content of the Articles will be made later in this chapter. They will be found in full on pp. 390-392 of this book, as they were appended to the Uniting Act being essential to the Basis and Plan of Union.

Act anent Spiritual Independence of the Church (1906).

(ii) From the United Free Church proceeded the next instrument to be mentioned as essential to the Constitution of the united Church. It had its origin in certain decisions of the House of Lords in the judgment of that Supreme Court of Appeal in civil actions affecting the Free Church of Scotland and the United Free Church of Scotland, delivered on 1st August 1904. An Act was passed by the General Assembly of the United Free Church "anent Spiritual Independence of the Church" in 1906, for the terms of which reference may be made to p. 392, this Act having also been printed as an appendix to the Uniting Act, and affirmed to be of equal validity with the Articles Declaratory of the Constitution of the Church of Scotland.

Act of Union (1929).

(iii) The third instrument which embodies or expresses in general outline the Constitution of the Church of Scotland was the work of neither section of the Church by itself, but the product of the two sections jointly. It is known as the Basis of Union. Having been drawn up in united conference, as well as after prolonged separate consideration, it was ultimately approved by the Presbyteries and ratified by the General Assembly of each of the Churches in May 1929, and, as a part of the Act of Union, was signed by the Moderators and Clerks of both Churches at the first Sederunt of the united General Assembly on 2nd October 1929. The Basis of Union is printed *in extenso* in the appendix (pp. 386-433).

It affirms certain historic documents, styled "leading documents," as those which set forth "the Constitution, standards, rules, and methods of the united Church" with regard to "the Principles of the Spirituality and Freedom of the Church and the National Recognition of Religion," as well as to the Doctrine, Government, Worship, and Discipline of the Church, stating the sense in which, and the extent to which, the said documents are to be interpreted and regarded as regulative and valid. The Basis of Union also mentions certain other documents whose general principles are held to be conserved, together with manuals of instruction and other instruments which, although not regarded as absolute standards, are held in honour because of the important place they have occupied and the valuable service they have rendered in the history of the Church, a place not yet lost and a service not yet ended.

(iv) Along with the Basis of Union, and included in the same Act by which it was made binding on the Church as united, there are the Preamble, the Questions, and the Formula prescribed to be used on every occasion of the ordination or induction of a minister. These, though adding nothing to the material of the Church's constitution, are of the highest importance with reference thereto, because in a measure they summarise the main elements of that constitution, and apply them to the particular occasion of the entrance of each of the office-bearers of the Church, at the time when it is of great moment that they should be thoroughly understood and accepted by him as a condition of his office. It may be added that the Formula is in the same Act appointed to be signed not only by the ministers, but by the ruling elders of the Church. Other Acts require it to be signed by licentiates, readers, and deacons, if ordained.

Preamble, Questions, and Formula (1929).

In addition to the matter contained in the "leading documents," which by the Act including the Basis of Union are declared to be standards of the Church, there must be included in the Constitution of the Church the body of standing laws, apart from merely administrative regulations, which have been brought into the common stock of the legislation of the Church by each of the uniting Churches through enactment in accordance with its own constitution previously, and have not been repealed or amended in accordance with the law of the Church as stated in the Basis of Union itself, or with any law constitutionally enacted since the event of Union. But inasmuch as there may be certain enactments of one section of the Church which conflict with those of the other on the same subject, it was laid down that any legislation necessary to bring the enactments into harmony should be brought about by the operation of the Barrier Act (see p. 15) after consideration by the Presbyteries of the united Church, and that any Act passed while such opinion of Presbyteries was being ascertained should be reckoned as only of an interim nature, and should not be adopted as a standing law of the Church until it had been approved by a majority of the Presbyteries, and subsequently by the General Assembly, in accordance with the said Barrier Act. This declaration was made to apply also to matters wherein the former practice, as distinct from the positive law, of the two Churches was materially different, and wherein there had not been adjustments of the difference by the "Plan of Union," which had, along with the Basis of Union, been approved by all the Presbyteries and thereafter ratified by the General Assembly of each uniting Church. This Plan of Union, it may be mentioned here, was also part of the uniting Act passed at the first Sederunt of the united General Assembly on 2nd October 1929; but it was in the same Act carefully and deliberately distinguished from the Basis of Union, on which alone it was stated that the two Churches had resolved to unite. Doubtless the reason for the distinction was that it was felt that experience might show the necessity or expediency of altering articles in the Plan which was provisionally adopted, while the occasion for alteration of the Basis was less likely to arise.

Passing from the documentary aspect of the Constitution of the Church of Scotland in the new chapter of history on which it has entered, we may outline the main principles of that Constitution, and show how these are expressed and upheld in the documents to which reference has been made.

Doctrine.

As to DOCTRINE, the Church of Scotland is, and must remain, a Christian Church, Trinitarian in its creed, evangelical in its character, maintaining, teaching, and promulgating the great facts of the faith once delivered unto the saints, in full accord with the Scriptures of the Old and New Testaments, as interpreted from time to time by the ever-living and quickening Spirit, whose office is to guide into truth. These principles are secured by the fact that in the Basis of Union they are "reaffirmed and set forth in a manner which is in accord with the convictions of both Churches." They are also distinctly declared in the first of the Articles Declaratory of the Constitution of the Church of Scotland in Matters Spiritual, appended to the Act on Basis of Union, as an inherent part thereof. Moreover, the second Article declares the principal subordinate standard of the Church to be the Westminster Confession of Faith approved by the General Assembly of 1647, and the Basis of Union itself gives it first place among its leading documents referring to doctrine, along with Declaratory Acts of the uniting Churches—viz., the United Presbyterian Church Declaratory Act, 1879; the Free Church Declaratory Act, 1892, with the Act 1894 referring thereto; and the Church of Scotland Act prescribing the Formula, 1910—which set forth the extent whereto adherence to that historic Confession is to be understood and interpreted as a standard subordinate to the Word of God contained in the Scriptures of the Old and New Testaments, which is declared to be the supreme standard of faith and life.

It is involved in what has been said that the Church of Scotland is Protestant in its testimony, or, to use a more correct phrase, reformed in its constitution. It has never swerved from the attitude of 1560, when it threw off the trammels and renounced the errors of the Papacy.

Government.

As to GOVERNMENT, the Church of Scotland is by constitution Presbyterian. There is no call in this chapter to compare Presbyterianism with other forms of Church government with respect either to origin or to history, nor yet to discuss the merits or disadvantages which it possesses when contrasted with Episcopacy on the one hand or Congregationalism on the other. It may suffice to say that in the first age of the Christian Church the presbyter and the bishop appear to have been identical, the former name having regard to qualification and the latter to function; and it was only in the development of the Church in subsequent centuries that gradually the bishop became exalted to a higher rank than the presbyter. It was the aim of the Reformers throughout Europe to recall the pristine simplicity and equality which were characteristic of the first age, so far as that might be gathered from Scripture; and, when the Papacy was overthrown in Scotland, those who were instrumental in that achievement, trained as their leaders had been in the school of Geneva, set up a Presbyterian polity in its place. Save for part of the following century, when Episcopacy was thrust upon Scotland against the will of the people, Presbyterianism has been consistently maintained by the Church of the nation. Since 1690 it has been recognised by the Crown, and its maintenance was ratified in the Treaty of Union, 1707, by an Act of Security, ever since which time the signing of the Oath of Security for the Church of Scotland in its Presbyterian polity has formed the first duty of the Sovereign on accession to the throne of Great Britain.

Among the leading documents mentioned in the Basis of Union is *The Form of Presbyterial Church Government and of Ordination of Ministers*, 1645. While it is thus included in the standards of the Church, it is stated to be "regarded as generally regulative and as of validity as . . . interpreted or modified by Acts of General Assembly or by consuetude."

Present in the Constitution of the Church certainly are the characteristic notes of Presbyterianism. There is parity of those who have been ordained to the office of the ministry for the administration of Word and Sacraments. No one is set in a position superior to that of his brethren in the ministry. If, for the orderly conduct of meetings of presbyters in the transaction of the affairs of the Church, one is called to preside, he is thereby raised to no higher rank, but is regarded for the time when he holds that position as merely *primus inter pares*, and is termed Moderator. So soon as his term of holding that office has expired, unless he be chosen for a further period, he ranks merely as other presbyters, and another is appointed moderator in his stead. For a brief period immediately after the Reformation, certain men, not in every case ministers, were nominated to act as superintendents, a word which by derivation is equivalent to bishops ; but their function was not really episcopal in character, and their appointment was merely a temporary expedient for the spiritual provision of large tracts of the country because of the paucity of men qualified to act as presbyters. Ere the sixteenth century closed, that defect had been remedied, the Presbytery, or conclave of presbyters in a definite area which developed into a Presbytery as we now know it, had been evolved, and the office of superintendent was allowed to lapse.

Another principle of Presbyterianism embedded in the Constitution of the Church of Scotland is that it is conciliar in polity. There is a system of Courts of the Church, inferior and superior, in an ascending scale. As the principle of parity distinguishes it from the hierarchical system of Episcopacy, so this principle makes it different from the individualistic system of independency or congregationalism. There is a linking together of the various congregations in mutual co-operation as organic members of the same body. Later pages of this book will deal in detail with the powers and regulations of the Courts of the Church, and at present it is enough to state what these are.

The lowest court is the Kirk Session, which concerns itself with the affairs of the Church in a parochial area, over which, as a rule, only one presbyter is placed to minister in spiritual things, with whom are associated ruling elders, to take counsel with him and give help to him in religious matters within the bounds of the parish.

The next court is the Presbytery, which consists of a group of such ministers as have been inducted to charges within a larger area, together with one ruling elder as representative of each charge. It includes likewise the theological professors, if these have been ordained to the ministry, and other ministers who qualify in terms of Act II, 1970. In the united Church not merely ministers in active service, but in most cases those who have retired from their charges, wholly or partially, are declared eligible for retention of seats in the Presbytery within which they last ministered. A certain number of additional ruling elders are, therefore, elected by the Presbytery itself to equalise the theological professors and those who hold various other clerical offices within the bounds, and also the senior colleagues and wholly retired ministers, who retain their seats in the Presbytery. It is a part of the Constitution as set forth in the Plan of Union, 1929, that " in all Presbyteries and Synods there shall be an equal number of ministers and elders when the roll is fully made up "; and this method of co-option of a number of elders from within the bounds, in addition to those who are chosen by Kirk Sessions to represent them, has been devised to make equality possible.

The next court in order of superiority is the Synod. It includes all the members of Presbytery within a still wider area, together with such corresponding members (a minister and an elder) as may be appointed from each of the adjacent Synods, who, when their commissions have been presented and sustained, have the same status and powers as the other members. No Synod has had fewer than three Presbyteries within its province, with this exception that the Presbytery of Orkney, the Presbytery of Shetland, and the Presbytery of England are in each case reckoned also as a Synod to the extent of being invested with Synodical powers.* The primary functions of the Synod are to exercise general superintendence of the Presbyteries comprised within its area of jurisdiction, and to act as an appellate court between the Presbytery and the General Assembly. By 1933, xviii. (as amended by 1947, viii. and 1962, xv.), the General Assembly, however, has enacted that finality of judgment should belong to the Synod in all cases of dissent and complaint, or of appeal, other than those involving doctrine, worship, or censure of a minister or other office-bearer, cases of licensing of students, and cases of unions and readjustments, the General Assembly remaining the Court of Appeal in these cases, and also in all cases where the Presbytery concerned possesses Synodical powers or is furth of Scotland.

Finally, there is the Supreme Court of the Church, called the General Assembly, to which are commissioned representatives, both ministers and elders in a fixed proportion, who are appointed by all the Presbyteries of the Church, including those which are fully constituted Presbyteries abroad. The right of the Church of Scotland to meet in General Assembly every year

* According to Act II, 1975, there are now certain Synods which have only two Presbyteries within their provinces—Editor.

at least, and oftener if occasion and necessity require, has been claimed from the first days of the Reformation period, and was explicitly recognised by the Scottish Parliament of 1592, a statute subsequently ratified by the Treaty of Union in 1707. It has been the almost invariable practice through its whole history that at the General Assembly of the Church of Scotland either the monarch in person or someone bearing his commission should attend the Assembly; but neither the Sovereign nor the Lord High Commissioner as such is a constituent member of the Assembly. The main functions of the Assembly are to dispose finally of appeals from the lower courts, and of petitions from individuals or external bodies; to deal with overtures from Presbyteries or Synods—that is, proposals that changes should be effected in the law or practice of the Church; to receive and consider reports as to the work and missionary enterprises of the Church at home and abroad; and generally to attend to all matters affecting the efficiency of the Church and the religious and spiritual condition of the nation. The Moderator is nominated some months previously by a Committee specially entrusted with this duty, but is actually elected by the Assembly themselves, when constituted by the Moderator of the preceding Assembly. It is for the Moderator to declare the dissolution of the Assembly and the day and place of the next meeting, which the Assembly themselves determine.

Some of the business which might otherwise fall to be considered by the Supreme Court in actual session may be discharged by the Commission of General Assembly, which hold two stated meetings during the period between one Assembly and another, and may meet at other times if specially convened. The membership of the Commission of General Assembly consists of all the commissioners of the appointing Assembly, and, in addition, one minister nominated by the Moderator of that Assembly. The Moderator of the Commission is chosen by the Commission themselves for all the meetings in the current year, and is usually but not necessarily the Moderator of the preceding Assembly. The Commission are not a Court of the Church, and cannot deal with business which has not been expressly devolved by the Assembly or is not implied in the terms of appointment. The findings of the Commission are liable to review by the next Assembly only if they should fail to act regularly or act outwith the powers entrusted to the Commission.

The third significant note of Presbyterianism is the share

given to the laity in the government of the Church. This also is inherent in the Constitution of the Church of Scotland, as is apparent from the description of the Courts of the Church above given, and as is more fully set forth in later pages of this book. It is essentially a democratic Church, in the management of whose affairs there is no respect of persons. In the lowest court, the Kirk Session, there must necessarily be a predominance of laymen, and in all the higher courts ruling elders are equal in number with teaching elders or presbyters.

In the appointment of ministers to parochial or other pastoral charges the Church of Scotland to-day holds the system of free election by all the members of the particular charge concerned, and the privilege is granted also to those who, though not communicants therein, are, under certain restrictions, admitted by the Kirk Session as adherents because of their personal interest or share in the work and worship of the congregation. The right of appointment by private or other patrons, generally known as patronage, after an unbroken sway since 1712, the exercise of which may be said to have been directly or indirectly the main cause of almost all the separations and secessions from the Church, ceased in 1874. In the year just mentioned an Act was passed by the legislature wholly abolishing the patronage system, compensation being paid by the Church to those private patrons who demanded it. In the Churches which separated themselves there was, of course, no patronage at all. Its abolition may be regarded as one of the most important steps toward reunion. Free election of pastors by the members and qualified adherents is now part of the Constitution of the Church, although the particular regulations by which such election is exercised are merely administrative, and form no part of the Constitution, but are subject to alteration as the General Assembly may determine. In view of the importance of such regulations, however, it is the practice of the General Assembly, before any change is effected, to submit it to the judgment of Presbyteries, and from time to time the whole code of regulations is submitted to revision by this method. The present code has been devised in accordance with principles laid down in the Plan of Union (1929, i), and will be found in Chap. XII. of this book.

Directory of Public Worship.

With regard to WORSHIP the standard of the Church is nominally the *Directory of Public Worship*, produced at the Westminster Assembly of Divines and approved by the

General Assembly of 1645. This is included among the leading documents mentioned in the Basis of Union, but, as no such directory can be expected to retain exclusive obligation on the Church after the age for which it was composed has passed, a note is added that it is to be "regarded as generally regulative and of validity as . . . interpreted or modified by Acts of General Assembly or by consuetude." The same qualifying phrase is used in Article II. of the Articles Declaratory of the Constitution already mentioned; and since the like right of legislating in matters of worship is claimed in the United Free Church Act of 1906, also appended to the Basis of Union, there can be no doubt that constitutionally the Church is entitled to modify its manner of worship as it feels guided by the Spirit of God, without the restraint of any form which is the product of a single age. A sufficient guarantee for the maintenance of purity of worship, and for the prevention of innovations of a superstitious or unseemly nature, is reckoned to exist in the words of the Formula, which every minister and elder is required to sign, and in which he undertakes to observe the order of worship and the administration of all public ordinances as the same are or may be allowed in this Church.

Discipline.

As to DISCIPLINE, in the special or technical sense of that word, which refers to correction of misdemeanour and avoidance or removal of scandal in the Church, the changes produced by the lapse of time in the manners and customs of the people and the moral standards of life, which are to some extent dependent thereon, have largely rendered out of date the *Form of Process* devised in 1707; and, although that still remains the disciplinary instrument of the Church, it is mentioned in the Basis of Union and in the Declaratory Articles appended thereto with the same qualifying remark noted with regard to the Directory above mentioned.[1]

Church and State.

One of the most important parts of the Constitution of the Church, especially from a historical point of view, is that which concerns the mutual relations of Church and State. Though the divisions which emerged were due in the first place to other causes, such as the exercise of patronage, yet the diverse views taken of ecclesiastical and civil government certainly accentuated and even widened these divisions, and it was only when a satisfactory concordat was reached

[1] The General Assembly of 1960 set up a Judicial Commission (App. XXIII., p. 653).

on this question that reunion became possible. It must be kept in mind that the whole conception of civil and religious economy has changed since the days of the Reformation, and even since the Revolution. There was then no such clearly defined boundary between the provinces of things ecclesiastical and things political as we discern to-day. With the passage of the centuries and the growth of civil and religious liberty in Scotland, there has come to be a more clear distinction between the magistrate and the minister, and there is a more manifest determination that neither should have authority in the domain of the other, in fulfilment of the precept: "Render unto Caesar the things which are Caesar's, and unto God the things that are God's."

There is no need to dwell on the controversies which are past. It is enough here to note that the matter is clearly and distinctly stated in the Articles Declaratory of the Constitution of the Church of Scotland, which have received the approval alike of the Church, in both its former sections, through Presbyteries and Assembly and of the State through both Houses of Parliament. Therein it is declared: "This Church, as part of the Universal Church, wherein the Lord Jesus Christ has appointed a government in the hands of Church office-bearers, receives from Him, its Divine King and Head, and from Him alone, the right and power, subject to no civil authority, to legislate, and to adjudicate finally, in all matters of doctrine, worship, government, and discipline in the Church. . . . Recognition by civil authority of the separate and independent government and jurisdiction of this Church in matters spiritual, in whatever manner such recognition be expressed, does not in any way affect the character of this government and jurisdiction as derived from the Divine Head of the Church alone, or give to the civil authority any right of interference with the proceedings or judgments of the Church within the sphere of its spiritual government and jurisdiction." (Article IV.)

"This Church acknowledges the divine appointment and authority of the civil magistrate within his own sphere, and maintains its historic testimony to the duty of the nation acting in its corporate capacity to render homage to God, to acknowledge the Lord Jesus Christ to be King over the nations, to obey His laws, to reverence His ordinances, to honour His Church, and to promote in all appropriate ways the Kingdom of God. The Church and the State owe mutual duties to each other, and acting within their respective spheres may signally promote each other's welfare. The Church and the State have the right to determine each for itself all questions concerning the extent and the continuance of their mutual relations in the discharge of these duties and the obligations arising therefrom." (Article VI.)

The acceptance of these Articles as satisfactory, alike by the ecclesiastical courts and by the Crown through Parliament, may be truly said to manifest that the problem of the right relations of the Church and the State has been solved, and that there is no Church in Christendom which can more fully claim to be at once national and free than the Church of Scotland to-day.

It ought to be remarked, however, in this connection that the Articles not only safeguard the present position of the Church of Scotland, but give it full liberty of determination with regard to future action within the limits of its Constitution, widely drawn as these are. It is not as in former days bound to the formularies devised in any particular era, even to those which appear adequate and accurate to this generation. So long as the Church remains true in its adherence to the worship of the Godhead and the essential facts of the faith once delivered to the saints as outlined in the First Article of the series, so long as it adheres to the principles of the Reformation which purged the Church of Popish error and superstition, so long as it rests on the Word of God as the supreme rule of faith and life, it is free, as it holds itself to be free, to modify the Articles that are now accepted as its manifesto ; and in Article VIII. there is laid down the definite procedure by which alone such freedom is to be exercised. In view of past experience also there is included in Article VII. liberty, without loss of its own identity, for the Church of Scotland to unite with any other Church which is imbued with the same aims and declares its loyalty to the same standards as its own ; and it is declared that union may be effected on such terms as, in the judgment of the Church of Scotland itself, are consistent with the Articles of its own Constitution.

Property. On the material side there is involved in the Constitution of the Church the tenure of its property. In a later chapter of this book (see p. 342) will be found a detailed outline of the property which the Church has inherited from the past, and is still accumulating, through the benefactions and contributions of its members. Whatever the source of the property, and whatever the method by which it is held or the persons in whom it is vested, though subject to the terms of the titles on which it is held, all the property of the Church is in its own absolute possession and under its sole control, and is not liable to any interference from without, or any alienation or diversion from the primary purpose for which it has been acquired, the purpose of serving the spiritual interests of the people of Scotland, and advancing through the Church the furtherance of the Gospel at home and abroad.

The Barrier Act.

It remains to be said that before any change can be made which affects the Constitution of the Church in its doctrine, government, worship, or discipline, a certain procedure must be followed, and the sanction of the whole Church must be obtained through the Presbyteries, which form its constituent courts for the purpose of such reference. The General Assembly cannot of themselves alone effect such a change. The procedure is known as the operation of the Barrier Act, and may be here briefly described. This Act, which is printed *in extenso* on p. 385, was passed in 1697. Its intention was to prevent hasty and ill-considered legislation, which might appear at the moment to be of value, but might prove to be really prejudicial to the best interests of the Church. Accordingly, in the year named the General Assembly, taking into consideration an Overture and Act of the previous year, made an Act to the effect that in future, before any Acts were passed which are "to be binding rules and constitutions to the Church," these should be first proposed by way of overture to the Assembly, and, if approved, should be remitted to Presbyteries for consideration, and for report to the following Assembly, "if the more general opinion of the Church thus had agreed thereto."

This Act has proved a most salutary measure. Dr Mair points out (*Digest of Church Laws*, Ed. iv., p. 62) that the Barrier Act is not itself part of the Constitution of the Church, though having an important share in the framing of that Constitution. If—a supposition extremely unlikely—the Church should desire to abolish the Act, and if, after a majority of the Presbyteries had reported approval of an overture to that effect, the Assembly should again resolve after the same fashion, the Act could and would be rescinded, and the position would become the same as before 1697. The Barrier Act, moreover, is required only in matters affecting the doctrine, government, worship, and discipline of the Church, and these categories do not include its whole legislation. In other matters the Church may pass, and has often passed, Declaratory Acts stating not what should be, but what *is*, the law; and so long as these Acts do not contravene anything which has already been enacted with regard to these categories, and do not contain anything inconsistent with the law as formerly existing, the Assembly are entitled to pass legislation and bring it immediately into effect. Moreover, even where legislation might have been thus immediately effective because it did not concern doctrine, worship, government, or discipline, but where it seemed advisable that the opinion of the Presbyteries should be obtained before a change in existing practice was made, the General Assembly of each of the now united Churches have not infrequently employed the machinery of the Barrier Act, although not compelled to do so. Further, as Dr Mair observes, "the Assembly is the interpreter of its own laws." They are accordingly the sole authority to determine whether any particular overture, or even less formal proposal, does or does not contain or involve matters which are inconsistent with existing laws in the four categories named.

It has been the practice of the Assembly, even after an overture has been approved by a majority of Presbyteries, but before passing it into "binding rules and constitutions to the Church," to make slight alterations in its terms which are not in any manner or to any extent inconsistent with the purport and provisions of the overture. Even when the operation of the Barrier Act is obligatory, the Assembly may find that an immediate change in the law is urgently necessary, and in these circumstances they hold themselves at liberty to pass an Interim Act to the effect desired, but at the same time the Assembly send it to Presbyteries in the form of an overture for their opinion. Such an Interim Act has force only till the next succeeding Assembly, which may then, if a majority of the Presbyteries have signified approval, make it permanent law, or in the contrary event may discharge it, so that it ceases to have validity. No Interim Act which has been disapproved by a majority of Presbyteries may be continued in the same form. If it should appear that the approval of Presbyteries has not been sufficiently strong, or that the majority has not been sufficiently large, to show that the measure has commended itself to the Church, it is competent for the General Assembly again to remit the measure for their opinion, either in the same or in an altered form, continuing it meanwhile as an Interim Act (see Chap. V., p. 104). Further, even when an overture sent to Presbyteries for their opinion has received the approval of a

Interim Acts.

majority of these courts, the succeeding Assembly do not automatically pass it into the "standing rules and constitutions to the Church," but are required again to put it to a vote of the Assembly for confirmation or rejection. An Interim Act, it may be remarked, should be passed only in a case of emergency, and urgency, for this reason at least, that it is liable to be set aside, if the overture which it expresses should be disapproved by a majority of Presbyteries, a procedure by no means unknown; and it is undesirable, as tending to confusion or possible injustice, that legislation on any matter should undergo change for only one year.

CHAPTER II.

THE CONGREGATION

SECTION I. *Membership*

"Charge." A "CHARGE" means a sphere of pastoral duty to which a Minister or Ministers may be appointed under terms of Section i of Act III, 1972. "As from the date of the passing of this Act a minister of the Church of Scotland admitted or inducted to a charge shall not be admitted or inducted *ad vitam aut culpam* but, except as hereinafter provided, on attaining the age of 70 years, his ministry shall terminate as if he had resigned his charge and such date appointed by the Presbytery of the bounds for the demission by the minister of his charge."* All charges within a former civil parish are of equal standing and are parish churches *quoad sacra* (Commission, Nov. 1929).

"Congregation." A "congregation" is a company of persons (members, adherents, and their children) associated together in a particular locality for Christian worship, instruction, fellowship and work (1957, xvii).

Members. The members of the congregation in full communion are those persons who have been admitted as such by the Kirk Session on profession of faith, on presentation of a certificate of transference from another congregation, or by special resolution (see p. 126). The names of all members of the congregation are placed on a Roll of Communicants which must be kept by every Kirk Session (p. 124). The names of those who have been removed from the Communion Roll without a Certificate of Transference and who continue to reside in the parish or district must be entered on a Separate or Supplementary Roll. The maintenance of such a Supplementary Roll is obligatory upon all Kirk Sessions (1938, vi; 1951, vi; p. 126).

Roll.

Supplementary Roll.

Baptised persons connected with the congregation, though not thus admitted to full communion, are members and are under the care and oversight of the Kirk Session. The General

* Where after the passing of this Act any minister, having been admitted to a parish *ad vitam aut culpam*, becomes the minister of a union or a linking involving the said parish, such admission shall not be construed as coming within the terms of this Act. (cf. Act XXI, 1974.)

Assembly has recommended that a Roll of Baptised Persons not Communicants should be kept (Oct. 1929, I.). Roll of Baptised Members.

It is the duty of members to give faithful attendance on Gospel ordinances; to give their minister all due honour and respect in the Lord; to submit to the Kirk Session as over them in the Lord; to cherish a brotherly spirit among themselves; to promote the peace and prosperity of the congregation; and to share with their minister the responsibility for Christian witness and Christian service. It is also their duty to take a lively interest in all that concerns the welfare of the whole Church and to give of their means, as the Lord shall prosper them, for the maintenance of the Christian Ministry and the furtherance of the Gospel at home and abroad; and to manifest a Christian spirit in all relationships of life. See Questions for Reception of Catechumens (Appendix XXXV, p. 783); Form of Call (Appendix XXXV, p. 817); and Question to be put to Congregation on Induction of a Minister (1958, xi, p. 568).

Members in full communion, and they only (subject to the exception below), have a right to take part in the business of congregational meetings. Persons whose names are on the Supplementary Roll may not do so (1951, vii).

A member, or group of members, desiring to bring any matter before the Kirk Session must do so by petition. For the procedure to be followed see Ch. V, p. 99.

Adherents. For the purpose of electing a minister adherents over twenty-one years of age, if they make claim in terms of Act ix, 1932, Section 5, (Ch. XII, p. 246), may have their names added to the Electoral Roll and take part in the business of all congregational meetings in connection with the vacancy in the same way as if they were members in full communion.

SECTION II. *Status of Congregation.*

Two or more congregations, or two collegiate charges, or a congregation or congregations and a mission station may be united to form one congregation and charge (1957, xvii).

Linking. Two or more congregations may be linked to form one "linked charge", and in such case there shall be one minister and one representative elder in Presbytery and Synod, but each congregation shall retain its identity, its courts, and its organisations. Such linking may be either of a temporary or of a permanent character (1957, xvii).

Transportation. A congregation may be "transported" from one place of worship to another, with or without a change of parish; or

Transference. "transferred" from the bounds of one Presbytery or Synod to another without change of site (1957, xvii).

Restricted Ministry. A "restricted ministry" means that a congregation is allowed to have a minister appointed under terms of Section i of Act III, 1972, but not under a stated age (1957, xvii).

Continued Vacancy. A "continued vacancy" is an interim arrangement to cover a period during which it is considered undesirable to suppress or reduce a charge, and readjustment negotiations are suspended (1957, xvii).

Suppression. "Suppression" is the withdrawal from a congregation of the right to have its minister appointed under terms of Section i of Act III, 1972. The work may thereafter be carried on under a Terminable Appointment when the congregation retains its Kirk Session, financial board, and representative elder, and continues to be liable for Presbytery, Synod, and Assembly dues (1957, xvii).

Reduction. Dissolution. A congregation may be "reduced" to a mission station, or its existence may be completely terminated by "dissolution" (1957, xvii).

For the procedure to be followed in erection, union, linking, transportation, transference, suppression, reduction, or dissolution of a congregation see Chapter VII, pp. 159, 182.

SECTION III. *Congregational Meetings* (1932, xviii).

Congregational meetings are of two kinds—those held for ecclesiastical and those held for temporal purposes.

A. MEETINGS FOR ECCLESIASTICAL PURPOSES.

All matters other than those concerning the ordinary finances of the congregation and the care and maintenance of its property are dealt with at meetings for ecclesiastical purposes. The erection or substantial alteration of church, hall, or manse buildings, or the installation of an organ, are matters of ecclesiastical business.

By whom called and conducted. Meetings for ecclesiastical purposes are called by the Kirk Session, presided over by the Moderator of Session, and the record is taken by the Clerk of Session and entered in the Session minute-book. In the absence of the Moderator any other minister of the Church authorised by him in writing or appointed by the Presbytery or by a superior court may preside. In the absence of the Session Clerk a Clerk is appointed by the meeting (1932, xviii).

The Presbytery or other superior court may at any time if it sees cause, summon a meeting of the congregation and appoint one of its members to preside.

The Interim Moderator in a vacancy has power, in virtue of his office, to summon meetings of the congregation in terms of the Regulations for the Election, Settlement and Translation of Ministers, and the same regulations empower the Clerk of Presbytery to summon a meeting of the congregation whose minister has received an Appointment and Call and to arrange that a minister of the Presbytery shall preside thereat (1932, ix and xviii ; and 1960, xxiii).

When a Presbytery appoints a Committee to confer with a congregation on any matter the Convener of such Committee has power to summon a meeting of the congregation in name of the Presbytery to deal with the remit received (1932, xviii)—*e.g.*, Visitation of a Congregation (1932, xvii), or readjustment negotiations.

All congregational meetings must be called by intimation to the congregation on the Lord's Day by the officiating minister or Session Clerk (1956, xvii). The intimation should clearly specify the business to be considered and should be attested by the officiating minister or Session Clerk as having been duly made by him. In the case of a meeting to consider an Appointment and Call (1932, ix 23), or of a meeting to consider readjustment proposals (except when a Basis of Union is to be submitted for approval) intimation on one Sunday is sufficient. In all other cases (including the meeting to consider a Basis of Union) intimation must be made on two separate Sundays (1932, xviii). How called.

It is not competent to raise any question in regard to the sufficiency of the notice calling a congregational meeting unless a petition specifying clearly the nature of the objection be sent to the Moderator of Kirk Session (or the Moderator of Presbytery if the meeting be held by order of the Presbytery or of a higher Court) within eight days after the meeting has been held (1932, xviii).

All congregational meetings are opened and closed with prayer. The object of the meeting is stated by the Chairman and the duly attested notice calling the meeting is laid on the table. Draft minutes are taken and submitted for approval after which they are initialled by Chairman and Clerk. They are subsequently engrossed in the Session Minute Book and signed by Chairman and Clerk. Opening and Closing.

If a vote be taken at a congregational meeting it shall be by standing up unless expressly appointed otherwise, as in the Voting.

case of the election of elders and deacons when the meeting may resolve to make use of voting papers (1932, x), or in the case of union when the vote may be taken by ballot (1932, xxii) in the following manner (1934, Rep. 285).

If at a congregational meeting when the question of union is being considered it is moved and seconded that the vote be taken by ballot and the Chairman is satisfied that the undernoted conditions can be complied with, he may accept the motion and put it to the meeting. Otherwise he shall not accept the motion and the normal method of voting by standing up shall be used. If the motion is carried the vote shall be taken as follows :—

(1) The vote shall be taken before the congregational meeting adjourns or ends.

(2) Only Voting Papers in the form approved and supplied by the Unions and Readjustments Committee shall be used (see p. 823).

(3) A copy of the Communion Roll as authorised by the Kirk Session shall be submitted and only to those persons whose names are on the Roll and who apply for them in person shall Voting Papers be issued.

(4) The Chairman shall be responsible for issuing, collecting, and counting the Voting Papers in an orderly fashion. Opportunity should be given to every voter to mark the paper in private.

(5) Voting Papers marked otherwise than with a cross placed opposite one or other motion shall not be counted.

(6) The Voting Papers after enumeration shall be given into the custody of the Clerk of the Presbytery, who shall retain them until the question of union is settled temporarily or otherwise, when they may be destroyed.

Plebiscite. In no case shall a vote by plebiscite be valid (1932, xxii).

Dissent. Any member present at a congregational meeting may enter his dissent from any part of the proceedings of which he disapproves, and, if he desires, may bring such decision or resolution against which he has dissented under review of the Presbytery by petition. For the procedure to be followed see Chapter V, Sect. III (*e*) (p. 99), and Model Deed (1965) article 19, (see p. 610).

B. Meetings for Temporal Purposes.

(a) *Where Finance is Managed by Kirk Session.*

Since the Kirk Session is not answerable to the congregation, but only to the superior courts, there is no obligation upon a Kirk Session to call congregational meetings for temporal purposes. There is, however, no reason why a Kirk Session should not summon a congregational meeting to deal with matters of finance, maintenance of property, etc., and if it does so the rules for meetings for ecclesiastical purposes dealt with above will apply.

(b) *Where there is a Deacons' Court or Congregational Board (U.F.).*

Annual Meeting.

It is required by Act of Assembly (F.C. 1846, vii ; 1932, xviii) that an Annual Congregational Meeting be called by the Deacons' Court or Congregational Board as soon as possible after the close of the financial year when the Court or Board reports on its activities in the past year, gives such explanations as may be asked for, and receives such suggestions as may be offered for its consideration with reference to the future distribution of the funds. The meeting should appoint two members to audit the accounts for the year and to report to next Annual Meeting (U.F.C., 1908). The Moderator of Kirk Session presides if present ; in his absence any office-bearer may be chosen to preside (1932, xviii).

Special Meetings.

Special meetings of the congregation are called by the Kirk Session when necessary and are presided over by the Moderator of Session or by a minister deputed by him in writing (F.C., 1847, xiv ; 1932, xviii).

The Clerk of the Court or Board acts as Clerk at all meetings for temporal purposes, and the minute is engrossed in the minute-book of the Court or Board as the case may be (1932, xviii). The rules anent intimation, opening and closing, dissent, and signing of minutes are the same as apply to meetings for ecclesiastical purposes.

(c) *Where there is a Congregational Board in terms of the Model Constitution for Congregations of the Church of Scotland* (1965, xxi).

Stated Annual Meeting.

Not later than 31st March (1955, iii) in each year a congregational meeting is called by pulpit intimation on the two immediately preceding Sundays. This is called the Stated Annual Meeting, and is held either in the Church or the Church Hall, or elsewhere as intimated, on a date fixed by the Kirk Session for the purpose of electing certain members of the congregation to act along with the minister and elders in administering the temporal affairs of the congregation. This meeting is presided over by the Moderator of Session, whom failing by a member of Presbytery specially authorised by him for the purpose, whom failing by a person elected by the meeting. The Clerk of the Congregational Board acts as Clerk and the minute of the meeting is engrossed in the minute-book of the Board.

Accounts. The congregational accounts, made up to 31st December, or such earlier date as the Congregational Board may decide in each year, and duly audited and containing *inter alia* a statement as to the application or disposal, or proposed application or disposal, of any balance on the Ordinary Revenue and Expenditure Account for the year in accordance with the Constitution, are submitted by the Board to the congregation at this meeting. After approval by the congregation they are to be laid (within a month thereafter) before the Presbytery for attestation that they are correct in accordance with the terms of the Constitution.

Should the Stated Annual Meeting not be held by the appointed time the Presbytery may, on application by the Kirk Session to that effect, direct such meeting to be called and held at any time thereafter during that year.

(d) *Where there is a Committee of Management.*

Ordinary Meetings. Ordinary meetings for temporal purposes are those held periodically in terms of the constitution of the congregation; they are called in name of the Committee of Management; the Preses of the Managers presides (in his absence, or at his request, one of the members—who may be the minister or an elder—chosen by the meeting presides); the Clerk of the Committee acts as Clerk and enters the minute in the Committee minute-book (1932, xviii).

Annual Meeting. The congregation holds an annual meeting as soon as convenient after the close of the financial year, pulpit intimation thereof being given on at least one Sunday immediately preceding. (The General Assembly recommend that the financial year should close at 31st December.) At this meeting the managers report their proceedings and management during the year and lay before the congregation an abstract of income and expenditure with a statement of the congregation's pecuniary affairs as they then stand; affording all relevant information required thereanent. The congregation then proceeds to the election of managers for the next year, or if these have already been elected by the use of Voting Papers the result of the vote is reported.

It is not competent to transact any special business at the annual meeting; but a special meeting may be held on the same day if regularly called and conducted in terms of the next paragraph.

Special meetings for temporal purposes can be called by the Committee of Management only with the concurrence of the Kirk Session. Such meetings must be the subject of at least two Sundays' intimation which must clearly specify the nature of the business. They are presided over by a chairman chosen by the meeting who may be the minister, the preses, an elder, or any member of the congregation. The Clerk of the Managers acts as Clerk and engrosses the minute in the minute-book of the Committee of Management. Special Meetings.

The rules anent opening and closing, attesting of minutes, and rights of dissent are the same as those that apply to meetings for ecclesiastical purposes.

(e) *Where there is a Special Constitution.*

There are a few congregations which have a special form of constitution and in these cases the provisions of such constitutions in regard to the holding and conducting of congregational meetings must be observed unless and until the constitution is competently altered (1932, xviii). See p. 253.

C. Congregational Meetings to appoint Trustees.

In certain congregations congregational meetings are held from time to time as provided in the constitution of the congregation for the purpose of electing trustees to hold the property of the congregation and other matters connected therewith. Congregations should be careful to ensure that there is always a sufficient number of trustees surviving and acting. Property Trustees.

In congregations where the appointment of trustees and other matters of property are not definitely regulated by a constitution, meetings may be held to deal with the property and these are regarded as meetings for ecclesiastical purposes.

For fuller information regarding matters of property reference should be made to Chapter XVII.

Section IV. *Congregations of Deaf Persons*

For many years prior to 1973 the Church had recognised the existence of congregations of deaf persons, which had been formed under the auspices of local welfare societies, to the extent of authorising the ordination of ministers for the specialised work of ministering to the deaf and dumb. In 1969 the General Assembly passed an Act regularising procedures for such ordinations (1969, xxiii). See Chapter XII, p. 268.

Since 1973 such special congregations may, after due procedure, be received by the appropriate Presbytery as congregations of the Church of Scotland (1973, iii).

CHAPTER III.

ADMINISTRATION OF CONGREGATIONAL FINANCES

INTRODUCTORY.

IN 1965 the General Assembly recommended and urged Congregations "which have not yet decided to adopt the Model Deed of Constitution to adopt the Model Deed now in its amended form." (Reports 1965 p. 640 and Act xxi, 1965.) However despite this exhortation of the General Assembly there are at time of publication more than six hundred congregations administering their temporal affairs according to constitutions other than the Model Deed and differing one from the other largely in terms of their historical origin. It will prove convenient in this chapter to deal first with the varying methods of administration (sections *A* to *F*), with the machinery for change in the method of administration (section *G*), and at the end of the chapter to deal with the more general questions.

It should be particularly noted that in all congregations, except those where there is a Deacons' Court or a Congregational Board according to the procedure of the United Free Church, collections for the poor and for the Schemes of the General Assembly are in control of the Kirk Session. In modern times it has become increasingly common for this control to be delegated to the financial court, but the responsibility for these matters must remain with the Kirk Session.

It is the duty of the Kirk Session to see that members of the congregation are fully informed, through circulation of 'Life and Work' and otherwise, about the work of the Church and its claims upon them.

In former *quoad omnia* parishes the Kirk Session has control of all financial matters. In parishes *quoad sacra* (which include all new parishes and most of those where a union has been effected) financial matters are administered by a Congregational Board which consists of the minister with all or a certain number of the elders and a corresponding number of communicant members elected by the congregation. In some congregations, particularly of the former Free Church, temporal affairs are the concern of the Deacons' Court consisting of the minister and elders together with a number of deacons (in some cases ordained for life, in other cases elected for a stated number of years). In some congregations, particularly of the former

United Presbyterian and Original Secession tradition, the temporal affairs are administered by a Committee of Management, all the members of which are elected by the congregation.

Apart from these four principal methods there are various other ways in which congregations may have their finances administered, and reference is made to these hereunder (see p. 45).

It should be particularly noted that the capital of a trust fund should not be drawn upon unless this is authorised by the deed of trust or gift.

A. The Kirk Session.

In former *quoad omnia* parishes (unless they have adopted the Model Constitution) the financial affairs are wholly under the control of the Kirk Session. For full particulars regarding meetings and conduct of business in Kirk Session see Ch. VI., p. 116.

By Act of Parliament (1845), the Kirk Session has the control and disposal of all ordinary collections. In terms of the Church of Scotland (Property and Endowment) Act, 1925, the right of allocating sittings, with or without payment therefor, and the right of disposal of the proceeds, if any, in churches transferred to the General Trustees, now belongs to the Kirk Session. It is, however, recommended by the General Assembly (Rep. 1927, p. 189) that the maintenance of an adequate local Fabric Fund should be a first charge on this income annually. The Assembly has further recommended (1944, 3) that the Fabric Fund should be such as to produce an annual income of not less than one-half per cent of the insurable value of the ecclesiastical property in the parish.

While the General Trustees are responsible as owners for payment of insurance premiums and of local rates and taxes on the property which they hold, these charges must be met by the Kirk Session in accordance with the instructions of the General Assembly (1928, 2).

After meeting the expenses detailed above, the Kirk Session has to apply the ordinary funds to the following purposes: stipend, or supplement to stipend, and travelling and other "listed" expenses of the minister (see p. 674); heating, lighting, cleaning of the church and other expenses connected with public worship; salaries of church officer, organist, and other officials; payments to the Aged and Infirm Ministers' Fund (p. 727); contributions made under the Mission and Service

Fund (p. 658); assessments levied by Presbytery, Synod, and General Assembly; and also any other fixed charges falling upon the Kirk Session or congregation.

When a Kirk Session holds property wholly or mainly for the benefit of the inhabitants of the parish, or any of them, "as such inhabitants"; and when forty years have expired since the foundation of the trust; and when it is neither ecclesiastical nor educational; the Kirk Session may (1) transfer it to the District or other appropriate Council (which need not accept it), or (2) appoint not more than three members to act with such number of persons appointed by the Council as the Secretary of State may approve—the joint body being "a committee of management of the property." If the Kirk Session number not less than six persons it must appoint; otherwise it need not (Local Government (Scotland) Act, 1947, section 359).

An "ecclesiastical charity" is for (*a*) theological instruction; (*b*) any person on the ground of ecclesiastical character or office; (*c*) the use, if a building, of a particular denomination; (*d*) the upkeeping of it or maintaining divine service in it; (*e*) the benefit of any particular denomination or members thereof as such. The benefit would thus (as regards individuals) have to be only members—a word undefined by the Act, and possibly undefined, if used, in the trust deed. Probably also a trust would not be held ecclesiastical, if it did no more than give a preference to persons of a particular church.

A charity endowment, other than a building, if it is only in part for those purposes, is "an ecclesiastical charity within the meaning of the 1947 Act."

When there are two or more churches in a parish the General Assembly may declare that one of these is to be deemed the church of the parish and its Minister, Elders, or Kirk Session the Minister, Elders, or Kirk Session of the parish for the purposes of any Act, Act of Sederunt, trust deed, scheme of administration, or other public or private instrument, deed, or document having reference to such Ministers, Elders, or Kirk Session as trustees. (Church of Scotland (Property and Endowments) Amendment Act, 1933, section 12.)

When the Kirk Session has control of the finances it is its duty to maintain in a proper state of repair all buildings vested in the General Trustees, but no extraordinary repairs, alterations or improvements are to be made without consent of the Presbytery and of the General Trustees (see p. 43 and p. 357).

Additionally, a Kirk Session may not without the consent of

Presbytery proceed with building operations or repairs to property whether or not application is to be made for financial assistance from the Home Board or from the Church generally (1971 Reg. 4).

When in connection with the church there is a churchyard no longer in use the Kirk Session may take over its management (P. 1925). Also if it so desired the Kirk Session may retain the custody and management of old ecclesiastical buildings situated within a churchyard which has been duly transferred to the County Council in terms of the Act (P. 1925, Rep. 1927, p. 160 ; also 1934, 11).

Whether or not it is alone responsible for financial administration within the congregation each Kirk Session should keep regular accounts of its intromissions with all church and trust funds under its charge and annually have them examined by (1) a professional auditor ; (2) themselves ; (3) some of their number ; or (4) others specially named for the purpose ; and should record in their minute-book that they have been so examined. An abstract of the duly audited accounts must be submitted annually to the Presbytery (1929, I.).

B. The Deacons' Court.

(F.C., 1846, vii. ; 1847, xiv.)

I. *Constitution and Officials.*

The Deacons' Court of a congregation consists of the minister, the elders, and the deacons, the deacons being elected—and in some cases ordained—to office for the purpose of assisting in the management of the temporal affairs of the congregation. Women may hold the office of deacon on the same terms as men (1935, viii.).

The Kirk Session determines when it is expedient to have an election of deacons, and determines also the number required, which ought to be conformable to the size and circumstances of the congregation. The deacons are elected by the members of the congregation in full communion.

There are two distinct ways, an older and a more recent, in which deacons may hold office. Under the older way the deacon is elected for life, is ordained to office by the Kirk Session, and continues in office till he ceases to be a member of the congregation, or his resignation is accepted, or he is deposed or otherwise removed from office. If a deacon has absented himself from the meetings of the court for more than a year without due cause satisfactory to the Kirk Session, the latter may, after giving him notice for his interest, declare that he has ceased to be a member of the Deacons' Court (1933, ix.). Deacons are, as all other members of the congregation, under the jurisdiction of the Kirk Session.

A congregation may resolve that its deacons shall be appointed according to the newer way. This provides that deacons shall be male or female members of the congregation in full communion and not less than eighteen years of age and that they shall be elected to the office for a period of three years. The regulations governing the appointment of members of a Congregational Board apply to the appointment of deacons according to this method. In this case the deacons are not ordained but on the first convenient Sunday after their election their names (if they accept office) may be read over to the congregation after which the minister should commend them in prayer to the grace of God for the work to which they have been appointed (1932, x.).

In the case of a congregation which has changed from the older to newer method, deacons who have been ordained on the basis of a life-tenure may, if they so desire, continue to hold office on the terms on which they were appointed (U.F.C., 1919, i. of Class I.; see also Ch. VI., p. 136).

The Minister, or Interim Moderator of session, presides in the Deacons' Court when he is present, and in his absence the court chooses one of its own number to preside. It is the chairman's duty to see that each meeting is opened and closed with prayer, to ensure that the business is properly ordered and recorded, to take the vote, and to announce the decisions of the court. He has a casting but no deliberative vote. He can, however, introduce business at the Deacons' Court and may address the members upon it.

The Deacons' Court appoints a clerk who, on his appointment, should take the oath *de fideli*. It is his duty to take regular minutes of all the proceedings, to engross these in a permanent record accessible to the members of the court at all reasonable times, to take charge of such of its papers, books and documents as are not entrusted to the custody of the treasurer, and to prepare and issue all extracts of the minutes and papers authorised by the court. In his absence from any meeting the court appoints a clerk *pro tempore*, whose appointment must be recorded in the minute. Each minute, when approved, must be signed in the permanent record by the chairman and clerk acting at the meeting at which the approval is given.

The Deacons' Court appoints a treasurer of the congregational fund who is to keep a congregational cash-book and record therein all moneys received and payments made. He is to lodge all money received in a separate bank account, identifying it as belonging to the congregation, and the court are entitled to require the production of this bank-book at any meeting. The court may also appoint treasurers of separate funds under their charge, particularly the Maintenance of the Ministry Fund.

The Church Officer acts as officer to the Deacons' Court, and is in attendance, if required, at the time of its meetings.

II. *Meetings and Procedure.*

Deacons' Courts normally meet once a month, but the frequency of meetings must depend largely upon local circumstances.

Three members—of whom the minister need not be one—form a quorum.

The Deacons' Court is normally called by intimation from the pulpit. It may be called by notice sent to each member, and in either case adequate time should be allowed for the attendance of the members. It is called by authority of the minister and any three members may requisition him to do so. During a vacancy in the pastoral charge the clerk of the court takes the place of the minister in this matter.

Meetings are opened and closed with prayer and both facts must be recorded under penalty of invalidating the meeting. Meetings are usually private, but the court may, if it see cause, hold meetings that are open to the congregation. The Deacons' Court cannot meet when the Kirk Session is sitting, nor, except for urgent business, at the time of an ordinary meeting of a superior court, without leave of that court. Meetings may be adjourned, and in this case the same rules apply as do in the case of the Kirk Session. (Chap. VI., p. 121.)

Immediately after the meeting is constituted the minutes of the previous meeting are read and the judgment of the court, approving or correcting them, has to be recorded. An extract minute must bear that the Deacons' Court was constituted, and must be certified by the clerk as having been extracted by him from the records of the court. Otherwise it will not be received. For further information regarding the keeping of minutes see Chap. V., p. 81.

Any member of a Deacons' Court may enter his dissent from any part of its proceedings of which he disapproves. (See Chap. V., p. 106.)

The Deacons' Court is entitled to certified extracts from the minutes of the Kirk Session in so far as these may affect its membership, officials, or duties; and such extracts must be engrossed in the records of the Deacons' Court.

III. *Powers and Functions.*

The Deacons' Court is required to apply spiritual principles to the management of temporal matters, but it is not authorised to exercise any kind of spiritual rule, nor to review the action of minister or Kirk Session. Being thus devoid of any power of discipline it cannot admit to the office of deacon or despose from it. It cannot even receive the resignation of a deacon, or deal with it in any way. (Chap. VI., p. 117.)

The Deacons' Court has the management and charge of the whole property belonging to the congregation or held for the congregation's use by trustees appointed in terms of deeds which the General Assembly has sanctioned. It has the responsibility of seeing that the place of worship and other ecclesiastical buildings are kept in good condition and repair and of taking steps to raise whatever funds may be necessary for this purpose. Building operations or repairs to ecclesiastical buildings should not be begun without the Presbytery's consent. (1971, Reg. 4.) The Deacons' Court has also full responsibility for the oversight of sittings and pews in the place of worship, and may let or allocate these as it sees fit.

The Deacons' Court is not entitled to grant the use of the place of worship or of any other ecclesiastical buildings belonging to the congregation, for any purpose whatever without the consent of the minister. It is not entitled to withhold the use of these buildings for meetings which are connected with the congregation or any of its organisations and which have the sanction of the minister, or for meetings of a religious, ecclesiastical or charitable nature which have the same sanction. But none of these buildings can be made use of, either by the minister or by others, for any meeting which is not of the character above specified, without the acquiescence of the Deacons' Court. (1932, xvii.)

The church officer is appointed by the Kirk Session, but it belongs to the Deacons' Court to determine his salary. (1931, xvii.) It appoints, dismisses, and fixes the salary and terms of service of doorkeepers and any other persons employed in attending to the convenience of the worshippers. The Deacons' Court fixes the salary of the leader of praise. The Kirk Session makes this appointment but it may, if it see fit, confer with the Deacons' Court before doing so. (1931, xvi.) (For suggested agreement with the leader of praise, see Appendix XXVI., p. 746.)

The Deacons' Court has the management and charge of all the congregation's temporal affairs. It is the duty of the court to ensure that feu-duties, cost of insurance, salaries of officials, Presbytery, Synod and Assembly charges, and current yearly expenses for the maintenance of public worship and the due administration of Gospel ordinances are met, that stipend and travelling and "listed" expenses are paid to the minister or the Maintenance of the Ministry Fund as may have been arranged, that a suitable sum in aid to the Maintenance of the Ministry Fund is paid, that the current charge for the Aged and Infirm Ministers' Fund is met, and that the requirements of the Mission and Service Fund are attended to.

The duty of attending to the temporal wants of poor persons connected with the congregation is specially assigned to the Deacons' Court, which may appoint special collections as often as may be necessary for this purpose.

The Deacons' Court is bound, as soon as possible after the auditing of the accounts, to call a meeting of the congregation. At this meeting the court presents a report of its proceedings for the previous year, gives such information and explanation as may be asked for, and receives any suggestions which may be offered by the members of the congregation for the consideration of the court with reference to the future administration of the funds.

It is recommended that the congregation should elect annually two members of the congregation as auditors of the accounts, who shall, previous to the next annual meeting, examine the treasurer's books and vouchers for the current year, and report thereon to said meeting. (U.F.C. 1908, I. of Class II.) Reference should also be made to Chap. II., p. 23.

IV. *Review of Decisions.*

While it is inexpedient to sustain complaints or appeals

against the ordinary administration of the Deacons' Court in temporal and financial affairs the said court is nevertheless subject to the review of the Presbytery in so far as it may take any step, or adopt any resolution, which the Presbytery can pronounce to be of a censurable nature, or in violation of any enactment of the General Assembly. (F.C. 1846, xiv.)

The Deacons' Court is bound to furnish extracts to parties concerned in its procedure in the same manner as the Kirk Session. (See Chap. V., p. 85.)

The record of the court, with the treasurer's account of income and expenditure for the year duly audited, has to be exhibited to the Presbytery as soon as possible after 31st December in each year for the purpose of being examined and attested by the Presbytery (1929, i.).

C. The Committee of Management.

"If the temporal affairs of the congregation are administered in accordance with a special constitution derived from and particular to the congregation itself, a copy of the said constitution shall immediately be given to those persons nominated." (Act III, 1970.)

The foregoing Act was passed in order to ensure that the minister or ministers nominated for election to a charge with a special constitution should be informed thereof as early as possible.

Each congregation of the former United Presbyterian Church had its own "Constitution," more properly described as "Rules for the Administration of the Temporal Affairs of the Congregation." This "constitution" derived from the congregation, which had powers to amend its terms (usually after a resolution to that effect entertained at one meeting and approved at a subsequent meeting) but always under authority of the Presbytery. What follows describes the usual pattern and must always, therefore, be read as subject to the condition that the individual congregational constitution may make other provisions, and that in that event the latter will prevail.

I. *Constitution and Officials.*

The Committee of Management consists of a definite number of managers, members of the congregation in full communion elected by the congregation.

The congregation determines the number of managers. It is not expedient that there should be fewer than six, and it is not usual for the number to exceed fifteen. The election is made at the annual meeting of the congregation; or by means of voting papers filled up and returned previous to the meeting and in accordance with a plan adopted by the congregation. Should any manager be suspended from membership or cease to be a member of the congregation he thereby ceases to be a manager.

Minister and elders are eligible as well as other members of the congregation. Women may be elected provided the congregation at a meeting duly called for the purpose resolves that all members on the roll of the congregation in full communion are eligible for membership of the Committee or Board administering its temporal affairs. Care must be taken to ensure that such a resolution is not at variance with the title deeds under which the property is held, or with the constitution according to which the affairs of the congregation are administered. (U.F.C. 1916, xii. of Class II.)

One-third of the managers retire annually by rotation, and their places, with those of any who may die or vacate office during the year, are filled at the annual meeting. The retiring managers are usually eligible for re-election. A manager elected in room of one who has died or vacated office retires at the expiry of the period for which the person in whose room he is elected was appointed. When it is considered necessary to fill a vacancy or vacancies in the number of managers during the year a special meeting of the congregation has to be called for the purpose.

It is recommended that the name of the managers who accept office be read over to the congregation on the first convenient Sunday after their election, and that the minister then commend them in prayer to the grace of God for the work to which they have been appointed.

The congregation either itself elects, or empowers the managers to appoint from their own number, a chairman or preses (of the managers, not of the congregation), a clerk, and a treasurer. The congregation also appoints annually two members of the congregation to be auditors of the accounts. It is the duty of the latter before next annual meeting to examine the treasurer's books and vouchers for the current year and to report thereon at the next annual meeting.

It is the duty of the chairman or preses to have each meeting opened and closed with prayer; to see that the business is properly ordered and recorded; to take the vote; and to announce the decisions reached. He may introduce any business to the managers and address them regarding it. He has a deliberative as well as a casting vote. In the absence of the chairman one of the other managers may be chosen to preside at a meeting.

It is the duty of the clerk to keep a regular minute-book, accessible to the managers at all reasonable times, wherein are engrossed the minutes of all meetings of the managers, and also of all meetings of the congregation held for temporal purposes.

It is the duty of the treasurer to keep a congregational cash-book, to enter therein a note of all moneys received and of all payments made, and to produce this at all annual meetings audited and docqueted by the auditors appointed by the congregation, or failing them by a committee of the managers, together with the vouchers. He is to lodge all money received in a bank account identified as belonging to the congregation, and to produce the bank pass-book whenever called upon to do so by the managers.

II. *Meetings and Procedure.*

The managers hold regular meetings at least once a quarter, and oftener when necessary. Meetings are called by authority from the chairman, or in his absence from the clerk, either by pulpit intimation or by written notice to individual managers. The chairman is bound to call a meeting if requisitioned to do so by one-third of the managers.

The number constituting a quorum is normally fixed by the constitution. If not so fixed it is three or not less than one-third of the number of managers, whichever is greater.

The rules for opening and closing meetings and for keeping and approving minutes are the same as for the Deacons' Court (p. 32).

III. *Powers and Functions.*

The management of the temporal affairs of the congregation —that is, the care of the church property, the ordering of repairs and alterations thereon, the letting of the seats and collection of the seat rents, the charge of all contributions for the support of ordinances, the payment of the minister's stipend, salaries of leader of praise or organist, church officer, and other expenses—is committed to the managers, who are bound to regulate their administration of these matters by the rules set forth in the congregational constitution, as well as to observe any special directions which may from time to time be given them by the congregation. It should be noted that management of temporal affairs does not include collections for the Mission and Service Fund or provision for the poor, which are the specific responsibilities of the Kirk Session.

The church officer is appointed and dismissed by the Kirk Session (1931, xvii.). The church officer gives attendance at managers' meetings, and takes charge of the place of worship in accordance with the instructions given him. (See also Chap. VI., p. 124.) Doorkeepers and other subordinate officials are appointed and dismissed by the managers.

The managers are not entitled to give the use of the place of worship, or of the other ecclesiastical buildings belonging to the congregation, for any purpose whatever, without the consent of the minister and Kirk Session. They are not entitled to withhold the use of these buildings for meetings which are connected with the congregation or any of its organisations, and which have the sanction of the minister, or for meetings of a religious, ecclesiastical or charitable nature, which have the same sanction. But none of these buildings can be made use of, either by the minister or by others, for any meeting which is not of the character above specified, without the acquiescence of the managers (1932, xvii.). The consent or acquiescence of the managers is not required for any use which may be made or given of any hall or premises apart from the church or place of worship and halls or buildings connected therewith which are used by the congregation or any missionary association or society of the congregation for carrying on mission or Sunday School or other congregational work, and which have not been placed under the charge of the managers, and for the care of which they are not responsible.

In congregations where provisions are made, either in a constitution approved by the Presbytery or in the title-deeds of the church or meeting-house of the congregation, with regard to the use of the church buildings which differ from what is stated above, the former, unless competently altered by the congregation, hold to the exclusion of the latter (1932, xvii.).

The managers report their proceedings and management during the year at the annual meeting of the congregation. A duly audited abstract of accounts must be produced annually to the Presbytery. (Oct. 1929, I.) (See Chap. II., p. 24.)

The managers when they deem it necessary, and having obtained the concurrence of the Kirk Session, can call special meetings of the congregation for temporal purposes. Intimation of such meetings, and of their purpose, must be made on the two preceding Sundays (1932, xviii.).

The managers have no power to contract debt on the security of the property belonging to the congregation, or for which it may be attached, without having secured the special authority of the congregation, given at a special meeting called for the purpose, and also the authority of the Presbytery where that is required. They are not to expend in any one year, on repairs or alterations, more than a sum fixed by the congregation, without its express authority, and no building operations or repairs to ecclesiastical buildings may be proceeded with without the consent of Presbytery.

The managers are required to apply spiritual principles to the management of temporal affairs, but they are not authorised to exercise any kind of spiritual rule, or to review the action of minister or Kirk Session, or to have any jurisdiction over the conduct of public worship in any of its parts.

The constitutional right of the Kirk Session to watch over all the interests of the congregation, and to interpose whenever, in its opinion, the welfare of the congregation calls on it to do so, by convening meetings for any purpose connected with congregational affairs, or in any other competent manner, is, in every congregational constitution, expressly reserved, and cannot be revoked by any resolution of the congregation.

D. The Congregational Board.

(as constituted under the Model Deed of Constitution, 1965, xxi) —(Constitution printed in full in Appendix XV., p. 610.)

I. *Constitution and Officials.*

The Congregational Board consists of the minister, with all or a certain number of elders, and a certain number of communicants elected at the Stated Annual Meeting of the congregation. (See Chap. II., p. 23.) Those so elected must be members, male or female, in full communion with the congregation, and over eighteen years of age. The number to be elected is decided by the congregation, but in no case must it exceed the number of elders at the date of election.

One-third of the elected members of the board retire annually, but are severally eligible for re-election. The order of retirement of the members is fixed by the board.

Power to reduce membership of Board.

In terms of Act XXI., 1965, it shall be in the power of the congregation by a resolution passed by not less than two-thirds of the members thereof present at a meeting of the congregation of which due notice of the intention to propose such resolution has been given, to resolve that the number of elders on the board should be reduced to a number specified in said resolution. The reduced number of elders shall be not less than 5 when the number of members on the Communion Roll does not exceed 200; shall be not less than 8 when the number of members on the Communion Roll exceeds 200 but does not exceed 400, and shall be not less than 12 when the number of members on the Communion Roll exceeds 400. In the event of such a resolution being passed (*a*) the elders who are to serve on the board shall be elected by the Kirk Session and shall be members of the board for such period as the Kirk Session may decide, and the Kirk Session shall fill any vacancy that occurs; (*b*) the number of members of the board elected by the congregation shall not exceed the number of elders specified in the resolution. If at the time such resolution is passed the number of members on the board elected by the congregation should exceed the reduced number of elders, the members elected by the congregation may decide among themselves by agreement or failing that by ballot or otherwise as the majority may wish which of them should demit office so as not to exceed the specified number of elders.

It shall be competent for the congregation at intervals of not less than one year after the passing of a resolution as aforesaid to review the matter and by a resolution passed by not less than two-thirds of the members thereof present at a meeting of which due notice of the intention to propose such a resolution has been given to rescind the resolution referred to in the preceding paragraph or to amend it by increasing or reducing the number of elders to serve on the board, provided that the minimum number shall be as before stated. In the event of the resolution referred to in the preceding paragraph being rescinded, all the elders shall thereupon become members of the board and the congregation shall have power to elect additional members of the board up to the total number of elders. In the event of the number of elders, however, being increased but still being less than the total number of elders on the Kirk Session, the Kirk Session shall elect additional members to serve on the board from their own number as before provided, and the congregation shall have power to elect additional members up to the total number of elders serving on the board. In the event of the number of elders being further reduced by said amending resolution, the Kirk Session shall decide which of the elders are to serve on the board, and the members of the board elected by the congregation shall decide by agreement or failing that by ballot or otherwise as the majority may wish, which of them should demit office so as to reduce their number to a number not exceeding the number of elders on the board.

In the event of any elected member of the board dying, or resigning, or becoming incapacitated to act, or having his or her name removed from the Communion Roll of the congregation, or being suspended from Communion, during the currency of his or her term of office, the board may appoint a duly qualified person to fill the vacancy, and the person so appointed holds office for the remainder of the predecessor's term, subject to confirmation at the next Stated Annual Meeting.

In the event of the Presbytery finding that the board, or a majority of its members, persist in disregarding the terms of the constitution after their attention has been drawn to the matter, the Presbytery may remove from the Board those who have been guilty of such contumacy, and declare them ineligible for re-appointment for a period of not less than three years, taking such steps as it may deem proper to fill the vacancy thus occasioned—having power itself to make appointments to the board in these circumstances.

The minister is *ex officio* the chairman of the board. In the event of his declining to accept office the board elects one of its number to act as chairman for the year. In the absence of the chairman from any meeting the members present appoint one of their number to act *pro tempore*. The chairman has a casting vote only.

It is the duty of the board at its first meeting to appoint a clerk and treasurer who need not be of its number and who may be the same person. Clerk and treasurer hold office during the pleasure of the board. The board also annually appoints an auditor or auditors of its accounts. These need not be of its own number.

It is the duty of the clerk to keep regular minutes of the proceedings of the board and also of the proceedings at the Stated Annual Meeting and to engross these in a permanent record in which each minute, when approved, is signed by the chairman and clerk.

It is the duty of the treasurer to keep a separate banking account in name of the board. All cheques drawn on the account should require to be signed by a member of the board as well as by the treasurer. Two or more members may be authorised so to sign, but only one signature besides that of the treasurer need be required.

II. *Meetings and Procedure.*

The board meets when summoned by authority of its chairman, either by pulpit intimation or by personal notice to each member, allowing reasonable time for attendance. The chairman is bound to call a meeting within ten days if requested to do so in writing by a quorum of the board. The first meeting of the board after election is called by authority of the minister within one month of the Stated Annual Meeting (1934, xii.).

Three is a quorum when the number of the board does not exceed nine, five when the number is between nine and twenty, seven when the number exceeds twenty.

The rules for opening and closing meetings and for keeping and approving minutes are the same as for the Deacons' Court (p. 32).

III. *Powers and Functions.*

The treasurer of the board keeps an account of the Ordinary Revenue and Expenditure of the Parish and Congregation, including in such Revenue under separate headings, *inter alia* (1) all sums (if any) received by him in respect of the statutory endowment and all other sums forming the stipend or further endowment of stipend, including all contributions made towards stipend; (2) seat rents; (3) ordinary church collections and donations in aid thereof; (4) contributions or donations for congregational purposes; (5) the income of any Congregational endowment for general or specific purposes; (6) contributions under the Mission and Service Fund; (7) collections for any other charitable or religious purpose except as after mentioned; and (8) revenue from any other source; but excluding from such revenue (1) Poor Fund (if any); and (2) any other funds or monies held or administered by the Kirk Session under Trusts or otherwise. The following charges shall also be stated under separate headings, and, except in so far as otherwise provided for, shall be met out of the said

Ordinary Revenue, *videlicet*: (1) the Stipend and Listed Expenses payable to the minister so far as the same are payable from congregational sources, which Stipend and Listed Expenses shall be a first charge on the said Ordinary Revenue, except in so far as the other charges hereinafter specified are by law entitled to rank prior thereto; (2) Communion expenses; (3) any other expenses necessarily incurred in the maintenance of public worship or in dispensing the ordinances of religion; (4) the cost of heating, lighting and cleaning the church and church hall (if any), and rates, taxes, feu-duty and insurance of same; (5) rates, taxes, feu-duty and insurance payable in respect of the manse (if any); (6) the amount fixed to be set aside annually towards a Fabric Fund Account; (7) the salaries of the church officer and of the precentor or choir-master and organist, and of any other like officials; (8) the cost of pulpit supply when it is the responsibility of the congregation; (9) General Assembly, Synod and Presbytery assessments; and (10) any additional annual charges authorised by the board. At the close of the year any balance standing at the credit of the Ordinary Revenue and Expenditure Account shall be dealt with as hereinafter provided (p. 44).

The Ordinary Revenue and Expenditure Account shall show, either inset or by note, the total stipend paid to the minister from all sources.

It is the duty of the board to take all appropriate steps to secure that the amount of stipend and the amount of aid to the Maintenance of the Ministry Fund promised in a Vacancy or Revision Schedule are met.

Maintenance of Properties.

It is the duty of the board to maintain in proper order and repair all congregational property whether vested in the General Trustees or otherwise, but no building operations or repairs to church buildings may be proceeded with without the consent of Presbytery. It is also its duty to keep such property fully insured against loss by damage or fire, in the case of property vested in the General Trustees the said insurance being effected in their name. Any sum fixed by the General Assembly, the Presbytery, or the board itself as necessary for the maintenance of the church fabrics may be taken annually from Ordinary Revenue. Repairs and improvements upon and material additions to property vested in the General Trustees or Local Trustees are not to be undertaken until the board receives the consent of the Presbytery and the General Trustees and has the necessary funds available or guaranteed without encroachment on Ordinary Revenue. Urgent repairs may be carried out without such consent, but the circumstances are to be reported at once to the Presbytery, and the General Trustees where the property is vested in them.

If at the close of any financial year there shall remain any balance at the credit of the Ordinary Revenue and Expenditure Account after making the payments, or setting aside the sums, specified or referred to above, the same shall be applied by the board in whole or in part, for congregational and/or general church purposes, which purposes shall include, *inter alia,* all or any one or more of the following—*videlicet* : (1) supplement to the minister to the extent necessary to provide the Appropriate Stipend and Listed Expenses if not already provided for; (2) addition to the Fabric Fund Account; (3) further contributions under the Mission and Service Fund to the Schemes of the Church; (4) a Reserve Fund to meet Extraordinary or Exceptional Expenditure in connection with the church properties, or for the furnishings thereof; and (5) a Reserve Fund for Stipend or further endowment. Any sum remaining thereafter may be carried forward to next year's account; provided always that where the congregation is in receipt of aid from the Maintenance of the Ministry Fund, any balance must be used in the first place for stipend so as to reduce the amount of aid drawn.

It shall be the responsibility of the Congregational Board on receiving intimation of the allocation on the congregation of the sum required each year under the Mission and Service Fund to take steps after conference with the Kirk Session to inform the congregation of the allocation, to raise at least the sum allocated along with the proposed minimum contributions to the Maintenance of the Ministry Fund and Aged and Infirm Ministers' Fund, to give members of the congregation full information with regard to the Mission and Service Fund, and to distribute literature, leaflets, etc., provided by the Stewardship and Budget Committee. The board shall also consult with representatives of the Woman's Guild to determine the proportion of the allocation which will be the responsibility of the Woman's Guild. If the Weekly Freewill Offering System or any similar system is in operation the board shall determine the allocation of the money thus raised in so far as such allocation has not been determined by the contributors.

It shall be the responsibility of the Kirk Session to afford the congregation convenient opportunities for contributing to any other objects for which the General Assembly shall have enjoined special collections and the Kirk Session shall also have power to make such collections as may be deemed necessary for the needs of the poor or other religious or charitable purposes, all of which shall be shewn in separate Accounts as previously indicated.

It shall be competent for the board to take steps to let or otherwise allocate the sittings in the church and to fix the rents or contributions payable therefor, where these are exigible—a pew being reserved for the family of the minister, and suitable accommodation being provided for the officiating elders.

The Kirk Session appoints the church officer and the precentor, choirmaster and organist and any other like officials, and defines their duties. The salaries of these officials are fixed by the board. Such officials are subject to the direction of the minister as regards the execution of their duties. The Kirk Session has power to suspend or terminate any such appointment, but it must give due intimation thereof to the board.

The Accounts of the congregation shall be made up to 31st December or such earlier date as the Congregational Board may decide in each year, and, after having been duly audited, shall be submitted by the board to the congregation for approval at the Stated Annual Meeting to be held not later than the 31st day of March following (or other date authorised by the Presbytery), and the same shall, *inter alia,* contain a Statement as to the application or disposal, or the proposed application or disposal, of any balance or surplus on the Ordinary Revenue and Expenditure Account for the year in accordance with the provisions of Article Eleventh of the Model Constitution. The said Accounts shall, after submission to and approval by the congregation, be laid before the Presbytery within one month thereafter, for examination and attestation to the effect that the Accounts are correct and are in accordance with the terms of this Constitution, and the same shall also be docqueted by the Presbytery with reference to the provisions of Article Eleventh of the Model Constitution. The board shall also satisfy itself that the Accounts kept by the several other agencies of the congregation, except in so far as such Accounts are under the control of the Kirk Session, have been duly audited and are in order.

IV. *Review of Decisions.*

If any question arise with reference to the election of the board, or the interpretation of any article of the Model Constitution, or the legality of any particular exercise of the powers therein contained, it is competent to any person or body interested to apply by petition to the Presbytery of the bounds to adjudicate upon the matter, and the judgment of the Presbytery upon such matter, or upon any question arising in connection with the annual audit as prescribed, is final; unless any party at the first ordinary meeting of the Presbytery held after the lapse of twenty-one days from the date of the judgment produce a certificate signed by the Procurator of the Church to the effect that the matter is one suitable for appeal to the Higher Courts of the Church, in which case an appeal or dissent and complaint may be taken in common form at such meeting as if the judgment of the Presbytery had only then been given.

The General Assembly has power at any time to alter, revoke, amend, or modify the Deed of Constitution.

E. The Congregational Board.

(Constituted in accordance with the procedure of the United Free Church of Scotland)

The Congregational Board consists of the minister, the ruling elders, and a definite number of other members elected to the board by the congregation for a fixed period.

The congregation determines the number of members to be elected by it, which ought to be suitable to the size and circumstances of the congregation. This number is not to be altered except at a congregational meeting summoned with due notice of the proposal to make such alteration.

One-third of the elected members retire annually by rotation and the rules for filling these places, for the eligibility of re-election, and for persons appointed to complete a term, are the same as those that apply in the case of the committee of management (see p. 36).

The rule as to the eligibility of women as members of a Congregational Board is the same as in the case of a committee of management. (U.F.C. 1916, xii. of Class II.)

It is recommended that the names of the elected members who accept office be read over to the congregation on the first convenient Sunday after their election, and that the minister then commend them in prayer to the grace of God for the work to which they have been appointed.

The rules relating to officials, meetings and procedure,

powers and functions are the same as those for the Deacons' Court (see p. 30).

F. Congregations with a Constitution approved by a Superior Court.

There are a few congregations which were formerly parishes *quoad sacra*, in which temporal affairs are regulated by special permission of the General Assembly, in accordance with a constitution adopted and approved prior to the Union, instead of by the 1931 constitution. For such cases reference may be made to Mair's 'Digest of Church Laws,' pp. 441-444 (1923 edition), and Rep., 1905, p. 531. In the case of congregations connected with the United Free Church of Scotland before Union, a congregation whose temporal affairs are regulated by rules or a constitution approved by a Presbytery which had jurisdiction over it before the union of the Free Church of Scotland and the United Presbyterian Church, or before its admission as a congregation of the United Free Church of Scotland, continues to be guided by these in the administration of its temporal affairs; but it has power to adopt at a congregational meeting called for the purpose, any one of the methods of administration approved by the General Assembly. Until one of these methods of administration has been adopted, it should observe the provisions laid down for the committee of management, unless special provision be made in its constitution for another method of appointing the officials (see section C.).

Congregations that have not formally adopted a constitution, but are guided by the model constitution approved by the United Presbyterian Synod, continue to administer their temporal affairs as hitherto, unless and until the congregation resolve to adopt one of the methods of administration before described. Until one of these methods is adopted, the congregation observes the provision laid down for the committee of management (see section C.).

A congregation whose temporal affairs are administered by managers acting under a constitution approved by the Presbytery which had jurisdiction over it before the union of the Free Church of Scotland and the United Presbyterian Church, or before its admission as a congregation of the United Free Church of Scotland, or under the model constitution approved by the United Presbyterian Synod, may by resolution adopted at a congregational meeting held after intimation from the pulpit specifying the object of the meeting and made on the two immediately preceding Sundays, and confirmed either at the annual congregational meeting or at a special meeting held at an interval not less than three weeks after the resolution was adopted, and in either case after similar intimation, resolve to adopt the method of administration by managers described in section C. of this chapter, and such resolution shall forthwith be reported to the Presbytery, and on being approved by the Presbytery the regulations contained in this chapter shall thenceforth supersede and come in place of those according to which their temporal affairs have previously been administered.

G. Change of Method of Administration.

The General Assembly of 1965 recommended and urged all congregations not having done so to adopt the Model Deed of Constitution as amended and approved by that Assembly. (Act XXI, 1965.)

Successive General Assemblies have recognised that the diversity in forms of constitution is frequently a cause of misunderstanding and confusion among both ministers and office-bearers, and a greater degree of uniformity in constitutions would make for ease of administration and saving of time and trouble at all levels.

Accordingly, in order to facilitate the adoption of the Model Constitution by congregations a revised Deed of Constitution was approved by the General Assembly of 1965 which superseded the Model Deed for Parishes *Quoad Sacra* (1931) and differed from it in the following important respects :—

1. The reference to " Church and Parish *Quoad Sacra* " was dropped so that the title now reads " Constitution of the Congregation of . . . of the Church of Scotland in the Presbytery of . . ."

2. The preamble, except in the case of former Church Extension charges being raised to full status, was greatly simplified.

3. Means were introduced by which the Congregational Board could be reduced in size.

4. By the repeal of section 2 of Act XIX, 1964, it became

no longer necessary to have any reference to congregational property except in the case of a former Church Extension charge being raised to full status.

Any congregation of the Church is at liberty to adopt the model constitution. A congregation connected with the United Free Church before union may adopt any of the methods of administering its temporal affairs described in this chapter in sections *B*, *C*, and *E* in place of the method existing at the time.

In any case where a change of constitution is to be adopted the following are the steps which must be followed.

1. When a Kirk Session judges it expedient to adopt a new method of managing the financial affairs of the congregation the Kirk Session shall summon a meeting of members of the congregation to consider the proposal and decide thereon. This meeting shall be intimated on the two Sundays preceding the meeting.

2. If the proposal be approved by the meeting of the congregation, the resolution shall be reported forthwith to the Presbytery of the bounds, which, having concurred therein, shall inform the Principal Clerk of General Assembly in order that the Delegation of General Assembly, or any other body to which such power is delegated, may issue the appropriate Model Deed of Constitution.

Where two or more congregations have been or shall be united and it is provided in the Basis of Union that the temporal affairs of the united congregation should be administered by a Congregational Board as in, or in accordance with, the Model Deed of Constitution as approved by the General Assembly but no express authority is given in the Basis of Union to the Delegation to issue the said Model Deed, it shall nevertheless be in the power of the Delegation of the General Assembly to issue the appropriate form of Model Deed of Constitution to the united congregation.

Where two or more congregations are to be united, and each of the uniting congregations administers its financial affairs according to the same constitution, the Presbytery may find it expedient to sanction the continued use of the said same constitution for the united charge.

It should be particularly noted that in the event of a congregation of either branch of the former United Free Church deciding to adopt the Model Constitution it may, if it care, elect to make over its property into the name of the General Trustees, but it is not under any obligation necessarily to do so.

General Considerations.

I. *Stipend, Ministerial Expenses, and Aid to the Fund.*

In every congregation the stipend to be paid to the minister is now regulated by the terms of a Vacancy Schedule completed in consultation between the congregational authority, the Presbytery and the General Assembly's Committee on the Maintenance of the Ministry, before the induction of the incumbent; or by a Revision Schedule completed in the same way but during an incumbency. This schedule shows (*a*) the amount proposed to be paid as stipend and the sources from which it is to come, (*b*) whether there is a manse, and if not what provision is to be made in lieu thereof, (*c*) what provision is to be made for meeting "listed expenses," (*d*) the amount of travelling allowance to be paid to the minister, and (*e*) the amount of aid to be given to, or received from, the Maintenance of the Ministry Fund. See p. 674 for "listed expenses."

The meeting of the obligations represented by the schedule must be regarded as a first charge upon congregational income.

Special collections may be ingathered (by monthly visitors or otherwise) for this purpose, but if these do not meet the sum required the balance must be a first charge on ordinary income. The figures for stipend and aid appearing in the schedule are to be regarded as minimum payments, but neither should be increased until the other has at least been reached.

II. *Aged and Infirm Ministers' Fund Contribution.*

The General Assembly of 1969 approved new regulations for the administration of the Aged and Infirm Ministers' Fund whereby congregations would contribute to the Fund each year a sum not less than 5 per cent of the stipend. Contributions unpaid at the end of the calendar year are subject thereafter to interest at the rate of 5 per cent per annum.

The payment of this sum, or of any sum which the General Assembly may subsequently determine in its place, is a first charge on the ordinary income of every congregation.

III. *Mission and Service Fund.*

The Kirk Session, Congregational Board, Deacons' Court or Board of Management, without detracting from the ultimate responsibility of the Congregational Court to meet its full allocation from congregational funds, shall consult with the Woman's Guild and other organisations within the congregation concerning their responsibilities towards the wider work of the Church and the education of members of such organisations in the purposes of the Mission and Service Fund. (Act XXXV, 1969, Sect. 6 (2).)

CHAPTER IV.

The Minister.

Section I. The Minister and his Parish.

Induction, &c.

A minister is admitted or inducted to his charge or introduced to his appointment by the Presbytery. "Certified intimation of the ordination and/or induction (or where applicable introduction) shall be sent (by the Presbytery Clerk) to the Session Clerk to be engrossed in the Minutes of the first meeting of Session thereafter" (1932, ix.). It should also be recorded at the first meeting of Session after the occurrence of a vacancy that the Church and parish became vacant, with date and occasion of vacancy.

Access to and use of Church Buildings.

"The place of worship and other ecclesiastical buildings connected with every charge are at the disposal of the minister for the purposes of his office." He "may use them and grant permission to others to use them for all purposes connected with the congregation or any of its organisations, and also for all purposes of an ecclesiastical, religious, or charitable nature, even if they be not connected with the congregation." All "subject to the control of the Presbytery." "The minister shall not use the buildings nor grant the use of them for any other purposes without the consent of the Kirk Session, Deacons' Court, Committee of Management, or Congregational Board, as the case may be" (1932, xvii.).[1]

Non-Residence.

The General Assembly (1582, 5) declares "non-residence and absence from his flock and office be the space of fortie days together in ane year without lawful impediment allowed by the Generall Assemblie" to be a cause of deprivation. There are several old Acts of Assembly dealing with this matter. The General Assembly of 1638 resolved that ministers be obliged to reside conform to those Acts. These Acts show the serious view taken regarding non-residence or absence. A minister rarely absented himself for more than six weeks continuously without the consent of his Presbytery. In cases of absence beyond forty days application for leave should therefore be made to the Presbytery.

[1] This appears to mean, consent of the Kirk Session where there is no Financial Board, but of the Financial Board where such exists. —Editor.

"When a manse is provided, the minister shall reside in it unless with the express consent of the Presbytery to reside elsewhere. In all cases the Presbytery shall require him to reside within a reasonable distance of the Church and sphere of ministry. A minister may be dealt with for non-residence" (1929, i.).

Entry into another's parish.

"A minister's field of ministerial work and responsibility lies within and does not extend beyond his own parish. The boundaries of a parish are determined by the Presbytery. A minister shall not be at liberty to overstep his own bounds and enter those of another to perform ministerial functions without the previous consent of the minister within the bounds of whose parish he proposes to enter, unless he be acting under special commission or order of the Presbytery of the bounds, or of a Superior Court having jurisdiction; provided always that a minister may enter the bounds of a parish other than his own for the purpose of ministering to members and adherents of his own congregation, or to officiate at a marriage or funeral by private invitation" (1933, viii.). A minister is not prohibited from accepting an invitation to conduct divine service in a church of another denomination.

Administration of the Sacraments.

Act XIII., 1964, as amended by Act IV., 1975, states :—

Administration of the Sacraments.

1. The Sacraments of the Church may be administered only by the following persons :—

   (*a*) a person who has the status of a Minister of the Church of Scotland and who (1) has been ordained by a Presbytery of the Church of Scotland ; or (2) has been inducted to a charge of the Church of Scotland, or (3) has been admitted by the General Assembly as a Minister of the Church of Scotland ;

   (*b*) a person who has the status of an ordained Minister of the United Reformed Church in England and Wales or any Presbyterian Church in Great Britain or elsewhere, whose Constitution is in agreement with the doctrine and practice of the Church of Scotland and who has been duly authorised to administer the Sacraments by the Presbytery of the bounds. Such authority may be given only in special circumstances (*e.g.*, *locum tenens*, exchange Minister) of which the Presbytery shall be the sole judge ;

(*c*) a person who has the status of an ordained Minister of one of the Lutheran and Reformed Churches in Europe along with Union Churches which grew out of them, and the related pre-Reformation Churches, the Waldensian Church and the Church of the Czech Brethren and who has been duly authorised to administer the Sacraments by the Presbytery of the bounds ; such authority may be given only in special circumstances (*e.g.*, *locum tenens*, exchange Minister) of which the Presbytery shall be the sole judge ;

(*d*) a person who has the status of an ordained Minister of a non-Presbyterian Church, who has obtained a certificate issued on the authority of the Committee on Admission of Ministers of other Churches to the effect that his ordination is in accordance with the standards of the Church of Scotland, and who has been duly authorised to administer the Sacraments by the Presbytery of the bounds. Such authority may be given only in special circumstances (*e.g.*, *locum tenens*, exchange Minister) of which the Presbytery shall be the sole judge.

2. Notwithstanding the foregoing provisions, Ministers of the Church of Scotland may occasionally invite Ministers of other churches whose orders are in accordance with the standards of the Church of Scotland to administer the Sacraments. Any Minister whose invitation to a Minister of another church in terms of this section has been accepted shall intimate the same in writing to the Clerk of Presbytery within fourteen days thereafter.

The General Assembly (1954, Sess. I.) have approved of Regulations governing the powers and duties of Special Chaplains as follows :—

1. The Chaplains dealt with in this Report include all officiating Service Chaplains, School and Industrial Chaplains, Prison and Borstal Chaplains, as well as Hospital Chaplains.

2. Under Act VIII. of 1933 the Presbytery of the bounds may permit one minister to enter the parish of another for the discharge of such limited ministerial functions including the administration of the Sacraments as the Presbytery may specially authorise. A Chaplain's appointment, therefore, should have the authority or approval of the Presbytery concerned and likewise the general scope of the Chaplain's duties.

3. *Admission to the Sacrament of the Lord's Supper.*—When a person under the Chaplain's care expresses the desire to be admitted to full Communion by Profession of Faith, the Chaplain should communicate with the minister of the congregation with which such person is connected and make arrangements for such person to receive as far as possible a short course of instruction for first Communicants, and where knowledge and profession are deemed satisfactory, for him to be received by the Kirk Session into the full Communion of the Church. Where such person has no Church connection, the Kirk Session to be approached should be that of the parish in which such person normally resides.

4. *Administration of the Sacrament of Baptism.*—Normally it is inadvisable for a Chaplain to administer baptism in connection with the work of his Special Chaplaincy. But, where in urgent or special circumstances he finds it necessary to do so, he should send particulars of the baptism to the minister of the parish, if known, within whose bounds the parents, or baptised person if adult, resides ; or the minister of the congregation with which connection is claimed. In cases of difficulty the Chaplain should send particulars to the Clerk of the appropriate Presbytery, with the request that he forward these particulars to the Keeper of the appropriate Baptismal Register.

5. *Duties of Industrial Chaplains.*—The duties of an Industrial Chaplain lie normally within the establishment to which he is appointed.

A minister should not refuse to perform ministerial functions for a person resident in his parish without sufficient reason.

Minister and Professor. A minister appointed to a professorship ought to resign his charge immediately on taking up his new office.

Public Worship and Instruction of the Young.

Public Worship and Administration of Ordinances. "The ministry of the Word, the conduct of public worship, the dispensing of the Sacraments, and the instruction of the young belong to the minister, subject to the control and direction of the Presbytery." The preparation of first communicants is his duty (Oct. 1929, i.; 1931, xvii.). In these matters he is responsible to his Presbytery. **Innovations.** Forbidden changes of worship are specified in Act, 1866, vii., and they include whatever is "a cause of division" in the congregation (1867, 6, Crieff; 1907, 9, Elgin).

Public Worship not to be conducted by unauthorised. The persons who are authorised to conduct public worship are Ministers, Probationers, regular Students of Theology, Deaconesses licensed to preach, approved candidates for licence who are regular students for the Diaconate (1960, 8), and Readers. The employment of any other persons in the conduct of public worship is prohibited, but the prohibition does not apply to the employment by the Home Board, with the approval of the Presbytery, of any lay missionary or evangelist responsible to the Committee, where special circumstances might render such arrangement necessary, or to the visit of any agent of a Committee of the Church on the occasion of giving an account of the work of that Committee (1933, 9), or to an exchange ministry sanctioned by the Presbytery.

Unqualified Persons. Any Minister, Interim Moderator, or Session Clerk employing a person not qualified as above for the conduct of public worship is required to intimate this in writing to the Clerk of Presbytery within fourteen days thereafter, giving the name, address, and occupation of the person employed, and stating whether before engaging him he had applied to one of the authorised agents for supply of a qualified substitute, and the Clerk of Presbytery is required to report all such cases so intimated to him at the next ordinary meeting of Presbytery (1934, ix.).

Baptism.

Baptism—Infants. Act XVII., 1963, regulates the administration of Baptism to Infants as follows:—

1. Baptism may be administered to a child—

(1) whose parents, one or both, have themselves been baptized, are in full communion with the Church, and undertake the Christian upbringing of the child;

(2) whose parents, one or both, having been baptized but not in full communion, are such that the Kirk Session is satisfied that he or she is an adherent permanently connected with the congregation and supporting the work and worship of the Church and will undertake the Christian upbringing of the child ;[1]

(3) whose parents, one or both, have themselves been baptized, profess the Christian faith, undertake to ensure that such child grows up in the life and worship of the Church and express the desire to seek admission to full membership in the Church. In such cases the Kirk Session shall appoint the Elder of the District in which the parents reside, or some other person, to shepherd them into full communion and to exercise pastoral care of the child concerned ;

(4) who, being of unknown parentage, or otherwise separated from his or her parents, is in the view of the Kirk Session under Christian care and guardianship.

2. Baptism may be administered only by Ministers authorised by the General Assembly to dispense the Sacrament of the Lord's Supper.

3. Baptism may be administered only after the parents or guardians have received such instruction in its meaning as the minister shall deem necessary.

4. No Minister shall baptize a child resident outwith his own Parish, whose parents are not members or adherents of his congregation, without consent of the Minister of that Parish or of the Presbytery.

5. Without the consent of the Presbytery, no Minister may administer Baptism in a case where to his knowledge another Minister has declined to do so.

6. Baptism shall normally be administered at a diet of public worship of the congregation of which the parents or guardians are members or adherents, or of the congregation of the Parish in which they normally reside. In exceptional circumstances Baptism may be administered elsewhere (*e.g.*,

[1] The General Assembly have advised that baptism may be administered to the children of adherents whose absence from public worship is due to causes which make such attendance a practical impossibility. (Reports 1964, p. 36 (17 (2)).)

at home, in hospitals or institutions). In every case an entry shall be made in the Register of Baptism kept by the Kirk Session of the congregation of which the parents or guardians are members or adherents, or in that of the Parish in which they normally reside, as the case may be.

7. Baptism shall be administered in the Name of the Father and of the Son, and of the Holy Ghost, with water, by sprinkling, pouring, or immersion. Other elements may not be used.

8. In all cases a Certificate of Baptism shall be given by the Minister.

9. Nothing in this Act shall be taken to mean that the Church of Scotland rejects Baptism in the Name of the Father, and of the Son, and of the Holy Ghost duly administered in accordance with the law and discipline of other Churches.

10. Act IV. of 1712, Act XVII. of 1951 and Section (1) of Act XXI. of 1956 are hereby repealed.

A person obtaining baptism of a child should produce to the Minister a certificate of the registration of birth.

How? The Minister is to use such words of instruction respecting this sacrament and of exhortation to the parent or sponsor as shall be for edification, requiring his promise for the fulfilment of his duty, and, after prayer, is to call the child by his name (not including the surname), and say, "I baptise thee in the name of the Father, and of the Son, and of the Holy Ghost." This done, he is to give thanks and pray. There is no authority for requiring assent to any of the Creeds.

Baptism—Adults. Baptism may also be administered to adults upon their profession of faith in Christ and obedience to Him (C.F. xxvii., 4; Shorter Catechism, Q. 95). Every communicant should be baptised. The Sacrament of the Lord's Supper does not supersede or include that of Baptism.

Tinkers. Baptism of the children of tinkers in church at time of public worship is desirable. If baptism at time of service is not possible it should at least take place in church and by the parish Minister. (Reports 1967, p. 12.)

Change of Name. A name given in baptism within twelve months of birth different from the registered name may also be inserted in the Register of Corrections on a certificate by the Minister before the expiry of two years from the date of birth of the child. A form of certificate may be obtained from the Registrar.

Baptismal Register. A Register of Baptisms must be kept, showing the names of the baptised, the names and designations of their parents, and the date of baptism (1856, vii.; 1890, xii.; 1929, i.). The date of birth may also be included. The Register is generally kept by the Minister, but it is a Kirk Session record, and the Session is responsible (1931, xvii.).

SECTION II. THE MINISTER AND MARRIAGE.

Banns and Marriage.

(App. XVI.-XIX., pp. 618-633.)

For the Acts anent the Proclamation of Banns, and forms for use by applicants for Proclamation, &c. (1932, xvi. and 1942, vi.; 1957, i.; 1966, i.; 1968, ii.; 1971, i.; 1975, i.), see Appendices XVI. and XVII., pp. 618, 624. Banns and Marriage.

Proclamation.

Act XVI., 1932, which regulates Proclamation of Banns has been amended (Act I., 1971) by the substitution of the following for the first sentence :—

" Proclamation of Banns shall, in ordinary cases, be made on two separate Sundays, and, wherever it can be conveniently done, shall be made from the pulpit or reading-desk by the Minister or his officiating substitute acting on his authority, at some time before the close of the service at the principal diet of Public Worship."

The General Assembly (1933, 12) instructed a Presbytery " to make arrangements for the Proclamation of Banns under which any method of rotation in appointed churches shall be avoided." Churches in which Proclamation may be made.

By the Age of Marriage Act, 1929, a marriage between persons either of whom is under the age of sixteen is void. The Act does not prohibit the proclamation of the banns of marriage of persons while they are under that age, but unless care is taken to ascertain the age of persons who wish banns to be proclaimed for their marriage it may become possible for them to participate in a ceremony of marriage which would be void. The prudent course in these circumstances is for Ministers to decline to make proclamation until the applicant has attained the age of sixteen, or at least until such date that the applicant will have attained that age when the Certificate of Proclamation is given out. As it is not certain whether a person ceases to be Age Limitation.

"under the age of sixteen" on the morning of the sixteenth anniversary of the date of his or her birth, or at the hour on that date when the birth occured, it is recommended that the marriage should not take place earlier than the day after the sixteenth anniversary.

Who signs Proclamation Certificate?

The Certificate of Proclamation shall be signed by the Minister, Session Clerk (or other person duly authorised by the Kirk Session), only of the congregation where Proclamation is made (Act II., 1968). Such certificate is valid in the case of a marriage to be solemnised in England, when one of the parties resides in Scotland (Marriage Act, 1949).

(Such Proclamation Certificate is valid for only three months from date of issue.)

The charge for the Proclamation of Banns has been declared by the General Assembly (1975, i.) to be the sum of seventy-five pence.

Residence—in Scotland.

The residential qualification for proclamation may be either "usual residence" or residence of fifteen clear days "immediately preceding" the date of application for proclamation, in a registration district in one of whose Churches proclamation is to be made.

—Furth of Scotland.

It is desirable, though not always practicable, that a resident furth of Scotland should show that the conditions required in his or her place of residence have been complied with. Failing this, the minister must satisfy himself "on such evidence as he shall deem sufficient" that the non-resident person is free to marry and that there is no impediment.

—In England or Wales.

Where a party to a marriage intended to be celebrated or contracted in Scotland—and to whose intended marriage there is no impediment recognised by the law of the Church—is residing in England or Wales, but has a parent[1] who has his or her usual residence in a registration district in Scotland, the banns of marriage may be proclaimed in like manner as if such a party had himself or herself resided in the aforesaid district for a period of fifteen clear days immediately preceding the application for proclamation.

In the case of such party proclamation shall be made in a church appointed for the registration district in which the parent of such party has his or her usual residence, and the minister shall satisfy himself on such evidence as he shall

[1] For the purposes of this Act any reference to a parent of a party to an intended marriage includes a reference to an adoptive parent (as defined by Adoption Act, 1950, 14 Geo. 6, Cap. 26) and any spouse, widow or widower of a parent or adoptive parent of that party.

deem sufficient that there is no impediment to the intended marriage (1957, ii.).

Names. The name used in proclamation should be that which the person habitually uses and by which he is known. If it be not his original name, it should be followed by the words " formerly ." If the original name does not appear to be obsolete, let that be the name, followed by the words, " commonly called ." Titled persons are proclaimed by their names, but their title should be added as probably better known. A widow should bear her deceased husband's surname, followed by " maiden surname ." If either party should have divorced, or have been divorced by, the spouse of a previous marriage, this fact must be stated in the application and entered in the register, but does not require to be announced when the proclamation is made in Church. In that announcement the woman should be designated by the surname she has habitually used and signed and by which she has been commonly known since the divorce.

Proclamation of divorced person. Since proclamation does not imply approval it ought not to be refused because the applicant has been divorced or for any other similar reason.

Objections offered. **Objections should be disregarded which are not stated in writing and subscribed in presence of the Session Clerk or the Minister.**

Certificates of proclamation of banns and of publication of notice by a Registrar (Marriage Act, 1939, App. XVIII., p. 626). Any Minister celebrating a marriage without the certificate (or certificates) of proclamation of banns issued by a Minister or Session Clerk or other person authorised by the Kirk Session or of publication of notice by a Registrar is liable to penalty. The certificate may be of proclamation in the case of one party and of publication in the case of the other, but there must be a certificate or certificates applicable to both. If the parties have residential qualification in the same Registration District one certificate is sufficient. The action of a Registrar in supplying a Marriage Schedule does not affect the responsibility of the Minister to require production of these certificates. By the Marriage Act, 1939, it is provided that where one party is resident in England or Wales and the other in Scotland, if the marriage is to take place in Scotland, publication of notice with regard to the former party may be made at the appropriate Superintendent Registrar's Office in England or Wales. The Superintendent Registrar's certificate of publication is valid for marriage in Scotland along with a certificate of proclamation of banns or publication of notice in respect of the party resident in

Scotland. If the marriage is to take place in England or Wales the party resident in Scotland may have either proclamation of banns in an appointed church or publication of notice in the appropriate Registration District in Scotland. It is understood, however, that if the marriage is a Church of England marriage both parties must proceed by the same form of preliminaries—*i.e.*, banns in both cases or notice in both cases. It should be noted that these provisions apply only to the case where one of the parties is resident in England or Wales, and do not apply to the case of one resident elsewhere furth of Scotland. In the latter case there must still be proclamation of banns — except where otherwise provided under the Marriage of British Subjects (Facilities) Acts, 1915 and 1916, or the Naval Marriages Act, 1908 (which has been repealed so far as it relates to marriages solemnised in England).

Marriage.

Table of Kinship and Affinity.

By the Marriage (Enabling) Act, 1960, a valid marriage may be contracted between a man and a woman who is the sister, aunt or niece of a former wife of his (whether living or not), or was formerly the wife of his brother, uncle or nephew (whether living or not): the Act applies to the specified degrees of kinship of the half-blood also, but does not validate a marriage either party to which is at the time of the marriage domiciled in a country which does not recognise the validity of a marriage between the parties. It may be assumed that the Church will take no disciplinary action against persons contracting, or ministers officiating at, marriages above enumerated.

In accordance with civil law, a man may not marry his—

1. Grandmother,
2. Grandfather's widow,
3. Deceased wife's grandmother,
4. Father's sister,
5. Mother's sister,
6. Mother,
7. Father's widow,
8. Deceased wife's mother,
9. Daughter,
10. Deceased wife's daughter,
11. Son's widow,
12. Sister,
13. Son's daughter,
14. Daughter's daughter,

15. Son's son's widow,
16. Daughter's son's widow,
17. Deceased wife's son's daughter,
18. Deceased wife's daughter's daughter,
19. Brother's daughter,
20. Sister's daughter.

The Church has expressed its mind on the Re-Marriage of Divorced Persons in 1959, xxvi., as follows :— Divorced Persons.

1. A Minister of the Church of Scotland may lawfully solemnise the marriage of a person whose former marriage has been dissolved by divorce and whose former spouse is still alive, provided that the said Minister adhere to the requirements stated hereunder.

2. A Minister shall not accede as a matter of routine to a request for the solemnisation of marriage of persons whose marriage has been dissolved by decree of divorce as aforesaid.

3. A Minister invited to celebrate such a second marriage shall, in order to enable him to make his decision, take all reasonable steps to obtain relevant information which shall normally include the following :—

(*a*) adequate information concerning the life and character of the parties to be married ; here the very greatest caution shall be exercised in cases where, for any reason, no pastoral relationship exists between the minister and either or both of the parties concerned ;

(*b*) the grounds and circumstances of the divorce case ;

(*c*) facts bearing upon the future well-being of any children concerned ;

(*d*) whether any other Minister of religion has declined to solemnise the proposed marriage ;

(*e*) the denomination to which the parties belong ; special care shall be taken in cases where one or both parties belong to a denomination whose discipline in this matter may differ from the Church of Scotland.

4. A Minister shall also consider whether there is any danger of scandal arising if he solemnise the re-marriage ; at the same time he shall take into careful consideration, before refusing to solemnise the re-marriage, the moral and spiritual effect of his refusal on the parties seeking such a marriage.

5. As the determinative factor, a Minister shall do all he can to assure himself that by word and deed there has been sincere repentance where guilt has existed in the past on the part of

any divorced person seeking re-marriage. He shall also give the most careful instruction, where this is needed, in the nature and requirements of a Christian marriage.

6. A Minister shall not be required to solemnise a re-marriage against his conscience.

7. Every Presbytery shall appoint certain individuals (who need not be members of the Presbytery concerned) with one of whom Ministers in doubt as to the correct course of action may consult if they so desire ; in such cases the final decision must rest with the Minister who has been asked to officiate.

8. A Minister shall submit annually to the Presbytery a return of the number of divorced persons who have been parties to marriages solemnised by him by virtue of this Act. Such return shall contain no details beyond the number of such persons.

9. The admission to Communion of persons who have contracted marriage after divorce, and any other matters effecting pastoral care, shall remain the responsibility of the Minister and Kirk Session involved.

The Marriage (Scotland) Act, 1939 (App. XIX., p. 629).

The Marriage (Scotland) Act, 1939, which came into operation on 1st July 1940, made considerable changes on the Law of Marriage in Scotland. By this Act two kinds of marriage are regarded as regular. Marriage can no longer be constituted by a mere declaration by a man and woman that they then and there take each other for husband and wife, nor by a promise to marry followed by sexual intercourse on the faith of that promise. The Act, however, does not abolish the type of irregular marriage which may be constituted by cohabitation with habit and repute. For the registration of this form of marriage a Decree of Declarator of the Court of Session is required.

Marriage by a Minister of Religion.

Regular marriage may be constituted in either of the following ways :—

(*a*) By a service performed by a Minister of religion, as heretofore, after proclamation of banns in an appointed church or publication of notice by a registrar. The place, the hour, and the nature of the ceremony are not prescribed, and no fee for the ceremony is required. The parties obtain from the Registrar, on production of a certificate (or certificates) of Proclamation of Banns or of Publication of Notice, a copy of the Marriage Schedule (*C*), which, duly completed, is produced to the Minister at the marriage ceremony, and is signed by the parties, the Minister, and two witnesses, not under fourteen years of age, and is thereafter returned to the Registrar for registration.

Marriage by Ministers not of Church of Scotland.

Ministers of other denominations temporarily in charge of Church of Scotland congregations may perform marriages according to the forms of the Church of Scotland, provided their names have been intimated to the Registrar-General by the Presbytery Clerk as being authorised to do so (1963, 1).

Civil Marriage before a Registrar of Births, Deaths, and Marriages.

(*b*) In the office of a *duly authorised* Registrar of births, deaths, and marriages, after such previous notice as is required by the Marriage Notice (Scotland) Act, 1878.

Licence by Sheriff.

The Act makes no alteration on previous practice with regard to marriage by a Minister of religion. The Act however introduces a new provision in regard to the preliminaries to marriage. Its second section provides that when, on account of the illness of one of the parties, or other unforeseen and exceptional circumstances, there has been reasonable excuse for failure to have proclamation of banns or publication of notice accomplished before the date of the intended marriage, the parties may jointly apply to the Sheriff who has jurisdiction in the area, and he may grant a licence which shall have the same effect and force as a certificate of publication. The Sheriff must be satisfied that one of the parties had his or her usual residence in Scotland, or had lived in Scotland for fifteen days immediately preceding the application for licence, and that there is no legal impediment to the marriage. This licence does not exempt from the necessity of procuring the Marriage Schedule from the Registrar of the district in which the marriage is to take place. A marriage warranted by this licence may be performed either by a Minister of religion in any place, at any hour, or contracted in the office of an authorised Registrar during the hours of his attendance. The validity of such a licence, however, extends for only ten days following its issue, after which it becomes void. Accordingly, the parties ought to make every endeavour to have proclamation or publication effected in the ordinary manner. They should not assume that the Sheriff's licence will be granted except in an emergency, when illness or other unforeseen circumstances make the ordinary procedure impossible. This is the only licence with regard to marriage in Scotland, and there is no such thing as a "special licence".

The following paragraphs are, by kind permission of the Church of Scotland Publications Committee, taken from an article by the Rev. Dr A. P. Sym in the 'Church of Scotland Year-Book,' 1939, pp. 41, 42, 43-45 :—

Proclamation of Sailors and Soldiers.

"In accordance with the Naval Marriages Act, 1908, banns of marriage may be published on board a ship *at sea* of His Majesty's Navy, in respect of officers and men actually on the ship.

Marriage Law in England.

"Those who wish to be married in England according to the rites of the Church of England should apply for information to the clergyman of the parish in which they are to be married. Proclamation should be made on three separate Sundays. The law of England, however, provides regulations whereby marriages can be celebrated with equal facility in non-Anglican churches. It is often stated, but incorrectly, that it is simpler and more expeditious to be married in England in a church of the Church of England. It has to be remembered that marriage in private houses, halls, or hotels is forbidden in England. Marriage must be either a religious ceremony in a church or other place of worship registered for marriages, or a civil ceremony in a registrar's office" (or elsewhere on special licence from the Registrar General).

In a non-Anglican Church, marriage may be :

"(1) *By Certificate.* In this case notice must be given by *each* party to the Superintendent Registrar or the District Registrar of Births, Marriages, and Deaths of the registration district in England in which he or she lives. Before giving notice the party doing so must have lived seven days in the district. If both live in the same district, one notice is sufficient. Twenty-one clear days in addition must then elapse, after which the Superintendent Registrar issues a certificate, and the marriage may take place any time thereafter within three months in the nearest place of worship of his or her denomination to the district in which one or other of the parties resides. It is not essential that the place of worship should be within the registration district, provided that the registrar is duly informed of that place when notice is given to him. In respect of a party resident in Scotland the certificate of proclamation of banns may be signed either by the minister or by the session-clerk (Marriage Act, 1939).

(2) *By Licence.* One notice only is necessary in this case, and either party may give the notice. The residential qualification required is one of fifteen clear days on the part of the person giving the notice. The marriage may then take place after one *clear* day. The second party to the marriage must be in England before the beginning of that one clear day. A Licence is issued at the end of the day, and the marriage may take place under the same conditions as 'By Certificate,'

as explained above. In this case, proclamation in Scotland is of no avail. In both cases (1) and (2) the period 'within three months' runs from the day on which notice is given. Here is the guidance given by the Registrar-General: 'The Registrar-General is advised that the period during which a Certificate for marriage without Licence or a certificate and licence for marriage by Licence remain valid authorities for marriage includes the day of the third calendar month corresponding to the day of the month upon which the notice of the marriage was entered in the Marriage Notice Book.'

Timely notice of the marriage must also be given to the registrar of the district in which the marriage is to take place, as, in the majority of cases, he has to be present with his books.

Parties desiring to be married in one of the churches of the Church of Scotland in England should communicate with one of the ministers thereof, whose names and addresses may be found in the 'Church of Scotland Year-Book.'"

Marriage Law in Northern Ireland.

"If the marriage of a person resident in Scotland is to take place in Northern Ireland, either in a Presbyterian Church certified as such under the Irish Marriage Act, 1845, or in a church of the Church of Ireland, or is to be solemnised according to the rites of the Church of Rome, no proclamation need take place in Scotland. If the marriage is to be celebrated in a registered place of worship of any other denomination (except Jews or Society of Friends) or in the office of a civil registrar, proclamation of banns in Scotland is necessary. The Act of 1846 requires that the certificate, which must be signed by the *Minister*, shall state that proclamation has taken place on *three separate Sundays*. Not earlier than seven days from the *date of issue* of this certificate it must be produced to the registrar of the district in Northern Ireland within which the other contracting party resides, and within which the marriage is to be celebrated, before the registrar can issue a licence for the marriage."

In Eire (Irish Free State).

In Eire (Irish Free State) "the law is the same as that for Northern Ireland."

Marriages of British Subjects abroad and Marriage with Foreigner in Britain.

"Ministers are sometimes consulted about marriages of British subjects abroad and marriage with a foreigner in Britain, and whether or not they are asked to perform the ceremony, they cannot be too careful in giving advice. A summary of the law on the whole subject of this paragraph in the form of the white paper dated 2nd October 1936 has been issued, a copy of which may be obtained from the Registrar-General for Scotland. Here it may suffice to state that in Germany, Norway, Sweden, Switzerland, the United States of America, and Venezuela, marriages can be validly celebrated only according to the local law, while in other countries the Foreign Marriage Act, 1892, with Orders in Council, 1913 and 1925, is applicable only under certain conditions described in the said Memorandum.

Marriages in Scotland of foreigners or of foreigners with British subjects, are, if performed in accordance with the requirements of Scottish law, valid throughout His Majesty's dominions; but it is important that it should be clearly understood that such marriages will not necessarily be valid in the countries to which the foreigners belong, *unless the legal requirements of those countries are also complied with.* Marriages duly solemnised in this country have, in many instances, been declared to be invalid abroad, and the wives, British by origin, and the children, have consequently found themselves abandoned in a foreign country. Steps should therefore be taken, prior to the marriage, to obtain from the Consul or from the diplomatic representative of the foreign State in this country satisfactory assurances that the requirements of that State have been complied with. Special arrangements exist with regard to French and Belgian subjects.

Marriages of British women with Hindus, Moslems, Chinese, African negroes, &c., even if valid in Britain, are not necessarily valid abroad, and on no account whatever should a minister celebrate such without careful consultation of the Memorandum mentioned. In such cases also satisfactory assurances should be obtained prior to the marriage from the accredited representative of the country concerned.

In the case of anyone leaving Scotland with the intention of being married abroad under the provisions of the Foreign Marriage Act, proclamation of the marriage must be made in an appointed Church of Scotland in the registration district in which the person is resident, and a certificate thereof obtained before departure from Scotland."

For an exposition of the whole subject of marriage, see 'Marriage in Scotland,' by Dr Sym, issued by authority of the General Assembly, 1933 (Fifth Edition, 1949).

Admission to Marriage Service. The marriage service should be in church, when possible. Admission to the service may be open or may be restricted to invited guests. It is not a public service.

U.S.A. Forces (1955, 1).

U.S.A. Forces. (*a*) *American Air Force Personnel.*—The regulations applicable to such personnel require that application should be made to the appropriate Commanding Officer for permission to marry. On receipt of such an application, the Commanding Officer causes an examination to be made of the Serviceman's record. Inquiries will also normally be made by him as to the Serviceman's fiancée, if necessary through the appropriate British authority. The couple will also normally be invited to have an interview with the base Chaplain. This procedure requires about six weeks to complete, and, if the Commanding Officer gives his approval, that approval is then reported to American Air Force Headquarters in the United Kingdom for their confirmation. The confirmation having been obtained, the Serviceman is then given the original and one signed copy of the Commanding Officer's statement of approval, bearing the endorsement of Headquarters, and he is required to present these to the minister who is to perform the marriage. The original of the statement of approval should thereafter be endorsed by such minister to show that the marriage has taken place, and should then be returned to the Serviceman for attachment to his service record. The signed copy should be retained by the minister (or his Session Clerk) for record purposes.

An American Serviceman who marries without the necessary approval is liable to be court-martialled, and his spouse may, if the marriage takes place without such approval, suffer loss of allotments, insurance or other benefits authorised for the wives of American Service personnel.

A woman who marries an American Serviceman does not become a United States citizen merely by virtue of her marriage, but is exempted from immigration quotas, and is entitled to speedier naturalisation.

(*b*) *American Naval and Army Personnel.*—It is understood that provisions similar to those applicable to the American Air Force apply also to the American Navy and Army.

(*c*) *Other Questions of American Law.*—On any question of doubt as to American law, and in particular as to immigration and naturalisation, and also as to military law affecting the United States Forces, application should, if necessary, be made to the American Consul-General in Scotland, 3 Regent Terrace, Edinburgh.

(*d*) *Proclamation of Banns.*—No proclamation of banns should be made unless there is produced, along with the application for proclamation, the original statement of approval and signed copy referred to in (*a*), showing that the Serviceman has permission to marry. If application for proclamation be made and no such approval is produced, the minister or Session Clerk should refuse meantime to make the proclamation.

SECTION III. THE MINISTER AND CIVIL DUTIES.

Minister as Notary.

Minister acting as Notary in execution of Wills.

A minister may, as any other, write another person's will. It need not embody the writer's name. The names and designations of witnesses need not be embodied, if their designations be appended to their signatures (not necessarily by themselves) before it is recorded or founded on in any Court.

A minister may act as notary in signing a will. "A minister of the Church of Scotland who has been appointed to a charge without limit of time or for a period of years to officiate as minister shall, in any parish in which such charge or any part thereof is situated, have the like power as regards the notarial execution of wills or other testamentary writings as is conferred by subsection (1) of Section eighteen of the Conveyancing (Scotland) Act, 1924, on a parish minister acting in his own parish. A certificate by one of the principal clerks, or the principal clerk, if there shall be only one, of the General Assembly, stating the parish in which the charge of any such minister is situated, shall be accepted as conclusive evidence thereof . . . the expression 'minister' shall include an assistant and successor or a colleague and successor of such minister." (Church of Scotland (Property and Endowments) Amendment Act, 1933, Sect. 13.)

The following form of notarial docquet is prescribed in Schedule I. (Sect. 18) of the Conveyancing (Scotland) Act, 1924, where granter of deed or testator is blind or cannot write:—

Form of Docquet.

Read over to, and signed by me for, and by authority of, the above-named A. B. (without designation), who declares that he is blind (or is unable to write), all in his presence, and in presence of the witnesses hereto subscribing.

M. N., *Witness.* G. H., *Minister* [*or Assistant* (*or Colleague*) *and Successor* to the Minister, of the Parish of ——]

P. Q., *Witness.*

The witnesses to the minister's signature may be designed in the testing clause; "but, if there be no testing clause, the designations of the witnesses may be added after their respective signatures, and, if desired, a specification of the place and date of signing may be added to the docquet." The deed is first to be read over by the minister to the granter before two witnesses who shall also hear or see authority given by the granter to the minister to sign on his behalf. The minister shall then, in presence of the granter and of the said two witnesses, add his own signature to the docquet, *which must also be written by him.* The will need not be written by the minister himself, but he must sign it on each page, and the witnesses on the last.

A minister cannot act as trustee or executor, nor can he receive benefit, under a will authenticated by him acting as notary (Chisholm, 1903, 11 S.L.T. 416). Minister cannot benefit.

The following is the opinion of the late Sir J. Randall Philip, Q.C. :—

> The law is now settled (1) that, where a notary is appointed a trustee under a will, or takes benefit thereunder, that interest disqualifies him from acting as notary in relation to the execution of the will, and, if he so acts, the execution of the will is invalid. *Finlay* v. *Finlay's Trustees*, 1948 S.C. 16 ; *Gorrie's Trs.* v. *Stiven*, 1952 S.C. 1 ; (2) that, if the notarial execution of a will is to be regarded as valid, the completion of the docquet, together with the signatures of the notary and the two witnesses, must be made *unico contextu* in the presence of the granter : *Hynd's Trustee* v. *Hynd's Trustees*, 1955 S.C. (H.L.) 1 ; and (3) that these rules apply to qualified parish ministers as to other persons authorised by law to act as notaries in relation to the execution of a will.

Civil Judicatories.

Formerly, ministers of the Church of Scotland were forbidden, under pain of losing their benefices, to be members of any civil or criminal judicatory or of Parliament. (1638, 25 ; 1735, ult. ; P. 1584, c. 133.) Among offices mentioned in the Act by way of example is that of Justice of the Peace, but in recent years there have been numerous cases where ministers have become Justices of the Peace. In at least one case a minister became a Deputy Lieutenant. Since 1959, however, after Barrier Act procedure this disability has been removed (1959, xxvii.), and there is now no Church impediment to a minister becoming a member of any civil or criminal Judiciary, or sitting in Parliament. There is, however, still a civil prohibition against ministers becoming members of the House of Commons, but none with regard to the House of Lords.

All ministers are exempted from serving on juries (Jurors (Scotland) Act, 1825, section 2).

Civil Employment.

The General Assembly has enacted that no minister in a regular charge shall undertake any contract for remunerative employment either within or outwith the jurisdiction of the Church without previously having obtained the approval of the Presbytery of the bounds or of a higher Court of the Church (1950, xxii.).

In a case where the minister of a regular charge had accepted the office of Town Clerk and continued to hold the same in conjunction with his charge, the Presbytery enjoined him to resign the Town Clerkship. The General Assembly affirmed the judgment of the Presbytery (1942, 9).

The General Assembly enjoin Presbyteries to exercise the utmost care in dealing with applications from ministers for permission to undertake contracts for remunerative employment, to obtain the opinion of the Kirk Session concerned, to satisfy themselves as to the number of hours involved and the suitability of the proposed employment, and to secure that a Minister will be free at any hour when pastoral duties are required, and that he will have adequate time for the proper discharge of all his ministerial responsibilities, including visitation, study and preparation for the pulpit, oversight of congregational organisations, and attendance at Church Courts (1950, 11).

Section IV. Miscellaneous.

Ministers Employed by Committees.

Standing Committees shall include in their annual Reports to the General Assembly a list of the ministers and probationers employed in non-parochial work under their supervision, indicating the nature of their service.

The General Assembly have made the following Regulation anent Ministerial Appointments by Committees :—

> Where it is proposed that a full-time appointment by a Standing Committee be filled by a minister (except in the case of agents to be centred in a particular localised field) the Committee or Department concerned shall confer with the Advisory Board as to (1) the necessity for a new

appointment and whether it should be filled by a minister; (2) any changes in the conditions, duties, and responsibilities of the office in question which may be desirable; (3) in the case of a new office its conditions, duties and responsibilities, and its relation to existing offices. The proposal shall be submitted to the General Assembly or Commission of Assembly for their approval by the Committee or Department before an appointment is made (1963, Reg. 9).

It is to be understood that the *person* to be appointed to any such non-parochial Ministry as is thus approved or confirmed by the General Assembly would, as at present, be selected by the Committee concerned (1949, 3).

The General Assembly recommend that standing Committees should not appoint ministers to such offices as can be filled equally suitably by laymen or women (1950, 11).

The General Assembly resolve that the pension scheme for future appointments of Assembly-appointed Secretaries be in accordance with the Regulations for the Aged and Infirm Ministers' Fund and the Pension Fund, employing Committees being instructed to pay a stipulated percentage of the annual salary to the Fund. Employing Committees may, like congregations, make additional provision for such Secretaries on retirement. The present pension arrangements shall remain unchanged in respect of the present male Assembly-appointed Secretaries and of women Assembly-appointed Secretaries (1962, 11.).

The pension arrangements for Secretaries appointed before 1962 are contained in the Regulations of the United Free Church (U.F.C., Acts and Proceedings, 1904, p. 573).

Bankruptcy.

The Court allowed an annual payment of £80 to a minister's creditors out of an income of £273 as a condition of his obtaining a discharge from sequestration, but then he had been under sequestration for over five years, during which time he had paid his creditors out of his stipend dividends amounting to at least 5s. in the £ (Feb. 20, 1900, Evie and Rendall). In a case decided a few years before (Kingoldrum, Nov. 23, 1888), an assistant and successor, whose total emoluments were just over £100, was allowed the benefit of *cessio bonorum* on assigning £20 annually to his creditors. In both cases the Court proceeded on the principle that it was bound to leave an income to the minister sufficient to enable him to discharge properly the duties of his office.

CHAPTER V.

THE COURTS OF THE CHURCH.

MATTERS IN COMMON.

SECTION I.

(*a*) MEETINGS OF THE COURTS.

WITH the exception of certain emergent meetings referred to below, every court except the Kirk Session must (and, of course, the Kirk Session may), before its rising, determine the time and place of its next meeting, and intimate this publicly. The usual terms of the resolution are, *e.g.*, "The Presbytery adjourned to meet," &c. For the General Assembly this form is appropriate only in passing from one session to another; at the conclusion of the General Assembly the time and place fixed in the Act appointing next General Assembly are as stated for another Assembly, so that adjournment to meet beyond the concluding sederunt is not possible. Its form is, "The next General Assembly of this Church is appointed to be holden, etc." At this moment, therefore, every court above the Kirk Session is either actually met, or has on its records a resolution to meet, at a fixed time and place understood to be publicly known within its bounds. From Meeting to Meeting.

A special meeting of a court can be called only by its moderator, unless there be exceptional enactment to the contrary, as on pp. 150, 187, where the clerk may act, if the moderator cannot. Details are dealt with under the various courts (pp. 120, 148-150, 186-187). The clerk may call a meeting "by order of the moderator," but not unless the circular bear these words. Calling Meetings.

Practice has settled the quorum in the inferior courts at three. In the case of the Kirk Session it has been definitely fixed at three—the moderator and two elders (Oct. 1929, i.). In the Presbytery and Synod only one of the three may be an elder, and his name must have been previously enrolled (1934, xi.). In the General Assembly and the Commission the quorum is thirty-one, of whom not less than sixteen must be ministers (S.O., 25). Quorum.

After the hour appointed for the meeting, the first act, as soon as there is a quorum, is to constitute the meeting with First acts.

prayer, after which (1) the sederunt is taken, (2) commissions are called for, (3) a new moderator is appointed, when necessary, and (4) minutes are submitted for approval.

Attendance obligatory. It is the duty of members to attend the meetings of the courts, which have the right to enforce attendance (*e.g.*, Assembly, 1709, vii.; Synod, 1817, 7; Presbytery, 1706, 12). A member is not blameable for what is done in his absence (1813, ult.); but nothing relieves from the blame of absence except a sufficient preventing cause. The minute may be—

Minute.

> resolved to require, and hereby do require to attend in his place at a meeting [*specified*], and to give due attendance at the meetings of the [*court*] henceforth, and the clerk was instructed to send him an extract of this minute.

Contumacy. If he fail to attend, or to send a satisfactory explanation of the failure, he should be cited to show reason why he should not be held contumacious for disregard of the order. After three citations contumacy may be found and sentence given.

Postal Vote. In the event of a General Election being held during a General Assembly ministers, unable to vote in person by reason of their attendance at the General Assembly, may apply for the right to vote by post. (Registration Appeal Court 1955, *Craig* v. *Rev. D. C. Mitchell,* 1955 S.C. 399.)

Opening and Closing. A meeting of court must be opened and closed with prayer. The closing prayer has in general practice taken the form of the benediction.

"Alone." The Kirk Session is presumed to be a close court, unless when it resolves to be open, which there is never necessity it should do, and which its business rarely permits. Deacons, if any, should not meet with the Session, unless they be specially invited by the moderator for a particular occasion, and should withdraw after the transaction of the business in which they are concerned. The minute should make this clear. The Kirk Session must determine its action by the vote of its own members. The other courts are presumed to be open, unless when they resolve to be close; but in a few matters their course, one way or the other, is prescribed, as will afterwards appear. A court is alone, *inter alia,* for all dealings with conscience; respect must always be had to the edification of the Church; reputations, especially of ministers, must be carefully guarded. When parties are "removed" from the bar, it is at the discretion of the court whether or not they shall hear the deliberation on their case.

A court must meet within its own bounds, except with permission of a higher court (1811, 5), in craving which it states the reason. For example, a Presbytery may meet at the seat of the Synod in an interval of business by instruction of the Synod, all the members of Presbytery being assumed to be present in accordance with their duty. No court can sit when any court superior to it is sitting, without that superior court's leave, in craving which it states the reason; for members must be free to attend the higher court. This implies also that sufficient time must intervene to allow attendance at both. A Kirk Session relatively to the General Assembly has standing leave when none of its members are members of Assembly, but it should not meet without urgent cause (1890, xiii.). **In their own bounds. Superior prevents Inferior. Kirk Session during Assembly.**

(*b*) Moderators.

In every court one of the members acts as moderator. The moderator of Kirk Session is the minister of the parish or charge, or one of the ministers, where there is a colleague, and, failing him, one appointed by the Presbytery. A moderator of a Kirk Session, in view of his unavoidable absence from a meeting or meetings of the Kirk Session, may, however, appoint a minister of the Presbytery or any other minister of the Church to act as moderator at such meeting or meetings, but such appointment must be in writing, and must specify the meeting or meetings to which such appointment relates and the business to be transacted, and the facts must be recorded in the minutes of the Kirk Session (1933, x.). **Election.**

In the other courts it is now the invariable practice to appoint a minister as moderator. Every court above the Kirk Session elects its own moderator (2 B. Dis., vii., 4). It is incompetent for a court to come to any resolution which would interfere with free election. "The moderator of a Provincial Synod shall be chosen from among the ministerial members of the court by free election. He shall hold office for one year at least, and shall be eligible for re-election.[1] During his term of office he may be appointed to visit the various

[1] This also applies to election of Moderator of Presbytery (1944, xxi.), with the added proviso "on the recommendation of the Business or other Committee of Presbytery".

districts within the bounds of the Synod, with a view to giving advice or stimulating interest in the work of the Church" (1933, xvii.).

When Elected. A retiring moderator retains the office only till the meeting, being constituted, has ascertained its membership and elected his successor.

Powers and Duties. The moderator is responsible for calling, or declining to call, a meeting when occasion seems to require. If the clerk issue notices for a special meeting, it should be on the moderator's instructions, and this fact should appear on the notice. The circular customarily issued for a meeting to be held pursuant to adjournment is merely a reminder, the meeting having been already summoned at the close of the previous sederunt.

Ruling. It is the moderator's duty to cause good order to be kept, to rule on points of order, and to refuse to allow motions to be put to the meeting which are irrelevant or offensive or otherwise incompetent. "A chairman is bound to decline to put from the chair a motion or amendment which is out of order" (Palgrave). The moderator's ruling is equivalent to a resolution of the court, and may be dissented from, and otherwise treated as any decision of the court may be.

Signature. His signature as moderator is understood to mean that he signs for the court and by its authority.

His vote. It has been the uniform practice that a moderator has a casting vote only. This was affirmed of Kirk Sessions (1870, 14). He cannot move or second a motion. If he do not give his casting vote, the question remains undecided, and may be raised again in future. The exception to this rule is where the Interim Moderator is Convener of a Vacancy Committee. (See Ch. XII., p. 249.)

The same rules are followed in Committees, unless they be instructed to the contrary. "A Committee follows the example of the appointing body" (Palgrave). The Speaker of the House of Commons, and consequently the Chairman of its Committees, have a casting vote only. When a Kirk Session has only two elders, and they make counter motions, it would probably be held that their being unseconded would not render the moderator's casting vote incompetent.

Leaving the Chair. The moderator of a superior court leaves the chair when an inferior court of which he is a member is called to its bar. He may do so also (except in the Kirk Session) in order to speak on a subject before the court; but in this case it is his duty immediately after the vote has been taken on the motion to which he has spoken to resume the chair, and he cannot competently vote except in the chair, giving a casting vote (1895, 7, Cairston).

(c) CLERKS.

Every court must have a clerk. The appointment is not for life, unless it be so specified, and then only *ad vitam aut culpam*. The age-limit for the retirement of Assembly Clerks is seventy (1938, Reg. 1). In absence of other provision, the court must be presumed to pay its own clerk. In the practice of the Church, his receiving a salary is not incompatible with his being a member of the court. Every court is required by its superiors to have its records properly kept. **Appointment and Payment.**

The office may be held by one who is not a member of the court. The law and practice of the Church assume that the offices of moderator and clerk are held by different persons—as are like offices in all other courts in the kingdom. **Eligible.**

At his appointment the oath *de fideli* (p. 80) ought to be administered to him. It is never omitted by the Assembly even in a temporary appointment, nor should it be in the inferior courts. It is to be kept in view, for example, that documents attested by him are admissible as evidence. **Oath.**

The clerk is the custodier of the court records, but this does not imply that records past and present, or any of them, are to be kept in his dwelling, or where he pleases. The court must be satisfied. The responsibility, however, is his, if anyone gets access to them without the authority of the court, or if they have been tampered with. He is the only legal extractor from the records. A clerk should be very cautious in giving extracts without the authority of his court. **Custodier.** **Extractor.**

He is custodier for the court, which is entitled to take the books and to put them into other custody pending an inquiry into his neglect or misconduct relative to them alleged on probable grounds (C.S., *Porter* v. *Auld* (1850) 13 D., 268). Doubtless, the court has power, which, however, should be exercised with great caution, and under safe conditions, if it see fit, to allow its records to be borrowed for a short time (*e.g.*, for literary purposes), or to be examined, but on no account to be taken out of Scotland. A signed and dated receipt should always be required of the borrower, and kept *in retentis* till the books are returned. **Borrowing of Records.**

A minister may, with consent of the Kirk Session, himself keep the Baptismal and/or Communion Rolls, or a member **Minister's Custody.**

of Kirk Session may be appointed to keep them, in which case all responsibility for these books will pass from the clerk to the minister, or the member so appointed.

Inventory. At the appointment of clerk an inventory of the books and papers of the court should be recorded in the minute-book. A higher court should not attest the records of a lower unless this has been done.

Relation to Superior Courts. It is to the clerk that the superior court gives orders as to bringing up records for inspection, and it holds him answerable for neglect; but the orders are required to be laid before his court, and may also be sent to the moderator (1804, 5; 1827, 4).

Signature. If a clerk signing any letter or paper append his official designation, this is understood to give to the writing the authority of his court. He ought, therefore, to be very careful that the writing carries the authority of the court. The misuse of it might involve serious responsibility.

Leaving the Desk. The clerk of a superior court leaves his desk when an inferior court of which he is a member is at the bar, for in the eyes of the law he is there himself.

Oath de fideli.

The form used in administering the oath of office, or oath *de fideli administratione officii*, is: "I swear that I will be faithful to the duties of [*name the office*]."

(*d*) Church Court Records.

Safe Custody. In 1960 an Agreement was made with the Keeper of the Records of Scotland whereby the Church Records were transmitted to him from the Highland, Tolbooth-St John's Church on loan for an indefinite period, and are housed in H.M. General Register House, Edinburgh (1960, Reg. 1).

The Agreement provides, *inter alia*, that "the Church Records shall, in the same way as the public records, be open without restriction to the public for legal or historical research, but shall be examined only in the public Search Rooms under the supervision of the Record Office staff. Access shall be free of charge and the public shall be allowed to have a photostat or microfilm copies on payment of the usual fees. These facilities and restrictions shall apply equally to the representatives of the Church or the Church courts.

" Any volume or document forming part of the Church records shall be re-transmitted by the Keeper to the Church or the appropriate court of the Church only on application by the Principal or Depute Clerk of the General Assembly of the Church on the ground that re-transmission is necessary for the purposes of the Church or such court. A request by a Kirk Session, Deacons' Court or similar body for re-transmission of any such volume or document shall be made in the first place to the Presbytery which, if satisfied that the business of the Kirk Session, Deacons' Court or other body requires the production of such volume or document, shall request the Principal Clerk or Depute Clerk of the General Assembly to make such application. Any such volume or document so re-transmitted shall be returned to the Keeper as soon as may be after it has ceased to be required for the purpose for which it was re-transmitted.

" The General Assembly again enjoin that all Records of Synods, Presbyteries, and Kirk Sessions of date prior to 1900, including those containing entries partly subsequent to that year, be transmitted to the Principal Clerk at the Church Offices for purposes of record and for transmission to H.M. Register House (1969, 1)." Transmission Enjoined.

The only exception from this injunction which is permitted (1968, Reg. 1) is where the General Administration Committee is satisfied that other arrangements have been made for the safe custody of such records.

Church courts being established by law, and what are called courts of record, their records belong to and are held inalienably by the courts for the benefit of the public. That being so, the records are *extra commercium*, and cannot be alienated so as to become private property by sale or gift; and the right of recovery cannot be cut off by lapse of time (C.S., *Presbytery of Edinburgh* v. *University of Edinburgh*, 1890, 28 S.L.R. 567). Inalienable.

If in a civil or criminal trial the court should give an order for the production of Church records, it has to be said, without discussing the law of the matter, that such a service to justice is a proper use of them. Subpœnaed.

A Church court should keep, in its minute-book, an up-to-date inventory of its records and also of its property.

(*e*) Minutes.

While " minute " as well as " minutes " is used to designate the record of the whole business of a meeting, it is used also Minute.

for any one piece of business. The less elaboration in a minute the better.

Framing and approving. The minute is to be taken down in scroll (in ordinary writing, not in shorthand), to be afterwards written out properly. It may be read out either part by part as business proceeds or at the close, and signed by the moderator (1813, 4), but the time so taken up may be grudged where the court has much business. In any case, where an important contentious matter is before the court, the minute relative thereto should be carefully adjusted to its satisfaction before the close of the meeting, and signed by the moderator. At next meeting the first business, after receiving commissions and appointing a new moderator when this is required, is to submit the extended minute in order that, after correction if necessary, it may be approved and ordered to be engrossed. The court ought afterwards to see that this is properly done, and the minute signed. In the larger Presbyteries and Synods, and in the General Assembly, the minutes of a meeting are generally printed and circulated among the members before the following meeting. The only competent question, when a minute is submitted for approval, is whether it accurately states what was done. A minute cannot be altered after it has been approved. The resolution of a court at once becomes operative; it is not necessary to await the approval of the minute at a subsequent meeting.

Essentials. The minutes of a meeting must bear the place and date, the names of all members present, and that it was constituted and closed with prayer, and must (1583, 15, in Oct.) be attested by the signatures of the moderator and clerk. In the larger Presbyteries and Synods, instead of the names of those present being entered in the ordinary minute, a record of the attendances of members is kept in a sederunt book, in which case the latter really becomes part of the minute, and should always be open to the inspection of members.

Form.

Aberdeen, July , 19 .

Which place and date the Presbytery of —— met, pursuant to adjournment [*or*, at call of the Moderator], and was constituted with prayer.

Sederunt, &c.

The Minute of meeting held on —— was approved.

Or thus:

At Aberdeen, July , 19 .

The Presbytery of —— met pursuant to adjournment [*or*, at call of the Moderator], and was constituted with prayer.

"Minutes of Church courts shall be signed by the moderator who occupies the chair at the time when the minutes are submitted for approval. They shall also be authenticated by the signature of the clerk of the court. A similar rule shall be followed in the case of the Standing Committees of the General Assembly. The minutes shall be signed by the chairman and clerk of the meeting at which they are approved" (1931, xv.). If for any reason the moderator be unable to sign a minute, or if his signature cannot be obtained after it has been engrossed in the permanent record, the court may appoint another member to sign, and along with his signature there should be written, "by authority of the [*name the court*] given on [*date*]."

Who signs.

Power in Minuting.

A court is entitled to say what shall have a place in its records (subject to overruling by a higher court); and, if a motion be made which it is resolved not to record, no reference should be made to it.

Unseconded Motions.

Unseconded motions should not be recorded (Erskine May, p. 277).

Rules for Clerks.

Minutes must be correctly written without blottings or interlinings, and must have a marginal index of subjects for the sake of reference. If words be struck out, the number of them, or of the lines, must be noted on the margin and signed both by the moderator and clerk, with the statement that the deletion was by authority of the court; and words to be inserted are to be written on the margin and signed by the clerk (1706, ix.; 1874, xiv.). Clerical errors may be attested by the initials of the clerk (Oct. 1929, i.). Care must be taken to avoid everything that would permit doubt of the authenticity of the record. The pasting of papers on the pages is irregular and undesirable. Such blank spaces ought not to be left as would give opportunity for unauthorised insertions.

Deleting Minutes.

It was always held incompetent for a court to *delete* its records without the authority of a superior (*e.g.*, 1817, 7), except, perhaps, when a case against a member ended in his favour. But now even in this case deletion cannot be authorised, and it is now incompetent for any court to delete or give authority to delete. The view of the Assembly in the legislation which here follows was that no writings should be expunged. (For loose-leaf records see Reg. 4, 1964.) (See Appendix XXXVII., p. 825.)

(*f*) RECORD APART (*Oct.* 1929, i.).

"To keep the ordinary records of the courts, which have to

be consulted and inspected for various purposes, free from the presence of undesirable matter, and to obviate their mutilation by the deletion of the proceedings, the principle of a Record Apart shall be adopted in all cases where moral delinquency is alleged. As far as the cases which ordinarily come before Kirk Sessions are concerned, involving communicants or baptised persons who are adherents, the desired end may be achieved by the use of a Minute-Book of Discipline as mentioned in the procedure recommended below. In all other cases, such as processes against office-bearers, the court of first instance shall resolve from the first to keep the proceedings of the case in a Record Apart, and said resolution shall be minuted in the Record Apart, and not in the ordinary record."

"When the judgment which finally disposes of the case, by whatever court of the Church pronounced, involves any degree of censure of the accused, then the court of first instance shall engross in its ordinary minute-book the first minute of the Record Apart, the libel, or a summary of each of the charges thereof, if a libel was served, and the final judgment. When a case has ended in entire acquittal, if there be a Record Apart in any court inferior to the General Assembly, it shall, with all papers in the case, so far as these do not affect the interests of third parties, be sealed up in presence of that court, docqueted with the name of the congregation and the date of final judgment, and kept *in retentis* for five years and thereafter destroyed. When a process ends in entire acquittal, the person whose innocence has been proved ought to have a certified copy of the judgment of the court delivered to him."

"If a record be kept by the Kirk Session of all cases of discipline, it shall be in a book reserved for this purpose alone. The names, and all that might lead to the identification of the parties, shall be rendered illegible after five years. In such cases the Kirk Session shall not, unless requested by the person accused, be required to keep a Record Apart, but in the event of an appeal or dissent and complaint to any superior court other than the General Assembly, a Record Apart shall be kept by that superior court."

Inventory of Process.

"In every case the inferior courts must keep an Inventory of Process, in which the clerk must enter and number all the documents."

If, in proceedings under the Act anent Congregations in an Unsatisfactory State (1960, xxi.) the Presbytery finds that the state of the congregation is unsatisfactory and that endeavours to effect a remedy are unavailing or have failed, the Presbytery must record the report of the Special Committee and its own findings thereon, and certain subsequent findings in a Record Apart.

(*g*) Extracts.

Essentials.

"Extract" is frequently used as a form of, or at least as equivalent to, "Extracted." An extract minute must give, in the very words of the minute, (1) the dating and constituting of the meeting (which does not include the sederunt); then (2), introduced by the words *inter alia*, the passage wanted.

Form of Attestation.

It is attested thus:

Extracted from the records of , on this and [*if more than one page*] the *so many* preceding pages, *so many* words deleted and *so many* inserted, by me this 7th day of May 19 years.

——, *Clerk*.

It must be signed on every sheet, and should be signed on every page.

Extract ordered.

When there is attached to a resolution an instruction to the clerk to send or give an extract of it, this should form part of the extract.

In retentis.

Papers *in retentis* are given in the form of a copy (1783, ult.), and attested: "A true copy. ——, *Clerk*."

Obtaining Extracts.

Parties in a case are entitled to full, but not to partial, extracts (and copies of papers) of the proceedings (1783, ult.). The form of crave as minuted is, "took instruments and craved extracts" (p. 107). But the omission to make the crave at the decision of the case is no bar to receiving extracts.

Borrowing.

The court may direct the clerk as to what documents, not being an original libel or the Inventory of Process, may be borrowed by a party, and for what period; the borrower must write on the Inventory of Process a receipt for the document and the date before which it shall be returned (1889, xix.).

Access to Productions.

Persons accused have the right of access to any productions in the case which are in the possession of the court (Oct. 1929, i.).

Refusing Extracts.

It is incompetent for a court to give a pledge that documents shall not be used in a superior court, and it cannot refuse extracts on the ground of having given such a pledge (1845, 8). Extracts in a cause which had been disposed of some years before were refused (1808, 6).

Caution.

It may be assumed that a court may at any time give an extract judgment on sufficient cause shown; but caution should be exercised in matters affecting private interests. In an appeal, also, if a party should apply for extracts to a court inferior to the one appealed from, it would be a question whether or not to give them without an order from the court of appeal, because the court from which the extracts are craved would be thereby practically dragged (so far as the party could) into the position of a party or a witness, while there is no provision for its appearing in either capacity.

Immediate Extracts.

Parties are entitled to extracts immediately, if they call for them; and Presbyteries are recommended to order the minutes of every sederunt to be read in hearing of the court before it rises, and authenticated by the signature of the moderator (1813, 4). In the previous year complainers had been held entitled to the jottings of the Presbytery as the only way of substantiating their complaint (1812, 9). Minutes unsigned by the moderator are unauthenticated, and stand only for what they may be thought worth. Appellants are entitled to extracts from authentic records. When, therefore, extracts are craved, it is specially the duty of the court to see there and then that the minute is satisfactory, and is signed by the moderator.

Charge for Extracts.

A court, through its clerk, is entitled to charge for extracts before furnishing them.

SECTION II.

Subordination of Courts.

Rule and Exceptions.

The courts of the Church are four—viz., General Assembly, Synod, Presbytery, and Kirk Session; and each has authority over those below it, and may review and reverse their proceedings when regularly before it. There are a very few matters excepted, well defined in their character, or by express enactment—*e.g.*, where a court is trustee for money for the poor or for bursaries. A Kirk Session's decision is final on claims for enrolment as adherents, and no court can interfere with a Presbytery in the exercise of the *jus devolutum*. A Presbytery's judgment also is final in certain *quoad sacra* matters, for which see Chap. III., *D.*, p. 46. In all cases which may come before a Synod by dissent and complaint, or by appeal, the judgment of the Synod is final, unless it be a case involving doctrine, worship, or censure of a minister or other office-bearer (1933, xviii.), the licensing of students (1947, viii.), or union or readjustment or other change in the status of a congregation (1962, xv.). At the same time a superior court has the right to satisfy itself that a trust, regulation, or

Act is being properly administered by a lower court. In a case of appeal relative to the administration of Act 1932, xvi., anent Proclamation of Banns, the Presbytery contended that "it is the Presbytery alone, according to the Act, which has the right to say which church or churches shall proclaim banns in a registration district; and the Act does not give to a higher court the right to review the decisions of the Presbytery in that matter." This contention was repelled by the Assembly (1933, 12).

Every court has power to send forth visitors to see how all things are ruled within its bounds (2 B. Dis., vii.). **Sending Visitors.**

It is an essential part of the constitution of the Church that the orders of a superior court unappealed from must be obeyed by an inferior court; and ministers and elders individually come under solemn obligations to such obedience. Disregard of orders is, therefore, held to be a grave offence (1733, v.; Cairston, 1895, 7). *Res noviter* in a case after the superior court's order has been given may affect the final judgment given by the inferior, but will not justify its neglect of the order. **Inferior must obey.**

SECTION III.

From Inferior Court to Superior.

PROCEDURE.

There are five ways in which the proceedings of a court may come before its superior. They are: (*a*) the records of the court, which are brought up annually to its immediate superior for inspection and attestation, and may be ordered up at any time; (*b*) reference by the court itself; (*c*) dissent and complaint by a dissatisfied member; (*d*) appeal by a party at the bar; (*e*) petition, when the petitioner could not competently have taken either of the two last-named courses, or was obstructed in the attempt to do so. There is also provision, (*f*), whereby an inferior court may by overture invite a superior court to take initiative in any matter requiring legislative or executive action.

(*a*) Inspection of Records.

Every book, including the Benefice Register, hitherto enjoined to be kept by any court is by one Act or another expressly ordered to be revised and attested yearly by the next superior court. **What books.**

"A competent number of the most fit and experienced ministers for that work" are to be appointed to examine (1700, ix.). **Who examine.**

What inspected for.

Books are inspected in order to see—

(1) If there be "nothing to challenge," "nothing appearing censurable" in the actings of the court (1700)—*i.e.*, if the proceedings be "in conformity with the law and practice of the Church" (1874); but in a matter affecting a private party this does not warrant the revival of a question the decision of which has become final (*e.g.*, a Synod, 1811, 4).

(2) If the records be exact and well kept, free from blottings and interlinings, and with a marginal index of subject; and if insertions be attested on the margin by the clerk, and words struck out (the number of words or lines being stated) be attested by the moderator and the clerk as being by authority of the court (1706, ix.).

(3) If the minutes be signed both by the moderator and the clerk (1931, xv.).

(4) If the advices marked in former attestations have been observed (1700 with 1713 and 1874).

(5) If the court have been diligent in executing all the Acts and recommendations of the Assembly (1712).

(6) If, in the case of a Kirk Session, the inventory of Church property be revised yearly (1931, xiv.).

(7) In the case of Presbyteries, Synods must satisfy themselves that the visitation of congregations and the care of ecclesiastical properties are effectively carried out (1931, xii., 1961, xxi.).

Any member of the examining court who is not a member of the examined court may complain against its actings as disclosed by its records. The court in question is entitled to be heard by its representatives present. Directions given to it are embodied in the attestation. Anything material that is censurable is to be recorded as censured both in the attestation and in the books of the examining court.

Forms.

The following are suggested as forms of attestation, each of the entries being followed in a new line by the words—

Attested by order of [*name the court*].

——, *Clerk*.

Satisfactory.

(*a*) These records, along with [*insert what other books*], have been examined from the date of last attestation and found satisfactory.

Faulty.

(*b*) *If there be fault*, after "satisfactory" insert "with the following exception [*or*, exceptions] ."

(*c*) *If aught be censurable,* after "satisfactory" insert "with the following exception [*or,* exceptions], which the [*name the court*] finds to be censurable ." Censurable.

(*d*) *If there be both faulty and censurable matter*, let the one follow the other in the statement of exceptions. Both.

(*e*) *If an instruction is to be given,* after the statement of the exceptions insert " and the [*name the erring court*] was instructed ." Instructions.

If anything implying censure is to be recorded, the erring court should be heard; and this may be minuted by inserting after the word "exception," "on which the members of the [*name the court*] were heard ." The erring heard.

It may be advisable for the examining court, after (or without) recording its strictures in the book, to send it without attestation to be corrected so far as this is practicable, and brought up again at next meeting. Graver fault.

Sufficient space must be left after the last *signed* minute in the Record for the attestation. Space for attestation.

If the sending up of records be neglected, it is the clerk that the superior court orders and holds answerable, but he is required to lay the order before his court, and it may be sent direct to the moderator also (1804, 5; 1827, 4). Unpresented.

(*b*) References.

Reference of any matter to the next superior court is made by a resolution of the court referring. The Kirk Session is required to refer to the Presbytery certain offences of the graver sort (p. 324). Any inferior court may take the same course in any matter, but only on sufficient cause; for generally the course is regarded with disfavour, as being an evasion of responsibility.

An extract of the minute embodying the resolution to refer is transmitted to the higher court with relative papers. If there be parties, they must be cited (1832, 6). If they be present when the resolution is come to, the citation may be *apud acta;* but acquiescence in the resolution will be sufficient. Members of the referring court retain their status as judges in the other. One who is a member of both courts may "state the reference" in his place in the superior; or, if the inferior court appoint for the purpose one of its members who is not a member of the superior, he speaks at the bar. His appointment, should he fail to appear, is no obstacle to the other course. The statement should show what the case is, and why it Procedure. Parties. The Referring Court—Not at Bar. Stating the case.

The Court referred to. is referred. Then the first question for the court referred to is, Shall the reference be sustained? If not, the whole goes back as it came; but, if it be sustained, the court enters on the case. In procedure the practice of the Assembly should be followed by the lower courts as far as possible (see S.O., 79). It may be that the resolution to "refer" has been complained or appealed against. If so, this must first be disposed of, and the disposing of it will involve the decision of the question of sustaining the reference.

Assembly. Where the matter of a reference has previously been under consideration of the Assembly, the reference shall state the date when the matter was previously before the Assembly, and shall narrate the Assembly's Deliverance thereon (S.O. 54).

Rejected. The Assembly rejected a reference from a Presbytery made on 7th March, because, a meeting of Synod in April having intervened, it ought to have been made to the Synod (1821, 6).

Irregular, but taken up. An exception was made to this rule, but not unanimously, in the particular circumstances of the Dunkeld Cathedral case, principally because it would come to the Assembly for final determination (1902, 4). In another case the Assembly "found that no sufficient ground has been stated for referring the cause, and that the Presbytery ought to have addressed themselves to the adjudication of the same"; but, considering the hardship of delay to parties, they proceeded with the case (1861, 4).

Rejected. A case from the Presbytery of Aberdeen (1891, 3) regarding the competency of proceeding to libel for acts of immorality committed before licence was rejected, partly on the ground of vagueness, and partly because of the unfairness of deciding a point of law in a proceeding in which the accused was not, and could not be, represented.

Minute in Higher Court. The minute of the higher court may be—

The [*Synod*] had transmitted to it a reference from the [*Presbytery*] of in regard to [*indicate the case briefly*].

Parties were called, when there appeared, &c. The reference was stated by .

It was moved and seconded—Sustain [*or*, Dismiss] the reference. [*If it be sustained, the court proceeds to the merits.*]

In Presbytery from Kirk Session. When a reference from a Kirk Session is in obedience to F.P., vi., there is no need to say "sustain the reference." The minute may run: "A reference under Form of Process,

Chap. VI., from the Kirk Session of was submitted by , who stated the reference." Then follows the Presbytery's action.

(*c*) Dissents and Complaints; (*d*) Appeals.

It is not competent in any court in the kingdom for a member of the court to appeal from its judgment, or for a party at the bar to dissent; but a member may dissent, and, in Church courts, may complain to a higher court, and a party at the bar may appeal. These principles are closely adhered to in the practice of the Church. An attempt to introduce an exception to the right of appeal failed (1902, 3, Primmer).

Essential nomenclature.

The member says, *I dissent and complain;* the party at the bar, *I appeal.* The member's document which brings up the case is a *Dissent and Complaint*; the party's an *Appeal.* The two documents are distinguished only by this nomenclature; but so important is this that either writing is incompetent and null for a person who ought to have used the other (1738, ult., Angus; 1812, 9, Meigle; 1827, 6, Macgillivray; 1838, 8, Strathbogie). The law and practice regarding them are the same (1889, xix.; 1907, 13, Primmer).

Obstruction.

There is no other course competent for either, unless he be obstructed in this one. In that case, but not otherwise, he may resort to petition. Obstruction is forbidden (1889, xix.).

The document. Leave.

A dissent and complaint or an appeal must be *a subscribed writing containing its reasons.* It must either be tabled on the spot, or the member must say, *I dissent and protest for leave to complain;* and the party, *I protest for leave to appeal.* This *protest for leave* was expressly provided (1648, 30; 1694, viii.), and has been declared to be for the purpose of meeting the usual case of unpreparedness to give in the writing on the spot (1889, xix.). While the leave lasts, it may be sent to the clerk or to the moderator. The leave cannot be refused when protested for; it expires when the tenth day expires (not including the day of the decision), and it cannot be extended (1694, viii.).

Misconceptions.

It is a misconception to regard the protest for leave as if it were (or were equivalent to) the complaint or appeal itself; or as if it could be refused; or as if it were a request for leave to appeal at all, whereas it is a request not to be forced to do it on the spot. It is indefensible to exact, or even to receive, a promise that the document itself or the portion of it which consists of the reasons shall be afterwards given in.

With-drawing. An appellant or complainer may withdraw his appeal or complaint at any time; and, when he has formed the intention of withdrawing, he ought to do it without delay.

"Instruments." The complainer or appellant "takes instruments, and craves extracts," and is entitled at any stage of a case to complete, but not to partial, extracts relative to the cause (p. 85). Omission to crave extracts will not disentitle to them.

Intermediate appeals. A complaint or appeal may be taken during the proceedings against any decision come to, or may be deferred till judgment is given on the merits (p. 96).

Minute. The entire minute is—

So-and-so protested for leave to appeal [*or*, dissented, and protested for leave to complain] to [name the court], took instruments, and craved extracts.

The clerk. When the subscribed writing containing its reasons is received by the clerk of the court whose proceedings are objected to, he should write upon it to the following effect:—

Received by me [*or*, at my house] on [*date*].

——, *Presb. Clk.*

In the rare (but, when possible, desirable) event of the document being given in on the spot, say—

A. B. protested and gave in his written appeal bearing the reasons thereof and subscribed [*or*, dissented and protested, and gave in his dissent and complaint, &c.], took instruments, and craved extracts. It was ordered to be kept *in retentis*.

Engrossing. A mere dissent with its reason may be engrossed under certain conditions (p. 106). But in a dissent and complaint or an appeal the engrossing of the judgment of the higher court serves all the proper ends of a record. To engross the complaint or appeal would lead to engrossing the discussion of the case.

Not lodged. If the document be not lodged within ten days, the fact is recorded, and the court acts as if it had never been mentioned. *E.g.*—

Minute. The clerk stated that he had not received from the [appeal] for which he took leave on [*date*]. *There may be occasion to add,* Whereupon the [*court*], proceeding upon their resolution of that date, &c.

If the business was from a lower court, that court will have to wait till the next meeting of its superior to see whether the appeal has been lodged (if only leave to lodge it was taken).

If the lower court is not then present to attend to its interests, the higher ought not to report to it that no appeal has been lodged, unless it should see cause to give some order.

Subscribers.

If it be the document of a class of people, the general designation (*e.g.*, parishioners, members, &c.) is best given at the beginning, and the individual designation at the signature. There is no need to mention the particular meeting of the appeal court; it must be the first, unless that is within ten days (p. 94), in which case it may be skipped, though it need not be.

Form.

I, the undersigned, appeal to [*name the court*] against a deliverance of [*name the court*] given on *such a date* regarding [*just enough to identify the matter*] for the following reasons: . . . [*Signature and designation*]. See *infra*.

No hindrances.

The absence of a counter motion does not make dissent and complaint incompetent. It is no doubt usual that reasons which result in a complaint have first led to a motion, but such reasons may arise too late for a motion; and, in any case, the Church makes no such bar to the right of complaint.

Explanatory.

The law and practice for a dissent and complaint being the same as for an appeal, it will be convenient in what follows to speak only of an appeal. The complainer will substitute the nomenclature applicable to himself.

On borrowing documents, see pp. 79, 85.

The following numbered paragraphs are relative and important sections of Act of Assembly on Forms and Procedure in Trials by Libel and in Causes generally (1889, xix.).

Appeal contents.

"5. An appeal need not contain such words as, 'for these and other reasons to be stated,' &c., but this shall be implied; and it shall not contain any crave, under penalty of being regarded as a petition, and dismissed as incompetent. Appellants are hereby charged to state their reasons with the utmost brevity, and to state only such as they deem of real importance.

Obstructing.

"6. It is hereby declared to be the law of the Church (1) that a dissent and complaint by a member of court is, *mutatis mutandis*, subject to all the rules applicable to an appeal by a party, and to no other; (2) that it is incompetent for any inferior court to refuse or obstruct an appeal against any of its judgments whatsoever." [*Note* 1.—This includes judgments even in matters which cannot themselves be competently dealt with by a superior court (p. 86). In such a case the court appealed from may consider itself bound to proceed on the assumption that execution of its sentence is not sisted. Before this is done it should be very clear that there was nothing in the subject-matter, or the procedure, or the judgment which justified the appeal. Appeals that are evidently frivolous may be regarded after the same manner, the court bearing in mind that only the court of appeal can dispose of them, and accepting the risk of what that court may say. *Note* 2.—While the enactment includes all judgments, it does not commit itself to all kinds of appeals. Every court is entitled to protect itself from evident insolence and contumacy, and outside parties from unnecessary injury, and may refuse to receive any document that involves such offences.] "(3) that the protest for leave to appeal is for securing the privilege during ten days, in case of present unpreparedness to give in (what alone is valid) the appeal written with the reasons thereof and subscribed; (4) that appeals shall be to the next superior court, not later than the first meeting thereof which is ten free days after the judgment in question; but if the appeal is to the Assembly, there is no such condition of time; and appeals which would have been to a meeting of Synod shall be to the Assembly if it meet earlier." [*Note.*—If the meeting of the court of appeal here prescribed should occur before the inferior court has concluded the case, does this enactment require appeals already taken in the course of procedure to be brought up? By the next section of this Act it is not necessary to take an appeal against any prior deliverance till the end. It would doubtless, therefore, be held that, if taken, it need not be brought up till the end. The other course, however, is open, and might at times be useful.] "(5) that in an appeal no document shall be read, or shall appear among the papers of the court (printed or written), unless it was before the court of first instance, or was offered to it and rejected, and has thence come up regularly; and no person shall be allowed at the bar unless he was at the bar of the court of first instance, or applied to be so and was refused, and has thence come up regularly, or unless he is a member of the next inferior court, complaining in the regular manner; (6) that written answers to appeals are not required."

A Court protects itself.

Leave.

What Higher Court.

What stage.

Documents.

Parties.

Answers.

Intermediate appeals.

"7. It shall not be necessary in any cause to take an appeal in any matter of incidental procedure, but an appeal on any part of the merits shall entitle any of the parties to bring up for review any prior relative deliverances given by the same court; but such prior deliverances shall in other respects be brought up according to the ordinary rules, by an appeal in writing with the reasons, and given in within the ten days claimed for giving in the appeal on the merits to which they relate."

[*Note.* 1.—With the first half of this section compare what is said under "Irregularities, Untimeous objection," p. 113. The appeal court will when necessary decide whether that or the foregoing shall rule. *Note* 2.—The form of an appeal under the provisions of this section would commence with the ordinary form (p. 93) relative to the principal judgment on the merits, and would state the general reason for that appeal, and thereafter proceed: "And further because of the following deliverances against which I also hereby appeal—viz., 1. The deliverance given on [*date, beginning with the earliest, and indicating the deliverance*] because [*give the reason or reasons*]; 2. The deliverance given on (*&c., as before*)."] Form.

"8. In cases of discipline a court appealed from may resolve, either *ex proprio motu* or on the application of a party, to transmit the Record Apart, if any, to the clerk of the court appealed to, and parties shall be informed of such resolution. All productions shall in every case be so transmitted and also the Inventory of Process. The provisions of this section shall not interfere with the right of any party to obtain on timely application extracts of the record or of any of the productions in accordance with present practice." [*Note.*—The first sentence deals with Records Apart (p. 83). The provision removes the necessity of copying or extracting it, and is practicable because the record is not in the minute-book. The second sentence deals with productions, and requires that in all cases the originals shall be transmitted. Both the Record Apart and originals can be sent only from clerk to clerk. "Process" consists of all documents and articles lodged. It will be safe for an appellant craving extracts to crave the court or clerk to transmit the Process, and to obtain satisfaction that this has been done, for it still rests with him (as laid down in the Kirkintilloch case, 1895, 8) to see that everything necessary is sent up.] Papers to Higher Court. [See p. 83.] [See p. 85.] Who sees to papers.

For time of lodging appeals, &c., coming before the Assembly, see S.O. 52, App., p. 587. Time of lodging.

"9. If a case has been printed for the Synod in a manner uniform with prints of cases for the Assembly, then in an appeal from the Synod a printed copy shall be held equivalent to the extracts or certified copies now in use, if it be attested by the Synod Clerk at the conclusion of the print in such terms as, 'This print of [135] pages is a copy of the case as it was laid before the Synod of .' But all productions in cases of discipline shall nevertheless be passed on to the General Assembly in accordance with the foregoing Synod printing.

section. A Synod may pass a Standing Order requiring certain cases to be printed for it, and giving such directions thereanent as shall seem good." [*Note.*—When a case for the Synod is to be printed locally the Clerks of General Assembly will direct as to the form and number of copies required, so that if appeal be taken to the Assembly the copies may be printed and sent with the MS. Minute of Synod to the Assembly's printer.]

Sisting. An appeal against a decision on part of a case or on a point of procedure does not sist procedure, unless it be expressly ordered otherwise. If no appeal be taken against the final judgment, all appeals taken previously fall.

An appeal sists execution of the sentence till it is disposed of, or becomes null because of not being prosecuted (1707, xi.); sentence is resolved on, recorded and intimated, and an appeal then taken sists its execution. In discipline when, for example, charges against a minister, which infer deposition, are found proven, the record ought to proceed to this effect :—

Minute. It was moved, seconded, and agreed that in respect of the charges found proven against him, Mr A. M. be now deposed from the office of the holy ministry. Parties were called in and judgment was intimated.

An appeal at this point sists execution of that sentence. If none be taken, the Presbytery will proceed to depose.

An error. "Sist procedure" must not be confused with "sist execution of sentence," as it was in the following cases, thereby causing much needless delay and trouble. When the Presbytery found the charges proven an appeal was taken, and the Presbytery mistakenly sisted procedure. The Synod also found the charges proven; but shrewdly no appeal was taken and so the case went back for judgment. When judgment was given, an appeal was taken. Meantime, the Assembly had passed by, and so a whole year was lost. (It may be added that the Presbytery, supported by the Synod, took upon it to refuse to receive this appeal. The Assembly (1892, 2) declared this to be "contrary to the law and practice of the Church," and "set aside as *funditus* null and inept" the whole subsequent procedure.) An earlier case (1875) is equally instructive. A Presbytery rejected the plea of insanity put in to bar the trial of a minister. This decision was appealed against, and no further part was taken by or for the accused. The Presbytery went on and found the libel proven, but mistakenly went no further. The appeal on insanity was the

Instances.

only part of the case which could come before the Assembly in ordinary course. The Presbytery therefore required to petition the Assembly to dispose of the case. The Assembly dismissed the appeal on insanity, and, in response to the petition, proceeded on the Presbytery's finding of proven, and pronounced sentence of deposition. The proper and regular course was for the Presbytery itself to have proceeded on its own finding and given sentence, and stopped there. If such a sentence were appealed against, this would bring the whole case before the Assembly. If not appealed against, it would be final as soon as the appeal on insanity was dismissed; protestation to that effect would be taken; and the solemnity of pronouncing sentence on the accused would then immediately take place.

Redress of the error.

If a Presbytery, notwithstanding the law above explained, have failed to go on and give sentence, and the accused do not appeal, or do not prosecute his appeal, it will have to trouble the Assembly with a petition to take up and dispose of the case; whereupon the Assembly will have to see that the petition is intimated, and so on—trouble begot by the procedure of the Presbytery. This course had to be taken in 1836, 1850, 1856, 1874.

A vacancy

Proceedings for filling a vacant charge go on to, but do not include, the fixing of a day for the admission (1732, v.; &c.).

Exception: doctrine.

When a libel is for doctrinal error an appeal against a judgment on relevancy sists procedure (1835, xi.; 1851, ix.).

Apparent exception: worship.

The Declaratory Act anent Changes in the Forms of Worship (1866, vii.) enjoins all to obey the orders of the Presbytery as to the performance of public worship and the administration of ordinances, "so long and in so far as the same remain unreversed and unvaried by the superior courts." Thus an appeal against an order of the Presbytery on these particular matters does not sist its execution. This is not an exception, but arises from the fact that the Presbytery is itself the party responsible for the worship—as the Act declares in accordance with P. 1592; and the ordinary rule operates on a judgment by the Synod, and sists its execution, if appealed against.

Appellant's absence.

An appeal not prosecuted at the prescribed time (p. 91) is held as fallen from (F.P., v. 1). It is proper, however, that protestation should be taken in the higher court that this is so (p. 99). Failure of an appellant to appear at the bar at the hour of cause is held to be desertion of the appeal (1743, ult.; &c.). But, with consent of parties, on a medical certificate and a minute by counsel for the appellant (Dr

Robert Lee) the Assembly (1867, 10) superseded consideration of the appeals, and left them for the consideration of next Assembly.

Appellant's death.

A minister died pending his appeal against deposition. His representatives were held entitled to insist in it. Sentence was reversed, and he was declared to have been minister of the parish at the time of his death (Com., Mar. 10, 1731).

Withdrawn at bar.

Should the appellant withdraw his appeal at the bar of the appeal court, the case will "take end," the other side, if it see cause, taking protestation before the court rises that the appeal is fallen from and that the judgment appealed against has become final (1902, 8, and ult.).

Parties at bar.

An appeal sists the court appealed from at the bar of the superior court; and any party, but not a court, who acquiesced in the judgment may also appear in defence of it. But the superior court may limit the number of those who speak either for or against (1824, 5; S.O., 72-77). Every party and all the members of the court appealed from are legally at the bar. Besides corresponding members from another Synod whose commissions have been sustained, these include all ministers admitted and all elders whose commissions to the inferior court had been sustained before it pronounced judgment. If the moderator or clerk of the appeal court be one of them he cannot act in that capacity because he is at the bar. Even if he should not be one of them, but only a commissioner to the Assembly from their court, it is seemly and customary that he should leave his chair of office. Elders of Kirk Sessions within the bounds, but not on the roll, of the Presbytery (or Synod) are not parties; and if, as often happens in the General Assembly, they are commissioners from another Presbytery, they are not precluded from deliberating and voting as members of the superior court to which appeal has been taken. Parties are sisted, arranged, and heard in the inferior courts as nearly as may be in accordance with the Standing Orders of the Assembly (App., p. 581).

In Higher Court.

When an appeal, which would be dismissed as incompetently or irregularly taken, is from a Kirk Session in such a cause as must always be finally determined by the Presbytery, this court may pass on to the merits without insisting on the *bene* or *male appellatum* (F.P., v. 2). With consent of parties this course may at times be followed with advantage in other circumstances and in other courts. An appeal cannot be dismissed on the ground of incompetency without the appellant being heard on that point (1897, 14, Primmer).

An appeal may be *sustained* either on account of irregularity of the procedure or the incompetency of the censure; and then, if further proceedings be necessary, the case is remitted to the proper court with particular instructions, or with the general instruction to proceed according to the laws of the Church, or with both. Care is to be taken that, while justice is done, the authority of the inferior courts is not weakened (F.P., v. 7). If the appeal be *dismissed* and further proceedings be necessary, the case is remitted to the proper court; but when all that remains to be done is to determine and pronounce judgment, this is done by the Assembly; or the Assembly may instruct the inferior court what sentence it shall pronounce in certain contingencies (Edward Irving, 1832, ult.; Kilmun, 1897, 12). **Appeal Court's decision.**

When an appeal or complaint is not proceeded with, it is proper that some member of the court appealed from, or a party, should take protestation in the appeal court that it is fallen from and that the decision of the inferior court has become final, taking instruments and craving extracts. **Protestation.**

I, , [*if authorised to act for a court, say,* for] hereby take protestation that *such and such* an appeal against *such and such* a judgment has been fallen from, and that said judgment has become final; and I take instruments and crave extracts. [*Signature*]. **Form.**

Protestation was taken by that *such and such* an appeal against *such and such* a judgment has been fallen from, and that said judgment has become final. **Minute.**

A protestation was presented that a Committee appointed by the preceding Assembly to answer Reasons of Dissent against a deliverance of that Assembly had given no answer; but it was held irregular and was disallowed (1883, ult.). **Irregular protestation.**

If a member be aggrieved by the decision of a congregational meeting, his remedy lies not in dissent and complaint. He must petition the Kirk Session or a superior court to intervene (see also Chap. II., p. 22). Where the Model Deed (1965) is in operation the procedure to be followed is set out in Article 19. **Remedy against decision of a congregational meeting.**

(*e*) Petitions.

It is not the proper use of petition to bring the proceedings of a subordinate court under review of its superior. In this it is severely restricted to such cases as when persons entitled **This use restricted.**

to have come by appeal or complaint have been obstructed in that course by the inferior court; or when persons could not have come by appeal or complaint (Auchtergaven, 1870, 14); or when a court in the conduct of a case finds itself in a position from which it can be extricated only by petitioning the higher court to take a specified step (p. 97).

Ordinary use. The ordinary use of petition is to initiate business in the court of first instance—the business generally concerning only the affairs of the petitioners. The General Assembly are in not a few things the court of first instance, as when the minister of another Church seeks admission; or when a court desires a change of its bounds, &c. But there are also matters of general interest within the bounds of a court, and competent for it, which may with propriety be brought up by petition from persons who—however suitable the subject is for overture—are not entitled to overture, and can only petition at the bar. The Assembly have, for example, frequently received a petition or "memorial" from an association. They rejected, however, a widely signed petition relating to alleged images at St Giles' Church because it disclosed matter for libel without reason for the ordinary course not having been taken (1889, 2).

Note.—If, *e.g.*, the Presbytery be the Court of first instance in a particular case, it is not necessary that the petition be transmitted through the Kirk Session.

In 1897 a "memorial from Dunfermline Protestant Defence Association" signed by its president and secretary, also a "Resolution from citizens of Dunfermline" at a public meeting, signed by its chairman, craved the Presbytery to deal with the ministers of the Abbey parish for permitting "a small excursionist band of ministers" to have in their church a performance called an "office" after a popish fashion. The Presbytery dismissed those documents. The Synod refused to hear the appellant (Mr Primmer). The Assembly disapproved of that; but found that "the deliverance of the Presbytery may be supported on the ground that the complaints were not at the instance of responsible individuals, but in name of a voluntary association and of a public meeting."

Hearing is not receiving. A petition must first (1) be *read*, or held as read. Then (2) the question is whether to *receive* it; and next (3) what shall be *the answer* to its prayer. The argument has been heard that it is unreasonable not to receive the petition of any petitioner within the bounds. This is to confound *reading* with *receiving*. It would be unreasonable not to read so much as will at least show its subject or its character. Either of these may be such, by reason of incompetency or impropriety, that the court immediately on the discovery decides not to receive it; but ordinarily, if the question of receiving it be raised, the petitioner ought to be heard thereon, and the safe rule is not to dispose of it without hearing him.

Not receivable. A petition is not to be received, unless some person appear at the bar in support of it (general principle and practice), or if it contain unbecoming, improper expressions (1765, 5); or if the matter of it be not cognisable by that court (1765, 5; 1950, 6; and 1956, 2); or if the matter ought to have been brought by another course—*e.g.*, by appeal (1756, 6; 1866, 4, Forfar), and even when indisposition is alleged to have prevented the other course (1801, 6); or if the petitioners might have appeared as parties before the inferior court, but did not (Com., June 2, 1835, Kilrenny; Com., June 3, 1845, Abertarff). In this last case the deliverance bore that "the Committee on Bills of the Synod ought not to have transmitted the petition."

Member petitioning. If a member of a court be a petitioner to it, singly or with others, he is, of course, at the bar during that business till it is disposed of.

For others. A member who is not a petitioner cannot present the petition of others, either in his place or at the bar.

Affecting others. When a petition affects the interest of others than the petitioner, and has been *received*, the court, if not satisfied that sufficient intimation has been made, orders the petitioner to serve a copy on them, with a citation to attend (pp. 109-111). To said copy a warrant is appended in ordinary form.

Warrant to. [*Place and date.*] Which day and place the [*court*], being met and constituted, did and hereby do grant warrant to serve the foregoing petition on *So-and-so*, and to cite him or them to appear for his or their interests at a meeting of said [*court, place, day, and hour*].

Signed by the Moderator and Clerk.

Against a minister. A petition affecting the character of a minister is not served upon him, for this matter can be dealt with only by libel; but he may be communicated with respecting it, and he will, of course, be heard upon it, and is entitled to take his ordinary part in the discussion of it.

The form of petition is familiar :—

Form.

Unto the Venerable [*for inferior courts,* Reverend] the General Assembly of the Church of Scotland [*needless to specify what meeting*]—
The Petition of

Humbly sheweth

That [*state succinctly and orderly the facts and reasons*].

May it therefore please your Venerable Court to [*state what is desired*], or to do otherwise as to your Venerable Court may seem good.

And your petitioner will ever pray.

If it be the petition of a class, the general designation—*e.g.*, parishioners, members, &c.—is best given at the beginning, and the individual designations at the signature. The concluding words are an expression of deference and of the attitude of waiting. A date is not necessary.

(*f*) Overtures.

Their use.

Overture is the designation given to the formal proposal submitted to a court by an inferior court, or by one or more members of the court itself, to initiate legislative or executive action of a general kind not limited to business of the overturers. Overtures dealing with a subject dealt with in the Deliverance on the Report of a Committee will not be transmitted to the Assembly. A simple amendment or countermotion to the Deliverance is the correct method and in normal cases supporters of the overture so rejected will be among the Commissioners to the Assembly (1962, 1). Though the Church is used to the overture in the General Assembly only, it is equally competent in the other courts, relative to matters within their province. The usual course for their own members is the more direct one of motion, preceded, in matters of importance, by notice of motion.

The General Assembly may, and frequently do, send overtures for the consideration of Presbyteries on their own initiative, or on the report of one of their Committees.

Overtures on the same or cognate subjects are grouped together and only one speaker is heard introducing each group (S.O. 70).

Incompetent overtures.

The question whether certain professors at St Andrews were members of Presbytery had been remitted to a Committee of Assembly to be reported on to next Assembly. The Presbytery of St Andrews overtured next Assembly to discourage any attempt to overturn decisions formerly given by the Assembly. The Committee on Bills and Overtures refused transmission to the Assembly, and an appeal against this was dismissed (1893, 2). The same took place in the case of an overture respecting the Baird Trust Deed, because the deed was not before the Assembly (1874, 2).

Who may overture. An overture may be promoted before a court only by a member, or members, thereof (1837, 4); or by an inferior court, in which case no member thereof can be heard, unless he be also a member of the court overtured (1780, 6), or has been specially appointed (S.O., 71). The parties entitled to overture the General Assembly do not include Kirk Sessions.

Supporting it. If no one appear to introduce the overture, it falls without a motion to that effect. Once introduced, even if the introducer do not support it (as when he acts for his Presbytery though not of its opinion), the overture is the property of the Assembly, and must be disposed of.

Form. All overtures from Presbyteries or Synods or from Commissioners which propose the introduction of new or the amendment of existing Acts (or Regulations) shall contain the precise terms of the legislation which they propose; and the Committee on Commissions shall not transmit to the Assembly any overture which is deficient in this respect: provided always that the Clerks and Procurator shall be available to assist with the framing of such proposals (S.O., 67).

The form might be:—

It is humbly overtured by the undersigned members of Assembly [*or*, by—*name the court*] to the Venerable the General Assembly to rescind *such and such a clause or Act*, and instead thereof to enact and ordain as follows: &c.

If reasons are to be advanced—though the more definite and complete the proposal the less will they be needed—begin with the reasons: "Whereas," &c.

How transmitted to General Assembly. Any overture from a Presbytery to the General Assembly must be transmitted through the Synod of the bounds, which shall forward it with or without comment, with approval or with disapproval (1961, xxiii.). A Synod is not entitled to refuse to transmit an overture which is presented in proper form. But a Presbytery has liberty to transmit an overture to the General Assembly direct in case of urgency when no regular meeting of Synod intervenes between the meeting of Presbytery at which it was adopted and the General Assembly (1933, xix.).

Overtures sent down to Presbyteries under the Barrier Act.

The General Assembly, in order to provide against "any sudden alteration, or innovation, or other prejudice to the Church, in either doctrine, or worship, or discipline, or government," passed an Act, 1697, ix., known as the Barrier Act, which requires that before the Assembly pass "any Acts which are to be binding rules and constitutions to the Church," they shall be proposed as overtures to the Assembly, and, being passed by them as such, shall be remitted to the consideration of the Presbyteries, and their opinion and consent reported to next Assembly, "which may then pass the same in Acts, if the more general opinion of the Church, thus had, agree thereunto" (see p. 105 and p. 385). This rule is also applied to any "Act recissory of any standing Acts" (1736, viii.).

Declaratory Acts.

The purpose and terms of the foregoing enactments are not applicable to the passing of Acts which only declare what the law of the Church is (and to this may be added that the Assembly alone interpret the laws of the Church), nor to making unimportant alterations in Acts or practice.

Interim Acts.

The Assembly may immediately convert an overture into an Interim Act, when this is "necessary for carrying out more effectually the subsisting regulations or forms of the Church" (1848, xiv.). In this case it is sent down as an "Overture and Interim Act," and continues in force till next Assembly. Since its first Assembly in 1843 the Free Church also passed Interim Acts from time to time. An Interim Act should be passed only in case of emergency for this reason at least, that it is liable to be set aside unless the overture embodying it be approved by a majority of Presbyteries. It is undesirable that legislation on any matter should be changed for only one year.

Treatment of overtures and other Acts.

"The draft of any proposed Declaratory or Interim Act, as also the draft of any Overture which it is proposed to transmit to Presbyteries in terms of the Barrier Act (other than any Overture printed and circulated in the volume of Reports), shall be printed and laid on the table of the Assembly and circulated among the Members at least one day before a Motion for the passing of such Declaratory or Interim Act, or for the transmission of such Overture to Presbyteries, is made in the Assembly" (S.O., 60).

When a proposal which requires the consent of Presbyteries is submitted to the Assembly by overture, the overture is either "dismissed," or it is "received" and "sent down" to Presbyteries in its original or in an amended form.

Schedule.

The opinion of Presbyteries is obtained by means of a

schedule with a column for the "Decision of the Presbytery," which may be "Approve" or "Disapprove"; and for "Remarks" (S.O., 30). Returns which do not bear "Approve" or "Disapprove" as the "Decision of the Presbytery" will not be counted on either side. Whether a Presbytery approve or disapprove, it is at liberty to make "Remarks," which may be reported for the consideration of the Assembly. If a Presbytery use the word "approve," with reservations so great as to affect adversely the scope of the measure proposed, it is liable to be held as disapproving the whole overture. If a proposed alteration in no way modifies the substance, sense, or intention of the overture, it is competent for the General Assembly, if it see cause, to adopt it (Oct. 1929, i.). If a majority of the Presbyteries approve, the Assembly either pass the overture into an Act, or resolve that it be not passed, or that it be sent down to Presbyteries in some amended form. It shall be the duty of the Committee reporting on the Returns to Overtures to report not only the number of Presbyteries approving or disapproving but also the numbers voting in the Presbyteries as reported in the printed schedule (S.O., 30).

If approved.

An "approved" overture may be passed into law notwithstanding such minor changes made by the Assembly as are not at variance with the spirit and purpose of the Barrier Act. This is not unusual in the Assembly.

If disapproved.

If half or more of the Presbyteries report disapproval, the overture is regarded as disapproved, and the official announcement of this to the Assembly is held to dispose of it (1881, 9; and 1961, Reports p. 887); but it may be sent down again in an altered form.

If indecisive.

If less than half the Presbyteries have pronounced on each side, the overture may be sent down again with or without change.

Of same year.

The returns from Presbyteries must all be of one year to one Assembly (1849, 9); and it is incompetent to pass an overture into law on the ground that it had been reported to the previous Assembly as approved by the Presbyteries (1895, 6).

Returns enjoined.

Presbyteries are imperatively enjoined to make returns to overtures (1865, xviii.).

Obedience.

"It is the duty of all ministers of this Church to give punctual and exemplary obedience to all the Acts and appointments of the Assembles thereof" (1697, viii.).

Overtures are sent to Presbyteries in England and on Continent.

Overtures sent down under the Barrier Act are also sent to the Presbytery of England and the Presbytery of Europe, and their returns have equal weight with those of the home

Presbyteries (1936, ix.). They may be sent to Kirk Sessions when so appointed (Oct. 1929, i.); but it is the verdict of the Presbyteries on which legislation depends.

Any proposal for a modification of or addition to the Articles Declaratory of the Constitution of the Church of Scotland in matters Spiritual (App., p. 390) which may be approved of by the General Assembly must, before it can be enacted by the Assembly, be transmitted by way of overture to Presbyteries in at least two successive years. Unless the overture receives the consent of not less than two-thirds of the Presbyteries the Assembly may not modify or add to the Articles. If the requisite consent is not received the same or a similar proposal may not be transmitted to Presbyteries until after an interval of five years.

(*g*) Dissents.

Members of a court are entitled to dissent, and to require their dissent to be recorded, if they find "the moderator refuse to put anything of importance to the vote," or if any resolution is come to which they "conceive to be contrary to the Word of God, the Acts of Assembly, or to the received order of this Kirk" (1644, 7). "Acts" include resolutions and decisions (see Glossary). Members now dissent for reasons much less serious than these, and without objection by the courts.

Reasons. No reasons need be given for a dissent. When given briefly and definitely as part of a dissent which is intimated immediately, it is the practice of the Church to record them (*e.g.*, 1865, 12; 1869, 3; 1873, ult.; Com., Jan. 14, 1873; 1889, 6); otherwise they are kept *in retentis*. The court may or may not frame answers, and may see fit to record them if the reasons have been recorded.

When reasons rejected. A court may reject reasons of dissent which are disrespectful to it (1803, 9 and ult.; 1845, 11), or injurious to a party (1803, 9). Everything that is fair in argument may be stated without offending in these respects. These are points which happen to have been tried and decided—there may be other grounds for rejection, though this is scarcely likely. There may also be grounds which, while not sufficient for the rejection of the dissent with its reasons, would justify a court in refusing to engross the reasons in its records, and in minuting only that the member dissented for reasons which were ordered to be kept *in retentis*. For general guidance to dissentients, therefore, the following observations may be useful: (1) other reasons of dissent than those founded on the Word of God, the Acts of Assembly, or the received order, as above quoted, can scarcely be entitled to the same degree of indulgence, when indulgence is needed, as those are; (2) even those reasons a court cannot well be expected to engross in its records, unless such reference be given to the Scripture or the Act or deliverance relied on as to make a reply possible; (3) nor can it be expected to load its pages with a discussion or a mass of matter. Reasons of dissent are not a discussion of the subject: they are to show the position of the dissentient, for his justification. In all the examples to which reference has been given above, and which are fair examples, the dissent and reason consist of a single, brief, definite, and simple statement in one sentence.

Object of reasons.

Dissent relieves of all the responsibility incurred, including expense (C.S., *Buist* v. *Taylor*, 1856, 18D. 596). It may be assumed that this would not be so if the dissent were incompetent or censurable.

Effect.

A dissent is censurable if found to be causeless (1644). It is incompetent and censurable when it is against carrying out an instruction of an Act or of a superior court, and members who will not take part in carrying out the instruction are liable to censure (1741, ult.; 1803, 5).

Censurable.

Who and when.

"Any Commissioner dissatisfied with a judgment of the Assembly, which has not been unanimous, has the right to enter his dissent against it; but no dissent can be given in until the matter to which it refers has, for that session, been disposed of, the Minute adjusted, and the Assembly is ready to proceed to other business (S.O., 102).

"When a dissent has been entered, it is in order for any other Commissioner present when that judgment was pronounced to adhere to such dissent. No other's adherence may be entered" (S.O., 103).

Adherence.

(*h*) Taking Instruments.

"Taking" has here the same sense as in "taking a step"; "Instrument" is the act or article by means of which anything is done. To take instruments is to perform a certain overt act, which by common consent signifies and evidences a completed and irrevocable transaction. There are, therefore,

What.

two parties to it; the court is one, acting in this by the hand of its clerk, though the moderator is to be addressed in this as in all things. There is no need to record that it is in the hands of the clerk (the Assembly does not), for if the court minute that instruments were taken, it acknowledges its part in the act. The transaction is the same as in the servant's arles, the soldier's shilling, the Israelite's shoe (Ruth iv. 7), the "striking of hands." Our mode is to pass a certain coin to the clerk—that at present in use is a five pence piece. Instrument money is not a fee; and it is an impediment to justice if the coin be not a small one.

When. When a party obtains a decision in his favour he acquiesces, takes instruments, and craves extracts; when (p. 91) a party appeals, or a member dissents and complains, he also takes instruments, and craves extracts. When a member of Assembly dissents, he must take instruments, though this act is not minuted. In the inferior courts it is not usual to take instruments in a mere dissent.

Minuting. The Assembly's form is "acquiesced, took instruments, and craved extracts, which were allowed" (or "granted"). This being so, we must assume that in the General Assembly there is some fitness in the last three words; but in the lower courts they are not only useless but misleading, in respect that they suggest some power of refusal while there is none. An instruction to the clerk to give them when called upon would be more to the purpose, if thought necessary.

Right to Extracts.

(i) Motions and Voting.

Method. There is no general rule laid down for voting in the courts. The method laid down in the Standing Orders of the Assembly furnishes a good guide for the inferior courts, and may be briefly stated. When there are *motions* inconsistent with each other, the first vote is a vote in favour of each of them, put in the order in which they were proposed, the result not being announced for one till it is announced for all. If any of them obtains a majority of those voting, it becomes the judgment; if none of them does so, the motion having fewest votes is struck off and the vote taken again, and so on. If the lowest two be equal, the moderator gives his casting vote on them. When *amendments* are proposed, that is, proposals not inconsistent with the general tenor of the motion, each may be disposed of immediately it has been moved, seconded, and spoken to, the vote on each being For or Against. Thereafter the motions (as amended, if amended) are voted on in the way already stated. On the casting vote, see p. 78. If this simple and excellent method were practised in all our courts and committees, the consequent familiarity with a uniform practice would save very much trouble (see S.O., 92-99).

Desirable practice.

It is unnecessary to move a direct negative to a motion. The same purpose is achieved by speaking and voting against the motion.

(*j*) CITATION (1707, xi., Chap. II.).

What

Citation is an authorised official act, authoritatively and distinctly calling the cited to a specified place and time for a specified purpose. The manner of it is never optional, but according to rule; and every matter has its own rule. Those rules will be found in this volume in connection with the matters to which they apply.

The Court's part.

In all cases where parties are concerned, the judicatory is to see that before it proceeds all are "sisted before it by a legal and timeous citation in writ bearing its cause," either at the instance of a party, or by order of the judicatory; and the execution of the summons "bearing its cause and made before witnesses insert" is to be returned by the officer in writing, and the persons cited called at the door (F.P., ii. 3).

It is *pars judicis*—belongs to the judge—to see that this has been done. The court on the application of a party will grant warrant to cite; and it may *ex proprio motu*, or in certain administrative procedure must, order a citation to be made; or it may give citation from the chair to a party present.

Modes of service.

Essentials.

It is essential to any citation that it shall be such as affords the party cited reasonable ground for believing it to be authentic, and that its execution can be proved to the court. The law of the Church above stated relates to citation of parties.

Civil law (P. 1882) in proceedings in a civil action allows citation both of parties and witnesses to be given by an officer of court or a law agent in a registered letter, or by recorded delivery service (P. 1962), the envelope of which must bear—

This letter contains a citation to [*or*, intimation from] [*here specify the court*]. If delivery of the letter cannot be made, it is to be returned to [*here insert the name and address of the clerk of court*].

To the writ, if there be any (*e.g.*, a petition), is appended the citation; then follows a certificate which is to be signed and returned along with the Post Office receipt by the office or agent, such as—

This [*designating the writ, if any*] with annexed citation was executed by me , Officer [*or*, Law Agent], by posting on between the hours of and at the Post Office at , a copy thereof in a registered (or recorded delivery) letter addressed as follows [*state address*].

Modes for Witnesses and Courts. The Church having prescribed no method of citing witnesses may doubtless authorise or sustain citation of this nature. It would appear that a similar course may be taken also in citing an inferior court; for the Form of Process never seems to include a court in the term "party"; nor does the term "cite" appear so appropriate here as language of the nature of an order, occasionally used by the Assembly when it "*appoints* [a court] to appear at the bar." The Assembly (1885, 2), at the instance of a petitioner who stated that his petition had been intimated to the Presbytery, appointed the Presbytery of Olnafirth to appear at the bar with all the documents in the case, and authorised intimation of that to be made "by telegraphic message." Also (1886, 2) the Assembly, on the crave of a member acting for the Synod of Glenelg, granted warrant to cite the Presbytery of Uist, through their moderator and clerk, to answer a petition at the instance of the Synod, and authorised the citation to be made in each case "by telegraph." In these cases the party craving the citation received an extract of the deliverance authorising to cite, and lodged with the Agent for the Church a certified copy of the telegram along with a certificate that it had been despatched.

Tele-graph.

Mode for parties. For parties, properly so called, the Church, as has been seen, has prescribed a mode of citation; and it would be very doubtful practice in a court to authorise or sustain any other. This certainly should not be done without, at the least, careful consideration of the circumstances of the particular case; and for a certain class of cases a weighty consideration is that even the State, while making many modifications, has not modified its old rule in criminal cases.

Court's power and bounds. A court has power to call before it any person residing within its bounds whom the ecclesiastical business before it concerns as party, witness, or otherwise; and if it desire to call a person residing in the bounds of another court of the same degree it applies to that court to cause the person to be cited (F.P., i. 5, 6). Of assistance from the civil courts, see p. 322.

Citation *apud acta* is citation in the proceedings—by the court in its presence. The minute is proof of it. *Apud acta.*

Citation by edict is citation by public intimation, and will be found prescribed only for citing a body or bodies, or an absconded minister. Edict.

Execution of a citation is a certificate of its having been served, given by the official who served it. In edictal citation it is written on the citation. Execution.

[*Place and date*] the foregoing [*or*, the within] citation was this day duly served by me. Form.

C. D., *Witness*. A. B. [*Designation*].
E. F., *Witness*.

The witnesses must be present at the public reading of it. For other executions see under the various occasions of citation.

A superior cites an inferior court to its bar by sending an extract resolution to that effect to the moderator and clerk. If either be present, though not at the bar, his court may be cited through him from the chair (1893, 2). Citing Inferior Court.

See also Chaps. XV. and XVI.

SECTION IV.

MISCELLANEOUS.

(*a*) RECKONING TIME.

"Month" is taken to mean a calendar month, if there be no specification to the contrary (P. 1859 and 1889).

"Free days," or "clear days," means days over and above the day of the initial and the day of the terminal act.

"Within" so many days—say ten—means that the time allowed, without counting the day of the initial act (the judgment, intimation, or the like), extends to the end (midnight) of the tenth day.

Sunday is always counted, except where otherwise provided (as, for example, in the Representation of the People Act, 1949).

(*b*) COMMISSIONS AND COMMITTEES.

Commissions and committees have much in common, but yet have points of distinction.

Commissions need in no case be confined to the membership of the commissioning court. Their character and powers Commissions.

must be defined by the commissioning court. They generally bear more of the character of a court than committees, and have authority to exercise higher functions. They never receive power to add to their number, and cannot sub-commit. But in this latter respect the Commission of Assembly appointed yearly is an exception (p. 201). A commission has been appointed by a Committee of Assembly after obtaining the approval of the Commission of Assembly (Com., Nov. 19, 1884).

Committees.

Committees are of every variety. For the business of the General Assembly during sederunts only Commissioners can be members of a committee. Speaking generally, committees that are appointed to service which is part of the official business assigned to the court by law must be composed of members of the court, and do not receive power to add to their number. Committees for work of which it may more correctly be said that the court has elected to manage it, or to lend the weight of its authority to it, may include others besides members of the court. Such Committees and their composition are as determined by the Standing Orders of the General Assembly (S.O. 107, 108). Not only Presbyteries, but General Assemblies have frequently appointed committees outside the number of commissioners, including some persons who never were members of the General Assembly.

Membership.

It is evidently essential, however, that every member, whether of a commission or a committee, be under the jurisdiction of the appointing court, so that such member may be called to account by it. If not on its roll, he should be within its bounds.

Chairman's vote.

It must be presumed, if no provision to the contrary be made, that the chairman of a committee is in the same position in respect of voting as the chairman of the body which appointed it. Accordingly in committees of the Church, as of the House of Commons, he gives only a casting vote (p. 78).

Time of sitting.

Committees cannot competently sit during the sitting of their court without leave. Assembly committees are under express orders to that effect (1846, ix.).

Of whole house.

When a court appoints a committee of the whole house, which the General Assembly have occasionally done, it then or afterwards adjourns, and at the adjourned meeting it calls, at time convenient, for the report of the committee.

The General Assembly have declared that Special Commissions and Committees appointed to deal with Union and Readjustment Cases should usually consist of not less than five members, that a Convener and a Vice-Convener should be appointed, and that such Special Commissions and Committees be empowered to act so long as the available membership is not less than four (1965, i., Rep. p. 6).

Ap-pealed from.

A commission or committee is not placed at the bar by the appeal of a party against its judgment (1813, 8). A dissent and complaint by a member of committee has always been held incompetent.

'Minority Report' incompetent.

A "minority report" is incompetent (1939, 3 and 7). The only remedy of a dissatisfied member is to approach the court which appointed by Petition, or, if a member of the court, to make an appropriate motion when the report of the committee is submitted. A committee may, however, incorporate in its report to the parent body a statement of the position of any dissentient members, if so determined (1962, 1, Rep. p. 19).

(*c*) Admissibility of Counsel.

"Parties may appear by, or have the assistance of, counsel or agents in any process depending before the Presbytery or any higher court, unless such court shall otherwise determine. They shall not be entitled to have such assistance in any process depending before a Kirk Session except with the special permission of the Kirk Session. Any parties appearing by counsel or agents shall not be entitled to be heard also by themselves" (Oct. 1929, i.).

In cases where the court decides to allow the assistance of counsel or agents, these should, if possible, be members of the Church (Oct. 1929, i.).

(*d*) Medical Certificate.

All courts require that a medical certificate shall be "on soul and conscience" (*e.g.*, "I hereby certify on soul and conscience"). Whatever may be the history of the form, it is now inveterate custom; and Acts of Parliament adopt it when scheduling forms of medical certificates.

(*e*) Irregularities. Untimeous Objection.

Irregularities in procedure committed unawares and in good faith, and not being such as to prejudice the result, will not invalidate the proceedings; if, however, they be such as would prejudice the result, or are committed deliberately, and especially if under any suspicion of partial purpose, it will be very different. In every case irregularities must be timeously challenged, otherwise *omnia praesumuntur rite et solemniter acta*—all things are presumed to have been done in due and customary form. In disputes over the election and appointment of a minister it was held that unwarrantable proceedings not appealed against at the time could not be pleaded as invalidating subsequent proceedings (1885, 15, Walls; 1888, 5, Halkirk). Yet the irregularities may be of such a kind, and the absence of challenge owing to such circumstances, as to overrule the general practice.

(*f*) NOBILE OFFICIUM.

There is a species of authority or power admitted to belong to the General Assembly, which is called the *nobile officium.* The same is true of the Court of Session, in which it has been more fully interpreted by practice, and to which it seems to have descended from the King's Council, into the place of which that court came. "So far as the *nobile officium* of the Court of Session is concerned, if I may state the position very shortly, it is an equitable power to modify and abate the rigour of the Law and to a certain extent to give a remedy where no remedy could be had in a court confined to strict Law. It is also confined, in practice, to a relatively limited sphere or spheres. So far as I am aware, it has never been used to create an entirely new form of process; or to deprive an individual of his legal rights; it has been used, rather, to give him equitable remedies which the strict Law would not give; again, it has never been used, so far as I am aware, to impose some penalty on an individual which the Law would not impose." (Sir Randall Philip, Q.C., Procurator—1953, 9.) In the General Assembly it is without definition or rules of action. But it is in short the power, which would seem naturally and necessarily to belong to a supreme court, to determine and order such things as are necessary to be done in a pending case, and for which there is no legal provision. It cannot overrule law, but only supply the want of it when necessary; and it belongs only to the supreme court. It was exercised by the Assembly 1837, ult., many members dissenting, and 1947, 9. It may also be called into exercise by petition in such circumstances as are here indicated.

(*g*) MAY A COURT REVIEW ITS OWN DECISIONS?

It is a principle of common law that a court cannot review its own decrees, which accordingly must stand till set aside by the authority of a competent court. *Presbytery of Deer* v. *Heritors of Pitsligo* (1876, 3 R., 974, L.P. 978). In the Auchterarder case (Nov. 23, 1903) the sheriff said the Presbytery's revision of its original order without consent of all possible parties was "an incompetency apparent on the face of" its judgment. The principle rules our Church courts in all matters, to the extent at least of embracing whatever is of the nature of a judicial deliverance—after a process has been begun by the citing of parties. It is not, however, strictly applied to non-judicial resolutions. For example, a Presbytery might resolve to proceed by libel, and might at any time before serving it rescind the resolution. Even in such cases a rescissory proposal is but the less of two evils, and should not be made by surprise, and would be unwisely pressed against formal opposition. If a court has passed a resolution contradictory of the order of a superior court, it ought certainly to pass from it, as not only incompetent but an offence (p. 88).

Pitsligo.

Auchterarder.

Insubordination.

CHAPTER VI.

THE KIRK SESSION.

SECTION I. *Constitution and Officials.*

Minister and Kirk Session.

THE Kirk Session in any congregation consists of the minister or ministers along with the ruling elders. Where a higher Court sends instructions to "minister and Kirk Session," thus including the minister twice, it covers any duty involved which belongs to the minister in his separate capacity as minister, as distinct from his function as moderator of Kirk Session.

Elders.

In 1966 the General Assembly after due procedure passed the following Act (XXVIII.):—

"Women members of a congregation shall be eligible for election and admission as elders on the same terms and conditions as men members of a congregation."

All members of Session are elders, ministers being teaching or preaching as well as ruling elders, the others being "ruling elders" only. (Ch. Gov.; F.P., i. 2; see also 'The Westminster Assembly' by Prof. A. F. Mitchell, D.D., 1883, p. 191 and App., Note G.) In practice the term "elder" or "ruling elder" is restricted to non-ministerial members. A minister is eligible for membership of the Courts of the Church only as a Minister. A Minister of the Church who is not in a charge or holding a terminable appointment or a chaplain in Her Majesty's Forces may be associated in the practical work of the Kirk Session of the congregation to which he has attached himself but shall not be a member of the Kirk Session (1961, xxiv.).

Ministers and elders have an equal voice on every subject as members of a church Court, and all have the same responsibility. Ruling elders in the Presbytery do not lay on hands at the ordination of a minister (1932, ix, 25 (3)) for this is outside of ruling; but they share in every step thereto.

The Office.

"The elderschip is a spirituall function as is the ministrie" (2 B. Dis., cap. vi.). The office of the elders is severally and conjunctly to watch over the flock committed to their charge, both publicly and privately, that no corruption of religion or manners enter therein. As "pastors and doctors" should be diligent in sowing the seed of the Word, so the elders should be careful in seeking the fruit of it in the people. It appertains to them to assist the minister in examining them that come to the Lord's Table. Elders ought to bring to the Kirk Session things they cannot correct by private admonition. As one of the remedies for profaneness, the Assembly resolved (1648, 38) that every elder should have a district assigned to him, that he might keep himself acquainted with and report to the Session; and the observance of this where practicable is as important as ever. It is no part of the elder's official duty to pray with the sick: "The office of the elder (that is, the pastor) is to pray for the sick, even in private," &c. (Ch. Gov.). Their principal office is to hold Kirk Session with the pastors and doctors who are also of their number, for establishing of good order and execution of discipline (2 B. Dis., vi; Ch. Gov.). See 1963, 12, Reports p. 757.

Admission to Office.

Ruling elders are elected in accordance with the provisions of Sect. IV. (p. 132), and they are ordained and admitted by the Kirk Session; ministers are ordained and inducted by the Presbytery, and are directly accountable to it for the discharge of all duties of their office.

Tenure of Office.

Elders are elected for life, and hold office till they cease to be members of the congregation, or their resignation is accepted, or they are deposed or otherwise removed from office. If an elder has absented himself from meetings of the Kirk Session for more than a year without due cause deemed satisfactory by the Kirk Session, the Session may, after giving him due notice for his interest, find he has ceased to be one of its members (1933, ix.). Elders, as all other members on the Communion Roll (except the minister) are under the jurisdiction of the Kirk Session. (See Chap. XV., p. 323.)

Number of Elders.

It belongs to the Kirk Session to determine the number of elders required by the circumstances of the congregation, and when expedient, to elect additional elders. (See Sect. IV., p. 132). It is, however, the duty of the Presbytery to see that all proper means are used in every charge to secure that the Kirk Session shall not only be a legal quorum, but in its opinion sufficient for the needs of the congregation, and this matter is the subject of special inquiry at the quinquennial visitation of each congregation (1931, xii.).

Number of Deacons.

The Kirk Session determines the number of deacons, when it is expedient to elect deacons, and deals with all cases of resignation or removal from office of deacons (1933, ix.). (See also Chap. III., p. 30).

Moderator.

The minister is *ex officio* moderator of the Kirk Session.

At the first meeting of Kirk Session after his admission to office by the Presbytery, a certified intimation of his induction forwarded by the Presbytery Clerk is read and engrossed in the minutes (1932, ix., Sect. 25 (3)). If there be colleagues, they preside alternately, or as may be agreed between them, or as appointed by the Presbytery. The minister not presiding sits and votes as an ordinary member, unless it be otherwise authoritatively regulated.

In the absence of the moderator, any other minister of the Church of Scotland may, if deputed by him in writing, with the business to be dealt with specified, preside *pro tempore* (1933, x.). No meeting of Kirk Session can be held without the presence of the moderator or of a minister deputed by him to act *pro tempore*, or appointed *ad interim* by the Presbytery or a superior Court.

Moderators' Duties.

The duties of the moderator are: to convene the meetings of Kirk Session, though the clerk may do this on the authority of the moderator; to preside thereat; to constitute and close each meeting with prayer; to see that the business is properly ordered and recorded; to take the vote and announce the decisions of the Kirk Session; to act for the Kirk Session in administering censure and in carrying out its decisions. (See also Chap. V., Sect. I. (*b*), p. 77.)

The moderator has a casting vote, but no deliberative vote, but he may introduce any business to the Kirk Session and address it thereanent. In common with other members he has the right of dissent and complaint against any decision. (See Chap. V., Sect. III. (*c*), p. 91.) He is not responsible to the Kirk Session for the discharge of his ministerial functions; but, if he seem to neglect these, or to encroach upon the functions of the Kirk Session, the Presbytery may be approached by petition. In practice, this is generally a petition of the elders (or any number of them), signing individually, not resolved on at a meeting of Session. If, for example, a minister should refuse to call a meeting of Kirk Session, or should dissolve meetings against their will, the Presbytery should be petitioned. Any member may so petition. Moreover, in all matters which the Kirk Session is entitled to decide, its decision is as truly binding on the minister as on any other person; he differs from others only in that his disregard has to be dealt with by the Presbytery. It will be the business of the Presbytery, if it see cause, to instruct or enjoin him; and thereafter, if necessary, to deal with disobedience to itself.

Complaint against Minister.

Clerk's Duties.

The Kirk Session appoints a Clerk, whose tenure of office

lasts during the pleasure of the Kirk Session, and whose duty it is to take regular minutes of the Session's procedure and engross the same in a permanent record, to take charge of all sessional documents, and to prepare and issue all extracts of minutes and papers authorised by the Session. In his absence from any meeting the Kirk Session appoints a clerk *pro tempore*, whose appointment must be recorded in the minute. The oath *de fideli* should be administered to the clerk on appointment. Each minute, when approved, must be signed in the permanent record by the clerk, as "clerk," or "clerk *pro tempore*," as well as by the moderator (1931, xv.). Failing the appointment of a clerk, it devolves on the moderator to perform the duties, and he signs as "moderator and clerk." The clerk need not be a member of the court, although it is advisable that he should.

Treasurer. If necessary, the Kirk Session appoints a treasurer to take charge of funds at its disposal. He holds office during the pleasure of the Session.

Officer. The Kirk Session may appoint an officer or beadle who waits upon its meetings and executes its orders. He should be a member of the congregation in full communion, or be one whom the Kirk Session is prepared to admit to membership. Suspension from membership carries with it suspension from office. The same person may be in charge of the place of worship. (See Chap. III., pp. 32, 34, 37, 45.)

Assessors. In the event of there being, from any cause, in a duly sanctioned congregation an insufficient number of ruling elders available to form a quorum, the Presbytery appoints one or more of its own number as assessors to act as members of the Kirk Session till a new election has taken place and a Kirk Session has been regularly constituted. The assessors so appointed may be either ministers or elders. The minister and the assessors must be taken to be the Kirk Session for all purposes (Sir William Chree, K.C., Procurator).

It is the duty of a supplemented Kirk Session immediately to seek the completion of the Session by the ordination of elders.

On the fulfilment of the purpose for which any assessor has been appointed, his duty ceases; and he ought to report to the Presbytery at its first meeting thereafter, and be discharged.

If occasion should bring a supplemented Kirk Session to the bar of the Presbytery, the assessors will be at the bar.

There is a Kirk Session in every regular charge, and also in every suppressed charge (1957, xvii.). In the case of a church extension charge a provisional Kirk Session is set up by the Presbytery, consisting of the minister of the extension charge, who is to be appointed moderator, and elders appointed by the Presbytery from other congregations in accordance with regulations anent Church Extension charges (p. 678). When the church extension charge has been granted full status, immediate steps should be taken to constitute a regular Kirk Session (1932, xiv.). When a congregation is reduced to a mission station, temporarily or otherwise, the Kirk Session ceases to function as a separate Court, but such elders as indicate their desire to remain in office are added to the Kirk Session of the parish (1932, 7; and Reports, 1932, p. 375).

Services, Kirk Sessions. For the institution of Kirk Sessions in Units of H.M. Forces reference should be made to p. 313 and the terms of Act, viii., 1952.

SECTION II. *Meetings and Procedure.*

Quorum. Unless the moderator or his regularly appointed substitute be present no meeting of Kirk Session can be held. Three, including the moderator, form a quorum (Oct. 1929, i.).

Mode of Convening. The Kirk Session is legally convened under the authority of the moderator, or the order of a superior Court, either by public intimation from the pulpit, or by personal notice given to each member. Such notice is held sufficient if a reasonable time be allowed for the attendance of all members.

Due Notice. If a Kirk Session be supplemented by an assessor (p. 119) from the Presbytery, individual notice must be sent to him. A meeting is always liable to be challenged if called without timeous notice, or without such notice that all members may know of it,—*e.g.*, if called from the pulpit to meet at the close of service, unless all members be present; or even to meet on a future day, if there be elders whose place of worship is a mission station.

Requisition to Moderator. The moderator is bound to call a meeting within ten days when requested by at least one-third of the elders, with a minimum of five when the number of elders exceeds nine. Such requisition must be in writing (Oct. 1929, i.), but if the requisition discloses that the business is incompetent the moderator is not bound to call the meeting (1950, 6. Appeal, *Presbytery of Melrose* v. *Synod of Merse and Teviotdale.*)

Meeting of a Superior Court. No meeting of Kirk Session can be held, except in connection with the administration of the sacraments or for urgent business, at the time of an ordinary meeting of a superior Court without the leave of that Court; but relative to the General Assembly the Kirk Session has standing leave to meet when none of its members is a member of Assembly but it should not meet without urgent cause.

Adjournment.

The Kirk Session may, if it see cause, adjourn to complete unfinished business to a time which must be fixed when the adjournment is made. In that case, unless the adjournment be made to a later hour of the same day, care should be taken that intimation is given to all members either *apud acta* or in one or other of the prescribed ways of calling a meeting. When intimation has been thus given, the Kirk Session may take up any competent business.

Opening and Closing.

Meetings of Kirk Session must be opened and closed with prayer, and both facts be minuted.

Minutes.

Immediately after the Kirk Session has been constituted the minutes of the previous meeting or meetings should be read, corrected if need be, and approved, and the approval duly recorded. The approval or correcting of the minutes does not imply any power to alter the acts or decisions of the meeting; the only question is the correctness of the minutes as a true account of what was done. For keeping, signing, correcting minutes, and the granting of extracts, see Chap. V., Sect. I., pp. 81-83.

Relation to other Sessions.

A Kirk Session is not entitled to interfere with, or review the action of, another Kirk Session. It may make friendly communication to another Kirk Session regarding any action of which it thinks it has cause to complain; but, if not satisfied, it can proceed further only by referring the matter to its own Presbytery.

Meetings usually Private.

The meetings of Kirk Session are not usually open to the congregation, but are private except where the Kirk Session resolve otherwise in any particular case. In many matters which come before the Session, it is necessary to proceed with great circumspection, especially in cases of discipline affecting the good name of members of the congregation; in all such, strict privacy ought to be observed. It may invite other office-bearers for advice and assistance, but in all cases the Kirk Session must determine its action by the vote of its own members.

In any matter of procedure not provided for, a discretionary power is left to Kirk Sessions, which may find guidance in the procedure applicable to superior Courts.

SECTION III. *Powers and Functions.*

It is the duty of the Kirk Session to maintain good order, to cause Acts of the Assembly to be put into execution, to administer discipline, to judge and determine cases, and to superintend the religious and moral condition of the parish (1931, xvii.).

Discipline. Of discipline in the Kirk Session, see Chap. XV., pp. 318-331.

Administration of Ordinances

Public Worship. It belongs to the Kirk Session in concurrence with the minister to regulate the hours of public worship and to fix the number of church services, while for the proper conduct thereof the minister is responsible to the Presbytery. The Kirk Session also appoints and provides for the administration of Baptism and the observance of the Lord's Supper. In addition to the stated church services the Kirk Session may appoint such occasional or special services as it judges desirable (1931, xvii.). One regular diet of worship at least should be provided each Sunday during holidays.

Administration of the Sacraments.

Baptism. Baptism is to be administered to adults upon their profession of faith in Christ and obedience to Him, and to infants in accordance with Act xvii., 1963 (see p. 56). A Certificate of Baptism must always be given by the minister and the baptism recorded in the Baptismal Register.

The Lord's Supper. The Kirk Session appoints and intimates the time and place for the observance of the Lord's Supper, and makes provision therefor. The elders assist the minister in the distribution of the elements at the Lord's Supper (1931, xvii.) but the Sacrament is a ministerial, not a sessional act, and the Session does not, accordingly, require to be constituted, unless it be necessary to hold a meeting for the admission of members or other business. Only members in full communion are entitled to participate; but the Kirk Session may grant occasional communion to members of other churches who desire it, when nothing is known concerning them inconsistent with their profession as members of the Church of Christ (1938, vi.). Permission is usually given by the minister as representing the Kirk Session. The Act anent Administration of the Sacraments (1956, xxi.) states: "The Sacrament of the Lord's Supper shall be celebrated in church at stated times. Exceptionally, the Sacrament may be administered in church or elsewhere at the discretion of a minister. Where the Sacrament is administered to the sick or infirm, the fact is to be noted in the Communion Roll."

The General Assembly (1909, 11) in regard to the question of the introduction of the individual cup charged ministers and Presbyteries to see that the harmony and peace of a congregation are not disturbed. It would be unwise of a minister to introduce, or to debar the use of, the individual cup without the consent and approval of the Kirk Session. Individual Cup.

Provision must be made to enable all who desire to do so to partake of Communion in the ordinary elements of bread and wine according to the use and wont of the Church (Barrhead Appeal, 1909, 13), with the reservation (1971, 5) that the problem of the alcoholic must be recognised as part of the pastoral concern of each individual minister. Variety of practice within the Church as a whole, and also within some congregations, should meet the individual situation. (1971, 5 and Reports p. 421.)

A Kirk Session wishing to sell surplus Communion Plate must apply for permission to do so to the General Assembly through the Committee on General Administration. (Reports, 1975, pp. 13-14.)

Appointment of Leader of Praise.

The appointment of the Precentor or Organist is made by the Kirk Session, which must be satisfied as to the Christian character of any applicant before he be recognised as eligible. A precise record of the terms of appointment must be entered in the minutes of the Kirk Session. (For suggested agreement, see Appendix, p. 746.)

The salary of the Precentor or Organist shall be determined by the Deacons' Court, Congregational Board or Committee of Management where such body exists. In all other cases it should be fixed by the Kirk Session. The Kirk Session is at liberty to consult the appropriate financial body with regard to the terms of appointment or the person to be appointed.

In the conduct of public worship the Precentor or Organist is under the direction and control of the minister (1931, xvi.), but the Kirk Session may dismiss the leader of praise if dissatisfied with his character or conduct, or with his behaviour or efficiency in the discharge of his duties. Resignation of office is given in to the Kirk Session.

Appointment of Church Officer.

The Church Officer is also appointed, and may be dismissed, if it see cause, by the Kirk Session (1931, xvii.). The terms of his appointment should be recorded in the minutes of the Kirk Session.

Oversight of Church Members.

Communion Roll.

The General Assembly (1938, vi.) passed an Act (amended by Act 1972, i.) anent Keeping of Communion Rolls and Pastoral Supervision as follows :—

(Reference may be made to Assembly Reports 1964, p. 12, *et seq.*)

1. There shall be a Communion Roll, made up and kept up by the Kirk Session of every parish, containing the names and addresses of the communicants. A record shall be kept in this Roll of the dates on which they communicated, together with the dates (1) of enrolment, (*a*) by profession as First Communicants, (*b*) by receipt of Certificates of Transference, (*c*) by special resolution of the Kirk Session ; and (2) of removals, (*a*) by death, (*b*) by issue of Certificates of Transference, (*c*) by special resolution of Kirk Session.

Form.

[Relevant thereto, by Act, 1933, xxiii., the Assembly stated that there is no objection to the loose-leaf system being employed by the Kirk Session for its own use, but the Roll as submitted to the Presbytery annually in terms of Act xviii., 1931, should be in the form of a consecutive list in alphabetical order. In 1952 the Assembly approved a recommendation of the General Administration Committee to the effect that the Roll must be of such a form as to be capable of being attested annually, and also of being a historical record of membership. It therefore recommended that the " consecutive list " referred to in Act xxiii. of 1933 should be contained or ultimately inserted in a bound volume. The Assembly in 1964 approved of the use of loose-leaf Church records including loose-leaf Roll of Communicants (1964, Reg. 4).] (See page 825.)

Certificates of Transference.

2. A communicant's name shall be transferred from the Communion Roll of one congregation to that of another congregation only by a Certificate of Transference, and such certificate shall not entitle to enrolment after the expiry of three years from the date which it bears, unless a satisfactory reason be given for delay. In the case of persons presenting

Certificates of Transference, the date of enrolment shall be the date of lodging the certificate ; and, in other cases, it shall be the date of the resolution of Kirk Session to add the name to the Roll. The date of removal shall be the date of death, or of the issue of a Certificate of Transference, or of a resolution of the Kirk Session to remove the name.

3. The Kirk Session shall revise and attest the Communion Roll, as at 31st December in each year, the attestation to include a statement of the number of names on the Roll after revision, and shall at the same meeting make an entry in the minutes that it did so. It is recommended that intimation be given from the pulpit on each of the two preceding Sundays that this procedure is to be taken. Revision of Communion Roll.

4. The Kirk Session shall have power, at the annual revision of the Communion Roll, to remove from the Roll the names of persons who are giving no evidence of real interest or are taking no share in the Church's Work and Worship. The names of persons whose names have been removed from the Communion Roll under this section may be restored to the Roll only by resolution of the Kirk Session. Removal of Names.

5. The name of no person whose address is known shall be removed from the Communion Roll under the preceding section until the Kirk Session has previously communicated with the person concerned. Kirk Sessions at the annual review of their Communion Rolls should not remove therefrom the names of persons who by reason of service in the Forces of the Crown may be absent from their congregations for a number of years, but should either retain the names of such persons on the Communion Roll of their own congregations or transfer them to the Forces Register. (Retained by Committee on Chaplains to H.M. Forces.) Notice of such transfer shall, if possible, be given by the Kirk Session to the person concerned.

6. The Kirk Session, with a view to lessening the danger of lapsing from Church connection, shall issue to every member in full Communion when leaving, or immediately after leaving, the parish or district to take up residence elsewhere, a Certificate of Transference, unless the communicant has expressed a definite desire to retain his connection with the congregation ; and, if his destination be known, shall intimate accordingly either to the minister of the parish within which the communicant is going, or has gone, to reside, or to the Presbyterial Correspondent. Kirk Sessions receiving Certificates of Transference shall acknowledge receipt of the same to the Kirk Session which has issued them. Members Leaving.

Supplementary Roll.

7. The Kirk Session, with a view to continued supervision, shall keep a separate or Supplementary Roll, on which shall be placed the names of those who have been removed from the Communion Roll without a Certificate of Transference and who continue to reside in the parish or district.

[Relevant thereto, the General Assembly (1951, vi.) declared that persons whose names are on the Supplementary Roll are in no way debarred from being admitted to the Sacrament of the Lord's Supper if they so desire, nor from being restored to the Communion Roll by special resolution of the Session. While their names are on the Supplementary Roll, they are not eligible to be elected as office-bearers or to take part in or vote in Congregational meetings. They may be admitted on application to the Electoral Register. If they remove to another parish, their names should be removed from the Supplementary Roll and intimation sent to the minister of the parish to which they have gone.]

Pastoral Supervision.

8. It being the duty of the Kirk Session to exercise pastoral supervision within the parish, the Kirk Session shall take steps to ascertain, as far as possible, the names of those within the parish who have no connection with any Church.

9. The Communion Roll shall be submitted once a year to the Presbytery of the bounds for attestation, and Presbyteries are enjoined to see that each Kirk Session keeps a Communion Roll in terms of this Act, and submits the same annually to the Presbytery.

Access to the Lord's Table.

10. Notwithstanding anything contained in this Act, access to the Lord's Table shall not be refused to any person who desires to communicate, provided such person has previously been admitted a member in full Communion and is not under discipline by a Court of the Church.

Reference may here be made to the regulations which govern admission to Holy Communion in the Forces of the Crown. (1970, Reg. 7, see p. 315.)

The right of the Kirk Session to admit to the Lord's Table a member of any Christian Church is expressly affirmed.

For forms of Transference Certificate, &c., authorised by the General Assembly, see p. 785.

Minister's Name on Roll.

The name of every minister, as a communicant, should appear on a Communion Roll—acting ministers on the Rolls of their own congregations, and others on the appropriate Rolls. It does not follow that a minister is subject to a Kirk Session in the matter of discipline ; exception is made in his case ; he can be subject only to the Presbytery.

On the occasion of a vacancy the Roll must be revised in terms of the Statute (1932, iv., see Chap. XII., pp. 246). This revision does not include removal of names for absence from communion, which ought to have been done at the annual revision of the Roll in terms of Act, 1938, vi., 3. The object is to ensure that the Roll is otherwise correct and in order.

The admission of members to the congregation belongs to the Kirk Session. They are admitted by certificate of Transference if already members of the Church, or upon profession of their faith. (For admission by Certificate, see above.) In the case of those desiring admission to full Communion for the first time, it is the duty of the Kirk Session to satisfy itself as to their profession of faith in Christ, their knowledge of the cardinal doctrines of Christian belief, and the nature and significance of Church ordinances; also to make proper inquiry to ascertain that, so far as known, their outward life is consistent with their profession. The instruction and preparation of first communicants is the special duty of the minister (1931, xvii.). The Kirk Session must take care that such as are ignorant or scandalous be not admitted to Church membership till it is satisfied as to their knowledge and repentance. It is necessary to ascertain whether applicants for admission to full Communion have been baptised, and, if they have not, they must be baptised before admission. If, after communicating, they are found not to have been baptised, the rite of baptism should be administered. (For suggested questions to applicants, see Appendix, p. 783.) In practice, adult baptisms often take place in the presence of two witnesses, one of whom should be an elder. Admission to full Communion.

A member desiring to leave one congregation and to connect himself with another is entitled, on application, to a certificate of transference unless he be under discipline, or unless there be matters connected with his conduct as a member of the church which seem to the Kirk Session to call for inquiry. In this latter case, he has a right to demand that inquiry be immediately entered upon, and brought to a conclusion without unnecessary delay. Such certificate does not entitle to enrolment after the expiry of three years from the date it bears. Ministers and Kirk Sessions are instructed to make use of the Transference Certificate books authorised by the General Assembly, and to report annually the number of persons in respect of whom Notices of Removal have been sent (1963, 1). Under Act vi., 1938, Transference Certificates should be signed by both minister and session clerk but Kirk Sessions Certificate of Transference.

may authorise either the minister or session clerk to act on their behalf in issuing such certificates (1961, Regs. 1). (For authorised forms of Transference and Notices of Removals, see App. p. 785.)

It is the duty of Kirk Session to see that members leaving the congregation are furnished with Transference Certificates, and letters of introduction should be given to adherents leaving.

Call. It is the duty of the Kirk Session (and not of the Vacancy Committee) to take charge of the call and to arrange for its being signed by members after a minister has been elected to a vacant charge (1932, ix.).

Elders' Districts. The Kirk Session should arrange for the division of the congregation into convenient districts, and appoint one or more of its members to have special spiritual oversight of each district (1648, v.). Each elder ought to have a correct list of all those thus entrusted to his charge, members and adherents, and to report to the Kirk Session regarding them; it is his duty to visit the families in his district as their spiritual overseer, specially the aged and those in affliction, to care for the young, and to deal privately and tenderly with any who are neglecting public worship, or are under discipline.

Supervision of Congregational Societies.

Supervision of Societies. All societies or associations of members or adherents in connection with the congregation are under the supervision of the Kirk Session (1931, xvii.); and no society or association can be sanctioned as congregational without first receiving the approval of the Kirk Session.

Woman's Guild. The Congregational Branch of the Woman's Guild at the beginning of each year's work should consult with the minister and Kirk Session (1935, ix.). For control of the finances of the branch, see pp. 662, 663.

Care of the Young.

Roll of Young. All baptised young persons in the congregation, being members of the Church not in full Communion, have special claims to supervision and care. Their names should be entered in a roll kept by the Kirk Session; and each elder should endeavour to make himself acquainted with the young in his district, and to promote their spiritual welfare (Oct. 1929, i.).

Such young persons on removing to another locality should be furnished with an introduction to the minister or session clerk of a congregation there. Where such is not given, notice regarding them should be sent to the minister or session clerk. Such introductions ought to be acknowledged to the Kirk Session furnishing them. Young Persons leaving.

It is the duty of the Kirk Session to see that parents attend to the godly upbringing of their children, and to aid them in this work by instituting a Sunday school. These schools are not intended to relieve parents of the duty of themselves instructing their children in the Scriptures and in Christian truth. All Sunday schools are under the supervision of the Kirk Session, which should take a particular interest in them, and use means to promote their efficiency by visitation and otherwise. The minister being in charge of the instruction of the young (1931, xvii.) is the head of the Sunday school, even where, as is common, another person acts as superintendent. Teachers should be persons of intelligence and piety, and, if possible, members of the Church, and their appointment should have the concurrence of the minister and Kirk Session. For the benefit of those more advanced there should also be a Bible class or classes under the charge of the minister or other qualified persons appointed by him. Sunday Schools.

Mission Work (1939, 3; Rep. 1939, pp. 427-430).

The formation of a Mission Station rests ordinarily with the minister and Kirk Session of the parish within whose bounds it is required, it being understood that the Presbytery may at any time take the initiatory steps towards the same. The Station has no separate constitution of its own, but is under the charge and supervision of the minister and Kirk Session of the parish. It is at the discretion of the Presbytery if found more convenient, and with consent of the said minister and Kirk Session, to place it under the supervision of those of another parish. Formation of a Mission Station.

The communicants worshipping in the Mission church or hall have their names upon the Communion Roll of the parish, unless the Presbytery see fit to make other arrangements, although it may be considered expedient to note these separately for financial and other purposes. Roll of Members.

Where an agent, licensed or lay, is appointed to the Station, he is subject to the authority of the minister and Kirk Session. Agent in Charge.

Committee of Management.

The Kirk Session may appoint a Committee of Management, responsible always to the Kirk Session, from within the Mission membership, of which the minister and at least one elder shall be members.

Wherever possible, one member of the Kirk Session should be drawn from the communicants worshipping in the Mission church or hall.

Grants-in-aid.

Where grants-in-aid are provided by Committees of Assembly, a separate financial statement in respect of the Mission, and bearing the attestation of the Kirk Session, is to be submitted to the Committees concerned.

While the ultimate responsibility for the Mission Station rests upon the minister and Kirk Session of the parish, the members worshipping in the Station should, as far as possible, accept their direct share of the burden of the maintenance of religious ordinances and the upkeep of the buildings.

Proclamation of Banns.

Banns.

The procedure to be followed in connection with the Proclamation of Banns is detailed in Chap. IV., pp. 58-69, and App. XVI., p. 618. The names, addresses, and designations of persons proclaimed are to be entered in a book kept for that purpose, open to public inspection. This book shall be produced, when required, to the Kirk Session, and must be submitted annually to the Presbytery for attestation (1932, xvi.).

Use of Church Buildings (1932, xvii.).

Use of Church Buildings.

As the minister is allowed, subject to his Presbytery, a large discretion in the methods of his ministry, the place of worship and other ecclesiastical buildings belonging to the congregation are at his disposal for the purposes of his office. He can use them, and grant permission to use them, for all purposes connected with the congregation or any of its organisations; and for purposes which are of a religious, ecclesiastical or charitable nature, though not connected with the congregation, subject only to the control of the Presbytery. But he cannot use them, or grant permission to use them, for any other purpose not connected with the congregation, without the acquiescence of " the Kirk Session, Deacons' Court, Committee of Management, or Congregational Board, as the case may be," where such bodies exist. (See footnote, p. 52.) On the other hand, neither the Kirk Session nor the Deacons' Court nor the Congregational Board can use them, or grant permission to use them, for any purpose whatever without the minister's consent. Nor can the managers use or grant the use of such buildings for any purpose without the acquiescence of the minister and Kirk Session. Provided always that in congregations where provisions are made, either in a constitution approved by the Presbytery or in the title deeds of the church or meeting-house of the congregation, with regard to the use of the church buildings which differ from what is here stated, the provisions of such constitution or title deeds shall remain in force to the exclusion of this rule in so far as it differs from these provisions, unless these provisions shall be completely altered by the congregation. For any use made of the church property the sacred character of the building shall be kept in view. During a vacancy or the time when a minister has leave of absence from his charge, the interim moderator of Kirk Session has the same rights as the stated minister in the use of the church buildings.

Where the Kirk Session is responsible for maintaining the ecclesiastical properties it shall observe the terms of 1961, xxi. (p. 774). Upkeep of Property.

Burials in a church are forbidden (1643, 9). This prohibition has been extended to the deposit of cremated remains within a church (1951, 1 and Holy Rude Case 1955, 12). Burials in Church.

Long Service Certificates.

A Long Service Diploma awarded to Sunday school teachers who have completed twenty-one or more years of service is issued by the Committee on Religious Instruction of Youth for presentation on the recommendation of the Kirk Session.

A Certificate of Long Service for office-bearers and members who have completed forty or more years of service or who being over seventy years of age have completed thirty years of service is similarly issued by the General Administration Committee.

Finance.

For the duties of the Kirk Session in regard to finance, See Chap. III., *A.*, pp. 28-30. Finance

SECTION IV. *Election and Admission of Elders and Deacons* (1932, x.; 1966, xxviii.).

The General Assembly has laid down the following requirements as to the character of one who is to be set apart to the office of elder or deacon.

Character. He must be of good life and godly conversation, tender and circumspect in his walk, punctual in attending on ordinances, strict in his observance of the Lord's Day and in keeping up the worship of God in his family; and one who will be careful of the flock, an example of sobriety, meekness, holiness, abstaining from all appearance of evil (1722, ix.). If his usual residence is in another parish, a certificate is to be produced from the Kirk Session thereof that such is his character (1816, x.).

A member of another Kirk Session is ineligible. Since a minister is eligible for membership of the Courts of the Church only as a minister he cannot be elected as an elder, but he may become associated in the practical work of the Kirk Session of the congregation of which he is a member (1961, xxiv.).

The following are the Regulations with regard to the election and admission of elders and deacons (1932, x.):—

ELDERS.

Act, 1932, x. 1. The Kirk Session shall determine the number of elders required for the oversight of the congregation, and the time when a new election is to take place. The Kirk Session shall determine the mode of election, which may be either by the choice of the Kirk Session itself as provided for in Regulation 2, or by the direct vote of the members of the congregation as provided for in Regulations 3 and 4.

Election by Resolution of Kirk Session.

2. The Kirk Session itself may elect as elders, when an addition to the number of elders is considered necessary, such persons as are deemed suitable for the office who shall be members of the congregation in full Communion and shall have attained the age of twenty-one years. In this case the Kirk Session shall confer with those who are so chosen, and upon obtaining their consent shall proceed to their ordination and admission in terms of Regulations 6, 7 and 8.

Election by Vote of the Congregation

3. When the Kirk Session has resolved that it is expedient to have an election of elders, and has fixed the number to be elected, and the date of the election, and has resolved that the method of election be by vote of the members of the congregation, due intimation thereof shall be made at the time of public worship, on the two successive Sundays preceding the date of election. It is desirable to give the congregation even earlier intimation of an intended election so that members may have time to inquire regarding persons suitable for the office, who shall be members of the congregation in full Communion and shall have attained the age of twenty-one years.

4. The election of elders by vote of the congregation may be made in either of the two following modes—viz. : (*a*) at a congregational meeting held in presence of the Kirk Session for the purpose of nominating persons for the office, to be voted upon, if necessary, as the meeting may determine ; (*b*) by signed lists. The Kirk Session shall determine in which of these ways the election shall be made ; and give directions to the members accordingly when intimating that the election is to be made. (*a*) When mode (*a*) is followed, intimation shall be made on at least two Sundays immediately preceding the meeting, that a congregational meeting will be held for the purpose of nominating persons for the office of the eldership ; with certification that if the number nominated does not exceed the number required, those nominated will be declared to be elected, subject to the judgment of the Kirk Session (see Regulation 5), and that if the number nominated exceeds the number required, a vote of the congregation on those nominated will be taken by standing up or by voting papers, as the meeting may determine. The Moderator of Kirk Session or a minister of the Church authorised by him in writing shall preside and open the meeting with devotional exercises. The names proposed and seconded shall be taken down. After full opportunity has been given for proposing names, the moderator shall ascertain whether any additional names are to be proposed, and if none be proposed he shall declare the leet closed. If the number on the leet do not exceed the number of elders required, the moderator thereupon shall declare them elected to the office of the eldership, subject to the judgment of the Kirk Session (see Regulation 5). If the number on the leet exceed the number required the moderator shall engage in prayer for the Divine guidance in

the election ; and the meeting shall decide whether the vote will be taken by standing up, or by voting papers issued to the members of the congregation. If it be agreed to vote by standing up, the names shall be submitted successively to the meeting in the order in which they have been nominated, and shall be voted upon by the meeting. No member shall vote for more than the number for which the congregation is asked by the Kirk Session to vote. Those, to the number required, having the highest number of votes shall be declared to be elected, subject to the judgment of the Kirk Session (see Regulation 5).

If the meeting resolve that voting papers be used, the meeting shall be closed. The Kirk Session thereafter shall cause voting papers to be prepared and distributed to the members of the congregation, containing the names of those on the leet arranged in alphabetical order, together with full instructions as to marking, signing, and returning the voting papers on or before a time appointed by the Kirk Session. The voting papers shall be examined, and the votes shall be counted by the Kirk Session ; and those, to the number required, who have the largest number of votes shall be declared to be elected, subject to the judgment of the Kirk Session (see Regulation 5).

(*b*) Where mode (*b*) is followed, the Kirk Session by intimation made from the pulpit shall request the members to give in lists containing the names, to a number not exceeding that which the congregation is asked to vote for, of members of the congregation in full Communion whom they desire to be elected ; each list being duly signed by the member or members voting by it, and being given in at the place and by the time fixed by the Kirk Session. The lists shall be examined, and the votes counted by the Kirk Session ; and those, to the number required, who have the largest number of votes shall be declared to be elected, subject to the judgment of the Kirk Session (see Regulation 5).

The Kirk Session, when intimating the number of elders required, may call upon the congregation to vote for a number as nearly as may be one-half more than the number required ; as six when four, or eight when five are required. If this is done, those to the number required who have the highest number of votes, whatever mode of voting is followed, shall be held to be elected ; but should the election of any of them be not sustained, or should any decline to accept office, the next highest shall be held to be elected, provided the

Session judges that a sufficient number of votes has been given for him; and so on, if necessary, until the whole number for which the congregation has been asked to vote is exhausted. Or should the Kirk Session think it advisable it may, when the result of the vote is ascertained, at once declare to be elected those for whom most votes are given, up to the number for which the congregation was asked to vote. (For Form of Intimation, see App. p. 821.)

5. The Kirk Session shall judge of the qualifications of those elected before sustaining their election. No one shall be admitted as a ruling elder if the Kirk Session be not satisfied with his qualifications, unless its judgment be reversed by a higher Court. When the Kirk Session is satisfied as to the fitness of the persons elected, and has sustained their election, it shall confer with them in regard to their acceptance of office; and on obtaining their acceptance it shall appoint the time of their ordination or admission, and shall proceed in terms of Regulations 6, 7, and 8.

6. The session clerk shall prepare an edict to be read from the pulpit on two Sundays giving intimation that if any person have objection to the life or doctrine of any of those proposed to be ordained or admitted, such objection must be given in to the Kirk Session at a meeting duly intimated in the edict, to be held not less than seven free days after the edict is first served, with certification that if no objection be given in, and substantiated at the time and place of which notice is given, the Kirk Session will proceed with the ordination or admission at the time appointed for it. (For Form of Edict, see App. p. 822.)

7. At the time and place intimated in the edict the Kirk Session shall meet to receive any objection which may be offered. The edict having been returned, certified as having been duly served, the Kirk Session shall intimate that it is prepared to hear objections. Any objection made shall refer to the life or doctrine of the elder-elect. If any objection is made, and forthwith substantiated, or if the Kirk Session judge that further inquiry is necessary, the Kirk Session shall not proceed to the ordination or admission of the person objected to until the objection is disposed of. Objections which in the judgment of the Kirk Session are frivolous or unsupported by evidence are to be set aside, and the ordination, or admission, proceeded with.

8. The ordination and admission to office shall take place in presence of the congregation, at a diet of public worship. The Kirk Session having been constituted, the moderator

shall narrate the steps that have been taken, and put the prescribed question. On receiving satisfactory answers and after the elders-elect have signed the Formula, he shall admit to office in the congregation any who have already been ordained to the eldership, and ordain by prayer and admit to the office of ruling elder in the congregation those not previously ordained, commending them to the grace of God for the work to which they are appointed; the right hand of fellowship shall be given by the moderator and other members of Kirk Session to the newly admitted elders, and the service concluded with suitable exhortations to them and to the congregation. Thereafter the newly ordained and admitted elders have their names added to the roll, and take their seats in the Kirk Session. (For Question and Formula, see App. X., pp. 568, 569.) *Note.*—This meeting is just as any other meeting, however called, and must be constituted in the usual manner.

Deacons.

9. The Kirk Session shall determine when it is expedient to have an election of deacons, and what number is required. The Kirk Session shall exercise precisely the same functions with reference to the election and ordination or admission of deacons as in the case of elders in accordance with the procedure outlined in Regulations 3-8. It is not desirable that a vote for election of elders and deacons be taken at the same time. (For Question and Formula, see App. X., p. 568.)

10. Minutes of all proceedings in connection with the election, ordination and admission of elders and deacons shall be recorded in the Minute Book of the Kirk Session.

11. In place of the above method of electing deacons, congregations may resolve that the office of deacon shall be held by persons, being male or female, members of the congregation in full Communion and at least eighteen years of age, who shall, without ordination, be appointed thereto for a term of years. Such terminable appointment to the office of deacon shall be for a period of three years, and the regulations governing the election and appointment of managers and members of a Congregational Board shall apply to the election and appointment of deacons after this method.

The names of deacons thus elected who accept office shall be read over to the congregation on the first convenient Sunday after their election, and the minister shall commend them in prayer to the grace of God for the work to which they have been appointed.

Resolutions involving changes in the constitution of a Deacons' Court shall be adopted either at a congregational meeting duly appointed by the Kirk Session and held for that express purpose, of which full intimation has been previously given on at least two Sundays; or by voting papers, the issue of which shall be similarly authorised and intimated by the Kirk Session. (See App. pp. 805, 822.)

When a proposal for changing the method of administering its temporal affairs is before a congregation, no step shall be taken by the Kirk Session toward the election of persons to any such office until the proposal for change has been disposed of.

In the event of a congregation making the above change as regards the persons eligible for the deaconship and the tenure of their office, such change shall be duly notified to the Presbytery.

In the case of congregations where the model constitution for *quoad sacra* parishes is in operation, it is the duty of the Kirk Session to appoint the day and hour when the congregation will meet to elect members to the Congregational Board (1931, xxxii.). See Chap. II. (*c*), p. 23.)

SECTION V. *Relation of Kirk Session to Superior Courts.*

The Kirk Session is subject in all its proceedings to the review and directions of the Presbytery and Superior Courts of the Church, and the Minute Book of the Kirk Session is to be submitted to the Presbytery, Synod, or General Assembly when called for. The Kirk Session is charged with carrying out the decisions of the Superior Courts in matters within its province, and furnishing to them such information as they may call for. It has direct access to the Presbytery by petitions and references, and through the Presbytery to the higher Courts (see Chap. V., Sect. III. (*b*) and (*e*), pp. 89, 100).

Review by Superior Courts.

Access to Superior Courts.

Records Enjoined.

The following records are ordered to be kept by the Kirk Session, and with the exception of the Supplementary Roll, must be annually submitted to the Presbytery for attestation:—

Records.

Record of proceedings—*i.e.*, Minute Book (1700, ix.; Oct. 1929, i.);
Communion Roll (1938, vi.);
Supplementary Roll (1938, vi.).
Roll of Baptised Persons not Communicants (1930, 10).

Property Register (1961, xxi.).
Register of Baptisms (1931, xvii.).
Register of Proclamation of Banns (1932, xvi.).
Abstract of Accounts (1929, i).

Visitation. At the quinquennial visitation of the congregation the Visiting Committee holds a separate meeting with the Kirk Session (1931, xii.; 1973, i.). See also Chap. VII., p. 170.

Records prior to 1900. All records prior to date 1900, including those containing entries partly subsequent to that year, are to be transmitted, by injunction of the General Assembly, to the Principal Clerk at the Church Offices for purposes of record and for transmission to H.M. Keeper of Records at H.M. Register House. This injunction has been relaxed as follows—" except where other arrangements satisfactory to the General Administration Committee have been made for their safe custody ". (1968, i.)

A request by a Kirk Session, Deacons' Court or other body for re-transmission of any such record or volume or document shall be made in the first place to the Presbytery, which, if satisfied that the business of the Kirk Session, Deacons' Court or other body requires the production of such record or volume or document, shall request the Principal Clerk or Depute Clerk of the General Assembly to make such application. Any such record, volume or document so re-transmitted shall be returned to the Keeper as soon as may be after it has ceased to be required for the purpose for which it was re-transmitted.

Inventory of Property. An inventory of all property held by the congregation should be made and a record entered at the back of the Minute Book of the Kirk Session. This should be kept up-to-date and all changes notified at once to the Keeper of the Benefice Register of the Presbytery.

At all vacancies the inventory should be checked and brought up-to-date and a copy should be placed in the hands of the new minister on his admission for the purpose of enabling him to ascertain that he has obtained the custody of all Church properties recorded therein.

Election of Representative Elder to Presbytery and Synod (1932, x.).

The General Assembly has made the following Regulations with regard to representation of Kirk Sessions in Presbytery and Synod :—

Representative Elder. Each Kirk Session shall elect annually one of its own number, or with the special sanction of the Presbytery any *bona fide* acting elder within the bounds of the Presbytery, to represent it in Presbytery and Synod. Where two or more congregations are linked together under the charge of one minister and each congregation has a separate Kirk Session, the Kirk Sessions shall meet together as one annually for the purpose of electing one representative elder in Presbytery and Synod. The election shall take place within two months of the close of the General Assembly, and commissions shall run from 1st July to 30th June. Commissions may be presented and sustained at any meeting of Presbytery, either ordinary, *in hunc effectum*, or *pro re nata*, held after the Assembly, but the elder shall not be entitled to take his seat till 1st July. After the expiry of two months from the close of the General Assembly, each Presbytery shall elect a sufficient number of elders to make the number of ministers and elders in the Presbytery equal. Such elders may be chosen from any Kirk Session within the bounds, and such elders shall, before taking their seat in the Presbytery, produce a certificate of *bona fide* eldership from the Kirk Session to which they belong. In the event of the death, resignation, or disqualification of any elder appointed to represent his Kirk Session in Presbytery and Synod the Kirk Session concerned may elect another elder to take his place within one month of such event. Similarly, in place of any elder elected by the Presbytery itself who may, during the year, die, resign, or become disqualified the Presbytery may elect another at its next or any subsequent meeting. Presbytery clerks shall send a list of the names and addresses of elders whose commissions have been sustained by the Presbytery to the Synod clerk annually not later than three months after the close of the Assembly, and shall intimate any changes which occur during the year. The synod may call for the production of the commissions if it shall see cause. (For Form of Commissions, see App. p. 786.)

Assembly Elder.

An elder elected by a Presbytery as one of its representatives to the General Assembly requires a certificate in the form appointed by the Assembly from the moderator and the clerk of the Kirk Session to which he belongs (1839, xii. ; 1934, 2). (For Form of Certificate, see App. p. 788.)

Overtures.

When an overture is transmitted to Presbyteries under the Barrier Act they are required to give Kirk Sessions within their bounds an opportunity of reporting their opinion thereon, when specially instructed to do so (Oct. 1929, i.).

CHAPTER VII.

The Presbytery.

Section I. Introductory.

The Presbytery is now the characteristic and in some sense the fundamental court of the Church since, on the one hand it directly superintends not only Kirk Sessions but the whole ecclesiastical activity within its bounds and on the other hand elects annually those ministers and elders who are to constitute the General Assembly. Yet the earliest framework of the Church of Scotland made provision in it for only "congregational, provincial and national assemblies." The Presbytery arose partly out of the "Weekly Exercise," a meeting appointed for bringing the ministers and people of a district together to read and interpret the Scriptures, and partly out of the need for Synods to delegate some of their duties (G. D. Henderson, *The Church of Scotland*). The General Assembly of 1581 set forth a regular pattern of presbyteries, the prototype of the existing organisation. From the time that Presbyteries were established the process began of devolving upon them the duties and responsibilities which had at first appertained to the Provincial Synods. This has now proceeded to so great an extent that periodically there appear proposals for the abolition of Provincial Synods.

It belongs to the General Assembly to unite, disjoin and erect Presbyteries, to alter their bounds and increase or decrease their number as changing populations or other circumstances may require. It is competent, however, for a Kirk Session to initiate proceedings for the transfer of a particular parish from one Presbytery to an adjacent one, the seat of which may have become more convenient. The procedure is laid down in Act 1957, xvii., p. 751.

Transfer of Charge to Another Presbytery.

Section II. Constitution and Officials.

Formation of Presbytery.

A Presbytery is formed by the General Assembly, and in the Act forming it the bounds thereof are defined, the designation fixed, and the place and time of the first meeting appointed (Oct. 1581, 2). The senior minister present presides at that meeting until the Presbytery has been duly constituted, the roll of members made up, and a moderator elected.

As the General Assembly have the power of uniting, disjoining and erecting Presbyteries at pleasure, their bounds may be altered or their number increased according to the change of circumstances (1699, iv.; 1703, xiii.; 1707, x.; 1724, v.; 1961, xxxi., &c.).

A Presbytery shall consist of ministers and elders.

The Membership of Presbytery is governed by Act II., 1970. (Schedule amended 1975, sess. 1.) **Membership.**

Act anent Membership of Presbyteries.

1. As from the date of the passing of this Act Presbyteries shall be composed of ministers and elders as provided hereunder.

2. Any one of the following persons and no other shall, for the purposes of this Act, be deemed to be a minister of this Church:— **Ministers.**

(*a*) A person who has been ordained to the office of the ministry by a Presbytery of the Church and who has not resigned, or been judicially deprived of, his status, and who has not entered the service and come under the jurisdiction of another Church.

(*b*) A person who, having been a minister of this Church and having left the service of this Church (either to enter the service of another Church or take employment outwith the jurisdiction of any Church), has left that service or employment and has obtained from the Committee on Admission of Ministers of Other Churches a Certificate of Eligibility.

(*c*) An ordained missionary of this Church who having entered the courts and come under the jurisdiction of the indigenous Church in the area where he worked has ceased to be under such jurisdiction and has been granted by the Overseas Council or its Executive a Certificate of Eligibility.

(*d*) A minister of another Church who on petition to the General Assembly has been accepted and granted the status of a minister.

(*e*) A person who having resigned, or been judicially deprived of, his status as a minister of this Church has had that status restored to him by the General Assembly.

3. Ministers as above defined who shall satisfy the requirements set forth in the following sub-sections (*a*) to (*o*) shall be members of Presbytery, and no other minister shall be entitled to sit as a ministerial member of Presbytery.

(*a*) A minister of this Church who has been inducted to the charge of a Church and Parish shall be a member of the Presbytery within whose bounds that charge is situated.

(*b*) A minister having a seat in Presbytery in terms of the immediately foregoing sub-section, (i) on demitting his charge on account of age or infirmity shall retain his membership of that Presbytery, and (ii) on demitting his charge in the interests of readjustment shall retain his membership of that Presbytery unless and until he accepts a full-time appointment (other than one of those in the Schedule to this Act) which is outwith the jurisdiction of this Church.

(*c*) A minister of this Church appointed to a charge of a Church and Parish for a period of years and introduced thereto by the Presbytery of the bounds shall be a member of that Presbytery.

(*d*) A minister who is a member of a Presbytery in terms of the immediately foregoing sub-section, when the appointment is terminated shall cease to be a member of Presbytery unless (i) at the time of the termination he is precluded by reason of age or infirmity from seeking another post, in which case he shall retain his membership of that Presbytery, or (ii) he had been eligible on other grounds to retain membership of his former Presbytery, in which case he shall be restored to its membership.

(*e*) A minister of this Church holding an appointment as a professor, reader, or lecturer in the Faculty of Divinity in a Scottish University may be a member of the Presbytery within whose bounds is situated the University in which he teaches.

(*f*) A minister who is a member of a Presbytery in terms of the immediately foregoing sub-section, on retiring from his post on grounds of age or infirmity shall retain his membership of that Presbytery.

(*g*) A minister of this Church appointed by a Committee of this Church to an overseas post shall, if he has not come under the jurisdiction of any other Church, be a member of the Overseas Presbytery in the area where he works ; or, if there is no Overseas Presbytery, of the Presbytery to which he belonged at the date of his appointment or, if he were ordained for the post, of the Presbytery which ordained him.

(*h*) A minister who is a member of a Presbytery in terms of the immediately foregoing sub-section, on retiring from his post on grounds of age or infirmity shall retain his membership of that Presbytery.

(*i*) A minister who had held an appointment under a Committee of the Church in virtue of which he was required to be a member of another Church, on retiring from that appointment on account of age or infirmity, if he takes up permanent residence in Scotland or England shall be a member of the Presbytery within whose bounds he resides provided he satisfies the requirements of Section 2 sub-section (*c*) above.

(*j*) A minister of this Church appointed to a commission as a chaplain to H.M. Forces (i) when serving in Scotland shall be a member of the Presbytery within whose bounds he is serving; (ii) when serving in England or in an area where there is an Overseas Presbytery shall be a member of the Presbytery of England or of the appropriate Overseas Presbytery as the case may be; and (iii) when serving elsewhere shall be a member of the Presbytery to which he belonged at the date of his appointment, or, if he were ordained for the post, of the Presbytery which ordained him.

(*k*) A minister who is a member of a Presbytery in terms of the immediately foregoing sub-section, on relinquishing his commission on grounds of age or infirmity, or on account of having attained the maximum age, or of having served the number of years permitted by the appropriate regulations, shall retain his membership of that Presbytery.

(*l*) A minister of this Church introduced by a Presbytery as an Associate Minister in an area declared by the General Assembly on the Report of the Committee on Unions and Readjustments to be a Special Area of Readjustment or in a parish in respect of which an Act of Assembly makes specific provision for such an appointment, shall be a member of that Presbytery.

(*m*) A minister of this Church appointed to a post, other than that of a parish minister or locum tenens for a minister, within the jurisdiction of the Church and under the direction and control of one of its courts or Committees may be a member of a Presbytery, and he may choose whether it shall be the Presbytery within whose bounds is situated (i) the parish in which he works, (ii) an office from which his work is wholly or partly carried out, or (iii) the congregation to which he shall attach himself.

(*n*) A minister of this Church appointed to one of the offices designated in the Schedule attached to this Act may, if he so elects, become a member of the Presbytery within whose bounds his sphere of work is situated, or of the Presbytery within whose bounds he shall reside, or of the Presbytery within whose bounds is situated the congregation to which he shall attach himself, as he may choose.

(*o*) A minister who is a member of a Presbytery in terms of any of the three immediately foregoing sub-sections (*l*), (*m*) or (*n*), on retiring or resigning from such an appointment on grounds of age or infirmity shall retain his membership of that Presbytery.

4. It shall be the duty of the Committee on General Administration at the end of each quinquennium after the passing of this Act to review its terms in so far as these define the classes of minister entitled to sit in Presbytery and to review the Schedule to the Act and to report to the General Assembly whether in their opinion any amendment of the Act or of the Schedule is called for.

5. A minister inducted to a parish, introduced to a terminable appointment or an Associate Ministry, or appointed to an overseas post or to a chaplaincy in H.M. Forces shall have his name added to the Roll of the appropriate Presbytery in virtue of such induction, introduction or appointment. A minister, other than a retired minister, entitled to a seat in Presbytery on grounds other than the foregoing shall present a Presbyterial Certificate and Certificate of Status, shall give a satisfactory answer to the question, "Do you declare your adherence to the vows which you took at your ordination?" and shall sign the Formula; and thereupon his name shall be added to the Roll of the Presbytery.

6. A minister who is entitled to be a member of a Presbytery on grounds of having demitted his charge or having resigned from an office as in Section 3 above may petition for transference from one Presbytery to another. Synods shall have power to deal with such petitions and their decision thereanent shall be final. Where two Synods are involved, the petition shall be presented to the Synod into whose province the

petitioner desires to transfer, and advance intimation shall be given by the petitioner to the other Synod and to the two Presbyteries involved. A minister so transferred shall have his name added to the Roll of the Presbytery on presentation of the relevant extract of Synod along with a Presbyterial Certificate and a Certificate of Status.

7. A minister of this Church shall be eligible for membership of the courts of the Church only as a minister.

8. A minister of this Church who does not come within the terms of sub-sections (*a*), (*c*) or (*l*) of Section 3 above may be associated in the practical work of the kirk session of the congregation to which he is attached but shall not be a member of the kirk session.

9. Nothing in this Act shall affect the existing rights of any minister who has demitted his charge or resigned his appointment prior to the Act coming into force.

10. For the purpose of this Act an elder shall be deemed to be a person who has been ordained to the office of elder in this Church and who, having been admitted to membership of a kirk session, has not been deposed, disqualified or otherwise removed from office therein. **Elders.**

11. Each kirk session within the bounds of a Presbytery shall within two months of the close of each General Assembly meet, and, with the exceptions undernoted, shall elect one of its own members (or, with permission of the Presbytery, any *bona fide* acting elder within the bounds of the Presbytery) to represent it in the Presbytery during the ensuing year. When two congregations are linked under the charge of one minister their kirk sessions shall meet together for this purpose and shall elect one elder to represent them both. When a collegiate arrangement provides for two charges within a congregation the kirk session concerned shall appoint two elders.

12. Commissions in favour of representative elders shall run from 1st July to 30th June and may be presented to any meeting of Presbytery held after the close of the General Assembly, providing a quorum is present apart from the elder whose commission is presented. On the commission being declared in order the elder concerned shall be entitled to take his seat.

13. A Presbytery shall itself elect such number of elders as may be required at the time when the Roll is made up to secure that the number of ministers and elders in the Presbytery shall be equal. Such elders shall be chosen from any kirk session within the bounds, and before taking their seats they

shall produce certificates of *bona fide* eldership from the kirk sessions to which they belong.

14. Acts of Assembly XXIV. 1960, XXIV. 1961, XIV. 1962, XIV. 1964, and Interim Act IV. 1968, in so far as inconsistent with the foregoing are hereby repealed.

SCHEDULE :—

Chaplains to Scottish Universities ;
Lecturers in Religious Studies in Scottish Universities ;
Principal lecturers and lecturers in Religious Education in Scottish Colleges of Education ;
Organisers and Assistant Organisers of Religious Broadcasting in Scotland ;
The Secretary of the Scottish Sunday School Union for Christian Education ;
The Secretary of the Scottish Churches Council ;
The Secretary of the National Bible Society of Scotland ;
The Scottish Secretary of the United Society for Christian Literature.

Transference of Membership (1960, xxiv.).

Transference of Membership.

1. Synods shall have power to receive and dispose of petitions by ministers who have demitted their charges on grounds of age or infirmity, for transference from one Presbytery to another.

2. Where a proposed transference involves two Synods, the petition shall be presented to the Synod in whose bounds is situated the Presbytery to which the petitioner wishes to be transferred, and intimation of the petition shall be made to the other Synod.

3. The decision of the Synod shall be final.

Replacement of Representative Elder.

In the event of the death, resignation, or disqualification of any elder appointed to represent his Kirk Session in Presbytery and Synod, the Kirk Session concerned may elect another elder to take his place within one month of such event. Similarly, in place of any elder elected by the Presbytery itself who may, during the year, die, resign or become disqualified, the Presbytery may elect another at its next or any subsequent meeting.

In the event of any Kirk Session being unable to replace a representative elder who has died, resigned or been disqualified the Presbytery may permit it to elect any *bona fide* acting elder within the bounds of the Presbytery or may itself elect an additional elder.

Each Presbytery Clerk shall lodge with the Clerk of Synod, not later than three months after the close of the General Assembly annually, a list of the names and addresses of elders whose commissions have been sustained by the Presbytery and shall intimate such changes as may occur during the year. The Synod may call for the production of the commissions if it shall see cause (1932, x.). (For Form of Commission, see Appendix, p. 786.)

For Presbyteries furth of Scotland reference should be made to Chap. XIV., p. 298.

Roll. It is the established practice of the Church that, as Steuart expresses it, "ministers are enrolled and have place only according to the seniority of their ordination," whatever character or station anyone holds. Elders follow.

Assessors. The Assembly have often appointed assessors to act along with a Presbytery: expressly with a vote (1717, 12); apparently with a vote (1842, Com., June 1); expressly "without a vote" (1888, 5); expressly "without a judicial vote" (1886, 10; 1897, 11); sometimes for specified business, as in 1717, 1842, 1888, 1897; sometimes in general, as in 1886.

Commissions to Presbytery. The Assembly has appointed commissions to perform duty laid on a Presbytery if it should neglect or refuse (1737, 6); to take proof in a case of libel, and report to next Assembly (1787, 6); to co-operate with the Presbyteries in certain duties (1840, xii.; 1841, xv.); to inquire how the members discharge their duties (1886, 10).

Corresponding Members. A Presbytery may invite any member of another Presbytery present at its meeting to be a corresponding member. A corresponding member has a right to speak, but not to vote, on any question before the court.

Ministers associated with Presbytery. It has been the practice to associate with the Presbytery at any particular meeting—*e.g.*, for ordination or induction—a minister present from another Presbytery, or from another communion, whose ordination is recognised by the Church.

Officials.

Moderator. The moderator shall be chosen from among the ministerial members of the court by free election, on the recommendation of the Business or other Committee of the Presbytery, and he shall hold office for a year at least and be eligible for re-election (1944, xxi.).

For the duties of the moderator in general, see Chap. V., p. 77.

In the absence of the moderator a previous moderator, and failing such the senior minister present, takes the chair and constitutes the meeting (Steuart, bk. 1, tit. 9). Thereafter the Presbytery may appoint any other ministerial member as moderator *pro tempore,* if it see cause. But if the moderator appears at any stage of the proceedings, he takes the chair, and the fact is recorded.

The Presbytery has power to appoint a minister to act as moderator *pro tempore* on any particular occasion.

If the moderator cease to be a member of Presbytery during his term of office, the duties immediately devolve upon the previous moderator until next ordinary meeting of Presbytery.

Clerks of Presbytery. The Presbytery appoints one or more clerks who hold office during the pleasure of the Presbytery.

For duties of Presbytery clerks, see Chap. V., p. 79.

In the absence of the clerk the Presbytery appoints one of its members to act as clerk *pro tempore.* The fact of the appointment is entered in the minutes, and the oath *de fideli* administered (see p. 80).

Should it be recorded in the minutes that the member of Presbytery thus appointed has already at a previous meeting of the court taken the oath *de fideli* as clerk *pro tempore* it does not appear necessary that this be repeated.

Officer. The Presbytery may appoint an officer to wait on its meetings and to execute its orders. At his appointment he promises to perform the duties of his office with fidelity. He receives a salary fixed by the Presbytery.

Presbytery Fund. The Presbytery has the right to assess the congregations under its jurisdiction, so as to obtain such funds as may be necessary for carrying on its business, and a treasurer is appointed to take charge of the Presbytery's funds. "Church assessments are not voluntary contributions. Their payment is a duty incumbent on loyal congregations of the Church" (Sir W. Chree, K.C., Procurator).

Section III. Meetings and Procedure.

Quorum. Three members of Presbytery form a quorum, provided that two of them are ministers (1934, xi.).

Meetings. The election of representatives to the General Assembly renders two meetings of Presbytery indispensable in the course of the year. (This does not apply to the Presbyteries of Europe and Jerusalem—see p. 644.) Apart from the special limitations imposed on Presbyteries with regard to those two meetings they have the power of meeting when they judge it expedient. In the exercise of this power it is necessary for them at each ordinary meeting to resolve when the next ordinary meeting shall be held, to enter the resolution in their minutes, and to cause public intimation of it to be made. If these requirements be neglected by a Presbytery, its powers and functions lapse altogether until revived in a constitutional manner (see p. 150).

Restriction on time of Meeting.

No meeting of Presbytery can be held while either the General Assembly or the Provincial Synod of the district is sitting, except when special leave to that effect has been granted by the Assembly or Synod respectively. Presbyteries within a radius of fifty miles of Edinburgh are prohibited from meeting on the days appointed for the stated meetings of the Commission of the Assembly.

An Ordinary Meeting.

An ordinary meeting of Presbytery is one which takes place in consequence of an express adjournment for ordinary business from a previous ordinary meeting, or in consequence of an express appointment by the General Assembly or the Provincial Synod, or in consequence of the lapsed powers and functions of the Presbytery having been revived in a constitutional manner (see p. 150).

Places of Meeting.

Every Presbytery fixes one or more places at which ordinary meetings are held (1932, xx.). If it is resolved to hold a meeting for ordinary business at any other place, or to transact ordinary business at a meeting appointed on account of special business, care must be taken that sufficient notice of the time and place of meeting be given to all the members.

When a Presbytery adopts a motion, of which due notice has been given, that it is desirable that it should name a place outwith its bounds at which its ordinary meetings may be held, it must petition the General Assembly for leave to meet outside its bounds.

An *in hunc effectum* Meeting.

An *in hunc effectum* meeting of Presbytery is a meeting specially appointed by the Presbytery for the transaction of specified business. This kind of meeting requires that the particular business and the time and place of meeting be specified in the minute of the meeting which appointed it, along with the resolution to meet *in hunc effectum*, and that public intimation thereof be made at that meeting. No business can be transacted at an *in hunc effectum* meeting except that for which it has been appointed. It may adjourn but only for the prosecution of the same business.

The only exception to this rule is that elders' commissions may be sustained at any meeting of Presbytery (see p. 145 (12)).

A *pro re nata* Meeting.

A *pro re nata* meeting is a meeting called during the interval between one ordinary meeting and another, in consequence of some unexpected business having arisen which requires immediate attention. Such a meeting may be called only by the moderator, either on his own initiative, or in consequence of a requisition addressed to him by at least three of the members. It is required that written notice of the meeting be given to every member, and that the specific business for which it is called be distinctly stated in the circular calling it, and no other business can be transacted at it. When the meeting takes place, the moderator must explain his reasons for calling it, and the Presbytery must pronounce judgment upon his conduct in doing so.

The Presbytery may adjourn, if necessary, to next ordinary meeting, or to a date previous to next ordinary meeting to complete the business. If the moderator declines to call a *pro re nata* meeting after a requisition to do so has been addressed to him, the whole circumstances of the case may be brought before the Presbytery at its next ordinary meeting. In the event of the death of the moderator, and until a successor is appointed, his rights and duties in connection with the calling of *pro re nata* meetings devolve upon the clerk.

Death of a Minister.

On the occasion of the death of a minister the Presbytery may meet without formal summons on the day of the funeral, and make arrangements for supply of the pulpit and for other necessary matters, unless intimation otherwise has been duly made to members by advertisement or by individual notice (1931, xx.).

On the death of a retired minister, or other minister not holding a pastoral charge, who is a member of the court, the Presbytery clerk is normally notified immediately and, in conjunction with the moderator, makes whatever arrangements circumstances may dictate for the Presbytery to be adequately represented at the funeral.

On the death of a minister, whether active or retired, it is the duty of the Presbytery clerk to make immediate intimation to the Church and Ministry Department.

It is the custom in most Presbyteries that a tribute to the deceased minister is read at the first ordinary meeting after the funeral.

Presbytery lapsed.

When from any cause the powers and functions of a Presbytery have lapsed, it shall be competent for any three or more of its members to address a requisition to the moderator, failing whom to the clerk, to call a meeting of the members of Presbytery for the purpose of appointing a day on which the Presbytery shall meet and proceed with ordinary business; and the moderator or clerk shall be bound to comply with such a requisition and to call a meeting, to be held on a day not less than ten nor more than fifteen days from the date of the requisition, by circular letter addressed to every member on the roll of the Presbytery. This meeting when held shall be considered a *pro re nata* meeting, at which no business can be transacted except the appointment of a day for an ordinary meeting (1863, x.; F.C., 1866, xii.). At the next ensuing meeting of the Provincial Synod, the Presbytery shall be bound to explain the causes that have necessitated its adopting this special procedure, and shall be liable to censure if the explanation be unsatisfactory.

For opening and closing of meetings, keeping and approving of minutes, see Chap. V., pp. 76, 81-86.

Order of Business. After the minutes are signed and the roll adjusted, all petitions, references, and papers of any kind to be submitted to the Presbytery, which have been previously put into the hands of the clerk, are laid on the table. The clerk intimates all causes and business to be brought before the court, and the Presbytery determines the order in which they are to be taken up. Business left over from a previous meeting has ordinarily precedence of new matters. Business appointed for a specified hour must be taken up at the time fixed. (Unless the Presbytery has adopted Standing Orders which make other provision, it is usual to allow any business which may be in progress at such "time fixed" to proceed, as in the General Assembly, for not more than thirty minutes.)

Presbytery in conference. For greater freedom in the discussion of important questions the Presbytery may resolve to meet in conference. The Presbytery may appoint its moderator or any other of its members to preside at such a conference or it may authorise the conference to appoint its own chairman. Resolutions framed and decisions taken at a conference are not recorded in the minutes of the court. The object of a conference is to ripen opinion for subsequent decision or action by the court or to influence public opinion.

Committee of Presbytery. For the consideration of any matter involving a variety of details or for other sufficient reasons, the Presbytery may resolve to meet in committee and appoint a chairman who may be the moderator or any other member. When this is done the ordinary rules of debate are understood to be suspended. When resolutions are framed or decisions adopted in this committee, they are reported to the Presbytery when it resumes, and they are usually adopted by the Presbytery without further discussion, the right of dissent, or of dissent and complaint, being reserved. (See Chap. V., pp. 91-99, 112.)

Committees. The Presbytery may appoint committees of its number for the more careful and minute consideration of those portions of business which seem to require such appointment, it being understood that these committees keep regular minutes and are to report to the Presbytery, which will record its own judgment upon the subjects of the several reports. Each committee has a convener who has a casting vote, but no deliberative vote. Committees cannot meet when the Presbytery is sitting except by leave of the court. Presbyteries are empowered to add women to their committees as they shall see cause. (U.F. Act, 1916, xii.)

Women Members.

Motions and Speaking. With a view to a Presbytery coming to a decision upon any question, a member of Presbytery must make a motion on the subject.

Notice of Motion. In cases in which parties are heard at the bar no previous notice of motion bearing on the merits of the case can be given. But in matters which do not involve the hearing of parties, and especially in matters of legislation, it is usual to give notice at a previous meeting of any motion which is to be brought forward.

Where Presbyteries send out to all members notices stating the business to be transacted at next meeting it is usual to regard a "Notice of Motion" printed on such "billet" as being adequate even if the member who proposes to move it did not give formal notice at the previous meeting of the court.

Rules of Debate. Any motion submitted to the Presbytery should be committed to writing and given in to the clerk. If, after the mover has addressed the Presbytery, the motion be not seconded, it falls to the ground without discussion. When it is duly seconded, it is open either for adoption or for discussion. No alteration can be made upon it without the leave of the Presbytery, or in the shape of an amendment, or second or third motion, proposed and seconded by other members who object to the first motion as it stands. A motion made and seconded cannot be withdrawn without the leave of the Presbytery.

In the discussion on motions a member is entitled to speak only once, but he may ask leave to explain something he has said which seems to be misunderstood. Leave is usually granted. The member who introduces the first motion, however, has a right to reply, but is not permitted to introduce any new matter into his reply. After the reply the discussion is held to be closed, and the vote is taken.

Call to order. Any member has a right to call a speaker to order; and immediately on his doing so the speaker stops until the question of order is determined. The member calling to order is then allowed to state briefly the grounds on which the call has been made; but no other member is entitled to speak to the point of order unless at the request of the moderator, with whom the decision rests. Members calling to order unnecessarily are liable to the censure of the court.

When the moderator has announced his decision with regard to a point of order, or to the competency of a motion submitted, the court in all ordinary circumstances accepts that decision as final, but any member is at liberty to dissent and complain against the ruling.

Voting. In voting a Presbytery is guided mainly by the principles noted in the standing orders of the Assembly. For further information as to voting in the courts of the Church, see Chap. V., p. 108.

Intimation of Decisions. Decisions of Presbytery are communicated to those whom they concern either *apud acta*, that is, orally to parties present, or by extracts.

Extracts. Parties in cases before Presbyteries are entitled to extracts from the record containing those parts of the minutes in which they are concerned. The parties who acquiesce in a judgment are equally entitled, with those who appeal against it, to crave extracts. Other parties desiring extracts crave the Presbytery for them. But the clerk is not at liberty to give extracts without the express leave of the Presbytery.

In all cases where extracts are craved, the clerk is entitled, before furnishing them, to such remuneration as the Presbytery may fix, unless such payment is already provided for in the clerk's salary. (See also Chap. V., p. 85.)

Dissents. When a cause has been concluded, the minute adjusted, and the decision announced by the moderator, it is competent for any member who has voted to crave leave to enter his dissent. (As to right of dissent, see further Chap. V., pp. 91-99, 101.)

An open Court. The Presbytery is an open court, but it may sit in private when it judges it necessary or expedient and must do so when required by the law of the Church, or by instruction of a superior court—*e.g.*, a Presbytery is required to sit in private when considering reports on the Quinquennial Visitation of any congregation within its bounds.

SECTION IV. POWERS AND FUNCTIONS.

Power and Duties. It belongs to the Presbytery to see that the Word of God is purely preached within its bounds, the sacraments rightly administered, and the discipline "intertenyit" (P. 1592,

c. 116); to maintain and enforce the existing laws and usages of the Church in matters connected with the performance of public worship and the administration of ordinances (1866, vii.); to oversee the conduct of ministers and the discharge of their professional duties, with power to libel, try, and sentence them; to cause ordinances made by the Synod and General Assembly to be kept and put in execution; to make rules for good order in the churches (altering no rule of the Synod or Assembly, and reporting what they have done to those courts); to supervise, examine, and license students of divinity; to judge appointments and calls, and reject or admit those appointed; to deal with matters brought before it by Kirk Sessions; to vindicate the Church's claim to funds or property; to guard them from injury or improper use, to consider questions of union and readjustment; to delimit ecclesiastical parishes, and alter bounds thereof, as occasion may arise; to determine in conjunction with the Maintenance of the Ministry Committee appropriate figures for stipend and aid for all charges within the bounds.

Three Divisions of Functions. These functions of a Presbytery may be comprehended under three divisions, embracing respectively the department of original action; the department of review; and the special relations of the Presbytery to the superior courts.

Division I. Department of Original Action.

Training of the Ministry.

Power as to admission and licensing. The Presbytery possesses the function in conjunction with the Committee on Education for the Ministry (see p. 216) of deciding whether applicants are qualified or not to be received into the number of enrolled students of theology, with a view to their becoming preachers of the Gospel, who may be called to the pastoral office. It has also the function of examining them as to their qualifications at any stage of their progress; of determining in due time whether or not they may be licensed to preach the Gospel; and of licensing them if they be found qualified. The Presbytery in the exercise of these functions is regulated by Acts of the Supreme Court of the Church.

For the regulations to be observed, see Chap. X., p. 214.

Oversight of Licentiates and Ministers without Charges.[1]

Licentiates. Licentiates remain under the supervision and subject to the authority of the Presbytery which licensed them, till they are regularly transferred to another Presbytery. A licentiate

[1] See Act 1973, xx., anent Presbyterial Supervision of Students, and Act 1935, x., Sections 9-22, anent Presbyterial Supervision of Probationers and Ministers, p. 634.

removing from the bounds of the Presbytery that licensed him, or within which he has been residing, and fixing his residence within the bounds of another Presbytery, shall present to that Presbytery an extract of his licence, and a presbyterial certificate of character from the Presbytery which he has left.

Ministers who are not members of any Presbytery are subject to the jurisdiction of the Presbytery within whose bounds they reside. They must within two months of taking up residence produce a certificate of status and a presbyterial certificate. Without these they are not permitted to exercise any function of the ministry (1933, xv.). Ministers.

Probationers who, for sufficient reason, have received ordination but have never been parochial incumbents, are "ministers without charge," being for all practical purposes in exactly the same position as a minister who has resigned from a charge without retaining membership of a Presbytery.

Any minister or Kirk Session intending to employ as assistant or as *locum tenens*, for more than four Sundays in any parish, a licentiate or minister of any other Church than the Church of Scotland, shall require such licentiate or minister to report himself to the clerk of Presbytery within whose bounds the parish is situated, and to submit for his inspection a certificate of licence or of ordination, as the case may be, or to give such other evidence of qualification as may be satisfactory to the Presbytery. The General Assembly further instruct all keepers of lists of licentiates or ministers available for pulpit supply that they shall not make engagements for such licentiates or ministers for more than four Sundays, whether in the same parish or in different parishes, without requiring them to produce evidence that they have reported themselves to the clerk of the Presbytery within whose bounds they reside in the manner aforesaid (1932, 9; see also p. 158).

Ordination of Licentiates.

(See also p. 268.)

Ordination should be granted to licentiates only for very good reasons.

A licentiate should not receive ordination until he has given at least six months' service and undertakes to remain for a period of not less than twelve months in the appointment for the work of which he is being ordained.

In the case of extra-parochial appointments, only where the Church has some control over or right to approve of the appointment and at least some continuing general oversight shall ordination be granted, and only where there is substantial and reasonable need for the person appointed regularly to baptise or celebrate Communion (1969, Reg. 1).

The salary of a Probationer shall be at the rate of 75 per cent of the Minimum Stipend as of 1st January of the year in which he commences his probationary period. Where a Probationer remains beyond a twelve month period, and the probationary period has been sustained, he shall be paid whether ordained or not at the rate of 80 per cent as operative 1st January of that year (1974, Reg. 5).

Public intimation should always be given of the Presbytery's intention to ordain; and the Edict, Narrative and Questions to the Ordinand modified where necessary (1955, i.).

Vacant Congregations.

Vacant Congregations.

It is the duty of the Presbytery to take a special oversight of a congregation in which the pastoral office is vacant; to see that ordinances are duly administered and discipline maintained; to appoint one of its ministers, whether he sits as a minister or elder in Presbytery, provided he is not a member of the vacant congregation (1948, ix), as *Interim* Moderator of the Session, and to carry out the laws of the Church as to filling up the vacancy. The General Assembly have instructed each Presbytery to appoint a Committee available for conference with Congregational Vacancy Committees and for consultation with the Assembly Committee on Probationers and Transference of Ministers (1943, 9).

The General Assembly have instructed that when an *Interim* Moderator is appointed the Presbytery shall also appoint three Assessors (one of whom shall be an elder) who must be consulted by the *Interim* Moderator with regard to the filling of the vacancy, and with whom the Vacancy Committee may consult at any time, such Assessors to have no voting powers when meeting with the Vacancy Committee (1967, xxi).

During a vacancy in the pastoral office the *Interim* Moderator of the Session is entitled and called upon, so far as he can do so consistently with the due performance of his own parochial duties, to execute all the functions that would otherwise appertain to the Minister of the parish. Where a congregation has a special constitution derived from and particular to the congregation it is the duty of the *Interim* Moderator to supply a copy thereof to the nominee or nominees for appointment to the vacant charge. (1970, iii.).

It is not his duty to take charge of convening the Deacons' Court, that duty being expressly assigned to the clerk of the Deacons' Court during a vacancy in the pastoral office; but, as representing the Presbytery, the *Interim* Moderator of Session stands in the same position as the stated Minister in regard to the use of the church and other ecclesiastical buildings.

For regulations to be observed in filling up vacant charges, see Chap. XII., pp. 242-280.

Colleagues and Successors.

It lies with the Presbytery to receive applications for the appointment of a colleague and successor and to transmit such applications to the General Assembly's Committee on the Aged and Infirm Ministers' Fund. (See p. 735.)

It is within the power of a Presbytery to grant a colleague and successor to a minister who proposes to retire partially and to continue to perform a substantial part of the ministerial duties of the charge, always provided that partial retirement shall not entitle a minister to apply for a grant from the Aged and Infirm Ministers' Fund, but on complete retirement from duty he shall demit charge and shall be eligible for the normal grant from the Aged and Infirm Ministers' Fund on condition that he satisfies the other regulations of the Fund (1946, viii).

It also falls to the Presbytery to deal with all applications by Ministers for leave to demit their charges. The procedure to be followed is detailed in Chap. XII., pp. 270-271.

Ministers of Other Churches.

Presbyteries have certain duties in connection with ministers of other Churches who may apply for admission to the Church of Scotland, for which see Chap. XI., pp. 234-240.

Public Worship.

It belongs to the Presbytery to regulate matters concerning the performance of public worship and the administration of ordinances, in accordance with the laws and settled usages of the Church; and they are to take cognisance of the alleged existence or proposed introduction of any innovation or novel practice coming regularly to their knowledge; and after inquiry, if this appears necessary, are to give such deliverance as seems to be warranted by the circumstances of the case and the laws and usages of the Church; and it is their duty to enjoin the discontinuance, or prohibit the introduction, of any novel practice inconsistent with the laws and settled usages of the Church, or a cause of division in the congregation, or unfit from any cause to be used in the worship of God, either in general or in the particular kirk (P. 1592; 1866, vii. with 1865, vii.). In the matter of worship the minister is

Charge of Worship.

not in the same relation to the Presbytery as in other matters. The Presbytery itself is the party directly responsible to the Church. The minister is its executive. From which it follows, and is enacted by the Assembly (1866, vii.), that in case of an appeal against its order, he and all must abide by the order till final judgment is given. See also *Directory for the Public Worship of God* (Mair, pp. 583-614).

It is to be noted that *The Book of Common Order* issued in 1940 by authority of the General Assembly and since revised periodically, expresses "the mind of the Church with regard to its offices of worship, in orders and forms which, while not fettering individual judgment in particulars, will set the norm for the orderly and reverent conduct of the various public services in which ministers have to lead their people." (B.C.O. Preface.)

Who may conduct.

For the conduct of public worship only the following may be employed—ministers, probationers, licensed deaconesses and approved students for the licensed diaconate, divinity students duly recognised, lay agents recognised by the Home Board and Readers (*cf.* 1875, ix). If an unqualified person be engaged to supply a pulpit, full particulars must be sent to the Presbytery clerk, who is to report the matter to the Presbytery (1934, ix.).

Special Services and Collections.

The Presbytery has the power of appointing special diets of worship, and special fast-days and days of thanksgiving. It can also appoint special collections for particular objects to be made in all the congregations under its jurisdiction. This power, however, requires to be exercised with great discretion and subject to the provisions relating to the Mission and Service Fund (p. 658).

General Supervision.

Presbyteries have, subject always to the laws of the Church, a duty of supervision in all matters affecting the spiritual welfare of the Church and of its members within their respective bounds, and may give counsel and admonition, and make public declarations of opinion on such matters, as they may see cause. In doing so they must be careful of the rights of Kirk Sessions and of individual members of the Church.

Administration of the Sacraments.

(See p. 53.)

The Sacraments may be administered only by ministers, but in special circumstances (*e.g.*, locum tenens, exchange ministers) and by authority of the Presbytery they may be administered by a minister of the United Reformed Church or of any Presbyterian Church, or of one of the Lutheran/Reformed Churches, or by a minister of a non-Presbyterian Church who has obtained a certificate from the Committee on Admission of Ministers of Other Churches. Notwithstanding, a minister of another Church, whose orders are in accordance with the standards of the Church of Scotland, may be invited occasionally to administer the Sacraments. Such invitation, if accepted, shall be intimated to the Presbytery Clerk within fourteen days (1964, xiii. ; 1975, iv).

Union and Linking of Congregations.

On the occurrence of a vacancy Presbyteries are enjoined to intimate the vacancy to the General Assembly's Committee on Unions and Readjustments, together with its opinion as to whether or not the question of readjustment should be raised. If the question be raised the Presbytery appoints a committee to confer with representatives of the Assembly Committee (1932, ix.). For the procedure to be followed thereafter reference should be made to Act xvii., 1957, which will be found in Appendix XVIII., p. 751. **Unions.**

When two congregations agree to unite or link under the present minister of one of them, and an explicit term of the basis of union or linking is that this Minister shall be the minister of the united or linked charge, no further vote of the members of the vacant charge is necessary to constitute the election of the Minister of the other charge to the united or linked charge. Induction is necessary where in the vacant charge the stipend is derived in whole or in part from sources outwith the control of the church (1957, xvii.).

A union may be effected by the Presbytery with the concurrence of the Committees on Unions and Readjustments and Maintenance of the Ministry, unless it involve any modification of a decree of the Court of Teinds or an Act of Assembly or a Scheme of the Scottish Ecclesiastical Commissioners (1957, xvii.) when the authority of the General Assembly is also required.

The General Assembly authorise the Committee in cases of union under the Minister of one of the uniting charges, where the stipend is the minimum, to make payment to the Minister of the minimum stipend plus such sum as may from time to time be determined by the General Assembly (1959, Reg. 2).

Dissolution of a Congregation (1957, xvii.).

The procedure to be adopted is as follows :—

Where the dissolution of a congregation involves any modification of arrangements set up by and existing under a decree of the Court of Teinds or an Act of the General Assembly, or a Scheme of the Scottish Ecclesiastical Commissioners, the Synod shall not be at liberty to decide the case, but shall report the case, with its judgment, to the General Assembly, or (except in the case of a modification of an Act of General Assembly or Scheme of the Scottish Ecclesiastical Commissioners) to the Commission of Assembly at one of their stated diets.

Dissolutions. When a Presbytery finds, after full inquiry, that from depopulation of a parish or from any other cause, it is not advisable to maintain the congregation, the Presbytery shall consider, in consultation with the General Assembly's Committees on Unions and Readjustments and the Maintenance of the Ministry and the Home Board, whether it should be discontinued or otherwise dealt with, and shall report its opinion thereanent to the Synod. A copy of such report and relative documents shall be supplied to the Kirk Session of the congregation reported on, that it may take all competent steps to be duly represented at the Synod when the Presbytery's report is heard. Except in the cases specified in Article 2 (see p. 752) the Synod, after hearing parties, shall decide whether the congregation should or should not be discontinued, and, in the event of its deciding to discontinue it, shall satisfy itself that there will be adequate provision for the pastoral oversight of the former parish.

Should the question be raised in a congregation as to its continuance or otherwise, the matter shall be reported forthwith to the Presbytery through the Kirk Session. The Presbytery shall without delay inquire into the whole circumstances of the congregation, meeting with the Minister, if any, the office-bearers, and the congregation. It shall formulate its opinion on the case, and report the case along with its opinion to the Synod.

The destination of the property shall, if possible, be settled before the dissolution of the congregation is finally determined, subject to the terms of the titles on which it is held.

In cases where no regular meeting of Synod intervenes, the Presbytery may refer the question of dissolution to the General Assembly, or to their Commission at any of the stated diets which may dispose of the case.

For suggested Basis of Dissolution of a Congregation and Memorandum thereanent, see Reg. 8, 1970, p. 759.

For reduction, continued vacancy, linking, restricted ministry, deferred union or linking, reference should be made also to 1957, xvii., p. 751 ; and 1961, xxii., p. 758.

Suppression of a Charge (1957, xvii.).

Suppression of a charge means the withdrawal from a congregation of the right to have its minister appointed without limitation of time (see Chap. II., p. 18). The work may be carried on under a terminable appointment by a Minister without charge, an Ordained Preacher, Licentiate or Lay Missionary. The congregation retains its Kirk Session and financial board, and shall be represented by an elder in Presbytery and in Synod, and be liable for Assembly, Synod and Presbytery dues. Suppression of a Charge.

A necessary condition is that the Presbytery and the Committee on Unions and Readjustments take the view that union or readjustment is desirable but for the time being not practicable.

The congregation does not sign a call, and the person appointed is not inducted but should be introduced by the Presbytery. Such arrangement is terminable by the Presbytery at the end of the stated period or on the question of union arising earlier. Suppression may be effected by the Presbytery with the concurrence of the Committee on Unions and Readjustments and the Committee on the Maintenance of the Ministry unless the suppression involve any alteration in a Decree of the Court of Teinds or an Act of Assembly, or a Scheme of the Scottish Ecclesiastical Commissioners. The right of appointment without restriction may be restored by the Presbytery with the concurrence of the two Committees.

A suppressed congregation should be given as full an opportunity as possible of selecting the Minister or other agent whom they desire from the list of these available.

Presbyteries should be careful to see that a precise record of the appointment made, including the financial terms, is engrossed in the minutes of the Presbytery, and a copy sent to the Secretary of the Committee on Unions and Readjustments.

Relation of Terminable Appointees to the Presbytery (1970, ii.).

A Minister who is introduced to a terminable appointment within the bounds of a Presbytery is during the continuance of that appointment a member of that Presbytery. If, on the termination of that appointment, he is called to a charge or appointed to a terminable appointment in another Presbytery he becomes a member of that Presbytery. Otherwise he resumes membership of his former Presbytery if he is eligible to do so in accordance with section 3 (*d*) of Act 1970, ii. (p. 142). Terminable appointees.

Any person appointed to minister to a congregation who is not a Minister of the Church of Scotland, shall not become a ministerial member of Presbytery, nor shall he be Moderator of Kirk Session. If the charge be vacant, or the arrangement be such as to accommodate an exchange ministry, the Presbytery shall appoint an Interim Moderator who shall be responsible to the Presbytery for the proper administration and oversight of the congregation.

Resignation of a Seat (1935, x.).

Resignation of Seat.

A minister who has retained his seat in Presbytery may resign the same by presenting a petition to that effect to the Presbytery. The petition should be forwarded to the Synod, which shall dispose of the case. If there be no Synod having jurisdiction, the Presbytery shall forward the petition to the General Assembly.

Transference of Ministers to another Presbytery (1970, ii.).

Transference of Ministers to another Presbytery.

Synods shall have power to receive and dispose of petitions by ministers who have demitted their charges on grounds of age or infirmity, for transference from one Presbytery to another.

Where a proposed transference involves two Synods, the petition shall be presented to the Synod in whose bounds is situated the Presbytery to which the petitioner wishes to be transferred, and intimation of the petition shall be made by the petitioner to the other Synod and to the two Presbyteries concerned.

The decision of the Synod shall be final.

Readers.

Readers.

During the 1914-18 War, when preachers were scarce, a proposal emanated from the Committee on Probationers that, for the time being, the ancient order of Readers should be revived. This was carried into effect by interim Act of Assembly, 1918, confirmed in 1919. The period of service was at first five years, but this was extended, and when, in 1933, the united Church anew sanctioned the order, no limit was enacted.

The current Act was passed in 1974 (xxviii.) and provides as follows :—

I. *Application and Acceptance of Candidature.*

(*a*) Members of the Church of Scotland may apply for training as Readers. Applications shall be submitted in writing to the Clerk of the Presbytery within whose bounds the applicant resides, or that of the congregation of which he or she is a member. The application shall be supported by a letter as to character and previous experience of Church work from the applicant's Minister and by extract minute of Kirk Session.

(*b*) The application will be considered by the Presbytery on the recommendation of its appropriate committee, which will first satisfy itself by interview and otherwise as to the applicant's general suitability for the office of Reader. If the Presbytery so resolve, the application may be referred to the Department of Education of the General Assembly.

II. *Training of Candidates.*

Training of Readers.

(*a*) An applicant accepted as a suitable candidate for the office of Reader will normally be required to complete to the satisfaction of Presbytery a course of education prescribed by the Department of Education of the General Assembly. A tutor shall be appointed by the Presbytery to supervise the work of each candidate.

(*b*) An accepted candidate shall be given reasonable opportunity of acquiring experience in the conduct of public worship. At least twice per year each candidate shall conduct two full services in the presence of his tutor or other assessor appointed by the Presbytery, who shall give written reports to the candidate and to the Presbytery's committee in charge of Readers.

(*c*) Before the completion of the prescribed course, there shall be submitted to the Department of Education a report from the tutor on the candidate's progress.

(*d*) When the whole prescribed course has been completed to its satisfaction the Presbytery will arrange a suitable occasion for the applicant to be admitted to the office of Reader.

III. *Admission to the office of Reader.*

Admission.

Presbyteries shall admit candidates to the office of Reader upon satisfactory answers being given to the following questions :—

(i) Do you believe in one God—Father, Son and Holy Spirit ; and do you confess the Lord Jesus Christ as your Lord and Saviour?

(ii) Do you believe the Word of God, which is contained in the Scriptures of the Old and New Testaments, to be the supreme rule of faith and life?

(iii) Do you believe the fundamental doctrines of the Christian Faith contained in the Confession of Faith of this Church?

(iv) Do you acknowledge the Presbyterian government of this Church to be agreeable to the Word of God; and do you promise to be subject to this Presbytery, or to any other Presbytery within whose bounds you may reside, and to the superior Courts of the Church?

(v) Do you promise to seek the unity and peace of this Church, to uphold the doctrine, worship, government, and discipline thereof, and to cherish a spirit of brotherhood towards all the followers of the Lord?

(vi) Are not zeal for the glory of God, love to the Lord Jesus Christ, and a desire for the salvation of men, so far as you know your own heart, your great motives and chief inducements to enter into the office of Reader?

(vii) Do you engage in the strength of the Lord Jesus Christ to live a godly and circumspect life; and faithfully, diligently, and cheerfully to discharge the duties of Reader, seeking in all things the advancement of the Kingdom of God?

After these questions have been answered satisfactorily, the Formula, which is the same as for ministers, shall be signed and the candidate shall be admitted to the office of Reader.

Readers so appointed shall be authorised to conduct public worship anywhere within the Church.

IV. *Superintendence.*

Superintendence of Readers.

(*a*) Supervision of Readers shall be exercised by Presbyteries, and shall include the annual appearance of Readers before their Presbytery.

(*b*) Readers shall attend at least once in every two years an in-service conference approved by the Department of Education.

(*c*) Each Presbytery shall maintain and shall revise annually a Roll of Readers under its supervision.

(*d*) Presbyteries shall send the names and addresses of those whom they admit to the office of Reader to the Committee on Probationers and Transference of Ministers and to the Editor of the Year Book.

(*e*) On leaving the bounds of a Presbytery, a Reader on request shall receive a certificate of status, which he may lodge with the Presbytery within whose bounds he becomes resident. The Reader's name shall then be added to the Readers' Roll of the latter Presbytery which shall notify the Committee on Probationers and Transference of Ministers.

V. *A List of Readers* shall be published annually in the Church of Scotland Year Book.

VI. *Supply Fee.* (The fee for services conducted by Readers shall be the regular pulpit supply fee.) (See p. 230.) **Supply Fee.**

Women shall be eligible to be set apart as Readers on the same terms and conditions as men (1970, i.).

Church Extension Charges

(1932, xiv.; 1939, 3; 1952, 3 and 7 and 1975, Reg. 1).

It lies with the Presbytery, in consultation with the Home Board of the General Assembly, to judge when a new congregation is necessary. The Kirk Session of the parish and neighbouring Kirk Sessions must be consulted. The Home Board, in consultation with the Presbytery, which takes steps to ascertain the mind of the congregation, appoints the first minister, and thereafter a Kirk Session is set up and a Financial Board. When a church extension charge is to be erected as a regular charge an application to that effect must be presented by the minister and provisional Kirk Session to the Presbytery for approval: thereafter the application, if approved, shall be forwarded to the Home Board which, after due procedure (see Regulations, p. 682) shall make appropriate recommendation to the General Assembly. **Church Extension.**

Until a church extension charge has been erected into a parish in full status its accounts require to be examined annually by two auditors appointed by the Presbytery of the bounds.

(See App. XXVI., p. 678, for the Regulations, and for Forms of Petition, &c.)

Cases of Discipline.

For procedure to be followed in cases of discipline, reference should be made to Chap. XV., Sects. III. and V., pp. 320-324.

Care of Church Property (1961, xxi., and 1969, xxvi.).

The General Assembly has deplored the deterioration into which much of the Church's property throughout the country has fallen, and has enjoined all Presbyteries to be more thorough in their examination of property and more insistent in seeing that necessary repairs are effected. **Property.**

The duties of Presbyteries are as follows :—

1. Each Presbytery shall set up a Fabric Committee to which it shall appoint one or more persons with technical knowledge and experience and shall empower the said Fabric Committee to co-opt such person or persons, or to obtain such assistance as it may deem necessary.

2. The Fabric Committee of the Presbytery shall have, *inter alia,* the duty of considering all schedules lodged by appropriate congregational authorities within the bounds in pursuance of this Act and of reporting thereon to the Presbytery.

3. At least once within each five-year period, beginning on 1st July 1972, the Fabric Committee of the Presbytery shall inspect on its own behalf and by whatever agency it deems wise the ecclesiastical properties of each congregation within the bounds and shall report thereon to the Presbytery. Reasonable notice of such intended inspection shall be given to the clerk of the appropriate congregational authority and to the minister of the charge, and it shall be their duty to afford all reasonable facilities for the carrying out of such inspection.

4. Not less than fourteen days before a report is to be submitted to the Presbytery concerning the ecclesiastical properties of any congregation, a copy of the report shall be sent to the clerk of the appropriate congregational authority, and the said appropriate congregational authority shall have the right, if so advised, to be represented by Commissioners at that meeting of Presbytery.

5. When the Presbytery takes into consideration reports in terms of the foregoing Articles 2 and 3, Commissioners from the appropriate congregational authority or other persons having an interest shall have the right to be heard thereon. The Presbytery shall thereupon record in a separate Property Record Book its findings thereanent, together with such recommendations or instructions as it may deem proper. A copy of the relevant entry shall be sent to the clerk of the appropriate congregational authority.

6. Within three months of receiving from the Presbytery, in terms of Article 5 above, a report and recommendations requiring action upon the part of the appropriate congregational authority, the clerk of the appropriate congregational authority shall lodge with the clerk of Presbytery a report setting forth how far such recommendations and instructions have received effect, and this shall be duly reported to the Presbytery.

7. In the event of any party having an interest being dissatisfied with the recommendations or instructions of the Presbytery made in terms of Article 5, above, they shall have the right to appeal to the Synod of the bounds, whose decision shall be final. Unless such an appeal is taken, it shall be the duty of the appropriate congregational authority to see that the instructions of the Presbytery are implemented without delay. Appeal shall include Dissent and Complaint.

8. Each Presbytery shall annually report to the Synod of the bounds its diligence under this Act.

For the full text of the Act and the duties of Presbyteries in regard to the erection of new buildings and alterations to existing buildings, &c., reference should be made to p. 774 and to Chap. XVII.

Collecting-books (1931, xxi.).

The General Assembly has enacted as follows:—

1. No one shall be recognised as entitled to collect outside the congregation with which he is connected for church, manse, hall, debt, or other local object, unless he has the written authority of the Presbytery of the bounds, and presents a collecting-book supplied by the Presbytery clerk. The whole details of the case shall, in the first instance, be submitted to the Presbytery of the bounds for its examination, and the deliverance of the Presbytery approving shall be embodied in the circular appealing for subscriptions, and shall be prefixed to the collecting-book used. Collecting Books.

2. All contributions received personally, or in answer to letters or circulars, shall be entered in the collecting-book. Letters or circulars applying for contributions shall refer to the book by its authority and date, and undertake that all sums received shall be duly entered in it.

3. The collecting-book (along with a written statement of receipts and disbursements, signed by the moderator and treasurer of the congregation) shall be returned to the Presbytery clerk within twelve months from the date of issue for examination by the Presbytery, and the fact shall be recorded in the minutes of the Presbytery.

4. If the purpose for which contributions are to be asked from the Church generally be the erection of a new church or manse, or alterations or repairs on church or manse, the Presbytery shall not issue a deliverance authorising an appeal for subscriptions until it has received intimation from the Church

and Manse Building Committee [1] and/or the General Trustees that they have approved of the plans and estimates and of the amount raised locally, and have granted leave to proceed. The deliverance of the Presbytery shall state that the Church and Manse Building Committee [1] and/or the General Trustees have approved. Further, the Presbytery shall report to the Church and Manse Building Committee,[1] immediately after the expiry of one year after authorising the issue of the appeal, the total sum raised, with certification that the account of receipts and disbursements have been audited, and the amount received duly applied to the purpose for which it was asked.

5. A second or subsequent collecting-book may be obtained, and shall be dealt with as in the case of a first book.

6. In the case of those collecting for any special scheme, home or foreign, the above regulations shall be enforced with the one difference, that the General Assembly's Committee, under whose oversight the scheme properly falls, shall be required to take the same responsibility as, in regard to local matters, is assigned to Presbyteries and to the Church and Manse Building Committee and/or the General Trustees.

Division II. Department of Review.

Right of Review.

The Presbytery's right of review extends not only to decisions and resolutions of congregational meetings, and the disposal of matters brought before it by reference, petition, protest and appeal, or dissent and complaint, but also to various other matters. As to the right of review of decisions of congregational meetings, see Chap. II., p. 22, and as to references, petitions, protests and appeals, and dissents and complaints, see Chap. V.

Records to be examined.

The Presbytery exercises the right of review through the periodical examination of the records of Kirk Sessions, Deacons' Courts, and Congregational Boards. Presbyteries are instructed to see that the Communion Rolls, Session Records, Roll of Baptised Persons not Communicants, Baptismal Registers, Registers of Banns, Property Registers, and Abstracts of Accounts of all congregations are attested annually by Kirk Sessions and produced to the Presbytery for attestation by the Presbytery or by a committee or committees appointed for this purpose (Oct. 1929, i.; 1930, 10; and see p. 137). It is also recommended that the records of Deacons' Courts, Committees of Management, and Congregational Boards be

[1] Now Home Board.

examined and attested annually; when such records are not examined annually they should be examined at the quinquennial visitation. After such examination the Presbytery comes to a finding regarding them. For duties of examining committees and attestation, see Chap. V., pp. 87-89.

The Presbytery may find that certain procedure of a Deacons' Court or Congregational Board has been *ultra vires*, or contrary to Acts of Assembly, and may declare it to be null and void, or order the minutes to be expunged. Before doing so, it must summon the Deacons' Court or Congregational Board to the bar, and hear them as parties. The Presbytery has no power of judgment with respect to those details of practical procedure in the Deacons' Court or Congregational Board which are within the province of that court or board, and consistent with the Acts of Assembly (F.C., 1847, xiv.). **Deacons' Court.**

An abstract of the accounts of all charges shall be submitted annually to the Presbytery for attestation. The accounts of charges where the 1965 Constitution is in operation shall be laid annually before the Presbytery and attested. **Examination of Accounts.**

Presbyterial Visitation of Congregations (1931, xii.; 1944, xx.; 1973, i.).

The following scheme is that which was adopted in 1931 as amended by Act XX., 1944, and Act I., 1973.

1. Every congregation of the Church shall be visited once at least in five years by a Committee of Presbytery. The five years' period shall begin with the Assembly of 1931. A special visitation shall be made when deemed necessary or expedient. **Quinquennial Visitation.**

The scheme of visitation shall wherever possible be under the direction of a Superintendence Committee of the Presbytery appointed for this purpose.

2. The object of the visitation is to strengthen the hands of the minister, Kirk Session, office-bearers and members, to advise them should anything appear to be unsatisfactory in the state of the congregation or not in accord with Church law and order, and in general to give counsel and encouragement as may be suitable to the circumstances of the case.

3. Every Presbytery shall prepare, as soon as possible, a rota whereby all the congregations may be visited. The work of visiting should be overtaken during the first four years in each quinquennium.

4. A Committee shall be appointed for the visitation of each

congregation. This should consist of not less than four members—say two ministers and two elders, on each Committee.

5. A printed schedule in the form hereto appended,[1] or in such other form as may be from time to time authorised by the General Assembly, shall be used in connection with the visitation, but the Committee of Presbytery may use their discretion in inquiring into other matters relevant to the state of the congregation.

6. The clerk of Presbytery or the convener of the Visitation Committee, after consultation with the minister, shall give notice of the date of visitation, which should be intimated to the congregation at public worship on two Sundays before the date of visitation. He shall at the same time send copies of the Visitation Schedule to the minister and session clerk. It is desirable that one of the ministers on the Committee conduct public worship at one or both diets of worship on the Lord's Day in connection with the visitation, or that he address the congregation on a week-day where found more convenient. He shall address to the congregation such counsels as may be considered appropriate and helpful for the promotion of Christian work and fellowship. Where possible the minister shall be present. Bible Classes, Sunday Schools, and similar organisations shall also be visited, if possible.

7. The Committee shall hold separate meetings with the Minister, the Kirk Session, the Financial Board (*i.e.*, Finance Committee, Deacons' Court, Committee of Management or Congregational Board), where such a body exists. The Minister is entitled to be present at all these meetings. The Convener of the Visitation Committee or his duly appointed Deputy shall take the chair at all aforementioned meetings.

8. The Visitation Committee shall report to the Presbytery, which shall in private take such report into its deliberate and careful consideration, and record in the Presbytery books its finding thereanent, together with such explanations or instructions as the Presbytery may deem proper. The Committee shall communicate its report or proposed finding to the Session of the congregation concerned timeously, and before it is dealt with by the Presbytery, and the Session or minister or any other party having an interest may claim to be heard by the Presbytery when the report is dealt with. In all cases where the scheme of visitation is under the direction of a Superintendence Committee, the Visitation Committee shall

[1] Appendix, p. 719.

report to the Superintendence Committee which shall communicate their own report or proposed finding to the Session of the Congregation before submitting the said report or proposed finding to the Presbytery.

Not later than six months after it has communicated its findings on the Visitation Committee's Report the Presbytery shall enquire of each congregation visited to what extent the recommendations and instructions have been implemented.

9. Every Presbytery shall report to the Synod of the bounds the result of each visitation. In the event of the Presbytery finding itself unable to express satisfaction with the state of any congregation, it shall be the duty of the Synod to appoint a Committee to make further inquiry in consultation with the Presbytery, and to endeavour to remedy what is deemed to be unsatisfactory. If, after this further visitation, it be found that matters are still unsatisfactory, the Synod shall forward a report to the General Assembly through the General Administration Committee, and the Assembly may take such further action as to its wisdom may appear best.

10. It shall be the duty of each Synod annually and immediately after the visitation of Presbytery records, to prepare and transmit to the General Assembly through the General Administration Committee a return showing distinctly and specifically whether each Presbytery has faithfully carried out the provisions of this Act.

11. The General Administration Committee shall annually appoint a Sub-Committee to receive returns from Synods and report.

The General Assembly direct Presbyteries to forward to the Synod of the bounds the schedules anent Presbyterial visitation in terms of Act xii., 1931, and subsequently amended, not later than the 31st day of March in each year, and the General Assembly instruct Synods to take these schedules into the most careful scrutiny and consideration with a view to the more effective supervision of the congregations of the Church. Act 1944, xx.

The General Assembly instruct Synods to send back to Presbyteries any schedules where there are omissions or inadequate answers to be properly completed, and returned for submission to next meeting of Synod.

The General Assembly urge Presbyteries, in carrying out visitation, to keep particularly in view the promotion of the spiritual well-being of the congregation visited and the efficiency of the congregational agencies.

Suggestions for the Guidance of Presbyteries in the Visitation of Congregations (1973, i.; Reports, p. 30).

The superintendence of congregations within its bounds is one of the functions of a Presbytery, and the scheme of five-yearly visitation is one of the methods whereby the General Assembly require that Presbyteries should exercise this function. All meetings in connection with a visitation are therefore called by authority of the Presbytery, whose Deputies attend these meetings as representatives of a superior Court. Accordingly, all meetings shall be constituted by a duly authorised Deputy of the Presbytery, who shall act as chairman throughout the proceedings.

Presbyteries may delegate this responsibility to a Superintendence Committee, with authority to choose Deputies, and assign them to individual congregations. The Chairman of the Deputies should be a man of maturity and experience, since the effectiveness of the visitation will largely depend on the manner in which it is conducted.

While the visitation must involve a rigorous examination of all aspects of a congregation's life, it must be conducted in a spirit of Christian charity, with a view to demonstrating the unity of the Church within the Presbyterian system of Church government, and the Deputies should endeavour at all times to give such positive help and encouragement as they can.

If any occasion of division or discontent within the congregation should come to the notice of the Deputies, they should make every effort to act impartially and to bring about a reconciliation. They should seek to act as arbitrators, with a view to settling the matter "out of court," before considering any formal report to the Presbytery.

Before conducting a visitation, Deputies should take steps to familiarise themselves with the state of the congregation, and in particular they should study the report of the previous visitation, as well as the statistical and financial returns of the congregation for the previous five years.

While the questions in the Schedule will form the basis of the visitation, and all the questions must be answered, the Deputies may ask further verbal questions on any particular matters of special situations which they consider important. A note of such questions and the answers given should be included in their report. Where appropriate, advantage might be taken of discussing the possibility of closer co-operation and association with neighbouring congregations—Church of Scotland and others.

In dealing with finance, Deputies should stress the importance of regular planned giving through Weekly Freewill Offering System, and of the principles of Christian Stewardship. Where necessary, the Deputies should give information about the assistance available from the Stewardship and Budget Committee.

While fabric is now the subject of separate reports and visitations, the Deputies should satisfy themselves that all is in order in this respect, by studying such reports before making their own visitation, and they should be prepared to discuss questions of principle with regard to the usefulness and relevance of buildings being maintained, as opposed to the manner of their maintenance.

Deputies should report definitely whether the congregation is fulfilling its purpose and should draw attention through the Presbytery to noteworthy experiments brought to the notice of Visitation Committees.

Visitation Committees (or Sub-Committees) should send copies of their proposed report to ministers or Kirk Sessions of congregations visited before it is submitted to the Presbytery. Not later than six months after the date of the visitation, they should be responsible, in consultation with the Presbytery Clerk, to ascertain what action has been taken by the congregations to implement any recommendation.

After Visitation Schedules have been carefully scrutinised by the Synod of the bounds in terms of Act XX., 1944, they should be returned to the Presbytery in order that visitors at the next visitation may be cognisant of the facts elicited at the previous visitation.

Congregations in an Unsatisfactory State (1960, xxi.).

The General Assembly have passed an Act anent Congregations in an Unsatisfactory State, as follows:—

1. If it should come to the knowledge of a Presbytery that the state of any congregation within the bounds is not considered to be satisfactory, either through a petition from office-bearers or members of the congregation concerned, or through

statements made by the minister of the congregation, or through the report of a quinquennial visitation, or through a remit from a superior court, or through other reports which the Presbytery deems to be such as require investigation, it shall be the duty of the Presbytery to appoint a Special Committee thereanent and to remit to such Committee, by means of special visitation, to inquire into the situation and to endeavour to remedy, by counsel and advice, anything which may appear to be unsatisfactory, such Committee to report back to the Presbytery on their inquiry and endeavours.

2. If, upon the report of such Committee, the Presbytery finds that the state of the congregation is unsatisfactory and that endeavours to effect a remedy are unavailing or have failed, the Presbytery shall record the said report and its own findings thereon in a record apart.

3. If the Presbytery be also of opinion that there are *prima facie* grounds for concluding that the unsatisfactory state of the congregation may be due (*a*) wholly or substantially to defects or errors personal to the minister, or (*b*) wholly or partly to the fault of any office-bearers or members specified, it shall record also its findings on the said *prima facie* grounds, along with the report and findings referred to in section 2, in the record apart. All further findings of the Presbytery in the matter shall likewise be recorded in the record apart.

4. (*a*) Where the Presbytery is of opinion that there are *prima facie* grounds for concluding that the unsatisfactory state of the congregation may be due wholly or substantially to defects or errors personal to the minister, a copy of the Special Committee's report and of the Presbytery's findings, certified by the clerk of Presbytery, shall be furnished to the minister, with a citation from the Presbytery to him to attend a meeting, not less than one month thereafter, at which the subject matter thereof is to be further considered by the Presbytery. Intimation of the said meeting shall also be given to such other parties as the Presbytery may think proper.

(*b*) At the said or a subsequent meeting, the Presbytery shall hear any statement which the minister may make and receive and record any relevant matter which he may tender to be recorded on his behalf. It shall also be competent for the Presbytery to hear statements from persons in the communion of the Church, who are or have been members of the congregation, bearing on the question whether the existing state of the congregation is attributable wholly or substantially to defects or errors personal to the minister. If the Presbytery be constrained to conclude that the ends of the ministry are not being served and that this state of matters is likely to continue, and further, that the unsatisfactory state of the congregation is due, either wholly or substantially, to defects or errors personal to the minister, it shall pronounce findings to that effect and the same shall be recorded in the record apart, together with a statement of the grounds thereof. The said findings shall be in numbered paragraphs and shall specify the said defects or errors.

(*c*) Thereupon the Presbytery may resolve to dissolve the pastoral tie and declare the charge vacant. In all cases in which the pastoral tie is dissolved, the Presbytery shall report to the Maintenance of the Ministry Committee all the circumstances known to it which ought to be in view of the Church in dealing with the question of a maintenance allowance for the minister during such period as he is in receipt of no other regular remuneration, and the Maintenance of the Ministry Committee shall report to the General Assembly and may make interim payments.

5. The procedure, findings, and final judgment of the Presbytery, except that part of the final judgment by which the Presbytery has resolved to dissolve the pastoral tie and declare the charge vacant, shall be subject to appeal or complaint only to the Judicial Commission of the General Assembly. Where the Presbytery has made findings in terms of section 2, it shall thereupon proceed in face of all appeals or complaints until it has disposed of all questions which may arise under sections 2, 3, and 4, except that where the Presbytery has resolved to dissolve the pastoral tie and to declare the charge vacant the appeal or complaint against that part of the said judgment shall be taken direct to the General Assembly, and shall suspend operation of the judgment of the Presbytery till the appeal or complaint has been disposed of. An appeal or complaint to the Judicial Commission shall entitle the appellant or complainer to submit for review any of the prior findings or procedure of the Presbytery.

6. (*a*) Where the Presbytery is of opinion that there are *prima facie* grounds for concluding that the unsatisfactory state of the congregation may be due wholly or partly to the fault of any office-bearers or members specified, a copy of the Special Committee's report and of the Presbytery's findings, certified by the clerk of Presbytery, shall be furnished to the parties specified, with a citation from the Presbytery to them to attend a meeting, not less than one month thereafter, at

which the subject matter thereof is to be further considered by the Presbytery. Intimation of the said meeting shall also be given to such other parties as the Presbytery may think proper.

(*b*) At the said or a subsequent meeting, the Presbytery shall proceed in the same manner, *mutatis mutandis*, as in the case of a minister. If the Presbytery be constrained to conclude that the unsatisfactory state of the congregation is due, either wholly or partly, to the fault of any one or more office-bearers or members specified, it shall pronounce findings to that effect and the same shall be recorded in the record apart, together with a statement of the grounds thereof. The said findings shall be in numbered paragraphs and shall specify the said fault. The Presbytery may in such case remove from office, or order transference certificates to be given, or suspend from Church membership, as the justice of the case and the interests of the congregation may require.

7. The procedure, findings, and final judgment of the Presbytery, except a judgment that an office-bearer be removed from office, or that a transference certificate be given to an office-bearer or member, or that an office-bearer or member shall be suspended from Church membership, shall be subject to appeal or complaint only to the Judicial Commission of the General Assembly. Where the Presbytery has made findings in terms of section 2, it shall thereafter proceed in face of all appeals or complaints until it has disposed of all questions which may arise under sections 2, 3, and 6, except that where the Presbytery has pronounced a final judgment involving any of the penalties referred to in section 6 (*b*), the appeal or complaint against the said judgment shall be taken direct to the General Assembly, and shall suspend the operation of the said penalties till the appeal or complaint has been disposed of. An appeal or complaint to the Judicial Commission shall entitle the appellant or complainer to submit for review any of the prior findings or procedure of the Presbytery.

8. No case shall be proceeded with under this Act if it is found by the Presbytery to involve, except to a minor extent, the moral character or doctrinal views of any minister, office-bearer, or member of the Church.

9. This Act shall not apply to the case of insanity in a minister.

10. All procedure in Presbytery under this Act shall be taken in private.

For Act 1960, xxii., anent the Judicial Commission see p. 653.

Procedure in the Case of Insanity in a Minister.

Regulations for the procedure to be followed by Presbyteries in cases where the Presbytery is satisfied by competent evidence that a minister is unable through mental illness to discharge his ministerial duties will be found in Chap. XII., pp. 275-278.

Mission and Service Fund.

The Scheme annexed to Act XXV., 1959, as amended by Act XIV., 1973, as further amended by Act XXVI., 1975 (see Appendix XXV., p. 658), directs that from 1st January 1961 "All Committees, Associations and other bodies whose funds have hitherto derived support from congregations in Scotland or England shall, with the exception of the Committee on the Maintenance of the Ministry and the Committee on the Aged and Infirm Ministers' Fund, cease to have right to appeal directly to such congregations for contributions to their funds. As from the operative date a co-ordinated appeal, now Mission and Service Fund, . . . shall be the sole method of appealing to such congregations." Act 1973, xiv, 1975, xxvi.

The Stewardship and Budget Committee is responsible for such publicity as may be necessary regarding the working of the Mission and Service Fund, but the duty of maintaining an efficient information and publicity service in order that members of the Church may be adequately informed of the work the Church is doing, still remains the responsibility of each appropriate Assembly Committee.

In its annual report to the General Assembly the Stewardship and Budget Committee shall include a statement of approved requirements from congregations and the proposed allocation of the total amount of such requirements among groups of congregations.

In its consideration of the allocation to groups of congregations, the Committee shall first of all examine the available balance figures for each congregation according to the information supplied by Presbyteries, shall thereafter group congregations according to the said figures, and then shall determine and allocate the proportion of the total budget required from each group, intimating to each Presbytery the amount allocated to and required from each group within that Presbytery.

Presbyteries' responsibilities within the Scheme.

1. Each Presbytery shall appoint a Stewardship and Budget Committee.

2. Each Presbytery shall be responsible for establishing, and for reporting by 30th April each year the available balance of each congregation, aid-receiving congregations and congregations making repayments for buildings to the National Church Extension Committee being given separate consideration.

3. On receipt of intimation of the share of the total amount allocated to each group within the Presbytery, the Presbytery's Stewardship and Budget Committee shall after due consideration proceed to make its proposed allocation of said amount to each congregation within the bounds within its relevant group so that the sum of such allocations will equal the proportion of the total budget required from that group. Presbyteries may ask for guidance from the Stewardship and Budget Committee.

In the event of any unions or readjustments having taken place within the Presbytery or any new congregation having come into existence, the Presbytery shall make such adjustments as in its discretion it considers appropriate.

4. Having made such allocation, the Presbytery's Committee shall report its allocation to the Presbytery clerk who shall communicate the particulars to individual members of Presbytery at least six days prior to the next meeting of Presbytery. The Presbytery either at that meeting or a subsequent meeting shall either confirm the allocation or make such amendments or adjustments thereto as in its sole discretion it thinks fit. The Presbytery's decision as to the allocation among congregations within its bounds shall be final in respect of the immediately ensuing calendar year.

5. After the allocation amongst congregations has been finally approved of by the Presbytery, the clerk of Presbytery shall, not later than 15th November in each year, notify each congregation of its allocation and afford information concerning the division of same amongst the several funds of the Church. The sums thus notified to congregations shall represent the minimum contributions they are expected to make. Presbyteries shall transmit copies of their allocations to congregations to the secretary of the Stewardship and Budget Committee.

6. The Presbytery's Stewardship and Budget Committee shall, in addition to undertaking the above-mentioned duties, take such steps as it may consider necessary to secure that every congregation shall attain its objective as allocated. To this end the Presbytery's Committee shall be required to

urge congregations to improve their methods of giving and generally to be responsible for the education of the membership to a fuller understanding of the real meaning of Christian stewardship.

7. In all cases where congregations fail to meet the requirements of the Mission and Service Fund the Presbytery's Stewardship and Budget Committee shall consult with the office-bearers.

Division III. Department of Special Relations to the Superior Courts.

A Presbytery can make no change in its designation without leave of the General Assembly. With a view to holding any meeting during the sittings of the Provincial Synod to which it belongs, or during the sittings of the General Assembly, a Presbytery must obtain the leave of the Synod or the Assembly to do so. Change of Name, &c.

If a Presbytery obtain leave or receive orders from the Synod to meet during an interval of business, as all the members are presumed to be there, the meeting may be competently announced from the chair. If a Presbytery receive leave or instructions from the General Assembly to meet, notice must be given to the members.

The Presbytery is responsible to the Synod for the correctness and accuracy of the permanent record of its proceedings. The minute-book must be submitted to the Synod when called for, which should be at least once a year. It is competent for the Synod, on examination of the Presbytery records, to take notice of any irregularity, omission, or error, not only in the language or form but also in the substance of the minutes, and to exercise their powers of review thereanent. Responsibility to Synod as to Record.

Benefice Register (1931, xiv., 1961, 1).

Every Presbytery must keep and annually revise a benefice register, containing all attainable information appertaining to every parish and chapel regarding the stipend and emoluments attached to the living, ecclesiastical property, trust funds, bequests, donations, mortifications, or charities, in which minister or Kirk Session, or trustees or managers of *quoad sacra* parishes or chapels, have an interest or any right of administration ; all relative writs, or registered copies Benefice Register.

thereof, to be produced if possible, and an inventory of them entered in the register with the names of their custodiers.

The Presbytery is responsible for the accuracy of the register, and must therefore as far as possible verify information furnished to it.

The benefice register of every Presbytery, after having been revised and brought up to date, shall be submitted annually for visitation by the Synod, and Synods shall report the diligence of Presbyteries to the General Assembly.

During vacancies, Interim Moderators of Kirk Sessions shall forthwith cause an inventory to be made of all Church properties which had been in the custody of the former Minister, and have the said inventory carefully compared with the record in the benefice register of the Presbytery.

On the admission of a Minister to a charge, the inventory made on the occurrence of the vacancy shall be placed in his hands for the purpose of enabling him to ascertain that he has obtained the custody of all Church properties recorded therein, and within three months after his induction he shall report to the Convener of the Benefice Register Committee of the Presbytery, or to such other person as the Presbytery may designate, whether he has ascertained it to be correct or otherwise.

No interference with another Presbytery.

A Presbytery cannot interfere with or review the procedure of another Presbytery. It may make a remonstrance thereanent, and endeavour by frank and friendly representation to have the matter put right. Where this is ineffectual the Presbytery which feels aggrieved can bring the matter by petition for redress before the Synod of the bounds, when both Presbyteries belong to the same Synod. When they belong to different Synods the petition must be addressed to the General Assembly.

Student Missionary.

When application is made to the Home Board on behalf of a station for aid, or by a congregation for aid towards the support of a missionary assistant or student missionary, the application must be forwarded through the Presbytery, which shall also report to the committee its judgment thereanent.

Grants.

A similar course is to be followed with applications for driving grants and, in general, with all applications for grants to the committees of the General Assembly.

Transference of Buildings, &c.

The consent of the Presbytery is required for the sale or transference of churches or manses, or other buildings which, by their title-deeds, have become the property of the Church of Scotland or are under the control of the General Assembly. The minute recording consent must, along with the application of the local parties, be forwarded to the General Trustees, or, in the case of properties belonging to the United Free Church before union, to the General Assembly or its Commission, which alone have power to sanction the sale or transference (1933, xxv.). Petitions must be lodged at least one month before the stated meetings of the Commission.

See also Chap. XVII., pp. 361-362, and Appendix, pp. 444-448.

Overtures under the Barrier Act.

Approval of Overtures under Barrier Act.

It is the right and duty of every Presbytery to take its part in the legislation of the Church, by approving or disapproving of overtures transmitted by the General Assembly, with a view to such overtures being passed into standing laws, in terms of 1697, ix., commonly known as the Barrier Act. (See Appendix I., p. 385.)

The Presbytery shall previously fix a day for the consideration of such overtures (1797, 8). If it be thought desirable, a committee may in the first instance be appointed to consider the overture, and to report.

Presbyteries must either approve or disapprove of the overture. Whether a Presbytery approve or disapprove it is at liberty to make remarks. These remarks should be sent on a separate sheet. If such remarks in no way modify the substance, sense or intention of the overture, it is competent for the General Assembly, if they see cause, to adopt the substance of them. A form to be used by Presbytery clerks in making returns is sent out by the clerks of Assembly, and all such returns must be transmitted to the clerks of Assembly not later than the 31st day of December in each year, or such date as the Assembly may appoint. (See Chap. V., p. 98.) The number of members voting for approval or disapproval must be given.

Overtures from Presbyteries.

Presbyteries are at liberty to overture the Synod, or the General Assembly through the Synod. In case of urgency, when no meeting of Synod intervenes, a Presbytery may transmit an overture to the General Assembly direct (1933, xix.) (For procedure to be followed, see Chap. V., pp. 102-106.)

Transference of Congregations (1957, xvii.).

The General Assembly has enacted as follows :—

1. When a Kirk Session desires that the charge should be transferred from one Presbytery to another, it shall present a petition to that effect to the Synod, through the Presbytery within whose bounds it is presently situated.

2. This petition shall be lodged with the clerk of the Presbytery in time for a meeting of Presbytery occurring not later than two months before the meeting of Synod, and it shall be the duty of the Kirk Session at the same time to intimate the petition to the other Presbytery involved.

3. If the Synod to which the petition is presented consists of not more than three Presbyteries, of which two are the Presbyteries involved, and these two Presbyteries are not in agreement as to the proposed transference, the Synod shall refer the petition to the General Assembly, or to their Commission at any of their stated diets, which may dispose of the case.

4. If the Presbytery to which transference is sought is within the bounds of another Synod, or if the transference involves any modification of the arrangements set up or existing under a decree of the Court of Teinds or an Act of the General Assembly or a scheme of the Scottish Ecclesiastical Commissioners, the petition, if approved by the Synod, shall be transmitted to the General Assembly.

5. Except as provided in sections 3 and 4 the decisions of the Synod upon such petition shall be final.

6. When a Presbytery desires that a charge within its bounds should be transferred to another Presbytery, it may, after consultation with the Kirk Session concerned, and with the concurrence of the Committee on Unions and Readjustments, present a petition for that purpose to the Synod, and it shall be the duty of the Presbytery at the same time to intimate the petition to the other Presbytery involved. Such petition shall be subject to the provision of sections 3, 4, and 5.

Election of Commissioners to the General Assembly.

Election of Representatives to Assembly.

The members of the General Assembly, other than those with *ex officio* status, are annually elected by the Presbyteries of the Church. Each Presbytery elects a definite number of ministers and elders as fixed by Act of Assembly to be its commissioners to the ensuing Assembly—the number of elders being equal to the number of ministers, and the number of each being one for every four or part thereof of the number of ministerial members on its roll. (See p. 193.)

By Act XXIV., 1969, Presbyteries are authorised to elect as Commissioners ex-Moderators who are members of the Presbytery so electing. Such ex-Moderators are in addition to the quota to which the Presbytery is entitled and an equalising elder shall be elected in respect of each such commissioner.

For directions in the election of representatives, see Chap. IX., pp. 193-194.

The Moderator of General Assembly, the Moderator Elect, the Procurator, the Clerks of Assembly, and the Law Agent are commissioners *ex officiis* (1956, xviii., xix.). It is recommended that Conveners of Assembly Committees be elected if possible (1944, 11).

Section V. Stated Annual Duties of Presbyteries.

1. To call for and examine the books of all Kirk Sessions, a certified abstract of the accounts of each congregation and the account books of all congregations where the model constitution is in operation.
2. To revise annually the Benefice Register.
3. To send immediately to the Committee on Probationers and Transference of Ministers and to the Committee on Education for the Ministry, the names of those who are licensed to preach the Gospel, of those probationers who are ordained otherwise than because of appointment to a charge and of those set apart as readers.
4. To produce annually to the Synod of the bounds: the records of the Presbytery; the Benefice Register; a report on the quinquennial visitation of congregations together with the schedules thereanent; a report anent the care of Church property.
5. To send monthly reports to the Committee on the Maintenance of the Ministry anent ordinations, inductions, demissions, deaths, and translations.
6. To send petitions for the sale of ecclesiastical property to the clerks of Assembly one month prior to each meeting of the Commission of Assembly.

Dated Duties.

By January 12. Returns of ministerial income to be sent to the Committee on the Maintenance of the Ministry.

By January 31. Statistical returns to be sent to the clerks of Assembly.

,, February. Returns to the Nomination Committee required.

,, March 15. List of ministers without charge resident within the bounds, who are not members of any Presbytery, to be sent to the Committee on Probationers and Transference of Ministers.

Applications to be received from students proposing to enter divinity halls.

,, April 24. Commissions, petitions, references and all other papers for the General Assembly to be in the hands of the clerks, commissioners having been elected in March or April at least ten free days after the date of resolution to elect.

List of candidates for theological training to be sent to the secretary of the Selection Board together with "any relevant information and observations and a commendation from the minister of each applicant."

,, May 1. Changes in the ministerial membership of Presbytery to be sent to the Trustees of the Churches and Universities (Scotland) Widows' and Orphans' Fund.

,, September 17. Names of students entering divinity halls to be sent to the Committee on Education for the Ministry.

,, November 1. Changes in the ministerial membership of Presbytery to be sent to the Trustees of the Churches and Universities (Scotland) Widows' and Orphans' Fund.

Two auditors to be appointed to audit the accounts of each church extension charge.

,, November 15. Congregations to be notified of allocations in terms of the Mission and Service Fund.

,, December 1. Reports on hospital chaplaincy work to be lodged with the Home Board.

,, December 31. Complete Roll of the Presbytery to be sent to the Clerks of Assembly.

CHAPTER VIII.

The Provincial Synod.

Section I. *Constitution and Officials.*

How formed.

The General Assembly determine the constituent Presbyteries of each Provincial Synod and approve the name thereof.

Membership.

A Provincial Synod consists of (1) all persons, both ministers and representative elders, who are on the Rolls of the several Presbyteries within the province (see Chap. VII., pp. 141-146); and (2) such corresponding members, both ministers and elders, as may have been appointed and commissioned by neighbouring Synods. A Provincial Synod may associate with itself in its deliberations, *pro tempore*, any minister who is present, but he cannot vote upon any question before the Court. Ministers and elders from other Synods may be added to the Synod by the General Assembly as assessors for special purposes. With reference to these purposes they have the rights of members during their appointment.

Elder's Commission.

The commission from a Kirk Session, which constitutes a representative elder a member of Presbytery, constitutes him also a member of Synod during the period for which that commission is valid. He cannot be allowed to take his seat in the Synod, unless his name appear in the roll of his Presbytery, as certified to the Synod by the clerk of Presbytery, or on production of a commission in proper form. The form of commission must bear that he is elected to represent the Session in the Synod as well as in the Presbytery. Presbytery clerks send a list of the names and addresses of elders whose commissions have been sustained by the Presbytery to the Synod clerk annually not later than three months after the close of the Assembly, and intimate any changes which occur during the year. The Synod may call for the production of the Commissions, if it see cause (1932, x.).

Corresponding Members.

At each meeting Synods may appoint corresponding members, a minister and an elder, to each neighbouring Synod. They can send only such as are within their own bounds (1836, 10). These corresponding members shall receive commissions from their own Synod, which, on being presented and sustained, shall constitute them members of the Synod to which they have been appointed for the period during which their commissions extend (1638, 23). The commission in common use is for the ensuing meeting and the several diets thereof. According to Mair (*Digest*, 4th edition, p. 167) their connection with the business of the Synod ceases at its rising. Corresponding members report their diligence to the next succeeding meeting of their Synod. (For Form of Commission, see p. 788.)

Receiving of Commissions.

Commissions to elders, or to corresponding members, may be received at any meeting of Synod.

It is incompetent for a Synod to appoint "correspondent members" to act with a Presbytery (1812, 7). This is entirely different from sending commissions as is done by the General Assembly, and as the Synod may do (see p. 147).

Moderator.

The Moderator shall be chosen from among the ministerial members of the court by free election. He shall hold office for a year at least, and shall be eligible for re-election. During his term of office he may be appointed to visit the various districts within the bounds of the Synod, with a view to giving advice or stimulating interest in the work of the Church (1933, xvii.).

Each Provincial Synod appoints one or more clerks (see pp. 79-80).

Synod Officer.

The Synod appoints an officer, who is in attendance at its meetings and executes its orders. At his appointment he promises to perform the duties of his office with fidelity. He has a salary fixed by the Synod.

Synod Fund.

Synods are entitled to assess the congregations under their jurisdiction in order to provide such funds as are necessary for carrying on their work. This may be done by assessment on Presbyteries which can then recover the amount due to the Synod from each congregation within their own bounds.

SECTION II. *Meetings and Procedure.*

Ordinary Meeting.

An ordinary meeting of Synod is held either under an Act of Assembly, or upon regular adjournment from the preceding ordinary meeting. Each Synod meets at least once a year, at such centres within its bounds as it may from time to time determine (1933, xvii.).

In hunc effectum Meeting.

A Synod may appoint a meeting *in hunc effectum*. The regulations for such meetings are the same as in the case of Presbyteries. (See Chap. VII., p. 149.)

Pro re nata Meeting.

During the interval between meetings of Synod the Moderator has the power, either on his own authority or on requisition from at least a quorum of members, to call a meeting *pro re nata*, to dispose of any business which has occurred, and which seems to require immediate attention (1647, 23). The first business after the Synod is constituted and the roll adjusted is the approval or disapproval of the Moderator's action in calling the meeting. No other business is to be entered upon except the particular business for which the meeting has been convened. The meeting is called by circular stating the special business, signed by the Moderator and the clerk, addressed to every minister of the Synod, and delivered or despatched through the post office in due time before the date fixed for the meeting. On receiving such notice, it is the duty of each minister to intimate the meeting to the member or members of his Kirk Session who are members of the Synod. The Presbytery clerk gives notice to the representative elders of vacant congregations. If the Moderator decline to call a *pro re nata* meeting after receiving a requisition to do so, the whole circumstances of the case may be brought before the Synod at its next ordinary meeting. In the event of the Moderator having ceased to be a member of the court, his duties and responsibilities in relation to convening a meeting *pro re nata* devolve upon the clerk.

A meeting of Synod may be duly constituted provided a quorum, consisting of three members, two of whom are ministers, have convened (1934, xi.). Quorum.

A quorum of members being assembled, the Moderator constitutes the Synod with prayer. In the event of the Moderator being absent or having ceased to be a member of the court, the next preceding Moderator who is present, or failing the presence of any ex-Moderator, the senior minister present constitutes the Synod. Synod constituted

The first act of the Synod after being constituted is to adjust its roll. This may be conveniently done by keeping the roll by itself and making the required changes on it—generally accomplished beforehand by the clerk. The names of those present are usually recorded in a separate register and not entered in the minutes. Thereafter the Moderator is elected if his predecessor's term of office has expired, and the minutes of last meeting of Synod read. Roll adjusted.

The Synod is an open court, but may meet in private when it judges it necessary or expedient. Reports on quinquennial visitation schedules are taken in private. An open Court.

It is now the usual custom for Synods to have a standing Business Committee which meets beforehand to suggest the order of business, and to act as a Committee on Bills and Overtures. The examination of Presbytery records may also be undertaken by such a Committee or by a Committee specially appointed for this purpose. If this course be followed, the whole of the Synod business may be transacted at one diet. Business Committee. Bills and Overtures. Presbytery Records.

Committee on Bills and Overtures.

Where there is no standing Business Committee there should be at least two diets at each ordinary meeting. At the first of these a Committee on Bills and Overtures is appointed, which meets in the interval between the first and second diets, and reports as soon as the second diet is opened. The Moderator and the clerk of the Synod are *ex officiis* convener and clerk of this Committee.

Opening and Closing.

Every diet of Synod is both opened and closed with prayer.

Examination of Presbytery Records.

Where there is no standing Business Committee or Committee for the Examination of Records, the records of Presbyteries are called for at the first diet. A Presbytery whose record is not produced is liable to censure, unless a satisfactory explanation be given. A Committee is appointed to examine the records produced and to report at the next diet.

Presbyterial Visitation.

It is the duty of each Synod annually and immediately after the visitation of Presbytery records to prepare and transmit to the General Assembly a return on Presbyterial visitation of congregations. A printed form is supplied for this purpose (1931, xii.).

Ecclesiastical Properties.

It is the duty of each Synod to prepare and transmit to the General Assembly through the General Administration Committee a report on the diligence of each Presbytery within its bounds in carrying out the provisions of the Act anent the Care of Ecclesiastical Properties (1961, xxi., and 1969, xxvi.).

Synods appoint such Committees as they deem necessary for the transaction of their business.

Intimation of Adjournment.

When there is more than one diet, intimation is publicly made, before each adjournment, of the time at which the next diet will commence.

Time and Mode of Transmission of Papers.

All business to be brought before the Synod should be intimated to the Synod clerk, and all papers and documents intended for transmission to the Synod should be in his hands, not less than ten days before the date fixed for the meeting of the Synod. No papers are received at a later date, unless reasons satisfactory to the court be assigned for the delay. The decision as to whether or not the papers in any cases coming before a Synod should be printed rests with the Business Committee or the moderator and clerk (or clerks) of Synod (1935, 2).

Printing of Papers.

Business Committee.

When there is a standing Business Committee, the clerk convenes that Committee at a suitable hour before the meeting of Synod; gives intimation of the time and place of its meeting to all parties in causes, all of whom have a right to attend the meeting for their interests; and submits to the Committee the whole causes sent up to the Synod, with the papers and documents in each cause. The Committee judges, subject to review of the Synod, as to the competency of each cause, and whether the papers and documents in connection with it be complete and in proper form, and decides upon its transmission or non-transmission accordingly. It reports to the Synod after the minutes have been approved.

When there is no standing Business Committee, the clerk lays all causes and papers before the Synod itself, which remits them to its Committee on Bills and Overtures with instructions to report at the beginning of the second diet.

Dissents anent Trans-mission.

Any member of Synod or party in a cause who is dissatisfied with the decision of the Business Committee or Committee on Bills and Overtures, or any member of the Committee who has entered his dissent, is entitled to be heard by the Synod when the report of the Committee is given in.

Order of Business.

When the report of the Business Committee or Committee on Bills and Overtures is disposed of, the Synod, having now its whole business before it, arranges the order in which the several causes are to be taken up, and proceeds to dispose of them.

New Causes.

The Synod may, for sufficient reason, receive any new cause during its proceedings, and may either itself judge of its competency or appoint the Committee to meet and report as to its transmission.

Records.

The Synod is responsible to the General Assembly for the keeping of its permanent record. It must be sent up to the Assembly for examination and attestation, and should be in the hands of the clerks of Assembly not later than the first day of the Assembly's sittings (S.O., 29).

At the conclusion of its business the Synod adjourns to meet at a stated time and place, which being publicly intimated the meeting is closed with prayer.

SECTION III. *Powers and Functions.*

Powers and duties.

The Synod cannot legislate; but it can give orders, having "power to handle, ordour, and redress all things omitted or done amiss" (P. 1592) in the courts below that come regularly before it, brought up by those courts, or parties, or Presbytery records. A Synod cannot review the conduct of a Presbytery respecting the attestation of a commission to the Assembly (1835, 3); whatever is alleged to affect the validity of a commission cannot be judged of by a court inferior to that to which the commission is addressed.

Causes with which it deals.

The Synod deals with the following causes in which its decision is final, except when otherwise specified as under:—

General super-vision.

(1) General supervision of the interests of the Church within its bounds, and promotion of the life of the Church.

Presby-tery Records.

(2) Supervision of Presbytery records. (See pp. 87, 179.) It must annually examine the minute-book and benefice register

of every Presbytery within its bounds (1700, ix.; 1766, ix.; 1931, xiv.), but in this examination it is not entitled to order up other papers for examination (1836, 8); and while it must have respect to the proceedings recorded, and is entitled to censure them, it is not to "revive a question affecting a private party, the decision of which has become final" (1811. 4).

Quinquennial Visitation Reports.

(3) Receiving and judging of reports of the quinquennial visitation of congregations by Presbyteries. (See Chap. VII., p. 169).

Every Presbytery reports to the Synod of the bounds the result of each visitation. In the event of the Presbytery finding itself unable to express satisfaction with the state of any congregation, it is the duty of the Synod to appoint a Committee to make further inquiry in conjunction with the Presbytery, and to endeavour to remedy what is deemed to be unsatisfactory. If, after this further visitation, it be found that matters are still unsatisfactory, the Synod forwards a report to the General Assembly through the General Administration Committee, and the Assembly may take such further action as may appear best (1931, xii.). (See also section II. of this Chapter, p. 188.) Alternatively the Synod may remit the case to the Presbytery to be dealt with under the Act anent Congregations in an Unsatisfactory State (1960, xxi.).[1]

Special Visitation.

(4) Special visitation of congregations. The Synod has power, in consultation with the Presbytery within whose bounds the congregation is situated, to visit any congregation when it is deemed expedient to do so from what appears in visitation reports or in Presbytery minutes, or from information reported by the Moderator or submitted in writing by another member of Synod, who is not a member of the Presbytery concerned (1933, 2, and Rep., p. 87).

Schemes of the Church.

(5) Supervision of the Schemes of the Church. The Synod exercises supervision over Presbyteries in connection with the Schemes of the Church; Presbyteries are required to report diligence in regard to the Maintenance of the Ministry Fund and the Mission and Service Fund.

Delimitation of Areas.

(6) Supervision of delimitation of areas. In any matter affecting delimitation of areas brought before the Synod by motion or by complaint of any member of Presbytery, the judgment of the Synod is final, unless the matter affect the bounds of the Synod itself, or the decision involves the modification of an arrangement set up by a decree of the Court of

[1] The General Assembly direct Presbyteries to forward to the Synod of the bounds the Schedules anent Presbyterial Visitation for examination (see 1944, xx., p. 717).

Teinds or an Act of the General Assembly (1933, 5, and Rep., p. 59).

(7) Transmission to the General Assembly of overtures originating in the Synod itself or transmitted from Presbyteries. Overtures from Presbyteries may be transmitted with or without comment, with approval or with disapproval. A Synod may not refuse to transmit an overture which is presented in proper form (1933, xix., as amended 1961, xxiii.). **Overtures.**

(8) Judging appeals and complaints from Presbyteries under limitation of right of appeal to the General Assembly in cases of doctrine, worship, or censure of a minister or other office-bearer (1933, xviii.); in cases of the licensing of students (1947, viii.); and in cases of union, readjustment and other changes in the status of congregations (1962, xv.). **Appeals and Complaints.**

(9) Transportation, reduction, and dissolution of charges. Except in cases where the change would involve any modification of arrangements set up by and existing under a decree of the Court of Teinds or an Act of General Assembly or a scheme of the Scottish Ecclesiastical Commissioners, the Synod deals with the transporting, reduction, and dissolution of charges, it being understood that, where grants are being asked from Assembly Committees, the approval of these Committees shall be obtained before any action is taken, and that such conditions are laid down as the General Assembly may determine from time to time (1957, xvii.). Where the transportation :— **Transportation, Reduction, and Dissolution of Charges**

(*a*) Concerns another Synod; or

(*b*) Concerns two Presbyteries out of a Synod consisting of not more than three, and these two Presbyteries are not in agreement as to the proposed transportation, the Synod shall refer the question to the General Assembly or their commission (1957, xvii.; 1958, xiii.). (See also p. 753.)

(10) Transference of charges from one Presbytery to another. Subject to the exceptions contained in par. (9) above, the Synod has power to transfer a charge from one Presbytery to another within the bounds of the Synod, on a petition to that effect from the Kirk Session of the charge concerned, transmitted through the Presbytery (1957, xvii.; 1958, xiii.). (See also p. 182.) **Transference of Charges.**

(11) Permitting ministers who have retained their seats to resign same on petition through the Presbytery (1935, x.). **Permitting ministers to resign their seats.**

(12) Receiving and disposing of petitions by ministers who have demitted their charges on grounds of age or infirmity, for transference from one Presbytery to another. Where the proposed transference involves two Synods, the petition is presented to the Synod in whose bounds is situated the Presby-

tery to which the petitioner desires to be transferred, and intimation of the petition is made to the other Synod, and to the two Presbyteries concerned (1960, xxiv.).

Appointments to Assembly Committees.

(13) Appointment of members to Standing Committees of the General Assembly. Each Synod appoints one member to the Committee on Education for the Ministry, who holds office for four years. Each Synod also appoints representatives to the Nomination Committee, who shall also hold office for four years (S.O., 107, 17, 3) in accordance with the instructions of the General Assembly. Each Synod appoints two ministers and two elders (the Presbyteries of Orkney, Shetland and England one minister and one elder) to be members, for a period of four years, of the Committee to nominate the Moderator of the General Assembly (S.O., 107, 25). Each Synod nominates members of the Judicial Commission of the General Assembly for a period of not more than four years (four from Lothian and Tweeddale; four from Clydesdale; two from each of the other Synods) (1960, xxii.).[1]

Draft Regulations.

(14) When the General Assembly send down to Presbyteries Draft Regulations (not under the Barrier Act) for suggestions, these are also sent to Synods, which may send in suggestions and express their judgment (1933, 5, Rep., p. 59).

Reports on work of Assembly Committees within bounds.

(15) (*a*) Reports on the activities of the General Assembly's Home Board, Committee on Social Responsibility, &c., carried on within the bounds are made periodically to the Synod (1933, 5, Rep., p. 59).

(*b*) Reports from the Agents of the General Assembly Committee on Parish Education, who are settled within the bounds, are also made periodically to the Synod (1933, 5, Rep., p. 59).

(*c*) Synods are expected to take direct interest in the various organisations of the Church, particularly those carried on within their own bounds. With this end in view they may arrange for the periodic visit to their statutory meetings of the agents employed by these organisations. Synods may send in suggestions to the Committee concerned (1933, 5, Rep., p. 59).

References to Commission of General Assembly.

The Commission of the General Assembly are empowered, at any of their stated diets, to take up and dispose of all References from Synods in matters connected with (1) calls, translations, retiral or settlement of ministers; and (2) the union and status of congregations and the readjustment of agencies falling under the scope of the Committee on Unions and Readjustments (1963, xxiii.).

[1] The Constitution of this Judicial Commission will fall to be revised consequent upon implementation of Act II, 1975.—Ed.

CHAPTER IX.

THE GENERAL ASSEMBLY.

SECTION I.

CONSTITUTION.

THE General Assembly is the Supreme Court of the Church. In matters spiritual the decisions of the Assembly are final, and are not subject to review by any civil court. "The membership of the General Assembly consists of commissioners elected by Presbyteries for each Assembly. These commissioners, being ministers (including theological professors) and ruling elders, are elected in proportion to the size of each Presbytery, one minister for every four, or part of four, ministers on the complete roll of the Presbytery, with additionally, by authority of Act XXIV., 1969, Ex-Moderators of General Assembly being members of the electing Presbytery, and an equal number of ruling elders. Ministers elected as commissioners must be members of the Presbyteries by which they are elected. Elders so elected must be *bona fide* acting members of Kirk Sessions within the Church" (Oct. 1929, i.).[1]

Membership.

By "the complete roll of the Presbytery" is meant "(1) the number of charges in the Presbytery, whether vacant or not; and (2) ministers who hold seats in Presbyteries in terms of Act anent Membership of Presbyteries (1970, ii.)."[2]

"Complete Roll."

The number and boundaries of Synods and Presbyteries in the Church are determined by the General Assembly. By Act II., 1975, the General Assembly effected a major reorganisation of the Synod and Presbytery structure as a result

[1] Vacancies should be filled up by free election and not according to a rota (1944, 11).

[2] A minister who demits his charge and retains his seat in the Presbytery retains also the rights and privileges of membership, including membership of the General Assembly.

of which there will be, as from 1st January 1976, 11 Synods and 50 Presbyteries, including the Presbytery of England and the Presbytery of Europe, with the Presbytery of Jerusalem in addition. This latter Presbytery has similar representation in the General Assembly, but it is not entitled to receive overtures sent down to Presbyteries under the Barrier Act (1936, ix.).

Ex-officio Members.

The clerks, procurator and law agent are members *ex officiis* of the General Assembly and they have all the rights and privileges of commissioners (1956, xviii.).

The Moderator of the General Assembly shall, upon his election, be, by virtue of his office, a member of the General Assembly, and shall also, by virtue of having held that office, be a member of the General Assembly during which his demission from office takes place (1956, xix.).

Corresponding Members.

Besides the Commissioners to Assembly the following have the privilege of sitting as corresponding members without a vote: (1) Missionaries at home on furlough, being ministers or elders ordained under the Home Formula or licentiates of the Church of Scotland ordained at a later date by a Church with which the Church of Scotland has a missionary connection through its Overseas Council, whether or not they be minister or elder of such other Church, who are certified by the Overseas Council or other Committee under whose auspices they have gone abroad, shall be corresponding members of the General Assembly; (2) Secretaries of Standing Committees being ministers or elders, and the editor of 'Life and Work,' being a minister or elder, shall, in years in which they are not elected as commissioners by a Presbytery be corresponding members of the General Assembly and of the Commission of the General Assembly (1962, Reg. 3).

There are other persons privileged to sit in the Assembly during the sittings of the General Assembly who may bring greetings from other churches or address the General Assembly when so invited: These are—(1) Delegates from other churches (*a*) Four duly commissioned representatives from the United Reformed Church in England and Wales; (*b*) Four duly commissioned representatives from the Presbyterian Church in Ireland; (*c*) Two duly commissioned representatives from the Presbyterian Church of Wales; (*d*) Representatives from other churches duly accredited by the Courts or equivalent authority of their churches. (2) Visitors. (*a*) Representatives of other churches who come to the General Assembly by special invitation from the Inter-Church Relations Committee;

Delegates.

Visitors.

(*b*) Brethren from other churches with letter of introduction from Assembly or Presbytery Clerks (1973, 6, Reports pp. 10, 11).

Within the quota of Commissioners to which a Presbytery is entitled it is recommended (1944, 11) that there be included Conveners of Assembly Committees.

Commissioners to the General Assembly are "answerable" to the body that appointed them, and must report their diligence on their return (1783, x.). Commissioners to report diligence.

The commissioners must be elected during the two calendar months next preceding that in which the General Assembly are to meet and ten clear days must elapse between the resolution to elect and the election (1877, vii.). If a commissioner resign, another may be appointed at any time before the Assembly meet (1877, vii.), and both commissions must be presented (1809, 3, 6). Presbyteries must send their full number, and be careful to choose such as can probably attend (1700, vii.; 1718, ix.). But the place of one who has become disqualified by being suspended cannot be supplied (1758, 6); nor of one who is found to have been disqualified for election (1789, 5, 6). Time of Election. "After Elections."

The commission of a minister translated after election is not thereby invalidated (1769, 4). Case of Commissioner translated.

In addition to their commission, elders require a certificate from moderator and clerk of the Kirk Session to which they belong of their being *bona fide* acting elders, and of their having signed the Formula (1839, xii.; 1934, 2). A form of certificate is provided by the clerks of the General Assembly. The clause in the certificate of each commissioner to the General Assembly that he has signed the Formula is, in the case of ministers and elders ordained previous to union, understood to mean that he has assented to the Formula in use in the church in which he was ordained (Form of Commission, p. 788). Elders' Certificate of *bona fide* Eldership.

The quorum of the General Assembly is thirty-one, not less than sixteen of whom must be ministers.

When the General Assembly have been constituted and have appointed their moderator, the Queen's Commissioner presents his commission. It has the crown seal for Scotland attached, and bears that the Queen authorises and appoints him to be her representative in all respects, and to be regarded as such. He then delivers to the General Assembly a letter from the Queen wherein she gives assurance anew of her affectionate regard and support and trust. The commissioner is not a The Queen's Commissioner.

member of Assembly, though he may be such in his private capacity, if he holds a valid commission from a Presbytery.

Moderator.

The General Assembly are presided over by a moderator, elected immediately after the constitution thereof. The Assembly may elect any one who has been ordained to the ministry. The moderator of each General Assembly is nominated by a committee consisting at present (1962, Reg. 5) of—

Method of Nomination.

(i) The ex-moderators.
(ii) The principal clerk (*ex officio*) who acts as secretary.
(iii) Four representatives—two ministers and two elders—from each Synod in Scotland, one minister and one elder from Orkney and Shetland and from Presbytery of England who shall be members of committee for four years, one-quarter of members retiring annually.
(iv) Elders equal in number to the number of ex-moderators, to be appointed by the General Assembly through their Nomination Committee.
(v) The convener shall be appointed by the General Assembly and hold office for the usual term.

The Committee meets usually in the month of October and intimates the nomination to the meeting in that month of the Commission of the General Assembly.

Although it is not essential it is highly desirable that consent should have been obtained before nomination at the Committee meeting (1967, Reg. 1).

Office, Function, and Duties of Moderator of General Assembly.

(1962, Reg. 5 (2).)

(*a*) To preside over the General Assembly and to perform those duties as stated in the Standing Orders.

(*b*) To visit Presbyteries according to the scheme of visitation sanctioned by the General Assembly (Reports, 1936, pp. 208, 209; 1936, 9).

(*c*) To perform such duties as may be directed by the General Assembly, and to represent the Church of Scotland on historic and national occasions, as they may arise.

(*d*) To undertake such other duties as he may choose during his term of office.

Ex-Moderator may preside in his absence.

At the moderator's request any member who has previously been moderator of the Supreme Court may occupy the chair in his absence.

1956, xix.

1. The moderator of the General Assembly shall be deemed to hold office from the time of his election by the General Assembly until he demits office upon the election of his successor. *Ex-officio* Membership.

2. The moderator of the General Assembly shall, upon his election, be, by virtue of his office, a member of the General Assembly, and shall also, by virtue of having held that office, be a member of the General Assembly during which his demission from office takes place.

3. A minister shall be eligible for election as moderator of the General Assembly notwithstanding that he may not, at the time of his election, be a commissioner to the General Assembly.

For further particulars regarding duties, see Standing Orders, App. XII., pp. 581 ff.

Former General Assemblies and their Membership.

At first all the ministers might sit in the Assembly, and many sat who were neither ministers nor elders. The first Assembly (Dec. 20, 1560) consisted of six ministers and thirty-five others designated commissioners, of whom two are also designated elders. Of the second there is no list. The third consisted of twenty ministers, and fifteen commissioners including two elders; the fourth, of twenty-two ministers, and fifteen commissioners of whom two were elders. In each, there were more than one commissioner from some places, and also commissioners who represented more bodies than one. The next extant roll is for 1590, showing 162 members, of whom 88 seem to be ministers. In 1598 it was ordained that from every Presbytery should be sent three at most of the wisest of the brethren, also one in name of Barrones, and one from every Burgh, but two from Edinburgh. Following a recommendation of P. 1693, 38, that commissioners from a Presbytery should be in due proportion to the number of its parishes, the Assembly in 1694 fixed the representation as it continued till 1894. Eight years after 1694 the roll shows from Presbyteries 119 ministers, 51 elders; from burghs, 5; from universities, 3. Presbyteries did not always send their full number, and even united in considerable numbers to make joint appointments. In 1709 Steuart gives the possible Assembly as, from Presbyteries, 180 ministers, 68 elders; and from burghs, 67 elders. He overlooks the universities. In the

United Presbyterian Supreme Court all ministers of charges were members ; in the United Free Church of Scotland one in every three. The General Assembly of 1933 consisted of 1602 commissioners from the home Presbyteries (including those from the Presbytery of the Synod in England), and 108 from Presbyteries in Europe and overseas—total, 1710. In 1974 the total was 1342.

After 1602 there was no regular Assembly till 1638. The six which had followed that of 1602 (1606, 1608, 1610, 1616, 1617, 1618) were declared in 1638, for distinct reasons assigned against each, to have all been "from the beginning unfree, unlawful, and null." From 1638 to 1649 inclusive regular Assemblies sat. There was an Assembly in 1650, and troubled meetings in 1651, 1652, 1653, the last of which was dispersed by the English troops. Those four are not recognised as lawful Assemblies. After the Revolution the Assembly met on Oct. 16, 1690. Intended meetings in 1691 and 1693 were prorogued or postponed. The next Assembly began on March 29, 1694, and Dec. 17, 1695. After this the meetings were at intervals of rather more than twelve months till thus the middle of May was reached in 1718.

Meetings.

Time and Place of Meeting.

It is now the practice of the General Assembly to meet on the first Tuesday after the 17th day of May. Before 1901 the day was Thursday similarly fixed. The place of meeting of the General Assembly of the Church of Scotland since the Revolution has been Edinburgh ; also of the Free Church of Scotland, with the following exceptions—viz. : Glasgow (Oct. 1843), Inverness (Aug. 1845, adjourned from May), Glasgow (1878), and Inverness (1888). The United Free Church Assembly met each year in Edinburgh, with the exception of 1902, when it met in Glasgow.

Section II.

Procedure.

Standing Orders.

For the Standing Orders of the General Assembly, see App. XII., pp. 581 ff. A copy of the Standing Orders is issued to each member along with other Assembly papers. These orders are for the Assembly only, but are usually taken as guides by inferior courts so far as applicable.

SECTION III.

POWERS AND FUNCTIONS.

The ordinary business of the Assembly consists mainly of two parts: (1) Reports from committees; (2) Matters brought up from the inferior courts. Members desiring to introduce any special subject for the consideration of the Assembly must do so in the form of an Overture from members. Ordinary Business.

Committees which report to the Assembly are of two classes: (1) Those which are appointed during the Assembly to report to a subsequent diet; (2) Those which are entrusted with business to be conducted by them in the course of the year. Regulations as to both classes of committees will be found in the Standing Orders. Committees.

It is usual to refer to committees of the first class all matters involving the preparation of documents, or the investigation of details, such, *e.g.*, as the preparation of an Address to Her Majesty and questions in dispute between parties in inferior courts which cannot conveniently be entered into at the bar of the Assembly. Several such committees are regularly appointed every year, and are named on the first or second day of the Assembly's meeting. But any special committee, which the Assembly may agree to appoint in the course of their proceedings, is not appointed till after the names proposed have appeared in the "Daily Proceedings," whether it be to report to the Assembly which appoint it, or to the Commission, or to the next Assembly.

Business brought from the inferior courts is introduced by the production of papers from these courts, which are printed according to regulations to be found in the Standing Orders. A Standing Committee, consisting of the clerks, procurator, and agent, is charged with the duty of examining these papers and reporting on their being in proper form for presentation to the Assembly. Production of Papers.

The functions of the Assembly are legislative as well as judicial and administrative. They deliberate on matters which concern the whole Church in her doctrine, worship, discipline, and government, and declare the mind of the Church thereupon, so as from time to time to determine and regulate constitutional and legal affairs. They may do so by way of what is called a Declaratory Act, which declares for the guidance of the Church what the Assembly hold the law of the Church Legislative Functions. Declaratory Acts.

to be on any point on which questions have been raised. Such an Act may be passed by the Assembly, without reference to Presbyteries; though Declaratory Acts on matters of difficulty or importance are often sent down to Presbyteries before the Assembly pass them. But when any proposal to pass an Act of Assembly, in any form, is such as involves "alteration or innovation in either doctrine or worship or discipline or government" of the Church, it must, in order to become a "binding rule" of the Church, be first sent down, under the Barrier Act, as an overture to the Presbyteries of the Church for their consideration, and can be finally passed only after the approval of a majority of Presbyteries has been obtained. Acts of immediate importance may be passed as *Interim Acts* until the approval of Presbyteries has been obtained (see p. 104).

Remit to a Special Commission.

The General Assembly may remit any cause to a special commission of members. The powers of such a special commission arise from, and are limited by, the Act or resolution of Assembly by which it is appointed, and should be carefully defined therein. The Assembly may instruct such a special commission to report to the ordinary Commission of Assembly at any of their stated diets, authorising the latter to deal with any appeal or question arising out of the report. But the ordinary Commission have no power to deal with the report beyond what may be conferred by the Assembly's deliverance.

Nobile Officium.

The General Assembly, being the supreme judicial, legislative, and administrative court of the Church, have a *nobile officium*. In virtue of this they may deal with and dispose of any matter which may arise and which is not otherwise provided for (see Chap. V., p. 114).

Decisions of General Assembly final.

The General Assembly being the Supreme Court of the Church, their decisions, whether on the merits of a cause or on matters of procedure, are final.

Dissents

Although there is no court to which an appeal from a deliverance of the Assembly can be carried, it is open to any member, who is dissatisfied, to have his dissent recorded in the minutes, provided he gives it in as soon as the decision has been pronounced and before the Assembly proceed to other business (S.O., 102).

Protestations.

At the last diet of the Assembly, after all other business is concluded, protestations are called for—that is, an opportunity is given to anyone to protest that some decision of an inferior court has become final because some party has failed to prosecute his appeal or complaint (see p. 99).

SECTION IV.

THE COMMISSION OF THE GENERAL ASSEMBLY (1963, xxiii.).

The practice of delegating to special commissioners the transaction of judicial and administrative business dates from the beginning of the General Assembly's history. With the single exception of legislation, there would appear to be no power belonging to the General Assembly which has not been exercised by commissioners. The Commission reponed ministers as well as deposed or suspended them; and there would seem to be no possible question in any process of discipline which has not been disposed of by the Commission. The disputed settlements thus determined are innumerable; sentences of inferior courts have been reversed as well as affirmed; committees have been appointed as freely as by the Assembly; and in fact the powers have been limited only by the terms of the Act constituting the Commission. In numerous instances judgments of the Commission have been overturned on the ground of irregularity in procedure, or acting in excess of power; but a long series of decisions warrants the statement that, *so long as the Commission act within the powers conferred by the Act and the procedure is regular,* the judgments are treated as final by the succeeding Assembly. The only case which seems to militate against the rule thus stated is the Cross case in 1888. In the Report of a Committee of Assembly appointed to report on the powers of the Commission of Assembly it is recorded in reference to this case: "The decision of the Assembly in that case may perhaps be supported (though it is believed that it was not advocated on that ground) upon the view that the Commission had not acted strictly in terms of the instructions given by the previous Assembly; but if it be taken, as it generally is, as a decision to the effect that the Assembly may review the proceedings of the Commission even when regular and *intra vires,* the committee must respectfully express their dissent from it, on the broad ground that it is at variance with a long and uniform course of practice. It was given by a majority of 9 in a vote of 235, and 32 members recorded their dissent." (Rep., 1893).

Its decisions final, so long as it acts within the powers entrusted to it and its procedure is regular.

The General Assembly, 1921, recalled a resolution of Commission of 1st December 1920, in so far as the same was inconsistent with the resolution of the General Assembly, 1920, and with previous resolutions on the subject (1921, 4).

A Resolution of Commission recalled.

Membership.

At first the Commission were a comparatively small body, and the members were elected without reference to the membership of the Assembly, but it was enacted in 1705 that Presbyteries should be proportionally represented on the Commission; in 1719 that only persons qualified to be members of the General Assembly should be members of the Commission; in 1736 that the proportion between ministers and elders should be the same as in the Assembly; and a few years later the membership of the Commission had settled down into being, as it is now, practically that of the Assembly. It has never, however, been exactly so. Persons excluded from the Assembly by reason of some informality in their commissions are always included; so in 1835 was the Royal Commissioner, Lord Belhaven, after the expiry of his commission, as ruling elder from the Presbytery of Hamilton; and from 1778 downwards it has been the practice, while still including the moderator himself, to name also a member of the Assembly "in place of the moderator," the object evidently being to admit of the latter being absent without incurring the appointed censure for absence (1705, vi.; 1742, v.).

Member "in place of the Moderator."

Act appointing.

An Act appointing the Commission is passed yearly at the last session of the General Assembly (for terms of Act, see App. XIII., pp. 605 ff.).

Moderator.

From an early date the Commission have been empowered to choose a moderator, who holds the office during the life of the Commission.

Meetings.

The Commission are appointed by the General Assembly to meet at Edinburgh on the first Thursday after the third Tuesday of October, and on the first Thursday after the third Tuesday of February, "and oftener when and where they shall think fit and convenient." It is "the duty of the Clerk of Assembly, on receiving a requisition signed by a quorum of the Commission, to call a meeting of the Commission, or on instruction from the General Administration Committee so to do." The Presbytery of Edinburgh, and all other Presbyteries within 50 miles of Edinburgh, are prohibited from meeting on any of the days appointed for the meeting of the Commission.

Quorum.

The quorum, since 1711, has been 31, of whom not less than 16 must be ministers.

Duties.

The Commission are to determine finally in every matter referred to them by the General Assembly; to receive any references and appeals that may be made to them from Synods in matters of doctrine, and to ripen such affairs for next

General Assembly; to make appointments on behalf of the Assembly to any governing body set up before the following Assembly; to contribute what they can to the suppression of vice and immorality; and to give all needed advice and assistance to Synods, Presbyteries, and Committees of Assembly upon application for that end; to receive information on the progress of the missionary schemes of the Church (motions on matters arising therefrom that may be controversial are incompetent except in terms of the Act).

Incompetent motions.

The Commission are empowered, at any stated diet, to take up and dispose of all References from Synods in matters connected with Calls, Translations, Retiral or Settlement of Ministers; and the Union and Status of Congregations and the Readjustment of Agencies falling under the scope of the Committee on Unions and Readjustments, provided always that all the papers in such References shall have been duly printed and made available to Members in the same way as if the References had been to the General Assembly, unless this be dispensed with by the Clerks and the Procurator.

They are empowered further to take up and dispose of cases brought by the Committee on Unions and Readjustments concerning the union and status of congregations and the readjustment of agencies falling under the scope of that Committee's appointment, in respect of which there has been no appeal to a Synod.

The Commission are empowered also to fill any vacancy in the membership or convenership of a Special Commission appointed to deal with a case of Readjustment, and to take up and dispose of References from Presbyteries, when no meeting of Synod intervenes, anent Transportation of Charges or Congregations. All such cases of Transportation must be reported to the next General Assembly.

They are empowered to take up and dispose of cases urgently requiring settlement in the spiritual interests of the parish concerned, where a minister is demitting his charge and financial arrangements for him require to be made, any action to be reported to next General Assembly.

They are empowered further, on report from the Law, Property Cases, and Discipline Committee, to dispose of all petitions for sale, burdening, or transfer of property. Such petitions should be lodged with the Principal Clerk of Assembly one month before the commission meet.

They are empowered also, at any stated diet, or at any meeting called *pro re nata*, to dispose of any matter brought before them, through the General Administration Committee, affecting the general interests of the Church at home or abroad, and requiring to be immediately dealt with, always with due regard to the limitations of their powers prescribed in the appointing Act. The General Administration Committee is authorised to take action in the name of the Church in any emergency affecting the interests of the Church when no meeting of the Commission of Assembly intervenes, so that the Church do not suffer or sustain any prejudice, the Committee to report its action to the General Assembly or their Commission in due course (1936, 5).

Obedience to it. Any court or party declining to give full execution to a sentence of the Commission is answerable to next Assembly.

Appeals. It is to be remembered that a judgment of the Commission is final unless they have exceeded their powers. Appeals or complaints against judgment are "no sufficient reason to justify a Presbytery's disobedience." (1750, 9, Kennoway). In this case the Presbytery itself did not appeal.

Status before Assembly. When the proceedings of the Commission are before the Assembly, members are not excluded because of having had a part in those proceedings as commissioners (1813, 8).

In 1946 the Commission, although not specially empowered, passed an Act, which was subsequently confirmed by the Assembly (1946, vii.).

Section V

The Committees of the General Assembly.

The general work of the Church at home and abroad, which is directly maintained and regulated by the General Assembly, requires constant administration throughout the year. This need was recognised in the Basis and Plan of Union, and the Committees, through whose service it is met, have a place and function in the constitution and organisation of the Church.

Standing Committees. The General Assembly appoint a certain number of Standing Committees which are grouped together into seven Departments and in connection with these Departments there are permanent officials appointed by the General Assembly whose status is that of Secretary and/or Deputy. These Committees discharge their functions under Acts passed, or Regulations approved by the General Assembly and report annually to the General Assembly.

A Deliverance on the Report of a Committee should not contain matter not dealt with in the Report. Report.

A synopsis of the functions of each Committee as then constituted is contained in the Plan of Union (Oct. 1929, i.). See pp. 417-423. (For details regarding the membership and method of appointment of these Committees, see S.O., 107, 108, pp. 596, 597.)

The General Assembly appoint also such temporary and occasional committees as it may judge necessary, and their function and powers depend upon the minute of their appointment. When the Assembly resolve that such a committee be appointed, it is not nominated till the following day, unless in case of urgency, and the names proposed by the Selection Committee are printed in the roll of business for the day. Temporary and Occasional Committees.

The opinion is here given that a person who is not either a minister or a *bona fide* acting elder is ineligible for membership of an Assembly Committee, unless there be a specific Act or Regulation of Assembly empowering such a Committee to have in its membership others specially designated.

Meetings of Committees and Sub-Committees should be called only by appointment of the Committee or Sub-Committee concerned, or by, or with the authority of, its Convener or Vice-Convener.

Section VI.

The Officials of the General Assembly.

Officials of the General Assembly, Clerks, Procurator and Solicitor, are appointed, subject to a retirement age limit of seventy. (The scale of retiring allowances for Secretaries of Committees applies to Clerks of Assembly, such retiring allowances, however, to be in addition to any retiring allowances to which the Clerks of Assembly may be entitled from other sources. No retiring allowance is payable to the other officials (1938, 5).)

They are *ex-officiis* members of Assembly, and it is convenient they should be.

They form a Standing Committee to report on commissions to the Assembly, and to report on returns of Presbyteries to overtures.

It is customary to appoint them, along with the Moderator, members of deputations representing the Church on ceremonial occasions.

The Clerks.

There are at present a Principal Clerk and a Depute Clerk.

1. The Principal Clerk of the General Assembly is *ex officio* Secretary of the General Administration Committee.

2. The Secretaryship of the General Administration Committee shall be a full-time appointment as an Assembly-appointed Secretary.

3. The duties of the Principal Clerk of the General Assembly shall be defined as hereunder, or as shall from time to time be delegated to him by the General Assembly, and in the discharge of these he shall be responsible solely to the General Assembly.

4. As Secretary of the General Administration Committee in the discharge of his duties he shall be responsible immediately to the Committee but ultimately to the General Assembly.

5. As Secretary of the General Administration Committee he shall receive the appropriate salary for an Assembly-appointed Secretary, including a house: and, in addition, as Principal Clerk of the General Assembly he shall receive an annual honorarium of £250 or of whatever sum may be authorised by the General Assembly on the recommendation of the General Administration Committee after consultation with the General Finance Committee.

6. He shall act as Secretary to the Moderator but without further remuneration.

7. The holder of the dual office of Principal Clerk of the General Assembly and Secretary of the General Administration Committee shall retire on reaching his seventieth birthday, but he may retire at an earlier age, retirement from one office always involving retirement from the other.

8. His pension and retiring allowance as Secretary of the General Administration Committee shall be governed by the Act of Assembly XXVIII., 1968, but, notwithstanding any provision in this Act, he shall be entitled to an additional retiring allowance as Principal Clerk of the General Assembly on the recommendation of the General Administration Committee after consultation with the General Finance Committee (1972, 1).

The duties of the Principal Clerk are: writing the minutes; preparing and printing them in the Daily Roll of Business; preparing, printing, and issuing the Abridgment of the Assembly Proceedings along with the Acts; and giving extracts.

He is the custodier of the Records and the legal extractor.

He also issues forms of commissions and Assembly papers, and advertises the meetings of the Assembly and of the Commission of Assembly; arranges with the Moderator and Purse-bearer; has charge of distributing papers and of printing the daily Lists of Business, &c.; and arranges for taking the vote at the meetings of the General Assembly and of the Commission. He is clerk to the Business Committee; and sees that all papers for the Assembly are regularly tabled. He also receives commissions to the Assembly; sends down overtures and Assembly schedules; prepares for the Assembly, and sends out, the volume of Reports, and (after the Assembly) prepares the volume of Assembly Papers (p. 212) for the Library; sends out printed copies of the Acts and Proceedings (p. 212); and arranges for meetings of the Commission of Assembly.

The Principal Clerk has power to arrange with the Depute Clerk as to the duties of the Depute Clerkship.

The Principal Clerk must be a minister; the Depute Clerk normally is a minister, but a layman is eligible for the office. The Depute Clerk has no preferential claim to the Principal Clerkship.

The Principal Clerk, as Secretary of the General Administration Committee, has power to arrange with the Depute Clerk as to the distribution of the secretarial work thereof. Both are *ex-officiis* members of the Committee (Reports, 1939, pp. 31-32).

The Principal Clerk and Depute Clerk are appointed by the General Assembly on the nomination of the General Administration Committee (1975, Sess. 1, Reports, pp. 17-18).

The Procurator.

The duties of the Procurator are summarised as follows (1969, 1):—

(1) He shall attend at meetings of the General Assembly and of their Commissions.

(2) He shall revise libels and other proceedings as required by Act of Assembly.

(3) He shall be a member of the General Administration Committee and a General Trustee, but he shall be expected to attend their meetings only when, in the opinion of the Principal Clerk or the Clerk to the General Trustees, as the case may be, matters are likely to arise requiring his advice.

(4) He shall conduct litigation as Senior Counsel on behalf of the Church.

(5) He shall give Opinions for the Church or any of its inferior Courts upon Memorials.

(6) He shall give advice, by Note or in Consultation, to inferior Courts of the Church, but requests for such advice shall first be submitted to the Principal Clerk for transmission, where relevant, to the Procurator.

(7) He shall not be required to give advice in any form to individual ministers or members of the Courts and congregations of the Church.

(8) He shall receive a General Retaining Fee, which shall be deemed to cover the duties defined under items (1), (2) and (3) above, and for work falling under items (4), (5) and (6) he shall be entitled to professional fees in ordinary course. Such fees, along with necessary expenses, shall be adjusted with his Clerk either at or about the time when instructions are given, or at convenient intervals each year as arranged, and shall be paid either by the parties concerned or the General Treasurer of the Church as the case may be.

It has been agreed that in future in the event of a vacancy in the office of Procurator the General Administration Committee shall bring forward a nomination to the General Assembly.

Solicitor of the Church of Scotland.

(Incorporating the Offices of Law Agent and Custodier of Titles.)
(1971., 1.)

The General Assembly resolved as follows (1937, 1) :—

(1) That a Law Department be formed in the Church Offices with a qualified Law Agent in charge, he to be known as the "Solicitor of the Church of Scotland," and with such clerical assistance as may be found necessary.

(2) That the work of the Law Department shall include the legal work of the General Trustees. The General Trustees shall be entitled to consult and employ another Solicitor in cases arising out of their particular work where that seems to them necessary.

(3) That the appointment of the Solicitor shall be a whole-time appointment at a fixed salary of £1,200 to £1,500, and on such other terms as may be arranged. He shall hold office during the pleasure

of the Assembly. His appointment shall not be regarded as falling under the Act anent Retiring Allowances to Officials in the Offices of the Church.

(4) That, in the event of the offices of Solicitor of the Church and of the General Trustees and Law Agent of the Church or any of them becoming vacant between the closing of one General Assembly and the opening of the next, the General Administration Committee shall be empowered, in conjunction with the General Finance Committee and the General Trustees, to make full provision for the carrying on of the work of the respective offices.

The salary of the Solicitor of the Church is determined from time to time by the General Finance Committee.

The London Agent.

(General Administration Committee's Minutes, 1937, pp. 48, 61 ; Rep. 1938, p. 29.)

There had long been an authorised Agent of the Church in London, with a salary of £21 ; but the arrangement was interrupted about 1843. Apparently on the recommendation of the Committee which reported on the Agency in 1855, it was revived.

His duties, for which he receives an annual retainer, plus expenses, are as follows :—

(1) The daily perusal of the Minutes of the House of Lords and the Votes and Proceedings of the House of Commons and attendances obtaining, and the perusal of all public Bills introduced into Parliament in which the interests of the Church are directly or indirectly affected ; writing with and forwarding to the Solicitor of the Church in Edinburgh all such Bills affecting Scotland, and also obtaining and forwarding to the Agent in Edinburgh any Minutes or Reports laid before either House of Parliament dealing with Scottish Ecclesiastical, Educational, and Trust Matters ; waiting in ordinary routine cases upon a Government Department or any Member of Parliament, in order to furnish information or explanation with reference to any matter affecting the Church in relation either to a Parliamentary Bill or Motion or to a question in either House.

(2) To receive any Deputation from the Church, and aid them in all their proceedings, including their attendance on Members of Parliament, Committees, and Government officials, but not including correspondence and attendance on Counsel.

(3) Advising any Committee of the Church, through the Procurator or Solicitor of the Church, as to the general nature of proceedings required for carrying out any matter by the assistance of Parliament or otherwise.

Any work not falling under the above headings to be charged for according to Parliamentary scale (Minutes, Committee on General Administration, 15th June 1937).

SECTION VII.

THE RECORDS OF THE ASSEMBLY AND THE COMMISSION.

1560-1638. Early in the struggles for the re-establishment of Episcopacy the Records of the Assembly (long called Registers) passed from their proper custodiers. They were discovered to be in the hands of Archbishop Adamson. In his recantation he confessed to the Synod of Fife in 1591 that he and others "rent out some leafes and destroyed sic things as made aganis our estate." No doubt such experiences taught the importance of transcripts.

On the subversion of Presbyterianism in 1605, they were again lost sight of till the Assembly of 1638, when the newly appointed clerk, Johnston (afterwards Lord Warriston), was able to announce that he had got many of them from persons connected by official duty with a former clerk, Nicholson; and the son of Nicholson's successor, Sandilands, produced two volumes, from 1590 to 1616, the only ones which had ever been in the custody of his father, who had received them from Archbishop Spottiswood. The following having been thoroughly examined were authenticated by the Assembly of 1638: two consecutive volumes, 1560-1572; [a vol., Mar. 1572–Mar. 1573, was produced to next Assembly]; one volume, 1574-1579; [awanting, 1580-1585]; one, 1586-1589; one, 1560-1590 (lent to Johnston by a minister), agreeing with the rest, and completing "all what is lacking in them, passing by what is mutilate in them"; two consecutive volumes from 1590 to 1616, which is called "to this present," for till now there had been no valid Assembly since 1602.

In 1650 the Records were in the Castle of Edinburgh for security, when it fell to the English; and the Commission of Assembly resolved that they should be taken to the Bass, except "the great volume" (1560-1590), which, being a duplicate, should be taken to another place, Dunnottar, not Dumbarton (Com. 1651, Jan. 24 and April 23), and it was apparently accompanied by the two subsequent volumes. When the Bass was taken, the House of Commons ordered the records found in it to be taken to the Tower of London, and after this, all is conjecture. From Dunnottar the rest were put into the safer keeping of Lord Balcarres. He would appear to have given them to the clerk, Ker; and after him, they are said to have been in his son's repositories when he died in 1677. They got into the hands of the Bishop of Edinburgh, and from him to one who disposed of them to Zion College, London. The Church labouring to recover them petitioned Parliament in 1828. By 1834 they had been well identified, and there was a near prospect of obtaining them when they were called for by a committee of the Commons on Patronage, and on Oct. 16, 1834, were consumed in the burning of the Houses of Parliament. 1638-1703.

By order of the Restoration Parliament a number of Church MSS. were brought together and burned.

From the report of a committee to the Assembly of 1703 we learn that on October 28, 1701, the records of the undernoted years were destroyed by a fire in the "Land-Market," Edinburgh (but that there was reason to believe much of the lost matter could be recovered from copies of parts in various quarters): 1638-1640; some years preceding 1650; 1690-1700; and part of 1701.

Apart from those which are known to have been destroyed, it is hard to say where MSS. of the Church, original or transcript, may be, as is suggested by some of the foregoing facts, and by similar ones. It is revealed in the minute of the commission, Jan. 21, 1708, that a register, Dec. 31, 1562–April 27, 1593, had been offered by the Earl of Cromarty, and received by a deputation appointed by the Assembly for the purpose. In 1739 it was reported to the Assembly that the registers of the commission, 1646-1653, had been purchased from a private gentleman; and these, being lent, were again amissing, and were restored but a few years ago. Again, the volume restored by the Earl of Cromarty disappeared for more than a century after being in the custody of Lord Prestongrange when he was clerk and procurator (as Mr Grant), reappeared among some of his books purchased by an Edin- General.

burgh bookseller, and was sold to Lord Rosebery, who restored it to the Church in 1905 (Rep., 1906, p. 1119).

Booke of the Kirk.

"The Booke of the Universall Kirk of Scotland" is the title by which has been known the Record from the Reformation to the temporary subversion of Presbyterianism, about half a century. The volumes in Zion College (1560-1616) were spoken of by this title. There is at present in Register House a folio MS. (1560-1608) bearing the same title, to which (after it had been "compared with a Register in the Theological Library at Edinburgh, subscribed by Mr Thomas Nicolson, then clerk of Assembly") is appended a minute of the Assembly of 1734, ordering it to be "attested to be a true Transcript of the original." The volume published by Peterkin under the same title (1839) agrees with it. But in every MS. the writer has made his remark on every blank as it occurs. The remarks quoted by Peterkin are not those in the Assembly transcript. It does not appear that he knew of it, or of its original, but wrought from another, apparently in the Advocates' Library.

Library.

"Assembly Papers."

In the Register House, the attested Records seem to be complete from 1702. From that date there are also "Assembly Papers" (cases, reports, &c.) bound up, and since 1872 in duplicate volumes. In the one volume there are only printed papers, which are placed together, followed by the printed Acts and Proceedings; and in the other, all papers, interspersed with the proceedings of the Assembly thereon as cut from the printed Acts and Proceedings. Papers in some important cases have also been arranged and bound, such as the case of Ebenezer Erskine and others, and those which led up to the Disruption of 1843.

Record Chamber.

The Records are now in the custody of the Keeper of the Records of Scotland (p. 80).

St Andrews.

In the Library of the University of St Andrews, also, the attested Records are complete from 1702, except 1793-1799 and 1801-1804.

What published.

The Acts and abridged proceedings of the following Assemblies have been published: 1638-1649; 1690 and 1692; 1694 onwards. So that the only want is for 1650, and the attempted or fragmentary meetings of the next three years before meetings were suppressed; but none of these Assemblies after 1649 are recognised as lawful. In 1691 and 1693 the meetings were prorogued or postponed.

Copies sent.

Pursuant to 1779, xii., one copy of the printed Acts and abridged proceedings of every Assembly is sent to the National Library, and to every University, Synod, and Presbytery

(1840, 7) to the Synod and Presbyteries in England; and to others.

The extant records of the Commission begin on June 18, 1646. After 1690 they resume on March 11, 1701, and continue without break. Their records from June 19, 1646, to June 28, 1650, were printed in two volumes in 1892 and 1896 for the Scottish History Society, edited by Professor Mitchell of St Andrews, and Dr Christie, the then Assembly's Librarian; and another volume from July 24, 1650, to May 30, 1653, edited by Dr Christie, with an Introduction by Lord Guthrie, was published in 1909. An abridgment of the proceedings of the Commission has been published annually along with that of the Assembly since 1830. Commission.

There is a complete set of the Minutes of the General Assembly of the Free Church of Scotland (1843-1900) in the Clerks' Room in the Offices of the Church and in the Library of the New College. The Minutes of the General Assembly of the United Free Church of Scotland (1900-1929) are also to be found complete in the same places. In the Library of the New College there is placed a set of the Minutes of the United Presbyterian Synod (1847-1900), and in the custody of the Keeper of the Records of Scotland there are to be found volumes of the Minutes of the United Presbyterian Synod from 1847 to 1886, as well as certain volumes of Minutes of the Associate Synod, the United Associate Synod, and the Relief Synod.

CHAPTER X.

THE MINISTRY.

Students and Probationers.

Section I. The Student.

Supply of Candidates (1959, 3).

A correspondent for the work of the Education for the Ministry Committee is appointed in each Presbytery, and it is strongly recommended that the scope of Students' Committees in Presbyteries include the recruitment of candidates for the Ministry.

Education and Training for the Ministry.

The General Assembly of 1973 by Act XX. codified all previous enactments and regulations governing the Education and Training for the Ministry.

The terms of Act XX., 1973, are as follows :—

Definition.

1. In these regulations " the Committee " refers to the Committee on Education for the Ministry as constituted and set up under Regulations 5 and 6 adopted by the General Assembly of 1970, or to such part of it as has been given powers to deal with selection of candidates or supervision of students or supervision of probationers in the terms of the constitution of the Committee approved by the General Assembly.

2. In all references to applicants or candidates " he " implies " she " as an alternative and so with all other personal pronouns.

3. A " candidate " is one who has been duly recognised as such by the Church (para. 8).

4. " Ordinary Candidates " are men and women who are under 23 years of age by 1st October of the year in which they begin their course.

5. " Mature Candidates " are men and women who are 23

years of age or over but under 40 years of age by 1st October of the year in which they begin their course.

6. "Pre-Divinity Students" are those "Mature Candidates" who are taking the Course for Mature Students and who are spending the first one or two years of their course as non-graduating students in certain university classes or specially arranged classes of a similar standard.

7. "Older Candidates" are men and women who are over 40 years of age by the 1st October of the year in which they begin their course.

Recognition as a Candidate.

8. A person seeking recognition as a candidate for the Ministry of the Church of Scotland must be a communicant member of the Church of Scotland. He must be accepted as a prospective candidate by the Committee on Education for the Ministry and must be nominated as a candidate by his Presbytery.

Acceptance by the Committee.

9. A person seeking such recognition who intends to take the Regular Course (paras. 37-38) shall apply to the Committee at any time before 31st January of the year in which he will start theological study.

10. A person seeking such recognition who intends to take the Alternative Course (paras. 39-41) or the Course for Mature Students (para. 42), and any applicant over 40, shall apply before 31st January of the year in which he will start upon his whole course.

11. The Committee shall obtain from the applicant such information as it shall deem necessary for the due consideration of the application and shall also inform the applicant's Presbytery, inviting the Presbytery to make such comments on the application as the Presbytery sees fit.

12. The Committee, under authority of the General Assembly, shall make suitable arrangements for the careful consideration of the applicant's character, motives and ability and shall be responsible for accepting or not accepting the applicant as a prospective candidate for the Ministry and shall inform the Presbytery of this decision.

Nomination by Presbytery.

13. A person seeking such recognition shall apply to Presbytery for nomination as a candidate for the Ministry of the Church of Scotland. Such application for nomination may be made at any time after his application has been lodged with the Committee, and if not made before being accepted by the Committee, must be made thereafter before the applicant starts his theological studies.

14. Application shall normally be made to the Presbytery within the bounds of which is situated the congregation of which the applicant is a communicant member.

15. In the case of an applicant resident within the bounds of one Presbytery and a communicant member of a congregation within the bounds of another Presbytery, the Committee shall inform both Presbyteries pending nomination.

16. In the case of a person who has no permanent residence in Scotland application for nomination shall be considered by the Presbytery within whose bounds is situated the University at which the applicant proposes to study, or by the Presbytery within whose bounds he fixes his residence.

17. Applicants taking the Regular Course shall seek nomination before starting theological study. Applicants taking the Alternative Course or the course for Mature Students shall seek nomination before starting their prescribed course.

18. Before considering an application for nomination the Presbytery shall satisfy itself that the applicant is a communicant member of the Church of Scotland and has been accepted as a prospective candidate by the Committee.

19. In considering an application the Presbytery shall satisfy itself as to the applicant's character, conduct, and beliefs.

20. If satisfied the Presbytery shall then nominate the applicant as a Candidate for the Ministry and shall give notice of such nomination to the Committee not later than 17th September of the year in which the applicant wishes to commence his theological studies.

Entrance Qualifications.

21. Ordinary candidates must possess such passes in the Higher and Ordinary grade examinations of the Scottish Certificate of Education or their equivalent as will qualify them for admission to the University.

22. Candidates whose qualifications are such as will enable them to gain entry to a University Faculty other than Divinity shall be encouraged to take the Regular Course.

23. Mature candidates shall be required before commencing the course to have passes in (*a*) two subjects on the Higher grade, one being English, and (*b*) one further subject on the Ordinary grade in the Scottish Certificate of Education examinations or other examinations deemed equivalent by the Scottish Universities Council on Entrance.

24. Mature candidates must, before starting the course of theological study, have completed the requirements for admission to a Faculty of Divinity in a Scottish University.

25. Mature candidates who possess at the outset the necessary qualifications for admission to a Scottish University shall be encouraged to take either the combined M.A./B.D. as in para. 38, or the Alternative Course as in para. 41.

26. Every applicant under 40 must be in a position during the current session to furnish himself with the necessary entrance qualifications before his application will be considered by the Committee.

27. Older candidates (applicants over 40) must be men of good educational qualifications or of recognised professional or vocational experience deemed satisfactory by the Committee.

General Requirements.

28. After due nomination by his Presbytery a candidate shall be eligible to begin his theological course without further examination by the Church.

29. Before completing his course the candidate shall satisfy the Committee as to his knowledge of the English Bible by passing such examinations as may be prescribed by the Committee.

30. In three of the years of theological study the candidate shall engage in such practical work as the Committee may prescribe.

Courses of Study.

Eligibility for Courses.

31. Training for the Ministry of the Church of Scotland shall normally require not less than six years of full-time study.

32. The candidate's intended course shall be considered and approved by the Committee.

33. Ordinary candidates are eligible for the Regular Course (paras. 37-38) or the Alternative Course (paras. 39-41) of full-time study lasting not less than six years.

34. Mature Candidates are eligible for the Regular Course (paras. 37-38) or the Alternative Course (paras. 39-41) of full-time study lasting not less than five years; or for the course for Mature Students (para. 42).

35. Older Candidates have courses of full-time study prescribed for them individually.

36. If after starting one course of study a candidate wishes to change to another he may do so only if the Committee after consultation with the Faculty of Divinity concerned approve such a change.

The Regular Course.

37. The Regular Course (paras. 33 and 34) shall consist of :—

(*a*) A first degree in Arts, Medicine, Science, Music or Law, or such other degree as may be approved as qualifying the candidate to study for the B.D. as a second degree at one of the Faculties of Divinity of the Universities of St Andrews, Glasgow, Aberdeen and Edinburgh or such equivalent professional qualifications as may be approved by the Committee; and

(*b*) A course of not less than three years' study leading to the attainment of the B.D. degree or the attainment of the L.Th. qualification at the Faculty of Divinity at one of the said Universities.

38. A candidate who completes a combined degree in Arts and Divinity in five years shall be required to take one year's further study as shall be prescribed by the Committee. A candidate who commences his Arts course after he attains the age of twenty-three shall be exempted from this requirement.

The Alternative Course.

39. The Alternative Course (paras. 33 and 34) shall consist of four years' study leading to the attainment of the B.D. as a first degree at one of the said Universities followed by the satisfactory completion of two years' further study as shall be approved by the Committee.

40. The nature of the two years' further study to be undertaken by the candidate on the attainment of the B.D. as a first degree shall be determined by the Committee before the end of the candidate's third year of study for the said degree, after consultation with the candidate.

41. In the case of a candidate commencing the First B.D. course after having reached the age of twenty-three years only one year's further study shall be required on the attainment of the said degree. The nature of this study shall be determined as in 40 above.

Course for "Mature Students"

42. The Course for Mature Students (paras. 6 and 34) shall offer the following options to candidates qualified as in Regulation 23 or Regulation 24 in addition to the provision in Regulations 38 and 41 :—

(*a*) Two years' study in a Pre-Divinity Course approved by the Committee and a course of three years' study leading to the attainment of the L.Th. qualification at the Faculty of Divinity at one of the said Universities ;
or

(*b*) One year's study in a Pre-Divinity Course approved by the Committee and a course of four years' study leading to the attainment of the B.D. as a First degree in one of the said Universities.

Special Courses.

43. The Committee shall consider the courses taken by a candidate for the Ministry who has pursued theological study at a University or College furth of Scotland and shall determine what further study shall be required of him. Such further study shall be for at least one academic year and shall normally be taken in the faculty of Divinity of one of the Scottish Universities.

44. Special courses of appropriate length and type shall be prescribed by the Committee for Older Candidates as defined in regulations 7 and 27.

45. The Committee may, at its discretion and in exceptional cases only, prescribe special courses for candidates under the age of forty years.

Content of Course.

46. A candidate studying for the B.D. degree or L.Th. qualification of one of the said Universities shall require to have his choice of classes and subjects of examination approved by the Committee through its appropriate academic sub-committee.

47. Such a course shall always include :—

The interpretation and use of Holy Scripture—both Old and New Testament.

The development and growth of the Church including special reference to the Church in Scotland.

The principal doctrines of the Christian Faith—their interpretation, their defence and their application.

The Principles of Christian Ethics.

The practice of the Ministry, attention being given to Public Worship, the Sacraments and preaching, the pastoral ministry, Christian education, spiritual discipline, Church law and procedure, and speech training.

48. Special courses in terms of regulations 43 and 44 are arranged by the Committee after consultation with the candidate so as to include as many of these studies as possible.

Supervision during Course.

49. A candidate shall remain under the supervision of the Presbytery which nominated him except as provided in 50-52 below.

50. If a candidate fix his permanent residence within the bounds of another Presbytery he shall within two months apply to the Presbytery within whose bounds he formerly resided for a certificate of transference, which on being granted he shall immediately present to the Presbytery within whose bounds his permanent residence is situated. This regulation shall not apply to married candidates who move house to a University centre for purposes of study, who shall be considered under 52.

51. If the candidate fails to make application within the appointed time, the Presbytery Clerk may then send the Certificate of Transference to the Clerk of the Presbytery to which he has removed and intimate accordingly to the candidate.

52. A candidate may, in exceptional circumstances, make application to be transferred to the supervision of the Presbytery within whose bounds is situated the University at which

he is studying or proposes to study. If his application be granted the same procedure shall be followed as in 51.

53. The supervising Presbytery shall confer regularly with each candidate on the progress of his studies and shall satisfy itself of his fitness as a candidate for the Ministry. The Presbytery shall report whether or not it is satisfied to the Committee each year not later than 17th September. If the Presbytery is not satisfied it shall have power to suspend or terminate his candidature.

54. The Committee shall consider annually the progress of each candidate and decide whether or not to sustain his year's study.

55. If the Committee is not satisfied with the progress of a candidate it may refuse to sustain that year's study, or may decide to bring the matter to the attention of his Presbytery and invite it to review his candidature.

56. The progress of each Pre-Divinity student shall be reported to the Committee annually by the governing body of the College concerned and his year, if thought fit, sustained by the Committee.

57. In all matters affecting the candidature of a duly nominated candidate for the Ministry the decision of the supervising Presbytery shall be final, with the reservation that any candidate shall have the right to petition the General Assembly to review his case.

Sustaining of Course.

58. Before sustaining a candidate's course the Committee shall satisfy itself that the requirements of paragraphs 28-30 have been fulfilled.

59. The Committee shall also be satisfied that the academic requirements of the prescribed course have been fulfilled.

60. A candidate who fails to attain the qualifications sought at the end of his prescribed course shall not have his course sustained or proceed to licence until he has successfully completed his nominated course. However, permission to proceed to licence may be given after full consultation by the Committee with the Faculty and candidate concerned, when this is considered to be in the best interests of the Church.

61. The Committee shall obtain from the Colleges, lists of those who have satisfactorily completed their prescribed course, and thereafter issue Certificates in their favour to their Presbyteries and advise them accordingly.

Licence.

Application for Licence.

62. Candidates entering on the last year of their courses in preparation for the Ministry shall intimate to the Committee not later than 31st October the Presbytery to which they intend to apply for Licence. The Committee shall draw up a list of such candidates and their Presbyteries and shall send a copy of the same, not later than 15th December in each year to the clerk of each Presbytery in the Church intimating that if no objections are received before 15th March from any other Presbytery by the Presbytery to which a candidate applies for licence, the said Presbytery may proceed to take such candidate on Trials for Licence.

63. Each candidate shall, not later than 30th November in the year preceding that in which he wishes to be licensed, make application to the Clerk of his own Presbytery to be taken on Trials for Licence.

64. If the name of any candidate has not been given in by him for insertion in the list referred to in para. 62, the Presbytery itself may call for an explanation and if satisfied may send his name to the other Presbyteries of the Church, with intimation that if no objections are received within three calendar months it will proceed to take him on Trials for Licence, the expense of such notice and intimation to be borne by the candidate himself.

65. Subject to para. 69, the Presbytery to whom application for Licence has been made may take a candidate on Trials for Licence at any time after 1st January in the last year of the candidate's course in preparation for the Ministry.

Trials for Licence.

66. The object of Trials for Licence shall be to enable the Presbytery to ensure that an applicant for Licence is acquainted with the present legal and sacramental practice and past tradition of the Church of Scotland, and that he is a fit person to proceed to the Ministry.

67. Trials for Licence shall consist of :—

Firstly, an oral examination in which each applicant is individually tested in his knowledge of the principles and practice of the Church of Scotland. A list of questions for the guidance of examiners shall be provided by the Committee.

Secondly, the conduct of Public Worship at the principal service on a Sunday in the presence and to the satisfaction of a Minister and Elder appointed by the Presbytery.

68. Thereafter, the examiners and those members of Presbytery who have supervised the candidate during his course shall confer and after consideration of all relevant facts shall decide whether or not to recommend to Presbytery that his Trials be sustained.

69. The Presbytery may not proceed to license an applicant until[1] :—

(*a*) it has received from the Committee a Certificate to the effect that the applicant has fulfilled the requirements detailed in 58-61 ; and

(*b*) it has sustained the applicant's Trials.

(Trials for Licence may be sustained before receipt of Exit Certificate.—*Ed.*)

Probationary Period.

70. Licentiates before becoming eligible for election or appointment to a home charge shall normally be required to spend a Probationary Period under the supervision of the Committee.

71. The Committee shall have power in special cases to grant exemption from this requirement.

72. If a Probationer's period of service as a Probationer starts between 1st April and 1st September the probationary period shall last from that date to 30th April of the year following, but if a Probationer's period of service as a probationer starts at any other time the Probationary Period shall last for at least ten months from that date, subject to the provisions in 78-81 below.

73. For his Probationary Period a Probationer shall be directed by the Committee to full-time employment in which he will be suitably trained for his future ministry.

74. The Committee shall be responsible for ensuring that the Probationer receives adequate supervision during his Pro-

[1] According to Section 3 of Act VIII., 1936, the Act of Licensing shall take place in public, and preferably in Church, not less than seven days after the Trials have been sustained.

bationary Period and that his terms of service and conditions of employment are satisfactory.

75. If in the opinion of the Committee the situation to which a Probationer has been directed proves unsatisfactory for the purpose of training, the Committee shall have power, after consultation with the Minister with whom the Probationer is working and the Presbytery and Kirk Session concerned to make alternative arrangements for the training and placement of the Probationer during the remainder of his Probationary Period.

76. The Committee shall have power to prescribe and provide supplementary training for Probationers.

77. In March of each year the Committee shall consider reports from each Probationer and the Minister with whom he is working and shall in each case determine whether or not the Probationary Period shall be sustained.

78. In the event of the Probationary Period being sustained the Committee shall send a certificate to this effect to the Committee on Probationers and Transference of Ministers. The Probationers concerned shall then be eligible for election or appointment to a home charge but shall not be inducted until after the conclusion of the Probationary Period on 30th April.

79. In the event of the Probationary Period not being sustained the Committee may prescribe a further period of training for the Probationer on the same conditions as in 67-68 above. On the completion of such further period of training the Committee shall consider whether or not to sustain the period as in 77-78 above.

80. On the issue of a certificate sustaining the Probationary Period the Committee shall cease to be responsible for the supervision or training of the Probationer concerned.

Repeal of Inconsistent Laws

81. The following Acts of previous General Assemblies are hereby repealed: VIII. 1945; VIII. 1936, Sections 1-2; X. 1935, Sections 1-8; VI. 1918.

The following Regulations of previous General Assemblies are hereby repealed; 11, 12, 1968; 8, 1967; 2, 3, 1965; 7, 8, 1963; 9, 1962; 5, 1953; 9, 11, 1949.

Section (B) of "Training for the Ministry" in the Plan of Union 1929 is hereby repealed.

The Regulations anent further use of Probationary Year approved by the General Assembly of 1964 (Reports p. 528) are hereby repealed.

All other Acts, Regulations and Deliverances of previous General Assemblies inconsistent with these provisions are hereby repealed.

Relevant hereto are the Regulations (1974, 5) *anent Payment and Expenses of Probationers :—*

1. *During the service of the Probationary Period a Probationer shall be paid at the rate of* 75 *per cent of the monetary payment of the Minimum Stipend as operative* 1st *January of the year in which he commences his Probationary Period.*
2. *The Probationer shall be entitled to claim out-of-pocket expenses incurred in travelling and in the duties of his office up to a limit of* £130 *per annum or* £200 *per annum where the Probationer provides his own car. All such expenses must be vouched for to the satisfaction of the Treasurer of the congregation. The rate per mile applicable to Ministers shall apply.*
3. *In addition to salary every Probationer shall be given occupation of a house or flat free of rates and rent, or a sum of* £300 *per annum in lieu thereof. The Probationer shall meet out of his own pocket the cost of the heating and lighting of any house he occupies.*
4. *A Probationer who has to move house because of his appointment shall be entitled to receive the amount expended in the removal of his household effects.*
5. *These payments and expenses shall be paid by the congregation of the parish where the Probationer serves as Assistant Minister. Congregations which feel unable to meet these payments in full may apply to the Home Board which shall in appropriate cases negotiate suitable arrangements with the Kirk Session concerned, in accordance with the resources available.*
6. *Where a Probationer remains beyond a twelve month period and the Probationary Period has been sustained he shall be paid regardless of ordination at the rate of* 80 *per cent of the Minimum Stipend as operative* 1st *January of that year.*
7. *The Committee on Education for the Ministry shall have powers in consultation with the Home Board to adjust rates of expenses in the light of prevailing conditions.*

Section II. Licentiates or Probationers.

1935, x., 9-16.

Nomenclature.

In the correct usage of the Church to-day there is no difference between a *licentiate* and a *probationer* with regard to status. Another synonym, employed in former times but not so common to-day, is *preacher of the gospel.* A still older word is *expectant.* Each term signifies one who, having completed his course as a student, has received authority to preach the Word, but has not yet been by ordination given authority to administer the Sacraments. Any distinction that exists is not in status but in outlook. A probationer desires, and intends if possible to obtain, promotion to a pastoral charge or other office, while a licentiate may be content with the seal set upon the completion of his studies and with the authority to conduct public worship, and may make no effort to enter on the other functions of the ministry. In earlier times not a few schoolmasters became licentiates of the Church without leaving the teaching profession; and even yet there are instances of men who in the ordinary way have received licence to preach, but who do not regard themselves as under probation for full ministerial status. For all practical purposes, however, the designations are identical.

While the Church has been chary of encouraging *ministerium vagum* (see p. 155), and therefore reluctant to grant ordination to those who are not about to enter on a settled charge, the General Assembly in 1896 called " the attention of Presbyteries to the discretionary powers which may be exercised in granting under suitable conditions ordination to probationers who are of sufficient experience, and are engaged in regular service." The person so ordained by laying on of hands is styled *ordained assistant,* being usually employed to aid the minister of a large or populous parish, or as *locum tenens* in special circumstances; but there may be other cases in which he is discharging such duties as to make it expedient that he should be ordained. In that event the term to be employed is *minister without charge.* It is important, in view of loose phraseology too often heard, to notice that no one is " ordained to a charge," pastoral or otherwise. He is ordained to the office of the ministry, and not to any particular sphere of exercise of that ministry. By the same token the term " ordained probationer " is clearly a contradiction in terms.

Relation of Licentiates to Presbytery.

Clerks of Presbyteries are required to send immediate intimation to the Secretaries of the Committee on Education for the Ministry and Probationers and Transference of Ministers Committee (see p. 228) of the names and addresses of those whom they have licensed. A student on receiving licence is entitled to receive from the Clerk of Presbytery an Extract of Licence (for Forms, see p. 789). During the Probationary Period Presbyteries exercise a conjoint supervision over licentiates within their bounds until such time as the Committee on Education for the Ministry issue a certificate sustaining the Probationary Period. Thereafter the Presbytery alone exercises supervision over licentiates within its bounds, keeping a careful note of the name, address, and employment of each, and is expected to show a friendly interest in them. It is the duty of the Probationer himself to see that his name has been reported as above for inclusion in the Register of Probationers kept by the Committee. The names of those qualified to conduct religious services in Gaelic are to be specially noted. A Licentiate whose Probationary Period has been sustained is solely under the jurisdiction of the Presbytery which licensed him, or of the Presbytery to which he has later been formally transferred. On leaving the bounds of a Presbytery, a licentiate should apply for a certificate of character from the Clerk of that Presbytery, and submit it as soon as possible, and in every case within two months, to the Clerk of the Presbytery within whose bounds he has come to reside, exhibiting also his Extract of Licence. When any Probationer appointed to a vacant parish or other charge has made application for a Presbyterial certificate, and when no meeting of Presbytery, ordinary or special, has been appointed to be held within seven days of receipt thereof, a certificate signed by the Moderator and Clerk, and two other members (or in absence of either Moderator or Clerk, by three other members), is reckoned sufficient, and the issue of the certificate is to be reported to the next ordinary meeting of Presbytery (1895, viii.).

The appointment of any Licentiate to be assistant is to be notified by the Minister of the charge, or in his name, to the next ordinary meeting of Presbytery (1883, 13). Any Minister or Kirk Session intending to employ as assistant or as *locum tenens* for more than four Sundays in any charge, a Licentiate or Minister of any other Church than the Church of Scotland, shall require such Licentiate or Minister to report himself to the Clerk of Presbytery within whose bounds the parish is situated, and to submit for his inspection a certificate of licence or of ordination as the case may be, or to give such other evidence of qualification as may be satisfactory to the Presbytery (1932, 9). (For the use of such persons in pulpit supply, see p. 229.)

For Licentiates from abroad or of other Churches, seeking to enter the Church of Scotland, see pp. 234-241.

Discipline with regard to Probationers is to be exercised in the same way as with regard to Ministers; but not more than five years must have elapsed between the date of the alleged offence and the date on which information regarding it is laid before the Presbytery, if the scandal have reference to a time before he was licensed (1707, xi., and 1894, xiii.).

Committee on Probationers.

A Committee of General Assembly, named the Committee on Probationers and Transference of Ministers, exists for, *inter alia*, attention to the welfare of Probationers generally, and in particular for distribution of supply of pulpits among those who are available, especially with a view to their settlement in vacant charges. Ordained Assistants, retired Ministers, and Ministers without charge, if they so wish, are to be included in the list for supply.

Probationers during their Probationary Period and Students for Divinity are for the purposes of their practical training entirely under the direction of the Committee on Education for the Ministry and may not engage in the supply of vacant pulpits without the consent of both the Committee on Education for the Ministry and the Committee on Probationers and Transference of Ministers.

Any Minister, Interim Moderator, or Session Clerk employing a person not qualified as a Minister, Probationer, Reader, or regular Student of Theology, or Lay Missionary recognised as an agent of the Home Mission Committee (1934, ix.), or Deaconess licensed to preach and approved candidates for licence, who are regular Students for the Diaconate (1960, 8), for the conduct of public worship, shall intimate this in writing to the Clerk of Presbytery within fourteen days thereafter, giving the name, address, and occupation of the person employed, and stating whether, before engaging him, he had applied to one of the authorised agents for supply for a qualified substitute;

and that the Clerk of Presbytery shall report all such cases at the next ordinary meeting of Presbytery. A Student of Theology shall have liberty to conduct ordinary services of public worship, but (1) the Committee on Education for the Ministry may, if it see cause, restrict or prohibit a Student from preaching, if it be reported to the Committee by the Faculty of Theology of the university in which the Student is studying or by his Presbytery, that such preaching is prejudicial to his proper studies, or is interfering with his regular attendance, or (2) if the Presbytery be not satisfied with his character and conduct as an aspirant to the Ministry (1935, x.).

If any serious misconduct on the part of a Probationer or other person employed under the scheme of pulpit supply, whether such supply be occasional or otherwise, be reported to the Convener, the Committee on Probationers and Transference of Ministers must hold a meeting within fourteen days; and, if sufficient cause be shown, it must transmit the information to the Clerk of the Presbytery of jurisdiction. Meanwhile it is in the Committee's power to instruct the supply agents to refuse employment till the Presbytery has dealt with the case (1918, vi.).

The Committee is in charge of a Fund for the benefit of Aged and Infirm Probationers, for particulars of which application should be made to the Secretary.

Scheme of Occasional Supply.

(Reports, 1930, pp. 1879-80; also 1933, p. 848.)

The Committee on Probationers and Transference of Ministers has charge of the arrangements for supply. It may be convenient to state first those for supply which is merely occasional, and thereafter to deal with the scheme for employment in vacant parishes with a view to settlement therein.

Supply agents are instructed to keep a list of those who are employed by them, indicating whether they are Ministers, Licentiates, Students, Licensed Deaconesses, or Readers of the Church of Scotland. The Committee on Probationers and Transference of Ministers is instructed to inspect these lists and report thereon to the General Assembly (1960, Reg. 8).

The keepers of lists are instructed that in providing pulpit supply preference be given to (i) probationers, (ii) ministers without charge, (iii) students who have completed two full sessions of their Theological course, and that no unauthorised person is to be sent. The scale of fees (1974, Reg. 4) is as follows :—

1. Where the stipend for the last full year did not exceed the minimum plus £200, the fee shall be £8.
2. Where the stipend for the last full year exceeded the minimum plus £200, the fee shall be £10.
3. A neighbouring Minister who supplies a vacant pulpit without providing supply for his own pulpit may receive an honorarium of £2·10 each Sunday, plus a refund of travelling expenses, but no fee.
4. Weekend board and lodging may be claimed at a maximum rate of £8 for the weekend (receipts should be exhibited). Travelling expenses (bus fare ; railway, 2nd class ; and steamer, cabin fare) shall be paid. Where there is no public conveyance the cost of hiring shall be paid, or a use of a private car shall be paid for at the rate of 3p per mile.

As these rates and expenses apply only in the case of pulpit supply in a vacancy, and in order to give some guidance to Ministers and office-bearers when considering the payment of pulpit supply fees during holiday periods and sickness, the General Assembly declare the above scale of fees to be the minimum applicable in the payment of holiday or sickness supply.

The fee payable to a Reader is the normal supply fee (1962, 8).

The fees are payable to the preacher supplying the pulpit, and should be handed to him before he leaves the place.

An office fee of 13p per Sunday is payable in advance when application is made to the supply agents in Edinburgh, Glasgow, Dundee, or Aberdeen (1950, Reg. 3). An additional office fee of 25p per Sunday is payable by ministers obtaining engagements through the said pulpit supply agent. (1958, Reg. 8.)

Regulations anent Probationers and Scheme for Transference of Ministers (1948, x.).

The General Assembly have instructed Interim Moderators and Presbytery clerks as follows :—

It shall be part of the duty of Presbytery clerks to intimate to the secretary of the Committee on Probationers and Transference of Ministers the names of Interim Moderators in vacancies immediately these are appointed ; and, whenever this information is received, instructions regarding the Transference of Ministers Scheme shall be sent to the Interim Moderators.

The General Assembly instruct Interim Moderators, at the first meeting of a Vacancy Committee, to make full intimation of the regulations of the Probationers and Transference of Ministers Committee and to point out the necessity of complying with these regulations.

Regulations anent Probationers
(1948, x. ; 1953, 6 ; 1967, 5 ; 1968, 10).

1. The Committee shall keep a Roll of Licentiates. All licentiates shall be placed on the roll on being licensed and the dates of their licence shall be recorded. The Committee shall also keep a Roll of Probationers who are eligible for appointments. This roll shall include Probationers who have received ordination but have not been admitted to a charge.

2. After each meeting of Presbytery at which students are licensed the clerk of the Presbytery shall immediately intimate the names and addresses of the Licentiates to the secretary of the Committee. If any licentiate is Gaelic-speaking, this should be indicated.

3. The employment of each licentiate during the first year of probation as approved by the Committee on Education for the Ministry shall be reported to the Committee by the secretary of the Committee on Education for the Ministry.

4. At the end of Probationary Period each Probationer shall report himself to the Committee, and shall appear, if required, for interview, consultation, and advice. A Probationer who does not report himself to the Committee for three successive years shall be removed from the Roll. A Probationer so removed shall only be restored to the Roll of Probationers by application to the Committee on Admission of Ministers of Other Churches for a Certificate of Eligibility or by Petition to the General Assembly.

5. Each Probationer when eligible for a charge shall receive appointments from the Committee to preach in vacancies. The Committee shall aim at securing equitable opportunities for all those on the list. Probationers may intimate that for a period in which they are otherwise employed they do not wish to receive such appointments.

6. Probationers who wish to receive appointments must

advise the secretary of the Committee of the addresses at which letters or telegrams will immediately reach them, and must acknowledge communications regarding appointments *by return of post.*

7. A record of all appointments to preach in vacancies shall be kept by the secretary of the Committee.

8. At the end of each year after licence, and until he is inducted to a charge, every Probationer shall complete and return to the Secretary the appropriate schedule of information. (1968, 10.)

9. Ministers, including Missionaries or Chaplains, ordained for special service at home or overseas who have completed such service satisfactorily shall be entitled to the privileges of Probationers as defined in these regulations, always provided that they satisfy the requirements of the Committee on Admission of Ministers.

10. Vacancy Committees desiring to consider Probationers must before doing so apply to the Probationers' Committee for a List of Probationers.

Should a congregation desire to consider Probationers not on the list submitted, their names shall be sent to the secretary of the Committee and the Committee shall, so far as is consistent with the equitable distribution of vacancies among those eligible and the interests of congregations, give effect to such a request (1953, 6).

11. Thereafter a Vacancy Committee which chooses a Probationer as a sole nominee, or as one of a leet, must apply to this Committee for his appointment to preach in the vacant charge. No one on the Probationers' Roll shall be eligible for a call to a vacant charge unless this permission has been received.

In order that due intimation may be given to congregations a Vacancy Committee shall make such request at least fourteen days before the date suggested for the candidate to preach (1953, 6).

Transference of Ministers (1948, x.; 1970, 4).

1. The Committee shall keep a List of Ministers who, having been in their present charges for not less than five years, have intimated their willingness to consider another sphere. In special cases, including those in which the desirability of a local union seems apparent, and where the Presbytery so recommends, it shall be in the power of the Committee to add to this list, at their own request, the names of Ministers who have not

completed five years in their present charge, always subject to Act VI. of 1945 (now 1959, xxiv.).

2. Names shall be retained on the list for five years. Ministers who wish to have their names retained thereafter must renew their applications.

3. In vacancies where it is proposed to hear a leet of Ministers in charges preaching in the vacant church the Committee shall make appointments from the list not more in number than those made by the congregation. The Committee reserves the right to modify this rule in cases where some or all of those nominated by the congregation are on the Transference List held by the Committee. If possible, those Ministers appointed by the Committee and those appointed by the congregation shall be heard on alternate Sundays. In the case of such appointments the Committee requires at least fourteen days' notice for the submission of names.

4. The Committee shall aim at securing equitable opportunities for all those on the list. Congregations proposing to hear ministers through deputations during a vacancy are recommended to apply to the Committee for names of ministers for consideration when a selection is being made (1970, 4).

5. The Committee, if it judges this course desirable, shall have power to forward to vacancy committees the names of Ministers on the list for their consideration (1970, 4).

Ministers Without Charge (1948, x.).

The Committee shall keep, apart from the Roll of Probationers, a List of Ministers without Charge, who fulfil the conditions of Acts of Assembly, 1933, xv., and 1935, x., and desire to preach in vacant charges with a view to election, and shall forward the said list on request to Interim Moderators in vacancies. The Committee may appoint Ministers from this list to preach as candidates in vacancies, as opportunity may arise, as well as from the List of Ministers under the Transference Scheme.

CHAPTER XI.

THE MINISTRY.

Admission of Ministers and Licentiates of Other Churches.

The following Regulations were adopted by the General Assembly (1965, Reg. 6) :—

All Acts, Deliverances, Schemes and Regulations of the General Assembly (including the Standing Orders thereof) shall be so construed that references therein to Ministers of the Word and Sacraments shall include women (Act XXV. (2), 1968).

1. Applicants for Admission to the Ministry of the Church of Scotland, including those who apply for removal of restrictions on status or for restoration of status of which they have been deprived, or which they have voluntarily resigned, shall approach the General Assembly by Petition submitted through the Committee on Admission of Ministers of Other Churches, whose duty shall be to examine each Petition, to have an interview with the Petitioner, to make such investigation and inquiry as may seem expedient in each case, and to transmit the Petition to the General Assembly, with a recommendation as to the judgment which in the opinion of the Committee ought to be pronounced, and whether the crave ought to be granted, partially granted, deferred, or refused. The Committee shall be empowered to make such Regulations for its procedure, and to require such Fees from Petitioners as it may deem fit, and to issue a statement of these Regulations and Fees in a separate pamphlet for the guidance of applicants and for orderly procedure in its own work.

2. The Petition in each case shall be as far as possible framed after a style to be set forth in the pamphlet issued by the Committee.[1] The Petition shall give full particulars as to the Petitioner's age, present Church connection, educational curriculum and ministerial career, with an explicit statement

[1] Forms A. and B.

of the reasons for which the Petitioner proposes to seek admission to this Church and what form of service he proposes to undertake in it. The Petition shall be accompanied by all documents required to substantiate the facts set forth. These documents shall be originals, or, if the originals be not available, copies or extracts from official records certified by the persons qualified to grant them. The Petition shall be lodged with the Secretary of the Committee not later than the first day of January preceding the meeting of General Assembly to which it is addressed.

3. Immediately after 1st January in each year, the Convener shall prepare a synopsis of each Petition received by that date, and shall cause it to be issued to the members of Committee at least a week previous to a Statutory Meeting to be held before 31st January, when the Petitioner shall appear for interview (unless in any particular case of an exceptional nature the Convener recommends the Committee to dispense with this requirement entirely, or to defer it till a subsequent meeting), and answer such questions as may be put to him bearing on the matters set forth in his Petition, or as may be relevant to the subject of his application. The Committee shall then deliberate as to the recommendation to be made to the General Assembly, but at this stage its resolution shall be provisional, and shall be confirmed, reversed, or varied at a later meeting. As soon as possible the resolution shall be communicated to the Petitioner, who shall be required to reply in writing whether he desires to adhere to his Petition as already presented, or to withdraw it, or to vary its crave in consequence of the said resolution. In exceptional cases, and for reasons to be stated in its report, the Committee may resolve to make no recommendation, but to refer the case *simpliciter* to the General Assembly, but otherwise the Committee shall not be required to assign to the Petitioner any reasons for its finding.

4. In order that the Courts of the Church may have their rightful place in the reception of those who are to become Ministers of the Church, and also in order that the Committee may have further opportunity of investigating the facts as set forth in the Petition, and be more fully persuaded of the desirability or otherwise of the admission of the Petitioner (*a*) intimation of the Petition shall be sent to all Presbyteries for information and comment ; and (*b*) the Petition itself shall be forwarded to the Presbytery of his residence ; but if he has not resided mainly within the bounds of any Presbytery in

Scotland for three months prior to 1st January, it shall be forwarded to the Presbytery of Edinburgh. It shall be accompanied by a copy of the synopsis already mentioned, and of the recommendation which the Committee has provisionally agreed to make. The Presbytery may, if it so desires, call on the Committee to forward also for inspection and return the documents on which the synopsis is based. The Petitioner shall be instructed to report himself to the Clerk of Presbytery, and to hold himself in readiness to appear before the Presbytery, if that Court should desire an interview. The Presbytery shall deal with the matter as soon as possible, and, after making such investigations and inquiries as it deems fit, shall communicate to the Secretary of the Committee its opinion on the case not later than the 15th day of April, and shall also intimate the same to the Petitioner.

5. As soon as possible thereafter, the Committee shall again meet, and, having anew considered each case with the opinion of the Presbytery thereanent and any comments or representations by other Presbyteries, shall come to a final decision as to the recommendation to be made to the General Assembly, and shall in this recommendation state whether or not the admission of the Petitioner would appear to be for the benefit of this Church. The decision shall forthwith be intimated to the Petitioner, who may, if he so desires, alter the crave of his Petition or may withdraw it, in which case the documents he has lodged in connection therewith shall be returned to him without delay.

6. When the Committee's report is presented to the General Assembly, each case shall be considered separately. The recommendations both of the Committee and of the Presbytery shall be included in the report. The Petitioner shall appear at the bar in support of his Petition, unless for cause shown and approved by the Committee or in exceptional circumstances by the Assembly. He shall have the right to be heard only with regard to any inaccuracy in the synopsis of the facts set forth in his Petition, or in reply to any relevant questions which may be put to him by any member of the General Assembly with permission of the Moderator. In the case of a Petition submitted to the Assembly *simpliciter* or in which there is an adverse recommendation by the Committee, the Petitioner shall be permitted to address the General Assembly briefly in support of his Petition. A copy of the synopsis shall be supplied to him at least seven days before the meeting of General Assembly.

7. If the Assembly resolve to grant the crave of the Petition and to admit the Petitioner, they shall remit the case to the Presbytery concerned, or to such other Presbytery as the Assembly may deem more expedient, in order that the appropriate steps may be completed, and the said Presbytery shall enrol him according to the status which the Assembly have granted; but the Presbytery shall not take these steps until any period of probation or interim-admission which the Assembly may have prescribed has been completed, and until a report on such period has been presented to the Assembly through the General Assembly's Committee.

8. The General Assembly, whether or not on the recommendation of the Committee, instead of granting full admission to a Petitioner immediately, may grant probation or interim-admission for a year, or for such other period as may seem expedient, during which period he shall not be permitted to officiate in a vacant charge or to administer either of the Sacraments, though he may exercise the other functions of the Ministry, this restriction being without prejudice to the validity of his orders. Further, the General Assembly, whether or not on the recommendation of the Committee, may require the Petitioner to attend additional classes in Arts or Theology with due performance of the work thereof, during which period he shall take part in the work and worship of a congregation of the Church of Scotland and be under the supervision of the Presbytery. Reports shall be submitted to the Committee by the Senate of his College and the Presbytery and the Minister under whom he has served, and the Committee shall include in its report to the ensuing Assembly a statement with regard to the case in these particulars.

9. Until the Petition of any applicant is actually submitted to the General Assembly, it (as well as all the other documents referring thereto) shall be regarded as confidential, and all procedure either by Committee or by Presbytery or other Court shall be taken in private; but this shall not debar the Committee (or a Presbytery to which the case has been referred) from pursuing its proper inquiries and investigations.

10. If a Minister who applies for admission to the Church of Scotland has already been ordained to the full status and function of the Ministry by a regularly constituted Presbyterian Church or by any regularly constituted branch of the Methodist Church, and if the General Assembly resolve to admit him to the Ministry of the Church of Scotland, he shall be admitted as a Minister. In any other case the Standing Committee shall

refer the matter to the General Assembly with its recommendation.

11. If a Minister who desires admission is already a Minister in full standing and the Minister, whether Emeritus or Acting, of a congregation of any regularly constituted Presbyterian Church and ordained by that Church, or holding an office recognised to be equivalent in status to a congregational charge, and has so served for a period of not less than five years, it shall not be necessary for him to make application in the manner aforesaid;[1] but he shall not be eligible for nomination and appointment to any charge in this Church until he has satisfied the Committee or its Executive[2] that he has taken a full course in Arts and Theology equal to that required of Licentiates of this Church, and that his character is in accordance with his profession; but after receiving a certificate[3] from the Committee or its Executive (in accordance with any regulations or conditions which that Committee may frame), he shall be eligible for nomination and appointment to a charge in this Church, or for being received by a Presbytery as a Minister residing or officiating in its bounds without a charge; provided always that in the latter event he shall not be entitled on this ground alone to a seat in the Presbytery. If the age of the applicant exceeds 45 years he shall not be eligible for a Certificate of Eligibility unless in exceptional cases.

12. If a Licentiate or Minister either of the Church of Scotland or of the United Free Church of Scotland before their union, or of the united Church subsequent thereto, have neither demitted nor been judicially deprived of the status he possessed, but has undertaken employment which is not subject to the jurisdiction of the Church as so united, he shall, on ceasing to be so employed, be eligible for appointment to a charge or other office in this Church, according to his status; provided that prior to nomination for such charge or office he shall have satisfied the Committee or its Executive[4] as to his status, record, and character, and shall have received from it a certificate[5] to that effect.

13. If an ordained Minister or Missionary of the Church of Scotland has, with the approval of the Overseas Council, entered the Courts of an indigenous Church as a full member, and has become subject to their jurisdiction, he shall, upon

[1] Special provisions obtain in the case of ministers of the former Presbyterian Church of England, for which see Chap. XII., § I., 10 (3) and (4), pp. 251, 252.

[2] Form D. or E. [3] Form F. [4] Form G. [5] Form H.

ceasing to be a member thereof and to be subject to such jurisdiction, be granted by the Committee or its Executive a Certificate of Eligibility for appointment to a charge or other office in this Church following satisfactory certification by the Overseas Council as to his status, record, and character. This Regulation shall also apply to a Licentiate of the Church of Scotland who, with the approval of the Overseas Council, has been ordained by an indigenous Church overseas.

A Certificate granted under Regulations 11 and 13 shall be valid for a period of one year but may be renewed on application to the Committee.

14. A Minister who has held an appointment under the Overseas Council which necessitated his being a Minister of another Church while holding that appointment and has now retired and taken up permanent residence within Scotland or within the bounds of the Presbytery of England shall be a member of the Presbytery within whose bounds he resides, provided he has received a Certificate of Eligibility [1] from the Committee on Admission of Ministers of Other Churches (Act XXIV., 1961).

15. It shall not be competent for the Committee to recommend to the General Assembly the admission of any Petitioner whose age on the 1st day of January preceding the meeting of Assembly exceeds 45 years, unless he has held a charge or charges in any regularly constituted Presbyterian Church for at least ten years; but this shall not preclude the Committee in exceptional cases from transmitting his Petition *simpliciter* if otherwise satisfactory, nor shall it preclude the General Assembly in the exercise of their *nobile officium* from granting admission; but in the latter event the Petitioner shall come under the ordinary regulations of the Aged and Infirm Ministers' Fund as regards annuity or retiring allowance.

16. When the crave of a Petition for admission (or readmission) is granted, an Extract of the General Assembly's Deliverance thereanent shall, within six months, be presented to the Clerk of the Presbytery appointed to take the necessary steps to complete admission, after which time the Deliverance shall cease to have effect; and where a Certificate of Readmission and Eligibility for Office in accordance with Regulation 12 has been issued by the Committee or its Executive, it shall be presented within three months to the Clerk of the Presbytery within whose bounds the person concerned is to reside or to officiate, after which time it shall be no longer valid; and

[1] Form I or J.

further, in each case when such Extract or Certificate is presented, the Clerk of Presbytery receiving it shall intimate forthwith accordingly to the Secretary of the Committee on Admission of Ministers of Other Churches.

17. A Petitioner may, along with his Petition, submit to the Committee a separate application [1] to be permitted to be employed in the meantime in connection with the Church. If the Committee resolves to grant the application, it shall be endorsed accordingly, and unless recalled shall be valid until the General Assembly have disposed of the Petition; provided (1) that the permission shall not entitle the Petitioner to administer either of the Sacraments or to be placed on the Register of Probationers, or to officiate in a vacant charge (excluding a terminable appointment or a continued vacancy); (2) that so soon as employment has been obtained the Petitioner shall submit the application as endorsed to the Clerk of the Presbytery within whose bounds the work is to be performed, and shall be deemed to be under the care and jurisdiction of that Presbytery, or of any other Presbytery to which he may be transferred; (3) that it shall be competent for the Committee or its Executive to recall the permission, or for the Presbytery to suspend its operation, at any time; (4) that the Presbytery within whose bounds he is employed shall report to the Committee within three weeks of such a report being requested, as to the manner in which he has performed his duties. Without production of the application as endorsed, it shall not be competent for a Petitioner to undertake, or for a Kirk Session to give, employment other than occasional supply while his case is pending. The same rules *mutatis mutandis* shall be observed by a Committee of the Church which may employ the Petitioner, and in this case the report to the Committee shall be made by the Convener of such Committee.

18. The foregoing principles and rules, together with such other regulations as the General Assembly may frame, while referring principally to Ministers of Other Churches in full status, shall be regarded as applying also to Licentiates of Other Churches, so far as capable of such application. Students who have been trained by other Churches, and who have not already been granted the status of Licentiates, shall not come within the scope of the procedure herein enacted, but shall report themselves to the Committee on Education for the

[1] Form C.

Ministry, which shall deal with such cases under its own regulations.

The General Assembly of 1946 directed Presbyteries, in taking steps to admit Ministers and Licentiates of other Churches, to satisfy themselves as to the knowledge of those admitted regarding the practice and procedure of the Church as contained in 'Practice and Procedure in the Church of Scotland,' Chapters I. to X. (1946, 9).

Fees for Lodging Petitions and Applications.
(Exclusive of V.A.T.)

(The amount of Fees may be altered as the Committee from time to time may determine.)

1. Ordinary Petitions from Ministers or Licentiates of Other Churches for admission: (*a*) as Minister, £12; (*b*) as Licentiate, £9.
2. Petitions from Ministers of the Church of Scotland for removal of restriction on their sphere of usefulness, £5.
3. Petitions of ordained Missionaries of the Church of Scotland for full status, or lay Missionaries for ordination, £4.
4. Petitions from Ministers or Licentiates of the Church of Scotland, who have lost or demitted status, for restoration: (*a*) as Minister, £9; (*b*) as Licentiate, £6.
5. Applications from Ministers of any regularly constituted Presbyterian Church for Certificates of Eligibility under Reg. 11, £8.
6. Applications from former Ministers or Licentiates of the Church of Scotland for Certificates of Eligibility under Reg. 12, £4.
7. Petitions continued to a subsequent General Assembly, whether or not for a period of interim admission, £3.

In cases 1, 2, 4, part (not exceeding one-half) may be returned if the Committee should resolve not to recommend the Petition, provided that the Petitioner withdraw the Petition not later than 21st April.

In cases 5 and 6, part (not exceeding one-half) may be returned if a Certificate of Eligibility be not granted.

No fee shall be charged for applications under Reg. 13.

Copies of the various Forms referred to in the preceding pages may be obtained on application to the Secretary of the Committee on Admission of Ministers of Other Churches, 121 George Street, Edinburgh.

CHAPTER XII.

THE MINISTRY.

ACT III., 1972 anent Admission of a Minister *ad vitam aut culpam*[1] states—

1. As from the date of the passing of this Act a minister of the Church of Scotland admitted or inducted to a charge shall not be admitted or inducted *ad vitam aut culpam* but except as hereinafter provided on attaining the age of 70 years, his ministry shall terminate as if he had resigned his charge and such date been appointed by the Presbytery of the bounds for the demission by the minister of his charge.

2. A minister over 70 years of age shall be eligible only for a terminable appointment and shall not be regularly admitted or inducted to any charge.

3. Nothing in this Act shall affect the existing rights of any minister who has been admitted to a charge *ad vitam aut culpam* pricr to this Act coming into force, nor be held to affect the existing law of the Church in matters of discipline.

ELECTION SETTLEMENT AND TRANSLATION OF MINISTERS (1932, ix.; 1945, vii.; 1948, ix.; 1958, xi.; 1959, xxiv.; 1960, xxiii.; 1961, xxii.; 1966, xxxi.; 1972, iii.; and 1974, ii., xxi.).

SECTION I. ELECTION AND APPOINTMENT OF MINISTERS.

THE Regulations for the election and settlement of ministers are contained in the Acts of General Assembly (1932, ix., Sections 1-21, as supplemented by the Acts abovementioned). They are as follows :—

Declaration of Vacancy and Appointment of Interim Moderator.

1. When a vacancy takes place in a charge, or an application by a minister for the appointment of a colleague and successor

[1] For the avoidance of doubt regarding the application in certain cases of the provisions of Act III., 1972, any minister who, having been admitted or inducted to a parish *ad vitam aut culpam,* becomes the minister of a new charge formed subsequently to May 1972 by a union or linking between the said parish and another parish or parishes shall be deemed to have an interest *ad vitam aut culpam* in the said new charge (Act XXI., 1974).

is agreed to, the Presbytery of the bounds shall, without delay, appoint one of the ministers, whether he sits in the Presbytery as a minister or elder, provided that he is not a member of the vacant congregation, to be interim moderator of the Kirk Session (1948, ix.), and to preside at all congregational meetings that may be held in connection with the vacancy, and shall instruct him to cause intimation of the vacancy to be made to the congregation on the first Sunday possible.

The date of the vacancy shall be:

(1) The day of the death of a minister; or
(2) The day of a minister's induction to another charge; or
(3) The day appointed by the Presbytery or a superior court for the demission by a minister of his charge, which day may be the day on which his resignation is accepted or a subsequent day fixed by the Presbytery or a superior court; or
(4) The day on which a minister is deposed or removed from his charge; or
(5) The day on which the application for a colleague and successor is agreed to.

The declaration of the vacancy shall be in terms of Schedule A., 1 (see Appendix, p. 813), and this declaration, as well as all other intimations prescribed in these Regulations, shall be attested by the person who makes them in terms of Schedule L. (see Appendix, p. 817). The interim moderator as the representative of the Presbytery shall make arrangements for the supply of the vacant pulpit in consultation with the Kirk Session and the Congregational Committee. (For payment of vacancy supply expenses, see p. 666.)

Notwithstanding the foregoing, it is lawful (1960, xxiii.) for the Presbytery to appoint the Interim Moderator before the date of the vacancy in the following cases:—

(1) Where a minister has been called to another charge; and
(2) Where a minister has intimated to the Presbytery his intention to demit office by resignation.

Where a minister has been called to another charge the Presbytery may appoint an Interim Moderator in the prospective vacancy as soon as the minister has accepted the appointment and call.

Where a minister has intimated to the Presbytery his intention to demit office by resignation the Presbytery may appoint an Interim Moderator in the prospective vacancy as soon as the resignation has been accepted.

Vacancy Committee.

In both of the foregoing cases the Presbytery for cause shown may grant leave to appoint a Vacancy Committee unless the question of readjustment is raised (1960, xxxiii.).

Assessors.

By a later Act of Assembly (1966, xxxi.) when an Interim Moderator has been appointed in a vacancy the Presbytery is required to appoint three Assessors (one of whom shall be an elder) who must be consulted by the Interim Moderator with regard to the filling of the vacancy, and with whom the Vacancy Committee may consult at any time ; such Assessors have no voting powers when attending meetings of the Vacancy Committee.

The Interim Moderator so appointed may call and preside at meetings of the Kirk Session and congregation only for the transaction of business relating to the prospective vacancy, and shall be associated with the minister until the date of the vacancy and shall subsequently take full charge.

After an Interim Moderator has been so appointed, it shall be lawful for all parties concerned to enter into conference with the Committee on Unions and Readjustments and the Maintenance of the Ministry Committee in terms of the provisions of Act IX. of 1932 as if the charge were actually vacant, but no final arrangements shall be entered into and no binding decisions shall be made with regard to the interests which are the concern of these Committees, until after the date of the vacancy.

Notwithstanding that the question of union or readjustment has been raised and procedure sisted in terms of Act, 1932, ix., it is the duty of the Interim Moderator to take all regular steps towards the attestation of an Electoral Register in terms of Sections 5, 6, and 7 of the said Act. Where the Interim Moderator is appointed before the date of the vacancy, the wording of Vacancy Schedules and Intimations shall be altered accordingly.

Death of Senior Minister —Proceedings *de novo*.

Note.—In the event of the death of a senior minister during the proceedings towards the election of a colleague or assistant and successor, and before an election has taken place, the procedure must be begun *de novo*, and the date of the occurrence of the vacancy is the date of the death of the minister, the election now being that of a minister.

Intimation of Vacancy to Standing Committees of the General Assembly.

2. The name of the Interim Moderator shall be sent by the Presbytery Clerk to the Secretary of the Probationers and Transference of Ministers Committee.

The Presbytery shall also communicate the occurrence of a vacancy to the Secretary of the Committee on Unions and Readjustments, together with its opinion as to whether the question of readjustment should be raised or not; and at the same time, in all cases of vacancies where in the opinion of the Presbytery a union or readjustment of agencies is worthy of consideration, it shall appoint a committee to confer with the representatives of that committee. When the question of union or readjustment is raised by the Presbytery it shall direct that procedure be sisted till this question is settled.

Approval of Financial Arrangements in the Vacancy.

3. When it has been agreed by the Unions and Readjustments Committee in consultation with the Presbytery that no question of union or readjustment does arise, a schedule shall be issued by the Maintenance of the Ministry Committee to be filled up by the office-bearers of the vacant congregation through which the Presbytery and the committee shall receive a statement of the proposed stipend arrangements and minimum contribution promised to the Maintenance of the Ministry Fund, and the Presbytery shall not sustain an appointment and call (see Regulation 20) till it and the committee are satisfied that these are in accordance with the resources of the congregation.

Time Limit for the Election of a Minister.

4. The time limit for the right of the congregation to elect a minister shall be calculated from the date when the Presbytery and the Unions and Readjustments Committee are agreed that the question of union or readjustment does not arise, and shall extend to six calendar months. If no appointment be made within that time, the Presbytery shall itself take steps towards the appointment of a minister; provided that, even after the date when the right of appointment has fallen to the Presbytery, it shall be competent for the Presbytery, according to the circumstances of the case, either to grant or to refuse the crave of a petition from the congregation for extension

of the period allowed or for a particular appointment to be made, and the decision of the Presbytery shall be final. *Unless in very exceptional circumstances, of which the Presbytery shall be the judge, the period of extension shall not exceed three months.* Any such petition as aforesaid shall clearly state the reason for which no appointment has been made within the prescribed period (1945, vii.).

The Kirk Session to make up the Electoral Register.

5. It shall be the duty of the Kirk Session, notwithstanding that the question of union or readjustment has been raised and procedure sisted (1960, xxiii.), to proceed to make up an electoral register of the congregation, which shall contain: (1) as communicants, all persons, not being under church discipline, whose names are upon the Communion Roll at the date of the occurrence of the vacancy after it has been corrected (if necessary) by the Kirk Session as at that date; as also those who are members in full communion with the Church of Scotland, and have given in certificates within the time intimated in terms of Schedule A., 2 (see Appendix, p. 813), provided such certificates are sustained; (2) as adherents, such other persons, being parishioners or seatholders at the date of the occurrence of the vacancy, and not under twenty-one years of age, and not members of any other congregation in Scotland at the time of the vacancy, as have claimed in writing within the time intimated as aforesaid, and in the form of Schedule B. (see Appendix, p. 813), to be placed on the electoral register, and in regard to whom the Kirk Session is satisfied that they desire to be permanently connected with the congregation, or are associated with it in its interests and work, and that no reason exists for refusing to admit them to the Sacrament of Holy Communion if they should apply. As regards adherents, the decision of the Kirk Session shall be final.

Hearing of Claims and preparing of Electoral Register.

6. At a meeting to be held not later than fourteen days after intimation has been made in terms of Schedule A., 2 (see previous paragraph), the Kirk Session shall decide on the claims of persons to be placed on the electoral register, such claims to be sent to the Session Clerk before the meeting. At

this meeting the Kirk Session shall hear parties having an interest if they desire; and shall forthwith prepare the list of the names and addresses of communicants and adherents which the Kirk Session proposes as the electoral register of the congregation, the names being arranged in alphabetical order.

Inspection and Final Adjustment of Electoral Register.

7. The list of persons proposed as the electoral register of the congregation having been prepared, the Interim Moderator shall cause intimation to be made from the pulpit at the first ordinary diet of public worship thereafter, in terms of Schedule C., 1 (see Appendix, p. 813), that on that day an opportunity will be given of inspecting the list in the session-house, or in the church after divine service, and that it will lie for inspection at such place or places and for such days and hours as the Kirk Session shall fix, due regard being had to the convenience of the congregation; and, further, that the Kirk Session will meet to hear parties having an interest, and will finally revise and adjust said list on a day to be appointed. At this meeting, or at any adjourned meeting to be held thereafter, the list, having been revised and adjusted, shall be attested by the Interim Moderator and clerk as the electoral register of the congregation, and this register or a certified copy thereof shall be forthwith transmitted for attestation to the clerk of Presbytery. The congregation for the purposes of these Regulations shall be the persons whose names are on the electoral register attested as aforesaid; and no person shall be entitled to vote under these Regulations whose name is not on said electoral register. On the electoral register aforesaid, or on the copy thereof to be transmitted for attestation to the clerk of Presbytery, the names shall be numbered, and marked with their numbers, consecutively in the order in which they stand on the electoral register. If, after the electoral register has been attested, any communicant receive a certificate of transference, which certificate during a vacancy shall only be granted on a written application, the Session clerk shall give intimation of such transference to the Interim Moderator who shall thereupon delete the name from the electoral register and initial the deletion.

Note 1.—It would be incompetent to add the name of a person whose certificate of transference had been deposited after the electoral register had been attested.

Note 2.—The electoral register should be attested by the Presbytery Clerk before a Congregational Committee is appointed.

Election of Congregational Committee.[1]

8. Unless special grounds exist for delay in filling up the vacancy, such as the question of readjustment being raised, the Presbytery may, on the date of agreement to a translation or demission, grant leave for the appointment of a Vacancy Committee, which in terms of Schedule C., 2, may be appointed and function in advance of the actual date of commencement of the vacancy. If this be not done, then having awaited the commencement of the vacancy, the Interim Moderator at the same time as the intimation in Schedule C., 1, is made from the pulpit, shall cause intimation to be made, in terms of Schedule C., 2 (see Appendix, p. 814), that a meeting of the congregation will be held (*a*) to appoint a committee of its own number for the purpose of nominating one or more persons to the congregation with a view to the election and appointment of a minister, and (*b*) to determine the method of election. A form of exhortation prepared by the General Assembly shall be read on one Sunday when this meeting is intimated, setting forth the duties and responsibilities in the election of a minister pertaining to all the parties concerned—namely, to the congregation, the Presbytery, and the person or persons put in nomination. (See Appendix, p. 819.) This meeting shall be intimated on two Sundays before it is held. The Interim Moderator shall preside at the meeting and the Session Clerk shall be clerk, but in his absence a clerk shall be appointed by the meeting. Only those whose names are on the electoral register shall be entitled to take part.

The procedure shall then be as follows:

(1) The first step necessary to be taken by the meeting being to fix a number which shall not be exceeded in electing a committee, this shall be determined according to the number of the congregation as shown by the electoral register; and the following is a scale which may ordinarily be adopted by congregations with advantage:—

Committee not to exceed	13 when the number on electoral register is under	500
	19 ,, ,, ,,	1000
	25 ,, ,, ,,	amounts to 1000, or more.

(2) The maximum number having been fixed by the meeting, the Interim Moderator shall next call for nominations. To

[1] The General Assembly have instructed each Presbytery to appoint a Committee available both for conference with Congregational Vacancy Committees and for consultation with the Assembly's Committee on Probationers and Transference of Ministers (1943, Reg. 3).

constitute a nomination, it is necessary that the name of a person be proposed and seconded. As it is of the utmost importance that sufficient opportunity should be given for hearing and judging of each name proposed, only one person shall be allowed to be nominated at a time. In the event of the name of anyone being proposed who is not present at the meeting, his proposer shall be able to state that, if elected, he will accept office, and act on the committee. The Interim Moderator shall have the names of the persons nominated taken down in writing in the order in which they are nominated.

(3) When the nominations appear to the Interim Moderator to be completed, he shall read to the meeting the list of the names of persons nominated; and he shall then ask, first, whether there be any further nominations, and second, whether there be any withdrawals. After he has allowed a sufficient opportunity to the meeting for responding to each question, and added further names nominated (if any), and deleted from the list the names withdrawn (if any), the election shall be proceeded with.

(4) If the number of persons nominated amount only to the maximum fixed by the meeting, or be less than the maximum fixed, such persons shall constitute the committee without any vote being taken. If the number of persons nominated, and not withdrawn, exceed the maximum fixed, the Interim Moderator shall take the votes of the meeting in their favour one by one in the order in which they stand on the list; and those for whom most votes are given, to the number fixed, shall constitute the committee. If any should have equal votes for the last place, a vote shall be taken as to who shall serve. Voting shall be by standing up, unless otherwise resolved. No member shall vote for more than the number agreed on by the congregation to serve on the committee.

(5) The meeting shall then determine by standing up whether the election of a minister shall be open or by ballot.

(6) After intimating the names of the persons elected to the committee, and announcing to them when they are to meet to appoint a convener and vice-convener, the Interim Moderator shall close the meeting with prayer.

The Interim Moderator shall be regarded as an assessor to the Vacancy Committee, in order that he may give advice and guidance. If the Committee so desire, he may act as its convener, but in no case shall he have a vote, either deliberative or casting.

Procedure of Vacancy Committee.

9. It shall be the duty of the Interim Moderator to summon the first meeting of the Vacancy Committee, which may be held at the close of the congregational meeting at which it is appointed. At this meeting a convener and vice-convener shall be appointed as well as a clerk, who shall keep regular minutes of the proceedings. The clerk need not be a member of the committee. The convener shall have a casting as well as a deliberative vote, unless he be the Interim Moderator. The committee in its proceedings shall have regard to the Regulations of the Probationers and Transference of Ministers Committee.

Any of the following methods may be adopted:

(*a*) The committee may determine to have no leet, but to make inquiries with a view to finding a minister who may preach before the congregation as sole nominee.

(*b*) Application may be made to the Probationers and Transference of Ministers Committee for a regular supply of probationers for a certain period. Particular probationers may be asked for up to half the number requested.

(*c*) The committee may resolve to hear a leet of ministers who shall preach in the vacant charge, and in this case the Probationers and Transference of Ministers Committee shall appoint a number of ministers to preach equal to that chosen by the Congregational Committee.

(*d*) It may be decided to hear a leet partly of ministers and partly of probationers. In this case the same rules shall apply as under (*b*) and (*c*).

Eligibility for Election as Ministers (1959, xxiv.).

1. No Presbytery shall sustain a Call to a minister in his first charge of a Church and Parish of the Church of Scotland until the expiry of at least five years from the date of his induction to that charge except in accordance with the provisions of this Act.

2. Before submitting to the congregation of a vacant charge any nomination of a minister in a first charge who has not completed five years therein the Interim Moderator shall be in possession of one or other of the following documents, viz.:—

(*a*) A Certificate in terms of the First Schedule to this Act signed by the Moderator, Clerk (or Depute Clerk), and two other Members of the Presbytery of which the minister is a member; or (*b*) a signed extract from the Minutes of the Presbytery of which the minister is a member in terms of the Second Schedule hereto.

3. The granting of a Certificate as in the First or Second Schedules to this Act shall be without prejudice to the right of the Presbytery to adjudge according to the usual law and practice of the Church the question of a specific translation if and when it arises.

(For Schedules see p. 823.)

10. Subject to the above the following classes of persons are qualified to be nominated, elected, called, and admitted as ministers of congregations in the Church of Scotland:

(1) All persons who have been licensed to preach the Gospel by any Presbytery of the Church, or of the Church of Scotland or United Free Church of Scotland before the Union, without any special limitation being attached to their licence, subject to the provisions of Sub-section (2).

(2) Licentiates or ministers either of the Church of Scotland or of the United Free Church of Scotland before their Union, or of the Church of Scotland subsequent thereto, who have neither demitted nor been judicially deprived of the status they possessed, but have undertaken employment which is not subject to the jurisdiction of the Church. These shall, on ceasing to be so employed, be eligible for appointment to office in the Church, according to their status; provided that prior to nomination for such office they shall have satisfied the Committee on Admission of Ministers of Other Churches or its Executive as to their status, record, and character, and shall have received from it a certificate to that effect. Provided also that any minister holding office under a religious society or in a charitable institution, if he be in full communion with the Church of Scotland, and if he have obtained the aforesaid certificate from the Committee on Admission of Ministers of Other Churches as to status, record, and character, may be nominated, elected, and called to a vacant charge, or other appointment; but it shall not be competent for a Presbytery to admit or induct him thereto, until he has given evidence of his resignation of the said office.

(3) Probationers and ministers of the Church of Scotland or any of its branches before the Union of 1929 who had been translated to charges in the former Presbyterian Church of England, provided that they produce a certificate of licence and that they hold a regular pastoral charge or professorial chair in

the United Reformed Church in England and Wales at the time of their appointment.

(4) Probationers and ministers of the former Presbyterian Church of England, provided that they produce a certificate from the appropriate Committee of the United Reformed Church in England and Wales that they have taken the full and regular course of study for the ministry as required by the former Presbyterian Church of England without any modification.

Pending the preparation of a mutual eligibility scheme between the Church of Scotland and the United Reformed Church in England and Wales the General Assembly of 1974 resolved as follows :—

> " In the meantime a Minister or Licentiate of the United Reformed Church shall be eligible for consideration in a vacancy only if he holds a Certificate from the Committee on Admission of Ministers that his educational curriculum has been in accordance with the requirements of the Church of Scotland " (1974, sess. 5.).

Ministers of the Presbyterian Church in Ireland are qualified to be nominated, elected, called and admitted as ministers of congregations of the Church of Scotland, provided they produce a certificate from the Clerk of their Assembly that they have been trained and ordained by that Church, and who have served in a charge or an appointment under the jurisdiction of that Church for a period of not less than five years prior to nomination.

(5) Ministers holding at the time a charge or office in any Presbyterian Church in Great Britain or Ireland, which adheres to the doctrine, government, and discipline of the Church of Scotland, or ministers emeriti of any such Church, *provided that*, prior to nomination, the Congregational Committee shall have received from the Committee on Admission of Ministers of Other Churches a certificate approving (i.) their course of study for the ministry both in arts and divinity as equal in extent and character to that required of licentiates of the Church of Scotland ; (ii.) their ordination as valid ; and (iii.) their presbyterial certificate as satisfactory.

(6) Ministers and probationers not included in the classes above mentioned who have been admitted by authority of the General Assembly of the Church or of any of its branches before Union to the status of ministers or probationers of the Church.

Nomination by the Vacancy Committee.

11. The Committee may resolve to nominate one person only for election, or it may name and propose more persons than one. If the temporal affairs of the congregation are administered in accordance with a special constitution derived from and particular to the congregation itself, a copy of the said constitution shall immediately be given to those persons nominated (1970, iii.). No one shall be nominated without his consent in writing. Notice shall immediately be given of the Committee's nomination to the Interim Moderator in the form of Schedule D. (see Appendix, p. 814).

Congregational Meeting for Election by Open Vote.

12. If the congregation have determined that the method of election be by open vote, the Interim Moderator, on receiving notice of the committee's nomination, shall summon on the first Sunday possible a meeting of the congregation to be held on an early day. This meeting shall be intimated to the congregation by the officiating minister or the Session Clerk on the two Sundays which immediately precede it, in the form contained in Schedule G. (see Appendix, p. 815).

At this meeting, when only one person has been nominated, the question shall be put, "Elect Mr —— or not." When more names than one have been proposed, they shall be put successively in the order in which they have been proposed; the name having fewest votes shall be dropped, and the vote shall be again taken on the remaining names, and so on till only one name remains. But if at any stage in the voting more votes shall be given for one person than for all the others collectively, the names of these others shall be dropped without further voting. The Interim Moderator shall then put the question, "Elect Mr —— or not," and if so resolved shall declare such person elected, subject to the judgment of the courts of the Church. He shall sign a declaration of the result in one of the forms of Schedule I. (see Appendix, p. 816).

The Interim Moderator shall invite those present to subscribe the call (Schedule M.) to the person elected, if an election take place, and the call shall be left in the hands of the Session for at least eight days for additional signatures. The Session shall make arrangements for such opportunities of signing the call (see Schedule K.). The call may be subscribed on behalf of members not present when mandates (Schedule N.) authorising such subscription are produced. Such names shall be initialled by the Interim Moderator or member of the Kirk Session appending them. Adherents over fourteen years of age shall be given the opportunity of signing a paper of concurrence in the call. The call and paper of concurrence shall be attested by the Interim Moderator at the congregational meeting, and by two elders on each occasion thereafter when signatures are appended. For forms of attestation, see Schedule O. For Schedules referred to, see Appendix, pp. 818-819.

If it be resolved not to elect—*i.e.*, if no name be accepted by the meeting, the procedure outlined in Regulation 17 shall be followed.

Election by Ballot Vote.

13. If the congregation have determined that the vote shall be by ballot, it shall be the duty of the Interim Moderator, upon receiving the minute of nomination, to see that it is read to the congregation by the officiating minister or the Session Clerk at the first ordinary diet of public worship after receipt. He shall at the same time fix the date and hour of election, having regard to the convenience of the electors. The time allowed for voting shall include a certain time during the day as well as in the evening, and an opportunity of voting at different places at different times may be given, where it is necessary. Due intimation thereof shall be made to the congregation by the officiating minister or Session Clerk on the two Sundays immediately preceding the election, in the form prescribed in Schedule E. or F. Where a further vote becomes necessary the same procedure shall be followed, except that intimation of the election on one Sunday will suffice. Election by ballot is the only method of election competent in the election of a minister to a vacant charge consisting of two or more congregations which have been Linked or which have agreed to a Deferred Union or a Deferred Linking. In such cases whenever reasonably possible and practicable, only one ballot box shall be used. In cases where more than one ballot box is used all boxes shall be opened at the same place and time and the voting papers mixed together before counting begins so that preponderence of votes in each congregation shall not be disclosed. In all other respects, however, these regulations apply to the election of ministers to such vacant charges (1961, xxii.).

Procedure at the Election by Ballot Vote.

14. (1) The Interim Moderator shall preside at the election,

and may be assisted by such persons as he shall appoint, not being persons whose names are on the electoral register. The election shall be by voting papers in one of the forms prescribed in Schedule H., which with their counterfoils shall be numbered consecutively, and which, as well as all means necessary to carry out the voting, shall be provided by the Kirk Session. The Interim Moderator shall have the electoral register at the place of voting, and he shall see that a voting paper is not supplied to any person whose name is not on the electoral register; and also that, as each elector receives a voting paper, the name of that elector is marked on the electoral register as having voted, and his number on the electoral register marked on the counterfoil of the voting paper supplied to him. He shall also arrange that the admission of electors is properly regulated, and that they retire after voting. Each elector, after receiving a voting paper, shall mark it as directed on the paper, and shall then place it in a ballot-box. The Interim Moderator, or his deputy, or the person or persons (if any) appointed under Regulation 18 by the Interim Moderator to superintend the voting along with himself, shall give assistance if desired by any elector in marking the voting paper, but no other person shall give such assistance, and care shall be taken that there be no interference with voters in marking their papers, and that they have an opportunity of marking them without divulging the vote given; provided always that the fact of a voting paper containing the means of identification shall not invalidate the vote, if it be otherwise sufficiently marked. The ballot-box and papers shall be under the charge of the Interim Moderator, who shall be responsible for their safe keeping. (For the special procedure in the case of election to a vacant charge consisting of two or more congregations which have been linked or which have agreed to a Deferred Union or Deferred Linking, see p. 758.)

(2) When only one person is voted on, if the number of qualified electors voting "For" such person exceed that of those voting "Against" him, he shall be held as elected and appointed, subject to the judgment of the courts of the Church; otherwise it shall be held that no election has been made.

(3) When more persons than one are voted on, an elector may vote for any one of such persons, or he may vote against them all. If one of the persons voted on receive a majority of the whole votes recorded, he shall be held as elected and appointed, subject to the judgment of the courts of the Church.

If no one of the persons voted on receive a majority of the whole votes recorded, there shall be struck off the names of all those persons whose total number of votes taken together does not amount to the number of votes recorded for the person standing next higher in said voting, but, if an equal number of votes be given for two or more of the persons having the lowest number of votes, and the total number of such votes exceeds the number of votes recorded for the person standing next higher, a second vote shall be taken, and the same procedure followed. Thereafter a further vote shall be taken on the person or persons remaining; and the same course shall, if necessary, be followed by successive votings until only one person remains. If such remaining person have not received a majority of the whole votes recorded at the last voting, the procedure with respect to him shall be the same as if he had been the only person originally nominated; and if at the final vote he do not receive a majority of the whole votes recorded, or if at any voting all the persons voted on have equal votes, or there be a majority of the whole votes recorded against all the persons voted on, it shall be held that no election has been made.

Withdrawal of Nominations.

15. When a person nominated intimates his withdrawal before the election notice is read from the pulpit, the fact of his withdrawal shall be announced when the said notice is read, and the wording of the notice may, if necessary, be altered so as to suit the altered circumstances. When a withdrawal is intimated after the election notice has been read from the pulpit, and before the voting commences, a notice of it, signed by the Interim Moderator or his deputy, shall be affixed to the door of the voting place, and, unless the person withdrawing be the sole original or remaining nominee, the voting shall proceed as if he had not been nominated, his name being struck out of the voting papers or nominations. In the event of the sole original or remaining nominee, or of all the original or remaining nominees, withdrawing, the convener of the committee, on being informed of the fact, shall forthwith call a meeting of the committee, and the committee at this meeting may make a new nomination, or resolve to take steps thereto, or to take no such steps. If it resolve to take no further steps, the Interim Moderator shall receive information without delay in writing of the resolution come to, and shall

proceed as directed by Regulation 17 in the case of a failure to nominate; but, if a new nomination be made or resolved on, the procedure prescribed in Regulations 11, 12, and 13 in regard to the making of the nomination and the intimation thereof and of the day of election shall be followed.

Counting and Declaration of the Votes and Call.

16. As soon as practicable, and at latest within twenty-four hours, after the close of the voting the Interim Moderator shall constitute the Kirk Session, and in presence thereof shall proceed with the counting of the votes, in which he may be assisted as provided in Regulation 14. He shall not count any papers in which, according to his judgment, the marking is uncertain. He shall, after the counting has been completed, make a declaration of the votes in one of the forms of Schedule I., said declaration to be forthwith affixed to the door or notice-board of the church. He shall also, after the counting is completed, seal up the voting papers used in the voting, and the counterfoils, and he shall transmit them, along with the documents specified in Regulation 19, to the Presbytery clerk, and after the settlement the Presbytery clerk shall destroy the voting papers and counterfoils and certify the same to the Presbytery at its first meeting thereafter.

The Interim Moderator shall cause intimation to be given from the pulpit, as soon as possible after an election and appointment has been made, that a call in the usual form will lie with the Session clerk, or other suitable person, for a certain time, being not less than seven free days, to receive the signatures of the members of the congregation. (See Schedule K.)

It shall be competent for any person who is unable to attend at the time or place fixed to have his or her name appended by the Interim Moderator, or by any member of Kirk Session, on application duly signed and submitted to the Session clerk. (Schedule N.) Such names shall be initialled by the Interim Moderator or member of Kirk Session appending them. There shall also be opportunity for persons over fourteen years of age who are connected with the congregation, but who are not members thereof in full communion, to sign a paper of concurrence in the call. (Schedule M. 3.) The signatures shall be attested in accordance with Schedule O. (For Schedules referred to, see Appendix, pp. 817-819.)

Failure to Nominate, and Failure to Elect.

17. If no minute of nomination from the Congregational Committee has been transmitted to the Interim Moderator within four months from the date of the election of the Committee, ten qualified electors may require the Interim Moderator to take steps with a view to a nomination being made. The Interim Moderator shall, upon receiving such requisition, intimate in writing to the clerk of the committee that, in the event of no minute of nomination being lodged with him within ten days from the date of writing, the committee will be regarded as failing to nominate. If the committee so fail to nominate, the Interim Moderator shall cause intimation to be made as soon as possible from the pulpit of the vacant church in terms of Schedule J. 1 that the congregation is to proceed of new to elect a committee; and the procedure which is hereinbefore prescribed for the election of a committee shall be followed, provided always that the date of that election shall be fixed by the Interim Moderator. The same course (except that the pulpit intimation shall be in terms of Schedule J. 2) shall be followed where, though there has been a nomination, there has been a failure to elect a minister, followed by a resolution of the committee to make no new nomination or to resign. In any other case of failure to elect, or in the case of the person elected intimating in writing to the convener of the committee that he declines to accept, the committee, unless it resign and intimate its resignation to the Interim Moderator, shall be held as continuing in office, and shall forthwith take steps with a view to making a new nomination; provided always that if, after any failure to elect, or the declinature of the person elected to accept, a requisition, signed by not fewer than one-tenth of the qualified electors, be lodged with the Interim Moderator before the expiry of the third free day, requiring him to call a meeting of the congregation to determine whether the committee shall continue, or to elect a new committee, he shall, at the first ordinary diet of public worship after receipt of such requisition, cause intimation to be made from the pulpit to that effect in terms of Schedule J. 3. (For Schedules referred to, see Appendix, pp. 816-817.)

Power of Interim Moderator to appoint Deputy and Assistants.

18. The Interim Moderator may, in case of unavoidable absence, authorise in writing a ministerial member of the Presbytery to act as his deputy, and he shall specify the

occasion on which he is to act. Also, where he deems the number of persons voting, in the election of a minister, to be so large as to render it necessary that more than one person should preside, he may in writing authorise one or more persons at his discretion (such persons not being on the electoral register) to superintend the voting along with himself.

Transmission of Documents to Presbytery.

19. After an election and appointment has been made, the Interim Moderator shall without delay transmit the relative documents to the clerk of the Presbytery of the bounds, to be laid before the Presbytery. The documents to be so transmitted shall be: minute of nomination by the Congregational Committee; all subsequent intimations to the congregation; and the declaration of the election and appointment given under the hand of the Interim Moderator, or the minute of the congregational meeting where the vote was taken.

The Interim Moderator shall also at the same time inform the Presbytery of the steps taken with reference to the call, and of the time during which it is to lie with the Session clerk or other person: and the Session clerk at the expiry of that time shall transmit it to the clerk of Presbytery.

These documents shall be laid before the Presbytery at its first ordinary meeting or at a meeting specially called for the purpose. It shall be the duty of the Interim Moderator to have intimation made of the meeting of the Presbytery to the vacant congregation either at the meeting when a minister is elected (Regulation 12) or on the Sunday when it is intimated that the call will lie for signature or on the Sunday immediately preceding the meeting of Presbytery. (See Schedule K.) There shall also be laid on the table of the Presbytery at the same time a letter of acceptance from the person elected, which shall include a statement that he has used no undue influence either by himself or others to secure the call and sufficient evidence that he is qualified to receive the appointment—viz.: extract of licence and Presbyterial certificate in the case of a probationer, a certificate of status and a Presbyterial certificate in the case of a minister without charge from the Presbytery having jurisdiction over him, the certificates specified in Act ii., 1974, in the case of a probationer or minister of the former Presbyterian Church of England, an extract minute of the General Assembly in the case of a probationer or minister received by the Supreme Court, or a certificate from the Committee on Admission of Ministers of other Churches in the case of a minister from another Presbyterian Church in Great Britain or a probationer or minister of this Church who has engaged in other service. If the person appointed be the minister of a regular charge of the Church of Scotland no certificate shall be required. If the vacant charge be one on the Assembly list of Gaelic-speaking charges, a certificate of competency to preach in Gaelic may be required.

(These documents should be secured before the meeting of Presbytery by the Presbytery Clerk.)

Judgment of Appointment and Call.

20. Having considered the relative documents, and having heard any parties who may be judged by the Presbytery to have an interest, the Presbytery shall decide whether or not to sustain the appointment and call. In such judgment the number of signatures appended to the call shall be a factor in the decision.

Jus Devolutum (1945, vii.).

21. If no appointment is made within six months from the time when leave to elect is given to the congregation, and no petition from the congregation for an extension of the time is granted, the Presbytery shall in terms of Regulation 4 take the necessary steps to appoint a minister to the vacant charge and shall intimate to the Vacancy Committee accordingly. For the procedure to be followed in the exercise of the *Jus Devolutum*, see below (see also p. 246). (*Note.*—No provision is made for the exercise of the *Jus Devolutum* in a case where the failure by the congregation is to exercise a restricted right of election.)

Appointment tanquam jure devoluto.

In the case of any appointment made by a Presbytery *tanquam jure devoluto* the following shall be the procedure:

(1) The Presbytery shall itself make choice of one duly qualified to be minister of the vacant charge, and shall record the appointment made in the minutes of Presbytery.

(2) The clerk of Presbytery shall intimate the appointment to the person concerned, and shall request him to forward a letter of acceptance and sufficient evidence that he is qualified to receive the appointment as set forth in Regulation 19 of the Regulations for the Election, Settlement, and Translation of Ministers.

(3) The clerk of Presbytery shall at the same time intimate to the minister appointed that he is required to conduct service in the vacant church on an early Sunday; and the clerk shall arrange the date of such service with the person appointed.

(4) The clerk of Presbytery shall cause intimation to be made in the form prescribed below[1] to the vacant congregation that the person appointed will conduct service in the vacant church, and that a call in the usual form will lie with the Session clerk, or other suitable person, for at least seven free days after the said service to receive the signatures of the members of the congregation.

(5) The provisions of Regulation 16 of the Regulations for the Election, Settlement, and Translation of Ministers with regard to Mandates and Paper of Concurrence shall apply in this case also.

(6) At the expiry of the time appointed by the clerk of Presbytery the call as signed shall be transmitted by the Session clerk to the clerk of the Presbytery, who shall lay it, with the documents specified in Section (2) of this Appendix, and the intimation made to the vacant congregation, before the Presbytery at its first ordinary meeting, or at a meeting specially called for the purpose. Intimation of this meeting shall be made to the vacant congregation.

(7) The procedure thereafter shall be in accordance with the Regulations for the Election, Settlement, and Translation of Ministers, Regulations 20, 22, 23, 24, and 25.

For guide to the Regulations, &c., see Appendix, pp. 576-580.

SECTION II. SETTLEMENT AND TRANSLATION OF MINISTERS.

Appointments and Calls to Probationers and Ministers not in Charges.

22. (1) If the Presbytery sustain an appointment and call to a probationer, and if there be no appeal or complaint tendered in due form against its judgment, the Presbytery shall appoint the day on which the ordination and induction shall take place.

(2) If the appointment and call which is sustained and accepted be to a minister of the Church of Scotland not having a fixed charge, the Presbytery shall, if there be no ecclesiastical impediment, proceed without delay to appoint the day for the induction.

[1] See page 821.

Probationary Period (*cf.* Act XX., 1973).

Licentiates before becoming eligible for election or appointment to a home charge shall normally be required to spend a Probationary Period under the supervision of the Committee on Education for the Ministry. The Committee on Education for the Ministry shall have power in special cases to grant exemption from this requirement. The provisions of this Act shall apply to all students who commence their theological curriculum after the General Assembly of 1973. In the case of a call to a probationer the Presbytery should satisfy itself that the requirements of this Act have been fulfilled.

Appointments and Calls to Ministers in Charges.

23. (1) If the sustained appointment and call be to the minister of a congregation of another Presbytery of the Church,[1] the induction shall not be proceeded with until a judgment has been obtained in favour of the translation, either from the Presbytery which has jurisdiction over the minister called, or from the superior court which has jurisdiction over that Presbytery. The Presbytery may, however, fix a provisional date for the induction. In the case of every such appointment and call, the Presbytery, immediately after sustaining it, or immediately after being officially informed that its judgment sustaining it has been affirmed by the superior court, may commission certain of its members to prosecute the call if it so desire. The clerk shall send the call, and along with it the relative extract minute of Presbytery sustaining the appointment and call, to the clerk of the Presbytery of which the minister called is a member, who shall acknowledge receipt of these documents, and intimate the time and place of the meeting of his Presbytery at which commissioners, if appointed, require to be present. The clerk of the latter Presbytery shall also intimate the call to the minister called and to the clerk of his Session. On the next or first suitable Sunday he shall cause the call to be intimated to the congregation and summon a congregational meeting, which may be held after

[1] The same procedure is followed in the case of translations to and from charges of the Presbyterian Church in Ireland and charges of the United Reformed Church which in the past were charges of the former Presbyterian Church of England. (See Acts 1931, x.; 1972, ii.; and 1974, ii.). A minister called by a congregation of another Church, other than a congregation of the former Presbyterian Church of England or a congregation of the Presbyterian Church in Ireland must demit his charge; he is not translated.

one Sunday's intimation, to consider the matter, and to appoint commissioners if so desired to appear for the interests of the congregation at the meeting of Presbytery at which the call is to be considered ; and he shall arrange that a minister of the Presbytery preside at that meeting. (For Form of Intimation, see Schedule P.) The commissioners prosecuting the call, if appointed, ascertain from the clerk of their own Presbytery the time and place of the meeting at which they require to appear.

(2) On the day and at the hour appointed, the Presbytery having met, all the parties shall be called and heard if they so desire. If no parties appear, they shall be held to acquiesce in the translation of the minister who is under call.

(3) The Presbytery shall decide, in the first instance, whether or not the call shall be presented to the minister. If the decision be in the affirmative, and there be no appeal or complaint, and if thereafter the minister acquiescing in the decision accept the call, the Presbytery shall give formal judgment to the effect that it agrees to the translation, and shall appoint the minister to await in that matter the orders of the Presbytery prosecuting the call, and shall instruct its clerk to send an extract of the finding to that Presbytery.

(4) In the event of translation being refused, the Presbytery prosecuting the appointment and call shall have the right to intimate an appeal to a higher court, and the minister who has received the appointment and call shall be entitled to dissent and complain if the Presbytery refuse to translate him.

(5) If a sustained call be to an ordained minister of a charge within the bounds of the same Presbytery which has sustained the call, the procedure shall be the same in principle as that adopted in the case already detailed.

(6) When the minister of a congregation accepts an appointment and call to another congregation in the United Kingdom or Ireland, he shall not be loosed from his charge till he has been inducted to his new charge. Until then he shall remain responsible for the due administration of ordinances, and shall continue to receive his stipend. When the call is to a congregation furth of the United Kingdom or Ireland, the minister shall be loosed from his charge when the call is accepted, or at such other date subsequent thereto as the Presbytery may determine.

(7) The Presbytery may, if it see cause, at the same meeting at which the minister has accepted an appointment and call, appoint an Interim Moderator of Session, who shall be associ-

ated with the minister until he is loosed from his charge, who shall act only in matters connected with the approaching vacancy, and shall subsequently take full charge. The Presbytery, having appointed an Interim Moderator, must also appoint three assessors (one of whom shall be an elder) whose duties are laid down in Act 1966, xxxi. (See p. 244.)

(8) By Act 1948, x., of the General Assembly appointments by the Committee on Probationers and Transference of Ministers for Probationers to preach in vacant charges or charges about to become vacant shall be made from the time when the Presbytery agrees to the translation.

24. The Commission of Assembly are empowered, at any of their stated diets, to take up and dispose of all references from Synods (or Presbyteries meeting subsequent to the Synods) in matters connected with calls, translations, or settlement of ministers which may be brought before them and which it is found desirable in the interest of the congregation concerned to dispose of without delay. In such cases the decision of the Commission shall be final (1933, xviii.).

Ordination and Induction.

25. (1) When the Presbytery has fixed a day for the ordination and induction of a probationer, or for the induction of a minister, it shall appoint an edict to be read to the congregation on the two Sundays immediately preceding the day fixed for the induction, which shall be attested each Sunday by the officiating minister or preacher. By the edict, public intimation is made that the day and hour named have been appointed for the ordination and induction, or for the induction, as the case may be, and that the Presbytery will proceed in due form to the settlement, if no objection to the life or doctrine of the probationer or minister be previously brought forward and substantiated. It shall be also intimated that the Presbytery will meet at a time and place appointed for the purpose of receiving and dealing with objections, if any, which meeting may be held on the same day as that fixed for the (ordination and) induction and at such previous hour as may be expedient. (For Forms of Edict and Attestation, see Appendix, pp. 820, 821.)

The General Assembly have instructed Presbyteries that when a congregation within the bounds is given leave to elect a minister its attention be drawn to the heavy costs of removal that a new minister may have to face, and that wherever possible the congregation should meet part, at least, of these expenses.

A grant may be obtained from the Maintenance of the Ministry Committee, not exceeding 50 per cent, of the total incurred in needful cases towards the removal expenses of a minister translated from Orkney or Shetland to a charge on the mainland of Scotland, provided he has served not less than seven years in such charges, and in cases of a minister who demits his charge either to retire from age or infirmity or to undertake the work of a terminable appointment on the mainland (1954, 7).

Note 1.—The importance of the Whitsunday Term, 15th May, in relation to the payment of annual rates to the Churches and Universities (Scotland) Widows' and Orphans' Fund, should be kept in view in fixing the date of an induction. If an induction take place shortly before 15th May, the first annual payment and the first instalment of entry money (in the case of a first induction) fall due on the first 15th May following the induction.

Note 2.—Objections may be called for either "at the most patent door of the Church" or in presence of the assembled congregation.

(2) At the time and place named in the edict, the Presbytery, having been constituted, shall call for "the return of the edict," with attestation that it has been duly served. Any objection at this last stage shall be substantiated immediately to the satisfaction of the Presbytery, in which case proceedings shall be sisted. When no objections are given in, or when they cannot be substantiated *instanter*, the Presbytery shall proceed with the (ordination and) induction, according to appointment. If the minister to be inducted is being translated from another charge, the minute of the Presbytery agreeing to his translation shall be laid on the table.

(3) The Presbytery shall then repair to the place of worship, where the minister appointed shall conduct devotional exercises and may preach a discourse suitable to the occasion. The clerk shall then read a brief narrative of the cause of the vacancy and the steps taken for the settlement, and the moderator, having read the Preamble appointed by the Basis of Union, shall put to the ordinand or minister to be inducted the questions therein prescribed, addressing him by name. (See App. X., p. 569.) These having been satisfactorily answered and the Formula having been signed, the ordinand shall kneel, and the Moderator, by prayer, with the imposition of hands in which all the ministers present join, shall ordain him to the office of the Holy Ministry. Prayer being ended, the Moderator, addressing him, shall say: "I now declare you to

have been ordained to the office of the Holy Ministry, and in the Name of the Lord Jesus Christ, the King and Head of the Church, and by authority of this Presbytery, I induct you to this charge; and in token thereof we give you the right hand of fellowship." The Moderator and other members of Presbytery present shall give to him the right hand of fellowship. The Moderator shall then put the prescribed question to the members of the congregation. Suitable exhortations shall then be addressed to the minister and afterwards to his people. The congregation shall then be dismissed, and as they retire the members shall have an opportunity of welcoming him as their minister. His name shall then be added to the roll of the Presbytery. Certified intimation of the ordination and induction shall be sent to the Session clerk to be engrossed in the minutes of the first meeting of Session thereafter.

(4) When one who has been already ordained to the ministry is to be inducted to the pastoral charge of a congregation, the act of ordination shall not be repeated, and the words "I now declare you to be ordained to the office of the Holy Ministry, and" in the declaration shall be omitted. In other respects the procedure shall be the same as that in an ordination.

(5) It is the duty of a Presbytery, after inducting to a charge within its bounds the minister of a charge under the jurisdiction of another Presbytery, either of this Church or of any other from which he has been duly translated, to give immediate intimation through its clerk to that Presbytery that the induction has taken place.

Ordination in Relation to Extra-Parochial Offices.

Caution. (6) Ordination which has no reference to a particular pastoral charge, or to some position or function held to be equivalent to that of a particular pastoral charge, shall not be conferred except when expressly authorised by the General Assembly or their Commission. But the right of a Presbytery to ordain a probationer as assistant to a minister within the bounds or to any other office the duties of which, in the judgment of the Presbytery, may be undertaken more effectively by a man ordained to the ministry, is hereby expressly affirmed. A Presbytery in Scotland may ordain a probationer who has been appointed to a pastoral charge overseas, or chaplaincy overseas when there is no local Presbytery having jurisdiction

Ordination of a Probationer.

over that charge; and missionaries to foreign parts may be ordained before they proceed to their spheres of labour. In these cases Presbyteries shall satisfy themselves with respect to the nature of the appointment, the position of the parties making it, the sphere of action proposed to be entered on, and the provision arranged or in prospect for the due support of the minister or missionary after he has entered on it. If they be satisfied regarding these points, they may proceed, and, as far as the act of ordination is concerned, they shall take the same steps as in ordinary cases. The serving of an edict may be dispensed with, but public notice of the Presbytery's intention shall be given, that there may be sufficient opportunity to bring forward and substantiate any objection to the life or doctrine of the person proposed to be ordained. (See also p. 155.)

The General Assembly of 1969 declared two principles to be regulative for this purpose (1969, Reg. 1.) :—

"Except in cases provided for in Acts of Assembly, such as Lecturers in Divinity or Chaplains to the Deaf :—

1. Only where the Church has some control over or right to approve of the appointment and at least some continuing general oversight of the way the 'charge' is being worked shall ordination be granted to a licentiate taking up the appointment.
2. And only where there is substantial and reasonable need for the person appointed to the 'charge' regularly to baptise or celebrate Communion shall ordination be granted.

If the appointment, on the other hand, is primarily for teaching, counselling or organising, the minister in the most convenient pastoral charge shall be the person called upon to administer the Sacraments and with his Kirk Session admit to full communion where this is required."

In making these proposals the General Assembly are aware that the cognate or related matter of ministerial membership of Presbytery is governed by Act II., 1970. It does not follow, however, that, because an appointment is listed on the schedule which if held by an already ordained person confers membership of Presbytery, this appointment would imply ordination to a licentiate if he were chosen to fill it.

It should be noted with regard to this regulation that any body intending to appoint a licentiate or any licentiate making application for an appointment would be well advised to consult with the Presbytery of the bounds as to the fulfilment of 1, provided always that the appointment involves the need specified in 2.

Ordination of Licentiates.

Ordination should be granted to licentiates only for very good reasons (either because of the size of the congregation in which they serve or the amount of pastoral or parochial work involved).

A licentiate should not receive ordination until he has given at least six months' service and undertakes to remain for a period of not less than twelve months in the appointment for the work of which he is being ordained. With regard to other offices, the duties of which might be undertaken more effectively by men ordained to the Ministry, the Committee recommends that Presbyteries should proceed with caution, and ordain only after full consideration of the necessity for ordination in view of the duties and responsibilities involved.

The general scale of salary paid to assistants both ordained and unordained is related to the Minimum Stipend which is declared each year and may be ascertained from the Committee on the Maintenance of Ministry (see p. 225).

Public intimation should always be given of the Presbytery's intention to ordain; and the Edict, Narrative and Questions to the Ordinand modified where necessary (1955, 1).

Work among the Deaf and Dumb.

Ordination for work among the Deaf and Dumb is regulated by Act XXIII., 1969 :—

1. A candidate for Licence with a view to Ordination and restriction to minister to the Deaf and Dumb shall (*a*) be a member of the Church of Scotland in full communion; (*b*) hold the Diploma of the Deaf Welfare Examination Board; (*c*) have attended satisfactorily classes at a Faculty of Divinity of a Scottish university in Divinity and Scottish Church History, for at least one session; and (*d*) have served with acceptance for at least five years in the employment of a Society for the Deaf.
2. Application on behalf of the candidate shall be made in the first instance by the local Society for the Deaf employing the candidate to the Presbytery of the bounds where

the Society's church is located, and shall have the approval of the Scottish Association for the Deaf. The Presbytery shall interview the candidate as to character, vocation and general suitability, and, if it approves the application, shall transmit it to the Home Board.

3. The Home Board shall confer with the Presbytery and the Committee on Education for the Ministry as to what, if any, supplementary course of training is required, and on the concurrence of the Home Board and the Presbytery in the application the candidate shall present a petition to the General Assembly.
4. If the crave of the Petition be granted, the General Assembly if so advised shall instruct the Presbytery to take the candidate on trials for Licence, with leave after Licence to proceed to Ordination to the Holy Ministry, with the restriction that he be not inducted to a charge of the Church of Scotland unless that charge be for work among the Deaf and Dumb.
5. Removal or alteration of the restriction shall be authorised only by the General Assembly. Any petition for the removal of restriction shall be accompanied by a recommendation from the Home Board.

Admission of a Professor.

University Professors of Theology who are ministers of the Church of Scotland may be admitted to membership of Presbytery in terms of Act II., 1970 (p. 142). In the case of Church Professors or Principals of Church Colleges appointed by the General Assembly, an Admission Service, in connection with their appointment must be arranged by the Presbytery within whose bounds they are to teach, and they are required to answer the questions to be put to ministers at their ordination and/or induction (see p. 570), and to sign the Formula (1936, 5).

A minister of the Church of Scotland, on his appointment to a Theological Chair or to the office of Principal of a Church College, must submit to the Presbytery within whose bounds he is to teach documentary evidence of his appointment, and, if a member of another Presbytery, an Extract Minute from the Presbytery of which he is a member, or, if a probationer, an Extract of Licence and a Presbyterial Certificate (1936, 5).

If at any time a licentiate of this Church shall be appointed to a Church or University Theological Chair or Lectureship in any of the Universities of Scotland or Colleges in connection with the Church of Scotland, or to a Lectureship in Biblical Studies in any of the said Universities or Colleges, the Presbytery within whose bounds he is to teach may ordain him as a minister of the Gospel as soon after his appointment thereto as may be conveniently arranged (1956, iii., and 1967, i.).

Theological Professors are entitled to be ministerial members of Presbytery. They may not become elders in the congregations to which they attach themselves (1970, ii.).

Appointment of Minister to a Church Extension Charge.

The appointment of a minister to a church extension charge lies with the General Assembly's Home Board in consultation with the Presbytery and local parties (1932, xiv.; 1955, Reg. 1). When a church extension charge is erected into a parish *quoad sacra* the Act of General Assembly provides that the minister of the church extension charge shall be the minister and that his successors shall be appointed in the same way as other ministers are.

Ministry in cases of Union or Linking.

When two congregations agree to unite or link under the present minister of one of them, and an explicit term of the basis of union or linking is that this minister shall be the minister of the united or linked charge, no further vote shall be necessary to constitute him minister of the united or linked charge. However he must be inducted in all cases when the vacant charge is a charge of the pre-union Church of Scotland and the stipend is derived in whole or in part from sources other than those vested in the General Trustees (1930, 15; 1957, xvii.).

Section III. Demission of Ministers.

Regular mode.

A minister's demission (resignation) must be offered to his Presbytery, which, before accepting it, must (*a*) ascertain and judge of his reasons, and (*b*) cite the parishioners and congregation for their interests (1820, 5; 1848, 7). The congregation must be cited even when the resignation includes the minister's status as a minister (1858, 3). Any members of the congregation may appear.

Irregularity fatal.

In a case (1820, 5) the Presbytery accepted the demission,

and had met to induct a successor, when the minister appeared, withdrew his demission, and protested against further procedure. The Presbytery did go on, however, and the Assembly set aside the whole, and declared the appellant to be still minister; because the Presbytery had accepted his demission before taking means to ascertain the state of his mind, and citing the congregation.

The demission of an assistant and successor was written in presence of the Presbytery, and accepted on the spot (the congregation not cited). Thirteen months afterwards the principal died. Two months later the Presbytery refused a petition from the demitted minister to be restored; and four months later still (when the papers of a new appointment were under consideration) it refused to hear an agent, or to receive his protest against going on with the induction, or to allow him to appeal. The Assembly found the Presbytery to have acted irregularly, but refused redress on the ground that the validity of the demission was not challenged timeously by any person having a title to do so (1885, 14). Irregularity with *mora*.

If the minister should put it out of the power of the Presbytery to judge of his reasons, it is absolved; he must take the consequences.

If he has absconded and then resigned, he should be treated as a deserter and deposed. Absconded.

For release to enter on a missionary appointment a minister demits, and the proceedings are those of an ordinary demission. For Mission Service.

A minister appointed to a professorship must tender his demission to his Presbytery (1817, vi.). For a Professorship.

A tendered demission may be withdrawn at any time previous to its acceptance (1901, 9). Demission may be withdrawn.

A demission may take place on the day on which the resignation is accepted or at a subsequent date fixed by the Presbytery or other court (1932, ix.). Date of Demission.

The importance of the Whitsunday Term, 15th May, in relation to the payment of annual rates to the Churches and Universities (Scotland) Widows' and Orphans' Fund, should be kept in view in fixing the date of a demission. If a minister demit shortly before 15th May and desire to retain his connection with the Fund, he must pay, personally, the rate due on 15th May; while, if the charge be vacant at that term, a rate of £7 for the vacant charge will be payable also by the Maintenance of the Ministry Fund or others liable.

If a minister offer to demit his status, such demission must be dealt with in the same way as demission of a charge (1966, 2.). Demission of Status.

Certificates for Ministers who demit their Charges (1933, xv.).[1]

The General Assembly has enacted as follows :—

Act 1933, xv. 1. Every minister on removal from his charge shall receive from his Presbytery (*a*) a Certificate of Status, bearing that he retains his status as a minister of the Church of Scotland, and (*b*) a Presbyterial Certificate, approving his character and conduct, unless the Presbytery shall see cause to withhold the same, in which case intimation shall forthwith be sent by the Presbytery to the Committee on Probationers and Transference of Ministers.

2. Except in the case of a minister who on demission of his charge retains his seat in the Presbytery, every minister without a charge shall, within two months of taking up residence within the bounds of a different Presbytery from that of which he was a member, report himself to that Presbytery by exhibiting the Certificate of Status, and by presenting the Presbyterial Certificate mentioned in Section 1, if this has been granted. If he again change his residence to the bounds of another Presbytery, he shall apply for a similar Presbyterial Certificate from the Presbytery whence he removes, and present it in like manner and within a like period. Without production of Certificate of Status and Presbyterial Certificate he shall not exercise any function of the ministry.

3. In the event of a Presbyterial Certificate being withheld, the minister concerned may, after the expiry of at least two years from the date when it was withheld, make application for the same to the Presbytery which formerly withheld it; and that Presbytery may, in the light of its own knowledge if the minister has continued to reside within its bounds, or, if he has ceased to do so, in the light of evidence that may be produced or that may be obtained by such inquiry as seems necessary, issue a Presbyterial Certificate in his favour, either immediately or after such period of supervision as may be determined, whether within its own bounds or as may be arranged with another Presbytery: always provided that if the minister has, during the period since his demission or since the Presbyterial Certificate was withheld, resided furth of Scotland, whether or not he has been in the employment of another Church, a Presbyterial Certificate shall not be issued without the consent of the Committee on Admission of Ministers of Other Churches or its Executive Sub-Committee, it being hereby declared that Section 12 of the Regulations

[1] Proposed new regulations (1975) have been sent down to Presbyteries for consideration under Barrier Act procedure.—*Ed.*

of that Committee enacted by General Assembly 1929 shall be construed in accordance with this Act.

4. A minister who has demitted his charge but does not hold a Presbyterial Certificate shall not be entitled to retain his seat in the Presbytery or Synod, and a minister from whom it is withheld shall not be eligible for associate membership in any Kirk Session.

Minister without Presbyterial Certificate not to retain seat in Presbytery or Synod.

5. Every Presbytery shall keep a list of ministers without a charge who reside within its bounds who are not members of another Presbytery, and who are not disqualified from exercising the functions of the ministry, and shall send a copy of this list annually in the month of March to the Clerks of the General Assembly and to the Secretary of the Committee on Probationers and Transference of Ministers.

The General Assembly in 1966 approved the following recommendations on ministers in appointments outwith the jurisdiction of the Church (Reg. 2) :—

Ministers may leave the parish ministry under one of the following categories :—

(*a*) There are those who leave the parish ministry (or who go as licentiates) to join the ministry of another Presbyterian Church (other than as in (*b*) below). These are regarded as having exchanged their status as ministers in the Church of Scotland, for status as ministers of the Church to which they go. If they wish to return they must acquire a Certificate of Eligibility before they can be elected to a parish or be received by a Presbytery as a minister without a charge, residing or officiating in its bounds.

(*b*) There are those who go abroad in the service of the Overseas Department. They may become members of the indigenous Church and may sit in its courts. They may go as licentiates and be ordained by the indigenous Church. So long as they remain under the direction and control of the Church of Scotland through its Overseas Department they may, on ceasing to be a member thereof, be granted a Certificate of Eligibility. On retiral such a minister, after receiving a Certificate of Eligibility, shall become a member of the Presbytery within which he resides.

(*c*) There are those who demit a charge (*a*) to become a professor or lecturer in a Divinity Faculty ; (*b*) to become a Chaplain to the Forces ; (*c*) to take up a non-parochial appointment within the jurisdiction of the Church ; (*d*) to take up one of the appointments outwith the jurisdiction of the Church which is listed in the Schedule to Act ii., 1970. These retain their full status as ministers and are given seats in Presbytery.

(*d*) There are those who demit a charge to take up an appointment which can be filled only by a minister but which is not within the jurisdiction of the Church and not included in the Schedule to Act ii., 1970. These have no seat in Presbytery but are under the discipline of the Presbytery within whose bounds they reside. In such cases it is easy for the Presbytery to maintain a fairly close degree of oversight, and ministers in this category, on resigning their appointment, can accept a call on production of a Presbyterial Certificate and Certificate of Eligibility.

(*e*) There are those who demit a charge to take up an appointment not requiring the service of a minister but (*a*) where a theological training is necessary or advantageous (teacher of religion, etc.) or (*b*) where pastoral experience is of value (welfare worker, marriage guidance counsellor, etc.). These are under the discipline of the Presbytery within whose bounds they reside. They must be careful to report their whereabouts and keep in touch generally with the Presbytery. They retain their full status as ministers and at any time can accept a call to a vacant parish provided they can produce a Presbyterial Certificate and a Certificate of Eligibility.

(*f*) There are those who demit a charge to take up an appointment not as defined in (*e*) above and in no way connected with their status and training. They also retain their full status as ministers and can accept a call to a vacant parish on production of a Presbyterial Certificate and Certificate of Eligibility. They are under the discipline of the Presbytery within whose bounds they reside, but the Presbytery must be kept informed of their whereabouts.

(*g*) Ministers of the Church of Scotland who wish to stand for election to the House of Commons must, by Civil law, demit status.

The General Administration Committee has recommended :—

(1) That no action be taken with reference to categories (*a*), (*b*), (*c*), (*d*) and (*e*).

(2) That when a minister demits a charge in circumstances which in the judgment of the Presbytery come under category (*f*) the Presbytery will request him to consider demission of status.

(3) That while any appointment is held under categories (*d*) and (*e*) and under (*f*) if demission of status has not taken place, the minister shall be required to report

annually his address and nature of employment to the Presbytery within whose bounds he resides.

(4) That in cases of a teaching appointment which in the judgment of the Presbytery carries an authentic chaplaincy involving a ministry of Word and Sacrament, a service of Introduction by the Presbytery is desirable.

Membership of Presbytery.

(See Chapter VII., p. 141-146.)

SECTION IV. FINANCIAL ARRANGEMENTS ON RETIREMENT.

(For Regulations of the Aged and Infirm Ministers' Fund, see Appendix XXVI., p. 730, and for the Regulations of the Pension Fund see Appendix XXVI., p. 737.)

SECTION V. INSANITY OF A MINISTER.

A. *Ministers admitted to pre-union Church of Scotland Charges before 1st June* 1933.

The following is the clause relating to insane ministers in the statute for removing doubts as to the powers of the Church courts, and for extending their powers (new title, Church of Scotland Courts Act, 1863), commonly known as Lord Belhaven's Act :—

For a Minister insane, Presbytery to appoint an assistant.

" When, in the course of any judicial process affecting the status of a minister, or on the representation of any party having interest, it has been established to the satisfaction of a Presbytery or other superior court of the Church, on a certificate by the sheriff of the county, which he is hereby authorised to grant after due investigation, that the minister of any parish is insane, and thereby disabled from discharging the duties of his office, it is hereby further declared and enacted, that it is and shall be the right of the Presbytery, unless an arrangement for the purposes after mentioned shall have been made on behalf of the said minister to the satisfaction of the Presbytery, to appoint a qualified assistant to perform the duties of the charge until the said minister shall be enabled to resume the same, or until the parish shall be declared vacant, and at the same time to apportion and fix, by their deliverance appointing such assistant, an allowance out of the stipend not exceeding one-half of the whole proceeds of the benefice, and which shall be payable so long as such assistant shall hold and continue to act on his appointment by the Presbytery ; and such deliverance, when duly intimated to the heritors or others liable in payment of the stipend, shall be equivalent to a legal and completed assignation by the minister to such assistant of the portion of the stipend specified in the deliverance so long as the said deliverance shall subsist : Provided, that it shall at all times be competent to such minister to apply to the Presbytery to be restored to the duties of his office on the ground of his recovery, and the Presbytery, on being satisfied that such minister has recovered, shall recall the deliverance, and from the date of such recall all right and interest under the deliverance shall cease and determine."

"A minister without charge who has been appointed qualified assistant in terms of the Church of Scotland Courts Act, 1863, shall be enrolled as a ministerial member of the Presbytery within whose bounds such appointment lies, and shall become interim moderator of the Kirk Session of the parish to which he has been appointed qualified assistant during his tenure of such appointment.

The provisions of Act 1932, xix., anent ministers without charge, shall apply *mutatis mutandis* to such appointments" (1938, v.).

For further information, reference may be made to Mair's *Digest of Church Laws* (4th edition), pp. 347-354.

B. *Ministers admitted to United Free Church Charges before 1st June* 1933.

Procedure in such cases is regulated by U.F.C., 1904, I. of Class I.

This Act is not printed as its provisions do not differ materially from the Act printed in C. below. For the exact terms of the Act, reference may be made to *Practice and Procedure in the United Free Church of Scotland* (1927 edition), pp. 67-68 and 153-154.

C. *Ministers admitted to Charges after 1st June* 1933 (1933, xvi.).

The General Assembly have enacted as follows :—

Act 1933, xvi. 1. When, in the course of any judicial process affecting the status of a minister or on the representation of any party having interest, a Presbytery is satisfied, by evidence laid before it, that the minister of any congregation within its bounds is unable, through mental illness, to discharge his ministerial duties, the Presbytery shall, as of its own authority, appoint an Interim Moderator of Session. The Presbytery shall not be warranted in taking such action except upon the independent certificates of two fully and legally qualified medical practitioners upon soul and conscience.

2. When it appears that such mental incapacity for duty may be regarded as only temporary, the Presbytery shall grant to the minister so incapacitated leave of absence for such time as it may judge expedient, and instruct the interim moderator to take all needful steps for the supply of ordinances and oversight of the congregation. When the expense of pulpit supply is not provided by the Presbytery itself by means of a Sick Supply Fund, or by the friends of the minister or by local parties, the Presbytery shall have power to fix the amount to be paid out of the minister's stipend. The Presbytery may, if it shall see cause, arrange for a temporary appointment.

3. When it appears that no improvement is to be expected, or if, after a year's leave of absence, there be no prospect of early recovery, the Presbytery shall take steps for the appointment of a colleague and successor,[1] or it shall, if deemed more expedient, refer the matter to the General Assembly: and the General Assembly, on such reference from the Presbytery, may grant leave to call a colleague, or may dissolve the pastoral tie, or may do otherwise in the circumstances as they shall deem expedient.

4. When the calling of a colleague and successor is sanctioned, the provision for each colleague shall be determined as in all other cases of colleagueships. When the pastoral tie is dissolved, the General Assembly shall arrange that suitable provision be made for the minister loosed from his charge. The relatives or legal representatives of a minister so incapacitated shall be entitled to be heard before any financial arrangement is approved.

5. The treasurer of the congregation, and the treasurers of any funds of the Church of Scotland, shall obtemper the orders of the Presbytery in the case of temporary financial arrangements (until the same are recalled or altered by a superior court), and shall act upon the directions of the court

[1] See Act VIII., 1946, and p. 157.

sanctioning the calling of a colleague, and fixing the emoluments of each colleague. A duly certified minute of such court shall be sufficient warrant to pay the amounts so appointed, and no treasurer of congregational or church funds so doing shall have any further liability to the minister so incapacitated or to his representatives.

6. In every claim for a grant from the Aged and Infirm Ministers' Fund, or other funds of the Church, and in all references of such cases to the General Assembly, all sources of ministerial income must be fully stated.

7. All grants which may be given in the case of a minister so incapacitated shall be subject to review in the event of the minister recovering his health to such an extent as to undertake ministerial duty or work of a remunerative nature.

8. The provisions of this Act shall apply to all ministers inducted to charges on and after the first day of June nineteen hundred and thirty-three years.

Section VI. Theological Professors.

University Nomination Boards and the Board of Nomination for Church Chairs.

(Reports, 1935, pp. 1147-48 ; 1936, pp. 27-29 ; 1946, p. 477 ; 1950, p. 488.)

Previous to the passing of the Universities (Scotland) Act, 1932, Professors in the University Faculties of Divinity were appointed by (*a*) the Crown, advised by the Secretary of State for Scotland after consultation with appropriate persons in Church and University ; (*b*) the Curators of Patronage (Edinburgh) and the University Court (Glasgow) after similar consultation ; and (*c*) the Synod of Aberdeen, with representatives of the University Senatus.

Professors in the Colleges of the United Free Church of Scotland were appointed by the General Assembly, on nomination by Presbyteries and Synods.

In the Universities (Scotland) Act, 1932, it was enacted with regard to the then existing Chairs in the Faculties of Divinity that the right of appointment to the Chairs should be transferred to the University Courts where that right was not already vested in these Courts, and that the powers previously conferred upon each of the University Courts should include power to make Ordinances " constituting a board of nomination composed of representatives elected in equal numbers by the University Court and by or under the authority of the General Assembly or otherwise in such manner as may be agreed on by the University Court and the General Assembly, and ordaining that a vacancy in any theological chair founded prior to the passing of this Act shall be filled by the appointment by the University Court of a person nominated by the aforesaid board"; and further, with regard to new or Church Chairs, "that appointment thereto shall be made by the University Court on the nomination of the General Assembly or of any Commission, Board, or other body to whom the General Assembly may delegate its power so to nominate."

The appropriate Ordinances having been made by the Universities, the General Assembly have sanctioned the following regulations:—

1. *Church Members on the several University Nomination Boards.*

The General Assembly shall appoint such members on report by its standing Nomination Committee. Members shall be appointed for six years, one member retiring annually from each Board. No member shall be eligible for re-election until after a period of one year, unless, as provided for in the Standing Orders of the General Assembly (No. 113), "there are exceptional circumstances which make re-election desirable."

2. *Method of Nominating Professors to the Chairs to be Provided and Maintained by the Church.*

(*a*) Nominations shall be made by the Board of Nomination set up for this purpose by the General Assembly.

(*b*) On the occurrence of a vacancy in a Church Chair which is not a University Chair, the Board shall make a nomination and shall forward the name agreed upon to the ensuing General Assembly or Commission of Assembly, which, after receiving the report, unless it shall resolve to reject the nomination, shall appoint the nominee to the Chair. The local Presbytery thereafter shall, as the case may require, ordain and induct, or induct, to his office the one so appointed.

3. In the filling of a vacancy in the office of Principal of Trinity College, Glasgow or of Master of Christ's College, Aberdeen the procedure laid down in 2 (*b*) shall be followed.

Vacancies in the University Nomination Boards.

When a vacancy occurs during the year among the Church representatives on any of the University Boards of Nomination (by reason of the resignation, death, or supervening incapacity of any individual member), the Committee on Education for the Ministry, after consultation with the Convener of the Nomination Committee, shall appoint a member to take the place of the member causing the vacancy. If such an appointment is for a longer period than one year, the appointment is to be reported through the Nomination Committee to the first General Assembly for confirmation (Reports, 1936, p. 777, and S.O. 129).

For Draft Agreements between University Courts and General Assembly see Rep. 1950, pp. 488-497. Under these Agreements the University Courts agree to institute ordinances regulating the appointment of Professors to Church Chairs in concurrence with the General Assembly.

CHAPTER XIII.

The Maintenance of the Ministry.

In 1929, when the principal component parts of the broken Church of Scotland were re-united, the General Assembly established the Committee on the Maintenance of the Ministry as one of their Standing Committees. Their remit to it was set forth in the "Basis and Plan of Union" 1929, under the heading "Property and Finance" with the sub-heading "Provision for the Ministry" (pp. 406-409).

While the whole of this part of the Plan of Union may be taken as the remit to the Committee, it is put concisely at its commencement (section I., paragraph 2) which runs: "The function of this Committee will be to carry on the various lines of development and work carried on by the Committees of both Churches."

These lines of development and work run through two main channels, which are (*A*) Endowment Funds, and (*B*) Annual Funds. These are complementary to each other. Each is indispensable and together they make up the Fund for the Maintenance of the Ministry.

Stipend.

Ministers in Scotland receive a stipend, which is not quite the same as a salary, nor is it wages. Before the Reformation the word changed its meaning slightly. At first it denoted the teind stipend only, which was the "spirituality" of the parish, but later it was commonly used to cover also the "temporalities," which included the glebe or glebe rent, any glebe moneys, and other official income of the minister—as, *e.g.*, from kirk lands and local bequests, if any. This was the meaning of the word at the time of the Reformation, but at that time the content was severely reduced. Ministers received only one-third of what the parish priest had received as the spirituality, which third was meant as a merely temporary measure in view of the life interests of the priests, but was never redressed, while practically the whole of the temporalities, except some glebes, were alienated from the Church.

About the middle of the eighteenth century, in consequence of the first secession, a new meaning was added to the word, namely the offerings of the supporters of, and sympathisers with, the ministers of the Secession Church, who had no other maintenance for themselves and their dependants. This source of stipend was destined to increase very greatly. Later new sources of stipend were opened including burgh church stipends, exchequer grants, the statutory stipends of parliamentary and *quoad sacra* parishes, and still later further endowments of one kind or another and many new glebe moneys arising from feus, minerals, &c.

From its beginning the Free Church in many cases had to supplement stipend from the local congregation with a grant from a central fund, and this happened later in the case of the United Presbyterian Church, as well as in the Church of Scotland. It is important to observe that in every one of the Churches these grants from the Church's funds for the purpose were not regarded as part of the stipend of the parish or charge, but as an addition to it. This meaning of the word "stipend" continued in common use in both the uniting Churches up to 1929, and in the modern Kirk of Scotland, in spite of the fact that the phrase "the minimum stipend" was also in common use, and often covered a payment from a central fund that was not properly "stipend" at all.

Recently there has occurred a change of another kind in the use of the word. Right up to modern times stipend has differed from a salary in that whereas a man's salary is his own and should not be subject, and usually is not subject, to deduction of expenses incurred by him in the course of his duty, a minister's stipend was liable for his necessary expenses first and foremost, and only the remainder could be used for the maintenance of himself and his dependants. There were three exceptions to this, the provision of a manse, a glebe, and a communion elements allowance.

The modern development of such exceptions is the conception of "listed expenses," which list includes six kinds of ministerial expense which should be paid by every congregation to, or on behalf of, the minister, and which payments by the congregation are not regarded as payments to his stipend (p. 674). As the listed expenses cover the majority of the necessary expenses of a minister, the old distinction between stipend and salary has more or less disappeared.

For all practical purposes "stipend" is the same as "ministerial income," but when the word is used in Acts of Parliament or of the General Assembly or any legal document, it should be construed in the ordinary sense in which the word was commonly used at the date of the Act or document.

(*A*) The Endowment Funds.

The principal part of the endowments for stipend of the Church of Scotland consists of standardised stipend, which is the modern form of the teinds of Scotland. These originated about the end of the eleventh century, and were the result of the consecration by the landowners of one-tenth of the produce of their lands to sustain a Christian ministry for the people on their estates. The custom spread rapidly, and in a remarkably short time for such a voluntary movement, it covered practically the whole country. Four and a half centuries later, in 1567, an Act of Council described the tenths or teinds as the "proper Patrimonie" of the Kirk, and they continued thereafter with little change for almost three centuries as the main, and almost the only, sustenance of the ministry.

A substantial change, however, in the teinds themselves took place in 1808 when an Act decreed that all victual stipends payable hitherto in kind, were thenceforward to be paid in money at fiars prices. No other change of consequence was made until 1925, when, under the Church of Scotland (Property and Endowments) Act of that year (p. 483), a process was begun of the standardisation of teind stipends. At Martinmas 1974 the last teind stipend was standardised. Under this Act all standardised stipend becomes a "standard charge" on the land "preferable to all other securities or burdens, not incidents of tenure" (1925 Act, section 12 (i.)).

The Act further provided (section 8) that on standardisation the teind stipend would be payable by the heritors no longer to the minister of the parish but to the General Trustees, and it proceeded (section 36) to establish a trust over these moneys in the declaration :—

> "All moneys received by the General Trustees with respect to any parish . . . shall be appropriated in the first place to meeting the proper requirements of that parish

or its neighbourhood (as such requirements may be determined by the General Assembly or by any body to which the General Assembly may delegate the necessary power), and any remainder after these requirements have been fully met shall form part of a general fund at the disposal of the General Assembly."

In this section four terms are used which require elucidation, namely (*a*) delegated body, (*b*) proper requirements, (*c*) parish or its neighbourhood, (*d*) remainders.

The Delegated Body.

The body to whom the General Assembly have delegated under section 36 of the 1925 Act the powers referred to, is the Committee on the Maintenance of the Ministry. This delegation was first made by the General Assembly in 1931, xli. This Act, however, was superseded by 1953, xxvii., which renewed the delegation but in addition laid down procedure to be followed by any interested parties who not only disagreed with, but also were not prepared to accept, a decision by the delegated body, and sought that the case be brought before the supreme court.

Proper Requirements.

The Act leaves the expression " proper requirements " undefined, but it makes clear where the power resides to determine the proper requirements of any parish or its neighbourhood—namely, in the General Assembly or in " any body to which the General Assembly may delegate the necessary power."

So far the General Assembly have not found it either necessary or desirable to take any action towards compiling an official list of what may, or may not, be regarded as " proper requirements " to be met out of the endowment. In one matter, however, the Committee has exercised its power. This concerned the ancient allowance for the provision of communion elements, which was paid by the heritors to the minister out of the teinds in addition to his stipend.

The General Assembly of 1939 noted the General Rule anent

Communion Elements Allowances adopted by the Committee under the powers of 1931, xli., and recorded their approval.

In no case in which the proper requirements of a parish or its neighbourhood have had a monetary value placed on them, either by the General Assembly or by their delegated body, can that determination be regarded as final or unchangeable. The determination is made invariably for the incumbency only. During an incumbency it may be increased, if more money becomes available, but it may not be decreased unless the full amount as at the time of the decision is no longer being received by the fund, or an equal sum from another source is substituted.

On the occurrence of a vacancy in the parish, a change in the determination may be called for. The real question that arises and has to be settled at that time is the proper distribution amongst the necessary congregations within the area of preference, in the light of all the relevant circumstances, of the parochial endowments that have become available.

Parish or its Neighbourhood.

Early in the administration of this trust, the Church found that the term "parish or its neighbourhood" was being interpreted in various ways. An opportunity was accordingly taken of submitting it for their opinion to leading Counsel, Messrs T. Graham Robertson, Q.C., and T. M. Cooper, Q.C., each of whom became subsequently a Judge of the Court of Session. That opinion was submitted to the General Assembly (Reports 1933, p. 994). It ran, "The area in question may be the civil parish, or the parish *quoad omnia*, or an area approximating to these units, for the significant qualification 'or its neighbourhood' absolves the General Assembly from the necessity of the paying exact regard to precise boundaries so long as the area which receives the preference substantially corresponds to the area contributing the funds or endowments to which the preference implies."

This interpretation was accepted by the General Assembly.

Remainders.

The probable intention of the clause that "any remainder after these requirements have been fully met shall form part of a general fund at the disposal of the General Assembly" was to secure the possession of these remainders by the Church. The Committee's practice has been to allocate any remainder to an aid-receiving congregation outwith the area of preference or to more than one such, thereby relieving *pro tanto* the Minimum Stipend Fund.

Other Endowments.

Besides standardised stipend, other endowments include burgh church stipends, exchequer moneys for exchequer grants and the stipends of parliamentary parishes, statutory stipends or initial endowments, further endowments of various kinds and basal endowments. Manse grants are also a form of endowment. Glebes and glebe moneys likewise are parochial endowments for the maintenance of the ministry.

Burgh Church Stipends.

Soon after the Reformation, church extension became necessary, the need being first felt in the growing cities and towns of Scotland. In all of them the City or Burgh Council was constrained to shoulder the responsibilities discharged by the heritors in the *quoad omnia* parishes. They built churches and maintained them, and also provided a stipend for the minister, or ministers, as well as a salary for other functionaries, the precentor, the beadle, doorkeepers, bell-ringers, cleaners and so on. It was a common practice to charge seat rents which were paid to the Corporation or Council in reduction of these expenses. The stipend as a rule was paid from the fund for the common good, but in some cases, including Edinburgh, certain taxes were levied on the citizens for the stipends. In the 1925 Act, Part II., a new body was set up of "Ecclesiastical Commissioners for Scotland," one of whose duties was to consider individually and separately each burgh church and to issue in each case an appropriate Order and Scheme which, *inter alia*, required the city or burgh to redeem the stipend and pay the redemption money to the General Trustees. In 1925 there existed forty-five such churches as enumerated in the ninth schedule to the Act.

Exchequer Moneys.

Under the Teinds Act, 1810, a sum of £10,000 p.a., increased by the Teinds Act, 1824, to £12,000 p.a., was payable out of the Consolidated Fund of the United Kingdom for the purpose of raising stipends of parishes of the Church of Scotland to £150 p.a. with manse and glebe, or to £180 p.a. with manse or glebe, or to £200 p.a. with neither manse nor glebe, in all parishes where the stipend was below these levels. This was the first minimum stipend fund of the Church.

Also under 5, George IV. (1824) cap. 90, there was set aside from the same source the sum of £5,040 p.a. for the payment of the stipends of forty-two of the parliamentary churches and manses enumerated in the tenth schedule to the Act of 1925.

Both these sums of £12,000 p.a., and £5,040 p.a., under Order and Scheme No. 1, dated 21st June 1926, of the Scottish Ecclesiastical Commissioners were redeemed by Parliament and the redemption money transferred to the General Trustees, since when they have been administered by the Church, and the exchequer grants of £12,000 p.a. are governed by special regulations approved by the General Assembly. These regulations were last amended by the General Assembly 1959, Reg. 4.

Statutory Stipends.

The endowment stipends of parliamentary parishes are regarded as the equivalent of the statutory stipends of *quoad sacra* parishes. From 1844 forwards until the 1925 Act became fully operative, practically all the new parishes in Scotland were erected under the provisions of the New Parishes Act, 7 & 8 Vic., cap. 44, after application to the Teind Court. Under this Act over 500 *quoad sacra* parishes were erected. It was necessary to satisfy the Teind Court that a stipend of at least £120 p.a. was provided in perpetuity by an endowment, though at first the endowment might be only £100 p.a., if there was also a manse and appurtenances.

The Teind Court was reluctant to accept as security for the stipend anything other than consols or feu-duties, and as consols were considerably more expensive than feu-duties, the Church in practice was restricted to investing the capital raised for the endowment of stipend in feu-duties.

The normal practice was that one-half of this capital had to be raised by the congregation, which in most cases received substantial help from the Baird Trust, and the other half was provided by the Endowment Committee, which was merged in 1920 into the Committee on Maintenance of the Ministry. The endowment thus provided became known as the "Statutory Endowment" because the necessity for it derived from the New Parishes Statute of 1844.

It was provided in section 34 of the 1925 Act that all statutory properties and endowments be transferred to the General Trustees, and from the time that this provision took effect the whole of the statutory endowments has been payable by the feuars to the General Trustees, and by the General Trustees to the Committee under 1931, xli., now 1953, xxvii., and by the Committee to the ministers as it became due.

After the 1925 Act it was no longer necessary for a church extension charge to apply to the Teind Court for erection into a *quoad sacra* parish, and so it became possible to simplify the procedure, and to ease the heavy financial burdens that lay on every new congregation.

The Committee decided, with the concurrence and co-operation of the Baird Trust, to relieve church extension congregations completely from the heavy cost of the endowment, and since 1930 the arrangement has been that instead of a statutory endowment, each would receive, on reaching a certain stage of development and making application, an original, or initial, endowment amounting to £150 p.a., of which the Committee provides £100 p.a. and the Baird Trust £50 p.a.

The regulations that now govern initial endowment will be found on p. 674, amongst the regulations of the Home Board anent church extension charges.

Further Endowment.

Another form of endowment of stipend that is encouraged and helped by the Committee, and that has superseded what were known formerly either as small living endowments or as additional endowments, is called further endowment. The benefits of this form of endowment are open to every congregation (1) that is recognised both by the Presbytery and by the Church and Ministry Department as a necessary congregation, including the case of a congregation that as soon as the possibility opens will be united with another, and the united congregation likely to be eligible for further endowment, and (2) the stipend of which from all sources does not exceed the limits set out in the regulations. The congregation qualifies for a grant for further endowment by raising new capital for the purpose, which local capital attracts a grant on a sliding scale that has the effect that the congregation with the greatest need gets the greatest help from the fund in respect of the capital raised.

The regulations are to be found at p. 664.

Basal Endowment.

A third form of direct endowment of congregations is restricted not only to necessary congregations in full status as described above under further endowment, but also to those of them that have no stipend endowments or relatively small endowments. Such a congregation would not, however, be regarded as eligible if its stipend exceeded the minimum stipend by £100 or more.

When the funds available for endowment grants appear to be more than sufficient to meet the calls likely to be made upon them in the near future for initial and further endowment and manse grants, the Committee may choose a charge that seems to be eligible for this particular form of endowment. It then ascertains whether its choice would be approved by the Presbytery. The intention in the usual case would be that a new endowment of £150 p.a. for the stipend would be provided.

No regulations have beeen framed to cover this type of endowment, because the initiative must lie with the Committee.

All the endowments described above are held either by the Church of Scotland General Trustees or by the Church of Scotland Trust, and the income is paid by these bodies into the Endowment General Fund and by the Committee to the ministers entitled.

Manse Grants.

The possession of a manse for the minister is a form of parochial endowment, and a congregation, if aid-receiving or just self-supporting, that has no manse and that has never had a manse, may apply to the Committee for a grant to help it either to build or to buy a house as a manse. In the pre-union Church of Scotland that grant did not exceed £400, today, however, the amount is £1,000. Most of the manse grants now made are paid to the National Church Extension Committee and reduce that Committee's expenditure on manses.

The grants are made on condition (1) that in the case of

building by a congregation the plans are approved by the Presbytery and the Church and Manse Building Committee, and in the case of buying by a congregation, the house has been approved by the Presbytery as suitable for a manse, and (2) that the title-deeds contain a stipulation that the manse may not be sold, or alienated otherwise, without the written consent of the Committee, which may impose any condition up to the limit of repayment to it of the manse grant made.

Any application by a congregation for a grant should be submitted in the first instance to the Presbytery for its approval. The form of minute to be endorsed on the title-deeds of a house that has been bought runs :—

> Whereas the Committee on the Maintenance of the Ministry of the Church of Scotland has made a grant of (£...........) sterling towards the purchase price of the subjects contained in the foregoing disposition, it is understood and agreed that in the event of the said subjects being sold, or otherwise disposed of, the amount of the said grant shall, if the said Committee so require, be repaid to the said Committee, and shall be a first charge on the proceeds of sale.

Procedure.

The procedure that has been developed in the Church of Scotland in respect of parochial endowments follows :—

(1) It is the duty of every Presbytery clerk (1932, ix. (2)) to send immediate intimation to the Church and Ministry Department of the occurrence of any vacancy, including a vacancy caused by the Presbytery's acceptance of an application for the appointment of a colleague and successor.

(2) Every vacancy in which any parochial endowments are involved is reported with the relevant information to the first meeting of the stipend sub-committee, which decides the recommendation it will make to the Committee as to whether or not it should raise the question of the future use of the endowments. If, however, the question of union or other readjustment arises, the question regarding the endowments is delayed until the prior question is settled.

This prompt action by the Committee on the occurrence of the vacancy or decision on union may save the Presbytery or a neighbouring congregation the odium it might have incurred if it had opened the question of the future use of the parochial endowments. In cases in which the Committee does not raise that question its action is without prejudice to the right of any other interested party to raise this question, and when that happens the question is considered as carefully and dispassionately as when the question is raised by the Committee. When there is no question of the use of the endowments, and when the question has been raised and settled so far as the vacant congregation is concerned, it proceeds to fill up the copies, with which it has been supplied, of the vacancy schedule, and in particular to enter the proposed stipend for a new minister, the amount to be contributed to that by the congregation, the method of payment, and the proposed annual contribution, if any, in aid to the fund.

(3) When the question of the use of the endowments is raised, the normal procedure is for the Committee to suggest an allocation to the Presbytery. The Committee may or may not adopt the Presbytery's recommendation and occasionally negotiations are prolonged before a decision is reached. Sometimes the case goes by petition to the General Assembly, whose decision is final. (For the procedure in this event see 1953, xxvii., 4, p. 532.)

In considering the use of balances, Presbyteries are not encouraged to undertake this duty until such time as the money has begun, or is about, to be free; except in the case above quoted for the special reason that a colleague and successor should know on his induction what his position in regard to the endowments will be when he succeeds to full charge.

The following points should be kept in mind: (*a*) that every necessary congregation in the area of preference (p. 285) has a valid claim on the parochial endowments, no matter what the stipend may be; (*b*) that a necessary aid-receiving congregation in the area of preference has a first claim on any balance; (*c*) that any allocation to a congregation outwith the area of preference can only be made if the congregation is aid-receiving to the amount of the proposed allocation at that time; it then becomes a legitimate allocation for the incumbency; (*d*) that any allocation outside the area of preference involves the determination as at that time of the proper requirements of the parish from which the endowments come; (*e*) that a balance does not become available for distribution until after an induction to the vacant charge, for up to that date it is vacant stipend; (*f*) that if the vacancy has been caused by death, there may be a prior charge on the balance of the endowments of a grant to a widow or other person near of kin to the deceased minister in lieu of ann of stipend (p. 671); (*g*) that the list of appropriate stipends and contributions is an invaluable guide in this work of allocation; and (*h*) that the Committee has made a rule for its own guidance that it will not approve the breaking up of a balance into small portions and allocating them amongst a number of claimants in token of the validity of their claims, for these token allocations seldom do any real good.

(4) All operative decisions anent parochial endowments are made only by the Committee on the Maintenance of the Ministry at a properly constituted meeting under the powers delegated to it by the General Assembly 1953, xxvii., in accordance with section 36 of the Church of Scotland (Property and Endowments) Act of Parliament, 1925, but any such decision by the delegated body, if the procedure of 1953, xxvii., has been followed, may be reviewed by the General Assembly.

Manse.

A manse is a parochial endowment and the right of a minister to occupy the manse emerges on his admission to the charge. Apart from any special arrangement, such as in a retirement for the sake of union, his right of occupancy terminates at the end of his incumbency. When the incumbency is ended by the death of the minister, his representatives are allowed a reasonable period before they are required to vacate the manse. They should, however, vacate it in time to permit of any repairs, renewals and maintenance work being completed before the admission of a new minister.

Glebe.

The minister's relation to a glebe is different from his relation to the manse. A case arose in which a minister declined to undertake the responsibilities of the glebe. As the charge had a stipend that exceeded the minimum stipend considerably and it was a parish in which there was more than one necessary charge, and no difficulty was experienced in finding another minister willing to undertake these responsibilities, the refusal was accepted by the Committee on the Maintenance of the Ministry, and the glebe with its rent was allocated to another.

The rent of a glebe forms part of the stipend. In many cases there are also glebe moneys, derived from minerals, feu-duties, &c., but it does not necessarily follow that the minister who receives the income from the agricultural glebe receives also the income from any glebe moneys.

The pre-1960 conditions of tenure followed by the additions of 1960 approved by the General Assembly will be found at pp. 668 and 670.

The Endowment Funds.

The actual funds for endowment in the books of the General Treasurer are (1) the Endowment General Fund; (2) the Uninvested Fund available for endowment grants; and (3) the Endowment Vacant Stipend Fund. There is also (4) a Capital Fund and some special funds.

The Endowment General Fund is the account into which is paid the annual income from all the endowments enumerated above and from which that income is paid out to the ministers entitled.

Fund available for Endowment Grants. Into this fund are paid all congregational contributions for endowment together with donations and grants for this purpose. It also receives all legacies destined by the testator for endowment, and a share (meantime £2,500) of the legacies to the Fund for the Maintenance of the Ministry received each year. Manse grants are paid in cash from this fund, but the rest of the free income is transferred as required to the general investment fund of the Church of Scotland Trust, and all other endowment grants are effected by appropriating the amount of capital needed from the sum at the credit of the Committee in that investment fund.

Vacant Stipend Fund. The Churches and Universities (Scotland) Widows' and Orphans' Fund Order Confirmation Act, 1930, 20 and 21 Geo. V., cap. cxxxiv., enacted in section 9 that after the passing of the Act the General Trustees would collect all vacant stipend from endowments, to much of which the Widows' Fund of the Church of Scotland had been entitled, and pay it to the Maintenance of the Ministry Fund. Under the same section the Committee on the Maintenance of the Ministry was bound to pay compensation to the Widows' Fund of £140,000 in forty annual instalments each of £3,500, payable in half-yearly instalments of £1,750 each. This arrangement was accepted by the Committee mainly with a view to assisting congregations, when they fell vacant, to meet their vacancy expenses. The scale on which these vacancy expenses are paid from this fund will be found on p. 666, where the regulations governing these payments are given. The first charge on this fund was the statutory compensation money to the Widows' and Orphans' Fund, but this came to an end at Martinmas 1969. The second charge are the Widows' grants (£150 each) in lieu of ann of stipend but all such are now discharged, and the third charge the vacancy expenses. Any balance is at the disposal of the Committee subject always to the General Assembly.

Special Funds. There are seven special funds, of which the largest by far is the munificent Trust for endowment created by the late Mr F. G. Salvesen, for which there are held investments valued at more than £64,000.

(*B*) The Annual Funds.

The annual funds of the Maintenance of the Ministry form a group made up of (I) The General Fund ; (II) The Minimum Stipend Fund ; and (III) The Supplementary Fund. These will be explained in that order.

Note.—The Commission of the General Assembly (February 1975) having been given powers, approved regulations for centralised payment of all stipends (Reports 1975).

I. The General Fund.

The General Fund and the Minimum Stipend Fund are closely integrated.

Into the General Fund there is paid the bulk of the congregational contributions sent to the General Treasurer for the support of the ministry. For certain purposes the bulk of donations should also be added. Most of these are from members or adherents of congregations who send in their contributions separately.

The congregational contributions to the annual funds for the Maintenance of the Ministry are of two kinds. They include contributions by the congregations to the stipend of its own minister and the contributions by the congregation in aid to the fund, which aid is used by the Committee for the minimum stipend.

Legacies.

An important item in the annual income of the fund is legacies. The practice of the Committee in regard to legacies destined simply to the Maintenance of the Ministry is that all the legacies received in the calendar year are lodged in a Legacy Suspense Account and the total treated at the end of the year as one legacy. From the total there is transferred the sum of £2,500 to the fund available for endowment grants. The whole of the remainder, after being divided into five equal parts, is transferred to the Legacy Distribution Account, and from that account one of the fifth parts of the sum transferred, together with a similar fifth of the legacies of each of the four preceding years, is paid to the ordinary income of the General Fund before its account for the year is closed.

II. The Minimum Stipend Fund (1965, Reg. 5).

By far the largest part of the income of the Minimum Stipend Fund comes from the General Fund, and is the credit balance on that fund at the end of the calendar year.

The aim of the Committee each year is to fix the minimum stipend at a figure that will use up the whole of that year's income. It carries forward from year to year a credit balance, known as the " cushion." This was begun by gradually saving £10,000 when the minimum stipend was £300 ; and when the minimum stipend was £800, it was increased to £15,000. This cushion was originally intended to be simply a protection against the grave possibility of a fall in the minimum stipend, or the possibility of a particular minimum stipend costing the fund more than had been expected ; but in practice, with a rising minimum stipend, it has been a great help in that it has enabled the Committee at times to take a risk that otherwise it might not have taken, and that has been to the advantage of the ministers on the minimum stipend. Nowadays it fulfils another useful function in reducing the debit balance on the Minimum Stipend Fund that accumulates throughout the year.

The Minimum Stipend Fund has certain other sources of income. It includes the interest of over £5,000 on the capital handed over by the Smaller Livings Association, and an annual sum of about £18,000 from the munificent legacy to the Church for its small livings from the late Mr F. G. Salvesen, besides that already mentioned (p. 293) for endowment.

The whole of this income is devoted to the one purpose of the minimum stipend. In order to fulfil its trust, the Committee has to be informed of the stipend from all sources received by every minister in a charge throughout the year or for any part of it. This is done by means of the ministers' "Return of Ministerial Income." Any obscurities having been cleared up, the Committee is in a position to authorise in each case that is eligible the appropriate grant, and all or almost all the payments are made on 31st March. In each case the grant is the sum required to bring the stipend up to a common level. There are, however, certain exceptions authorised and approved by the General Assembly. They are: (1) The special city minimum stipend payable to ministers in city charges who were inducted to their present charge prior to 30th June 1960 (£50 extra—1960, Reg. 6); (2) The special minimum stipend for a minister under whose ministry a union or linking of a congregation has taken place (£150 extra—1959, Reg. 2); (3) The special minimum stipend for a church extension charge (see p. 680); and (4) The special minimum stipend for certain remote districts designated as special areas (£50 extra—1960 Reg. 6).

III. The Supplementary Fund.

The Supplementary Fund was raised by the United Free Church, not for stipend but for purposes ancillary to stipend such as driving grants, removal expenses and the like. It was a capital fund, the income from which was to relieve ministers whose stipend was the minimum or little more and who were hard pressed to meet heavy costs incurred in the way of duty.

In 1960 the General Assembly approved the transfer to the capital of this fund of the invested funds, which amounted to

£3,307, of the Personal Interest Reserve Account, the residue of a fund raised in 1908 to facilitate the combination of the Sustentation and Augmentation Funds of the United Free Church.

Apart from the interest on the Capital above, the responsibilities of this Fund are now met from the General Fund.

CHAPTER XIV.

FURTH OF SCOTLAND.

WHEN opening the chapter with this title in his *Digest of Church Laws*, Dr Mair says: "The territory of the Church of Scotland's jurisdiction is Scotland." The Union of 1929 has made that statement subject to important modification. There are relations in which this Church stands to Churches which carry on their work in other lands, to congregations outside its own borders, as well as to its members and office-bearers sojourning abroad.

The Church of Scotland has many members and adherents living in communities far from the home country—communities which claim and maintain connection with the mother Church. As a mother, she has to make provision for their welfare and to exercise control over them. The measure of this responsibility differs largely according to the growth and circumstances of her offspring. There are, however, certain matters which they share in common, and this fact suggests some observations before the various spheres to which they have gone are considered separately.

Right of Appeal.

Any member of an Overseas Presbytery may dissent and complain to the General Assembly against the judgment of the Presbytery in respect of any matters referred to in sect. 8, 1936, ix. (*vide* p. 641). Notice of any such dissent and complaint, or appeal, must be given to the Overseas Council (1936 ix., sec. 9).

Presbyteries are recommended not to grant ordination to those who go furth of Scotland when their call or other appointment is only for a limited period or when there is insufficient security for their permanent provision. Ordination for those whose curriculum has not entitled them to licence cannot be granted without consent of the General Assembly, or, in certain cases, the Commission of Assembly.

Right to license.

Presbyteries overseas have the right to license those who are adjudged fit in respect of training and character for work within their own bounds; but the status so given is not valid beyond these bounds, and one holding it is not eligible for appointment to office in Scotland unless and until the General Assembly grant the crave of a petition to that effect, submitted through the Committee on Admission of Ministers of Other Churches in accordance with its regulations. Ordination by a Church abroad may be conferred on a licentiate of a Presbytery in Scotland only if he produce an extract of his licence, accompanied by a Presbyterial certificate of character down to the time of his leaving Scotland; but if so ordained, he has all rights and privileges of a minister of the Church. With others than such licentiates the case is different. They have no eligibility for appointments in Scotland—or for service abroad as ministers of the Church of Scotland in full status (see case of Mr Francon Williams, 1932)—until the General Assembly have granted the crave of a petition submitted through the Committee on Admission of Ministers of Other Churches.

Status of licentiate.

Right to ordain.

Status of person ordained.

It is competent for the Assembly's Overseas Council to present a call to missionary service to any minister in a regular charge, and to prosecute the same before the Presbytery of which he is a member (1936, ix., sec. 10 (*b*)). The procedure in transference of a minister from a charge in Scotland to one furth of Scotland, but adhering, though not belonging, to the Church of Scotland, is not by translation but by demission from the former and admission to the latter. When his connection with another Church abroad (not merely with a particular charge therein) ceases, he reverts to the cognisance and jurisdiction of the Church of Scotland. A minister or licentiate of the Church of Scotland, or of either of its pre-union branches, who has undertaken employment which is not under the jurisdiction of the Church of Scotland—as, *e.g.*, in the service of a Church of another denomination—before regaining status as a minister of the Church of Scotland, and eligibility for nomination for appointment to office therein, must satisfy the Overseas Council as to his status, record, and character (Oct. 1929, i.). This does not apply to ministers or licentiates of the Church of Scotland who have held office for a period in the former Presbyterian Church of England. In translations to and from the Church just mentioned the same procedure is followed *mutatis mutandis* as if the respective charges had both been in Scotland (1931, x.). Since 1972 the same principle of mutual eligibility is observed with the Presbyterian Church in Ireland (1972, ii.).

Position of a Minister transferred from a charge in Scotland to one furth of Scotland.

For procedure in the case of missionaries who enter the

Courts of the Church in India or other indigenous Church as full members and thereafter return to the Church of Scotland, see pp. 238, 239.

Section I. England.

Historical. The Presbytery of England owes its origin wholly to the desire of the Scottish people who went across the Border to preserve for themselves and for their children the faith and worship to which they had been accustomed, and who preferred to remain distinct from the Presbyterians of purely English origin. Before the end of the eighteenth century Scottish Presbyteries were to be found in London, Lancashire, Northumberland, and elsewhere, which maintained the traditions of the mother Church, and steadfastly adhered to its constitution. (See minutes of Presbytery of London, 1804.) In 1834 the Presbytery of Lancashire apparently approached the General Assembly for recognition as a Presbytery of the Church of Scotland, and a Committee on Presbyterian Churches in England was appointed, which reported on 1st June 1835. The report, which was adopted, included the following words: "recommend to the several Presbyteries in England, at present in communion with this Church, to form themselves into one or more Synods, as they shall see fit; assuring the said Presbyteries that so soon as the measure recommended shall have been carried into execution, on principles in accordance with the Constitution and Laws of the Church of Scotland, the General Assembly will enter into such communication with them as may distinctly mark their recognition of them as a branch of this Church, and will otherwise promote their interests by all lawful means within their power." The Assembly further resolved "to consider in what manner the difficulties which stand in the way of closer communion with these churches may be removed."

In accordance with this resolution the Synod was formed at Manchester on 4th May 1836, styled "The Synod in England of the Presbyterian Church in connection with the Church of Scotland,"[1] and the General Assembly in the same month recognised it as a branch of this Church to the effect of receiving its ministers into ministerial communion with this

[1] At different periods the Synod has borne varying titles, but is now styled "The Presbytery of England"—("of the Church of Scotland" being understood).

Church. Other Presbyteries united themselves with the Synod, making five in all, and in 1839 the General Assembly expressed "satisfaction at the formation of a Synod as a superior judicatory of the Church in England," resolved that the two Churches should interchange "communications by deputations to and from their respective Supreme Judicatories," and appointed a deputation to attend the Synod and explain the purport of the deliverance, and assure the members of the "affection with which the Church regards the allied Church of which they are the Supreme Court." This deliverance, however, did not fulfil the expectation that the constituent Presbyteries would be recognised by the Assembly as giving to the Synod the status of a court of the Church of Scotland.

The Disruption of 1843 wrought a change. Most of the congregations in the Synod threw in their lot with the Free Church, and renounced connection with the parent Church; but a few maintained their allegiance. Under the direction of the Assembly, which rescinded its decision of 1836, three scattered charges with their ministers and sessions were formed into a Presbytery, "recognised as heretofore as the Scots Presbytery of London" by 1845, xvii. Later, in 1850, two additional Presbyteries, and a Synod, were formed, and in 1866 another brought the number to four, comprising seventeen congregations. To a large extent the Synod was an autonomous body, but it maintained close and intimate relations with the General Assembly through a Committee of Assembly on Correspondence, and was careful to retain the phrase "in connection with the Church of Scotland" in its title. In doctrine, worship, government, and discipline it recognised the same standards, followed the same methods, and was guided by the same rules as the parent Church. Its members were regarded as being in full communion with the Church of Scotland; and its ministers, having been either licensed by the Presbyteries or admitted by the Assembly of that Church, held the full status thereof. Though they were under the jurisdiction of the Synod itself, the judgments of the Synod were recognised by the Church courts in Scotland. This is illustrated by instances quoted in Mair's *Digest*, that of Irving occurring, indeed, in 1833, before the Synod was formed, but a later case, in 1857, being to the same effect.

While actual incorporation of the Synod with the Church of Scotland was not found possible, close relations were maintained. Copies of the title-deeds of property of the churches of the Synod were deposited in the Assembly library.[1] The Committee on Correspondence from time to time received the proceeds of a collection appointed to be made in the churches in Scotland, and expended the money in aiding the congregations in England as might be found expedient; and in other ways the Assembly expressed its unfailing interest in and sympathy with the Synod in all its work. On the other hand, the Synod reported each year by letter and by deputy, and ordered collections for the Foreign Mission work of the Assembly, and otherwise showed its respect and regard for its mother Church. Another sign of the alliance was that the Assembly ordered its chaplains and ministers, when they went to reside in England, to report to the nearest Presbytery, and also instructed them on returning to Scotland to obtain certificates from a Presbytery of the Synod.

Certain disabilities, however, resulted from the impossibility of including the Synod as an integral part of the Church of Scotland. Ministers inducted to its charges, unless they had formerly been inducted to parishes in Scotland, were not eligible to become contributors to the Ministers' Widows' Fund, or to receive benefit from the Aged and Infirm Ministers' Fund, and a minister was unable to become a commissioner to the General Assembly. In 1888 a suggestion that members of the Synod might be allowed to sit in the Assembly without vote in judicial cases, was rejected on constitutional grounds; and in a later year, 1914, the claim of one of its ministers to become a commissioner, in the capacity of an elder sent by a Presbytery in Scotland, was refused, on the ground that, being minister of a charge, he could not competently hold the office of ruling elder.

The Presbytery of the Synod of England now an integral part of the Church of Scotland.

The Union of the Scottish Churches in 1929 and its implications made a great change in the nature of the relation of charges furth of Scotland, and of those belonging to the Synod in England in particular, to the Church as united. In preparation for the Union, the General Assembly in 1927 enacted "that, with the concurrence of the Scottish Synod in England, the congregations embraced in that Synod shall be attached to such Presbyteries as may be determined by the General Assembly" and have "the same status as that which belongs to each such Presbytery." The incorporation was not to take effect until the necessary financial and other implications had been mutually agreed upon by the General Assembly and by the Scottish Synod in England, and finally

[1] These are now missing.

approved by the General Assembly. This method of solving the problem was ultimately not carried out. In 1929 the Assembly enacted and ordained that the Synod should be represented by two ministers and two elders resident within the bounds of the Synod, nominated by the Synod. This, however, not being Presbyterial representation, was superseded by a new Act (v) passed by the Assembly of 1934, the effect of which is to repeal the Act of 1929 (which itself had repealed the Act of 1927), and to provide that the nature and extent of representation shall be similar to that exercised by every other Presbytery of the Church of Scotland—viz.: "The Presbytery of the Synod of England shall return as commissioners to the General Assembly one-fourth (or such portion as the General Assembly may determine) of the ministers on the complete roll, with an equal number of elders, who, if not available within the bounds of the said Presbytery, may be selected from the whole eldership of the Church" (1934, v.). There remained certain questions of funds belonging to the Synod, which have now been finally adjusted. The Presbytery of England is thus an integral part of the Church of Scotland (1934, vi.).

The General Assembly of 1952 passed an Act anent Constituent Presbyteries of the Synod in England as follows :—

1. The three constituent Presbyteries of the former Synod in England in connection with the Church of Scotland—*videlicet*: the Presbytery of the North of England; the Presbytery of the West of England; and the Presbytery of London are hereby dissolved; but this provision is without prejudice to :—

(*a*) the position, status, and functions of the Presbytery of the Synod in England as an integral and constituent Presbytery of the Church of Scotland under the Act of the General Assembly, 1934, vi.; and

(*b*) any acts or proceedings of the said three constituent Presbyteries before such dissolution.

2. The Presbytery of the Synod in England shall hereafter be designed: "The Presbytery of England." (1952, vii.)

In 1957 the Presbytery of England was granted Synodical powers as follows :—

Whereas the Presbytery of England is not within any Synod of the Church of Scotland, and, for the better government of the Church of Scotland in England, it is necessary and desirable that the Presbytery of England should be granted Synodical Powers:

Now therefore the Presbytery of England is hereby authorised to exercise within its bounds, in addition to its jurisdiction and powers as a Presbytery, the jurisdiction and powers of a Synod of the Church of Scotland. (1957, xviii.)

SECTION II. CONTINENTAL AND OVERSEAS (1936, ix.).

For a brief history of the Church's work on the Continent of Europe and Overseas reference may be had to previous editions.

There are two Presbyteries furth of Great Britain—the Presbytery of Europe and the Overseas Presbytery of Jerusalem.

The Churches in the former mission areas abroad are now known as indigenous Churches and they have become independent and self-governing. In their courts the ordained servants of the Church of Scotland may sit by express invitation either as full members or as assessors, with or without a vote as may be determined. On production of commissions their delegates are received by the General Assembly, as corresponding members thereof, and the Church of Scotland in turn maintains fellowship with them by correspondence or by appointment of delegates as opportunity may offer.

Corresponding members of Assembly.

Missionaries at home on furlough, being ministers or elders ordained under the Home Formula or licentiates of the Church of Scotland ordained at a later date by a Church with which the Church of Scotland has a missionary connection through its Overseas Council, whether they be minister or elder of such other Church, or not, who are certified by the Overseas Council under whose auspices they have gone abroad, shall be corresponding members of the General Assembly (S.O. 34).

The appointment of ministers to charges furth of Scotland is made by the Overseas Council.

A decision of the General Assembly to discontinue any such charge or to displace it from the position as a sanctioned charge *ipso facto* terminates the appointment of a minister.

Ministers and missionaries overseas are expected to interest themselves in the life and work of the Presbyterian Church, where such exists.

In the Presbytery of Europe are included the Scots congregations in Amsterdam and Rotterdam. These cases are abnormal. Technically they belong to the Reformed Church of the Netherlands, but their ministers, though as such members of the Dutch Classis, require the status of ministers of the Church of Scotland, and are accordingly reckoned as members of Presbytery.

Any ordained missionary or licentiate of the Church of Scotland who, with the approval of the Overseas Council, enters the courts of an indigenous Church as a full member and becomes subject to the jurisdiction thereof, shall, upon his ceasing to be a member thereof and to be subject to such jurisdiction, be granted by the Committee on Admission of Ministers of Other Churches or its Executive a Certificate of Eligibility for appointment to a charge or other office in the Church of Scotland following satisfactory certification by the Overseas Council to his status, record, and character (Reg. 6, 1965). Cf. p. 238 (13).

Relation of missionaries and ministers furth of Scotland to Aged and Infirm Ministers' Fund and to Widows' Fund.

In respect of a capital sum paid many years ago to the Aged and Infirm Ministers' Fund, a certain number of United Free Church Colonial, Continental, and Jewish missionaries and their successors acquired the right to obtain annuities, if they were otherwise qualified under its regulations. As to the relation of missionaries and ministers furth of Scotland to the Widows' Fund, see pp. 560-567.

Most of the foregoing regulations and remarks apply to missions to the Jews at the various stations where that work is prosecuted. Appointments are made by the Overseas Council, in the first instance for a three years' period, new engagements under fresh conditions extending thereafter for four years. After a maximum of thirty-five years' service the engagement ends without previous notice on either side. Subject to approval by the Council, appointments of subordinate agents, such as teachers, evangelists, &c., may be made by Mission Councils, where such exist.

List of Committee Reports, Relative Assembly Deliverances, and Acts of Assembly bearing upon matters dealt with in this Chapter.

1. Report of Foreign Mission Committee to General Assembly of 1930. Part III., I. 2, Vol. of Reports, p. 695, with Deliverance thereanent, par. 6, page 709.

2. Report of Overseas Consultative Board to General Assembly of 1931. Vol. of Reports, pp. 1047-1063, with Deliverance thereanent, page 1063.

3. Report of Overseas Consultative Board to General Assembly of 1932. Vol. of Reports, pp. 903-905, with Deliverance thereanent, page 905.

4. Report of Overseas Consultative Board to General

Assembly of 1933. Vol. of Reports, pp. 985-986, with Deliverance thereanent, page 986.

5. Act of General Assembly 1931, xxvi., "Overture and Interim Act anent Overseas Presbyteries."

6. Act of General Assembly 1931, xxviii., "Repeal of Act I., 1917, of the General Assembly of the United Free Church of Scotland regarding the Constitution of Mission Councils."

7. Act of General Assembly 1931, xxix., "Act anent ministers accepting appointments overseas and Presbytery membership."

8. Act of General Assembly 1931, xxx., "Act anent regulations for the election of commissioners to the General Assembly by Overseas Presbyteries." (With relative Schedule.)

9. Act of General Assembly 1932, xii., "Act anent repeal of Act x., Church of Scotland General Assembly, 1927" (involving abolition of the appointment of representatives to the General Assembly by the Synod in India).

10. Report of General Administration Committee to G.A., 1934. Vol. of Reports, p. 11, and Appendix A., p. 25, with Deliverance thereanent, p. 67.

11. Act of General Assembly, 1934, vii., anent Overseas Presbyteries.

12. Reports of Special Committee on Overseas Presbyteries to General Assembly (Reports, 1935, pp. 1055-1058, and 1936, pp. 1119-1122).

13. Act of General Assembly, 1936, ix., anent Presbyteries furth of Great Britain.

14. Deliverance of General Assembly, 1951, 3, anent Belize, British Honduras (Rep. p. 475).

15. Deliverance of General Assembly, 1951, 3, anent suppression of Florence, Mentone, Nice and Cannes (Rep. p. 475).

16. Act 1955, xxiv., anent dissolution of Presbytery of Calabar.

17. Act 1952, xv., dissolving Presbytery of Manchuria.

18. 1955. Union of Kenya Churches (Rep., p. 839; 1955, 5).

19. Act 1956, xxii., anent dissolution of Presbytery of Rajputana.

20. Act 1957, xix., authorising change of name of Presbytery of Gold Coast to Presbytery of Ghana.

21. Act 1957, xx., dissolving Presbytery of the Punjab and North-West Frontier Province.

22. Act 1959, xxiii., dissolving Presbytery of Eastern Himalaya.

23. Act 1961, xxv., dissolving Presbytery of Ghana.

24. Act 1961, xxvi., dissolving Presbytery of Blantyre, Nyasaland.

25. Act 1962, xvi., dissolving Presbytery of Bengal.
26. Act 1962, xvii., dissolving Presbytery of Western India.
27. Act 1962, xviii., dissolving Presbytery of Madras.
28. Act 1962, xix., dissolving Presbytery of Jamaica.
29. Act 1962, xx., dissolving Presbytery of South Africa.
30. Act 1963, xvi., dissolving Presbytery of Livingstonia.
31. Act (Oct.) 1963, dissolving Presbytery of Guiana.
32. 1974, Act 1, creating Presbytery of Europe.

Section III. Chaplains to H.M. Forces.

There are chaplains to Her Majesty's Forces, with regard to whom some notes may be useful in this chapter.

Royal Navy.—In the Royal Navy the Church of Scotland and the English Free Churches form one administrative unit. They are under the direction of a Principal Chaplain appointed by the Board of Admiralty on the advice of the Advisory Committee on Naval Chaplaincy Services. The Convener of the Committee on Chaplains to H.M. Forces represents the Church of Scotland on this Admiralty Committee.

Appointment as a naval chaplain is made on the recommendation of the Committee on Chaplains to H.M. Forces to the Principal Chaplain who then nominates the minister to the Admiralty. Appointments are made in the first instance for four years after which a chaplain may be granted a sixteen-year pensionable commission which may, in certain circumstances, be extended until he reaches the age of fifty-five.

A naval chaplain must be prepared to serve ashore or afloat in any part of the world.

The number of chaplains allowed is determined by a census of religious denominations. The present number of chaplains allowed to the Church of Scotland is seven.

Appointments are also made as chaplains of the Royal Naval Reserve. Whilst these are generally with Royal Naval Reserve Divisions in Scotland it is possible that an appointment might be held furth of Scotland and all Reserve Chaplains might, in certain circumstances, be required to serve anywhere with the Royal Navy.

Regular Army.—The establishment of the Royal Army Chaplains' Department is fixed from time to time by the Army Council, and the number of chaplains allocated to each denomination is approximately in proportion to the number of men of the respective denominations serving with the troops.

Appointments are made by the War Office on the recommendation of the Committee on Chaplains to H.M. Forces. In the first instance, the commission is temporary, but, on a vacancy occurring in the permanent establishment, the chaplain receives a permanent commission entitling him to pension and other rights which are fixed by War Office from time to time. The number of commissioned Presbyterian chaplains is, on a peace-time establishment, twenty-one, seventeen of whom are ministers of the Church of Scotland.

Territorial Army.—Though normally chaplains of this class do not come within the scope of the chapter, they may in certain circumstances be required to proceed overseas. The War Office requires all applications for a commission as chaplain in the Territorial Army to receive the approval of the Church authorities. With this in view, the General Assembly in the deliverance on the Report of the Committee on H.M. Forces, 1931, resolved that the consent of the Church authorities to the service abroad of ministers acting as chaplains is to be given by the Committee after obtaining the approval of the Presbytery to which the chaplain belongs (1931, 5).

The Royal Air Force.—The Church of Scotland is represented by one member on the Advisory Board on Chaplaincy Services in the Royal Air Force. Within the Royal Air Force, chaplains of the Presbyterian, Methodist, Baptist and Congregational Churches work as one group, and day-to-day administration and control are in the hands of the Principal Chaplain (P.M.U.B.) at Headquarters. He is chosen from any of these Churches after consultation with the Advisory Board, and acts under the guidance of the Advisory Board members of the several Churches. Appointments to commissions in the Chaplains' Branch of the Royal Air Force are made by the Royal Air Force, but no applicant will be commissioned who is not approved and nominated by his own denomination. The Principal Chaplain accordingly informs the Committee on Chaplains to Her Majesty's Forces of vacancies for Church of Scotland chaplains as such arise, in order that the Committee may select and nominate suitable candidates.

Relation to Presbyteries.

In Act ii., 1970, the General Assembly made the following provisions regarding membership of Presbyteries :—

(*j*) A minister of this Church appointed to a commission as a chaplain to H.M. Forces (i) when serving in Scotland shall be a member of the Presbytery within whose bounds he is serving; (ii) when serving in England or in an area where there is an Overseas Presbytery shall be a member of the Presbytery of England or of the appropriate Overseas Presbytery as the case may be; and (iii) when serving elsewhere shall be a member of the Presbytery to which he belonged at the date of his appointment, or, if he were ordained for the post, of the Presbytery which ordained him.

(*k*) A minister who is a member of a Presbytery in terms of the immediately foregoing section, on relinquishing his commission on grounds of age or infirmity, or on account of having attained the maximum age, or having served the number of years permitted by the appropriate regulations, shall retain his membership of that Presbytery.

For Regulations for Service of Introduction of a chaplain, see p. 570.

Kirk Sessions in Units of H.M. Forces.

Act anent the institution of Kirk Sessions in Scottish Units of Her Majesty's Forces (1952, viii.).

1. Where members of the Church of Scotland serving in any embodied unit of Her Majesty's Forces desire authority for the constitution of a Services Kirk Session in their unit, they may apply to the Committee on Chaplains to Her Majesty's Forces requesting the Committee to take steps to that effect.

2. On receiving any such application, the Committee shall first satisfy itself—

(i) that the unit in question comprises a sufficient number of persons who are or may desire to become members of the Church of Scotland;

(ii) that a Services Kirk Session, if constituted in that unit, would have a reasonable prospect of continuing in existence for a material period; and

(iii) that the application has the approval of the Church of Scotland chaplain concerned and of the Commanding Officer of the unit;

and, if satisfied of these matters, may take steps to authorise the constitution of a Services Kirk Session in the unit.

3. A Services Kirk Session shall consist of the Church of Scotland chaplain of the unit, or failing him, of any other

Church of Scotland chaplain, as moderator, and also of not less than two duly ordained elders of the Church of Scotland who are members of the unit. Nothing herein contained shall prevent a Church of Scotland chaplain from acting as moderator of more than one Services Kirk Session.

4. Notwithstanding the foregoing provisions, for the purpose of enabling a Services Kirk Session to be constituted in any unit of Her Majesty's Forces where there is available no, or only one, duly ordained elder of the Church of Scotland, the Committee on Chaplains to Her Majesty's Forces shall appoint as assessors not less than three duly ordained elders, and any of these elders may act along with the Church of Scotland chaplain of the unit, or failing him, any other Church of Scotland chaplain, and any elder in the unit, as an interim Services Kirk Session for that unit to enable the election, ordination, and admission to the eldership of a sufficient numbers of members of the Church of Scotland in the unit to constitute a Services Kirk Session as provided for by section 3; and, in any such case, the ordination and admission of the said elders shall be conducted by such chaplain with any available elders in the unit, after approval of the election has been given by the said assessors as well as by the said chaplain and any available elders in the unit.

5. Before any Services Kirk Session, or interim Services Kirk Session, is constituted, it shall first be authorised by the Committee on Chaplains to Her Majesty's Forces.

6. A Services Kirk Session may itself elect further elders when an addition to its numbers is considered necessary. Any elder so elected shall be a member of the Church of Scotland and also a member of the unit.

7. The ordination and admission of an elder to office in a Services Kirk Session shall take place at a diet of public worship.

8. Intimation by edict in common form of the election of any person as elder by a Services Kirk Session or Interim Services Kirk Session shall not be necessary, but it shall be the duty of any Chaplain, before ordaining or admitting any such person to office as elder in such Kirk Session, to take all steps reasonable and practicable in the circumstances to satisfy himself that no objection exists to such person's life or doctrine, and, in discharging this duty, the chaplain shall consult with any available elder.

9. Each Services Kirk Session shall be associated with a Presbytery of the Church of Scotland. Where the unit has a

depot in Scotland the Services Kirk Session of that unit may elect to be placed on the roll of the Presbytery of the bounds. In other cases, the Services Kirk Session shall be placed on the roll of the Presbytery of Edinburgh.

10. The placing of a Services Kirk Session on the roll of a particular Presbytery shall not affect the existing membership of Presbytery of any Chaplain to His Majesty's Forces.

11. The Committee on Chaplains to Her Majesty's Forces shall keep a Register of Services Kirk Sessions authorised by the Committee.

12. The Committee on Chaplains to Her Majesty's Forces shall report each year to the General Assembly on the state of its Register of Services Kirk Sessions.

Regulations for the Institution and Maintenance of Registers of Baptisms and Admissions to Holy Communion in the Forces of the Crown (1970, Reg. 7).

1. The Committee on Chaplains to Her Majesty's Forces (hereinafter in these Regulations referred to as " the Committee ") shall institute and maintain a Register of Baptisms (hereinafter in these Regulations referred to as " the Forces Register of Baptisms ") and shall record therein the names of all Church of Scotland personnel or the wives and families of such personnel baptised by chaplains serving in Her Majesty's Forces ministering to Church of Scotland personnel.

2. The Committee shall institute and maintain a Register of Admissions to Holy Communion (hereinafter in these Regulations referred to as " the Forces Register ") and shall record therein the names of all Church of Scotland personnel or the wives and families of such personnel who after due preparation have been admitted to Holy Communion by chaplains serving in Her Majesty's Forces ministering to Church of Scotland personnel.

3. The Committee shall on request issue Certificates of Baptism or Certificates of Admission to Holy Communion in accordance with the Registers. On receipt of a Certificate of Admission to Holy Communion a parish minister may without further instruction or preparation and by resolution of the Kirk Session add the name of the person to whom the Certificate relates to his Congregational Roll.

4. Kirk Sessions at the annual review of their Communion Rolls should not remove therefrom the names of persons who

by reason of service in the Forces of the Crown may be absent from their congregations for a number of years, but should either retain the names of such persons on the Communion Roll of their own congregations or transfer them to the Forces Register. Notice of such transfer shall, if possible, be given by the Kirk Session to the person concerned.

5. When a member leaves his congregation to serve in the Forces of the Crown the minister of the congregation to which he belongs shall if so desired issue to him a letter certifying that he is in full Communion with the Church of Scotland so that such member may present such letter to the chaplain of the unit or establishment which he joins or in which he may serve from time to time.

6. The form of the Registers to be kept by the Committee as aforesaid, the procedure to be adopted in the maintenance thereof and the form of the certificates to be issued in connection therewith shall be such as may be agreed from time to time by the Committee in consultation with the General Administration Committee and the senior chaplains and may be varied from time to time in the light of experience.

7. The Committee shall report each year to the General Assembly the number of persons added to the Forces Register of Baptisms, distinguishing between adult baptisms and infant baptisms, and the number of persons added to the Forces Register, distinguishing between those added by transfer from Congregational Rolls and those admitted to Holy Communion for the first time.

Sundry Matters.

Marriage.—For regulations as to banns and as to marriage of persons coming to Scotland or leaving Scotland to be married abroad, see pp. 65-69. Full information is given in the revised manual entitled *Marriage in Scotland*; obtainable at Church of Scotland Offices, Edinburgh, and Book Depots of Committee on Publications in Glasgow, Aberdeen, and Dundee.

Admission of Ministers and Licentiates of Other Churches.—See pp. 234-240.

Ministers and Licentiates called to Charges Abroad.—See p. 304.

Transference of Members and Adherents.—The General Assembly have given instructions that ministers and Kirk

Sessions should provide communicants with Certificates of Transference when leaving, or immediately after leaving, the parish (1938, vi.) for immediate presentation to ministers when they take up residence. The General Assembly have urged ministers and session clerks, when members have gone abroad, to notify the Overseas Council of the name and overseas address. The Overseas Council endeavours to inform the Churches and ministers in the particular overseas area to which the member has gone.

Widows' Fund.—Commissioned Chaplains are eligible to be contributors to the Widows' and Orphans' Fund in the same way as parish ministers (Widows' and Orphans' Fund Order Confirmation Act, 1954).

CHAPTER XV.

DISCIPLINE.[1]

SECTION I. GENERAL PRINCIPLES AND CENSURES (see Oct. 2, 1929, i.; 1935, vii.; 1960, xxii.; App. XXII. and XXIII., pp. 646-657).

DISCIPLINE in the government of the Church is of scriptural authority. The ends contemplated by it are the glory of God, the purity of the Church, and the spiritual benefit of members. It is to be administered in faithfulness, meekness, love, and tenderness.

Discipline consists in the administration of the appropriate censures of the Church to those whose conduct shall have given occasion for it.

Nothing is to be admitted as the ground of a process for censure but what is declared censurable by the Word of God, or by some Act or universal custom of the Church.

The subjects of discipline are those who hold office in the Church, communicants, and baptised persons who are adherents.

Censures. The censures of the Church are admonition, rebuke, suspension, deposition from office, and excommunication, and they are administered only on confession or proof of sin or of offence.

Admonition. Admonition consists in addressing the offender, placing his sin or offence before him, and exhorting him to greater rectitude. In the case of a minister or a probationer this is done in the Presbytery or the Synod or the General Assembly; in other cases, in or by authority of the Session or other court; and in each case by the moderator of the court. Private admonition, which is not a judicial censure, may in certain cases meet the ends of discipline.

Rebuke. Rebuke, which is always accompanied with admonition, is a severer form of censure involving reproof.

Suspension from full Communion. Suspension from full communion, as a censure, is a temporary exclusion from the privileges of sealing ordinances and other rights of membership. Suspension may or may not be for a specified period, and is removed as soon as sufficient

[1] *Note.*—For Form of Process, see Mair, pp. 547-573.

cause for its removal appears. This is to be distinguished from suspension during the investigation of a charge, which is not to be considered as of the nature of a censure at all.

Suspension from office, as a censure, debars from the privileges and duties of the office. It is either for a specified period or *sine die*. In neither case is it removed until sufficient cause appear for doing so, and in the former case it is not removed before the expiry of the period specified. Suspension of an office-bearer from the privilege of full communion is uniformly accompanied with suspension from office, but there may be cases in which the latter is expedient, while no sufficient grounds exist for the former. In the case of a minister suspension from office may be, and suspension *sine die* is, accompanied by removal from his charge. Suspension from the office of the holy ministry means that the suspended minister is debarred from discharging any of the functions of the ministry, including the conduct of public worship. Suspension from Office.

Deposition consists in depriving an office-bearer of the office with which he is invested, and is resorted to only in very serious cases. Deposition.

Excommunication or exclusion from the fellowship of the Church is resorted to only in cases of peculiar aggravation, when all other means of reclaiming the offender have failed, and when he continues impenitent and contumacious. Excommunication.

The proceedings or judgment of a civil court, as in a suit for damages involving immoral conduct, can be no substitute for due process in a Church court, but may occasionally aid in determining whether to enter on a process. In discipline Church courts form their own judgments independently of proceedings in other courts. Civil and Church Courts.

The courts have power to summon any persons within their bounds as party, witness, or otherwise, and to examine them, and to determine in cases orderly brought before them (1707, xi.). Courts' powers.

SECTION II. RECORD OF PROCEEDINGS (see Oct. 2, 1929, i.).

To keep the ordinary records (of the courts) free from the presence of undesirable matter, and to obviate their mutilation by the deletion of the proceedings, Kirk Sessions may, in cases which ordinarily come before them involving communicants or baptised persons who are adherents, use a Minute-book of Discipline. In all other cases where moral delinquency is alleged the court of first instance shall resolve Minute-book of Discipline. Record Apart.

to keep the proceedings of the case in a record apart, and this resolution shall be minuted in the record apart and not in the ordinary record.

When the judgment which finally disposes of the case, by whatever court of the Church pronounced, involves any degree of censure of the accused, then the court of first instance shall engross in its ordinary minute-book the first minute of the record apart, the libel, or a summary of each of the charges thereof, if a libel had been served, and the final judgment.

When a case has ended in entire acquittal, if there be a record apart in any court inferior to the General Assembly, it shall, with all papers in the case, so far as these do not affect the interests of third parties, be sealed up in presence of the court, docqueted with the name of the congregation and the date of final judgment, and kept *in retentis* for five years and thereafter destroyed.

When a case has ended in entire acquittal, the person whose innocence has been established ought to have a certified copy of the judgment of the court delivered to him.

Inventory of Process.

In every case the courts inferior to the General Assembly shall keep an inventory of process in which the clerk shall enter and number all the documents.

Right of access to productions.

Persons accused have the right of access to any productions in the case which are in the possession of the court.

Counsel or Agents.

Parties may appear by, or have the assistance of, counsel or agents in any process depending before the Presbytery or any higher court, unless such court shall otherwise determine. They shall not be entitled to have such assistance in any process depending before a Kirk Session, except with the special permission of the Kirk Session. Any parties appearing by counsel or agents shall not be entitled to be heard themselves.

Section III. Procedure Common to Kirk Sessions and Presbyteries as Courts of First Instance.

Where any charge is made against any person in a Church judicatory, whether by information, petition, or otherwise, the court must in the first place consider whether it be proper for it to entertain the matter or to prepare it for a superior court. All courts should endeavour to shorten their work as much as is possible consistently with the performance of their duty and the edification of the Church (1707, xi.).

Fama.

"There seems to be no need of accusers or informers in

ecclesiastical process." If a *fama* be rife, the Kirk Session or the Presbytery may take the matter up (1707, xi.).

Sometimes it is advisable that a party under or suspected of a scandal should be privately spoken to before he is cited to appear before a Church court (1707, xi.).

In all cases before a Church court where any party or parties are concerned the court must ensure that the parties are duly cited to appear before the court (1707, xi.). **Parties to be duly cited.**

The various methods of citation are as follows:— **Methods of citation.**

Personal.—By the delivery of a written citation to the person concerned (accused or witness) by a person authorised by the court.

At the dwelling-place.—By delivery at the dwelling-place of the person concerned of a written citation by a person authorised by the court.

By registered post or recorded delivery service, a letter posted to the last known address of the person concerned containing a schedule of citation subjoined to the service copy of the writ; or, in the case of a witness, a citation.

The execution of citation must be returned to the court by the person effecting the citation.

Apud acta is citation of the person concerned by the court in its presence. The minute is proof of it.

Edictal citation is citation by public intimation and is used only for citing a body or bodies, or for citing a minister who has absconded. In this case the execution is written on the citation.

A superior court cites an inferior court to its bar by sending an extract resolution to that effect to the moderator and clerk. If either be present, though not at the bar, his court may be cited through him from the chair (1893, 2).

In cases before the Kirk Session, if pastoral dealing fail to bring about voluntary compearance, an ordinary registered or recorded delivery letter may be sent to the accused, stating that, unless he make known to the minister within a specified time that he is willing to submit to discipline, he will be suspended from the privileges of the Church till such submission is made.

If a minister or probationer served with a libel intend to lead evidence in his defence, he must lodge with the clerk or joint-clerks of Presbytery a list of his witnesses and his productions within twenty-one days from the service of the libel. If he have a special defence, he must within the same number of days lodge with the said clerk or clerks a notice thereof along with a list of witnesses and productions (1935, vii.).

Forty-eight hours, if within the parish, is the *induciæ* in the citation of a person cited to attend the meeting of a court.

Execution of citation.

Execution of citation is a certificate, stating that the writ (whatever it may be) has been served, given by the official who has served it.

Failure to appear.

If the party cited do not appear, a second and a third citation should be given by order of the court, either personally or at the dwelling-house, before the party is declared contumacious. If the party has already appeared before an inferior court and has been cited *apud acta*, or has been declared contumacious, there is no need of more than one citation to appear before a superior court, if the matter be brought there by appeal or by reference (1707, xi.).

Contumacy.

All citations *apud acta* are peremptory, and, if instructed, infer contumacy if not obeyed (1707, xi.).

Evidence anent truth of scandal.

If the party do not appear on the third citation, or upon a citation *apud acta*, and no relevant excuse be adduced and verified, though in such case he may be censurable for contumacy, yet the court may proceed to consider evidence either from witnesses or from writ, regarding the truth of the scandal alleged against the accused, before proceeding to censure him for contumacy (1707, xi.).

Essential for Censure. Contempt.

A fault cannot be visited with judicial censure unless it has been confessed to the court or regularly proven. Only contempt of court committed in presence of the court may be dealt with on the spot.

Names of witnesses to be supplied if desired.

If the party appear, then the moderator is to inform him of the reason why he is called before the court, and shall give him, if desired, a short written statement thereof with the names of the witnesses (if these names have not been previously given to him) who are to give evidence regarding the charge (1707, xi.).

Citation of witnesses.

Witnesses should be cited, and if, after three citations, they refuse to appear, they may be dealt with as contumacious (1707, xi.) or, if desired, application may be made to the civil courts for a warrant ordaining them to appear (*Presbytery of Lewis* v. *Fraser*, C.S. (1874) 1 R. 888).

Relevancy of charge.

Before a proof is allowed, the accused should be summoned before the court and the relevancy of the charge against him discussed. The accused may object to the relevancy of the charge (1707, xi.). If the charge be found not relevant, it is dismissed.

If the charge be found relevant, it may then be decided to proceed to proof. The accused is entitled to be present at the proof. Proof.

In the Presbytery the accused is entitled to be present at every stage of the proceedings, beginning with the preliminary inquiry.

If the accused propone a defence to the charge against him, the relevancy of his defence is to be considered, and, if found relevant, he is entitled to a warrant from the moderator and the clerk to cite witnesses to support his defence at his own expense. Defence.

If witnesses cannot subscribe their names to their depositions, the clerk is to mark that they declare they cannot write. The moderator is to subscribe all depositions, whether the witnesses can subscribe or not (1707, xi.). Depositions.

A Presbytery or higher court may appoint the evidence led before it to be taken down by a shorthand writer, to whom they administer the oath *de fideli*. The shorthand record is written or typed out in full by the shorthand writer, and when certified by the moderator and clerk is held to be the record of the evidence (Church of Scotland Courts Act, 1863, sec. 4). Evidence may be taken by a shorthand writer.

After the evidence for both sides has been led and parties have addressed the court, the parties are removed and the court proceeds to discuss its judgment.

Section IV. Cases in which the Kirk Session is the Court of First Instance.

In the case of elders, deacons, communicants, and baptised persons who are adherents, the Kirk Session is the court of first instance.

When a person in any of the above classes is under scandal and refuses to submit to discipline, notwithstanding such pastoral dealing as appears to the Kirk Session sufficient, the Kirk Session may, instead of formal citation, intimate to him by registered or recorded delivery letter by its clerk that, unless within thirty days he shall make known his willingness to submit to discipline (or if the charge be denied, to discipline or trial), he will be suspended from privileges till such submission is made and disposed of, or till the Kirk Session is otherwise satisfied (Oct. 1929, i.).

When an accused person has made known his willingness to submit to discipline, the Kirk Session may remit the case to the moderator alone, or to the moderator and one of Case may be remitted.

the elders, to deal with the accused and report to the Kirk Session, which may then dispose finally of the case (Oct. 1929, i.).

It is not competent for a Kirk Session to follow any procedure other than that prescribed by the Form of Process in its original form or as modified by subsequent Acts.

Gross Scandal. When information concerning gross scandal comes before the Kirk Session, it is to consider it according to the rules prescribed for it, and, if it find good grounds for a process, it is to deal with the person accused to confess.

Confession. If confession be made, the Kirk Session refers the case, and sends an extract of their procedure, to the Presbytery (1707, xi.).

When no confession is made, the Kirk Session is not to proceed to hear proof till an account of the matter be brought by reference to the Presbytery, and the Presbytery thereupon appoints the Session to proceed with proof. After proof has been led, it shall be brought before the Presbytery, which may inflict what censure it may see fit (1707, xi.).

Kirk Sessions shall afford facilities for the transference of cases from one Kirk Session to another, when this would be for the convenience of parties and Kirk Sessions (Oct. 1929, i.).

Section V. Procedure before Presbytery as a Court of First Instance.

Preliminary Inquiry. When a *fama* has arisen against a minister or a probationer, who is subject to the jurisdiction of a Presbytery, it shall be the duty of the Presbytery to institute a preliminary inquiry (1935, vii.).

Jurisdiction. All processes against a minister or probationer begin before the Presbytery to which he belongs.

Example. It was stated in the Assembly that, on the previous day, an intoxicated minister had attempted to enter the Hall, and had been in the same condition in the streets. A Committee was appointed to inquire and report. The minister being found to be present was called to the bar, and cited *apud acta* to appear at an appointed time. At that time the convener of the Committee, having reported, moved that the minister be heard at the bar. This done, the Assembly transmitted the precognitions taken by the Committee to his Presbytery (Skye) with instructions to libel, and to apply to the Presbytery of Edinburgh to examine witnesses within its bounds, or who from their distance could not be expected to appear before the

Presbytery of Skye, and to report to the commission, which it empowered to dispose of the case. The Assembly also appointed the Presbytery to meet on a certain day to serve the libel, and cited the minister *apud acta* to appear before that meeting (1838, *ult.*).

Caution necessary.

Since a scandal against a minister (or probationer), even though groundless, is not easily wiped off, a Presbytery should consider well by whose information and complaint it comes before it, and it is not to cite or begin a process except (1) some reliable person either (*a*) in writing subscribed by him, or (*b*) orally, in presence of the Presbytery, give in a complaint with some account of its probability, and undertake by sufficient evidence to make good a libel; or (2) there be a *fama clamosa* so great that the Presbytery for its own vindication finds it necessary to begin the process without an accuser (1935, vii.). In the last-mentioned case it should first carefully inquire into the rise, occasion, broachers, and grounds of the *fama clamosa* (1707, xi.).

Duty and Privilege in Presbytery.

It is the duty of the Presbytery to attend to a *fama* of a serious kind against a minister or probationer. A member of Presbytery has a duty and right to inform the Presbytery, if he should know, or have information, of an offence committed by another member, and is therefore protected in doing so (*A*. v. *B*., C.S. (1895) 22 R 984).

The protection afforded to a witness in the witness-box extends to him under precognition (*Watson* v. *McEwan*, H.L. (1905) 7 F (H.L.) 109).

Revival of Scandal.

If a scandal have subsided and lain dormant for a period of five years, it should not be revived nor be the subject of consideration and discussion except in very exceptional circumstances (1935, vii.).

Confession.

If the accused confess, and the matter confessed be of a scandalous nature, censurable in others, such as the sin of uncleanness, or some other gross scandal (whatever be the nature of his penitence, though all be convinced of it), the Presbytery is *instanter* to depose him *ab officio* (1707, xi.). A probationer in such circumstances is deprived of his licence.

Failure to appear when cited.

If the accused be cited to appear before his own Presbytery, and absent himself by leaving the place and be contumacious, without making any relevant excuse, after a new public citation and intimation made at his own church when the congregation is met, he is to be holden as confessed, and to be deposed and censured *instanter* with the lesser excommunication, but, if after some time he do not return and subject himself to the censures of the Church, he may be proceeded against till he be censured with the greater excommunication, if the Court see cause for it (1707, xi.).

Trial by Libel.

If the offence be denied, and after a preliminary inquiry there still appear ground for investigation, the Presbytery shall proceed to a trial by libel (1935, vii.).

Record apart.

In all cases of libel a record apart shall be required (1935, vii.).

General Assembly's Committee on Law, &c.

If called upon by the Presbytery to do so, the General Assembly's Committee on Law, Property Cases, and Discipline is, if it think fit, entitled to afford all help in its power in cases of trial by libel or itself to undertake the conduct of the case if it shall so decide.

The General Assembly appoints annually a Board of Assessors whose names are available for selection by Presbyteries or Synods to assist in the conduct of trials by libel and who act as members of the court to which they are appointed. When requested by any Presbytery to do so, the Committee on Law, Property Cases, and Discipline appoints two of the members of the Board of Assessors to deal with any case unless the Committee has either advised upon the case or itself undertaken the conduct of the same, in which event the appointment of assessors is made by the General Administration Committee.

The Committee on Law, Property Cases, and Discipline is not bound either to advise or to enter upon the conduct of any case, and it is entitled to withdraw from the conduct of any case, if entered upon, at any time. Presbyteries may enter upon, sist themselves to, or depart from any process without reference to the Committee, and may proceed notwithstanding the withdrawal of the Committee.

If it be decided to proceed to trial by libel, the libel is prepared by the Presbytery, or by any person or persons appointed by the Presbytery for that purpose, and, before service, the libel is revised by the Procurator for the Church. A certified copy of the libel is served upon the accused along with a list of the witnesses to be called by or on behalf of the Presbytery, and of the productions to be made on its behalf.

Presbytery may commit the trial to a Committee.

After the libel has been adjusted and signed, the Presbytery may commit the whole conduct of the trial to a Committee of its number, consisting of not less than three nor more than five of its members, with the addition, if desired by the Presbytery, of two members of the Board of Assessors.

The accused is entitled to lodge a notice of a special defence (*e.g.*, *alibi*, insanity, bodily infirmity, &c., at the time of the offence charged) within twenty-one days from the date of the service of the libel upon him. If the accused desire to lead evidence in his defence, he must lodge a list of the witnesses to be called for him and also a list of productions to be made on his behalf along with the notice of special defence if lodged. If no notice of special defence be lodged, the list of witnesses and productions must nevertheless be lodged within twenty-one days after the date of service of the libel.

Special defence.

Lists of Witnesses and of productions.

After the service of the libel and the expiry of the days within which notice of a special defence falls to be lodged, the Presbytery (or the Committee if the Presbytery has appointed a Committee for the purpose of conducting the trial) fixes a date for the first sitting of the court. Not less than seven clear days' notice of such sitting must be given to the accused.

The first question that the court must decide is the relevancy of the libel—that is, whether the offences charged are censurable offences in the eye of the law, for, if they be not, it would be useless to investigate whether the accused had committed them.

Relevancy of Libel.

Sometimes the question of relevancy is the laborious part of the case; sometimes the question whether the accused committed the offence which has been found relevant. For example, drunkenness is so obviously a censurable offence that finding relevancy is little more than a form: the burden of the case lies in proving that it took place. On the other hand, in the case of doctrine to find that the statement libelled is a censurable offence is to find it to be error, and this may be the burden of the case: the subsequent step of proving that the statement was made by the accused is generally little more than a form, for this is usually admitted or is beyond dispute.

A Presbytery after citation *apud acta* found relevancy in absence, appointed next meeting for probation, and cited the accused to attend. He did so, and gave his excuse for former absence. Finding it unsatisfactory, the Presbytery resolved to deal with him for this at next meeting, and cited him *apud acta*. At this meeting it resolved to depose him for contumacy. On appeal, the Assembly ordered it to proceed to probation of the libel (1850, 8). It had not only found relevancy and resolved on probation, but his presence afterwards shows that his contumacy must have been very mild. The case would have been unworthy of notice, had not others referred to it without showing its character.

With-drawal of Libel.

The Presbytery may not allow libellers to withdraw a libel that has been served and present another, but it may dismiss or discharge it, and receive another (1805, 8). Libellers may not withdraw a libel which has been found relevant (1805, ult.). A Presbytery may withdraw its libel, and the parishioners present one in its place (1812, 8). Where the sentence of a Presbytery is null because of its illegal procedure, the Presbytery or others are at liberty to proceed *de novo*, if so advised (1843, ult.).

Amend-ment of Libel.

Libellers may be allowed to amend vague charges in a libel, by giving a particular condescendence of the special offences, or to present a new libel, the first having been discharged. An additional libel based on matters unknown when the first was served is competent.

Irrele-vant portion of Libel.

If the libel be irrelevant, it is dismissed. An irrelevant portion of the libel may be struck out, if this can be done without altering the nature of the charge.

Failure to appear.

If the accused do not appear before the court after three citations, or one citation *apud acta*, he may be treated as contumacious.

Proof.

If the libel be found relevant, and no appeal be taken, the case proceeds to proof. In such a case the court has the right to enjoin the accused to abstain from the exercise of all the functions of his office till the libel is disposed of. In certain cases provision may be made for providing ordinances by the Maintenance of the Ministry Committee (1931, xix.).

Evidence in support of the charge is first led, and thereafter the accused is entitled to lead evidence in his defence.

All the charges in the libel served must be disposed of; when the libel is at the instance of the Presbytery, it must lead proof on all the charges that are denied (1870, 14).

At the proof each party is entitled to cross-examine the witnesses adduced by the others; then follows re-examination on new matter raised in cross; and at the conclusion of each witness's evidence questions, allowed by the court, may be put to the witness through the moderator.

Evidence to be recorded in full.

The evidence shall be taken down in shorthand and recorded in full.

Sentence.

If the Presbytery shall itself have heard the case and the evidence, it delivers judgment forthwith.

When case is heard by a Committee of Presbytery.

If the case has been heard by a Committee appointed by the Presbytery, the Committee reports its findings on the whole matter, including its findings on the facts, but it is not obliged to do so immediately after the proof or hearing. It may intimate that it will take time to consider its findings.

The findings of the Committee on the facts, if unanimous, are final as regards the Presbytery, and not subject to reversal or alteration by that body. The Committee's report must (1) embrace the Committee's decision on the whole subject-matter of the libel, and (2) state whether the findings are unanimous, and, if not unanimous, the state of the vote. The Presbytery may resolve either to decide in terms of the findings of the majority of the Committee or to appoint the evidence to be printed and of new to hear parties thereon. As soon as practicable thereafter the Presbytery considers the report. It may either (*a*) adopt the report and agree with the decision of the Committee; (*b*) alter and amend the decision of the Committee, if not unanimous, on the subject-matter of the cause or any legal question involved; or (*c*) set aside the decision of the Committee and issue an independent judgment. If the judgment of the Presbytery be against the accused, the Presbytery determines the appropriate censure and directs what steps are to be taken for carrying the censure into effect.

Sentence in absence. Sentence in absence is competent in any court. The defender ought, of course, to be called at the door three times—the assumption being that sentence is addressed to him.

The Presbytery ought not to sist process because of an appeal against a decision of "Proven." Its duty is to proceed to the end, resolving on the sentence. An appeal against this latter resolution sists its execution. It should be noted that, where the trial is concerned with doctrinal error only, an appeal against a judgment on relevancy sists procedure (1835, xi.).

All cases proceed in name of Presbytery (or Synod). All cases undertaken by the General Assembly's Committee proceed in the name of the Presbytery (or the Synod) on whose behalf the Committee is acting, and counsel and agents employed by the Committee shall be treated as acting for the Presbytery (or the Synod) for which the Committee is acting (1935, vii.).

When not competent for an Assessor to take part in the judgment. It is not competent for any assessor appointed to act on a panel to take part in the judgment in any case which has been dealt with by such assessor in a lower court and is being prosecuted before a higher court of which he is also a member (1935, vii.).

Deposition. Deposition from office does not *ipso facto* suspend from Church privileges.

A deposed minister cannot hold the office of an elder (1770, 3).

Reponement. A deposed minister is not to be reponed, except on such evidence of penitence and an example so convincing as to have worn out and healed the wound the scandal gave (1707, xi.).

L 2

In 1748, 6, the Assembly ratified and confirmed its laws and regulations "whereby Presbyteries are bound up from reponing ministers deposed." This applies also to licentiates.

No reordination. No proposal to reordain the deposed has ever been mooted in the Church; and the Form of Process does not refer to any degree of restoration short of reponement. Thus practically the cause of deposition is regarded as a temporary backsliding.

Partial restoration inadvisable. The Assembly have in several cases restored a minister partially by giving the status of a licentiate. When this is done, he may be elected by a congregation; but, as there is no reordination, and as the Presbytery cannot repone, it must delay to sustain the appointment till the Assembly meet. The person appointed proceeds by petition, but the Presbytery also brings up the case by reference, with its opinion (1905, 9, Carfin Chapel; 1906, 3, John Knox's, Aberdeen). It were well that the Assembly should never give partial restoration, but adhere to real reponement. If it should shrink from *ministerium vagum*, it might instruct the reponed minister to refrain from those services which are competent only to a minister till he be inducted into a charge (see Rep., 1906, p. 1221; 1911, p. 1183).

Section VI. Appeal.

For procedure in cases of Appeal, see Chap. V., pp. 91-99.

Appeals from Kirk Sessions. When an appeal is taken from Kirk Session to Presbytery in such a case as must be finally determined by the Presbytery, the latter may pass to consider the merits without insisting upon the discussion of the competency (1707, xi.).

In cases where decision of Kirk Session final. If, however, the case be such that the decision of the Kirk Session is final upon it, and the Kirk Session have neither broken the rules of orderly procedure nor imposed an incompetent censure, the Presbytery is not to sustain the appeal (1707, xi.).

Unnecessary and frivolous appeals. In a case where the Presbytery does not sustain an appeal, but finds that there has been "some fault, passion, or culpable mistake in the appellant," the Presbytery is to inflict some censure on the appellant, in order to prevent unnecessary appeals, and to endorse the censure of the Kirk Session if it be already inflicted, and, if not inflicted, "to sist themselves during the process, if it be depending" (1707, xi.).

In a case where the appeal is sustained, and yet upon proceeding the Presbytery find the appellant censurable, the Presbytery should, in addition to inflicting censure itself, order the appellant to undergo censure before the Kirk Session in order to discourage frivolous appeals (1707, xi.).

If, on the other hand, the Presbytery find that the Kirk Session has unwarrantably proceeded either in contributing to the raising of a scandal, or inflicting censure without a sufficient cause, and thereby the appellant has been injured, the Presbytery shall not only assoilzie the appellant, but take such steps as may be proper and necessary to vindicate his innocence (1707, xi.). **Where Kirk Session at fault.**

In so doing, the Presbytery must exercise great prudence; and, while doing justice to the innocent party, must take care not to weaken the authority of the Kirk Session in the congregation (1707, xi.).

In such circumstances the Presbytery may give the Kirk Session suitable injunctions, or private admonitions, or may call for a visitation of its Session register (1707, xi.).

The same rules as are prescribed for appeals from Kirk Sessions to Presbyteries are to be followed in appeals from Presbyteries to Synods, and from Synods to General Assemblies (1707, xi.).

By 1940, vii., the General Assembly established a Judicial Commission for the hearing of appeals against the judgment of inferior courts in cases of trial by libel affecting the character or conduct of ministers and probationers. The Act was repealed by 1960, xxii. (p. 653), which substantially re-enacted the 1940 Act, and extended the jurisdiction of the Judicial Commission to include the hearing of certain appeals arising under the Act anent Congregation in an Unsatisfactory State (1960, xxi., p. 173). The Judicial Commission cannot hear appeals taken only against sentence or penalty. **Judicial Commission.**

CHAPTER XVI.

EVIDENCE.

So far as it has not made laws, or established precedents of its own, the practice of the Church is generally on the lines of the law and practice of civil government.

SECTION I. WITNESSES.

Witnesses Admissibility.

All persons, whose powers of observation and memory and whose knowledge of the duty to speak the truth are so far developed that they will be likely to give trustworthy evidence, are admissible as witnesses.

To comprehend and undertake the obligation of an oath requires more maturity of intellect and some education. Accordingly children, however young, may be examined on facts within their comprehension ; but the oath is commonly administered to persons over fourteen years of age only. Even where the witness is over fourteen the oath is not administered if the judge think the witness is not able to undertake the obligation involved.

To children under twelve the oath is not administered, nor to those between twelve and fourteen, unless the judge be satisfied as to the capability of the witness.

If the oath be not administered, the witness is asked whether he knows it is wrong to tell a lie, and is cautioned that he must tell the truth.

When a person qualified to take the oath objects to do so, on the ground that he has no religious belief or that taking an oath is contrary to his religious belief, he is allowed to make a solemn affirmation of his intention to tell the truth.

Competency.

As regards competency the general rule is that all persons capable of giving evidence are competent and compellable witnesses. This general rule suffers exception in the following cases :—

(*a*) The husband or wife of a person accused is a competent, but not invariably a compellable, witness. Husband and wife.

1. During the subsistence of the marriage neither a spouse nor a third party can be compelled to disclose communications between husband and wife against the will of the spouse having the interest to object. This privilege does not apply—

(1) Where the spouses waive the objection; (2) where the conduct of the spouses towards each other is the subject of the inquiry—*e.g.*, in actions of divorce or of judicial separation.

2. The husband or wife of a person accused is not a compellable witness at the instance of the prosecutor or a co-accused, against the will of the spouse accused except (1) where he or she is the injured party, in which case he or she is a competent and compellable witness, and (2) in the case of prosecutions for certain offences where statutes contain express provision making them competent and compellable.

In the case of statutory offences, unless it be provided to the contrary, the husband or wife, though competent as witnesses for the prosecutor against the will of the accused, is not compellable against his or her own will.

Where the husband or wife of the accused is a competent witness for the prosecutor by reason only of the Criminal Evidence Act, 1898, he or she is not a compellable witness against his or her own will.

In any case, unless where the husband and wife are compellable witnesses, the accused does not lose the right to plead privilege as to communications passing between the accused and the other spouse. Where a husband or wife is admissible at common law as a witness for the prosecution, he or she is also compellable and has not the option of declining to give evidence.

The husband or wife of an accused person is a competent witness for the defence. If he or she is to be called, his or her name must be entered on the list of witnesses. The failure of husband or wife to give evidence for the defence cannot be made the subject of comment by the prosecution.

(*b*) A minister, a priest, or a physician is not exempt; but the Court has shown a desire to respect the aversion of a minister or a priest to give evidence regarding communications made by the accused. There is no rule exempting a physician. A law agent is compelled to disclose what has been com- Persons in confidential relation.

municated to him in his professional capacity, only if his own client have adduced him or waives privilege.

Crime. (*c*) A witness is not bound to answer any question the answer to which may reasonably be held to expose him, or tend to expose him, to a criminal charge of any description.

Adultery. (*d*) In any proceedings instituted in consequence of adultery, no witness is liable to be asked, or is bound to answer, any question tending to show that he or she has been guilty of that adultery, provided he or she has not in the same case given evidence in disproof of his or her adultery.

Judge. (*e*) Judges of the Supreme Court would probably be held exempt from giving evidence upon any matter taking place before them in their judicial capacity.

Prosecutor. (*f*) The prosecutor should not give evidence against the accused, although he is not an incompetent witness by reason only of his being a party.

Evidence of a *Socius*. Where the offence is not committed by one person only, the prosecutor may, in his discretion, call one or more of the *socii* as witnesses to prove the charge against the others. He is entitled to do this in the following circumstances :—

(1) Where he refrains from charging such person or persons ; (2) where the trials are separated ; (3) where the *socius* the prosecutor proposes to call has either been acquitted of the charge, or has been found guilty under a separate libel at a separate diet, or where he has pled guilty ; and (4) where the prosecutor abandons, or withdraws, the charge as regards this *socius*.

In any case, the mere fact of his being examined as a witness for the prosecution renders him immune from prosecution in that case.

In cases where more than one person is charged, each one is a competent witness in his own defence ; but he is not entitled to call his co-accused as a witness on his behalf, except where such co-accused has been convicted, or discharged, or pled guilty, or the trials have been separated.

If an accused give evidence to exculpate himself, and in doing so directly or indirectly should inculpate any of the co-accused, he is liable to be cross-examined by that co-accused as well as by the prosecutor. The prosecutor has the right to cross-examine last in order, and he may ask questions of the accused giving evidence, which tend to show he has committed, been convicted of, or charged with, another offence than that with which he is then charged, or that he is of bad character.

The examination of a member of a Presbytery as a witness does not disqualify him from being a judge, provided the party proposing to examine him states to the Presbytery the particular matter on which he proposes to examine him; and the Presbytery give permission (1747, ult.; 1850, xii.; 1858, 9). Member of a Presbytery as a witness.

The general rule is that witnesses should not be allowed to be present in Court until they give evidence; but the Court may decide whether a witness, who has not given his evidence, may be present during the examination of another. Witnesses excluded from Court.

Evidence of persons about to leave the country may be taken and sealed up after a libel has been served, but not before (1834, 5; 1848, 5). Evidence of persons about to leave the country.

Church Courts, being Courts of the realm, are not liable for the expenses of witnesses cited by them, either at their own instance or at the instance of parties (Ayr Sheriff Court, Mar. 21, 1901, Tarbolton K.S.). Expenses of witnesses.

Examination *in initialibus* has respect to the admissibility and credibility of a witness, that he may be "purged of malice, bribe, or good deed done or to be done, and of partial counsel." It does not require that any objection shall have been taken against the witness. It is now in abeyance, but it is competent in all Courts, and is resorted to when required by the Court or by the opposite party. The examination is on oath. Examination *in initialibus.*

Either party may object to a witness before or after his examination *in initialibus* and before his examination *in causa* (1850, xii.). A defender may, besides, send in objections to witnesses along with his defences. If he desire at once to bring proof of his objections, and if they be relevant, he must be allowed to do so, and to examine the witnesses objected to on the objections brought against them. Objections.

If the objector cannot proceed to proof at once *in initialibus*, he protests for reprobator, which he must do before examination of the witness *in causa* (1850, xii.). The examination *in causa* then proceeds, and is kept *in retentis*, until after the reprobatory proof is led. The decision in the cause is held up until the decision on the reprobatory proof is issued.

No protest for reprobator is necessary in the case of an application to lead additional evidence in respect of *res noviter*.

The result of the examination *in initialibus*, or of the reprobatory proof, may be to admit or reject the witness, or to admit him *cum nota*.

No lists of witnesses are exchanged. In this, as in other respects, this proof differs from a proof on the merits where a list of witnesses is supplied to the accused when the libel is Lists of witnesses.

served on him, and he must give in a list of witnesses within twenty-one days after the libel is served, if he should desire to lead evidence in his defence. In the ordinary case, if the accused wish to get a warrant to cite witnesses, he must give in a list along with his defences.

Section II. Evidence at the Trial.

At the proof on the merits the prosecutor first leads the evidence against the accused. On the conclusion of this evidence the accused is entitled to lead evidence for his defence.

Each witness, after taking the oath or affirmation, is examined in chief by the person conducting the prosecution or the defence, according as the witness is for the prosecution or for the defence. Upon the conclusion of his evidence in chief, the person conducting the case for the other side is entitled, if he desire, to cross-examine the witness, and thereafter re-examination on new matter brought out in cross may take place by the person who took the evidence in chief.

After re-examination the cross-examiner may put further questions with the leave of the Court.

Leading questions.

Leading questions are not allowed in examination in chief. In cross-examination leading questions may be put.

Witnesses may refer to their papers to refresh their memories on details, but they must have some recollection of the matter spoken to, and the writing must have been made at or about the time of the event in question.

What a party has said extrajudicially may be proved against him provided that his earlier statement was made voluntarily.

Discrediting a witness by proof of prior contradictory statement.

Questions may be put to a witness in order to prove that he has made statements at a time and place, and in the presence of named persons, contradictory of the evidence he is giving.

Recall of witness.

The Court may on the motion of either party recall a witness for the purpose of removing ambiguity or palpable error in the evidence already given or as to matters which could not have been foreseen.

Questions must be relevant.

All questions should be strictly relevant to the question at issue. A slight deviation from this rule may occasionally be permitted in cross-examination when the object is to test the credibility of the witness.

Evidence led must be competent.

The evidence led must be competent. This consideration brings into operation what is known as "the best evidence rule." Under it (1) writing is in general held to be better than oral evidence; (2) original evidence is preferred to secondary evidence—*e.g.*, copies of documents are admitted in certain defined situations only; (3) oral evidence must be original—viz., that of the witness who has experienced the facts deponed to, and not derivative; hence the rule that hearsay oral evidence is excluded.

Hearsay.

"Hearsay" character does not always attach to what was said by another. Such evidence is competent where the words spoken by another form part of the *res gestae*, or when they were spoken in the presence of the accused, or the party against whom the evidence is given. In offences against women and children statements made by them outwith the presence of the accused may be proved if made *de recenti* although not forming part of the *res gestae*. When something heard by the witness led him to take steps relevant to the cause, it is competent to put a question of the following nature: "In consequence of what you heard from [someone], did you [do something or go somewhere]?"

Disallowance of evidence.

When tendered evidence of importance has been disallowed, and an Appeal Court decides that it should have been allowed, the Appeal Court is not to proceed to consider the merits, but is to remit to the Court of first instance in order that the rejected evidence be led, unless the party in whose favour the rejected evidence was tendered do not insist on a remit.

Written evidence.

Written evidence may be divided into three classes: (1) public writings; (2) private writings; (3) copies of writings.

(1) Public writings.

(1) Public writings include *inter alia* Acts of the British Parliament, and statutory instruments made thereunder which do not require to be proved: Colonial Acts proved by production of a copy thereof purporting to be printed by the Government printer; enactments of foreign States require proof by expert witnesses in the same way as other principles of foreign law; records of Courts of Law authenticated by the judge or by the Clerk of Court, being probative, are competent evidence of what the Court has done; extracts of deeds registered in the books of Council and Session and other public registers are probative; extract of an entry in the Register of Births, Marriages, and Deaths produced and referred to by one witness is evidence of the entry without any further or other proof.

(2) Private writings.

(2) Private writings may be properly described as "written evidence" when they prove themselves, and thus become

immediately admissible in evidence. They acquire this character either by reason of the solemn form in which they are executed by the parties, or on account of the favour extended by law to writings holograph of the maker, or to the writings of a particular class. The first class, called probative deeds, establish their own admissibility by reason of their execution being in conformity with the requirements of our law; and they are accepted as the authentic deeds of the parties whose signatures are on them.

Probative.

Holograph.

Holograph writings are not, strictly speaking, probative, as they do not themselves prove that they were executed by the person bearing to be the granter. But when they are admitted or proved to be in the handwriting of the granter, they acquire the qualities and effects of probative deeds.

Writs in *re mercatoria* do not prove their execution by the maker, but, in the absence of challenge of their authenticity, they are admissible in evidence without further proof of their execution.

(3) Copies of writings.

(3) Copies of documents have not in themselves any recognised evidentiary value. In many cases, however, copies are accepted as equivalent to the principals—*e.g.*, extracts from various public registers; copies of various documents certified in the manner prescribed by statute declared to be equivalent to principals; copies made by a commissioner appointed by the Court for recovery of documents. Parties frequently agree to hold copies as equivalent to principals. In practice the message sent out by the Post Office to the addressee is accepted as equivalent to the original telegram unless challenged, when the original can be recovered and produced.

Real evidence.

Material objects are the basis of what is known as real evidence. Where the actual appearance of a particular object is a material element in any inquiry, there ought to be evidence of it. This is done by producing the object in Court and getting a witness or witnesses to speak to the aspect or feature of it that is of value as evidence in the case.

Sufficiency of evidence.

Written evidence.

Writings which are immediately admissible in evidence—*e.g.*, probative or holograph writings, or writings otherwise privileged, form in themselves sufficient evidence in law of the statements and final relationships embodied in them. When a writing of this kind has been admitted in evidence, the Court may competently hold that what it purports to record has been proved. The distinction between writings of the kind mentioned and those which are admissible as adminicles, and so merely items of evidence to be taken into account in estimating the value of the evidence as a whole, should be kept in view.

The uncorroborated testimony of one witness is not in itself sufficient in law.

Oral testimony becomes sufficient in law when it is corroborated, and sufficient corroboration may take place in the following circumstances:— Oral evidence.

The evidence of two or more credible witnesses testifying to the same fact is sufficient corroboration.

The evidence of one credible witness corroborated as regards its material elements by facts and circumstances is sufficient.

Facts and circumstances contributed from independent sources may in themselves, when sufficiently established, be sufficient evidence of facts which cannot be otherwise proved.

Section III. Citation.

The Church has not prescribed any forms for the purpose of citation of witnesses or others. In the Kirk Session oral citation by the beadle is regarded as sufficient. A citation should state who is pursuer (if that be not the Court itself); what is the ground of action; also whether the citation be on the application of defender or prosecutor, unless the prosecutor be the Court.

The "certification" in such documents means that the party addressed must abide the legal consequences of neglecting them. Certification.

The warrant to cite witnesses may run as follows:— Warrant to cite witnesses.

"In the name of [state the Court] I authorise and require A. B., officer of the Court, and any competent officer, to cite witnesses to compear before the said [name the Court, the place, the day, and the hour], with continuation of days to bear true witness in a process depending before said Court against , for the offence of ; and this is done on the application of , defender [*or*, prosecutor] in said case; with certification as effeirs. Given under my hand, this [date],

——— *Clerk.*"

The safe course is to cite a witness by serving a citation upon him personally in the presence of witnesses. Personal citation.

The citation may run:—

"I, officer of the [name the Court], by virtue of a warrant from said Court dated , do hereby cite you, The citation.

, to compear before the said Court [state place, day, and hour], with continuation of days, to bear true witness [&c., as in the warrant], with certification as effeirs. This I do on [the date], before these witnesses [names, designations, and residences].

——— *Officer*."

Execution of citation [by officer].

The execution is the report under the hand of the officer setting forth the facts of the service of the citation. It is proof of the service. The witnesses do not attest the officer's signature, but the truth of his narrative, and therefore must be present at the serving.

The execution.

The execution of citation may run :—

" On [date], by virtue of a warrant from [name the Court], I, , did lawfully cite C. D. to compear [&c., as in the warrant and citation] ; with certification conform to the said warrant, a written citation to the effect foresaid, I delivered to the said C. D. [*or*, I left for the said C. D., at his dwelling-place at , because I could not find him] ; which citation was subscribed by me and by [give names and designations and addresses of the witnesses], in whose presence it was given, and who hereto subscribe with me.

——— *Witness*. ——— *Officer*."
——— *Witness*.

Citation by registered letter.

Citation by registered letter or recorded delivery is now competent, and in cases where personal citation is not considered necessary this method may be adopted.

In the Civil Courts it is executed " by an officer of the Court from which (the) summons, warrant, or judicial intimation was issued, or other officer who, according to the present law and practice, might lawfully execute the same, or by an enrolled law agent."

Any of the Church Courts would probably authorise the clerk or an agent for the defender or other party to execute postal citation.

In such circumstances it would be effected by the clerk, or other person authorised by the Court, sending to the witness at his last known address a registered or recorded delivery letter containing a citation.

The citation must specify the date of posting and the *induciæ ;* the latter are reckoned from twenty-four hours after the time of posting.

Execution of citation by registered letter.

When the citation has been made by registered or recorded delivery letter, the execution, written on a copy of the citation which is lodged in Court, along with the Post Office receipt, runs as follows :—

"This citation executed by me [name of the person sending the registered letter or recorded delivery] by posting on last, between the hours of and , at the Post Office of a copy of the citation to [name, designation, and address of the witness] in a registered [recorded delivery] letter addressed as follows, viz. :—

[Signature of the official.]"

On the back of the registered or recorded delivery letter, in addition to the address, there must be written or printed the following notice, or a notice to the like effect :—

"This letter contains a citation to [name the Court]. If delivery of the letter cannot be made, it is to be returned immediately to [give the official name and office or place of business of the Clerk of Court].

These forms, with the appropriate alterations, may be used in serving a libel, or other writ, or intimation.

Witnesses in a trial are sworn in the following manner :—

The witness, standing and holding up his right hand, repeats the words of the oath after the person whose duty it is to administer it, as follows : "I swear by Almighty God, as I shall answer to God at the great day of judgment, that I will tell the truth, the whole truth, and nothing but the truth." Oath.

The Church has not yet spoken on the subject of accepting the "affirmation." Presumably it would be accepted, as in the Law Courts. Affirmation.

The form of the affirmation is : "I do solemnly, sincerely, and truly declare and affirm that I will tell the truth, the whole truth, and nothing but the truth."

This has the same legal effect as the oath, and the same relation to perjury as the oath.

CHAPTER XVII.

Property and Funds.

Section I. Property of Church of Scotland as constituted before Union.

A. Position prior to Act of 1925.

This property fell under two main divisions—parishes *quoad omnia* and parishes *quoad sacra,* but in each of these divisions the property was of various descriptions, which may be shortly summarised as follows :—

Parishes quoad omnia.

(*a*) Stipends payable out of teinds including as supplementary thereto grants from Exchequer under Acts of Parliament.

(*b*) Stipends of burgh churches.

(*c*) Churches and manses erected and maintained by the heritors or by Town Councils of Burghs.

(*d*) Glebes. The history of their origin and of their designation by Presbyteries under statutory powers is involved and complicated. The glebes were usually held without any written title except the designation by the Presbytery ; and the minister was entitled to the possession during his incumbency, but, apart from special statutory powers in a few instances, had or could confer no right to possession after the termination of his incumbency except for the purpose of reaping crops sown during it. In the Glebe Lands (Scotland) Act, 1866, ministers were empowered, subject to obtaining certain consents, to grant leases of short duration, to sell servitudes for fixed annual payments, and, on obtaining the authority of the Teind Court, to feu or grant building leases of the glebe or part thereof. In addition to the glebes thus designed, there were in some instances large areas of land with, it might be, salmon fishings, enjoyed by the minister under some mortification or other special title.

Parishes quoad sacra.

These were erected by the Court of Teinds, acting under statutory powers (7 & 8 Vict. cap. 44, 31 & 32 Vict. cap. 30, and 39 & 40 Vict. cap. 11), by disjunction of an area or areas from one or more parishes. The normal condition of such erection was that a church should be built and inalienably secured as the church of the new parish in connection with the Church of Scotland, and due provision made for the future maintenance of the fabric, and that an endowment of specified minimum amount should be provided in all time coming with a suitable manse inalienably secured, or, if there were not a manse, then a correspondingly larger minimum stipend. In addition to these statutory endowments there frequently were other endowments held in trust by individual or *ex officiis* trustees.

In addition to parishes *quoad omnia* and *quoad sacra* there were in the Highlands and Islands a small number of parliamentary churches, whose ministers were supported by the income of funds voted by Parliament under Statute (4 Geo. IV. cap. 79 and 5 Geo. IV. cap. 90). Some of these were later erected as parishes *quoad sacra.*

The above was, very briefly, the state of matters before The Church of Scotland (Property and Endowments) Act, 1925, which was passed with a view to the union effected in 1929, came into force on May 8, 1925. For fuller information on this subject, which is now largely one of historical interest, reference may be made to Duncan's 'Parochial Ecclesiastical Law of Scotland.'

FUNDS OF COMMITTEES OF CHURCH.

In addition to the property already referred to, funds of large amount and derived from various sources were held by the Committees of the Church. These funds, consisting of heritable properties and securities, and of investments in moveable property, were frequently held in the names of individuals as trustees, whose deaths or resignations from time to time necessitated transfers or other legal proceedings involving considerable expense and inconvenience. With a view to obviating this, the Church in 1921 obtained a Provisional Order, confirmed by Act of Parliament, known as The Church of Scotland (General Trustees) Order Confirmation App. VI.,
Act, 1921, incorporating The Church of Scotland General *A.*, p. 474.
Trustees. The Order provided for the transfer to this corpora-

tion of the various properties, securities, and investments specified in a Schedule to the Order, and for its accepting from, and holding on behalf of, any committee or association making a report to the General Assembly any funds, properties, or investments belonging to it. The properties and investments so transferred to and vested in the General Trustees are now vested in The Church of Scotland Trust incorporated by The Church of Scotland Trust Order Confirmation Act, 1932 (22 & 23 Geo. V. cap. 21), the position of which is explained later (p. 364). That Order (s. 29), on the other hand, empowers the General Trustees to receive and hold any property or funds held by any person or body of trustees in connection with any church, chapel of ease, or mission chapel, manse, church hall, or other property belonging to or connected with the church or held by any body, committee, or association connected with the Church where such person or body of trustees or such body, committee, or association desires to convey the same to the General Trustees.

App. VII., p. 535.

The powers of investment contained in that Order were extended by the Church of Scotland General Trustees Order Confirmation Act, 1957.

B. The position as altered by the Acts of 1925 and 1933 (pp. 483-530).

A. *Parishes* quoad omnia

(a) *Stipend.*

Under the law before 1925, stipends modified out of teinds were fixed mainly in quantities of victual—*i.e.*, meal, barley, wheat, &c., payable according to the highest fiars' prices of the year, and thus fluctuating greatly in value. Under the Act of 1925 (s. 1) stipends have now all been standardised. As a consequence of standardisation the stipends are payable in fixed sums of money to the General Trustees.

An important change effected by the Act is the entire change of the nature of stipend. It was formerly a personal debt by the heritor by whom it was payable. The teind roll shows the precise sum payable by each heritor. On the roll being completed and declared final (Fifth Schedule, s. 8), that sum becomes (s. 12)—subject to the heritor's right to redeem the payment, if exceeding £1, on terms specified, or, if over a shilling but under £1, on easier terms, or its being extinguished if not exceeding a shilling (sub-sec. (1))—" a standard charge," or real burden on the lands from which it is payable, " preferable to all other securities or burdens not incidents of tenure."

(b) *Burgh Churches and payments out of Exchequer.*

Under schemes framed by the Ecclesiastical Commissioners appointed under the Act of 1925, the sums formerly paid by the magistrates or Town Council of any burgh in respect of the stipends of the burgh churches have been redeemed by capital payments to the General Trustees. The payments out of Exchequer have also been redeemed by payments to the General Trustees in pursuance of the Act (s. 39).

(c) *Churches and Manses.*

The Act of 1925 provided (s. 27) that no proceedings against the heritors for enforcement of their obligations of maintenance and repair should thereafter be instituted. The sheriff was directed to grant, on the prescribed conditions being satisfied, a certificate that all obligations of the heritors with regard to the subjects specified in the schedule to this certificate had been fulfilled, and the certificate might be recorded in the Register of Sasines. On the certificate being so recorded, all liability on the heritors came to an end, and all rights of property in the subjects were fully vested in the General Trustees (s. 28 (3)).

Burgh Churches.

In the case of the burgh churches, forty-five in number scheduled to the Act, provision was made for the churches and manses or other subjects connected therewith being vested in the General Trustees along with any property held for the benefit of the minister of any burgh church by way of stipend. These churches and manses have in virtue of the Act all now been vested in the General Trustees (s. 22) under schemes framed by the Ecclesiastical Commissioners. The schemes framed by the Ecclesiastical Commissioners contain provisions (1) for the protection of the interests of Town Councils as regards sittings in the burgh churches, the right to have church bells rung on special occasions, and for the preservation of any other similar right or privilege previously enjoyed by the Town Councils; and (2) for the General Trustees, before selling or otherwise disposing of any burgh church and its site, giving the Town Council an opportunity of acquiring them (s. 22 (2) *h*).

(d) *Glebes.*

Under the Act of 1925 (s. 30) glebes became vested in the General Trustees by virtue of Orders and relative Schemes issued by the Ecclesiastical Commissioners. Glebe feu-duties and investments resulting from the sale of glebe lands were also vested in the General Trustees by these Orders and Schemes. By virtue of the Act of 1925 (s. 37), the General Trustees can sell or feu a glebe, subject to the directions of the General Assembly and to the right of adjoining heritors, to purchase or take it in feu on such terms as may be agreed by the General Trustees and the heritors, or, failing agreement, determined by an arbiter appointed by the sheriff. A number have been sold or feued.

Administration of Glebes.

I. Act XXXIII., 1966.

The General Assembly, in order to give authoritative effect to the existing practice in relation to Glebe land and superiorities, etc., held for endowment purposes, and moneys derived therefrom, enact and ordain as follows :—

Declare and direct that all Glebe land held or to be held by the Church of Scotland General Trustees, and all superiorities, ground annuals, ground rents, etc., held or to be held by the said General Trustees or the Church of Scotland Trust for endowment purposes, shall not be expended without distinction between capital and income, and that only the income shall be expended. In particular, but without prejudice to said generality, declare and direct (*a*) that in the event of any Glebe land being sold or disposed of for a consideration consisting wholly or partly of a capital sum, the net proceeds of sale or of such capital sum shall be subject to a restriction that these shall be invested and that only the income derived from the investment shall be expended ; (*b*) that in the event of any Glebe land being feued or leased, only the income derived from such feu or lease shall be expended ; (*c*) that with regard to all existing superiorities, ground annuals and ground rents held for endowment purposes by the said General Trustees or the

Church of Scotland Trust, only the income derived therefrom shall be expended ; and (*d*) that in the event of the sale of any such superiorities, ground annuals or ground rents or in the event of a capital sum being received in consideration of discharging restrictive conditions in any Feu, Writ, Contract of Ground Annual, Lease or other document, the net proceeds of sale or of such capital sum as the case may be shall be invested and shall be subject to the restriction that only the income thereof shall be expended.

II. Act XXVII., 1968.

1. The General Assembly authorise and empower The Church of Scotland General Trustees or other Trustees in whom the relevant subjects are vested at any time to sell or otherwise dispose of :—

(1) Any ground attached or pertaining to any of the churches and manses of the parishes *Quoad Omnia* mentioned in the Eighth Schedule to the Church of Scotland (Property and Endowments) Act, 1925, or any Glebe land connected therewith.

(2) Any ground attached or pertaining to any of the churches and manses mentioned in the Ninth Schedule to the said Act of 1925.

(3) Any ground attached or pertaining to any of the churches and manses mentioned in the Tenth Schedule (as amended) to the said Act of 1925 or any Glebe land connected therewith.

(4) Any ground attached or pertaining to any church, hall, manse or other building or any Glebe land which forms part of the statutory properties and endowments of any parish *Quoad Sacra*.

(5) Any ground attached or pertaining to any church, hall, manse or other building or any Glebe land which forms part of the non-statutory properties and endowments of any parish *Quoad Sacra* as mentioned in Section 3 of the Church of Scotland (Property and Endowments) Amendment Act, 1933 (where the consent of the General Assembly is necessary) ; and

(6) Any ground attached or pertaining to any Chapel of Ease, mission church or church hall as mentioned in Section 4 of the said Act of 1933 (where the consent of the General Assembly is necessary) ;

but in any case only where the sale price payable for such ground or Glebe land does not exceed £500 and that on such terms and conditions as the said General Trustees or other Trustees as the case may be having regard to the circumstances of each case shall think fit subject, however, to their consulting with and obtaining the approval of the relevant Congregational Board (or other congregational body responsible for the maintenance and oversight of properties and endowments) and the Presbytery of the bounds.

2. The General Assembly direct :—

(1) that the proceeds of sale of such Glebe land shall be held and the income thereof applied for stipend purposes ; and

(2) that the proceeds of sale of such ground other than Glebe lands shall be held and applied as a fabric fund for the ecclesiastical buildings of the congregation concerned ; declaring that in the event of the sale of ground vested in the said General Trustees such proceeds shall be held and applied as a fabric fund only for such ecclesiastical buildings as are vested in them.

III. Regulations (1972) anent Glebes.

1. For the removal of any doubt, no Minister shall have the right to the possession or lease of such land, other than such right as may have been or be granted to him by the General Trustees.

2. The General Trustees shall be entitled to grant a lease or right of possession to any Minister, Kirk Session or Congregational Board of such land on such terms and conditions as shall be mutually acceptable to the parties.

3. Subject to the following provisions hereof, the Conditions of Tenure of Glebes approved by the General Assembly of 1933 (Appendix C), and the regulations in regard to the question of the amount which Ministers in occupation of glebes should return as part of their ministerial income approved by the General Assembly of 1960 (regulations 7) are revoked.

4. Nothing herein contained shall affect the interests of a Minister or the assistant and successor of a Minister who, at the passing of the Church of Scotland (Property and Endowments) Act 1925, was the incumbent of the benefice of any Parish.

5. Nothing herein contained shall affect the interests or obligations of a Minister, Kirk Session or Congregational

Board in any case where, at the passing hereof, a Minister is in occupation of such land, or has entered into an arrangement where such land is being worked by the Kirk Session or Congregational Board and in respect of which a returnable rent has been fixed; and accordingly in such cases the Conditions of Tenure of Glebes and the Regulations of 1960 shall continue to apply.

6. From the date of passing hereof no Minister shall be entitled to grant any lease or right of possession of such land.

7. The General Trustees, before selling, feuing or otherwise disposing of such land or leasing or granting any right of possession thereof, shall take steps to consult with the Minister of the Parish and (except in the case of seasonal grazing or mowing lets or other lets carrying no security of tenure for a period exceeding three years) the Presbytery of the bounds.

Other Matters affecting Glebes.

(*a*) *Glebe Rents.*

Rents now payable, due to reviews carried out by the General Trustees, assisted by Presbyteries, reflect the economic value of such lands, and periodic reconsiderations ensure that these glebe rents do not fall behind prevailing values. Any cases requiring review should be brought to the attention either of the General Trustees or of the Glebes Committee of the Presbytery. The Agricultural Holdings Acts enable rents to be referred to arbitration if there has been no change in the amount for five years.

(*b*) *Glebe Fences, &c.*

(i) *When Glebe is in occupation of Minister.*—When a Minister is himself in occupation of the glebe he is responsible for maintenance and when necessary the renewal of fences, gates, walls, ditches, &c. In the case of boundary fences or walls the adjoining proprietors will be responsible for one-half of the cost. The Minister is also responsible for the maintenance in good order and repair of the drainage of the glebe and any pipes or other works connected with the water supply thereof in so far as there may not be other proprietors jointly responsible. The maintenance of buildings on the glebe or used in connection with the working of the glebe are also the responsibility of the Minister.

(ii) *When the Glebe is let.*—All leases of glebes are effected by the General Trustees who generally consult with the Minister before entering into missives of let. Normally a glebe tenant is made liable in the lease or missive of let for the maintenance of fences, walls, gates, ditches, drains, water supply, buildings, &c., but prior to 1948 many glebes were let by Ministers without entering into any formal leases or missives and in such cases the tenant may not be liable, particularly where wear and tear is the cause of the repairs, &c., being necessary.

It should be added that Kirk Sessions may relieve Ministers of their obligations in relation to the above matters as well as local rates payable for the glebe, and it is understood that it is a growing practice for Kirk Sessions to do so.

The proper maintenance of glebe fences, gates, walls, ditches and other fixed equipment is of great importance.

Whether or not the Minister or Kirk Session is responsible, a regular inspection should be made. If fences, gates, walls, &c., fall into a state of neglect and require renewal, the cost is often out of all proportion to the rent obtainable. Regular attention to the fences, &c., can avoid a great deal of unnecessary expenditure.

In accordance with the Rules of the Maintenance of the Ministry Committee, a Minister is entitled to deduct from the income of the glebe in his Ministerial Return for the year expenses incurred by him with the approval of the Presbytery and the General Trustees under the headings (i) and (ii) above. The Minister of an aid-receiving congregation may receive a refund of these approved expenses on application to the Maintenance of the Ministry Committee. If the Minister receives a refund the amount should not then be deducted from the glebe rent in his Return of Ministerial Income.

(*c*) *Glebes in the occupation of Ministers.*

Since 15th May 1961 glebes let or used for agricultural purposes have not appeared in the Valuation Roll. In conference with the Maintenance of the Ministry Committee the General Trustees have framed regulations as to how the annual value of glebes in the occupation of Ministers are fixed for the purpose of their annual Returns of Ministerial income to the Maintenance of the Ministry Committee. For these regulations (1960, Reg. 7), see Appendix XXVI., p. 668.

(*d*) *Glebes worked by the Kirk Session.*

Subject to the approval of the General Trustees, a Minister may enter into an arrangement whereby the Kirk Session will work the Glebe and apply the net proceeds for Church purposes, subject to paying the Minister an appropriate sum in lieu of rent. As from 15th May 1961 the sum to be paid in lieu of rent is to be arrived at on the basis of the current lettable value of the glebe in accordance with regulations approved of by the General Assembly of 1960. (See under (*c*)). In cases where the Kirk Session is working the glebe it will be responsible for relieving the Minister of all the obligations of maintenance, &c., referred to under (i) of head (*b*).

(*e*) *Cutting of Trees.*

In general a Minister has no right or authority to cut down or sell trees growing on the glebe. In every case the Minister should intimate to the General Trustees any proposal to cut down a tree or trees on the glebe. The General Trustees will consider the Minister's request and, if they have any difficulty in the matter, they will consult with the Presbytery and, if considered necessary, take experienced advice before reaching a decision. In the case of a tree or trees that are clearly rotten or otherwise in a dangerous condition and there is urgency in dealing with them, the Minister may deal with these on his own responsibility, subject to intimating his action immediately to the General Trustees. In the case of glebes the question of the felling of trees is a matter between the Minister and the General Trustees and one with which a Kirk Session has no direct concern, although it is advisable that the Kirk Session should be consulted.

B. *Parishes* quoad omnia *erected under the New Parishes (Scotland) Act,* 1844, s. 15.

Schedule Eighth of the Act of 1925 contains a list of ten parishes in this position erected during the years 1844 to 1865. Under the Act (ss. 21 & 24) the Ecclesiastical Commissioners have by Order and Scheme in each case transferred the Church and Manse with the glebe, if any, to the General Trustees. By Section 6 of the Act of 1933 the General Trustees are empowered, notwithstanding anything contained in the titles under which any of them are held, subject to the consent of the General Assembly declared by Act of Assembly, to sell or otherwise dispose of such churches or manses or any glebes or other subjects connected therewith vested in them.

C. *Parishes* quoad sacra.

Under the Act of 1925 (s. 34) the statutory properties and endowments of parishes *quoad sacra* erected before the passing of the Act were transferred to the General Trustees. For what is meant by " the Statutory properties and endowments " see s. 34 (4) of the said Act.

Under the Act of 1933 (s. 3) the General Trustees can require that non-statutory properties of parishes *quoad sacra* be vested in the General Trustees or in a permanent body of Local Trustees, usually the Minister and Session clerk and treasurer of the congregation, or clerk of the Congregational Board *ex officiis*.

The statutory properties and endowments vested in the General Trustees or in other Trustees may in terms of the Act of 1925 (s. 37), as amended by the Act of 1933 (s. 1), be sold or otherwise disposed of, if the General Assembly shall by Act of Assembly at any time so direct. The other properties and endowments may, subject to the provisions of any Trust under which they are held and to the approval of the Presbytery of the bounds, be sold or otherwise disposed of, but the consent of the General Assembly declared by Act of Assembly is also required, unless under the titles on which they are held they may be sold or disposed of without such consent (Act of 1933, s. 3 (2) (i)).

D. *Parishes other than* quoad omnia *and* quoad sacra.

In addition to parishes *quoad omnia* and *quoad sacra* there were in the Highlands and Islands a certain number of parliamentary churches and manses whose ministers were endowed with the income of funds voted by Parliament under Statutes (4 Geo. IV. cap. 79 and 5 Geo. IV. cap. 90), some of which were later erected as parishes *quoad sacra* under the Act 7 & 8 Vict. cap. 44, s. 14. These parliamentary churches (forty-three in all) are enumerated in the Tenth Schedule to the Act of 1925.

By Section 15 of the Act of 1933 it was provided that Section 23 and the Tenth Schedule of the Act of 1925 should apply to the churches in eight of these parishes where the manses alone were contained in the Schedule in like manner in all respects as if they were mentioned in the Schedule.

All these churches and manses were transferred to the General Trustees by Order and Schemes issued by the Ecclesiastical Commissioners.

By Section 5 of the Act of 1933 the General Trustees were empowered, subject to the consent of the General Assembly declared by Act of Assembly, and subject to the provisions of any Deed of Trust, Conveyance, or other Deed applicable thereto, to sell or otherwise dispose of any parliamentary church or manse or any other subjects connected therewith vested in them under Section 23 of the Act of 1925, and to apply the proceeds thereof for such ends, uses, and purposes as the General Assembly may direct.

E. *Appropriation of Endowments.*

The Act of 1925 (s. 36) provides that "all moneys received by the General Trustees with respect to any parish under or in pursuance of the provisions of this Act relating to stipend and any church, manse, glebe, or other property heritable or moveable situated in, or forming part of, the endowments of any parish transferred to, or received by, the General Trustees by or in pursuance of this Act, and the proceeds of any such moneys, property, or endowments shall be appropriated in the first place to meeting the proper requirements of that parish or its neighbourhood (as such requirements may be determined by the General Assembly or by any body to which the General Assembly may delegate the necessary power), and any remainder after these requirements have been fully met shall form part of a general fund at the disposal of the General Assembly." By Act xxvii., 1953, the General Assembly has meantime delegated the power to the Committee on the Maintenance of the Ministry (App. VI., p. 532). (For further information see Chapter XIII., p. 284.)

Section II. Property which before the Union belonged to the United Free Church of Scotland.

This comprises (*a*) Property which before the Union of 1900 belonged to the Free Church of Scotland, (*b*) Property which before that date belonged to the United Presbyterian Church, and (*c*) Property thereafter acquired by the United Free Church of Scotland. They will be dealt with in that order.

(a) *Property which belonged to the Free Church of Scotland.*

The properties belonging to congregations of the former Free Church of Scotland prior to 1900 were for the most part held by local Trustees for the respective congregations, these Trustees being generally the minister and office-bearers of the congregation. In a few cases, however, the title was taken in favour of the General Trustees of the Free Church of Scotland. Practically the whole of these titles were granted in terms of the Model Trust Deed of the Free Church of Scotland, by which it was, *inter alia,* declared that the Trustees holding the properties had no power to burden them with debt or to sell, alienate or dispose of the same or any part thereof unless for the purpose of providing another place of worship or manse, and then only with the consent of the General Assembly. A few congregations, however, held their property on titles which were not under the Model Trust Deed, and they had under these titles power to dispose of their property without the consent of the General Assembly.

After the Union of 1900 and the decision of the House of Lords, the Commissioners appointed under the Churches (Scotland) Act, 1905, allocated a very large majority of the properties of Free Church congregations to the United Free Church of Scotland, and granted Orders of Allocation for each of the properties so allocated. By these Orders the Commissioners allocated to the United Free Church of Scotland, to be used for the purpose of and in connection with a congregation of the said Church, the whole property (including the property described in a Schedule thereto) which at 30th October 1900 was vested in or held by or on trust for the same congregation of the Free Church of Scotland, and transferred the property thereby allocated to the General Trustees of the United Free Church of Scotland for behoof of the said congregation in the cases where the title had been in name of the General Trustees of the Free Church of Scotland, and in cases where the original title had been in favour of local Trustees transferred the said properties to the ministers, Session clerks and clerks of the Deacons' Courts of the respective congregations to which they were allocated, and their successors in their respective offices, and such other persons as individuals or *ex officiis* as might be appointed as thereby provided, and, as regards management and disposal of the heritable property subject to the regulation and direction of the General Assembly, the Trustees having, subject to such regulation and direction, in the case of heritable property, power to sell or otherwise dispose of the whole or any part of the property, and to burden it with debt ; but, where prior to the Union the titles did not give to the General Assembly of the Free Church any power of regulation and direction as to the management and disposal of the property, the Trustees were empowered to sell or otherwise dispose of the property or burden it with debt without the authority of the General Assembly. The proceeds of the properties were to be held for and applied and appropriated to the purposes mentioned in the Order. It further provided that the General Assembly of the United Free Church and the congregation to which the property was allocated might jointly grant to and confer on the Trustees such powers of management and disposal of the property or any part thereof and with and under such conditions and trusts as might be jointly agreed upon. The Schedule to each Order specified the property allocated. In some cases the form of the Order was modified to suit special circumstances or to bring it into harmony with the allocation by the Commissioners.

The full terms of an Order of Allocation, of which the foregoing is a summary, will be found in Appendix IV., *A.*, p. 444.

The procedure to be adopted in the case of proposed sale or transference of properties belonging to congregations of the Church of Scotland which were properties of congregations of the Free Church of Scotland are regulated by Act 1940, viii., as amended Act 1959, xxviii. These are printed in Appendix IV., *H.*, p. 465.

(b) *Property which belonged to the United Presbyterian Church.*

The congregational properties were vested in Trustees for the congregation who were either (*a*) the ministers, elders, members of the Committee of Management or other office-bearers of the congregation, with, in a few cases, the moderator and the clerk, for the time being, of the Presbytery, or (*b*) individuals, elected by the members of the congregation from time to time, whose appointment fell on their ceasing to be in full communion with the congregation, or removing beyond its fellowship with the view of permanent residence, or connecting themselves with any other congregation, or ceasing from whatever cause to be members of the congregation. Any of the Trustees, other than the moderator and clerk of Presbytery were entitled to resign office at any time, and might be removed by a general meeting of the congregation. The Trustees in many cases hold on the terms specified in a Model Trust Deed dated 5th and registered in the Books of Council and Session 9th May 1892. The trust purposes, which contain provisions applicable to the cases of splits or divisions and unions, are printed in Appendix IV., *C.*, p. 449.

(c) *Properties acquired by Congregations of the United Free Church of Scotland after the Union on 30th October* 1900.

The titles of these properties, when acquired by formerly United Presbyterian congregations, were as a rule taken in the same terms as the titles of the existing properties of the congregation.

In other cases they were taken in name of the minister, Session clerk, and Deacons' Court of the congregation, and their successors in office, as Trustees for the congregation. It is normally provided that the Trustees are, as regards the management and disposal of the properties, subject to the regulation and direction of the General Assembly of the Church for the time being, and, subject to such regulation and direction, have power to sell or burden with debt.

The procedure in the case of proposed sale or transference is also regulated by Act viii. of the General Assembly of 1940, as amended by Act 1959, xxviii., before referred to and printed in the Appendix, p. 465.

In addition to the churches, manses, and other congregational buildings as already referred to, the United Free Church of Scotland possessed at the date of the Union in 1929 other heritable properties belonging to the Church both at home and abroad, and properties and investments of large amount belonging to various Committees, and other ecclesiastical associations, bodies, and missions. The titles to these were vested in the General Trustees of that Church, the United Free Church of Scotland Trust, incorporated under the Companies Acts, or Trustees acting under a variety of other Trusts, or individual persons holding for behoof of the Church. These properties and investments so far as formerly vested in the said General Trustees and the said Trust, and in certain cases in other trusts and in the names of individual persons, are all now vested in The Church of Scotland Trust, of which an account is given *infra*, p. 364.

By virtue of the union between the Free Church of Scotland and the United Presbyterian Church in 1900, and of the union between the Church of Scotland and the United Free Church of Scotland in 1929, the properties belonging to the United Free Church of Scotland and its branches now belong to the reunited Church of Scotland.

Where any congregation is being dissolved, or united with another congregation, and any congregational property is in consequence no longer required for purely congregational purposes, and is being sold, the General Assembly (1933, xxvi.) have enjoined the Presbytery to take steps to secure that the importance of applying funds arising from such sale (where this is permissible under the title) towards church extension in neighbouring districts, or for the provision of church hall accommodation for neighbouring congregations which are not fully equipped, shall be timeously and appropriately represented to the congregations concerned, with a view to their adopting a plan of allocation towards such purposes of the sums at their disposal, which can be approved of by the Presbytery and by the General Assembly (see Appendix IV., *I*., p. 468).

Since the Union of 1929 many properties of the former United Free Church have been transferred by congregational trustees to the General Trustees for behoof of the congregations concerned. The General Trustees are always ready to hold such titles if required.

Section III. Titles to Property.

The General Assembly have directed that in all cases where grants are received by a congregation from the Home Mission Committee, and/or Property Committee of the Home Board, or any other Committee in use to make such grants out of general Church Funds, all such grants shall be made on condition that the Title to the Ecclesiastical Property concerned either be transferred into the name of the Church of Scotland General Trustees, subject to the directions and control of the General Assembly, or, alternatively, be vested in a body of Local Trustees, *ex officiis*, under the express stipulation that the properties towards which such grants are made shall not be capable of sale, disposal, or burdening with debt by such Local Trustees, *ex officiis*, except with the consent of the General Assembly upon an application made for that purpose (1935, 2 ; Reports, 1935, pp. 43-46).

Section IV. Care, Upkeep and Administration of Property.

It is the duty of the Kirk Session, Deacons' Court, Committee of Management, or Congregational Board, as the case may be (see Chap. III.), to see that the Church property is kept in a proper state of repair. Under Act 1961, xxi., anent the Care of Ecclesiastical Properties (Appendix XXXII., p. 774), Fabric Committees must be appointed in every congregation to inspect or have inspected all ecclesiastical properties each year. A property register must be kept and submitted to the

Presbytery and attested annually. Each Presbytery must appoint a Fabric Committee to consider all schedules submitted and in addition arrange for an inspection on its own behalf and submit a report to the Presbytery. This Presbyterial inspection to be done at least once every five years. Each Presbytery must report annually to the Synod and each Synod to the General Administration Committee, which shall report to the General Assembly (1961, xxi.; 1969, xxvi., p. 776).

In the case of all pre-union Church of Scotland charges every congregation is expected to institute and maintain a local Fabric Fund proportionate in amount to the value of the buildings in accordance with a specified scale [1] (1927, 4 and 7).

In the case of Church Extension charges a capital sum of £50 is to be provided by the congregation itself towards the nucleus for the local Fabric Fund, and the nucleus must yield £6 annually (1932, xiv.). No building operation or repairs to ecclesiastical buildings shall be made without the consent of the Presbytery and, where appropriate, the General Trustees. Sufficient funds must be raised for such purposes without encroaching on the ordinary revenue of the congregation before the work is begun. Any urgent repairs may be carried out by the Board without consent, but a report as to the necessity of such a course must be made immediately to the Presbytery and, where appropriate, to the General Trustees, and in no case may the cost be defrayed out of ordinary revenue (1931, xxxii.). See further Regulations of Home Mission and of Property Committees in Appendix XXVI., p. 688.

The following are excerpts from a Memorandum issued in 1961 by the General Trustees with reference to properties vested in them :—

(1) Care of Ecclesiastical Buildings.

It is the duty of the Kirk Session [2] to see that the Church and Manse are kept in good repair and to this end these essential points should be observed :—

1. The buildings should be thoroughly inspected, outside and inside, at regular intervals, a careful look-out being kept for signs of woodworm and dry-rot.

[1] One half of one per cent of insurable value of the ecclesiastical properties concerned.

[2] References in this Memorandum to Kirk Sessions should be read as applying also to Congregational Boards, Deacons' Courts, Boards of Management, &c., where they are in charge of the temporal affairs of the congregation.

2. Any visible signs of disrepair between inspections should be attended to without delay.
3. The Church should be well ventilated after services. This will prevent dampness and consequent dry-rot.
4. Rhones, downpipes, gutters (especially behind parapets and between parallel roofs) should be kept clear of obstructions and regularly cleaned out.
5. Electrical installations should receive careful attention to see that they conform with modern standards of safety. Water pipes and drains should be examined, especially during and after frost, as a precaution against flooding.
6. Outside woodwork should be repainted at regular intervals to prevent deterioration.
7. Every Kirk Session should have a Fabric Committee, including, if possible, men with technical knowledge and experience. It is on the Kirk Session's careful and conscientious observance of the ordinary precautions against neglect that the condition of the Churc hand Manse depend and unnecessary expense is prevented.

(2) Repairs, Alterations, Additions, and Improvements to Ecclesiastical Buildings.

It is essential in all cases where a Kirk Session desires to effect any alteration, addition or improvement to existing Ecclesiastical Buildings, to demolish any redundant or ruinous building or outbuilding, or to erect any new building on ground vested in the General Trustees, that the proposal be referred for consideration and approval in the first place to the Presbytery and thereafter to the General Trustees, with any relevant specification, estimate and plan of the proposed work, and that the consent of the Presbytery and the General Trustees be obtained before any contract is entered into for the carrying out of the work.

(3) Memorials in Churches.

Where buildings are vested in the General Trustees, all proposals and designs should be submitted to them, through the Presbytery, before any work is put in hand.

The General Trustees and the Advisory Committee on Artistic Questions have recently been greatly concerned over the question of Memorials in Churches as a consequence of proposals and designs submitted to them. These proposals or designs have been considered unsuitable in themselves or because of the proposed inscription, or as failing to reach the high standard proper to the House of God. After conferring with the Advisory Committee, the Trustees drafted the following suggestions which were approved by the General Assembly 1960 and are now offered to Ministers who may be consulted by intending donors of Memorials or other gifts to be placed in Churches :—

1. Donors should be encouraged and if possible persuaded to present gifts which may be of use in the services of the Church or which will add to its beauty, rather than Tablets. A small and inconspicuously placed inscription could be added if necessary.
2. Tablets to the memory of private individuals should be discouraged, unless to commemorate someone who has shown singular devotion to his (or her) Church or to the service of his fellow-men.
3. Memorials of whatever form should be of real artistic value designed by a competent authority, should harmonise with their surroundings and enhance the atmosphere of worship. Anything of an assertive character which conflicts with the general character of the Church should be ruled out.
4. Where a stained-glass window is proposed the design should be by a recognised artist who will have regard to the character of the Church and any other windows already in position.

The General Trustees will be glad to furnish Ministers or intending donors with the names of competent Artists, Church Furnishers, &c. The following list of possible Memorials and gifts may be used for guidance : Alms Dish and Offering Plates, Communion Table, Chairs, Pulpit, Pulpit Fall, Baptismal Font, Lectern, Table Lectern, Stained-glass Window, Reredos or Panelling, Gates.

Burials in Churches.

It should be noted that burial in Churches has been prohibited by the General Assembly as has also the depositing of cremated remains. (See p. 131.)

(4) Insurances.

All properties vested in the General Trustees must be insured through them. They effect the Insurance through the Church of Scotland Insurance Trust which ensures that the risk is shared by a number of leading Insurance Companies. The General Trustees send annually to each Kirk Session a note of the Premiums due. These should be remitted to the General Trustees who account for them to the Insurance Trust.

Owing to the increasing cost of building work, it is very important that Kirk Sessions should review the amount of their Insurance covers from time to time. The General Trustees, where they deem it to be necessary, have authority to arrange for a survey of any property vested in them with a view to getting advice as to the adequacy of the cover (1974, sess. 5).

An increasing number of Kirk Sessions consider that Fire Insurance cover is not enough and have taken out through the General Trustees Comprehensive cover which gives protection against damage by storm or flooding, breakage of glass, burglary, &c. The General Trustees recommend this course and will be glad to obtain Premium quotations for the extra cover required. Boiler Insurance is also important.

The organ and other furnishings in Churches and Church Halls, although not belonging to the General Trustees, can be insured through them.

(5) Letting of Vacant or Redundant Manses, &c.

In every case where a Manse or other property is vested in the General Trustees it is essential that the General Trustees should be approached in regard to any proposed letting arrangement—even where a let for a period of a few months only may be contemplated—*e.g.*, during the period of a vacancy in a parish. As owners of the Manse or other property the General Trustees are the only parties who can grant a valid let.

In the case of prolonged vacancies it is very desirable that a Manse should be occupied and kept properly fired and aired and the grounds kept in good order. If occupation is considered advisable, to prevent creating a regulated tenancy, the only safe course is to arrange for a caretaker to occupy the house on a rent-free basis. Even in that case the proposed arrangement should be submitted for approval to the General Trustees before any action is taken.

Manse gardens should not be let as market gardens.

(6) Sale of Ecclesiastical Properties.

In all cases where it is desired that an ecclesiastical property vested in the ownership of the General Trustees should be sold, whether it be a Church, Church Hall, Manse or Glebe, no step should be taken by the Minister or Kirk Session to proceed with the sale arrangements on their own responsibility. In such cases the sale arrangements fall to be carried through by the General Trustees. The correct procedure, whenever a decision has been taken locally that the property should be sold, is for the Minister or Kirk Session to inform the General Trustees of the decision taken and then to refer the question of sale to the Presbytery for its consideration and approval. If the Presbytery approve of the sale and the Trustees also approve, the Trustees, subject to obtaining any necessary consents of Superiors or adjoining proprietors, will normally obtain a report upon and valuation of the subjects for sale from a professional Valuer for guidance in adjusting a price and other terms of sale with prospective purchasers. After the Report and Valuation has been considered by the Trustees and the local parties and their views obtained as to the manner of sale—*i.e.*, whether by public or private bargain—the Trustees will proceed to advertise the property. In certain cases an Act of Assembly is necessary before a sale can be effected.

(7) Purchase of Ecclesiastical Properties.

It is also important to keep in view that if a congregation should desire to purchase a property—*e.g.*, a Manse—the Presbytery must be consulted beforehand. If the property to be purchased is to take the place of a property at present vested in the General Trustees and it is proposed that the latter property should be sold, it is essential that the General Trustees should also be consulted before any step is taken.

SECTION V. THE CHURCH OF SCOTLAND GENERAL TRUSTEES.

The Church of Scotland General Trustees were created under The Church of Scotland (General Trustees) Order Confirmation Act, 1921, for the purpose of "holding" property and investments belonging to the Church of Scotland and the Committees of the General Assembly. Their powers and responsibilities were greatly extended under The Church of Scotland (Property and Endowments) Act, 1925, when they became an administrative, as well as a holding, body, and were still further extended by The Church of Scotland (Property and Endowments) Amendment Act, 1933, which enabled the Trustees to deal with various matters, and overcome certain technical difficulties which they had previously experienced in dealing with various properties and endowments belonging to the Church, or to which the Church had right. The General Assembly of 1935 approved of an increase of their number to thirty.

Churches, Manses, and Glebes.

The General Trustees now hold, under the 1925 Act, all the Churches, Manses (where these form part of the statutory property or Endowment), and Glebes of *quoad omnia* (old), Burgh, and Parliamentary Charges. All these Churches, Manses, and Glebes (878 in number) have become the absolute property of the Church.

The General Trustees hold also, under the Act, the Churches and, where they form part of the *statutory* endowment, the Manses of *quoad sacra* parishes ; and also all the Parliamentary Churches and Manses. They may also hold *non-statutory* and other properties which may be transferred to them by local trustees.

The General Trustees are responsible for any feus, sales or lets of Churches, Manses, and Glebes which they hold. They are responsible also, as owners, for payment of Insurance Premiums and of rates and taxes on the Ecclesiastical Buildings, but, as they have no funds, these charges must be met by the congregations concerned, in accordance with the injunction of the General Assembly. (See excerpts from Memo. in this section.)

Stipends.

The General Trustees collect all "standardised" Stipends and the Stipends of *quoad sacra* parishes whose endowments have been transferred to them in terms of the 1925 Act.

The General Assembly of 1931 passed an Act (1931, xli.) which provides that the General Trustees shall pay over all Stipends and Fruits of Benefices (including the Rents and Feu-duties of Glebes), as and when (*a*) the Stipends of Parishes become standardised, (*b*) the Statutory Properties and Endowments of the *quoad sacra* parishes are transferred, and (*c*) the Glebes are likewise transferred to the General Trustees, together with the Stipends of the Burgh Churches, and of such other Churches or Parishes as fall to be collected by them in terms of the 1925 Act, to the Maintenance of the Ministry Committee, which shall make payment to the Ministers of the Parishes. The only exception is the payment of the Stipends of the Edinburgh Burgh Churches, which shall continue to be made direct to the ministers. Act xli. of 1931 has now been superseded by 1953, xxvii. (App. VI., p. 532).

General Trustees' Expenses.

At the present time (1975) the General Trustees are authorised to make a charge of 4½ per cent in respect of commission on all funds ingathered by them for stipend and other purposes.

Where the administrative expenses of the General Trustees are not met by the percentage indicated above the General Finance Committee are empowered to bring forward to the General Assembly recommendations for meeting any actual or anticipated deficit.

Section VI. The Church of Scotland Trust.

At the date of their union, the Church of Scotland and the United Free Church of Scotland each possessed, in addition to churches and manses and other congregational properties, large funds belonging to Committees of the Churches or to the Churches generally and vested in Trustees. Each Church had a body of General Trustees. In the Church of Scotland these were incorporated by the Order of 1921, before referred to. In the case of the United Free Church of Scotland there were the General Trustees of the United Free Church of Scotland, appointed by Act of Assembly dated 31st October 1900, and subsequent Acts of Assembly as such General Trustees or in some cases as individuals; and there was also the United Free Church of Scotland Trust incorporated under the Companies Act on 18th February 1917. Each Church also had properties and investments, the titles to which stood in the names of various persons or sets of persons, either as trustees or as individuals. With a view to all these properties and investments being held by a single body of Trustees for the Church of Scotland, The Church of Scotland Trust was on 16th June 1932 incorporated by the Church of Scotland Trust Order 1932 (Sect. 2), confirmed by the Church of Scotland Trust Order Confirmation Act, 1932, and amended by the Church of Scotland Trust (Amendment) Orders Confirmation Acts, 1948 and 1958 (Appendix VII., *A*. and *B*., pp. 535-549). For Byelaws and Regulations, see Appendix VII., *C*., p. 550.

The Order (Sect. 9), vested in the Trust all the properties and investments detailed in a Schedule along with all rights, obligations, claims, and demands relative to all the properties and investments.

The various properties (Sect. 10) are to be held by the Trust for the same ends, uses, and purposes for which they were held by the Trustees in whom they were formerly vested, where such are expressed or defined, and, failing such expression or definition, subject to the direction of the committee, association, fund, or scheme on whose behalf they were so held, or of the General Assembly.

The general treasurer of the Church is (Sect. 12) *ex officio* the treasurer of the Trust. In the event of a vacancy the Trust appoints an interim treasurer of the Trust until a new general treasurer is appointed. A secretary and clerk is (Sect. 13) appointed by the Trust.

In addition to the properties and investments transferred to the Trust under Sect. 9, the Trust may (Sect. 15) accept from and hold on behalf of any committee, association, trustees, or body of persons connected with the Church, or with any congregation, Kirk Session, Deacons' Court, Committee of Management, or Congregational Board, or other ecclesiastical body or organisation of the Church, or the minister of any congregation of the Church as such, any properties or investments which they may desire to transfer to the Trust. Upon being so accepted they shall be held by the Trust subject to the directions of the committee or other body or minister on whose behalf they are held, or failing such direction then subject to the directions of the General Assembly.

The Trust may also (Sect. 16) receive on behalf of the Church or the General Assembly or any committee, association, fund, or scheme of the Church, any gift, legacy, or bequest to which they have become entitled, or payment of any capital sum or income thereof, annuity or annual payment, and by the hands of the treasurer grant receipts therefor.

It has power (Sect. 17) on behalf of the Church or of the General Assembly or of any committee, association, fund, or scheme of the Church to sue for and recover all property or funds to which they may be entitled, and to enforce, compromise, settle, or refer to arbitration all or any claims relating to such property or funds at the instance of or against the Church or other such body.

Funds held by the Church of Scotland Trust for behoof of Committees, congregations, &c., are held either in the Special Investment Account or in the General Investment Fund or in the Deposit Fund. The investments held in the Special Investment Account are held specially for behoof of the respective Committees, congregations, &c., and under their direction (see Byelaws and Regulations, p. 550). The investments held under the General Investment Fund are held in a common pool in the form of a Unit Trust (see Byelaws and Regulations, p. 552). (See also pp. 364, 365 below.) The investments held in the Deposit Fund are part of a common pool invested in accordance with the Bye-laws and Regulations (see p. 554).

SECTION VII. INVESTMENT OF CONGREGATIONAL FUNDS —THE TRUSTEE INVESTMENTS ACT, 1961.

PART I.

Investment by Kirk Sessions, &c., otherwise than through The Church of Scotland Trust.

The Church of Scotland Trust has had occasion to consider the terms of the above Act in so far as the investment of funds held by congregations is concerned.

Kirk Sessions, &c., Trustees for their Congregations.

Kirk Sessions, Congregational Boards, Boards of Management, &c., are Trustees for their congregations and therefore this question is of importance to them in cases where invested funds are held.

Investment position prior to 1961 Act.

Hitherto, the investment of such funds has been restricted to the very limited range of investments authorised by the Trusts (Scotland) Act, 1921. Owing to the fact that such investments yielded a fixed rate of interest, the real value of these investments in a period of inflation declined. It was from consideration of such circumstances that the Trustee Investments Act, 1961, was passed into law.

This Act provides that a Trustee may divide the Trust Funds into two parts of equal value, the "narrower-range" part and the "wider-range" part.

Provisions in 1961 Act.

The "narrower-range" part consists of all the investments previously authorised by the Trusts (Scotland) Act, 1921, and some additional fixed interest securities of local and public authorities in the Commonwealth and Debentures in United Kingdom Companies conforming to certain conditions and Trustee Savings Banks.

The "wider-range" part may consist of (1) Ordinary and Preference Shares and Stock of Companies incorporated in the United Kingdom which have an issued paid up capital of at least £1,000,000 and which have paid a dividend on all Ordinary

Shares for the preceding five years provided that the Shares are fully paid up and are quoted on a recognised Stock Exchange, (2) Shares in designated Building Societies, and (3) Unit Trusts in respect of which there is in force an Order of the Board of Trade under the Prevention of Fraud (Investments) Act, 1958.

Where a division of the fund has been made into two parts of equal value, the parts are to remain separate and no transfer may be made from one part to the other without a compensating or balancing transfer of equal value.

> *Note.*—It should be mentioned that it is not advisable for Kirk Sessions, &c., to invest in Building Societies as Income Tax is paid by the Societies and cannot be recovered. It should also be kept in mind that in the case of certain Companies and Unit Trusts which have interests abroad, only a portion of the Income Tax deducted from dividends can be recovered.

Investments—advice not required.

Under the Act, Trustees may invest funds in certain investments without obtaining advice. These are (1) Defence Bonds, National Savings Certificates and Ulster Savings Certificates, and (2) deposits in the Post Office Savings Bank, ordinary deposits in a Trustee Savings Bank and deposits in a Bank or Department thereof certified under Sub-section 3 of Section 9 of the Finance Act, 1956.

Investments—advice required.

In the case of *all other investments*, whatever their form, the Trustees are required to obtain *written* advice from a person who is reasonably believed by the Trustees to be qualified by his ability in and practical experience of financial matters before making any investment. Such persons would include Stockbrokers who are members of a Stock Exchange and Solicitors, Chartered Accountants and Bankers experienced in such matters and willing to advise. The Act also requires that Trustees are to have regard to the need for diversification of investments and the purpose of the Trust.

Separate Trust Funds.

Where Trustees hold funds for Trust purposes which are not identical with those on which other funds are held, such funds fall to be treated separately. For example, a Kirk Session may hold a Poor Fund and may also administer a Fund under a charitable bequest. Such Funds should be treated separately, and not more than 50 per cent of each of the Funds can be invested in "wider-range" investments.

It will be understood that the foregoing is merely an outline of the main provisions of the Act and, before exercising the extended powers of investment under the Act, Kirk Sessions, &c., must obtain advice from some person qualified to give it.

At present, when sound ordinary Stocks and Shares are

Duties of Trustees to review existing Investments.

generally yielding much less than fixed interest Stocks, Kirk Sessions, &c., may be unwilling to proceed in terms of the new Act, as this might result in an immediate and substantial reduction of income. Even so, this opportunity is taken to remind Kirk Sessions and others acting as Trustees for their congregations that they have a duty to review their investments at regular intervals; it also behoves them to consider periodically the possibility or desirability of exercising the extended powers of investment made available to them by the Act.

PART II.

Investment by Kirk Sessions, &c., through The Church of Scotland Trust.

General.

So far, we have dealt solely with the position of Trustees under the new Act. There is, however, a further option available to Kirk Sessions, &c., of congregations of the Church of Scotland. In 1948 The Church of Scotland Trust promoted a Provisional Order whereby widely extended powers of investment were given to the Trust.

Special Investment Account.

One of the functions of this Trust is to hold investments for congregations, when requested to do so. Another function is to accept capital from congregations for investment in a particular security. Such investments are held under the Special Investment Account (1960, Reg. 2).

General Investment Fund.

The Church of Scotland Trust also operates the General Investment Fund which at present holds capital amounting to approximately £8,000,000 for Committees of the General Assembly and Congregations. The investment of these funds is conducted by an Investment Committee composed mainly of professional and business men with wide experience in such matters. The Funds, as authorised by the General Assembly in 1960 (Reg. 3), is managed in the form of a Unit Trust by a firm of professional Investment Managers in Edinburgh. Units may be bought or sold by Committees, Kirk Sessions, &c., according to the current market value of the Unit. The portfolio of investments affords all investors a share in a wide range of investments, much wider than could be obtained by any single Committee or Congregation acting alone. Approximately 36 per cent of the Fund is invested in first-class Ordinary Stocks and Shares. This spread of investments affords a degree of protection against loss which in most cases could not otherwise be obtained by individual congregations.

Congregations are at liberty to invest in this Fund to an unlimited extent. It is specially constituted for the investment of Church Funds which are more or less of a permanent nature and the purpose for which the capital is held is "charitable" within the sense of the Income Tax Acts. These conditions satisfied, the capital may be admitted to the Fund and income distributed at a rate determined from time to time by the Trust without deduction of Income Tax, half-yearly at Whitsunday and Martinmas. No expenses are incurred either in making an investment or in realising it. These are important advantages to investors in the General Investment Fund of The Church of Scotland Trust.

Advantages of Investment in General Investment Fund.

This Fund is commended to congregations having capital available for investment as the facilities afforded thereby, specially created for the convenience of congregations, are preferable to the extended powers of investment offered by the Trustee Investments Act, 1961, with all its attendant restrictions and conditions.

The Deposit Fund is a medium for the short-term investment by congregations and committees. Investments are in multiples of £5 with a maximum of £25,000. Investment in the first instance is for a minimum period of three months but thereafter withdrawal is available on seven days notice being given. There is no capital loss on withdrawal and interest is paid half-yearly and gross. A copy of the Bye-laws and Regulations is set out on page 554.

Copies of the Byelaws and Regulations made by the General Assembly in 1961 (see App. VII., *C.*, p. 550), and further information about the Special Investment Account and the General Investment Fund with Forms of Application can be obtained from the General Treasurer of the Church who, with his staff, are also prepared to give advice to Kirk Sessions, &c., on investment questions generally.

Byelaws and Regulations.

SECTION VIII. THE BAIRD TRUST.

Since the inception of the Trust in 1873 the Baird Trust has made, and may continue to make, grants for (*a*) the erection of churches, (*b*) the erection of church halls, (*c*) the enlargement, renovation, and improvement of churches and church halls, and (*d*) the endowment and further endowment of churches. It has been the custom to insert in the titles a condition that the subjects are inalienably secured to the Church of Scotland. Some of these properties and endowments are or will be vested in the General Trustees; and others vested in trustees other than the General Trustees are held by them subject to the direction and oversight of the General Assembly. The General Trustees and the General Administration Committee of the Church, acting under the authority of the General Assembly (Reports 1931, pp. 21 and 113), have respectively granted letters to the Baird Trust undertaking, (1) in the event of its being desired to sell any church or church hall to which the Trust has given a grant, to communicate and consult with it as to the terms of sale, and (2) before rearranging, transferring, and disposing of the endowments of any parish to which they have given a grant, to communicate and consult with it as to the rearrangements proposed (in both cases without prejudice to the right of the Church to act on the direction of the General Assembly), and undertaking, in the event of the Baird Trust not acquiescing, to repay them the grant, if required to do so. (For Letter of Obligation, see Appendix IV., pp. 464, 465.)

SECTION IX. THE WIDOWS' FUND.

The Churches and Universities (Scotland) Widows' and Orphans' Fund Order Confirmation Act, 1954, *and (Amendment) Order Confirmation Act,* 1967.

Constitution of Fund

In 1744 a Fund was established for the benefit of the widows and children of ministers of the Church of Scotland and professors in the Scottish Universities. A similar Fund was instituted in 1846 for the benefit of widows and children of ministers of the Free Church of Scotland and of professors of the colleges of that Church. These two Funds were amalgamated by The Churches and Universities (Scotland) Widows' and Orphans' Fund Order, 1930, with effect as from 2nd October 1929. The combined Fund followed the pattern of the former Free Church Fund, with new entrants paying the same contributions as were paid by contributors to that Fund to secure corresponding benefits, and the former Church of Scotland Fund, with four classes of contribution, four classes of widow's annuity and varying children's provisions became, as from the above date, a separate closed section of the Fund.

The 1930 Order was superseded by the Churches and Universities (Scotland) Widows' and Orphans' Fund Order, 1954 (*vide* Appendix, p. 560). The principal changes effected by the

1954 Order were the extension of the Trustees' power of investment, the admission of chaplains to H.M. Forces to membership of the Fund, the entitlement of legally adopted children to the benefits of the Fund, and the introduction of a right to contributors on retirement or on ceasing to hold a charge or office in the Churches or Universities to discontinue further contributions to the Fund.

By an Amendment Order (*vide* Appendix, p. 560) which came into operation on 14th July 1967 University professors (other than ministers of either of the Churches appointed to Chairs in the Divinity Faculties of the four original Scottish Universities or in the Colleges of the Churches, *i.e.*, Church professors) ceased to be eligible for admission to membership of the Fund and University professors, active and retired, then in membership of the Fund were given the opportunity, if they so wished, to discontinue membership on the basis of a refund of contributions. The Amendment Order (Section 7) also provides for the eventual discontinuance of the Universities' representation on the board of Trustees of the Fund when, in the opinion of the Trustees, such representation is considered to be no longer expedient. University Professors no longer eligible for admission to membership.

The affairs of the Fund are now regulated by the 1954 Order as amended by the 1967 Order. Unless otherwise stated, marginal references are to sections of the 1954 Order.

The whole property and assets of the Fund are vested in twenty Trustees as a body corporate, of whom twelve are appointed by the General Assembly of the Church of Scotland, four by the General Assembly of the Free Church of Scotland, and four by the University Court of the University of Edinburgh. One-fourth of the Trustees in order of seniority retire by rotation annually but are eligible for reappointment, and vacancies are filled by the respective General Assemblies and the University Court referred to by reappointment or the appointment of new Trustees. Trustees of the Fund (Secs. 4-10).

Every minister or missionary on induction or appointment to a permanent charge of the Church of Scotland or of the Free Church of Scotland (which in the case of a minister may include an appointment declared by the General Assembly to be the equivalent of a "charge" for the purposes of the Widows' Fund) and every Church professor (not already in membership) on admission to a Chair in the Divinity Faculty of any of the Universities or in the Colleges of either of the Churches is obliged as at the date of his induction or appointment to join the Fund, involving payment of the following contributions to Membership of Fund.

secure certain provisions in the form of annuities for his wife and children in the event of his death, viz. :—

Contributions. 1954 (Sec. 29). 1967 (Sec. 12).

(1) *Entry Money.—Age last birthday at entry* — *Amount payable*

Age last birthday at entry	Amount payable
Up to 34	£10
35–44	25
45–49	40
50–54	60
55–59	80
60 & Over	100

Entry money of £10, £25 or £40 is payable in two equal annual instalments, and entry money of £60, £80 or £100 by three, four or five equal annual instalments respectively ; the first instalment being payable at the first term of Whitsunday (15th May) after date of admission and the remaining instalments at the succeeding terms of Whitsunday thereafter.

1954 (Sec. 29). 1967 (Sec. 12).

(2) *Marriage Tax.*—If married on admission, or when marriage takes place thereafter, and on the occasion of every subsequent marriage, a Marriage Tax is payable in accordance with the following scale :—

Wife older, the same age or not more than 5 years younger than husband	£10
Wife more than 5 but not more than 10 years younger than husband	£20
Wife more than 10 but not more than 15 years younger than husband	£35
Wife more than 15 but not more than 20 years younger than husband	£50
Wife more than 20 years younger than husband	£75

Marriage tax of £10, £20, £35 or £50 is payable by two equal annual instalments and Marriage Tax of £75 by three equal annual instalments, payable the first instalment at the first term of Martinmas (11th November) occurring after three months from the date of the marriage or, if then married, from the date of admission and the second and third instalments at the succeeding term or terms of Martinmas.

The above scales of Entry Money and Marriage Tax apply to entrants after 15th May 1970. The Marriage Tax for entrants prior to that date is £5 plus the sum of £1 for each complete year by which the husband's age exceeds that of his wife.

(3) *Annual Rate.*—An annual rate, at present £16·80 for new entrants, payable at Whitsunday (15th May) annually, the first payment being due at the first term of Whitsunday after date of admission, and thereafter at Whitsunday yearly during the lifetime of the member, but with the right on ceasing to hold a permanent charge or office in the Churches or Universities to discontinue further contributions. In that event, however, all prior contributions paid are forfeited and the contributors' dependants cease to be entitled to the benefits of the Fund. (Secs. 22-25.)

Under a scheme introduced by the Trustees in July 1972 in terms of Section 31 of the 1954 Order any member (other than a contributor to the former Church of Scotland Fund) may at any time elect to make an increased annual payment to cease at age 65 years in place of the ordinary annual rate for life or to commute his future liability to make payment of the ordinary annual rate by a single payment in accordance with Tables prepared by the Actuary of the Fund.

A member on leaving the service of the Churches or Universities connected with the Fund may continue membership of the Fund, even if he enters other employment unconnected with any Church or University.

All contributions to the Fund qualify for income tax relief and, by concession, this relief is extended to members who after retirement continue contributions to preserve the right of their dependants to the benefits of the Fund.

Importance of date, 15th May.

The importance of the date 15th May in relation to inductions and resignations under consideration shortly before that date should be specially noted, particularly by Presbyteries. If an induction takes place shortly before 15th May the first annual rate and the first instalment of entry money (in the case of a first induction) fall due at 15th May immediately following the induction. If a minister resigns shortly before or on 15th May and desires to continue his connection with the Fund he must pay personally the rate due at 15th May; while, if the charge is vacant at that term, a vacancy rate will also be payable by the Maintenance of the Ministry Fund or others liable. If no other considerations are involved, the induction or resignation should be deferred until after 15th May.

Collection of Contributions (Sec. 22).

In general the regulations provide for the payment of all contributions, whether of entry money, marriage taxes or annual rates, due in respect of active ministers, missionaries and college professors of the Churches connected with the Fund direct from the sources of their stipends or emoluments, so that in the Church of Scotland the fund for the Maintenance of the Ministry, the funds of the mission committees, the college funds or the funds of non-participating congregations, as the case may be, are primarily responsible for payment of all such contributions to the Fund. In accordance with established practice the contributions are recovered from the ministers, missionaries or professors in respect of whom they are paid, by deduction from their stipends or other emoluments. A non-participating congregation, as defined in sec. 3, means, briefly, a congregation of the Church of Scotland the minister of which does not receive any payment, or receives only a nominal payment, by way of stipend from the fund for the Maintenance of the Ministry—*i.e.*, a self-supporting congregation which is directly responsible for payment of its minister's stipend.

(Sec. 23.)

A minister, missionary or professor on ceasing to hold a charge or office in the Churches, whether on retirement or on leaving the service of the Churches, becomes personally responsible for payment of his annual rate direct to the Fund. Ministers introduced to suppressed charges or inducted to certain non-participating congregations, relatively few in number, which have forfeited their connection with the Fund, likewise become personally responsible for payment of their annual rates direct to the Fund so long as they continue in such charges.

Vacancy Rates (Sec. 27).

If a charge is vacant at 15th May when the annual rate becomes payable, the Maintenance of Ministry Fund or others liable become responsible for payment to the Fund of an annual rate in respect of the vacancy in the charge, thus ensuring continuity of contributions to the Fund when charges are vacant. The vacancy rate amounts to £7 or such higher annual sum as was paid for or in respect of the incumbent of the charge before the vacancy occurred. Where the incumbent has opted to make an increased annual payment to cease at age 65 or has commuted his former annual rate by a single payment, the vacancy rate is the amount of the annual rate for life formerly paid by the incumbent.

This payment is not due, however, on the death, translation, resignation, or deprivation of a colleague and successor, or assistant and successor, or the holder of an appointment declared by the General Assembly to be the equivalent of a charge, or in the case of a suppressed charge, or in respect of any charge linked or united with some other charge, or any charge which has forfeited its connection with the Fund.

Benefits consist of provisions in the form of annuities to widows and children of members, payable in half-yearly instalments on 15th May and 11th November. The widow's annuity continues until the term of payment immediately preceding death or remarriage and the child's annuity, equal in amount to one-half of the widow's annuity, or three-fourths if the child is or becomes an orphan, until the term of payment immediately preceding the attainment of eighteen years of age or earlier death. Benefits of Fund (Secs. 37 and 38).

The widow's annuity qualifies as "earned income" for income tax purposes, provided the husband was not engaged in other employment outwith the service of the Churches or Universities connected with the Fund at the time of his death.

Statistics relating to the numbers of contributors to the Fund and widows and children in receipt of the benefits of the Fund are compiled annually at 15th May, and each member is required to complete and return to the clerk and treasurer of the Fund in July annually a schedule recording any changes which have taken place in the state of his family during the preceding year. Failure to comply with this requirement may involve suspension of payment of the stipend or other emoluments to which the member is entitled. Statistics of Fund. (Sec. 16.)

Presbytery clerks are required to furnish to the Trustees half-yearly reports as at 1st April and 1st October of all changes that may occur within the bounds of the Presbytery with respect to the induction, translation, resignation, deprivation and death of any minister and any additional particulars required for the information of the Trustees, together with excerpts from the appropriate minutes when unions, suppressions, reductions and linkings, also restorations after suppressions in terms of 1957, xvii., have taken place. Synod minutes are required in cases of dissolutions. Certain unions and all dissolutions of unions require the authority of the General Assembly or the Commission of Assembly (1957, xvii.). In a case of suppression it is essential that the Presbytery minute should record "the withdrawal from a congregation of the right to have its minister appointed without restriction." (Sec. 15.)

The affairs of the Fund are subject to periodical actuarial investigation, the latest investigation having been made at Actuarial Investigation (Secs. 44 and 45).

15th May 1969. The Trustees, subject to obtaining an interim report from the actuary of the Fund, are empowered to make temporary annual additions to annuities and such additions have been made annually since 1952. Such additions are separate from and do not form part of the basic annuities and are subject to review at any time by the Trustees.

(Sec. 53.) The Trustees are obliged to prepare and lay annually before the General Assemblies of the Churches and also annually before the University Courts of the Universities a report on the state and progress of the Fund.

Rates &c.; Privileged Debts (Sec. 34). All contributions due to the Fund—*i.e.*, annual rates, entry money, and marriage tax, with interest thereon, are privileged debts and preferable to all other debts of the contributors, except imperial taxes and local rates.

Annuities Alimentary (Sec. 42). The annuities payable to widows and children are alimentary and not affectable by their debts or deeds nor subject to arrestment or other legal diligence at the instance of creditors.

Estate Duty on Annuities. Under the law as it is at present the capitalised value of the annuity to which a widow becomes entitled from the Fund on the death of her husband does not attract liability to Estate Duty but should be reported separately from her husband's personal estate and as an estate by itself.

NOTES

APPENDIX I.

THE BARRIER ACT, 1697.

THE General Assembly, taking into their consideration the Overture and Act made in the last Assembly concerning innovations, and having heard the report of the several commissioners from Presbyteries to whom the consideration of the same was recommended, in order to its being more ripely advised and determined in this Assembly; and considering the frequent practice of former Assemblies of this Church, and that it will mightily conduce to the exact obedience of the Acts of Assemblies, that General Assemblies be very deliberate in making of the same, and that the whole Church have a previous knowledge thereof, and their opinion be had therein, and for preventing any sudden alteration or innovation, or other prejudice to the Church, in either doctrine or worship, or discipline, or government thereof, now happily established; do, therefore, appoint, enact, and declare, that before any General Assembly of this Church shall pass any Acts, which are to be binding Rules and Constitutions to the Church, the same Acts be first proposed as overtures to the Assembly, and, being by them passed as such, be remitted to the consideration of the several Presbyteries of this Church, and their opinions and consent reported by their commissioners to the next General Assembly following, who may then pass the same in Acts, if the more general opinion of the Church thus had agreed thereunto.

APPENDIX II.

THE BASIS AND PLAN OF UNION, 1929.

BASIS OF UNION.

UNITING ACT.

I.

THE Church of Scotland and the United Free Church of Scotland, as branches of the Holy Catholic or Universal Church, believing that it is the will of their Lord for His disciples that they all should be one, acknowledge that the witness borne to the Lord by the Catholic Visible Church and the particular Churches which are members thereof, is obscured, and that His work is hindered by division and separation therein :

And WHEREAS in the Church of Scotland, which was reformed by Presbyters in 1560, and whose outward and visible unity continued for long time thereafter unbroken, separations have taken place among those who alike claimed to share in the common heritage and adhered to the common traditions and standards, whereby :—

> In 1690 certain members thereof, being unable to consent to the Revolution Settlement of the Church, continued independent ordinances and ultimately became known as the Reformed Presbyterian Church in Scotland :
>
> And in 1733 certain brethren, on grounds duly set forth and made public at the time, separated themselves from the jurisdiction of the Church of Scotland, and in due course formed the Secession Church in Scotland :
>
> And in 1761 certain other brethren, for grounds and reasons similarly declared and published, formed the Relief Church in Scotland :
>
> And in 1843 there occurred the cleavage in the Church of Scotland historically known as the Disruption, when a large section of the Church, severing ecclesiastical connection with the State on grounds set forth and recorded in the Claim, Declaration, and Protest of the General Assembly, 1842, and the Protest, 1843, formed the Free Church of Scotland :

And WHEREAS the obligation resting upon the followers of Christ to manifest their inward and spiritual unity to the world, in a common profession of faith and observance of the ordinances of Christ, has never ceased to be acknowledged by the Scottish Church throughout all her branches, so that not only were these separations contemplated and carried through with profound reluctance and in hope of ultimate reunion, but further, as the way was opened in God's Providence, various unions took place from time to time, and in particular those effected under and in terms of the several Uniting Acts following—viz., the Articles forming the Basis of Union of the United Secession and Relief Churches to form the United Presbyterian Church in 1847; the Act of Union of the Free Church of Scotland and the Reformed Presbyterian Church in 1876; and the Uniting Act with Declarations anent Union of the Free Church of Scotland and the United Presbyterian Church to form the United Free Church of Scotland in 1900:

And WHEREAS the Church of Scotland and the United Free Church of Scotland, maintaining alike the common historic heritage, and steadfastly desiring reunion, agreed, in 1909, through their General Assemblies, to enter into "unrestricted conference on the ecclesiastical situation in Scotland and the main causes which keep the Churches apart, in the earnest hope that by God's blessing, misunderstandings and hindrances may be removed, and the great object of Presbyterian reunion in Scotland be thereby advanced":

And WHEREAS in the course of conference it appeared that the main obstacles to reunion were concerned with differences which had arisen in regard to certain aspects and applications of the principles, common throughout their history to both Churches, of the National Recognition of Religion and the Spiritual Freedom of the Church under Christ, the only King and Head thereof:

And WHEREAS in the Articles Declaratory of the Constitution of the Church of Scotland in Matters Spiritual adopted by the General Assembly of 1926, and in the United Free Church Act anent the Spiritual Independence of the Church, 1906 (which Articles and Act are appended to the present Act), these principles are reaffirmed and set forth in a manner which is in accordance with the convictions of both Churches:

And WHEREAS these Churches, deeply conscious of the evils of disunion, and being increasingly impressed with the urgent need for reunion in order to meet more adequately the religious requirements of the people, welcomed the opportunity thus afforded for the readjustment of their relations to each other, and in the General Assemblies of 1926 agreed to confer together on the formation of a Basis of Union, and generally on the whole matters to be arranged before an incorporating union could be carried through successfully:

And WHEREAS representative Committees having been appointed and having communicated to one another the existing standards, rules, and methods of the Churches, it appeared that in regard to doctrine, worship, government, and discipline as therein set forth substantial agreement obtained between them:

And WHEREAS certain further necessary adjustments have now been made; and in particular Questions and a Formula to be used at the Ordination and Induction of Ministers, the constitution of the Courts of the united Church, provision for the support and for the training of the Ministry, and arrangements for combining the methods and work of the two Churches, have been agreed upon, and have been duly authorised by the Courts of the two Churches:

NOW THEREFORE THE GENERAL ASSEMBLY OF THE CHURCH OF

SCOTLAND AND THE GENERAL ASSEMBLY OF THE UNITED FREE CHURCH OF SCOTLAND, devoutly acknowledging the mercy and long-suffering shown by Almighty God to themselves and to their fathers, rendering humble and hearty thanks for the gracious guidance bestowed upon them in this their endeavour to heal the divisions in His Church and to promote His glory, and entreating Him to pour out His Spirit upon His servants and upon those who shall come after them, that as good stewards of the manifold grace of God they may with growing power minister to the people of this land and to the nations that have not yet received the Gospel, DO HEREBY, in terms and in pursuance of Deliverances of their respective General Assemblies, with approval of the Presbyteries of the respective Churches in accordance with the provisions of the Barrier Act, ENACT AND DECLARE THAT THESE CHURCHES, being historic branches of the Reformed Church in Scotland, DO AND SHALL HENCEFORTH CONSTITUTE ONE CHURCH, and that the name of the united Church shall be THE CHURCH OF SCOTLAND.

II.

The General Assembly of the Church of Scotland and the General Assembly of the United Free Church of Scotland enact that the Churches enter into union in view of the following DECLARATIONS, viz. :—

1. The various matters of agreement between the Churches with a view to union are accepted and enacted without prejudice to the inherent liberty of the united Church as a branch of the Church of God to determine and regulate her own constitution and laws as duty may require, in dependence on the grace of God and under the guidance of His Word and Spirit, all as more particularly set forth in the aftermentioned *Act*, 1906, and *Articles*, 1926.

2. The following are leading documents setting forth the constitution, standards, rules and methods of the united Church, viz. :—

GENERAL CONSTITUTION, including the Principles of the Spirituality and Freedom of the Church, and the National Recognition of Religion.

United Free Church Act anent Spiritual Independence (1906).

Articles Declaratory of the Constitution of the Church of Scotland in matters Spiritual (1926).

DOCTRINE.

The Westminster Confession of Faith (1647).

United Presbyterian Church Declaratory Act (1879).

Free Church Declaratory Act (1892) with *Act* (1894) relative thereto.

The Church of Scotland Act on the Formula (1910).

GOVERNMENT.

The Form of Presbyterial Church Government and of Ordination of Ministers (1645).

WORSHIP.

A Directory for the Public Worship of God (1645).

DISCIPLINE.

The Form of Process (1707).

Which *Form of Presbyterial Church Government, Directory for the Public Worship of God,* and *Form of Process* respectively are to be regarded as generally regulative and as of validity, as these have been interpreted or modified by Acts of General Assembly or by consuetude.

3. The following *Uniting Acts* are historic documents the general principles whereof are held to be conserved in the united Church :—

Articles forming the Basis of Union of the United Secession and Relief Churches to form the United Presbyterian Church (1847).

Act of Union of the Free Church of Scotland and the Reformed Presbyterian Church (1876).

Uniting Act with Declarations anent Union of the Free Church of Scotland and the United Presbyterian Church to form the United Free Church of Scotland (1900).

4. *The Larger and Shorter Catechisms* prepared by the Westminster Assembly of Divines, sanctioned by the General Assembly in 1648 and for long approved as manuals of instruction, continue to be held in honour in the united Church.

5. The following documents are also held in honour as having an important place in the history of Scottish Presbyterianism :—

Scots Confession (1560).
First Book of Discipline (1560).
Second Book of Discipline (1578).
Book of Common Order (1564).

6. As this Union takes place on the footing of maintaining the liberty of judgment and action heretofore recognised in either of the Churches uniting, so in particular it is hereby declared that members of both Churches shall have full right, as they shall see cause, to assert and maintain the views of truth and duty which they had liberty to maintain in the said Churches.

7. The Churches, in entering into Union, under a sense of responsibility as a branch of the Church of God, acknowledge afresh the obligation resting on the Church to provide the ordinances of religion to the people of Scotland through a territorial ministry and to labour for the universal diffusion of the Gospel, and the duty of her members to contribute, according to their ability, both by their service and their means, for the support of the ordinances of religion in this land and the extension of the Kingdom of Christ throughout the world.

III.

The General Assembly of the Church of Scotland and the General Assembly of the United Free Church of Scotland enact and ordain that all previous enactments and regulations of the General Assemblies of either uniting Church in force at the passing of this Act, unless in so far as modified by the Basis and Plan of Union, shall continue in force in the same manner as prior to the passing of this Act, so long as they shall not have been repealed or amended in accordance with the law of the united Church: provided always that where any such enactments or regulations are found in conflict or where the former practice of the two Churches is materially different and has not been adjusted by the Basis and Plan of Union, any necessary legislation to which the procedure of the Barrier Act is appropriate shall be by interim Act only, which shall be transmitted to Presbyteries in accordance with the provisions of the Barrier Act for consent or suggestions before its adoption as a standing law of the Church.

IV.

The General Assembly of the Church of Scotland and the General Assembly of the United Free Church of Scotland enact and ordain that the General Assembly of the Church of Scotland and the General Assembly of the United Free Church of Scotland, when they have met for the purpose of consummating the Union, and have adopted the Uniting Act, shall thereafter have the powers of a General Assembly of the united Church, and may do and authorise all things necessary or proper and lawful to be done with a view to the orderly inauguration and conduct of the affairs of the united Church, and in consistency with the terms of Union agreed upon.

APPENDIX TO UNITING ACT.

Articles Declaratory of the Constitution of the Church of Scotland in Matters Spiritual.

I. The Church of Scotland is part of the Holy Catholic or Universal Church; worshipping one God, Almighty, all-wise, and all-loving, in the Trinity of the Father, the Son, and the Holy Ghost, the same in substance, equal in power and glory; adoring the Father, infinite in Majesty, of whom are all things; confessing our Lord Jesus Christ, the Eternal Son, made very man for our salvation; glorying in His Cross and Resurrection, and owning obedience to Him as the Head over all things to His Church; trusting in the promised renewal and guidance of the Holy Spirit; proclaiming the forgiveness of sins and acceptance with God through faith in Christ, and the gift of Eternal Life; and labouring for the advancement of the Kingdom of God throughout the world. The Church of Scotland adheres to the Scottish Reformation; receives the Word of God which is contained in the Scriptures of the Old and New Testaments as its supreme rule of faith and life; and avows the fundamental doctrines of the Catholic faith founded thereupon.

II. The principal subordinate standard of the Church of Scotland is the Westminster Confession of Faith approved by the General Assembly of 1647, containing the sum and substance of the Faith of the Reformed Church. Its government is Presbyterian, and is exercised through Kirk Sessions, Presbyteries, Provincial Synods, and General Assemblies. Its system and principles of worship, orders, and discipline are in accordance with "The Directory for the Public

Worship of God," "The Form of Presbyterial Church Government," and "The Form of Process," as these have been or may hereafter be interpreted or modified by Acts of the General Assembly or by consuetude.

III. This Church is in historical continuity with the Church of Scotland which was reformed in 1560, whose liberties were ratified in 1592, and for whose security provision was made in the Treaty of Union of 1707. The continuity and identity of the Church of Scotland are not prejudiced by the adoption of these Articles. As a national Church representative of the Christian Faith of the Scottish people it acknowledges its distinctive call and duty to bring the ordinances of religion to the people in every parish of Scotland through a territorial ministry.

IV. This Church, as part of the Universal Church wherein the Lord Jesus Christ has appointed a government in the hands of Church office-bearers, receives from Him, its Divine King and Head, and from Him alone, the right and power subject to no civil authority to legislate, and to adjudicate finally, in all matters of doctrine, worship, government, and discipline in the Church, including the right to determine all questions concerning membership and office in the Church, the constitution and membership of its Courts, and the mode of election of its office-bearers, and to define the boundaries of the spheres of labour of its ministers and other office-bearers. Recognition by civil authority of the separate and independent government and jurisdiction of this Church in matters spiritual, in whatever manner such recognition be expressed, does not in any way affect the character of this government and jurisdiction as derived from the Divine Head of the Church alone, or give to the civil authority any right of interference with the proceedings or judgments of the Church within the sphere of its spiritual government and jurisdiction.

V. This Church has the inherent right, free from interference by civil authority, but under the safeguards for deliberate action and legislation provided by the Church itself, to frame or adopt its subordinate standards, to declare the sense in which it understands its Confession of Faith, to modify the forms of expression therein, or to formulate other doctrinal statements, and to define the relation thereto of its office-bearers and members, but always in agreement with the Word of God and the fundamental doctrines of the Christian Faith contained in the said Confession, of which agreement the Church shall be sole judge, and with due regard to liberty of opinion in points which do not enter into the substance of the Faith.

VI. This Church acknowledges the divine appointment and authority of the civil magistrate within his own sphere, and maintains its historic testimony to the duty of the nation acting in its corporate capacity to render homage to God, to acknowledge the Lord Jesus Christ to be King over the nations, to obey His laws, to reverence His ordinances, to honour His Church, and to promote in all appropriate ways the Kingdom of God. The Church and the State owe mutual duties to each other, and acting within their respective spheres may signally promote each other's welfare. The Church and the State have the right to determine each for itself all questions concerning the extent and the continuance of their mutual relations in the discharge of these duties and the obligations arising therefrom.

VII. The Church of Scotland, believing it to be the will of Christ that His disciples should be all one in the Father and in Him, that the world may believe that the Father has sent Him, recognises the obligation to seek and promote union with other Churches in which it finds the Word to be purely preached, the sacraments administered according to Christ's ordinance, and discipline rightly exercised; and it has the right to unite with any such Church without loss of its identity on terms which this Church finds to be consistent with these Articles.

VIII. The Church has the right to interpret these Articles, and, subject to the safeguards for deliberate action and legislation provided by the Church itself, to modify or add to them; but always consistently with the provisions of the first Article hereof, adherence to which, as interpreted by the Church, is essential to its continuity and corporate life. Any proposal for a modification of or addition to these Articles which may be approved of by the General Assembly shall, before it can be enacted by the Assembly, be transmitted by way of overture to Presbyteries in at least two immediately successive years. If the overture shall receive the approval, with or without suggested amendment, of two-thirds of the whole of the Presbyteries of the Church, the Assembly may revise the overture in the light of any suggestions by the Presbyteries, and may transmit the overture when so revised to Presbyteries for their consent. If the overture as transmitted in its final form shall receive the consent of not less than two-thirds of the whole of the Presbyteries of the Church, the General Assembly may, if it deems it expedient, modify or add to these Articles in terms of the said overture. But if the overture as transmitted in its final form shall not receive the requisite consent, the same or a similar proposal shall not be again transmitted for the consent of Presbyteries until an interval of five years after the failure to obtain the requisite consent has been reported to the General Assembly.

IX. Subject to the provisions of the foregoing Articles and the powers of amendment therein contained, the Constitution of the Church of Scotland in matters spiritual is hereby anew ratified and confirmed by the Church.

United Free Church Act anent Spiritual Independence of the Church (1906).

"Whereas the General Assembly judged it necessary in the circumstances of the Church to pass the following Act, and although the principles set forth therein involve no new departure and are not in any sense a constitutional novation, but have been always accepted and maintained by this Church, yet in respect of the importance of making manifest to all that the whole Church explicitly adheres to these principles, the General Assembly deemed it right to send it down as an Overture under the Barrier Act: the General Assembly hereby, with consent of a majority of Presbyteries, declare and enact, as follows:—

"Considering the situation created by the decisions of the House of Lords on 1st August 1904, in the Cases of *Bannatyne and Others* v. *Lord Overtoun and Others*, and *Young and Others* v. *Macalister and Others*, and the grounds on which these decisions were based; considering also the Resolutions relative thereto of the Commission of Assembly at its ordinary Meeting on 10th August 1904, of which Resolutions the Assembly hereby approve; and considering that it is needful to make clear the position in which the United Free Church of Scotland stands in reference to the questions thus raised, the General Assembly resolve and declare as follows:—

1. "They assert and protest that those branches of the Church of Christ in Scotland now united in this Church have always claimed, and this Church continues to claim, that the Church of Christ has under Him as her only Head independent and exclusive jurisdiction and power of legislating in all matters of doctrine, worship, discipline, and government of the Church, including therein the right from time to time to alter, change,

add to, or modify, her constitution and laws, Subordinate Standards, and Church Formulas, and to determine and declare what these are.

2. "The General Assembly accordingly declare anew and enact that it is a fundamental principle and rule of this Church that, in dependence on the grace of God, recognising the authority of the Word of God, contained in the Scriptures of the Old and New Testaments, as the supreme unchangeable Standard, and looking to the Head of the Church for the promised guidance of the Holy Spirit, this Church has the sole and exclusive right and power from time to time, as duty may require, through her Courts to alter, change, add to, or modify, her constitution and laws, Subordinate Standards, and Formulas, and to determine and declare what these are, and to unite with other Christian Churches; always in conformity with the Word of God, and also with the safeguards for deliberate action and legislation in such cases provided by the Church herself—of which conformity the Church herself, acting through her Courts, shall be the sole judge—and under a sense of direct responsibility to the ever-living Head of the Church, and of duty towards all the Church's members.

3. "The General Assembly also declare and enact that in all the Courts of the Church a decision of the Court given either unanimously, or by a majority of its members present and voting, is the decision of the Court, and the decision of the General Assembly so reached is final. With respect to Acts which are to be binding Rules and Constitutions of the Church, the Assembly shall have regard to the safeguards referred to in the foregoing resolution.

4. "The General Assembly further declare that the Church holds her funds and property, present and future, in conformity with these principles; the Church reserving her right to accept and hold benefactions, subject to specific conditions attached to them by the donor, when and so long as she judges these conditions to be consistent with her liberty and her principles, and to be expedient in the circumstances of the time."

PREAMBLE, QUESTIONS, AND FORMULA.

Preamble.

The Narrative shall be read and, the Ordinand having taken his place before the Presbytery, the Moderator shall declare as follows :—

In the name of the Lord Jesus Christ, the King and Head of thr Church, Who, being ascended on high, hath given gifts unto men foe the edifying of the body of Christ, we are met here as a Presbytery to ordain A. B. to the office of the Holy Ministry by prayer and the laying on of hands by the Presbyters to whom it doth belong, and to induct him into the pastoral charge of . . . .

In this act of ordination the Church of Scotland, as part of the Holy Catholic or Universal Church worshipping One God—Father, Son, and Holy Spirit—affirms anew its belief in the Gospel of the sovereign grace and love of God, wherein through Jesus Christ, His only Son, our Lord,

Incarnate, Crucified, and Risen, He freely offers to all men, upon repentance and faith, the forgiveness of sins, renewal by the Holy Spirit, and eternal life, and calls them to labour in the fellowship of faith for the advancement of the Kingdom of God throughout the world.

The Church of Scotland acknowledges the Word of God which is contained in the Scriptures of the Old and New Testaments to be the supreme rule of faith and life.

The Church of Scotland holds as its subordinate standard the Westminster Confession of Faith, recognising liberty of opinion on such points of doctrine as do not enter into the substance of the Faith, and claiming the right, in dependence on the promised guidance of the Holy Spirit, to formulate, interpret, or modify its subordinate standards: always in agreement with the Word of God and the fundamental doctrines of the Christian Faith contained in the said Confession—of which agreement the Church itself shall be sole judge.

Then the Moderator, addressing the Ordinand or Minister to be inducted, who is to stand and make answer to the questions put to him, shall say :—

A. B., in view of this Declaration, you are now required to answer these questions :—

Questions to be put to Ministers before their Ordination or Admission to a Charge.

1. Do you believe in one God—Father, Son, and Holy Spirit; and do you confess anew the Lord Jesus Christ as your Saviour and Lord?
2. Do you believe the Word of God, which is contained in the Scriptures of the Old and New Testaments, to be the supreme rule of faith and life?
3. Do you believe the fundamental doctrines of the Christian faith contained in the Confession of Faith of this Church?
4. Do you acknowledge the Presbyterian Government of this Church to be agreeable to the Word of God; and do you promise to be subject in the Lord to this Presbytery and to the superior Courts of the Church, and to take your due part in the administration of its affairs?
5. Do you promise to seek the unity and peace of this Church; to uphold the doctrine, worship, government, and discipline thereof; and to cherish a spirit of brotherhood towards all the followers of the Lord?
6. Are not zeal for the glory of God, love to the Lord Jesus Christ, and a desire for the salvation of men, so far as you know your own heart, your great motives and chief inducements to enter into the office of the Holy Ministry?
7. Do you engage in the strength of the Lord Jesus Christ to live a godly and circumspect life; and faithfully, diligently, and cheerfully to discharge the duties of your ministry, seeking in all things the advancement of the Kingdom of God?
8. Do you accept and close with the call to be Pastor of this charge, and promise through grace to study to approve yourself a faithful Minister of the Gospel among this people?

The questions having been answered to the satisfaction of the Presbytery, and the Formula having been signed, the Ordinand shall kneel, and the Moderator, by prayer with laying on of hands, in which all the Ministers present join, shall ordain him to the Office of the Holy Ministry.

Thereafter the Moderator, except in cases in which there is no induction to a pastoral charge or any office, shall add these words :—

I now declare you to have been ordained to the office of the Holy Ministry, and in the Name of the Lord Jesus Christ, the King and Head of the Church, and by authority of this Presbytery, I induct you to this charge ; and in token thereof we give you the right hand of fellowship.

The following Question shall then be addressed to the Congregation, who are asked to signify assent by rising and standing in their places :—

Do you, the members and adherents of this Congregation, receive A. B., whom you have called to be your Minister, promising him all due honour and support in the Lord, and will you give of your means, as the Lord shall prosper you, for the maintenance of the Christian Ministry and the furtherance of the Gospel ?

Formula.

I believe the fundamental doctrines of the Christian faith contained in the Confession of Faith of this Church.

I acknowledge the Presbyterian government of this Church to be agreeable to the Word of God, and promise that I will submit thereto and concur therewith.

I promise to observe the order of worship and the administration of all public ordinances as the same are or may be allowed in this Church.

This Formula shall also be that to be signed by Elders on admission to office.

PLAN OF UNION.

CONSTITUTION AND POWERS OF COURTS.

The General Assembly.

1. The General Assembly is the Supreme Court of the Church. In matters spiritual its decisions are final, and are not subject to review by any Civil Court

2. The membership of the General Assembly consists of Commissioners elected by Presbyteries for each Assembly. These Commissioners, being Ministers (including Theological Professors) and Ruling Elders, are elected in proportion to the size of each Presbytery, one Minister for every four or part of four Ministers on the complete Roll of the Presby-

tery, and an equal number of Ruling Elders. Ministers elected as Commissioners to the General Assembly must be members of the Presbyteries by which they are elected. Elders so elected must be *bonâ fide* acting members of Kirk Sessions within the Church. The quorum of the General Assembly shall be 31, of whom not less than 16 shall be Ministers.

3. Each General Assembly is presided over by a Moderator elected by itself from among its own members. It is the duty of the Moderator to preside at meetings of Assembly and apply the Standing Orders for the conduct of business. He alone declares the dissolution of the Assembly and intimates the day appointed by the General Assembly for the meeting of the next Assembly. At the close of the Assembly he delivers an Address; and preaches at the opening of the next Assembly, constituting the Court, which shall then proceed to elect its Moderator.

The Moderator of the Assembly at which Union takes place shall be nominated by mutual agreement between the Committees on Union of the Church of Scotland and the United Free Church of Scotland. The first Assembly shall nominate the Moderator of the second Assembly, and the second Assembly shall determine the future method of nomination of Moderators of Assemblies.

4. The General Assembly will loyally welcome the Sovereign should it be the royal pleasure to attend in person: or, failing the Sovereign, a Lord High Commissioner as the royal representative. Neither the Sovereign nor the Lord High Commissioner as such is a constituent member of the Assembly.

5. The Commission of Assembly shall consist of the members of the Assembly with one member added, who shall be nominated by the Moderator; its quorum shall be the same as that of the General Assembly; it shall appoint its own Chairman, and it shall deal with such business as has been made statutory for the Commission by the law of the Church or has been remitted to it by the Assembly.

Presbyteries and Synods.

1. In all Presbyteries and Synods there shall be an equal number of Ministers and Elders when the Roll is fully made up.

2. Every Minister inducted to a charge within the bounds of the Presbytery shall be a member of the Presbytery. The Kirk Session for each charge shall elect annually a representative Elder from amongst their own number (of which intimation shall be made to the Presbytery within three months of the close of the General Assembly), or with the special permission of the Presbytery from any Kirk Session within the bounds.

3. Ministers to whom Assistants and Successors or Junior Colleagues have been appointed prior to 31st May 1932 shall continue to be members of Presbytery, as well as their Assistants and Successors or Junior Colleagues, and Ministers and Theological Professors of either the Church of Scotland or the United Free Church of Scotland who prior to the Union had demitted their charges on account of age or infirmity, and Ministers and Theological Professors so demitting their charges prior to 31st May 1932 may, if they so desire, remain members of the

Presbyteries which accepted their demission (or in the case of Ministers of the Church of Scotland may, if they so desire, return as members to such Presbyteries), it being understood that the question of the extension of this right to Ministers having Junior Colleagues appointed to them or Ministers and Theological Professors so demitting their charges subsequent to 31st May 1932, is meantime reserved for determination of the General Assembly with the consent of the Presbyteries of the Church. Ministers who have demitted their charges for any other reason may remain members of the Presbyteries which accepted the demission of their charges, subject to the approval of the Synod. When the Presbytery which accepted the demission has ceased to exist, or the charge which the Minister demitted has been severed from it, "the Presbytery which accepted the demission" shall be construed as meaning the Presbytery in which after the said date his said charge is situated.

4. Theological Professors who are Ministers of the united Church shall be members of the Presbytery within whose bounds is situated the College or University in which they teach.

5. Ministers in Colonial or Continental Charges, Missionaries who are ordained Ministers, Chaplains to His Majesty's Forces, and Chaplains on the Indian Establishment who have retired from active service, may remain members of the Presbyteries of which they were members at the date of their retirement on the same conditions as Ministers of home charges.

6. Ministers of the united Church who are temporarily appointed by or with the sanction of the Presbytery for a period of not less than twelve months to the charge of congregations, shall be received as members of the Presbytery within whose bounds they labour for the period during which they hold such temporary appointment, their membership in any other Presbyteries being meantime suspended, due intimation being made to the other Presbyteries concerned.

7. In order to maintain the equal number of Ministers and Elders in the Constitution of the Court, the Presbytery shall elect as members such a number of Elders as may be necessary for this purpose, such Elders to be chosen at the will of the Presbytery from any of the Kirk Sessions within the bounds.

8. With regard to Ministers of Charges furth of Scotland, the situation shall be accepted as it exists at present, and it shall be left to the united Church to make such readjustments as may be considered advisable.

Functions and Powers of Synods.

A Supplementary Report was sent down to Presbyteries in accordance with the Deliverance of the General Assembly. In response suggestions were received, but it has been agreed that any important change in functions and powers of Synods is a matter which would most suitably be considered and decided upon by the united Church. (See App. XIV., pp. 607-609.)

Functions, Constitution, and Powers of Kirk Sessions.

Until otherwise determined by the united Church through its General Assembly, after due consultation with Presbyteries, the method of election to and the powers and duties of Kirk Sessions shall continue in each congregation of the united Church to be governed by the regulations presently applicable to such congregation according to the branch of the united Church to which it belonged prior to the Union, except that the Formula to be signed by Elders on admission to office shall be the Formula hereinbefore provided for Ministers.

The same shall apply to Deacons' Courts, Committees of Management, Congregational Boards, &c.

TRAINING OF THE MINISTRY.

The General Assembly shall take immediate steps towards the adjustment and co-ordination of the system of Training for the Ministry and Theological Teaching upon the lines of the subjoined Report subject to such readjustments as may be approved of by the General Assembly with consent of Presbyteries, and so far as the Universities are interested, subject to the completion of negotiations and the obtaining of the necessary sanctions for a scheme on the lines set forth in the said Report with such readjustments as may be approved of as aforesaid. The General Assembly shall make such interim arrangements as shall be found expedient. (See App. VIII., p. 557.)

(*A*)

Relation of Divinity Halls to the Universities.

In the Report which was presented to the last General Assembly with regard to the Training of the Ministry and the Future Relations of Theological Teaching to the Universities, it was stated that meetings had been arranged with the four University Courts for the purpose of discussing future relations between the Universities and the united Church. Repeated conferences have since taken place, and have resulted in the adjustment of the Scheme which is printed as an Appendix hereto.

The Committee gratefully acknowledge the helpful and accommodating spirit in which the requirements of the Church were considered by the various Courts, and, in particular, the services rendered by the Principals of Glasgow and Edinburgh Universities in the actual drafting of the Scheme.

The negotiations were conducted on the basis of the three general principles which were enunciated in the previous Report and accepted by the General Assemblies of both Churches—viz. : (1) that the existing University Theological Chairs, freed from statutory tests, should be continued in a form in which they would still be serviceable to students of the Church ; (2) that the relations between the Theological Colleges and the Universities should be as close as possible ; and (3) that the Church must retain effective control over those to whom the doctrinal instruction of its ministry is entrusted.

The main features of the Scheme which has been adjusted are :—

(1) That in the case of the existing University Theological Chairs, while statutory tests should be abolished, appointments to these Chairs should be made by an Electoral Board equally

representative of the Church and the University. A two-thirds majority would be necessary for an appointment, thus ensuring that no Chair could be filled by a Professor whose teaching was repugnant to the Church. Powers would be taken to admit of other Churches being represented on the Board.

(2) That the Professors of the United Free Church Colleges holding office at the date of Union should become Professors in one of the University Faculties of Theology, provided that the Church guarantees payment of their stipends; and that, under a similar guarantee, their successors should be appointed by the Church. The University must, of course, be satisfied with the academic qualifications of any person nominated to a University Chair, and for that purpose every nomination would be subject to confirmation by the University. It would also be a necessary qualification for the tenure of these new Chairs, the stipends of which would be wholly provided by the Church, that the Professor should be and continue to be an ordinand or ordained minister of the Church The holders of both classes of Chairs would constitute, and would deliberate as, one University Faculty, and at the same time the necessary control of the Church over its teachers would be secured.

(3) That on a vacancy occurring, either in an existing University Chair or in any new Chair, the necessity for modifications in the subject-matter of its teaching (and in the case of a new Chair the necessity for its continuation) should be considered by the Church and the University with the assistance of a joint Advisory Committee representative of both. Any possible overlapping resulting from the immediate association of the two staffs would thus be gradually eliminated, and provision could then be made for any desirable extensions of the curriculum.

(4) That as the teachers of the Church would thus acquire the status of University Professors, students preparing for the Ministry would be matriculated students of the University. At the same time, the existing United Free Church Colleges would be maintained as Colleges of the united Church, and the buildings and libraries made available for the purposes of the enlarged Faculty. The corporate life which is regarded as a valuable feature of these Colleges would thus be preserved.

(5) That the Joint Advisory Committee already referred to would advise as to partition of class fees, arrangements for the maintenance and use of buildings and libraries, and other administrative details.

The Committee recommend this Scheme as one which satisfactorily meets the requirements set forth in their previous Report. They would, however, point out that the circumstances of the four Universities vary a good deal, and the detailed provisions of the Scheme are more directly applicable to Glasgow and Edinburgh. The Courts of both these Universities have intimated that they approve of it as a basis for action. In St Andrews, on the other hand, there is no United Free Church College, and in Aberdeen also the conditions are somewhat different; so that, in the case of these two Universities, some adjustments in the application of the Scheme may have to be made. This contingency is covered by the following resolution passed at a conference between the four University Courts held at Glasgow on 23rd July 1927: "That as far as possible the four Universities should proceed on common lines, regard being had to particular differences of conditions in the several Universities." At the same time it was minuted: "That in the opinion of the conference the general plan outlined in the Proposals and Memorandum presented to the University Courts of Edinburgh and Glasgow affords a suitable basis for action on the part of the Universities, certain members from Aberdeen reserving their opinion on the proposed abolition of University Tests."

In these circumstances the Committee consider that a sufficient measure of agreement with regard to the future of theological teaching has now been attained. No binding agreement can be made until Union takes place, because the Scheme involves acts of third parties —*e.g.*, the legislation necessary to abolish tests, the relinquishment by the present patrons of their rights of patronage and the approval by the Universities Committee of the Privy Council of the conditions of tenure of the new Chairs, which cannot be obtained *ab ante*. All that the Committee could hope to attain at this stage is substantial agreement between the two Churches and the Universities as to the lines upon which provision for theological instruction should be made, and substantial agreement has been reached.

SCHEME.

1. It is desired that, in respect of theological teaching, the closest possible relations should be established between the united Church and the University, by means of an enlarged and readjusted Faculty of Theology.

2. It is desired that the existing University Theological Chairs should be retained, but free from their present statutory tests, and subject to certain readjustments.

3. It is desired that—

(1) The Church shall retain control of the Course of theological training prescribed by it for its own candidates for the ministry.

(2) As far as practicable, facilities should be provided for the theological training of students of other Churches.

(3) Having regard to the necessary increase in the number of students, and the greater variety of their requirements, the Faculty should be enlarged, with a view to its greater efficiency and comprehensiveness.

(4) It is accordingly proposed to arrange (*a*) for a permanent association with the University of such Professorships of Theology now in the United Free Church College as should be maintained subject to any desirable modifications; and (*b*) for an immediate association with a University of those Professors who occupy Chairs in the United Free Church College at the time when the Union of the Churches takes effect.

4. To further these ends, it is suggested that, in regard to the existing University Chairs—

(1) The Crown and the University should relinquish their respective rights of patronage.
(2) Future appointments should be made by an Electoral Board, containing, say, five representatives appointed by the University Court and five representatives appointed by the Church. Powers should be taken to allow the Electoral Board to be enlarged should circumstances arise which make it desirable to admit representatives of other churches.
(3) Professors appointed by the Board should be subject to no statutory tests.
(4) An appointment by the Board to any Professorship shall require to be approved by at least two-thirds of the whole number of members of the Board.
(5) The University should have power to assign the duties of the Theological Professors, so as to permit of the possible alteration or redistribution of their subjects.
(6) On any Chair falling vacant, the University should make such readjustments as, in consultation with the Advisory Committee, seem desirable.

5. With regard to the Chairs in the United Free Church College, arrangements are required under both sub-heads (*a*) and (*b*) of Clause 3 (4) above.

Powers should be taken by the University under which any Professor of the United Free Church College holding office as such at the date of the Union will become a Professor of a University in the Faculty of Theology, provided the united Church guarantees payment of his present stipend and appropriate superannuation charge. He will be subject to the age-limit and other regulations prescribed for Professors of the University.

When his Chair falls vacant, the Advisory Committee named in Clause 10 below will report whether the Professorship should be continued with or without modification of subject-matter or other conditions. It will be open to the Advisory Committee, if they think fit, to recommend the substitution of a Lectureship.

If, in accordance with such report, the Church agrees to continue the Professorship as a Chair in the University, provided by the Church, she will undertake to maintain it by providing the necessary stipend and superannuation charge, under the following conditions:—

(1) The nomination to any such new Chair to be made by the Church, subject to confirmation as a University appointment by the University Court.
(2) The endowment of the new Chair to consist of the provision of an annual stipend and superannuation benefit, agreed to by the University with the approval of the Universities (Scotland) Committee of the Privy Council, and duly guaranteed by the Church.
(3) A necessary qualification for appointment to and tenure of the new Chair to be that the Professor be and continue to be an ordinand or ordained minister of the Church.

(4) In other respects the Professor to be subject to the direction and discipline of the University Court in the same manner as other Professors.

In the event of the Church's undertaking to maintain a Lectureship, the conditions as to appointment and tenure will be adjusted by agreement with the University Court on the recommendation of the Advisory Committee.

6. It is suggested that the present Colleges of the United Free Church in Edinburgh and Glasgow, together with their buildings, libraries, and other equipment, shall be maintained as Colleges of the united Church, and shall be available for the purposes of teaching, examination, study, and research by the enlarged Faculties.

It is contemplated that holders of the existing Theological Chairs in the University shall be associated in the closest possible way with the governing body of the Colleges.

7. In case the Church shall consider it desirable to maintain an administrative head of the College, powers should be taken to admit the Principal or other officer appointed to act in that capacity to a seat on the Faculty and the Senatus; and the provisions of Clause 5 above shall apply *mutatis mutandis* to such administrative officer as well as to the occupants of Chairs.

8. It is understood that all Fellowships, Scholarships, Bursaries, and Prizes open to students in the existing Faculty shall be open (subject to the conditions, if any, of their respective Trust Deeds) to students in the enlarged Faculty.

9. All students in the enlarged Faculty preparing for the ministry of the Church should be required to be matriculated students of the University.

10. For the purpose indicated in Clauses 4 (6) and 5, and also for the purpose of discussing and reporting to Church and University respectively on questions of common interest, or other matters referred to it by the University Court or the Church, a Joint Advisory Committee should be established, consisting of three members appointed by the Court and an equal number of members appointed by the Church, with the Principal of the University as Convener. The same Committee will advise as to the incidence of class expenses, the partition of fees, and any other administrative details in the work of the enlarged Faculty.

(*B*)

After careful consideration of the Regulations presently in operation in the Church of Scotland and the United Free Church respectively, the following suggestions are made for the future training of the Ministry in the united Church:—

I. The Supervising Committee.

A Committee shall be appointed by the united Church—to be named "The Committee on Education for the Ministry"—to which shall be entrusted the work of supervising all matters pertaining to the Training of Candidates for the Ministry.

This Committee shall consist of 49 members or thereabouts, and shall be constituted as follows :—

1 member from each Synod of the Church ;
12 members from the Teaching Staffs of the Divinity Halls, 3 being appointed from each ;
24 members appointed by the General Assembly, 12 of whom shall be laymen.

Normally the period of service on the Committee shall be four years, but it shall be open to the respective electing bodies to recommend the reappointment of any retiring member on good cause shown for such period as they may determine.

The following sub-committees shall be appointed, each with its own convener, to take oversight of the matters specified, and report to the parent Committee :—

(*a*) A sub-committee on Examination, Scholarships, and Bursaries.
(*b*) A sub-committee on Petitions, Courses, and Status of students.
(*c*) A sub-committee on Supply of students, including Gaelic-speaking students.
(*d*) A sub-committee on Finance.

The Powers and Functions of the Committee shall include :—

(*a*) The general supervision of the procedure of students towards the Ministry of the Church.
(*b*) The general oversight of the curriculum, including Pastoral Institutes.
(*c*) The supervision of the properties and finances of the Colleges.
(*d*) The investigation of any question which may arise relative to the status or discipline of any member of the Teaching Staffs, and, without invasion of the right of a Presbytery to raise such a question, the advising as to the initiation of any process against such a member.
(*e*) The consideration of the salaries and retiring allowances of the professors appointed by the Church.
(*f*) The dealing with appeals and petitions of students.
(*g*) The arrangement and superintendence of examinations, together with the adjudication of the results.
(*h*) The nomination to the General Assembly of Examiners and Assessors, who need not be members of the Committee, though they must be members of the Church.

It shall fall to the Committee to report to the General Assembly upon all matters, whether arising within the Church or not, which have a bearing upon the education of the Church's students, and their progress towards the Ministry. Petitions by students with reference to their curriculum shall be in the first instance submitted to the Committee, and after consideration the Committee shall present a report to the Assembly of each case, appending to each their recommendation as to how it should be disposed of.

II. The Students.

A. *Entrance on the Study of Divinity.*

Before entering on the study of Divinity in any of the Theological Faculties of a Scottish University, candidates for the Ministry of the Church must satisfy the Presbytery with which they are connected of their character, and the motives which have actuated them to seek entrance into the work of the Ministry. They must further produce certificates showing that they are in full communion with the Church, and be nominated by their Presbyteries for admission as candidates for the Ministry.

During their course of theological study they shall remain under the supervision of the Presbytery which nominated them, except in so far as their permanent place of residence shall fall within the bounds of another Presbytery, in which case that Presbytery shall exercise supervision over them. The supervising Presbytery shall confer with them at least once during each recess on the progress of their studies, as shown by their class certificates, and shall satisfy itself of their fitness to go forward to the office of the Ministry; it shall also, as it sees fit, test their theological attainments, or require them to deliver a discourse; but there shall be no Presbyterial examinations upon prescribed books, either before certification for admission to the theological course, or between the various sessions of that course.

All intending students, before admission to a regular theological course qualifying for the Ministry of the Church, shall be required to pass an Entrance Examination; and this examination shall embrace five subjects, the first four of which shall be compulsory—namely, Scripture Knowledge, Hebrew, Greek, and Moral Philosophy; while the fifth may be chosen from the following: English, Latin, French or German, Mathematics (Pure or Applied), Economics, Gaelic.

In order to be admitted to this examination, a student must be a graduate in Arts, Medicine, Science, or Law of a Scottish University, or of some other University whose curriculum is recognised for this purpose by the General Assembly; or he must have completed in a Scottish University a curriculum qualifying for graduation in Arts, with or without honours, after having passed the Arts Preliminary Examination in the manner required by University regulations. Candidates shall be exempted from examination in any prescribed subject in which they have passed the University Degree Examination.

No student who fails in Scripture Knowledge in the Entrance Examination shall be permitted to enter on a course of theological study. But a student who fails in one subject, other than Scripture Knowledge, may so enter by special permission of the Committee, which shall have regard to the standard he has reached in the other subjects. The subjects in which he has satisfied the examiners will be credited to him as a pass in these subjects; and an opportunity will be given him at the next Entrance Examination, or at an earlier date if the Committee so determine, to qualify in the subject in which he has failed. If he succeeds in completing his examination, his work of the previous session, should it have satisfied his professors, will be regularised as part of his theological course. No one shall be enrolled as a regular student in the second session who has not completed his Entrance Examination and had his first session sustained.

The Entrance Examination will be held annually in the month of September, and a small fee will be charged from the candidates.

There being at present in operation in the United Free Church a shortened course of study in Arts for men of maturer years, with permission to enter the theological curriculum without having passed the University Preliminary Examination, and the principle of such a course having already been approved by the General Assembly of the Church of Scotland, it is suggested by the sub-committee that it should be continued and maintained in the united Church.

B. *Curriculum and Course of Study in Divinity.*

In the present position of the question of the relation between the Church and the Universities the Committee consider that many matters bearing on the future curriculum can only be finally determined by the Church after Union. And they are also of opinion that, since the new arrangements can only be gradually brought into operation and must be the subject of negotiation between Church and University, it would be unwise to enter into details on the subject at present and so give the appearance of finality to what must at this stage be only tentative.

Accordingly they have limited themselves to setting down what appear to be the essential subjects which are required for the adequate training of their students for the Ministry and what is the curriculum demanded from all.

The normal period of study shall consist of three winter and three spring terms, with, in addition, such use of summer terms as the Church shall from time to time prescribe.

The essential disciplines are the five leading subjects :—

1. *Old Testament*—Language, Literature, and Religion.
2. *New Testament*—Language, Literature, and Theology
3. *Church History*—Especially that of the Early Church, of the Reformation, and of Scotland.
4. *Systematic Theology*—Including Apologetics, Dogmatics, and Principles of Christian Ethics.
5. *Practical Theology* :—
    - (*a*) Homiletics.
    - (*b*) Public Worship, Pastoral Duties, and Church Music.
    - (*c*) Government and Discipline of the Church.
    - (*d*) Principles and Methods of Religious Education and Care of the Young.
    - (*e*) Christian Missions.
    - (*f*) Practical Application of Christian Principles.

    This Department will be under the charge of a professor, assisted, it is hoped, by lecturers.

There are other subjects which the Committee desire to receive fuller treatment in the Faculties, and the teaching of which the enlarged Faculties will be able to undertake. While these would be available for the more thorough training of all students, they would especially meet the needs of B.D. students and of advanced students who desire to take a longer curriculum than that of three years. They would also offer the opportunity for the Church at a future time to consider and provide for the institution of alternative courses for the students generally.

The subjects alluded to are specially Philosophy of Religion ; History of Religion ; Church History in its larger scope ; Hellenistic Greek ; and Semitic languages, such as Aramaic, Syriac and Post-Biblical Hebrew.

PROPERTY AND FINANCE.

Provision for the Ministry.

On the Provision for the Ministry the following *Joint Memorandum and Plan of Amalgamation* has been agreed to, with an accompanying explanation of the procedure that will be necessary in regard to the adjustment of stipend in the united Church :—

Memorandum.

I.

1. It may be taken for granted that the united Church will create an Assembly Committee responsible for ingathering from the General Trustees and all other available sources, and for their distribution, all funds destined for stipend.

2. The function of this Committee will be to carry on the various lines of development and work carried on by the Committees of both Churches.

3. Its relation to the General Trustees and to other Trustees, in so far as they may hold and distribute funds for stipend, will be similar to the relation which has existed between the Churches and the Ferguson Bequest Trustees. When the Ferguson Bequest Trustees make a grant to stipend, this becomes part of the stipend from " local sources " in relation to which distribution from stipend funds is made.

II.

The stipend funds of the two Churches shall be amalgamated at the date of Union, subject to the following considerations :—

1. Interests of Ministers in regular charges in both Churches, existing at the date of Union, remain unaffected.
2. On the expiry of such interests, standardised stipends and all other stipend funds other than those held under private trusts will become available for distribution among the necessary churches in each parish or neighbourhood, due regard being had to the necessity for making sufficient provision, by endowment or otherwise, for the maintenance of ordinances : it being understood that any remainder, after these requirements have been fully met, shall form part of a General Fund at the disposal of the General Assembly for stipend purposes.

3. It will be the duty of each congregation of the Church to contribute annually in accordance with its resources towards the Maintenance of the Ministry Fund of the Church.
4. While it is a duty incumbent upon all members of the Church to contribute according to their ability, and likewise the duty of the Church to take whatever measures are necessary to ensure that every congregation shall contribute according to its ability for the support of the ordinances of religion, the claim of a parish or neighbourhood to its proper requirements from the standardised stipend shall not be dependent upon, or affected by, the amount to be contributed either to the stipends of ministers or to the Maintenance of the Ministry Fund.
5. In order to avoid hardship or difficulty that might arise consequent on any schemes for amalgamation or readjustment and for allocation of stipend, and in order to meet the case of such congregations as have not hitherto been bearing the burden of stipend and the expenses of upkeep of fabrics, and to provide a limited period in which they would become accustomed to the duty of providing a substantial portion of the whole stipend, special consideration shall be given to the circumstances of the formerly benefiting Parish Churches at the occurrence of the earlier vacancies after Union.

III.

Proposed Plan of Amalgamation.

1. The united Church shall have a Fund, to be called "The Maintenance of the Ministry Fund," to secure the maintenance of religious ordinances throughout the land, so that the strong may be enabled to help the weak in a systematic as well as a brotherly manner. The Fund shall be administered by a Committee representative of the whole Church, to be called "The Maintenance of the Ministry Committee."

2. The Committee shall consist in the first instance of the Church of Scotland's Maintenance of the Ministry Committee with representatives from the Association for Augmenting the Smaller Livings of the Clergy added, and the Central Fund Committee of the United Free Church. The Committee thus formed shall be subject to such reduction in numbers as the General Assembly shall determine.

3. The Committee shall administer the income from all capital Funds at present administered by the above Committees and Association in accordance with the trusts under which the same were acquired.

4. The Committee shall aim at providing such an annual amount as shall secure for all regular charges of the Church a minimum stipend of not less than £400 and a manse, in so far as this has not been provided otherwise.

5. It shall be the duty of the Presbytery in consultation with the Committee to take measures to secure that every congregation shall contribute annually to the Fund in a measure adequate to its resources; in particular when a charge is vacant the Presbytery and the Committee shall receive a statement of the proposed stipend arrangements and minimum contribution promised to the Fund, and the Presbytery

shall delay the filling of the vacancy until they and the Committee are satisfied that these are in harmony with the resources of the congregation.

6. The charges on the Fund shall be :—

(*a*) All payments such as office expenses and various grants which ought to be a charge on any of the funds amalgamated.

(*b*) The provision of the average stipend enjoyed for seven years prior to 1st January 1928 to all ministers in smaller living or aid receiving charges at the date of the Union.

(*c*) The provision of a Standard Minimum Stipend, to be fixed each year, to all Ministers inducted to a charge whose ministerial income for the year from all other sources shall be less than the minimum fixed.

7. In all matters of administration not provided for by these general rules the Committee shall exercise its discretion under guidance from the Regulations of the different Funds amalgamated.

8. The Committee shall present to the General Assembly for approval, at as early a date as possible after Union, Regulations which shall control the administration of the Funds available for Stipend in the united Church.

Explanation of Procedure.

The Joint Committee, in submitting the accompanying Memorandum on the Provision for the Ministry, desire to explain the procedure that will be necessary in regard to the adjustment of stipend in the united Church, subject to the continuance of all life interests.

1. The General Assembly will have to appoint a Committee whose duty, on the occurrence of a vacancy or other opportunity, will be to consider in concert with the Presbytery and local parties the whole circumstances of the parish and neighbourhood, and endeavour to secure such amalgamation of charges or other readjustment of agencies as shall further the efficient discharge of the Church's work.

2. The General Assembly will further have to remit to Presbyteries and the Committee on the Maintenance of the Ministry Fund to consider and deal with standardised stipend in accordance with the provisions of the Act, 1925. In regard to this matter there will have to be considered the decision on readjustment and the total amount of standardised stipend available, as well as the circumstances of each congregation in the parish or neighbourhood.

3. Thereafter the Presbytery and the Committee on the Maintenance of the Ministry Fund, acting in concert, will be called upon to deal with the congregations involved in any alteration of stipend, especially those in which a vacancy has occurred, in regard to :—

(1) The amount of stipend available from standardised stipend or local endowment.

(2) The amount of contribution to the minister's stipend which the congregation are prepared to make. It will be the duty of the Committee to endeavour to maintain the stipend at not less than £400 and a manse. In cases in which before Union the stipend was less than that sum, the endeavour will be to maintain it at not less than the level previously existing.

(3) The amount of contribution to the Maintenance of the Ministry Fund which the congregation are prepared to give.

(4) The total amount of stipend which the minister is to receive, with the amount of help, if any, which may be necessary from the Maintenance of the Ministry Fund.

4. It is not proposed that there should be uniformity of stipend throughout the Church, except where help is given towards the total from the Maintenance of the Ministry Fund ; in such cases the principle of a standard minimum stipend will operate.

5. It is confidently expected that a wiser use of the available resources will enable the Church to meet more effectively the religious needs of the people, and to provide a minimum stipend beyond the sum of £300 and a manse, which both uniting Churches have regarded as inadequate support for the work of the ministry.

Provisional Proposals for certain Congregations which may desire to depend wholly for Stipend on the Freewill Offerings of the people.

1. It shall be open to any congregation to declare within three months after the date of Union its intention to depend for stipend entirely on Freewill Offerings, and these congregations, for the guidance of the Courts and Committees of the Church in relation to questions of stipend and readjustment, shall be formed into a group. It shall be in the option of any of these congregations, with the approval of the Presbytery, to withdraw from the group at any time.

2. In order to meet the situation thus created, the Maintenance of the Ministry Committee shall keep two separate accounts, (1) for funds received from Standardised Stipend and any other funds derived from endowments, and (2) for funds derived solely from the Freewill Offerings of the people. Congregations in the above group shall share only in the funds included in the second account. The auditors of the Committee's accounts shall certify in each year that no part of the standardised stipend or interest from endowment funds has been allocated to any of the congregations within the group. These financial arrangements shall be revised only on request being made to the General Assembly by Overture to that effect, and after the mind of the Church has been ascertained by consultation of Presbyteries.

Aged and Infirm Ministers' Funds.

Proposed Plan of Amalgamation.

1. There shall be one governing and administration Committee, to be called the Aged and Infirm Ministers' Fund Committee.

2. There shall be one fund, composed of the two funds amalgamated as to capital and interest and other sources.

3. The charges on the Fund shall be :—

(*a*) All payments of expenses, &c., which have been customary in connection with either Fund.

(*b*) All grants to annuitants hitherto authorised in either Church under the Regulations in force when the grants were made.

(c) The provision of retiring allowances to ministers inducted prior to the union applying after the date of union, to an amount as far as possible similar to that to which they would have been entitled, inclusive of bonus payments, from the separate funds of the two Churches, provided the applicant is qualified for a grant by age or infirmity within fifteen years of the date of union.

(d) Provision of an allowance from the Fund for all other ministers at a rate to be fixed by the General Assembly on the report of the Committee.

4. All new grants from the Fund shall be made by the Committee, which shall meet four times in the year at stated dates for the purpose of dealing with applications. At these meetings a certificate shall be submitted by the Secretary, who may receive assistance from a professional adviser, of the amount of money available for the purpose of making additional grants. No grants shall be made unless there is a balance available for it.

5. In the event of there not being sufficient funds available to make grants to all the applicants on any occasion, consideration shall be given to age, degree of infirmity, length of service, and the resources of each congregation involved.

6. In all matters of administration not provided for by these general rules the Committee shall exercise its discretion under guidance from the Regulations of the different Funds amalgamated.

7. The right of a minister who at the date of union is in receipt of the stipend of the parish to claim three-tenths of the stipend on retirement is reserved subject to the conditions in the Regulations of the Aged and Infirm Ministers' Fund of the Church of Scotland.

8. The Committee shall present to the General Assembly for approval, at as early a date as possible after union, Regulations which shall control the administration of the Aged and Infirm Ministers' Fund.

9. While the aim of the Committee shall be to provide a reasonable retiring allowance in complete independence of the Maintenance of the Ministry Fund, the Committee may receive assistance from that Fund by authority of the General Assembly given from year to year, so that a minimum retiring allowance of £155, or such higher sum as the Church shall fix, may be provided for all ministers retiring through age or infirmity.

Pension Fund of the Church of Scotland.

The relation of the united Fund to the Pension Fund shall be as defined in the Constitution of the Church of Scotland's Aged and Infirm Ministers' Fund.

Excerpt from Constitution of the Aged and Infirm Ministers' Fund and Pension Fund of the Church of Scotland : A contributor to the Pension Fund shall not be precluded from receiving an annuity from the Aged and Infirm Ministers' Fund Department in addition to (1) the pension to which he is entitled from the Contributors' Fund, and (2) the appropriate share of the divisible income from the Pension Capital Fund, provided always that the share of such divisible income shall not in any one year exceed £50, or, alternatively, one-half of the annuity which he may receive from the Aged and Infirm Ministers' Fund, whichever is greater.

Missionary Funds.

In regard to the amalgamation of missionary and other funds (Home, Highlands and Islands, Foreign, Jewish, Colonial and Continental, Youth, &c.), full information has been exchanged between the Committees, and they are satisfied that the amalgamation of these funds presents no difficulty either of principle or of administration, and can be easily and effectively dealt with as a consequence of the adjustment of the varied work of the two Churches under appropriate Committees.

Church and Congregational Properties and Finance.

The Joint Committee are of opinion that if the identity of each uniting Church is preserved in the united Church, which must be safeguarded by the uniting Act, Church properties and funds not held under private trusts will become the properties and funds of the united Church, and similarly congregational properties and funds will remain the properties and funds of the congregations. Subject to Presbyterian order congregations in entering into the Union carry with them their existing rights in the possession and control of their property, and in the administration of congregational affairs under their respective constitutions.

Widows' and Orphans' Funds.

In regard to the Widows' and Orphans' Funds the Joint Committee propose that a Sub-Committee in conjunction with representatives of the Trustees of both Funds should be asked to consider what changes may be necessary in relation to the right of ministers inducted for the first time into a charge in the united Church, and of missionaries (as provided for under Churches (Scotland) Act, Commission Order No. 19, Widows' and Orphans' Fund, Section 3) to join one or other of these Funds, and the possibility of their amalgamation. The rights of ministers and missionaries already connected with either Fund will not be affected by the union of the Churches. (See App. IX., p. 560.)

RULES AND FORMS OF PROCEDURE.

Until a Manual of Procedure has been prepared by the united Church, it is understood that Presbyteries, Sessions, and Congregations are at liberty to follow any of the methods of procedure in use in either of the Churches except in so far as modified by the Plan of Union, provided always that in cases where there is uncertainty in any Congregation or Kirk Session as to which rules should be followed (as, for example, in cases of amalgamation of charges), the question shall be referred to the Presbytery, whose decision shall be final.

Election and Appointment of Ministers.

1. In the case of a vacancy the Presbytery shall appoint an interim Moderator of Kirk Session, and the Congregation shall appoint a Vacancy Committee.
2. Those persons shall be entitled to vote for a Minister (i) who are members of the Congregation in full communion, and (ii) as adherents, such other persons being parishioners or seatholders at the date of the occurrence of the vacancy, not under twenty-one years of age, and not members of any other Congregation in Scotland at the time of the vacancy, as have claimed in writing to be placed on the Electoral Register, and in regard to whom the Kirk Session is satisfied that they desire to be permanently connected with the Congregation, or are associated with it in its interests and work, and that no reason exists for refusing to admit them to the communion if they should apply. As regards adherents, the decision of the Kirk Session shall be final.
3. No person shall be nominated without previous intimation to him in writing.
4. The vote may be either open or by ballot. A decision on this point shall be made by the Congregation at the meeting at which the Vacancy Committee is appointed.
5. When a vacancy takes place intimation thereof shall be made by the Presbytery to the General Interests (or other similar) Committee, which shall have opportunity, acting in concert with the Presbytery, to intervene where it is thought there may be need for readjustment of agencies.
6. There shall be a time limit for the right of the Congregation to elect a Minister. The period of this right shall begin with the date when leave to elect is announced to the Congregation, and shall extend to nine calendar months, provided that at the end of six months notice shall be sent to the Congregation by the Presbytery that if no appointment is made within three months the Presbytery will itself take steps towards the appointment of a Minister; provided also that, even after the date when the right of appointment has fallen to the Presbytery, it shall be competent for the Presbytery, according to the circumstances of the case, either to grant or to refuse the crave of a petition from the Congregation for extension of the period allowed or for a particular appointment to be made.
7. Every appointment or call by a Congregation shall be subject to the judgment of the courts of the Church; and in such judgment the number of signatures appended to the call in proportion to the membership of the Congregation, as shown by the roll of communicants, shall be a factor in the decision of the Presbytery whether or not to sustain the appointment or call.
8. Arrangements for the signing of the call, as soon as the election has been completed, shall be made by the Kirk Session. It shall be competent for any person who is unable to attend at the time or place fixed to have his or her name appended by the Moderator, or by any member of Kirk Session authorised by the Moderator to do so, on application duly signed and sub-

mitted to the Session Clerk. Such names shall be initialled by the Moderator or member of Kirk Session appending them.

9. There shall also be opportunity for persons over fourteen years of age who are connected with the Congregation, but who are not members thereof in full communion, to sign a paper of adherence to the call.

Function, Ordination, and Induction of Ministers.

1. The ministry of the Word, the conduct of Public Worship, and the dispensing of the Sacraments belong to the Minister, subject to the control and direction of the Presbytery.
2. The ordination of a Minister is the solemn setting apart by prayer and the laying on of hands by Presbyters of a person already licensed to preach the Gospel, to the office and function of the Holy Ministry with a view to the exercise of that Ministry in a particular sphere.
3. Induction is admission to a particular charge of one who has been previously or on the same occasion ordained in accordance with the standards of the uniting Churches.

Sundry Matters.

1. *Records of Church Courts.*—Material alterations shall be attested by both Moderator and Clerk; clerical errors by the initials of the Clerk.
2. *Convening of Kirk Session.*—It is the function of the Moderator to call meetings of Kirk Session. He shall be bound to do so within ten days if requested in writing by a majority of the elders, or where these exceed nine in number by at least one-third with a minimum of five.
3. *Quorum of Kirk Session.*—This shall be three, the Moderator and two Elders.
4. *Assessors to Kirk Session.*—If there be not a sufficient number of Elders available to make a quorum, or in cases of difficulty at the discretion of the Presbytery, Assessors may be appointed by the Presbytery with or without a vote according to the terms of their appointment.
5. *Rolls, Registers, &c.*—Those persons who, at the annual revisal of the Communion Roll, are found to have been absent from Communion for three consecutive years without a sufficient reason known to the Kirk Session, shall be deemed not to be communicants, and their names shall be removed from the Roll; and the names of such persons can be restored to the Roll only by a resolution of the Kirk Session to that effect duly recorded in its Minutes. Provided always, that if at the annual revisal of the Roll any communicant, whose address is known, is found to have been absent from Communion for two consecutive years without a sufficient reason known to the Kirk Session, it shall take such means as shall seem best to inform the said communicant of this enactment.

   A Register of Baptisms shall be kept by the Minister in each charge, and it is recommended that a Register of baptised persons, not communicants, be also kept.

The Rolls, Registers, and Records shall be examined annually by the Presbytery, and an abstract of the congregational accounts (after being audited) shall be examined and attested by the Presbytery.

Every Presbytery shall keep a Benefice Register of the property belonging to each Charge within the bounds.

6. *Presbyterial Visitation.*—The principle of periodic visitation of all Congregations is affirmed.

7. *Overtures.*—In their return to Overtures, remitted for their consideration in accordance with the provisions of the Barrier Act, 1697, IX., Presbyteries shall be required to state clearly and categorically whether they approve or disapprove, but they shall have the opportunity of appending remarks or suggestions. If any alteration so proposed in no way modifies the substance, sense, or intention of the Overture, it shall be competent for the General Assembly to adopt it. It shall be competent for a Presbytery among its remarks to indicate approval of the principle of an Overture while disagreeing with the method in which it is proposed to carry out that principle. In this case, however, it shall be reckoned to disapprove. When so instructed by the General Assembly, Presbyteries shall give to Kirk Sessions the opportunity of stating their opinion on Overtures.

8. *Non-residence.*—When a Manse is provided, the Minister shall reside in it unless with the express consent of the Presbytery to reside elsewhere. In all cases the Presbytery shall require him to reside within a reasonable distance of the Church and sphere of ministry. A Minister may be dealt with for non-residence.

9. *Proclamation of Banns.*—In parishes where there is more than one church, the banns shall be duly published if proclaimed in such church or churches in the parish as shall be selected for the purpose by the Presbytery within whose jurisdiction the parish is situated. Until the Presbytery has made a selection, the existing practice shall continue, and proclamation of banns shall be made in the church or churches in the parish where it was in use to be made before Union.

10. *Parishes and Other Territorial Areas.*—For the purposes of effective pastoral work on a territorial basis, it shall be an early duty of Presbyteries after Union to readjust parochial and other areas where necessary, and assign spheres of pastoral labour and responsibility to the Ministers of particular charges.

Until this has been done (1) for the purposes of the immediately preceding article the boundaries of parishes shall remain as at the date of Union, and (2) existing arrangements, whereby parochial or other areas are assigned or recognised as spheres of pastoral labour and responsibility, shall continue.

DISCIPLINE.

I. Applicable to all Courts.

Principles.

Discipline in the government of the Church is of Scriptural authority. The ends contemplated by it are the glory of God, the purity of the Church, and the spiritual benefit of her members. It is to be administered in faithfulness, meekness, love, and tenderness.

Discipline consists in the administration of the appropriate censures of the Church to those whose conduct shall have given occasion for it.

Nothing is to be admitted as the ground of a process for censure but what is declared censurable by the Word of God, or by some Act or universal custom of this Church.

The subjects of discipline are those who hold office in the Church, communicants, and baptised persons who are adherents.

Censures.

The Censures of the Church are Admonition, Rebuke, Suspension, Deposition from office, and Excommunication, and they are administered only on confession or proof of sin or offence. Private admonition, which is not a censure, may in certain cases meet the ends of Discipline.

Suspension of a person under scandal from performance of duties, or even from sealing ordinances during the investigation of the scandal, is not a Censure as long as the charge is not judicially confessed or proven.

Suspension from office *sine die* involves removal from the office held.

Record Apart.

To keep the ordinary records of the courts, which have to be consulted and inspected for various purposes, free from the presence of undesirable matter, and to obviate their mutilation by the deletion of the proceedings, the principle of a Record Apart shall be adopted in all cases where moral delinquency is alleged. As far as the cases which ordinarily come before Kirk Sessions are concerned, involving communicants or baptised persons who are adherents, the desired end may be achieved by the use of a Minute Book of Discipline as mentioned in the procedure recommended below. In all other cases, such as processes against office-bearers, the court of first instance shall resolve from the first to keep the proceedings of the case in a Record Apart, and said resolution shall be minuted in the Record Apart, and not in the ordinary record.

When the judgment which finally disposes of the case, by whatever court of the Church pronounced, involves any degree of censure of the accused, then the court of first instance shall engross in its ordinary Minute Book the first Minute of the Record Apart, the libel, or a summary of each of the charges thereof, if a libel was served, and the final judgment. When a case has ended in entire acquittal, if there is a Record Apart in any court inferior to the General Assembly, it shall, with all papers in the case, so far as these do not affect the interests of third parties, be sealed up in presence of that court, docqueted with the name of the congregation and the date of final judgment, and kept *in retentis* for five years and thereafter destroyed. When a process ends in entire acquittal, the person whose innocence has been proved ought to have a certified copy of the judgment of the court delivered to him.

In every case the inferior courts shall keep an Inventory of Process, in which the clerk shall enter and number all the documents.

Persons accused have the right of access to any productions in the case which are in the possession of the court.

Parties may appear by or have the assistance of Counsel or Agents in any process depending before the Presbytery or any higher court, unless such court shall otherwise determine. They shall not be entitled to have such assistance in any process depending before a Kirk Session except with the special permission of the Kirk Session. Any parties appearing by Counsel or Agents shall not be entitled to be heard also by themselves.

II. Processes in which the Kirk Session is the Court of First Instance.

When a person under scandal refuses to submit to discipline, notwithstanding such pastoral dealing as appears to the Kirk Session sufficient, the Kirk Session may intimate to *him* (or *her*) by registered letter by its clerk that, unless within thirty days *he* shall make known *his* willingness to submit to discipline (or, if the charge is denied, to discipline or trial), *he* will be suspended from privileges till such submission is made and disposed of, or till the Kirk Session is otherwise satisfied.

When an accused person has made known *his* willingness to submit to discipline, the Kirk Session may remit the case to the Moderator alone, or to the Moderator and one of the elders.

If a record be kept by the Kirk Session of all cases of discipline, it shall be in a book reserved for this purpose alone. The names, and all that might lead to the identification of the parties, shall be rendered illegible after five years. In such cases the Kirk Session shall not, unless requested by the person accused, be required to keep a Record Apart, but in the event of an appeal or dissent and complaint to any superior court other than the General Assembly, a Record Apart shall be kept by that superior court.

Kirk Sessions shall afford facilities for the transference of cases from one Kirk Session to another when this would be for the convenience of parties and Kirk Sessions.

III. Processes in which the Presbytery is the Court of First Instance.

When a *fama* has arisen against an office-bearer (minister or probationer) who is subject to the jurisdiction of a Presbytery, it shall be the duty of the Presbytery to institute a preliminary inquiry, and if the offence is denied, and there still appears ground for investigation, the court shall, except in the case of a minister who demands that a libel be served on him, proceed to a formal inquiry or a trial by libel. In such cases a Record Apart is required.

Alike in the case of such a formal inquiry and of a trial by libel, there are certain principles to which it is desirable to give effect :—

(*a*) It is the right of the courts of the Church to adjudicate in all matters of discipline, and the court should not be both prosecutor and judge.

(*b*) The difficulties occasioned by the numerical size of Church courts ought to be recognised, and such procedure adopted as will ensure that findings on matters of probation will be reached only by those who have heard the whole of the case.

Accordingly there shall be a Committee on Cases against ministers (or probationers) appointed by the General Assembly, who shall advise with the Presbytery if it so desires as to the scope of a formal inquiry, and furnish prosecutors to conduct the inquiry; or in cases where a libel is instituted, who shall prepare the libel and prosecute it, after it has been submitted to and revised by the legal adviser of the Church.

There shall also be a Committee of Assessors appointed annually by the General Assembly, and when evidence has been appointed to be taken either in a formal inquiry, or in a trial by libel, the Presbytery shall commit the hearing of the evidence to a Committee of its own number, or to a panel consisting of, say, three or five of its own number and two assessors, who may hear the whole case, and report to the Presbytery their findings on the extent of probation of the various charges, stating whether they are unanimous or with how many dissentients, and whether their findings are acquiesced in or appealed against by the accused.

It will be for the Presbytery to judge of the report, and to determine the degree of censure appropriate to the extent of the offence found to have been proved. In the event of an appeal to a higher court, this finding shall be transmitted with the other documents in the case.

CONSTITUTION AND ADMINISTRATIVE REGULATIONS OF ASSEMBLY COMMITTEES.

According to the Scheme submitted the Administrative work of the united Church is arranged in Departments. Within each Department are placed the various Committees of Assembly which in field or function have more or less affinity. The present freedom of action enjoyed by each Committee in relation to the Assembly in matters remitted to it by the Supreme Court remains unimpaired. Many of the Committees have at present their own secretarial arrangements, and these abide. As vacancies occur, however, it will be for the Committees within each Department to review the situation as it then presents itself, and under guidance of the Assembly consider any new appointment in relation to the Department as a whole, and with a view to securing the most effective service of that Committee within the Department to which it belongs. The Scheme is not complete in every detail, but the General Assembly, guided by the experience within the united Church, will develop or modify it as in its wisdom it deems best.

Proposals bearing upon unifying the practice of the two Churches in respect of the position, duties, and methods of appointment of Secretaries are not meantime submitted; these require further consideration and will be presented to the next Assembly.

Note.—In the following Scheme dealing with the grouping of the Committees it is to be understood that each Committee carries its respective duties into the new arrangement within the united Church.

A.—CONSTITUTION OF ASSEMBLY COMMITTEES.

I. GENERAL INTERESTS DEPARTMENT. To include the work of the following Committees :—

CHURCH OF SCOTLAND.

(*a*) The General Committee in the matter of Law and Libels ; also certain Arrangements for the General Assembly.
(*b*) Assembly Arrangements.
(*c*) Synodical Reports.
(*d*) Constitution of *Quoad Sacra* Parishes.
(*e*) Benefice Register and Church Records.
(*f*) Statistics.
(*g*) Committee on Overtures.

UNITED FREE CHURCH.

(*a*) Assembly Arrangements.
(*b*) Law.
(*c*) Assessors in Cases of Discipline.
(*d*) Property Cases.
(*e*) Reports of Synods anent Presbyterial Visitation.
(*f*) Statistics.
(*g*) General Interests, so far as not concerned with "Re-adjustment of Agencies" and Union of Congregations.
(*h*) Nomination.
(*i*) Church and State.

It is suggested that the work of this Department be grouped in these three Committees :—

1. *General Administration.*—To include—

From Church of Scotland, *b, c, d, e, f,* and *g.*
From United Free Church, *a, e, f, g,* and *i.*

2. *Law, Property Cases, and Discipline.*—To include—

From Church of Scotland, *a.*
From United Free Church, *b, c,* and *d.*

3. *Nomination.*

II. FINANCE DEPARTMENT.—To include the work of the following Committees :—

The General Committee in the matters of :—

CHURCH OF SCOTLAND.

Administration of General Purposes Fund.
Arrangement of the Assessments.
Supervision of Banking Operations.
Finance and Annual Budget.
Freewill Offerings.
Affairs of the Offices of the Church.
Affairs connected with Office at Assembly Hall.

UNITED FREE CHURCH.

Finance.
Systematic Giving and Ingathering of Funds.

The necessary subdivision of the work of above Department to be determined later.

III. CHURCH AND MINISTRY DEPARTMENT.—To include the work of the following Committees:—

CHURCH OF SCOTLAND.	(a) Maintenance of the Ministry. (b) Aged and Infirm Ministers' Fund and Pension Fund, including Aged and Infirm Probationers' Fund.
UNITED FREE CHURCH.	(a) Central Fund. (b) Aged and Infirm Ministers' Fund. (c) General Interests—so far as it acts as a Readjustment of Agencies Committee.

It is suggested that the work of this Department be grouped in these three Committees:—

1. Maintenance of Ministry.
2. Aged and Infirm Ministers' Fund and Pension Fund, including Aged and Infirm Probationers' Fund.
3. Union of Congregations and Readjustment of Agencies.

IV. HOME DEPARTMENT.—To include the work of the following Committees:—

1. *Home Mission*—

CHURCH OF SCOTLAND.	(a) The work of its present Home Mission Committee. (b) The Evangelistic enterprise of the Christian Life and Work Committee—*i.e.*, Work among Fisher-folk and Mission Weeks. (c) Moderator's Visits and Assembly Deputies.
UNITED FREE CHURCH.	(a) The present work of the Home Mission and Church Extension Committee. (b) The Visitation Work of the Church Life and Social Problems Committee.

Connected with the Home Mission Committee these three related Committees which follow—viz., 2, 3, and 4.

2. *Church and Manse Building*—

CHURCH OF SCOTLAND.	Such matters in connection with churches and manses as are not undertaken by the General Trustees.
UNITED FREE CHURCH.	Church and Manse Building Fund.

This Committee shall apply the regulations of the Assembly in respect of grants given on the recommendation of Presbyteries for the erection and repair of ecclesiastical buildings. In cases where grants are applied for, it shall withhold its consent to the undertaking proposed until assured that this is structurally sound, and that a sum is in hand sufficient to warrant the work being carried out without an undue debt remaining upon the congregation. It shall also, in such cases as require it, provide expert counsel or advice.

This Committee shall be composed in one-half of its membership of men possessed of professional or other special qualifications, and nominated by the Nomination Committee; the other half of its membership shall be nominated by the Home Mission and Highlands and Islands Committees in the proportion of three to one respectively.

3. *Committee for the Highlands and Islands, including the operations of the Royal Bounty Committee of the Church of Scotland.*

Take oversight of Gaelic-speaking areas, also Orkney and Shetland Islands; superintend, in conjunction with the Home Mission Committee, Mission Stations, Mission Agents, and Evangelists within these areas; advise with Presbyteries as to Church Extension in the Highlands and Islands; act as a Highland Probationers' Committee within these Gaelic-speaking areas; render assistance to Gaelic-speaking students preparing for the ministry.

Representation on this Committee shall consist of one-third of its members nominated by the Home Mission Committee; in regard to the other two-thirds, the Nomination Committee shall take special care in regard to the selection of members with a knowledge of Gaelic and the Gaelic-speaking areas; to these shall be added eight members from the Ladies' Highland Associations. The Superintendent of Highland Missions to be *ex officio* a member of the Home Mission Committee.

These two Committees, 2 and 3, to manage their own affairs, including the raising and control of their own funds, and to report direct to the General Assembly.

4. *Women's Home Mission.*—To include :—

CHURCH OF SCOTLAND. Work of the Women's Associations for Home Missions, including the Direction of the Order of Parish Sisters, also Direction of such Deaconesses as enter into the employment of the Committee.

UNITED FREE CHURCH. Work of the Women's Home Mission, including the enterprises conducted by them in various parts of the Home Field; also the Direction of the Order of Deaconess and Church Sister at present under charge of the Home Mission Committee.

Note 1.—The membership of this Committee as a Committee closely related to the Home Mission Committee yet to be determined.

It shall have power to raise and control its own finances, and shall report to the General Assembly through the Home Mission Committee.

Note 2.—The Order of Deaconess within each Church shall remain for the period of three years under the direction of its present Committee. The two Committees concerned shall present at the close of that period a Scheme which secures unity in the regulations which bear upon their admission to the Order and upon their employment in the service of the Church. (For present scheme, see 1962, Reg. 8, pp. 694-715.)

5. *Christian Life and Work.*—To include:—

Work of Woman's Guild, and Direction of the Order of Deaconess with its related Institutions at present under charge of the Christian Life and Work Committee of the Church of Scotland.

6. *Social Work.*

To continue the work of the Social Work Committee of the Church of Scotland—*i.e.*, Rescue and Preventive Work Farm Colonies, and Orphanages, &c.

7. *Church and Nation.*—To include:—

CHURCH OF SCOTLAND.	Church and Nation.
UNITED FREE CHURCH.	Church Life and Social Problems with the exception of Visitation Work.

8. *Temperance.*

This Committee to include not only the Temperance Committee of both Churches, but also the Women's Temperance Association of the Church of Scotland.

V. FOREIGN MISSIONS DEPARTMENT.

This Department to include in one Committee the Foreign Missions Committee of each Church, also the incorporation of the work of the Women's Association for the Foreign Missions of the Church of Scotland. This Committee to be left to form its own Special Sub-Committees.

VI. CHURCHES OVERSEAS DEPARTMENT.—To include the work of the following Committees:—

CHURCH OF SCOTLAND.	(*a*) Church Overseas. (*b*) Jewish Missions. (*c*) Women's Association for Jewish Missions. (*d*) Correspondence with other Reformed Churches. (*e*) Chaplains to H.M. Forces. (*f*) Faith and Order.
UNITED FREE CHURCH.	(*a*) Colonial and Continental. (*b*) Jewish Missions. (*c*) Women's Jewish Missions. (*d*) Chaplains to H.M. Forces. (*e*) Faith and Order.

Work of this Department to be undertaken by these four Committees:—

1. Colonial Churches; Chaplaincies and Churches in India.
2. Jewish Missions, including Jewish Mission Work undertaken by the two Women's Organisations.
3. Work on the Continent and Relations with other Churches, this to include work of Faith and Order Committee.
4. Chaplains to H.M. Forces.

VII. PREPARATION FOR THE MINISTRY DEPARTMENT.—To include the work of the following Committees :—

CHURCH OF SCOTLAND.	(*a*) Education for the Ministry. (*b*) Board of Pastoral Institutes. (*c*) Library of the General Assembly. (*d*) Probationers. (*e*) Admission from other Churches.
UNITED FREE CHURCH.	(*a*) College. (*b*) Probationers and Transference of Ministers. (*c*) Petitions and Status.

The work of this Department to be undertaken by these three Committees :—

1. Education for the Ministry.

Note.—All Trust Funds of the respective Colleges of the United Free Church shall remain meantime under present administration.

2. Probationers and Transference of Ministers.
3. Admission of Ministers from other Churches and all questions of Status.

VIII. YOUTH AND EDUCATION DEPARTMENT.—To include the work of the following Committees :—

CHURCH OF SCOTLAND.	(*a*) Religious Instruction of Youth. (*b*) Education.
UNITED FREE CHURCH.	(*a*) Youth, including the Federation of Young People's Societies. (*b*) Education.

The work of this Department to be undertaken by these three Committees :—

1. Religious Instruction of Youth.
2. Education.
3. Societies of Young Men and Women.

Note.—The Joint Conveners of the Union Sub-Committee shall call together in conference representatives of the different Societies of Young People in both Churches, and of the Committees concerned, with a view to reaching some adjustment whereby these Societies shall be brought into a direct relationship with each other and their common service be secured for the united Church.

In addition to the foregoing Departments these two Committees (unrelated) :—

1. *Committee on Public Worship and Aids to Devotion.* To include :—

CHURCH OF SCOTLAND.	(*a*) Psalmody and Hymns. (*b*) Aids to Devotion.
UNITED FREE CHURCH.	(*a*) Praise. (*b*) 'Book of Common Order.'

2. *Committee on Publications.* To include :—

CHURCH OF SCOTLAND.	Church Magazines as conducted by "Christian Life and Work" and by "Religious Instruction of Youth" Committees.
UNITED FREE CHURCH.	(*a*) Publications and Records. (*b*) Magazines conducted by the Committee on Youth.

Note 1.—The Committees of the united Church which are interested in Publications shall be given adequate representation upon the Publications and Records Committee.

Note 2.—A Profit and Loss Account shall be kept for each Committee interested in Publications, any ascertained balance, after the expenses of the Department have been made, to be paid over to, or by, the respective Committees.

B.—ADMINISTRATIVE REGULATIONS OF ASSEMBLY COMMITTEES.

1. The Presbytery shall be the Court from which the "representative" element shall be drawn.

2. The Committees which raise funds from congregational sources shall be the Committees on which representatives of Presbyteries shall be placed.

(Exception is made of the Church and Manse Building and of the Women's Home Mission Committees.)

3. The "representative" element and the "nominated" element shall be practically equal.

(Exception is made of the Nomination Committee, the Education for the Ministry Committee, and the Admission of Ministers Committee.)

4. The numbers of each Committee shall be according to requirements, and on a general arrangement yet to be worked out; but until experience suggests otherwise, these four Committees—"Maintenance of the Ministry," "Home Mission," "Foreign Mission," and "Youth of the Church"—shall have a membership not exceeding 120; other Committees dealing with funds shall have a membership not exceeding 80, the remaining Committees shall have a membership not exceeding 60.

5. The representation from Presbyteries shall be according to the number of congregations within the bounds, and in a proportion yet to be determined.

6. Membership of Committees shall be for a period of four years.

7. Conveners of Committees shall hold office for five years, and Vice-Conveners for three years.

8. Ministers and elders shall be placed upon Committees as far as possible in equal numbers. In committees which carry a representation of women, the proportion shall be 40 per cent ministers, 40 per cent elders, and 20 per cent women, an exception to this being made in the case of the Foreign Mission Committee.

9. Committees shall meet as a rule in June, October, December, February, and April. They shall be free to meet on other months as business may require. The third Tuesday of the month, and if need be the days following, shall be regarded as the selected day or days.

10. Expenses incurred by members of Committees, consisting of travel charges and a sum for maintenance when required, shall be defrayed; the source from which these expenses shall be drawn shall be determined later.

11. The Nomination Committee of Assembly shall consist, to begin with, of forty-eight members, two-thirds nominated by Synods and one-third by the Assembly through its Selection Committee. Membership of the Nomination Committee of Assembly shall be for four years. No member shall be open for re-election until after a period of four years, except for special cause shown. The Convenership of this Committee shall be for three years.

RELATIONS WITH OTHER CHURCHES.

1. The Conferring Churches in Relation to Other Presbyterian Churches.

(a) *General Relations.*

Both Churches are constituent members of the Alliance of Reformed Churches holding the Presbyterian System (a federation instituted fifty years ago and inaugurated in Edinburgh, and now embracing almost every Presbyterian Church in the world), and contribute annually substantial sums towards its maintenance. Their membership in the Alliance implies a public recognition of the Sister Churches as forming one ecclesiastical family, without determining such questions as mutual elegibility and identity of orders.

Through the Committee on Correspondence with Other Reformed Churches, and in relation to Churches in the British Dominions and Dependencies, through the Committee on the Church Overseas, the Church of Scotland sends and receives official delegates, provides bursaries for Continental students preparing for the Ministry, and in several instances sends financial assistance where required. The United Free Church acts in the same way through one Committee, the Colonial and Continental Committee.

Both Churches through their Foreign Mission and Overseas Committees maintain fraternal relations with autonomous Churches in Mission fields in Africa, Asia, and the West Indies, some of which are now united Churches, including ministers and members who formerly belonged to other denominations—*e.g.*, Congregational, Methodist. These united Churches are as follows :—

United Church of Northern India.
United Church of India, South.
Bantu Presbyterian Church of South Africa
Church of Central Africa, Presbyterian.
Presbyterian Church of Jamaica.
United Church of Christ in China.

In these Churches Scottish missionaries are for the most part full members of the Church Courts, and the Mission Councils have a close relationship to the Churches in Scotland.

It is recommended that all the foregoing relations, which are practically identical for both Churches, be continued, after union, with a redistribution of the provinces and activities of the Standing Committees mentioned above.

(b) *Recognition of Orders and Admission of Ministers.*

In 1911 the Special Committee of the Church of Scotland on the Petition of the Rev. J. A. D. J. Macdonald, a Wesleyan Minister who had served the Church as Minister to the Scotsmen in the mills upon the Hoogly, gave in unanimously, through the Rev. George Gardiner, D.D., an extremely valuable and comprehensive report on this subject (Assembly Report, pp. 1149-1198), reviewing the Doctrine, Law, and Practice of the Church. Among the Committee's conclusions, which were not questioned and may be held as authoritative, the following (p. 1192) regarding Ministers already ordained are here relevant :—

"*Doctrine*, § 3. A Minister who hath been an ordained presbyter of the Church of England or of 'other Reformed Church' is to be admitted without reordination."

"*Doctrine*, § 4. The Ordination of an ecclesiastical union whose constitution is not that of a court governing the several congregations represented in it does not satisfy the requirements of the doctrinal standard of our Church."

"*Law*, § 2. The orders of other regularly constituted Presbyterian Churches are recognised as valid."

"*Practice*, § 1. With very few exceptions, and these all prior to 1850, Presbyterian Ministers (*i.e.*, already ordained) have been admitted either as ordained Ministers or as licentiates who were to be admitted (*i.e.*, inducted) without ordination on being called to a pastoral charge. This latter practice ceased in 1875. Only one case has been found of the reordination of a Presbyterian Minister."

No similar document is available in the United Free Church, but the above findings are in accord with its Doctrine, Law, and Practice.

The conferring Churches have at no time drawn up complete lists of the Presbyterian Churches whose orders are held as sufficient to qualify for admission. They have both been content to deal with particular cases of application as they emerged. The procedure in each Church is by petition to the General Assembly through the Standing Committee on Admission of Ministers of Other Churches, which reports on the applicant's orders and theological training and character, &c., and his avowed reason for seeking admission.

Section IX. of the Church of Scotland Act (XI., 1907) decrees that "Ministers admitted from Churches whose ordination of probationers of the Church of Scotland is recognised as valid under Act XV., 1902, and Ministers of Presbyterian Churches in Scotland, shall be enrolled in the list of ministers (*i.e.*, ordained ministers). The Churches specified in Act XV., 1902, without prejudice to others that may be so recognised, are the Presbyterian Churches of England, Ireland, Canada, United States (North and South), Australia, New Zealand and South Africa, the Reformed Church in America (Dutch), the United Presbyterian

Church of North America, the Dutch Reformed Church of South Africa, and the Reformed Church of the Netherlands."

In the United Free Church, as stated in the Manual of Practice and Procedure, a similar position is held, the Churches specified, without prejudice to others, being the Presbyterian Churches of Canada, Australia, New Zealand, and South Africa.

It is recommended (i) that as at present in both Churches a Standing Committee (to be named the Committee on Admission and Status of Ministers) be entrusted with the supervision of applications for admission by licentiates, ministers, and professors from other Churches; and (ii) that it be held not advisable to draw up a list of Churches whose training for the ministry and whose orders are to be deemed valid for the purpose of admission, but that individual cases of application be considered by the Committee on Admission and Status of Ministers as they arise in accordance with the standards of the united Church.

(c) *Eligibility for Direct Election and Appointment.*

In the case of an ordained minister "holding at the time a regular congregational charge of any Presbyterian Church in Great Britain or Ireland adhering to the doctrine, government, and discipline of this Church," the Act VIII. of Assembly 1921, Church of Scotland, declares that it shall be competent for a Congregational Committee to nominate him with a view to an election and appointment to a vacant Parish, "provided that, prior to such nomination he shall have received from the Committee on the Admission of Ministers of Other Churches a Certificate approving his course of study for the Ministry, both in Arts and in Divinity, as equal in extent and character to that required of a licentiate of this Church." That requirement being fulfilled, election, appointment, and call may competently follow in the same manner as in the appointment of an ordained minister of this Church. And provision is made for the application of this rule to cases of Presbyterial appointment *tanquam jure devoluto*, and to appointment by the Presbytery of Edinburgh to stations under the Colonial, Foreign Mission, and Jewish Mission Committees. By this Act the relevant Acts of 1886 and 1911 were repealed.

In the United Free Church ordained ministers of the Presbyterian Churches in England and in Ireland have been recognised as eligible.

It is recommended that in the united Church it shall be competent for a congregational committee to nominate, with a view to election to a vacant charge, an ordained minister holding at the time a charge or office in any Presbyterian Church in Great Britain and Ireland which adheres to the doctrine, government, and discipline of the united Church, provided that, *prior to such nomination, the congregational committee shall have received from the Committee on Admission and Status of Ministers a certificate approving (i) his course of study for the ministry both in Arts and Divinity as equal in extent and character to that required of licentiates of the united Church;*

(ii) his ordination as valid; and

(iii) his presbyterial certificate as satisfactory. This requirement being fulfilled, election, appointment, and call may competently

follow as in the appointment of an ordained minister of the united Church.

This rule, it is further recommended, shall also apply to appointments made tanquam jure devoluto, *and by the Foreign Mission, Jewish Mission, Chaplains, and Overseas Committees, as well as to appointments to vacant theological chairs.*

A probationer of the Church of Scotland, ordained by a Presbyterian Church furth of Scotland, who has not expressly demitted, or been judicially deprived of, his status as a probationer of this Church, does not on his return to Scotland require to apply to the Standing Committee on the Admission of Ministers of Other Churches, nor has an ordained minister of the Church, similarly returning after service in another Church, been required so to apply.

It is recommended that probationers and ordained ministers of either conferring Church, who return to Scotland from other countries where they have held office as ministers or missionaries or professors outside the jurisdiction of the Church which licensed them, shall be eligible for nomination with a view to appointment to office in the united Church, provided (1) *that they have not expressly demitted their status as licentiates or been judicially deprived of it, and* (2) *that they shall have satisfied the Committee on Admission and Status of Ministers as to their character, record, and standing, and shall have received from that Committee a certificate to that effect.*

2. The Conferring Churches in Relation to Churches holding other Systems.

(a) *The Roman Catholic Church.*

Thomas Abernethie, Roman Catholic priest and Jesuit, was received into communion after "abjuration of Poperie" in 1638, and was admitted by reordination to the charge of Hounam in 1640.

But James Tyrie, a Roman Catholic priest, received in 1735, seems to have been admitted to an Orkney charge without reordination.

So recently as 1884, Dr Browne, priest of the same Church and Professor of Metaphysics, was admitted by the Church of Scotland as a minister.

No cases of admission from the Roman Catholic Church have occurred in the United Free Church.

It is recommended that any cases of application be dealt with by the united Church as they arise in accordance with her standards.

(b) *Anglican and Moravian Churches.*

Ministers of these Episcopal Churches have been admitted by the Church of Scotland without reordination. No case has arisen in the United Free Church.

It is recommended that any cases of application be dealt with by the united Church as they arise in accordance with her standards.

(c) *Wesleyan and Other Methodist Churches.*

(i) *Church of Scotland Practice.*

In 1872 a Wesleyan minister was admitted as a probationer in British Guiana, the Assembly having declined to interfere beyond advising the Presbytery to "use extreme caution in the exercise of the power to admit to the status of a probationer."

In 1876, John Gunson of the Methodist Free Church was admitted as a licentiate at the same time as George Chute of the Church of England was admitted as an ordained minister; and two years later the same action was taken with a Primitive Methodist minister, Lewis Frederick Armitage, followed by Arthur Jenkinson, United Free Methodist, in 1885.

In 1898 reordination was required by the Assembly in the case of John Robbins, minister of the Wesleyan Methodist Church in Canada from 1875, admitted in 1885 to the Presbyterian Church in Canada, and in 1896 inducted to a charge at Watford by the Presbytery of London (Scottish Church in England).

In 1911, in the case of J. A. D. J. Macdonald, above cited, the Special Committee was equally divided on the question of admitting him as an ordained minister, but by the casting vote of the Convener recommended adherence to the previous Assembly's resolution to admit as a licentiate. "In those circumstances," it is reported, "and in view of the fact that no application has been made, or indication given, by the Wesleyan Methodist Church that this Church should review its history, or give judgment as to the orders of its ministers, your Committee deem it unnecessary and undesirable to pronounce on these matters." The General Assembly "gave no opinion on the Report," but resolved by a majority, "without calling in question the validity of Mr Macdonald's ordination," that it was inadvisable to alter its former decision in this case.

(ii) *United Free Church of Scotland.*

Since 1916 seven Methodists have been admitted as ordained ministers.

It is recommended that any cases of application be dealt with by the united Church as they arise in accordance with her standards.

(d) *Congregational and Baptist Churches.*

(i) *Church of Scotland.*

Prior to 1866 no admission is recorded. From 1866 to 1882 practice varies as to the status granted on admission.

In 1873, W. M. Metcalfe, Congregational minister at Ayr, was admitted as a licentiate *not to be reordained.* Similarly in 1874 William Mackay, of the same denomination at Alexandria, and in 1875 R. H. Hutchieson. In 1877 and 1878 five Congregational ministers were received as licentiates to be subsequently reordained. Since 1880 all Congregational ministers admitted have been given licentiate status only, with two exceptions in 1882 in whose favour reordination was dispensed with.

Applicants from Evangelical Union Churches and from Baptist Churches have in all cases been received as probationers *simpliciter.*

(ii) *United Free Church of Scotland.*

Since 1916 sixteen Congregational and seven Baptist ministers have been admitted, not seldom without reordination.

It is recommended that any cases of application be dealt with by the united Church as they arise in accordance with her standards.

3. The Conferring Churches in Relation to the United Church of Canada.

The United Church of Canada is composed of Presbyterian, Methodist, and, in a very small proportion, Congregational elements, with the first of which the conferring Churches have been in fellowship. This Church claims to be Presbyterian in doctrine, government, orders, and worship, and desires to have the same relations with the united Church of Scotland as the Presbyterian Church in Canada maintained with the conferring Churches.

It is recommended that fraternal relations be maintained with this Church, and that, in the event of applications being made for admission by ministers in it, each case should be considered on its merits in accordance with the standards of the united Church, as already recommended in connection with applications from ministers of other Churches outside the British Isles.

It is also recommended that regulations be drawn up to guide the Committee which is to be entrusted with the supervision of admissions and re-admissions as above mentioned.

4. The Conferring Churches in Relation to Wider Union Movements.

(*a*) The Churches are both official participants in the *Faith and Order Movement*, contributing financially, and represented regularly on the Continuation Committee and ecumenical gatherings through the Assemblies' Committees on "World Conference on Faith and Order." Their freedom of action is expressly reserved.

(*b*) They are both official participants on similar terms in the *Life and Work Movement*, through the Church of Scotland Assembly's Committee on Church and Nation, and the United Free Church Assembly's Committee on Church Life and Social Problems, without financial obligation.

(*c*) The same is true of the *World Alliance for Promoting International Friendship through the Churches*, to whose British National Council the Assemblies appoint representatives.

(*d*) The Churches are also regularly represented through the same Committees on the *Scottish Churches Council*, an essentially deliberative and advisory body, numbering delegates from practically all the Scottish Churches except the Roman Catholic and the Free.

(*e*) The Churches have both returned favourable replies to the overtures of the Church of England suggesting conference with the Episcopal Church in England and Scotland on the Lambeth proposals towards a larger reunion, though they have asked, as was courteously anticipated by the Archbishop of Canterbury, that conference be deferred until the prior obligations of their pending union have been discharged.

(*f*) The General Assemblies have both welcomed distinguished representatives bringing ecclesiastical greetings from the Lutheran Churches of Sweden and Finland, on the introduction of the Committee on Correspondence with Other Reformed Churches and the Colonial and Continental Committee, as well as Archbishops and Bishops of the Anglican Church.

It is recommended that the above wider relations be maintained as hitherto through the appropriate Committees of the united Church.

SCHEME FOR ADMISSION OF MINISTERS AND LICENTIATES OF OTHER CHURCHES.

1. Applicants for Admission to the Ministry of the united Church shall approach the General Assembly by Petition submitted through the Committee on Admission and Status of Ministers, whose duty shall be to examine each Petition, to have an interview with the Petitioner, to make such investigation and inquiry as may seem expedient in each case, and to transmit the Petition to the General Assembly, with a recommendation as to the judgment which in the opinion of the Committee ought to be pronounced, and whether the crave ought to be granted, partially granted, deferred, or refused. The Committee shall be empowered to make such Regulations for its procedure, and to require such Fees from Petitioners as it may deem fit, and to issue a statement of these Regulations and Fees in a separate pamphlet for the guidance of applicants and for orderly procedure in its own work.

2. The Petition in each case shall be as far as possible framed after a style to be set forth in the pamphlet issued by the Committee. The Petition shall give full particulars as to the Petitioner's age, present Church connection, Educational Curriculum and Ministerial Career, with an explicit statement of the reasons for which the Petitioner proposes to seek admission to the united Church, and shall be accompanied by all documents required to substantiate the facts set forth. These documents shall be originals, or, if the originals are not available, copies or extracts from official records certified by the persons qualified to grant them. The Petition shall be lodged with the Secretary of the Committee not later than the first day of January preceding the meeting of General Assembly for which it is intended.

3. Immediately after 1st January in each year, the Convener shall prepare a synopsis of each Petition received before that date, and shall cause it to be issued to the members of Committee at least a week previous to a Statutory Meeting to be held before 31st January, when the Petitioner shall appear for interview (unless in any particular case of an exceptional nature the Convener recommends the Committee to dispense with this requirement entirely, or to defer it till a subsequent meeting), and answer such questions as may be put to him bearing on the matters set forth in his Petition, or as may be relevant to the subject of his application. The Committee shall then deliberate as to the recommendation to be made to the General Assembly, but at this stage its resolution shall be merely provisional, and liable to be confirmed,

reversed or varied at a later meeting. As soon as possible the resolution shall be communicated to the Petitioner, who shall be required to reply in writing whether he desires to adhere to his Petition as already presented, or to withdraw it, or to vary its crave in consequence of the said resolution. In exceptional cases, and for reasons to be stated in its Report, the Committee may resolve to make no recommendation, but to refer the case *simpliciter* to the General Assembly, but otherwise the Committee shall not be required to assign to the Petitioner any reasons for its finding.

4. In order that the Courts of the Church may have their rightful place in the reception of those who are to become Ministers of the Church, and also in order that the Committee may have further opportunity of investigating the facts as set forth in the Petition, and be more fully persuaded of the desirability or otherwise of the admission of the Petitioner, the Petition shall then be forwarded to the Presbytery of his residence; but if he has not resided mainly within the bounds of any Presbytery in Scotland for three months prior to 1st January, it shall be forwarded to the Presbytery of Edinburgh. It shall be accompanied by a copy of the synopsis already mentioned, and of the recommendation which the Committee has provisionally agreed to make. The Presbytery may, if it so desires, call on the Committee to forward also the documents on which the synopsis is based for inspection and return. The Petitioner shall be instructed to report himself to the Clerk of Presbytery, and to hold himself in readiness to appear before the Presbytery if that Court should desire an interview. The Presbytery shall deal with the matter as soon as possible, and, after making such investigations and inquiries as it deems fit, shall communicate to the Secretary of the Committee its opinion on the case not later than the 15th day of April, and shall also intimate the same to the Petitioner.

5. As soon as possible thereafter, the Standing Committee shall again meet, and, having anew considered each case with the opinion of the Presbytery thereanent, shall come to a final decision as to the recommendation to be made to the General Assembly, and shall in this recommendation state whether or not the admission of the Petitioner seems to be for the benefit of the united Church. The decision shall forthwith be intimated to the Petitioner, who may, if he so desires, withdraw the Petition (in which case the documents he has lodged in connection therewith shall be at once returned to him) or may alter its crave.

6. When the Committee's Report is presented to the General Assembly, each case shall be considered separately. The recommendations alike of the Committee and of the Presbytery shall be included in the Report. The Petitioner shall appear at the bar in support of his Petition, unless for cause shown and approved by the Committee or in exceptional circumstances by the Assembly. He shall have the right to be heard only with regard to any inaccuracy in the synopsis of the facts set forth in his Petition, of which synopsis a copy shall be supplied to him at least seven days before the meeting of Assembly.

7. If the Assembly resolves to grant the crave of the Petition and to admit the Petitioner, it shall remit the case to the Presbytery concerned, or to such other Presbytery as the Assembly may deem more expedient, in order that the appropriate steps may be completed, and the said Presbytery shall enrol him according to the status which the Assembly has granted; but the Presbytery shall not take these steps until any

period of probation or interim-admission which the Assembly may have prescribed has been completed, and until a report on such period has been presented to the Assembly.

8. It shall be competent for the General Assembly, whether or not on the recommendation of the Committee, instead of granting full admission to a Petitioner immediately, to grant probation or interim-admission for a year, or for such other period as may seem expedient, during which period he shall not be permitted to officiate in a vacant charge or to administer either of the Sacraments, though he may exercise the other functions of the Ministry, this restriction being without prejudice to the validity of his orders. Further, it shall be competent for the General Assembly, whether or not on the recommendation of the Committee, to require the Petitioner to attend additional classes in Arts or Divinity with due performance of the work thereof. During this period of probation or interim-admission, the Petitioner shall be required to make such report to the Committee as its Regulations may state, alike as to the work in which he has been engaged and as to the classes, if any, which he has been required to attend, and the Committee shall include in its Report to the ensuing Assembly a statement with regard to the case in these particulars.

9. Until the Petition of any applicant is actually submitted to the General Assembly, it (as well as all the other documents referring thereto) shall be regarded as confidential, and all procedure either by Committee or by Presbytery or other Court shall be taken in private; but this shall not be deemed a hindrance to the Committee (or to a Presbytery to which the case has been referred) in pursuing its proper inquiries and investigations.

10. If a Minister who applies for admission to the united Church has already been ordained to the full status and function of the Ministry by any Presbyterian Church, whose orders are recognised by the united Church, and if the General Assembly resolves to admit him to the Ministry of the united Church, he shall not on such admission be re-ordained; but in any other case the Standing Committee shall refer the matter to the General Assembly with their recommendation.

11. If a Minister who desires admission is already a Minister in full standing and the Minister, whether Emeritus or Acting, of a congregation of any Presbyterian Church in Great Britain or Ireland whose orders are recognised by the united Church, it shall not be necessary for him to make application in the manner aforesaid; but he shall not be eligible for appointment to any charge in the united Church until he has satisfied the Committee or its Executive that he has taken a full course in Arts and Theology equal to that required of Licentiates of the united Church, and that his character is in accordance with his profession; but after receiving a certificate from the Committee or its Executive (in accordance with any Regulations or conditions which that Committee may frame) he shall be eligible for translation from his present charge to a charge in the united Church, or for being received by a Presbytery as a Minister residing or officiating in its bounds without a charge; provided always that in the latter event he shall not be entitled on this ground alone to a seat in the Presbytery.

12. If a Licentiate or Minister either of the Church of Scotland or of the United Free Church of Scotland before their union, or of the united Church subsequent thereto, has neither demitted nor been judicially deprived of the status he possessed, but has undertaken employment

which is not subject to the jurisdiction of the Church as so united, he shall, on ceasing to be so employed, be eligible for appointment to office in the united Church, according to his status ; provided that prior to nomination for such office he shall have satisfied the Committee or its Executive as to his status, record, and character, and shall have received from it a certificate to that effect.

13. It shall not be competent for the Committee to recommend to the General Assembly the admission of any Petitioner whose age on the 1st day of January preceding the Meeting of Assembly exceeds 45 years, unless he has held a charge or charges in any Presbyterian Church in Great Britain or Ireland or the Dominions for at least ten years ; but this shall not preclude the Committee in exceptional cases from transmitting his Petition *simpliciter* if otherwise satisfactory, nor shall it preclude the General Assembly in the exercise of its *nobile officium* from granting admission ; but in the latter event the Petitioner shall come under the ordinary regulations of the Aged and Infirm Ministers' Fund as regards annuity or retiring allowance.

14. A Petitioner may, along with his Petition, submit to the Committee a separate application to be permitted to be employed in the meantime in connection with the Church. If the Committee resolves to grant the application, it shall be endorsed accordingly, and unless recalled shall be valid until the General Assembly has disposed of the Petition ; provided (1) that the permission shall not entitle the Petitioner to administer either of the Sacraments or to be placed on the Register of Probationers, or to officiate in a vacant charge ; (2) that so soon as employment has been obtained the Petitioner shall submit the application as endorsed to the Clerk of the Presbytery within whose bounds the work is to be performed, and shall be deemed to be under the care and jurisdiction of that Presbytery, or of any other Presbytery to which he may be transferred ; (3) that it shall be competent for the Committee or its Executive to recall the permission, or for the Presbytery to suspend its operation, at any time ; (4) that the Presbytery within whose bounds he is employed shall report to the Committee within three weeks of such a report being requested, as to the manner in which he has performed his duties. Without production of the application as endorsed, it shall not be competent for a Petitioner to undertake, or for a Kirk Session to give, employment other than occasional supply while his case is pending. The same rules *mutatis mutandis* shall be observed by a Committee of the Church which may employ the Petitioner, and in this case the report to the Committee shall be made by the Convener of such Committee.

15. The foregoing principles and rules, together with such other regulations as the General Assembly may frame, while referring principally to Ministers of other Churches in full status, shall be regarded as applying also to Licentiates of other Churches, so far as capable of such application. Students who have been trained by other Churches, and who have not already been granted the status of Licentiates, shall not come within the scope of the procedure herein enacted, but shall report themselves to the Committee on Education for the Ministry, which shall deal with such cases under its own regulations.

APPENDIX III.

CERTAIN DECLARATORY AND UNITING ACTS REFERRED TO IN THE BASIS OF UNION (Oct. 1929, i.).

A.—CHURCH OF SCOTLAND ACT ON THE FORMULA (1910, xiii.).

Edinburgh, 30th May 1910. *Sess.* 7.

WHEREAS it is expedient to amend the Formula of Subscription to the Confession of Faith required from ministers and preachers of this Church, and from persons appointed to Chairs of Theology in the Scottish Universities, and the Principal of Saint Mary's College, Saint Andrews, respectively, the General Assembly, with the consent of the majority of Presbyteries, declare and enact that in lieu of the present Formula of Subscription to the Confession of Faith, which is prescribed by Act XVII. of General Assembly 1889, the following shall be the Formula of Subscription by ministers at their ordination and by probationers when receiving licence, viz. :—

> I hereby subscribe the Confession of Faith, declaring that I accept it as the Confession of this Church, and that I believe the fundamental doctrines of the Christian faith contained therein.
>
> As likewise I own and acknowledge Presbyterian Church government, as now and for long time settled by law, to be the only government of this Church, and I will submit thereto and concur therewith, and never endeavour, directly or indirectly, the prejudice or subversion thereof. As also I will observe that uniformity of worship and of the administration of all public ordinances in this Church, as the same are at present performed and allowed, or shall be hereafter declared by the authority of the same.

And further, the General Assembly declare and enact that Subscription of the Confession of Faith, which has been made in terms of the Formula at present in use, or which may be so made prior to the 1st July after the passing of this Act, by ministers, preachers, or other persons above-named, shall be held to be equivalent to Subscription of the Formula herein enacted.

B.—Declaratory Act of the United Presbyterian Synod.

(*Adopted May* 1879.)

Whereas the formula in which the Subordinate Standards of this Church are accepted requires assent to them as an exhibition of the sense in which the Scriptures are understood: Whereas these Standards, being of human composition, are necessarily imperfect, and the Church has already allowed exception to be taken to their teaching or supposed teaching on one important subject: And whereas there are other subjects in regard to which it has been found desirable to set forth more fully and clearly the view which the Synod takes of the teaching of Holy Scripture: Therefore, the Synod hereby declares as follows:— Declaratory Act, 1879.

1. That in regard to the doctrine of redemption as taught in the Standards, and in consistency therewith, the love of God to all mankind, His gift of His Son to be the propitiation for the sins of the whole world, and the free offer of salvation to men without distinction on the ground of Christ's perfect sacrifice, are matters which have been and continue to be regarded by this Church as vital in the system of Gospel truth, and to which due prominence ought ever to be given.
2. That the doctrine of the divine decrees, including the doctrine of election to eternal life, is held in connection and harmony with the truth that God is not willing that any should perish, but that all should come to repentance, and that He has provided a salvation sufficient for all, adapted to all, and offered to all in the Gospel; and also with the responsibility of every man for his dealing with the free and unrestricted offer of eternal life.
3. That the doctrine of man's total depravity, and of his loss of "all ability of will to any spiritual good accompanying salvation," is not held as implying such a condition of man's nature as would affect his responsibility under the law of God and the Gospel of Christ, or that he does not experience the strivings and restraining influences of the Spirit of God, or that he cannot perform actions in any sense good; although actions which do not spring from a renewed heart are not spiritually good or holy—such as accompany salvation.
4. That while none are saved except through the mediation of Christ, and by the grace of His Holy Spirit, who worketh when, and where, and how it pleaseth Him; while the duty of sending the Gospel to the heathen, who are sunk in ignorance, sin, and misery, is clear and imperative; and while the outward and ordinary means of salvation for those capable of being called by the Word are the ordinances of the Gospel: in accepting the Standards, it is not required to be held that any who die in infancy are lost, or that God may not extend His grace to any who are without the pale of ordinary means, as it may seem good in His sight.
5. That in regard to the doctrine of the Civil Magistrate, and his authority and duty in the sphere of religion, as taught in the Standards, this Church holds that the Lord Jesus Christ is the

only King and Head of the Church, and "Head over all things to the Church which is His body"; disapproves of all compulsory or persecuting and intolerant principles in religion; and declares, as hitherto, that she does not require approval of anything in her Standards that teaches, or may be supposed to teach, such principles.

6. That Christ has laid it as a permanent and universal obligation upon His Church, at once to maintain her own ordinances, and to "preach the Gospel to every creature"; and has ordained that His people provide by their free-will offerings for the fulfilment of this obligation.

7. That, in accordance with the practice hitherto observed in this Church, liberty of opinion is allowed on such points in the Standards, not entering into the substance of the faith, as the interpretation of the "six days" in the Mosaic account of the creation: the Church guarding against the abuse of this liberty to the injury of its unity and peace.

C.—Declaratory Act of the General Assembly of the Free Church, 1892—Anent the Confession of Faith.

Declaratory Act, 1892.

Whereas it is expedient to remove difficulties and scruples which have been felt by some in reference to the declaration of belief required from persons who receive licence or are admitted to office in this Church, the General Assembly, with consent of Presbyteries, declare as follows:—

That, in holding and teaching, according to the Confession, the Divine purpose of grace towards those who are saved, and the execution of that purpose in time, this Church most earnestly proclaims, as standing in the forefront of the revelation of Grace, the love of God, Father, Son, and Holy Spirit, to sinners of mankind, manifested especially in the Father's gift of the Son to be the Saviour of the world, in the coming of the Son to offer Himself a propitiation for sin, and in the striving of the Holy Spirit with men to bring them to repentance.

That this Church also holds that all who hear the Gospel are warranted and required to believe to the saving of their souls; and that in the case of such as do not believe, but perish in their sins, the issue is due to their own rejection of the Gospel call. That this Church does not teach, and does not regard the Confession as teaching, the fore-ordination of men to death irrespective of their own sin.

That it is the duty of those who believe, and one end of their calling by God, to make known the Gospel to all men everywhere for the obedience of faith. And that while the Gospel is the ordinary means of salvation for those to whom it is made known, yet it does not follow, nor is the Confession to be held as teaching, that any who died in infancy are lost, or that God may not extend His mercy, for Christ's sake, and by His Holy Spirit, to those who are beyond the reach of these means, as it may seem good to Him, according to the riches of His grace.

That, in holding and teaching, according to the Confession of Faith, the corruption of man's whole nature as fallen, this Church also maintains that there remain tokens of his greatness as created in the image of God; that he possesses a knowledge of God and of duty; that he is responsible for compliance with the moral law and with the Gospel; and that, although unable without the aid of the Holy Spirit to return to

God, he is yet capable of affections and actions which in themselves are virtuous and praiseworthy.

That this Church disclaims intolerant or persecuting principles, and does not consider her office-bearers, in subscribing the Confession, committed to any principles inconsistent with liberty of conscience and the right of private judgment.

That while diversity of opinion is recognised in this Church on such points in the Confession as do not enter into the substance of the Reformed Faith therein set forth, the Church retains full authority to determine, in any case which may arise, what points fall within this description, and thus to guard against any abuse of this liberty to the detriment of sound doctrine, or to the injury of her unity and peace.

D.—F.C. Act IX., 1894.—Anent Declaratory Act, 1892, on Confession of Faith.

The General Assembly enact and declare as follows:—

Whereas the Declaratory Act, 1892, was passed to remove difficulties and scruples which had been felt by some in reference to the declaration of belief required from persons who receive licence, or are admitted to office in this Church, the Assembly hereby declare that the statements of doctrine contained in the said Act are not thereby imposed upon any of the Church's office-bearers as part of the Standards of the Church; but that those who are licensed or ordained to office in this Church, in answering the questions and subscribing the Formula, are entitled to do so in view of the said Declaratory Act. Declaratory Act, 1894.

E.—Articles forming the Basis of Union of the United Secession and Relief Churches to form the United Presbyterian Church.

(*Adopted May* 1847.)

1. That the Word of God, contained in the Scriptures of the Old and New Testament, is the only rule of Faith and Practice. Articles forming Basis of Union, 1847.

2. That the Westminster Confession of Faith, and the Larger and Shorter Catechisms, are the confession and catechisms of this Church, and contain the authorised exhibition of the sense in which we understand the Holy Scriptures; it being always understood that we do not approve of anything in these documents which teaches, or may be supposed to teach, compulsory or persecuting and intolerant principles in religion.

3. That Presbyterian Government, without any superiority of office to that of a teaching presbyter, and in a due subordination of church courts, which is founded on and agreeable to the Word of God, is the government of this Church.

4. That the ordinances of worship shall be administered in the united Church as they have been in both bodies of which it is formed; and that the Westminster Directory of Worship continue to be regarded as a compilation of excellent rules.

5. That the term of membership is a credible profession of the Faith

of Christ as held by this Church—a profession made with intelligence, and justified by a corresponding character and deportment.

6. That with regard to those Ministers and Sessions who may think that the 2nd Section of the 26th chapter of the Confession of Faith authorises free communion—that is, not loose or indiscriminate communion, but the occasional admission to fellowship in the Lord's Supper, of persons respecting whose Christian character satisfactory evidence has been obtained, though belonging to other religious denominations—they shall enjoy in the united body what they enjoyed in their separate communions—the right of acting on their conscientious convictions.

7. That the election of office-bearers of this Church, in its several congregations, belongs, by the authority of Christ, exclusively to the members in full communion.

8. That this Church solemnly recognises the obligation to hold forth, as well as to hold fast, the doctrine and law of Christ, and to make exertions for the universal diffusion of the blessings of His Gospel at home and abroad.

9. That as the Lord hath ordained that they who preach the Gospel should live of the Gospel—that they who are taught in the Word should communicate to Him that teacheth in all good things—that they who are strong should help the weak—and that, having freely received, thus they should freely give the Gospel to those who are destitute of it—this Church asserts the obligation and the privilege of its members, influenced by regard to the authority of Christ, to support and extend, by voluntary contribution, the ordinances of the Gospel.

10. That the respective bodies of which this Church is composed, without requiring from each other any approval of the steps of procedure by their fathers, or interfering with the rights of private judgment in reference to these, unite in regarding as still valid the reasons on which they have hitherto maintained their state of secession and separation from the Judicatories of the Established Church, as expressed in the authorised documents of the respective bodies, and in maintaining the lawfulness and obligation of separation from ecclesiastical bodies in which dangerous error is tolerated, or the discipline of the Church or the rights of her ministers or members are disregarded.

The united Church, in their present most solemn circumstances, join in expressing their grateful acknowledgment to the Great Head of the Church for the measure of spiritual good which He has accomplished by them in their separate state—their deep sense of the many imperfections and sins which have marked their ecclesiastical management—and their determined resolution, in dependence on the promised grace of their Lord, to apply more faithfully the great principles of church fellowship—to be more watchful in reference to admission and discipline, that the purity and efficiency of our congregations may be promoted, and the great end of our existence as a collective body may be answered with respect to all within its pale, and to all without it, whether members of other denominations, or the world lying in wickedness. And in fine, the united Church regard, with a feeling of brotherhood, all the faithful followers of Christ, and shall endeavour to maintain the unity of the whole body of Christ, by a readiness to co-operate with all its members in all things in which they are agreed.

F.—UNITING ACT, 1876.

ACT OF UNION OF THE FREE CHURCH OF SCOTLAND AND THE REFORMED PRESBYTERIAN CHURCH OF SCOTLAND.

(F.C., 1876, III.)

Whereas the General Assembly of the Free Church of Scotland, on the 30th May 1874, upon Overtures from Presbyteries, declared the cordial satisfaction with which they would contemplate a scriptural union with the Reformed Presbyterian Church, and authorised their Commission, at any stated diet, to entertain any communication from the Reformed Presbyterian Church to that effect: And the Commission, on the 18th November, received a communication from a Committee on Union, appointed by the Reformed Presbyterian Synod, requesting the appointment of a Committee on the part of the Free Church, for conference with respect to Union; and such a Committee was appointed accordingly by the said Commission: and in the months of January and February of the year 1875, statements on the part of the Committees were exchanged, setting forth the principles and historical position of both Churches, and the terms on which Union was contemplated on either side, and especially on the part of the Reformed Presbyterian Church, with reference to the second Reformation and Revolution Settlement: And whereas upon the report of its Committee, the Reformed Presbyterian Synod, at its meeting in May 1875, resolved to transmit to Presbyteries and Sessions an Overture wherein, *inter alia*, the Synod, considering, "as the result of more recent conferences, there is the hope that the Free Church may be prepared for union with this Church as such, on terms which would leave its members free to retain and abide by the views and principles embodied in the statement" by its Committee above referred to, agreed to union with the Free Church, and appointed a Committee to take such steps as might be needful to accomplish the object of the Overture, with due regard to the regulations of the Church, and to all its interests, spiritual and temporal; and the General Assembly of the Free Church, at its meeting in May 1875, on the report of their Committee, adopted and transmitted to Presbyteries, in terms of the Barrier Act, an Overture, wherein, after reciting previous steps, and declaring that the report of the Committee was satisfactory on the question of the views expressed by the Committee of the Synod of the Reformed Presbyterian Church, so far as the question of union with the Free Church is concerned; and also that it appeared that the Reformed Presbyterian Synod were willing to accept, without reserve, the existing Formula of the Free Church of Scotland, on the understanding that the Act of Assembly, August 27, 1647, and the preamble to the Act XII. Assembly 1846 are held to be in force as interpreting the said Formula, and also to allow the name of the united Church to be the Free Church of Scotland, so as to involve no change by that Church in that respect: "Therefore the General Assembly, with consent of a majority of Presbyteries, hereby enact and ordain that an incorporative union may now be effected by the Assembly, upon the terms above indicated, it being understood that the united Church may be declared to consist of the Free Church of Scotland, as existing

Act of Union, 1876.

previously to the Union, and of the Reformed Presbyterian Church, as existing previously to the Union, under the common designation of the Free Church of Scotland simply, and that other secondary details may be adjusted in such manner as to the Assembly may seem meet, provided the adjustment be consistent with the terms specified in the previous parts of this Act": And whereas the Reformed Presbyterian Synod, at its meeting in March 1876, having found that the Overture sent down by them had received the approval of all the Presbyteries, and of all the Sessions reporting, with the exception of two, declared that the said Overture had become the Resolution of the Church in accordance with its law and practice, and empowered its Committee to take steps with a view to the adjustment of all remaining details; and the General Assembly of the Free Church, at its present meeting, having found the Overture before mentioned to have been unanimously approved by the Presbyteries of the Church reporting, passed the same into a standing law; and the General Assembly of the Free Church, and the Synod of the Reformed Presbyterian Church having severally passed the Acts necessary in order to prepare for the consummation of the designed Union, on the terms agreed upon, have severally resolved to meet together for that purpose, and are now met accordingly.

Now, THEREFORE, the said General Assembly and Synod thus met, first of all desire to express their devout thankfulness to the great Head of the Church for the spirit of love and concord which has prevailed during these negotiations for Union; humbly acknowledge their entire dependence on the mercy of God for all the happy results which they hope for in connection with it; and entreat the Divine blessing on the step now to be taken, and on all the congregations and people under their charge; and the General Assembly of the Free Church of Scotland and the Synod of the Reformed Presbyterian Church, empowered as aforesaid, do hereby, in terms and in pursuance of the deliverances of their respective Church Courts, ENACT and DECLARE that the two Churches do and shall henceforth constitute one united Church in all matters spiritual and ecclesiastical; that the said Church shall include and consist of the Free Church of Scotland as existing previously to the union, and of the Reformed Presbyterian Church of Scotland as existing previously to the union; that the name of the united Church shall be "The Free Church of Scotland"; and that its supreme Court shall be designated "The General Assembly of the Free Church of Scotland"; but reserving to the said Reformed Presbyterian Church of Scotland its separate name and existence in so far as regards the civil rights and property now belonging, or which may hereafter accrue or belong to it, or to any of its congregations, with full power to the Ministers and Elders of its congregations, and to the successors of such Ministers and Elders for the time being, to meet hereafter as the Courts of the Reformed Presbyterian Church of Scotland with the necessary officers as heretofore, but only in order to deal with the said civil rights and property now belonging, or which hereafter may accrue or belong to that Church as aforesaid, and with power to make all arrangements and do and perform all acts and deeds proper and necessary to preserve and protect said civil rights and property.

G.—Uniting Act.

(U.F.C., November 1900, I.)

I.

Whereas the Synod of the United Presbyterian Church, at its meeting in May 1896, upon a proposal of the General Assembly of the Free Church of Scotland for closer co-operation of the two Churches in their common work, cordially approved of the proposal, and, further, adopted a resolution in favour of taking steps towards a Union with the Free Church of Scotland, and appointed a Committee, which was reappointed at the meeting of the Synod of 1897, to prosecute that object; and whereas the Free Church Assembly, having, in 1896, appointed a Committee to consider the subject, did, in 1897, reappoint the said Committee, with powers to confer with the Committee of the United Presbyterian Church; and whereas these Committees having met and communicated to one another the existing doctrinal standards, rules, and methods of the two Churches, it appeared that in regard to doctrine, government, discipline, and worship therein set forth, a remarkable and happy agreement obtained between them, as also in particular in the views of the two Churches with respect to the spirituality and freedom of the Church of Christ, and her subjection to Him as her only Head, and to His Word as her Supreme Standard, and that an incorporating union might harmoniously be accomplished: and whereas Questions and a Formula to be used at ordination and induction, as also arrangements for the support and training of the ministry and for combining the methods and work of the two Churches, have been agreed upon, and have been considered by the inferior Courts of the two Churches—and in particular— Uniting Act, 1900.

Whereas the Synod of the United Presbyterian Church, at its meeting in May 1899, had before it the Report of the Joint Union Committee submitting Questions and Formula as these had been revised in the light of suggestions from Presbyteries and Sessions; also proposals relating, first, to the Provision for the Ministry; second, to the Training of the Ministry; third, to the Aged and Infirm Ministers' Fund; fourth, to the Constitution of the General Assembly; fifth, to Rules and Forms of Procedure; sixth, to Administration of Missions; seventh, to Arrangements for Home Work; and eighth, to Government Grants for Training Colleges and Mission Schools; and the Synod, having approved of the proposals submitted under the several heads of said Report as providing a satisfactory scheme for an incorporating Union of the two Churches, remitted them to Presbyteries and Sessions for final approval, and reappointed its Committee to continue Conference with the Free Church Committee on the practical matters still requiring consideration and adjustment, including the Uniting Act;

And in like manner the General Assembly of the Free Church of Scotland, at its meeting in the same month of May 1899, sent down an Overture to Presbyteries reciting the steps previously taken in regard to Questions and Formula, which, having been under consideration of Presbyteries, were adjusted and approved by the Assembly; and further specifying proposals submitted by the Joint Union Committee relating, first, to the Provision for the Ministry; second, to the Training of the Ministry; third, to the Aged and Infirm Ministers' Fund; fourth, to the Constitution of the General Assembly; fifth, to Rules and Forms of Procedure; sixth, to Administration of Missions; seventh, to Arrangements for Home Work; eighth, to Government Grants for Training Colleges and Schools, and also proposals for Rearrangement of Presbyteries and Synods, which were still subject to adjustment; after all which the Overture proceeded: "Therefore the General Assembly, with consent of a majority of Presbyteries, hereby enact and ordain that the plan of Union set forth in the proposals hereinbefore referred to, including the rearrangement of Presbyteries and Synods as that may be approved by next or any subsequent Assembly, is authorised and accepted by this Church with a view to an incorporating Union with the United Presbyterian Church as a plan to come into operation as soon as a Uniting Act shall have been passed by the General Assembly with consent of a majority of Presbyteries of the Church, it being understood that the united Church may be declared to consist of the Free Church of Scotland as existing previously to the Union, and the United Presbyterian Church as existing previously to the Union, under such common designation as may be agreed upon; and that secondary details may be adjusted as to that Assembly may seem meet";

And WHEREAS the Synod of the United Presbyterian Church, at its meeting in May 1900, adopted the proposals which had been remitted in the previous year to Presbyteries and Sessions, and by them finally approved of; and further, having approved of the proposals respecting Presbyteries and Synods, and the other practical matters agreed on as necessary to complete the arrangements for entering into Union with the Free Church of Scotland, and having also approved of the proposed Uniting Act, and of certain express Declarations which the Churches have in view in entering into Union, the Synod remitted said Act and Declarations for final approval to Presbyteries and Sessions;

And in like manner the General Assembly of the Free Church of Scotland, at its meeting in the same month of May 1900, approved of the proposals respecting Presbyteries and Synods as finally adjusted, and passed the foresaid Overture, with consent of a majority of Presbyteries, into a standing law; and approved of the said proposed Uniting Act, and also of the foresaid Declarations, and remitted the same in the form of an overture to Presbyteries;

And WHEREAS in this month of October the General Assembly of the Free Church of Scotland, with consent of a majority of Presbyteries, and the Synod of the United Presbyterian Church, have now sanctioned the form of a Uniting Act and also adopted the aforesaid Declarations, and having now severally passed all Acts necessary for the consummation of the Union on the terms agreed upon, have severally resolved to meet together for that purpose, and are now met accordingly;

Now, therefore, the said General Assembly of the Free Church of Scotland and the Synod of the United Presbyterian Church thus met, first of all desire to express their devout thankfulness to the great Head of the Church for the spirit of love and concord which has prevailed during those negotiations for Union; humbly acknowledge their entire dependence on the mercy of God for all the happy results which they hope for in connection with it; and entreat the Divine blessing on the step now to be taken, and on all the congregations and people under their charge;

AND

the General Assembly of the Free Church of Scotland, and the Synod of the United Presbyterian Church, empowered as aforesaid, do hereby, in terms and in pursuance of the deliverances of their respective Church courts, enact and declare that the Free Church of Scotland and the United Presbyterian Church do and shall henceforth constitute one united Church; that the name of the united Church shall be "The United Free Church of Scotland," and that its Supreme Court shall be designated "The General Assembly of the United Free Church of Scotland."

II.

That the General Assembly of the Free Church of Scotland and Synod of the United Presbyterian Church, when they have met for the purpose of consummating the Union, and have adopted the Uniting Act, shall thereafter have the powers of a General Assembly of the united Church, and may do and authorise all things necessary or convenient to be done with a view to the orderly inauguration and conduct of the affairs of the united Church, and in consistency with the terms of Union agreed upon.

DECLARATIONS ANENT UNION.

The Assembly declares that the Church enters into this union and authorises it in view of the following express Declarations, viz.:—

1. The various matters of agreement between the Churches with a view to Union are accepted and enacted without prejudice to the inherent liberty of the united Church, as a Church of Christ, to determine and regulate its own constitution and laws as duty may require, in dependence on the grace of God and under the guidance of His Word.

2. The Larger and Shorter Catechisms of the Westminster Assembly, received and sanctioned by the General Assembly of 1648, and heretofore enumerated among the doctrinal standards of the United Presbyterian Church, continue to be received in the united Church as manuals of religious instruction long approved, and held in honour by the people of both Churches.

3. As this Union takes place on the footing of maintaining the liberty of judgment and action heretofore recognised in either of the Churches uniting, so, in particular, it is hereby declared that members of both Churches, and also of all Churches which in time past have united with either of them, shall have full right as they see cause, to assert and maintain the views of truth and duty which they had liberty to maintain in the said Churches.

4. While thankfully owning the goodness of God in time past, in moving the hearts of their people to provide means for carrying on the work of the Gospel, the Churches in entering into Union, and under a sense of their present and future responsibilities as a Church of Christ, desire afresh to acknowledge the obligation resting on the Church to labour for the universal diffusion of the Gospel, and the duty of its members to contribute, according to their ability, for the support of the Gospel and the extension of the cause of Christ throughout the world.

APPENDIX IV.

DEEDS, FORMS, AND ACTS ANENT PROPERTY AND SALES OF PROPERTY AND APPLICATION OF PROCEEDS.[1]

A.—FORM OF ALLOCATION ORDER MADE BY THE CHURCHES (SCOTLAND) ACT COMMISSION.

FORMER FREE CHURCH CONGREGATIONS.

ORDER No.......:—..

At Edinburgh the day of Nineteen Hundred and Eight Years.

Form of Allocation Order.

WHEREAS by The Churches (Scotland) Act, 1905 (5 Edw. 7, Ch. 12), the Commissioners appointed by His Majesty under the said Act are empowered to allocate between the Free Church of Scotland and the United Free Church of Scotland "All property which, on the Thirtieth day of October Nineteen Hundred, was vested in or held by or on trust for, or was payable to or for behoof of the Free Church, or was held for the purposes of any school, scheme, mission, or other special object of the said Church, or, where any such property has been disposed of since that date, the proceeds of sale thereof or any investments representing the same, including any revenue or accumulations of any such property, proceeds of sale, or investments accruing since the said date," and "Such rights, duties, and liabilities (including the right of appointing representatives on bodies of trustees or other boards) as belonged or attached to the Free Church on the Thirtieth day of October Nineteen Hundred," and also "Any legacies, bequests, or conveyances of property under testamentary writings made before the Thirtieth day of October Nineteen Hundred, by testators who died thereafter and before the commencement of this Act, in dispute between the Free Church and the United Free Church": And WHEREAS the Commissioners have resolved, after inquiring into the circumstances, to make the following allocation :—

THEREFORE THE COMMISSIONERS acting under the said Act pronounce this Order :—

1. THE COMMISSIONERS HEREBY ALLOCATE as from and after the Thirtieth day of October Nineteen Hundred, or in the case of any

[1] For pre-union Church of Scotland Property see App. VI., B. and C., and App. VII. pp. 483-530, 535-546; also G., p. 464 of this App.

legacies, bequests, or conveyances of property under testamentary writings made before the said date by testators who died thereafter and before the commencement of the said Act, in dispute between the Free Church and the United Free Church, from and after the date of vesting of the same, to THE UNITED FREE CHURCH OF SCOTLAND to be used for the purposes of and in connection with the Congregation of the said United Free Church of Scotland known as the

United Free Church of Scotland Congregation

the whole property (including the property described or referred to in the Schedule hereto annexed), which at said date or dates respectively was vested in or held by or on trust for or was payable to or for behoof of the Congregation known as the Free Church of Scotland Congregation, or the Trustees, Kirk Session, Deacons' Court, Minister, or any other organisation or office-bearers of or connected with that Congregation, or any member or members thereof as such, or which was then held for the purposes of any School, Scheme, Mission, or other special object of or in connection with that Congregation; DECLARING—

(1) That the conditions and provisions of any Model Trust Deed or other title under which the said property was at the said Thirtieth day of October Nineteen Hundred held in connection with the Free Church of Scotland and the said Congregation thereof, and any conditions and provisions determining or affecting the relations between the said Free Church of Scotland Congregation and the Free Church of Scotland and the General Assembly thereof with reference to the said property shall cease to apply thereto; and such property shall be held, in terms of the said Act, for the purposes of and in accordance with the Constitution of the United Free Church of Scotland: Provided always that in so far as such property, or any part thereof, was at the commencement of the said Act appropriated to any special Church purposes, the same shall be thenceforth appropriated to the same or similar purposes of or in connection with the United Free Church of Scotland.

(2) That the said property is so allocated, subject to any bonds, burdens, and debts thereon, or in respect thereof; and any person or persons who have come under personal obligation or liability in connection therewith shall have all the like remedies against such property, and the United Free Church of Scotland, and the said Congregations thereof, as they would have had against such property and the Free Church of Scotland and the said Congregation thereof, had this allocation not been made.

2. For the purpose of carrying the present allocation into effect, THE COMMISSIONERS hereby TRANSFER the property by this Order allocated from all persons in whom such property or any part thereof is at present vested, to the Reverend

Minister,

Session Clerk, and

Clerk of the Deacons' Court, all of the said United Free Church of Scotland Congregation, and their successors in their said respective offices, and such other persons as individuals or *ex officiis* as may be appointed in manner after mentioned, all as Trustees, who shall hold the same for the purposes herein expressed, and subject to the declaration after mentioned in this section shall, as regards the management and disposal of the heritable property hereby allocated, be subject to the regulation and direction of the General Assembly of the said United Free Church of Scotland for the time being, and shall (subject to such regulation and direction in the case of heritable property) have power to sell, or otherwise dispose of the whole or any part of the property hereby allocated, and to burden the same with debt: Declaring, however, that where any property allocated and transferred by this Order as aforesaid was at the Thirtieth day of October Nineteen Hundred held by Trustees upon titles which did not give to the General Assembly of the Free Church of Scotland any powers of regulation and direction as to the management and disposal of such property, nothing contained in this Order shall confer on the General Assembly of the United Free Church of Scotland any powers of regulation and direction in regard to such property; and the Trustees to whom such property is by this Order transferred shall in that case have power without the authority of the General Assembly of the United Free Church of Scotland to sell such property or otherwise to dispose of it or to burden it with debt: Provided always that any proceeds arising from the exercise of the said powers or any of them shall be held for and applied and appropriated to the purposes mentioned in this Order, and shall in all respects be subject to this Order, and that purchasers from or lenders to the said Trustees shall not be entitled to inquire into, and shall have no responsibility in regard to, the application of the money paid by them to the said Trustees. Provided further that the members of the said United Free Church of Scotland Congregation, at a meeting duly convened, may from time to time appoint other persons as individuals or *ex officiis* to be Trustees in addition to the Trustees *ex officiis* before mentioned, or in succession to or in the place of any appointed Trustee or Trustees, and that the minute of such meeting, or a copy or extract thereof, purporting to be signed by the chairman and clerk of the meeting, shall be sufficient evidence of such appointment. The Trustees holding office for the time being shall be entitled to act by a majority as a quorum; and no act of the Trustees shall be open to question or objection because of the existence of a vacancy or vacancies in the Trusteeship at the time when such act was done.

3. This Order shall, as regards the property described or referred to in the Schedule hereto annexed, be equivalent to and have the effect of a Disposition, Assignation, Transfer, or other special conveyance of such property, with all rights and pertinents thereof, as more particularly described in the title-deeds thereof, executed in legal and appropriate form by a person duly vested in the same by a title completed in legal and appropriate form, in favour of the said Trustees herein named and their successors in office and any other Trustees who may be appointed in manner before mentioned, or otherwise be equivalent to and have effect of a general conveyance, transfer, or assignation of the property described or referred to in the

Schedule hereto annexed, and the titles, writs, and evidents thereof, granted by the person or persons last vested with or in right of the same in favour of such Trustees as aforesaid ; and further this Order shall, as regards any other property hereby allocated and transferred of whatever kind and wherever situated, and the titles, writs, and evidents thereof, also be equivalent to and have the effect of a general conveyance, transfer, or assignation of the same granted in manner foresaid ; And the production of this Order or of a copy thereof or excerpt therefrom, purporting to be certified by the Secretary to the Commissioners, or of an official Extract thereof from the Books of Council and Session, shall be a sufficient warrant to the Registrar, Directors, or other Officials of any Corporation, Firm, Company, or Concern as well out of Scotland as in Scotland, to enter the said Trustees upon the Register thereof as proprietors of the property hereby allocated or any part thereof, and to grant and issue all Certificates and other deeds or writings which may be requisite or usual as evidence of their title ; and upon such production all persons holding such property or any part thereof shall be bound at the expense of the said Congregation of the United Free Church of Scotland to pay or deliver the same to the said Trustees or to grant such conveyances or transfers thereof as the said Trustees may require.

4. Subject and without prejudice to the provisions of Sub-section 1 of Section 1 of this Order, the General Assembly of the United Free Church of Scotland and the said Congregation of that Church may jointly grant to and confer upon the Trustees herein named and their foresaids and any other Trustees who may be appointed in manner before mentioned, or any new Trustees whether as individuals or *ex officiis* who may be appointed by the said General Assembly and Congregation jointly, such powers of management and disposal of the property hereby allocated or any part thereof and with and under such conditions and trusts, as the said General Assembly and Congregation may jointly agree upon ; and the Trustees herein named and their foresaids, and any other Trustees who may be appointed in manner before mentioned, shall thereupon hold such property or such part thereof with the powers and under the conditions and trusts so granted and agreed upon, or may convey the same to themselves or to other trustees to be jointly appointed as aforesaid to be held with the said powers and under the said conditions and trusts ; And the exercise of the powers hereby conferred upon the said congregation and General Assembly respectively shall be sufficiently evidenced by the minute of a duly convened meeting of the members of the congregation, or a copy or extract thereof purporting to be signed by the chairman and clerk of such meeting, and by an Act or Minute of said General Assembly, or a copy or extract thereof purporting to be signed by one of the Clerks or the Depute Clerk of said Assembly.

5. THE COMMISSIONERS hereby ALLOCATE and TRANSFER all such rights, duties, and liabilities (including the right of appointing representatives on bodies of trustees or other boards, or acting as such representatives or trustees) as belonged or attached to the said Free Church of Scotland Congregation, and to any organisation minister or other office-bearers or members thereof as aforesaid, on the Thirtieth day of October Nineteen Hundred (including the rights described or referred to in the Schedule hereto annexed), to the said United Free Church

of Scotland Congregation, and to the corresponding organisation minister or other office-bearers or members of the said congregation.

6. In this Order, the expression "property" includes property heritable and moveable and all interests therein; and the expression "rights" includes powers, privileges, and immunities.

NOTHING IN THIS ORDER shall prejudice or affect any rights, duties, and liabilities as regards the property hereby allocated other than those of the Free Church and the United Free Church.

IN WITNESS WHEREOF these presents and the Schedule hereto annexed are signed in accordance with the Determinations of the Commission for the Regulation of Procedure, in terms of the Churches (Scotland) Act, 1905, Section 3, sub-section 5.

Note.—In the Schedule to each Order the congregational property was specified. In some cases the form of the Order was modified to suit particular circumstances, or to bring it into harmony with the allocation by the Commissioners.

B.—CLAUSES FOR CONGREGATIONAL TITLES.

UNITED FREE CHURCH.

To the Reverend , Minister; , Session Clerk; and Clerk of the Deacons' Court, all of the Congregation of the United Free Church of Scotland at present known as the United Free Church Congregation of , and their successors in their said respective offices, and such other persons as individuals or *ex officiis* as may be appointed in manner after mentioned as trustees for the said United Free Church Congregation, to act in the trust after specified, and to the acceptors and acceptor and survivors and survivor, the majority of the accepting and surviving trustees for the time being always a quorum; and to the assignees and disponees of the said accepting and surviving trustees, whether named or to be appointed as aforesaid, in life for the time, or of their quorum, heritably and irredeemably, All and Whole

[*Here follows the description.*]

Which subjects hereby disponed are, so long as possessed by trustees for said congregation, to be used for the purposes of and in connection with the said United Free Church Congregation of and in accordance with the constitution of the said United Free Church of Scotland. Declaring always that the said trustees before mentioned, or to be appointed as said is, shall, as regards the management and disposal of the said subjects, be subject to the regulation and direction of the General Assembly for the time being of the said United Free Church of Scotland, and shall, subject to such regulation and direction, have power to sell or otherwise dispose of and to burden with debt said property; and purchasers from and lenders to the said trustees shall not be entitled to inquire into and shall have no responsibility in regard to the application of the money paid by them to the said trustees. Also declaring always that the said trustees before named, and any trustees to be appointed as said is, shall be bound, on being required by the General Assembly of the United Free Church of Scotland, or by the said Congregation of the United Free Church of Scotland, to convey the said subjects to themselves or to such other trustees as may be appointed by the said congregation, to be held by them under the conditions and provisions of any trusts which may be prescribed by the said General Assembly. Declaring always that the members of the said congregation, at a meeting duly convened by intimation from the pulpit on the two Sabbaths immediately preceding the day of meeting—such intimation specifying the business to be dealt with—may from time to time appoint other persons to be trustees, in addition to the trustees hereinbefore mentioned, or in succession to, or in place of, any of them, or of any trustees to be hereafter appointed. Declaring further that the exercise of the powers hereby conferred upon the said congregation and the said General Assembly respectively, shall be sufficiently evidenced by the minute of a duly convened meeting of the members of the congregation, or a copy or extract thereof, purporting to be signed by the chairman and clerk of such meeting, and by an Act or Minute of the said General Assembly, or a copy or extract thereof, purporting to be signed by one of the Clerks, or Depute Clerk, of said Assembly.

C.—Model Trust Deed of the United Presbyterian Church, with Forms and Instructions.

(a) Model Trust Deed.

(Dated 5th, and registered in the Books of Council and Session, 9th May 1892.)

We, the Rev. James Black, Doctor of Divinity, minister of Wellington United Presbyterian Church, Glasgow, present Moderator, and the Rev. Thomas Kennedy, Doctor of Divinity, minister of North Richmond Street United Presbyterian Church, Edinburgh, and the Rev. William Blair, Doctor of Divinity, minister of the United Presbyterian Church in Dunblane, present Clerks, all of the Synod of the United Presbyterian Church, considering that the said Synod, at a meeting held at Edinburgh on the fifth day of May in the year 1892, resolved that it was advisable that a deed should be made and executed setting forth the purposes for which the said Synod recommends that the heritable properties now belonging to or held for behoof of, or which may hereafter belong to or be held for behoof of, the various congregations which now are or may hereafter be in connection with or under the superintendence of the said Synod, should be held by the trustees in whom they are or shall be vested, and also the duties, powers, and privileges which the said Synod recommends should be conferred on and possessed by such trustees; and that the deed so to be made and executed should be registered in the Books of Council and Session for preservation, and in order that ready access to its terms might be had by congregations and others interested: And further considering that these presents having been submitted to the said Synod and considered by them, the said Synod at its said meeting on the said fifth day of May in the year 1892 approved thereof, adopted the same as containing a statement approved of by them of the said purposes, duties, powers, and privileges, and authorised us, the present

Model Trust Deed of United Presbyterian Church.

Moderator and Clerks of the said Synod, to subscribe the same on their behalf, and directed the same, on being completed, to be registered in the Books of Council and Session for preservation: THEREFORE We, the said James Black, Thomas Kennedy, and William Blair, Moderator and Clerks foresaid, do hereby, for and on behalf of and as authorised as aforesaid by the said Synod, DECLARE that these presents shall be called and known, and may be referred to, as "The Model Trust Deed of the United Presbyterian Church"; and that in these presents the following words or expressions shall have the following meanings—viz. the word "congregation," in the case of each congregation in connection with and under the superintendence of the Synod of the United Presbyterian Church who shall adopt this Model Trust Deed, either without or with any variation, shall mean the persons, male and female, whose names are from time to time on the communicants' roll of the congregation, kept by the minister or session thereof, or who are recognised and held to be members in full communion by the said session or by the superior judicatories of the United Presbyterian Church; and the expression "trust subjects" shall mean the ground, buildings, or other heritable or real property or subjects belonging to or held for behoof of the congregation, and with reference to which the congregation shall adopt this Model Trust Deed; and the expression "the trustees" shall mean the trustees in whom the trust subjects shall from time to time be vested, whether they shall consist of office-bearers, or of individuals named or elected and appointed as trustees, or partly of office-bearers and partly of individuals named or elected and appointed as trustees: AND FURTHER, We do hereby, for and on behalf of, and as authorised as aforesaid by, the said Synod, DECLARE that the trust subjects shall be vested in the trustees, in trust, for the purposes, and with the powers, privileges and immunities after mentioned, viz.:—*First*, The trust subjects shall be held in trust for the use and behoof of the congregation; and in case of any split or division taking place in the Synod of the United Presbyterian Church whereby the members composing the said Synod may be separated into two or more bodies, or in the event of the said Synod uniting or resolving to unite with any other religious judicatory or denomination, the trust subjects shall be held in trust for the use and behoof of those members of the congregation, male and female, who shall adhere to and remain in connection with the body composed of those who adhere to the majority of the ministers and ruling elders who voted on the occasion of such division; or with the body composed of those who adhere to the Synod in the event of there being no division, or to the majority of the Synod in the event of there being a division, along with the ministers and ruling elders and members of any other body with which they may unite, as the case may be; and subject to the Synod or Assembly representing such body or bodies, to the exclusion of all other members or persons, so long as such members as shall adhere and remain as aforesaid shall be recognised as a congregation by the Presbytery of the bounds; and in case the members of the said congregation, or those adhering to and remaining in connection with the United Presbyterian Church, or the body or bodies hereinbefore described as aforesaid, and subject to the Synod or Assembly representing the same, shall, with any who may join them, be so few as not to be recognised as a congregation by the Presbytery of the bounds, or in case the whole members of the said congregation shall separate from and renounce their connection with the United Presbyterian Church, or the body or bodies hereinbefore described, either of which cases shall be conclusively proved by an order of the Presbytery of the bounds to drop the name of the said congregation from the Roll of the Presbytery, the trust subjects shall be held for behoof of the Synod or Assembly forming the Supreme Court for the time of the United Presbyterian Church, or of the body or bodies hereinbefore described, as the case may be; and shall be dealt with and sold or otherwise disposed of or used, and the proceeds used or applied, all as such Synod, Assembly, or Supreme Court shall direct or authorise: and in case of any split or division taking place in the congregation itself, the trust subjects shall be held in trust for the members of the congregation, male and female, who may adhere to and remain in connection with, and subject to the United Presbyterian Church, or the body or bodies hereinbefore described. *Second*, The management, repair, and occupation of the trust subjects, and every transaction relative thereto, shall be conducted and performed by or with the consent of the committee of management, or of a body of deacons if any be, chosen by the congregation and appointed for such purposes from time to time, in conformity with its rules and regulations for the management of its secular and civil affairs; and the trustees acting for the time being shall be bound, so far as may be required of them, to act along with and give their sanction to the acts and deeds of such committee of management or deacons as the case may be, in all matters and things lawfully done by them in execution of the powers and duties entrusted to them. *Third*, It shall not be lawful to nor in the power of the trustees, excepting with the consent thereto of the congregation, previously had and obtained at a general meeting thereof, to make any extensive alteration or repair on the trust subjects; nor, excepting with such consent, and also with the consent and approval of the Presbytery of the bounds, to sell, lease for more than nineteen years, or otherwise dispose of the trust subjects, or to burden or affect them with debt. *Fourth*, Any special business relating to the administration of the trust, or requiring the consent and authority of the congregation, shall be decided on by a general meeting of the members of the congregation. *Fifth*, The trustees shall each year render a report of their management to the annual meeting of the congregation, to be held in terms of the rules or constitution of the congregation, accompanied with a statement of their acts and management and intromissions if any; DECLARING that the trustees shall not be liable for omissions, nor for one another, but each of them for his own actual intromissions only, deducting his necessary expenses and disbursements in the premises: and the trustees shall be entitled to be freed and relieved out of the trust subjects of any advances they may have lawfully made, and of any obligations or engagements they may have come under, in the necessary or proper discharge of the trust; but they shall not be entitled to require a discharge of their obligation for the feu-duty or rent and consequents so far as irredeemable, but only to be freed and relieved from the consequences thereof as the same may arise. *Lastly*, All meetings of the congregation for the purposes hereof shall be general meetings, whether annual or special, of the members, male and female, of the congregation, called by competent authority, and whereof intimation shall have been given at the regular and ordinary diets of public worship of the congregation immediately before the congregation is dismissed on the two Sabbaths next preceding the day on which the meeting is to be held; such intimation specifying all the purposes of the meeting except the submitting of the report and statement provided for by the immediately preceding article; and the acts and deeds of a majority of the persons qualified as members, male and female, who may assemble in virtue of an intimation made as aforesaid, shall be held valid and binding as the acts and deeds of the congregation; and a copy of the minute of such meeting, under the hand of the preses and clerk, narrating such intimation, shall be conclusive evidence of such intimation having been made, and of the resolutions come to at such meeting: ALL which purposes, duties, powers, and privileges, and conditions, provisions, and declarations shall remain binding on the trustees for the congregation, and on all others concerned, until and unless altered as hereinafter mentioned, and if so altered they shall as altered remain binding as aforesaid until again so altered. No such alteration shall be made by the congregation excepting by a majority as after mentioned at two consecutive meetings of the members of the congregation to be called as above provided for this special purpose, which majority shall be not less than three-fourths of the members present at each meeting, and the second of which meetings shall be held at an interval of not less than three weeks after the time of holding the first; and no such alteration shall take effect or be operative until it shall have been approved of by the Presbytery of the bounds, and such approval shall have been confirmed by the said Presbytery at a subsequent meeting held at an interval of not less than ten days after the meeting at which the approval shall have been given; and if the Presbytery of the bounds shall not approve of such alteration within three months of the second congregational meeting aforesaid, or shall not confirm their approval within three months of their meeting at which they approve of the alteration, such alteration shall not take effect nor become operative. AND WE, for and on behalf foresaid, and as authorised as aforesaid, CONSENT to registration hereof for preservation.—IN WITNESS WHEREOF, these presents, written on this and the three preceding pages by Peter M'Murray, clerk to William Robson, Solicitor in the Supreme Courts of Scotland, Edinburgh, are subscribed by us, the said James Black, Thomas Kennedy, and William Blair, all at Edinburgh, upon the fifth day of May in the year eighteen hundred and ninety-two, at a meeting of the said Synod, in presence thereof and before these witnesses, the said William Robson and John Knox Crawford, also Solicitor in the Supreme Courts of Scotland, Edinburgh.

WILLIAM ROBSON, *Witness.*	JAMES BLACK, D.D., *Moderator.*
J. KNOX CRAWFORD, *Witness.*	THOMAS KENNEDY, D.D., *Clerk.*
	WILLIAM BLAIR, D.D., *Clerk.*

(*b*) FORMS OF DISPOSITION.

1. *Form of Disposition in favour of Office-Bearers and Managers.*

I, A. B., heritable proprietor of the subjects after disponed, in consideration of the sum of   instantly paid to me by C. D., treasurer of the United Presbyterian Congregation of as the price and value of the said subjects, of which I hereby acknowledge the receipt, and discharge the said C. D. and all others concerned, do hereby SELL, ALIENATE, and DISPONE to and in favour of the Reverend E. F., present minister, G. H., I. J., etc., present elders, and K. L., M. N., etc., present members of the committee of management (or presently deacons) of the said congregation, while they respectively continue to hold the said offices of minister, elders, and members of the committee of management (or deacons) foresaid, and their successors in office, the minister or ministers, elders, and members of the committee of management (or deacons) of the said congregation for the time being, duly elected and appointed in terms of the rules and practice of the United Presbyterian Church, and the Reverend O. P., presently moderator, and the Reverend Q. R., presently clerk of the United Presbyterian Presbytery of , under whose inspection the said congregation are, while they continue to hold the said offices of moderator and clerk aforesaid, and their successors in office, the moderator and clerk for the time being of the said Presbytery, while the said congregation shall remain under the inspection of the said Presbytery, or the moderator and clerk for the time being of any other or different Presbytery with which the said congregation may afterwards be connected, or under whose inspection they may be placed, as trustees for the use and behoof of the said United Presbyterian Congregation of , in connection with and under the inspection of the Synod of the United Presbyterian Church and Presbyteries thereof, as a site for a church or place of worship (or "for a manse or dwelling-house for the minister," or otherwise as the case may be), and to the assignees of the said trustees, heritably and irredeemably : ALL and WHOLE (*here describe the property*), together with all my right, title, and interest present and future therein : BUT that IN TRUST always for behoof of the said congregation, for the purposes, with the powers, privileges, and immunities, and subject to the duties set forth and specified in the Model Trust Deed of the United Presbyterian Church, executed by the Reverend James Black, Doctor of Divinity, then Moderator, and the Reverend Thomas Kennedy, Doctor of Divinity, minister of North Richmond Street United Presbyterian Church, Edinburgh, and the Reverend William Blair, Doctor of Divinity, minister of the United Presbyterian Church in Dunblane, then Clerks, all of the Synod of the United Presbyterian Church, for and on behalf of, and as authorised by, the said Synod, dated 5th, and registered in the Books of Council and Session 9th May 1892, which is hereby adopted as the statement of the purposes for which the said subjects shall be held by the said trustees, and of the powers, privileges, immunities, and duties of the said trustees, without prejudice to any further powers, privileges, and immunities possessed by or pertaining to them by law, and not inconsistent with those contained in the said Model Trust Deed : With entry at the term of (*here specify the date of entry, and continue the deed in usual form*).

2. *Form of Disposition in favour of Individuals as Trustees.*

I, A. B., heritable proprietor of the subjects after disponed, in consideration of the sum of instantly paid to me by C. D., treasurer of the United Presbyterian Congregation of as the price and value of the said subjects, of which I hereby acknowledge the receipt, and discharge the said C. D. and all others concerned, do hereby SELL, ALIENATE, and DISPONE to and in favour of E. F., G. H., etc., and such other person or persons as may be elected and appointed in manner after specified, and the Reverend J. K., present moderator, and the Reverend L. M., present clerk, of the United Presbyterian Presbytery of   , under whose inspection the said congregation are, while they continue to hold the said offices of moderator and clerk aforesaid, and their successors in office, the moderator and clerk for the time being of the said Presbytery, while the said congregation remain under the inspection of the said Presbytery, or the moderator and clerk for the time being of any other or different Presbytery with which the said congregation may afterwards be connected, or under whose inspection they may be placed, as trustees for the use and behoof of the said United Presbyterian Congregation of   , in connection with and under the inspection of the Synod of the United Presbyterian Church and Presbyteries thereof, as a site for a church or place of worship (or "for a manse or dwelling-house for the minister," or otherwise as the case may be), and to the assignees of the said trustees, heritably and irredeemably: ALL and WHOLE (*here describe the property*), together with all my right, title, and interest present and future therein: BUT that IN TRUST always for behoof of the said congregation, for the purposes, with the powers, privileges, and immunities, and subject to the duties set forth and specified in the Model Trust Deed of the United Presbyterian Church, executed by the Reverend James Black, Doctor of Divinity, then Moderator, and the Reverend Thomas Kennedy, Doctor of Divinity, minister of North Richmond Street United Presbyterian Church, Edinburgh, and the Reverend William Blair, Doctor of Divinity, minister of the United Presbyterian Church in Dunblane, then Clerks, all of the Synod of the United Presbyterian Church, for and on behalf of, and as authorised by, the said Synod, dated 5th, and registered in the Books of Council and Session 9th May 1892, which is hereby adopted as the statement of the purposes for which the said subjects shall be held by the said trustees, and of the powers, privileges, immunities, and duties of the said trustees, without prejudice to any further powers, privileges, and immunities possessed by or pertaining to them by law, and not inconsistent with those contained in the said Model Trust Deed: DECLARING FURTHER, that in case any of the said trustees other than the moderator and clerk for the time being of the said Presbytery, or of those who may be elected in manner hereinafter mentioned, shall cease to be in full communion with the said congregation, or shall remove beyond the fellowship of the said congregation with the view of permanent residence, or shall connect himself with any other congregation, whether in the same or any other communion, or shall cease from whatever cause to be a member of the said congregation, such trustee or trustees shall be *ipso facto* disqualified, and cease to be a trustee in the same way as if he were naturally dead: AND FURTHER, that it shall, on the one hand, be lawful to and in the power of any of the trustees, other than the moderator and clerk for the time being of the said Presbytery, original or elected, to resign office at any time; and, on the other hand, it shall be lawful to and in the power of the members of the said congregation for the time being, assembled at any general meeting of the congregation to be called and intimated as prescribed in the said Model Trust Deed, to supersede and remove any trustee or trustees, original or to be elected as aforesaid, other than the moderator and clerk for the time being of the said Presbytery; and in the event of a resolution to that effect being passed at such meeting, such trustee or trustees shall be disqualified from further acting, and shall cease to hold office in the same way as if he or they were naturally dead; AND FURTHER DECLARING, that the said trustees shall not have power to assume new trustees, but that it shall be lawful to and in the power of the members of the said congregation for the time being, assembled at any general meeting thereof, called and intimated as aforesaid, to elect and appoint any person or persons, being members of the said congregation at the time, to be trustee or trustees along with the trustee or trustees who may be surviving and remaining qualified, or in place of any or all who may have been disqualified, or have deceased, or been removed; and any person or persons who may be so elected and appointed shall, in virtue of such appointment, and of "The Titles to Land Consolidation (Scotland) Act, 1868," sect. 26, be *ipso facto* vested with the same rights of property, and the same powers, on the same conditions and for the same purposes, as the trustees named and designed in these presents: With entry at the term of (*here specify the date of entry, and continue the deed in usual form*).

(c) FORMS IN CONNECTION WITH ELECTION OF TRUSTEES AND ADOPTION OF RULES.

1. *Form of Intimation for calling a Meeting to elect Trustees.*

Notice is hereby given, that in consequence of an order from the Session, a general meeting of this congregation will be held in this place on the evening of , the day of curt., at o'clock, for the purpose of electing new trustees.

Note.—In reference to the time of the meeting, etc., regard must be had to any provisions on the subject in the trust-deed or constitution of the congregation.

2. *Form of Certificate of Intimation.*

I, A. B. [*designation*], hereby certify that I officiated as minister [*or precentor, as the case may be*] of the United Presbyterian[1] Congregation of on Sunday, the day of , and that on that occasion, immediately after public worship, and before the congregation had retired, in consequence of an order to that effect from the Session of said congregation [*or otherwise, as the case may be*], I intimated that a general meeting of the said congregation would be held, etc. [*repeating words of intimation*].

C. D., *Witness.* (Signed) A. B., *Minister,*
E. F., *Witness.* *or Precentor.*

[1] See note at end of this Section, p. 460.

3. *Form of Minutes of Election of New Trustees*

At , and within the church there of the United Presbyterian[1] Congregation of , the day of , Nineteen hundred and years, at o'clock, in consequence of an intimation from the pulpit [*or, desk*] last Lord's day,—the said United Presbyterian[1] congregation [*where necessary, add,* "*formerly called or known by the name of* "] met. The meeting having been constituted by prayer, A. B. was elected preses, and C. D. was chosen clerk, with authority to sign these minutes in name and behalf of the meeting.

The names and designations of the trustees as they stood at the day of , being the date of the last election, were read over, and it was found that the following, viz. :—

A. B., merchant in M——, and C. D., farmer in N——, have died ;
That E. F., grocer in M——, and G. H., mason in P——, have become incapacitated ;
That I. J., weaver in O——, has been removed ;
And that K. L., merchant in P——, M. N., farmer in E——, and O. P., wright in O——, remain in office.

It was resolved in these circumstances to elect new trustees, to act along with the said K. L., M. N., and O. P.—and the following persons were proposed and seconded, and were, and hereby are, duly elected accordingly, viz. :—

R. S., merchant in E——,
S. T., baker in ——,
U. V., etc.,

making the trustees in whom, and in the survivors or survivor of them, the heritable property belonging to the congregation becomes now legally vested in terms of [*here specify the last disposition and infeftment or lease*], and of the "Titles to Land Consolidation (Scotland) Act, 1868" ; or, if the trustees' infeftment is prior to 1st January 1869, in place of the "Titles to Land Consolidation (Scotland) Act, 1868," insert "the Act 13 and 14 Vict. cap. 13, intituled 'An Act to render more simple and effectual the titles by which congregations or societies, associated for purposes of religious worship or education in Scotland, hold real property acquired for such purposes,'" the said K. L.,
M. N.,
O. P.,
R. S.,
S. T.,
U. V., etc,

In witness whereof, this minute, written by the said C. D., clerk, on this and the preceding pages, is subscribed by the said A. B., preses of the said meeting, and the said C. D., clerk thereof, in presence of E. F. and G. H. (*designing them*) witnesses, present at said meeting.

E. F., *Witness.* A. B., *Preses.*
G H., *Witness.* C. D., *Clerk.*

[1] See note at end of this Section, p. 460.

4. *Form of Minutes of Congregation called for the Adoption of Rules.*

The notice of the meeting and certificate of intimation should be in the terms given above, with the necessary alterations as to the object.

At , and within the church there of the United Presbyterian[1] Congregation of , the day of , Nineteen hundred and years, at o'clock, in consequence of an intimation from the pulpit [*or desk*] last Lord's day,—the said United Presbyterian[1] congregation [*where necessary, add,* "*formerly called or known by the name of* "] met. The meeting having been constituted by prayer, A. B. was elected preses, and C. D. was chosen clerk, with authority to sign these minutes in name and behalf of the meeting.

It was moved and seconded, That, seeing the title-deeds simply declare that the trustees [*or, office-bearers*] therein mentioned, and their successors in office, are vested in the subjects therein contained, in trust for (*quote the words from the title*), it is expedient that the purposes of the trust should be more explicitly declared, and that rules and regulations should be adopted for the guidance of said trustees in the management of the trust, and to regulate the mode of appointment of their successors; and that the following declarations and rules and regulations should now be enacted, viz. (*here insert them as in Form 5 below*). This motion having been duly considered, and the proposed declarations and rules and regulations having been carefully gone over, article by article, the same were, and hereby are, adopted and enacted as the conditions and declarations, and rules and regulations, of the trust accordingly, to be henceforth as binding on the trustees now elected [*or,* "*at present in office*"], and their successors, as if the same had been contained in the title-deeds thereof.

In witness whereof, this minute, written by the said C. D., clerk, on this and the preceding pages, is subscribed by the said A. B., preses of the said meeting, and the said C. D., clerk thereof, in presence of E. F. and G. H. (*designing them*) witnesses, present at said meeting.

E. F., *Witness.*	A. B., *Preses.*
G. H., *Witness.*	C. D., *Clerk.*

5. *Rules to be adopted by Congregations whose Title-Deeds do not specify Mode of electing Trustees, etc.*

1. The said trustees and their successors in office are vested in the said subjects, and shall hold the same in trust for behoof of the congregation for the purposes, with the powers, privileges, and immunities, and subject to the duties set forth and specified in the Model Trust Deed of the United Presbyterian Church, executed by the Reverend James Black, Doctor of Divinity, then Moderator, and the Reverend Thomas Kennedy, Doctor of Divinity, minister of North Richmond Street United Presbyterian Church, Edinburgh, and the Reverend William Blair, Doctor of Divinity, minister of the United Presbyterian Church in Dunblane, then Clerks, all of the Synod of the United Presbyterian Church, for and on behalf of and as authorised by the said Synod, dated 5th, and registered in the Books of Council and Session 9th May 1892, which is hereby adopted as the statement of

[1] See note at end of this Section, p. 460.

the purposes for which the said subjects shall be held by the said trustees, and of the powers, privileges, immunities, and duties of the said trustees, without prejudice to any further powers, privileges, and immunities possessed by or pertaining to them by law, and not inconsistent with those contained in the said Model Trust Deed.

2. The said trustees shall not have power to assume new trustees, but it shall be lawful to and in the power of the congregation assembled at any general meeting thereof, called and intimated as prescribed in the said Model Trust Deed, to elect and appoint any person or persons, being members of the congregation at the time, to be trustee or trustees along with the trustee or trustees who may be surviving and remaining qualified, or in place of any or all who may have been disqualified, or have deceased or been removed, and any person or persons who may be so elected and appointed shall, in virtue of such appointment, and of "The Titles to Land Consolidation (Scotland) Act, 1868," sect. 26 (*or*, the Act 13 and 14 Vict. cap. 13, intituled "An Act to render more simple and effectual the titles by which congregations or societies, associated for purposes of religious worship or education in Scotland, hold real property acquired for such purposes," *as the case may be*), be *ipso facto* vested with the same rights of property, and the same powers, on the same conditions, and for the same purposes, as any individual trustee who is actually named and designed in the titles and who may be infeft under the same—subject always to the whole conditions, provisions, and declarations set forth in the said Model Trust Deed, or contained in the title-deeds.

3. In case any of the said trustees, or of those who may be elected in manner herein above mentioned, shall cease to be in full communion with the congregation, or shall remove beyond the fellowship of the congregation with the view of permanent residence, or shall connect himself with any other congregation, whether in the same or any other communion, or shall cease from whatever cause to be a member of the congregation, such trustee or trustees shall be *ipso facto* disqualified, and cease to be a trustee or trustees in the same way as if he or they were naturally dead.

4. It shall, on the one hand, be lawful to and in the power of any of the trustees, original or elected, to resign office at any time; and, on the other hand, it shall be lawful to and in the power of the members of the congregation assembled at any general meeting of the congregation, to be called and intimated as aforesaid, to supersede and remove any trustee or trustees, original or to be elected as aforesaid; and in the event of a resolution to that effect being passed at such meeting, such trustee or trustees shall be disqualified from further acting, and shall cease to hold office in the same way as if he or they were naturally dead.

(*d*) General Directions for the Guidance of Congregations.

Revised in 1892 by the Law Advisers of the Synod.

1. Titles to congregational property may now, in virtue of the Act 31 and 32 Vict. cap. 101, sect. 26 ("The Titles to Land Consolidation (Scotland) Act, 1868"), be taken (1) in favour of the moderator, minister, kirk-session, deacons, managers, or other office-bearers, and of their successors in office; (2) or of individuals specially named as

trustees, and their successors in office; and the rights so taken will vest in their successors, "without any transmission or renewal of investiture whatsoever," provided that in other respects the provisions of the Act apply. Titles taken before the passing of the Act have the same privilege if the same conditions be fulfilled. The directions which follow will thus apply to all titles, old and new. The Synod recommends that in all cases where it can be done, office-bearers of the congregation, as such, rather than individuals, be appointed as trustees.

2. In order to obtain the benefit of the Act, it is necessary that the party or parties in whose favour the trust is originally created, or who have been assumed, should have been infeft in the property, if the nature of the right be one requiring infeftment.

3. It is also important (1) that the deeds should expressly bear that the trust is for behoof of the congregation; and (2) that the intended *use* of the property should be stated. (See the whole section of the Act, page 460.)

4. If these conditions are complied with, it will follow that, after the death or resignation or removal from office of the party or parties infeft, the right vests in their "successors in office for the time being."

5. If the title is taken to office-bearers of the congregation as such, and to their successors in office as trustees, the election of new office-bearers completes their title as trustees without any further formality.

6. If the title is taken to individuals specially named as trustees and their successors in office, regard would be had to the following directions, viz.:—

(*a*) It is important that the mode of appointment of successors in office should be prescribed in the title-deeds, and exactly followed in every election, and a record thereof carefully preserved.

(*b*) When the title-deeds do not prescribe the mode of appointment of successors in office, the congregation ought, at a meeting regularly called for the purpose, to adopt rules to regulate the matter. (See Forms 4 and 5, pages 457-458.)

(*c*) In order that there may be evidence as to who are the successors in office of the trustees, the congregation ought to keep a book in which there are inserted (1) the rules for the election of successors prescribed in the title-deeds, or adopted by the congregation; (2) the successive minutes of election themselves, or duplicates thereof, duly attested. These minutes should be prepared in a formal and accurate manner, and should be regularly signed by the preses of the meeting and clerk, and by two witnesses. (See Form 3, page 456.)

(*d*) The designation given to the congregation in the title-deeds should be carefully inserted in the minutes. In cases of congregations that existed before the Union in 1847, if the titles describe the congregation as "The United Associate Congregation of A——," or "The Relief Congregation of A——," the minute should repeat the designation, and add, "now known as the United Presbyterian Congregation of A——," or, reversing the order, "The United Presbyterian Congregation of A——, formerly called the United Associate Congregation of A——," or "The Relief Congregation of A——," as the case may be. (See Form 3, page 456.)

(*e*) Evidence should also be preserved that the meeting has been duly called in conformity to the rules either prescribed in the titles, or adopted by the congregation. A certificate under the hands of the minister or precentor who made the intimation, and by two witnesses, will serve for this purpose. (See Forms 1 and 2, page 455.)

7. [1] It is important that the title-deeds should contain an agreement with the superior for a payment in lieu of every kind of casualties, as, where this is not done, the Act 31 and 32 Vict. cap. 101, sect. 113, provides that a sum corresponding to what would be demandable on the entry of a singular successor shall be payable every twenty-fifth year. This provision is re-enacted by Section 5 of the Conveyancing (Scotland) Act of 1874 (37 and 38 Vict. c. 94), and it is thereby further provided that where a composition is by the titles payable at each sale or transfer, as well as on the death of each vassal, trustees must pay a composition every fifteen years instead of every twenty-five years, as above stated. Where, therefore, an agreement has not been inserted in the titles, an arrangement should be made with the superior on as favourable terms as possible. By Section 15 of the same Act (1874), all casualties may be redeemed by a single payment, and by Section 17 they may be converted into an annual payment at the rate of four per cent on the amount required to redeem them. In feus constituted after 1st October 1874, it is enacted by Section 23 that casualties are not claimable by a superior unless by special stipulation, which, therefore, it is better to avoid if possible.

8. In order that title-deeds may be securely kept, it is very strongly recommended that they be put, for safe custody, into the hands of the Synod's Finance Committee, who shall grant a proper receipt for them.[2]

9. The Synod recommends congregations to adopt the Model Trust Deed, and the trust purposes therein set forth, as regulating the terms on which their property shall be held.

> *Note.*—In the case of meetings held subsequent to the Union of the Church of Scotland and the United Free Church of Scotland in 1929, care should be taken to see that the congregation is correctly named in the forms given in Section (*c*) 2, 3, 4, *i.e.*, Church, formerly called or known by the name of United Free Church or United Presbyterian Church.

D.—Acts of Parliament referred to in Model Trust Deeds and Directions.

1. Act 31 and 32 Vict. 1868, Cap. 101.

Titles to Land Consolidation Act, 1868.

An Act to Consolidate the Statutes relating to the Constitution and Completion of Titles to Heritable Property in Scotland, and to make certain changes in the Law of Scotland relating to Heritable Rights (31st July 1868).

> *N.B.*—It is important to notice that this Act repeals, *inter alia*, the Act 13 and 14 Vict. 1850, cap. 51, entitled "An Act to render more simple and effectual the Titles by which Congregations or Societies associated for purposes of Religious Worship or Education in Scotland hold real property required for such purposes."

[1] Now superseded owing to recent legislation.

[2] Titles may now be deposited with the Custodier of Titles, who will grant a proper receipt for them.

The following are portions of this Act (1868) which relate to ecclesiastical or school property :—

Section 3 (the Interpretation section) provides that "the word 'Lands' shall extend to and include all Heritable Subjects, Securities, and Rights."

Section 26. Wherever lands have been or may hereafter be acquired by any congregation, society, or body of men associated for religious purposes, or for the promotion of education, including the General Assemblies, Synods, and Presbyteries of the Established Church of *Scotland*, and of all other Presbyterian Churches in *Scotland*, as a chapel, meeting-house, or other place of worship, or as a manse or dwelling-house for the minister of such congregation or society or body of men, or offices, garden, or glebe for his use, or as a schoolhouse or schoolmaster's house, garden, or playground, or as a college, academy, or seminary, or as a hall or rooms for meeting for the transaction of business, or as part of the property belonging to such congregation, society, or body of men, and wherever the conveyance or lease of such lands has been or may be taken in favour of the moderator, minister, kirk-session, vestrymen, deacons, managers, or other office-bearers or office-bearer of such congregation or society, or body of men, or any of them, or of trustees appointed, or to be from time to time appointed, or of any party or parties named in such conveyance or lease in trust for behoof of the congregation or society or body of men, or of the individuals comprising the same, such conveyance, when recorded with warrant of registration thereon in terms of this Act, or when followed by notarial instrument expede, and with warrant of registration thereon recorded in terms of this Act, or such lease, shall not only vest the party or parties named therein in the lands thereby feued, conveyed, or leased, but shall also, after the death or resignation or removal from office of such party or parties, or any of them, effectually vest their successors in office for the time being chosen and appointed in the manner provided or referred to in such conveyance or lease, or if no mode of appointment be therein set forth or prescribed, then in terms of the rules or regulations of such congregation or society or body of men, in such lands, subject to such and the like trusts, and with and under the same powers and provisions as are contained or referred to in the conveyance or lease given and granted to the parties, disponees, or lessees, therein, and that without any transmission or renewal of the investiture whatsoever, anything in such conveyance or lease contained to the contrary notwithstanding: And the provisions of this section shall apply also to all trusts for the maintenance, support, or endowment of ministers of religion, missionaries, or schoolmasters, or for the maintenance of the fabric of churches, chapels, meeting-houses, or other places of worship, or of manses or dwelling-houses or offices for ministers of the gospel, or of schoolhouses or schoolmasters' houses, or other like buildings.

2. Act 37 and 38 Vict. Cap. 94.

An Act relating to Land Rights and Conveyancing, and to facilitate the Transfer of Land in Scotland (7th August 1874).

Sect. XLV. When by the tenor of the title to any estate in land held in trust duly completed in favour of the trustee or trustees therein named, or any of them, and recorded in the appropriate register of Conveyancing (Scotland) Act, 1874.

sasines, the office of a trustee has been or shall be conferred upon the holder of any place or office, or proprietor of any estate, and his successors therein, any person subsequently becoming a trustee by appointment or succession to the place or office or estate to which the office of trustee has thus been or shall be annexed, shall be deemed and taken to have a valid and complete title by infeftment in the estate, in the same manner and to the same effect as if he had been named in the completed and recorded title, without the necessity of any deed of conveyance or other procedure.

E.—ABSTRACT OF "FREE CHURCH OF SCOTLAND SCHOOL PROPERTIES ACT, 1878."

(*Report of Special Commission*, 1879.)

School Properties Act, 1878.

The deacons' court of each congregation, for whose behoof or in connection with which any school property is held, may, with the consent of the General Assembly, appropriate such school property, or any part thereof, to such educational uses, including Sabbath Schools, libraries, lectures, etc., in connection with such congregation as such deacons' court may think fit, notwithstanding any restrictions or conditions with respect to the use, or reversion, or forfeiture thereof, contained or referred to in the titles under which it is held.

In case of school property held under a title granted under the powers of the Act of Parliament of 1840, or of the Act of 1841, the continued use of the dwelling-house attached to such school property, as a dwelling-house requires the consent of the granter of such title or his successor.

If the deacons' court of the congregation, or the General Assembly, shall consider that the school property cannot be, or at any time has ceased to be, beneficially appropriated to educational uses, or may with greater advantage be sold or let for other purposes, such deacons' court may, with the consent of the General Assembly, but subject to the provisions contained in the Act, sell, at the highest price that can be obtained, such school property; or the deacons' court, with the consent of the General Assembly, may from time to time let the same at the highest rent which can safely be obtained, and the free proceeds of the sale of such school property, if sold, or the proportion thereof falling to the congregation, and the free rents of the school property, if let, shall be held and applied in the manner provided by the Act.

Provisions are inserted for the protection of proprietors of estates, of which sites of school properties are held by a title under which, either by reference to the Act of 1840 or to the Act of 1841, or otherwise than by incorporation of or reference to the terms and conditions of the Model Trust Deed, the use of such school property is restricted, or any right reserved to the person from whom such school property was acquired.

In the event of the sale of any school property the free proceeds, after deducting the reasonable expenses of and consequent upon the sale, and the repayment to Government of any grant which may have been made out of public money towards the purchase, erection, or furnishing of such school, shall, where the General Assembly has contributed any part of the original cost of the school, in cases where such free proceeds shall not amount to the aggregate sums contributed by the General Assembly or by the congregation for whose behoof or in connection with which such school property is held respectively, be divided between the General Assembly and the deacons' court of such congregation in proportion to the respective amounts contributed towards such cost by the General Assembly on the one hand and by such congregation on the other hand ; and in cases where such free proceeds shall amount to or exceed the aggregate sums contributed by the General Assembly and by such congregation respectively, such free proceeds shall be applied in the first place in payment to the General Assembly of the sum contributed by them, and the balance shall be paid over to the deacons' court of such congregation. Where no part of such cost was contributed by the General Assembly, the whole of the free proceeds shall be paid over to the deacons' court.

The portions of the free proceeds of sale received by the General Assembly shall be applied by them towards such of the following purposes, in relation to educational interests in connection with the Free Church, as they may appoint, that is to say, towards the granting of pensions or allowances to retired teachers (so far as the same are not paid by deacons' courts), the support of normal schools, the payment of fees of normal school students attending universities or colleges, the foundation of scholarships or bursaries, or the establishment or maintenance of a school or schools.

The free proceeds or portions of free proceeds of sale, and the rents received by such deacons' court as aforesaid, shall be applied by them towards such purposes as aforesaid, in connection with their congregation or with the Free Church, as may be sanctioned by the General Assembly, or towards the establishment or maintenance of a Sabbath School or Sabbath Schools, and of a library where deemed expedient, or for school prizes ; provided always, that if there shall be a retired teacher of a school attached or which may have been attached to such congregation, to whom the General Assembly shall have granted a pension or allowance, the payment thereof shall, to such an extent as may be agreed upon between the General Assembly and such deacons' court, form a primary charge on the sums received by such deacons' court.

It is specially provided that no part of the capital sums arising from the free proceeds of sale of school properties shall be applied to any of the aforesaid purposes, except the establishment of schools or libraries, and, except so far as applied to the last-mentioned purposes, such capital sums shall be invested by the General Assembly, or the respective deacons' courts, as the case may be, in the manner pointed out by the Act.

F.—Deliverance of Assembly anent Application of Proceeds of Sales of Properties no longer used by Congregations.

(U.F.C. *Assembly*, 1923.)

Application of Proceeds of Sales of Properties no longer used by Congregations.

The Assembly, on the Report of the Law Committee, hereby approve of the proposed scheme, and enact and ordain that each of the funds mentioned in the schedule annexed hereto, with all interest thereon, shall be held by the General Trustees at the disposal of, and the said General Trustees shall pay over the same on the joint directions of, the Presbytery indicated under the corresponding number in the second column of the said schedule, and of the Church and Manse Building Fund Committee of said Church, and failing agreement between these two bodies, on the directions of the General Assembly, for the purpose only of providing a new church and manse or other congregational building within the bounds of the said Presbytery, or for the extension, improvement, or repair of any church, manse, or other congregational building within the bounds of the said Presbytery, or for the repayment of any debt affecting the same, or for the redemption of any feu-duty, casualty, ground annual, duplicand, or other periodical payment affecting any such church, manse, or other congregational building or the site thereof, reserving full power to deal with any further sums that may be realised from the sale of the property of dissolved congregations as the Assembly may afterwards determine.

SCHEDULE.

Properties from the Sale of which Funds derived.	Presbytery within which Properties situated.	Sums held on 30th December 1922.
1. Church at Creetown . .	Wigtown and Stranraer .	£480 19 0
2. Church, Manse and Stable belonging to Congregation of Kinnettles	Arbroath and Forfar .	1086 8 5
3. Church and Manse at Nenthorn	Jedburgh and Kelso .	204 2 3
4. Manse of Saltoun and Bolton .	Haddington and Dunbar	509 2 1
5. Church and Manse at Slains .	Deer	445 18 11

G.—Letter of Obligation to the Baird Trust.

(Rep., 1931, pp. 113, 122; 1931, 3 and 12.)

By instruction of the General Assembly the following Letter of Obligation has been given by the General Trustees and the General Administration Committee to the Trustees of the Baird Trust.

A similar undertaking must be given in the case of properties not held by the General Trustees by the Trustees in whom the property is vested as a condition of receiving grants from the Baird Trust. In the case of properties of congregations not standing in the names of the General Trustees, but held by Trustees for each respective congregation, the Baird Trustees and the Home Board, as a condition of their giving grants, require that the property in respect of which the grants are given shall be transferred by a Disposition by the present Trustees holding the property to Trustees for the congregation, on condition, *inter alia,* that the building shall be used exclusively in connection with work of the Church of Scotland generally and the work of the congregation of the Church of Scotland particularly, and that the Trustees in whose favour the Disposition is granted will consult with the Baird Trustees or the Home Board who are making the grant, before they sell or dispose of the property. Where such property is held under a title which provides that the congregation shall only have power to sell or otherwise dispose of, or to burden with debt, such property, subject to the consent of the General Assembly, the permission of the General Assembly must be obtained to the insertion of the Baird Trust and Home Board clauses in the said Disposition.

LETTER OF OBLIGATION.

Stamp 6d.

To

THE TRUSTEES OF THE BAIRD TRUST,
182 BATH STREET,
GLASGOW, C.2.

We, THE CHURCH OF SCOTLAND GENERAL TRUSTEES, incorporated by the Church of Scotland (General Trustees) Order Confirmation Act, 1921, CONSIDERING that you have since the inception of the Baird Trust in 1873, made grants, and may continue to make grants, towards—

(*a*) the erection of Churches *Quoad Omnia*, *Quoad Sacra*, and Mission;
(*b*) the erection of Church Halls;
(*c*) the enlarging, renovation and improving of Churches and Church Halls; and
(*d*) the endowing and further endowing of Churches *Quoad Omnia* and *Quoad Sacra*.

HEREBY AGREE AND UNDERTAKE—

1. That in the event of it being desired to sell or dispose of any church or church hall to which you have given a grant or grants, following upon a condition inserted in the titles that the subjects are inalienably secured to the Church of Scotland, we, before so selling or disposing of these subjects, which have been provided wholly or partly from grants given by you, shall, without prejudice to the right of the Church to deal with its property on the direction of the General Assembly, communicate and consult with you as to the terms of sale; and in the event of your not acquiescing the Church of Scotland will repay the grant if required.
2. Before rearranging, transferring and disposing of the endowments of any Parish to which you have given grants, we shall, without prejudice to the right of the Church to deal with the endowments subject to the direction of the General Assembly, communicate and consult with you as to the rearrangements proposed, and in the event of your not acquiescing the Church of Scotland will repay the grant if required.

In witness whereof

H.—ACT (1940, VIII.), AS AMENDED BY 1959, XXVIII, ANENT SALES AND TRANSFERENCES OF PROPERTIES OF CONGREGATIONS OF THE CHURCH WHICH WERE PROPERTIES OF CONGREGATIONS OF THE FORMER FREE CHURCH OF SCOTLAND AND OF CONGREGATIONS OF THE FORMER UNITED FREE CHURCH OF SCOTLAND WHERE THE TITLE WAS TAKEN IN TERMS OF THE "CLAUSES FOR CONGREGATIONAL TITLES" APPROVED OF FOR USE IN THE CASE OF PROPERTIES ACQUIRED AFTER 30TH OCTOBER 1900.

Edinburgh, May 21, 1940. *Sess.* 1.

The General Assembly hereby declare and enact as follows:—

1. All petitions for the sale or transference of properties belonging to Congregations of the Church of Scotland which were properties of

Congregations of the former Free Church of Scotland and of Congregations of the former United Free Church of Scotland where the title was taken in terms of the "Clauses for Congregational Titles" approved of for use in the case of properties acquired after 30th October 1900, or for the application of the proceeds of such sales, shall proceed from the Deacons' Court or other Body in a Congregation having charge of the property of the Congregation, with concurrence of the Kirk Session and Congregation, and shall have obtained the sanction of the Presbytery of the bounds.

2. All such Petitions, on being received by the Clerks of the General Assembly, shall be communicated to the Committee on Law, Property Cases, and Discipline, in order that they may advise the General Assembly or its Commission with reference to these Petitions.

3. The said Petitions and the Minutes of the Congregations and Courts of the Congregations submitted therewith shall state the purposes to which the Congregation desire the proceeds to be applied, provided always that the same shall be subject to the approval of the General Assembly.

4. Where property is to be sold and the proceeds are forthwith to be applied to the purchase of other property which is substituted in lieu of the property intended to be sold, the Law Agents of the Church or other person or persons to whom the General Assembly shall have committed the custody of the Titles of the Congregational Properties referred to in the first Article hereof shall be directed to see the transaction carried into effect and also to see that the title-deeds of the new property are taken in such terms that the said Congregation and the Trustees holding the property shall, as regards the management and also as regards the disposal of the same, be subject to the regulation and direction of the General Assembly of the Church of Scotland, and that such Congregation and Trustees shall (subject to such regulation and direction) have power to sell or otherwise dispose of the whole or any part of such new property and to burden the same with debt in all cases where such control by the General Assembly was contained in the title of the property sold or intended to be sold.

4a. Where property is to be sold or disposed of by a Congregation and the price or consideration does not exceed £250 in value it shall not be necessary to present a Petition to the General Assembly but such sale or disposal and the application of the proceeds thereof may be authorised by the Assembly Committee on Law, Property Cases and Discipline on a request to that effect being made by letter signed by the Chairman and Clerk of the Deacons' Court or other body in the Congregation having charge of the property of the Congregation and addressed to the Convener of the said Committee provided that such application be accompanied by Extract Minutes of the Congregation, Kirk Session and Presbytery approving of the sale or disposal and the proposed application of the proceeds thereof. In the event of the said Committee authorising the said sale or disposal but not the proposed application of the said proceeds the sale or disposal may proceed and the price shall be remitted to the General Treasurer to retain on behalf of the Congregation until the General Assembly, or its Commission, direct otherwise (1959, xxviii.).

5. Where the proceeds of the property to be sold or of any property intended to be transferred under the authority contained in this Act are not forthwith to be expended as mentioned in Article 4 hereof,

or for any other congregational purpose or purposes specified or referred to under Article 6 hereof, the same shall be transmitted to the General Treasurer of the Church and placed by him on Deposit Receipt until such time as arrangements have been made for the investment thereof, and the said proceeds to be invested shall be invested at the option of the congregation interested either (*a*) in an investment in which Trustees have power to invest under the Trusts (Scotland) Acts as may be suggested by the congregation interested and approved of by the General Treasurer to be taken in the name of the Church of Scotland Trust for behoof of the congregation, or (*b*) under the General Investment Account of the Church of Scotland Trust.

6. The General Assembly hereby further enact the following Rules and Regulations with regard to the purposes or any of the purposes for which the proceeds of the sales of such properties may be applied in all those cases in which the consent of the General Assembly is required to such sale, viz. :—

I. The purposes for which the same may be applied shall be as follows :—

(*a*) For the provision of a new church, manse, or hall, or other congregational building where such is required by the Congregation.

(*b*) For the extension, improvement, or repair of any church, manse, or hall or other congregational building belonging to or in the occupation of the congregation or minister, or to which they respectively may remove.

(*c*) For making due provision for the maintenance of the church, manse, or hall or other congregational building ; for the repayment of any debt affecting the same ; for the redemption of any feu-duty, ground annual or other such periodical payment affecting the congregational property or any part thereof, or providing a capital sum to be invested against meeting such feu-duty, ground annual or other periodical payment as aforesaid, and also for making due provision for other outgoings in connection with such property.

(*d*) Any balance remaining over, after making provision for any of the purposes above named, shall be used for any other purpose or purposes of and in connection with the Congregation, subject to the approval of the General Assembly ; or, where this shall be permissible under the terms of the title under which the property sold or transferred was held then for such purposes as, although not congregational, may be beneficial to the Church of Scotland, and which shall be agreed to by the Congregation, with the approval of the General Assembly.

II. Where the proceeds of sale or transference are to be applied in whole or in part for the maintenance of or repairs to buildings belonging to the Congregation, they shall be placed to a Fabric Fund, and such proceeds shall be retained as capital and the income only applied for the said maintenance or repairs, except in so far as any payment from capital shall be authorised by the General Assembly or the Assembly Committee on Law, Property Cases and Discipline (1959, xxviii.) on application made to that effect.

III. Where any part of the Capital of the proceeds is authorised by the General Assembly or the Assembly Committee on Law, Property Cases and Discipline to be applied to repairs or to alterations or to improvements of the buildings of the Congregation or towards the erection of new buildings such repairs, alterations and improvements, and such erection of buildings shall be carried out subject to the approval and under the supervision of the Presbytery, and on production to the General Treasurer of accounts, certified by the Clerk of the Presbytery, the General Treasurer shall release such sum as may be required to meet these accounts from the funds in his hands belonging to the Congregation.

IV. Where the property sold was School Property held under the Model Trust Deed for Schools of the Free Church of Scotland, reference shall be made to the Free Church of Scotland School Properties Act, 1878 (41 & 42 Vict., Ch. CCXX.), for the purposes to which the proceeds thereof may be applied.

V. The General Assembly reserve full power to modify these rules and regulations or any of them in any case in which the Assembly may think that special circumstances require this to be done.

7. The General Assembly enjoin Presbyteries to see that the abovementioned rules and regulations have been duly complied with previous to their transmission of the Petitions and papers in the case to the Clerks of Assembly.

8. It shall be the duty of the Law Agents of the Church or other person or persons to whom the General Assembly shall have committed the custody of the Titles of the Congregational Properties referred to in the first Article hereof to report annually to the General Assembly through the Committee on Law, Property Cases and Discipline how far in each particular case of sale or transference of property the provisions of this Act and the instructions of the General Assembly have been observed.

9. It is hereby declared that no authority granted by the General Assembly for the sale or transference of any property such as is hereinbefore referred to or any power given to borrow in respect of such property shall be acted upon after the lapse of five years from the date of the granting of such authority unless upon a new application being made to the General Assembly, and where authority is given to borrow it shall be implied that every effort shall be made to repay the amount borrowed within five years from the date of the loan being obtained.

I.—ACT (1933, XXVI.) ANENT APPLICATION OF PROCEEDS OF SALES OF PROPERTIES NO LONGER USED BY CONGREGATIONS.[1]

Edinburgh, May 23, 1933. *Sess.* 2.

The General Assembly declare and enact as follows :—

The General Assembly enjoin Presbyteries in cases in which a Congregation is being dissolved or where a union with another Congregation is being effected to take steps (1) to secure that the importance of applying the funds arising therefrom or from the sale or sales of any Property of the Congregation concerned consequent upon such dissolution or Union (where this shall be permissible under the terms of the title to the congregational properties) towards Church Extension purposes in neighbouring districts, or for the provision of Church hall accommodation for neighbouring Congregations which are not fully

[1] It is not lawful for any congregation to resolve to devote the proceeds of the sale of a church or a manse to secular or non-church purposes (Appendix IV. (1)).

equipped, shall be timeously and appropriately represented to the Congregation concerned—with a view to their adopting a plan of allocation towards such purposes of the sums at their disposal which can be approved by the Presbytery and the General Assembly, and (2) to remind all Congregations that, in the possession of their property, they are stewards of the liberality of former members of the Church, and are in honour bound, in their disposal of the proceeds of property no longer necessary for purely congregational purposes, to keep in view the general needs of the Church, and to consider whether they will not best give effect to the intentions of the donors through whose generosity the property was originally acquired, by supporting plans for Church Extension or for the provision of Manse or Hall accommodation such as aforesaid which have been approved of by the Presbytery.

Act 1964, VIII. anent Application of Proceeds of Sale of Properties ceasing to be used by Congregations on Transportation to New Housing Areas.

The General Assembly enact and ordain as follows :—

When a Congregation is transported to a new Housing Area and new buildings are provided by the Home Board (Church Extension Sectional Committee) the free proceeds of the sale of the ecclesiastical properties (other than the Manse) belonging to or held for the transported Congregation shall, subject to the titles on which these are held, be applied as follows :—

(1) The first charge on the free proceeds of sale shall be applied in meeting the Congregation's normal share of repayment of the cost of the new ecclesiastical buildings (other than the Manse) provided by the Home Board (Church Extension Sectional Committee).

(2) The remainder of the free proceeds of sale shall normally be applied in the following manner and order of priority :—

(*a*) In the establishment of a Fabric Fund of £1,000 for the maintenance of the buildings (including the Manse) of the transported Congregation ;

(*b*) towards the purchase or erection of a Manse for the transported Congregation if a Manse should be required in the new area, but only in so far as the cost of the new Manse is not out of the proceeds of sale of the former Manse ; and

(*c*) in such manner and for such purposes as may be agreed between the Congregational Board (or other body having charge of the temporal affairs of the transported Congregation) the Presbytery of the bounds, the Home Board (Church Extension Sectional Committee) and the Church of Scotland General Trustees, due regard being given to the cost of the new buildings provided or to be provided as aforesaid, and, failing agreement, in such manner and for such purposes as may be determined by the General Assembly.

See also Act 1968, iii., dispensing with printing of Petitions in certain cases.

APPENDIX V.—*A.*

THE CHURCH OF SCOTLAND ACT, 1921.

[11 & 12 Geo. 5.]

CHAPTER 29.

A.D. 1921. *An Act to declare the lawfulness of certain Articles declaratory of the Constitution of the Church of Scotland in matters spiritual prepared with the authority of the General Assembly of the Church.*

[*28th July* 1921.]

Whereas certain articles declaratory of the constitution of the Church of Scotland in matters spiritual have been prepared with the authority of the General Assembly of the Church, with a view to facilitate the union of other Churches with the Church of Scotland, which articles are set out in the Schedule to this Act, and together with any modifications of the said articles or additions thereto made in accordance therewith are hereinafter in this Act referred to as "the Declaratory Articles":

And whereas it is expedient that any doubts as to the lawfulness of the Declaratory Articles should be removed:

Be it therefore enacted by the King's most Excellent Majesty, by and with the advice and consent of the Lords Spiritual and Temporal, and Commons, in this present Parliament assembled, and by the authority of the same, as follows:—

Effect of Declaratory Articles.

1. The Declaratory Articles are lawful articles, and the constitution of the Church of Scotland in matters spiritual is as therein set forth, and no limitation of the liberty, rights, and powers in matters spiritual therein set forth shall be derived from any statute or law affecting the Church of Scotland in matters spiritual at present in force, it being hereby declared that in all questions of construction the Declaratory Articles shall prevail, and that all such statutes and laws shall be construed in conformity therewith and in subordination thereto, and all such statutes and laws in so far as they are inconsistent with the Declaratory Articles are hereby repealed and declared to be of no effect.

Other Churches not to be prejudiced.

2. Nothing contained in this Act or in any other Act affecting the Church of Scotland shall prejudice the recognition of any other Church in Scotland as a Christian Church protected by law in the exercise of its spiritual functions.

Jurisdiction of civil courts.

3. Subject to the recognition of the matters dealt with in the Declaratory Articles as matters spiritual, nothing in this Act contained shall affect or prejudice the jurisdiction of the civil courts in relation to any matter of a civil nature.

Citations and commencement.

4. This Act may be cited as the Church of Scotland Act, 1921, and shall come into operation on such date as His Majesty may fix by Order in Council after the Declaratory Articles shall have been adopted by an Act of the General Assembly of the Church of Scotland with the consent of a majority of the Presbyteries of the Church.

SCHEDULE.

A.D. 1921.

ARTICLES DECLARATORY OF THE CONSTITUTION OF THE CHURCH OF SCOTLAND IN MATTERS SPIRITUAL.

I. The Church of Scotland is part of the Holy Catholic or Universal Church; worshipping one God, Almighty, all-wise, and all-loving, in the Trinity of the Father, the Son, and the Holy Ghost, the same in substance, equal in power and glory; adoring the Father, infinite in Majesty, of whom are all things; confessing our Lord Jesus Christ, the Eternal Son, made very man for our salvation; glorying in His Cross and Resurrection, and owning obedience to Him as the Head over all things to His Church; trusting in the promised renewal and guidance of the Holy Spirit; proclaiming the forgiveness of sins and acceptance with God through faith in Christ, and the gift of Eternal life; and labouring for the advancement of the Kingdom of God throughout the world. The Church of Scotland adheres to the Scottish Reformation; receives the Word of God which is contained in the Scriptures of the Old and New Testaments as its supreme rule of faith and life; and avows the fundamental doctrines of the Catholic faith founded thereupon.

II. The principal subordinate standard of the Church of Scotland is the Westminster Confession of Faith approved by the General Assembly of 1647, containing the sum and substance of the Faith of the Reformed Church. Its government is Presbyterian, and is exercised through Kirk Sessions, Presbyteries, Provincial Synods, and General Assemblies. Its system and principles of worship, orders, and discipline are in accordance with "The Directory for the Public Worship of God," "The Form of Presbyterial Church Government," and "The Form of Process," as these have been or may hereafter be interpreted or modified by Acts of the General Assembly or by consuetude.

III. This Church is in historical continuity with the Church of Scotland which was reformed in 1560, whose liberties were ratified in 1592, and for whose security provision was made in the Treaty of Union of 1707. The continuity and identity of the Church of Scotland are not prejudiced by the adoption of these Articles. As a national Church representative of the Christian Faith of the Scottish people it acknowledges its distinctive call and duty to bring the ordinances of religion to the people in every parish of Scotland through a territorial ministry.

IV. This Church, as part of the Universal Church wherein the Lord Jesus Christ has appointed a government in the hands of Church office-bearers, receives from Him, its Divine King and Head, and from Him alone, the right and power subject to no civil authority to legislate, and to adjudicate finally, in all matters of doctrine, worship, government, and discipline in the Church, including the right to determine all questions concerning membership and office in the Church, the constitution and membership of its Courts, and the mode of election of its office-bearers, and to define the boundaries of the spheres of labour of its ministers and other office-bearers. Recognition by civil authority of the separate and independent government and jurisdiction of this Church in matters spiritual, in whatever manner such recognition be expressed, does not in any way affect the character of this government and jurisdiction as derived from the Divine Head of the Church alone, or give to the civil authority any right of interference with the proceedings or judgments of the Church within the sphere of its spiritual government and jurisdiction.

V. This Church has the inherent right, free from interference by civil authority, but under the safeguards for deliberate action and legislation provided by the Church itself, to frame or adopt its subordinate standards, to declare the sense in which it understands its Confession of Faith, to modify the forms of expression therein, or to formulate other

A.D. 1921. doctrinal statements, and to define the relation thereto of its office-bearers and members, but always in agreement with the Word of God and the fundamental doctrines of the Christian Faith contained in the said Confession, of which agreement the Church shall be sole judge, and with due regard to liberty of opinion in points which do not enter into the substance of the Faith.

VI. This Church acknowledges the divine appointment and authority of the civil magistrate within his own sphere, and maintains its historic testimony to the duty of the nation acting in its corporate capacity to render homage to God, to acknowledge the Lord Jesus Christ to be King over the nations, to obey His laws, to reverence His ordinances, to honour His Church, and to promote in all appropriate ways the Kingdom of God. The Church and the State owe mutual duties to each other, and acting within their respective spheres may signally promote each other's welfare. The Church and the State have the right to determine each for itself all questions concerning the extent and the continuance of their mutual relations in the discharge of these duties and the obligations arising therefrom.

VII. The Church of Scotland, believing it to be the will of Christ that His disciples should be all one in the Father and in Him, that the world may believe that the Father has sent Him, recognises the obligation to seek and promote union with other Churches in which it finds the Word to be purely preached, the sacraments administered according to Christ's ordinance, and discipline rightly exercised; and it has the right to unite with any such Church without loss of its identity on terms which this Church finds to be consistent with these Articles.

VIII. The Church has the right to interpret these Articles, and, subject to the safeguards for deliberate action and legislation provided by the Church itself, to modify or add to them; but always consistently with the provisions of the first Article hereof, adherence to which, as interpreted by the Church, is essential to its continuity and corporate life. Any proposal for a modification of or addition to these Articles which may be approved of by the General Assembly shall, before it can be enacted by the Assembly, be transmitted by way of overture to Presbyteries in at least two immediately successive years. If the overture shall receive the approval, with or without suggested amendment, of two-thirds of the whole of the Presbyteries of the Church, the Assembly may revise the overture in the light of any suggestions by Presbyteries, and may transmit the overture when so revised to Presbyteries for their consent. If the overture as transmitted in its final form shall receive the consent of not less than two-thirds of the whole of the Presbyteries of the Church, the General Assembly may, if it deems it expedient, modify or add to these Articles in terms of the said overture. But if the overture as transmitted in its final form shall not receive the requisite consent, the same or a similar proposal shall not be again transmitted for the consent of Presbyteries until an interval of five years after the failure to obtain the requisite consent has been reported to the General Assembly.

IX. Subject to the provisions of the foregoing Articles and the powers of amendment therein contained, the Constitution of the Church of Scotland in matters spiritual is hereby anew ratified and confirmed by the Church.

APPENDIX V.—*B.*

STATUTORY RULES AND ORDERS.

1926, No. $\frac{841}{\text{S. } 31}$.

THE CHURCH OF SCOTLAND ORDER IN COUNCIL, 1926.

At the Court at Buckingham Palace, the 28th day of June 1926.

PRESENT,

The King's Most Excellent Majesty in Council.

WHEREAS it is provided by the Church of Scotland Act, 1921 [1] (hereinafter referred to as the Act), that the Act shall come into operation on such date as His Majesty may fix by Order in Council after the Declaratory Articles shall have been adopted by an Act of the General Assembly of the Church of Scotland with the consent of a majority of the Presbyteries of the Church:

And whereas the said Declaratory Articles have been adopted by an Act of the General Assembly of the Church of Scotland with the consent of a majority of the Presbyteries of the Church:

Now, therefore, His Majesty is pleased, by and with the advice of His Privy Council, to order, and it is hereby ordered, as follows:—

1. This Order may be cited as the Church of Scotland Order in Council, 1926.

2. The 28th day of June, 1926, is hereby fixed as the date on which the Act shall come into operation.

M. P. A. Hankey.

[1] 11 & 12 Geo. 5. c. 29.

APPENDIX VI.—*A*.

CHURCH OF SCOTLAND (GENERAL TRUSTEES) ORDER CONFIRMATION ACT, 1921.

[11 & 12 Geo. 5, cxxv.]

CHAPTER 125.

A.D. 1921.

An Act to confirm a Provisional Order under the Private Legislation Procedure (Scotland) Act 1899 *relating to the Church of Scotland (General Trustees).* [*8th November* 1921.]

Whereas His Majesty's Secretary for Scotland has made the Provisional Order set forth in the schedule hereunto annexed under the provisions of the Private Legislation Procedure (Scotland) Act 1899 and it is requisite that the said Order should be confirmed by Parliament:

62 & 63 Vict. c. 47

Be it therefore enacted by the King's most Excellent Majesty by and with the advice and consent of the Lords Spiritual and Temporal and Commons in this present Parliament assembled and by the authority of the same as follows:—

Confirmation of Order in schedule.

1. The Provisional Order contained in the Schedule hereunto annexed shall be and the same is hereby confirmed.

Short title.

2. This Act may be cited as the Church of Scotland (General Trustees) Order Confirmation Act 1921.

SCHEDULE.

Church of Scotland (General Trustees).

Provisional Order to incorporate the Church of Scotland (General Trustees) to vest in the corporation the heritable properties and investments held by the different sets of trustees on behalf of the committees of the General Assembly of the Church of Scotland and for other purposes.

Whereas the general work of the Church of Scotland beyond the local spheres of kirk sessions presbyteries and synods is directed and controlled by the General Assembly of the Church of Scotland through standing committees appointed for the purpose : A.D. 1921.

And whereas these committees comprise among others the following :—

The General Committee of the Church ;
The Committee on the Endowment of Chapels of Ease sometimes called the Committee for the Endowment of Chapels of Ease ;
The Committee on Small Livings sometimes called the Small Livings Committee ;
The Committee on the Aged and Infirm Ministers' Fund ;
The Committee on the Home Mission Scheme ;
The Committee on Proposed Pension Fund for Ministers ;
The Committee on Christian Life and Work ;
The Committee on Social Work ;
The Committee for the Better Endowment of Theological Chairs ;
The Colonial Committee ;
The Committee on the Conversion of the Jews ;
The Foreign Mission Committee sometimes called the Committee for the Propagation of the Gospel in Foreign Parts especially in India ;
The Education Committee sometimes called the Committee for increasing the means of Education and Religious Instruction in Scotland ;
The Committee on Correspondence with other Reformed Churches ;
The Committee on Psalmody and Hymns ;
The Committee on Maintenance of the Ministry :

And whereas each of the committees before named makes an annual report to the General Assembly which expresses approval or otherwise thereof and gives instructions thereon :

And whereas each of the said committees has funds under its charge which have been invested in heritable properties and investments the titles to which have been taken in the names of different sets of individual trustees for behoof of such committees respectively :

And whereas the said heritable properties and investments held by each of the said committees with the names of the trustees in whom they are at present vested are detailed in the schedule annexed to this Order :

And whereas the committee of the General Assembly of the Church of Scotland called the General Committee of the Church which is entrusted with the administration of the general business of the Church so far as not administered by any other committee in its report to the General Assembly of the Church of Scotland which met in Edinburgh on the eighteenth day of May one thousand nine hundred and twenty drew the attention of the General Assembly to the inconvenience and unnecessary expense caused through the holding of heritable properties and investments on behalf of the several committees of the Church in names of different sets of individual trustees and stated that the transference of such heritable properties and investments to official trustees of the Church appeared to be the obvious method to adopt but such transference would require the authority of a Provisional Order :

And whereas the General Assembly having considered the report of the General Committee of the Church appointed a special committee to consider the whole question and instructed the special committee to

A.D. 1921.

report to the Commission of Assembly in November one thousand nine hundred and twenty:

And whereas the Act of the General Assembly appointing the Commission of Assembly contained among others the following clause "The "commissioners are also empowered to appoint general trustees for the "Church of Scotland to hold the heritable properties investments and "securities presently vested in and held by trustees on behalf of com-"mittees of the General Assembly of the Church and to approve of the "draft of a Provisional Order to be promoted for incorporating such "trustees and vesting in the corporate body the said heritable properties "investments and securities":

And whereas the said special committee having taken up the remit of the General Assembly and considered the whole question gave in a report to the Commission of Assembly which was received and considered and upon which the Commission of Assembly on the seventeenth day of November one thousand nine hundred and twenty pronounced the following deliverance:—

"The Commission of Assembly having considered the report of the "special committee appointed by the General Assembly with "regard to the appointment of general trustees for the Church "for the purpose of holding the heritable properties investments "and securities vested in trustees on behalf of committees of the "Church and to the promotion of a Provisional Order for the "purpose of incorporating such trustees and vesting in the "corporate body the said heritable properties investments and "securities—

"Resolve that the following persons be general trustees of the Church "and have their names inserted in section 4 of the draft Pro-"visional Order submitted to the meeting namely:—

"The Reverend William Main Edinburgh;
"The Very Reverend David Paul D.D. LL.D. Edinburgh;
"The Reverend William Seath Provand Glasgow;
"James Laidlaw Ewing LL.D. Edinburgh;
"John James Herdman W.S. Edinburgh;
"William Mackay M'Lachlan W.S. Edinburgh;
"William Mackay LL.D. Inverness;
"David Macbeth Moir Milligan advocate Aberdeen;
"Timothy Warren writer Glasgow;
"The Honourable William Watson K.C. Edinburgh; and
"William Whitelaw Hatton Kirknewton:

"Approve of the said draft Provisional Order for incorporating said "trustees and vesting in the corporate body the said heritable "properties investments and securities and instruct the General "Committee to proceed with the said Provisional Order":

And whereas the purposes aforesaid cannot be effected without an Order of the Secretary for Scotland confirmed by Parliament under the provisions of the Private Legislation Procedure (Scotland) Act 1899:

Now therefore in pursuance of the powers contained in the last-mentioned Act the Secretary for Scotland orders as follows:—

Short title.

1. This Order may be cited for all purposes as the Church of Scotland (General Trustees) Order 1921.

2. This Order shall come into operation at the date of the passing of the Act confirming the same which date is herein referred to as "the commencement of this Order." Commencement.

3. In this Order the following words and expressions have the meanings hereby assigned to them respectively unless there be something in the subject or context repugnant to such construction :— Interpretation.

"The Church" means the Church of Scotland;

"The General Assembly" means the General Assembly of the Church;

"Heritable properties" means lands houses buildings feu duties ground annuals ground rents heritably secured perpetual annual payments tack duties bonds of relief and dispositions in security and bonds and dispositions in security which are heritable and other heritable rights;

"Investments" means personal or moveable property of any nature whatever not included under the term "heritable properties";

"Treasurer" includes interim treasurer;

"Clerk" includes interim clerk;

"Committee" means committee of the General Assembly.

4. On the commencement of this Order and subject to the provisions thereof the Reverend William Main Edinburgh the Very Reverend David Paul D.D. LL.D. Edinburgh the Reverend William Seath Provand Glasgow James Laidlaw Ewing LL.D. Edinburgh John James Herdman W.S. Edinburgh William Mackay M'Lachlan W.S. Edinburgh William Mackay LL.D. Inverness David Macbeth Moir Milligan advocate Aberdeen Timothy Warren writer Glasgow the Honourable William Watson K.C. Edinburgh and William Whitelaw Hatton Kirknewton and the survivors and survivor of them and their and his successors and any additional members to be nominated and appointed as hereinafter provided (hereinafter referred to as "the members of the corporation") shall be and they are hereby incorporated by the name of "The Church of Scotland General Trustees" (hereinafter referred to as "the corporation") and by that name shall be a body corporate with perpetual succession and a common seal and may sue and be sued and may purchase acquire hold and sell feu or otherwise dispose of lands and other property heritable and moveable and borrow on the security thereof and shall have all other privileges of a body corporate. Incorporation.

5. Each of the members of the corporation shall be either a minister or an elder of the Church and in the event of any person who is a member of the corporation ceasing to be a minister or elder of the Church he shall thereupon cease to be a member of the corporation. Qualification of members of corporation.

6.—(1) The corporation shall report to the General Assembly all vacancies in the membership of the corporation. Appointment and removal of members of corporation.

(2) The General Assembly shall have the power to remove any member from the office of member of the corporation.

(3) Any General Assembly shall have the power to nominate and appoint members of the corporation either as additional members of the corporation or in place of members of the corporation who have died resigned or become disqualified or been removed.

A.D. 1921.

Transfer to corporation of heritable properties and investments belonging to committees.

7. From and after the commencement of this Order the following provisions shall have effect: —

(1) Without prejudice to the provisions of subsection (2) of this section any trustees or persons in or by whom any heritable property and investment is at the commencement of this Order vested or held for and on behalf of any of the committees mentioned in the first column of the schedule annexed to this Order shall as soon as conveniently may be after the commencement of this Order transfer to the corporation such heritable property and investment and all interests and rights therein and shall do and concur in doing all acts and things necessary or proper for effectually vesting such heritable property and investment in the corporation:

(2) Subject to payment of stamp duty as provided in the immediately following section each of the heritable properties and investments detailed and set forth in the second column of the schedule annexed to this Order and vested in or held by the trustees or persons named opposite thereto in the third column of the said schedule for behoof of the committee named opposite thereto in the first column of the said schedule and all rights obligations claims and demands relative thereto including all accrued income or interest and all arrears of income or interest shall by virtue of this Order *ipso facto* and without any disposition assignation or transfer other than this Order be deemed and taken to be validly transferred to and vested in the corporation to the same effect as if particular dispositions assignations or transfers of the same as the case may be had been granted in favour of the corporation and where necessary had been recorded in the appropriate division of the register of sasines or burgh register and this Order shall be and be deemed to be a valid title thereto and shall not be challengeable or open to objection on the ground that any of the said heritable properties or investments or that any of the said trustees or persons are inaccurately insufficiently or erroneously described or named in the said schedule so long as such property or investment was in truth vested in or held by such trustees or persons for behoof of such committee. Further without prejudice to the foregoing provisions of this subsection all feu-duties ground rents ground annuals tack duties and heritably secured perpetual annual payments (including additional feu-duties ground rents ground annuals tack duties and heritably secured perpetual annual payments and augmentations of feu-duties ground rents ground annuals tack duties and heritably secured perpetual annual payments created either upon the granting of allocations the redemption of casualties the dischargingof building conditions or upon any other ground) vested in or held by trustees or persons for behoof of the following committees viz. the Committee on the Endowment of Chapels of Ease the Committee on Small Livings the Committee on the Aged and Infirm Ministers' Fund the Committee on the Home Mission Scheme the Committee on Christian Life and Work and the Foreign Mission Committee and all rights obligations claims and demands relative thereto and all accrued feu-duties ground rents ground annuals tack

A.D. 1921.

duties and heritably secured perpetual annual payments and all arrears thereof shall by virtue of this Order *ipso facto* and without any conveyance or assignation other than this Order be deemed and taken to be validly transferred to and vested in the corporation to the same effect as if particular dispositions and assignations of the same as the case may be had been granted in favour of the corporation and had been recorded in the appropriate division of the register of sasines or burgh register and this Order shall be and be deemed to be a valid title thereto:

(3) Without prejudice to the immediately preceding subsection and for the purpose of enabling the corporation if thought fit to complete a title to any of the heritable properties and investments detailed and set forth in the second column of the schedule annexed to this Order or to any part thereof by expeding and recording a notarial instrument this Order shall be deemed to be and may be used as a general disposition or assignation as the case may be of such heritable properties and investments in favour of the corporation:

(4) The production of a copy of the Act confirming this Order shall be sufficient warrant to the registrar directors or other officials of any corporation firm company or concern as well out of Scotland as in Scotland to enter the corporation upon the register thereof as proprietor of the investment transferred to and vested in the corporation under this Order without the production of any particular assignation or transfer and to grant and issue to the corporation a certificate or other writing as evidence of the title of the Corporation to such investment: Provided always that this subsection shall not apply to an investment which is only transferable in manner prescribed by or under Act of Parliament or by or under the constitution or rules of the particular corporation firm company or concern which excepted investment shall be by the appropriate means transferred to and vested in the corporation and the instrument by which such investment is transferred shall be liable to the stamp duty in force at the date of execution.

Payment of stamp duty.

8. In place of the stamp duties which would have been payable upon the dispositions assignations or transfers which in case this Order had not been made would have been required to transfer the heritable properties and investments vested in or held for and on behalf of any of the committees mentioned in the first column of the schedule to this Order and vest the same in the corporation there shall be paid a stamp duty of five pounds and such duty shall be impressed upon a copy of the Act confirming this Order and the corporation shall produce such stamped copy to the Commissioners of Inland Revenue within three months after such Act has been printed by His Majesty's Printers.

Heritable properties and investments transferred to and vested in corporation to be held for same purposes as held by trustees.

9. The heritable properties and investments transferred to and vested in the corporation under the section of this Order of which the marginal note is "Transfer to corporation of heritable properties and investments "belonging to committees" shall be held by the corporation for the same ends uses and purposes as those for which they were held by the trustees or persons in whom they were vested or by whom they were held prior to their being transferred to the corporation where these are

A.D. 1921.

expressed or defined and failing such expression or definition subject to the directions of the committee on whose behalf they are held or of the General Assembly.

Trustees in whom heritable properties and investments vested discharged of actings.

10. The trustees and persons in whom the heritable properties and investments detailed and set forth in the second column of the schedule annexed to this Order were invested or by whom they were held before being transferred to and vested in the corporation are hereby as soon as they are divested of the said heritable properties and investments absolutely finally and for ever exonerated and discharged of their actings transactions intromissions and management and of all omissions if any in relation to the said heritable properties and investments.

Treasurer of corporation.

11. The treasurer of the Church shall *ex officio* be the treasurer of the corporation. In the event of a vacancy in the office of treasurer of the Church the corporation shall appoint an interim treasurer of the corporation who shall vacate office immediately on a treasurer of the Church being appointed. The corporation shall have power to grant powers of attorney mandates or other authorities necessary for the collection and distribution of the income and interest upon the heritable properties and investments transferred to and vested in the corporation.

Clerk of corporation.

12. The corporation shall appoint a clerk who shall keep minutes of all meetings of the corporation and also a record of all deeds and documents to which the seal of the corporation has been adhibited.

Meetings of corporation.

13. The clerk of the corporation whom failing the treasurer of the corporation shall call meetings of the corporation and shall call a meeting of the corporation on being requested to do so by a convener of a committee. Not less than five days' notice shall be given for a meeting of the corporation. At all meetings of the corporation three of the members of the corporation shall be a quorum and any meeting at which a quorum is present shall be competent to exercise all or any of the authorities powers and discretions exercisable by the corporation. Each meeting of the corporation shall appoint its own chairman who shall in the event of an equality of votes have a casting vote in addition to his deliberative vote.

14. [Repealed by Church of Scotland Trust Confirmation Act 1932, sec. 28, see p. 546.]

Seal of corporation and execution of deeds, &c.

15. The seal of the corporation shall be kept in the office of the treasurer of the corporation and shall not be affixed to any deed or document of whatever nature the same may be unless such deed or document shall have been signed by one member of the corporation and by the treasurer of the corporation or the clerk of the corporation and all deeds whether relating to heritable or moveable property or of whatever other nature shall be valid and effectual if signed by one member of the corporation and by the treasurer of the corporation or the clerk of the corporation and sealed with the seal of the corporation and such execution on behalf of the corporation shall be equally binding and effectual whether attested by witnesses or not and it shall not be necessary that such execution should take place at a meeting of the corporation.

Cheques &c. how signed and endorsed.

16. All cheques of the corporation upon the bankers of the corporation for the time being shall be signed and all deposit receipts shall be endorsed on behalf of the corporation by two members of the corporation or by one member of the corporation and by the treasurer of the corporation whom failing by the clerk of the corporation. All cheques dividend warrants interest warrants and other like documents in favour

of the corporation shall be endorsed on behalf of the corporation by a member of the corporation or by the treasurer of the corporation whom failing by the clerk of the corporation.

Powers of investment.

17. The corporation may invest funds in any of the following investments namely:—

(1) Investments in which trustees are authorised to invest trust funds according to the law of Scotland or the law of England for the time being:
(2) In the purchase of or on security of heritable property land or real estate in any part of the world:
(3) Stocks or public funds of the United Kingdom:
(4) Debentures debenture stock mortgages or other securities or obligations of any local authority corporation commissioners or other public body being either municipal county district parochial general or otherwise in the United Kingdom:
(5) Debentures deposit receipts debenture stock mortgages or other securities or obligations or the guaranteed stock of any company incorporated or registered either under Royal Charter Act of Parliament or the Companies (Consolidation) Act 1908 or any Act amending the same:
(6) Public or Government or municipal stock funds or securities of India or of any colony or dependency of the United Kingdom:
(7) Stocks or shares of Indian railways the dividends of which are guaranteed by the British or Indian Government:
(8) Policies of life assurance or on the security thereof:
(9) Vested reversionary contingent reversionary or other estate or interest with or without life assurance:
(10) Any investments or security heritable or moveable of any kind or nature whatever not included in the foregoing list provided always the General Committee of the Church has approved thereof:

Provided always that the corporation may retain and hold any heritable property investment or security which has been or may hereafter be transferred to the corporation under the provisions of this Order even though not included in the foregoing list.

Titles certificates &c. to be taken in corporate name of corporation.

18. The titles certificates and all other documents of title of all heritable properties and investments transferred or which may hereafter be transferred to the corporation under this Order as well as the titles certificates and all other documents of title of all heritable properties and investments in which the corporation may invest funds under the powers contained in this Order shall be taken in the corporate name of the corporation.

Costs of management and administration.

19. All expenses incurred in the management or administration of the corporation shall be paid in the first instance by the General Committee of the Church and the General Committee of the Church shall have power and authority to determine each year how such expenses shall be apportioned among the committees of the Church and other committees or associations having heritable properties and investments held in the corporate name of the corporation and to apportion the same accordingly and the said committees and other committees or associations shall each year repay to the General Committee of the Church the portions of such expenses which have been so apportioned upon them on being called upon by the General Committee so to do.

A.D. 1921.

Questions or disputes referred to General Committee.

20. In the event of any question or dispute arising between the corporation and any committee or other committee or association having funds heritable properties and investments held in the corporate name of the corporation the same shall be referred to the General Committee whose decision shall be final and binding on all parties.

Corporation immune from liability.

21. The corporation shall not be liable for the acts receipts neglects defaults or frauds of any member of the corporation or of any treasurer clerk agent officer or servant of the corporation or for any loss or expense resulting through the depreciation or loss of any investment or through the insufficiency or deficiency of title of any heritable property or investment.

22. [Repealed by Church of Scotland Trust Confirmation Act 1932, sec. 28, see p. 546.]

Byelaws and regulations may be made.

23. It shall be lawful for the General Assembly from time to time to make byelaws and regulations to be observed by the corporation in the discharge of its duties under this Order.

Costs of Order.

24. The costs charges and expenses of and incidental to the preparing for obtaining and confirming of this Order or otherwise in relation thereto shall be paid by the General Committee of the Church.

APPENDIX VI.—*B*.

CHURCH OF SCOTLAND (PROPERTY AND ENDOWMENTS) ACT, 1925.

[15 & 16 GEO. 5. CH. 33.]

ARRANGEMENT OF SECTIONS

A.D. 1925.

PART I.

STIPEND AND TEIND.

PART II.

SCOTTISH ECCLESIASTICAL COMMISSIONERS.

A.D. 1925.

PART III.

TRANSFER OF PARISH CHURCHES, MANSES, GLEBES AND CHURCHYARDS.

PART IV.

GENERAL.

CHAPTER 33.

An Act to amend the law relating to Teinds and to the Stipends of Ministers of the Church of Scotland, and the tenure of the Property and Endowments of that Church, and for purposes connected therewith.

[28th May 1925.]

BE it enacted by the King's most Excellent Majesty, by and with the advice and consent of the Lords Spiritual and Temporal, and Commons, in this present Parliament assembled, and by the authority of the same, as follows :—

PART I.

STIPEND AND TEIND.

1. Subject to the provisions of this Act, every stipend which in any way or to any extent depends upon fluctuations in the price of victual (hereinafter in this Act referred to as " victual stipend ") shall cease

so to depend, and shall be payable only in money at the standard value thereof as hereinafter defined.

The substitution of the standard value of a victual stipend for the value thereof according to the present law and practice is hereinafter in this Act referred to as the "standardisation" of the stipend and the expressions "standardised" and "date of standardisation" have corresponding meanings.

Standard value of victual stipend.

2.—(1) The value in money of victual stipend shall for each county in Scotland be determined by adding to the former county average value of the different kinds of victual in which such stipends are localled an increase of five per centum of that average value, and for the purposes of this section the former county average value of any kind of victual shall be deemed to be the average value of that kind of victual for that county for the fifty years 1873 to 1922, as ascertained—

(*a*) In the case of the kinds of victual mentioned in the First Schedule to this Act, by reference to the values set out therein, or where for any county the value of any such kind of victual is not so set out, then by reference to the value of such other kind of victual for that county or to the value of the same kind of victual for such other county or counties as the Court of Session may select, and by Act of Sederunt prescribe, as being most suitable in the circumstances of the case; and

(*b*) In the case of any kind of victual not mentioned in the First Schedule to this Act, in accordance with the provisions set out in the Second Schedule to this Act.

(2) In the application of the foregoing provisions of this section to a particular parish, regard shall be had to any special method of calculation of stipend customary in that parish (including calculation of a stipend localled in Bear by reference to the fiars price for first or second Barley) and the sheriff may give such instructions to the Clerk of Teinds as he may deem to be necessary or proper for this purpose upon application made to him by any minister or presbytery or heritor concerned at any time before the expiry of six months after the date of standardisation. If no such application is then made in respect of any parish, this subsection shall not have effect with respect to that parish. Intimation of any such application shall be made to such persons as the sheriff may appoint. The decision of the sheriff shall be final unless an appeal therefrom shall be taken to the Lord Ordinary by the applicant or by any person appearing in the application in manner provided by the Ecclesiastical Buildings and Glebes (Scotland) Act, 1868, with respect to appeals from the sheriff to the Lord Ordinary under that Act, and the provisions of that Act relating to such appeals, shall with the necessary modifications, apply to appeals under this subsection, and the clerk to the process in appeals under this subsection shall be the Clerk of Teinds.

31 & 32 Vict. c. 96.

(3) The value in money of any victual stipend, as the same may be determined under subsection (1) of this section subject to any variation under subsection (2) thereof along with the value of any money stipend is in this Act referred to as the "standard value" of that stipend.

Date of standardisation of stipend.

3. The date of standardisation of a stipend shall be the term of Martinmas which shall first occur not less than six months after the date when the benefice becomes actually vacant or is deemed to have become vacant by election or by notification as hereinafter provided.

A.D. 1925.

In the case of a benefice which is actually vacant at the passing of this Act the date of standardisation shall be the term of Martinmas, nineteen hundred and twenty-five.

The words " becomes actually vacant " shall not include the occasion where a minister is succeeded by an assistant and successor appointed to him before the passing of this Act, but shall include the occasion where a minister is succeeded by an assistant and successor appointed to him after such passing.

Standardisation by election.

4. Any minister who at the passing of this Act is entitled to a victual stipend may elect that the stipend shall be standardised, and if he so elects he shall intimate his election in writing in the form set forth in the Third Schedule to this Act or in a similar form to the heritors to the clerk of the presbytery and to the General Trustees, and in such case the benefice shall for the purposes of this Act be deemed to have become vacant by election at the date of the said intimation.

Where at the passing of this Act an assistant and successor has been appointed to a minister entitled to a victual stipend, either the minister or the assistant and successor with the consent of the assistant and successor or of the minister (as the case may be), or failing such consent with the authority of the presbytery may elect and intimate his election as aforesaid.

Standardisation by notification.

5.—(1) It shall be lawful for the General Trustees to intimate in writing to the minister of any parish who is entitled to victual stipend and to the clerk of the presbytery and to the heritors that the victual stipend is to be standardised and in such case the benefice shall for the purposes of this Act, but subject as hereinafter in this section provided, be deemed to have become vacant by notification at the date of the said intimation: Provided that the General Trustees before making such intimation shall have given to the minister an undertaking that (notwithstanding such standardisation) the amount of his stipend according to the present law and practice will continue to be paid to him by the General Trustees until he ceases to be minister of the parish and that the right (if any) of his widow or other representatives to Ann will, in the event of his death, be satisfied, and the obligations contained in any such undertaking shall be duly fulfilled by the General Trustees, who shall be indemnified by the General Assembly to such extent (if any) as may be necessary having regard to the amount of money at the disposal of the Trustees for that purpose: Provided always that if at any time during the currency of such an undertaking the minister intimates to the General Trustees in terms of the section of this Act relating to standardisation by election, his election that his stipend should be standardised, such intimation shall have effect as in that section provided and the undertaking shall cease to operate.

(2) In the application of the foregoing subsection to a benefice where an assistant and successor has been appointed to the minister before the passing of this Act, the word " minister " shall include and refer to that assistant and successor as well as the minister: Provided that the undertaking to be given by the General Trustees to the assistant and successor shall include his interest in the stipend so long as he remains assistant and successor as well as after he succeeds the minister should that event occur, but shall not include any right with respect to Ann.

Collegiate charges.

6. With respect to a parish where separate benefices exist and both the ministers are entitled to victual stipend, except where in such parish there are no surplus teinds, the foregoing provisions of this Act shall

have effect subject to the following modification, namely, that neither of the benefices shall be deemed to be or to become actually vacant or to have become vacant by election or notification, unless the other benefice was actually vacant at the passing of this Act, or shall thereafter have become actually vacant or been deemed to have become vacant by election or notification.

Vesting of standardised stipend.

7. Any stipend which has been standardised under the provisions of this Act shall as on and from the date of standardisation vest *de die in diem* in the minister entitled thereto without prejudice to the payment of any stipend vested in him or in any former incumbent of the benefice according to the present law and practice and subject to the satisfaction of any claim for Ann on the part of the widow or other representative of a deceased incumbent: Provided that in the case of a benefice which is deemed to have become vacant by notification the foregoing provision shall not have effect unless and until the benefice becomes actually vacant or is deemed to have become vacant by election.

Payment of standardised stipend.

8.—(1) As from the date of standardisation any stipend which has been standardised under the provisions of this Act shall be payable by the heritors to the General Trustees half-yearly at the terms of Whitsunday and Martinmas each half-yearly payment being in respect of the half-year preceding the date of payment subject to the following exceptions, namely—

(*a*) that the first half of the standardised stipend for the year beginning on the date of standardisation shall not become payable until the term of Lammas in that year; and

(*b*) that the second half of the standardised stipend for that year shall not become payable till the term of Candlemas in the following year.

(2) Where as hereinafter in this Act provided the standard value of the stipend as shown by the teind roll is constituted a real burden or has been redeemed or extinguished as the case may be, the provisions of this section shall cease to have effect, and with respect to payments under this section due or payable before that event, the General Trustees shall have all the powers of recovery which according to the present law and practice a minister has with respect to his stipend.

Provisions as to Ann.

9.—(1) Neither the widow nor any other representative of any minister admitted after the passing of this Act to any benefice in the Church of Scotland shall be entitled to Ann.

(2) The foregoing provision shall, so far as respects any right in name of Ann to any stipend standardised under the provisions of this Act, apply to the widow and other representatives of any minister admitted before the passing of this Act where the benefice is deemed to have become vacant by election and the minister survives the date of standardisation by one year or more.

(3) Save as in this Act expressly provided, nothing contained therein shall affect or be construed to affect the right which the widow or other representatives of a deceased minister has or have by the present law and practice to one half year's stipend in name of Ann.

Augmentation of stipend.

10.—(1) On the passing of this Act the present law relating to augmentation of stipend shall cease to have effect without prejudice to any application for augmentation competently made before such passing or to anything following on such application or done therein.

A.D. 1925.

(2) The minister or the General Trustees as the case may be to whom a stipend or a standardised stipend is payable may—

(*a*) if not less than twenty years shall have elapsed since the date of the last application for augmentation of the stipend; or

(*b*) upon the expiry of twenty years from the date of the last application for augmentation of the stipend or upon the expiry of ten years from the passing of this Act, whichever of these two events shall first occur;

apply to the Lord Ordinary to find whether there are surplus teinds available for an augmentation. No such application may be made after the expiry of eleven years from the passing of this Act.

(3) If the Lord Ordinary (whose decision shall be final and not subject to review) finds that there are surplus teinds so available, the minister or the General Trustees, as the case may be, shall be entitled to receive as from the first term of Martinmas following the date of the application an augmentation according to the following scale:—

(*a*) Where the stipend as last modified by the Court of Teinds does not exceed twenty-five chalders, an augmentation of six chalders; and

(*b*) Where the stipend as so modified exceeds twenty-five chalders but is less than thirty chalders, an augmentation of five chalders; and

(*c*) Where the stipend as so modified is thirty chalders or upwards, an augmentation of four chalders.

The foregoing augmentation of six, five or four chalders, as the case may be, shall be converted and localled in sterling money according to the standard value, the order of allocation being in accordance with the present practice.

If the amount of the available surplus teinds as ultimately ascertained in the localling of the augmentation among the heritors is insufficient to meet the foregoing augmentations, the augmentations shall be limited to the amount so ascertained.

(4) As from the date when a minister or the General Trustees, as the case may be, becomes or become entitled to an augmentation under this section, the amount of the augmentation shall be added to the stipend and shall be payable and recoverable in like manner.

(5) The provisions set out in the Fourth Schedule to this Act shall have effect with respect to augmentations under this section and any decree of locality following thereon.

(6) An augmentation under this section shall come in place of all future rights of augmentation and shall be final.

(7) In the event of the Lord Ordinary finding that there are no surplus teinds available for an augmentation, neither the minister nor the General Trustees shall be entitled to make any further application.

(8) In the application of this section to a parish where separate benefices exist and both ministers are entitled to victual stipend—

(*a*) the expression " the date of the last application for augmentation of the stipend " shall, in cases where applications for augmentation were last made at different dates, mean the later of those dates; and

A.D. 1925.

(*b*) the expression "the stipend as last modified by the Court of Teinds" shall mean the stipend of each or either of the two benefices taken separately.

Teind rolls.

11.—(1) There shall be prepared by the Clerk of Teinds for every parish in Scotland a teind roll specifying in sterling money—

(*a*) The total teind of that parish; and

(*b*) The amount of that total applicable to the lands of each heritor; and

(*c*) The value of the whole stipend payable to the minister, so far as payable out of teinds including vicarage teinds payable as stipend and surrendered teinds so payable; and

(*d*) The proportion of that value payable by each heritor in the parish.

(2) The said teind rolls shall be prepared and issued as soon as may be practicable, and the provisions of the Fifth Schedule to this Act shall have effect with respect to the preparation, issue, and adjustment of the teind rolls.

(3) The Court of Session shall make by Act of Sederunt, with the approval of the Treasury, such rules and regulations as may in the judgment of the Court from time to time be necessary to regulate the amount of the fees to be paid to the Clerk of Teinds in connection with the preparation, issue, and adjustment of the teind rolls and the time and place of the payment of the said fees. The expenses of the preparation, issue, and adjustment of the teind roll, including where a state of teinds is necessary the expense of the preparation thereof, shall be apportioned among the heritors (including any heritors whose teinds have been valued and surrendered before the date of standardisation) in proportion to the amount of the total teind applicable to the lands of each heritor. The share of such expenses apportioned to any heritor, other than a heritor whose teinds have been valued and surrendered as aforesaid shall be payable by such heritor, and the share of such expenses apportioned to any heritor whose teinds have been valued and surrendered as aforesaid shall be payable by the General Trustees.

Charge to be substituted for liability for stipend exceeding one pound.

12.[1] Where the standard value (as shown by the teind roll of a parish) of the stipend exigible from the teinds of any lands of a heritor in that parish which are comprised in one entry in the teind roll exceeds the sum of one pound—

(1) the amount of such standard value shall by virtue of this Act be constituted as at and from the first term of Whitsunday or Martinmas which shall occur after the date when the teind roll becomes final a real burden (in this Act referred to as the "standard charge") on the lands from the teinds of which the said stipend is exigible in favour of the General Trustees preferable to all other securities or burdens not incidents of tenure;

(2) the amount of the standard charge shall be payable by equal half-yearly instalments at the terms of Whitsunday and Martinmas each half-yearly instalment being in respect of the half-year preceding the date of payment and the said instalments shall be recoverable by the same means and in the like manner as any feu-duty out of the said lands would be recoverable;

[1] Charge not to be an interest in land for compulsory purchase (Town and Country Planning (Scotland) Act, 1947, Sched. of para. 3 (2).

A.D. 1925.

(3) the standard charge over any lands may at any time after the completion of the teind roll be redeemed by and in the option of the heritor of those lands or other person liable in respect of the standard charge either (*a*) for such consideration or in such manner as may be agreed upon between the person liable and the General Trustees, or (*b*) at any term of Whitsunday or Martinmas after three months' notice either (i) by payment to the Trustees of such a sum as would if invested at the time of payment in Consolidated 2½ per cent annuities produce an annual sum equal to the standard charge, or (ii) by transfer to the General Trustees of such an amount of Consolidated 2½ per cent annuities as would produce an annual sum equal to the standard charge ;

(4) upon the redemption of the standard charge as aforesaid any claim upon the heritor or other person in respect of such standard charge shall cease and be extinguished and the lands from which the same was exigible shall be disburdened thereof in all time coming and an entry to that effect shall be made in the teind roll which shall be sufficient evidence of the discharge of the burden.

Allocation of standard charge.

13. A standard charge shall from its constitution continue a real burden on the whole of the lands subject thereto, and on every part of those lands notwithstanding any disposition of the lands or any part thereof unless and until intimation of an allocation of the standard charge has been made in writing by the General Trustees and the disponer or his representatives to the Clerk of Teinds, who upon receiving such an intimation shall forthwith make the necessary entry in the teind roll.

If as the result of any such allocation the portion of a standard charge so allocated upon the lands disponed or remaining a real burden on the lands retained by the disponer does not exceed one pound, the disponer or his representatives shall within three months after the date of the entry in the roll redeem the same payment to the General Trustees of a sum equal to the amount so allocated or remaining a burden multiplied by twenty ; and if the portion of the standard charge so allocated or remaining a burden exceeds one pound but is less than fifteen pounds, that portion of the standard charge shall as from the date of entry in the teind roll be increased by five per centum.

Provisions where stipend does not exceed one pound.

14. Subject to the provisions of the next succeeding section of this Act, where the standard value (as shown by the teind roll of a parish) of the stipend exigible from the teinds of any lands of a heritor in that parish which are comprised in one entry in the teind roll does not exceed the sum of one pound :—

(1) the heritor or other person liable in payment of the said stipend shall redeem the same either

(*a*) at the first term of Whitsunday or Martinmas which shall occur not less than three months after the date on which the teind roll of the parish becomes final for such consideration or in such manner as may be agreed upon between the person so liable and the General Trustees ; or

(*b*) by payment to the General Trustees at the said term of Whitsunday or Martinmas of a sum equal to the standard value of the said stipend multiplied by eighteen ; or

(c) by payment to the General Trustees, along with each half-yearly payment of the said stipend during a period of eighteen years commencing at the said term of Whitsunday or Martinmas, of a redemption instalment equal to seventy-five per centum of the half-yearly payment of the stipend, which redemption instalment shall be recoverable by the General Trustees in the same manner as the half-yearly payment of the stipend :

(2) Upon the redemption of a stipend as aforesaid any claim upon the heritor or other person in respect of such stipend shall cease and be extinguished and an entry to that effect made in the teind roll shall be sufficient evidence of the redemption.

Extinction of liability for stipend not exceeding one shilling.

15. Where the standard value (as shown by the teind roll of a parish) of the stipend exigible from the teinds of all the lands of a heritor in that parish, whether those lands are comprised in one or in more than one entry in the teind roll does not exceed the sum of one shilling, any claim for or in respect of the stipend upon the heritor or other person liable in payment thereof (other than a claim for payments already due) shall, notwithstanding any law or practice to the contrary, cease and be extinguished as at the first term of Whitsunday or Martinmas which shall occur not less than three months after the date on which the teind roll of the parish becomes final.

Valuation and surrender of teinds.

16.—(1) After the passing of this Act, the provisions set out in the Sixth Schedule to this Act which relate to the obtaining of valuations of teinds and the surrender of valued teinds shall have effect for those purposes and the present law and practice relating thereto shall cease to apply but without prejudice to any proceedings taken before the passing of this Act or to any proceedings which may be taken within three years after the passing of this Act for the approbation of reports of sub-commissioners relating to the valuation of teinds.

(2) Where the annual agricultural value of any lands has been ascertained in accordance with the provisions set out in the said schedule one-fifth part of that value shall be the valued teind of those lands in all time coming.

(3) Where no application for the ascertainment of the annual agricultural value of any lands, the teinds of which have not been valued, is made in accordance with the said provisions and within the period thereby prescribed, the value of such teinds specified in the teind roll for the parish in which the lands are situate shall be deemed to be accepted by acquiescence, and shall be the valued teind of those lands in all time coming.

Deduction of stipend in question with titular.

17. As from the date of standardisation of any stipend which has been standardised under the provisions of this Act, the heritor of any lands from the teinds of which the stipend or any part thereof is exigible shall, in any accounting in respect of those teinds with the titular thereof, be entitled to deduct the amount of the standardised stipend exigible from those teinds, or of any standard charge coming in place of such stipend or any part thereof, whether or not such stipend or part thereof, or standard charge, has been redeemed or extinguished.

Sale of surplus teinds.

18. Notwithstanding anything contained in the Act of the Scots Parliament, 1693, c. 23 (an Act renewing the commission for plantation of kirks and valuation of teinds), or in any other enactment or in any charter, grant or deed, it shall be lawful after the passing of this Act for

A.D. 1925.

the titular or any person having right of titularity to sell surplus teinds on such terms as may be agreed upon between him and the heritor.

Nothing in this section shall prejudice or affect the provisions of the Acts of the Scots Parliament, 1633, c. 17 (anent the rate and price of teinds), and 1690, c. 23 (concerning patronages), or any other enactment at present in force authorising the sale of surplus teinds.

Provisions as to certain payments out of the Consolidated Fund.

19.—(1) The charges and payments described in the Seventh Schedule to this Act and any other payments to or on behalf of the Church or the General Assembly or any committee or institution of the Church or any minister which at the passing of this Act are charged on and payable out of the Consolidated Fund of the United Kingdom shall thenceforth be paid to the General Trustees in such manner as may be directed by the Treasury.

(2) The Treasury may at any time contract for the redemption of all or any of the payments referred to in the preceding subsection by payment to the General Trustees of such capital sum or sums as may be agreed between the Treasury and the General Trustees.

(3)—(i) The Treasury may from time to time borrow from the National Debt Commissioners and those Commissioners may lend to the Treasury such capital sum or sums as may be necessary for carrying into effect any contract made in pursuance of the immediately preceding subsection.

(ii) For the purpose of repaying any such loan the Treasury may create in favour of the National Debt Commissioners a terminable annuity for a period not exceeding twenty years from the date of the loan to be calculated with interest at such rate as may be agreed.

(iii) Such annuity shall be notified by certificate under the hand of the Comptroller or Assistant Comptroller and the Actuary of the National Debt Office and shall be charged upon the Consolidated Fund of the United Kingdom or the growing produce thereof.

PART II.

SCOTTISH ECCLESIASTICAL COMMISSIONERS.

Constitution, powers and procedure of Scottish Ecclesiastical Commissioners.

20.—(1) Such persons not exceeding five in number as His Majesty may appoint shall be Commissioners under this Act for the purposes aftermentioned, and shall be styled the Scottish Ecclesiastical Commissioners. One of the Commissioners being a person who holds or has held judicial office shall be appointed Chairman.

(2) The Commissioners shall hold office during His Majesty's pleasure. If a vacancy occurs in the number of the Commissioners by reason of death, resignation, incapacity or otherwise, His Majesty may appoint some other person to fill the vacancy, and so from time to time as occasion requires.

(3) The Commissioners may act by any one or more of their body and notwithstanding any vacancy in their number; but if any person aggrieved by an order or decision of one Commissioner so requires, the order or decision shall be reconsidered on re-hearing by not less than three Commissioners.

(4) The procedure, place of meeting, and authentication of documents of the Commissioners shall be regulated in such manner as the Commissioners determine.

(5) The Commissioners may examine witnesses on oath, and for enforcing the attendance of witnesses, the examination of witnesses and the production of books and documents, shall have all such powers, rights, and privileges as are vested in any of His Majesty's Courts of Law.

(6) The Commissioners may appoint or employ a secretary and such other officers and persons and with such remuneration as they think necessary, and may remove any person so appointed or employed.

(7) The salaries and remuneration of any persons so appointed or employed, and all expenses of the Commissioners incurred in the execution of this Act, shall be paid out of moneys to be provided for that purpose by the General Assembly.

Orders of Commissioners.

21.—(1) The Commissioners may, after such inquiry in each individual case as they may think fit, make such orders as they may consider necessary or proper for any of the following purposes, that is to say:

(*a*) for giving effect to the schemes framed by the Commissioners under the provisions of this Act relating to burgh churches, including the modification of the Act 23 & 24 Victoria, chapter 50, entitled "An Act to abolish the annuity tax in Edinburgh and Montrose, and to make provision in regard to the stipends of the ministers in that city and burgh, and also to make provision for the patronage of the church of North Leith," and of any other local or personal Act, decree of the Court of Session or Court of Teinds or agreement relating to the burgh churches;

(*b*) for the transfer to the General Trustees of the parliamentary churches and manses under the provisions of the section of this Act relating to parliamentary churches and manses;

(*c*) for the transfer to the General Trustees of the churches and manses of the parishes mentioned in the Eighth Schedule to this Act;

(*d*) for the transfer to the General Trustees of endowments referred to in the section of this Act relating to endowments in certain parishes *quoad omnia*;

(*e*) for framing and giving effect to schemes relating to churches and manses with respect to which the sheriff may, as hereinafter provided, find and declare that the case ought to be dealt with by the Commissioners;

(*f*) for giving effect to the provisions of the section of this Act relating to the transfer of rights in glebes;

(*g*) for framing and giving effect to a scheme or schemes under the provisions of the section of this Act relating to allocation by General Trustees of certain moneys to be received from Treasury;

(*h*) for the protection and preservation of any church or other ecclesiastical building which is for the time being used for ecclesiastical purposes, and which the Commissioners may, upon application made to them by the Royal Commission on Historic Monuments in Scotland or any person interested, consider to require special provisions in the public interest with respect to maintenance and access;

(*i*) for the transfer to and administration by the General Trustees of any capital sum fixed or awarded and invested by way of commutation of fish teinds under the provisions of the Fish Teinds (Scotland) Act, 1864; 27 & 28 Vict. c. 33.

A.D. 1925.

(j) for the transfer to a kirk session of communion plate or other ecclesiastical furnishings in use in a church or by a congregation in any case in which a right of property in the plate or other furnishings is claimed by any public body;

(k) for any other matter or thing which the Commissioners consider to be necessary or proper in connection with any of the purposes aforesaid.

(2) Any such order shall have effect as if enacted in this Act, and may be recorded in the Register of Sasines.

(3) In respect that the Act 23 & 24 Victoria, chapter 50, imposed an obligation on the town council of Edinburgh to grant a bond of annuity for the annual sum of four thousand two hundred pounds to the Edinburgh Ecclesiastical Commissioners for the purposes of the said Act, and in respect that the Act 33 & 34 Victoria, chapter 87, empowered the said town council to redeem the said bond of annuity by a payment to the said Commissioners of the sum of fifty-six thousand five hundred pounds and that the said bond of annuity was so redeemed by the payment of the said sum to the said Commissioners, nothing contained in this Act or in any order to be made by the Commissioners under the provisions of this section shall impose or be deemed to impose any further financial obligation or liability on the said town council in relation to the burgh churches situated within the burgh of Edinburgh, and any liability or obligation incumbent on the said town council in connection with the upkeep and maintenance or restoration or renewal of the burgh churches situated within the said burgh or payment of stipend to the ministers thereof shall be deemed to have been fulfilled and shall be at an end.

Burgh churches.

22. With respect to the churches mentioned in the Ninth Schedule to this Act (in this Act referred to as "burgh churches") the following provisions shall have effect [1]:—

(1) As soon as conveniently may be after the passing of this Act the Commissioners shall inquire into all circumstances relating to existing rights of property in the fabrics and sites of the burgh churches, and any manses or other subjects connected therewith, and in any churchyards connected with the burgh churches, the stipends of the ministers thereof and any funds, endowments, pew rents or assessments from which the stipends of the ministers, the maintenance of the churches and other subjects and any other expenditure in connection therewith is defrayed, and shall thereafter frame schemes for the future ownership, maintenance, and administration of the burgh churches and other subjects and the payment of stipend to the ministers:

(2) Every such scheme shall make provision for—

(a) the transfer to the General Trustees of all rights of property vested in or belonging to the magistrates or the town council of any of the burghs within which the burgh churches are situated in the fabrics and sites of the burgh churches and of any manses and other subjects connected therewith, and in any churchyards connected with the burgh churches, and for the transfer to the General Trustees of the duty of maintaining any property so transferred;

(b) the transfer to the General Trustees of all or any property held for church purposes by or on behalf of the magis-

[1] See p. 522.

trates or the town council of any of the burghs within which the burgh churches are situated ;

(*c*) the periodical payment to the General Trustees of all sums which are at present paid or payable by the magistrates or town council of any of the said burghs in respect of the stipends of the ministers of the burgh churches and (so far as the Commissioners consider this to be equitable and reasonable) of all sums which are at present paid or payable by the magistrates or town council of any of the said burghs in respect of the ownership and maintenance of the fabrics and sites of the churches and manses, or other subjects connected therewith ;

(*d*) the redemption of such periodical payments by the payment to the General Trustees of a capital sum or by the creation of terminable annuities or of sinking funds ;

(*e*) the transfer to the General Trustees of any property heritable or moveable held by any public body (whether statutory or otherwise) or person other than the magistrates or town council for the benefit of the minister of any of the burgh churches by way of stipend ;

(*f*) the protection of the interests of the ministers or assistants and successors who at the passing of this Act are incumbents of the benefices of the burgh churches ;

(*g*) the protection (so far as the Commissioners consider this to be practicable) of the interests of town councils in the burgh churches as regards sittings allotted to the town councils for their use, the right to have the church bells rung on special occasions, and the preservation of any other similar right or privilege hitherto enjoyed by the town councils ;

(*h*) [1] the General Trustees before selling, feuing, or otherwise alienating a burgh church, and the site thereof, giving to the town council of the burgh in which such burgh church is situated an opportunity of acquiring the same on such terms and conditions as may be agreed upon or as, failing agreement, may be determined by an arbiter to be appointed by the sheriff on the application of either party provided as follows :—

(i) The price to be paid to the General Trustees by the town council shall not exceed such sum as would be necessary to reinstate the church on a new site within the municipal boundaries of the burgh in which such burgh church is situated, should it in the judgment of the General Trustees be necessary to provide at the time a new church within the municipal boundaries of such burgh ;

(ii) In the event of it being unnecessary in the judgment of the General Trustees to provide at the time a new church such as aforesaid the price to be paid to the General Trustees by the town council shall not exceed such a sum as would be necessary to reimburse the General Trustees for all expenditure incurred by them subsequent to the passing of this Act, and within forty years prior to the date of the sale, for the repair, enlargement, or renewal of such burgh

[1] See note on p. 522.

A.D. 1925.

church, or part thereof, or as the case may be to liquidate any outstanding debt or obligation incurred or undertaken by the General Trustees relative to any such repair, enlargement, or renewal (so far as such expenditure, debt, or obligation has not been met out of any periodical payment made by the magistrates or town council of such burgh for the maintenance of such burgh church, or out of any capital sum, terminable annuity, or sinking fund paid in respect of the redemption thereof), and to meet the expenses of the necessary conveyance :

(3) The General Trustees shall not be entitled to sell, feu, or otherwise alienate any of the burgh churches or the site thereof to any person unless they shall have previously offered to convey such church or site to the town council of the burgh in which such church is situated, on the same terms and conditions as they may be prepared to accept from such person, and the town council have failed to reply to the offer within a period of one month from the date thereof, or have within that period declined to accept the offer :

(4) The provisions of this Act in regard to the transfer to the General Trustees of all rights of property in any churchyards connected with the burgh churches, and the duty of maintaining any churchyards so transferred, shall not apply to the churchyards of Greyfriars and Canongate in the burgh of Edinburgh, or to the churchyard of St David's or Ramshorn in the burgh of Glasgow, or to the churchyards of St Nicholas and St Clements in the burgh of Aberdeen, which churchyards shall continue to belong to and be maintained by the town councils of the said burghs, respectively :

(5) In the application of paragraphs (*b*), (*c*), and (*d*) of subsection (2) of this section to any scheme framed with respect to any of the burgh churches the Commissioners shall have regard to the conditions contained in the decree of disjunction and erection of the burgh church :

(6) When all matters contained in the scheme relating to a burgh church have been duly carried out and implemented all liability or obligation incumbent on the magistrates and town council of the burgh in which a burgh church is situated, in connection with the upkeep and maintenance of such burgh church and payment of stipend to the minister thereof, shall be deemed to have been fulfilled and shall be at an end, subject only to the payment of any capital sum, terminable annuity, or sinking fund for the redemption of any periodical payment made by such magistrates or town council in connection with the maintenance of such church and the stipend of the minister thereof.

Parliamentary churches and manses.

23. With respect to the churches [1] and manses mentioned in the Tenth Schedule to this Act (which together with any land whether described as churchyard, glebe, or otherwise connected with the said churches and manses are in this Act referred to as "parliamentary churches and manses") the following provisions shall have effect :—

As soon as conveniently may be after the passing of this Act the Commissioners shall inquire into all circumstances relating to existing rights of property in the fabrics and sites of the parliamen-

[1] Amended 1933, ss. 9 (3), 15. See pp. 528, 530.

tary churches and manses, and to the maintenance thereof whether under the provisions of the Act 5 George IV., Chapter 90, and any conveyance or other deed relating to any of the said churches and manses in favour of the Commissioners under the said Act or under any decision of the Court of Teinds or otherwise, and the Commissioners shall thereafter by order provide for the transfer to the General Trustees of the fabrics and sites of the said churches and manses, and of all powers and duties with respect to the maintenance and repair of the said fabrics and the allocation of sitting accommodation in the said churches.

Churches and manses of certain parishes erected under Act of 1844.

24.[1] With respect to the churches and manses of the parishes *quoad omnia* mentioned in the Eighth Schedule to this Act, the following provisions shall have effect:—

As soon as conveniently may be after the passing of this Act the Commissioners shall inquire into all circumstances relating to existing rights of property in the fabrics and sites of the churches and manses of the parishes aforesaid, and to the maintenance thereof whether under any existing titles relating to the said churches and manses or otherwise, and the Commissioners shall thereafter by order provide for the transfer to the General Trustees of the fabrics and sites of the said churches and manses, and of all powers and duties with respect to the maintenance and repair of the said fabrics, and the allocation of sitting accommodation in the said churches.

Mortifications and Endowments in certain parishes *quoad omnia*.

25.[2] Where in the case of a parish *quoad omnia* (not being one of the parishes *quoad omnia* mentioned in the Eighth Schedule to this Act) there exists any mortification or other endowment not derived from teinds which is for the benefit of the minister or parish either by way of stipend or by way of provision of a manse, glebe or other subjects, the Commissioners shall upon application made to them by the General Trustees, inquire into all circumstances relating to such mortification or endowment and may thereafter, by order, provide for the transfer of the mortification or endowment or of the properties forming the subject of such mortification or endowment to the General Trustees:

Provided that, except in the case of a benefice which is actually vacant at the passing of this Act, any order made by the Commissioners under this section shall not take effect unless or until the benefice shall have become actually vacant after such passing.

PART III.

TRANSFER OF PARISH CHURCHES, MANSES, GLEBES AND CHURCHYARDS.

Parish churches, manses, glebes and churchyards.

26. With a view to the transfer to and vesting in the General Trustees of all rights of property in and duties of maintenance or extension with respect to the churches, manses, and glebes of parishes *quoad omnia* (other than the churches and manses of the parishes *quoad omnia* mentioned in the Eighth Schedule to this Act), the transfer to and vesting in the respective parish councils of all such rights in and duties with respect to the churchyards of such parishes, and the extinction of all such rights and duties as aforesaid heretofore belonging to and incumbent upon heritors or ministers, the following provisions of this Part of this Act shall have effect, and shall apply to such parishes only.

[1] See section 6 of 1933 Act, p. 525.
[2] Substituted for original section 25 by 1933 Amending Act, section 16.

A.D. 1925.

Proceedings relating to matters mentioned in section 3 of 31 & 32 Vict. c. 96.

27. No proceedings relating to any of the matters mentioned in section three of the Ecclesiastical Buildings and Glebes (Scotland) Act, 1868, shall be instituted or entertained before or by any presbytery or any court of law or the Commissioners except as hereinafter in this Act provided. The foregoing provision shall be deemed to have had effect as on and from the first day of February, nineteen hundred and twenty-five, but without prejudice to any proceedings instituted before that date or to the enforcement of any order, finding, judgment, interlocutor, or decree made, given, or pronounced therein, or to any contract or agreement made by heritors before that date or to any resolution passed by heritors to levy an assessment to meet expenditure incurred in pursuance of such contract or agreement, and any such assessment shall be recoverable as if this Act had not been passed.

Transfer of rights in parish churches and manses.

28.—(1) Where the General Trustees are of opinion that any church or manse is not in a reasonable state of tenantable repair and that the duty of executing repairs is incumbent upon heritors, the General Trustees may agree with the heritors concerned for the repair of the same by or at the expense of the heritors or for the payment by the heritors to the General Trustees of a sum of money in lieu of repair, and failing agreement the General Trustees may within three years after the passing of this Act apply to the sheriff for an order directing the heritors to carry out such repairs (if any) not involving structural alterations as he may consider necessary, or if the General Trustees so require to pay to the General Trustees such sum of money in lieu of repair as the sheriff may determine. The sheriff shall deal with any such application in a summary manner and his decision shall be final.

(2) Any heritor concerned or the General Trustees may apply to the sheriff for a certificate that all obligations incumbent on the heritors with respect to the church or manse of a parish have been fulfilled, and the sheriff shall deal with the application in a summary manner and shall issue a certificate to that effect if the General Trustees state or admit that all such obligations have been fulfilled, or if failing such statement or admission, he is satisfied either that any agreement or order made as aforesaid has been implemented, or that notwithstanding the absence of any such agreement no application has been made for such an order within three years after the passing of this Act, or that any application for an order so made has been refused. The certificate may be in or as nearly as may be in the form set out in the Eleventh Schedule to this Act, and shall contain or refer to a description of the subjects whether church or manse to which it relates and may be recorded by the General Trustees or by any heritor concerned in the appropriate Register of Sasines.

(3) When a certificate issued by the sheriff under this section has been recorded as aforesaid—

(*a*) any liability or obligation incumbent on any heritor in connection with the subjects to which the certificate relates shall be at an end except the obligation or liability to assess or to be assessed for the repayment of any debt existing at the date of the certificate; and

(*b*) all rights of property in the said subjects shall by virtue of this Act and without the necessity of any further conveyance vest in and belong to the General Trustees, to the same effect as if a complete feudal title holding of the Crown in free blench farm for payment of a penny Scots yearly if asked only had been duly constituted in favour of the General Trustees. A.D. 1925.

(4) Whereas in certain parishes, town councils in their capacity as town councils, or other public bodies (whether statutory or otherwise) or kirk sessions or persons are under the present law and practice or by Royal Warrant, charter, agreement or custom liable along with or in place of the heritors in obligations relating to the church or manse, it shall be lawful, in any such case, for the presbytery or the General Trustees or any other person concerned to apply to the sheriff to find and declare that the case ought to be dealt with by the Commissioners, and if the sheriff so finds and declares the provisions of this section shall have no further application to the case, and the Commissioners shall as soon thereafter as conveniently may be inquire into all circumstances relating to existing obligations in respect of the fabric and site of such church or manse and the maintenance of such fabric, and by order provide for the transfer to the General Trustees of the said fabric and site, and of all powers and duties with respect to the maintenance and repair of the said fabric.

(5) If in any application to the sheriff under this section a question arises as to whether or not the church or manse to which the application relates is the church or manse of a parish within the meaning of this section, that question shall be determined by the sheriff in a summary manner, and his determination shall be final.

(6) Whenever in any parish it shall be necessary in consequence of anything done, or agreed, or ordered to be done under or in pursuance of this section to impose any ecclesiastical assessment upon lands and heritages in the parish, and such assessment is imposed according to the real rent thereof, the following provisions shall have effect, in lieu of the provisions of section three of the Ecclesiastical Assessments (Scotland) Act, 1900:— 63 & 64 Vict. c. 20.

(*a*) No part of such assessment shall be imposed or levied upon lands and heritages occupied solely as the church and accessory buildings or burying-ground attached of any religious body, or as the dwelling-house with offices or garden or glebe land attached of the minister of such church;

(*b*) The rental on which each heritor shall be assessed shall be his total rental within the parish as appearing in the valuation roll (whether such rental consists of one or more subjects), but subject to deduction of the sum of thirty pounds;

(*c*) The amount of the deficiency created in the total amount of the assessment, by allowing the said deduction of thirty pounds to every heritor, shall be defrayed by the General Trustees;

(*d*) No heritor, who by reason of any exemption or deduction allowed by this subsection is relieved altogether from assessment in respect of the execution of any repair, or in respect of any payment by the heritors in lieu of repair, shall be entitled at any meeting of the heritors to take part in the discussion of, or to vote upon, any question concerning any plans for or the execution of the said repair, or the defraying of the expenses of the same, or any question concerning an agreement involving payment by the heritors in lieu of repair.

(7) Whenever in any parish it shall be necessary in view of anything

A.D. 1925.

to be done or agreed, or in consequence of anything done or agreed, or ordered to be done under or in pursuance of this section to call a meeting of heritors, a circular letter containing an intimation of the meeting shall be sent twenty-one clear days before the meeting to every known heritor whose total rental within the parish as appearing in the valuation roll (whether such rental consists of one or more subjects) exceeds the sum of thirty pounds, and intimation of the meeting shall also be given by advertisement in a newspaper circulating in the parish once during each of two successive weeks and within the said period of twenty-one days.

(8) Subject to the modifications in the two immediately preceding subsections of this section the existing law and practice relating to heritors' meetings and ecclesiastical assessments shall apply to meetings of heritors to be held and ecclesiastical assessments to be imposed under, or in consequence, or pursuance of this section.

Rights with respect to sitting accommodation in parish churches.

29. On the expiry of one year from the date on which any church is by or in pursuance of this Act transferred to the General Trustees the right of allocating sitting accommodation in the church, whether with or without payment therefor, and the right of disposal of any proceeds therefrom shall belong to the kirk session, or to such other body as the General Assembly may direct and any existing right to such accommodation shall cease and terminate.

Transfer of rights in glebes.

30. With respect to glebes, the following provisions shall have effect:—

(1) It shall be the duty of the clerk of every presbytery within one year after the passing of this Act to furnish to the Commissioners a list of the glebes appropriated to the ministers of the parishes in the presbytery, and of any cases where a minister has accepted or is entitled to any annual payment in place of glebe, and at the same time to intimate in which cases (if any) it is claimed by the presbytery (whether on the representation of the minister concerned or otherwise) that the heritors concerned have not fully implemented the obligations incumbent on them according to the present law and practice with respect to the provisions and enlargement of a glebe:

(2) As soon as conveniently may be after the receipt of the said lists, the Commissioners shall inquire into all circumstances relating to existing rights of property in the glebes, and in any payments in place of glebe, and shall thereafter make orders relating to the glebes and payments:

(3) Every such order shall make provision for—

(*a*) the implement by the heritors of any obligations incumbent on them as aforesaid which have not already been implemented; and

(*b*) the transfer to and vesting in the General Trustees of the ownership of the glebes; and

(*c*) the preservation of the existing rights of all persons other than the heritors or the minister of the parish who, under or in pursuance of any general or local Act of Parliament or otherwise, have acquired any right in any glebe or any part thereof, whether as purchasers, feuars, or tenants, and the payment of any feu-duties, casualties, or rent to the General Trustees in place of the minister; and

A.D. 1925

(d) the manner in which—
(i) any burden upon the glebe created under section eighteen of the Glebe Lands (Scotland) Act, 1866; and 29 & 30 Vict. c. 71.
(ii) any of the costs, charges and expenses referred to in that section which have not been made a burden on the glebe
may be dealt with, discharged and extinguished; and

(e) the transfer to the General Trustees of any feu-duties and Government or other securities or investments representing the price or consideration received for any glebe or part thereof or right therein under or in pursuance of the Glebe Lands (Scotland) Act, 1866, the Feudal Casualties (Scotland) Act, 1914, or any other general or local Act of Parliament, or any decree of the Court of Teinds, or any grant or contract validly made by a minister and held by any persons acting as trustees in trust for the payment of the income to the minister of the parish; and 4 & 5 Geo. 5. c. 48.

(f) the conversion into a money payment of any right of pasturage over any lands which is possessed by the minister as minister of the parish, and the redemption of that money payment, if the heritor or heritors concerned so desire, in such manner as may be agreed upon between the General Trustees and such heritor or heritors, or as, failing agreement, may be fixed by the Commissioners; and

(g) the protection of the interests of the ministers or assistants and successors who at the passing of this Act are incumbents of the benefice of any parish.

Redemption of feu-duty affecting glebe.

31. Where the glebe or any part thereof has been feued to the proprietors of conterminous lands in terms of section seventeen of the Glebe Lands (Scotland) Act, 1866, and the feu-duty payable therefor has been transferred to the General Trustees by an order made by the Commissioners, the said proprietors or their successors shall be entitled to redeem the feu-duty affecting the glebe or any part thereof—

(a) for such consideration or in such manner as may be agreed upon between the person liable and the General Trustees; or

(b) at any term of Whitsunday or Martinmas after three months' notice either—
(i) by payment to the Trustees of such a sum as would, if invested at the time of payment in Consolidated $2\frac{1}{2}$ per cent annuities, produce an annual sum equal to the feu-duty; or
(ii) by transfer to the General Trustees of such an amount of Consolidated $2\frac{1}{2}$ per cent annuities as would produce an annual sum equal to the feu-duty.

Transfer of parish church-yards.

32.—(1) The property of any churchyard heretofore held by the heritors of any parish shall as at and from the passing of this Act by virtue of this Act and without the necessity of any further conveyance be transferred from the heritors and vested in the parish [1] council to the same effect as if the churchyard had been as at that date transferred by the heritors to the council in pursuance of subsection (6) of section thirty of the Local Government (Scotland) Act, 1894: Provided that due regard and respect shall be had by the parish [1] council to the memory of the dead and the wishes of their relatives before any ground already allo- 57 & 58 Vict. c. 58.

[1] Now the Regional Council (Local Government (Scotland) Act, 1973).

A.D. 1925. cated as a burial-ground shall be treated as being vacant and unoccupied ground and re-allocated by the parish[1] council as the burial-place for another family or for the interment of another body: Provided also that in addition to the powers and duties by the said subsection transferred from the heritors to the parish[1] council the power or duty of enlarging or extending the churchyard and assessing for the cost of such enlargement or extension shall also be so transferred and for the purpose of providing ground for such enlargement or extension or additional accommodation in a suitable and convenient situation, the parish[1] council shall have and may exercise all the powers relating to the acquisition of land for burial-grounds contained in the Burial-Grounds (Scotland) Act, 1855, and the costs of providing, maintaining, and managing ground so acquired, so far as they require to be defrayed out of any rate, shall be a charge on the poor rate or the assessment under the said Act of 1855, as the parish[1] council may determine: Provided further that where any churchyard transferred to a parish[1] council by or in pursuance of this Act surrounds or adjoins any church or other ecclesiastical building vested in the heritors or in the General Trustees or in any other body holding the same in trust for the purpose of worship or for preservation as an ancient or historic monument—

18 & 19 Vict. c. 68.

(*a*) the churchyard shall be held subject to a right of access to the minister and the congregation attending the church, and such other persons as may resort thereto for the purpose of public or private worship, or of inspecting or repairing the church, or for any other lawful purpose; and

(*b*) no funeral shall be allowed to take place during the usual time of the ordinary services in the church; and

(*c*) any road or path through the burial-ground shall be kept in good and sufficient repair by the parish[1] council; and

(*d*) where the use of part of the churchyard is required for the enlargement or repair of the church it may be so used in any case where it might lawfully have been so used if this Act had not been passed and subject to the like conditions and restrictions, and where used for the purpose of the enlargement of the church the part so used shall thereupon vest in the heritors or the General Trustees or other body holding the church as aforesaid.

(2) The provisions relating to the sale of the right of burial contained in section eighteen of the Burial-Grounds (Scotland) Act, 1855, shall apply to any churchyard transferred to a parish[1] council by or in pursuance of this Act, and to any enlargement or extension thereof.

(3) Where the powers and duties conferred and imposed by the Burial-Grounds (Scotland) Act, 1855, are exercised and carried out by a local authority other than the parish[1] council, the foregoing provisions of this section shall, with the necessary modifications, have effect as if that authority were named therein instead of the parish[1] council, and any expenses of the local authority due to the operation of this section shall be defrayed in the same manner as expenses under the said Act of 1855. Where in any parish the powers and duties conferred and imposed by the said Act of 1855 are carried out by more than one local authority, this subsection shall be held to refer to the local authority carrying out the said powers and duties within the district where the churchyard is situated.

(4) Where the property of a churchyard is held by the kirk session of

[1] See note on previous page.

A.D. 1925.

the parish the foregoing provisions of this section shall, with the necessary modifications, have effect as if the kirk session were named therein and in subsection (6) of section thirty of the Local Government (Scotland) Act, 1894, instead of the heritors.

(5)—(*a*) Where a churchyard of a parish has been closed—

(i) either before or after the passing of this Act under the Burial-Grounds (Scotland) Act, 1855, or as a result of proceedings under the Public Health (Scotland) Act, 1897; or 60 & 61 Vict. c. 38.

(ii) before the passing of this Act by resolution of the heritors on the ground that no accommodation for further interments remains available therein; or

(iii) by desuetude during a period of twenty years or upwards prior to the passing of this Act;

the kirk session of the parish may, within ten years after the passing of this Act, in the case of a churchyard which has been closed before the passing of this Act, or within ten years after the date of the closing of a churchyard in the case of a churchyard closed after the passing of this Act, intimate in writing to the parish [1] council or other local authority to whom the churchyard has been transferred that the kirk session desire to take over the custody, maintenance, and control of such churchyard, and the parish [1] council or other local authority, as the case may be, shall, on receiving such intimation, transfer the custody, maintenance, and control of such churchyard to the kirk session, subject always to such conditions (if any) as the parish [1] council or other local authority may appoint with respect to the public right of access to the churchyard free of charge.

(*b*) Where a churchyard of a parish which has been transferred to a parish [1] council or other local authority has been closed, or has ceased to be used for interment, the parish [1] council or other local authority, as the case may be, may at any time, upon the application in writing of the kirk session of the parish, transfer the custody, maintenance, and control of such churchyard to the kirk session.

(*c*) Where the custody, maintenance, and control of a churchyard have, in pursuance of this subsection, been transferred to the kirk session, the kirk session shall thenceforward be responsible for such custody, maintenance, and control, and for any expense in connection therewith.

Preservation of monuments, &c., in churches and churchyards.

33. For the preservation and maintenance of any family burying ground, or enclosure, tombstone, monument, or other memorial to the dead, in any parish churchyard or parish church, any person who, in the case of a parish churchyard, satisfies the parish [1] council or other body to whom the parish churchyard or the control thereof is transferred, and in the case of a parish church satisfies the General Trustees that he has an interest in such burying ground, enclosure, tombstone, monument, or other memorial, on the ground of relationship to the deceased person or persons therein buried or thereby commemorated, shall be entitled, with the approval of the parish [1] council or other body to whom the parish churchyard or the control thereof is transferred, or the General Trustees, as the case may be, to provide for the preservation and maintenance of the same.

[1] See note on p. 501.

A.D. 1925

PART IV.

GENERAL.

Provisions relating to *quoad sacra* parishes.

7 & 8 Vict. c. 44
31 & 32 Vict. c. 30.
39 & 40 Vict. c. 11.

34. With respect to parishes *quoad sacra* erected under the New Parishes (Scotland) Act, 1844, the United Parishes (Scotland) Act, 1868, and the United Parishes (Scotland) Act, 1876 (other than parishes *quoad sacra* erected under section fourteen of the said Act of 1844), the following provisions shall have effect:—

(1) In the case of a parish erected before the passing of this Act—

(*a*) The statutory properties and endowments of the parish shall be transferred to the General Trustees as in this section provided;

(*b*) As soon as conveniently may be after the passing of this Act there shall be prepared by the General Trustees and certified by the Clerk of Teinds with respect to each parish, an inventory referring to this section of this Act and setting out the statutory properties and endowments of the parish, and each such inventory shall specify—

(i) the name of the parish;

(ii) each property or security forming part of the said statutory properties and endowments; and

(iii) the name or names of the person or persons in whom the same is vested;

(*c*) Without prejudice to the provisions of the immediately following paragraph of this subsection any person in whom any property or security specified in any such inventory is vested shall if so required by the General Trustees, and at their expense, transfer such property or security to the General Trustees, and do and concur in doing all acts and things necessary for that purpose;

(*d*) Upon any such inventory in so far as the same relates to heritable properties or securities being recorded in the appropriate register of sasines the heritable properties and securities specified in such inventory shall by virtue of this Act and without the necessity of any further conveyance be deemed and taken to be validly transferred to and vested in the General Trustees as if a disposition or assignation by the person or persons in whom the said heritable properties or securities were vested had been granted in favour of the General Trustees and had been recorded in the appropriate register of sasines;

(*e*) (i) The Clerk of Teinds shall make available to the General Trustees, so far as may be necessary for the purposes of this section, all or any title deeds, certificates, or other documents which are in his custody as keeper of the records of the Court of Teinds relating to any properties or securities specified in any such inventory;

(ii) Upon the completion of the transfer of any such properties and securities to the General Trustees the Clerk of Teinds shall hand over to the General Trustees any title deeds, certificates, or other documents relating to the same which are in his custody as aforesaid upon a receipt therefor being given by the General Trustees; A.D. 1925.

(*f*) The General Assembly, or any body to which the General Assembly may delegate the necessary power, may at any time after the completion of the transfer to the General Trustees of the properties and securities specified in any such inventory alter the existing deed of constitution of the parish to which the inventory relates, or annul the said deed and grant a new deed of constitution in place thereof;

(*g*) the statutory properties and endowments of the parish transferred to the General Trustees under or by virtue or in pursuance of this subsection shall be held by the General Trustees for the same ends, uses and purposes as those for which they were held by the trustees or other persons in whom they were vested prior to their being so transferred, or, if the General Assembly shall by Act of Assembly at any time so direct, shall be sold or otherwise disposed of, and the proceeds shall be held and applied by the General Trustees (or by any body to whom the General Assembly may delegate or may have delegated the necessary powers) in accordance with the provisions of section thrity-six of this Act. Provided that no ground used as a burial-ground shall be put to any other use (1933 Act, Section 1, p. 523).

Amendment of principal Act, by 23 & 24 Geo. 5. c. 44. s. 1.

(2) In the case of a parish erected after the passing of this Act—

(*a*) the titles, deeds, certificates, and other documents of or relating to the statutory properties and endowments of the parish shall be taken in the name of the General Trustees;

(*b*) the original deed of constitution shall be in such terms as the General Assembly, or any body to which the General Assembly may delegate the necessary power, may direct, and the General Assembly or any such body may subsequently alter the said deed or annul the same and grant a new deed of constitution in place thereof:

(3) Nothing in this section shall apply to any permanent endowment secured from teinds under section thirteen of the New Parishes (Scotland) Act, 1844:

(4) In this section—

the expression "the statutory properties and endowments of the parish" means—

(i) the church erected as a parish church for the parish under the aforesaid Acts of 1844, 1868, and 1876; and

(ii) where a manse or glebe has been permanently provided under the said Acts as part of the endowment of the minister of the parish, such manse or glebe; and

(iii) any feu-duties, ground annuals, bonds of annual rent, or other heritable securities permanently provided and secured at the time of erection or subsequently substituted with the sanction of the Court of Teinds for the minister of the parish or for the maintenance of the church or manse or payment of the feu-duty thereon; and

(iv) any Government securities or other securities or in-

A.D. 1925.

vestments (not being heritable securities) permanently provided and secured or substituted as aforesaid;

the expression "church" includes the fabric and site of the church and hall (if any) and any ground used as a burial-ground in connection therewith;

the expression "manse" includes the dwelling-house and offices and appurtenances thereof.

Provisions relating to the allocation and redemption of bonds of annual rent held for behoof of *quoad sacra* churches.

35.—(1) Where the debtor under any bond and disposition in security, bond of annual rent, or other heritable security, whereby the payment of any annual sum is secured over land in favour of the minister of any parish *quoad sacra* erected under the New Parishes (Scotland) Act, 1844, the United Parishes (Scotland) Act, 1868, and the United Parishes (Scotland) Act, 1876, or in favour of the trustees acting under the deed of constitution of any such parish or of the General Trustees as coming in place of such minister or trustees (such minister or trustees or the General Trustees, as the case may be, being hereinafter in this section referred to as "the creditor") sells or has sold any portion of such land the debtor shall be entitled to allocate upon the portion of such land so sold such a proportion of such annual sum as may be agreed upon between the debtor and the creditor, or, failing agreement, as may be fixed by the sheriff of the county in which such land is situated upon the application of the debtor.

(2) If, as a result of any such allocation as is provided in the preceding subsection, the proportion of such annual sum so allocated, or the proportion of such annual sum remaining unallocated, does not exceed one pound in amount, the debtor shall forthwith redeem the same by payment to the General Trustees of a sum equal to the proportion of such annual sum so allocated, or to the proportion of such annual sum remaining unallocated, as the case may be, multiplied by twenty, and if the proportion of such annual sum so allocated, or the proportion of such annual sum remaining unallocated, exceeds one pound but is less than fifteen pounds in amount, such proportion shall be increased from the date when such allocation takes effect by five per cent.

(3) Where the debtor and the creditor have agreed upon, or the sheriff has fixed, the proportion of such annual sum to be allocated the debtor shall be entitled to obtain from the creditor a memorandum of allocation in or as nearly as may be in the form of the Thirteenth Schedule to this Act, and upon such memorandum of allocation being recorded in the appropriate register of sasines the allocation contained therein shall be binding on all having interest.

(4) Such annual sum or an allocated proportion thereof exceeding one pound may at any time be redeemed by and in the option of the debtor either

(*a*) for such consideration or in such manner as may be agreed upon between the debtor and the creditor; or

(*b*) at any term of Whitsunday or Martinmas after three months' notice either

(i) by payment to the creditor of such a sum as would, if invested at the time of payment in Consolidated $2\frac{1}{2}$ per cent annuities, produce a yearly amount equal to the annual sum to be redeemed, or

(ii) by transfer to the creditor of such an amount of Consolidated $2\frac{1}{2}$ per cent annuities as would produce a yearly amount equal to the annual sum to be redeemed.

(5) Upon such annual sum or the allocated proportion thereof being redeemed by the debtor, as in this section provided, the debtor shall be entitled to obtain from the creditor a deed or other document disburdening the land over which the same is secured, which shall be recorded on behalf of the debtor in the appropriate register of sasines. A.D. 1925.

(6) The whole expenses of any allocation of such annual sum and of the redemption of such annual sum or a proportion thereof shall be defrayed by the debtor.

(7) In this section the word "debtor" includes the original debtor, his successor in such land, any uninfeft or infeft purchaser of such land or portion thereof, or any disponee to whom such land or portion thereof may be disponed.

Requirements of parish to be first charge on endowments.

36. All moneys received by the General Trustees with respect to any parish under or in pursuance of the provisions of this Act relating to stipend and any church, manse, glebe or other property heritable or moveable situated in, or forming part of, the endowments of any parish transferred to, or received by, the General Trustees by or in pursuance of this Act, and the proceeds of any such moneys, property, or endowments shall be appropriated in the first place to meeting the proper requirements of that parish or its neighbourhood (as such requirements may be determined by the General Assembly or by any body to which the General Assembly may delegate the necessary power), and any remainder after these requirements have been fully met shall form part of a general fund at the disposal of the General Assembly: Provided[1] that except where a benefice is actually vacant at the passing of this act or has become actually vacant thereafter—

(a) all payments received by the General Trustees from heritors in respect of a stipend or standard charge until the same is redeemed, and the income from the redemption money in respect of the stipend or standard charge, shall be appropriated to the payment of that stipend after deduction of a sum not exceeding two per centum of the said payments and income to meet the expense of administration; and

(b) the determination of the General Assembly shall not be exercised so as to decrease the amount of stipend, or the income from, or in respect of, any property transferred to the General Trustees as aforesaid to be received by the incumbent of a benefice nor so as to diminish the benefit to be derived by the incumbent from the use or occupation of any such property.

Powers of General Trustees.

37. In addition to any powers which they already enjoy, the General Trustees shall have power to hold, maintain, administer, and dispose of any property of whatsoever description transferred to, or received by, or vested in them under, or in pursuance of this Act, subject always to the provisions of this Act and to the directions of the General Assembly: Provided that the General Trustees before selling or feuing a glebe or any part thereof shall give to the heritor or heritors whose lands adjoin such glebe or part an opportunity to purchase or take the same in feu at such price or feu-duty and on such terms as may be agreed upon between the General Trustees and the heritor or heritors, or as may, failing agreement, be determined by an arbiter appointed by the sheriff on the application of either party. Without prejudice to the foregoing generality, the General Trustees shall have power, subject as aforesaid,

[1] Amended by Church of Scotland (Property and Endowments) Act, 1957, see p. 531.

A.D. 1925.

to compromise or settle any claim against or by any heritor or other person arising out of anything contained in this Act or done thereunder.

Additional powers of General Trustees.

38.—(1) The General Assembly shall have power to appoint from among the General Trustees a chairman and a vice-chairman of the General Trustees who shall respectively hold office for such period with such powers and duties, and subject to such conditions as the General Assembly may determine, and such chairman and vice-chairman or either of them may receive such remuneration as the General Assembly may from time to time fix. Such chairman, whom failing such vice-chairman, shall when present act as chairman at all meetings of the General Trustees, and when so present shall come in place of any chairman falling to be appointed under section thirteen of the Church of Scotland (General Trustees) Order, 1921, and shall have the like voting powers. Without prejudice to the provisions of the said section with respect to the manner in which meetings of the General Trustees may be called, the chairman or the vice-chairman appointed by the General Assembly may direct that meetings of the General Trustees shall be called.

(2) The General Trustees shall have power to appoint or employ (either from among their own number or otherwise) a solicitor or legal adviser to the General Trustees and such additional officers, attorneys, and persons as they may consider necessary for the proper conduct of the business of the General Trustees, and to pay to such solicitor or legal adviser or other officers, attorneys, or persons employed by them suitable remuneration for their services.

(3) Any intimation to the General Trustees shall be competently made if addressed to the clerk or the chairman or vice-chairman of the General Trustees on their behalf at the known address of the General Trustees in Edinburgh, and any intimation by the General Trustees shall be competently made by the clerk or the chairman or vice-chairman on their behalf.

(4) The General Assembly shall have power to determine from time to time the number of General Trustees who shall form a quorum at meetings of the General Trustees, provided always that the number so determined shall in no case be less than three as prescribed in section thirteen of the Church of Scotland (General Trustees) Order, 1921.

(5) All expenses incurred by the General Trustees in the discharge of their duties under this Act, so far as such expenses are not otherwise provided for under this Act, shall be defrayed in such manner as the General Assembly may determine, and the provisions of section nineteen of the said Order of 1921 shall not apply to such expenses.

(6) The General Assembly may from time to time make byelaws and regulations to be observed by the General Trustees in the discharge of their duties under this Act.

Allocation by General Trustees of certain moneys to be received from Treasury.

39.—(1) As soon as conveniently may be after the passing of this Act the Commissioners shall frame a scheme or schemes for the allocation by the General Trustees of the annual sums of twelve thousand pounds and five thousand and forty pounds mentioned in the Seventh Schedule to this Act, and of the income from any capital sum or sums received by them in redemption of the said annual sums, or either of them, and for the payment by the General Trustees of the various amounts so allocated.

(2) In framing any such scheme the Commissioners shall provide for the protection of the interests of the ministers who at the passing of

this Act are entitled to augmentations of stipend under the Teinds Act, 1810, and the Teinds Act, 1824, or to stipend under the Act 5 Geo. 4. c. 90, and the right in name of Ann of the widow or other representatives of any such minister, and for that purpose the Commissioners shall have regard to the provisions of the aforesaid Acts, notwithstanding any repeal of those provisions under this Act.

A.D. 1925.

50 Geo. 3 c. 84.
5 Geo. 4. c. 72.

(3) Pending the making by the Commissioners of an Order giving effect to a scheme under this section, the General Trustees may, out of the annual sums or the income from any capital sum or sums aforesaid, pay to any minister or assistant and successor, or widow or other representative of a deceased minister, or to the Collector of the Church of Scotland Ministers' and Scottish Universities' Professors' Widows' Fund, as the case may be, such half-yearly sum or sums, as in the judgment of the General Trustees, would have been payable under the aforesaid Acts to such minister or assistant and successor, or widow or other representative, or Collector if this Act had not been passed.

Redemption of manse maill, &c.

40.—(1) Where in any parish manse maill is at the passing of this Act payable in lieu of a manse the heritors legally liable in payment thereof shall redeem the manse maill by payment to the General Trustees of a sum equal to the annual amount thereof multiplied by twenty, such redemption payment to be made within five years after the passing of this Act.

(2) Where a manse has been sold and the price invested and the income from the investments representing the price paid to the minister, those investments shall within five years after the passing of this Act be transferred to the General Trustees, and on the completion of the transfer any liability of the heritors in respect thereof shall cease.

Provisions relating to Court of Teinds.

31 & 32 Vict. c. 100.

41. Notwithstanding anything in the Court of Session (Scotland) Act, 1868, the Court of Teinds may meet at such hours as may be convenient on such days as the Court of Session may by Act of Sederunt prescribe, and section one hundred and six of the said Act of 1868 (which relates to Acts of Sederunt) shall, for the purposes of Acts of Sederunt relating to the Court of Teinds, have effect as if references to that Act in the said section included references to this Act.

Application to Crown lands.

42. This Act shall be binding on the Crown and the provisions of this Act shall apply to lands vested in His Majesty in right of the Crown, and to lands vested in any Government Department for public purposes, and to the teinds of any lands so vested in His Majesty or in any Government Department.

43. [Repealed by Local Government (Scotland) Act, 1929.]

Provisions with respect to certain registration districts.
Provisions for preservation of heritors' records.

44.[1] Whereas in consequence of the transfers of rights of property and the transfer or termination of obligations in connection therewith effected or to be effected by or under or in pursuance of this Act, the powers and duties of heritors (including the power and duty to impose and levy heritors' assessments) will in due course be extinguished, it shall be the duty of the clerk to the heritors of any parish where such extinction has been effected to make intimation thereof in writing to the Secretary for Scotland, who may by order under his hand give such direction as he may think necessary or proper with respect to the preservation and permanent custody of the books of the heritors or any records or documents in their possession as heritors or in the possession of their clerk.

[1] Amended by 1933 Act, section 17, see p. 530.

A.D. 1925.

Saving for obligations of relief.

45. Nothing in this Act shall prejudice or affect any obligation to relieve the heritor of any lands from liability in respect of any stipend or augmentation thereof exigible from the teinds of such lands, and any such obligation shall extend to relief from liability in respect of any standard charge over those lands or in respect of any payments under the section of this Act relating to provisions where stipend does not exceed one pound.

Saving for superiors.

46. Nothing in this Act shall affect or be deemed to affect the rights of superiors of the sites of the churches mentioned in the Ninth Schedule to this Act, where the superiorities are not held by or on behalf of town councils, to payment of their feu duties from the parties in whom the dominium utile of the said sites is vested by this Act or otherwise, and to all other rights and privileges vested in such superiors prior to the passing of this Act.

Interpretation.

47.—(1) In this Act, unless the context otherwise requires—

"The Church" means the Church of Scotland;

"The General Assembly" means the General Assembly of the Church;

"The General Trustees" means the Church of Scotland General Trustees incorporated by the Church of Scotland (General Trustees) Order, 1921;

"The Commissioners" means the Scottish Ecclesiastical Commissioners to be appointed under this Act;

"Minister" means a minister of the Church;

"Stipend" means the stipend of a minister, including any allowance for communion elements payable by heritors out of teinds;

"Glebe" means the lands appropriated to a minister as his glebe, and shall be deemed to include grass glebe or minister's grass, servitudes, right of pasturage, or other heritable rights belonging to the minister and forming part of the benefice, or any money payments in use to be made to the minister in respect of the said rights or any of them, and any land settled in perpetuity on the minister for the time being;

"Court of Teinds" has the same meaning as in the United Parishes (Scotland) Act, 1876;

"Manse" and "Lord Ordinary" have the same meanings as in the Ecclesiastical Buildings and Glebes (Scotland) Act, 1868.

(2) For the purposes of this Act the surrendered teinds of any lands payable as stipend shall be deemed to be stipend exigible from the teinds of those lands.

27 & 28 Vict. c. 114.

(3) The reference to "teinds" in section fifty-nine of the Improvement of Land Act, 1864, shall be construed so as to include standard charges.

Repeal.

48. The enactments specified in the Twelfth Schedule to this Act are hereby repealed to the extent specified in the third column of that Schedule,[1] and so much of any Act as is inconsistent with this Act is also hereby repealed.

Short title.

49. This Act may be cited as the Church of Scotland (Property and Endowments) Act, 1925.

[1] Repealed, Statute Law Revision Act, 1950.

SCHEDULES.

A.D. 1925.

Section 2.

FIRST SCHEDULE.

TABLE A.—FIARS PRICES FOR THE COUNTIES OF SCOTLAND.

Average 1873 *to* 1922 *inclusive.—Showing the value of One Boll of Meal and One Boll of Barley in each county according to these prices, and the average value of the Double Boll of Meal and Barley, and the average value of the Chalder in each county.*

County.	Meal. Average Value of 1 Boll for crops and years 1873-1922.			Barley. Average Value of 1 Boll for crops and years 1873-1922.			Value of the Double Boll of Meal and Barley.			Value of 1 Chalder calculated to nearest Penny.		
	£	s.	d.	£	s.	d.	£	s.	d.	£	s.	d.
1. Aberdeen	0	16	$11\frac{9}{12}$	1	3	$5\frac{9}{12}$	2	0	$5\frac{6}{12}$	16	3	8
2. Argyll	1	0	$5\frac{8}{12}$	1	3	6	2	3	$11\frac{8}{12}$	17	11	9
3. Ayr.	0	18	$6\frac{9}{12}$	1	5	$0\frac{8}{12}$	2	3	$7\frac{5}{12}$	17	8	11
4. Banff	0	16	$11\frac{3}{12}$	1	4	7	2	1	$6\frac{3}{12}$	16	12	2
5. Berwick	1	0	$1\frac{1}{12}$	1	4	$11\frac{4}{12}$	2	5	$0\frac{5}{12}$	18	0	3
6. Bute	0	19	$6\frac{11}{12}$	1	3	$11\frac{10}{12}$	2	3	$6\frac{9}{12}$	17	8	6
7. Caithness	0	17	$2\frac{9}{12}$	1	0	$5\frac{2}{12}$	1	17	$7\frac{11}{12}$	15	1	3
8. Clackmannan	0	18	$9\frac{7}{12}$	1	4	$0\frac{2}{12}$	2	2	$9\frac{9}{12}$	17	2	6
9. Dumbarton	1	0	6	1	3	$1\frac{4}{12}$	2	3	$7\frac{4}{12}$	17	8	11
10. Dumfries	0	18	$3\frac{7}{12}$	1	4	$8\frac{11}{12}$	2	3	$0\frac{6}{12}$	17	4	4
11. Edinburgh or Mid Lothian	0	19	$0\frac{3}{12}$	1	5	4	2	4	$4\frac{3}{12}$	17	14	10
12. Elgin or Moray	0	17	$7\frac{6}{12}$	1	5	$1\frac{4}{12}$	2	2	$8\frac{10}{12}$	17	1	11
13. Fife.	0	19	$3\frac{6}{12}$	1	4	$0\frac{3}{12}$	2	3	$3\frac{9}{12}$	17	6	6
14. Forfar	0	18	10	1	2	$4\frac{4}{12}$	2	1	$2\frac{4}{12}$	16	9	7
15. Haddington or East Lothian	1	0	$3\frac{3}{12}$	1	8	$3\frac{4}{12}$	2	8	$6\frac{7}{12}$	19	8	5
16. Inverness.	0	18	$5\frac{2}{12}$	1	5	$0\frac{6}{12}$	2	3	$5\frac{8}{12}$	17	7	9
17. Kincardine	0	17	$10\frac{3}{12}$	1	2	$1\frac{3}{12}$	1	19	$11\frac{6}{12}$	15	19	8
18. Kinross	0	19	$5\frac{8}{12}$	1	2	$6\frac{5}{12}$	2	2	$0\frac{1}{12}$	16	16	1
19. Kirkcudbright	0	17	$10\frac{4}{12}$	1	4	$6\frac{5}{12}$	2	2	$4\frac{9}{12}$	16	19	2
20. Lanark	1	0	$4\frac{9}{12}$	1	4	11	2	5	$3\frac{9}{12}$	18	2	6
21. Linlithgow or West Lothian	0	19	$7\frac{9}{12}$	1	4	$7\frac{6}{12}$	2	4	$3\frac{3}{12}$	17	14	2
22. Nairn	0	18	$9\frac{5}{12}$	1	5	$2\frac{3}{12}$	2	3	$11\frac{8}{12}$	17	11	9
23. Orkney	0	15	$2\frac{3}{12}$	0	16	$7\frac{9}{12}$	1	11	10	12	14	8
24. Peebles	1	1	$3\frac{8}{12}$	1	5	$4\frac{9}{12}$	2	6	$8\frac{5}{12}$	18	13	7
25. Perth	0	19	$5\frac{2}{12}$	1	3	$6\frac{10}{12}$	2	3	0	17	4	0
26. Renfrew	0	19	$9\frac{7}{12}$	1	4	$11\frac{8}{12}$	2	4	$9\frac{3}{12}$	17	18	2
27. Ross and Cromarty	0	18	$3\frac{3}{12}$	1	4	$5\frac{5}{12}$	2	2	$8\frac{8}{12}$	17	1	5
28. Roxburgh	0	19	$8\frac{10}{12}$	1	4	7	2	4	$3\frac{10}{12}$	17	14	7
29. Selkirk	0	19	$0\frac{6}{12}$	1	4	$2\frac{8}{12}$	2	3	$3\frac{2}{12}$	17	6	5
30. Stirling	1	0	$0\frac{4}{12}$	1	4	$1\frac{9}{12}$	2	4	$2\frac{1}{12}$	17	13	6
31. Sutherland	0	19	$2\frac{3}{12}$	1	4	$1\frac{5}{12}$	2	3	$3\frac{8}{12}$	17	6	9
32. Wigtown	0	17	$3\frac{5}{12}$	1	3	$6\frac{7}{12}$	2	0	10	18	6	1

A.D. 1925.

1st Sch. —*cont.*

Table B.—Fiars Prices for the Counties of Scotland.

Average 1873 *to* 1922 *inclusive.—Showing the value of one quarter of Wheat, Oats, Bear and Barley in each county according to an average of the fiars prices struck for the* 50 *years* 1873 *to* 1922.

County.	Wheat per Quarter.			Oats per Quarter.			Bear per Quarter.			Barley per Quarter.		
	£	s.	d.	£	s.	d.	£	s.	d.	£	s.	d.
1. Aberdeen . .	1	18	$1\frac{5}{12}$	1	2	$1\frac{10}{12}$	1	3	11	1	12	$2\frac{11}{12}$
2. Argyll . . .	2	1	$2\frac{4}{12}$	1	4	$1\frac{9}{12}$	1	11	$1\frac{6}{12}$	1	12	$3\frac{3}{12}$
3. Ayr. . . .	1	16	$11\frac{4}{12}$	1	2	$0\frac{5}{12}$	1	5	7	1	14	$4\frac{11}{12}$
4. Banff . . .	1	18	$8\frac{8}{12}$	1	2	$10\frac{9}{12}$	1	9	1	1	13	$9\frac{3}{12}$
5. Berwick . . .	1	19	$7\frac{10}{12}$	1	5	$8\frac{8}{12}$		—		1	14	$3\frac{1}{12}$
6. Bute . . .	2	3	$1\frac{3}{12}$	1	4	$0\frac{3}{12}$	1	8	$9\frac{11}{12}$	1	12	$11\frac{4}{12}$
7. Caithness . .		—		1	0	$3\frac{3}{12}$	1	6	$5\frac{5}{12}$	1	8	$0\frac{9}{12}$
8. Clackmannan . .	1	15	$10\frac{5}{12}$	1	4	$1\frac{3}{12}$		—		1	12	$11\frac{9}{12}$
9. Dumbarton . .	1	16	$1\frac{3}{12}$	1	3	$9\frac{11}{12}$	1	8	$11\frac{8}{12}$	1	11	$8\frac{11}{12}$
10. Dumfries . .	1	19	$3\frac{5}{12}$	1	3	$6\frac{8}{12}$		—		1	13	$11\frac{9}{12}$
11. Edinburgh or Mid Lothian . .	1	17	$10\frac{5}{12}$	1	5	$3\frac{7}{12}$		—		1	14	$9\frac{5}{12}$
12. Elgin or Moray .	1	17	$7\frac{9}{12}$	1	2	$9\frac{11}{12}$		—		1	14	$5\frac{10}{12}$
13. Fife. . . .	1	15	$10\frac{8}{12}$	1	2	$11\frac{5}{12}$	1	3	$11\frac{3}{12}$	1	12	$11\frac{11}{12}$
14. Forfar . . .	1	15	$8\frac{6}{12}$	1	2	10	1	4	$6\frac{9}{12}$	1	10	$8\frac{7}{12}$
15. Haddington or East Lothian . .	2	1	$9\frac{8}{12}$	1	8	$7\frac{6}{12}$		—		1	18	10
16. Inverness. . .	2	1	2	1	2	$11\frac{11}{12}$	1	12	$2\frac{8}{12}$	1	14	$4\frac{9}{12}$
17. Kincardine . .	1	15	$11\frac{7}{12}$	1	2	$3\frac{10}{12}$	1	3	$7\frac{5}{12}$	1	10	$4\frac{3}{12}$
18. Kinross . . .	2	1	$0\frac{3}{12}$	1	2	$11\frac{1}{12}$		—		1	10	$11\frac{5}{12}$
19. Kirkcudbright. .	1	17	$4\frac{9}{12}$	1	2	$7\frac{1}{12}$		—		1	13	$8\frac{4}{12}$
20. Lanark . . .	1	17	$1\frac{3}{12}$	1	3	$8\frac{3}{12}$		—		1	14	$2\frac{8}{12}$
21. Linlithgow or West Lothian . .	1	17	$4\frac{1}{12}$	1	4	$2\frac{6}{12}$		—		1	13	$9\frac{11}{12}$
22. Nairn . . .	1	19	$7\frac{11}{12}$	1	2	$10\frac{5}{12}$		—		1	14	$7\frac{2}{12}$
23. Orkney . . .		—			—		1	2	$10\frac{3}{12}$	1	2	$10\frac{3}{12}$
24. Peebles . . .	2	0	0	1	5	$2\frac{3}{12}$		—		1	14	$10\frac{7}{12}$
25. Perth . . .	1	17	$3\frac{3}{12}$	1	3	8		—		1	12	$4\frac{5}{12}$
26. Renfrew . . .	1	17	$0\frac{7}{12}$	1	3	$10\frac{11}{12}$		—		1	14	$3\frac{7}{12}$
27. Ross and Cromarty .	1	19	$1\frac{6}{12}$	1	3	$3\frac{7}{12}$		—		1	13	$6\frac{11}{12}$
28. Roxburgh . .	1	18	$5\frac{2}{12}$	1	4	$10\frac{3}{12}$		—		1	13	$9\frac{2}{12}$
29. Selkirk . . .	2	13	$5\frac{3}{12}$	1	4	$5\frac{10}{12}$		—		1	13	$3\frac{2}{12}$
30. Stirling . . .	1	17	$2\frac{9}{12}$	1	3	$10\frac{8}{12}$		—		1	13	$1\frac{10}{12}$
31. Sutherland . .	2	0	$0\frac{11}{12}$	1	3	$6\frac{10}{12}$	1	1	$3\frac{11}{12}$	1	13	$1\frac{5}{12}$
32. Wigtown. . .	1	16	$3\frac{8}{12}$	1	1	$6\frac{7}{12}$	1	8	$3\frac{7}{12}$	1	12	$4\frac{1}{12}$

Section 2.

SECOND SCHEDULE.

Provisions relating to the County average Value of kinds of Victual not mentioned in the First Schedule.

A.—*Where the Value of the kind of Victual is given in the Official Returns of Fiars Prices.*

1. The minister of a parish, the whole or part of whose victual stipend has been localled in any kind of victual not mentioned in the First Schedule to this Act or the clerk of the presbytery where the benefice is

vacant or any heritor concerned, may apply to the Clerk of Teinds to fix the former county average value (in this Schedule referred to as the "average value") of such kind of victual. In any such application by the minister or the clerk of the presbytery the applicant shall give the names of the heritors on whose lands the whole or part of such stipend has been so localled.

2. Thereafter the average value of the kind of victual in question for the fifty years one thousand eight hundred and seventy-three to one thousand nine hundred and twenty-two shall be fixed by the Clerk of Teinds by reference to the official returns of fiars prices for the county in which the parish is situated or where no value for that kind of victual is given in those returns then by reference to the official returns of fiars prices for such other county or counties as the Clerk of Teinds may select as being most suitable in the circumstances of the case.

3. The average value as so fixed shall be intimated by the Clerk of Teinds to the minister or the clerk of the presbytery where the benefice is vacant and to the common agent of the heritors, and the Clerk of Teinds shall at the same time enter the said value in a book to be kept by him in the Teind Office for the purpose, the said book being available for inspection by any member of the public at the Teind Office during the official hours of opening thereof.

B.—*Where the Value of the kind of Victual is not given in the Official Returns of Fiars Prices.*

1. The minister of a parish the whole or part of whose victual stipend has been localled in any kind of victual not mentioned in the First Schedule to this Act or the clerk of the presbytery where the benefice is vacant or any heritor concerned may apply to the sheriff to fix the average value thereof.

2. The sheriff after intimation of any such application to such persons as he may appoint and after such inquiry as he thinks fit shall fix the said average value.

3. The said average value as so fixed shall be intimated by the sheriff to the Clerk of Teinds who shall enter the value in the book mentioned in paragraph 3 of Head A of this Schedule which shall be open for inspection as therein mentioned.

THIRD SCHEDULE.

Section 4.

Form of Intimation of Election that Stipend shall be Standardised.

Date.

I, ...Minister (*or as the case may be*) of the Parish of.. in the Presbytery of ....hereby intimate that I elect that the stipend to which the Minister of the said Parish is entitled shall be standardised in accordance with the provisions of the Church of Scotland (Property and Endowments) Act, 1925.

FOURTH SCHEDULE.

Section 10.

Provisions relating to Augmentation of Stipend.

1. In ascertaining the amount of the available teinds the victual teind and stipend shall be converted according to the average of the fiars prices for the five years preceding the year in which an application is made:

A.D. 1925.

4TH SCH. —*cont.*

Provided that—

(*a*) if in the case of victual teind that average is less than the value as determined in accordance with paragraph 3 of the Fifth Schedule to this Act, the victual teind shall be converted in accordance with that paragraph; and

(*b*) if in the case of victual stipend that average is less than the standard value, the victual stipend shall be converted according to the standard value.

2. Any application to the Lord Ordinary, and the localling of any augmentation, and any decree of locality following thereon shall, subject to the provisions of this Act, be made and dealt with in such manner as the Court of Session by Act of Sederunt may prescribe.

Section 11.

FIFTH SCHEDULE.

Provisions relating to the Preparation, Issuing, and Adjustment of Teind Rolls.

1. Where a benefice is actually vacant at the passing of this Act or where, after the passing of this Act, a benefice becomes actually vacant or is deemed to have become vacant by election or notification the clerk of the presbytery shall forthwith intimate the vacancy to the Clerk of Teinds, who shall communicate the intimation to any titular who has previously notified the Clerk of Teinds in writing that he desires to receive such intimation.

2. Where a benefice is actually vacant at the passing of this Act or where, after the passing of this Act, the benefice becomes actually vacant or is deemed to have become vacant by election or notification it shall be the duty of the heritors concerned forthwith to prepare and lodge in the Teind Office a state of teinds unless in any case the Lord Ordinary shall on the application of any party dispense therewith.

3. For the purposes of the teind rolls the value in sterling money of teind valued in victual shall be determined :—

(*a*) Where a basis of conversion has been specified in the decree of valuation by reference to that basis; and

(*b*) In any other case by reference to the former county average value within the meaning of section two of this Act.

4. Effect shall be given in the teind roll by the Clerk of Teinds to any augmentation of stipend or to any reduction of stipend following upon a surrender of teinds, made in accordance with the provisions of the Sixth Schedule to this Act. The Clerk of Teinds may also give effect in a teind roll to an extra-judicial surrender made before the passing of this Act on intimation from or on behalf of the heritor concerned that such a surrender has been made and on production to him of evidence thereof.

5. Where a heritor is entered in the teind roll separately for different subjects belonging to him in the same parish for teinds of the same class only, he shall be entitled to have the said entries or some of them consolidated into one entry, and on receiving from the heritor an application to that effect before the teind roll is made final, the Clerk of Teinds shall give effect thereto.

6. Where stipend is payable to the minister of one parish from the teinds of lands situated in another parish the Clerk of Teinds shall in the teind roll of the parish where stipend is so payable specify the value of the stipend so payable and in the teind roll of the parish wherein the lands are situated the teinds of those lands shall be stated under deduction of any stipend payable as aforesaid.

7. Where the Clerk of Teinds has prepared a teind roll for any parish he shall report the same to the Lord Ordinary who shall take the roll

into consideration and make such order as he thinks fit with respect to the intimation of the roll (including where necessary an order for the appointment of a common agent by the heritors concerned) and with respect to the subsequent adjustment and completion of the roll. The date of the Lord Ordinary's interlocutor ordering intimation of the teind roll is hereinafter in this Act referred to as the "date of issue of the teind roll."

8. Subject to the provisions of this Act relating to valuation and surrender of teinds no objection to a teind roll shall be competent unless the same is lodged with the Clerk of Teinds before the expiry of eighteen months after the date of issue of the teind roll and so soon as any such objection and any application for the valuation of teinds has been disposed of and any surrender of teinds has received effect and any necessary adjustment of the teind roll has been made, the Lord Ordinary shall by interlocutor declare the roll to be final. As on and from the date of such interlocutor the roll shall for the purposes of this Act be final, subject to such alterations and adjustments as may be necessary in consequence of changes of ownership or in consequence of redemption.

9. The Court of Session shall make by Act of Sederunt such rules and regulations as may in their judgment from time to time be necessary with respect to the preparation, reporting, adjustment, disposal and custody of the teind roll.

10. Nothing in this Act shall affect the right of the titular to lodge a state of teinds should he elect to do so, provided that the expense of the preparation of the said state by the titular shall be payable by the titular.

SIXTH SCHEDULE.

Section 16.

Provisions relating to the Valuation of Teinds and the Surrender of Valued Teinds.

1. Any heritor whose teinds in any parish are wholly or partly unvalued, or the titular of any such teinds, or any minister whose stipend is wholly or partly exigible from unvalued teinds or where the benefice is vacant the General Trustees may at any time not later than the expiry of twelve months after the date of issue of the teind roll for the parish apply to the sheriff to appoint a valuer for the purpose of fixing the annual agricultural value of the lands the teinds of which have not been valued, and in estimating that value the valuer (who shall be appointed by the sheriff at his own hand) shall have regard to the following directions, that is to say: Where the lands are *bona fide* let for a term of years, the rent payable under the lease (so far as it represents agricultural rental) and where the lands are not so let the agricultural rent at which the lands might, in the opinion of the valuer, be reasonably expected to be let shall be deemed to be the annual agricultural value:

Provided that in either case there shall be deducted from the rent—

(*a*) interest on expenditure by the heritor or his predecessors, upon permanent improvements within twenty years prior to the date of valuation, where such expenditure is shown to the satisfaction of the valuer to have increased the annual agricultural letting value of the land; and

(*b*) interest on any other improvement expenditure made by the heritor or his predecessors which, in the opinion of the valuer, has increased such letting value as at the date of valuation.

2.—(*a*) Any heritor or titular who applies to the sheriff as aforesaid shall so soon as the appointment of a valuer has been made give written notice thereof to the minister of the parish in which the lands are situate, or if the benefice is vacant to the General Trustees, and any

A.D. 1925. — 6TH SCH. —*cont.*

minister or the General Trustees so applying shall in like manner give notice to the heritor of the lands.

(*b*) The minister, or the General Trustees or the heritor, as the case may be, receiving such notice may within fifteen days after the date of the notice intimate in writing to the valuer that he or they desires or desire to be heard.

3. The valuer shall after such inquiry as he may think necessary, including the hearing of the parties where a desire to be heard has been intimated as aforesaid, issue a certificate of valuation showing the annual agricultural value of the lands.

4. The provisions set out in the Second Schedule to the Agricultural Holdings (Scotland) Act, 1923, relating to the removal of arbiter, evidence, statement of case and expenses shall, with the necessary modifications, apply to any inquiry by a valuer appointed by the sheriff under this Schedule. The Court of Session shall from time to time by Act of Sederunt make such regulations as they may think necessary for regulating the fees of valuers so appointed.

5.—(*a*) Where the annual agricultural value of the lands, as shown by the certificate issued by the valuer, does not exceed fifty pounds the certificate shall be final. Where the said value exceeds fifty pounds—

(i) The applicant for the appointment of the valuer, or the heritor, or the minister, or the General Trustees, as the case may be, interested in the valuation, if not satisfied with the said valuation, may within fifteen days after the issue of the certificate by the valuer, appeal to the Lord Ordinary, who after such inquiry as he thinks necessary (including if the Lord Ordinary so directs, a remit to a skilled valuer) may either approve or modify the certificate, and the certificate so approved or modified shall thereupon become final. In estimating the annual agricultural value of the land the Lord Ordinary shall have regard to the provisions in that behalf contained in paragraph 1 of this Schedule, which for this purpose shall apply with the substitution of the Lord Ordinary for the valuer.

(ii) If no such appeal has been intimated before the expiry of fifteen days from the issue of the certificate by the valuer, the certificate shall upon such expiry become final.

6.—(*a*) Where the annual agricultural value of the lands as shown in the certificate issued by the valuer does not exceed fifty pounds the applicant for the appointment of the valuer shall within ten days after the issue of the certificate lodge the same at the Teind Office for registration.

(*b*) Where the said value exceeds fifty pounds the certificate issued by the valuer shall be so lodged within ten days of the date when the same becomes final—

(i) by the applicant if the certificate has not been modified by the Lord Ordinary; and

(ii) by the appellant if the certificate has been so modified.

(*c*) When a certificate has been lodged as aforesaid the Clerk of Teinds shall issue a certificate of the amount of the valued teind and such certificate shall be recorded in the Teind Office, and when so recorded shall be evidence of the valuation to the same effect as an exact decree of valuation of the Court of Teinds issued in accordance with the present practice.

7.—(*a*) Any heritor or titular whose teinds have been valued either in accordance with the present practice or in accordance with the provisions of this Schedule, and whether there is or is not a depending process of locality may, so soon as the decree of valuation has been extracted or the certificate of the amount of the valued teinds has been recorded, as the case may be, and within the period hereinafter limited in that behalf, surrender the amount of such valued teind to the minister or the General Trustees, as the case may be. Such surrender shall be as nearly as may be in the form presently in use in the Court of Teinds, and if there is a process of locality pending may be embodied in a minute of surrender lodged in that process, and if there is no depending process of locality the surrender may be signed by the heritor or his agent or the titular or his agent (as the case may be) and lodged at the Teind Office. Any heritor whose teinds have been valued in accordance with the present practice may exercise the powers of this paragraph, notwithstanding that such valuation comprises the teinds of a heritor other than the heritor named in the surrender, but only where there has been an agreement between the parties interested with respect to the division of the cumulo valuation.

(*b*) Surrender of valued teinds shall not be competent unless the minute of surrender is lodged in a process of locality or the surrender is lodged at the Teind Office as aforesaid before the date hereinafter mentioned (that is to say) :—

(i) In cases where the teinds are valued before the date of issue of the teind roll for the parish in which the lands are situate, before the expiry of six months after the date of the said issue ; and

(ii) In cases where the teinds are valued after the date of issue of the teind roll for the parish in which the lands are situate, before the expiry of two months after the issue by the Clerk of Teinds of a certificate of the amount of the valued teinds ; and

(iii) In cases where the value of teinds specified in the teind roll for the parish in which the lands are situate is deemed to be accepted by acquiescence as hereinbefore in this Act provided, before the expiry of fifteen months after the date of issue of the teind roll for that parish.

(*c*) The heritor or the titular shall at the same time as the minute of surrender or the surrender, as the case may be, is lodged as aforesaid send a copy thereof to the minister of the parish, or if the benefice is vacant to the General Trustees, and the Clerk of Teinds shall, as soon as may be after the lodging of the minute or of the surrender, examine the state of the teinds in the parish and calculate what deficiency of stipend (if any) would ensue if the surrender took effect, and shall notify the result of his examination and calculation to the minister or to the General Trustees, as the case may be. Within twenty-one days after the date of such notification the minister or the General Trustees, as the case may be, may lodge objections to the surrender, which shall be finally disposed of by the Lord Ordinary ; but if no such objection shall be so lodged the surrender shall have effect at the expiry of the said period of twenty-one days.

(*d*) It shall not be a valid objection to a surrender made under the provisions of this Schedule that the decree of locality on which the stipend has been paid up to the date of the surrender has not been made final.

8. Where a surrender made under the provisions of this Schedule has become effectual, whether no objection has been lodged or any objection lodged has been disposed of, and a deficiency of stipend amounting to not less than ten pounds per annum is caused thereby, the minister of the parish, or if the benefice is vacant the General Trustees may within thirty days after the date when the surrender has become effectual, intimate in writing to the Clerk of Teinds that he or they claims or claim that the deficiency of stipend shall be re-allocated among those heritors in the parish (if any) who have unexhausted teinds not yet allocated for stipend. The Clerk of Teinds on receiving intimation of the claim shall notify the same to the common agent of the heritors, and if any heritor

A.D. 1925.

6TH SCH. —*cont.*

within thirty days after the date of such notification lodges with the Clerk of Teinds a written objection to the claim the matter shall be finally disposed of by the Lord Ordinary. But if no such objection be lodged, the re-allocation shall be made by the Clerk of Teinds, who shall issue to the minister or to the General Trustees, as the case may be, a certificate specifying the amounts of stipend payable by the heritors whose teinds are affected by the re-allocation.

9. Any calculation as to the amount of any deficiency of stipend caused by a surrender in accordance with the provisions of this Schedule or as to the amounts of unexhausted teinds available to meet such deficiency shall be made—

(*a*) so far as the stipend is concerned, on the basis of the standard value thereof ; and

(*b*) so far as the value of the teind is concerned, in accordance with paragraph 3 of the Fifth Schedule to this Act.

10. A heritor may have his unvalued teinds valued or surrender valued teinds in accordance with the provisions of this Schedule, whether he has or has not a heritable right to such teinds :

Provided that—

(*a*) Where the heritor proposes to have valued or to surrender any teinds to which he has no heritable right, he shall at the time when he gives notice of the appointment of a valuer or lodges a minute of surrender or a surrender as aforesaid intimate the appointment or the surrender in writing to the titular of the teinds who shall have the same rights of objection and appeal as are by the provisions of this Schedule conferred upon the minister of the parish or the General Trustees ;

(*b*) When a heritor receives from a minister or the General Trustees notice of the appointment of a valuer with respect to lands to the teinds of which he has no heritable right, he shall forthwith intimate the appointment in writing to the titular of the teinds, who shall in such case have the same rights of objection and appeal as are by the provisions of this Schedule conferred upon the heritor.

Sections 19 and 39.

SEVENTH SCHEDULE.

PAYMENTS OUT OF THE CONSOLIDATED FUND.

(1) The annual sum of £12,000 on account of augmentations of stipends chargeable on and payable out of the Consolidated Fund of the United Kingdom, under the Teinds Act, 1810, and the Teinds Act, 1824.

(2) The annual sum of £5040 on account of stipends, chargeable and payable, as aforesaid, under the Act 5 George IV., chapter 90.

(3) The annual sum of £2000 chargeable and payable as aforesaid to the General Assembly for itinerant preachers.

(4) The annual sum of £1100 chargeable and payable as aforesaid towards the expenses of the General Assembly.

(5) The annual sum of £86, 3s. 1d. land revenue allowances, chargeable and payable as aforesaid to certain precentors and ministers.

(6) The annual payment under Royal Warrant to the minister of Dunkeld and Dowally of an amount fixed by reference to Fiars Prices, chargeable and payable as aforesaid.

A.D. 1925.

EIGHTH SCHEDULE.

Sections 21 and 24.

LIST OF CERTAIN PARISHES *QUOAD OMNIA* ERECTED UNDER THE NEW PARISHES (SCOTLAND) ACT, 1844.

PARISH.	DATE OF ERECTION.
North Bute	26th June 1844.
Shettleston	30th June 1847.
Calton	11th July 1849.
Teviothead	20th February 1850.
Maryhill	10th July 1850.
Kirkhope	25th June 1851.
Springburn	14th June 1854.
Ardoch	21st February 1855.
Colonsay	27th February 1861.
Coll	15th March 1865.

NINTH SCHEDULE.

Sections 22 and 46.

LIST OF BURGH CHURCHES.

1. East Kirk, Aberdeen.
2. Greyfriars, Aberdeen. Manse.
3. North Kirk, Aberdeen.
4. South Kirk, Aberdeen.
5. St Clement's, Aberdeen. Manse.
6. West Kirk, Aberdeen. Manse.
7. Greyfriars, Dumfries.
8. St Clement's, Dundee.
9. St David's, Dundee. Manse.
10. St John's, Dundee.
11. St Paul's, Dundee. Manse.
12. Canongate, Edinburgh.
13. Greenside, Edinburgh. Manse.
14. Greyfriars New, Edinburgh.
15. Greyfriars Old, Edinburgh.
16. High Kirk (St Giles'), Edinburgh.
17. Lady Yester's, Edinburgh.
18. New North (West St Giles'), Edinburgh. Manse.
19. St Andrew's, Edinburgh.
20. St George's, Edinburgh.
21. St John's, Edinburgh.
22. St Mary's, Edinburgh.
23. St Stephen's, Edinburgh. Manse.
24. Trinity College, Edinburgh.
25. Tron, Edinburgh.
26. College or Blackfriars, Glasgow. Manse.
27. St Andrew's, Glasgow.
28. St David's or Ramshorn, Glasgow. Manse.
29. St George's, Glasgow. Manse.
30. St James', Glasgow.
31. St John's, Glasgow.
32. St Paul's, Glasgow.
33. Tron, Glasgow.
34. East Kirk, Greenock.
35. Middle Kirk, Greenock. Manse.
36. High Kirk, Kilmarnock.
37. High, Paisley. Manse.

A.D. 1925.

9TH SCH. —*cont.*

38. Laigh, Paisley. Manse.
39. Middle, Paisley. Manse.
40. St John's, Perth. Manse.
41. St Paul's, Perth.
42. St Mark's, Perth. Manse.
43. Queensferry.
44. North, Stirling.
45. West, Stirling.

Section 23.

TENTH SCHEDULE.[1]

LIST OF PARLIAMENTARY CHURCHES AND MANSES.

Name of Place.	Parish or Island.	County.
1. Loch-Gilphead	Glassary	Argyll.
2. Muckairn (manse only)	Muckairn	do.
3. Duror	Appin	do.
4. Kilmeny (manse only)	Islay Island	do.
5. Portnahaven	do.	do.
6. Oe or Oth	do.	do.
7. Kinlochspelvie	Mull Island	do.
8. Salen (manse only)	do.	do.
9. Tobermory	do.	do.
10. Ulva	Ulva Isle	do.
11. Iona	Iona Isle	do.
12. Strontian	Ardnamurchan	do.
13. Acharacle	do.	do.
14. North-Ballachulish	Kilmallie	Inverness.
15. Ardgour (no manse)	do.	Argyll.
16. Rothiemurchus (manse only).	Rothiemurchus	Inverness.
17. Tomintoul	Kirkmichael	Banff.
18. Inch (manse only)	Kingussie	Inverness.
19. Steinsholl (in Trotternish)	Skye Island	do.
20. Halen (in Waternish)	do.	do.
21. Trumisgarry	N. Uist Isle	do.
22. Bernera Isle	Harris	do.
23. Plockton	Lochalsh	Ross and Cromarty.
24. Shieldaig	Applecross	do.
25. Carnoch, Strath-Conan	Contin	do.
26. Kinloch-Luichart	do.	do.
27. Poolewe	Gairloch	do.
28. Croich	Kincardine	do.
29. Ullapool	Loch-Broom	do.
30. Cross (Ness District)	Lewis Island	do.
31. Knock (Eye District)	do.	do.
32. Rhuistore	Assynt	Sutherland.
33. Kinloch-Bervie	Edrachilles	do.
34. Strathy	Farr	do.
35. Berriedale	Latheron	Caithness.
36. Keiss	Wick	do.
37. Deerness (manse only)	St Andrew and Deerness.	Orkney and Shetland.

[1] Amended by 1933 Act, section 15, see p. 530.

A.D. 1925.

10TH SCH. —*cont.*

Name of Place.	Parish or Island.	County.
38. N. Ronaldshay (manse only).	Cross and Burness .	Orkney and Shetland.
39. Sandwick (manse only) .	Dunrossness . .	do.
40. Quarff	Quarff . . .	do.
41. Interwick, or Innerwick (in Glenlyon).	Fortingall . .	Perth.
42. Rannoch . . .	do. . .	do.
43. Kirktown of Foss . .	Dull . . .	do.

Note.—For additions to this Schedule see p. 530.

ELEVENTH SCHEDULE.

Section 28.

CERTIFICATE OF SHERIFF UNDER THE CHURCH OF SCOTLAND (PROPERTY AND ENDOWMENTS) ACT, 1925.

County of
Parish of

I, , sheriff of as authorised by the Church of Scotland (Property and Endowments) Act, 1925, hereby certify that all obligations incumbent on the heritors of the said parish, with respect to the subjects mentioned in the Schedule annexed hereto have been fulfilled.

[*Signature and date.*]

SCHEDULE.

Church or manse

(*Insert or refer to a description of the church, and the site thereof, or the manse (with pertinents, if any) and the site thereof, or both of the said subjects (as the case may be) to which the certificate relates.*)

TWELFTH SCHEDULE.

[Repealed, Statute Law Revision Act, 1950.]

THIRTEENTH SCHEDULE.

Section 35.

FORM OF MEMORANDUM OF ALLOCATION.

The proportion of the annual sum of £ created by (*particulars of deed*) allocated upon all and whole (*description of land*) is hereby fixed at £ (*and if an increase is payable, add*) with £ of increase making a total of £ per annum.

[*To be signed by minister or trustees under deed of constitution or the General Trustees, as the case may be, or by an agent on behalf of the minister or trustees or General Trustees, respectively.*]

A.D. 1925.

NOTE ON SECTION 22 (2) (*h*) (i) AND (ii) AND (3) (pp. 470-472).

In connection with the sale of Lady Yester's Parish Church (a Burgh Church) to the Town Council of Edinburgh, a Memorial by the Church of Scotland General Trustees and the Presbytery of Edinburgh was submitted in 1939 to the Procurator for the Church, Mr J. F. Strachan, K.C., for his opinion. The memorialists submitted the following questions :—

On consideration of the terms of Section 22 (2) (*h*) (i) and (ii) and (3) of the Act of 1925 as incorporated in the Scheme of the Scottish Ecclesiastical Commissioners and of the whole facts and circumstances as narrated above (in the Memorial) and as disclosed in the correspondence with the Corporation, is the Procurator of opinion—

(*a*) that the proceeds of the sale of Lady Yester's Church must be applied for the purpose of the erection of a new Church within the municipal boundaries of the city ? or

(*b*) that sub-clause (2) (*h*) (1) of Section 22 as incorporated in the Scheme is a provision for the ascertainment or limitation of a price without importing any obligation that the price is to be applied for said purpose ?

The Procurator answered (*a*) in the negative, and (*b*) in the affirmative.

APPENDIX VI.—*C.*

CHURCH OF SCOTLAND (PROPERTY AND ENDOWMENTS) AMENDMENT ACT, 1933.

[23 & 24 Geo. 5. Ch. 44.]

ARRANGEMENT OF SECTIONS.

A.D. 1933.

CHAPTER 44.

An Act to amend the Church of Scotland (Property and Endowments) Act, 1925, to make further provision with regard to the properties and endowments of the Church of Scotland, and for purposes connected therewith. [*28th July* 1933.]

Be it enacted by the King's most Excellent Majesty, by and with the advice and consent of the Lords Spiritual and Temporal, and Commons, in this present Parliament assembled, and by the authority of the same, as follows :—

1. [Section 1 substituted for Section 34(1)(g) of 1925 Act, see page 505.]

A.D. 1933.

Transfer of churchyards attached to parishes *quoad sacra*, and parliamentary churches.

2.—(1) Notwithstanding anything contained in paragraph (*g*) of subsection (1) of section thirty-four of the principal Act, and without prejudice to anything therein contained, the trustees or other persons by whom any churchyard forming part of the statutory properties and endowments of a parish *quoad sacra* or connected with a parliamentary church is held, or the General Trustees if any such churchyard shall have become vested in them, may by notice in writing require the local authority to take over such churchyard, and as from the date of such notice such churchyard shall, without the necessity of any further conveyance, be transferred to and vested in the local authority, and the provisions of section thirty-two of the principal Act shall apply to any churchyard so transferred in like manner as they apply to a churchyard transferred under that section.

(2) For the purposes of this section the expression "local authority" shall as regards any churchyard, mean the council of the county or burgh within which the churchyard is situated, or, in the case of a churchyard situated partly in a county and partly in a burgh, the council of the county and the council of the burgh as regards the parts of the churchyard respectively situated in the county and in the burgh.

Non-statutory properties and endowments of *quoad sacra* parishes.

3.—(1) The trustees or other persons in whom any properties or endowments, whether heritable or moveable, of a parish *quoad sacra*, other than the statutory properties and endowments of the parish, are vested shall, if so required by the General Trustees, convey or transfer such properties and endowments (hereinafter referred to as non-statutory properties and endowments) or any of them in the option of such Trustees or other persons as aforesaid to the General Trustees or to any other body authorised for the purpose by the General Assembly, or to a permanent body of local trustees, and on their so conveying or transferring the same, such trustees or other persons as aforesaid shall be thereby fully exonered and discharged of the trust under which the said properties and endowments were held without the necessity of any further release, discharge or exoneration.

(2) The General Trustees shall as regards any non-statutory properties and endowments vested in them, and any trustees or other persons shall as regards any such properties or endowments vested in them, have power, subject to the provisions of any deed of trust, conveyance or other deed applicable thereto and to the approval of the presbytery of the bounds, to sell or otherwise dispose of such properties and endowments and to apply the proceeds thereof in the first place to meet the proper requirements of the parish as such requirements may be determined by the General Assembly, or by any body to which the General Assembly may delegate the necessary power, and any remainder after these requirements have been fully met shall be applied for such ends, uses and purposes as the General Assembly may direct:

Provided always that—

(i) the consent of the General Assembly declared by Act of Assembly shall be required to the sale or disposal of any such properties and endowments, except where by the terms of the deed of trust, conveyance or other deed under which any such properties and endowments are held the General Trustees or any trustees or other persons holding the same have power to sell or to dispose thereof without such consent; and

(ii) where it is proposed under the authority of the General Assembly

A.D. 1933.

to transfer the statutory properties and endowments of a parish *quoad sacra* to a new area, the non-statutory properties and endowments of such parish, or the proceeds of the sale of the same, if sold, may, with the like approval of the presbytery of the bounds and of the kirk session of the parish concerned, also be transferred along with the statutory properties and endowments of such parish to such new area.

Chapels of ease and mission churches.

4. Any trustees or other persons in whom any chapel of ease, mission church or church hall is vested or the General Trustees if the same shall be vested in them shall have power, subject to the provisions of any deed of trust, conveyance or other deed applicable thereto, to sell or otherwise dispose of the same and to apply the proceeds thereof for such ends, uses and purposes as the General Assembly may direct. Provided always that the consent of the General Assembly declared by Act of Assembly shall be required to the sale or disposal thereof, except where by the terms of the deed of trust, conveyance or other deed under which any chapel of ease, mission church or church hall is held the trustees or other persons or the General Trustees holding the same have power to sell or to dispose thereof without such consent.

Parliamentary churches and manses, &c.

5. Notwithstanding anything in the Act 5 George IV., chapter 90, or in the principal Act, the General Trustees shall, subject to the consent of the General Assembly, declared by Act of Assembly, have power, subject to the provisions of any deed of trust, conveyance or other deed applicable thereto, to sell or otherwise dispose of any parliamentary church or manse, or any other subjects connected therewith vested in them under section twenty-three of the principal Act and to apply the proceeds thereof for such ends, uses and purposes as the General Assembly may direct. Provided always that no ground used as a burial-ground shall be put to any other use.

Power to dispose of certain churches and manses erected under the Act of 1844.

6. Notwithstanding anything contained in the titles under which any of the churches or manses of the parishes *quoad omnia* referred to in section twenty-four of the principal Act and specified in the Eighth Schedule thereto are held, the General Trustees shall, upon the same becoming vested or having become vested in them, in terms of the said section of the principal Act, have power, subject to the consent of the General Assembly, declared by Act of Assembly, to sell or otherwise dispose of any of the said churches or manses or any glebes or other subjects connected therewith, so far as such glebes or other subjects shall be vested in the General Trustees, and the General Trustees shall apply the proceeds thereof in the first place to meet the proper requirements of the parish as such requirements may be determined by the General Assembly, or by any body to which the General Assembly may delegate the necessary power, and any remainder after these requirements have been fully met shall be applied for such ends, uses and purposes as the General Assembly may direct: Provided always that no ground used as a burial-ground shall be put to any other use.

Suppression or union of parishes.

7. Notwithstanding anything contained in any Act of Parliament, decree of the Court of Session or Court of Teinds, or deed of constitution or in the titles, deeds or certificates relating to any parish *quoad sacra* or any parish *quoad omnia* included in the Eighth Schedule to the principal Act, the General Assembly or any body to which the General Assembly may have delegated the necessary powers may, by Act of Assembly or by resolution of such body, suppress any such parish or alter or extend

A.D. 1933.

the bounds of any such parish or unite any such parish with any other parish or parishes, and on the suppression of any such parish *quoad sacra* or *quoad omnia* the area or district thereof shall be united to and form part of such other parish or parishes as the General Assembly or such body as aforesaid (as the case may be) may direct; or if no such direction is given, such area or district shall be reunited to and form part of the parish from which it was disjoined on the erection of the parish suppressed, or where such area or district was disjoined from more than one parish then the several parts thereof shall be reunited to and form parts of the parishes from which they were respectively so disjoined:

Provided that—

(i) the consent of the minister of any such parish who was appointed thereto prior to the passing of the principal Act shall be necessary to any suppression of that parish or to any union thereof or of any part thereof with any other parish or parishes, or to any union therewith of any part of the area or district of any other parish; and

(ii) no such parish the stipend whereof is payable out of teinds shall be suppressed or united with any other parish or parishes, nor shall any part of any area or district be united with any such parish, until a teind roll therefor shall have been made up in terms of the provisions of the principal Act and shall have become final.

Application of properties and endowments on suppression or union of *quoad sacra* parishes.

8. Upon the suppression of any parish *quoad sacra* or of any parish *quoad omnia* included in the Eighth Schedule to the principal Act, or upon the alteration or extension of the bounds of such parish or the uniting of the same with any other parish or parishes by the General Assembly or by such body as aforesaid, whether such suppression or uniting shall have taken place prior to the commencement of this Act or shall take place at any date subsequent thereto, the following provisions shall have effect:—

(1) Any obligation by any third party contained in any bond or other deed or document representing or making provision for part or the whole of the statutory endowments of the parish being a parish *quoad sacra*, or any obligation at common law for payment of the stipend or part of the stipend of the parish being a parish *quoad omnia*, shall not be prejudiced or affected by such suppression or union or alteration or extension of bounds, but shall remain in full force and effect unless and until expressly discharged or otherwise dealt with by the General Trustees, and the statutory properties and endowments of the parish being a parish *quoad sacra* shall be held, or if the General Assembly by Act of Assembly so direct, shall, subject to the provisions of any deed of trust, conveyance or other deed applicable thereto, be sold or otherwise disposed of by the General Trustees, and the income of such properties and endowments or the proceeds thereof, if sold or otherwise disposed of as well as the income of such proceeds, shall be applied by the General Trustees, subject to the provisions of section thirty-six of the principal Act, for such ends, uses and purposes as the General Assembly may direct. Provided always that—

(*a*) Any bond of annual rent or other heritable security

permanently provided or secured for the maintenance of the church or manse of any parish *quoad sacra* shall, if such church or manse is sold or otherwise disposed of, be discharged by the General Trustees as regards the subject so sold or disposed of, quoad the obligation for such maintenance, unless the debtor in such bond or other heritable security consents to such obligation remaining in full force and effect; but that without prejudice to any obligations for payment of stipend or otherwise contained in such bond of annual rent or other heritable security such as aforesaid, or for the maintenance of any church or manse remaining unsold or undisposed of and falling to be retained for any ecclesiastical purpose; and

(*b*) no ground used as a burial-ground shall be put to any other use:

(2) The non-statutory properties and endowments (if any) of the parish being a parish *quoad sacra* may, subject to any provisions applicable thereto contained in any deed of trust, conveyance or other deed relating to any such non-statutory property or endowment, be sold or otherwise disposed of and the income of such properties and endowments and the proceeds thereof, if sold or otherwise disposed of as well as the income of such proceeds, shall be applied by the trustees or other person in whom the same may then be vested for behoof of the parish or district concerned, or by the General Trustees, if the same shall then have become vested in them, in the first place to meet the proper requirements of the parish as such requirements may be determined by the General Assembly, or by any body to which the General Assembly may delegate the necessary power, and any remainder after these requirements have been fully met shall be applied for such ends, uses and purposes as the General Assembly may direct. Provided always that the consent of the General Assembly declared by Act of Assembly shall be required to the sale or disposal of any such properties and endowments, except where by the terms of the deed of trust, conveyance or other deed under which any such properties and endowments are held the General Trustees or any trustees or other persons holding the same have power to sell or to dispose thereof without such consent:

(3) Without prejudice to the provisions of section five of this Act, where the church or manse in the parish being a parish *quoad sacra* is a parliamentary church or manse, such church or manse and any other subjects connected therewith and situated within the parish shall after the transfer thereof to the General Trustees under the principal Act be held by the General Trustees, or if the General Assembly by Act of Assembly so direct, shall, subject to the provisions of any deed of trust, conveyance or other deed applicable thereto, be sold or otherwise disposed of by the General Trustees and the proceeds thereof shall be applied for such ends, uses and purposes as the General Assembly may direct. Provided always that no ground used as a burial-ground shall be put to any other use.

Rights of superiors and others.

9.—(1) Nothing in this Act contained shall prejudice or affect the patrimonial rights or interests of superiors or other persons conferred by

A.D. 1933.

or reserved under any Act, Decree of the Court of Session or Court of Teinds, deed of constitution, deed of trust, or any feu charter, feu contract, deed, conveyance or other document relating to the properties and endowments, whether statutory or non-statutory, of any parish or to any chapel of ease, mission church or church hall, or to any parliamentary church or manse or any other subjects connected therewith, and all such rights and interests shall continue to have the like force and effect as if this Act had not passed.

(2) Where any ground has been feued for a nominal feu-duty for the site of the church or manse of any parish and where nothing is stated in the feu charter, feu contract or other deed under which such ground is feued as to the feu-duty which is to be payable by the vassal in the event of the church or manse being sold or disposed of for other than any ecclesiastical purpose, the feu-duty to be payable for the said ground after such sale is effected shall be such sum as shall be agreed upon between the superior and the General Trustees or other vassal, or such sum as, failing agreement, shall be determined by an arbiter to be appointed by the sheriff.

(3) Before selling or otherwise disposing of the ground or any part thereof on which any church or manse included in the Tenth Schedule to the principal Act as extended by section fifteen of this Act has been erected, the General Trustees shall give to any heritor whose lands adjoin such ground or part and by whose predecessor in title such ground or part was originally granted or disponed without valuable consideration for the erection of the church or manse, an opportunity to purchase or take in feu such ground or part at such price or feu-duty and on such terms as may be agreed upon between the General Trustees and such heritor, or, as failing agreement, may be determined by an arbiter appointed by the sheriff on the application of either party.

Vesting of stipends of ministers of burgh churches, &c.

10. The stipend payable to the minister of any burgh church or parliamentary church or the church of any parish *quoad omnia* mentioned in the Eighth Schedule to the principal Act shall, as from the date of the passing of this Act, if the benefice shall then be vacant, and, if the benefice shall not then be vacant, as from the occurrence of the first vacancy after the said date, be deemed to vest *de die in diem* in the minister entitled thereto without prejudice to the payment of any stipend vested in him or in any former incumbent according to the law and practice existing at the passing of this Act, and subject to the satisfaction of any claim for Ann on the part of the widow or other representatives of a deceased incumbent:

Provided that the minister of any such church as aforesaid, being the incumbent of the benefice at the date of the passing of this Act, or where an assistant and successor has been appointed to such minister, either the minister or the assistant and successor, with the consent of the assistant and successor or of the minister (as the case may be), or, failing such consent, with the authority of the presbytery, may elect, by intimation in writing addressed to the General Trustees, that the provisions of this section shall apply to his stipend, and in such cases the benefice shall for the purposes of this section be deemed to have become vacant as at the date of the said intimation.

Vesting of glebe feu-duties, &c.

11.—(1) Where the General Trustees or the minister of any parish is entitled to receive payment of any feu-duties or rents in respect of the glebe of the parish, or the income of any Government or other securities

A.D. 1933.

or investments representing the price or consideration received in respect of the sale of the glebe or part thereof, or of any right therein, including any rents or royalties received in respect of or under any lease or agreement applicable to any minerals underlying such glebe or part thereof or of any mineral wayleaves, such feu-duties, rents, royalties, or income shall be deemed to vest *de die in diem* any law or practice to the contrary notwithstanding, and neither the widow nor any other representative of such minister shall have any claim thereto after his death in name of Ann.

(2) This section shall not take effect until all rights in or in relation to the glebe specified in section thirty of the principal Act shall have been transferred to the General Trustees in accordance with the provisions of that Act, and, except in the case of a benefice which is or was actually vacant at the date of such transfer, unless and until a vacancy in the benefice occurring after that date shall have been filled:

Provided however that the minister being the incumbent of the benefice at the date of such transfer, or, where an assistant and successor has been appointed to such minister, either the minister or the assistant and successor, with the consent of the assistant and successor or of the minister (as the case may be) or, failing such consent, with the authority of the presbytery, may elect, by intimation in writing addressed to the General Trustees, that the provisions of this section shall take effect as if a vacancy in the benefice had occurred, and in such case the benefice shall, for the purposes of this section, be deemed to have become vacant as at the date of the said intimation.

General Assembly may specify parish church.

12. Where in any parish, parochial district or area as defined by the General Assembly, or by any body to which the General Assembly may have delegated or may hereafter delegate the necessary powers, there are two or more separate churches or benefices, it shall be competent for the General Assembly to declare that such one of the churches within the parish, district or area concerned as the General Assembly may specify shall be deemed to be the church of the parish, and that the minister and elders or kirk session of such church shall be deemed to be the minister and elders or kirk session thereof for the purposes of any Act, Act of Sederunt, trust deed, scheme of administration or other public or private instrument, deed or document having reference to the minister or to the elders or to the kirk session (as the case may be) of the parish as trustee or trustees *ex officio*, and, where the General Assembly shall have so declared, the church so specified shall be deemed to be the church and the minister and elders or the kirk session thereof for the time being shall be deemed to be the minister and elders or kirk session (as the case may be) for the purposes aforesaid.

Notarial execution by minister of wills, &c.

13.—(1) A minister of the Church of Scotland who has been appointed to a charge without limit of time or for a period of years to officiate as minister shall, in any parish in which such charge or any part thereof is situated, have the like power as regards the notarial execution of wills or other testamentary writings as is conferred by subsection (1) of section eighteen of the Conveyancing (Scotland) Act, 1924, on a parish minister acting in his own parish.

14 & 15 Geo. 5. c. 27.

(2) A certificate by one of the principal clerks, or the principal clerk if there shall be only one, of the General Assembly, stating the parish in which the charge of any such minister is situated shall be accepted as conclusive evidence thereof.

(3) In the foregoing provisions of this section the expression

A.D. 1933.

"minister" shall include an assistant and successor or a colleague and successor of such minister.

(4) Any reference in subsection (1) of section eighteen of the Conveyancing (Scotland) Act, 1924, to an assistant and successor shall be deemed to include a reference to a colleague and successor.

Appointment of interim chairman or vice-chairman of General Trustees during a vacancy.

14. In the event of the death, resignation or incapacity of the chairman or vice-chairman of the General Trustees between the close of one General Assembly and the meeting of the next General Assembly, the General Trustees are hereby authorised to appoint an interim chairman or vice-chairman (as the case may be) until the first meeting of the General Assembly occurring thereafter, or in the case of incapacity such earlier date as may be specified.

Amendment of principal Act with regard to parliamentary churches.

15. Section twenty-three of and the Tenth Schedule to the principal Act shall apply to the following churches in like manner in all respects as if they were mentioned in the said schedule, viz.: Muckairn, Kilmeny and Salen, in the county of Argyll; Rothiemurchus and Inch in the county of Inverness; and Deerness, N. Ronaldshay and Sandwick, in the county of Orkney and Shetland; and accordingly the said schedule shall have effect as if the words "manse only" wherever they occur were omitted.

16. [Section 16 substituted for Section 25 of 1925 Act, see p. 497.]

Amendment of principal Act, s. 44.

17. Section forty-four of the principal Act in so far as it empowers the Secretary of State to give direction with respect to the preservation of books, records or documents, shall apply in any case where the Secretary of State is satisfied that the powers and duties of the heritors of a parish have been extinguished, notwithstanding that intimation of such extinction may not have been made by the clerk to the heritors of the parish in pursuance of the said section.

Interpretation.

18. In this Act, unless the context otherwise requires, the expression "the Church" means the Church of Scotland as now constituted by the Union of the said Church with the United Free Church of Scotland on the second day of October 1929; the expression "The General Assembly" means the General Assembly of the said Church as now so constituted; the expression "the statutory properties and endowments of the parish" has the meaning assigned to it in section thirty-four of the principal Act; the expression "parliamentary church or manse" means any church or manse mentioned in the Tenth Schedule to the principal Act, together with any land whether described as churchyard, glebe or otherwise, connected with any such church or manse; and other expressions have the like meaning as in the principal Act.

Citation.

19. This Act may be cited as the Church of Scotland (Property and Endowments) Amendment Act, 1933, and the principal Act and this Act may be cited as the Church of Scotland (Property and Endowments) Acts, 1925 and 1933.

APPENDIX VI.—*D.*

CHURCH OF SCOTLAND (PROPERTY AND ENDOWMENTS) AMENDMENT ACT, 1957.

An Act to amend section thirty-six of the Church of Scotland (Property and Endowments) Act, 1925, *in its application to benefices with more than one incumbency.* [*6th June* 1957.]

A.D. 1957.

Be it enacted by the Queen's most Excellent Majesty, by and with the advice and consent of the Lords Spiritual and Temporal, and Commons, in this present Parliament assembled, and by the authority of the same, as follows:—

Amendment of 15 & 16 Geo. 5. c. 33, s. 36.

1. For the purposes of the proviso to section thirty-six of the Church of Scotland (Property and Endowments) Act, 1925 (in this Act referred to as "the principal Act"), a benefice with more than one incumbency, being a benefice which was not actually vacant at the passing of the principal Act and which has not become actually vacant before the passing of this Act, shall be deemed to become actually vacant—

(*a*) if at the passing of this Act there were more incumbents than one of the benefice, on the termination of the interest of that one of them who last ceases to be an incumbent of the benefice; or

(*b*) if at the passing of this Act there was only one incumbent of the benefice, on the termination of the interest of that incumbent;

and from the date on which such a benefice as aforesaid is by virtue of this section deemed to have become actually vacant the said section thirty-six shall, in relation to that benefice, have effect as if the proviso thereto were omitted.

Short title construction and citation.

2. This Act may be cited as the Church of Scotland (Property and Endowments) Amendment Act, 1957, and shall be construed as one with the principal Act; and the Church of Scotland (Property and Endowments) Acts, 1925 and 1933, and this Act may be cited together as the Church of Scotland (Property and Endowments) Acts, 1925 to 1957.

APPENDIX VI.—*E*

ACT ANENT POWERS DELEGATED TO THE COMMITTEE ON MAINTENANCE OF THE MINISTRY (1953, xxvii.).

Edinburgh, May 25, 1953. *Sess.* 10.

A.D. 1953. The General Assembly repeal Act 1931, xli., and, in place thereof, enact and ordain as follows :—

Section 1.—The General Assembly, with reference to the provisions of Section 36 of the Church of Scotland (Property and Endowments) Act, 1925, hereby nominate and appoint the Committee on the Maintenance of the Ministry (hereinafter referred to as "the said Committee") as the body to whom the General Assembly hereby delegate all the powers conferred upon the General Assembly by the said Section of said Act so far as relating to stipend (including all sums to be paid over by the Church of Scotland General Trustees to the said Committee as hereinafter provided) ; the General Assembly hereby further authorise, direct, and empower the Church of Scotland General Trustees to pay over to the said Committee as and when the same shall be received by them, or at such dates or terms as may be arranged between them and the said Committee, all Standardised Stipends which they are empowered to collect under the provisions of said Act, together with the Stipends of all Parishes *Quoad Sacra*, as and when the Statutory Properties and Endowments thereof shall have been transferred to the said General Trustees in accordance with the provisions of said Act ; as also the Stipends payable to the Ministers of the Burgh Churches named in the Ninth Schedule to said Act (other than and except those of the Ministers of the Burgh Churches of Edinburgh, which for the present fall to be specially dealt with) ; as also the Stipends of the Burghal-Landward Churches, Parliamentary Charges, and Exchequer Livings, and of the Parishes named in the Eighth Schedule to said Act —in so far as the said General Trustees are directed and empowered by said Act, or under the provisions of any Orders and Schemes issued by the Scottish Ecclesiastical Commissioners thereunder relative to the above-named Churches, Parliamentary Charges and Exchequer Livings, and the Parishes named in the said Eighth Schedule to said Act, to receive the Stipends of the said Parishes, Churches, Parliamentary Charges and Exchequer Livings, and of the said Parishes named in the said Eighth Schedule to said Act, or some of them, and to pay the same over to the Ministers thereof according to the specific amounts named in the said Orders and Schemes, where such amounts are named therein—the said Committee being bound, in respect of the authority and direction, to the said General Trustees (unless and until the General Assembly shall otherwise direct)—duly to pay over the said Stipends to the Ministers entitled thereto in accordance with the provisions of the said Act, and the said Orders and Schemes.

Further, the General Assembly hereby authorise the said General Trustees to pay over to the said Committee the free income of all Glebes, or of any Mortifications or Endowments not derived from teinds referred to in Section 25 of the said Act, which shall have been transferred or which may hereafter be transferred to and vested in them the said General Trustees under the provisions of the said Act, or of any relative Orders and Schemes issued by the Scottish Ecclesiastical Commissioners with reference thereto, together with the income derived or hereafter to be derived from the feuing or from the proceeds of sale of Glebes or parts thereof—as forming together part of the emoluments of the Parishes or fruits of the Benefices, but that subject always to the rights of existing incumbents under said Act, or under said Orders and Schemes; and also any income derived from the proceeds of sale of Churches or Manses in so far as the same may have been or may hereafter be appropriated to the augmentation of Stipend, the free income derived from the various sources above referred to being paid over to and applied by the said Committee (unless and until otherwise directed by the General Assembly) in the same manner as is hereinbefore provided in relation to Stipend—so that the said Committee may hereafter be, with the exception before specified, the sole distributing body in relation to such Stipends, Income derived from Glebes or the sale of Glebes, Mortifications or Endowments, or such other fruits of the Benefices as are hereinbefore referred to, or are intended to be comprised and included in this present Act.

Section 2.—Before exercising the powers delegated to it under Section 1 and proceeding to make an appropriation or allocation under these or any other powers thereanent, the said Committee shall consult with the Presbytery or Presbyteries concerned with a view to endeavouring to reach agreement thereon.

Section 3.—In the event of the said Committee and the Presbytery or Presbyteries concerned failing to reach agreement on any appropriation or allocation, the said Committee shall nevertheless have power to issue its determination thereon.

Section 4.—(1) Notwithstanding the provisions of Sections 1 and 3, any Presbytery concerned or any Minister, Kirk Session, Congregational Board, Deacons' Court, or Board of Management having title and interest may, within two months of receipt by the Clerk of the Presbytery of notice of the determination of the said Committee and, subject to compliance with the Standing Orders of the General Assembly, lodge with the Clerks of Assembly a Petition to the General Assembly for review of any appropriation or allocation made by the said Committee as distributing body under the powers delegated to it; and if written notice be given to the Clerk of the Presbytery of the bounds of any such Petition the prayer of which if granted would reduce the appropriation or allocation to a vacant charge, or if the Presbytery of the bounds itself should present such a Petition, the Presbytery shall, pending disposal of the Petition, sist any proceedings towards the induction of a Minister of such charge unless the Petition should meanwhile be withdrawn.

(2) On receipt by the Clerk of Presbytery of notice of the determination of the said Committee, it shall be the duty of the Clerk of Presbytery to intimate the same forthwith to the Minister and Session Clerk of any congregation or congregations directly affected by the appropriation or allocation and also of any other congregation whose parochial area

A.D. 1953. is contiguous with the parochial area or areas of the said first-mentioned congregation or congregations.

Provided always :—

(i) that, where after any such appropriation or allocation for the period of the incumbency the Presbytery of the bounds has not timeously presented such a Petition and, in the absence of any such written notice as aforesaid, has inducted a Minister to the charge, such appropriation or allocation shall not be subject to reduction until a vacancy next occurs in the said charge ; and further

(ii) that in any circumstance review shall be competent only if the Petition therefor shall be presented to the General Assembly next occurring after such appropriation or allocation ; or, if the appropriation or allocation has been made by the said Committee within two months before such General Assembly, then only to the said General Assembly or the next succeeding General Assembly ; and, except as aforesaid, any such appropriation or allocation made by the said Committee in the exercise of the said delegated powers shall be final until a vacancy next occurs in the charge.

Section 5.—The General Assembly reserve power to amend, alter, or rescind this Act at any time, as they shall think proper.

Section 6.—The repeal of Act 1931, xli., shall not affect the operation of the said Act previous to its repeal or anything duly done or suffered under the said Act.

APPENDIX VII.—*A*.

CHURCH OF SCOTLAND TRUST ORDER CONFIRMATION ACT, 1932.

[22 & 23 GEO. 5.]

CHAPTER xxi.

An Act to confirm a Provisional Order under the Private Legislation Procedure (*Scotland*) *Act* 1899 *relating to the Church of Scotland Trust.* A.D. 1932.
[16*th June* 1932.]

WHEREAS the Provisional Order set forth in the schedule hereunto annexed has been made by one of His Majesty's Principal Secretaries of State under the provisions of the Private Legislation Procedure (Scotland) Act 1899 as read with the Secretaries of State Act 1926 and it is requisite that the said Order should be confirmed by Parliament: 62 & 63 Vict. c. 47 16 & 17 Geo. 5. c. 18.

Be it therefore enacted by the King's most Excellent Majesty by and with the advice and consent of the Lords Spiritual and Temporal and Commons in this present Parliament assembled and by the authority of the same as follows:—

1. The Provisional Order contained in the schedule hereunto annexed is hereby confirmed. Confirmation of Order in schedule.

2. This Act may be cited as the Church of Scotland Trust Order Confirmation Act 1932. Short title.

SCHEDULE.

CHURCH OF SCOTLAND TRUST.

Provisional Order to incorporate the Church of Scotland Trust to vest in the Trust certain heritable properties and investments belonging to the Church and for other purposes.

WHEREAS the Church of Scotland and the United Free Church of Scotland were by Act of Union adopted by the General Assembly of the Church of Scotland and the General Assembly of the United Free Church of Scotland met together in joint session on the second day of October one thousand nine hundred and twenty-nine united and constituted one Church under the name of "The Church of Scotland":

And whereas the heritable properties and investments pertaining or belonging to the various committees of the General Assembly of the Church of Scotland as that church existed and was constituted prior to

A.D. 1932. the second day of October one thousand nine hundred and twenty-nine were by the Church of Scotland (General Trustees) Order 1921 transferred to and vested in the Church of Scotland General Trustees incorporated by the said Order and are subject to the powers contained in the said Order and to the provisions of the Church of Scotland (Property and Endowments) Act 1925 held by the said General Trustees for the same ends uses and purposes as those for which they were held by the trustees or persons in whom they were vested or by whom they were held prior to their being transferred to the said General Trustees where these ends uses and purposes are expressed or defined and failing such expression or definition subject to the directions of the committee on whose behalf they are held or of the General Assembly of the Church of Scotland :

And whereas since the commencement of the said Order other heritable properties and investments have been acquired by the said General Trustees and are now held by and vested in them on behalf of various committees of the said General Assembly :

And whereas by virtue of the Church of Scotland (Property and Endowments) Act 1925 certain of the heritable properties and investments previously held by the said General Trustees under the said Order are now held for the purposes of the said Act of 1925 :

And whereas under and in pursuance of the said Act of 1925 there have been or will be transferred to the said General Trustees other heritable properties and investments to be held and administered by them for the purposes of that Act and for purposes set out in orders and schemes issued by the Scottish Ecclesiastical Commissioners appointed thereunder :

And whereas the greater part of the heritable properties and investments representing the funds pertaining or belonging to the United Free Church of Scotland as that Church existed and was constituted prior to the second day of October one thousand nine hundred and twenty-nine and also certain other heritable subjects belonging to the said Church are at present held by and vested in the General Trustees of the United Free Church of Scotland appointed by Act of the General Assembly of the United Free Church of Scotland dated the thirty-first day of October one thousand nine hundred and subsequent Acts of the said Assembly as such General Trustees or in some of them as individuals :

And whereas by Act of the General Assembly of the United Free Church of Scotland dated the first day of October one thousand nine hundred and twenty-nine it was enacted and declared in contemplation of the union between the Church of Scotland and the United Free Church of Scotland that the General Trustees of the United Free Church of Scotland should continue to act as such trustees and also as a body of General Trustees for the united Church after the union (meaning thereby the Church of Scotland as constituted by the said union) for the purposes of administering receiving and transferring to the General Trustees to be created or incorporated by Act of Parliament or otherwise appointed for the said united Church when and so soon as they should be so created or incorporated or otherwise appointed any property or funds which might be in or might come into the hands of the said General Trustees of the United Free Church of Scotland or into their hands as a body of General Trustees for the said united Church but that always as a body of trustees separate from the Church of Scotland General Trustees until the said new body of trustees to be created or incorporated or otherwise appointed as aforesaid should be so created incorporated or otherwise appointed and be in a position to act as such trustees: A.D. 1932.

And whereas by Act of Assembly of the Church of Scotland as reconstituted after the union of the Church of Scotland with the United Free Church of Scotland dated the second day of October one thousand nine hundred and twenty-nine the General Assembly of the Church of Scotland ratified confirmed and approved of the said Act of the General Assembly of the United Free Church of Scotland dated the first day of October one thousand nine hundred and twenty-nine and confirmed and adopted the appointment or continuance of the General Trustees of the United Free Church of Scotland as formerly constituted made or continued by and under the said last mentioned Act of Assembly and the whole terms and provisions thereof in all respects:

And whereas certain of the remaining heritable properties and investments representing the funds of the United Free Church of Scotland as formerly constituted are at present held by and are vested in the United Free Church of Scotland Trust incorporated under the Companies Acts 1908 to 1917 on the eighteenth day of February one thousand nine hundred and twenty-seven:

And whereas certain funds belonging to the Church of Scotland or to the United Free Church of Scotland as formerly constituted and now to the united Church have been invested in heritable properties and investments the titles to which have been taken in the names of different persons or sets of persons either as trustees or as individuals all hereinafter referred to as " the individual trustees ":

And whereas it is desirable and expedient that—

(1) the whole heritable properties and investments at present held by or vested in the Church of Scotland General Trustees under the provisions of the Church of Scotland (General Trustees) Order 1921 (so far as these do not fall under the provisions of the Church of Scotland (Property and Endowments) Act 1925) as these are set out in Part I. of the Schedule to this Order;

(2) the whole heritable properties and investments at present held by or vested in the General Trustees of the United Free Church of Scotland as these are set out in Part II. of the said schedule;

(3) the whole heritable properties and investments at present held by or vested in the United Free Church of Scotland Trust as these also are set out in Part II. of the said schedule; and

(4) the whole heritable properties and investments at present held by or vested in the individual trustees as these are set out in Part III. of the said schedule;

should be held by a single body of trustees for the Church of Scotland:

And whereas having regard to the statutory duties and responsibilities imposed upon the Church of Scotland General Trustees by the Church of Scotland (Property and Endowments) Act 1925 it is expedient to transfer to them the heritable properties and investments set forth in Parts II. and III. of the said schedule:

And whereas in the circumstances above recited it is expedient that the heritable properties and investments set forth in the said schedule should be transferred to a new body of trustees constituted and incorporated for that purpose as in this Order provided:

And whereas the purposes aforesaid cannot be effected without an

A.D. 1932. Order confirmed by Parliament under the provisions of the Private Legislation Procedure (Scotland) Act 1899:

Now therefore in pursuance of the powers contained in the said last-mentioned Act as read with the Secretaries of State Act 1926 the Secretary of State orders as follows:—

Short title. 1. This Order may be cited for all purposes as the Church of Scotland Trust Order 1932.

Commencement. 2. This Order shall come into operation at the date of the passing of the Act confirming the same which date is herein referred to as "the commencement of this Order."

Interpretation. 3. In this Order the following words and expressions have the meanings hereby assigned to them respectively unless there be something in the subject or context repugnant to such construction:—

"The Church" means the Church of Scotland as constituted by the union of the Church of Scotland and the United Free Church of Scotland on the second day of October one thousand nine hundred and twenty-nine;

"The General Assembly" means the General Assembly of the Church;

"The Commission" means the Commission of the General Assembly appointed to meet from time to time between the closing of one General Assembly and the meeting of the next General Assembly;

"The General Trustees" mean the Church of Scotland General Trustees incorporated by the Church of Scotland (General Trustees) Order 1921 and also acting under the provisions of the Church of Scotland (Property and Endowments) Act 1925;

"The United Free Church General Trustees" mean the General Trustees of the United Free Church of Scotland as acting prior to the union between the Church of Scotland and the United Free Church of Scotland on the second day of October one thousand nine hundred and twenty-nine and continuing in office after that date for the purposes in that behalf mentioned in this Order;

"The United Free Church of Scotland Trust" means the United Free Church of Scotland Trust incorporated under the Companies Acts 1908 to 1917 on the eighteenth day of February one thousand nine hundred and twenty-seven;

"The Trust" means the Church of Scotland Trust incorporated by this Order;

"Individual trustees" mean and include all persons or sets of persons in whom funds invested in heritable properties or investments belonging to the Church of Scotland or to the United Free Church of Scotland as these churches were constituted prior to the second day of October one thousand nine hundred and twenty-nine or to any committee association fund or scheme of the said churches and now to the united Church or to any committee association fund or scheme thereof are vested either in their individual names or as trustees but do not include the General Trustees the United Free Church General Trustees or the United Free Church of Scotland Trust or any local trustees holding for particular congregations any churches manses halls or other ecclesiastical properties or local trustees holding any investments for behoof of particular congregations;

"Heritable properties" mean lands houses buildings feu-duties ground annuals ground rents tack duties bonds of relief and dispositions in security bonds and dispositions in security which are heritable in their nature securities constituted by *ex facie* absolute dispositions long leases and other heritable rights or real property of whatsoever nature whether situated in Scotland or England or elsewhere ; A.D. 1932.

" Investments " mean personal or moveable property of any nature whatever and wheresoever situated not included in the term " heritable properties " ;

" The general treasurer of the Church " includes any interim general treasurer ;

" Treasurer " includes interim treasurer and " secretary and clerk " includes interim secretary and clerk ;

" Committee " means a committee of the General Assembly.

4. Subject to the provisions of this Order the following thirty-eight ministers and elders of the Church viz. :— Incorporation.

The Reverend James Taylor Cox D.D.
William Whitelaw LL.D.
General Sir Charles Fergusson Bart K.C.B.
The Very Reverend James Harvey D.D.
Francis Archibald Brown Douglas advocate.
John Archibald Roxburgh.
Sir Ralph William Anstruther Bart.
Honourable Lord Sands D.D. LL.D.
Daniel Macfarlane Inglis.
Robert Walker Wallace W.S.
Henry Moubray Cadell D.L.
Frederick Lewis Maitland Moir.
The Very Reverend Charles Laing Warr D.D.
David Meiklereid.
Colonel Norman MacLeod C.M.G. D.S.O.
The Very Reverend Robert James Drummond D.D.
Sheriff Robert Low Orr K.C.
John Parker Watson W.S.
The Very Reverend John White D.D. LL.D.
Sir Malcolm Smith K.B.E.
William Cockburn Laing Stark S.S.C.
The Very Reverend Andrew Nisbet Bogle D.D.
Hugh Barnett.
Hugh Reid Buchanan S.S.C.
The Reverend James Hutchison Cockburn B.D.
James Macfarlane LL.D.
Archibald Brown Campbell W.S.
The Reverend Andrew Kerr Walton M.A.
William Galbraith W.S.
George William Service.
Steuart Bayley Hog.
Archibald Campbell Black K.C.
James Brown Adshead.
Thomas Miller.
Robert Edwin Boyd.
Andrew Wallace Cowan.
Sheriff John Lean Wark K.C.
James Caldwell Scott S.S.C.

and the survivors and survivor of them and their and his successors in office and any additional members to be nominated and appointed as hereinafter provided (all hereinafter referred to as " the members of the Trust ") shall be and are hereby incorporated by the name of " The

A.D. 1932.

Church of Scotland Trust" and by that name shall be a body corporate with perpetual succession and a common seal and may sue and be sued and may purchase acquire hold sell teu let or otherwise dispose of lands and other property heritable and moveable and borrow on the security thereof and shall have all the other privileges of a body corporate.

Qualification of members of Trust.

5. Each of the members of the Trust shall be either a minister or an elder of the Church and in the event of any person who is a member of the Trust ceasing to be a minister or elder of the Church he shall thereupon cease to be a member of the Trust.

Retirement of members of Trust.

6. Six members of the Trust other than the chairman and vice-chairman shall retire annually from the membership of the Trust on the thirty-first day of May in each year but shall be eligible for reappointment by the General Assembly as hereinafter provided. Provided that the order in which the members named in the section of this Order of which the marginal note is "Incorporation" shall retire shall be the order in which their respective names appear in the said section and that the order in which any other members of the Trust to be hereafter appointed shall retire shall be the order in which after the date of their respective appointments as members of the Trust they are entered on the roll of trustees.

Appointment and removal of members of Trust.

7.—(1) The Trust shall report to the General Assembly all vacancies in the membership of the Trust.

(2) The General Assembly shall have power to remove any member from the office of member of the Trust.

(3) The General Assembly shall annually nominate and appoint or reappoint six persons to be members of the Trust in room and place of the six members of the Trust who retire in terms of this Order. The General Assembly shall also have the power to nominate and appoint persons to be members of the Trust in place of members of the Trust who have died resigned or become disqualified or been removed from office and likewise at any time to appoint persons to be additional members beyond the number specified in the section of this Order of which the marginal note is "Incorporation."

Appointment of chairman, &c.

8.—(1) From among the members of the Trust the General Assembly or the Commission shall have power to appoint a chairman and vice-chairman of the Trust with or without remuneration for a period of five years from the date of such appointment in each case and subject to such conditions as the General Assembly or the Commission shall determine and the General Assembly or the Commission shall have power to renew or extend such appointments or either of them for any period not exceeding five years.

(2) In the event of a vacancy occurring in the office of chairman or vice-chairman whether by expiry of the term of appointment or otherwise the General Assembly or the Commission shall have power to appoint a new chairman or vice-chairman as the case may be subject to such conditions as the General Assembly or the Commission shall determine.

(3) In the event of a vacancy occurring in the office of chairman or vice-chairman and pending such appointment by the General Assembly or the Commission the members of the Trust may elect an interim chairman or vice-chairman as the case may be.

Transfer to Trust of heritable properties and investments.

9.—(1) Each of the heritable properties and investments detailed and set forth in—

(i) Part I. of the schedule to this Order and presently vested in or held by the body of trustees or persons named in the said Part of the said schedule for behoof of the committee association or body or for the purpose also named or set forth in the said Part of the said schedule; A.D. 1932.

(ii) Part II. of the said schedule and presently vested in or held by the body of trustees trust or persons named in the said Part of the said schedule for behoof of the body or for the purpose also named or set forth in the said Part of the said schedule; and

(iii) Part III. of the said schedule and presently vested in or held by the individual trustees or persons named in the said Part of the said schedule for behoof of the body or for the purpose also named or set forth in the said Part of the said schedule;

and all rights obligations claims and demands relative to the whole of the heritable properties and investments set forth in the said schedule including all accrued rents income or interest and all arrears of rents income or interest shall by virtue of this Order *ipso facto* and without the necessity of any disposition assignation conveyance or transfer other than this Order be deemed and taken to be validly transferred to and vested in the Trust to the same effect as if particular dispositions assignations conveyances or transfers of the same (as the case may be) had been granted in favour of the Trust and where necessary had been recorded in the appropriate division of the general register of sasines or burgh register of sasines and this Order shall be and be deemed to be a valid title thereto and shall not be challengeable or open to objection on the ground that any of the said heritable properties or investments are inaccurately or insufficiently or erroneously described in the said schedule so long as such properties or investments were in truth vested in or held by the General Trustees the United Free Church General Trustees the United Free Church of Scotland Trust or individual trustees or other persons whomsoever for behoof of such committee association or body or for the purpose or purposes before referred to as the case may be.

(2) Without prejudice to the immediately preceding subsection and for the purpose of enabling the Trust if thought fit to complete a title to any of the heritable properties or investments detailed and set forth in Parts I., II. and III. of the schedule to this Order or to any part thereof by expeding and recording a notarial instrument or notice of title or by obtaining or granting a conveyance assignation or transfer thereof this Order shall be deemed to be and may be used as a general disposition or assignation as the case may be of such heritable properties or investments in favour of the Trust.

(3) The production of a copy of the Act confirming this Order shall be sufficient warrant to the registrar directors or other officials of any corporation firm company or concern as well out of Scotland as in Scotland to enter the Trust upon the register thereof as proprietor or holder of the investment transferred to and vested in the Trust under this Order without the production of any particular assignation conveyance or transfer thereof and to grant and issue to the Trust a certificate or other writing as evidence of the title of the Trust to such investment. Provided that in the case of any investment which is only transferable in a particular manner prescribed by or under Act of Parliament or by or under the constitution or rules of any particular corporation firm company or concern such investment shall be transferred to and vested in the Trust in the prescribed manner.

A.D. 1932.

Heritable properties and investments transferred to and vested in the Trust to be held for same purposes as held by trustees trust bodies or persons from whom transferred.

10. The heritable properties and investments transferred to and vested in the Trust under the section of this Order of which the marginal note is "Transfer to Trust of heritable properties and investments" shall be held by the Trust for the same ends uses and purposes as those for which they were held by the General Trustees the United Free Church General Trustees the United Free Church of Scotland Trust or any individual trustees or persons as the case may be in whom they were vested or by whom they were held prior to their being transferred to the Trust where such ends uses and purposes are expressed or defined and failing such expression or definition subject to the directions both as to the management realisation or disposal of capital and as to the application of income of the committee association fund or scheme on whose behalf they were so held or of the General Assembly and wherever in the trust deed fund or scheme under which such heritable properties and investments were held at the first day of October one thousand nine hundred and twenty-nine the words "United Free Church of Scotland" "Free Church of Scotland" or "United Presbyterian Church" occur there shall be substituted the words "Church of Scotland."

Trustees trust and persons in whom heritable properties and investments vested discharged of their actings.

11. The bodies of trustees trust or individual trustees or persons in whom the heritable properties and investments detailed and set forth in Parts I., II. and III. of the schedule annexed to this Order were vested or by whom they were held before being transferred to and vested in the Trust are hereby so soon as they are respectively divested of the said heritable properties and investments absolutely finally and for ever exonerated and discharged of their actings intromissions and management and of all omissions if any in relation to the said heritable properties and investments.

Treasurer of Trust.

12.—(1) The general treasurer of the Church shall *ex officio* be the treasurer of the Trust. In the event of a vacancy in the office of general treasurer of the Church the Trust shall appoint an interim treasurer of the Trust to fill the vacancy who shall vacate office immediately on a general treasurer of the Church being appointed.

(2) The Trust shall have power to grant all powers of attorney mandates or other authorities necessary for the collection and distribution of the rents of or the income and interest upon the heritable properties and investments transferred to and vested in the Trust.

Secretary and clerk of Trust.

13. The Trust shall appoint a secretary and clerk who shall keep minutes of all meetings of the Trust and also a record of all deeds and documents to which the seal of the Trust has been adhibited.

Meetings of Trust.

14.—(1) The secretary and clerk of the Trust whom failing the treasurer of the Trust shall call all meetings of the Trust and shall also call a meeting of the Trust upon being requested in writing to do so by not less than five members of the Trust.

(2) Not less than five days' notice shall be given for a meeting of the Trust.

(3) At all meetings of the Trust five of the members of the Trust shall be a quorum and any meeting at which a quorum is present shall be competent to exercise all or any of the authorities powers and discretions exercisable by the Trust.

(4) In the absence of the chairman and vice-chairman from any meeting of the Trust the meeting shall appoint its own chairman.

(5) The chairman presiding at any meeting of the Trust shall in the event of an equality of votes have a casting vote in addition to his deliberative vote.

Trust may hold heritable properties and investments belonging to any committee, &c

15.—(1) Without prejudice to the operation of the section of this Order of which the marginal note is "Transfer to Trust of heritable properties and investments" the Trust may accept from and hold on behalf of any committee association trustees or body of persons connected with the Church or with any congregation kirk session deacons' court committee of management or congregational board or other ecclesiastical body or organisation of the Church or the minister of any congregation of the Church as such minister any funds heritable properties or investments which such committee association trustees or body of persons congregation kirk session deacons' court committee of management congregational board or other ecclesiastical body or organisation or minister may desire to transfer to them.

A.D. 1932.

(2) The said funds heritable properties or investments upon being accepted by the Trust shall be held by the Trust subject to the directions of the committee association trustees or body of persons congregation kirk session deacons' court committee of management congregational board or other ecclesiastical body or organisation or minister on whose behalf they are held or failing such directions then subject to the directions of the General Assembly.[1]

Trust may receive gifts, bequests, &c. on behalf of Church.

16. In the event of the Church the General Assembly or any committee association fund or scheme of the Church being or becoming entitled to any gift legacy or bequest or to payment of any capital sum or to payment of the income of any capital sum annuity or annual payment it shall be competent for the Trust to receive such gift legacy or bequest or such capital sum or such income annuity or annual payment on behalf of the Church or of the General Assembly or of such committee association fund or scheme as the case may be and by the hand of the treasurer to grant a receipt discharge or other writing therefor and a receipt discharge or other writing so granted in favour of any person or persons paying or transferring to the Trust any such gift legacy or bequest or making payment of such capital sum or of such income annuity or annual payment shall be a full and complete discharge to such person or persons and such person or persons shall have no concern with the application of such gift legacy or bequest or capital sum or of such income annuity or annual payment.

Trust entitled to sue for and recover property or funds, &c.

17. The Trust shall without prejudice to the right and title of the General Trustees as regards any property or funds now vested or hereafter becoming vested in them be entitled on behalf of the Church or of the General Assembly or of any committee association fund or scheme of the Church to sue for and recover all property or funds to which the Church or the General Assembly or such committee association fund or scheme as the case may be may be entitled and also to enforce compromise settle or refer to arbitration all or any claims relating to such property or funds at the instance of or against the Church or the General Assembly or any committee association fund or scheme of the Church.

Trust may hold property acquired by Church.

18. Without prejudice to anything hereinbefore in this Order contained where any heritable properties investments or funds are hereafter acquired by or on behalf of the Church the General Assembly or any committee association fund or scheme of the Church whether by purchase bequest donation or otherwise (other than any properties or endowments to which the Church of Scotland (Property and Endowments) Act 1925 applies) such heritable properties investments or funds may be held by the Trust for behoof of the Church the General

[1] The General Assembly of 1960 adopted Byelaws and Regulations to be observed by the Trust in accepting investments belonging to any Committee, &c. The Trust, if it see cause, is empowered to decline to accept any such investment. (See Article 7, p. 551, and Article 12, p. 554.)

A.D. 1932.

Assembly or such committee association fund or scheme as the case may be.

Trustees to be entitled to transfer to Trust property or funds held for behoof of Church, &c.

19.—(1) Where any trustee or body of trustees shall hold any property or funds for behoof of the Church or of any committee association fund or scheme thereof or for behoof of any of the ministers thereof by way of augmentation of stipend or for behoof of any parishes ecclesiastical districts churches or congregations by way of or towards the maintenance improvement or repair of any ecclesiastical buildings belonging or attached to such parishes districts churches or congregations under any deeds of trust gift or appointment whether granted *inter vivos* or *mortis causa* and the trustee or body of trustees acting for the time under any such deed of trust gift or appointment shall desire to be relieved of the trust thereby constituted or created it shall be competent for such trustee or body of trustees unless expressly prohibited by the terms of such deed of trust gift or appointment to denude themselves or himself of such trust and to pay or transfer and convey the whole property or funds held thereunder to and in favour of the Trust or to and in favour of the General Trustees to be held by the Trust or by the General Trustees as the case may be for the same ends uses and purposes as such property or funds was or were held prior to the date of such payment or transfer and conveyance.

(2) Upon such payment or transfer and conveyance as aforesaid being completed the trustee or body of trustees making the same shall be fully exonerated released and discharged of the trust constituted or created by such deed of trust gift or appointment as aforesaid by any receipt discharge release or other writing to be granted by the Trust or by the General Trustees (as the case may be) under their hand and seal to and in favour of such trustees or trustee in respect of any sum or sums so paid over or of any property or funds paid transferred and conveyed by them or him as aforesaid.

Trust to come in place of United Free Church General Trustees in trust deeds, &c.

20. In all trusts created under any trust deeds dated prior to the second day of October one thousand nine hundred and twenty-nine and in all schemes of administration of legacies bequests or funds or of bursaries scholarships or other educational endowments settled prior to that date where the United Free Church General Trustees are mentioned or referred to as the donees of or as the body charged with the administration of any heritable property trust property legacies bequests or funds or of any bursaries scholarships or other educational endowments the Trust shall on the commencement of this Order be substituted for and take the place of the United Free Church General Trustees and shall in relation thereto have all the powers responsibilities and duties of the United Free Church General Trustees.

Seal of Trust and execution of deeds.

21. The seal of the Trust shall be kept in the office of the secretary and clerk of the Trust and shall not be affixed to any deed or document of whatever nature the same may be unless such deed or document shall have been signed by one member of the Trust and in addition by the secretary and clerk of the Trust or by the treasurer of the Trust and all deeds whether relating to heritable or moveable property or of whatever other nature the same may be shall be valid and effectual if signed by one member of the Trust and by the secretary and clerk or the treasurer of the Trust and sealed with the seal of the Trust and such execution on behalf of the Trust shall be equally binding and effectual whether attested by witnesses or not and it shall not be necessary that such execution should take place at a meeting of the Trust.

Cheques &c. how endorsed.

22. All cheques dividend warrants interest warrants and other like documents in favour of the Trust shall be validly endorsed if so endorsed on behalf of the Trust by the treasurer of the Trust or by the secretary and clerk of the Trust or by the chairman or vice-chairman thereof all for the time being.

Powers of investment.

23.[1] The Trust may invest the whole or any part of the funds belonging to or held by the Trust from time to time in or upon all or any of the following investments securities and obligations (namely) :—

(1) Investments in which trustees are authorised to invest trust funds according to the law of Scotland or the law of England for the time being :

(2) On the security of heritable or real property in Scotland or England :

(3) In the purchase of heritable or real or leasehold property in any part of the world to be used for any purpose in connection with the carrying out of the purposes and objects of the Church or of any committee association mission or organisation thereof or in any way connected therewith :

(4) In or upon the public stocks or funds or Government securities of the United Kingdom of Great Britain and Northern Ireland or any part of His Majesty's dominions or of the territories under His protection or the United States of America :

(5) In or upon the deposit receipts bonds debentures debenture stock mortgages or securities of any corporation company or body whether municipal railway public-utility commercial industrial investment trust mortgage insurance banking or otherwise registered or incorporated in the United Kingdom of Great Britain and Northern Ireland or any part of His Majesty's dominions or of the territories under His protection or the United States of America or in or upon the guaranteed lien preference or preferred or ordinary or deferred or common stocks or shares of any such corporation company or body or upon any securities whatsoever issued or guaranteed by any such corporation company or body and in the case of banks and insurance companies whether or not there is liability for calls or other payments :

Provided that the Trust may retain and hold any heritable properties or investments which may be transferred to the Trust under any of the provisions of this Order notwithstanding that such properties or investments may not be of the nature authorised by any of the provisions of this section.

Titles certificates &c. to be taken in name of Trust.

24. The titles certificates and all other documents of title to all heritable properties and investments transferred or which may hereafter be transferred to or which may be acquired or held by the Trust under this Order as well as the titles certificates and all other documents of title to all heritable properties and investments in which the Trust may invest funds under the powers contained in this Order shall be taken in the name of the Trust unless in any cases where it shall be necessary in accordance with the laws of any British dominion colony or dependency or the Empire of India or any of the states thereof or of any foreign country or state to take such titles certificates or other documents of title in another form.

[1] Substituted for original section 23 by section 3 of Church of Scotland Trust (Amendment) Order Confirmation Act, 1948 (11 & 12 Geo. 6, Ch. ix.).

A.D. 1932.

Costs of management and administration.

25. The whole costs charges and expenses of executing the Trust or incidental to or arising out of the execution of the same shall form a first charge upon the income of the trust funds and estate held and administered under the provisions of this Order except in so far as the same may in the discretion of the Trust form a proper charge against any special or separate fund property or estate whether heritable or moveable forming part of such trust funds and estate or in so far as such costs charges and expenses shall be provided by the General Assembly.

Questions or disputes referred to general administration committee.

26. In the event of any question or dispute arising between the Trust and any committee association body of trustees individual trustees congregation kirk session deacons' court committee of management congregational board minister of any congregation as such minister or other person on whose behalf funds heritable properties or investments are held by the Trust the same shall be referred to the general administration committee of the General Assembly or to any special committee who may be appointed by the said last-mentioned committee or by the General Assembly or the Commission for the purpose and the decision of the general administration committee or of such special committee if and when so appointed shall be final and binding on all parties unless an appeal against such decision shall within the space of twenty-one days from the date of such decision be taken or intimated by any party or parties concerned to the then ensuing General Assembly.

Trust immune from liability

27. The Trust shall not be liable for the acts receipts neglects defaults or frauds of any member of the Trust or of any treasurer clerk law agent or other agent officer or servant of the Trust or for any loss or expense resulting through any depreciation or loss arising upon any heritable property or investment taken or held by the Trust or through the insufficiency or deficiency of title of or to any heritable property or investment.

Repeal.

28. As from the date of the commencement of this Order section 14 (Corporation may hold heritable properties and investments belonging to any committee &c.) and section 22 (Receipt of Corporation to be full exoneration to persons paying funds &c. to corporation) of the Church of Scotland (General Trustees) Order 1921 shall be and the same are hereby repealed.

Powers of General Trustees to take and hold property held for behoof of any church, &c.

29. Notwithstanding anything contained in this Order or in the Church of Scotland (General Trustees) Order 1921 and in addition to the powers thereby conferred the General Trustees may receive take and hold any property or funds vested in or held by any person or body of trustees in connection with any church chapel of ease or mission chapel manse church hall or other property belonging to or connected with the Church or vested in or held by any body committee or association connected with the Church where such person or body of trustees or such body committee or association may desire to convey transfer or make over the same to the General Trustees.

Byelaws and regulations may be made.

30. It shall be lawful for the General Assembly from time to time to make byelaws and regulations to be observed by the Trust in the discharge of its duties under this Order.

Costs of Order.

31. The costs charges and expenses of and incidental to the preparation obtaining and confirming of this Order or otherwise in relation thereto shall be paid by the general finance committee of the Church out of the general purposes fund or other funds of the Church.

APPENDIX VII.—*B*.

CHURCH OF SCOTLAND TRUST ORDER CONFIRMATION ACT, 1958.

[7 ELIZ. 2.]

CHAPTER i.

An Act to confirm a Provisional Order under the Private Legislation Procedure (*Scotland*) *Act* 1936 *relating to the Church of Scotland Trust.* [*18th December* 1958.] A.D. 1958.

WHEREAS the Provisional Order set forth in the schedule hereunto annexed has been made by the Secretary of State under the provisions of the Private Legislation Procedure (Scotland) Act 1936 and it is requisite that the said Order should be confirmed by Parliament: 26 Geo. 5. & 1 Edw. 8. c. 52.

Be it therefore enacted by the Queen's most Excellent Majesty by and with the advice and consent of the Lords Spiritual and Temporal and Commons in this present Parliament assembled and by the authority of the same as follows:—

1. The Provisional Order contained in the schedule hereunto annexed is hereby confirmed. **Confirmation of Order in schedule.**

2. This Act may be cited as the Church of Scotland Trust Order Confirmation Act 1958. **Short title.**

SCHEDULE.

CHURCH OF SCOTLAND TRUST.

Provisional Order to authorise the Church of Scotland Trust to transfer to such trusts authorities and organisations of or constituted by the Christian churches or to such other authorities in Asia Africa and the West Indies as may be approved by the said Trust certain properties held by them for the purposes of foreign missions and for other purposes.

WHEREAS the Church of Scotland Trust (hereinafter referred to as " the Trust ") was incorporated by the Church of Scotland Trust Order 1932 (hereinafter referred to as " the Order of 1932 ") and by the Order of 1932 the properties described in the schedule to the Order of 1932 were transferred to and vested in the Trust to be held by the Trust for the same ends uses and purposes as those for which they were held by the several trustees or persons by whom they were held before such transfer and the Trust was also authorised to accept and hold such other properties as any organisation or minister of any congregation of the Church of Scotland (hereinafter referred to as " the Church ") might desire to transfer to the Trust:

A.D. 1958.

And whereas the properties transferred to the Trust in pursuance of the Order of 1932 or subsequently vested in the Trust include lands churches institutions missionary residences and other properties situated in Asia Africa and the West Indies which are held by the Trust for the purposes of the foreign missions of the Church:

And whereas it is the policy of the Foreign Mission Committee of the General Assembly of the Church that the work for which they are responsible should progressively become an integral part of the life and work of the Christian churches which have been and are being established in the said continents and territories and the said policy has been approved by the General Assembly of the Church:

And whereas it is expedient that in pursuance of the said policy the Trust should be authorised to transfer by gift from time to time to such trusts authorities and organisations of or constituted by the Christian churches or to such other authorities in the said continents and territories as may be approved by the Church such of the lands churches institutions missionary residences and other properties hereinbefore referred to and such of any lands buildings or other properties which may after the confirming of this Order be vested in and held by the Trust for the purposes of foreign missions as they may think fit:

And whereas it is expedient that certain gifts of property held for the purposes of foreign missions which have been made by the Trust to the trusts authorities and organisations of or constituted by the Christian churches in the said continents and territories should be sanctioned and confirmed:

And whereas the purposes aforesaid cannot be effected without an Order confirmed by Parliament under the provisions of the Private Legislation Procedure (Scotland) Act 1936:

Now therefore in pursuance of the powers contained in the said Act the Secretary of State orders as follows:—

Short and collective titles.

1. This Order may be cited for all purposes as the Church of Scotland Trust Order 1958 and this Order and the Church of Scotland Trust Orders 1932 and 1948 may be cited together as the Church of Scotland Trust Orders 1932 to 1958.

Interpretation.

2. In this Order the following words and expressions have unless there is anything in the subject or context repugnant to such construction the meanings hereby assigned to them respectively (that is to say):—

"appropriate authority" in relation to the transfer of a foreign mission property means—

(*a*) any trust authority or other organisation in the country or territory in which that foreign mission property is situated which is legally incorporated and as to which the committee and the Trust are satisfied that it is properly constituted for the purpose of holding property on behalf of the Christian church or other Christian body with which the missionary work of the Church in such country or territory has been or is being integrated or associated; or

(*b*) a governmental or local authority;

"Church" has the same meaning as in the Order of 1932

"committee" means the Foreign Mission Committee of the General Assembly of the Church;

"foreign mission property" means any of the properties described in (*a*) Part II of the schedule to the Order of 1932 and numbered 685 to 716 inclusive and (*b*) Part III of the said schedule and numbered 725 to 727 inclusive together with any other lands churches institutions missionary residences or other properties situated in Asia Africa or the West Indies vested in the Trust after the commencement of the Order of 1932 or which may become vested in the Trust after the confirming of this Order and which are for the time being held by the Trust for the purposes of the foreign missions;

"Order of 1932" means the Church of Scotland Trust Order 1932;

"Trust" means the Church of Scotland Trust incorporated by the Order of 1932.

Powers of Trust to transfer foreign mission properties to appropriate authorities.

3.—(1) The trusts upon which foreign mission property is held by the Trust or has been held by the Trust or shall from time to time be held by the Trust and the Order of 1932 shall empower and shall be deemed always to have empowered the transfer by the Trust of foreign mission property by way of gift to an appropriate authority.

(2) A transfer of a foreign mission property under this section shall not be made unless (*a*) the committee has by minute requested the Trust to proceed with the transfer of such foreign mission property and (*b*) the committee and the Trust have been satisfied as to the standing of the appropriate authority to which the property referred to in the said minute is to be transferred.

Discharge of trustees and officials in respect of previous transfers of foreign mission property.

4. All members of the Trust and their predecessors and the treasurer and the secretary and clerk of the Trust and all other persons holding office in pursuance of the Order of 1932 and the heirs executors and representatives of any of them who have predeceased or may predecease the confirming of this Order are hereby exonerated acquitted and simpliciter discharged in relation to the trusts referred to in subsection (1) of the immediately preceding section and in relation to the provisions of the Order of 1932 of their whole actings transactions intromissions and management in any way and in whatever capacities in respect of any transfer by way of gift of foreign mission properties made by the Trust before the confirming of this Order.

Costs of Order.

5. The costs charges and expenses of and incidental to the preparation obtaining and confirming of this Order or otherwise in relation thereto shall be paid by the Trust out of the funds of the Trust held for the committee.

APPENDIX VII.—*C.*

THE CHURCH OF SCOTLAND TRUST.

Special Investment Account.

BYELAWS and REGULATIONS made by the General Assembly of the Church of Scotland on 24th May 1960 with reference to investments already held and which may be held by The Church of Scotland Trust on Special Investment Account, in exercise of powers contained in Section 30 of the Church of Scotland Trust Order Confirmation Act, 1932.

1. These Byelaws and Regulations shall operate as from 24th May 1960 and supersede the Rules and Regulations made by the General Assembly on 22nd May 1951 so far as applicable to the Special Investment Account.

2. Interpretation :—

" the Trust " means The Church of Scotland Trust.

" Church " means the Church of Scotland.

" investor " means the Church or the General Assembly of the Church or any committee, association, trustees or body of persons connected with the Church or with any congregation, kirk session, deacons' court, committee of management or congregational board or other ecclesiastical body or organisation of the Church or the minister of any congregation of the Church, as such minister.

" investment " means all or any of the investments, securities and obligations in which the Trust may invest in terms of Section 3 of the Church of Scotland Trust (Amendment) Order Confirmation Act, 1948, and includes not only stocks, shares, debentures, &c., but also feu-duties, ground annuals, and heritable, real and leasehold properties.

3. These Byelaws and Regulations shall apply to all existing investments held by the Trust on Special Investment Account for behoof of an investor as at 24th May 1960 and to all investments so held by the Trust after that date.

4. The Trust may accept from or on behalf of any investor any money held by such investor for any Church purpose which the investor desires to be separately invested on behalf of such investor. Such investment when made shall be held by the Trust on Special Investment Account and shall be separately earmarked or designated in the books of the Trust as held for behoof of such investor.

5. The Trust may also accept from or on behalf of any investor the transfer, assignation or conveyance of any existing investment which an investor desires the Trust to hold on behalf of the investor in terms of the Church of Scotland Trust Order Confirmation Acts, 1932 to 1958. Such investment shall be held by the Trust on Special Investment

Account, and shall be separately earmarked or designated in the books of the Trust as held for behoof of such investor.

6. Before any money is invested or any change of investment is made, the Trust shall consult the investor, and the consent of the investor shall be obtained in writing to the proposed investment or new investment.

7. The Trust may, if it think fit, decline to accede to the desire of an investor with regard to the investment of any money handed to the Trust to be held on Special Investment Account, in which case the money shall be returned to the investor; and the Trust may, if it think fit, decline to accept the transfer, assignation or conveyance of an investment under Article 5, or to continue to hold any existing investment, in which case such investment shall be either transferred to the investor or sold and the proceeds re-invested subject to the conditions of Article 6.

8. The Trust shall collect and pay over to each investor all or any dividends, interest or other revenue which may be received by the Trust on account of or in respect of the investment held for such investor, subject to deducting any expense which the Trust has incurred.

9. An investor may at any time withdraw from the Trust any investment held on behalf of such investor or require the Trust to realise an investment held on behalf of such investor and to pay to the investor the net proceeds of such investment, subject always to the Trust being given reasonable notice and being relieved by the investor of any expense incurred in the matter.

10. An investor by handing money to the Trust for investment to be held on Special Investment Account, or by transferring an existing investment to the Trust to be held on that Account, does not thereby cease to have responsibility for the adequacy or sufficiency of the investment made or transferred, but shall have a continuing responsibility with such investment.

11. Neither the Trust nor its members or officials shall have any responsibility for the adequacy or sufficiency of any investment held or which may be held by the Trust or otherwise in connection therewith, or for advice given or which may be given to any investor with regard to an investment. An investor shall have no claim on any reserve fund or any other fund held by the Trust.

12. Each investor shall be under obligation to relieve and indemnify the Trust and its members in respect of all obligations or liabilities attaching to the investment held by the Trust on behalf of such investor and in respect of any expenses incurred by the Trust in connection with such investment.

13. Articles 11 and 12 of these Byelaws and Regulations shall apply to all heritable, real or leasehold properties (including Churches, halls, manses, homes and other institutions, secretaries' houses, furlough houses, offices and business premises) which are or may in future be held by the Trust for behoof of investors, notwithstanding that such properties are not held on Special Investment Account.

14. Nothing in these Byelaws and Regulations shall be held to relieve the Trust of its duties and responsibilities under or by virtue of Section 19 of the Church of Scotland Trust Order Confirmation Act, 1932, notwithstanding that any property or funds which have been or may in future be transferred to the Trust under that Section are or may be held on Special Investment Account.

15. The General Assembly shall have power at any time to amend, alter, add to or revoke all or any of the foregoing Articles or to substitute new Articles in whole or in part.

In the event of the Trust proposing to recommend to the General Assembly any amendment, alteration, addition to or revocation of any Article or Articles or the substitution of new Articles, it shall be under obligation before approaching the General Assembly to consult the General Finance Committee of the General Assembly of the Church.

General Investment Fund.

Byelaws and Regulations made by the General Assembly of the Church of Scotland on 24th May 1960 and amended 23rd May 1964, with reference to the General Investment Fund of The Church of Scotland Trust, in exercise of powers contained in Section 30 of the Church of Scotland Trust Order Confirmation Act, 1932, and amended 1964, Reg. 2.

1. These Byelaws and Regulations shall operate as from 24th May 1960 and supersede the Rules and Regulations made by the General Assembly on 22nd May 1951 so far as applicable to the General Investment Account.

2. Interpretation :—

" the Trust " means The Church of Scotland Trust.

" Church " means the Church of Scotland.

" investor " means all or any of the following bodies or persons who shall be investors in the General Investment Account as at 24th May 1960, or who shall invest in the General Investment Fund thereafter, viz. : the Church or the General Assembly of the Church or any committee, association, trustees or body of persons connected with the Church or with any congregation, kirk session, deacons' court, committee of management or congregational board or other ecclesiastical body or organisation of the Church or the minister of any congregation of the Church, as such minister.

" investment " means all or any of the investments, securities and obligations in which the Trust may invest in terms of Section 3 of the Church of Scotland Trust (Amendment) Order Confirmation Act, 1948, and includes not only stocks, shares, debentures, &c., but also feu-duties, ground annuals, and heritable, real and leasehold properties.

3. As from 24th May 1960 the existing General Investment Account of the Trust shall be known as the General Investment Fund. The investments held on that date by the Trust in the General Investment Account shall be held for the General Investment Fund, and shall, together with all investments made by the Trust after that date for the General Investment Fund be regarded as made for the common behoof of the investors.

4. The Trust may accept from or on behalf of any investor any money held by such investor for any Church purpose which the investor desires to invest in the General Investment Fund.

5. The General Investment Fund shall be divided into units. Investors

in the General Investment Account as at 24th May 1960 shall be credited with one unit of the General Investment Fund in respect of each £5 which they have respectively invested in the General Investment Account and which remains invested in the Account at that date. In the case of fractions of £5 the investor shall have the option of making up the fraction to £5 or of receiving payment of the fraction in cash. Any such fractions which are not so made up or paid over shall be held for the common behoof of the investors.

6. The Trust shall prepare a Statement quarterly as at 31st March, 30th June, 30th September, and 31st December (hereinafter called "quarter dates") showing (*a*) the total number of units held by investors, and (*b*) the total market value as estimated by the Trust of the investments held for the General Investment Fund including any cash balance whether representing Capital or Income (due allowance being made for sums over-invested).

7. The price per unit at each of the quarter dates shall be determined to the nearest penny by dividing such total market value, including any cash balance as aforesaid, by such total number of units.

8. Intending investors wishing to invest money in the General Investment Fund on or after 24th May 1960 shall invest in the desired number of units at a price to be determined by the Trust in accordance with Article 7. Such investment may only be made as at one of the quarter dates, and not less than two weeks' notice shall be given prior to the quarter date of the intention to invest and of the approximate sum intended to be invested. The intending investor shall be informed of the price per unit as soon as possible after completion of the quarterly valuation made in accordance with Article 6 and shall then have the option, to be exercised forthwith, of either making the investment (in whole or in part) or intimating his or their intention not to invest. If the investor fails to exercise such option within a week of being informed of the price per unit, the Trust may decline to accept the money for investment.

9. Investors wishing to withdraw money on or after 24th May 1960 shall realise the desired number of units at a price to be determined by the Trust in accordance with Article 7. Such withdrawal may only be made as at one of the quarter dates. (See also Article 11.)

10. All income received in respect of investments held for the General Investment Fund shall, after deduction of expenses, be carried to a General Income Account. The Trust in consultation with the General Finance Committee of the Church shall have power to make such transfers as it thinks desirable out of income to the income reserve or capital reserve and similarly to make transfers to income out of income reserve. A dividend shall be declared half-yearly by the Trust in consultation with the General Finance Committee of the General Assembly of the Church out of the balance in the General Income Account after such transfers. Investors in the General Investment Fund shall participate in proportion to the number of units held at the due date of the dividend.

11. The General Investment Fund is intended for investors seeking permanent investment. In the event of an investor desiring to withdraw money in terms of Article 9 the investor may be required by the Trust to state the reasons for desiring to do so, and, depending on the reasons given, the Trust may require that such period of notice, ending on one of the quarter dates, should be given as the Trust may determine.

The period of notice, however, shall not exceed six months and shall not be less than two weeks. The investor shall be informed of the price per unit as soon as possible after completion of the valuation made in accordance with Article 6 as at the quarter date on which the withdrawal is due to be made. The investor shall then have the option, to be exercised forthwith, of either completing the withdrawal or cancelling the request therefor, in which latter case such request shall lapse. If the investor fails to exercise such option within a week of being informed of the price per unit, the Trust shall be entitled to treat the request for withdrawal as having lapsed.

12. The Trust shall also in its discretion be free to decline to accept any money offered to it for investment in units in the General Investment Fund.

13. The General Assembly shall have power at any time to authorise the winding up of the General Investment Fund. In the event of a winding up of the Fund, the whole investments and other assets of the Fund (including any balance on General Income Account) or the proceeds of sale thereof shall, less expenses of winding up, be divided among the investors in the Fund *pro rata* according to the number of units then held by the respective investors in the Fund and subject to such Byelaws and Regulations as may be made by the General Assembly for regulating the winding up of the Fund.

14. Neither the Trust nor its members or officials shall have any responsibility for the adequacy or sufficiency of the investments held or which may be held by the Trust for the General Investment Fund.

15. The General Assembly shall have power at any time to amend, alter, add to or revoke all or any of the foregoing Articles or to substitute new Articles in whole or in part.

In the event of the Trust proposing to recommend to the General Assembly any amendment, alteration, addition to or revocation of any Article or Articles or the substitution of new Articles, it shall be under obligation before approaching the General Assembly to consult the General Finance Committee of the General Assembly of the Church.

Deposit Fund.

Byelaws and Regulations made by the General Assembly of the Church of Scotland on 27th May 1967 and amended on 24th May 1969 and 27th May 1972 with reference to the Deposit Fund of The Church of Scotland Trust in exercise of powers contained in Section 30 *of the Church of Scotland Trust Order Confirmation Act,* 1932.

1. These Byelaws and Regulations shall operate as from 30th September 1967.

2. Interpretation :—

" the Trust " means The Church of Scotland Trust.

" Church " means the Church of Scotland.

" depositor " means all or any of the following bodies or persons who shall deposit money in the Deposit Fund, viz.: the Church or the General Assembly of the Church or any committee, association, trustees, or body of persons connected with the Church or with any congregation, kirk session, deacons' court, committee of management or congregational board or other ecclesiastical body or organisation of the Church or the minister of any congregation of the Church, as such minister.

"investment" means all or any of the investments in—

(*a*) the narrower range of investments as contained in Parts I and II of the First Schedule of the Trustee Investments Act, 1961;

(*b*) deposit receipts, bonds, debentures, debenture stock, mortgages or securities of any corporation, company or body whether municipal, railway, public-utility, commercial, industrial, investment trust, mortgage, insurance, banking or otherwise registered or incorporated in the United Kingdom of Great Britain and Northern Ireland.

3. As from 30th September 1967, the Trust shall create a Deposit Fund, and from that date shall have power to invest money deposited in the Fund in investments coming within the above definition.

4. The Trust may accept from or on behalf of any depositor any money held by such depositor for any Church purpose. The Trust, however, shall not have powers to accept more than a total sum of £25,000 from any one depositor, except in cases where the money is held for or on behalf of a Parish or congregation or for analogous purposes in such circumstances as shall be acceptable in the sole discretion of the Trust.

5. Deposits shall be made in multiples of £5 and the minimum deposit shall be £100. No deposit shall normally be accepted for a period of less than three months, except in cases where the money is held for or on behalf of a Parish or congregation or for analogous purposes in such circumstances as shall be acceptable in the sole discretion of the Trust.

6. The Trust shall prepare a Statement quarterly as at 31st March, 30th June, 30th September and 31st December showing (*a*) the total deposits and (*b*) the value of the investments held for the Deposit Fund, due allowance being made for any sums over or under invested.

7. Depositors wishing to withdraw sums in the Deposit Fund shall give one week's notice of their intention to withdraw.

8. All income received in respect of investments held for the Deposit Fund shall, after deduction of expenses, be carried to a Deposit Fund Income Account. The Trust in consultation with the General Finance Committee of the Church shall have power to make such transfers as it thinks desirable out of income to the income reserve or capital reserve and similarly to make transfers to income out of income reserve. A rate of interest shall be declared for each half-year to 31st March and 30th September by the Trust in consultation with the General Finance Committee of the Church out of the balance in the Deposit Fund Income Account. Interest at the rate so declared shall be remitted to depositors at 15th May and 11th November of each year.

9. The Trust shall in its discretion be free to decline any money offered to it for investment in the Deposit Fund.

10. The General Assembly shall have power at any time to authorise the winding up of the Deposit Fund, subject to such Byelaws and Regulations as may be made by the General Assembly for regulating

the winding up of the Fund. In the event of a winding up of the Fund, the whole investments and other assets of the Fund or the proceeds of sale thereof shall, less expenses of winding up, be applied *pro rata* in the repayment of deposits in the Fund with interest due thereon. Any excess remaining thereafter shall be applied as the General Assembly may determine.

11. Neither the Trust nor its members or officials shall have any responsibility for the adequacy or sufficiency of the investments held or which may be held by the Trust for the Deposit Fund.

12. The General Assembly shall have power at any time to amend, alter, add to or revoke all or any of the foregoing Articles or to substitute new Articles in whole or in part.

In the event of the Trust proposing to recommend to the General Assembly any amendment, alteration, addition to or revocation of any Article or Articles or the substitituon of new Articles, it shall be under obligation before approaching the General Assembly to consult the General Finance Committee of the Church.

APPENDIX VIII.

UNIVERSITIES (SCOTLAND) ACT, 1932.

(Amended by Universities (Scotland) Act, 1966)

[22 & 23 Geo. 5.] [1]

CHAPTER 26.

A.D. 1932.

An Act to transfer to the University Courts the right of presentation or appointment to certain chairs or professorships in the faculties of divinity or theology in the universities of Scotland; to remove restrictions as regards appointment to chairs or professorships in the said universities; to extend the powers of the University Courts of the said universities with regard to the making of ordinances, and for purposes connected therewith. [*16th June* 1932.]

Be it enacted by the King's most Excellent Majesty, by and with the advice and consent of the Lords Spiritual and Temporal, and Commons, in this present Parliament assembled, and by the authority of the same, as follows:—

Transfer of right of appointment to theological chairs in the Scottish Universities.

1. The right of presentation or appointment to any theological chair in any of the Scottish Universities which, according to the law existing immediately prior to the passing of this Act, was vested in His Majesty or in any body or person other than the University Court shall, subject to the provisions of the immediately succeeding section, be transferred to and vested in the University Court of the university to which the chair belongs.

Extension of powers of University Courts to make ordinances. 52 & 53 Vict. c. 55.

2.—(1) The powers conferred on the University Court of each of the Scottish Universities by the Universities (Scotland) Act, 1966, shall include power to make and to alter or revoke such ordinances as the University Court think fit:—

(*a*) constituting a board of nomination composed of representatives elected in equal numbers by the University Court and by or under the authority of the General Assembly or otherwise in such manner as may be agreed on by the University Court and the General Assembly, and ordaining that a vacancy in any theological chair founded prior to the passing of this Act shall be filled by the appointment by the University Court of a person nominated by the aforesaid board if such nomination is agreed to by two-thirds of the whole number of the members of the board, and is intimated to the University Court within twelve months after the occurrence of the vacancy, and that failing such intimation within the said period the University Court may

[1] *Note.*—For appointment to Theological Chairs, Boards of Nomination, etc., see pp. 278-280.

A.D. 1932.

proceed to make an appointment without further consultation with the Board of Nomination;

(*b*) Section 1 (*b*) of this Act has been superseded by the provisions of the Universities (Scotland) Act, 1966.

(*c*) altering, with the consent of the General Assembly or of any commission, board, or other body to which the General Assembly may delegate the power so to consent, the name of any chair founded in pursuance of this section, or the scope of teaching, duties, and conditions of appointment of the professor, or, with the consent of the General Assembly, abolishing such chair, provided that no such ordinance shall authorise such alteration or abolition, except on the occurrence of a vacancy, or with the consent of the holder of the chair for the time being;

(*d*) in the case of the University of St Andrews, separating the Principalship of St Mary's College in that University from the Primarius Professorship of Divinity in the said College, and making such division of the emoluments attached to the said Principalship and Professorship conjointly prior to such separation, as the University Court may think fit.

(2) Any ordinance made by the University Court of the University of Aberdeen under paragraph (*a*) of subsection (1) of this section may provide that the nomination board constituted under such ordinance may, in the case of a nomination for the Chair of Systematic Theology in the said University, follow the procedure established by the deed of erection relating to such Chair.

(3) Section (3) has been superseded by the provisions of the Universities (Scotland) Act, 1966.

(4) When an ordinance under paragraph (*d*) of subsection (1) of this section separating the principalship from the professorship therein referred to has come into operation, the right of presentation or appointment to the said principalship and to the said professorship shall be vested in the University Court, subject in the case of the professorship to the provisions of paragraph (*a*) of the said subsection (1).

(5) Nothing in the foregoing provisions of this section, or of any ordinance made thereunder, shall prejudice any rights reserved to the Free Church of Scotland by the Order entitled "Assembly Records, Libraries, &c.," and dated the twenty-ninth day of November, nineteen hundred and nine, made by the Commissioners under the Churches (Scotland) Act, 1905.

5 Edw. 7. c. 12.

Provision regarding bursaries or scholarships in United Free Church of Scotland.

45 & 46 Vict. c. 59.

3. Notwithstanding anything contained in any deed of foundation establishing bursaries or scholarships tenable by students of theology in the former United Free Church Colleges or in any scheme made or approved by the Court of Session or in any scheme under the Educational Endowments (Scotland) Act, 1882, or in any order under the Churches (Scotland) Act, 1905, regarding such bursaries or scholarships, it shall be lawful for the trustees, patrons or administrators under such deed of foundation or under such scheme or order to provide and declare by deed of declaration under their hands that such bursaries or scholarships shall be tenable by students of theology preparing for the Ministry of the Church of Scotland or of the United Free Church of Scotland (Continuing) and attending any Scottish University or a specified Scottish University and such provision and declaration shall be of the

like force and effect as if it had been contained in the deed of foundation or in such a scheme or order as aforesaid: Provided that, where by the terms of the deed of foundation or of any such scheme or order as aforesaid any such bursary or scholarship is tenable only by students attending a specified former United Free Church College, no deed of declaration under this section shall, except with the consent of the Church of Scotland given in such way as the General Assembly may appoint, provide or declare that such bursary or scholarship shall be tenable at any university other than that in the burgh in which such college is situated:

Provided also that, where any bursary or scholarship which, in pursuance of a deed of declaration under this section is tenable at a Scottish university, is awarded to a student of theology preparing for the ministry of the United Free Church of Scotland (Continuing), any period not exceeding one year during such student's tenure of the bursary or scholarship which he may spend as a student in the College of the United Free Church of Scotland (Continuing) shall, for the purposes of the said deed of declaration, be deemed to be spent at the university.

Agreements for admission of teachers of theology to university status.

4. Nothing in this Act contained shall restrict any University Court from entering into agreements with any Christian Church or Association of Christians whereby teachers of theology may be admitted to university status or privileges.

Declaration in Act of Queen Anne not to be required of principals or professors in Scottish Universities.

5. It shall not be necessary for any person who shall have been, or shall be, elected, presented or provided to the office of principal, professor, regent, master or other office in any of the universities or colleges in Scotland to make and subscribe the acknowledgment or declaration mentioned in an Act passed in the fourth session of the first Parliament held in Scotland by Her Majesty Queen Anne, intituled "Act for securing the Protestant religion and Presbyterian Church Government."

Interpretation.

6. In this Act, unless the context otherwise requires:—

"General Assembly" means the General Assembly of the Church of Scotland;

"Theological chair" means the chair of any professor who for the time being is included as a professor in the faculty of theology or divinity in any of the Scottish Universities;

"Former United Free Church College" means a college which, prior to the Union of the United Free Church and the Church of Scotland on the second day of October, nineteen hundred and twenty-nine, belonged to and was administered by the United Free Church of Scotland or which was associated with that church, and which since that date has belonged to and been administered by the Church of Scotland or has been associated with that church;

and other expressions shall have the like meaning as in the Universities (Scotland) Acts, 1858 to 1922.

Extent, short title and repeal.

7.—(1) This Act shall extend to Scotland only and may be cited as the Universities (Scotland) Act, 1932, and the Universities (Scotland) Acts, 1858 to 1922, and this Act may be cited together as the Universities (Scotland) Acts, 1858 to 1932.

(2) [Repealed by Statute Law Revision Act, 1950.]

(For the application of the Amendments authorised in the following Act reference may be had to the text of the 1954 Act which is printed at length as Appendix IX in the Fifth Edition of this Volume.)

APPENDIX IX.

CHURCHES AND UNIVERSITIES (SCOTLAND) WIDOWS' AND ORPHANS' FUND (AMENDMENT) ORDER CONFIRMATION ACT, 1967.

A.D. 1967.

1967 CHAPTER xv.

An Act to confirm a Provisional Order under the Private Legislation Procedure (Scotland) Act, 1936, relating to the Churches and Universities (Scotland) Widows' and Orphans' Fund (Amendment).

[14th July 1967.]

WHEREAS the Provisional Order set forth in the schedule hereunto annexed has been made by the Secretary of State under the provisions of the Private Legislation Procedure (Scotland) Act, 1936, and it is requisite that the said Order should be confirmed by Parliament: (1936 c. 52.)

Be it therefore enacted by the Queen's most Excellent Majesty, by and with the advice and consent of the Lords Spiritual and Temporal, and Commons, in this present Parliament assembled, and by the authority of the same, as follows:—

Confirmation of Order in schedule.

1. The Provisional Order contained in the schedule hereunto annexed is hereby confirmed.

Short title.

2. This Act may be cited as the Churches and Universities (Scotland) Widows' and Orphans' Fund (Amendment) Order Confirmation Act, 1967.

SCHEDULE

CHURCHES AND UNIVERSITIES (SCOTLAND) WIDOWS' AND ORPHANS' FUND (AMENDMENT)

Provisional Order to amend the provisions of the Churches and Universities (Scotland) Widows' and Orphans' Fund Order, 1954, in their application to certain professors and for other purposes.

WHEREAS by the Churches and Universities (Scotland) Widows' and Orphans' Fund Order, 1954 (hereinafter referred to as "the Order of 1954") the Trustees of the Churches and Universities (Scotland) Widows' and Orphans' Fund (hereinafter referred to as "the Trustees") were reincorporated and the Churches and Universities (Scotland) Widows' and Orphans' Fund as constituted by the Churches and Universities (Scotland) Widows' and Orphans' Fund Order, 1930 (which was repealed by the Order of 1954) was transferred to and vested in the Trustees:

And whereas provision was made by the Order of 1954 for the payment of annuities and benefits to the widows and children of ministers, professors and missionaries of the Church of Scotland and the Free Church of Scotland and of professors in the Universities of St Andrews, Glasgow, Aberdeen and Edinburgh:

A.D. 1967.

And whereas owing to changes, since the coming into operation of the Order of 1954, in the circumstances obtaining with regard to the remuneration and superannuation of professors in the said universities and in view, further, of the establishment in Scotland of additional universities (to which the provisions of the Order of 1954 do not apply) it is no longer necessary or expedient for provision to be made as heretofore for the payment of annuities and benefits to the widows and children of professors hereafter appointed to office in the said universities and it is expedient that the Order of 1954 should be amended accordingly:

And whereas in the case of professors now contributing to the said fund and whose widows and children would be entitled to the benefits thereof it is expedient that such professors should, if they so desire, be entitled to elect that the provisions of the Order of 1954 (with the benefits thereof) should cease to apply to them and that in such event the sums paid by them into the said fund should be repaid to them:

And whereas it is expedient that the Order of 1954 should be further amended as provided in this Order and that the other provisions contained in this Order should be enacted:

And whereas the purposes aforesaid cannot be effected without an Order confirmed by Parliament under the provisions of the Private Legislation Procedure (Scotland) Act, 1936: 1936 c. 52.

Now therefore in pursuance of the powers contained in the last-mentioned Act the Secretary of State orders as follows:—

Short title.

1. This Order may be cited as the Churches and Universities (Scotland) Widows' and Orphans' Fund (Amendment) Order 1967, and this Order and the Churches and Universities (Scotland) Widows' and Orphans' Fund Order, 1954, may be cited together as the Churches and Universities (Scotland) Widows' and Orphans' Fund Orders, 1954 and 1967.

Commencement of Order.

2. This Order shall come into operation on the date of the passing of the Act confirming this Order, which date is in this Order referred to as "the commencement of this Order".

Interpretation.

3. (*a*) In this Order, unless there is something in the subject or context repugnant to such construction:—

words and expressions to which meanings are assigned by the Order of 1954 shall have the same respective meanings; and

"church professor" means a minister of either of the churches holding the office of professor in the faculty of divinity in any of the universities or in any college in Scotland connected with either of the churches at the commencement of this Order or appointed to such office on or after the commencement of this Order; and

"Order of 1954" means the Churches and Universities (Scotland) Widows' and Orphans' Fund Order, 1954.

(*b*) The Order of 1954 shall be read and have effect as if, after the definition of "office" in section 3 (Interpretation) thereof, there were inserted the following definition:—

"'the Order of 1967' means the Churches and Universities (Scotland) Widows' and Orphans' Fund (Amendment) Order, 1967."

Provisions of Order of 1954 not to apply to certain professors.

4. As from the commencement of this Order the provisions of the Order of 1954 shall no longer apply with respect to persons appointed for the first time to office as professors in any of the universities (other than persons appointed as church professors) and the sections of the

A.D. 1967.

Order of 1954 of which the numbers and marginal notes are set out in column 1 of the Schedule to this Order shall have effect subject to the amendments specified in relation to those sections respectively in column 2 of the said schedule.

Certain professors to be entitled to elect to discontinue membership of the Fund.

5.—(1) As soon as may be practicable after the commencement of this Order (and in any event not later than 1st January, 1968), the Trustees shall, by notice sent by registered post or recorded delivery service, intimate to every professor to whom this section applies that he shall within six months from the receipt of such notice be entitled, on giving notice to the treasurer, to elect that the provisions of the Order of 1954 as amended by this Order shall cease to apply to him.

(2) (*a*) In any case where any professor to whom this section applies elects that the provisions of the Order of 1954 as amended by this Order shall cease to apply to him:—

(i) his widow and children shall no longer be entitled to the benefits of the Fund;

(ii) he shall be entitled to the payment to him (or in the event of his death to his executors), not later than one month from the expiry of the said period of six months, of an amount equal to the sums paid by him to the Fund from the date of his admission, less an amount equal to any income tax in respect thereof for which the Fund may be accountable.

(*b*) Any dispute as to the amount payable as aforesaid shall be determined by an arbiter to be appointed by the President of the Institute of Chartered Accountants of Scotland.

(3) In the event of any professor failing to exercise the right of election conferred on him under this section within the said period the provisions of the Order of 1954 as amended by this Order shall continue to apply to him.

(4) Every notice sent by the Trustees as aforesaid shall set out the effect of the foregoing provisions of this section.

(5) This section shall apply to every professor (other than a church professor) holding office as such at the commencement of this Order and to every professor (other than a church professor) who ceased to hold office as such before the commencement of this Order unless any such professor (not being a contributor) has, before the commencement of this Order, elected pursuant to section 25 (Discontinuance of payments) of the Order of 1954 to discontinue to make to the Fund the payments specified in the Order of 1954.

Savings for rights of widows and children of deceased professors.

6. Nothing in this Order shall affect the rights of the widow or children of any professor to whom the immediately preceding section of this Order applies who died before the commencement of this Order or who shall die after the commencement of this Order unless such professor shall die during the period of six months referred to in the said section and shall, in any such case, before his death have elected, pursuant to the provisions of the preceding section, that the provisions of the Order of 1954 as amended by this Order shall cease to apply to him.

Constitution of Trustees may be altered by the Secretary of State.

7.—(1) In the event of the Trustees being of opinion that it is no longer expedient that four professors of any of the universities appointed by the University Court of the University of Edinburgh pursuant to section 8 (Rotation of trustees) of the Order of 1954 should be trustees in accordance with the provisions of section 4 (Reincorporation of trustees) of the Order of 1954 they may so represent to the Secretary of State and the Secretary of State may, on such representations being made and as may appear to him expedient, by order alter the constitution of the Trustees by reducing the number of professors who are to be Trustees or by providing that the membership of the Trustees shall no longer include professors appointed as aforesaid and any such order may make all such amendments and adaptations of the Order of 1954 and of this Order as seem to him necessary in consequence of such alteration of the constitution of the Trustees.

(2) The power to make orders conferred on the Secretary of State by this section shall be exercisable by statutory instrument and no such order shall be made unless a draft thereof has been laid before Parliament and has been approved by resolution of each House of Parliament.

(3) Any such order may be amended or revoked by a subsequent order made in like manner and subject to the like conditions.

Amendment of section 3 of Order of 1954.

8. Section 3 (Interpretation) of the Order of 1954 as amended by this Order shall be read and have effect as if in the definition of " charge " or " benefice " for the words from " and in the case of " to the end there were substituted the words " In the case of :—

(*a*) ministers, 'charge' shall include an appointment held by a minister which has been or shall hereafter be declared by the General Assembly of the Church of Scotland or of the Free Church of Scotland as the case may be to be the equivalent of a 'charge' for the purposes of this Order ;

(*b*) chaplains, 'charge' means a commission to Her Majesty's regular forces ;

(*c*) missionaries, 'charge' shall include an appointment held by a missionary in a definite area or country without parochial limitation."

Amendment of section 22 of Order of 1954.

9. Section 22 (Annual payments to Fund in respect of ministers, professors and missionaries) of the Order of 1954 as amended by this Order shall be read and have effect as if in subsection (1) (iv) at the end of paragraph (*b*) the word " and " were omitted and the following paragraph were added :—

" (*bb*) by every minister who shall hold an appointment which has been declared by the general assembly of either of the Churches to be the equivalent of a 'charge' unless or until he receives payment from the fund for the maintenance of the ministry or the sustentation fund as the case may be ; and ".

Amendment of section 23 of Order of 1954.

10. Section 23 (Provisions as to annual payments) of the Order of 1954 shall be read and have effect as if in subsection (2) for the words " and (*b*) " there were substituted the words " (*b*) and (*bb*) " and there were inserted after the word " ministry " the words " or the sustentation fund as the case may be ".

Amendment of sections 25 and 29 of Order of 1954.

11.—(1) Section 25 (Discontinuance of payments) of the Order of 1954 shall be read and have effect as if—

(*a*) the following paragraph were substituted for paragraph (*a*) thereof :—

" (*a*) a minister professor or missionary who ceases to receive any payment (other than a retirement allowance or

A.D. 1967.

retirement pension) from any of the funds specified in the said section ; or "

and as if the words " (other than as aforesaid) " were inserted after the words " before he ceased to receive any payment " occurring therein ; and

(*b*) at the end of paragraph (*c*) the word " or " were added and after paragraph (*c*) the following paragraph were added :—

" (*d*) a minister ceasing to hold an appointment declared by the General Assembly of either of the Churches to be the equivalent of a ' charge ' for the purposes of this Order."

and as if after the words " or before he ceased to hold an office " there were inserted the words " or before he ceased to hold an appointment ".

(2) Section 29 (Entry money and marriage tax) of the Order of 1954 as amended by this Order shall be read and have effect as if the words " (other than of a retirement allowance or retirement pension) " were inserted after the words " to be entitled to payment " occurring in the proviso to sub-paragraph (ii) of paragraph (*a*) of subsection (2) thereof.

Further amendment of section 29 of Order of 1954.

12. Section 29 (Entry money and marriage tax) of the Order of 1954, as amended by this Order, shall be read and have effect as if :—

(*a*) in subsection (1) after paragraph (*d*) (ii) the following paragraph were added :—

" (iiA) by every minister who after the commencement of this Order shall hold an appointment which has been declared by the General Assembly of either of the Churches to be the equivalent of a ' charge ' for the purposes of this Order and who is not receiving payment from the fund for the maintenance of the ministry or the sustentation fund as the case may be " ; and

(*b*) the following subsection were added thereto :—

" (4) The Trustees may, if they think fit, from time to time increase or reduce the sums payable under the foregoing provisions of this section in respect of entry money and marriage tax or either of them and may vary as they think fit the manner of and dates for payment thereof in the case of ministers, professors to whom the said section 29 as amended by the Order of 1967 applies and missionaries first admitted after a date to be determined by the Trustees when resolving on any such increase or reduction."

Amendment of section 27 of Order of 1954.

13. Section 27 (Payments to Fund in respect of vacant charges) of the Order of 1954 shall be read and have effect as if the said section were subsection (1) thereof and as if :—

(*a*) at the end of the provisos to the said subsection the following proviso were added—

" (iv) that payment as for a vacant charge shall not be made on the death, translation, resignation or deprivation of any minister holding an appointment which has been declared by the General Assembly of the Church of Scotland or of the Free Church of Scotland as the case may be to be the equivalent of a ' charge ' for the purposes of this Order " ; and (*b*) the following subsection were inserted at the end thereof :— A.D. 1967.

" (2) For the purposes of this section 'annual sum' shall not in any case where the Trustees under the provisions of section 31 (Commutation of payments) of this Order have allowed or shall allow any minister, professor or missionary to commute the ordinary annual payments for which provision is made in this Order by the payment of increased annual payments to cease on his attaining a specified age, be construed as meaning such increased annual payments."

Amendment of section 37 of Order of 1954.

14. Section 37 (Payment of expenses and provisions for widows and children) of the Order of 1954 as amended by this Order shall be read and have effect as if in subsection (1) after paragraph (*c*) (iv) the following sub-paragraph were added :—

" (iva) every minister hereafter holding an appointment which has been declared by the General Assembly of either of the Churches to be the equivalent of a 'charge' for the purposes of this Order ".

Costs of Order.

15. All costs, charges and expenses preliminary to and of and incidental to the preparing for, obtaining and confirming of this Order or otherwise in relation thereto shall be paid out of the Fund.

SCHEDULE

AMENDMENTS OF ORDER OF 1954

(1) Section	(2) Amendments
3 Interpretation . .	The words " but shall not include any professor who has elected pursuant to section 5 (Certain professors to be entitled to elect to discontinue membership of the Fund) of the Order of 1967 that the provisions of this Order shall not apply to him ; " shall be inserted at the end of the definition of " contributor ".
6 Existing fund transferred to Trustees	The words " and of the Order of 1967 " shall be inserted at the end of the section.
15 Returns to be made to treasurer	At the beginning " (1) " shall be inserted and at the end the following subsection shall be inserted :— " (2) Paragraph (*a*) and sub-paragraph (i) of paragraph (*b*) of the preceding subsection shall not apply to the appointment of any professor (other than a church professor) for the first time after the commencement of the Order of 1967 and the provisions of the said paragraph (*a*) relative to the translation,

A.D. 1967.

(1) Section	(2) Amendments
	resignation, deprivation or death of professors and of sub-paragraph (ii) of the said paragraph (*b*) relative to the making of annual returns shall not apply to professors who have elected pursuant to section 5 (Certain professors to be entitled to elect to discontinue membership of the Fund) of the Order of 1967 that the provisions of this Order as amended by the Order of 1967 shall cease to apply to them."
22 Annual payments to Fund in respect of ministers professors and missionaries	For paragraph (v) of subsection (1) there shall be substituted the following :— " (v) by every professor who at the commencement of this Order has been or is thereafter appointed to an office not being (*a*) a professor admitted to a share of the college funds, (*b*) a professor who has pursuant to section 5 (Certain professors to be entitled to elect to discontinue membership of the Fund) of the Order of 1967 elected that the provisions of this Order as amended by the Order of 1967 shall cease to apply to him or (*c*) a professor (other than a church professor) appointed for the first time after the commencement of the Order of 1967."
29 Entry money and marriage tax	After paragraph (*e*) of subsection (3) the following paragraph shall be inserted :— " (*f*) any professor (other than a church professor) appointed for the first time after the commencement of the Order of 1967 or any professor who has elected pursuant to section 5 (Certain professors to be entitled to elect to discontinue membership of the Fund) thereof that the provisions of this Order as amended by the Order of 1967 shall cease to apply to him."
37 Payment of expenses and provisions for widows and children	(*a*) The words " except in any case where a contributor, being a professor, has elected pursuant to section 5 (Certain professors to be entitled to elect to discontinue membership of the Fund) of the Order of 1967 that the provisions of this Order as amended by

(1) Section	(2) Amendments
	the Order of 1967 shall cease to apply to him." shall be added at the end of paragraph (*a*) of subsection (1).
	(*b*) The words " or (not being a contributor) elected in pursuance of section 25 (Discontinuance of payments) of this Order to discontinue making to the Fund payment of the annual sum referred to in the said section or elected, pursuant to section 5 (Certain professors to be entitled to elect to discontinue membership of the Fund) of the Order of 1967, that the provisions of this Order as amended by the Order of 1967 shall cease to apply to him." shall be added at the end of the proviso to paragraph (*c*) of subsection (1).

APPENDIX X.

PREAMBLE, QUESTIONS, AND FORMULA TO BE USED FOR ADMISSION TO OFFICE IN THE CHURCH.

SECTION I. PREAMBLE AND QUESTIONS.

1. Preamble and Questions for Use at Ordination and Induction of a Minister (Oct. 1929, i.).

Preamble.

The Narrative shall be read and, the Ordinand or Minister to be inducted having taken his place before the Presbytery, the Moderator shall declare as follows :—

In the name of the Lord Jesus Christ, the King and Head of the Church, Who, being ascended on high, hath given gifts unto men for the edifying of the body of Christ, we are met here as a Presbytery [to ordain A. B. to the office of the Holy Ministry by prayer and the laying on of hands by the Presbyters to whom it doth belong and] [1] to induct him into the pastoral charge of...........

In this act of ordination [2] the Church of Scotland, as part of the Holy Catholic or Universal Church worshipping One God—Father, Son, and Holy Spirit—affirms anew its belief in the Gospel of the sovereign grace and love of God, wherein through Jesus Christ, His only Son, our Lord, Incarnate, Crucified, and Risen, He freely offers to all men, upon repentance and faith, the forgiveness of sins, renewal by the Holy Spirit, and eternal life, and calls them to labour in the fellowship of faith for the advancement of the Kingdom of God throughout the world.

The Church of Scotland acknowledges the Word of God which is contained in the Scriptures of the Old and New Testaments to be the supreme rule of faith and life.

The Church of Scotland holds as its subordinate standard the Westminster Confession of Faith, recognising liberty of opinion on such points of doctrine as do not enter into the substance of the Faith, and claiming the right, in dependence on the promised guidance of the Holy Spirit, to formulate, interpret, or modify its subordinate standards : always in agreement with the Word of God and the fundamental doctrines of the Christian Faith contained in the said Confession—of which agreement the Church itself shall be sole judge.

[1] The words in brackets to be omitted if there be no ordination.
[2] Or induction.

Then the Moderator, addressing the Ordinand or Minister to be inducted, who is to stand and make answer to the questions put to him, shall say :—

A. B., in view of this Declaration, you are now required to answer these questions :—

QUESTIONS TO BE PUT TO MINISTERS BEFORE THEIR ORDINATION OR ADMISSION TO A CHARGE.

1. Do you believe in one God—Father, Son, and Holy Spirit; and do you confess anew the Lord Jesus Christ as your Saviour and Lord?

2. Do you believe the Word of God, which is contained in the Scriptures of the Old and New Testaments, to be the supreme rule of faith and life?

3. Do you believe the fundamental doctrines of the Christian faith contained in the Confession of Faith of this Church?

4. Do you acknowledge the Presbyterian Government of this Church to be agreeable to the Word of God; and do you promise to be subject in the Lord to this Presbytery and to the superior Courts of the Church, and to take your due part in the administration of its affairs?

5. Do you promise to seek the unity and peace of this Church; to uphold the doctrine, worship, government, and discipline thereof; and to cherish a spirit of brotherhood towards all the followers of the Lord?

6. Are not zeal for the glory of God, love to the Lord Jesus Christ, and a desire for the salvation of men, so far as you know your own heart, your great motives and chief inducements to enter into the office of the Holy Ministry? [1]

7. Do you engage in the strength of the Lord Jesus Christ to live a godly and circumspect life; and faithfully, diligently, and cheerfully to discharge the duties of your ministry, seeking in all things the advancement of the Kingdom of God?

8. Do you accept and close with the call to be Pastor of this charge, and promise through grace to study to approve yourself a faithful Minister of the Gospel among this people? [2]

The questions having been answered to the satisfaction of the Presbytery, and the Formula having been signed, the Ordinand shall kneel, and the Moderator, by prayer with laying on of hands, in which all the Ministers present join, shall ordain him to the office of the Holy Ministry.

Thereafter the Moderator, except in cases in which there is no induction to a pastoral charge or any office, shall add these words :—

[I now declare you to have been ordained to the office of the Holy Ministry, and] [3] in the name of the Lord Jesus Christ, the King and Head of the Church, and by authority of this Presbytery, I induct you to this charge; and in token thereof we give you the right hand of fellowship.

[1] The words "to enter into the office of the Holy Ministry" are to be altered to read "to enter into this Ministry" in cases where the person about to be Inducted has already been Ordained to the Holy Ministry (1943, 8).

[2] Question 8 and the question to the congregation are to be omitted when there is no induction to a pastoral charge—*e.g.*, in the case of a Presbytery ordaining an assistant or admitting one who has been received by the General Assembly with the status of a minister, or in the case of ordination as a Foreign Missionary. For Church Professor or Principal, see p. 570.

[3] The words in brackets to be omitted if there be no ordination.

The following question shall then be addressed to the congregation, who are asked to signify assent by rising and standing in their places :—[1]

Do you, the members and adherents of this congregation, in receiving N. N., whom you have called to be your Minister,[2] promise him all due honour and support in the Lord; and in view of the pastoral and missionary obligations of this congregation, do you each now agree to share with your Minister the responsibility for Christian witness and Christian service, and will you give of your means, as the Lord shall prosper you, for the maintenance of the Christian Ministry and the furtherance of the Gospel? (1958, xi.).

Will you signify your assent by standing?

QUESTION (8) TO PRINCIPAL OR CHURCH PROFESSOR.

" In accepting this call and appointment to hold office in the Church of Scotland as a teacher in Theology or as the Principal or Master of   College, do you engage yourself as a minister of the Lord Jesus Christ, and as God by His Holy Spirit shall enable you, to maintain the truth of His Gospel, and in loyalty to the doctrine of this Church faithfully to train the students entrusted to your care for the office of the Holy Ministry and the edifying of the Body of Christ?"

II. REGULATIONS FOR SERVICE OF INTRODUCTION OF A CHAPLAIN TO DUTIES WITH HER MAJESTY'S FORCES (1962, REG. 10).

1. A Service of Introduction shall be held when a Minister becomes a Chaplain in Her Majesty's Forces.

2. At this Service questions 1 to 7 in the ordinary Induction Service shall be put to the Minister with the addition of the following questions:—

" Do you promise through grace to study to approve yourself a faithful Minister of the Gospel in the Office of Chaplain in Her Majesty's Forces serving in the Royal Navy (or the Army or the Royal Air Force), to which you have been called and appointed?"

3. When a Probationer is to be commissioned as Chaplain he shall be Ordained and the Form and Order for the Ordination of a Minister shall be used, with the substitution of the above question for question number 8.

4. The Service of Introduction shall be carried out by the Presbytery of Edinburgh or other appropriate Presbytery.

III. ADMISSION TO PRESBYTERY.

In the case of a Service of Introduction or Admission to Membership of a Presbytery otherwise than by Induction, the following question is asked :—

" Do you declare your adherence to the vows which you took at your ordination?"

The Formula must then be signed (1961, xxiv.).

[1] Question 8 and the question to the congregation are to be omitted when there is no induction to a pastoral charge—*e.g.*, in the case of a Presbytery ordaining an assistant or admitting one who has been received by the General Assembly with the status of a minister, or in the case of ordination as a Foreign Missionary.

[2] In the case of the Introduction of a minister the words " whom you have called to be your Minister " are deleted and the words " who has now been introduced as Minister without charge " substituted

IV. Service of Linking (1958, Reg. 9).

Narrative and Questions to be used at Service of Linking of Two Congregations under the Minister of one of them.

The General Assembly approve the following Narrative and Questions to be used at Service of Linking of Two Congregations under the Minister of one of them :—

Questions, etc., at Linking Service.

Narrative.

Consequent upon the Resolution of the Presbytery of .... to link the Parish of .... to the Parish of .... as from .... under the ministry of Mr A. B. we are met as a Presbytery to instal Mr A. B. to this additional sphere of pastoral service on which he now enters.

To the Minister : Mr A. B.

In view of the added responsibility which this linking lays upon you, you are required to answer the following questions :—

Do you promise through grace to study to approve yourself a faithful Minister of the Gospel among this people of the Parish of .... as you have already so promised to do among the people of the Parish of .... ?

Moderator.

In the Name of the Lord Jesus Christ and by authority of this Presbytery I now declare you to be Minister of the Parish of .... in addition to the Parish of .... now linked as one charge.

To the Congregation.

Brethren of the Congregation for as much as this solemn act involves obligations on your part, I put to you the appointed question :—

Do you, the members and adherents of this Congregation, in receiving A. B. as your Minister, promise him all due honour and support in the Lord ; and in view of the pastoral and missionary obligations of this Congregation, do you each now agree to share with your Minister the responsibility for Christian witness and Christian service, and will you give of your means, as the Lord shall prosper you, for the maintenance of the Christian Ministry and the furtherance of the Gospel ?

V. Preamble and Questions for use at the Licensing of Probationers (1932, xi.).

Preamble.

The Candidates for Licence having taken their places before the Presbytery, the Moderator shall declare as follows :—

In the name of the Lord Jesus Christ, the King and Head of the Church, Who, being ascended on high, hath given gifts unto men for the edifying of the body of Christ, we are met here as a Presbytery to license M. (*and* N.) as preachers of the Gospel, and probationers for the Holy Ministry.

In this act the Church of Scotland, as part of the Holy Catholic or Universal Church worshipping One God—Father, Son, and Holy Spirit—affirms anew its belief in the Gospel of the sovereign grace and love of God, wherein through Jesus Christ, His only Son, our Lord, Incarnate,

Crucified, and Risen, He freely offers to all men, upon repentance and faith, the forgiveness of sins, renewal by the Holy Spirit, and eternal life, and calls them to labour in the fellowship of faith for the advancement of the Kingdom of God throughout the world.

The Church of Scotland acknowledges the Word of God, which is contained in the Scriptures of the Old and New Testaments, to be the supreme rule of faith and life.

The Church of Scotland holds as its subordinate standard the Westminster Confession of Faith, recognising liberty of opinion on such points of doctrine as do not enter into the substance of the Faith, and claiming the right, in dependence on the promised guidance of the Holy Spirit, to formulate, interpret, or modify its subordinate standards: always in agreement with the Word of God and the fundamental doctrines of the Christian Faith contained in the said Confession—of which agreement the Church itself shall be sole judge.

Then the Moderator, addressing the Candidate or Candidates, who are to stand and make answer to the questions put to them, shall say :—

In view of this Declaration, you are now required to answer these questions :—

1. Do you believe in One God—Father, Son, and Holy Spirit; and do you confess anew the Lord Jesus Christ as your Saviour and Lord?
2. Do you believe the Word of God, which is contained in the Scriptures of the Old and New Testaments, to be the supreme rule of faith and life?
3. Do you believe the fundamental doctrines of the Christian faith contained in the Confession of Faith of this Church?
4. Do you acknowledge the Presbyterian government of this Church to be agreeable to the Word of God; and do you promise to be subject in the Lord to this Presbytery, or any Presbytery within whose bounds you may reside, and to the superior Courts of the Church?
5. Do you promise to seek the unity and peace of this Church; to uphold the doctrine, worship, government and discipline thereof; and to cherish a spirit of brotherhood towards all the followers of the Lord?
6. Are not zeal for the glory of God, love to the Lord Jesus Christ, and a desire for the salvation of men, so far as you know your own heart, your great motives and chief inducements to enter into the office of the Holy Ministry?
7. Do you engage in the strength of the Lord Jesus Christ to live a godly and circumspect life; and faithfully, diligently, and cheerfully to discharge the duties of your ministry, seeking in all things the advancement of the Kingdom of God?

The questions having been answered to the satisfaction of the Presbytery, and the Formula having been signed, the Moderator shall engage in prayer.

Thereafter the Moderator shall say :—

In the name of the Lord Jesus Christ, the King and Head of the Church, and by authority of this Presbytery, we do now license you to preach the Gospel of the grace of God, and to exercise your gifts as a Probationer (*or* Probationers) for the Holy Ministry.

VI. Preamble and Question for use at Ordination and Admission of Elders (1932, x.).

Preamble.

The narrative shall be read and, the Elders-elect having taken their places before the Session, the Moderator shall declare as follows :—

In the name of the Lord Jesus Christ, the King and Head of the Church, Who, being ascended on high, hath given gifts unto men for the edifying of the body of Christ, we are met here as a Kirk Session to ordain A, B, C, D, &c., to the Eldership, and to admit E, F, G, H, &c., into that office in this congregation.

In this act of ordination [1] the Church of Scotland, as part of the Holy Catholic or Universal Church worshipping one God—Father, Son, and Holy Spirit—affirms anew its belief in the Gospel of the sovereign grace and love of God, wherein through Jesus Christ, His only Son, our Lord, Incarnate, Crucified, and Risen, He freely offers to all men, upon repentance and faith, the forgiveness of sins, renewal of the Holy Spirit and eternal life, and calls them to labour in the fellowship of faith for the advancement of the Kingdom of God throughout the world.

The Church of Scotland acknowledges the Word of God, which is contained in the Scriptures of the Old and New Testaments, to be the supreme rule of faith and life.

The Church of Scotland holds as its subordinate standard the Westminster Confession of Faith, recognising liberty of opinion on such points of doctrine as do not enter into the substance of the Faith, and claiming the right, in dependence on the promised guidance of the Holy Spirit, to formulate, interpret, or modify its subordinate standards: always in agreement with the Word of God and the fundamental doctrines of the Christian Faith contained in the said Confession—of which agreement the Church itself shall be sole judge.

Then the Moderator, addressing the Elders-elect, who are to stand and make answer to the question put to them, shall say :—

In view of this Declaration you are now required to answer this question :—

Do you believe the fundamental doctrines of the Christian Faith; do you promise to seek the unity and peace of this Church; to uphold the doctrine, worship, government, and discipline thereof; and to take your due part in the administration of its affairs?

The question having been answered to the satisfaction of the Session, and the Formula having been signed by the Elders-elect, the Moderator, by prayer, shall ordain them to the office of the Eldership.

Thereafter the Moderator shall add these words :—

[I now declare you to have been ordained to the office of the Eldership, and] [2] in the name of the Lord Jesus Christ, the King and Head of the Church, I admit you to office in this congregation. In token thereof we give you the right hand of fellowship.

[1] And/or admission.
[2] To be omitted where there is no ordination.

VII. Preamble and Question for use at Ordination and Admission of Deacons (1932, x.).

When Deacons are appointed for life the same Preamble and Question are used as in the case of Elders with the exception that the word "Diaconate" is used in the Declaration in place of the word "Eldership."

VIII. Questions for use at the Admission of Readers (1974, xxviii).

Presbyteries shall admit candidates to the office of Reader upon satisfactory answers being given to the following questions :—

(i) Do you believe in one God—Father, Son and Holy Spirit ; and do you confess the Lord Jesus Christ as your Lord and Saviour ?

(ii) Do you believe the Word of God, which is contained in the Scriptures of the Old and New Testaments, to be the supreme rule of faith and life ?

(iii) Do you believe the fundamental doctrines of the Christian Faith contained in the Confession of Faith of this Church ?

(iv) Do you acknowledge the Presbyterian government of this Church to be agreeable to the Word of God ; and do you promise to be subject to this Presbytery, or to any other Presbytery within whose bounds you may reside, and to the superior Courts of the Church ?

(v) Do you promise to seek the unity and peace of this Church, to uphold the doctrine, worship, government, and discipline thereof, and to cherish a spirit of brotherhood towards all the followers of the Lord ?

(vi) Are not zeal for the glory of God, love to the Lord Jesus Christ, and a desire for the salvation of men, so far as you know your own heart, your great motives and chief inducements to enter into the office of Reader ?

(vii) Do you engage in the strength of the Lord Jesus Christ to live a godly and circumspect life ; and faithfully, diligently, and cheerfully to discharge the duties of Reader, seeking in all things the advancement of the Kingdom of God ?

SECTION II. FORMULA.

(Oct. 1929, i. ; 1932, ix., x., xi. ; 1933, xiii.).

(To be signed by all who are admitted to any office in the Church.)

I believe the fundamental doctrines of the Christian Faith contained in the Confession of Faith of this Church.

I acknowledge the Presbyterian government of this Church to be agreeable to the Word of God, and promise that I will submit thereto and concur therewith.

I promise to observe the order of worship and the administration of all public ordinances as the same are or may be allowed in this Church.

SECTION III. PROCEDURE IN THE ADMISSION OF LICENTIATES AND MINISTERS FROM OTHER CHURCHES.

When Petitions are received from Ministers and Licentiates from other Churches for admission to the Ministry of the Church of Scotland by the General Assembly through the Committee on Admission of Ministers of Other Churches (for Regulations, see Chap. XI., p. 234), should the General Assembly see fit to grant the crave of the Petition the formal act of reception does not take place in the General Assembly. The General Assembly remit this either to the Presbytery in which the Petitioner resides, or to the Presbytery of Edinburgh if he has no fixed residence in Scotland.

The Minute of Assembly is as follows :—

> "The General Assembly grant the crave of the Petition, and remit to the Presbytery of   to take the necessary steps for the admission of the Petitioner to the status of a Licentiate (or Minister) of the Church of Scotland."

An Extract Minute is supplied to the Petitioner and it is his duty to make application to the Presbytery concerned, presenting the Extract Minute. This he must do within six months after the Assembly, otherwise it becomes void.

Before admission the Presbytery must satisfy itself as to the knowledge of those admitted regarding the practice and procedure of the Church as contained in 'Practice and Procedure in the Church of Scotland,' Chapters I.-X. (1946, 9).

In the case of those admitted from other Churches by the General Assembly to the status of Licentiates, the Act of Licensing should not be repeated.

The usual questions should be put, the Formula signed, and the Moderator should declare as follows :—

> "Inasmuch as the General Assembly have received you as a Licentiate, and you have signed the Formula, in the name of the Lord Jesus Christ, the King and Head of the Church, we do now admit you to the status of a Licentiate of the Church of Scotland."

The Minute of Presbytery should be in such terms as follow :—

> "There was submitted extract minute of the General Assembly of date   , the tenor whereof follows :
>
> After the usual questions were put to Mr   to which explicit and satisfactory answers were given, and after he had signed the Formula, as required by the General Assembly, the said Mr   was admitted to the status of a Licentiate of the Church in accordance with the instructions of the General Assembly."

In the event of candidates being licensed at the same time, care must be taken to make a distinction.

The Declaration on the part of the Moderator should, in such a case, be as follows :—

> "In the name of the Lord Jesus Christ, the King and Head of the Church, and by authority of this Presbytery, we do now license you, A. B., C. D., &c., to preach the Gospel of the Grace of God and to exercise your gifts as a Probationer (or Probationers) for the Holy Ministry and inasmuch as the General Assembly have received you, E. F., as a Licentiate and you have signed the Formula, we do now admit you to the status of a Licentiate of the Church of Scotland."

In the case of a Petitioner who is received as a Minister, the same procedure is followed, except that the word "Minister" is substituted for "Licentiate" both in the Declaration of the Moderator and the Minute of Presbytery.

APPENDIX XI.

GUIDE TO THE PROCEDURE FOR THE ELECTION, SETTLEMENT, AND TRANSLATION OF MINISTERS (1932, ix.; 1948, ix.; 1957, xvii.; 1960, xxiii.; 1961, xxii.).

(For Regulations see p. 242 ff.; for Schedules see p. 813 ff.)

The following Synopsis [1] of the Duties of those concerned in the Election, Settlement and Translation of Ministers has been prepared by the General Administration Committee, and is issued for the guidance of Presbyteries, Kirk Sessions and others.

A.—Duties of Presbytery.

1. Appoint Interim Moderator together with three Assessors with whom the Interim Moderator must consult with regard to filling the Vacancy. The Interim Moderator shall be instructed to declare the Vacancy. (Reg. 1. Sch. A.) (1948, ix., 1960, xxiii., 1961, xxi.)

2. Decide if question of union or readjustment of agencies arises. (Reg. 2.)

If it be decided that the question of union or readjustment be considered, procedure shall be sisted and thereafter regulated in accordance with the Memorandum prepared by the General Assembly's Committee on Union of Congregations and Readjustment of Agencies, which may be obtained from the Secretaries of that Committee (see pp. 244 and 751).

3. Intimate Vacancy to the Committee on Probationers and Transference of Ministers. (Reg. 2.)

4. Consider financial arrangements, when submitted by the office-bearers of the vacant charge, and transmit Schedule to the Maintenance of the Ministry Committee. (Reg. 3.)

5. Attest Electoral Register. (Reg. 7.)

6. If no election take place within six months from the date at which the Presbytery and the Union of Congregations Committee are agreed that no question of readjustment should be raised, intimate to the vacant congregation that, if no election takes place within the next three months, the Presbytery may take steps to fill the vacancy. (Reg. 4.)

7. If no election take place within the time specified above, and no petition for an extension of time be granted, proceed to make an appointment *tanquam jure devoluto*. (Regs. 4 and 21. Appendix VI.)

8. Judge Appointment and Call. (Regs. 19 and 20.) No election can be sustained till the Presbytery and the Committee on the Maintenance of the Ministry have each approved the financial arrangements.

[1] The references are to 1932, ix., except where otherwise stated.

9. Fix date of ordination, if a Probationer; of induction, if a Minister without charge; or prosecute the Call before his Presbytery, if a Minister in a charge. (Regs. 22 and 23.)

10. Proceed to Ordination or Induction. (Reg. 25.)

11. A copy of the Deliverance of the Committee on the Maintenance of the Ministry on the financial arrangements shall be given to the newly inducted Minister.

B.—DUTIES OF THE INTERIM MODERATOR OF KIRK SESSION.[1]

1. If appointed before the actual vacancy, call meeting and proceed as allowed by 1960, xxiii.

2. Arrange for declaration of vacancy. (Reg. 1. Sch. A.)

3. Arrange for supply of vacant pulpit in consultation with Kirk Session and Congregational Committee. (Reg. 1.)

4. Supply the place of a stated Minister in so far as is compatible with his duty to his own congregation.

5. Make an inventory of all church property in the custody of the former Minister in terms of 1931, xiv.

6. Call a meeting of Kirk Session to make up Electoral Register unless the Presbytery has sisted procedure. (Regs. 5 and 6. Sch. A. 2 and B.)

7. Cause intimation to be made of the Register having been made up, and of meeting of Session for final adjustment. (Reg. 7. Sch. C., 1.)

8. Cause intimation to be made on the two Sundays preceding the meeting, that a meeting of the congregation will be held to appoint a Congregational Committee, and to determine the mode of electing a Minister. (Reg. 8. Sch. C., 2.)

The Exhortation to Vacant Congregations (Appendix II.) should be read on one of the Sundays on which the meeting is intimated.

9. Preside at meeting above-mentioned, and follow procedure outlined in Reg. 8.

10. Summon first meeting of Congregational Committee, preside thereat till a Convener be appointed; give such help and guidance as may be required; act as Convener, if the Committee so determine. (Reg. 9.)

11. Receive notice of Committee's recommendations. (Reg. 11. Sch. D.)

12. Provide those so recommended by the Congregational Committee with a copy of the Constitution of the Congregation if such Constitution be of a special nature or peculiar to the congregation itself.

13. Consult with Assessors regarding those recommended by the Congregational Committee.

14. Appoint meeting for election, intimate accordingly and preside thereat, if the congregation has decided that the mode of election be by open vote. (Reg. 12. Sch. G.) (1956, xvii.)

or,

Make arrangements for the election by ballot vote, in consultation with the Kirk Session; intimate accordingly; preside at the election; and thereafter count votes in presence of the Session. (Regs. 13, 14, 16.

[1] The Interim Moderator should impress upon the Kirk Session and Financial Board the necessity of maintaining in full operation the arrangements for ingathering the offerings of the people for the Mission and Service Fund, and keeping manse garden and grounds in good order during the vacancy.

Sch. E. or F. and 1956, xvii.) (See 1961, xxii., in cases of Linking, &c., p. 758.)

15. Declare result of election. (Regs. 12 and 16. Sch. I.)

16. In the event of nominees withdrawing, or of failure to nominate, or failure to elect, follow procedure set forth in Regs. 15 and 17. Sch. I. and J.

17. Appoint Deputy or Assistants, where deemed needful. (Reg. 18.)

18. Make arrangements for signing Call, Mandates, &c., in conjunction with the Kirk Session, due intimation thereof to be given. (Regs. 12 and 16. Sch. K., M., N., O.)

19. Transmit Documents to the Clerk of Presbytery. (Reg. 19.)

20. Ascertain from Presbytery Clerk when the Appointment and Call will be dealt with by the Presbytery, and intimate accordingly to the vacant congregation on the Sunday preceding Presbytery meeting. (Reg. 19. Sch. K.)

C.—Duties of the Kirk Session.

1. Make up Electoral Register, decide on claims of those who apply to be put on same and transmit the Register or a certified copy thereof to the Clerk of Presbytery for attestation. (Regs. 5, 6 and 7.)

2. Arrange for Pulpit Supply under the direction of the Interim Moderator and in conjunction with the Congregational Committee. (Reg. 1.)

3. See that an adequate contribution is promised to the Fund for the Maintenance of the Ministry. (Reg. 3.)

4. Provide Voting Papers and other necessary material, if the Election be by Ballot Vote. (Reg. 14.)

5. Arrange, in conjunction with the Interim Moderator, for opportunities for signing Call, &c.; attest signatures, and transmit Call to the Clerk of Presbytery. (Regs. 12 and 16.)

D.—Duties of Deacons' Court, Congregational Board, or Committee of Management.

1. Fill up Schedule stating what contribution is promised for Stipend of Minister, or to the Maintenance of the Ministry Fund. (Reg. 3.) This Schedule must be approved by both Presbytery and the Maintenance of the Ministry Committee before the appointment can be sustained.

E.—Duties of Congregational Committee.

1. Appoint Convener and Clerk. (Reg. 9.)

2. Follow any of the methods indicated in Reg. 9.

3. Note: (*a*) time limit for election of Minister (Reg. 4); (*b*) Regulations of Probationers and Transference of Ministers Committee (Reg. 9); (*c*) classes of persons eligible for election (Reg. 10); (*d*) procedure to be followed, if nominees withdraw, or if there be failure to nominate or elect. (Regs. 15 and 17.)

4. Intimate nomination or nominations to the Interim Moderator. (Reg. 11. Sch. D.)

Suggestions for the Guidance of the Congregational Committee.

On the appointment of a Committee for the purpose of taking steps for the election of a Minister to a vacant charge, applications and testimonials may be sent by persons desirous of being elected to the vacancy. This in itself is probably inevitable; but there is reason to apprehend that some Committees, in making choice of those whom they have nominated to the congregation for election, have limited themselves entirely to the persons who have sent applications. This is a practice which is to be deprecated. The function with which the Committee are entrusted by the congregation is the large one of proposing a person or persons whom they regard as well fitted for the vacant charge; and it is not justified in narrowing its inquiry so as to embrace only those who have applied. It should be remembered that many who are well qualified for appointment to a vacant charge will not send applications or credentials, while, at the same time, they are willing to be nominated, if the initiative comes from the Committee. It is therefore incumbent on the Committee not to limit their selection to those only who may have sent in applications; but, while paying due attention to their claims, to institute independent inquiry also, with the view of finding out the most suitable person or persons for nomination.

While the duty of instituting inquiry in order to make a suitable nomination (whether from among those who have applied or those who have not) is one which imposes considerable labour on the Committee, it should bear in mind that it is really on its conducting this part of its work with earnestness and thoroughness that its success and the future welfare of the congregation mainly depend.

If the preliminary inquiries made by the Committee be of this careful and thorough character, it will do much to obviate an evil which has been made the subject of frequent representation to the General Assembly. The evil referred to is connected with what has been designated 'Competitive Preaching.' It is, no doubt, only right that, before being called on to take part in the election of a Minister, a congregation should have an opportunity of hearing, and forming their own opinion of, the person or persons who may be nominated. But at the same time, if this practice is carried to excess—if many persons, as is sometimes the case, be brought to officiate to the congregation with a view to the appointment—the effect cannot but be prejudicial to the spiritual tone of the congregation. Besides, it is not at all conducive to a satisfactory decision being arrived at. The congregation, during a protracted period of hearing, naturally become perplexed and divided by the multiplicity of men and gifts brought before them, and this is apt to lead to unfortunate consequences. It lies with the Committee to prevent an evil which has been so much complained of, and is of such a serious character. It should make its preliminary inquiries in such a thorough manner as to be able to confine this practice within moderate limits. If it can select *one*, whom it regards as specially well fitted for appointment to the vacant charge, and on whom the congregation as a whole is likely to unite, it should arrange for his being alone heard by the congregation. This may not always be possible; and if it be not possible, the Committee should at all events reduce its selection of persons for hearing by the congregation to a very small number, whom, after full inquiry, it considers to be the most suitable.

The observations which have now been made on the propriety of the Committee limiting the number of persons to be heard by the congregation apply equally to the number of persons to be nominated to the congregation with a view to election. It is in every way undesirable that the minute of nomination by the Committee should contain many names. This can only lead to confusion and misunderstanding. If the Committee have performed its work of preliminary investigation carefully, and have taken pains to ascertain the feelings of the congregation, it will, as a rule, have no difficulty in avoiding this evil. If it be of opinion that there is not sufficient unanimity in the congregation to justify it in confining its nomination to one name only, it should exceed that number to the smallest possible extent. In very many cases in which a single nomination is impracticable, it is known beforehand that the choice of the majority of the congregation will rest on one or other of two persons. In these circumstances the Committee should limit its nomination to them. Indeed, it were well that Committees should, in every instance where a division is inevitable, make it their aim to arrive at a selection of the two names only which in their judgment commend themselves most to the congregation. This would obviate the evils arising from the issue presented to the congregation being needlessly complicated by the proposal of a number of names.

Advisory Committee.

Congregational Committees will find it profitable to consult with the Advisory Committee appointed, as instructed by the General Assembly, by the Presbytery in connection with vacancies.

APPENDIX XII.

STANDING ORDERS, GENERAL ASSEMBLY 1975.

I. COMMISSIONS.

1. *Roll of Presbytery.* Each Presbytery Clerk shall, by 31st December of each year, transmit to the Clerks of Assembly the complete Roll of the Presbytery, that is, the number of charges (whether vacant or not), and the number of Theological Professors, Retired Ministers, and other ministers who have seats in the Presbytery. **Standing Orders.**

2. *Presbyterial Representation.* The General Administration Committee, or a Sub-Committee thereof, shall meet in January of each year for the purpose of considering the said Rolls and of ascertaining the effect, as regards representation, of any changes in Presbyteries which have occurred in the course of the previous year. The Clerks of Assembly shall immediately thereafter intimate to Presbyteries what will be their representation in the ensuing Assembly.

The decision of the General Administration Committee or Sub-Committee, so intimated to Presbyteries, shall be subject to review by the Assembly on Petition by the Presbytery concerned.

3. *Question Arising.* Should there arise between the month of February and the opening of the Assembly any question regarding representation not provided for in these Orders the General Administration Committee shall have power to dispose thereof.

4. *Furnishing of Forms.* The Clerks of Assembly shall furnish Presbytery Clerks with printed copies of the approved Form of Commission and also of the Certificate of *bona fide* Eldership to be used by Kirk Sessions according to Acts of Assembly in respect of Elders who are elected to be Commissioners to the Assembly.

5. *Transmission of Commissions.* The names, in alphabetical order, and full postal addresses of Commissioners from Presbyteries shall be transmitted by Presbytery Clerks to the Clerks of Assembly not later than 31st March in each year, so far as they have been elected by that time.

Commissions and Certificates of *bona fide* Eldership shall be transmitted by Presbytery Clerks so as to be in the hands of the Clerks of Assembly not less than one week before the opening of the Assembly.

6. *Committee on Commissions.* The Clerks of Assembly shall, on a day not later than four days previous to the opening of the Assembly, submit for examination to the Committee on Commissions, all Commissions and Certificates transmitted to them. The Committee on Commissions shall consist of the Clerks, the Procurator, and the Law Agent; and the Principal Clerk shall be Convener. The said Committee shall prepare and print a List of Commissioners.

Along with the said List shall be printed the Standing Orders of the Assembly; and a copy of this print shall be made available for each member.

The Clerks shall arrange to forward to each Commissioner, at least one week before the opening day of the Assembly, a copy of the volume of Reports and Proposed Deliverances, a Membership Card, with a book of consecutively numbered Voting Papers attached, and a copy of all Assembly Papers then available.

7. *Objections.* The Committee on Commissions shall, if called upon, or if it shall appear to it necessary or expedient so to do, hear any person whose Commission is objected to in support of his Commission, and also any person or persons who may object to such Commission.

8. *Late Commissions.* It shall be competent at any time during the sitting of the Assembly to lodge with the Clerks of Assembly Commissions and Certificates which have not previously been transmitted to them; and such Commissions shall be submitted by the Clerks to the Assembly at the first session on the day next after that on which the Commissions have been lodged, and shall be disposed of by the Assembly as may seem proper.

II. CONDUCT OF BUSINESS.

(*a*) Opening Session.

9. *Convening.* The Commissioners elected to serve in the Assembly shall convene in the Assembly Hall, on the day fixed for the meeting of the Assembly, at the usual hour and after Sermon according to the present practice, and, after prayer by the Moderator of the preceding Assembly, the List of Commissioners shall be laid on the table.

10. *Election of Moderator.* The election of a Moderator shall then be made.

11. *Her Majesty's Commission.* Her Majesty's Commission to the Lord High Commissioner may then be read and ordered to be recorded.

12. *Her Majesty's Letter.* Her Majesty's Letter to the Assembly may then be read and a Committee shall be appointed to prepare an answer thereto.

13. *Standing Orders.* The Standing Orders shall be laid on the table.

14. *Committee on Commissions.* The Report of the Committee on Commissions (S.O. 6) shall be called for, and disposed of.

15. *Order of business.* The General Administration Committee shall prepare and submit to the opening Session an Order of Business for the first and second days. At the same diet the Assembly shall appoint a Business Committee, and the Convener and Vice-Convener thereof.

(*b*) Business Committee.

16. (i) The Business Committee shall consist of forty Commissioners with the Moderator, Clerks, Procurator, and Law Agent as additional members *ex officiis*.

(ii) The General Administration Committee shall suggest names of Commissioners to form the Business Committee.

(iii) The Convener shall be nominated by the General Administration Committee at its stated meeting in February, and the nomination shall hold for a period not exceeding four years. The General Assembly shall consider this nomination and make the appointment each year at the Opening Session.

(iv) The Vice-Convener shall be appointed each year on the nomination of the General Administration Committee.

17. *First Meeting.* The Business Committee shall meet on the opening day of the Assembly at the close of the first session—approximately 4.30 p.m.—and thereafter as business may require. At its first meeting it shall consider the Draft Order of Business which shall have been prepared by the General Administration Committee for the business of the Assembly subsequent to the first and second days, and shall be wholly responsible therefor.

18. *Selection Committee.* The Business Committee shall nominate a Selection Committee whose function it shall be to select and submit to the Assembly for their approval names of persons to serve on all Special Commissions and Committees appointed during the sittings of the Assembly. Such persons need not be Commissioners.

19. *Communications.* All letters addressed to the Moderator for the purpose of being communicated to the Assembly shall, in the first instance, be laid before the Business Committee, which shall advise the Moderator as to the way of disposing of them.

20. *Permission to Speak.* All applications from Deputations for permission to address the Assembly shall be submitted to, and reported on by, the Business Committee. (See also S.O. 36, 37, and 41.)

21. *Papers through Boxes.* Requests for permission to distribute material through Members' boxes should be submitted to the General Administration Committee before the General Assembly, and requests received thereafter be submitted to the General Assembly. Any Committee concerned should be informed and supplied with copies, if available, of the material to be distributed.

(*c*) Devotional Exercises.

22. *The Lord's Supper.* The Assembly shall celebrate the Sacrament of the Lord's Supper at the commencement of the first diet of the second day of their meeting.

23. *Special Devotional Exercises.* Any proposal for a pause in the Assembly's proceedings to allow of engaging in special devotional exercises shall be made to the Assembly only through the Moderator; and, for the purpose of arranging diets of prayer and the devotional exercises of the Assembly generally, the Moderator may, at his discretion, associate with himself a few Members of Assembly to serve as a Devotional Exercises Committee.

(*d*) Miscellaneous.

24. *Minutes.* The Minutes of each day's proceedings, if available, together with the Agenda for the following day, intimations of meetings of Committees, and Notices of Motion, shall be printed from day to day as the "Daily Proceedings," and shall be made available for all Members.

The Minutes, being taken as read and full opportunity having been given for correction, shall be approved each day or as available.

It shall always be in order at the close of any particular item of business to require that the Minute thereanent be adjusted and approved.

Before the dissolution of Assembly a small Committee, appointed for the purpose, shall be authorised to approve the Minutes not already approved by the General Assembly.

25. *Quorum.* The quorum of the Assembly shall be thirty-one, of

whom not less than sixteen shall be Ministers. Any Member may at any time call the attention of the Moderator to the fact that there is not a quorum present, and if, on a count being made, it is found that such is the case, it shall be the duty of the Moderator to suspend or adjourn the session.

26. *Tellers.* The General Administration Committee shall submit for the approval of the Assembly at their first diet a proposed Panel of Tellers. (See S.O. 101.)

27. *Vacancy.* Where there is a vacancy in any of the offices of the ordinary office-bearers of the Assembly, such steps as to the Assembly may appear proper shall be taken for supplying the same.

28. *Printing of Acts.* The Committee on Commissions (S.O. 6) shall arrange for the printing of the Acts of Assembly and shall lay on the table at the forenoon diet of the second last day an Interim Report thereon, and this, having been printed in the "Daily Proceedings," shall be considered at the forenoon diet of the last day of the Assembly.

29. *Visitation of Records.* Synod Books, Minutes of Standing Committees of Assembly, and the Record of the Commission of Assembly shall be called for at the second session of the first day of the Assembly and the Assembly shall appoint a Committee for visiting the same. The Visiting Committee shall complete a schedule with the information required by the Assembly regarding each book, and this shall be returned on the Saturday, and on the second Tuesday the Report of the Committee shall be called for.

A copy of the Report, as sustained by the Assembly, and of the relevant schedules, shall be transmitted to the Synod, Assembly Committee, or Assembly Clerks as the case may be, and the said Report shall be engrossed in their respective records.

30. *Returns to Overtures.* When any Overture has been transmitted to Presbyteries by the Assembly, whether under the Barrier Act or not, the Return by each Presbytery shall be made upon the printed schedule sent to the Presbytery Clerk for the purpose, and shall be transmitted by him as soon as possible to the Clerks of Assembly, who shall submit the Returns to the Committee on Commissions (which shall also form a Committee for Classifying Returns to Overtures) to be classified and reported not later than the third day of the Assembly. It shall be the duty of the Committee to report not only the number of Presbyteries for and against an Overture, but also the numbers voting in the Presbyteries as reported in the printed schedule.

The Report of the Committee shall include the text of such Overtures as have been approved by a majority of Presbyteries.

31. *Closing of Assembly.* When the business set down for the last day of the sitting of the Assembly has been disposed of, the Assembly shall be closed by addresses by the Moderator to the Assembly and to the Lord High Commissioner, and by an address by the Lord High Commissioner to the Assembly, followed by devotional exercises, and dissolved according to the ancient practice of the Church.

III. MEMBERS NOT COMMISSIONERS.

(*a*) MEMBERS *ex officiis.*

32. These are the Moderator of the Assembly, upon his election, and his predecessor in office, the Clerks, Procurator, and Law Agent.

They have all the rights and privileges of Commissioners.

(*b*) Corresponding Members, Delegates, and Visiting Brethren—Definition.

33. *Corresponding Members.* Missionaries, Secretaries and President of the Woman's Guild as stated in Standing Order No. 34.

Delegates from other Churches. Representatives of other Churches, duly accredited by the Courts, or equivalent authority, of their Churches.

Visitors. (i) Representatives of other Churches who come to the General Assembly by special invitation from the Inter-Church Relations Committee; and (ii) as in Standing Order No. 39.

34. *Missionaries, Secretaries and President of the Woman's Guild.* (1) Missionaries at home on furlough, being Ministers or Elders ordained under the Home Formula or licentiates of the Church of Scotland ordained at a later date by a Church with which the Church of Scotland has a missionary connection through its Overseas Council, whether they be Minister or Elder of such other Church or not, who are certified by the Overseas Council or other Committee under whose auspices they have gone abroad, shall be Corresponding Members of the General Assembly.

(2) Secretaries of Standing Committees, being Ministers or Elders, and the Editor of 'Life and Work,' being a Minister or Elder, shall, in years in which they are not elected as Commissioners by a Presbytery be Corresponding Members of the General Assembly.

(3) The President of the Woman's Guild shall be a Corresponding Member of the General Assembly.

35. *Status.* Corresponding Members of Assembly shall be entitled to attend all sessions of the same and to speak on any matter before the Assembly, but shall not have the right to vote.

(*c*) Delegates.

36. *Reception.* (i) Delegates appointed by the United Reformed Church, the Presbyterian Church in Ireland, and the Presbyterian Church of Wales, shall be received and welcomed by the Moderator on the opening day of Assembly; and one Delegate from each of these Churches shall be offered an opportunity of briefly addressing the Assembly at the second session on the same day.

Conveners of Committees shall keep in view to give any of these Delegates who are conversant with a particular subject an opportunity of taking part in the subsequent business of the Assembly.

(ii) Delegates from other Churches shall be received and welcomed by the Moderator. Such of the Delegates as may be invited by the Committee on Inter-Church Relations may have an opportunity of addressing the Assembly at later Sessions.

37. *Status.* Delegates to the Assembly shall have the right to attend all sessions and to speak on all matters before the Assembly, but shall not have the right to vote.

38. *Oversight.* The officials of the Overseas Council and other Committees who may be interested in Delegates shall see that invitations to Assembly functions are procured for the Delegates, and that the Members of Assembly shall do everything in their power to make the visits of all the Delegates pleasant and profitable.

(*d*) Visitors.

39. *Status.* (i) Representatives of other Churches who come to the General Assembly by special invitation of the Inter-Church Relations

Committee; and (ii) Brethren from other Churches with Letter of Introduction from Assembly or Presbytery Clerks shall have the privilege of seats in the Assembly but without the right to speak or to vote.

(*e*) DEPUTATIONS.

40. *Reception.* Deputations from other Churches, Societies, or Public Bodies shall, on their arrival, give in their Commissions or Letters of Introduction to the Clerks of Assembly, who shall report the same to the Business Committee that arrangements may be made, if possible, for receiving them at a convenient time. Due care shall be exercised in restricting the number of such Deputations, so that the dispatch of the proper business of the Assembly be not hindered thereby.

(*f*) GUEST SPEAKERS.

41. *Procedure.* Where any Committee wishes that some person not a Member of Assembly should have an opportunity of addressing the Assembly in connection with the discussion of its Report, the Convener shall submit the name of such person for approval to the General Administration Committee before the Assembly opens, or to the Business Committee during the sittings of the Assembly, and the decision of the General Administration or Business Committee shall be final, unless the Assembly themselves shall resolve in terms of S.O. 132 hereof to dispense with the observance of Standing Orders in respect of that particular matter.

IV. COMMITTEE REPORTS.

42. *Transmission.* Reports of all Committees reporting to the Assembly shall be transmitted to the Clerks of Assembly not later than the first Monday after the third Tuesday in February each year. All such Reports shall be accompanied by the Deliverance to be proposed to the Assembly, and when the Proposed Deliverance exceeds two sections each section shall be numbered consecutively.

43. *Printing.* It shall be the duty of the Clerks to arrange for all such Reports and Proposed Deliverances to be printed in the octavo form, to be stitched together, paged, and provided with an alphabetical index for reference, and a copy to be forwarded to each Member of Assembly at least one week before the day of meeting. All Reports so distributed shall be held as read.

Each Committee shall immediately after the rising of the Assembly furnish the publisher of the Reports with the number required for circulation.

44. *Verbal Reports and Reports of Sub-Committees.* Verbal Reports shall not be received, and no Sub-Committee shall give in any Report to the Assembly.

45. *In Retentis.* Reports shall not be engrossed in the Minutes, but two copies of each printed Report, certified by one of the Clerks as being that given to the Assembly, shall be kept *in retentis*; and the Reports thus collected shall be bound up in volume to be preserved among the other Records of the Assembly.

46. *Questions and Discussion.* After the Deliverance on the Report of any Committee has been moved and seconded the Assembly, before dealing with any other motions or amendments thereon, shall have

opportunity for general discussion of the Report, and asking questions thereon, this being without prejudice to the right of members to put questions, with the leave of the Assembly, at any subsequent stage.

47. *Questions.* It shall be in order to ask questions of the Convener regarding any matter in the care of the Committee to which no reference is made in the Report, but in such cases timeous notice shall be given to the Convener.

48. *Deliverance.* The final Deliverance of the Assembly upon the Report of any Committee shall follow immediately after the consideration of that Report, except in the event of a special reason for the contrary having been approved by the Assembly and recorded in the Minutes.

49. *New Expenditure.* Not less than two days' notice shall be given to the Clerks of any Proposed Deliverance, Motion, or Amendment which would involve new expenditure. This order shall not apply to proposals which have been circulated in the volume of Reports. In all cases an estimate of the expenditure involved shall be given.

50. *Late Reports.* Reports of Committees appointed during the sittings of Assembly, if they propose any motion not already printed, shall be put into the hands of the Clerks of Assembly at least one day prior to their being considered, and printed in the "Daily Proceedings."

V. CONDUCT OF CAUSES.

(*a*) Lodging of Papers.

51. *Overtures.* All Overtures from Presbyteries and Synods passed on or before 24th April shall be sent to the Clerks of Assembly not later than that date in each year, and shall be in the form of certified extracts from the Minutes of the Court which is promoting the Overture.

Overtures from Commissioners shall be lodged with the Clerks not later than the Monday during the meeting of Assembly, unless the Assembly for special reason decide otherwise.

52. *Appeal; Dissent and Complaint; Petition.* The papers in all cases intended to be brought before the Assembly, whether Appeals or Dissents and Complaints against the judgment of inferior courts, or Petitions, should be lodged with the Clerks of Assembly not later than 24th April, and must be lodged not less than fourteen days before the opening meeting of Assembly; except in the case of judgments pronounced within sixteen days of the meeting of Assembly, in which case they shall be lodged within forty-eight hours of the judgment being pronounced.

53. *Reference.* In the case of Reference of a matter from an inferior court for the judgment of the Assembly the same limits as to time for lodging of papers in the case shall apply as in S.O. 52.

54. *Reference of Matter Previously Considered.* Where the matter of a Reference has previously been under consideration of the Assembly, the Reference shall state the date when the matter was previously before the Assembly and shall narrate the Assembly's Deliverance thereon.

(*b*) Printing of Papers.

55. It shall be the duty of the Clerks on receiving papers that are to come before the Assembly in connection with cases—Memorials, Peti-

tions, except Petitions under Act VIII. of 1940 as amended by Act XXVIII. of 1959 or any Act amending the same or Petitions under Act III. of 1968 or any Act amending the same, Applications, References, Overtures, Appeals, Dissents and Complaints, Minutes of the Judicial Commission, Extracts of Minutes of inferior courts relative thereto, Reasons of Appeal or of Complaint—to arrange to have these printed in demy octavo (8½″ by 5½″) form and stitched together, and shall be paged and provided with an alphabetical index for reference. The Printing of Petitions under said Acts shall be dispensed with unless the Clerks, after consultation with the Convener of the Committee on Law, Property Cases and Discipline, decide that printing of any particular Petition submitted in terms of said Acts is necessary.

56. *In Private.* Papers relating to business dealt with by Presbyteries or Synods in private, or which the Committee on Commissions (S.O. 6) consider should be taken in private, shall be printed separately and may be dealt with by the Assembly in private.

57. *Cost of Printing.* In cases of discipline brought before the Assembly by the Judicial Commission, by Reference from a Presbytery or Synod, or by Complaint by a minority of the Court, the expense of printing shall be borne by the General Administration Committee; in other circumstances by the Complainer or Appellant. In all other cases the expense of printing in sufficient numbers for the use of Commissioners shall be borne by the party having interest in the same or desiring a Deliverance from the Assembly.

58. *In Retentis.* Two copies of every printed paper shall be kept by the Clerks of Assembly to be bound up and retained among the Records of Assembly.

(*c*) Circulation of Papers.

59. *Date of Dispatch.* A copy of all papers transmitted to the Clerks of Assembly not later than 24th April shall be forwarded by them to each Member of Assembly at least one week before the opening day of the Assembly.

60. *Declaratory or Interim Act.* The draft of any proposed Declaratory or Interim Act, as also the draft of any Overture which it is proposed to transmit to Presbyteries in terms of the Barrier Act (other than any Overture printed and circulated in the volume of Reports), shall be printed and laid on the table of the Assembly and circulated among the Members at least one day before a Motion for the passing of such Declaratory or Interim Act, or for the transmission of such Overture to Presbyteries, is made in the Assembly.

61. *In Private.* The Clerks of Assembly shall not issue in advance to Members the papers in cases which they think require to be conducted with closed doors, until specially instructed by the Assembly so to do; but shall report such cases to the Convener of the Business Committee, for the information of his Committee, immediately after its appointment.

(*d*) Intimation to Parties.

62. *Appeal; Dissent and Complaint.* In all cases coming before the Assembly by Appeal or Dissent and Complaint it shall be the duty of the Clerks of Assembly to inform the parties on both sides as soon as possible of the time at which such case is likely to be taken by the

Assembly. Such intimation shall, unless in a specific case the Assembly determine otherwise, be regarded as sufficient notice.

The Clerks shall further be bound, on application made to them for the purpose, to supply six copies of all prints made in pursuance of the foregoing Orders to the opposite party or parties in any cause, or to his or their duly accredited Agents.

63. *Petition.* In every Petition it shall be the duty of the Petitioner to make such intimation of the Petition as may be necessary having regard to the nature of the Petition. Such intimation shall be made not more than seven days later than the time when the Petition is lodged with the Clerks of Assembly as provided in S.O. 52 above; and along with the Petition there shall be lodged a certificate signed by the Petitioner or his Agent setting forth the names of the parties to whom such intimation has been made or is to be made. The Assembly may refuse to dispose of any Petition if in their opinion sufficient intimation thereof has not been made.

(*e*) Transmission to Assembly.

64. *Committee on Commissions.* All papers lodged with the Clerks in causes of every sort in terms of the foregoing Orders shall be laid by them before the Committee on Commissions, which shall consider the same and report to the Assembly.

65. *Decision not to Transmit.* If the Committee on Commissions shall decide not to transmit to the Assembly any papers in causes duly lodged with the Clerks of Assembly it shall report the same to the Assembly at their first Session, or at the Session next after such decision, with its reasons for not transmitting the papers; and parties shall be entitled to be heard thereon at the bar of the Assembly. Intimation of a decision not to transmit papers shall be made to the parties concerned as soon as possible, and in time to allow of their being represented at the bar when the decision not to transmit is reported to the Assembly.

66. *In Private.* The Business Committee shall, in its first Report, specify any case which in its judgment requires to be conducted with closed doors, and any case which does not appear to it to be of that character although the Clerks of Assembly may have reported it as such. The Assembly shall thereupon determine, by a special Deliverance, at what stage in the proceedings the papers in such a case shall be issued to the Commissioners. In every case which the Assembly appoint to be conducted with closed doors the instruction to issue the papers shall be accompanied by a special exhortation to the Commissioners to keep them private.

67. *Proposed Legislation.* All Overtures from Presbyteries or Synods or from Commissioners which propose the introduction of new or the amendment of existing Acts (or Regulations) shall contain the precise terms of the legislation which they propose; and the Committee on Commissions shall not transmit to the Assembly any Overture which is deficient in this respect: provided always that the Clerks and Procurator shall be available to assist with the framing of such proposals.

(*f*) Hearing of Causes.

68. *Announcement.* Before parties are heard in any contentious Cause the Clerk shall read the following announcement, viz.: "The Commissioners are reminded that justice requires the pleadings at the bar

to be heard by all those who vote in the Cause, and that, in particular, no Commissioner ought to vote against either side at the bar who has not heard the pleadings on that side."

69. *Overture : When Taken.* Overtures relating to matters under the care of Committees of the Church whose Reports are on the Agenda for either of the first two days of the Assembly shall be assigned by the General Administration Committee (unless the Committee on Commissions decides not to transmit) to the place in the discussion at which they shall be introduced to the Assembly. In other cases this shall be done by the Business Committee.

70. *Overtures : Grouping.* Overtures on the same or cognate subjects shall be grouped by the General Administration or Business Committee and only one speaker shall be heard introducing each group.

71. *Overture : Introduction.* An Overture from a Presbytery may be introduced by any Member of that Presbytery, specially appointed for the purpose, at the bar ; or by any one of its Commissioners to the Assembly in his place as a Commissioner.

An Overture from a Synod may be introduced by any Member of that Synod, specially appointed for the purpose, at the bar ; or by any one of the Commissioners of a Presbytery within its bounds in his place as a Commissioner.

72. *Appeal ; Complaint ; One Appellant.* In Causes brought before the Assembly by Appeal, where there is only one appellant (or one set of appellants concurring in the same reasons of Appeal) and only one respondent (or one set of respondents concurring in the same answers to the reasons of Appeal) the case for the appellant (or set of appellants) shall be stated by himself or by his counsel, who at the same time shall submit such argument upon the case as he shall think fit. The party or counsel so stating the Appeal shall be followed by the respondent or his counsel who likewise shall submit such argument upon the case as he shall think fit. At the close of the statement for the respondent the appellant shall be entitled to be again heard, and the respondent shall also be entitled to be heard in answer to the second speech for the appellant and if, in his final answer, the respondent shall state any fact or submit any argument not adverted to in his answer to the opening statement for the appellant, the appellant shall be entitled to a reply upon the new matter introduced in the final answer for the respondent. With the exception of this right of reply, so limited, more than two speeches shall not be allowed to any party at the bar.

73. *Appeal ; Complaint ; More than One Appellant.* In such Causes as those referred to in S.O. 72 if there is more than one appellant (or set of appellants) insisting on the Appeal, or more than one respondent (or set of respondents) supporting the judgment appealed against, (*a*) on different grounds, or (*b*) in separate reasons or answers, each appellant shall be entitled to open and state his separate case, and each respondent shall be entitled to make his separate answer, and the debate shall be closed with a reply for the several appellants. Provided always that it shall be competent to the parties, with consent of the Assembly, to make any arrangement for conducting the debate other than herein prescribed, if it shall have the effect of limiting, further than is herein done, the number of speeches to be made from the bar.

74. In S.O. 72 to 77, " Appeal " includes " Dissents and Complaints " and " Appellant " includes " Complainer."

75. *Appeal; Complaint; Who May Appear.* Any Member of an inferior court whose judgment is brought under review of the Assembly may appear at the bar in support of the judgment; but, when Commissioners have been specially appointed by the inferior court to support its judgment, the Assembly shall not hear any Member of such court other than the Commissioners so appointed, unless any Member not so appointed but wishing to be heard can show a separate and peculiar interest to support the judgment; and in all such cases it shall be competent to the Assembly to limit the number of Members of an inferior court who shall be heard in support of the judgment under review.

76. *Appeal; Complaint—Judgment of Synod.* When a judgment of a Synod affirming the judgment of a Presbytery is brought under review of Assembly the Members of Presbytery shall have no status as parties at the bar except in the character of Members of the Synod; but when a reversal of a judgment of a Presbytery by a Synod is under review the Presbytery may appear and be heard at the bar of the Assembly as appellants against the judgment: provided always that they comply with the regulations herein contained regarding Causes brought under review of the Assembly by Appeal.

77. *Appeal; Complaint—Presbytery* v. *Synod.* When a Synod, on a Dissent and Complaint, reverses a judgment of a Presbytery, and the Presbytery appeals against the reversal, the complainers in the Dissent and Complaint to the Synod may appear and be heard at the bar of the Assembly as respondents to the Appeal for the Presbytery.

78. *Petition.* In Causes brought before the Assembly as the court of first instance, by Petition, the party promoting the application shall, subject to the proviso hereinafter contained, be entitled to be heard in support of the same; and the Assembly shall also hear an answer from any party at the bar claiming to be heard whom it shall consider to be a proper respondent, and the debate at the bar shall be closed with a reply from the person promoting the application: providing always that, except where a Petition relates to a personal grievance, or complaint against the action of a Church court, the Assembly may, if they see fit, order the Petition to lie on the table, without hearing the party promoting the application.

79. *Reference.* In Causes brought before the Assembly by reference from a Presbytery or Synod the reference shall be stated to the Assembly by a Member of the referring court, specially appointed for the purpose, at the bar if not a Commissioner, or in his place as a Commissioner if a Commissioner from the Presbytery, or from a Presbytery within the bounds of the Synod, making the reference. The Assembly shall thereafter hear the parties in the Cause referred in such order as the nature of the case may seem to require, keeping in view the regulations in S.O. 72 to 77.

VI. ORDER OF DEBATE.

(*a*) Order of the Day.

80. When the Assembly have resolved that a case or other piece of business shall be taken up at a certain hour mentioned in the Order of Business, such case or other piece of business shall be taken at the hour fixed, and the business before the Assembly, if not finished at the hour

named, shall be adjourned: provided that if, in the opinion of the Moderator, it would be in accordance with the general convenience of the Assembly, he may allow the transaction of the business then actually under discussion to continue for a period of not more than 30 minutes beyond the specified time; but no fresh business shall be commenced.

(*b*) Motions.

81. *Right to Move.* Any Commissioner to the Assembly may make a motion upon any matter coming regularly before the Assembly; and on rising to do so he shall read the terms of his motion and hand the same in writing to the Clerks.

When a motion has been duly seconded it shall not be competent to withdraw it, or to make any alteration upon it, without the permission of the Assembly.

82. *Priority.* The Deliverance on the Report of a Committee shall take precedence of any other motion on that subject.

83. *Committee Convener.* The Convener of a Committee when a Commissioner, on giving in the Report of his Committee, shall move the Deliverance proposed in terms of S.O. 42. A Convener, when not a Commissioner, shall be allowed to submit the Report of his Committee and to give explanations in the subsequent discussion. In such a case the Principal Clerk, whom failing, the Depute Clerk, shall formally move the Deliverance, and the seconder shall have the right of replying to the debate.

84. *Notice of Motion.* Any Commissioner may, during the sittings of the Assembly, give Notice of Motion on any subject due to come regularly before the Assembly, other than a contentious cause. Notices of Motion so given in shall be printed in the "Daily Proceedings" not later than the day before that on which the business is to be taken. Such printed Notice of Motion shall confer no right of priority of moving same, the Moderator being the sole judge of the order in which Members are entitled to address the Assembly.

(*c*) The Debate.

85. *The Chair.* Every speaker shall address the Assembly through the Moderator, and the correct address is "Moderator."

86. *In Support.* When a motion or motions have been made and seconded, any Member may take part in subsequent debate.

87. *One Speech Only.* Except as provided in S.O. 89 no Member may speak twice on the same matter except in explanation, and then only by special permission of the Assembly.

88. *Point of Order.* Any Member may rise to speak to a Point of Order. A speaker is not to be interrupted unless upon a call to order. When so interrupted he shall cease speaking, and resume his seat until the point of order is decided. The Member calling to order shall state the grounds on which he makes the call; and the speaker who has been interrupted may briefly reply in explanation, to show that he is not out of order, but no other Member may speak to the point of order unless with the permission or at the request of the Moderator, with whom the decision of the point rests, though he may put the point to a vote of the Assembly.

89. *Right of Reply.* The Commissioner who makes the first motion

on any matter shall be entitled to reply to the debate but must not introduce new matter into his reply. The debate will then be closed.

90. *Time Limits.* All speeches shall be limited to 5 minutes with the following exceptions:

(i) COMMITTEES.

Convener giving in the Report of his Committee and moving thereon	15 minutes
Seconder thereof	7 "
Movers of Amendments or Counter-Motions . .	10 "

(ii) OVERTURES.

Introducing an Overture and, when the Introducer is a Commissioner, moving thereon	10 minutes
Mover of other Motions in relation to Overture .	10 "

(iii) PETITIONS.

Speeches of Petitioners	15 minutes

(iv) DEPUTIES.

When Deputies from other Churches, introduced by a Convener of a Committee, are invited to address the Assembly, the Convener of such Committee shall be responsible for informing them that the limit of each address shall be 15 minutes.

(v) MISSIONARIES.

When Missionaries in the service of the Church, introduced by the Convener of the Committee under whose supervision they are employed, address the Assembly the limit of each address shall be 15 minutes.

91. *No Time Limit.* The time limits shall apply, except in the following cases:

(*a*) when the Assembly are debating specific proposals for change under Barrier Act procedure;
(*b*) when the Assembly are exercising judicial functions;
(*c*) in Petitions when, for special reasons, the Committee on Commissions reports that the circumstances demand an extension, and when the Assembly adopt that opinion;
(*d*) in any other matter when the General Administration Committee (in respect of the Order of Business for the first two days) or the Business Committee (in respect of the Order of Business for the subsequent days) declares that, in its opinion, such matter is of exceptional importance, and when the Assembly adopt that opinion.

(*d*) DEALING WITH MOTIONS.

92. *Character of Motions.* Motions shall be considered as belonging to one of the following categories, and shall be dealt with as prescribed, viz.:—

(1) The original Motion.
(2) Counter-Motions—being Motions contradictory or negative of the original Motion or of a substantial part of the original Motion.

(3) Amendments—being Motions not substantially contradictory of the original Motion or Counter-Motion, but for making deletions, alterations, or additions thereto without defeating its main object.

(4) Amendments on amendments already moved and seconded.

93. *Moderator to Judge.* The Moderator shall be judge of the category to which any Motion shall be considered to belong, and his ruling shall be final.

94. *Grouping of Amendments.* When to any Proposed Deliverance there has been given notice of amendments which differ from each other only slightly in their general tenor, the Moderator shall decide whether or not to permit more than one of such amendments to be moved.

95. *Voting on Amendments.* Immediately after an amendment on an amendment (Category 4) has been proposed, seconded, and spoken to, the Moderator shall take a vote "For" or "Against." He shall thereafter take a vote "For" or "Against" any amendment (Category 3) amended or unamended as the case may be.

96. *Voting on Motions.* After all amendments, if any, have been disposed of, the Moderator shall take a vote between all Motions in Categories (1) and (2), and in doing so shall adopt the following procedure. A vote shall be taken, in one of the methods provided below, between all the Motions in the order in which they were made, beginning at the first. Each Commissioner may vote for one Motion only. If, on the numbers being announced, one Motion has obtained a clear majority of votes, all the other Motions shall fall; but if no Motion has obtained a clear majority, the Motion having the smallest number of votes shall be struck off and a vote taken between the remaining Motions; and so on until one Motion receives a clear majority on a vote. The Motion which has received a clear majority shall then be put from the Chair to the Assembly, and, if challenged, shall be voted on "For" or "Against." If a majority vote for it, the Motion shall become the judgment of the Assembly. If a majority vote against it, the Motion shall fall, and further procedure in the matter shall be as the Assembly may determine.

97. *Voting for Appointments.* In the case of voting for appointments to vacant offices in the Church, where there are more than two nominations the Assembly shall vote separately on all the names proposed, and, unless there be a majority in favour of one over all the others combined, the one having the lowest number shall be dropped, and the Assembly shall again vote on those that remain.

98. *Voting in Cases heard by the Judicial Commission.* In cases reported to the Assembly by the Judicial Commission, after an opportunity has been given to Commissioners to ask questions, the question shall be put by the Moderator with regard to each Finding—"Do the General Assembly approve this Finding of the Judicial Commission—Yes? or No?" Immediately after the question has been put the Assembly, without debate on the Finding, shall vote. (1960, xxii., Section 6 (*h*).)

After the Assembly shall have resolved whether any Finding or Findings of the Judicial Commission be approved or not approved, the Assembly shall determine what further action, if any, shall be taken, but before any decision is made or any sentence pronounced the Appellant shall be entitled to be heard either personally or through his counsel or solicitor on a plea in mitigation. (Section 6 (*i*).)

99. *Casting Vote.* If in any division there shall be an equality of votes for two proposals before the Assembly, the Moderator shall have power to give a deciding vote; and if in the course of the voting as provided in S.O. 96 and 97 above, there should be an equality of votes for the two Motions having fewest votes, the Moderator shall have power to give a deciding vote and the Motion for which he shall vote shall be retained for the purpose of the next vote of the Assembly.

(*e*) Taking the Vote.

100. *Vote by Standing.* The Moderator may, if he deem fit, ascertain the mind of the Assembly by asking the Commissioners to stand in their places, and he shall intimate to the Assembly on which side there is in his opinion a majority. Unless the opinion of the Moderator so intimated is at once challenged it shall become the decision of the Assembly. If any Commissioner challenge the opinion of the Moderator the Assembly shall proceed to take a Vote by Papers as provided in S.O. 101.

101. *Vote by Papers.* If the Moderator is not prepared to give an opinion on the result of a Vote by Standing, or if his opinion is challenged, the Assembly shall proceed to take a Vote by Papers, and that in the following manner:—

The Moderator shall intimate which number of Paper is to be used, and Tellers shall be appointed from the Panel (S.O. 26) to each block of seats. As the vote is taken for each competing Motion, those voting therefor shall stand in their places and shall hand the appropriate Voting Paper to the Tellers who shall count these and deliver them to one of the Clerks. After the votes on all competing Motions have been counted the Moderator shall intimate the result of the voting. It shall be in order for any Commissioner thereupon to challenge the count, and in such a case the Clerks shall count the Voting Papers in their possession; but in no circumstances shall a second vote be taken on a matter which has already been the subject of a Vote by Papers. The doors shall be closed during a Vote by Papers.

(*f*) Dissents.

102. *Entering.* Any Commissioner dissatisfied with a judgment of the Assembly, which has not been unanimous, has the right to enter his dissent against it; but no dissent can be given in until the matter to which it refers has, for that session, been disposed of, the Minute adjusted, and the Assembly is ready to proceed to other business.

103. *Adhering.* When a dissent has been entered, it is in order for any other Commissioner present when that judgment was pronounced to adhere to such dissent. No other's adherence may be entered.

104. *Reasons.* A person dissenting may do so with or without giving in reasons of dissent. If he dissent for reasons given in at the time, or to be afterwards given in, such reasons shall, if received by the Assembly as proper and relevant, and provided they are given in before the close of the next Session (or, when made on the last day of the Assembly, before the close of the same Session), be recorded in the Minutes.

105. *Answers.* If the Assembly appoint a Committee to prepare

answers to reasons of dissent, the Report of the Committee shall, except on the last day of the Assembly, be printed in the "Daily Proceedings"; and, as approved by the Assembly, shall be printed in the Minutes, if the reasons of dissent have been so printed.

106. *Record of Dissents.* Reasons of dissent and answers thereto, when not entered in the Minutes, shall be kept in a separate Record of Dissents.

VII. COMMITTEES AND THEIR MEMBERS.

(*a*) COMMITTEES.

107. *Departments.* For administrative purposes the following Standing Committees shall be grouped together in the Departments indicated :—

DEPARTMENT.	COMMITTEES.
	A. ADMINISTRATIVE
I. *Administration and General Interests* .	1. General Administration. 2. Nomination of Moderator. 3. Judicial Commission. 4. Law, Property Cases and Discipline. 5. General Trustees. 6. Nomination. 7. Church of Scotland Trust. 8. General Finance. 9. Stewardship and Budget. 10. Advisory Board.
	B. SPECIAL INTERESTS
	11. Church and Nation. 12. Panel on Doctrine. 13. Public Worship and Aids to Devotion. 14. *Ad hoc* Committees appointed by the General Assembly.
II. *Church and Ministry*	15. Maintenance of the Ministry. 16. Unions and Readjustments. 17. Aged and Infirm Ministers' Fund. 18. Probationers and Transference of Ministers. 19. Admission of Ministers of Other Churches. 20. Oxford Chaplaincy Consultative Committee. 21. Chaplains to H.M. Forces. 22. Trustees of Ministers' War Memorial and Orphan Funds.
III. *Home* . . .	23. Home Board. (*a*) Home Mission. (*b*) National Church Extension. (*c*) Property.
	24. Advisory Committee on Artistic Questions. 25. Deaconess Board. 26. Iona Community Board.
IV. *Social Responsibility*	27. Social Responsibility.

DEPARTMENT.	COMMITTEES.
V. *Overseas Mission and Inter-Church Relations.*	28. Overseas Council. (*a*) Europe, Israel and the Americas. (*b*) Africa. (*c*) Asia and Australasia. (*d*) Christian Aid. 29. Inter-Church Relations.
VI. *Education* . .	30. Board of Education. 31. Education. 32. Education for the Ministry. 33. Board of St Colm's. 34. Parish Education. 35. University Boards of Nomination.
VII. *Publicity and Publication.*	36. Publicity. 37. Publications.

108. *Representation.* The Assembly's Standing Committees shall be classified as follows. They shall have the membership after stated.

CLASS I. STANDING COMMITTEES ON WHICH PRESBYTERIES ARE REPRESENTED.

	Membership.	*From Assembly.*	*From Presbyteries.*	*Members.*
9. Stewardship and Budget .	81	30	48	3
15. Maintenance of the Ministry	89	41	48	...
23. Home Board . . .	113	40	48	25
27. Social Responsibility .	92 [1]	28	48	16
28. Overseas Council . .	116	40	48	28
34. Parish Education . .	108	60	48	...

CLASS II. STANDING COMMITTEES ON WHICH PRESBYTERIES ARE NOT REPRESENTED.

Membership.

1. General Administration 45

Forty appointed by the General Assembly through the Nomination Committee.

The Moderator, Clerks of Assembly, Procurator, and Law Agent shall be additional members *ex officiis.*

2. Nomination of Moderator

The ex-Moderators, the Principal Clerk, four representatives from each Synod (two Ministers and two Elders), one Minister and one Elder from Orkney and Shetland and the Presbytery of England. Elders equal in number to the ex-Moderators to be appointed through the Nomination Committee.

[1] The President of the Woman's Guild shall be an additional member *ex officio.*

Membership.

3. Judicial Commission 48

Ministers and Elders—forty-eight in number—to be appointed by the General Assembly. Thirty-two members to be nominated from Synods (two from each and four from Synod of Clydesdale and Synod of Lothian and Tweeddale) and sixteen nominated by the General Administration Committee.

4. Law, Property Cases and Discipline 22

Eighteen appointed by the General Assembly through the Nomination Committee.

The Clerks of Assembly, Procurator, and Law Agent shall be additional members *ex officiis*.

6. Nomination 47

Twenty-four nominated by Synods and twelve by the Assembly through the Nomination Committee. Two Ministers and two Elders from the Synod of Clydesdale; two Ministers and one Elder or one Minister and two Elders alternately from the Synod of Lothian and Tweeddale; one Minister and one Elder from each of the Synods of Ayr, Perth and Stirling, Fife, Angus and Mearns, and Aberdeen; one Minister or one Elder alternately from each of the other Synods and from each of the Presbyteries of Orkney and Shetland, the alternate order to be determined by the Nomination Committee. In addition one member appointed by each of the following Committees, viz.:—General Administration, General Finance, Maintenance of the Ministry, Home Board, Social Responsibility, Church and Nation, Overseas Council, Education for the Ministry, and Parish Education. Membership of the Nomination Committee of Assembly shall be for four years. No member shall be open for re-election until after a period of four years, except for special cause shown. The Convenership of this Committee shall be for three years.

8. General Finance 43

Forty appointed by the General Assembly through the Nomination Committee.

The Clerks of Assembly and Law Agent additional members *ex officiis*.

10. Advisory Board 31

Twelve Ministers and twelve Elders appointed by the General Assembly; the Moderators of the three preceding General Assemblies; the Conveners of the General Administration and the General Finance Committees, the Principal Clerk of the General Assembly and the General Treasurer are corresponding members.

11. Church and Nation 57

Forty-two members, including eight women, appointed by the General Assembly on the nomination of the Nomination Committee, and one from each Synod and the Presbyteries of Orkney and Shetland.

12. Panel on Doctrine 15

Four Ministers and four Elders appointed by the General Assembly through the Nomination Committee, one member appointed by the Faculty of Divinity in each of the four Scottish Universities where there is such Faculty, with the Principal Clerk, the Procurator, and Convener of General Administration Committee *ex officiis*.

13. Public Worship and Aids to Devotion 36

Thirty-six members appointed by the General Assembly through the Nomination Committee.

Membership.

16. Unions and Readjustments 105

Ninety-six members appointed by the General Assembly through the Nomination Committee.

And in addition, the Conveners of the Committees on Law, Property Cases, and Discipline; General Finance; Maintenance of the Ministry; Aged and Infirm Ministers' Fund; Home Board; National Church Extension Committee; and Probationers, with the Secretary and Secretary-Depute of the Home Board.

17. Aged and Infirm Ministers' Fund 48

Forty-eight members appointed by the General Assembly through the Nomination Committee.

18. Probationers and Transference of Ministers 27

Twenty members appointed by the General Assembly through the Nomination Committee.

The four Professors of Practical Training in the Theological Colleges shall be additional members *ex officiis*, and three members from the Church and Ministry Department.

19. Admission of Ministers of Other Churches 15

Thirteen members appointed by the General Assembly through the Nomination Committee. The Clerks of Assembly shall be additional members *ex officiis*.

20. Oxford Chaplaincy Consultative Committee 3

Three members appointed by the General Assembly on the nomination of the General Administration Committee.

21. Chaplains to H.M. Forces 26

Twenty-four members appointed by the General Assembly through the Nomination Committee.

24. Artistic Questions 24

Twenty-four members—twelve Ministers and eight Elders, of whom two shall be representatives from the Home Board (including one from the Church Extension Sectional Committee), and four lay members with special knowledge and experience.

25. Deaconess Board 21

The Board shall consist of: four Ministers, four Elders, and four women members; the President and Vice-President of the Deaconess Council, *ex officiis*; the Secretary, *ex officio*; six other Deaconesses.

Two representatives of the Women's Home Mission Committee, one woman representative of the Overseas Council, one representative from each other Department or Committee of the Church with which a Deaconess is serving and the Principal of St Colm's College shall be entitled to attend the meetings of the Board as corresponding members without right to vote.

The four Ministers, four Elders, and four women members shall be appointed by the General Assembly in accordance with its Standing Orders.

The six Deaconesses shall be appointed by the Deaconess Council on a territorial basis for a period of three years. Two shall retire each year and shall not be eligible for immediate re-election.

The Convener shall be a Minister designated by the General Assembly, and shall hold office for five years.

The President of the Deaconess Council shall be Vice-Convener of the Board.

The Secretary of the Board shall be a Deaconess appointed by the Board as Secretary of the Board and Secretary of the Council.

Membership.

26. Iona Community Board 24

One member each from the Home Board, the Overseas Council, the Parish Education Committee, the Committee on Education for the Ministry, one representative from each of the four Liaison Committees appointed by the Committee on Education for the Ministry.

Eight other members appointed by the General Assembly, one of whom shall be from the Presbytery of Lorn and Mull, and one from the Presbytery of Glasgow, to serve four years, two changing each year.

Six members of the Board shall be nominated by the Iona Community, two changing each year, and also one of the Trustees of the Iona Community.

The Leader of the Iona Community shall be *ex officio* a member. The Clerk to the Presbytery of Lorn and Mull shall also be *ex officio* a member.

29. Inter-Church Relations 60

Thirty, including eight women, appointed by the General Assembly through the Nomination Committee; one appointed by each Synod; four appointed by the Overseas Council; four appointed by the General Administration Committee; two appointed by each of the following: Home Board, Education Department, Panel on Doctrine, Woman's Guild, Church and Nation Committee.

In addition: Church of Scotland representatives on Divisions, permanent Commissions and Committees of the World Council of Churches, World Alliance of Reformed Churches, Conference of European Churches, and on the Executive of the British Council of Churches and Scottish Churches Council, with the exception of members of the British Churches Committee of the World Alliance of Reformed Churches.

30. Board of Education 46

Twelve members appointed by the General Assembly, four of whom to be Ministers and eight Elders; sixteen representatives from the Committee on Parish Education; eight representatives from the Committee on Education; and four representatives from the Board of St Colm's College.

31. Education 28

Twenty-eight members appointed by the General Assembly through the Nomination Committee.

32. Education for the Ministry 40

One representative from each Synod of the Church, including the Presbyteries of Orkney and Shetland; eight members of the Teaching Staffs of the Divinity Halls, two being appointed from each; thirteen Ministers and five Elders appointed by the General Assembly through the Nomination Committee.

33. Board of St Colm's College. 19

Eight appointed by the General Assembly; four appointed by the Overseas Council and four by the Home Board; one appointed by each of the Deaconess Board, the Social Responsibility, and the St Colm's House Guild; one appointed to represent the Students of the College who shall hold office for one year. The Principal of the College, the Secretary of the Board and the Parish Minister of the bounds shall be members *ex officiis*.

Membership.

35. University Board of Nomination 27

Twenty-four appointed by the General Assembly through the Nomination Committee (six in respect of each of the Scottish Universities where there is a Faculty of Divinity) together with the following if not otherwise members of the Board: the Moderator, the Convener of Committee on Education for the Ministry; the Principal of the Divinity College especially concerned in a Nomination, acting *ad hoc*.

36. Publicity 27

Eight persons appointed by the General Assembly, two from Stewardship and Budget Committee, Woman's Guild, General Administration Committee, Church and Ministry Department, Home Department, Social Responsibility Committee, Overseas Mission, Inter-Church Relations Department, Education Department and Publications Committee.

37. Publications 40

Twenty Ministers, sixteen Elders and four members all appointed by the General Assembly.

109. *Meetings.* Committees shall meet as a rule in June, October, February, and April. They shall be free to meet on other months as business may require. The third Tuesday of the month, and if need be the days following, shall be regarded as the selected day or days, but they shall be free to meet on other days as business may require.

(*b*) MEMBERS.

110. *Period of Service.* All Members of each of the Standing Committees shall retire after serving for four years. Presbyteries and Committees entitled to appoint representatives shall be permitted to make changes in their representation for special reasons in any year when making their return by 1st March (S.O. 121). In the case of the University Boards of Nomination the period of service shall be six years. (S.O. 129.)

111. *Non-attendance.* The name of a Member shall be removed from any Standing Committee which has met three times or oftener between 1st June and 1st March unless he has attended one-third of the meetings held within that period. Attendance at meetings of Sub-Committees shall for this purpose be reckoned as equivalent to attendance at the meetings of the Committee itself.

112. *Replacement.* When a Minister, Elder, or Woman Member of any Standing or Special Committee is unable to accept the appointment, or where from any cause vacancies occur in Committees during the year, that Committee, after consultation with the Convener of the Nomination Committee, may appoint a Member to take the place of the Member whose retirement has caused the vacancy.

All such appointments, if for a longer period than one year, shall be reported for confirmation through the Nomination Committee to the General Assembly.

113. *Re-election.* A member retiring by rotation, or having his name removed for non-attendance, from a Committee, shall not be eligible for re-election to that Committee until the expiry of one year thereafter, unless the Assembly are satisfied, on the Report of the Nomination Committee, on information submitted to it by the Committee concerned,

that there are circumstances which make re-election desirable, but in no case shall more than one-half of the retiring Members be so re-elected. No member shall normally serve for more than two consecutive terms of office. (If possible 20% of the Assembly appointed members of committees should be under the age of 35 at the time of their appointment.) A Member appointed in the room of one deceased, resigned, or removed, or of one appointed as Convener or Vice-Convener, shall serve for the remainder of the period for which the person was appointed whose place he takes, and on retiral shall be eligible for re-election if he has not served for more than two years.

114. *Eligibility.* No person shall be a Member of more than three Standing Committees at the same time. Appointments *ex officio* and membership of the Advisory Board shall not be reckoned in this number. This rule shall not apply to those for whom the Nomination Committee is prepared to give special reasons to the Assembly for their appointment to more than three Committees.

The Nomination Committee shall not nominate for Committees any of its own number except in the case of those who are nominated by Presbyteries or Committees for representation, or in special circumstances which must be stated to the Assembly.

115. *Secretaries and Deputies.* Secretaries and Deputies shall be members *ex officiis* of their respective Committees, unless otherwise determined by the Assembly.

116. *Expenses.* Expenses incurred by Members of Committees, consisting of travel charges and a sum for maintenance when required shall be defrayed.

(*c*) CONVENERS AND VICE-CONVENERS.

117. *Appointment.* Conveners and Vice-Conveners of Standing Committees shall be appointed by the Assembly. Conveners shall hold office for not more than four consecutive years (in the case of the Nomination Committee, three consecutive years, in the case of the Advisory Board the Convener and Vice-Convener shall not be Conveners of any Departmental Board or Standing Committees of the General Assembly) ; and Vice-Conveners shall hold office for not more than three consecutive years, unless the Assembly are satisfied that there are exceptional circumstances which make the reappointment of Conveners and Vice-Conveners desirable. The period of reappointment shall be for one year only. Conveners and Vice-Conveners on their appointment shall serve for four years and three years ; and if at the time of appointment they are already Members of the Committee another Member shall be appointed in their room for the remainder of the period of their original appointment.

118. *Replacement.* In the event of the death, resignation, or supervening incapacity of the Convener of any Standing or Special Committee, the Committee concerned, after consultation with the Convener of the Nomination Committee, may appoint an Interim Convener. Such appointment shall be reported by the Committee to the Assembly, or to the Commission of Assembly at either of the stated diets and the Assembly or the Commission shall make such order as the situation may require.

(*d*) Presbytery Appointments.

119. *Right of Representation.* Presbyteries shall be entitled to appoint one representative to each of the following Standing Committees, viz.: Maintenance of the Ministry, Home Board, Social Responsibility, Overseas Council, Stewardship and Budget, and Parish Education. Such representative may be either a Minister or an Elder, but Presbyteries should bear in mind the adequate representation of elders on these Committees. Elders may, if necessary, be chosen from any Presbytery of the Church.

120. *Translation of Representative.* When a Minister appointed to represent his Presbytery on Committee is translated to another Presbytery, he shall cease to hold the position of representative from the first Assembly following.

121. *Intimation of Appointments.* Intimation of representatives appointed by Presbyteries shall be sent in to the Nomination Committee by 1st March in each year in order that that Committee may have these before it in making its nominations to the Assembly, and that the names of those so appointed may be submitted in due course to the Assembly.

122. *Period of Service.* S.O. 110 and 113 shall apply to all Presbyterial appointments.

(*e*) Nomination Committee.

123. *List of Nominations.* The Nomination Committee shall include in its Report its list of nominations to be submitted to the Assembly. The Report, so prepared, shall be included in the volume of Reports issued to Members of Assembly.

124. *Nomination of Conveners.* When the Convener or Vice-Convener of a Committee is completing his term of office, the Committee shall be invited by the Convener of the Nomination Committee to suggest the name of one who may be appointed in his room.

125. *Conveners to Attend Meeting.* Conveners of Standing Committees not represented on the Nomination Committee shall be entitled to be present at meetings of Nomination Committee when the composition of their respective Committees is under consideration, but not to vote.

126. *Inter-Committee Nominations.* Appointments made by other Standing Committees to the Nomination, Inter-Church Relations, Stewardship and Budget Committees, and any others to which they have the right of appointment shall be intimated to the Nomination Committee by 1st March in each year. (S.O. 110 and 113 shall apply to all inter-Committee appointments.)

127. *Amendment to Report.* No amendment to the Report of the Nomination Committee shall be in order of which due notice has not been given.

All notices of proposed amendments on the Report, including such as propose the omission or insertion of any name or names, or the addition of a name or names where the full number eligible has not been nominated by the Committee, must be given in to the Clerks before the close of the forenoon Session of the Saturday, signed by the Member or Members giving them.

All such notices of proposed amendment shall, with the names of those signing them, be printed in the "Daily Proceedings" issued on the

Monday morning and on the morning of the day the Report is to be called for.

(*f*) Missionaries and Chaplains.

128. *Representation.* Missionaries and Chaplains on furlough shall be corresponding members of the Overseas Council with liberty to speak but not to vote.

(*g*) University Boards of Nomination.

129. *Vacancy.* When a vacancy occurs during the year among the Church representatives on any of the University Boards of Nomination (by reason of the resignation, death, or supervening incapacity of any individual Member), the Committee on Education for the Ministry, after consultation with the Convener of the Nomination Committee, shall appoint a member to take the place of the Member whose retirement has caused the vacancy.

In such a case if the appointment is for more than one year it shall be reported for confirmation through the Nomination Committee to the Assembly.

130. *Amendment on Report.* No amendment on the Report of the Boards of Nomination for Church Chairs in the Universities, where names are nominated for vacant Chairs, or office of Principal of any Church College, shall be in order unless Notice of Motion be given in to the Clerks of Assembly at least three days before the day on which the Report is to be taken up.

VIII. STANDING ORDERS.

Printing and Adoption. See S.O. 13 hereof.

131. *Alteration.* Any proposal for alteration of the Standing Orders shall be either (*a*) on the Report of the General Administration Committee and printed in the volume of Reports or (*b*) by Overture and the subject of at least one day's notice in the "Daily Proceedings." This Standing Order shall not apply to Standing Orders 107 and 108 which may be amended by the Principal Clerk in accordance with the decisions of the General Assembly.

132. *Suspension.* It shall always be competent for the Assembly, on the Motion of any Commissioner, and on cause shown, summarily to dispense with the observance of the Standing Orders, or any part of them, in any particular case: provided that such Motion shall receive the support of not less than two-thirds of those voting on the question when put from the Chair, and that such suspension shall not contravene any Act of Assembly.

APPENDIX XIII.

ACT APPOINTING THE COMMISSION OF THE GENERAL ASSEMBLY.

1. The General Assembly hereby appoint a Commission of the General Assembly, consisting of the Members of this Assembly with the addition of the Rev. , named by the Moderator, with power to meet at Edinburgh at 11 a.m. on the first Thursday after the third Tuesday of October and February respectively next to come, and oftener, when and where they shall think fit and convenient, with the following powers:—

(*a*) To choose their own Moderator.

(*b*) To dispose of every matter referred to them by or in view of any Act or Order of the General Assembly.

(*c*) To advert to the interests of the Church so that the Church may not suffer or sustain any prejudice which they can prevent, provided that this power shall not extend to particular affairs or processes before Synods or Presbyteries, that are not of Universal concern to or influence upon the whole Church. A decision reached at one diet shall not be alterable at the other stated diet, but shall stand till disapproved by the General Assembly.

(*d*) To dispose of any matter brought before them through the General Administration Committee affecting the general interests of the Church at home and abroad and requiring to be dealt with immediately.

(*e*) To receive any References or Appeals from Synods in matters of Doctrine and to ripen such affairs for the next General Assembly.

(*f*) To give all needful advice and assistance to Synods, Presbyteries, and Committees of Assembly upon their application.

(*g*) To appoint representatives on behalf of the General Assembly where such appointments are required before the next General Assembly.

(*h*) To receive statements from any Standing Committee relative to the sphere of such Committee.

(*i*) To take up and dispose of (*a*) cases brought before them by the Committee on Unions and Readjustments, (*b*) references by Synods, and (*c*) references by Presbyteries when no meeting of Synod intervenes, in all matters connected with (1) calls, translations, retiral and settlement of Ministers, and (2) union and status of Congregations and the readjustment of Agencies falling under the scope of the Committee on Unions and Readjustments, provided always that all papers in such references shall have been duly printed and made available to members as if the References had been made to the General Assembly, unless this is dispensed with by the Clerks and Procurator.

(*j*) To arrange on the request of the Overseas Council, or any Committee thereof, for the ordination of such Missionary Agents as shall be deemed suitable, provided that those thus ordained shall not be eligible for a charge at home without the special sanction of the General Assembly.

(*k*) To dispose of all Petitions for the sale, burdening or transfer of property, and the disposal of the proceeds of such sales, provided that such Petitions shall have been lodged with the Principal Clerk of Assembly at least one month before the date of the sitting of the Commission, that he has transmitted them to the Committee on Law, Property Cases and Discipline, that the said Committee has considered them and that after conference with parties if necessary, the said Committee has reported on them to the Commission; provided always that the authority hereby conferred shall not interfere in any way with the statutory powers and duties possessed by or imposed upon the Church of Scotland General Trustees under or by virtue of the provisions of the Church of Scotland (General Trustees) Order Confirmation Act 1921, the Church of Scotland (Property and Endowments) Act 1925, and any Acts amending the same.

2. The quorum of the Commission shall be 31, whereof 16 must be Ministers.

3. The Commission shall continue in office until another shall be appointed.

4. The Commission shall proceed in accordance with the Constitution of the Church and Acts of the General Assembly, and their decisions shall be final, but the Commission shall do nothing contrary thereto, or to the prejudice of the same and shall not entertain or deal with any matters other than those that are referred to them as herein provided, as they shall be accountable to and censurable by the next General Assembly.

5. Synods, Presbyteries, and Kirk Sessions shall not meet on either of the dates mentioned in Section 1 hereof, or on either of the days immediately preceeding and following the said dates in cases where members would be prevented from attending these Courts.

6. If any Synod, Presbytery or Kirk Session should decline to comply with a decision of the Commission, or to execute the same in full, the matter shall lie over until the ensuing General Assembly to which such Synod, Presbytery or Kirk Session, as the case may be, shall be answerable for its conduct.

7. The Principal Clerk of Assembly shall, on receiving a requisition signed by a quorum of the Commission, or an instruction from the General Administration Committee, forthwith issue a notice to all members of the Commission summoning them to a meeting to be held not sooner than ten clear days after the date of the notice. The notice shall state the business for which the meeting of the Commission is desired, and no other business shall be considered at the meeting.

APPENDIX XIV.

REGULATIONS ANENT POWERS AND FUNCTIONS OF PROVINCIAL SYNODS (1933 Rep., p. 58; 1933, xviii., xix.; 1947, viii.; 1961, xxiii.; 1962, xv.).

I. General.

1. The Moderator shall be chosen from among the ministerial members of the Court by free election. He shall hold office for a year at least, and shall be eligible for re-election. During his term of office he may be appointed to visit the various districts within the bounds of the Synod, with a view to giving advice or stimulating interest in the work of the Church.

2. At each meeting Synods may appoint corresponding members, a Minister and an Elder, to each neighbouring Synod. These corresponding members shall receive Commissions from their own Synod, which, on being presented and sustained, shall constitute them members of the Synod to which they have been appointed for the period during which their Commissions extend. Corresponding members report their diligence to the next succeeding meeting of their Synod.

3. Synods shall have power to hold their regular meetings in various centres within their bounds, as they themselves may determine.

4. Synods may take up and consider in conference questions dealing with the spiritual, moral, and social well-being of the Church.

II. Finality of Judgment.

1. Synods shall adjudicate finally in all cases of appeal, with the exception of cases involving doctrine, worship, or censure of a Minister or other office-bearer, the licensing of students,[1] and cases of Union and Readjustment.[2]

2. For Presbyteries with Synodical powers and for Foreign Presbyteries the General Assembly shall be the Court of final appeal.

III. Legislative and Deliberative Functions of Synods.

1. Subject to the terms of Subsection 2 below, any Overture from a Presbytery to the General Assembly shall be transmitted through the Synod of the bounds, which shall forward it either with or without comment, with approval or with disapproval (1961, xxiii.). A Synod shall not be entitled to refuse to transmit an Overture which is presented in proper form.

2. A Presbytery shall have liberty to transmit an Overture to the General Assembly direct in case of urgency, when no meeting of Synod intervenes between the meeting of Presbytery at which it was adopted and the General Assembly.

[1] 1947, viii. [2] 1962, xv.

3. A Synod may transmit to the General Assembly any Overture originating in the Synod itself.

4. When the General Assembly sends down to Presbyteries Draft Regulations (not under the Barrier Act) for suggestions, these shall also be sent to Synods, which may send in suggestions, and express their judgment.

IV. Superintendence Functions of Synods.

1. Synods shall annually visit Presbytery Records and Benefice Registers, and their decisions thereanent shall be final.

2. Under the scheme of Presbyterial visitation, each Presbytery shall annually report to the Synod the result of visitation undertaken during the year, and the Synod shall take action, if the report in any case be unsatisfactory. Synods shall have power, in consultation with the Presbytery within whose bounds the congregation is situated, to visit that or any congregation when it is deemed expedient to do so from what appears in visitation reports or in Presbytery Minutes, or from information reported by the Moderator or submitted in writing by other member of Synod, who is not a member of the Presbytery concerned.

3. Synods shall exercise supervision over Presbyteries in connection with the Schemes of the Church; Presbyteries shall be required to report diligence in regard to the Maintenance of the Ministry Fund, and the Mission and Service Fund.

4. In any matter affecting delimitation of areas brought before the Synod by motion or by complaint of any member of Presbytery, the judgment of the Synod shall be final, unless the matter affect the bounds of the Synod itself, or the decision involves the modification of an arrangement set up by a decree of the Court of Teinds or an Act of the General Assembly.

V. Administrative Functions of Synods.

1. Reports on the activities of the General Assembly Committees on Home Mission, Social Responsibility, &c., carried on within the bounds shall be made periodically to the Synod.

2. Reports from the Agents of the General Assembly Committees on Parish Education and Social Responsibility, who are settled within the bounds, shall also be made periodically to the Synod.

3. Synods shall be expected to take direct interest in the various organisations of the Church, particularly those carried on within their own bounds. With this end in view they may arrange for the periodic visit to their statutory meetings of the agents employed by these organisations. Synods may send in suggestions to the Committee concerned.

4. Except in cases where the change would involve any modification of an arrangement set up by a decree of the Court of Teinds or an Act of General Assembly, Synods shall have full powers to adjudicate on the action of Presbyteries in regard to the transporting and dissolution of charges, it being understood that, where grants are being asked from Assembly Committees, the approval of these Committees shall be

obtained before any action is taken, and that such conditions are laid down as the General Assembly may determine from time to time. The decision of the Synod shall be final.[1]

5. Subject to the exceptions contained in Section V. (4) above, Synods shall have power to transfer a charge from one Presbytery to another within the bounds of the Synod, on a petition to that effect from the Kirk Session of the charge concerned. The decision of the Synod shall be final.

6. Synods shall continue to appoint members to Committees of the General Assembly, as the General Assembly may determine.

Note.—Attention is called to the following Extract from the Act (1963, xxiii.) appointing the Commission of the General Assembly :—

" The General Assembly empower the Commission, at any of its stated diets, to take up and dispose of all References from Synods and from Presbyteries when no meeting of Synod intervenes, in matters connected with (1) Calls, Translations, Retiral or Settlement of Ministers ; and (2) the union and status of congregations and the readjustment of agencies, falling under the scope of the Committee on Unions and Readjustments, provided always that all the papers in such References shall have been duly printed and made available to Members in the same way as if the References had been to the General Assembly, unless this be dispensed with by the Clerks and the Procurator."

[1] This sentence does not now apply (1962, xv.).

APPENDIX XV.

THE CHURCH OF SCOTLAND

DEED OF CONSTITUTION

OF

THE CONGREGATION OF.......................................
OF THE CHURCH OF SCOTLAND

IN THE PRESBYTERY OF........................

Constitution of Congregational Board.

First, The control of the financial and other temporal affairs of the Congregation shall (subject as hereinafter mentioned, or to any Regulations or Directions which may hereafter be enacted by the General Assembly) be vested in a Congregational Board (hereinafter referred to as "the Board"), which shall consist of the Minister, the Elders, and a certain number of Communicants of years eighteen * of age or over to be elected by the Congregation as hereinafter provided. The number so to be elected shall be determined by the Congregation, but in no case shall it exceed the number of Elders of the Congregation as at the date of such election.[1]

Election of Board.

Second, In the month of January first occurring after the date of issue of this Constitution, or within the period of one month from the delivery hereof by the Delegation of the General Assembly, and not later than the 31st day of March in each year thereafter, a Meeting of all those whose names are on the Communion Roll of the Congregation shall be called by intimation made from the Pulpit on the two Sundays immediately preceding the Meeting. The said Meeting (which shall be designated the Stated Annual Meeting of the Congregation) shall be held in the Church or Church Hall or elsewhere as may be intimated (the Moderator or Interim Moderator of the Kirk Session, whom failing a Member of the Presbytery specially authorised by him for the purpose, whom failing some person to be elected by those present at the Meeting, presiding) on a date to be fixed by the Kirk Session in the case of the first such Meeting and subsequently by the Board, for the purpose of electing certain of their number to act along with the Minister and the Elders on the Board in administering the financial and other temporal affairs of the Congregation. In the event of any of such Meetings not being held within the said appointed times, the Presbytery may, on application by the Kirk Session to that effect, direct such Meeting to be called and held at any time thereafter during that year. One-third of the Members of the Board so elected shall retire annually, but they shall be severally eligible for re-election.[2] The order of retirement of such one-third of the Members shall be fixed by the Board.

* Act V of the General Assembly of 1968 refers.

[1] There is an exception to this rule in cases where the number of Elders is less than six—See Note 1, page 616.

[2] Deacons for life who have been members of a Deacons' Court immediately prior to the adoption of the Model Deed are in a special position—See Note 2, page 617.

Third, Notwithstanding the foregoing, it shall be in the power of the Congregation by a resolution passed by not less than two-thirds of the Members thereof present at a Meeting of the Congregation (whether the Stated Annual General Meeting or not) of which due notice of the intention to propose such resolution has been given, to resolve that the number of Elders on the Board should be reduced to a number specified in said resolution. The reduced number of Elders shall be not less than 5 when the number of Members on the Communion Roll does not exceed 200; shall be not less than 8 when the number of Members on the Communion Roll exceeds 200 but does not exceed 400, and shall be not less than 12 when the number of Members on the Communion Roll exceeds 400. In the event of such a resolution being passed (*a*) the Elders who are to serve on the Board shall be elected by the Kirk Session and shall be Members of the Board for such period as the Kirk Session may decide, and the Kirk Session shall fill any vacancy that occurs; (*b*) the number of Members of the Board elected by the Congregation shall not exceed the number of Elders specified in the resolution. If at the time such resolution is passed the number of Members on the Board elected by the Congregation should exceed the reduced number of elders, the Members elected by the Congregation may decide among themselves by agreement or failing that by ballot or otherwise as the majority may wish which of them should demit office so as not to exceed the specified number of Elders. Power to reduce membership of Board.

It shall be competent for the Congregation at intervals of not less than one year after the passing of a resolution as aforesaid to review the matter and by a resolution passed by not less than two-thirds of the members thereof present at a Meeting of which due notice of the intention to propose such a resolution has been given to rescind the resolution referred to in the preceding paragraph or to amend it by increasing or reducing the number of Elders to serve on the Board, provided that the minimum number shall be as before stated. In the event of the resolution referred to in the preceding paragraph being rescinded, all the Elders shall thereupon become Members of the Board and the Congregation shall have power to elect additional Members of the Board up to the total number of Elders. In the event of the number of Elders, however, being increased but still being less than the total number of Elders on the Kirk Session, the Kirk Session shall elect additional Members to serve on the Board from their own number as before provided, and the Congregation shall have power to elect additional Members up to the total number of Elders serving on the Board. In the event of the number of Elders being further reduced by said amending resolution, the Kirk Session shall decide which of the Elders are to serve on the Board, and the Members of the Board elected by the Congregation shall decide by agreement or failing that by ballot or otherwise as the majority may wish, which of them should demit office so as to reduce their number to a number not exceeding the number of Elders on the Board.

Fourth, In the event of any Member of the Board who has been elected by the Congregation dying or resigning, or becoming incapacitated to act, or having his or her name removed from the Communion Roll of the Congregation, or being suspended from Communion during the currency of his or her term of office, the Board may appoint a duly Filling of Vacancies.

qualified person to fill the vacancy, and the person thus appointed shall hold office for the remainder of the period for which such predecessor was elected, subject to confirmation at the next Stated Annual Meeting of the Congregation.

Quorum and Chairman.

Fifth, So soon as the Board has been constituted, three shall be a quorum where the number of the Board does not exceed nine, and five shall be a quorum where the number exceeds nine and does not exceed twenty. Where it exceeds twenty, seven shall be a quorum. The Minister of the Congregation (or the Interim Moderator of the Kirk Session during a vacancy) shall be *ex officio* the Chairman of the Board, and in the event of his declining to accept office, the Board shall elect one of their own number as Chairman for the year. If the Chairman (either *ex officio* or elected) shall be absent from any Meeting, the Members of the Board present shall elect one of their own number as Chairman for that Meeting. The Chairman shall have a casting vote only.

Appointment of Officials of Board.

Sixth, It shall be the duty of the Board at their first Meeting to appoint a Clerk and a Treasurer, who may or may not be of their own number, and both offices may be held by the same person. The Treasurer if holding only that office need not be a member of the Congregation. The person or persons so appointed shall hold office during the pleasure of the Board, but in any event shall not hold office longer than three years unless reappointed by the Board, which reappointment may be for a period not exceeding three years but may be renewed thereafter for periods not exceeding three years at a time. The Board shall also appoint annually an Auditor or Auditors of the accounts of the Board, who many or may not be of their own number and who need not be a Member or Members of the Congregation. There shall be a minimum of two Auditors except where the audit is conducted on a professional basis by a duly qualified accountant.

Minutes and Banking Account.

Seventh, It shall be the duty of the Clerk to keep regular Minutes of the proceedings of the Board, and also of the proceedings at the Stated Annual Meeting of the Congregation, and to engross or bind these in a permanent Record, in which each Minute, when approved, shall be signed by the Chairman and the Clerk. It shall be the duty of the Treasurer to keep a separate banking account in the name of the Board, and all cheques drawn thereon shall be signed by the Treasurer and by one Member to be authorised by the Board from time to time for that purpose. Two or more Members may be so authorised, but it shall only be necessary for one of them to sign along with the Treasurer.

Accounts.

Eighth, The Treasurer of the Board shall keep an account of the Ordinary Revenue and Expenditure of the Parish and Congregation, including in such Revenue under separate headings *inter alia* (1) all sums (if any) received by him in respect of the statutory endowment and all other sums forming the stipend or further endowment of stipend, including all contributions made towards stipend; (2) seat rents; (3) ordinary Church collections and donations in aid thereof; (4) contributions or donations for Congregational purposes; (5) the income of any Congregational endowment for general or specific purposes; (6) contributions under the Co-ordinated Appeal to the Schemes of the

Church; (7) collections for any other charitable or religious purpose except as aftermentioned; and (8) revenue from any other source; but excluding from such revenue (1) Poor Fund (if any) and (2) any other funds or monies held or administered by the Kirk Session under trusts or otherwise, The following charges shall also be stated under separate headings, and, except in so far as otherwise provided for, shall be met out of the said Ordinary Revenue—*videlicet:* (1) the Stipend and Listed Expenses payable to the Minister so far as the same are payable from Congregational sources, which Stipend and Listed Expenses shall be a first charge on the said Ordinary Revenue, except in so far as the other charges hereinafter specified are by law entitled to rank prior thereto; (2) Communion expenses; (3) any other expenses necessarily incurred in the maintenance of public worship or in dispensing the ordinances of religion; (4) the cost of heating, lighting and cleaning the Church and Church Hall (if any), and rates, taxes, feu-duty and insurance of same; (5) rates, taxes, feu-duty and insurance payable in respect of the Manse (if any); (6) the amount fixed to be set aside annually towards a Fabrics Fund Account; (7) the salaries of the Church Officer and of the Precentor or Choirmaster and Organist, and of any other like officials; (8) the cost of Pulpit supply when it is the responsibility of the Congregation; (9) General Assembly, Synod and Presbytery assessments; and (10) any additional annual charges authorised by the Board. At the close of the year any balance standing at the credit of the Ordinary Revenue and Expenditure Account shall be dealt with as hereinafter provided under Article Eleventh hereof.

The Ordinary Revenue and Expenditure Account shall show, either inset or by Note, the total stipend paid to the Minister from all sources.

Provision for Stipend, etc.

Ninth, When on a vacancy occurring in the pastoral charge the Congregation is allowed to proceed to the election of a Minister, the Board shall complete the Vacancy Schedule showing how it is proposed to provide the Appropriate Stipend and Listed Expenses of the charge subject to the approval of the Presbytery and the Committee on the Maintenance of the Ministry—which Appropriate Stipend and Listed Expenses the Board shall use all necessary means to secure; Provided that if the Board should desire to increase the Stipend and/or Listed Expenses for the charge at any time, they shall be entitled to do so with the consent and approval of the Presbytery and of the said Committee; but always without prejudice to the right of the Presbytery, either at the request of the existing Minister or on its own initiative, with the consent and approval of the said Committee, or the right of the said Committee with the consent and approval of the Presbytery, to direct the Board to provide an amended Appropriate Stipend and Listed Expenses for the charge.

Maintenance of Church Properties.

Tenth, Without prejudice to the provisions of Article Eighth hereof, it shall be the duty of the Board to maintain the fabrics of all properties vested in the Church of Scotland General Trustees and/or belonging to the Congregation in proper order and repair, and fully insured against loss or damage by fire,—such insurances to be effected in name of and by the Church of Scotland General Trustees, in so far as the subjects insured are vested in them. Any sum or sums which may be or may have been fixed by the General Assembly or by the Presbytery or by the Board itself in terms of Article Eighth hereof, as necessary for the maintenance of the fabrics of the said Church properties, shall be taken annually from the Ordinary Revenue where not provided for in the original endowment, or obtained from voluntary or other sources. No extraordinary repairs or improvements upon the Church properties shall be undertaken, and no material additions thereto shall be made, until the Board shall have received the consent thereto of the Presbytery, and also of the General Trustees in the case of properties vested in them, and sufficient funds shall have been raised or guaranteed for the purpose without encroaching upon the Ordinary Revenue of the Parish and Congregation. Further, no material additions to the furnishings for the Church or Church Hall shall be provided until the monies required to meet the cost of the same shall have been similarly raised or guaranteed. Any urgent extraordinary repairs to properties may be executed by the Board without such consent as aforesaid, but the necessity for the same shall be immediately reported by the Board to the Presbytery, and to the General Trustees where the property is vested in them.

Application of balance at credit of Ordinary Revenue and Expenditure Account.

Eleventh, If at the close of any financial year there shall remain any balance at the credit of the Ordinary Revenue and Expenditure Account after making the payments, or setting aside the sums, specified or referred to in Article Eighth hereof, the same shall be applied by the Board in whole or in part, for Congregational and/or general Church purposes, which purposes shall include, *inter alia,* all or any one or more of the following—*videlicet :* (1) supplement to the Minister to the extent necessary to provide the Appropriate Stipend and Listed Expenses if not already provided for ; (2) addition to the Fabrics Fund Account ; (3) further contributions under the Co-ordinated Appeal to the Schemes of the Church ; (4) a Reserve Fund to meet Extraordinary or Exceptional Expenditure in connection with the Church properties, or for the furnishings thereof ; and (5) a Reserve Fund for Stipend or further endowment. Any sum remaining thereafter may be carried forward to next year's Account. Provided always, notwithstanding anything hereinbefore contained in this Article, that in any year in which aid is received from the Fund for the Maintenance of the Ministry in order to raise the Stipend or emoluments of said Parish to the Minimum Stipend of the Church of Scotland for the year in question, any balance foresaid shall be applied, primarily and as a first charge, as supplement to the Stipend in order to reduce the amount received by way of aid from the said Fund for the Maintenance of the Ministry during such year.

Contributions to Co-ordinated Appeal, etc.

Twelfth, It shall be the responsibility of the Congregational Board on receiving intimation of the allocation on the Congregation of the sum required each year under the Co-ordinated Appeal to take steps after conference with the Kirk Session to inform the Congregation of the allocation, to raise at least the sum allocated along with the proposed minimum contributions to the Maintenance of the Ministry Fund and Aged and Infirm Ministers' Fund, to give members of the Congregation full information with regard to the Co-ordinated Appeal, and to distribute literature, leaflets, etc., provided by the Stewardship and Budget Committee. The Board shall also consult with representatives of the Woman's Guild to determine the proportion of the allocation which will be the responsibility of the Woman's Guild. If the Weekly Freewill Offering System or any similar system is in operation the Board shall determine the allocation of the money thus raised in so far as such allocation has not been determined by the contributors.

It shall be the responsibility of the Kirk Session to afford the Congregation convenient opportunities for contributing to any other objects for which the General Assembly shall have enjoined special collections and the Kirk Session shall also have power to make such collections as may be deemed necessary for the needs of the poor or other religious or charitable purposes, all of which shall be shewn in separate Accounts as required under Article Eighth hereof.

Audit of Accounts and submission thereof to Congregation and Presbytery.

Thirteenth, The Accounts of the Congregation shall be made up to 31st December or such earlier date as the Congregational Board may decide in each year, and, after having been duly audited,[3] shall be submitted by the Board to the Congregation for approval at the Stated Annual Meeting to be held not later than the 31st day of March following (or other date authorised in terms of Article Second hereof), and the same shall, *inter alia,* contain a Statement as to the application or disposal, or the proposed application or disposal, of any balance or surplus on the Ordinary Revenue and Expenditure Account for the year in accordance with the provisions of Article Eleventh hereof. The said Accounts shall, after submission to and approval by the Congregation, be laid before the Presbytery within one month thereafter, for examination and attestation to the effect that the Accounts are correct and are in accordance with the terms of this Constitution, and the same shall also be docqueted by the Presbytery with reference to the provisions of Article Eleventh hereof. The Board shall also satisfy themselves that the Accounts kept by the several other agencies of the Congregation, except in so far as such Accounts are under the control of the Kirk Session, have been duly audited and are in order.

Seat Rents, etc.

Fourteenth, It shall be competent for the Board to take steps to let or otherwise allocate the sittings in the Church and to fix the rents or contributions payable therefor, where these are exigible,—a pew being reserved for the family of the Minister, and suitable accommodation being provided for the officiating Elders.

Appointment and Salaries of Church Officials.

Fifteenth, The Kirk Session shall appoint the Church Officer, and the Precentor or Choirmaster and the Organist, and any other like officials, and shall define their duties. The salaries of all such officials shall be fixed by the Board. Such Officials shall each and all be subject to the direction of the Minister as regards the execution of their duties. The Kirk Session shall have power to suspend or terminate the appointments of all or any of the said officials, due intimation of such suspension or termination being given by them to the Board.

Vesting and Payment of Minister's Stipend.

Sixteenth, The Stipend, including that derived from the statutory endowments, shall vest *de die in diem* in the Minister, and, until the General Assembly shall otherwise determine, shall be payable to him monthly.

[3] A form of docquet which it is recommended should be signed by the Auditor or Auditors is given in Note 3, page 617.

Existing functions of Minister and Kirk Session reserved.

Seventeenth, Nothing herein contained shall interfere with the functions assigned to the Minister and to the Kirk Session respectively by the common law of the Church of Scotland or by any Acts of the General Assembly applicable thereto.

Powers of Presbytery where Board disregard terms of Constitution.

Eighteenth, In the event of the Presbytery finding that the Board constituted in terms hereof, or a majority of its Members, persist or shall have persisted in disregarding the terms of this Constitution after their attention has been called to the matter, the Presbytery may remove from the Board those who have been guilty of such contumacy, and declare them ineligible for reappointment for a period of not less than three years, and shall thereafter take such steps as they may deem proper to fill up the vacancies thus occasioned, with power to the Presbytery, if that Court should itself find it necessary or expedient to do so, to make appointments to the Board.

Interpretation.

Nineteenth, If any question shall arise with reference to the election of the Board, or to the interpretation of any Article of this Constitution or the legality of any particular exercise of the powers herein contained, it shall be competent to any person or body interested to apply by Petition to the Presbytery to adjudicate upon the matter, and the judgment of the Presbytery upon such matter, or upon any question arising in connection with the annual audit provided for in Article Thirteenth hereof shall be final, unless any party shall, at the first ordinary meeting of the Presbytery held after the lapse of twenty-one days from the date of the judgment, produce a certificate under the hand of the Procurator of the Church to the effect that the matter is one suitable for appeal to the Higher Courts of the Church, in which case an appeal or dissent and complaint may be taken in common form at such meeting as if the judgment of the Presbytery had only then been given.

Powers reserved to General Assembly.

Twentieth, It shall be in the power of the General Assembly at any time, or from time to time, to alter, revoke, amend, or modify this Deed of Constitution, in whole or in part, or to substitute a new Model Deed of Constitution for this Deed of Constitution, subject always to such conditions and provisions relative thereto as the General Assembly shall determine ; provided that nothing shall thereby be done to require that the titles of the heritable properties of the Congregation be transferred from the existing Trustees to any other body of Trustees.

Given under our hands this day of 19 , and Signed and Delivered by us, as duly authorised by the General Assembly of the Church of Scotland, and as a Quorum of the Delegation appointed by the said General Assembly for, *inter alia,* that purpose.

NOTES

Note 1

In cases where the number of Elders is less than six and the Presbytery is satisfied that there is no immediate prospect of that number being augmented, the Presbytery may permit that a number of communicants in excess of the number of Elders be elected to the Congregational Board, subject, however, in such cases to the total number of Members of the Congregational Board other than Elders not exceeding six. The Presbytery shall, subject as aforesaid, decide the number to be so elected and shall report each decision to the Delegation of the General Assembly.

Note 2

It is enacted by Act XIX of the General Assembly of 1964, Section 3, as follows :—

Notwithstanding the terms of the Model Deed of Constitution, in cases where the Model Deed shall in future be issued to a Congregation whose financial or temporal affairs immediately prior thereto have been administered by a Deacons' Court consisting wholly or partly of Members ordained or commissioned for life or otherwise holding office for life, such Members of the former Deacons' Court, if they so wish, shall, without election, become Members of the Congregational Board for life or for as long as they wish to remain Members thereof, provided always that their names remain on the Communion Roll. While any such persons are Members of the Congregational Board the number of Members elected to the Board by the Congregation shall be reduced accordingly, and the provisions in the Model Deed of Constitution for the retiral of Members by rotation shall apply only to elected Members. Any life Member of the Congregational Board who ceases to be a Member of the Board during his lifetime owing to resignation or some other cause, shall if subsequently elected to the Board be an ordinary Member thereof.

Note 3

Recommended form of Auditors' docquet :—

We have examined the foregoing Accounts for the period from .... to .... and we have to report that we have obtained all the information and explanations we have required. The Accounts have been properly vouched and instructed and we have verified the Cash Balances and also the Balances on Bank Accounts as shown by the Treasurer's Books at the close of the period. We have seen Certificates or other evidence of the Investments held for behoof of the Congregation as at the close of the period and we are satisfied that they are in order. In our opinion the Accounts exhibit a true state of affairs as shown by the Treasurer's Books.

APPENDIX XVI.

ACT ANENT PROCLAMATION OF BANNS OF MARRIAGE (1932, xvi., as amended by 1942, vi., 1959, iii., 1971, i., and 1975, i.).

Edinburgh, June 1, 1932. *Sess.* 12.

THE General Assembly declare and enact as follows :—

1. The General Assembly hereby repeal, as from the date hereof, Act XIII. of the General Assembly, 1931, anent the Proclamation of Banns, and re-enact the same with the amendments thereon shown below, which amendments the General Assembly hereby approve of and adopt, and that in the same manner and to the same effect as if they had been originally contained and enacted in the said Act XIII. of the General Assembly, 1931.

2. The General Assembly also hereby re-enact the First and Second Schedules to the said Act XIII. of the General Assembly, 1931, without alteration, except as regards the First Schedule to the extent shown in the said Appendix to said Report, and declare them to be effectual as the First and Second Schedules to the said Act as now amended.

The Act, as amended, follows :—

WHEREAS it is expedient, in view of the reunion of the Church of Scotland and the United Free Church of Scotland under the name of "The Church of Scotland," and the provisions of the Act of Assembly No. I. of date 2nd October 1929, approving of and adopting the Basis and Plan of Union of the said Churches (being the Uniting Act) that provision should be made relative to the Proclamation of Banns of Marriage in the said reunited Church ;

AND WHEREAS it is laid down in the said Plan of Union that the place or places where Banns are to be proclaimed fall to be determined by Presbyteries ;

THE GENERAL ASSEMBLY THEREFORE ENACT AND ORDAIN AS FOLLOWS :—

1. The General Assembly hereby repeal Act VIII. of the General Assembly, 1880, anent the Proclamation of Banns, and also rescind or amend all previous Regulations of Assembly in relation to the said matter, and in particular those contained in the Acts of 1699, 1782, and 1784, in so far as the same are inconsistent with what is hereinafter enacted and ordained.

2. The Regulations printed in the First Schedule hereto with regard to residence in a Registration District and otherwise shall receive effect in the same manner and to the same extent as if the said Regulations had been printed in and formed part of the provisions of this Act.

3. (1) The Presbyteries of the Church shall forthwith consider, determine, and appoint, after consultation with the Ministers and Kirk Sessions, or representatives thereof, the Churches or Church within the bounds of each Registration District, as delimited for the registration of Births, Deaths, and Marriages, in which Proclamation of Banns shall henceforth be made, or otherwise as provided in subsection (2), and they are hereby directed to see that proper Regulations are framed relative thereto, and adequate arrangements made for receiving Notices

of Proclamation in each case: Provided always that it shall be competent for any Presbytery to determine that Proclamation in any of the Churches within the Registration District in which they are situated shall be valid and effectual.

(2) Where no Church belonging to the Church of Scotland exists within any Registration District the Presbytery concerned shall, after consultation as aforesaid, determine and appoint a Church or Churches convenient or adjacent thereto for the purposes of Proclamation, and make all other necessary arrangements in connection therewith, and where any Church has for ecclesiastical purposes an area attached thereto which is situated within an adjoining Registration District, the Presbytery may, if they shall deem it expedient, appoint the said Church for the purposes of Proclamation in respect of persons residing in the said area.

(3) Intimation shall be given by all Presbytery Clerks to the Registrars of Births, Deaths, and Marriages within the bounds of their respective Presbyteries, and also to the Registrar-General, as to the Churches or Church within the bounds of each Registration District, as above defined (or as regards any cases falling under subsection (2) hereof then to the Registrar or Registrars of the adjoining District or Districts and to the Registrar-General), which shall have been determined and appointed by the Presbytery concerned for the purpose of receiving and making Proclamation of Banns. Provided always that in the event of any Presbytery subsequently making any alteration as regards the appointed Churches or any of them within the bounds of such Presbytery, intimation of any change or changes so made shall forthwith be intimated by the Clerk or Clerks of such Presbytery to the Registrar-General, and also to the District Registrar or District Registrars concerned.

(4) Until each Presbytery shall have determined and appointed, as above set forth, the existing practice shall continue within the bounds of each Presbytery, and Proclamation of Banns shall be made in the Church or Churches where the same was in use to be made before Union.

4. Proclamation of Banns of Marriage in any Church or Churches thus determined and appointed by the Presbyteries shall, as from and after the date of such determination and appointment by the respective Presbyteries, constitute a valid and sufficient Proclamation of the Banns of such Marriage. Provided always that in the event of any party or parties being by inadvertence proclaimed in a Church not so determined and appointed in respect of the Registration District of qualifying residence, but being an appointed Church in an adjoining Registration District, such Proclamation shall nevertheless be valid and effectual.

5. Notwithstanding the terms of this Act, or anything done in pursuance of this Act, the *Quoad Omnia* Parishes of the Church of Scotland as existing at the date of the passing of the Church of Scotland (Property and Endowments) Act, 1925, shall remain unaltered as regards any question affecting the teinds, or the Stipends or standard charges payable out of the teinds, of such Parishes, and the rights of the Ministers of such Parishes or of the Church of Scotland General Trustees under and in virtue of the said last-mentioned Act (as the case may be) to raise and pursue processes of Augmentation, Modification, and Locality of the Stipends of such Parishes, or for the preparation of Teind Rolls

applicable to such Parishes (as the case may be) shall likewise remain unaltered.

6. (1) The charge for the Proclamation of Banns in any Church in which such Proclamation is made in terms of this Act shall be the sum of 75p (1975, i.).[1]

(2) The Form of Application for Proclamation of Banns and the requisite Certificates to be granted in relation thereto shall be those in, or as nearly as may be in, the terms printed in the Second Schedule hereto.

FIRST SCHEDULE.[2]

Regulations with regard to Residence in a Registration District, Etc.

1. Persons proposing to marry—and to whose marriage there is no impediment recognised by the laws of the Church—shall be entitled to have the banns of the marriage proclaimed in a Church or Churches which shall have been appointed by the Presbytery for that purpose, provided that—

(*a*) Each of the parties to the intended marriage has his or her usual residence, or has resided for a period of fifteen clear days immediately preceding the application for proclamation, in a registration district in Scotland; or

(*b*) In a case where one of the parties is resident furth of Scotland the other party has his or her usual residence, or has resided for the period of fifteen clear days as aforesaid, in a registration district in Scotland.

Unless the above-mentioned conditions are satisfied, no proclamation of banns shall be allowed except in cases falling within the Emergency Provisions of Act VI. of the General Assembly, 1940,[3] or within Section 2 of Act VI. of the General Assembly, 1942,[3] or within Act II. of the General Assembly, 1957 (1957, ii.), p. 624.

In order to due proclamation of banns in any case where the two parties to the intended marriage have their usual residence or have resided for the period aforesaid in different registration districts in Scotland, proclamation shall be made in each registration district in one or other of the Churches appointed by the Presbytery for the purpose. In any case where both of the parties have their usual residence or have resided for the said period in the same registration district it shall be sufficient if proclamation is made in one of the Churches appointed for that registration district. In a case where one of the parties is resident furth of Scotland, proclamation shall be made in a Church appointed for the registration district in which the other party has his or her usual residence or has resided for the said period, and the Minister shall satisfy himself on such evidence as he shall deem sufficient that there is no impediment to the intended marriage (1942, vi.). Where there is no Church belonging to the Church of Scotland within any Registration District, residence in that Registration District shall constitute sufficient residence for Proclamation of Banns in the Church or Churches in any adjoining Registration District or Districts as determined and appointed by the Presbytery concerned under the provisions of Section 3 (2) of the foregoing Act, and where a Church is appointed in terms of

[1] This charge is altered from time to time by the General Assembly.
[2] This Schedule has been amended by Act 1940, vi., and by Act 1942, vi.
[3] The emergency provisions and section 2 of 1942 (vi.) expired on 31st December 1947 (1946, vii.).

said section in respect of an area attached thereto, but which is in an adjoining Registration District, residence in that area shall constitute sufficient residence for Proclamation of Banns in such last-mentioned Church; and such Proclamation shall constitute sufficient Proclamation in terms of the foregoing Act: Provided always that if only one of the parties shall be so resident Proclamation in respect of the other party shall at the same time be made in an appointed Church in the appropriate Registration District in accordance with the provisions of section 3 (1) of the foregoing Act.

2. Applicants for Proclamation of Banns shall lodge their applications, along with the requisite particulars, with the person or persons to be appointed by the Presbytery for each Registration District for the purpose of receiving the same, and such person or persons shall transmit each application to the Minister or Session Clerk of the Church or one of the Churches where Proclamation of Banns have been determined and appointed by the Presbytery to be made. The Minister or Session Clerk receiving the application shall enter the names, designations, and places of residence of the persons to be proclaimed, as required by the Act of Assembly, 1784, in a book to be kept for the purpose. This book shall be open to public inspection, and shall, if required by the Kirk Session, be laid before them from time to time, and the same shall also be submitted once a year for examination and attestation to the Presbytery of the bounds, whose duty it shall be to see that the Law of the Church on this subject is duly observed. Where it is necessary to do so, Special Regulations shall be made by the Presbytery concerned for dealing with applications for Proclamation of Banns and otherwise in relation to any cases falling under Section 3, subsection (2), of the foregoing Act.

3. Proclamation of Banns shall, in ordinary cases, be made on two separate Sundays, and, wherever it can be conveniently done, shall be made from the pulpit or reading-desk by the Minister or his officiating substitute acting on his authority, at some time before the close of the service at the principal diet of Public Worship.[1] When this cannot be conveniently done, the Proclamation shall be made in such manner as may be agreed upon by the Minister and Kirk Session, but always, except as provided for in the immediately succeeding Article, in presence of the Congregation. The Certificate of Proclamation shall be delivered on the day following the completion of the Proclamation, except in the case of persons engaged in War Service (1940, vi.), when such Certificate may be delivered at any time after Proclamation has been made.

4. When through unavoidable circumstances there is no service in the Church or any of the Churches appointed by the Presbytery, or in any building or buildings temporarily authorised by the Presbytery for Public Worship in lieu of such Church or Churches on any Sunday, a Proclamation by the Minister or the Session Clerk at the door of the Church or of one of the Churches so appointed at the usual hour of service for the first diet of Public Worship in presence of at least two witnesses, together with a written Proclamation signed by the Minister or the Session Clerk posted on the door of the said Church, on the Sunday or Sundays on which it is desired that Proclamation should be made, shall be equivalent to Proclamation from the pulpit or reading-desk of such Church in presence of the Congregation. No such Proclamation shall, however, be competently made except on a Sunday at the hour and place above specified, unless in any case falling under the provisions of the said Act VI. of the General Assembly, 1940.

5. It shall always be in the power of the Minister (but shall not be obligatory upon him) to complete the Proclamation of Banns on a single

[1] Act 1971, i.

Sunday in the case of persons who are known to him, or in regard to whom he has reason to be satisfied, on the information of others, that there is no impediment recognised by the Laws of this Church to the proposed Marriage, or for any other reason sufficient to the Minister. In such case, however, the Certificate of Proclamation shall not be granted or delivered to the parties until the expiry of a period of forty-eight hours after Proclamation has taken place, but, when it is so granted and delivered, it shall have the same legal effect as if Proclamation had been made on two separate Sundays.

6. While it shall be the duty of the Ministers of the Church of Scotland to celebrate Marriages, recognised by the Church as lawful, on the production of a Session Clerk's Certificate, or Session Clerk's Certificates, of the Proclamation of Banns having been duly made in proper form, within the period of three months immediately preceding, they shall not be bound, but shall be at liberty, if they see fit, to receive as a valid notice of marriage a Registrar's Certificate granted within the same period of three months under the Act of Parliament entitled "Marriage Notice (Scotland) Act, 1878," or any certificate which by virtue of any enactment is of the same force and effect as a Certificate under the last-named Act (1940, vi.).

7. No Minister of the Church shall be entitled to recognise as valid any Certificate of Proclamation of Banns of Marriage or Registrar's Certificate of Notice of Marriage granted more than three months prior to the proposed date of the celebration of the Marriage, and he shall not proceed to the solemnisation of the same until due and proper republication of the Banns shall have been made or a new Certificate of Notice by the Registrar has been obtained.

8. The fee or charge for Proclamation payable in terms of Section 6 (1) of the foregoing Act shall, unless and until the Presbytery shall otherwise direct, be paid to the Kirk Session of the Church where the Proclamation is made.

SECOND SCHEDULE.

Forms for use by Applicants, Etc.

I. *Application for Proclamation of Banns.*

(1) Application by Parties.

Date

State full Name and Occupation, and whether Bachelor or Widower.

State full Name and Occupation, if any, and whether Spinster or Widow.

There is a purpose of marriage between residing at in the Registration District of and residing at in the Registration District of

To be Signed by the Party or Parties about to be Married resident in District where the Proclamation is made.

Application for Proclamation is made by

Signature ....

Note.—In cases falling under Section 3 (2) of the foregoing Act the Form of Application and relative Certificate Nos. (2) and (3) may be altered so far as necessary.

(2) Certificate of Householders (1942, vi.)

in respect of both parties.

Date,

We, householder, residing at , and householder, residing at

do hereby certify that the parties above named are personally known to us, and that they * (1) have their usual residence in the Registration District of ; * (2) have resided for a period of fifteen clear days immediately preceding the above date in the Registration District of ; and that we have good reason to believe them to be unmarried persons, not related to each other within the forbidden degrees, and not under sixteen years of age.

......................Householder.
......................Householder.

* Delete whichever is not applicable.

* *Note.*—Where only one of the parties is so resident, the certificate will be altered so as to apply to the circumstances as actually existing, and separate certificates for each party may be required. (See succeeding form.)

(3) CERTIFICATE OF HOUSEHOLDERS (1942, vi.)
in respect of one party.

Date,

We, householder, residing at , and householder, residing at , do hereby certify that one of the parties above named, is personally known to us, and that he/she * (1) has his/her usual residence in the Registration District of ; * (2) has resided for a period of fifteen clear days immediately preceding the above date in the Registration District of . We further certify that we have good reason to believe him/her to be an unmarried person, that the said parties are not related to each other within the forbidden degrees, and that the said is not under sixteen years of age.

......................Householder.
......................Householder.

* Delete whichever is not applicable.

II. *Certificate to be endorsed on Form No. 1, and signed by the Minister when the Proclamation is to be made on one Sunday.*

I, Minister of the Church of hereby authorise the Proclamation of the Banns of the parties within named to be completed on one Sunday, in terms of Act of Assembly, 1932.

Signature......................

III. *Certificate of Proclamation.*

At *the* *day of* 19

It is hereby certified, That and , have been duly proclaimed in the Church of on in order to marriage, and that no objections have been offered.

Signature...................{*Minister or Session Clerk.*

Note.—Certificates Nos. (2) and (3) may be dispensed with in the discretion of the Minister where the parties are personally well known to him.

APPENDIX XVII.

ACT ANENT PROCLAMATION OF BANNS OF MARRIAGE (1957, ii.).

WHEREAS the Marriage (Scotland) Act, 1956 (4 & 5 Eliz. 2 Cap. 70) has amended the law with regard to civil notice of marriage intended to be celebrated or contracted in Scotland, to the effect of enabling a party residing in England or Wales, but having a parent whose usual residence is in Scotland, to give notice of intended marriage to the registrar of the parish or district in which that parent has his usual residence: And Whereas it is expedient to amend the law of the Church so that such party should likewise be enabled to have the banns of such marriage proclaimed: Now therefore the General Assembly enact and ordain as follows:—

1. Notwithstanding anything contained in the existing Acts anent Proclamation of Banns of Marriage:—

(1) Where a party to a marriage intended to be celebrated or contracted in Scotland—and to whose intended marriage there is no impediment recognised by the law of the Church—is residing in England or Wales, but has a parent (as hereinafter defined) who has his or her usual residence in a registration district in Scotland, the banns of marriage may be proclaimed in like manner as if such party had himself or herself resided in the aforesaid district for a period of fifteen clear days immediately preceding the application for proclamation.

(2) In the case of any such party such proclamation shall be made in a Church appointed for the registration district in which the parent of such party has his or her usual residence, and the Minister shall satisfy himself on such evidence as he shall deem sufficient that there is no impediment to the intended marriage.

2. In this Act any reference to a parent of a party to an intended marriage includes a reference to:—

(1) any person who has adopted that party by virtue of an adoption order within the meaning of the Adoption Act, 1950 (14 Geo. 6 Cap. 26), or any enactment repealed by that Act, or any similar order pronounced by a competent court elsewhere than in Great Britain (in this section referred to as an " adoptive parent "), and

(2) any spouse, widow, or widower of a parent or adoptive parent of that party.

3. (1) Paragraph 1 of the First Schedule to Act XVI. of 1932, as amended by Act VI. of 1942, is hereby further amended by the insertion after the words " or within section 2 of Act VI. of the General Assembly, 1942," of the words " or within Act II of the General Assembly, 1957."

(2) Notwithstanding anything contained in section 6 (2) of Act XVI. of 1932, the Certificate of householders to be granted in relation to an application for proclamation of banns under this Act shall be in, or as nearly as may be in, the form set forth in the Schedule hereto.

SCHEDULE.

CERTIFICATE OF HOUSEHOLDERS.

Date ....

WE, ..., householder, residing at .... and ...., householder, residing at ...., do hereby certify that one of the parties above-named, namely ...., is personally known to us and that he/she is residing in England/Wales. We further certify that .... is the .... and, as such, a parent of the above-named party within the meaning of Act II. of the General Assembly, 1957, and has his/her usual residence at .... Scotland. We further certify that we have good reason to believe that the said party is an unmarried person, that the parties intending marriage are not related to each other within the forbidden degrees, and that the said .... is not under sixteen years of age.

......................*Householder.*
......................*Householder.*

Note.—The " parent " of a party to an intended marriage within the meaning of Act of the General Assembly, 1957, includes :—

(1) any person who has adopted that party by virtue of an adoption order within the meaning of the Adoption Act, 1950 (14 Geo. 6 Cap. 26), or any enactment repealed by that Act, or any similar order pronounced by a competent court elsewhere than in Great Britain (in this section referred to as an " adoptive parent "), and

(2) any spouse, widow, or widower of a parent or adoptive parent of that party.

APPENDIX XVIII.

MARRIAGE ACT, 1939.

[2 & 3 Geo. 6.]

CHAPTER 33.

An Act to facilitate marriages in cases where one party resides in Scotland and the other in England and to make further provision as respects notices of marriage between parties one of whom resides in Scotland or England. [13*th July* 1939.]

Be it enacted by the King's most Excellent Majesty, by and with the advice and consent of the Lords Spiritual and Temporal, and Commons, in this present Parliament assembled, and by the authority of the same, as follows :—

Notices and Certificates where one party resides in Scotland and the other in England.

1.[1]—(1) Where it is intended that a marriage shall be solemnised in England, or that a regular marriage shall be contracted or celebrated in Scotland, between parties of whom one is residing in Scotland and the other is residing in England, the following provisions shall have effect :—

41 & 42 Vict. c. 43.

(*a*) the party residing in Scotland may, subject to and in accordance with the provisions of section seven of the Marriage Notice (Scotland) Act, 1878, give notice of the intended marriage as if the parties were residing in different parishes or districts in Scotland and (where the marriage is to be solemnised in England) as if it were intended to be contracted or celebrated in Scotland, and the provisions of that Act relating to notices of intended marriages and the granting of certificates of due publication thereof shall apply accordingly :

6 & 7 Will. 4. c. 85.

(*b*) the party residing in England may, subject to and in accordance with the provisions of section four of the Marriage Act, 1836, as amended by any subsequent enactment, give notice of the intended marriage as if the parties were residing in different districts in England and (where the marriage is to be contracted or celebrated in Scotland) as if it were intended to be solemnised in England, and the provisions of the Marriage Acts, 1811 to 1934, relating to notices of marriage and the issue of certificates for marriage shall apply accordingly ;

(*c*) where the marriage is to be solemnised in England—

(i) a certificate of due publication of a notice of the intended marriage granted in Scotland by virtue of para-

[1] Repealed as far as it relates to marriages solemnised in England (Marriage Act, 1949, Schedule 5 I.).

graph (*a*) of this section shall, for the purpose of the marriage, have the like force and effect in all respects as a certificate for marriage issued by a superintendent registrar in England under the Marriage Acts, 1811 to 1934 ; and

(ii) for the purpose of any enactment limiting the time within which the marriage may be solemnised by reference to the day of entry of the notice, the notice shall be deemed to have been entered by a superintendent registrar in England on the day on which it was given :

(*d*) where the marriage is to be contracted or celebrated in Scotland, a certificate for marriage issued in England by virtue of paragraph (*b*) of this section shall, for the purpose of the marriage, be of the like force and effect in all respects as a certificate granted by a registrar in Scotland under section nine of the Marriage Notice (Scotland) Act, 1878.

(2) This section shall come into operation on the first day of October nineteen hundred and thirty-nine.

Power to accept notices and issue certificates where one party is residing in England or Scotland.

2.—(1) Where—

(*a*) a marriage is intended to be solemnised in England between parties of whom one is residing in England, and

(*b*) by virtue of any enactment to which this subsection applies, a certificate issued to the other party otherwise than by a superintendent registrar in England may be treated for the purpose of the marriage as if it had been issued by such a registrar,

the superintendent registrar of the district in which the first-mentioned party is residing shall have power, and shall be deemed always to have had power, to accept notice of the marriage given by that party, subject to and in accordance with the provisions of section four of the Marriage Act, 1836, as amended by any subsequent enactment, as if both parties were residing in different districts in England, and the provisions of the Marriage Acts, 1811 to 1934, relating to notices of marriage and the issue of certificates for marriage shall apply, and shall be deemed always to have applied, accordingly.

(2) Where—

(*a*) it is intended that a marriage shall be contracted or celebrated in Scotland between parties of whom one is residing in Scotland, and

(*b*) by virtue of any enactment to which this subsection applies, a certificate issued to the other party otherwise than by a registrar in Scotland may be treated for the purpose of the marriage as if it had been issued by such a registrar,

the registrar of the district or parish in Scotland in which the first-mentioned party is residing shall have power, and shall be deemed always to have had power, to accept notice of the marriage given by that party, subject to and in accordance with the provisions of section seven of the Marriage Notice (Scotland) Act, 1878, as if both parties were residing in different parishes or districts in Scotland, and the provisions of that Act relating to notices of intended marriages and the granting of certificates of due publication thereof shall apply, and shall be deemed always to have applied, accordingly.

5 & 6 Geo. 5. c. 40.

(3) The enactments to which subsection (1) of this section applies are .... [repealed by Marriage Act, 1949, Sched. 5 I.], and paragraph (*a*) of subsection (1) of section one of the Marriage of British Subjects (Facilities) Act, 1915, and the enactments to which subsection (2) of this section applies are the said section three and the said paragraph (*a*) as those enactments apply to Scotland.

3. [Repealed by Marriage Act, 1949, Sched. 5 I.] [1]

Short title and citation.

4.—(1) This Act may be cited as the Marriage Act, 1939.

(2) This Act, so far as it relates to England, may be cited together with the Marriage Acts, 1811 to 1934, as the Marriage Acts, 1811 to 1939.

[1] *Note.*—By section 13 of the Marriage Act 1949, for the purpose of a marriage in England a Certificate of Proclamation of Banns according to the law or custom of Scotland is sufficient.

APPENDIX XIX.

MARRIAGE (SCOTLAND) ACT, 1939.

[2 & 3 Geo. 6.]

CHAPTER 34.

An Act to amend the law relating to the constitution of marriage in Scotland. [*13th July* 1939.]

Be it enacted by the King's most Excellent Majesty, by and with the advice and consent of the Lords Spiritual and Temporal, and Commons, in this present Parliament assembled, and by the authority of the same, as follows :—

1.—(1) Any two persons who desire to be married to each other in Scotland, may contract a marriage in the office of an authorised registrar in accordance with the following provisions :— Marriage before registrar.

(i) on production to an authorised registrar of valid certificates of due publication under the Marriage Notice (Scotland) Act, 1878, of notice of the intended marriage, or of a valid certificate of such publication, applicable to both parties, the registrar shall supply a copy of the First Schedule to this Act, and shall, so far as possible, fill up the same according to the information supplied by the parties to the best of their knowledge and belief ; 41 & 42 Vict. c. 4.

(ii) the parties shall thereafter, in the presence of the registrar and of two persons of the age of sixteen years or upwards as witnesses, declare that they know of no legal impediment to their marriage, and that they accept each other as husband and wife ;

(iii) the registrar shall then complete the filling up of the copy of the aforesaid Schedule and it shall be signed [1] by the parties, the registrar and the witnesses.

(2) The registrar shall cause the particulars of every marriage contracted under this section in his presence as such particulars are set forth in the copy of the aforesaid Schedule to be entered as soon as possible in the register, and the copy of the Schedule shall be transmitted to the Registrar-General for preservation.

(3) The registrar shall be entitled in respect of a marriage contracted under this section in his presence to a fee of five shillings.

(4) Any marriage contracted in accordance with the foregoing pro-

[1] Any person whose signature is required for the purpose of a marriage and who by reason of blindness or any other cause is unable to write may sign by adhibiting a cross or other mark in presence of the registrar or two witnesses, provided the registrar or witnesses shall duly subscribe a declaration relative to such cross or mark as having been so adhibited by such person in their presence. (Marriages (Scotland) Act, 1878, section 16 ; Marriage (Scotland) Act, 1942, section 4.)

visions of this section shall, unless there be a legal impediment thereto, be a valid and regular marriage in all respects.

18 & 19 Vict. c. 29. (5) Section three of the Registration of Births, Deaths and Marriages (Scotland) Act, 1964 (which confers power to make regulations), shall extend to the making of regulations regarding the discharge of the duties imposed on registrars by this section, including, without prejudice to the foregoing generality, the hours during which registrars shall be required to give attendance for the purposes of this section.

(6) In this section the expression "authorised registrar" means a registrar authorised for the purposes of this section by the Registrar-General, and it shall be the duty of the Registrar-General, in pursuance of the power hereby conferred, to authorise at least one registrar in each large burgh and one registrar in each small burgh or in the registration district comprising such burgh, and to authorise in the landward areas of counties such number of registrars as the Registrar-General may, after consultation with the county councils, think necessary in order to afford reasonable facilities in every part of Scotland for marriages in accordance with this section. Where any registrar is authorised in pursuance of this subsection, the assistant to that registrar shall, unless the Registrar-General otherwise directs, be deemed to be an authorised registrar.

(7) The power conferred by the last foregoing subsection may be exercised from time to time as the Registrar-General shall think fit, and shall include power to revoke an authorisation thereunder.

Marriage by licence. 2.—(1) Where on a joint application to the sheriff by the parties to any marriage intended to be contracted within his jurisdiction it appears to the sheriff—

(a) That one of the parties has his usual residence in Scotland or has lived in Scotland for fifteen days immediately preceding the presentation of the application;

(b) that there is no legal impediment to the marriage;

(c) that proclamation of banns of the marriage or publication of notice thereof under the Marriage Notice (Scotland) Act, 1878, could not be obtained till after the day on which it is intended that the marriage shall take place; and

(d) that, in respect of the illness of one of the parties or other unforeseen and exceptional circumstance, there is reasonable excuse for the failure of the parties to take the necessary steps to secure such proclamation or publication and to obtain a certificate thereof before the said day;

the sheriff may grant a licence for such marriage, and such licence shall, for all purposes, be of the like force and effect as a certificate of notice of marriage applicable to both parties granted under section nine of the aforesaid Act.

(2) If any marriage for which a licence has been granted under this section does not take place within ten days after the grant thereof, the licence shall be void.

Amendment of s. 5 of 41 & 42 Vict. cap. 43. 3. Section five of the Marriage Notice (Scotland) Act, 1878, shall apply to a marriage contracted and solemnised in Scotland according to the usages of the Society of Friends, commonly called Quakers, if either of the parties to such marriage is a member of the said Society or an attender associated therewith, in like manner as the said section applies to a marriage so contracted and solemnised between persons who are both members of the said Society.

4. The validity of a regular marriage which has been registered under the Registration of Births, Deaths and Marriages (Scotland) Acts, 1854 to 1938, shall not be questioned in any legal proceedings whatsoever, on the ground that the person by whom such marriage was celebrated or solemnised was not competent or qualified to do so. **Validity of registered regular marriage.**

5. No irregular marriage by declaration *de presenti* or by promise *subsequente copula* contracted after the commencement of this Act shall be valid. **Abolition of irregular marriage by declaration and by promise *subsequente copula*.**

6.—(1) Where decree of declarator establishing an irregular marriage has been granted in the Court of Session, the Principal Clerk of Session shall forthwith cause the decree and the names, designations and addresses of the parties to be intimated to the Registrar-General, and on receipt of such intimation the Registrar-General shall cause the marriage to be registered. **Registration of irregular marriages by declarator.**

(2) Sections forty-eight and forty-nine of, and Schedule (K.) annexed to, the Registration of Births, Deaths and Marriages (Scotland) Act, 1854, are hereby repealed.

7. In this Act unless the context otherwise requires— **Interpretation.**

the expression "Registrar-General" means the Registrar-General of Births, Deaths and Marriages in Scotland;

the expression "register" means register of Marriages for a registration district kept under the Registration of Births, Deaths and Marriages (Scotland) Act, 1964, and "registration district" has the same meaning as in that Act.

the expressions "large burgh" and "small burgh" have the like meanings as in the Local Government (Scotland) Act, 1929; **19 & 20 Geo. 5. c. 25.**

any reference to a certificate of due publication under the Marriage Notice (Scotland) Act, 1878, of notice of an intended marriage shall include a reference to any certificate which, by virtue of any enactment, is of the same force and effect as a certificate under the said Act.

8. [Repealed by Statute Law Revision Act, 1950.] **Repeal.**

Without prejudice to the provisions of section thirty-eight of the Interpretation Act, 1889, nothing in this repeal shall affect any irregular marriage contracted before the commencement of this Act. **52 & 53 Vict. c. 63.**

9. This Act may be cited as the Marriage (Scotland) Act, 1939.

SCHEDULES.

Section 1.

FIRST SCHEDULE.

SCHEDULE OF MARRIAGE.

Pursuant to Marriage (Scotland) Act, 1939, sec. 1.

When, Where and How Married.	Names (in full) of Parties with Signatures. — Rank or Profession and whether Bachelor, Spinster, Widower, Widow or Divorced.	Age	Usual Residence.	Name, Surname and Rank or Profession of Father. — Name and Maiden Surname of Mother.	Signature of Registrar and Signatures and Addresses of Witnesses.	When and Where Registered and Signature of Registrar.
19 .	(Name in full)				*	19 .
on the						
day of	(Signature)					
						at
					†	
					Witness	
After	(Name in full)				†	
In the office of the Registrar for the parish of and in the presence of the said Registrar in accordance with the Marriage (Scotland) Act, 1939.	(Signature)				Witness	Registrar.

* Signature of Registrar. † Signature and Addresses of two Witnesses.

SECOND SCHEDULE.

Section 8.

[Repealed by Statute Law Revision Act, 1950.]

APPENDIX XX.

ACT ANENT PREPARATION FOR THE MINISTRY—1973, XX.

(See pp. 214-225)

ACT ANENT PRESBYTERIAL SUPERVISION OF STUDENTS, PROBATIONERS, AND MINISTERS

(1935, X, Sections 9-22.).

Licentiates or Probationers.

9. (1) The Trials for Licence of Students shall be such as the General Assembly may from time to time prescribe.

(2) At the request of the student, it shall be competent to any Presbytery to transfer to another Presbytery the receiving of the Trials or any part thereof, certifying to the Presbytery to which the transference is made whether the student has been regularly received for Trials, and what part (if any) of his Trials has already been sustained.

(3) The Presbytery shall be alone when dealing with any matter regarding the preliminary business as to students who are proposed for licence, and when discussing their Trials for Licence, but the proceedings at the actual time of licensing shall not be in private.

10. Besides passing a judgment, sustaining or not sustaining each part of the Trials separately, the Presbytery shall also, after all have been sustained separately, pass a judgment on the whole by a regular vote, "Sustain or not sustain these Trials." The Trials having been sustained, the student shall be required to answer the questions, and to sign the relative formula, prescribed in Act XI., 1932. If it be resolved to proceed to licence, the Moderator shall, after prayer, address the student as follows: "In the Name of the Lord Jesus Christ, the King and Head of the Church, and by authority of this Presbytery, we do now license you to preach the Gospel of the Grace of God, and to exercise your gifts as a Probationer for the Holy Ministry." The Moderator, or another Minister deputed by the Presbytery, shall then address suitable counsels to the licentiate, and conclude with prayer. The Clerk of Presbytery shall furnish the licentiate with an extract of his licence. He shall also, within a week after the student has been licensed, send the name and address of the licentiate, with the date of his licence, to the Clerk of the Committee on Probationers and Transference of Ministers.

11. A Probationer shall remain under the supervision and under the authority of the Presbytery which licensed him, unless and until he be transferred to another Presbytery.

12. If a Probationer undertake work or fix his residence within the bounds of another Presbytery for a longer period than two months, he

shall within that time report himself to the Clerk of the Presbytery into whose bounds he has come, and shall immediately thereafter submit to the Presbytery an Extract Minute of his licence and a Presbyterial Certificate from the Presbytery which he has left. In the event of there being no meeting of that Presbytery to be held immediately after application is made for such a certificate, the Moderator and Clerk (or, failing one of these, two members of Presbytery) may issue the certificate, and the circumstances shall be reported to next meeting of Presbytery. The same course shall be followed on each occasion on which he may remove to another Presbytery.

13. If a Probationer be elected to a vacant charge within the bounds of a Presbytery other than the Presbytery having supervision over him, he shall, before his ordination, submit to the Presbytery an Extract Minute of his licence and a Presbyterial Certificate; the latter may be granted in accordance with the provisions of Section 12 above.

14. A Probationer from the Presbyterian Church of England may be received by a Presbytery as a Probationer of the Church, and his name and address forwarded to the Secretary of the Probationers and Transference of Ministers Committee, provided that he produce to the Presbytery (i) a certificate from the College Committee of his Church that he has taken the full and regular curriculum without any modification whatever, (ii) an Extract Minute of his licence, (iii) a certificate from the Presbytery within whose bounds he last resided that his character and conduct are in accordance with his profession. A Probationer of the Presbyterian Church of England, who is elected to a vacant charge in the Church, shall produce the same documents unless he has already been received as a Probationer of this Church.[1]

15. If the General Assembly resolve to admit any person to the status of a Probationer of the Church, there shall be presented to the Presbytery of his residence, or to such other Presbytery as the General Assembly may appoint, within six months, an Extract of the General Assembly's Deliverance. The Presbytery shall thereafter put to the person concerned the Questions appointed to be put to Probationers by Act XI., 1932, and the formula shall be signed. His name shall immediately be forwarded to the Clerk of the Probationers and Transference of Ministers Committee. If he afterwards remove to another Presbytery, the provisions of Sections 13 and 14 of this Act shall apply, except that there shall be produced, instead of an Extract of Licence, an Extract of the General Assembly's Deliverance, and of the Minute of Presbytery anent his admission.

16. If a Probationer shall engage in work not under the jurisdiction of the Church, before being again recognised as a Probationer he shall produce to the Presbytery within whose bounds he resides a certificate from the Committee on Admission of Ministers from Other Churches, or its Executive, that it is satisfied as to his status, record, and character, unless he has remained under the supervision of a Presbytery or Presbyteries of the Church during the whole term of such work in accordance with Sections 12 and 13 of this Act. The certificate shall be produced within three months of its being granted.

MINISTERS.

17. The General Assembly instruct that any minister or Kirk Session intending to employ as assistant or as *locum tenens* for more than four

[1] See Act 1974, ii.

Sundays in any parish, a licentiate or minister of any other Church than the Church of Scotland, shall require such licentiate or minister to report himself to the Clerk of Presbytery within whose bounds the parish is situated, and to submit for his inspection a certificate of licence or of ordination, as the case may be, or to give such other evidence of qualification as may be satisfactory to the Presbytery. The General Assembly further instruct all keepers of lists of licentiates or ministers available for pulpit supply that they shall not make engagements for such licentiates or ministers for more than four Sundays, whether in the same parish or in different parishes, without requiring them to produce evidence that they have reported themselves to the Clerk of Presbytery within whose bounds they reside, in the manner aforesaid. Any such employment shall be immediately intimated to the Committee on Probationers and Transference of Ministers by the minister or Kirk Session concerned, with statement of the name, denomination, and status of the person employed.

18. A minister who is a member of a Presbytery is under the jurisdiction of the Presbytery of which he is a ministerial member, no matter where he may reside ; but he must within two months report himself to the Clerk of the Presbytery within whose bounds he has come to reside.

19. A minister who has retained his seat in Presbytery and Synod in terms of Act XIII., 1932, may at any time resign his seat, if he so desire. In such an event he shall present a petition to the Presbytery craving leave to resign his seat, which petition shall be forwarded by the Presbytery to the Synod of the bounds with the opinion of the Presbytery, and the Synod shall give final judgment in the case. If there be no Synod having jurisdiction the petition shall be transmitted by the Presbytery to the General Assembly. Upon the prayer of such a petition being granted the provisions of the next section shall apply, unless the minister at the same time shall resign his status.

20. A minister without charge shall be under the jurisdiction of the Presbytery within whose bounds he resides. He shall observe the provisions of Act XV., 1933, and, in particular, he shall produce a certificate of status and a Presbyterial Certificate from the Presbytery he leaves, within two months of his removing to another Presbytery, except in the case covered by Act XIX., 1932, Section 2.

21. The provisions of Section 16 of this Act shall apply *mutatis mutandis* to any person who is admitted by the General Assembly to the status of a minister.

22. It shall be the duty of every Presbytery to report any contravention of this Act which is brought to its knowledge to the Presbytery having supervision over the person who is alleged to have violated the terms of this Act, in order that proper disciplinary action may be taken.

Students.

In all matters relating to the nomination and supervision of students, without prejudice to the Regulations adopted by the General Assembly on 29th May 1944 anent a Central Board for the Selection and Supervision of Candidates for the Ministry, *the decision of a Presbytery shall be final, with the reservation that any student or intending student concerned shall have the right to petition the General Assembly to review his case.* Any such Petition shall be in the first instance submitted to the Committee on Education for the Ministry, and, after consideration, that Committee shall present a report to the General Assembly appending its recommendation as to how it should be disposed of (1947, ix.).

The Assembly resolved that, with a view to facilitating the work of the Selection Board in relation to Presbyteries, all candidates for entrance to the Theological Course be required to indicate their desire to be recognised as students training for the Ministry of the Church of Scotland to the Clerk of the Presbytery within whose bounds their normal residence is situated not later than the 31st day of March in any year.

With the same purpose in view, nominations by the Presbyteries must be in the hands of the Joint Secretary of the Committee not later than 31st July (1948, Reg. 8.).

APPENDIX XXI.

ACT ANENT PRESBYTERIES FURTH OF GREAT BRITAIN

(1936, IX.).

Edinburgh, May 27, 1936. *Sess.* 12.

THE General Assembly, with consent of a majority of the Presbyteries of the Church, enact and ordain as follows :—

1. Presbyteries in connection with the Church of Scotland furth of Great Britain shall be as detailed in Schedules A., B., and C., appended to this Act, or as the General Assembly may from time to time determine. The General Assembly may constitute such other Presbyteries, or suppress or alter the bounds and membership of any Presbytery furth of Great Britain as they shall see fit, without reference to the Presbyteries of the Church under the Barrier Act.

2. (1) (*a*) Except in the cases falling under subsection (5) of this section, every minister who at the date of the passing of this Act is actually serving, or who hereafter may accept an appointment, furth of Great Britain under a Committee of this Church, is or shall become a member of the Presbytery which comprises the area wherein he is serving or is to serve for the time being ;

(*b*) If his charge or sphere of duty be not included in any Presbytery, he shall remain a member of the Presbytery to which he belonged at the date of his appointment ;

(*c*) If at that date he was not on the roll of any *Home* Presbytery, he shall be enrolled in such Presbytery as the General Assembly or its Commission may decide, on application by the Committee concerned ;

(*d*) In the case of a probationer who has accepted an appointment overseas, and for whom the Committee concerned desires ordination, arrangements shall be made by mutual agreement between the Committee and any Presbytery at home or abroad which the Committee concerned may deem appropriate, for his ordination by such Presbytery ;

(*e*) If there be no Presbytery overseas by which such probationer may be ordained, or to which he may be transferred, he shall be enrolled as a member of the Presbytery which ordained him ;

(*f*) It shall be the duty of any Committee appointing a missionary, minister, or chaplain for service overseas to intimate his acceptance of appointment to the Presbytery within which he is to serve, in order that if and when ordained as before provided (where such ordination shall take place) he may be enrolled as a member thereof : provided always that in the case of a chaplain appointed to the Indian Ecclesiastical Establishment, the Presidency Senior Chaplain concerned shall make this intimation.

(2) When a ministerial member of any Overseas Presbytery goes on furlough, or when a chaplain is appointed to service outwith the bounds of any Presbytery within which he has been serving for the time being, he shall remain a member of the Presbytery in which he was so serving until he is formally transferred to another Presbytery.

(3) Retired ordained missionaries, ministers, and chaplains may continue to be members of the Presbyteries in which they were serving at the date of their retiral, as provided for in sections 4 (*b*) and (5) (*d*) of this Act.

(4) Where any new Presbytery is constituted by the General Assembly under the powers contained in this Act, the Committee or Committees concerned shall give effect to the decision of the Assembly, and shall make arrangements for the first meeting of the Presbytery.

(5) Chaplains to His Majesty's Forces (but not chaplains appointed to the Indian Ecclesiastical Establishment), when serving furth of Great Britain, shall remain members of the *Home* Presbytery from which they proceeded or by which they were ordained, or of such Presbytery as the General Assembly or the Commission of Assembly may appoint.

3. Presbyteries furth of Great Britain shall consist of the following, viz.:—

(*a*) *Continental Presbyteries—i.e.*, Presbyteries constituted on the Continent of Europe as detailed in Schedule A. to this Act, or as enlarged or modified by the General Assembly under the provisions of section 1 hereof;

(*b*) *Overseas Presbyteries—i.e.*, Presbyteries constituted in Africa, China, the West Indies, and India (or elsewhere outwith Europe), all as set forth in Schedule B. to this Act, or as enlarged or modified in terms of section 1 hereof; and

(*c*) *Presbyteries with a Special Constitution recognised by the General Assembly*, all as set forth in Schedule C. to this Act, or as enlarged or modified in terms of section 1 hereof.

4. The membership of *Continental Presbyteries* shall consist of:—

(*a*) Ministers of the charges specified in Schedule A. to this Act, or of such charges as the General Assembly may at any time determine in the exercise of its powers of constituting Presbyteries or altering the bounds or membership thereof in terms of section 1 hereof, provided that such ministers are regularly settled and are not holding a temporary appointment for less than one year;

(*b*) Ministers *emeriti* of any such charges, who desire to retain their seats in the Presbytery in which they were serving at the time of retirement, provided that they have retired on account of old age, infirmity, or sickness, as attested by a satisfactory medical certificate;

(*c*) Former ministers of any such charges who have been permitted to retain their seats in the Presbytery concerned by authority of the General Assembly on a petition to that effect presented to the General Assembly;

(*d*) One elder appointed by each Kirk Session within the bounds;

(*e*) Elders appointed by the Presbytery itself in such numbers as to make the number of ministers and elders equal.

5. The membership of *Overseas Presbyteries* shall consist of:—

(*a*) All ordained missionaries appointed by a Committee of the General Assembly, being ministers of the Church of Scotland and serving within the bounds of the Presbytery concerned;

(*b*) Ministers of congregations of the Church of Scotland overseas serving within the bounds of the Presbytery concerned;

(*c*) Chaplains appointed to the Indian Ecclesiastical Establishment;

(*d*) Retired missionaries, ministers, and chaplains of the above three classes who desire to retain their seats in the Presbytery in which they were serving at the time of retirement, provided that they have retired on account of old age, infirmity, or sickness, as attested by a satisfactory medical certificate, or on account of their attaining the maximum age or number of years of service permitted by the Regulations of the Committee under which they serve.

(*e*) Former missionaries, ministers, and chaplains of the above three classes who have been permitted to retain their seats in the Presbytery by authority of the General Assembly on a petition to that effect presented to the General Assembly;

(*f*) Missionaries or agents appointed by a Committee of the General Assembly who have been ordained as elders under the Home formula;

(*g*) One representative elder from each duly constituted Kirk Session of a congregation or charge of the Church of Scotland within the bounds of each such Presbytery.

6. The following Presbyteries shall continue under the constitutions hitherto recognised by the General Assembly:—

(*a*) *The Presbytery of British Guiana*, as set forth in Schedule C. The provisions of the Government Ordinance of 1872 entitled "An Ordinance for the Better Government of the British Guiana Branch of the Established Church of Scotland" as modified by Ordinance No. 46, 1932, shall continue to apply to the Presbytery of British Guiana. This Presbytery shall have no right or power to appoint Commissioners to the General Assembly, nor the right to receive or make returns to Overtures sent down under the Barrier Act. The provisions of section 2 of this Act shall not apply in the case of this Presbytery.

(*b*) *The Presbytery of Kenya*, otherwise known as *The Presbytery of British East Africa*. This Presbytery shall continue under the constitution approved by the General Assembly of the Church of Scotland in 1918 until such time as the General Assembly shall determine otherwise. It shall have no right or power to appoint Commissioners to the General Assembly, nor the right to receive or make returns to Overtures sent down under the Barrier Act. European ministers serving within the bounds of this Presbytery shall be attached to a Home Presbytery in terms of section 2 of this Act.[1]

7. (1) *Continental Presbyteries*, as before defined, shall have similar powers to those of the Home Presbyteries, including the right to receive Overtures sent down to the Presbyteries of the Church under the Barrier Act, and to make returns thereon, which returns shall have equal weight with those of the Home Presbyteries, the right to make suggestions on other matters directed to be sent down to Presbyteries, but not under the Barrier Act, and the right to appoint Commissioners to the General Assembly, in accordance with the Regu-

[1] This section rescinded by 1936, xvi.

lations contained in Schedule E. to this Act. There being no Synod having jurisdiction, any Dissent and Complaint, or Appeal, against a judgment of a Continental Presbytery shall be made to the General Assembly direct. Notice of any such Dissent and Complaint, or Appeal, shall be given to the Committee on Work on the Continent and Relations with other Churches, and the Committee shall have a right to be heard in its interests before the Assembly or any Committee thereof appointed to deal with the subject-matter of the Dissent and Complaint, or Appeal.

(2) The appointment of ministers or other agents to charges within the bounds of Continental Presbyteries shall lie with the General Assembly's Committee on Work on the Continent and Relations with Other Churches, or with such other Committee of the General Assembly as the General Assembly may from time to time or at any time determine. Such appointments shall be made in accordance with the Regulations contained in Schedule D. to this Act, or as the same may be altered or modified by the General Assembly on the report of the Committee concerned. These Regulations may be so altered or modified without reference to the Presbyteries of the Church under the Barrier Act.

8. *Overseas Presbyteries*, as before defined, shall have the following powers:—

(*a*) Ecclesiastical oversight in matters of discipline of all agents, being members of the Church of Scotland, nominated, appointed, or sent overseas by the Home Church through any of its Committees, except chaplains appointed to the Indian Ecclesiastical Establishment, who shall remain under the jurisdiction of the Presbytery of Edinburgh;

(*b*) Oversight of the congregations of the Church of Scotland in their respective areas similar to that exercised by Home Presbyteries, the Presbytery being in each case the superior judicatory of such congregations and of their Kirk Sessions;

(*c*) The right to send Overtures to the General Assembly;

(*d*) The right to forward Petitions to the General Assembly, except in regard to (1) any matters specified under section 9 of this Act, and (2) any questions affecting the constitution, government, doctrine, or worship of the Church;

(*e*) The right to send Commissioners to the General Assembly in accordance with the Regulations contained in Schedule E. to this Act, or as these Regulations may, from time to time, be modified by the General Assembly. Provided always that the General Assembly may alter or modify these Regulations as they may deem necessary without any reference to Presbyteries under the Barrier Act;

(*f*) The right to license and/or ordain medical and other lay missionaries when requested so to do by one of the Mission Committees of the General Assembly, after permission for such action has been granted by the General Assembly or by the Commission of Assembly at any of its stated Diets. In carrying out such ordination, Presbyteries shall observe the Regulations approved by the General Assembly on 28th May 1932, as contained in Schedule F. to this Act, or such other Regulations as the General Assembly may, from time to time, approve of or enact;

(*g*) The right to exercise such other functions or perform such additional or other duties as the General Assembly may, from time to time, or at any time specially direct.

9. (*a*) Unless the General Assembly shall instruct otherwise, *Overseas Presbyteries* shall not be entitled to receive or to make returns to Overtures sent down to the Presbyteries of the Church under the Barrier Act, nor shall such Overtures or any other matters which may be directed to be sent down to Presbyteries, though not under the Barrier Act, be sent down to Overseas Presbyteries unless the General Assembly shall specially instruct otherwise;

(*b*) Overseas Presbyteries shall not have power to appoint missionaries or local agents, or to terminate their engagements except in cases of discipline as provided for in section 8, subsection (*a*) hereof, nor shall they have any power to determine the duties or spheres of labour of missionaries or other agents, such powers being hereby expressly committed to the *Foreign Mission Committee* or other appropriate *Mission Committee* of the General Assembly in conjunction with Mission Councils set up in terms of Act XXVIII., 1931, where such Councils exist;

(*c*) It shall be competent for any member of an Overseas Presbytery to dissent and complain to the General Assembly against a judgment of the Presbytery in respect of any matters arising in connection with any causes or questions affecting any of the matters referred to under section 8 hereof. Notice of any such Dissent and Complaint, or Appeal, shall be given to the Foreign Mission Committee or any other Committee of the General Assembly concerned, and such Committee shall have a right to be heard in its interests before the Assembly or any Committee thereof, appointed to deal with the subject-matter of the Dissent and Complaint, or Appeal.

10. (*a*) Each Assembly Committee making appointments overseas shall have power to make Regulations with reference to all or any matters affecting the appointment and service of its missionary agents, and to alter or modify the same from time to time as it may deem necessary;

(*b*) It shall be competent for any such Committee to present a Call to missionary service to any minister in a regular charge, and to prosecute the same before the Presbytery of which he is a member. The Presbytery concerned, if so resolved, shall loose the minister from his charge as from a date to be fixed by the Presbytery and instruct him to wait upon the Committee concerned as to the time of his taking up the appointment. Where it is necessary the minister shall be transferred to the appropriate Presbytery furth of Great Britain, in accordance with the provisions of section 2 of this Act.

11. Nothing in this Act with regard to the formation of Presbyteries furth of Great Britain shall affect the relation in which missionaries and ministers of the Church of Scotland stand at present to the Committees which appointed them, or to indigenous Churches on the Mission Fields or to their Courts, nor shall the present organisation of the indigenous Churches be affected thereby.

Provided always and it is hereby declared that a missionary appointed as aforesaid shall remain under the jurisdiction and discipline of the Presbytery of the Church of Scotland in which he is enrolled as a member.

Nothing in this Act shall affect the special relations of chaplains appointed to the Indian Ecclesiastical Establishment to the Presbytery of Edinburgh, as these are set forth in the Government of India Act, 1935 (25 & 26 Geo. 5, ch. 42), Section 269, subsection (3).

12. All previous legislation inconsistent with the provisions of this Act is hereby repealed.

SCHEDULE A.

CONTINENTAL PRESBYTERY.

Presbytery of Europe.

Charges.

Amsterdam.	Malta.
Brussels.	Paris.
Geneva.	Rome, St Andrew's.
Genoa.	Rotterdam.
Lausanne.	

SCHEDULE B.

OVERSEAS PRESBYTERY.

Jerusalem (1941, vi.).

SCHEDULE C.

REGULATIONS OF GENERAL ASSEMBLY ANENT APPOINTMENTS TO SANCTIONED CHARGES ON THE CONTINENT.

Whereas the membership of the congregations of the Church on the Continent of Europe is of a fluctuating nature, and adaptation on the part of ministers labouring in such spheres is accordingly of peculiar importance; *whereas* the appointment of ministers to those charges that were under the pre-Union Free Church and United Free Church of Scotland was regulated by Act XVI. of 1894 (Act anent Sanctioned Charges on the Continent, No. 12 of Class II.); *whereas* no Assembly Regulation existed for appointments to ministers to pre-Union Church of Scotland charges on the Continent; and *whereas* it is now desirable that appointments to all the Sanctioned Continental charges of the Church be uniformly regulated, the General Assembly hereby enact and ordain as follows:—

1. That the appointment of ministers, which shall be in the hands of the Continental Committee, shall continue for not more than five years from the date of ordination or induction to the charge.

2. That if the question of the minister's continuance in the charge be not raised by the Committee or the Presbytery of the bounds at least nine months before the expiry of the term of appointment, he shall be understood to enter upon a second engagement of the same duration as the first, subject to the continuance of the charge by the Assembly, and so at the close of each successive term.

3. That if the Committee, with the concurrence of the Presbytery of the bounds, shall decline to reappoint him, his membership of the Presbytery (unless he retains his seat as minister-emeritus or by special permission of the General Assembly) and all rights to the use of the Church and Manse, and to the emoluments pertaining to his appointment

shall cease and determine: Provided always that if the minister concerned, or the Presbytery, do not acquiesce in the Committee's decision not to reappoint, the case shall be referred to the General Assembly.

4. That the General Assembly reserves to itself the right to raise at any time the question of the continuance of any charge on the Continent; and its decision to close the Church, or to displace the charge from the position as a sanctioned charge shall *ipso facto* terminate the appointment of the minister and his connection with the Presbytery (unless he retains his seat as minister-emeritus or by special permission of the General Assembly), just as and to all effects as if his term of appointment had expired.

SCHEDULE D.

REGULATIONS ANENT ELECTION OF COMMISSIONERS TO THE GENERAL ASSEMBLY.

1. Continental and Overseas Presbyteries (as defined in this Act) shall return as Commissioners to the General Assembly one-fourth (or such proportion as the General Assembly may determine) of the number of ordained ministers on the roll of the Presbytery who are eligible to be returned as Commissioners, with an equal number of elders, who, if not available within the Presbytery, may be selected from the whole eldership of the Church of Scotland.

2. Each Presbytery shall hold at least one stated meeting yearly.

3. A notice of the meeting at which Commissioners to the General Assembly are to be elected shall be sent to each member of the Presbytery concerned.

4. The Minute recording the appointment of representative ministers and elders shall (*a*) contain the sederunt of meeting, (*b*) bear that the meeting was constituted, (*c*) state that the notice calling the meeting contained due intimation of the purpose to elect, and (*d*) be signed by the Moderator and the Clerk.

5. The Commission shall be forwarded to the Secretary of the Committee on Work on the Continent and Relations with Other Churches in the case of Continental Presbyteries, or to the Secretary of the Foreign Mission Committee or other Committee of the General Assembly concerned in the case of Overseas Presbyteries.

6. The election of representatives shall be made annually in time for the Minute recording their appointment to reach the Secretary of the Committee concerned not later than 10th April.

7. The Commissions of such duly elected representatives shall be forwarded duly certified by the Secretary of the Committee concerned to the Clerks of the General Assembly, so as to be in the hands of the latter by 24th April.

8. The elders appointed as representatives, whether in congregations abroad or congregations at home, shall be duly certified by the Moderator and Clerk of the Kirk Session of which they are members as *bona fide* acting elders who have signed the Formula; and those elders ordained under the Home Formula, who are agents appointed by a Committee of the General Assembly, shall be similarly certified by that Committee. It shall be the duty of the Clerks of the Presbyteries to inform all elders so elected from the overseas fields of the necessity of obtaining such certificate, and the duty of the Secretary of the Committee concerned to inform all elders in the Church at home of their election in order that they may obtain and forward such certificates to the Clerks of the General Assembly.

9. After-elections may be made at meetings of Presbytery, duly summoned by timeous notice.

10. Missionaries at home on furlough, being ministers or elders

ordained under the Home Formula or licentiates of the Church of Scotland ordained at a later date by a Church with which the Church of Scotland has a missionary connection through its Foreign Mission Committee, whether they be minister or Elder of such other Church or not, who are certified by the Foreign Mission Committee or other committee under whose auspices they have gone abroad, shall be corresponding members of the General Assembly (1962, Reg. 3).

APPENDIX XXII.

ACT ANENT TRIALS BY LIBEL (1935, vii.).

Edinburgh, May 22, 1935. *Sess.* 3.

WHEREAS prior to their Union in 1929 there were differences of procedure in Cases of Discipline in the Church of Scotland and the United Free Church of Scotland and provision was made in the Plan of Union for the preparation of a Manual of Procedure applicable to the Church of Scotland as united and for certain changes of procedure, and it is now necessary to amend, consolidate and declare the law of the Church in said matters.

The General Assembly, with consent of a majority of Presbyteries, enact and ordain as follows :—

PART I.

1. Since a *fama* against a Minister or a Probationer, even though groundless, is not easily extinguished, a Presbytery shall consider well at whose instance and by whose " information " and complaint it comes before them, and they shall not begin a process unless (1) some reliable person either, (*a*) in a writing subscribed by him or (*b*) orally and in presence of the Presbytery, gives in a complaint, with some account of its probability, and undertakes by sufficient evidence to make good a libel ; or (2) there is a *fama clamosa* so great that the Presbytery, for its own vindication, shall find it necessary to begin proceedings without an accuser.

2. If a *fama* has subsided and lain dormant for a period of five years, it shall not be revived nor form the subject of discussion, unless in very grave and exceptional circumstances.

3. Ministers residing beyond the bounds of the Presbytery of which they continue to be members shall remain subject to the jurisdiction of that Presbytery. Ministers who are not members of any Presbytery shall be subject to the jurisdiction of the Presbytery within whose bounds they reside.

Probationers shall be subject to the jurisdiction of the Presybtery which licensed them, or to which they have been transferred, until they are regularly transferred to another Presbytery.

4. Should a *fama* arise, or allegation be made, concerning the doctrine or conduct of a Minister or a Probationer, and be such as appears to call for inquiry, and if the same shall come under the notice of a Presbytery other than that which has jurisdiction over him, the Presbytery under whose notice such *fama* or allegation comes, shall communicate the same, together with all information thereanent in its

possession, or to which it may have access, to the Presbytery having jurisdiction over such Minister or Probationer, in order that it may deal with the case.

5. When a *fama* relating to a Minister or a Probationer has been brought to the notice of the Presbytery having jurisdiction over such Minister or Probationer, the Presbytery, after giving notice to the person concerned, shall either itself or by a Committee hold a Preliminary Inquiry.

6. The accused shall be entitled to be present throughout the whole course of such preliminary inquiry and shall be given full opportunity of defending himself against the allegations in relation to such *fama* made against him.

7. If, after such preliminary inquiry, the Presbytery shall decide to take no steps against the accused, then, in a case where the Presbytery has itself instituted the inquiry, any member dissatisfied with the decision may dissent and complain to the next higher Court: and in a case where a third party has been the complainer he may take an appeal to the next higher Court.

8. When, as a result of the preliminary inquiry provided for under Article 5 hereof, it appears to the Presbytery that there is reason to proceed further in the case, it shall forward to the person concerned a full and precise Statement of the heretical opinions or of the sinful or improper conduct (as the case may be) attributed to him, and shall request him to state in writing whether he admits or denies the allegations, or any of them, contained in such Statement.

9. The person concerned may state in writing Objections to the terms, or to the sufficiency, of the Statement submitted to him, and the Court, after consideration of these Objections, may amend and add to the Statement, or in its discretion adhere to the Statement as originally framed and submitted to such person.

10. If the person concerned shall admit all or any of the allegations contained in said Statement, the Presbytery shall take such steps as may seem to it to be necessary and proper according to the nature and extent of the allegations admitted by such person.

11. If the person concerned shall on the other hand deny all the allegations contained in said Statement, the Presbytery shall, having regard to the terms of Section 8 hereof in relation to such case, thereupon proceed to a Trial by Libel of such person.

12. The Libel shall be prepared by the Presbytery, or by any person or persons appointed by the Presbytery for that purpose, and, before service thereof, such Libel shall be revised by the Procurator of the Church. It shall, as nearly as possible, be in the form contained in Schedule A. hereto and shall be subscribed by the Moderator and the Clerk or Joint-Clerks of the Presbytery.

13. Service of a copy of the Libel, certified by the Clerk or Joint Clerks of the Presbytery, shall be made upon the accused by any person duly authorised by the Presbytery to that effect. Along with the certified copy of the Libel a list of the witnesses to be called by or on behalf of the Presbytery, and of the productions to be made on its behalf, shall be transmitted to the accused.

14. After the Libel has been adjusted and signed, the Presbytery, if it shall so determine, may commit the whole conduct of the Trial to a Committee of its number, which Committee shall consist of not less than

three nor more than five of its members, with the addition, if desired by the Presbytery, of two members of the Board of Assessors to be appointed in terms of Article 31 hereof: Provided always that whether the Presbytery itself, or a Committee of its number to be appointed as aforesaid,—and whether with or without Assessors,—shall conduct the Trial the same shall form " the Court " for the Trial of the Cause.

15. The accused shall be entitled to lodge Notice of a Special Defence within 21 days from the date of the service of the Libel upon him. If the accused should desire to lead evidence in his defence he shall lodge with the Clerk or Joint Clerks of Presbytery a list of the witnesses to be called for him, and also a list of productions to be made on his behalf, along with such Notice, or, if he shall lodge no such Notice then such lists shall nevertheless be lodged by him within 21 days from the date of the service of the Libel as aforesaid.

A " Special Defence " shall be deemed to mean and include a Statement of an *alibi* or of the insanity or other infirmity of the accused which is alleged by him or on his behalf to have been the cause or occasion of his having committed the offence charged against him, or any other Statement which shall amount to substantially more than a denial of his having committed the offence charged.

16. The accused shall have a right to borrow any documents produced in process by or on behalf of the Presbytery, upon him or his Agent granting a borrowing receipt therefor and being responsible for the care and protection of such documents and their due return to the process whenever called for.

17. After the service of the Libel and the expiry of the days within which Notice of a Special Defence falls to be lodged, the Presbytery (or the Committee if the Presbytery shall have appointed a Committee of their number specially for the purpose of conducting the Trial) shall fix a date for the first sitting of the Court, and shall give not less than seven clear days' notice of such sitting to the accused.

18. The Presbytery shall appoint suitable persons to act as Prosecutors in the case. The Prosecutors to be so appointed shall be not less than two nor more than three members of the Presbytery, and such Prosecutors may employ agents and counsel to act on their behalf, or may in their discretion themselves conduct the prosecution. The accused shall likewise have the right to employ agents and counsel for his defence if he so desire.

19. At the first sitting of the Court the accused shall be invited to state Objections, if he have any, to the competency of the proceedings, the constitution of the Committee (if such shall have been appointed for the Trial of the Cause), or the relevancy of the Libel, or any other Objections which he may desire to state.

20. If no such Objections shall be stated by the accused, or if such as he has stated shall be repelled, the Court shall pronounce a finding holding the Libel relevant.

21. If any material Objection stated by the accused shall be upheld as valid by the Court, the Court shall thereupon find the Libel irrelevant, and dismiss the same, and the accused shall forthwith be entitled *ipso facto* to discharge the duties of his office, unless the Court shall find sufficient grounds otherwise for suspending him from the exercise of his office, which it shall have power to do notwithstanding the finding of the Libel irrelevant as aforesaid.

22. Notwithstanding anything contained in the immediately preceding Article, it shall nevertheless be competent for the Court, either at the instance of the Prosecutors or otherwise, to strike out any irrelevant portions of the Libel and to hold the remaining portions thereof as relevant.

23. If the Libel shall be found relevant either in whole or in part, and the accused shall still deny the charges contained therein, the Court shall appoint the Cause to go to Proof on a specified date or dates, but with power to the Court, on cause shown, to postpone any date or dates so fixed. Upon the Libel being held relevant, either in whole or in part as aforesaid, the Presbytery may at any time thereafter before the completion of the Trial, enjoin the accused to abstain from the exercise of all the functions of his office as Minister until the Libel is finally disposed of. During such suspension of the accused ordinances shall be administered in such manner as shall be arranged by the Presbytery in the same way as if the charge were vacant: provided always that the Minister's right to the Stipend or other emoluments of the benefice shall be in no way affected by such suspension. The Court shall also fix a date not less than 21 days thereafter on which the Proof shall proceed.

24. At the Diet of Proof all evidence shall be given on oath. Evidence in support of the charge shall be first led, and thereafter the accused shall be entitled to lead evidence in his defence. Each party shall be entitled to cross-examine the witnesses of the other, and each may re-examine their witnesses on any new matter brought out in cross-examination. On the conclusion of the parties' examination of a witness, any member of the Court may put questions to the witness on his own behalf, or on the suggestion of either party.

The whole evidence shall be taken down in shorthand and recorded in full.

25. On the conclusion of the evidence, a person representing the prosecution shall first address the Court, and thereafter the accused or any person representing him may address the Court upon the evidence led,—the prosecutors having a right of reply upon any points in the evidence with regard to which the Court may, in its discretion, direct such reply to be made.

26. If the Presbytery shall itself have heard the case and the evidence thereon, it shall deliver judgment forthwith. If the case shall have been heard by a Committee appointed by the Presbytery as hereinbefore provided for, the Committee shall report its findings on the whole matter, including its findings on the facts, to the Presbytery, but it shall not be obliged to do so immediately after the Proof or Hearing, and may intimate that it will take time to consider its findings. Its findings on the facts, if unanimous, shall be final as regards the Presbytery, and shall not be subject to reversal or alteration by the latter.

Such Report shall (1) embrace the Committee's decision on the whole subject-matter of the Libel; and (2) state whether the findings are unanimous, and, if not unanimous, the state of the vote. The Presbytery may thereafter resolve either to decide in terms of the findings of the majority of the Committee, or to appoint the evidence to be printed and of new to hear parties thereon.

27. The Presbytery shall as soon as practicable thereafter consider the Report. It may either (*a*) adopt the Report and agree with the

decision of the Committee; (*b*) alter and amend the decision of the Committee if not unanimous on the subject-matter of the Cause or any legal questions involved therein; or (*c*) (but subject always to the provisions of Section 26 hereof as to the finality of unanimous findings on the facts) set aside the decision of the Committee and issue an independent judgment, and also determine what its judgment shall be. Should the judgment be against the accused, it shall determine the appropriate censure and direct what steps shall be taken for carrying the censure into effect.

28. In all cases of Trial by Libel a Record Apart shall be kept.

29.[1] In the event of an Appeal being taken by the accused, or, where a third party has been the Complainer, of an Appeal being taken by such third party,—to a higher Court, or of a Dissent and Appeal by a Member of the Presbytery to such higher Court, the whole record of proceedings and the documents and other productions, if any, shall be transmitted forthwith by the Clerk or Joint Clerks of Presbytery to such higher Court.

PART II.

30. If called upon by a Presbytery to do so, the General Assembly's Committee on Law, Property Cases, and Discipline shall, if it think fit, be entitled to afford all help in its power in cases of Trial by Libel or itself to undertake the conduct of the Case if it shall so decide.

31. The General Assembly shall annually appoint a Board of Assessors whose members shall be available for selection by Presbyteries or Synods to assist in the conduct of Trials by Libel, and to act as members of the Court to which they are appointed.

When requested by any Presbytery concerned to do so, the Committee on Law, Property Cases, and Discipline shall appoint two of the members of the Board of Assessors as Assessors to deal with the case in terms of this Section unless such Committee shall have either advised upon the case or itself undertaken the conduct of the same in accordance with the powers conferred upon it under the immediately preceding Section hereof, in which case the appointment of Assessors in terms of this Section shall be made by the General Administration Committee of the Church.

32. Without prejudice to the terms of Section 30 hereof the General Assembly's Committee on Law, Property Cases, and Discipline shall not be bound either to advise or to enter upon the conduct of any case, and it shall also be entitled to withdraw from the conduct of any case, if entered upon, at any time: Provided always that nothing in this Act shall prevent Presbyteries from entering upon, sisting themselves to, or departing from, any process without reference to the said Committee, or from proceeding after the withdrawal of the said Committee from any Case.

33. In a Trial by Libel no member of the Court shall vote or take any part in the decision unless he shall have been present during the whole time that evidence was being led and has also heard the parties thereon.

34. Where a Dissent and Complaint or an Appeal, whether on a preliminary plea or on the merits of the case, is taken from a Presbytery to the Synod or from the Synod to the General Assembly, the said

[1] Such appeals are heard by the Judicial Commission (1960, xxii., see p. 653).

General Assembly's Committee on Law, Property Cases, and Discipline, if requested either by the Presbytery or by the Synod concerned to do so, may, if so advised, take charge of the prosecution in the higher Court to which such Dissent and Complaint or such Appeal is taken,—on behalf of such Presbytery or Synod.

35. All cases undertaken by the said General Assembly's Committee shall proceed in the name of the Presbytery or of the Synod (as the case may be) on whose behalf the said Committee is acting, and Counsel or Agents employed by the said Committee shall be treated by the Court before which the case is pending as being instructed by or on behalf of the Presbytery or of the Synod (as the case may be) for which the said Committee is acting.

36. It shall not be competent for any Assessor appointed to act on a Court under Section 31 hereof, and who has so acted, to take any part in any further proceedings in connection with the case under a Dissent and Complaint or an Appeal to any higher Court of the Church.

37. In any proceedings relative to a case of alleged errors in doctrine or worship on the part of any Minister or Licentiate of the Church, only such sections of this Act as shall, in the opinion of the Procurator of the Church for the time being, be properly applicable to cases of that nature shall be deemed to apply to the case in question.

38. The expenses incurred by the said General Assembly's Committee on Law, Property Cases, and Discipline or by any Assessors appointed as aforesaid shall be defrayed by the General Administration Committee, which shall also pay such legal expenses of Presbyteries and/or Synods incurred in the conduct of prosecutions as shall be certified by the said General Assembly's Committee, or where the said General Assembly's Committee and the Presbytery or the Synod (as the case may be) shall have differed in regard to the conduct of the case, then by the Procurator of the Church, to have been reasonably incurred.

Part III.

Miscellaneous.

39. If any case shall arise for which there is no specific provision contained in this or in any other Act of the General Assembly, either the Court concerned or the General Assembly or the Commission thereof at any of its stated Diets, or at any Special Diet of the Commission, shall have power to make such Order or Orders as may seem just in the circumstances. Such Order or Orders, if issued, shall be obligatory both upon the parties conducting the prosecution and on the accused.

40. If, in the course of a case, a situation shall arise for which there is no provision regulating procedure contained in this or in any other Act of the General Assembly, the same rule as in Section 39 hereof shall *mutatis mutandis* apply and be applicable to such case, and the General Assembly or the Commission thereof shall have power to issue an Order or Orders directing the procedure to be followed. Such Order or Orders, if issued, shall be obligatory both upon the parties conducting the prosecution and on the accused.

41. Act XXI. of General Assembly, 1933, and all prior Acts of Assembly in so far as any of the provisions thereof are inconsistent with this Act are hereby repealed.

SCHEDULE A.

Name and Designation (*e.g.*, A. B., Minister of the Parish of C.). You are indicted at the instance of (The Presbytery of D.—or if the Prosecutors are private persons, name and design them) and the Charge against you is [specify clearly and shortly the offence charged—*e.g.*, that you were in a state of intoxication on (specify date and place)]. If there be any aggravations, specify them (*e.g.*, that you were admonished for drunkenness by the Presbytery of   on (date) which is an Aggravation).

Note.—Numerous other examples will be found in Schedule to Act XIX. of 1889 of the Church of Scotland.

APPENDIX.

(List of witnesses and their addresses, and of productions.)

APPENDIX XXIII.

ACT ANENT A JUDICIAL COMMISSION OF THE GENERAL ASSEMBLY (1960, xxii.).

The General Assembly, with the consent of a majority of Presbyteries, enact and ordain as follows :—

1. The Judicial Commission for the hearing of appeals in cases of Trial by Libel, affecting character or conduct (but not doctrine) against a Minister or Probationer of the Church, shall also hear Appeals in certain cases arising under the Act anent Congregations in an Unsatisfactory State under the Constitution and with the Functions and Powers hereinafter set forth.

2. (*a*) The Judicial Commission shall consist of Ministers and Elders forty-eight in number, to be appointed by the General Assembly. Two-thirds of this number shall be nominated by Synods—four from the Synod of Lothian and Tweeddale, four from the Synod of Clydesdale, and two from each of the other Synods, including the Presbyteries of Orkney and Shetland ; and the remaining one-third shall be nominated by the General Administration Committee.

(*b*) Members shall not hold office for more than four years, and no member shall be eligible for reappointment until after the lapse of one year, except upon special cause shown.

(*c*) Eight of the members appointed on the nomination of Synods and four of those appointed on the nomination of the General Administration Committee shall retire annually all according to the dates of their appointments, whether the same are before or after the date of this Act.

(*d*) It shall not be necessary that any or all of the persons nominated shall be members of the General Assembly making the appointments.

(*e*) The General Assembly shall appoint one of the members to be Chairman, and another to be Vice-Chairman, of the Judicial Commission, and they shall hold office for five years, notwithstanding anything contained in subsections (*b*) and (*c*).

(*f*) In the event of the death or resignation or supervening incapacity of any member of the Judicial Commission, the General Administration Committee shall appoint another in his place to hold office until the close of next Assembly.

(*g*) In the event of a member of the Judicial Commission who is due to retire being then engaged in the hearing of an appeal, he shall, even if not reappointed, continue in office, but only for the purpose of that particular Appeal, until the Judicial Commission has recorded its finding or findings in the Appeal in question.

(*h*) Any twenty-four members shall form a quorum and the Chairman shall have a casting vote only. No appeal shall be begun unless at least thirty members are present at the commencement thereof.

(*i*) In the event of the Chairman or Vice-Chairman being unable to preside at any Sederunt of the Judicial Commission, the members present shall elect one of their number to act as Chairman, who shall continue to act until the close of that Appeal.

(*j*) The Procurator of the Church shall not be eligible for membership of the Judicial Commission. The Clerks of the General Assembly shall act as Clerks to the Judicial Commission, though not necessarily members thereof, but the duties may be carried out by one of them. If it be not possible for any one of them to be present, the Judicial Commission shall appoint a substitute, whether or not a member thereof, to act as Clerk of the Commission during the sittings thereof, and the oath *de fideli* shall be administered to him and recorded.

(*k*) No member of any Court whose decision is under review, nor anyone who has taken part in the cause at any stage as Counsel or Assessor, shall act as a member of the Judicial Commission when an Appeal in such cause is being heard. The General Administration Committee shall appoint for such particular Appeal Ministers or Elders, one or more, to act in the place of the member or members so disqualified.

(*l*) No member of the Commission shall vote or take any part in the finding or findings of the Judicial Commission, unless he shall have been present during the whole proceedings in the Appeal.

(*m*) An Appellant shall have the right on special cause shown to object to any member of the Commission acting when his Appeal is being heard, and such objection, if sustained, shall disqualify the member or members objected to from acting in that Appeal: provided that such objection shall be stated and disposed of at the commencement of the hearing of the Appeal, and the members of the Commission then present, other than the member or members objected to, shall be the sole judges as to whether the objection is to be sustained or repelled, and their decision on this matter shall not be subject to review.

3. The Judicial Commission shall hear Appeals (1) against the Judgment of Inferior Courts in all cases affecting the character or conduct of Ministers and Probationers proceeded against under Libel, and (2) against the procedure, findings, and final judgment of Presbyteries acting under the Act anent Congregations in an Unsatisfactory State (Act XXI. 1960 or any Act amending the same) in cases where the findings of the Presbytery include a finding that the unsatisfactory state of the congregation is due (*a*) wholly or substantially to defects or errors personal to the Minister, or (*b*) wholly or partly to the fault of any office-bearers or members specified.

4. (*a*) The Judicial Commission shall not have jurisdiction to hear any Appeal:—

(1) taken only against the sentence pronounced in a case of Trial by Libel, or

(2) taken only against that part of the final judgment of the Presbytery by which the Presbytery has resolved—

(i) to dissolve the pastoral tie and to declare the charge vacant; or

(ii) to remove an office-bearer from office; or

(iii) to order a transference certificate to be given to an office-bearer or member, or to suspend an office-bearer or member from Church membership.

(*b*) Appeals referred to in the preceding subsection shall be taken direct to the General Assembly.

(*c*) The Judicial Commission shall not have jurisdiction to propose, determine or pronounce sentence or penalties.

5. (*a*) The Judicial Commission shall have all the powers and privileges of the General Assembly in relation to the conduct and hearing of Appeals, including power, where necessary, to require the attendance of witnesses, to examine witnesses on oath, and to call for the production of all books and documents connected with or relevant to the Appeal; and the procedure before the Commission shall be similar to that followed in Appeals to the General Assembly.

(*b*) The procedure in Appeals heard by the Judicial Commission shall be in accordance with the Rules of Procedure set forth in the Schedule hereto annexed. Such rules shall be construed and have effect as part of this Act. The Judicial Commission may recommend alterations to the said Rules of Procedure, but such alterations shall not come into force until they have been approved by the General Assembly.

6. (*a*) Appeals shall be transmitted to the Clerks of the Judicial Commission within fourteen days of the receipt of the same by the Clerk of the Court against whose judgment the Appeal has been taken.

(*b*) Upon receipt of an Appeal the Clerks of the Judicial Commission shall forthwith intimate the same to the Chairman, whom failing to the Vice-Chairman of the Judicial Commission, who shall forthwith arrange for the hearing of the Appeal, and shall instruct the Clerks of the Judicial Commission to give the necessary intimations to the parties concerned. Not less than seven clear days' notice shall be given to the parties.

(*c*) The hearing of an Appeal shall proceed *de die in diem* without interruption until concluded, provided always that it shall be in the power of the Judicial Commission, if in its opinion the justice of the case demands it, or for any other reason which may appear to be sufficient, to adjourn the hearing either *ex proprio motu*, or at the request of any party on cause shown, and subject to such conditions as it may think proper to impose.

(*d*) The Judicial Commission shall decide at any stage of the proceedings whether these shall be taken in private.

(*e*) The appellant shall first address the Judicial Commission, and thereafter the respondent may address the Commission. The appellant shall have the right of reply. Normally the parties will not be permitted to lead the evidence of witnesses, but the Commission shall have power on cause shown to allow new evidence to be given in addition to that given in the Inferior Court.

(*f*) The Minutes of the Judicial Commission shall enumerate each count in the Libel, or, as the case may be, each item in the procedure, findings, and final judgment of the Presbytery, which are the subject of the Appeal, and shall show the Finding of the Commission on each count or item and the grounds on which the Finding has been reached. The Minutes shall also show the state of the vote of the Members of the Commission on each count or item, but not the names of those voting, and the state of the vote on each count or item in the Inferior Court, if these have been recorded.

(*g*) Upon the conclusion of the hearing of an Appeal the Minutes of the Judicial Commission shall be engrossed in a Sederunt Book, and signed by the Chairman or acting Chairman and reported to the next General Assembly, or if the General Assembly be in Session, to that General Assembly on the first available Sederunt Day.

(*h*) When the Minutes of the Judicial Commission are reported to the

General Assembly, and after an opportunity has been given to Members of the General Assembly to ask questions, the question shall be put by the Moderator with regard to each Finding : " Do the General Assembly approve this Finding of the Judicial Commission 'Yes' or 'No'?" Immediately after the question has been put, the General Assembly, without debate on the Finding, shall vote.

(*i*) After the General Assembly shall have resolved whether any finding or findings of the Judicial Commission be approved or not approved the General Assembly shall determine what further action, if any, shall be taken, but before any decision is made or any sentence pronounced the appellant shall be entitled to be heard either personally or through his Counsel or Solicitor on a plea in mitigation.

7. In construing this Act " Appeal " shall include " Dissent and Complaint " and " Appellant " shall include " Complainer."

8. The expenses of the members and of the proceedings of the Judicial Commission shall be defrayed out of the General Purposes Fund of the Church, unless and until the General Assembly shall determine otherwise.

9. Act VII. of 1940 is hereby repealed. The repeal of the said Act shall not effect its operation previous to this repeal or anything duly done or suffered under the said Act, and proceedings begun under the provisions of the said Act, and not completed at the date of its repeal shall be continued under this Act as if they had commenced thereunder.

Schedule.

Rules of Procedure.

1. All appeals to the Judicial Commission shall be formally stated in ordinary form.

2. An appellant shall have the right to borrow any documents produced in the Inferior Court, upon him or his agent granting a borrowing receipt therefor and being responsible for the care and protection of such documents and their due return whenever called for.

3. The provisions of the said Act of Assembly on Forms and Procedure in Trials by Libel and in Causes Generally (1889, XIX.) shall apply *mutatis mutandis* to appeals from Inferior Courts which are heard by the Judicial Commission.

4. In appeals arising under the Act anent Trials by Libel, the Clerk of the Inferior Court shall within fourteen days of the receipt by him of the written statement of appeal transmit to the Clerks of the Judicial Commission the written statement of appeal, the Libel, Notice of Special Defence, if any, productions, transcript of evidence, and the whole record of proceedings. In appeals under the Act anent Congregations in an Unsatisfactory State, the Clerk of Presbytery shall within fourteen days of the receipt by him of the written statement of appeal transmit to the Clerks of the Judicial Commission the said written statement of appeal together with the Record Apart, and all productions.

5. On receipt of an appeal the Clerks of the Judicial Commission shall within seven days intimate the same to the Chairman, whom failing to the Vice-Chairman of the Judicial Commission who shall forthwith arrange for the hearing of the appeal, and shall instruct the Clerks of the

Judicial Commission to give intimations to the parties concerned. Not less than seven clear days' notice shall be given to parties.

6. The parties to an appeal before the Judicial Commission may employ Counsel or Solicitors to act on their behalf, or may in their discretion conduct their case themselves or delegate one of their number to do so. The Inferior Court whose decision is appealed against shall be entitled, if it so desire, to have the assistance of the Law, Property Cases, and Discipline Committee of the General Assembly.

7. In appeals where the Judicial Commission deems it necessary to hear evidence, witnesses shall be cited in ordinary form by the Clerks of the Judicial Commission. Such witnesses shall be examined on oath, as the Judicial Commission shall direct, by the party adducing them. Thereafter the witness may be cross-examined by the other party and the party adducing the witness may thereafter re-examine the witness on any new matter brought out in cross-examination. On the conclusion of the parties' examination of a witness, any member of the Judicial Commission may put questions to the witness on his own behalf, or on the suggestion of either party. The evidence of such witnesses may be taken down in shorthand.

8. The appellant shall first address the Judicial Commission, and thereafter the respondent may address the Commission on any evidence led before the Inferior Court or the Commission, and on the whole subject matter of the Appeal. After the respondent has addressed the Commission as aforesaid, the appellant may exercise the right of reply upon any points on the evidence with regard to which the Commission may, in its discretion, direct such reply to be made.

APPENDIX XXIV.

ACT ANENT GAELIC-SPEAKING CHARGES (1948, viii.).

THE General Assembly rescind Act XII., 1944, anent Gaelic-speaking Charges and enact and declare that the Home Board shall each year, after consultation with Presbyteries, fix in which charges it is *necessary* that public worship should be regularly conducted in Gaelic and in which it is *desirable* that the minister should have a knowledge of Gaelic The General Assembly instruct Presbyteries in the Gaelic areas to consult the Kirk Sessions concerned within their bounds.

APPENDIX XXV.

ACT AMENDING THE SCHEME ANNEXED TO ACT XXV., 1959, ANENT A CO-ORDINATED APPEAL AS APPROVED BY THE GENERAL ASSEMBLY, 1973, AND FURTHER AMENDED BY ACT XXVI., 1975.

Annexation.

Scheme for a Co-ordinated Appeal to Congregations for the Support of the Work of the Church to be known as The Church of Scotland Mission and Service Fund.

1. *Co-ordination of Appeals.*

As from 1st January 1961 (hereinafter referred to as " the operative date ") all Committees, Associations or other bodies whose funds have hitherto derived support from congregations in Scotland or England shall, with the exception of the Committee on the Maintenance of the Ministry and the Committee on the Aged and Infirm Ministers' Fund, cease to have right to appeal directly to such congregations for contributions to their funds. As from the operative date a Co-ordinated Appeal, to be known as the Church of Scotland Mission and Service Fund, made through the medium of the Stewardship and Budget Committee shall be the sole method of appealing to such congregations by any Committees, Associations or other bodies, with the above exceptions.

The appeal to be made through the medium of the Stewardship and Budget Committee shall be confined to the branch of income known as congregational contributions. While, after the operative date, Committees, Associations and other bodies within the Scheme shall cease to have right to appeal direct to congregations in Scotland or England for contributions, nothing in this Scheme shall prevent them from making appeals for funds from other sources. In the event of any emergency arising which necessitates a Committee, Association or body making a special appeal to congregations of the Church for contributions, the Stewardship and Budget Committee may grant permission for such an appeal to be made and state conditions on which it is to be made.

2. *Stewardship and Budget Committee.*

(1) *Membership.* The Stewardship and Budget Committee shall be made up as follows :—

(*a*) Fifteen members to be appointed by the General Assembly on the recommendation of the Nomination Committee.

(*b*) Four members to be appointed by the General Finance Committee.

(*c*) Eleven members to be appointed by the Committees of the General Assembly as follows :—

Two by the Home Board.
Two by the Overseas Council.
Two by the Department of Social Responsibility.
Two by the Department of Education.
One by the Woman's Guild.
Two by the Church and Ministry Department.

(*d*) One representative to be appointed by each Presbytery in Scotland, and by the Presbytery of England.

All the members to be appointed under (*b*), (*c*) and (*d*) must be members of the respective bodies by whom they are appointed.

In the event of a vacancy occurring, the vacancy shall be filled as soon as possible by the body by whom the member ceasing to act was appointed or whom he represented.

(2) *Status.* The Committee shall be a Standing Committee of the General Assembly within the Administration and Special Interests Department.

(3) *Functions.* The Committee's functions shall include the following :—

(*a*) To educate the membership of the Church in the spiritual basis of Christian giving and in the adoption of the best methods of ingathering and systematic giving.
(*b*) To prepare such co-ordinated publicity as may be required.
(*c*) To prepare a draft Act each year for submission to the General Assembly showing the details of the sums required by Committees, Associations and other bodies from congregational contributions in the ensuing year.
(*d*) To allocate the total Budget as approved by the General Assembly amongst Groups of congregations.
(*e*) To compare the response by congregations with the allocations made and to direct special attention to areas where the response is regarded as inadequate.
(*f*) To devise such methods as it may see fit for the allocation of the total requirements provided that, before such methods are put into operation, the authority of the General Assembly shall be obtained.
(*g*) To give guidance to Presbyteries on any special problems that may be raised by them in connection with the Scheme.

(4) *Secretary and Staff.* The Secretary of the Committee (who may be either a minister or a layman) shall be appointed by the General Assembly or should the General Assembly so decide by their Commission and will be a Secretary with Assembly status who shall hold office during the pleasure of the General Assembly.

Subject to the approval of the General Finance Committee, the Committee will have power to appoint such staff as may be necessary.

(5) *Administrative Expenses.* At the end of each financial year the Committee shall prepare a statement of its administration expenses for

that year, and the said expenses shall be met by the Committees, Associations or other bodies who come within the Scheme *pro rata* according to the contributions they have respectively received from congregations during that year.

(6) *Meetings, etc.* The Committee shall meet as often as required, but at least twice each year. From its members the Committee may appoint with or without powers such Sub-Committees as it may consider necessary or advisable.

3. *Preparation of the Budget.*

(1) Each year on a date to be determined by the Stewardship and Budget Committee, each Committee, Association or body within the Scheme shall submit to the Stewardship and Budget Committee a budget of its estimated income and expenditure for the ensuing calendar year. Such budget shall be prepared on a realistic basis, having due regard to the essential needs of the work of the Committee, Association or body.

(2) The budget submitted by each Committee, Association or body shall be carefully considered by the Stewardship and Budget Committee, not with the object of questioning or objecting to the ordinary operating expenditure but with the obligation to satisfy itself in regard to extraordinary or additional expenditure.

(3) Where a Committee, Association or body is not represented on the Stewardship and Budget Committee, it shall be entitled to appoint a representative to attend the meetings of the Stewardship and Budget Committee for the purpose of giving information and explanations regarding its budget.

(4) If at the time of submission of any budget under this Scheme a Committee has a debt, such debt may be spread over such a period and in such proportions as the Stewardship and Budget Committee shall determine, having due regard to the additional burden which such sums shall place upon congregations.

(5) If, after the operative date, any Committee, Association or other body within the Scheme has a deficit at the end of the year, the amount of the deficit as agreed with the Stewardship and Budget Committee shall be added to the next estimated amount required by the said Committee, Association or body.

(6) The Stewardship and Budget Committee shall include in the total amount of its annual budget an amount to provide for contingencies.

4. *Submission of Budget to General Assembly.*

(1) In its Report to the General Assembly the Stewardship and Budget Committee shall include a statement of approved requirements from congregations of each Committee, Association or body in the Scheme for the ensuing year. These particulars shall be incorporated in a draft Act of Assembly to be submitted along with the Report for approval by the General Assembly.

(2) The Stewardship and Budget Committee shall state how the total Budget is to be apportioned among the several funds of the Church.

5. *Allocation of total Budget.*

(1) The Stewardship and Budget Committee shall allocate the total

Budget as approved by the General Assembly by determining the proportion of the total Budget required from each Group of congregations.

(2) In its consideration of the allocation to Groups of congregations, the Stewardship and Budget Committee shall first of all examine the Available Balance figures for each congregation according to the information supplied by Presbyteries as hereinafter stated and shall thereafter group congregations according to the said figures.

(3) The Stewardship and Budget Committee shall intimate to each Presbytery the amount allocated to and required from each Group within that Presbytery.

6. *Presbyteries' Responsibilities within the Scheme.*

(1) Each Presbytery shall appoint a Stewardship and Budget Committee.

Preparation of Available Balance figures for each congregation.

(2) Each Presbytery shall be responsible for establishing from and in the manner indicated by a Financial Schedule as formulated and approved by the General Finance Committee from time to time and completed in respect of each congregation within its bounds :—

(*a*) Normal Recurring Income for the general purposes of the congregation.
(*b*) Net cost of Maintenance of the Ministry.
(*c*) The Available Balance for the Mission and Service Fund and local Congregational Expenditure.

(3) In the case of (*a*) Aid-receiving congregations and (*b*) congregations making repayments for buildings to the National Church Extension Committee, such special arrangements shall apply as shall be agreed from time to time between the Stewardship and Budget Committee, and the Committee on the Maintenance of the Ministry and the Home Board respectively. In the event of failure to agree reference will be made to the General Assembly on the Report of the Stewardship and Budget Committee.

(4) Each Presbytery shall make a return to the Stewardship and Budget Committee prior to 30th April each year giving Available Balance figures for each congregation within its bounds.

(5) In the event of a congregation not submitting its Financial Schedule in time to enable the Presbytery to include an Available Balance figure for the congregation, the Presbytery Stewardship and Budget Committee shall have power to submit an estimated figure for the congregation's Available Balance, on the basis of which that congregation's allocation shall be determined.

(6) In the event of a Presbytery not submitting figures for Available Balances for congregations within its bounds in time to allow the Assembly Stewardship and Budget Committee to proceed with the calculation of allocations of the Mission and Service Budget, the Assembly Stewardship and Budget Committee shall have power to estimate figures for the Available Balances of congregations within the bounds of the said Presbytery on the basis of which the congregations' allocations shall be determined.

Allocation of Share of Budget

(7) On receipt of intimation of the share of the Total Budget allocated to each Group within the Presbytery, the Presbytery's Stewardship and Budget Committee shall, after due consideration, proceed to make its proposed allocation of the said amount to each congregation within its relevant Group, so that the sum of such allocations will equal the proportion of the Total Budget required from that Group. The Presbytery may ask for guidance from the Stewardship and Budget Committee.

In the event of any unions or readjustments having taken place within the Presbytery or any new congregation having come into existence, the Presbytery shall make such adjustments as in its discretion it considers appropriate.

(8) Having made such allocation, the Presbytery's Committee shall report its allocation to the Presbytery Clerk who shall communicate the particulars to individual members of Presbytery at least six days prior to the next Meeting of the Presbytery. The Presbytery either at that meeting or a subsequent Meeting shall either confirm the allocation or make such amendments or adjustments thereto as in its sole discretion it thinks fit. The Presbytery's decision as to the allocation among congregations within its bounds shall be final in respect of the immediately ensuing calendar year.

(9) After the allocation amongst congregations has been finally approved of by the Presbytery, the Clerk of the Presbytery shall, not later than 15th November in each year, notify each congregation of its allocation and afford information concerning the division of same amongst the several funds of the Church. The sums thus notified to congregations shall represent the minimum contributions they are expected to make. Presbyteries shall also transmit copies of their allocations to congregations to the Secretary of the Stewardship and Budget Committee in November each year.

(10) The Presbytery's Stewardship and Budget Committee shall, in addition to undertaking the above-mentioned duties, take such steps as it may consider necessary to secure that every congregation shall attain its objective as allocated. To this end the Presbytery's Committee shall be required to urge congregations to improve their methods of giving and generally to be responsible for the education of the membership to a fuller understanding of the real meaning of Christian stewardship.

(11) When Vacancy and Revision Schedules are being completed, Presbyteries will arrange that representatives of the Presbytery's Stewardship and Budget Committee have opportunity to be present along with representatives of the Presbytery's Maintenance of the Ministry Committee in order that office-bearers may have in mind at the same time the congregation's allocation to the Mission and Service Fund and the necessity for encouraging adequate Christian liberality for all Church purposes.

(12) In all cases where congregations fail to meet the requirements of the Mission and Service Fund, the Presbytery's Stewardship and Budget Committee shall consult with the office-bearers, giving opportunity for representatives of the Presbytery's Maintenance of the Ministry Committee to be present.

7. *Responsibilities of Congregations, Kirk Sessions, etc.*

(1) It will be the responsibility of each Kirk Session, Congregational

Board, Deacons' Court or Board of Management, on receiving intimation of the allocation, to take steps to inform the congregation of the allocation, to raise at least the sum allocated along with promised minimum contributions to the Maintenance of the Ministry Fund and Aged and Infirm Ministers' Fund, to give members of the congregation full information with regard to the Mission and Service Fund and to distribute literature, leaflets, etc., provided by the Stewardship and Budget Committee so that each member may be made fully aware of the new system.

(2) The Kirk Session, Congregational Board, Deacons' Court or Board of Management, without detracting from the ultimate responsibility of the congregational Court to meet its full allocation from congregational funds, shall consult with representatives of the Woman's Guild and other organisations within the congregation concerning their responsibilities towards the wider work of the Church and the education of members of such organisations in the purposes of the Mission and Service Fund.

(3) Each congregation shall transmit each quarter by Bank Transfer or directly to the General Treasurer of the Church, 121 George Street, Edinburgh, its minimum contribution as notified to it duly allocated. Where a congregation raises more than the minimum required, it shall be at liberty to allocate the excess amongst the funds of the Church in such manner as it or its responsible Financial Board thinks fit.

8. *General.*

(1) Notwithstanding the introduction of the Co-ordinated Appeal, it shall be the duty of each Assembly Committee to maintain an efficient information and publicity service in order that members of the Church may be adequately informed of the work the Church is doing in the wider field of Christian evangelism and service.

(2) The Stewardship and Budget Committee shall, in light of experience, review this Scheme at yearly intervals and submit to the General Assembly any recommendation for the amendment of the Scheme or otherwise.

APPENDIX XXVI.

ADMINISTRATIVE REGULATIONS OF GENERAL ASSEMBLY COMMITTEES.

I. Regulations of the Committee on the Maintenance of the Ministry of the Church of Scotland.

MINIMUM STIPEND PAYMENTS.

(See p. 295 ; 1965, Reg. 5.)

ENDOWMENT BRANCH.

For New Charges see Church Extension Regulations, p. 677.

Further Endowment.

1956 (Reg. 3) Regulations, amended by the General Assembly in 1958 (Reg. 4) and applicable to *all* charges in the Church.

1. *Charges Eligible for a Grant.*

An Endowment Grant will be given only to a charge :—

(1) Which in the opinion of the Presbytery and of the Committee on Unions and Readjustments is a necessary charge. An exception may be made in a case where a union is probable, and the stipend of the united charge is likely to be in accordance with these regulations.

(2) Whose stipend from all sources is under £2,100 and a manse, and whose stipend from endowment is under £900.

(Figures applicable from 1st January 1975.)

Note.—For the purpose of this scheme a stipend is computed by taking the average of the three years preceding the application, excluding any aid received. A permanent endowment secured within the three years is regarded as if it had existed throughout the three years. The Committee reserves the right to compute the stipend in cases where a vacancy has occurred within the preceding three years or other exceptional circumstances exist. The Committee also reserves the right to decline a grant in a case in which the Further Endowment in whole or in part will not be used either to increase the stipend or to relieve the aid drawn from the Fund for the Maintenance of the Ministry.

2. *Conditions of Grants.*

A charge qualifies for a grant by raising local capital. The certificate on the form of application that no debt nor obligation of repayment of any kind exists in connection with it must be duly completed. The local capital will be paid to the Committee, and it, together with the Committee's grant, will be held by The Church of Scotland Investment Trust for the Committee on behoof of the charge. The income arising from the endowment so constituted will be paid by the Committee to the incumbent on a *de die in diem* basis. It will be administered during a vacancy, or during the suspension of a minister, as other vacant stipend. An endowment so obtained ranks as a private endowment in the Plan of Union.

Note.—Existing endowments (except such capital as has been obtained in connection with the Further Endowment Scheme) or/and any capital obtained by the sale of property, &c., do not qualify for a grant.

3. *Amount of Grants.*

A grant will be given only in respect of the difference between the stipend of the charge and the limits of Regulation I., Condition (2). Where the endowed stipend is less than £700, the amount of the Grant will be 2 units in the Church of Scotland Trust for each unit purchased by the congregation. Where the endowed stipend is between £701 and £900, the Grant will be unit for unit.

Note.—The Interest shall be at the rate allowed on the General Investment Fund of the Church of Scotland Trust.

4. *Method of Application.*

Before a congregation proceeds to raise capital for this purpose, approach shall be made to the Presbytery to learn whether any objection under Regulation I., Condition (1) will be taken to an application by it. The Presbytery will ascertain the view of the Committee on Unions and Readjustments.

The Secretaries of the Committee will give any information required regarding the amount of local capital that should be raised etc. They will also provide a form of application, which should be submitted to the Presbytery along with copies of the Congregational Balance Sheets for each of the last three years, when there is near prospect of the capital being raised.

When the application, attested by the Presbytery, is submitted, a grant may be voted, but the income will not begin to vest in the incumbent until the first quarterly investment date following receipt of the Local Capital.

5. *Travelling Expenses.*

Provided funds are available, the Committee may in certain cases consider application to provide Travelling Expenses up to a limit of £240 per annum, when the Grant will be three units for every two units put up by the Congregation for investment. (Reports, 1968, p. 224.)

Addendum to Endowment Regulations (1961, Reg. 3).

A charge which has been transported with full status to a new housing area, or a charge which has been transported with full status and united with a Church Extension Charge, and having Endowments exceeding £50 but not exceeding £150, and having very few assets may be granted an Original Endowment of an amount required to bring the total Endowments up to £150.

A charge which has been transported with full status to a new housing area, or a charge which has been transported with full status and united with a Church Extension Charge, and having Endowments exceeding £50 but not exceeding £150, but having considerable assets may be granted a Basal or Further Endowment of an amount required to bring the total Endowments up to £150, the Congregation providing its share of the capital required out of these assets, or otherwise.

REGULATIONS GOVERNING THE REPAYMENT OF VACANCY EXPENSES (1952, Reg. 2).

1. *Congregational Contributions.*—Congregations during a vacancy are expected to collect and remit their contributions to the Fund for the Maintenance of the Ministry fully and regularly, but see 2 (*d*).

2. *Liability for Expenses.*—The pulpit supply expenses will be met by the Committee and by the congregation in the proportion of their respective liability for stipend. In ordinary cases the stipend will be reckoned as in the last full year :—

(*a*) *Where the whole stipend is payable by the Committee*, the Committee will be responsible for the whole of the expenses incurred according to these regulations.

(*b*) *Where the whole stipend is paid direct by the congregation*, the congregation is itself responsible for the whole of its pulpit supply expenses, and there will be no refund by the Committee.

(*c*) *Where the Committee pays only the Basic Stipend*, its liability is the same proportion as the basic Stipend bears to the total stipend of the charge, provided that the congregation continues to remit to the Fund its share of the Basic Stipend.

(*d*) Alternatively a *congregation on the Basic Stipend* may intimate at the beginning of the vacancy that during its course the contributions to the Basic Stipend will cease. In this event the refund by the Committee will be in accordance with (*e*).

(*e*) *Where the stipend is paid partly by the Committee* from endowments and/or Minimum Stipend and partly direct by the congregation (plus any sum paid through the Basic Stipend during an incumbency, but not during a vacancy as provided for under (*d*) above), the refund by the Committee will be the same proportion of the pulpit supply expenses incurred according to the regulations as the stipend from endowments and/or Minimum Stipend payable by the Committee bears to the total stipend.

(*f*) Where there is an *endowment for stipend that is not available during a vacancy*, its amount is deducted both from the total stipend and from the share paid, in order that the respective liabilities may be calculated.

(*g*) *In exceptional cases*, such as unstandardised teind stipends, special arrangements will require to be made, and the interim Moderator or the Treasurer should communicate with the Secretaries of the Department.

3. *Permitted Expenses.*—(1973, Reg. 3.) (1) Where the stipend for the last full year did not exceed the minimum plus £200, the fee shall be £8. (2) Where the stipend for the last full year exceeded the minimum plus £200, the fee shall be £10. (3) A neighbouring minister who supplies a vacant pulpit without providing supply for his own pulpit may receive an honorarium £2·10p each Sunday, plus a refund of travelling expenses, but no fee. (4) Weekend board and lodging may be claimed at a maximum rate of £8 for the weekend (receipts should be exhibited). Travelling expenses (bus fare; railway, second-class; and steamer, cabin fare) shall be paid. Where there is no public conveyance the cost of hiring shall be paid, or a use of a private car shall be paid for at the rate[1] 3p per mile.

No other expense in connection with the vacancy is to be charged.

When a candidate preaches in a neighbouring pulpit, and a claim is made for the supply on that Sunday of the vacant pulpit, the fee due to the candidate and his expenses are a liability of the congregation only.

Instead of weekly supply a *locum tenens* may be employed by the congregation.

Where the stipend includes endowments, the remuneration of a *locum tenens* and the refund to be made by the Committee should be determined *only after consultation with the Secretaries of the Department.*

4. *Expenses of the Interim Moderator.*—In all normal cases *the expenses incurred by the Interim Moderator are a liability of the vacant congregation and should be repaid by it to him.*

In charges that are very remote and whose resources are limited, and also in cases where the resources are limited and the work of the congregation is being carried on by a lay missionary under a short-term appointment, a grant may be made towards the expenses of the Interim Moderator on application by the Treasurer of the congregation, when the claim is approved by the Presbytery.

5. *Refund.*—The normal procedure is that the Treasurer pays the supply out of congregational funds and periodically claims refund from the Committee of its share. It is recommended that claims be sent in quarterly. The name of the minister supplying each Sunday must be given and the name of his charge if he has one. In no case will a congregation be paid beyond its actual outlays certified by the Interim Moderator and Treasurer. In cases under 2 (*a*) above, the voucher system may be used, and on request a book of vouchers will be sent. Similarly in a case in which the part of stipend paid direct by the congregation is small, the voucher system may be used, provided that the financial court undertakes to refund the Committee its share of the expenses.

[1] This amount is subject to increase from time to time.

REGULATIONS *RE* GLEBES
(Reg. I., 1972.)

1. For the removal of any doubt, no Minister shall have the right to the possession or lease of such land, other than such right as may have been or be granted to him by the General Trustees.

2. The General Trustees shall be entitled to grant a lease or right of possession to any Minister, Kirk Session or Congregational Board of such land on such terms and conditions as shall be mutually acceptable to the parties.

3. Subject to the following provisions hereof, the Conditions of Tenure of Glebes approved by the General Assembly of 1933 (Appendix C), and the regulations in regard to the question of the amount which Ministers in occupation of Glebes should return as part of their ministerial income approved by the General Assembly of 1960 (Regulation 7) are revoked.

4. Nothing herein contained shall affect the interests of a Minister or the Assistant and Successor of a Minister who, at the passing of the Church of Scotland (Property and Endowments) Act 1925, was the incumbent of the benefice of any Parish.

5. Nothing herein contained shall affect the interests or obligations of a Minister, Kirk Session or Congregational Board in any case where, at the passing hereof, a Minister is in occupation of such land, or has entered into an arrangement where such land is being worked by the Kirk Session or Congregational Board and in respect of which a returnable rent has been fixed ; and accordingly in such cases the Conditions of Tenure of Glebes and the Regulations of 1960 shall continue to apply.

6. From the date of passing hereof no Minister shall be entitled to grant any lease or right of possession of such land.

7. The General Trustees, before selling, feuing or otherwise disposing of such land or leasing or granting any right of possession thereof, shall take steps to consult with the Minister of the Parish and (except in the case of seasonal grazing or mowing lets or other lets carrying no security of tenure for a period exceeding three years) the Presbytery of the bounds.

CONDITIONS OF TENURE OF GLEBES
(1933, App. C.).

I.

In cases where the Glebe of a parish is allocated to or retained by the Minister as part of his emoluments, he will be responsible for :—

1. The maintenance of the Fences of the Glebe or the renewal thereof where this is required, except in so far as boundary fences are concerned, in which case he will be liable for one-half of the cost of the maintenance or renewal thereof jointly with the adjoining Proprietor or Proprietors.
2. The maintenance in good order and repair of the drainage of the Glebe and the Pipes or other works connected with any Water Supply thereto, in so far as such cost of maintenance may not be mutual with other parties interested in the Water Supply.

3. The farming and treatment of the Glebe according to the rules of good husbandry in cases where it is in the Minister's own occupation.
4. The maintenance of any buildings erected and necessary for the working of the Glebe, and of any cottages, etc., which form part of the Glebe property.
5. The payment out of the Rent, Feu-duties or other Income of the Glebes of all Rates (if any) and Taxes exigible therefrom, unless otherwise provided.

The Kirk Session or Congregational Board may relieve the Minister of all, or part, of the cost of maintenance of the Glebe as well as Rates.

A Minister may enter into arrangement whereby the Kirk Session or Congregational Board will work the Glebe and apply the net profits for Church purposes subject to paying the Minister an appropriate sum in lieu of rent. The General Trustees should be informed and approve of any such arrangement.

Rates when paid by the Minister may be deducted from the Minister's Return of Ministerial Income.

The Minister is also entitled to deduct from the income of the Glebe in his Return of Ministerial Income for the year, expenses incurred by him, with the approval of the Presbytery and the General Trustees. in connection with items 1-4 above.

The Minister of an aid-receiving congregation may receive refund of these approved expenses on application to the Fund for the Maintenance of the Ministry, and the amount should not then be deducted from the Glebe Rent in the Return of Ministerial Income.

In general a Minister has no right or authority to cut down or sell trees growing on the Glebe. In every case the Minister should intimate to the General Trustees any proposal to cut down a tree or trees on the Glebe. The General Trustees will consider the Minister's request and, if they have any difficulty in the matter, they will consult with the Presbytery and, if considered necessary, with the Kirk Session, Congregational Board or Deacons' Court as the case may be, before reaching a decision. In the case of a tree that is clearly rotten or otherwise in a dangerous condition and there is urgency in dealing with it, the Minister may deal with it on his own responsibility, subject to intimating his action immediately to the General Trustees.

The Agricultural Holdings (Scotland) Act, 1949, laid new responsibilities on owners of land. Special attention is drawn to the fact that, unless for seasonal grazing for a fixed period of less than a year, no Glebe is to be let, except by the General Trustees. A Minister who himself lets a Glebe, will therefore be acting *ultra vires*, and may easily find himself burdened with unexpected and heavy responsibilities (*vide* Assembly Reports, 1948, pages 572 and 583; and 1950, page 635).

On a Glebe becoming vacant, the General Trustees should be notified without delay. Notice terminating the tenancy of a Glebe (other than a seasonal grazing let) can only be given by the General Trustees. Neither Glebes nor Manse Gardens should be let as market gardens.

If a Glebe is let at a rent which the Minister considers inadequate, or if the Tenant of the Glebe is failing to fulfil the obligations incumbent on him, the Minister should report the circumstances to the General Trustees.

II.

Joint recommendations of the General Trustees and the Maintenance of the Ministry Committee in regard to the question of the amount which Ministers in occupation of Glebes should, as from 16th May 1961, return as part of their ministerial income; which recommendations were approved by the General Assembly, 1960, Reg. 7:—

1. Where on 16th May 1961 or any time thereafter a Minister is in occupation of the whole or part of a Glebe, or has entered into an arrangement whereby the Glebe is being worked in whole or in part by the Kirk Session or Congregational Board, the amount of the rent which should be returned by the Minister to the Committee on the Maintenance of the Ministry as part of his Ministerial Income (hereinafter called "the returnable rent") shall be considered by the Glebes Committee of the General Trustees along with representatives of the Committee on the Maintenance of the Ministry (hereinafter referred to as "the joint Committee").
2. The joint Committee, after obtaining such information as it thinks necessary, shall determine what the returnable rent should be on the basis of the current lettable value of similar land in the neighbourhood after taking into account any special circumstances relating to the Glebe. The amount of the returnable rent so determined shall be intimated to the Minister and also to the Kirk Session or Congregational Board if working the Glebe. If the Minister and the Kirk Session or Congregational Board if involved agree to the proposed figure or do not object within three weeks from the date of intimation, such figure will become the amount of the returnable rent as from 16th May 1961 or from such later date as the Minister takes over the occupation of Glebe land or arranges for the Kirk Session or Congregational Board to work it.
3. If the Minister, or the Kirk Session or Congregational Board if involved, should object to the proposed figure within three weeks from the date of intimation and if a mutually satisfactory figure cannot be adjusted, the determination of the amount of the returnable rent on the basis referred to in Paragraph 2 shall be referred to a neutral person mutually appointed, or, in the event of failure or delay in making a mutual appointment, to a neutral person appointed by the General Trustees, and the figure determined by such neutral person will become the amount of the returnable rent as from 16th May 1961 or such later date as is mentioned in Paragraph 2.
4. When the amount of the returnable rent has been fixed under either Paragraph 2 or 3 it will continue at that figure for a minimum period of five years subject to any adjustment which might require to be made in the event of a sale, feu or let of parts of the Glebe. After the elapse of five years, however, it will be open to the joint Committee, the Minister or the Kirk Session or Congregational Board if involved, to have the amount of the returnable rent reviewed, in which case the same procedure will be followed as under Paragraphs 2 and 3 and the figure

may again be reviewed in the same manner and in accordance with the same procedure at not less than five-yearly intervals thereafter.

5. In making his Return of Ministerial Income, the Minister will be entitled to deduct from the amount of the returnable rent such expense as he is entitled to deduct under the Regulations relating to Conditions of Tenure of Glebes made by the Committee on the Maintenance of the Ministry as these may be amended from time to time.

6. Where a Glebe is being worked by a Kirk Session or Congregational Board by arrangement with the Minister and he is paid by them a sum in lieu of rent, the amount of such sum to be paid to the Minister as from 16th May 1961 (or such later date as is mentioned in Paragraph 2) will be not less than the amount of the returnable rent determined as above.

7. If a Minister, while technically in occupation of his Glebe, lets the Glebe in whole or in part for seasonal grazing, the amount of the returnable rent for such Glebe or part will as hitherto be the rent which the Minister received for such seasonal grazing less appropriate expenses.

WIDOW'S GRANT.

On the death of a minister who, at the time of his death is in a charge or in receipt of an annuity, a grant which is determined from time to time by the General Assembly is made to his widow or next of kin keeping house for him (1930, 3; 1960, 7).

For loans to widows, see A. & I. Report, 1765, p. 161 (6).

CAR GRANTS (1948, Reg. 6; 1959, Reg. 3; 1973, Reg. 1).

1. A grant towards the cost of a car may be made to the minister of a parish certified by the Presbytery, and approved by the Committee as a parish where the work cannot be effectively undertaken without a car.

The grant will not exceed £400, and will not exceed two-thirds of the cost if less than £600. A second-hand car may not be bought until an independent professional opinion on the reliability, general condition, and price asked is regarded as satisfactory by the Committee, and a report received from a qualified motor engineer on the appropriate form (obtainable on request).

If the applicant has already had a Car Grant, the maximum grant will be reduced by the amount of the Committee's interest in the old car, ascertained as in Regulation 5.

An application for a grant should be submitted through the Presbytery.

2. As the grant is made in respect of the parish, the minister, if translated or retiring, will not be entitled to take away the car without the sanction of the Committee.

3. Subject to the provision of the foregoing article, the car is the property of the minister and he is responsible for comprehensive insurance, licence, and all running costs, repairs and replacements.

4. The minister will submit for inspection the receipt for the purchase of the car and, if required, for any year or years, or part of a year, the total mileage run, the mileage on parochial duty, and the cost of repairs and replacements.

5. In the event of the arrangement between the Committee and the minister coming to an end, the car will be professionally valued, and its value apportioned between the Committee and the minister, in accordance with their respective shares of the purchase price. The general rule shall be that the middle price as published in Glass's Guide for the car in question at the date of demission, translation or death, as the case may be, shall be accepted.

6. The Committee shall be free either to buy out the minister's share or sell its share to the minister, as it may decide.

7. The minister shall in accepting the grant accept the foregoing conditions.

8. Grants are made at the sole discretion of the Committee.

9. Car grants will not be made in a case in which the congregation does not pay the Travelling Expenses of its minister or the appropriate share of the Driving Grant as the case may be.

CAR LOAN FUND (1965, Reg. 4).

1. The Fund, the capital of which amounts to £21,000, shall be called the Ministers' Car Loan Fund. The Committee on the Maintenance of the Ministry (hereinafter referred to as "the Committee") shall have power to increase the capital out of such funds as may be available for the purpose.

2. The Committee shall be the Trustees and Administrators of the Fund and its decision in all matters relative to the Fund, to the granting of loans and the administration of the Fund generally, shall be final. The Committee shall have power to make such rules as it may think fit for the suitable administration of the Fund.

3. The object of the Fund shall be the granting of a Loan to the Minister of a charge of the Church of Scotland in Scotland or England considered as a "Car Essential Charge" by the Presbytery and the Committee, preference being given to Ministers in remote areas who do not qualify for a Car Grant. The Loans shall be for the purpose of assisting such Ministers to purchase cars and the money shall be used only for that purpose.

4. Only a Minister whose ministerial income does not exceed the Minimum Stipend shall be eligible to receive a Loan (cf. p. 674, 6 (*b*)).

5. The Committee shall decide the amount of each Loan, but the maximum Loan shall be £300, and no Loan shall be made on any vehicle which is subject to a Hire Purchase Agreement or any other loan or rental arrangement. A Loan shall not be made in respect of a second-hand car.

6. Unless otherwise agreed in any particular case, a Loan shall be repaid over three years in equal monthly instalments commencing on the last day of the month following payment of the Loan.

7. The Committee shall have right to deduct from any Stipend

payments due to the borrower from its funds the amounts required to meet instalments of repayment.

8. If a borrower is not paid by the Committee such part of his stipend as will meet the instalments of repayment, he shall himself make monthly repayments to the Committee.

9. Loans shall be free of interest; provided, however, that if the borrower should fail to make any instalment repayment within one month after it is due or should be in breach of any of these Regulations, the Committee shall have the right to demand interest at 5 per cent per annum on the balance of the loan then outstanding, and shall also have right to demand immediate repayment of the whole of such balance with interest.

10. In the event of the borrower ceasing to hold a pastoral charge of the Church of Scotland in Scotland or England, he shall immediately repay any balance of the loan outstanding. Likewise, in the event of the death of the borrower, the whole balance of the loan outstanding shall be immediately repayable, and shall form a debt against his Estate. In either of those events, if any sums should be due to the borrower, or his Estate as the case may be, from funds or other moneys held by the Committee or the General Treasurer of the Church, the Committee shall be entitled to apply such sums so far as necessary in reduction of the borrower's or his Estate indebtedness to the Fund.

11. The car for which a loan is made can only be traded in or sold or otherwise disposed of after the loan has been repaid in full.

12. The borrower shall forthwith (unless otherwise agreed in writing by the Committee) insure the car, and while any part of the loan remains unpaid, shall keep the car insured under a fully comprehensive policy without any excess or restrictions (unless otherwise agreed by the Committee) issued by an insurance company approved by the Committee and shall advise the insurance company of the interest of the Committee in the car and shall have such interest endorsed on the policy and produce such policy to the Committee upon demand. The borrower shall forthwith notify the Committee of any occurrence which shall or may give rise to a claim under such policy of insurance and shall not agree to the settlement of any such claim without the concurrence of the Committee. Any moneys received under any such insurance shall be paid by the insurers to the Committee to the extent of the loan outstanding, and the borrower hereby irrevocably authorises the Committee to give a good discharge to the insurers for any such moneys.

13. The amount of the loans in any one year shall not exceed one-half of the capital in the Fund at the time.

14. As the loan is made in respect of the charge, the minister, if translated or retiring, shall not be entitled to take away the car without the sanction of the Committee, except in cases where the loan is repaid in full.

15. Subject to the provision of the foregoing article, the car is the property of the minister and he is responsible for Comprehensive Insurance, licence and all running costs, repairs and replacements.

16. By accepting a loan from the fund, the borrower shall be held to have accepted it under the foregoing Regulations and shall be bound to comply with the foregoing Regulations and to fulfil all obligations imposed on him thereunder.

17. No alterations shall be made on the foregoing Regulations except

by authority of the General Assembly, and that only after any proposed alterations have been considered and reported on by the Committee.

Notes.—Loans of not more than £400 may be made to ministers in receipt of stipends in excess of the Basic Minimum Stipend but not exceeding the Minimum plus £150 in the year prior to the application being made, or in the current year as the case may be. In these cases interest at the rate of 6 per cent p.a. shall be charged, and the loan shall be recovered in thirty-six equal monthly instalments. (Reports 1972, p. 251, and Reports 1974, p. 200.)

All communications addressed to the Secretary of the Committee on the Maintenance of the Ministry in reference to this Fund should be marked " Private ".

LISTED EXPENSES (1961, 7; 1963, 7; 1967, p. 274).

1. (*a*) The Communion Expenses incurred.

(*b*) Any fee or expenses due to a visiting minister at Communion Seasons if such payment be authorised by Kirk Session.

2. (*a*) The rates on the Manse.

(*b*) The rates on any house owned or rented by the minister, and occupied by him in lieu of a Manse, the rates in such cases to be calculated on a rateable value limited to £60 in ordinary cases and £100 in the four large cities.

3. One month's holiday supply, and supply during the minister's attendance at the General Assembly as a Commissioner.

4. Telephone Rental and Calls incurred in performance of ministerial duties where the Presbytery deems a telephone necessary.

5. Notepaper and postage stamps for his official use.

6. (*a*) In parishes which receive a Driving Grant, the remaining proportion of the cost of transport (if any) as may be approved by the Committee on the Maintenance of the Ministry shall be a charge on the congregation.

(*b*) In congregations where no Driving Grant is payable from Central Funds, and where the Committee and the Presbytery agree that the work of the parish involves the minister in travelling expenses, the congregation shall pay on the same basis as the Committee's grants the cost of such travelling either by car or public transport, as may be approved by the Committee (see p. 672).

II. HOME BOARD REGULATIONS (1967, REG. 11).

CONSTITUTION OF HOME BOARD.

1. The function of the Home Board is to extend the Kingdom of God in Scotland by assisting congregations to prosecute more effectively their missionary task in their own parochial areas and communities and by promoting evangelistic enterprises aimed at bringing all types and conditions of men and women under the obedience of Christ, and by such other work as the General Assembly shall from time to time determine.

2. The membership of the Home Board shall consist of:—

(*a*) One representative nominated by each presbytery of the Church.

(*b*) Twenty ministers, twenty elders and twenty-five members, including the Convener and two Vice-Conveners (one of whom shall be a woman), appointed by the General Assembly.

(*c*) The Secretary and Secretary-Depute of the Board.

3. The Home Board shall be responsible for the oversight of all work hitherto carried on through the Home Mission, Women's Home Mission, Church Extension, Highlands and Islands, and Church and Manse Building Committees.

4. The Home Board shall establish a number of Committees responsible for promoting all the work with which the Board has been, or may be, charged, and determine the function of the various Committees from time to time.

These Committees will submit recommendations regarding items remitted to their care to the Home Board for its decision, except in respect of particular matters remitted to them with powers.

5. The Home Board shall be responsible for the oversight of the expenditure of all monies received in respect of work carried on under its control and shall exercise care to ensure that all existing and future funds and monies, whether congregational contributions, legacies, or gifts, are expended for the purpose for which they have been, or may be, given. Each year, the Home Board shall submit to the Stewardship and Budget Committee a statement of anticipated expenditure in respect of all aspects of its work, according to Assembly Regulations.

6. Any reference to a former Sectional Committee of the Home Board in Title Deeds of properties shall, in future, be held to apply to the Home Board and not to the Sectional Committees, and the Home Board shall be entitled to grant authority for sale, let or disposal of such properties, subject to obtaining the authority of the General Assembly where, in terms of the Title Deeds, that is necessary.

7. The Home Board shall request each Presbytery to appoint one or more members of the Presbytery to represent and further the interests of the Board within its bounds. The Board shall keep such representatives regularly informed in regard to its work.

8. The Convener, Vice-Conveners, Secretary and Secretary-Depute of the Home Board shall be members *ex officiis* of all Committees of the Board.

REVISED STRUCTURE OF HOME BOARD

1. The Board shall appoint three Committees and a Convener's Committee.

(*a*) A Home Mission Committee consisting of 60 members, together with those appointed *ex officio* (cf. Constitution, Clause 8). Of the 60 members, at least 15 shall be women, and at least 10 shall be Elders.

The function of the Committee will be to promote and develop the work presently carried out by the Home Mission, Women's Home Mission, and the Highlands and Islands Sectional Committees, with the exception of all matters relating to the maintenance of Church property.

To further particular aspects of its work, the Committee will set up the following Sub-Committees :—

(a) A Rural and Highlands Sub-Committee (8 members plus Co-options).

(b) A Hospital Chaplaincy Sub-Committee (8 members plus Co-options).

(c) A Parochial Assistance and Grants Sub-Committee (15 members plus Co-options).

(d) A Church and Industry Sub-Committee (10 members plus Co-options).

(e) A Church Extension Appointments Sub-Committee (6 members plus Co-options).

(f) St Ninian's, Crieff, Sub-Committee (6 members plus Co-options).

(g) An Elm Row Sub-Committee (6 members plus Co-options).

(*b*) A National Church Extension Committee comprising 55 members (including at least 10 women and 10 Elders). The remit of this Committee will be to promote and develop the work carried out by the Committee on Church Extension.

(*c*) A Property Committee comprising 50 members (including at least 5 women and 10 Elders). The remit of this Committee will be to promote and develop the work carried out by the Church and Manse Building Committee and the former Home Mission Grants Committee, and to maintain all mission and house properties owned by the Home Board and by the former Highlands and Islands, Home Mission, and Women's Home Mission Sectional Committees.

(*d*) A Convener's Committee consisting of the *ex officio* members (cf. Constitution, Clause 8), together with the Conveners of the Home Mission, Church Extension, and Property Committees and 10 members appointed by the Board (of whom 3 at least should be Elders and 3 at least should be women).

The function of the Convener's Committee is to advise the Board regarding matters which are of general concern to the Board, and which are not dealt with by any of its Committees. In particular, it will give consideration to the financial needs of the various fields of the Board's work, and make recommendations regarding Executive Staff whose work relates to more than one of the Board's Committees (*e.g.*, Publicity Officer, Architect).

2. Conveners of Committees appointed by the Home Board will hold Office for a four-year period.

3. A Women's Home Board Council will be established comprising representatives of Presbyterial Councils of the Woman's Guild. Its function will be educational and consultative.

A Council Executive will be formed, comprising 15 members appointed by the Home Board from its own membership.

The function of this Executive will be to make arrangements for the meeting of the General Council, and for the annual Home Board Women's meeting to be held at Assembly time ; and to consider ways and means of promoting Home Mission work in local areas.

The woman Vice-Convener of the Home Board will be *ex officio* Convener of the Council and its Executive.

4. The Home Board Secretariat will consist of a Secretary, Secretary-Depute, and two Assistant Secretaries (one man, one woman).

5. The structure as outlined above shall be regarded as provisional, pending discussion with the other bodies constituting the Home Department.

REGULATIONS *RE* LAY MISSIONARY (1961, Reg. 2).

1. The Lay Missionary is an agent of the Home Board appointed to preach and exercise pastoral care, under the direction of a Minister and Kirk Session.

2. A candidate for the post of lay missionary must be a man of strong Christian conviction and character and a member of the Church of Scotland. His candidature must be approved by the Presbytery in which he is normally resident at the time of his application. At the direction of the Home Board a candidate may require to submit himself for a course of training before acceptance.

3. All appointments to particular parishes are made by the Home Board through the appropriate sectional Committee, with the concurrence of the Minister and Kirk Session concerned, and the lay missionary, at the discretion of appropriate sectional Committee, may be transferred at any time from one sphere of work to another. The Board undertakes to inform the Presbytery or Presbyteries concerned when such transfers are made.

4. A candidate for the post of lay missionary serves for one probationary year, and the Committee, if satisfied, then requests the General Assembly, or such subordinate court as may be named by the General Assembly, to commission him as a lay missionary of the Church. When he is transferred from one sphere of work to another, he is introduced to his new field of labour at a service held in the Parish or Mission Church and conducted by the Parish Minister.

5. A lay missionary may be elected as an elder in the congregation in which he serves. As such he is eligible for membership of Presbytery. If the lay missionary is not serving as an elder, the Kirk Session or the Presbytery may, at their discretion, invite him to attend and speak at meetings of these Courts, without voting powers. If he is serving as an elder without being a representative member of Presbytery, the Presbytery may invite him to attend and speak at its meetings, but without voting powers.

6. The lay missionary receives a salary determined by the Home Board (£500 per annum in 1961) with a house or an appropriate sum of money in lieu of a house. Termination of appointment of a lay missionary may take place on three months' notice on either side.

7. The lay missionary shall retire at the age of 70, though in special cases his period of service may be continued at the discretion of the Board. A non-contributory pension, the amount of which is determined by the Board (£208 in 1960) shall be made available to all missionaries who retire at the age of 70 or over if they have served the Committee for a period exceeding 15 years. Special consideration will be given to cases of men who retire on grounds of infirmity.

In 1963 a non-contributory pension scheme was instituted by arrangement with a life assurance company, and included all the missionaries under the age of 50 at that time.

Church Extension Charges

(1955, Reg. 1, 1969, Reg. 9 and 1975, Reg. 2, except where otherwise stated.)

(A) *New Charges.*

1. The initial steps towards the formation of a Church Extension Charge shall ordinarily rest with the minister and Kirk Session of the Parish within the bounds of which it is required, it being understood that the Presbytery may at any time take the initial steps towards the same.

2. It shall lie with the Presbytery, in consultation with the Home Board (National Church Extension Sectional Committee), to judge whether, having regard to the necessities of any area within its bounds, a new charge is called for.

3. The Presbytery shall consult with local authorities as to suitable sites for new buildings, and shall transmit its findings to the Home Board (National Church Extension Sectional Committee) which, if so advised, shall authorise negotiation for the acquisition of the proposed site.

4. Before the Presbytery agrees to the formation of a new congregation as a Church Extension Charge, it shall consult with the ministers and Kirk Sessions of contiguous parishes.

5. Before proposals to erect church buildings or to appoint a minister for the charge are approved, the Presbytery shall delimit the bounds of the parish to be allotted to it and the Home Board (National Church Extension Sectional Committee) shall be satisfied that the population in the area is or will be sufficient to justify the further steps proposed.

(B) *Appointment of Ministers.*

1. The appointment of the minister of a Church Extension Charge shall lie with the Home Board (Home Mission Sectional Committee), after consultation with the Presbytery and the congregation, should a congregation have been formed. The procedure shall be as follows :—

(*a*) In cases where no congregation exists, the Home Board (Home Mission Sectional Committee) shall nominate a minister and submit his name to the Presbytery, inviting it to concur in his appointment.

(*b*) In cases where a congregation exists :—

(i) Before taking steps towards the settlement of a minister in the Church Extension Charge, the Presbytery shall consult the Home Board (Home Mission Sectional Committee) with whom shall lie the duty of suggesting the name of a suitable minister.

(ii) The Home Board (Home Mission Sectional Committee) may confer with local parties should that course seem desirable.

(iii) If the appropriate committee of the Presbytery is satisfied with the name suggested, the interim moderator shall arrange that the nominee preach to the congregation (1962, Reg. 7).

(iv) The interim moderator or other person appointed by the Presbytery shall take immediate steps thereafter to learn the mind of the congregation and shall intimate the result of the inquiry to the Home Board (Home Mission Sectional Committee) (1962, Reg. 7).

(v) If the Home Board (Home Mission Sectional Committee) is satisfied that the nominee is acceptable to the congregation it shall make the appointment subject to the concurrence of the Presbytery (1962, Reg. 7).

(*c*) In the event of the minister thus appointed being a probationer or a minister without charge, the Presbytery shall take the necessary steps for ordination, if required, and admission to the charge.

(*d*) In the event of the minister thus appointed being the minister of a charge in another Presbytery, the Home Board (Home Mission Sectional Committee) shall intimate the appointment to both Presbyteries, each of whom thereafter shall follow as closely as possible the normal procedure of prosecuting and receiving a call and arranging for a translation and settlement.

(*e*) In the event of the minister first proposed being unacceptable, the Home Board (Home Mission Sectional Committee) shall suggest another name, and the same procedure shall be followed as in the first case.

(*f*) Should a third nomination be required, and it prove to be equally barren in respect of an accepted settlement, the Home Board (Home Mission Sectional Committee) shall consult with the Presbytery on the selection of a suitable minister who shall be appointed to the charge.

2. The minister inducted to a Church Extension Charge shall be responsible with the Kirk Session for the pastoral oversight of the area allotted to the charge. He shall have full ministerial standing in the Presbytery, and shall be directly responsible in the usual way to that Court.

(C) *Administration of Spiritual and Temporal Affairs.*

1. The administration of the spiritual affairs of a Church Extension Charge shall be in the hands of a Provisional Kirk Session, of which the minister shall be Moderator, and to which the Presbytery shall appoint a number of elders from other congregations as assessors.

Presbyteries should endeavour to ensure that assessors have adequate instruction and information on their duties as assessor elders and should endeavour to have them released for other duties in their own congregations.

2. In cases where the membership of the Church Extension congregation includes elders who have been ordained for service in other congregations, such members may at any time be admitted to the eldership of the Church Extension Charge in addition to the elders appointed as assessors from other congregations.

3. The Presbytery shall exercise its discretion as to the number of Assessors to be appointed in the first instance, and may increase or decrease this number, from time to time, according to its estimate of the

needs of the Charge and having regard to any representations which the Provisional Kirk Session may make.

After eighteen months (which may be reduced to twelve months at the discretion of the Presbytery) from the date of the formation of a Church Extension Charge, the Presbytery may sanction the ordination of a specified number of new Elders from the membership of the Church Extension congregation; and after three years from the formation of the Church Extension Charge, the Kirk Session itself may authorise the ordination of further Elders at its own discretion.

> *Note.*—In the case of a transportation, where an adequate number of elders of the transported charge are continuing to function as elders in the new area, the Presbytery may deem it unnecessary to appoint assessor elders (or to restrict the appointment of new elders).

4. The Kirk Session of a Church Extension congregation, composed wholly or partly of elders appointed as assessors by the Presbytery from other congregations, shall have the right to appoint a representative elder to Presbytery and Synod.

5. The temporal affairs of a Church Extension Charge shall be managed by a Committee composed of the Kirk Session, together with a number of members, over the age of 18, elected by the congregation at a meeting duly called for the purpose, the number of members thus elected not to exceed the number of the Kirk Session. One-third of the elected members shall retire annually by rotation but shall be eligible for re-election. At the first meeting of the congregation to elect office-bearers, following the raising of the Charge to full status, all elected members shall retire, but shall be eligible for re-election. The Minister shall normally be chairman of this Committee, but should he not wish so to act, the Committee may elect one of its members as chairman for the ensuing year. He shall be eligible for re-election at the end of each year.

(D) *Payment of Stipend.*

1. The Committee on the Maintenance of the Ministry shall pay the Minimum Stipend (or City Minimum in cases where still payable) to the Minister of a Church Extension Charge. The Home Board shall pay a supplement to the Minimum Stipend of £200 per annum to Ministers of all Church Extension Charges.

2. This supplement may also be paid to Ministers of Charges which are transported in full status to new housing areas on the same conditions as apply to former Church Extension Charges granted Full Status (see Section F11), always provided that the total Stipend of the Charge shall be restricted to the Minimum Stipend (or City Minimum where applicable) plus the supplement.

(E) *Financial Responsibility of Church Extension Charges.*

(1959, Reg. 6, 1965, Reg. 1 and 1975, Reg. 2.)

1. A Church Extension Charge shall from the beginning provide for its

ordinary expenses. It should endeavour to contribute to the Mission and Service Fund in accordance with the allocations made by the Presbytery. In making these allocations Presbyteries should bear in mind the stage which the Church Extension Charge has reached and that it has two immediate financial obligations :—

(*a*) The contribution of as large a proportion as possible of the Stipend guaranteed by the Home Board (Home Mission Sectional Committee) and the Committee on the Maintenance of the Ministry ; and

(*b*) The repayment of a proportion of the cost of its buildings to the Home Board (National Church Extension Sectional Committee) in accordance with paragraph 2 below.

2. The repayment obligations of a Church Extension Charge or a Charge transported with full status in respect of buildings provided by the Home Board (National Church Extension Sectional Committee) shall be as follows:—

(*a*) Except as provided below, three-tenths of the total cost of the church buildings (including church, hall-church, halls, etc.) and the manse.

Note.—In any case, where this sum would exceed existing obligations, the repayment will be limited to the existing obligations.

(*b*) If a manse has not been provided by the Committee, the repayment obligations will be one-fifth of the cost of the church buildings.

(*c*) The Home Board (National Church Extension Sectional Committee) shall have power to vary the terms of repayment in exceptional cases and to determine a maximum sum (*e.g.*, £20,000) which any congregation should repay.

3. The Presbytery, through its Church Extension Committee and/or any others appointed by the Presbytery for the purpose, will be consulted before purchase or erection of any house for use as a manse.

Local parties will be consulted before purchase or erection when this is possible or practicable, but the Home Board (National Church Extension Sectional Committee) shall determine the nature of the accommodation, fittings and specification of new manses to be erected, and the nature of alterations and expenditure on manses purchased for use as manses.

If a manse is sold before repayment has been completed, any loss on the sale shall normally be borne by the congregation, while any profit shall be applied primarily towards reduction of the congregation's debt to the Committee. The Home Board (National Church Extension Sectional Committee) shall have power to modify this regulation in exceptional cases.

4. The Home Board (Home Mission Sectional Committee) shall have a general control over the entire expenditure of a Church Extension Charge, and the annual budget and statement of accounts shall be submitted to it for examination and approval, subject to the following conditions :—

(*a*) In cases where a minister is inducted to a new Church Extension Charge, or a congregation is transported to a new area with the status of a Church Extension Charge, it shall be intimated either at the induction or at the transportation, as the case may be, that a Schedule will be issued by the Committee on the Maintenance of the Ministry in two years' time, by which time the congregation will be expected to make a contribution agreeable to the Committee on the Maintenance of the Ministry and the Home Board.

(*b*) In cases where a congregation is transported with full status, a Revision Schedule will be issued by the Committee on the Maintenance of the Ministry at the beginning of the year occurring not less than twelve months after the transportation.

Note.—In furtherance of the control vested in the Home Board (Home Mission Sectional Committee) by this regulation, the Committee has directed that the accounts of Church Extension Charges shall be audited by two auditors approved by the Presbytery and outwith the membership of the congregation and Kirk Session.

(F) *Application for Full Status.*

1. It shall be open to a Church Extension Charge to apply for full status at any time after it has been in existence for five years, and, in normal circumstances, it is expected to do so before the eleventh anniversary of its inception.

It shall likewise be open, at any time, to the Presbytery, with the agreement of the Home Board and the Committee on the Maintenance of the Ministry, to take the initiative towards the erection of full status of any Church Extension Charge within its bounds.

2. An application by a Church Extension Charge for full status shall be submitted, in the first instance, to the Presbytery of the bounds. If the Presbytery is of opinion that the application merits consideration at that time, it shall forward the application to the Home Board, together with information relative to the following factors. If the Presbytery is of opinion that a Church Extension Charge should be raised to full status, although an application has not been received, it may also advise the Home Board accordingly and likewise forward the same following information :—

(*a*) whether the number of communicant members in relation to the size and circumstances of its delimited area is sufficient to justify a full Charge.

(*b*) whether an adequate number of suitable men and women are available as elders and office-bearers from its own membership, and whether the leadership of agencies is satisfactory.

(*c*) whether the Charge has a suitable building for worship and other activities, and a suitable manse, and whether these are being properly maintained.

(*d*) whether the Minister and the Charge are endeavouring to fulfil an effective and necessary role in the parochial area.

(*e*) whether the Charge is making the Appropriate contribution to Stipend as fixed by the Maintenance of the Ministry Committee acting in concert with the Presbytery of the bounds.

(*f*) whether the Charge has made repayments which are considered reasonable, in the light of its circumstances, towards its ultimate share of the cost of the buildings provided by the Home Board, and has in operation a satisfactory scheme of ingathering funds for this purpose which will not prejudice, or be prejudiced by, its contributions to the Maintenance of the Ministry Fund or the Mission and Service Fund.

(*g*) whether the Charge has met its allocation by the Presbytery to the Mission and Service Fund in previous years, and gives evidence of intention to make contributions in the future according to its resources.

(*h*) general progress and harmony.

3. The Home Board will then consult with the Committee on the Maintenance of the Ministry on the merits of the case in the light of the information provided and, if both Committees are satisfied, may agree to recommend to the General Assembly that the Church Extension Charge be granted full status. Alternatively, these Committees may seek further conference with the Presbytery and the Charge concerned by visitation or otherwise before reaching a decision on their recommendation. Only in exceptional circumstances will a recommendation to grant full status be withheld after the Charge has been in existence for ten years.

4. The Committee on the Maintenance of the Ministry shall accept from a Church Extension Charge proceeding to full status, as it does from any aid-receiving charge, an application for a manse grant in a case where it is proposed to build or purchase a manse.

5. A Church Extension Charge shall repay to the Home Board (National Church Extension Sectional Committee) as soon as possible after it has been granted full status, any outstanding balance of its total financial liability as set out in Section (*e*).

6. (*a*) The full details of the arrangements with regard to Stipend that are proposed shall be submitted, on a schedule that will be supplied for the purpose, to the Committee on the Maintenance of the Ministry at least ten days before the meeting of the Committee in the month of February prior to the General Assembly to which the application or recommendation is to be submitted, and a Minute of the Committee shall be laid on the table of the General Assembly.

(*b*) The proposed Stipend arrangements shall include an application to the Committee on the Maintenance of the Ministry for a grant for Initial Endowment unless there are reasons approved by the Committee for not so applying.

(*c*) Provided sufficient endowment funds are available, the Committee on the Maintenance of the Ministry will grant an endowment yielding not less than £100 per annum at the time when the grant is made (exclusive of any grant towards endowment which may be made by the Baird Trust or otherwise). Normally this endowment shall attach to the charge as long as it remains in full status, but, like other endowments for Stipend, it will be administered under Act XXVII., 1953.

(*d*) In the event of funds not being immediately available for a capital endowment, the Committee may give an undertaking (i) pending such funds being available to provide an annual sum of not less than £100 for the Stipend of the charge; and (ii) to provide, as early as possible, a capital endowment yielding not less than £100 per annum at the time when the capital is provided. The Minute of the Committee on the Maintenance of the Ministry embodying this undertaking shall be accepted as equivalent to the capital endowment for the purposes of the erection of the Church Extension Charge into a full charge.

7. When a recommendation is to be made to the General Assembly to raise a Church Extension Charge to full status, the Home Board shall incorporate in its Report information about the Charge which will enable the General Assembly to make a judgement, and will include in its draft deliverance a paragraph in the following terms:—

> "The General Assembly resolve to raise the Church Extension Charge(s) of   into (a) parish(es) *quoad sacra* and to pass an Act(s) thereanent in terms of the draft in Appendix   to the Report."

The proposed Act shall be in the style of the draft Act appended to these Regulations.

The Church Extension Charge may be represented at the Bar of the General Assembly for its interest.

8. When an Initial Endowment is to be provided, there shall be attached thereto the nucleus of a Fabric Fund. Towards the capital required for this purpose the Committee on the Maintenance of the Ministry shall provide a capital sum of £50, and the congregation shall deposit with the Committee on the Maintenance of the Ministry a capital sum of £50.

9. The titles to the existing heritable properties of the charge, and if no Churchis erected at the date of the Act of Assembly after-mentioned, the titles of the Church when erected or acquired, shall be taken in name of the Church of Scotland General Trustees.

10. As a regular charge it shall have a Kirk Session and such method of management as is provided by the Deed of Constitution. After the Church Extension Charge has been constituted a Regular Charge and erected into a Parish *quoad sacra*, as aforesaid, the elders appointed as assessors by the Presbytery from other congregations shall no longer be members of the Kirk Session.

11. The Home Board may continue to supplement the Stipend, after full status is granted, in the same way as for Church Extension Charges during the incumbency of the Minister of the Charge at the date of being granted full status. This supplement will cease on the occurrence of a vacancy and, in any case, not later than three years after the Stipend first ceases to be aided by the Committee on the Maintenance of the Ministry during which period the supplement may be paid on a reducing annual scale. The rights of Ministers receiving supplements, after attaining full status, under earlier regulations, will be preserved.

12. Applications from Church Extension Charges and recommendations from Presbyteries for erection to full status must be received by the Home Board by 30th November if they are to be submitted to the next General Assembly and intimation of the intention to erect a Church Extension Charge into a Church and Parish *quoad sacra* shall be given by the Home Board to the Delegation of Assembly on or before the 31st day of January preceding the meeting of the General Assembly, at which the recommendation is to be considered.

13. The Solicitor of the Church shall, under the direction of the Delegation, thereafter proceed with the preparation of the necessary documents, so that they may be ready for signature immediately after the passing of the Act of Assembly.

14. After the passing of the Act of Assembly, it must be shown to the satisfaction of the Delegation that the existing heritable properties of the charge are duly vested in the Church of Scotland General Trustees, that the Initial Endowment has been duly provided in a form approved of by the General Assembly, subject to Regulation (F) 5 (*d*), and that the nucleus of a Fabric Fund has been duly provided and secured.

15. The Delegation shall thereafter issue the new Deed of Constitution with effect as from the date of issue. The Act of Assembly shall (unless otherwise provided in the Act itself) take effect at the date of issue of the Deed of Constitution.

16. The whole procedure shall, if possible, be completed by 1st July immediately following the passing of the Act of the General Assembly. The whole expenses in connection with the Application and Act, including *inter alia*, the conveyance of properties, the setting aside and securing of the Initial Endowment and the nucleus of the Fabric Fund and the preparation and issue of the Deed of Constitution, shall be borne in equal shares by the congregation and by the General Assembly.

17. On the Church Extension Charge being constituted as a regular charge, the Presbytery shall make formal intimation of the change to the congregation, and take such steps in connection therewith as may seem to that Court appropriate.

18. Former Church Extension Charge raised to full status, and Charges transported to new housing areas in full status, shall submit annually to the Home Board and the Committee on the Maintenance of the Ministry a copy of their audited accounts not later than 31st March following the close of the financial year, to which these pertain, until such time as they have discharged their liability for their share of the cost of the buildings provided by the Home Board, and cease to draw aid from the Fund for the Maintenance of the Ministry.

APPENDIX.

ACT ANENT ERECTING CHURCH EXTENSION CHARGE TO FULL STATUS.

EDINBURGH, *May* 19 *Sess.*

The General Assembly enact and ordain as follows :—

1. Disjoin an area from the Parishes of and in the Presbytery of situated approximately in the and parts of the said Parishes respectively and the boundaries of which area are

more particularly described in the Minute of the said Presbytery dated Provided always that the Presbytery of shall have power to revise or alter the boundaries of the said area from time to time.

2. Erect the said area as so disjoined together with the Church at into a Parish *quoad sacra* of the Church of Scotland to be called the Parish of *quoad sacra*, and designate the said Church to be the Church of the said Parish *quoad sacra*.

3. Declare the said Parish of *quoad sacra* to be wholly within the jurisdiction of the Presbytery of in the Synod of .

4. Find and declare that the Minister and Elders of the said Church and Parish as so erected shall have and enjoy the status and have all the powers, rights and privileges of a Parish Minister and Elders in connection with the Church of Scotland and shall form together the Minister and Kirk Session of the said Parish.

5. Provide and declare that any existing rights of the Ministers of the Parishes of and shall in no way be affected by the erection of the said Parish of *quoad sacra*.

6. Appoint as a Constitution for the said Parish a Deed of Constitution in the form of the Model Deed approved by the General Assembly on 20th May 1965 (as amended) as applicable to new Parishes *quoad sacra*, and remit to the Delegation of the General Assembly to execute and deliver the same after it is satisfied as to the vesting of the Church, Hall and Manse and endowment for stipend and fabric all in terms of the Regulations; provided always as it is hereby specially provided and declared, that this Act shall not come into operation until the date of issue of the said Deed of Constitution.

REGULATIONS GOVERNING GRANTS.

(*a*) Parochial Evangelism.

Grants may be given to Congregations for the employment of Agents (Ordained Assistants, Probationers, Student Assistants, Lay Missionaries). Such grants shall only be given where the Presbytery attests that the Parish concerned requires such help.

(*b*) Hall Grants (Home Mission Committee) (1966, Reg. 4).

1. The Committee shall each year set aside a sum of money which may be disbursed in grants to congregations undertaking the erection of new church halls or the extension of existing halls.

2. Applications for such hall grants shall be made on the prescribed schedule, and each application must have the approval of the presbytery of the bounds before submission to the committee.

3. In determining whether a grant shall be given, and the amount, the committee will take into account in particular the need of the parish for new or increased hall accommodation and the local financial resources available.

4. In no case will a grant be given exceeding one-sixth of the total sum set apart by the committee in terms of Clause 1.

5. Any grant voted will be regarded as having lapsed if not claimed within three years of the date of voting.

(c) Property Grants (Property Committee).

(1) *Inspection of Buildings.*

1. Under terms of Act XXI., 1961, it is the duty of Presbyteries to carry out a five-yearly inspection of ecclesiastical properties and to include in their reports a deliverance on the state of repair of the buildings belonging to the congregations visited; and Presbytery Clerks shall transmit a copy of this deliverance in each case to the Secretary of the Home Board.

2. In the case of poorer congregations in which Presbyteries may require professional advice, they shall report to the Home Board which may supply such advice or assistance as the case requires.

(2) *Issue of Collecting-Books.*

Should a congregation desire to appeal to the Church generally for subscriptions in aid of any building or renovation scheme, it may do so only by means of a Collecting-book issued on these following conditions:—

1. The use of a Collecting-book shall be authorised by the Presbytery after being satisfied from its knowledge of all the circumstances of the case that the congregation is justified in making such an appeal.

2. The Presbytery's judgment shall be set forth in a deliverance which shall be embodied in any circular issued in connection with the appeal, and prefixed to the Collecting-book itself.

3. The Presbytery shall have received intimation from the Church and Manse Building Committee of its approval of the plans and estimates in the case, its satisfaction with the amount raised locally, its permission to proceed, and its concurrence in the issue of a Collecting-book.

4. The total cost for which an appeal is to be made shall not be under £50.

5. All subscriptions received personally or in answer to letters or circulars shall be entered in the Collecting-book.

6. The Collecting-book, along with a statement of receipts and disbursement signed by the Moderator and Session Clerk and the Treasurer of the congregation, shall be returned to the Clerk of Presbytery within twelve months from the date of issue, and after due examination an abstract of said statement shall be engrossed in the Minute of Presbytery.

WOMEN'S HOME MISSION.

The practice of the Women's Home Mission Committee is contained in Reports 1963, pp. 279-282, with regard to the employment of Deaconesses.

DRIVING GRANTS (1948, Reg. 5).

ADMINISTRATION.

1. A Standing Joint Committee shall be appointed consisting of three members from each of the Committee on the Maintenance of the Ministry, the Home Mission and the Highlands and Islands Committees, which shall consider all applications for Driving Grants, the revision of existing grants and applications for capital expenditure, and submit recommendations to the Committees concerned, who shall vote all grants.

2. The general principles governing Driving Grants are :—

(*a*) That they are applied to parishes where the stipend is small and the local conditions such that the Minister cannot serve the parish adequately without incurring greater expense on transport than he can reasonably be expected to bear.

(*b*) That as the money available for such grants is strictly limited, a grant is not intended to meet the whole cost, except in certain readjustment cases and for Missionaries. Part should be borne by the congregation.

(*c*) That the money available is allocated on as fair a basis as possible.

REGULATIONS.

I. Grants shall be voted only on an application attested by the Presbytery.

II. Grants are valid only for one year unless specially designated otherwise, and shall date from 15th August to 14th August, and be paid quarterly.

III. Grants may be voted to enable Ministers or Missionaries to provide ordinances in places where by reason of remoteness or otherwise a stated Service is required for a group of people.

IV. Grants may also be voted, if funds permit, to enable Ministers and Missionaries to pay pastoral visits in remote districts in order that they may keep up personal contact with the people in their homes.

V. Grants may be voted where two or more congregations are served by one agent, or where in cases of readjustment of agencies the provision of a Driving Grant is required.

VI. Grants may be voted for a Service which entails travelling a distance of not less than 10 miles for the double journey, or in cases where two or more Services are necessarily held at times which demand motor transport.

VII. Grants shall not cover the whole cost, and are voted on the understanding that the remainder of the cost shall be a charge on the parties benefiting—namely, the members of the congregations.

VIII. In special cases arising from Union of Congregations, the Regulations as to distance and cost may be modified.

IX. In cases where a Minister or Missionary owns a car or motor-cycle, grants shall be voted on a mileage basis (subject to Regulations VII. and XI.) as follows :—

Motor-car	5p a mile.
Motor-cycle	3p a mile.

X. Claims for payment of grant on the mileage basis shall be dealt with only when forwarded on the form provided for this purpose.

XI. When hiring is necessary, *the grant shall not exceed two-thirds of the account rendered, except in special cases arising from local unions.* Where a mileage allowance is given, *the grant shall not exceed the sum due for three-fourths of the total mileage for Sunday Services, except in cases arising from local unions.* The Committee shall be satisfied that in all hiring arrangements the most economical estimate has been accepted.

XII. In connection with any grant a statement may at any time be called for, showing the number of journeys made by the Minister or Missionary to the districts served.

Regulations anent Prison Chaplaincies (1964, Reg. 5).

1. The General Assembly shall set up a Prison Chaplaincies Board consisting of seven persons, of whom six shall be appointed annually by the General Assembly on the nomination of the Home Board, the Secretary of the Home Board being *ex officio* a member and Secretary of the Board. Two of the six appointed members shall in the first instance serve for two years, two for three years, all other appointments being for four years. Members retiring will not be eligible for reappointment until after the lapse of one year.

2. Subject to the procedure outlined in the following paragraphs, this Board will have full and final authority in tendering advice to the Director of Prison and Borstal Services regarding the appointment, duration, and terms of service of Prison and Borstal Chaplains.

3. When a vacancy occurs in a Prison or Borstal chaplaincy the agreed procedure is that the Director of Prison Services communicates with the Secretary of the Prison Chaplaincies Board, stating the conditions of appointment and the remuneration and duties involved. The Secretary of the Board shall inform the Presbytery concerned. Thereafter the Board together with three representatives of the Presbytery within whose bounds the vacant chaplaincy is located, will consider a recommendation or recommendations from the Presbytery for the post and then nominate a minister to the Director of Prison Services.

4. The appointment of a chaplain shall be initially for a period of five years, of which the first year shall be a probationary year. Before the expiry of this initial five-year period the Director will communicate with the Secretary of the Board, and thereafter the Board in conjunction with the three representatives of the Presbytery of the bounds may nominate the minister for a second five-year period of service. Only in exceptional circumstances will the Prison Chaplaincies Board recommend that appointments be extended beyond ten years, and any such appointment will be subject to annual review.

5. Whenever possible, a minister beginning work as a chaplain will serve a minimum of two months with the retiring chaplain, or with some other minister experienced in the work.

6. It will be the duty of each chaplain to prepare annually a written report on his work which shall be submitted to the Presbytery of the bounds before 30th November. The Presbytery Clerk will thereafter transmit it with any comments from the Presbytery to the Secretary of the Prison Chaplaincies Board before 31st December. The latter shall prepare a general report on the work of Prison and Borstal Chaplains in Scotland to be submitted to the General Assembly as part of the Report of the Home Board.

7. The Prison Chaplaincies Board will arrange an annual meeting of chaplains to confer on their work and any matter relating to their chaplaincy service.

8. In the event of a serving chaplain, or a group of chaplains, or a Presbytery being of opinion that some revision or modification of the terms of service of chaplains is called for, such opinion shall be passed to the Secretary of the Board, for consideration by the Board, which may, if it sees fit, make representations to the Director of Prison Services on the matter.

9. Subject to the rights of Church Courts and of Commissioners to the General Assembly, any amendment to this scheme or any alternative scheme shall be presented by the Home Board to the General Assembly for approval.

10. The foregoing procedure will apply in the case of all new chaplaincy appointments and of all chaplains in post, except in those cases where special arrangements have been made by the Home and Health Department.

III. Regulations anent Probationers, Scheme for Transference of Ministers, and Scale of Fees.

Note.—The purpose of the following provisions is to secure a system which will enable the Church to make the most effective use of its ministerial resources, not only in the interests of Probationers and Ministers on the Transference List, but also in relation to the needs of the Church as a whole. At the same time they are intended to safeguard the interests of vacant Congregations by ensuring that Probationers or Ministers are heard only with the consent of the Congregation concerned.

(1948, x.)

The General Assembly withdraw, as from 30th September 1948, the existing Regulations anent Probationers and Scheme for Transference of Ministers contained in Appendix V. to Act IX., 1932, and in place thereof ENACT and DECLARE as follows, the new provisions to come into operation as from the 1st day of October 1948 :—

Instructions to Interim Moderators and Presbytery Clerks.

It shall be part of the duty of Presbytery Clerks to intimate to the Secretary of the Committee on Probationers and Transference of Ministers the names of Interim Moderators in vacancies immediately these are appointed ; and, whenever this information is received, instructions regarding the Transference of Ministers Scheme shall be sent to the Interim Moderators.

The General Assembly instruct Interim Moderators, at the first meeting of a Vacancy Committee, to make full intimation of the Regulations of the Probationers and Transference of Ministers Committee and to point out the necessity of complying with these Regulations.

A.—REGULATIONS ANENT PROBATIONERS.

1. The Committee shall keep a Roll of Licentiates. All Licentiates shall be placed on the Roll on being licensed, and the dates of their licence shall be recorded. The Committee shall also keep a Roll of Probationers who are eligible for appointments. This Roll shall include Probationers who have received ordination but have not been admitted to a charge.

2. After each meeting of Presbytery at which students are licensed, the Clerk of the Presbytery shall immediately intimate the names and addresses of the Licentiates to the Secretary of the Committee. If any Licentiate is Gaelic-speaking, this should be indicated.

3. The employment of each Licentiate during the first year of Probation, as approved by the Board of Practical Training, shall be reported to the Committee by the Secretary of the Board.

4. At the end of one year after licence each Probationer shall report himself to the Committee, and shall appear, if required, for interview, consultation, and advice.

> *Note.*—In the case of students who have been engaged in approved National Service and who may not be required to fulfil a year of Probation, this Regulation shall apply immediately after licence.

5. Each Probationer, when eligible for a charge, shall receive appointments from the Committee to preach in vacancies. The Committee shall aim at securing equitable opportunities for all those on the List.

Probationers may intimate that for a period in which they are otherwise employed they do not wish to receive such appointments.

6. Probationers who wish to receive appointments must advise the Secretary of the Committee of the addresses at which letters or telegrams will immediately reach them, and must acknowledge communications regarding appointments *by return of post.*

7. A record of all appointments to preach in vacancies shall be kept by the Secretary of the Committee.

8. At the end of each year after licence, and until he is inducted to a charge, every Probationer shall complete and return to the Secretary the appropriate schedule of information (1968, Reg. 10).

9. Ministers, including Missionaries or Chaplains, ordained for special service at home or overseas, who have completed such service satisfactorily shall be entitled to the privileges of Probationers as defined in these Regulations, always provided that they satisfy the requirements of the Committee on Admission of Ministers.

10. Vacancy Committees desiring to consider Probationers must before doing so apply to the Probationers' Committee for a list of Probationers.

Should a congregation desire to consider Probationers not on the list submitted, their names shall be sent to the Secretary of the Committee and the Committee shall, so far as is consistent with the equitable distribution of vacancies among those eligible and the interests of congregations, give effect to such a request (1953, Reg. 6).

11. Thereafter a Vacancy Committee which chooses a Probationer as a sole nominee, or as one of a leet, must apply to this Committee for his appointment to preach in the vacant charge. No one on the Probationers' Roll shall be eligible for a call to a vacant charge unless this permission has been received.

In order that due intimation may be given to congregations a Vacancy Committee shall make such request at least 14 days before the date suggested for the candidate to preach (1953, Reg. 6).

B.—SCHEME FOR TRANSFERENCE OF MINISTERS (1948, x. 1970, Reg. 4).

1. The Committee shall keep a List of Ministers who, having been in their present charges for not less than five years, have intimated their willingness to consider another sphere. In special cases, including those in which the desirability of a local union seems apparent, and where the Presbytery so recommends, it shall be in the power of the Committee to add to this List, at their own request, the names of Ministers who have not completed five years in their present charge, always subject to Act VI. of 1945.[1]

[1] Now replaced by 1959, xxiv.

2. Names shall be retained on the List for five years. Ministers who wish to have their names retained thereafter must renew their applications.

3. In vacancies where it is proposed to hear a leet of Ministers in charges preaching in the vacant Church, the Committee shall make appointments from the List not more in number than those made by the Congregation. The Committee reserves the right to modify this rule in cases where some or all of those nominated by the Congregation are on the Transference List held by the Committee. If possible, those Ministers appointed by the Committee and those appointed by the Congregation shall be heard on alternate Sundays. In the case of such appointments the Committee requires at least fourteen days' notice for the submission of names.

4. The Committee shall aim at securing equitable opportunities for all those on the List. Congregations proposing to hear Ministers through deputations during a vacancy are recommended to apply to the Committee for names of Ministers for consideration when a selection is being made.

5. The Committee, if it judges this course desirable, shall have power to forward to vacant Congregations the names of Ministers on the List for their consideration.

C.—MINISTERS WITHOUT CHARGE (1948, x.).

The Committee shall keep, apart from the Roll of Probationers, a List of Ministers without Charge, who fulfil the conditions of Acts of Assembly XV., 1933, and X., 1935, and desire to preach in vacant charges with a view to election, and shall forward the said List on request to Interim Moderators in vacancies. The Committee may appoint Ministers from this List to preach as candidates in vacancies, as opportunity may arise, as well as from the List of Ministers under the Transference Scheme.

D.—REVISED SCALE OF PULPIT SUPPLY FEES AND EXPENSES IN A VACANCY (1974, Reg. 3).

1. Where the Stipend for the last full year did not exceed the Minimum plus £200, the fee shall be £8.

2. Where the Stipend for the last full year exceeded the Minimum plus £200, the fee shall be £10.

3. A neighbouring minister who supplies a Vacant Pulpit without providing supply for his own pulpit may receive an honorarium of £2·10 each Sunday, plus a refund of travelling expenses, but no fee.

4. Weekend Board and Lodging may be claimed at a maximum rate of £8 for the weekend (receipts should be exhibited). Travelling expenses (bus fare; railway, 2nd class; and steamer, cabin fare) shall be paid. Where there is no public conveyance the cost of hiring shall be paid, or a use of a private car shall be paid for at the rate of 5p per mile.

As these rates and expenses apply only in the case of pulpit supply in a vacancy, and in order to give some guidance to ministers and office-bearers when considering the payment of pulpit supply fees during holiday periods and sickness, the General Assembly declare the above scale of fees to be the minimum applicable in the payment of holiday or sickness supply.

E.—REGULATIONS ANENT EMPLOYMENT OF LICENTIATES AND MINISTERS OF OTHER CHURCHES (1935, x.).

17. Any Minister or Kirk Session intending to employ as assistant or as *locum tenens*, for more than four Sundays in any parish, a Licentiate or Minister of any other Church than the Church of Scotland, shall require such Licentiate or Minister to report himself to the Clerk of Presbytery within whose bounds the parish is situated, and to submit for his inspection a certificate of licence or of ordination, as the case may be, or to give such other evidence of qualification as may be satisfactory to the Presbytery. The General Assembly further instruct all keepers of lists of Licentiates or Ministers available for pulpit supply that they shall not make engagements for such Licentiates or Ministers for more than four Sundays, whether in the same parish or in different parishes, without requiring them to produce evidence that they have reported themselves to the Clerk of the Presbytery within whose bounds they reside in the manner aforesaid.

F.—EMPLOYMENT OF PERSONS NOT QUALIFIED.

See Chap. X., p. 228, as to the employment of a person not qualified.

IV. Scheme for Deaconesses appointed by the General Assembly (1962, Reg. 8).

(Amended 1968, Reg. 4; 1969, Reg. 7; 1970, Reg. 3; 1971, Reg. 3.)

1. The Office of Deaconess.

A Deaconess is one who has, under a call from God, pledged herself to the service of Jesus Christ and His Church, and has been trained and commissioned thereto in conformity with the doctrine and discipline of the Church of Scotland.

The office of Deaconess is recognised by the Church to be a distinctive office, and to be agreeable to the Word of God.

2. The Function of a Deaconess.

The function of a Deaconess is to exercise a ministry of an evangelistic, pastoral, educational or social nature in one or more of the following spheres, namely :—

(*a*) service under a Department, or with a Committee or Court of the Church. Such service would include taking part in the work of a parish—in worship, evangelism, pastoral care, teaching, and training for leadership and service—and as Sunday School Organiser, Youth Leader, Hut and Canteen Worker, and assistant to chaplains in hospitals and prisons ;

(*b*) service in a chaplaincy in university, college, school or H.M. Forces, and, if otherwise qualified, lecturer in religious education or specialist teacher of Scripture in school, and in similar spheres ;

(*c*) other service which is approved by the Deaconess Board (see Section 17), with the concurrence of the Presbytery concerned.

A Deaconess may be licensed to preach the Word. The regular preaching of the Word and regular participation in the conduct of public worship by Deaconesses shall belong only to Deaconesses so licensed.

3. Qualifications.

A Deaconess must

(*a*) be a communicant member of the Church of Scotland, and over twenty-one years of age ;

(*b*) possess the preliminary qualifications hereinafter required of all candidates ;

(*c*) have undergone training appropriate to her particular service ;

(*d*) be commissioned by Presbytery, and, in the case of a Deaconess qualified and trained to preach the Word, be licensed by Presbytery.

4. Candidature.

Preliminary qualifications.—An applicant must have a true sense of vocation, a required standard of education, and be medically fit.

Application—Application shall be made to the Deaconess Board by the applicant herself.

An applicant who has been accepted for training by a Department or Committee of the Church, or other body, may make application to the Board to be considered as a Deaconess-in-training as soon as she has been so accepted.

Interview—The Deaconess Board shall interview all applicants and satisfy itself that they have the preliminary qualifications.

Acceptance—Intimation to Presbytery—The Deaconess Board shall, if it decides to accept an applicant as a Deaconess-in-training, notify the appropriate Presbytery for its interest.

In the case of a candidate accepted for theological training with a view to being licensed to preach, the Deaconess Board shall commend her to the Presbytery within whose bounds she is to undergo her training, or such other Presbytery as seems appropriate, and the Presbytery shall, if satisfied, nominate her as a regular theological student at the theological college of her choice, recognise her as a Deaconess-in-training for commission and licence, and have an interest in her progress.

Appeal—In any of the cases above-mentioned, a candidate, if dissatisfied with the decision of the Deaconess Board, may petition the General Assembly. Without prejudice to her right so to do, she may, in the first instance, invite the Presbytery and Department or Committee of the Church or other organisation with which she is to serve to make representations on her behalf to the Deaconess Board.

5. Training.

General.—All Deaconesses must have a knowledge of the Bible, Christian Doctrine and Church History, and an understanding of the Church, and be able to relate these to man's individual and corporate life to-day. They must also have practical experience and understanding of Christian education and the communication of the Gospel to different ages and groups.

Special.—Subject to the above general requirement, the training of Candidates for Commissioning shall be governed by the regulations of the Department, Committee or other body with which they intend to serve, and the training for Commissioning and Licensing shall be governed by regulations of the Deaconess Board. (See Appendix E.)

6. Probationary Period.

The Deaconess Board may prescribe for any candidate a probationary period. In all such cases it shall notify the appropriate Presbytery. The Deaconess Board may, if not satisfied, extend the probationary period.

7. Recommendation.

The Deaconess Board, having obtained a Certificate from the Department, Committee or other body concerned and if itself satisfied, shall recommend the candidate for commissioning, and, in the case of a candidate for licence, for licensing also, to the Presbytery within whose bounds she has been a Deaconess-in-training or served a probationary period or such other Presbytery as seems appropriate.

8. Commissioning.

General.—A candidate to be commissioned must be a communican member of the Church of Scotland and be over 21 years of age.

Procedure.—It belongs to Presbytery to commission to the office of Deaconess.

In order to ensure a general standard of qualification and training for the office throughout the Church, a Presbytery may commission a candidate to this office only if it is furnished with a recommendation from the Deaconess Board.

Service.—The service of commissioning shall, wherever possible, take place at a diet of worship to which a congregation can be invited and at a time when it is possible for members of Presbytery to attend.

An Order of Service, approved by the General Assembly, is available in print.

The Commission.—A Deaconess on being commissioned shall have the authority of the Church to exercise her appointed ministry, with right to the title "Deaconess" and to append the letters "D.C.S." (Deaconess of the Church of Scotland) after her name, and to wear the badge and uniform of a Deaconess.

All Deaconesses, irrespective of their qualifications and particular spheres of service, have equal status within the Church.

A Deaconess may resign her commission.

A Deaconess may be deprived of her commission only by decision of Presbytery, in the first instance, with right of appeal to Synod and General Assembly.

9. Licensing to Preach.

A Presbytery may, on recommendation by the Deaconess Board of a candidate, and on being satisfied as to her ability and qualifications, license her to be a preacher of the Word.

Commissioning as a Deaconess shall precede licensing as a preacher, but licensing may take place at the same service as commissioning.

A Deaconess already commissioned may, if recommended by the Deaconess Board, apply to the Committee on Education for the Ministry to have prescribed for her such additional training as would qualify her for Licensing as a Preacher of the Word, and she shall comply with such of the above regulations as the Deaconess Board may prescribe.

An Order of Service, approved by the General Assembly, for commissioning and licensing is available in print. The General Assembly authorise Presbyteries to adapt this service in the case of a Deaconess who is already licensed to preach, such adaptation to be done in consultation with the Principal Clerk.

10. Responsibility for Life and Doctrine.

A Deaconess shall be responsible for her life and doctrine to the Presbytery within whose bounds she is serving, or, if not serving within the bounds of any Presbytery, to the Presbytery which commissioned her.

11. Responsibility for Service.

A Deaconess shall be responsible for the due performance of her service as follows, namely :—

(*a*) A Deaconess serving within a Department, or with a Committee, of the Church, shall be responsible to that Department or Committee;

(*b*) A Deaconess licensed to preach serving as Assistant in a Parish shall be responsible to the Minister and Kirk Session;

(*c*) A Deaconess serving with a secular organisation shall be responsible to that organisation.

12. The Roll of Deaconesses.

The Deaconess Board shall keep a Roll of Deaconesses containing the following lists:—

1. A list of Deaconesses actively engaged in service. This list shall be known as "The Active List."
2. A list of Deaconesses retired from service on account of age or ill-health. This list shall be known as "The Retired List."
3. A list of Deaconesses who have, for reasons other than age or ill-health, ceased to be actively engaged in service. This list shall be known as "The Supplementary List."

 Deaconesses on the Supplementary List shall, on undertaking full-time service, be transferred to the Active List.

 Deaconesses commissioned by the Church of Scotland who go to serve overseas as members of another Church shall be considered corresponding members of the Local Association of which they were last members, or of the Local Association in the area where their home in Scotland is situated, whichever is appropriate. When on furlough they shall be entitled to attend all meetings of the Deaconess Council as corresponding members without the right to vote. On relinquishing their appointment overseas and becoming again communicant members of the Church of Scotland they may apply to the Deaconess Board to have their names put on the appropriate list of Deaconesses.

 In case of doubt as to the list on which a Deaconess's name should be placed, the decision of the Deaconess Board shall be final.

The Deaconess Board shall, in December of each year, check the Roll with Presbyteries.

13. Relation to Presbytery.

Roll of Deaconesses.—Every Presbytery shall, in addition to exercising the functions and discharging the responsibilities set forth herein, keep a Roll of Deaconesses on active service, and a note of Deaconesses-in-training and Deaconesses serving a probationary period, within its bounds. In the case of a Deaconess serving furth of Scotland, her name shall be kept on the Roll of Deaconesses of the Presbytery which commissioned her, or such other Presbytery of the Church of Scotland as she may choose.

Reception.—At an ordinary meeting at least once a year, a Presbytery should receive the Deaconesses on its Deaconess Roll, those in training, and those serving a probationary period.

Transfer.—In the event of a Deaconess being transferred from residence or service in one Presbytery to residence or service in another Presbytery she shall be granted a Certificate regarding her life and doctrine by the former Presbytery.

14. Place in Courts of Church.

Acts and deliverances of the General Assembly anent the place of Deaconesses in the Courts of the Church are contained in Appendix C.

15. Service, Salaries, Insurance, and Pensions.

The terms and conditions of service shall be determined by the Department, Committee or other organisation with which the Deaconess is to serve.

16. Uniforms.

Responsibility for the provision of uniforms shall belong to the Deaconess Board.

17. Organisation and Administration.

A. The Deaconess Board.

The Deaconess Board shall be a Standing Committee of the General Assembly.

Functions.

The functions of the Deaconess Board hereinafter constituted shall include the following:—

(1) *General.*—The Board shall have as its primary concern the welfare of Deaconesses.

(2) *Deaconess Council.*—The Board shall, without prejudice to its responsibility to the General Assembly, act as the executive of the Council.

The Board shall act on behalf of the Council between Council meetings, provided always that a majority of the Deaconesses on the Board approve of its so doing.

The Board may initiate business at the Council.

(3) *Finance.*—The Board shall be responsible for all financial arrangements regarding its own administration and that of the Council, and shall annually submit a budget to the Stewardship and Budget Committee for inclusion in the Co-ordinated Appeal.

(4) *Roll of Deaconesses.*—The Board shall keep a Roll of Deaconesses in manner herein provided, and shall, in December each year, check the lists with Presbyteries.

(5) *Co-ordination.*—The Board may as occasion arises confer with Departments and Committees of the Church, and, if required, with other organisations, with which Deaconesses are serving.

(6) *Information.*—The Board shall keep constantly before the Church the opportunities of service which the Church offers to women, and, in particular, to Deaconesses, and the service rendered by them.

(7) *Policy.*—It is the duty of the Board to discuss with other interested bodies any matters affecting the general interests of Deaconesses and their part in the life of the Church.

Constitution.

Membership.—The Board shall consist of—

Four ministers, four elders, and four women members ;
The President and Vice-President of the Deaconess Council, *ex officiis* ;
The Secretary, *ex officio* ;
Six other Deaconesses.

Three representatives of the Home Board, one representative of the Overseas Council, one representative from each other Department or Committee of the Church with which a Deaconess is serving and the Principal of St Colm's College shall be entitled to attend the meetings of the Board as corresponding members without right to vote.

Appointment.—The four ministers, four elders, and four women members shall be appointed by the General Assembly in accordance with its Standing Orders.

The six Deaconesses shall be appointed by the Deaconess Council on a territorial basis for a period of three years. Two shall retire each year and shall not be eligible for immediate re-election.

The Convener shall be a minister designated by the General Assembly, and shall hold office for five years.

The President of the Deaconess Council shall be Vice-Convener of the Board.

Secretariat.—The Secretary of the Board shall be a Deaconess appointed by the Board as Secretary of the Board and Secretary of the Council.

The Secretary shall have the assistance of an Office Secretary.

Meetings.

The Board shall meet each year in June, November, January and March, and at such other times as it may appoint.

Committees.

The Board shall, for the better exercise of its functions, appoint the following Committees, of which the Convener and Vice-Convener of the Board and the Secretary shall be members, *ex officiis* :—

1. *Administration Committee*—

Function.—To deal with Council business and any matters remitted to it by the Board.

Membership.—The Administration Committee shall consist of all Deaconesses who are members of the Board, and not more than four of those members of the Board who are appointed by the General Assembly. The Vice-Convener of the Board shall be Convener, and the Convener of the Board shall be Vice-Convener.

2. *Candidates Committee*—

Function.—To interview candidates and make recommendations to the Board concerning recruitment, training, probationary period, commissioning and licensing.

Membership.—The Candidates Committee shall consist of four Deaconesses who are members of the Board, the Convener and three others of the members of the Board appointed by the General Assembly, the President, Vice-President and Secretary of the Council, and the corresponding members of the Deaconess Board with right to vote.

One of the members of the Board appointed directly by the General Assembly shall be Convener.

3. *Deaconess House Committee*—

Function.—To maintain and manage Deaconess House, Edinburgh, and administer its affairs.

Membership.—This Committee shall consist of the four women appointed by the General Assembly to the Board, three Deaconesses who are members of the Board, two representatives from each of the Women's Home Mission Committee and Women's Foreign Mission, and two women Foreign Missionaries. One of the four women first-mentioned shall be Convener.

4. *Finance Committee*—

Function.—To administer the funds in the General Account and the Deaconess House Account, the Batterflats Endowment Fund, and any other funds in which Deaconesses have an interest, in accordance with the terms and conditions governing the same.

Membership.—The Finance Committee shall consist of the four elders on the Board, one of whom shall be Convener, two ministers, members of the Board ; two women, members of the Board, one of whom shall be the Convener of the Deaconess House Committee ; and three Deaconesses, members of the Board.

The Board may appoint such other Committees as it may deem necessary.

Report.

The Deaconess Board shall each year report directly to the General Assembly on its own work and on the work of the Deaconess Council.

B. The Deaconess Council.

Functions.

The functions of the Deaconess Council hereinafter constituted shall be—

(*a*) to formulate and express the collective views of its members;
(*b*) to make contacts with those engaged in like work at home and overseas;
(*c*) to make recommendations, through the Deaconess Board, to interested bodies on matters concerning Deaconesses and the wider interests of the Church.

Constitution.

The Council shall consist of—

(i) All Deaconesses on the Active List.
(ii) Ex-Presidents of the Council who have retired from active service.
(iii) A number of Deaconesses on the Retired List elected by postal vote, the number to be in proportion of one Retired Deaconess for every eight Deaconesses on the Active List.
(iv) The members of the Deaconess Board appointed by the General Assembly.

Deaconesses commissioned by the Church of Scotland who are serving overseas as members of another Church shall be entitled when on furlough to attend all meetings of the Council as corresponding members but without right to vote.

Two representatives of the Women's Home Mission Committee, one representative of the Women's Foreign Mission, one representative from each other Department or Committee of the Church with which a Deaconess is serving and the Principal of St Colm's College shall be entitled to attend the public meetings of the Council as corresponding members. They may be invited to speak, but shall not be entitled to vote.

Office-bearers.

The Office-bearers shall be—

A President, who shall hold office for three years, and not be eligible for re-election.
A Vice-President, who shall hold office for two years, and not be eligible for re-election.
A Secretary, who shall also be Secretary of the Deaconess Board.

The President and the Vice-President shall be elected by the Council in manner specified in the Standing Orders appended hereto.

The Secretary shall be the Deaconess appointed by the Deaconess Board as Secretary of the Board and Secretary of the Council.

Committees.

Business Committee.—A Business Committee to attend to business during the meetings of the Council may be constituted in manner provided in Standing Orders. (Cf. Appendix A.)

Other Committees.—The Council shall have power to appoint, if it so desires, other Committees to facilitate its business and to consider various aspects of the service undertaken by Deaconesses.

Meetings.

The Council shall meet each year for two days in June and for one day in January.

The Council shall meet in public or in private as the Business Committee may decide, provided that at least one meeting in June be a public meeting.

The Council may in exceptional circumstances meet at such other times as the Deaconess Board may appoint.

Procedure.

Meetings shall each day be opened, and the Council closed, with prayer.

Other procedure shall be as set forth in Standing Orders. (Cf. Appendix A.)

Finance.

The expenses of the Council, including the travelling expenses of full members of the Council, shall be met by the Deaconess Board.

C. Local Associations of Deaconesses.

The Council shall set up Local Associations of Deaconesses, which shall have the following aims:—

(*a*) to provide a fellowship for Deaconesses;
(*b*) to be the only channel through which Deaconesses may communicate to the Deaconess Council matters concerning Deaconesses or the wider interests of the Church;
(*c*) to give an opportunity to Deaconesses to express their views on matters of public interest;
(*d*) to be the body to have liaison with the Presbytery and such local groups as the Presbyterial Council of the Woman's Guild, and women's secular organisations;
(*e*) to do all things necessary for or incidental to the attainment of these aims.

Local Associations shall be governed by the Constitution appended hereto.

18. Regulations.

The Deaconess Board may make Regulations for the due discharge of the responsibilities committed to it by this Scheme, always subject to the approval of the General Assembly.

19. Alteration of Scheme.

Any alteration to this Scheme may be made only by the General Assembly.

Any proposal by the Deaconess Council for alteration of the provisions of this Scheme must be approved by a two-thirds majority of the Deaconess Council.

Any Appendix may be altered in manner therein specified.

APPENDICES.

APPENDIX A.

THE DEACONESS COUNCIL.
STANDING ORDERS.

Procedure at Meetings.

The President, or in her absence the Vice-President, shall preside, whom failing, the Council shall appoint its own Chairman.

Proceedings each day shall be opened with prayer.

Business.

The business of the Council shall include :—

(1) Election of Office-bearers, Committees and Representatives on the Deaconess Board, such election to take place at the meeting of the Council in June.
(2) Reports from Local Associations, Committees of the Council, and the Deaconess Board.
(3) Initiation of discussion on any matters which concern Deaconesses and the wider interests of the Church.
(4) Address by Deputy appointed by the General Assembly.

Election of Office-bearers.

Nominations for the election of the President and Vice-President shall be sent in by Local Associations. Each Local Association shall send in a maximum of four nominations, selected from the whole membership of the Council, and those nominated must have been commissioned for at least seven years. The President, Vice-President, Secretary and other Deaconess members of the Deaconess Board shall draw up a short leet, which shall be sent to all Deaconesses on the Active List for their postal vote.

Election of Representatives on the Deaconess Board.

Nominations for the election of representatives other than the President and Vice-President shall be sent in by Local Associations as follows: Edinburgh and Glasgow shall send in four each, Aberdeen and Dundee shall send in two each. Voting shall take place at a meeting of the Deaconess Council, and shall be by paper ballot, each member having votes corresponding to the number of vacancies, and due consideration being given to territorial representation.

Business Committee.

The President, Vice-President, Secretary and Presidents of the Local Associations shall constitute the Business Committee, with the Vice-President as Convener.

Other Committees.

Any Committee appointed by the Council by virtue of the power conferred on it in the Scheme shall be given a specific remit, and shall report to the Council.

Finance.

Any proposal involving finance shall, before action is taken, be referred to the Deaconess Board for confirmation.

Minutes.

The Minutes of each day's proceedings of the Council shall be read over and approved at the first session of the following day's proceedings. The Minutes of proceedings of the final day, or of a single day, shall be approved by the Business Committee. Full Minutes of the proceedings of the Council shall be circulated to Local Associations for information.

Reports.

Reports from Local Associations and Committees of the Council shall reach the Secretary at least seven days before the meeting of the Council.

Resolutions arising from Reports.

In submitting any report the first speaker shall speak to any resolution which it may be intended to put to the Council as arising therefrom. When the report has been submitted, there shall be a time for questions and general discussion. When the President rules that a resolution be now put, the first speaker shall formally move it, and it shall be seconded.

Such resolutions shall normally be in the hands of the members of Council, in print or typescript, prior to being considered, but if circumstances prevent this, they shall be given to members by the Secretary at dictation speed. Where there are two or more resolutions, they shall be numbered consecutively in paragraphs. It shall be competent for any member of Council to move an amendment or addendum to any resolution, provided that thereby no new matter is introduced. Such amendments or addenda must be handed to the Secretary in writing, and must be seconded before discussion.

New Business.

It shall be competent for new business or matters not covered by any report to be introduced in one of three ways :—

(*a*) *By Overture from Local Association.*—Such Overture shall have been passed by a majority in the Local Association and shall have been transmitted to the Secretary of the Council not less than four weeks before the meeting at which it is to be submitted. It shall be put into the hands of members in print or typescript before discussion.

(*b*) *By Overture signed by ten members of Council during the first day of the Council's meeting.*—Such overture shall be given to the Secretary not later than 4 o'clock P.M. on the first day, and shall be in the hands of the members in print or typescript, or read at dictation speed, before discussion on the second day.

(*c*) *By the suspension of Standing Orders*, which shall be carried by a two-thirds majority of those present.

Length of Speeches.

In the discussion of subjects brought before the Council by report of a Committee or a Local Association, or by an Overture, or on the hearing of matters concerning Deaconesses or the wider interests of the Church, the following regulations as to the length of speeches shall have effect :—

The Convener or representative of a committee giving in the report of her committee	15 minutes
The President of a Local Association giving in the report of her Association	15 ,,
Other speeches thereon	5 ,,
Introducing an Amendment, Addendum or Overture	10 ,,
Seconding Amendment, Addendum or Overture .	5 ,,
Introducing a discussion on wider issues . . .	10 ,,
Other speeches thereon	5 ,,

Resolutions.

All resolutions requiring action by the Deaconess Board must be accompanied by voting numbers.

Closing of the Council.

When the business set down for the final day of the session of the Deaconess Council has been completed, the Council shall appoint the date and place of its next meeting. Thereafter the President shall address the members and close the Council with prayer.

Alteration of Standing Orders.

Fourteen days' notice having been given, these Standing Orders, with the exception of the paragraph on Finance, may be altered by a vote of the majority of Deaconesses present at a meeting of the Council.

APPENDIX B.

LOCAL ASSOCIATION OF DEACONESSES—CONSTITUTION.

1. The name shall be " Church of Scotland Deaconesses .... Local Association."

2. Aim

(*a*) To provide a fellowship for Deaconesses.

(*b*) To be the only channel through which Deaconesses may communicate to the Deaconess Council matters concerning Deaconesses or the wider interests of the Church.

(c) To give an opportunity to Deaconesses to express their views on matters of public interest.

(d) To be the body to have liaison with the Presbytery and such local groups as Presbyterial Council of the Woman's Guild, and women's secular organisations.

3. This Aim shall be reached by—

(a) holding at least four statutory meetings each year ;

(b) providing an opportunity for corporate worship, retreat and help for the devotional life of Deaconesses throughout the year ;

(c) submitting to the Council a report which will include matters referred to the Local Association by the Council ;

(d) initiating business for the Council.

4. Membership

All Deaconesses, including those who are retired, shall be full members of the Association.

Deaconesses serving a probationary period shall be fully associated with the Association but without voting power.

Candidates engaged in full-time practical training with a view to Commissioning may be associated with the Association without voting power.

Deaconesses commissioned by the Church of Scotland who are serving overseas as members of another Church may be corresponding members, and when on furlough may attend meetings but may not vote.

5. Office-bearers

The Association shall appoint its own office-bearers and committee in accordance with accepted rules of procedure.

6. Subscriptions and Meetings

The Association shall fix the amount of subscription and arrange the time and character of its meetings.

7. Report for Council

The adoption of the Association's Report for the Council shall be moved by one of the office-bearers and seconded briefly by a non-committee member.

After adoption by the Association, the Report shall be dispatched so as to be in the hands of the Secretary of the Council seven days before the meeting of the Council.

8. Individual Business

Any business brought forward by an individual Deaconess, if rejected by the Association, shall, if desired by the sponsor, be forwarded by the Association with full comments to the Secretary of the Council.

9. Election of President and Vice-President of Council

On the occasion of the election of a President or Vice-President of the Council, the Association shall send to the Secretary of the Council by the end of February not more than four nominations for each office. Nominees shall be selected from the whole membership of the Council and must have been commissioned for not less than seven years.

10. Change of Constitution

Any change in this constitution proposed by the Association shall be notified to all other Local Associations, and shall become effective only when approved by the Council and the Deaconess Board.

APPENDIX C.

ACTS AND DELIVERANCES OF THE GENERAL ASSEMBLY.

1. *Act anent the Licensing of Deaconesses as Preachers of the Word.*

Whereas under the Draft Scheme for the Order of Deaconesses submitted to the General Assembly of 1955 it is proposed that certain Candidates for membership of the Order of Deaconesses, who have the required qualifications, shall receive a course of theological training which will fit them to act as Assistants in parishes, Chaplains in universities and training colleges, Teachers of religious instruction in schools and colleges and similar spheres of service, it is hereby enacted and ordained :—

(*a*) That such Candidates on the completion of their theological training shall be recommended, if found suitable by the Committee on the Order of Deaconesses, to a Presbytery for commissioning as Deaconesses and, at the same time, shall be presented for licence as Preachers of the Word in the way at present prevailing for students for the Ministry, but omitting reference to probation for the Holy Ministry.

(*b*) That the regular preaching of the Word and regular participation in the conduct of public worship by Deaconesses shall belong only to Deaconesses so qualified and licensed.

(*c*) That it shall be open to other Deaconesses to apply to the Committee on Education for the Ministry, if they are suitably commended, to have such additional training prescribed for them as would qualify them for a similar licence to Preach the Word.

1956, xx.

2. *Deliverance anent Place of Deaconesses in Courts of Church.*

The General Assembly " recommend as immediate practical steps without prejudice to any future decisions :—

(*a*) That Parochial Deaconesses be invited to attend session meetings when matters affecting their work are under consideration.

(*b*) That Presbyteries appoint Deaconesses as members of suitable Presbytery Committees.
(*c*) That the Nomination Committee consider the appointment of Deaconesses as members of Committees on which women at present serve."

1958, 3.

3. *Deliverance anent Pulpit Supply.*

The General Assembly amended the Regulations anent Pulpit Supply, adding "Deaconesses licensed to preach, and approved Candidates for licence, who are regular students for the Diaconate" to the list of those available for Pulpit Supply.

1960, Reg. 8.

APPENDIX D.

REGULATIONS GOVERNING COMMISSIONING.

These regulations do not apply to persons desiring to become Deaconesses licensed as Preachers of the Word. There are separate regulations governing such persons which should be consulted by those intending this special qualification.

1. General.

Any person desiring to become a Deaconess of the Church of Scotland must possess certain preliminary qualifications, be willing to undergo an approved course of training, and make application to be accepted as a candidate in the manner prescribed in these regulations.

2. Preliminary Qualifications.

The following preliminary qualifications are required of any person applying to be recognised as a candidate for Commissioning as a Deaconess :—

(*a*) The applicant must have a true sense of vocation.
(*b*) The applicant must possess a required standard of education.
(*c*) The applicant must be medically fit.

3. Application and Acceptance.

Every applicant shall complete and return to the Deaconess Board an Application Form, obtainable from the Secretary to the Board, along with a certificate of character from her own minister.

In the case of an applicant accepted for training with a view to service with a Department or Committee of the Church, or other body, application may be made as soon as she has been so accepted. The applicant shall then be interviewed by the Deaconess Board, who, if satisfied as to the preliminary qualifications mentioned in Section 2 above, will nominate her as a Deaconess-in-training, will notify the appropriate Presbytery for its interest, and will itself take an interest in her progress.

In the case of any other applicant, including an applicant already serving with a Department or Committee of the Church or in any other recognised service, application may be made at any time. The applicant shall then be interviewed by the Deaconess Board, which shall satisfy itself as to the preliminary qualifications mentioned in Section 2 above and as to the requirements mentioned in Section 4 below.

4. Training.

(*a*) Every candidate must satisfy the Deaconess Board that she has a knowledge of the Bible, Christian Doctrine, Church History (and particularly of Scottish Church History), and an understanding of the Church and is able to relate these to individual and corporate life to-day, and that she has practical experience and understanding of Christian Education and the communication of the Gospel to different ages and groups.

Training in these subjects shall normally be taken at St Colm's College, and the Deaconess Board may require a certificate from St Colm's College or other recognised training college.

(*b*) In addition, every candidate must undergo such training as may be prescribed by the Department or Committee of the Church, or other recognised body with which she is serving or by which she has been accepted for training with a view to service. The Deaconess Board must obtain a certificate from the Department or Committee or other body that the candidate has satisfactorily completed such training.

(*c*) Before commissioning a candidate must be a communicant member of the Church of Scotland and over 21 years of age.

5. Probationary Period.

The Deaconess Board may prescribe for any candidate a probationary period. In all such cases it shall notify the appropriate Presbytery. The Deaconess Board may, if not satisfied, extend the probationary period.

6. Recommendation.

The Deaconess Board, having obtained the necessary Certificate from the Department, Committee or other body concerned and if itself satisfied, shall recommend the candidate for commissioning to the Presbytery within whose bounds she has been a Deaconess-in-training or served a probationary period, or such other Presbytery as seems appropriate.

7. Commissioning.

The Service of Commissioning by Presbytery shall, wherever possible, take place at a diet of worship to which a congregation can be invited and at a time when it is possible for members of Presbytery to attend.

A copy of the Order of Service approved by the General Assembly may be obtained from the Secretary to the Deaconess Board.

A Deaconess, on being commissioned, may proceed to exercise the functions of her office with right to the title " Deaconess " and to append the letters " D.C.S." (Deaconess of the Church of Scotland) after her name, and to wear the badge and uniform of a Deaconess.

8. Service.

The terms and conditions of service shall be determined by the Department, Committee or other organisation with which the Deaconess is to serve.

A Deaconess may only engage in the particular service for which she has been trained. In the event of her wishing to transfer to another sphere of service, she shall undergo such further training as may be required of her by the Department, Committee, or other body with which she is to serve.

A copy of the Order of Service approved by the General Assembly for the Introduction of a Deaconess to a new appointment may be obtained from the Secretary to the Board.

9. Uniform.

The regulation uniform as supplied is a tailored suit and coat of dark grey worsted material, a grey felt hat, and a blue terylene blouse. Uniform should be worn by Deaconesses on the following occasions: Meetings of the General Assembly, Presbytery, and the Deaconess Council; Commissioning Services; Woman's Guild and Women's Meetings, and on public occasions.

10. Alteration of Regulations.

These regulations may be altered only by the General Assembly.

APPENDIX E.

REGULATIONS GOVERNING COMMISSIONING AND LICENSING TO PREACH.

These regulations apply only to persons desiring to become Deaconesses licensed as Preachers of the Word.

1. General.

Any person desiring to become a Deaconess of the Church of Scotland licensed as a Preacher of the Word must possess certain preliminary qualifications, be willing to undergo an extensive course of theological and other study, and make application to be accepted as a candidate in the manner prescribed in these regulations.

2. Preliminary Qualifications.

The following preliminary qualifications are required of any person applying to be recognised as a candidate for Commissioning as a Deaconess and for Licensing as a Preacher of the Word:—

(*a*) The applicant must have a true sense of vocation.
(*b*) The applicant must possess a University certificate of attestation of fitness.
(*c*) The applicant must be medically fit.

3. Application and Acceptance.

Every applicant shall complete and return to the Deaconess Board an Application Form, obtainable from the Secretary to the Board, along with a certificate of character from her own minister.

Application may be made at any time, but in any case before 1st March in the year in which it is intended to begin the course of Theological Study. In the case of an applicant who has completed a University Degree Course, or is presently engaged in such a course and who intends to proceed to the study of Theology, the application should be accompanied by a letter from the Presbytery within whose bounds the applicant normally resides commending her as a student in Theology in the same way as obtains for students intending the ministry.

The applicant shall then be interviewed by the Deaconess Board, who, if satisfied as to the preliminary qualifications mentioned in Section 2 above, will accept her as a Deaconess-in-training for Commissioning and Licensing as a Preacher of the Word, and will notify the appropriate Presbytery.

The candidate will remain under the supervision of the Deaconess Board and the Presbytery throughout her Theological Course.

4. Training.

(*a*) Every candidate must satisfactorily complete a Degree Course in Theology, or other course approved by the Committee on Education for the Ministry. The course may be taken at any college chosen by the candidate herself, and approved by the Committee on Education for the Ministry.

(*b*) Every candidate at the commencement of her Theological Course shall consult the Principal of St Colm's College, Edinburgh, or other person appointed by the Deaconess Board, who, along with the appropriate Professor of Practical Theology or other specialist adviser, will ensure that the candidate receives the practical training appropriate to her requirements, and will report thereon to the Board. Normally this training will include a period of residence and attendance at some classes at St Colm's College, Edinburgh.

(*c*) A candidate taking a student assistantship is recommended to do so during her second year.

(*d*) Every candidate must, during her Theological Course, satisfactorily complete any inter-sessional exercises prescribed by the Presbytery and the Committee on Education for the Ministry.

(*e*) Before commissioning, a candidate must be a communicant member of the Church of Scotland and over 21 years of age.

> Attention is called to the Regulations anent Pulpit Supply which provide that a candidate is eligible for pulpit supply during her theological course. Any candidate interested should intimate her interest to the Secretary to the Committee on Probationers and Transference of Ministers, 121 George Street, Edinburgh, or to the local Pulpit Supply Agent.

5. Probationary Period.

The Deaconess Board, if not satisfied as to suitability for Commissioning, may prescribe a probationary period for any candidate. In all such cases it shall notify the appropriate Presbytery. The Deaconess Board may extend the probationary period.

6. Recommendation.

The Deaconess Board, if assured that the conditions set out in Section 4 above have been fulfilled and if itself satisfied, shall recommend the candidate for Commissioning as a Deaconess to the Presbytery which has had supervision of her during her Theological Course. The Presbytery shall satisfy its own requirements anent Trials for Licence.

> A candidate must be commissioned as a Deaconess before she is licensed as a Preacher of the Word, though Commissioning and Licensing may take place at the same service.

7. Commissioning and Licensing to Preach.

The Service of Commissioning and Licensing by the Presbytery, or of Licensing, shall, wherever possible, take place at a diet of worship to which a congregation can be invited and at a time when it is possible for members of Presbytery to attend. A copy of the Order of Service approved by the General Assembly may be obtained from the Secretary to the Deaconess Board.

A Deaconess on being commissioned and licensed may proceed to exercise the functions of her office, with right to the title Deaconess with Licence to Preach the Word. She shall also be entitled to append the letters "D.C.S." (Deaconess of the Church of Scotland) after her name, and to wear the badge and uniform of a Deaconess.

8. Service.

A Deaconess commissioned and licensed to preach may serve in the following ways :—

(*a*) As Assistant in a Parish in manner similar to that of a Licentiate Probationer for the Ministry. She may also serve, under the supervision of the Interim Moderator, in a vacant parish. Her salary will, for the first five years, be at a rate not less than the rate for a Licentiate Probationer, and thereafter at the rate for an Ordained Assistant.

Uniform will be supplied, and an Insurance Policy taken out to safeguard her retirement, by the Deaconess Board.

(*b*) As Parish Deaconess, with authority to conduct worship and preach regularly as required. Such an appointment is dependent on her application to and acceptance by the Women's Home Mission Committee.

(*c*) In a chaplaincy in university, college, school or H.M. Forces, and, if otherwise qualified, as lecturer in religious education or specialist teacher of Scripture in schools and in similar spheres of service. A Deaconess licensed to preach wishing to engage in such service should consult the Deaconess Board.

(*d*) In service which, though outside the immediate work of the Church, is approved by the Deaconess Board, with the concurrence of the Presbytery concerned.

A Deaconess wishing to transfer from one sphere of service to another shall undergo such further training as may be required of her by the Department, Committee or other organisation with which she is to serve.

9. Uniform.

The regulation uniform as supplied is a tailored suit and coat of dark grey worsted material, a grey felt hat, and a blue terylene blouse. Uniform should be worn by Deaconesses on the following occasions; Meetings of the General Assembly, Presbytery, and the Deaconess Council; Commissioning Services; Woman's Guild and Women's Meetings, and on public occasions.

10. Alteration of Regulations.

These regulations may be altered only by the General Assembly.

V. Presbyterial Superintendence—Acts and Deliverances of the General Assembly. (1931, xii., 1973, i.)

Scheme of Visitation.

The General Assembly enact and ordain as follows :—

1. Every Congregation of the Church shall be visited once at least in five years by a Committee of Presbytery. The five years' period shall begin with the Assembly of 1931. A Special Visitation shall be made when deemed necessary or expedient. The scheme of visitation shall, wherever possible, be under the direction of a Superintendence Committee of the Presbytery appointed for the purpose.

2. The object of the Visitation is to strengthen the hands of the Minister, Kirk Session, Office-bearers, and Members, to advise them should anything appear to be unsatisfactory in the state of the Congregation or not in accord with Church Law and Order, and in general to give counsel and encouragement as may be suitable to the circumstances of the case.

3. Every Presbytery shall prepare, as soon as possible, a rota whereby all the Congregations may be visited. The work of visiting should be overtaken during the first four years in each quinquennium.

4. A Committee shall be appointed for the Visitation of each Congregation. It is desirable that there be four members, say two Ministers and two Elders, on each Committee.

5. A printed Schedule in the form hereto appended, or in such other form as may be from time to time authorised by the General Assembly, shall be used in connection with the Visitation, but the Committee of

Presbytery may use their discretion in enquiring into other matters relevant to the state of the Congregation.

6. The Clerk of Presbytery or the Convener of the Visitation Committee, after consultation with the Minister, shall give notice of the date of Visitation, which should be intimated to the Congregation at public worship on two Sundays before the date of Visitation. He shall at the same time send copies of the Visitation Schedule to the Minister and Session Clerk. It is desirable that one of the Ministers on the Committee conduct Public Worship at one or both diets of worship on the Lord's Day in connection with the Visitation, or that he address the Congregation on a week-day, where found more convenient. He shall address to the Congregation such counsels as may be considered appropriate and helpful for the promotion of Christian work and fellowship. Where possible the Minister shall be present. Bible Classes, Sunday Schools, and similar organisations shall also be visited, if possible.

7. The Committee shall hold separate meetings with the Minister, the Kirk Session, the Financial Board (*i.e.*, Finance Committee, Deacons' Court, Committee of Management, or Congregational Board), where such a body exists. The Minister is entitled to be present at all these meetings. The Convener of the Visitation Committee or his duly appointed Deputy shall take the chair at all aforementioned meetings.

8. In all cases where the scheme of visitation is under the direction of a Superintendence Committee, the Visitation Committee shall report to the Superintendence Committee which shall communicate its own report or proposed finding to the Session of the Congregation before submitting the said report or proposed finding to the Presbytery.

Where there is no Superintendence Committee, the Visitation Committee shall report to the Presbytery, which shall in private take such Report into their deliberate and careful consideration, and record in the Presbytery books their finding thereanent, together with such explanations or instructions as the Presbytery may deem proper. The Committee shall communicate its Report or proposed finding to the Session of the Congregation concerned timeously, and before it is dealt with by the Presbytery, and the Session or Minister or any other party having an interest may claim to be heard by the Presbytery when the Report is dealt with.

Not later than six months after it has communicated its findings on the Visitation Committee's Report the Presbytery shall enquire of each Congregation visited to what extent the recommendations and instructions have been implemented.

9. Every Presbytery shall report to the Synod of the bounds the result of each Visitation. In the event of the Presbytery finding itself unable to express satisfaction with the state of any Congregation, it shall be the duty of the Synod to appoint a Committee to make further enquiry, in conjunction with the Presbytery, and to endeavour to remedy what is deemed to be unsatisfactory. If, after this further Visitation, it be found that matters are still unsatisfactory, the Synod shall forward a report to the General Assembly through the General Administration Committee, and the Assembly may take such further action as to their wisdom may appear best.

10. It shall be the duty of each Synod annually, and immediately after the Visitation of Presbytery Records, to prepare and transmit to

the General Assembly through the General Administration Committee a return showing distinctly and specifically whether each Presbytery has faithfully carried out the provisions of this Act.

11. The General Administration Committee shall annually appoint a Sub-Committee to receive returns from Synods and report.

(ACT XX. GENERAL ASSEMBLY, 1944.)

The General Assembly enact and declare, as follows :—

The General Assembly direct Presbyteries to forward to the Synod of the bounds the Schedules anent Presbyterial Visitation in terms of Act XII, 1931, not later than the 31st day of March in each year, and the General Assembly instruct Synods to take these Schedules into the most careful scrutiny and consideration with a view to the more effective supervision of the Congregations of the Church.

The General Assembly instruct Synods to send back to Presbyteries any Schedules where there are omissions or inadequate answers to be properly completed, and returned for submission to next meeting of Synod.

(DELIVERANCE OF THE GENERAL ASSEMBLY, 1946, i)

The General Assembly urge Presbyteries, in carrying out Visitation, to keep particularly in view the promotion of the spiritual wellbeing of the Congregation visited and the adequate efficiency of the Congregational Agencies.

SUGGESTIONS FOR THE GUIDANCE OF PRESBYTERIES IN THE FIVE-YEARLY VISITATION OF CONGREGATIONS.
(REVISED BY THE GENERAL ASSEMBLY, 1973.)

The Superintendence of Congregations within its bounds is one of the functions of a Presbytery, and the Scheme of Five-yearly Visitation is one of the methods whereby the General Assembly require that Presbyteries should exercise this function. All meetings in connection with a Visitation are therefore called by authority of the Presbytery, whose Deputies attend these meetings as representatives of a Superior Court. Accordingly, all meetings shall be constituted by a duly authorised Deputy of the Presbytery, who shall act as chairman throughout the proceedings.

Presbyteries may delegate this responsibility to a Superintendence Committee, with authority to choose Deputies, and assign them to individual Congregations. The Chairman of the Deputies should be a man of maturity and experience, since the effectiveness of the Visitation will largely depend on the manner in which it is conducted.

While the Visitation must involve a rigorous examination of all aspects of a Congregation's life, it must be conducted in a spirit of Christian charity, with a view to demonstrating the unity of the Church within the Presbyterian system of Church government, and the

Deputies should endeavour at all times to give such positive help and encouragement as they can.

If any occasion of division or discontent within the Congregation should come to the notice of the Deputies, they should make every effort to act impartially and to bring about a reconciliation. They should seek to act as arbitrators, with a view to settling the matter " out of court ", before considering any formal report to the Presbytery.

Before conducting a Visitation, Deputies should take steps to familarise themselves with the state of the Congregation, and in particular they should study the report of the previous Visitation, as well as the statistical and financial returns of the Congregation for the previous five years.

While the questions in the Schedule will form the basis of the Visitation, and all the questions must be answered, the Deputies may ask further verbal questions on any particular matters of special situations which they consider important. A note of such questions and the answers given should be included in their report. Where appropriate, advantage might be taken of discussing the possibility of closer co-operation and association with neighbouring Congregations—Church of Scotland and others.

In dealing with Finance, Deputies should stress the importance of regular planned giving through Weekly Freewill Offering System, and of the principles of Christian Stewardship. Where necessary, the Deputies should give information about the assistance available from the Stewardship and Budget Committee.

While Fabric is now the subject of separate reports and visitations, the Deputies should satisfy themselves that all is in order in this respect, by studying such reports before making their own Visitation, and they should be prepared to discuss questions of principle with regard to the usefulness and relevance of buildings being maintained, as opposed to the manner of their maintenance.

Deputies should report definitely whether the Congregation is fulfilling its purpose and should draw attention through the Presbytery to noteworthy experiments and activities brought to the notice of Visitation Committees.

The Superintendence Committee (or Visitation Committee) shall send copies of their report and proposed finding to the Kirk Sessions of Congregations visited before it is submitted to the Presbytery. Not later than six months after it has communicated its findings on the Visitation Committee's Report the Presbytery shall ascertain what action has been taken by the Congregations to implement any recommendations and instructions.

After Visitation Schedules have been carefully scrutinised by the Synod of the bounds in terms of Act XX, 1944, they should be returned to the Presbytery in order that Visitors at the next Visitation may be cognisant of the facts elicited at the previous Visitation.

SCHEDULE.

(*Revised* 1973.)

Presbytery of................. *Congregation of*................

Names of Committee............ *Date of Visitation* ....

Points for Consideration and Inquiry.

A. *Conference with the Minister.*

1. Divine Service:—	
(1) What Services are held in church on Sunday?	(1)
(2) What steps are taken to encourage children to attend Church?	(2)
(3) If any other Services are held beside those in church, state nature.	(3)
(4) What Services are held regularly on weekdays?	(4)
2. Pulpit Supply:—	
(1) Is pulpit supply in Minister's absence in accordance with the General Assembly regulation as regards—	(1)
(*a*) the Fee paid?	(*a*)
(*b*) the proper ecclesiastical status of the preacher employed?	(*b*)
(2) If the ordinary Services in church have ever been omitted since last visitation, state circumstances.	(2)
3. Christian Education:—	
(1) What part does the Minister take in work among the young?	(1)
(2) How does he supervise—	(2)
(*a*) Sunday Schools?	(*a*)
(*b*) Bible Class?	(*b*)
(*c*) training of teachers for above activities?	(*c*)
(3) What arrangements are made for work among young people after Bible Class?	(3)
(4) What method of teaching is used in—	(4)
(*a*) Sunday School?	(*a*)
(*b*) Bible Class?	(*b*)
(5) What instruction is given to those offering themselves for full membership of the Church?	(5)

4. Administration of the Sacraments:—	
(1) Baptism:—	(1)
(*a*) Is the Sacrament of Baptism administered in church unless in exceptional circumstances?	(*a*)
(*b*) In the case of Infant Baptism, what steps are taken to explain to parents the meaning and responsibility of Baptism?	(*b*)
(*c*) Is the Sacrament of Baptism administered in accordance with Act XVII, 1963 (anent the Administration of Baptism to Infants)?	(*c*)
(*d*) Are questions as approved by the General Assembly used at Baptism?	(*d*)
(2) Are the questions as most recently authorised by the General Assembly used at Services of Admission of new members?	(2)
(3) The Lord's Supper—	(3)
(*a*) Is there a Preparatory Service on a weekday or Sunday?	(*a*)
(*b*) Is the Minister satisfied with the frequency of Services of Holy Communion?	(*b*)
5. Pastoral Care:— How does the Minister exercise pastoral care over—	
(*a*) parish?	(*a*)
(*b*) congregation?	(*b*)
(*c*) sick and aged in both?	(*c*)
6. Presbytery:—	
(1) Does the Minister—	(1)
(*a*) attend meetings of Presbytery regularly?	(*a*)
(*b*) take his due part in the affairs of the Courts of Church?	(*b*)
(2) Is there a local Council of Churches?	(2)
7. Chaplaincies:—	
(1) Does the Minister act as—	(1)
(*a*) School Chaplain?	(*a*)
(*b*) Industrial Chaplain?	(*b*)
(*c*) Hospital Chaplain?	(*c*)
(*d*) Prison or Borstal Chaplain?	(*d*)
(*e*) Chaplain to any other institution?	(*e*)
(2) Does the Congregation take the opportunity of sharing in this work?	(2)

8. Community Service:—	
(1) In what other ways does the Minister serve in the Community?	(1)
(2) Are new opportunities for service opening up?	(2)
9. Manse:—	
(1) Is the Manse conveniently situated?	(1)
(2) Is it a comfortable and workable house?	(2)
(3) Is there a large garden?	(3)
(4) Are there extensive grounds?	(4)
(5) Does the Congregation take any responsibility for their upkeep?	(5)
10. Special Features:— Are there any special circumstances connected with the parish or Congregation or any difficulties tnat should be reported?	

B. *Conference with the Kirk Session.*

1. Kirk Session:—	
(1) How often does the Kirk Session meet?	(1)
(2) State the number of elders.	(2)
(3) Is this number sufficient?	(3)
(4) If not, are steps being taken to secure others?	(4)
(5) What arrangements are being made for the selection, training and appointment of Elders?	(5)
(6) (*a*) Have all Elders districts?	(6) (*a*)
(*b*) Have all districts Elders?	(*b*)
(7) How many times a year do they visit them?	(7)
(8) Does the Session appoint an Elder each year to represent it in Presbytery and Synod?	(8)
(9) Does the representative Elder attend regularly the meetings of these Courts, and does he report to Kirk Session?	(9)
(10) Do Elders take any special part in the work of the Congregation?	(10)
(11) Is the Communion Roll attested by the Kirk Session each year?	(11)

2. Congregation:—	
(1) What was the membership of the Congregation in each of the four preceding years?	(1) 19... 19... 19... 19...
(2) How many communicated at least once during each year?	(2)
(3) State average attendance at normal Sunday Services.	(3)
(4) What is the approximate turn-over of members?	(4)
(5) Are new members admitted by resolution of the Kirk Session?	(5)
(6) Are all new members admitted in face of the Congregation?	(6)
(7) What steps are taken to welcome new members into the Congregation?	(7)
(8) Are there any factors likely to affect the Congregation in the next five years?	(8)
3. Administration of the Lord's Supper:—	
(1) How often is this Sacrament celebrated?	(1)
(2) Does this give sufficient opportunity for participation in the Sacrament?	(2)
(3) State average attendance.	(3)
4. Prevention of Lapsing:—	
(1) Are members given Transference Certificates on leaving the parish or district in accordance with Act VI, 1938? Are Notices of Removal sent concerning such members?	(1)
(2) Are newcomers visited as soon as possible after they come to reside in the parish?	(2)
5. Church Discipline:—	
Is pastoral concern exercised with regard to—	
(*a*) scandalous conduct?	(*a*)
(*b*) unsatisfactory attendance at public worship and lack of interest and support for the work of the Congregation?	(*b*)
6. Organisations:—	
(1) For men.	(1)
(2) For women—	(2)
(*a*) Is there an affiliated Branch of the Woman's Guild?	(*a*)
(*b*) Is there an affiliated Branch of the Young Wives' and Mothers' Group?	(*b*)
(3) For children and young people.	(3)
(4) Is there periodical visitation of each organisation by members of the Kirk Session?	(4)
(5) Is the Kirk Session satisfied that all agencies are in a satisfactory condition?	(5)

7. Christian Education:—	
(1) How does the Kirk Session encourage and direct the work of Christian Education among all sections of the Congregation?	(1)
(2) Does the Kirk Session ensure that funds are available for the equipping of Sunday School and the training of teachers and other leaders?	(2)
(3) What efforts have been made to promote Christian Education among the adult membership?	(3)
(4) What courses have been attended by adult members to further their Christian knowledge?	(4)
8. Congregational Praise:—	
(1) Is there a choir?	(1)
(2) Are regular choir practices held?	(2)
(3) Is there a junior choir?	(3)
(4) What means are taken to develop congregational praise?	(4)
(5) What praise books are in use?	(5)
9. Congregational Mission:—	
(1) What parish Visitation or other special efforts have recently been carried out?	(1)
(2) Has special material prepared and provided by Stewardship & Budget Committee been used?	(2)
10. Service to Community:—	
(1) In what ways does the Congregation serve the community?	(1)
(2) Are all possible ways covered?	(2)
11. Church Buildings:—	
(1) Are existing Church and Hall accommodation adequate for requirements?	(1)
(2) List existing accommodation available.	(2)
(3) To what extent is Hall accommodation used by—	(3)
(*a*) Church organisations?	(*a*)
(*b*) other organisations?	(*b*)
12. Neighbouring Congregations:—	
In what ways does the Kirk Session encourage co-operation with neighbouring Congregations?	

13. Ministerial Assistance:— (1) Is there Ministerial Assistance, *e.g.*, Probationer, Deaconess, Home Missionary? (2) If not, does the Kirk Session think Ministerial Assistance is necessary? (3) Is secretarial assistance provided for the Minister?	(1) (2) (3)
14. Official Communications:— (1) Are all communications and schedules authorised by the General Assembly and their Committees submitted to the Kirk Session and noted in the Minutes? (2) Are all communications from the Presbytery submitted to the Kirk Session and noted in the Minutes?	(1) (2)
15. Custody of Records:— (1) State place of custody of records currently in use, and if protected from fire and other damage. (2) Have all records prior to 1900 been deposited in accordance with the instructions of the General Assembly?	(1) (2)

C. *Conference anent Finance, Kirk Session (or Finance Committee of Kirk Session), Deacons' Court, Committee of Management, or Congregational Board.*

Note.—In Congregations where all or any of the matters referred to are under the charge of the Session, the Committee will deal with these while conferring with the Session.

1. Congregational Finances:— (1) By what body are the Financial affairs of the Congregation managed? (2) If by the Kirk Session, has the adoption of a Model Constitution, 1965, been considered? (3) Has a Stewardship Promoter been appointed? (4) Is there an Annual Business Meeting of the Congregation?	(1) (2) (3) (4)

2. Methods of Contributing:—	
(1) Is the W.F.O. in use?	(1)
(2) What proportion of the Congregation use it?	(2)
(3) How many members give by Covenant?	(3)
(4) Is the Christian liberality of the Congregation commensurate with the Congregation's resources?	(4)
(5) What means are taken to encourage and increase interest and support for the wider work of the Church?	(5)
3. Congregational Contribution towards:—	
(1) Mission and Service Fund—	(1)
(*a*) Allocation for this year.	(*a*) £
(*b*) Allocation for each of four preceding years.	(*b*) 19 19 19 19 £ £ £ £
(*c*) Amount contributed in each of the four years.	(*c*) 19 19 19 19 £ £ £ £
(*d*) Are the amounts sent quarterly as requested?	(*d*)
(2) Maintenance of the Ministry:—	(2)
(*a*) Appropriate Stipend.	(*a*) £
(*b*) Appropriate Aid (to be attained by 19).	(*b*) £
(*c*) Contributions for each of four preceding years—	
(i) To stipend.	(i) 19 19 19 19 £ £ £ £
(ii) To Maintenance of Ministry Fund.	(ii) 19 19 19 19 £ £ £ £
(iii) To Aged and Infirm Ministers' Fund.	(iii) 19 19 19 19 £ £ £ £
(*d*) Have all the above payments been made when they became due?	(*d*)
(3) Congregational Accounts—	(3)
(*a*) What was the Income in the four preceding years in the Congregational Accounts?	(*a*) 19 19 19 19 £ £ £ £
(*b*) What is the amount of the debit or credit balance in the Congregational Accounts?	(*b*) £
(*c*) Are there any reserve funds? Give particulars.	(*c*)
(*d*) Does the Congregation pay Listed Expenses 1-6?	(*d*)
(*e*) What payment is made in respect of secretarial assistance for the Minister?	(*e*) £
(*f*) What is the amount directed annually towards Christian Education—Sunday School equipment, teacher training etc.?	(*f*) £
(4) Does the Congregation expect any difficulty in meeting the necessary commitments over the next five-year period?	(4)

4. Maintenance of Fabric:— (1) State amount of Fabric Fund. (2) Is there a Fabric or Property Committee? (3) Is care taken to maintain the Church, Hall and Manse in good order? (4) If Manse grounds are large does the Congregation take any responsibility for upkeep? (5) Is the amount spent on buildings realistically related to the life of the Church and to Mission and Service obligations? (6) Is the adequate maintenance of all fabric likely to be within the means of the Congregation for the next five years?	(1) £ (2) (3) (4) (5) (6)
5. Trustees and Titles:— (1) Are vacancies among Trustees regularly filled? (2) Where are the Title Deeds of Property deposited?	(1) (2)
6. Property, Trusts, Endowments:— (1) Is inventory of all property revised annually? (2) Are all Securities for Investments in safe custody and the place of custody recorded in the Minutes?	(1) (2)
7. Circulation of Literature:— (1) How many copies of the following are circulated?— (*a*) 'Life and Work'. (*b*) Other Church publications. (2) How are they distributed? (3) Is there a Congregational magazine or supplement?	(1) (*a*) (*b*) (2) (3)
8. Official Communications:— Are communications anent Finance received from the General Assembly and from the Presbytery duly submitted to the Financial Board and noted in the Minutes?	

Report by Committee.

Note.—Attention should be called in the Report to all omissions, &c., and recommendations should be carefully stated.

....

....

Signature of Convener of Committee.

DELIVERANCE OF PRESBYTERY.

Note.—All recommendations should be recorded in the Presbytery Minutes and enquiry made within six months as to whether or not they have been implemented.

At on the day of
the Presbytery of met and was constituted.

Inter alia :—..
....

Extracted from the Records of Presbytery by

....

Presbytery Clerk.

VI. CONSTITUTION AND REGULATIONS OF THE CHURCH OF SCOTLAND HOUSING AND LOAN FUND FOR RETIRED MINISTERS AND WIDOWS OF MINISTERS.

1. *Name and Object.*

The Church of Scotland Housing and Loan Fund for Retired Ministers and Widows of Ministers (hereinafter referred to wherever the expression "the Fund" is used) is established by the General Assembly to facilitate the provision of housing accommodation for aged or infirm Ministers and Widows of Ministers.

2. *The Funds.*

The Capital of the Fund shall consist initially of a sum of £25,000 provided by the Committee on the Maintenance of the Ministry, together with a sum of £ provided by the Committee on the Aged and Infirm Ministers' Fund and Pension Fund and a sum of £ provided by "The Baird Trust" acting under The Baird Trust Orders of 1939 and 1957, as confirmed by The Baird Trust Order Confirmation Acts 1939 and 1957. Such initial provisions, together with all receipts by the Fund in respect of donations, legacies, interests, and all loans or other assets of whatever description are hereinafter referred to as "the funds."

3. *Management and Administration.*

The management and administration of the funds shall be under the control of the Trustees of the Fund (hereinafter referred to wherever the expression "the Trustees" is used). The whole funds shall be vested in the Trustees. The Trustees shall be ten in number, being :—

(1) The Convener and Vice-Convener *ex officiis* of the Committee on the Maintenance of the Ministry ; with one further person nominated and appointed by that Committee ;

(2) The Convener and Vice-Convener *ex officiis* of the Committee on the Aged and Infirm Ministers' Fund and Pension Fund ; with one further person nominated and appointed by that Committee;

(3) The Chairman *ex officio* of The Baird Trust, with one further person nominated and appointed by The Baird Trust; and

(4) The Secretary of the Church and Ministry Department and the Secretary of The Baird Trust, both *ex officiis*.

The following Rules shall apply to the conduct of the Trust hereby constituted :—

(*a*) Regular meetings of the Trustees shall be held at such places as may be appointed by the Trustees, and such meetings shall be called by a notice sent by the Secretary or Chairman appointed as after-mentioned stating generally the purposes of the meeting and addressed to each of the Trustees and posted at least five clear days before the date of the meeting, provided however that in exceptional circumstances it shall be competent with the consent of a quorum of the Trustees as after-mentioned to call a meeting of the Trustees on shorter notice.

(*b*) The Trustees shall appoint one of their number to be Chairman at meetings of the Trustees, and the Chairman appointed shall serve as such until the meeting following the third anniversary of his appointment when he may be reappointed or a new Chairman appointed as may be decided by the Trustees. In the event of the Chairman being absent from a meeting of the Trustees then the Trustees present at such meeting shall appoint one of their number to act as Chairman at that meeting.

(*c*) On a vote a resolution carried by a majority of the Trustees present at a meeting of the Trustees shall be the finding of the meeting and in the case of equality the Chairman at the meeting shall have a casting vote in addition to a deliberative vote.

(*d*) The Minutes of Meeting of the Trustees shall be submitted for approval at the following meeting of the Trustees and, if approved, shall be signed by the Chairman who presides at that following meeting and the Secretary and shall thereafter be recorded as duly authenticated as evidence of the views therein stated.

(*e*) Five Trustees shall be a quorum at meetings.

4. *Officials.*

The General Treasurer of the Church and the Secretary of the Church and Ministry Department shall be the Treasurer and the Secretary respectively of the Fund. The Trustees may further appoint such other officials as from time to time they may consider necessary for the proper administration of the Fund and may define the duties of all officials.

5. *Legacies and Donations.*

Legacies and donations to the Fund shall be validly discharged by the Treasurer.

6. *Expenses.*

The expenses of management of the Fund each year shall be due and payable from the funds.

7. *Accounts.*

The Accounts of the Fund shall be made up each year as at 31st December, submitted to the Auditor of the Church and reported to the succeeding General Assembly.

8. *Management of Funds.*

The Trustees shall utilise the funds or such part thereof as may be required :—

(1) in the making at their discretion of loans to Ministers and the Widows of Ministers for the purpose of assisting such Ministers or Widows in the purchase of housing accommodation for their own occupation. Such loans may be made of such amount and on such terms as to interest (including non-liability to interest), repayment, *etcetera* as the Trustees in the particular case shall determine. The Trustees shall have discretion as to whether loans shall, in the particular circumstances of each case, be heritably secured ; and

(2) in the acquisition of suitable heritable property for the provision at their discretion of housing accommodation for Ministers and the Widows of Ministers. Such property may be made available on such terms as to rent (including non-liability to rent) *etcetera* as the Trustees, in the particular case, shall determine.

The balance of funds not required for the aforementioned purposes may be invested by the Trustees in any investment in which Trustees in Scotland are at such time entitled to invest funds according to law. The Trustees shall also have power to lodge the funds with The Church of Scotland Trust incorporated by the Church of Scotland Trust Order Confirmation Act 1932 for investment by them in terms of their powers.

The Trustees shall have power to vary the investments from time to time.

9. *Eligibility for Benefit of Fund.*

The following shall be eligible for benefit :—

(1) Retired Ministers of the Church of Scotland who are qualified to receive an Annuity from the Aged and Infirm Ministers' Fund and Pension Fund ; and

(2) The Widows of Ministers of the Church of Scotland ; declaring that on remarriage such Widows shall no longer be eligible for benefit. References in this Constitution and Regulations to Ministers or Widows shall be construed according to the rules of this Section.

VII. Regulations of the Aged and Infirm Ministers' Fund and the Pension Fund and Life Assurance Scheme for Ministers (1968, Reg. 6, 1969, Reg. 8).

1. *Name and Object.*

The Aged and Infirm Ministers' Fund, with the Pension Fund for Ministers and the Life Assurance Scheme, are established by the General Assembly to facilitate the retirement of ministers when aged or infirm and thus enable the spiritual care of the parishes to be efficiently maintained.

2. *Departments.*

(*a*) The Aged and Infirm Ministers' Fund and the Pension Fund for Ministers shall together provide the retiring allowance for ministers who are eligible to receive it.

(*b*) The Supplementary Fund, Part I, from which payments have been made to retired ministers ineligible to receive a National Retirement Pension shall be incorporated in the Aged and Infirm Ministers' Fund as from the date on which these Regulations become operative. The benefits hitherto payable from this Fund shall continue to be incorporated in the additional payments made to retired ministers who are ineligible to receive a National Retirement Pension. The Supplementary Fund, Part II, which has been used for the purpose of assisting ministers to purchase a house on retiring, shall be incorporated in the Church of Scotland Housing and Loan Fund for behoof of Retired Ministers and Widows of Ministers as from the date on which these Regulations become operative.

(*c*) The accounts of each Fund in respect of Capital and Income shall be kept separate.

(*d*) The contributions of congregations shall form part of the income of the Aged and Infirm Ministers' Fund.

3. *Administrative Body.*

The management and administration of the Funds shall be (under the control of the General Assembly) in the hands of a Standing Committee to be appointed each year by the General Assembly, and to be named "The Committee on the Aged and Infirm Ministers' Fund and Pension Fund", hereinafter referred to as the Committee.

4. *Officials.*

The General Assembly may appoint such officials as from time to time they may consider necessary for the proper administration of the Funds, may define their duties, and make provision out of the Funds for their remuneration. The General Treasurer of the Church shall be the Treasurer of the Funds.

5. *Administration.*

The Funds, Capital and Revenue, shall be administered by the Committee according to these Regulations.

The Capital, present and future, of the Funds shall be held for behoof of the Committee by The Church of Scotland Trust incorporated by The Church of Scotland Trust Order Confirmation Act, 1932, as amended by

The Church of Scotland Trust (Amendment) Order Confirmation Act, 1948, and any subsequent amendments.

The Committee shall report each year to the General Assembly.

6. *Legacies.*

(1) Legacies and Donations to the Funds or to the Committee shall be validly discharged by the Treasurer.

(2) Legacies bequeathed " to the Aged and Infirm Ministers' Fund and Pension Fund " shall be divided between the Funds in the proportion of 75 per cent thereof to the Aged and Infirm Ministers' Fund, and 25 per cent thereof to the Capital Pension Fund, unless there be any specific destination to a particular Fund by the benefactor.

7. *Expenses.*

The expenses of management of the Funds each year shall be shared by the Funds in such proportions as the Committee may from time to time determine.

8. *Accounts.*

The Accounts of the Funds shall be made up as at 31st December of each year, submitted to the Auditor of the Church, and reported to the Committee and to the General Assembly.

9. *Benefits Declared Alimentary.*

The Retiring Allowance provided from the Aged and Infirm Ministers' Fund, the Capital and Contributors' Pension Funds, the Fund for Early Disablement and the Assurance Fund shall not be assignable by the beneficiaries, nor attachable for their debts or deeds, nor liable to the diligence of their creditors, but shall be alimentary provisions in their favour.

10. *Incapacity of an Applicant or Beneficiary.*

(1) In the event of an applicant for an annuity being unable through infirmity to sign a form of application, it shall be competent for the Committee to accept an application signed by a person approved by the Presbytery of the bounds as representing the applicant for this purpose.

(2) In the event of a receipt being required from a beneficiary who is unable through infirmity to grant such a receipt for it, and failing intimation of the appointment of a legal representative, the Treasury shall pay the amount on the discharge of such person as an official of the Committee may approve on receiving an undertaking in writing that the money will be applied for behoof of the beneficiary. The receipts granted by such payee shall completely discharge the Funds and the Committee of all claim for the benefits so paid.

11. *No Personal Liability.*

Contributors or beneficiaries shall not have any claim against the individual members of the General Assembly or their officials, or against the members of the Committee.

12. *Saving of Rights of Ministers, etc.*

Nothing connected with the Funds shall interfere with the rights of ministers, the jurisdiction or rights of Presbyteries, or the law and practice of the Church in regard to discipline.

13. *Power to Make By-Laws.*

The Committee shall have the power to make, and from time to time to alter, by-laws in relation to the management of the Funds, provided these are not inconsistent with these Regulations and are reported to, and approved by, the General Assembly.

14. *Changes in Regulations.*

No alteration on these Regulations shall be made except by the General Assembly after report by the Committee.

15. *Date of Commencement.*

These Regulations shall come into operation on the 1st day of July 1968.

THE AGED AND INFIRM MINISTERS' FUND

16. *Capital.*

(1) The Capital of the Aged and Infirm Ministers' Fund consists of the funds at the credit of the Capital Account to which shall be added Legacies and Donations directed by the Testators and Donors to be capitalised, and such sums as the Committee in its discretion may add from Legacies and Donations not so directed by the Testators or Donors, or otherwise in terms of Regulation 17.

(2) The Capital shall not be encroached upon for the purpose of paying annuities, but any legal or other expense incurred in connection with any capital sum, investment, or bequest may be charged against Capital.

17. *Legacies.*

All legacies received in each year, except such as are bequeathed to the Capital Fund by the Testator, shall be credited to a Legacies Suspense Account. The Committee shall be entitled in each year to transfer to the General Account such sum as it considers necessary for the payment of annuities. The Committee may, in its discretion, use any balance remaining in the Legacies Suspense Account towards the provision of an Annuity Reserve Account or to making an addition to the Capital Account.

18. *Revenue.*

(1) The revenue of the Aged and Infirm Ministers' Fund shall consist of :—

Contributions from congregations and other bodies as defined in Regulation 19 (1) ;

Contributions from Income from Capital and from other Invested Moneys ;

Donations not otherwise destined by the donor ;
Legacies transferred from the Legacies Suspense Account ;
Moneys received from Trusts or other sources.

(2) The annual revenue shall be applied to the payment of the annuities and expenses. Any deficiency in the amount available for such payments in any year shall be a first charge on the Annuity Reserve Fund failing which it shall be a first charge on the income of the following year. Any surplus shall be carried forward in the Revenue Account to the following year, or transferred in whole or in part to an Annuity Reserve Account at the discretion of the Committee.

19. *Contributions Required.*

(1) The Standard Contribution shall be 5 per cent of the stipend or salary as defined in Regulation 19 (2) or such other percentage as may be decided by the General Assembly on the Report of the Committee.

All Church of Scotland congregations and all other bodies under which a minister holds an extra-parochial appointment approved by the General Assembly and the Committee shall pay the Standard Contribution to the Fund each year.

(2) The stipend shall be reckoned as the amount of the ministerial income as agreed by the Committee on the Maintenance of the Ministry for the previous Calendar Year, exclusive of manse or manse allowance at the recognised rate and exclusive of the listed expenses as calculated for the purposes of the Maintenance of the Ministry. In a vacancy the stipend shall be reckoned at the figure for the last full Calendar Year, but in Minimum Stipend charges it shall be reckoned as the Minimum Stipend for the previous Calendar Year. From the beginning of a new incumbency and during the first full Calendar Year the stipend shall be reckoned at the figure proposed in the Vacancy Schedule. In a collegiate charge, excluding any in which there is a colleague and successor, the stipend shall be reckoned as the total of the two stipends.

Any sum in addition to the normal retiring allowance, paid to a retired minister by the congregation from which that minister has retired, shall be excluded from the reckoning while so paid.

The payment due in respect to a minister holding an extra-parochial appointment shall be calculated on the salary received in the previous Calendar Year, or the Minimum Stipend whichever is the greater. From the beginning of a new appointment and during the first full Calendar Year the salary shall be reckoned at the figure at which the minister was appointed.

(3) Contributions shall be payable in quarterly instalments to the General Treasurer both during an incumbency and during a vacancy; and contributions unpaid at the end of the Calendar Year shall be subject thereafter to interest at 5 per cent.

(4) Congregations who desire to contribute in excess of the required percentage may do so.

(5) Where appropriate, in these Regulations the expressions "Standard Contribution" and "Contribution" shall be deemed to include :—

(*a*) Contributions paid under Scheme A of the Regulations for the Administration of the Aged and Infirm Ministers' Fund, the

Supplementary Fund and the Pension Fund for Ministers adopted by the General Assembly of 1950.

(*b*) Contributions paid under the Regulations of the Aged and Infirm Ministers' Fund and the Pension Fund and Life Assurance Scheme for Ministers approved and enacted by the General Assembly of 1961, and

(*c*) Contributions paid under these Regulations.

20. *Eligibility for Benefits.*

(1) Every ordained minister of the Church of Scotland who has served for at least fifteen years in one or more of the charges or appointments defined in (2) and (3) and has demitted such a charge or retired from such an appointment on or after attaining the age of sixty-five or earlier because of permanent disability as provided in Regulation 24 is eligible for benefit.

The following charges or appointments qualify :—

(2) (*a*) Any parish or church extension charge in Scotland or in the Presbytery of England.

(*b*) Every charge abroad which has been accepted as a Church of Scotland charge.

(*c*) Terminable appointments where it has been agreed by the Presbytery and the Committee concerned that the work of the congregation be carried on by a minister without charge under such an arrangement.

(*d*) Service as parochial assistant or associate minister (except by a minister in receipt of an annuity under Regulation 21).

(*e*) Every extra-parochial appointment approved by the General Assembly and the Committee for the purpose of a retiring allowance.

(3) Every ordained minister who has demitted a charge or resigned from a non-parochial appointment within the jurisdiction of the Church of Scotland and who has been permitted to retain status by a Court of the Church on taking up an appointment outwith the jurisdiction of the Church which either :—

(*a*) qualifies for membership of Presbytery by any Act of Assembly ; or

(*b*) has been approved by petition to the General Assembly, such petition to be intimated to the Aged and Infirm Ministers' Committee not later than 31st January in the year in which the petition is to be presented,

and in respect of which the Fund has received each year from the employing body a sum not less than the Standard Contribution, is eligible for benefit.

21. *Amount of Annuity.*

(1) The Standard Annuity shall be such sum as the Committee may from time to time determine. Annuities shall be payable monthly, but not in advance. In fixing the amount of the Standard Annuity regard

shall be had to the note on the Regulation defining the Amount of Pension, in the Pension Fund Regulations.

Every annuitant shall receive 1/40th of the Standard Annuity for every complete year of service, subject to a minimum of fifteen years' service as provided in Regulation 20 (1). No service for which a Standard Contribution has not been received shall be reckoned towards the period of service on which the amount of the relevant annuity is calculated.

(2) A minister who qualifies for an annuity and continues in a charge or appointment after reaching the age and service which qualifies shall receive an additional 1/40th of the Standard Annuity for every complete year of service thereafter, up to a maximum of an additional 5/40ths.

(3) A minister who on 30th June 1968 was in a charge or appointment from which application could be made for an annuity may elect, at the time of retirement, to have the annuity calculated in terms of the regulations in force on 30th June 1968.

(4) A minister who has entered the Ministry in accordance with the provisions of Regulation 9, General Assembly, 1949, and who cannot normally, because of age at entry to the Ministry, complete fifteen years' qualifying service may, at or after age sixty-five and retiring, apply for an annuity and the Committee may grant an annuity of such amount as in its sole discretion it may determine in the light of the years of service and personal circumstances at the time of retirement.

A congregation that is self-supporting, or a Committee of the Church, shall be free to undertake to augment from its own resources the retiring allowance payable to its retired minister, or official as the case may be, from its Funds, subject to the approval of the Presbytery, the Committee on the Maintenance of the Ministry and this Committee, provided that, in the case of congregations, the stipend for the new minister is regarded as adequate by the Presbytery and the Committee on the Maintenance of the Ministry.

22. *Procedure in Applications.*

Applications, for which the appropriate schedules can be obtained from the Church and Ministry Department, are to be submitted to the Deacons' Court, Committee of Management, or Congregational Board, if any, and to the Kirk Session and the Presbytery, and afterwards lodged with the Committee together with relevant Extract Minutes of the proceedings of these bodies. It should be the duty of the Presbytery to consider and approve the proposed financial arrangements for the retiring minister and any successor.

23. *Application Subsequent to Retirement.*

Any minister who has had not less than fifteen years' ordained service in a charge or charges who may demit the charge, and who does not at the time make application for an annuity, shall be entitled to make application therefor at or after reaching the age of sixty-five ; or earlier on production of medical evidence approved by the Committee's Medical Adviser.

24. *Early Disablement.*

(1) A Medical Certificate, on soul and conscience, is required from all applicants under the age of sixty-five. In addition, the medical

practitioner who has signed the above certificate shall submit a confidential certificate for consideration by the Committee's Medical Adviser. Forms of both certificates may be obtained from the Church and Ministry Department. The Committee's Medical Adviser, or a doctor nominated by the Committee, shall also be entitled to examine any applicant under sixty-five years of age.

(2) A minister demitting a charge or appointment on the grounds of ill-health before completing the qualifying service and attaining to the age of sixty-five shall be granted an annuity in the same proportion as the years of service bear to forty years with a minimum annuity of 15/40ths if the service has not exceeded fifteen years. Where the annuitant has not been able to take other employment, the Committee may, at its discretion, increase the annuity by annual instalments in special circumstances shown to it.

In the event of the annuitant recovering and being admitted to a charge or undertaking other full-time salaried employment the annuity shall cease during the time of such employment.

25. *Annuitants taking up other Duties or Leaving Church.*

(1) An annuitant accepting an appointment to regular ministerial or other remunerated work of a permanent nature shall intimate forthwith to the Committee acceptance of such appointment; and the Committee after inquiry into the circumstances may continue, or withdraw, or reduce the amount of the annuity, or suspend it during the tenure of such appointment.

(2) In the event of an annuitant ceasing to be a member of the Church of Scotland, the Committee, after inquiry into the reasons, may continue, reduce, or withdraw the annuity.

26. *Commencement, Payment and Duration of Annuities.*

(1) Annuities shall commence at the date on which stipend or salary ceases to be payable to the applicant. Annuities for which application has been made subsequent to retirement shall commence at the date of authorisation by the Committee, or on cause shown at a date determined by it.

(2) The legal representatives of a deceased annuitant shall be entitled to receive the difference between the sum already paid and the due proportion of the retiring allowance up to the last day of the month in which death occurred.

27. *Comity Agreements.*

A minister demitting a charge to enter the service of another Church which has entered into a comity agreement with this Committee may, on completing forty years' ordained service and on reaching the age of sixty-five, or on becoming permanently incapacitated for duty at an earlier age, apply for an annuity, and the Committee may grant an annuity of 1/40th of the Standard Annuity in respect of every year of service in a charge or charges of the Church of Scotland.

28. *Widow's Pension Option*

A minister qualified to receive an annuity and retiring at or after reaching the age of sixty-five may elect, at the time of retirement, to receive a reduced annuity during his lifetime in order that a pension may be provided for his widow, or next of kin who has kept house for him during the later years of his ministry. The amount of annuity which he must give up in exercise of this option shall be determined on an actuarial basis according to the age of the annuitant and of his wife (or next of kin as defined above) at the time of his retirement. The maximum pension which an annuitant may provide for his widow (or next of kin as defined above) shall not exceed the total amount of retiring allowance from the Annuity Fund and the Pension Fund that remains to him during his own lifetime. The option once exercised cannot be recalled.

29. *Exceptional Cases.*

If in any exceptional case hardship arises from the application of these Regulations, the Committee shall have power to consider and report the facts to the next General Assembly for authority to deal therewith, and in a case of urgent need the Committee shall have power to make a temporary arrangement.

THE PENSION FUND FOR MINISTERS AND THE LIFE ASSURANCE SCHEME

30. *Pension Fund.*

The Pension Fund shall comprise the following :—

Contributors' Pension Fund.
Capital Pension Fund.
Early Disablement Pension Fund.

Separate investments and accounts shall be kept for each of these Funds and the share of the expenses of management falling upon the Pension Fund shall be divided amongst the separate Funds in such proportions as the Committee may from time to time determine.

31. *Contributors' Pension Fund.*

The Contributors' Pension Fund shall consist of :—

(i) the Contributors' Pension Fund as existing at 1st January 1961 ;
(ii) the contributions paid by ministers to the Pension Fund in terms of these Regulations ;
(iii) the interest on the investments of the Fund ;

less sums applied in payment of pensions and expenses.

32. *Capital Pension Fund.*

The Capital Pension Fund shall consist of :—

(i) the Capital Pension Fund as existing at 1st January 1961 ;
(ii) all sums that may be given or bequeathed to or on behalf of the Church of Scotland Pension Fund ;
(iii) the interest on the investments of the Fund ;

less sums applied in payment of pensions and expenses and proportion of the net income transferred to Early Disablement Fund.

33. *Early Disablement Pension Fund.*

The Early Disablement Pension Fund shall consist of :—

(i) the Special Fund for this purpose as existing at 1st January 1961 ;

(ii) annual sums equal in any year to one-twentieth (or such other proportion as the Committee may from time to time determine) of the net income of the Capital Pension Fund ;

(iii) the interest on the investments of the Fund ;

less sums applied in payment of pensions and expenses.

34. *Life Assurance Scheme.*

The Life Assurance Scheme shall provide for the payment of a capital sum on the death of a member before attaining age sixty-five or on his sixty-fifth birthday should he survive to that date.

For the purpose of this Scheme the Committee shall have power to effect policies with such Assurance Company or Companies as it thinks fit.

35. *Eligibility, Membership and Contributions.*

(*a*) Eligibility to join the Pension Fund, the Life Assurance Scheme, or both, and the contributions payable, shall be determined according to the classification set out in Table 1 hereafter. For the purpose of this classification a qualifying charge shall mean any charge or appointment as defined in Regulation 20 whether in Scotland or furth of Scotland, but excluding appointments under the Foreign Mission Committee other than appointments under its short-service scheme. Where a nil entry appears under " Pension Fund " or under both columns of " Life Assurance Scheme ", ministers in the class to which the entry relates shall not be eligible to join the Fund or Scheme. For those eligible the date of entry shall be the first day of January following the date of admission to a qualifying charge or appointment.

TABLE 1.

	Annual Contributions payable to		
		Life Assurance Scheme	
	Pension Fund	(i) Endowment	(ii) Convertible Policy for Widows and Dependents
Ministers admitted on or after 1st January 1969 to a qualifying charge for the first time who at the date of admission are:—			
(*a*) not over 50 years of age .	£3	£18	£12
(*b*) over 50 but not over 55 years of age at the birthday following admission to their charge . .	Nil	33	Nil
(*c*) over 55 years of age .	Nil	Nil	Nil

(*b*) For existing members who were members prior to the date of these Regulations coming into effect, the old Table 1 as it appears in the 1961 Regulations, with the amendments introduced with effect from 1st January 1966, will continue to apply.

36. *Payment of Contributions.*

Contributions to the Pension Fund shall be payable from the date of entry and will cease at the date of retirement at age sixty-five or, at the minister's option, at any later retirement date up to age seventy.

Contributions to the Life Assurance Scheme shall be payable from the date of entry until age sixty-five but contributions by existing members at the date these Regulations come into force will continue until age seventy, subject to the minister's option to retire at any time between age sixty-five and age seventy and accept reduced benefits.

In cases in which stipend exceeding a sum sufficient for the purpose is paid from the Fund for the Maintenance of the Ministry the contribution of £33 per annum will be deducted in monthly instalments from the payment of that stipend and transferred to the Pension and Assurance Funds, unless the statutory dues of the minister to the Widows' and Orphans' Fund leave, in one year, insufficient margin, on which occasion his contribution will be paid by others responsible for the payment of stipend.

In other cases the contributions of the minister will be deducted by those responsible for the payment of stipend and paid to the General Treasurer by the person responsible for the deduction.

37. *Payment of Pensions.*

(i) If a member retires on or after reaching age sixty-five payment of pension shall be due from the date of his retirement.

(ii) If a member retires before reaching age sixty-five payment of pension shall be due from the date of his sixty-fifth birthday, except as provided in Regulation 39.

(iii) If a member, after reaching age sixty-five, shall be granted a Colleague and Successor payment of pension shall be due from the date of induction of the Colleague and Successor.

All pensions shall be payable monthly on a *de die in diem* basis. Any balance of pension unpaid at the death of a member shall be payable to his legal representatives.

38. *Amount of Pension.*

(1) *Contributors' Pension Fund.*

(*a*) For entrants on or after 1st January 1969 the amount of pension payable on retiral at age sixty-five shall be determined by age on the birthday following the date of admission or on the date of admission should that be the birthday, in accordance with Table 2 below (but see Regulation 42).

TABLE 2.

Age next birthday at time of joining	*Amount of Pension*	*Age next birthday at time of joining*	*Amount of Pension*	*Age next birthday at time of joining*	*Amount of Pension*
26 or under	£34·20	34	£21·30	43	£11·65
		35	20·05	44	10·80
27	32·30	36	18·80	45	10·00
28	30·50	37	17·60	46	9·25
29	28·80	38	16·50	47	8·50
30	27·15	39	15·45	48	7·80
31	25·60	40	14·40	49	7·15
32	24·10	41	13·45	50	6·50
33	22·65	42	12·50		

A minister has the option to delay retirement for up to five years while continuing contributions and if he does so the pension will be increased in accordance with the following rule :—

To find the equivalent pension payable on retirement after sixty-five in respect of a contribution of £3 per annum, multiply the pension to which the member is entitled at age sixty-five (including any additions to pension made out of surplus under Regulation 42) by the appropriate factor from the table given below and thereafter add 45p for each complete year by which the age of retirement exceeds sixty-five.

Age last birthday at date of retirement	*Factor*
66	1·112
67	1·241
68	1·391
69	1·564
70	1·767

Note.—These benefits apply to male lives and figures for female lives will be quoted as required.

(*b*) For existing members who were members prior to the date on which these regulations come into effect the old Table 2, as it appears in the 1961 Regulations, will apply to retirement at age seventy, but such members may retire at any time between age sixty-five and age seventy in which case the pension will be reduced in accordance with the following rule :—

To find the equivalent pension payable on retirement before seventy in respect of a contribution of £3 per annum with return of contributions on death (or of £2 per annum without return of contributions on death) deduct from the amount of pension to which the member is entitled at age seventy (including any additions to pension made out of surplus) 45p for each complete year by which his age at retirement is less than seventy and multiply the pension so reduced by the appropriate factor from the following table :—

Age last birthday at date of retirement	*Factor*
65	·565
66	·630
67	·700
68	·785
69	·885

For (i) contributions of £6 per annum with return on death (or £4 per annum without return on death) and (ii) contributions of £9 per annum with return on death (or £6 per annum without return on death), the same rule will apply except that the deductions from pension will be (i) 90p and (ii) £1·35 for each complete year by which the age at retirement is less than seventy.

(*c*) In the event of a contributor, who has paid contributions repayable on death before entering on a pension, dying after becoming entitled to pension and before the payments of Contributors' Fund pension made to him have equalled the amount of the contributions paid by him, the excess of the contributions without interest, over the Contributors' Fund pension payment shall be payable to his legal representatives.

(2) *Capital Pension Fund.*

The Capital Pension Fund, after deduction of the sum payable to the Early Disablement Pension Fund as provided in Regulation 32 and payment of the expenses of management charged to the Fund or such part of it as the Committee may from time to time determine, shall be available to provide pensions to retired members of the Contributors' Pension Fund. The pensions shall depend on the age at retirement and will be in accordance with the following scale :—

Age last birthday at date of retirement	*Amount of Pension per annum*
65	£30·50
66	34·00
67	37·80
68	42·40
69	47·80
70	54·00

subject to any alterations resulting from the periodical investigations under Regulation 42.

Note.—To comply with Inland Revenue requirements the total of the pensions payable from the Aged and Infirm Ministers' Fund and from the Pension Fund for Ministers to a minister on retirement shall not exceed (*a*) two-thirds of his earnings, (*b*) one-sixtieth of his earnings for each year of service as defined in Regulation 20, or such greater sum as may be approved by the Commissioners of Inland Revenue. For this purpose earnings shall be defined as the yearly average of total actual emoluments of any three or more consecutive years of the last ten years before the normal retirement date.

39. *Early Disablement Fund.*

A member of the Contributors' Pension Fund shall qualify for a pension from the Early Disablement Fund if he is :—

(*a*) under the age of sixty-five years, and
(*b*) receiving an annuity from the Aged and Infirm Ministers' Fund on account of ill-health or permanent incapacity (Regulation 20).

The amount of the Early Disablement Fund Pension shall be determined by the Committee from time to time on the advice of the Actuary. If a minister is receiving a proportionate annuity from the Aged and Infirm Ministers' Fund on account of Early Disablement (Regulation 24) he shall be entitled to a pension from the Early Disablement Fund which bears the same proportion to the full Early Disablement Fund Pension as the annuity he is receiving from the Aged and Infirm Ministers' Fund bears to the full annuity payable by that Fund.

Grants from the Special Fund shall commence at the date of demission of charge or office ; shall continue at the discretion of the Committee ; shall be payable monthly on a *de die in diem* basis ; and shall cease at the date of death, or on attainment of the age of sixty-five years, when ordinary pension begins.

40. *Ministers entering the Service of Another Church.*

(1) A contributor who (*a*) leaves the service of the Church of Scotland in order to become a minister of another Church, or (*b*) leaves the service of the Church of Scotland in order to undertake full-time employment outwith the Church (unless that employment has been sanctioned by the Committee at the time when it was undertaken) shall cease to be a contributor to the Pension Fund, but he shall be entitled to receive (i) a pension from the Contributors' Fund of an amount determined by the Committee on the advice of the Actuary having regard to the number of years' contributions he has made to the Pension Fund and (ii) a pension from the Capital Pension Fund similarly determined.

These pensions shall commence at age sixty-five, or at the date of retirement, whichever is later.

If he retires before age sixty-five and be admitted to an annuity from the Aged and Infirm Ministers' Fund on grounds of ill-health he shall be entitled to a grant from the Early Disablement Pension Fund of an amount to be determined by the Committee on the advice of the Actuary. Such pension shall cease at age sixty-five.

(2) A contributor who leaves the service of the Church of Scotland in order to undertake full-time employment which is not sanctioned by the Committee at the time when it is undertaken shall cease to be a contributor to the Pension Fund, but he shall be entitled on the attainment of age sixty-five to receive a pension from the Contributors' Fund of an amount determined by the Committee on the advice of the Actuary having regard to the number of years' contributions he has made to the Pension Fund.

41. *Benefits payable under the Life Assurance Scheme.*

Ministers who are eligible to become members of the Life Assurance Scheme in terms of Regulation 35 shall be entitled to do so without producing evidence of their state of health.

The amounts of the benefits payable under this Scheme will depend upon the terms negotiated from time to time with the Assurance Company or Companies chosen to underwrite the Scheme. The benefits available under the Endowment Assurance Scheme from the date on which these Regulations come into effect are as shown in the following table:—

Age next birthday at entry	Sums Assured secured at age 65 by Annual Contributions of £9 to Endowment Assurance Scheme (*These benefits apply to male lives: benefits for female lives will be quoted*)		
	Without Profits	With Profits	
		Basic Sum Assured	Estimated Maturity Value (At Age 65) See Note 2
24	£712	£339	£1,486
25	683	331	1,393
26	658	323	1,306
27	631	315	1,223
28	604	307	1,145
29	580	299	1,071
30	553	290	999
31	529	283	937
32	505	274	872
33	481	267	817
34	458	259	762
35	435	252	713
36	414	244	664
37	392	235	615
38	371	226	569
39	351	217	526
40	331	211	493
41	312	203	456
42	293	194	420
43	275	186	388
44	258	178	358
45	241	169	328
46	225	161	301
47	209	151	272
48	194	143	249
49	180	134	225
50	166	126	204
51	152	117	183
52	139	109	165
53	127	101	147
54	114	92	130
55	102	84	115

Note 1.—For annual contribution other than £9 the benefits will be in proportion.

Note 2.—These figures include bonuses, the amount of which will depend on future profits. The figures quoted here, which are based on the latest bonus declaration of the office, are given for illustrative purposes only and are not in any way guaranteed.

Note 3.—If a member does not retire at age sixty-five contributions cease, but the maturing benefit must remain on deposit at interest with the Insurance Company to age seventy or any earlier age at which retirement or death takes place.

The benefits available under the Scheme for widows and dependents arise from a special type of convertible policy under which substantial sums will become payable to the dependents of a minister who dies before the age of fifty-five. Examples of the benefits are :—

Age at Entry	*Sum Assured*
25	£3,946
30	3,370
35	2,667
40	2,182
45	1,720
50	1,388

This Scheme provides very substantial life cover up to age fifty-five, which will normally be the period when family responsibilities are greatest. At any time before attaining age fifty-five, the member has the option to convert this benefit into an endowment policy maturing at age sixty-five or into another form of policy, such as Whole Life Assurance, which may accord with his requirements. After conversion the sum assured will be reduced to an extent depending on the alternative type of policy selected. It is a condition of the Scheme that the annual premium of £12 be paid up to age fifty-five *so long as the member remains in the service of the Church.*

BEFORE EXERCISING THE OPTION TO CONVERT, MINISTERS MUST WRITE TO THE SECRETARY OF THE AGED AND INFIRM MINISTERS' FUND COMMITTEE WHO WILL BE PLEASED TO PROVIDE ALL THE NECESSARY DETAILS.

Members who were in the Life Assurance Scheme before these Regulations came into effect will continue payment of premiums up to age seventy and to be entitled to benefits maturing at age seventy, but on retirement at any time between age sixty-five and age seventy they may, if they so desire, cease payment of the contributions and receive payment of reduced benefits.

42. *Periodical Investigations.*

(1) An investigation into the financial position of the Fund shall be made at the termination of each period of five years from 31st December 1962, or of such other suitable periods of years as may be fixed by the Committee. The Committee may postpone in exceptional circumstances any particular investigation for one year or more, but must report its action to the ensuing General Assembly. Each of these investigations shall be made by an Actuary appointed by the Committee, who shall be either a Fellow of the Faculty of Actuaries in Scotland or a Fellow of the Institute of Actuaries. It shall be the duty of the Actuary to consider, *inter alia,* whether or not any alterations are required in the rates of pension mentioned in the tables or in the rates of pension to ministers who became contributors at ages over sixty under the original Regulations, so that the value of the liabilities of the Fund may not be greater than the value of its assets and to make any recommendation on the subject that he may think fit.

(2) It shall be the duty of the Committee to consider the Actuary's Report, and it is empowered to take all such steps as in its judgment may be required to maintain or place the Fund in a sound financial position. In particular, the Committee may alter the rates of pension given in the above-mentioned tables, and the rates so altered shall thereafter supersede for all purposes the rates previously in force. Similarly, the

Committee may alter the rate of pension corresponding to the contributions paid by ministers who became contributors at ages over fifty under the original Regulations.

VIII. Procedure Recommended in Appointment of Organist and Choirmaster.

Attention is drawn to the first section of Act xvi. of the General Assembly, 1931, anent Precentor or Organist, which provides :—

The appointment of the Precentor or Organist shall be made by the Kirk Session, which must be satisfied as to the Christian character of any applicant before he be recognised as eligible.

I. On occurrence of a vacancy the Kirk Session should immediately decide

(*a*) whether they will themselves consider the qualifications of Applicants ; or

(*b*) appoint an Advisory Committee representative of themselves, the Congregation, and the Choir, such Committee, or an Executive appointed by it to examine Applications and Testimonials and hear suitable candidates in their own Churches, make recommendations to the Kirk Session of a Short Leet of Candidates, and ultimately recommend a particular candidate for appointment ;

> *Note.*—It is desirable, where possible, that Candidates on a Short Leet should each take the Choir Practice in presence of the Committee and also the Services on the following Sunday.

or (*c*) appoint a duly qualified person to consider the musical qualifications of Applicants and make a recommendation.

II. The Kirk Session should also prepare a List of the Duties of the Organist and Choirmaster, a copy of which should be sent to each applicant who is to be interviewed.

In preparing the List the following points should be considered :

(1) Tenure of the appointment.
(2) Relation to the Minister.
(3) Amount of Salary and how payable.
(4) Duties at diets of Public Worship.
(5) Choir Training.
(6) Sunday School and Juvenile Choir (if thought desirable).
(7) Holiday.
(8) The use of the Organ for pupils.
(9) Rate of payment for additional services, *e.g.*, Marriages and Funerals—responsibility for collecting which not to rest with the Kirk Session.

When the List has been finally adjusted with the Organist and Choirmaster, the provisions should be embodied in a formal Agreement which, when completed, should be engrossed in the Minutes of the Kirk Session (1931, xvi.).

III. It is recommended that when a new Organist and Choirmaster is installed, his appointment should be intimated to the Congregation, and he should be publicly welcomed. It is further desirable that prayers should be offered during the service on his behalf and for the welfare of the work to which he has been called.

IX. Scottish Federation of Organists.

Suggested form of contract between the Organist and Kirk Session.

N.B.—Where brackets appear in the text of the suggested form of contract they mean that the enclosed words may be amended or omitted if not applicable or not required.

An AGREEMENT made this day 19 between the Kirk Session of Church and of hereinafter named "the Organist".

1. Until the termination of this Agreement by the giving of due notice shall act as the Organist and Choirmaster of Church.

2. The salary of the Organist shall be the annual sum of £ . The salary shall be paid (monthly), and shall be reviewed every two years.

3. Subject to the control of the Minister the Organist shall have the direction of the music in the Church.

4. The Organist shall play the organ at the ordinary Sunday services, (the Sunday School) and at such special services as the Kirk Session may require. He shall not be obliged to play on week-days at times which interfere with his week-day employment.

5. The Organist shall be responsible for the recruitment, training and discipline of the Choir(s). He shall conduct (weekly) practices during the period from (September) to (April) each year.

6. The Organ shall normally be reserved for the personal use of, and the giving of lessons by, the Organist; also for the practice of a recognised assistant or deputy; also for the practice of the Organist's pupils. A charge of per hour will be made to pupils for the use of the organ for practice. This charge shall be collected by the Organist and accounted to the Church Treasurer. The charge shall be reviewed every two years.

7. The Organist shall play at Wedding and Funeral services and all other services not specified in para. 4 of this Agreement and shall be paid the proper fee by those who engage him. The fee shall be and shall be reviewed every two years. The Organist may waive his right to play at any such services if so requested, but shall, if available, be entitled to his fee.

8. The Organist shall have weeks' holiday each year, to be taken at such times as shall be mutually agreed between him and the Kirk Session. His deputy shall be paid by the Church Treasurer. Other leave of absence shall be the subject of arrangement with the Kirk Session and the Organist shall provide and pay a competent deputy.

9. (If the Organist be incapacitated by illness he shall at the discretion of the Kirk Session be paid his normal salary for a period or periods not exceeding in total (thirteen) weeks in any consecutive twelve months period. A deputy during such illness shall be paid by the Church Treasurer, when payment is required.)

10. The Organist shall be entitled to claim from the Church Treasurer a refund of the cost of postages, stationery, telephone calls and other expenses reasonably incurred in the pursuit of his duties Such expenses shall not include the cost of organ music (or travel). The Organist shall keep a record of his expenses and obtain the approval of the appropriate Financial Court before incurring any large or unusual expenditure.

11. A sum of not more than   shall be made available annually for the purchase of choral music which shall remain the property of the Congregation. The Organist shall make purchases at his discretion and present the appropriate accounts to the Church Treasurer. The amount of the allocation shall be reviewed every two years.

12. This Agreement may be terminated by either party giving to the other   calendar months' notice in writing.

APPENDIX XXVII.

PROCEDURE IN NEGOTIATIONS FOR CONGREGATIONAL UNIONS.

Committee on Unions and Readjustments.

The General Assembly have legislated regarding the uniting, linking, transporting, suppressing, reducing and dissolving of congregations in Act 1957, xvii., Act 1958, xiii., and Act xxiv., 1966, which are printed on p. 751. (See Memo. on Readjustment 1966, Reports pp. 288-303.)

Model Basis of Union for Uniting Two Congregations.

Model Basis of Union.

THE CONGREGATION OF (formerly {Church of Scotland / United Free Church of Scotland}) AND THE CONGREGATION OF (formerly {Church of Scotland / United Free Church of Scotland}).

PRESBYTERY OF .

1. (*a*) *Act of Union, Name of Congregation.*—The and Congregations shall be united as from the day of 19 .

(*b*) The name of the united congregation shall be .

2. *Transference of Property and Funds.*—The property and funds belonging to or held on behalf of each congregation shall belong to or be held on behalf of the united congregation and any transference necessary shall be duly effected.

3. *Place of Worship.*—The Church at present used and occupied by the congregation shall be the place of worship of the united congregation. The Church at present used by the congregation shall be sold, let or otherwise disposed of subject to the titles on which it is held, subject to the approval of the Presbytery, and, if necessary, the General Trustees or the General Assembly. The free proceeds of any such sale or let shall be held as a Fabric Fund for the Maintenance of the Fabric of the Church of the united congregation.

If the property to be sold or let is vested in the General Trustees and the property to be retained is not vested in them, the latter property will require to be transferred to the General Trustees before they can make available for its improvement or maintenance the proceeds of sale or rent of the property which has been sold or let. However, the General

Assembly have authorised the General Trustees to disburse interest accruing on the proceeds of sale of properties vested in them to meet the cost of maintenance work approved by the General Trustees on properties not so vested.

4. *Territorial Responsibility.*—The bounds to be served by the united charge shall be .

Note.—Definite bounds should be given and the sentence should end " or as the Presbytery shall determine."

5. *Kirk Session.*—The elders of both Kirk Sessions shall form with the minister or ministers the Kirk Session of the united congregation.

6. *Congregational Management.*—(1) the temporal affairs of the united congregation shall be administered by the Kirk Session ; or

(2) The temporal affairs of the united congregation shall be administered by a Congregational Board constituted as in the Deed of Constitution of Quoad Sacra Churches, 1931 ; or as in the Constitution for Quoad Omnia Churches, 1933, and the Delegation of Assembly is hereby authorised to issue the appropriate Deed of Constitution to the united congregation.

7. *Minister.*—(1) The Rev. , the present minister of shall be the minister of the united charge ; or

(2) In the event of the Rev. retiring his interests being conserved by the Church, the united congregation shall proceed to the election of a new minister ; or

(3) Both charges being vacant the united congregation shall proceed to the election of a minister.

8. *Manse.*—The Manse of the congregation shall be the Manse of the united congregation. The Manse of the congregation shall be sold, let or otherwise disposed of, subject to the titles on which it is held, and subject to the approval of the Presbytery, and, if necessary, of the General Trustees or the General Assembly. The free proceeds of any such sale or let shall be held as a Fabric Fund for the maintenance of the Manse of the united congregation.

9. *Ministerial Support.*—The stipend shall be such as is sanctioned by the Presbytery in conjunction with the Committee on the Maintenance of the Ministry.

Note.—While discussion as to the stipend in the united congregation may enter into the negotiations for union, no figure may be inserted in the Basis of Union.

10. *Power to Readjust.*—While these articles and terms shall form a Basis of Union for the two congregations now uniting, the united congregation shall be free, like other congregations, to adjust arrangements under authority of the Presbytery except for Clause 1 (*a*) as need may arise.

Note.—In a union involving a *Quoad Sacra* parish, Article 10 should conclude with " provided that the General Assembly sanction any change proposed in the statutory provisions of the parish." It is not necessary, however, to obtain the sanction of the General Assembly for addition to the area of a *Quoad Sacra* parish.

Model Basis of Linking.

THE CONGREGATION OF (formerly {Church of Scotland / United Free Church of Scotland}) AND THE CONGREGATION OF (formerly {Church of Scotland / United Free Church of Scotland}).

PRESBYTERY OF .

1. *Act of Linking.*—The congregation of and the congregation of shall be linked as from the day of 19 .

2. *Transference of Property and Funds.*—The property and funds belonging to or held on behalf of each congregation shall remain the property and funds of each congregation as at present.

3. *Places of Worship.*—Both Churches at present used and occupied by the congregations shall be the places of worship of the linked congregations. Services shall be conducted in Church at and in Church at each Sunday. (Or at times to be decided by the Minister and the Kirk Sessions, subject to the approval of the Presbytery.)

4. *Territorial Responsibility.*—The bounds to be served by the linked charge shall be .

Note.—Definite bounds should be given and the sentence should end " or as the Presbytery shall determine."

5. *Kirk Session.*—The minister of the linked charge shall be Moderator of each Kirk Session. The two Kirk Sessions shall meet as one annually to elect a representative elder to Presbytery and Synod. They may meet together at other times as they may deem it desirable.

6. *Congregational Management.*—The temporal affairs of each congregation shall be administered as at present.

7. *Minister.*—The Rev. the present minister of shall be the first minister of the linked charge; or , .

In the event of the Rev. retiring, his interests being conserved by the Church, the linked congregation shall proceed to the election of a new minister; or .

Both charges being vacant the linked congregations shall proceed to the election of a minister.

8. *Manse.*—The Manse of congregation shall be the Manse of the linked congregation. The Manse of congregation shall be sold, let or otherwise disposed of subject to the Titles on which it is held, and subject to the approval of the Presbytery and, if necessary, of the General Trustees or the General Assembly. The free proceeds of any such sale or let shall be held as a Fabric Fund for the maintenance of the Manse of the linked charge (or partly for the maintenance of the Manse and partly for the maintenance of the Church at).

9. *Ministerial Support.*—The stipend shall be such as is sanctioned by the Presbytery in conjunction with the Committee on the Maintenance of the Ministry.

10. *Power to Readjust.*—While these articles and terms shall form a Basis of Linking for the two congregations now linking, the linked congregations shall be free like other congregations, to adjust arrangements under authority of the Presbytery except for Clause (1) as need may arise.

Note 1.—In a linking involving a *Quoad Sacra* parish, Article 10 should conclude with "provided that the General Assembly sanction any change proposed in the statutory provisions of the parish." It is not necessary, however, to obtain the sanction of the General Assembly for addition to the area of a *Quoad Sacra* parish.

Note 2.—If payment of any endowment depends on induction then this should be provided for in the Basis of Linking.

APPENDIX I.

ACT ANENT UNIONS, READJUSTMENTS, AND OTHER CHANGES IN THE STATUS OF CONGREGATIONS (1957, xvii., 1966, xxiv.).

Preamble.

Whereas unions and readjustments and other changes in the status of congregations have been regulated by a series of Acts and Deliverances of the General Assembly, and it is desirable to clarify and amend the law.

Now therefore the General Assembly with consent of a majority of Presbyteries, hereby enact, ordain, and declare as follows :—

Interpretation.

1. For the purposes of this Act the following words and expressions shall be deemed to have the meaning hereby assigned to them :—

(*a*) A "charge" shall mean a sphere of pastoral duty to which a minister or ministers are appointed *ad vitam aut culpam.*[1] Such a sphere is referred to in this Act as a Parish.

(*b*) A "congregation" is a company of persons associated together in a particular locality for Christian worship, instruction, fellowship, and work, consisting of members in full communion—*i.e.*, those whose names appear on the Communion Roll kept by the Kirk Session, who alone are entitled to vote at congregational meetings—and adherents who have no vote except in the case provided for in Act IX. of 1932, Section 5.

(*c*) "Union" shall mean the joining of two or more congregations, or the joining of two collegiate charges of one congregation, so that two or more charges, where these exist, are made into one unless otherwise specifically provided. It includes the union of a congregation with a mission station.

(*d*) "Linking" shall mean the joining of two or more congregations as one charge under one minister, with each congregation retaining its own identity, courts, services and organisations. A linking may be either of a temporary or of a permanent character.

(*e*) A "Deferred Union" or "Deferred Linking" shall mean agreement to a Basis of Union or Linking between the congregation

[1] Cf. Act iii, 1972

of a vacant charge and another congregation, which Basis shall not be put into effect until a vacancy occurs in the other charge, and then under a minister who has been elected by both congregations to the first-mentioned vacant charge.

(*f*) " Transportation " shall mean the moving of a congregation from one place of worship to another with or without a change of parish.

(*g*) " Transference " shall mean the change of a congregation and its parish from the bounds of one Presbytery or Synod to the bounds of another without any change of site.

(*h*) A " Restricted Ministry " shall mean the ministry of a congregation that is permitted to call a minister *ad vitam aut culpam*[1] but who is not under a stated age, or a minister or Probationer whose name is on the Special List ;

(*i*) A " Continued Vacancy " shall mean an interim arrangement to cover a period during which it is considered undesirable to suppress or reduce a charge, and negotiations towards union or readjustment are suspended.

(*j*) " Suppression " of a charge shall mean the withdrawal from a congregation of the right to have its minister or ministers appointed *ad vitam aut culpam*. The work of the congregation may be carried on under a terminable appointment by a minister without charge, or licentiate. The congregation shall retain its Kirk Session and financial board and shall be represented by an Elder in Presbytery and in Synod, and be liable for Assembly, Synod, and Presbytery dues.

(*k*) " Reduction " shall mean the alteration of the status of a congregation to that of a mission station.

(*l*) " Dissolution " shall mean the termination of the existence of a congregation.

(*m*) " Special List " shall mean a list of ministers, whose translation would open the way to readjustment involving their charge, and certain Probationers.

Cases in which Action by the General Assembly is necessary.

2. Where a union, transportation, reduction, dissolution, or other change in the status of a congregation involves any modification of arrangements set up by and existing under a decree of the Court of Teinds or modification of an Act of the General Assembly, or a scheme of the Scottish Ecclesiastical Commissioners, the union, transportation, reduction, or other change shall be effected only by the General Assembly, or (except in the case of a modification of an Act of General Assembly or Scheme of the Scottish Ecclesiastical Commissioners) by their Commission at one of their stated diets.

The Presbytery of the bounds, with the concurrence of the Committee on Unions and Readjustments, shall normally institute the necessary proceedings for this purpose.

Procedure towards Union.

3. Except in the cases specified in Section 2, a union may be effected by the Presbytery of the bounds, with the concurrence of the Committee on Unions and Readjustments and of the Committee on the Maintenance

[1] Cf. Act iii, 1972.

of the Ministry, or failing such concurrence, by or under the authority of the General Assembly, or their Commission at one of the stated diets.

Dissolution of Union.

4. A Union shall be dissolved only by or under the authority of the General Assembly or their Commission at any of the stated diets. The dissolution may be effected by a deliverance on a Report of the Committee on Unions and Readjustments, after due intimation.

Linking Arrangements.

5. Where a union is regarded as desirable, but only a linking arrangement is practicable at the time, such arrangement shall be regarded as a temporary expedient only and as a step towards union.

Where two or more congregations are at such a distance from each other as to make impracticable united worship, and to make difficult the effective working of united congregational courts and organisations, but where one minister can serve the congregations they may be permanently linked and share a minister and a representative elder.

While congregations are linked they become one charge. Each congregation shall retain its own Kirk Session and financial board, but, for the purpose of electing a representative elder to the Presbytery and Synod, the two Kirk Sessions shall meet together as one annually, in accordance with the last paragraph of Act X. of 1932. The provisions of this Act with regard to unions shall apply to linkings, except that a temporary linking arrangement may be broken in order to effect a union, or in favour of a new linking arrangement, by the Presbytery of the bounds, with the concurrence of the Committee on Unions and Readjustments and of the Committee on the Maintenance of the Ministry.

Deferred Unions and Deferred Linkings.

6. As the purpose of a Deferred Union and a Deferred Linking is to protect an existing life interest, and at the same time to make sure of a union or linking at the first opportunity, the basis of union or linking shall be recorded by the Presbytery and by the Committee on Unions and Readjustments and shall be put into effect by the Presbytery on the opportunity arising. In the event of a second vacancy occurring in the charge that was vacant, before the Deferred union or Deferred linking takes place, the agreement to the Deferred union or Deferred linking shall not prejudice an immediate union, or linking, under the existing minister or any other readjustment if so agreed.

Transportation.

7. (i) Except in the cases specified in Section 2, and as after provided in this section, the transportation of a charge of a congregation from one Parish to another, may be effected by the Synod of the bounds.

(ii) Where the transportation—

(*a*) concerns another Synod ; or

(*b*) concerns two Presbyteries out of a Synod consisting of not more than three, and these two Presbyteries are not in agreement as to the proposed transportation ;

the Synod of the bounds shall refer the question to the General Assembly, or to their Commission at any of their stated diets, which may dispose of the case.

(iii) Where no regular meetings of the Synod intervenes, or in the event referred to in head (*a*) of the foregoing subsection, the Presbytery of the bounds may refer the question to the General Assembly, or to their Commission at any of their stated diets, which may dispose of the case.

(iv) The Presbytery of the bounds, with the concurrence of the Committee on Unions and Readjustments, may institute the necessary proceedings for transportation.

Transference.

8. (i) When a Kirk Session desires that the charge should be transferred from one Presbytery to another, it shall present a Petition to that effect to the Synod, through the Presbytery within whose bounds it is presently situated.

(ii) This Petition shall be lodged with the Clerk of the Presbytery in time for a meeting of Presbytery occurring not later than two months before the meeting of Synod, and it shall be the duty of the Kirk Session at the same time to intimate the Petition to the other Presbytery involved.

(iii) If the Synod to which the Petition is presented consists of not more than three Presbyteries, of which two are the Presbyteries involved, and these two Presbyteries are not in agreement as to the proposed transference, the Synod shall refer the Petition to the General Assembly, or to their Commission at any of their stated diets, which may dispose of the case.

(iv) If the Presbytery to which transference is sought is within the bounds of another Synod, or if the transference involves any modification of the arrangements set up or existing under a decree of the Court of Teinds or an Act of the General Assembly or a scheme of the Scottish Ecclesiastical Commissioners, the Petition, if approved by the Synod, shall be transmitted to the General Assembly.

(v) When a Presbytery desires that a charge within its bounds should be transferred to another Presbytery, it may, after consultation with the Kirk Session concerned, and with the concurrence of the Committee on Unions and Readjustments, present a Petition for that purpose to the Synod, and it shall be the duty of the Presbytery at the same time to intimate the Petition to the other Presbytery involved. Such Petition shall be subject to the provision of Sub-sections (iii) and (iv) of this section.

Restricted Ministry.

9. A Restricted Ministry may be imposed on a vacant charge by the Presbytery of the bounds, with the concurrence of the Committee on Unions and Readjustments, either with a view to another vacancy occurring in the charge about the time when a neighbouring charge is likely to become vacant, or because the Presbytery has decided that the work of the vacant charge can be adequately done by a Minister not under a stated age, or by a Minister or Probationer whose name is on the Special List.

Continued Vacancy.

10. A Continued Vacancy may be declared by decision of the Presbytery of the bounds, with the concurrence of the Committee on Unions and Readjustments. The charge shall remain under an Interim Moderator as in an ordinary Vacancy.

Suppression.

11. Except in the cases specified in Section 2—

Suppression may be effected by the Presbytery of the bounds, with the concurrence of the Committee on Unions and Readjustments and of the Committee on the Maintenance of the Ministry. A necessary condition shall be that the Presbytery and the Committee on Unions and Readjustments take the view that union or readjustment is desirable but for the time being not practicable.

The Congregation shall not sign a call, and the person appointed shall not be inducted, but may be introduced by the Presbytery. Such arrangements shall be terminable by the Presbytery at the end of the stated period, or on the question of union arising earlier.

The restoration to a congregation of the right to have a minister appointed *ad vitam aut culpam*[1] so that the charge is revived may be effected by the Presbytery of the bounds, with the concurrence of the Committee on Unions and Readjustments and of the Committee on the Maintenance of the Ministry.

Reduction.

12. (i) When a Presbytery finds, after full inquiry, that from depopulation of a Parish, or from any other cause, it is not advisable to maintain a congregation, the Presbytery shall consider, in consultation with the General Assembly Committees on Unions and Readjustments and the Maintenance of the Ministry and the Home Board, whether it should be reduced to a Mission Station, or otherwise dealt with, and shall report its opinion thereanent to the Synod. A copy of such report and relative documents shall be supplied to the Kirk Session of the congregation reported on, that it may take all competent steps to be duly represented at the Synod when the Presbytery's report is heard. Except in the cases specified in Section 2, the Synod, after hearing parties, shall decide whether the congregation should or should not be reduced.

(ii) Should the question be raised in a congregation as to its reduction or otherwise, the matter shall be reported forthwith to the Presbytery through the Kirk Session. The Presbytery shall without delay inquire into the whole circumstances of the congregation, meeting with the minister, if any, the office-bearers, and the congregation. It shall formulate its opinion on the case, and report the case along with its opinion thereon to the Synod.

(iii) In cases where no regular meeting of Synod intervenes, the Presbytery may refer the question of Reduction to the General Assembly, or to their Commission at any of the stated diets, which may dispose of the case.

(iv) A mission station may be raised or restored by the General Assembly or their Commission at any of their stated diets.

The Presbytery of the bounds, with the concurrence of the Committee

[1] Cf. Act iii, 1972.

on Unions and Readjustments, and of the Committee on the Maintenance of the Ministry, shall normally institute the necessary proceedings for this purpose, and the raising or restoration may be effected by a Deliverance on a Report of the Committee on Unions and Readjustments, after due intimation.

Dissolution.

13. (i) When a Presbytery finds, after full inquiry, that from depopulation of a Parish, or from any other cause, it is not advisable to maintain the congregation, the Presbytery shall consider, in consultation with the Committees on Unions and Readjustments and the Maintenance of the Ministry and the Home Board, whether it should be discontinued, or otherwise dealt with, and shall report its opinion thereanent to the Synod. A copy of such report and relative documents shall be supplied to the Kirk Session of the congregation reported on, that it may take all competent steps to be duly represented at the Synod when the Presbytery's report is heard. Except in the cases specified in Section 2, the Synod, after hearing parties, shall decide whether the congregation should or should not be discontinued, and in the event of its deciding to discontinue it, shall satisfy itself that there will be adequate provision for the pastoral oversight of the former Parish.

(ii) Should the question be raised in a congregation as to its continuance or otherwise, the matter shall be reported forthwith to the Presbytery through the Kirk Session. The Presbytery shall without delay inquire into the whole circumstances of the congregation, meeting with the minister, if any, the office-bearers, and the congregation. It shall formulate its opinion on the case and report the case along with its opinion to the Synod.

(iii) The destination of the property shall, if possible, be settled before the Dissolution of the congregation is finally determined, subject to the terms of the titles on which it is held.

(iv) In cases where no regular meeting of Synod intervenes, the Presbytery may refer the question of Dissolution to the General Assembly, or to their Commission at any of the stated diets, which may dispose of the case.

(See Memorandum pp. 759, 760.)

Reporting of Readjustments.

14. All Unions and Linkings, Deferred Unions and Deferred Linkings, Transportations, Restricted Ministries, Continued Vacancies, Suppressions, Reductions, and Dissolutions shall be reported annually to the General Assembly by the Committee on Unions and Readjustments. Reductions may be reported also by the Home Board. It shall be the duty of the Clerk of the Presbytery or the Clerk of the Synod, as the case may be, to inform the Committee concerned of any action taken in pursuance of this Act.

A Retired Minister.

15. The position and status of a minister who demits his charge in the interests of union or readjustment shall be in no way affected by such union or readjustment. He shall continue to be a member of the Presbytery to which he belonged at the date of his demission, and shall

remain Minister Emeritus or Senior Minister of his former congregation, although it is no longer a separate entity.

Agreement to Union or Linking under an Incumbent.

16. When two congregations agree to unite or link under the present minister of one of them, and an explicit term of the Basis of Union or Linking is that this minister shall be the minister of the united or linked charge, no further vote of the members of the vacant charge shall be necessary to constitute the election of the minister of the other charge to the united or linked charge, and to entitle him to be inducted thereto.

A service of induction, or of introduction as may be appropriate, shall be conducted in all such cases of union or linking.

17. No Court of the Church (including the Commission of the General Assembly) may approve any form of Union or Readjustment unless due intimation has been made to every congregation affected thereby. Every such congregation shall be entitled to appear in its interest.

18. In any case where any proceedings of a Presbytery under this Act are made the subject of appeal or complaint, the Presbytery shall inform the General Assembly's Committees on Unions and Readjustments and on the Maintenance of the Ministry of this fact and these Committees shall defer consideration of the said case until final judgment has been given upon the said appeal or complaint.

Repeal.

19. The Act of 29th May 1930 anent union under the minister of one of the uniting congregations, and Acts XX. of 1933, XV. and XVI. of 1951 are hereby repealed.

Validity of all action taken under the Acts now repealed and Deliverances.

20. The repeal of the Acts mentioned in Section 17 shall not affect the operation of the said Acts (or Deliverances of the General Assembly in pursuance thereof) prior to the repeal of the said Acts, or anything duly done or suffered under the said Acts and Deliverances, and any right or obligation so acquired or incurred thereunder shall have effect as if the said Acts had not been repealed.

ACT AMENDING ACT XVII. OF 1957 (1958, xiii.).

The General Assembly enact and ordain that Section 17 of Act XVII. of 1957 be amended by including Act XII. of 1933 among the Acts thereby repealed.

APPENDIX II.

EXTRACT FROM ACT 1932, ix.

The Presbytery shall also communicate the occurrence of a vacancy to the Secretary of the Committee on Unions and Readjustments, together with its opinion as to whether the question of readjustment should be raised or not; and at the same time, in all cases of vacancies where in the opinion of the Presbytery a union or readjustment of agencies is worthy of consideration, it shall appoint a Committee to confer with the representatives of that Committee. When the question of union or readjustment is raised by the Presbytery, it shall direct that procedure be sisted till this question is settled. Informal conference may take place before the charge is actually vacant (1960, xxiii.).

APPENDIX III.

BALLOT REGULATIONS (1934, Reg., App. D.).

If at a congregational meeting where the matter of union is being considered it is moved and seconded that the vote be taken by ballot, the Chairman shall first satisfy himself that the following regulations can be observed. If the regulations cannot be carried out the motion shall not be accepted, and the normal method of voting openly shall be used. If the motion is accepted by the Chairman, and carried, the vote shall be taken as follows:—

(1) The vote shall be taken before the Congregational Meeting adjourns or ends.

(2) Only Voting Papers in the form approved and supplied by the Committee shall be used.

(3) A copy of the Communion Roll as authorised by the Kirk Session shall be submitted, and a Voting Paper shall be issued to each person whose name is on the roll and who applies for it in person, but to no one else.

(4) The Chairman shall be responsible for issuing, collecting, and counting the Voting Papers in an orderly fashion. Opportunity should be given to every voter to mark the paper in private.

(5) Voting Papers marked otherwise than with a cross placed opposite one or other motion shall not be counted.

(6) The Voting Papers after enumeration shall be given into the custody of the Clerk of the Presbytery, who shall retain them until the question of union is settled temporarily or otherwise, when they may be destroyed.

APPENDIX IV.

ACT ANENT ELECTION OF MINISTERS IN CASES OF LINKED CONGREGATIONS, DEFERRED UNIONS, AND DEFERRED LINKINGS (1961, xxii.).

The General Assembly, with the consent of a majority of Presbyteries, enact and ordain as follows:—

1. Notwithstanding the terms of Act IX. of 1932 the election of a Minister to a vacant charge which consists of two or more congregations which have been linked, or which have agreed to a Deferred Union or a Deferred Linking shall be by ballot, and not by open vote.

2. Whenever reasonably possible and practicable in such cases only one ballot box shall be used. In cases where more than one ballot box is used all boxes shall be opened at the same place and time and the voting papers shall be mixed together before counting begins so that the preponderance of votes in each Congregation shall not be disclosed.

3. In all other respects Act IX. of 1932 shall apply *mutatis mutandis* to the election of Ministers to the vacant charges referred to in Section 1 hereof.

APPENDIX V.

MEMORANDUM IN CONNECTION WITH THE DISSOLUTION OF CONGREGATIONS OF THE CHURCH OF SCOTLAND

I. *Notes in connection with Proposed Dissolutions.*

1. Dissolution terminates the existence of a Congregation. Generally speaking, dissolution renders void trust moneys, legacies, etc., otherwise payable to the Congregation. It can also produce difficulties with regard to heritable property. Union of Congregations, on the other hand, usually produces no such difficulties, as neither of the uniting Congregations loses, in law, its identity. From this point of view, therefore, dissolution should only be contemplated as a last resort. Where dissolution is eventually decided upon, however, a detailed Basis should be drawn up and agreed in order to obviate or minimise resulting difficulties.

2. A proposed Basis of Dissolution should be approved by the following :—

(1) Kirk Session.
(2) Congregational Board, Deacons' Court or Board of Managers, etc.
(3) Congregation.
(4) Presbytery.
(5) The General Assembly's Committee on the Maintenance of the Ministry.
(6) The General Assembly's Committee on Unions of Congregations and Readjustment of Agencies.
(7) Home Board.
(8) The General Trustees (where properties vested in them are concerned).

3. The dissolution of a Congregation is normally effected by the Synod but in the case of certain Congregations (principally some Congregations of the pre-1929 Church of Scotland) only the General Assembly can effect dissolution and grant the necessary authority for the disposal of property and the application of proceeds. The General Assembly has legislated on the matter—see the Act anent Unions, Readjustments and other Changes in the Status of Congregations (XXIX, 1966).

II. *Suggested Headings of Basis of Dissolution.*

Basis of Dissolution of the Congregation of in the Presbytery of .

1. *Act of Dissolution.*

The Congregation of shall be dissolved as at a date to be appointed by the Presbytery of .

2. *Minister.*

Here if applicable detail the position with regard to the Minister, how his interests are being conserved on retiral, etc.

3. *Territorial Responsibility.*

Here will be given details of how the Presbytery proposes to deal with the pastoral care of the parish of the Congregation to be dissolved.

4. *Heritable Property.*

Here detail the arrangements for the disposal of heritable property and application of proceeds. The heritable properties will normally consist of :—

(1) Church.
(2) Halls.
(3) Manse.
(4) Any other properties.

The titles to heritable properties (even of the same Congregation) may be held in differing ways and the following points should be borne in mind :—

(1) Where property is vested in the General Trustees, the latter must be consulted with regard to any matter involving disposal, application of proceeds, etc. The Solicitor of the General Trustees should be consulted.
(2) Where property is vested in local Trustees, a Solicitor should be consulted for his advice on the effect which dissolution would have on the title-holding. The Trusts imposed in such titles may well require, for example, specific authority to dispose of property given at a Meeting of the Congregation summoned in a particular way, etc. The Solicitor of the Church will be pleased to advise in all such cases.

5. *Endowments.*

Here detail the arrangements with regard to endowments. This matter affects principally the Maintenance of the Ministry Committee in the allocation of statutory endowment in terms of Act XXVII., 1953.

6. *Moveable Property.*

Here detail the arrangements for disposal of :—

(1) Cash, Funds in bank, marketable securities, etc.
(2) Furniture, etc.
(3) Memorials.

7. *Congregational Trusts.*

Here detail the arrangements for the future of Congregational Trusts. If the Congregation is to dissolve it may well be outwith the power of the Congregation to secure the future position of these Trusts. Legal advice should be taken on this matter.

APPENDIX XXVIII.

SCHEME RELATING TO THE UNIVERSITY NOMINATION BOARDS AND THE BOARD OF NOMINATION FOR CHURCH CHAIRS

(1935, 12; Rep. 1935, pp. 1147-48).

1. Church Members on the several University Nomination Boards.

The General Assembly shall appoint such members on report by its Standing Nomination Committee. Members shall be appointed for six years, one member retiring annually from each Board. No member shall be eligible for re-election until after a period of one year, unless, as provided for in the Standing Orders of the General Assembly (No. 113), "there are exceptional circumstances which make re-election desirable."

2. Method of nominating Professors to the Chairs to be Provided and Maintained by the Church.

(*a*) Nominations shall be made by the Board of Nomination set up for this purpose by the General Assembly.

(*b*) The Board shall consist of the Church representatives on the University Nomination Boards along with the following, if not otherwise members of the Board: the Moderator of the General Assembly for the time being, who shall act as Chairman; the Convener of the Committee on Education for the Ministry; and the Dean of the Faculty of Divinity in the University specially concerned in a particular nomination acting *ad hoc*.[1]

(*c*) On the occurrence of a vacancy in a Church Chair which is not a University Chair, the Board shall make a nomination and shall forward the name agreed upon to the ensuing General Assembly or Commission of Assembly, which, after receiving the report, unless it shall resolve to reject the nomination, shall appoint the nominee to the Chair. The local Presbytery thereafter shall, as the case may require, ordain and induct, or induct, to his office the one so appointed.

3. In the filling of a vacancy in the Principalship of Trinity College or of Master of Christ's College, Aberdeen, the procedure laid down in 2 (*c*) shall be followed.

In the filling of a vacancy in the post of Principal of New College, Edinburgh, the University Board of Nomination for Theological Chairs shall nominate a person, being a member of the Faculty of Divinity and also a Minister of the Church of Scotland, to be recommended to the General Assembly as Principal of the College and to the Faculty as Dean. The Principalship of New College is a terminable appointment of four years.

[1] In the case of a Church Chair which is not a University Chair the Principal or Master of the Church College takes the place of the Dean of the Faculty of Divinity (1946, 11).

APPENDIX XXIX

THE CHURCH OF SCOTLAND WOMAN'S GUILD CONSTITUTION (1975).

CONSTITUTION.

The aim of the Woman's Guild of the Church of Scotland is to unite the women of the Church in the dedication of their lives to the Lord Jesus Christ through worship, fellowship and service.

The aim of the Young Woman's Group of the Woman's Guild of the Church of Scotland is to encourage Christian home and family life and to unite its members through worship, fellowship and service.

ORGANISATION.

1. (*a*) *Congregational—The Branch/Group.* Membership of the Woman's Guild is open to all women who accept the Aims. Members are united in the Branch/Group within the congregation.

(*b*) *Presbyterial—The Council.* Branches and Groups are united in the Presbyterial Council within the bounds of the Presbytery.

(*c*) *Central—The Central Committee.* Councils are united in the Central Committee, which is the executive body of the Woman's Guild.

2. A Woman's Guild Branch is formed with the consent of the Minister and Kirk Session, and is under its jurisdiction.

3. A Young Woman's Group may be formed with the consent of the Minister and Kirk Session, and is under its jurisdiction.

4. On the formation of a Branch/Group it shall be registered with the Organising Secretary, at 121 George Street, Edinburgh EH2 4YN, who makes intimation to the Secretary of the appropriate Presbyterial Council.

5. The Branch/Group shall report annually by means of Schedules supplied by the Central Committee, one copy to be submitted to the Central Committee, and one to the Presbyterial Council.

THE BRANCH.

6. The Woman's Guild Branch shall appoint a Committee, which shall consist of :—

(*a*) A President.
(*b*) A Vice-President.
(*c*) A Secretary.
(*d*) A Treasurer.
(*e*) Delegates to the Presbyterial Council in the interests of the Church at home and overseas.
(*f*) Two representatives nominated by the Young Woman's Group Committee.
(*g*) Additional members according to the size of the Branch.

Each member of committee shall hold office for not more than three consecutive years, being eligible for re-election after the lapse of one year. If a change of office occurs the term of office may be six consecutive years.

Two members of the Committee shall be appointed as representatives to the Committee of the Young Woman's Group.

7. The Branch shall be represented at the Presbyterial Council by its President, Secretary and Delegates.

THE PRESBYTERIAL COUNCIL.

8. The Presbyterial Council shall consist of :—

(*a*) Branch Presidents.
(*b*) Branch Secretaries.
(*c*) Branch Delegates.
(*d*) Two representatives from each Young Woman's Group.
(*e*) Women members of Assembly Committees resident in the area.
(*f*) Women members of the Central Committee resident in the area.
(*g*) A representative from the Presbytery.
(*h*) A representative of Deaconesses serving in the area.
(*i*) The Convener and Secretary of each Presbyterial Council Committee.
(*j*) Such other members as the Council may wish to co-opt.

Care should be taken to ensure that the Council includes an Ecumenical Contact and a Parish Education Representative.

9. Within the Council there shall be three Committees—Home, Social and Moral Welfare and Overseas. Each Committee shall nominate a Convener and appoint a Secretary.

10. The Presbyterial Council shall appoint as Office-Bearers :—

(*a*) A President.
(*b*) Three Vice-Presidents, who shall be the Conveners of the above Committees.
(*c*) A Secretary.
(*d*) A Treasurer.

The Office-Bearers shall hold office for not more than three consecutive years, being eligible for re-election after the lapse of one year. If a change of office occurs, the term of office may be six consecutive years.

The President and Secretary of the Council shall be members of all Council Committees *ex officio*.

11. The Presbyterial Council shall appoint a Business Committee, annually, which shall be responsible for the arrangements and oversight of Council business.

The Business Committee shall consist of :—

(*a*) The Office-Bearers.
(*b*) The Secretary from each of the three Committees.
(*c*) A Young Woman's Group Representative.
(*d*) The Parish Education Representative.
(*e*) The Ecumenical Contact.
(*f*) A Literature Secretary.
(*g*) Additional members not exceeding six in number.

12. Each Presbyterial Council shall appoint a representative, preferably the President, to the Central Committee. This appointment shall take effect from the first meeting of the Central Committee after the General Assembly.

The Young Woman's Group Representatives from the Presbyterial Councils shall be appointed to the Central Committee to serve for two years, on a rota basis. (Councils to be notified.)

If the Young Woman's Group Representative to the Central Committee is not already on the Presbyterial Council Business Committee, she shall be co-opted on to said Committee.

THE CENTRAL COMMITTEE.

13. The executive authority and general administration of the Woman's Guild shall be vested in the Central Committee.

14. The Central Committee shall consist of :—

(*a*) *Representative Members.*

One from each Presbyterial Council who shall serve for a term of three years.

Twenty representatives from Young Woman's Groups, who shall serve for a term of two years, on a rota basis.

(*b*) *Nominated Members.*

Four nominated by the General Administration Committee and appointed by the General Assembly, who shall serve for a period of three years.

Eight from the following Committees, appointed by the Central Committee after nomination as follows :—

Two from the Home Board.

Two from the Women's Committee on Social and Moral Welfare.

One from the Committee on Parish Education.

Three from the Overseas Council.

(*c*) *Co-opted Members.*

Not exceeding twelve in number, nominated by the Business Committee, and appointed by the Central Committee, for a period of three years.

(*d*) *Associate Members.*

Secretaries of Edinburgh and Glasgow Co-ordinating Committees.

The Church Press Officer.

The Editor of " Spotlight ".

Associate members shall have no voting powers.

Membership shall take effect from the first meeting after the General Assembly.

15. The Central Committee shall appoint :—

(*a*) An honorary President, if so desired.

(*b*) A National President, who shall be the Convener of the Central Committee, of its Business Committee, and a member of all Sub-Committees, *ex officio*.

(*c*) Six National Vice-Presidents :—

Three elected by the Central Committee.

The Woman Vice-Convener of the Home Board.

The Convener of the Women's Committee on Social and Moral Welfare.

The Woman Convener of the Overseas Council.

The President and Vice-Presidents shall hold office for not more than three consecutive years, being eligible for re-election after the lapse of one year. If a change of office occurs, the term of office may be six consecutive years.

16. The Central Committee shall appoint :—

(*a*) An Organising Secretary who shall be a member *ex officio* of the Central Committee and of all sub-committees, unless otherwise determined.

(*b*) Other secretarial assistants as necessary.

17. The Central Committee shall meet on statutory dates, or as business may require.

The President, or a Vice-President in the Chair shall have a deliberative as well as a casting vote.

Any member of the Central Committee who fails to attend at least one meeting during the year shall be regarded as having lapsed from membership.

Vacancies which occur during the period of membership may be filled by the appropriate nominating body.

18. The Central Committee shall appoint a Business Committee annually, and sub-committees as required.

The Business Committee shall be responsible for the preparation of the Central Committee business.

The Business Committee shall consist of :—

(*a*) The National President.
(*b*) The six National Vice-Presidents.
(*c*) The Organising Secretary, *ex officio*.
(*d*) Three Secretaries—one from each of the three Women's Committees.
(*e*) Twelve members from the Central Committee to include :—
A Young Woman's Group Representative.
The Parish Education Representative.
The Editor of "Spotlight", *ex officio*.

19. There shall be a President's Group which shall consist of —

(*a*) The National President.
(*b*) The six National Vice-Presidents.
(*c*) The Organising Secretary, *ex officio*.

This is a consultative Group, and has no executive powers.

20. The Central Committee may appoint members to confer, consult and co-operate with representatives of other Church Committees.

21. Minutes shall be kept of all meetings of the Central Committee, of the Business Committee, and of all Sub-Committees. A Statement of Accounts shall be prepared as at 31st December each year, and shall be audited by the Church Auditor.

22. The Woman's Guild shall report annually to the General Assembly.

23. The Central Committee shall have the power to make by-laws, or to alter those which exist, after notice has been given in writing to a meeting of the Central Committee and approval has been given by two-thirds of the members present at the subsequent meeting. By-laws shall deal with the administration in Branch/Group, Council and the Central Committee, and with contributions from Branches/Groups and Councils to Central Expenses Fund.

24. Any woman belonging to a parish or congregation in which there is no Branch/Group of the Woman's Guild may become a member by applying to the Organising Secretary and being enrolled. Names and addresses of such individual members shall be sent by the Organising Secretary to the Secretary of the appropriate Presbyterial Council.

25. The Central Committee shall have the power to change this Constitution only after notice of the proposed change has been given in writing to a meeting of the Central Committee, and approval given by :—

(*a*) Two-thirds of members present at the subsequent meeting of the Central Committee.
(*b*) The majority of the Presbyterial Councils.
(*c*) The General Assembly.

APPENDIX XXX

INCOME TAX.

EACH year, after 5th April, ministers, in common with other taxpayers, are required to complete an Income Tax return. The Finance Act each year regulates the rate of tax, allowances, etc., but the minister has certain special allowances which it may be helpful to mention here.

I. MINISTERS' PERSONAL INCOME TAX ALLOWANCE.

Ministers are assessed to Income Tax under Schedule E and are allowed under Section 194 of the Income and Corporation Taxes Act 1970, to deduct expenses incurred " wholly, exclusively and necessarily " in the performance of their duties as ministers. The duty of ministers cannot be precisely defined but is reasonably interpreted by the Inland Revenue. The following particular types of expenses where borne by a minister out of his emoluments are regarded by the Inland Revenue as *prima facie* eligible :—

(1) Upkeep of motor-car, motor-bicycle or cycle necessarily used in the course of ministerial duties. If no such conveyance is used, bus, tram and train fares or other transport costs are allowed.

Where a minister uses his own motor-car, &c., the claim should include appropriate allowance for depreciation, and, where a rent is paid for garaging the vehicle, such rent, or part thereof, is a legitimate claim.

(2) Expenses incurred and not refunded in attending meetings of Church Courts and Committees where it is the minister's duty to attend.

(3) Cost of stationery, stamps, and telephone incurred in the course of ministerial duties, less any refund.

(4) Heating, cleaning, lighting, &c., of study *except when paid by the Church*. Cost of repairing or replacing the study furnishings.

(5) The cost or part cost of a servant, to the extent that the minister is necessarily involved by the performance of his duties in expenditure on domestic help that would not otherwise be incurred.

(Where instead of employing domestic help the minister pays his wife wages commensurate with her work in cleaning his study or the part of the house used mainly or substantially for the purposes of his duty, the payments are admissible as a deduction.)

(6) Cost of repairing or replacing robes.

(7) Pulpit Supply. The amount entirely borne by a minister out of his own income in providing a *locum tenens* during an illness which incapacitates him from performing his duties personally, or during vacation.

(8) The cost of Communion elements where these are borne by the minister and not refunded by the congregation.

(9) In the event of the minister himself paying the whole or part of the rates of the house which he occupies and uses as a Manse, a deduction not exceeding one-quarter of the amount paid by him may be claimed.

(10) In the event of the minister himself paying rent for the house which he occupies and uses as a Manse, a deduction not exceeding one-quarter of the rent may be claimed.

(11) Cost of reasonable entertainment of visitors on official occasions—*e.g.*, the Moderator of General Assembly, visiting ministers, members of Church organisations, &c.

(12) Cost of secretarial assistance necessarily incurred in the performance of duties (including the cost of repair or replacement of typewriters, filing cabinets, &c.).

(If the minister finds it necessary to employ assistance in the performance of his own duties and pays his wife a reasonable amount for such assistance, a deduction may be admitted provided the wages are, in fact, paid and are commensurate with the duties performed. No deduction can be allowed in respect of work done by the minister's wife as an active member of his Church—*e.g.*, as the leader of a women's meeting.)

(13) If the Church provides the minister with a house from which to perform the duties of his office and he bears expenses in its maintenance, repair, insurance and management, one-quarter of those expenses may be claimed; where more than one-quarter of such expenses are wholly, exclusively and necessarily incurred in the performance of the minister's duties, then that higher proportion may be claimed.

II. Manses—Expenses of Heating, Lighting, and Cleaning the Manse and maintaining the Manse Garden.

If the Church or the Congregation meets, or reimburses the minister for, any part of the cost of the provision of living accommodation for the minister,[1] in premises provided for him by the Church from which to perform his official duties, the amount so paid or reimbursed does not form part of the minister's taxable income. Where, therefore, a minister occupies a Manse provided by the Church or Congregation, and the Church or Congregation meets the whole or part of the expenses of heating, lighting and cleaning the Manse and maintaining the Manse garden, or reimburses the minister in respect of these expenses or reimbursement should not be included in his return of income for income tax purposes as emoluments of his office.

If such an arrangement is made on behalf of a Congregation, the Kirk Session, Congregational Board or other body concerned will in each case need to pass a resolution undertaking as from that date to meet, or reimburse the minister for, some or all of the expenses referred to. P.A.Y.E. should not thereafter be applied to such payments or reimbursements. Repayment of tax deducted from any sums paid as stipend and later claimed to be reimbursements cannot be made. Any

[1] This applies also to ordained assistant ministers.

payment to which P.A.Y.E. has been applied is, *prima facie*, a payment of stipend, and is not intended to be a payment in respect of such expenses.

Ministers' Stipends are now paid wholly by or through the Maintenance of the Ministry Committee. The practice is that a basic stipend is paid monthly to the minister by the Committee. The total of the monthly payments in each year is less than the stipend, and it has been the practice in March of the following year to remit the balance required to bring the minister's stipend for the year ending 31st December up to the agreed figure.

The Committee is prepared to reimburse *after the end of the year* reasonable sums expended by such ministers in the lighting, heating, and cleaning of the Manse and servicing the Manse garden on the following terms :—

(i) that the minister sends in *receipted* accounts not later than 31st March.

(ii) that the reimbursements be limited to the amount available to the minister as balance of stipend for the previous year.

The minister's stipend for the year in question will, of course, be reduced by the amount reimbursed. If this sum is applied by the Committee in or towards meeting the expenses referred to, the stipend for the year in question will be reduced by that amount, and this is the figure which should be returned for income tax purposes. The minister may be able to claim a deduction for tax purposes in respect of any balance of expenditure not met or reimbursed (see Head I (4) above).

If a minister wishes the Committee to undertake this arrangement for him, he should notify the Committee *as soon as possible*. If he wishes, he may intimate that he is prepared to accept a smaller monthly remittance of stipend so as to leave a larger sum available at the end of the year, out of which the expenses referred to can be reimbursed. In such a case he should state by what amount he is prepared to have the monthly sum reduced.

In all cases the Committee will be prepared to advise if requested.

It is specially pointed out that if, owing to the amount of his personal and other allowances, no income tax is payable by a minister, the foregoing arrangement cannot help him ; it will put both himself and the Congregational Treasurer to unnecessary trouble if he asks that it be undertaken for him.

III. Assistant Ministers.

Assistant ministers, whether ordained or not, in making returns of income tax can claim the expenses listed under Head I above where applicable.

Where an ordained assistant minister is given rent-free occupation of a house belonging to the Church or Congregation for the purpose of performance of his duties, what is stated under Head II above will apply, with necessary adaptations, to such houses.

IV. Retirement for the sake of Union.

In the case of a minister retiring for the sake of Union where, on account of special circumstances, a lump sum payment out of the Athol Gordon Fund is made, it should be noted that such a receipt in the hands of the minister is not Income for Income Tax purposes. Accordingly, it should not be included in the minister's Income Tax Return.

APPENDIX XXXI.

BONDS OF ANNUITY.

Memorandum.

A Bond of Annuity is an obligation to pay a specified sum for a period of more than six years. Normally, the obligation endures for seven years, but it can be made terminable on the death of the Contributor. General.

To avoid any additional cost to himself the Contributor must have income taxed at the basic rate, at least equivalent to the gross amount of the annual contribution.

A Certificate of Deduction of Tax (Income Tax Form RI85 (AP)), signed by the Contributor, is required in respect of each payment made under the Bond.

Bonds may be granted in favour of The Church of Scotland, or the local congregation, as desired.

Bonds may be granted in either of two ways as illustrated by the following examples which are based on Income Tax at 30 per cent :—

1. *After deduction of Tax*—

The Contributor provides by the Deed for an annual contribution of such sum as, after deduction of tax, will yield, say, £10. This means that a cash payment is made by the Contributor of	£10·00
Tax would be recoverable by the Church at 33 per cent on the gross amount of the contribution . .	4·93
Gross Contribution	£14·93

2. *Before deduction of Tax*—

The Contributor provides by the Deed for the payment of an annual contribution of, say, £10, before deduction of tax. This means that there is payable by the Contributor the sum of	£6·70
Tax would be recoverable by the Church at 33 per cent on the gross amount of the contribution . .	3·30
Gross Contribution	£10·00

In the first example the amount of the annual cash donation by the Contributor is fixed ; in the second, it will vary if the Basic Rate of Income Tax changes.

From the foregoing it will be realised that by contributing in this way considerable additional benefit is conferred on the Funds of the Church. It will be noted that with Income Tax at the Basic Rate of 33 per cent an additional 49p is recovered for every £1 paid in cash by the Contributor.

Contributions need not necessarily be paid in one annual instalment; they may be made under the Weekly Freewill Offering System or otherwise, by arrangement. Income Tax is recoverable only on contributions made after the date on which the Bond is signed.

Points in procedure to be carefully observed.

Particular attention should be given to the following points:—

(*a*) It is recommended that Bonds should be accepted only from persons who are liable to pay Income Tax at the basic rate on an amount at least equivalent to the gross annual amount of their contribution under the Bond.

(*b*) The *first* payment due thereunder must be *subsequent* to the date on which the Bond is signed.

(*c*) A Tax Certificate on Form R185 (AP) must be obtained from the Contributor at the time of payment of the contribution.

(*d*) A Bond of Annuity may either be signed by the donor in the presence of two witnesses who must also sign or alternatively, a Bond may be signed by the donor without witnesses provided that he adds in his own writing the words "Adopted as holograph" above his signature.

Forms.

Two forms of Deeds are normally used.

Form "C": (*a*) General.

Form "C" is suitable for Contributors who wish to help Congregational Funds. The annual contribution is paid to the local Church Treasurer. In such cases the local Church Treasurer recovers Income Tax from the Inland Revenue direct.

(*b*) How to reclaim the Tax.

H.M. Chief Inspector of Taxes, Claims Branch, Lothian House, Lothian Road, Edinburgh, will, on application, supply the necessary form of Claim R235 (Scotland). After completion, the Claim should be forwarded to the Chief Inspector of Taxes with the Income Tax Certificates and, in the first year, the Bonds of Annuity should be exhibited. The Bonds will be returned in due course and should be retained in safe custody. When the Claim has been passed by the Revenue, a cheque will be sent to the local Church Treasurer with form of Claim for use on the next occasion. The normal practice is to lodge Claims for repayment of Tax once every year, or perhaps twice yearly if the Bonds are numerous.

Form "T": (*a*) General.

Form "T" is also suitable for Contributors who wish to help Congregational Funds. This form, however, provides for the continuation of their Bonds notwithstanding the possible transference of the Contributor's membership from one congregation to another while the Bond subsists. In such cases the Bond *must* be taken in favour of The Church of Scotland but the cash contribution may be paid to the local Church Treasurer.

(*b*) Procedure relating to Tax Certificates.

When using this form of Bond the Tax Certificates require to be sent to the General Treasurer of the Church for inclusion in his quarterly Claims for repayment of Income Tax to 31st March, 30th June, 30th September, and 31st December. Income Tax Certificates are included in the Claim appropriate to the date on which the annual contribution is completed, *e.g.*, the Certificate relating to a payment due on 15th June should be in the General Treasurer's Office by 30th June.

(*c*) The Tax recovered.

The amount of Tax recovered is either credited as a congregational contribution to the Funds of the Church as instructed by the local

Church Treasurer (in which case an advice note will be sent) or the amount recovered is remitted to the local Church Treasurer under deduction of $2\frac{1}{2}$ per cent of the sum recovered to meet expenses.

It must here be emphasised that to ensure regular and speedy clearance of Claims all local Church Treasurers involved in this matter are required to procure the necessary Income Tax Certificates as and when these are due and to send them to the General Treasurer of the Church immediately thereafter or not later than the appropriate quarterly dates abovementioned. The Inland Revenue make no repayment without production of the necessary Income Tax Certificates. **(*d*) The responsibility of the Church Treasurer.**

From the information given above concerning the two types of Form "C" and "T", it will be recognised that the ultimate result in each case is the same so far as the carrying out of the intention of the Contributor is concerned.

Subject to what is stated in the foregoing Memorandum, contributors under the Weekly Freewill Offering System may grant a Bond of Annuity for the amount stated in the Promise Card. The local Church Treasurer must be in a position at the end of the year to verify that the full amount has been contributed before calling upon the contributor to sign an Income Tax Certificate. **The Weekly Freewill Offering System.**

On the expiry of a Bond the Contributor may be invited to grant a fresh Bond. To this end Congregational Treasurers will find it useful to record particulars of all Bonds in a Register. **Renewal of Bonds.**

APPENDIX XXXII

ACT ANENT THE CARE OF ECCLESIASTICAL PROPERTIES (1961, xxi.).
(Amended by Act 1969, xxvi.)

Duties of Congregations.

1. The Kirk Session, Deacons' Court, Committee of Management, Congregational Board, or other congregational authority responsible for the maintenance of the congregation's ecclesiastical properties (hereinafter referred to as the appropriate congregational authority), shall in each congregation set up a Fabric Committee and shall appoint to act thereon one or more persons with technical knowledge and experience or shall empower the said Committee to co-opt such person or persons or to obtain such assistance.

2. The Fabric Committee of each congregation shall carry out or cause to be carried out a thorough inspection of all ecclesiastical properties belonging to that congregation at some time before 1st January 1962 and thereafter at least once in each year.

3. After the passing of this Act, and before 1st January 1962, there shall be completed a Schedule in the form annexed hereto (Form A.) or in such other form as may from time to time be authorised by the General Assembly, unless a Schedule in terms of Act II. of 1955 has already been completed. In cases where a congregation has built or acquired new premises since a Schedule in terms of Act II. of 1955 was completed, a Schedule in the form annexed hereto (Form A.) shall be completed in respect of the new premises. Thereafter Form A. shall be submitted to the appropriate congregational authority and attested by the Clerk, and a copy thereof shall be lodged with the Clerk of Presbytery within one month of the date of attestation. The particulars therein shall be entered in the Property Register of the congregation referred to in Article 6 hereof.

4. In addition to the Regular inspections referred to in Article 2 above, special inspections may be carried out by the Fabric Committee of the congregation when deemed necessary or expedient by it, and shall be carried out when required by the Presbytery and on the occurrence of a vacancy in the charge.

5. Once in each five-year period, a report shall be prepared in the form of the Schedule annexed hereto (Form B.), or in such other form as may from time to time be authorised by the General Assembly. Form B. shall be submitted and attested as above by the Clerk of the appropriate congregational authority, and a copy thereof shall be lodged within one month of attestation with the Clerk of Presbytery. The particulars therein shall be entered in the Property Register of the congregation.

6. The appropriate congregational authority of each congregation shall keep a register of all the ecclesiastical properties attached to the congregation (referred to in this Act as "The Property Register") and shall record in it the particulars (*a*) of each Schedule lodged with the Clerk of Presbytery in terms of this Act; (*b*) of all recommendations and instructions of the Presbytery in respect of its properties; (*c*) of any alterations, repairs, or reconstructions effected in pursuance of such recommendations or instructions, or otherwise; and (*d*) of the dates and results of all inspections of properties carried out in terms of Articles 2 and 5 above.

7. The Clerk of the appropriate congregational authority shall enter in the Property Register the names and designations of the persons or bodies (*e.g.*, the General Trustees) in whose name the title to each heritable property attached to the congregation is registered and the place where the title-deeds are kept.

8. The Property Register shall be submitted and attested as above annually by the Clerk of the appropriate congregational authority, and shall thereafter be submitted to the Presbytery for inspection by the Fabric Committee of the Presbytery.

9. The period beginning 1st January 1967 shall continue until 30th June 1972, and thereafter each quinquennium shall commence on 1st July.

Duties of Presbyteries.

9. Each Presbytery shall set up a Fabric Committee to which it shall appoint one or more persons with technical knowledge and experience and shall empower the said Fabric Committee to co-opt such person or persons, or to obtain such assistance as it may deem necessary.

10. The Fabric Committee of the Presbytery shall have, *inter alia*, the duty of considering all Schedules lodged by appropriate congregational authorities within the bounds in pursuance of this Act and of reporting thereon to the Presbytery.

11. At least once within each five-year period the Fabric Committee of the Presbytery shall inspect on its own behalf and by whatever agency it deems wise the ecclesiastical properties of each congregation within the bounds and shall report thereon to the Presbytery. Reasonable notice of such intended inspection shall be given to the Clerk of the appropriate congregational authority and to the Minister of the charge, and it shall be their duty to afford it all reasonable facilities for the carrying out of such inspection.

12. Not less than fourteen days before a report is to be submitted to the Presbytery concerning the ecclesiastical properties of any congregation, a copy of the report shall be sent to the Clerk of the appropriate congregational authority, and the said appropriate congregational authority shall have the right, if so advised, to be represented by Commissioners at that meeting of Presbytery.

13. When the Presbytery considers reports in terms of the foregoing Articles 10 and 11, Commissioners from the appropriate congregational authority or other persons having an interest shall have the right to be heard thereon. The Presbytery shall thereupon record in a separate Property Record Book its findings thereanent together with such

recommendations or instructions as it may deem proper. A copy of the relevant entry shall be sent to the Clerk of the appropriate congregational authority.

General.

14. Within three months of receiving from the Presbytery, in terms of Article 13 above, a report and recommendations requiring action upon the part of the appropriate congregational authority, the Clerk of the appropriate congregational authority shall lodge with the Clerk of Presbytery a report setting forth how far such recommendations and instructions have received effect, and this shall be duly reported to the Presbytery.

15. In the event of any party having an interest being dissatisfied with the recommendations or instructions of the Presbytery made in terms of Article 13 above, they shall have the right to appeal to the Synod of the bounds, whose decision shall be final. Unless such an appeal is taken, it shall be the duty of the appropriate congregational authority to ensure that the instructions of the Presbytery are implemented without delay. Appeal shall include Dissent and Complaint.

16. Each Presbytery shall annually report to the Synod of the bounds its diligence under this Act.

17. Each Synod shall annually prepare and transmit to the General Assembly through the General Administration Committee a report upon the diligence of each Presbytery within its bounds in carrying out the provisions of this Act.

18. The General Administration Committee shall annually appoint a Sub-Committee, with power to co-opt representatives from the Church of Scotland General Trustees, and from the Church and Manse Buildings Sectional Committee of the Home Board, to consider the reports from Synods and to report. The General Administration Committee shall report to the General Assembly.

19. This Act shall not apply to congregations and Presbyteries outwith the United Kingdom, but these Presbyteries shall take such steps as they deem wise in their own circumstances for the inspection and proper maintenance of all properties belonging to the Church within their bounds.

20. The period beginning 1st January 1967 shall continue until 30th June 1972, and thereafter each quinquennium shall commence on 1st July.

APPENDIX XXXIII.

LIST OF PRINCIPAL CLERKS; SUB- OR DEPUTE-CLERKS; PROCURATORS; AGENTS.

CHURCH OF SCOTLAND.

PRINCIPAL CLERKS OF THE GENERAL ASSEMBLY.

Circa 1572. Mr John Gray, succeeded by
,, 1589. Mr James Ritchie, succeeded by
Mr Thomas Nicolson, succeeded by
Mr Sandilands.
1638–1639. Mr Archibald Johnston of Warriston. (Also Advocate for the Church.)
1690–1694. Mr John Spalding.
1694–1695. Mr Robert Park, Advocate.
1695–1701. Mr John Bannatyne, Minister at Lanark.
1701–1703. Mr David Dundas, Advocate.
1703–1731. Mr John Dundas of Philipstoun, Advocate. (Also Procurator from 1706.)
1731–1746. Mr Wm. Grant, Advocate—afterwards Lord Prestongrange (Also Procurator.)
1746–1778. Dr George Wishart, Minister at Tron, Edinburgh.
1778–1785. Dr George Wishart and Dr John Drysdale (Assistant and Successor), Minister at Tron, Edinburgh.
1785–1788. Dr John Drysdale.
1789–1807. Mr Andrew Dalzell, Professor of Greek, University of Edinburgh.
1807–1827. Dr Andrew Duncan, Minister at Ratho.
1828–1859. Dr John Lee, Principal of University of Edinburgh.
1859–1861. Dr Alex. Lockhart Simpson, Minister at Kirknewton.
1862–1874. Dr John Cook, Minister of First Charge, Haddington.
1875–1886. Dr John Tulloch, Principal of St Mary's College, St Andrews.
1886–1893. Dr Wm. Milligan, Professor of Biblical Criticism, University of Aberdeen.
1894–1907. Dr Robert Herbert Story, Principal of University of Glasgow.
1907–1911. Dr Norman Macleod, Minister at Inverness (First Charge).
1912–1926. Dr David Paul, Minister at Grange, Edinburgh.
1926–1927. Dr James Alexander M'Clymont.
1928–1929. Dr James Taylor Cox, Minister at Dyce.

AFTER UNION OF THE CHURCHES.

Senior Clerks.

1929–1939. Dr James Taylor Cox and
1929–1939. Dr James Harvey, *Joint Clerks.*

Principal Clerks.

1939–1946. Dr James Taylor Cox.
1946–1948. Dr Louis Carrick Phillips.
1949–1953. Dr Thomas Caldwell.
1953–1955. Dr William MacNicol.
1955–1972. Dr James Boyd Longmuir.
1972. Rev. Donald Farquhar Macleod Macdonald.
1968–1969 (*pro tem.*). Rev. Charles Adamson Smith.

SUB- OR DEPUTE-CLERKS OF THE GENERAL ASSEMBLY.

After 1589. Mr Robert Winrame.
1638. Mr Alex. Blair.
1701–1738. Mr Nicol Spence.
1738–1743. Mr Nicol Spence and Mr Robert M'Intosh.
1743–1753. Mr Robert M'Intosh and Mr John Baillie.
1753–1754. Mr John Baillie and Mr Jas. Edmonston.
1754–1781. Mr Jas. Edmonston.
1781–1802. Dr Wm. Gloag, Minister at West St Giles, Edinburgh.
1802–1808. Dr David Ritchie, Minister at St Andrew's (Second Charge), Edinburgh; afterwards Professor of Logic in the University of Edinburgh.
1808–1826. Dr Thos. M'Knight, Minister at Old Kirk, Edinburgh.
1826–1828. Dr Thos. M'Knight and Dr John Lee, Principal of University of Edinburgh.
1828–1836. Dr Thos. M'Knight and Dr Alex. Lockhart Simpson, Minister at Kirknewton.
1836–1859. Dr Alex. Lockhart Simpson.
1859–1862. Dr John Cook, Minister at Haddington.
1862–1875. Dr John Tulloch, Principal of St Mary's College, St Andrews.
1875–1886. Dr William Milligan, Professor of Divinity and Biblical Criticism, University of Aberdeen.
1886–1894. Dr Robert Herbert Story, Principal of University of Glasgow.
1894–1907. Dr Norman Macleod, Minister at Inverness (First Charge).
1907–1912. Dr John Gillespie, Minister at Mouswald.
1912–1913. Dr Wm. Simpson, Minister at Bonhill.
1914–1926. Dr James Alexander M'Clymont.
1926. Dr James Nicoll Ogilvie.
1927–1928. Dr James Taylor Cox, Minister at Dyce.
1928–1929. Mr Duncan Cameron, Minister at Kilsyth.

AFTER UNION OF THE CHURCHES.

Junior Clerk.

1929–1938. Dr James Gordon Sutherland.

Depute Clerks.

1939–1946. Dr Louis Carrick Phillips.
1946–1949. Dr Thomas Caldwell.
1949–1953. Dr William MacNicol.
1953–1955. Rev. James Boyd Longmuir.
1955–1971. Rev. Donald Farquhar Macleod Macdonald.
1971– Rev. Alexander Gordon McGillivray.

ADVOCATES AND PROCURATORS FOR THE CHURCH.

1638. Mr Archibald Johnston of Warriston. (Also Clerk.)
1706–1731. Mr John Dundas. (Also Clerk.)
1731–1745. Mr William Grant (afterwards Lord Prestongrange). Also Clerk.)
1746–1778. Mr David Dalrymple.
1778–1806. Mr William Robertson (afterwards Lord Robertson).
1806–1831. Sir John Connell.
1831–1856. Mr Robert Bell.
1856–1869. Mr Alexander Shank Cook.
1869–1880. Mr Robert Lee (afterwards Lord Lee).
1880–1886. Mr William Mackintosh (afterwards Lord Kyllachy).
1886–1891. Sir Charles Pearson (afterwards Lord Pearson).
1891–1906. Sir John Cheyne.
1907–1918. Sir C. N. Johnston (afterwards Lord Sands).
1918–1922. Hon. William Watson (afterwards Lord Thankerton).
1923–1929. Sir William Chree.

After Union of the Churches.

Procurators.

1929–1936. Sir William Chree.
1936–1937. Sir Archibald Campbell Black.
1938–1948. James Frederick Strachan (afterwards Lord Strachan).
1949–1957. Sir James Randall Philip.
1957–1968. Thomas Pringle McDonald.
1969–1972. William Robertson Grieve (afterwards Lord Grieve).
1973– Charles Kemp Davidson.

AGENTS FOR THE CHURCH.

1690–1706. Mr John Blair.
1706–1722. Mr John Blair and Mr Nicol Spence, *Joint Agents.*
1722–1738. Mr Nicol Spence.
1738–1743. Mr Nicol Spence and Mr Robert M'Intosh, *Joint Agents.*
1743–1753. Mr Robert M'Intosh and Mr John Baillie, W.S., *Joint Agents.*
1753–1754. Mr John Baillie and Mr James Edmonston, *Joint Agents.*
1754–1781. Mr James Edmonston.
1781–1795. Mr George Cairncross.
1795–1809. Mr William Murray.
1809–1831. Mr William Murray and Mr John Murray.
1831–1855. Mr William Young, W.S.
1855–1868. Mr John Beatson Bell, W.S.
1868–1905. Sir William J. Menzies, W.S.
1906–1925. Mr Alan Lockhart Menzies, W.S.
1926–1929. Mr John Alexander Stevenson Millar, W.S.

After Union of the Churches.

Agents.

1929–1938. Mr John Alexander Stevenson Millar, W.S.
1929–1949. Mr Edward John M'Candlish, W.S.; and
1929–1955. Mr Arthur Henry M'Lean, W.S., *Joint Agents.*
1951–1954. Mr David Blyth Bogle, W.S., *Joint Agent.*
1955–1971. Mr David Blyth Bogle, W.S.

Note.—It may be noted: (1) that Mr Archibald Johnston of Warriston, Mr John Dundas, and Mr William Grant held the offices both of Clerk of Assembly and Procurator for the Church; (2) that the office of Principal Clerk was, with one exception, held by a layman up to 1746, and again from 1789 to 1807, and similarly that of Sub-Clerk up to 1781.

FREE CHURCH OF SCOTLAND.

PRINCIPAL CLERKS OF ASSEMBLY.

1843–1854. Dr Thomas Pitcairn, Minister at Cockpen.
1843–1867. Dr Patrick Clason, Minister at Edinburgh.
1855–1883. Sir Henry Wellwood Moncrieff, Bart., D.D., Minister at Edinburgh.
1868–1888. Dr William Wilson, Minister at Dundee.
1884–1900. Dr Andrew Melville, Minister at Glasgow.
1888–1900. Dr Archibald Henderson, Minister at Crieff.

DEPUTE-CLERKS.

1843–1863. Mr James Crawford, W.S.
1864–1876. Mr George Meldrum, C.A.
1877–1900. Sir Robert Russell Simpson, W.S.

LEGAL ADVISERS.

1843–1870. Mr Alex. C. S. Murray Dunlop, LL.D., Advocate.
1870. Mr Andrew Jamieson, Advocate, Assistant.
1871–1874. Mr Thomas Cleghorn, Advocate.
1875–1883. Mr Neil C. Campbell, Advocate.
1883–1900. Mr Charles J. Guthrie, Advocate.

LAW AGENTS.

1843–1863. Mr James Crawford, W.S.
1864–1872. Mr Patrick Dalmahoy, W.S.
1873–1900. Mr John Cowan, W.S.

UNITED PRESBYTERIAN CHURCH.

CLERKS OF SYNOD.

1847–1861. Mr David Ronald, Minister at Saltcoats.
1847–1861. Dr David Crawford, Minister at Portobello.
1847–1874. Mr David Thomas, Minister at Mauchline.
1861–1878. Mr William Beckett, Minister at Rutherglen.
1874–1883. Mr William Wood, Minister at Campsie.
1879–1900. Dr Thomas Kennedy, Minister at Edinburgh.
1884–1900. Dr William Blair, Minister at Dunblane.

LEGAL ADVISERS.

1847–1864. Mr Adam G. Ellis, W.S.
1847–1874. Mr James Peddie, W.S.
1847–1883. Mr James Mitchell, LL.D.
1853–1890. Mr James Burns Kidston.
1865–1868. Mr Robert Ellis, W.S.
1883–1900. Mr John Baird Smith.
1883–1900. Mr John Colin Mitchell.
1886–1900. Mr Wm. Robson, S.S.C.
1886–1900. Mr J. Knox Crawford, S.S.C.
1886–1900. Mr John Smart, S.S.C.
1892–1900. Mr Thos. Stark Brown.

UNITED FREE CHURCH OF SCOTLAND.

CLERKS OF ASSEMBLY.

1900–1902. Dr Thomas Kennedy, Minister at Edinburgh.
1900–1907. Dr William Blair, Minister at Dunblane.
1900–1906. Dr Andrew Melville, Minister at Glasgow.
1900–1916. Dr Archibald Henderson, Minister at Crieff.
1907–1916. Dr Charles Jerdan, Minister at Greenock.
1916–1929. Dr James Harvey, Minister at Edinburgh.
1920–1929. Dr James Gordon Sutherland, Minister at Galston.

DEPUTE-CLERK.

1900–1923. Sir Robert Russell Simpson, W.S.

LEGAL ADVISER.

1900–1902. Sheriff Charles J. Guthrie, K.C. (afterwards Lord Guthrie).

LAW AGENTS.

1900–1927. Mr John Cowan, W.S.
1900–1913. Mr William Robson, S.S.C.
1914–1929. Mr Arthur H. M'Lean, W.S.
1927–1929. Mr Edward J. M'Candlish, W.S.

APPENDIX XXXIV.

NOTE ON DESIGNATIONS AND PRECEDENCE OF MODERATORS AND EX-MODERATORS OF THE GENERAL ASSEMBLY.

In 1895 Her Majesty Queen Victoria issued an order that, in the *English* Table of Precedence, the Moderator of the General Assembly of the Church of Scotland should take his place after the Bishops of the Church of England and before Barons. Consequential on this the title " Right Reverend " seems to have been informally adopted.

In 1904, on the recommendation of the Secretary for Scotland, His Majesty King Edward VII. granted to the Moderator of the General Assembly precedence, *in Scotland* and during his term of office, next after the Lord Chancellor of Great Britain.

In 1910 the Scottish Office decided that the designations " Right Reverend " for Moderators and " Very Reverend " for ex-Moderators should be officially recognised.

It may be noted that the General Assembly has never given any decision regarding the use of these designations. Although the Moderator continues to be styled " The Right Reverend the Moderator of the General Assembly " till a successor is appointed, strictly speaking he ceases to be Moderator of the General Assembly when the Assembly closes and ceases to exist.

It may be stated here that the Moderator may, on certain official occasions, be accompanied by the Clerks of Assembly, Procurator, and Law Agent in the order named. Ex-Moderators have no official status, but they usually occupy seats on the platform at the opening and closing diets of the Assembly, and an ex-Moderator occupies the Chair of the Assembly in the temporary absence of the Moderator, although it may be competently occupied by any ministerial member.

In reference to the appointment of clergymen to the higher classes of Orders, King Edward VII. decided to confer on them the Insignia of the Order, without the accolade. His Majesty's idea seems to have been that the emblems belonging to a Knight were a sword, spurs, and belt, which were unsuitable for a man in Holy Orders. In one case, at least, the accolade was conferred before it was discovered that the recipient was a clergyman. A clergyman recipient of any Knighthood is not entitled to the title " Sir " nor his wife to that of " Lady."

(The Editor is largely indebted to Sir Francis J. Grant, K.C.V.O., LL.D., former Lord Lyon King, for the above information.)

PLACE OF CLERGY.

On such important public occasions as that of the Proclamation of the Accession to the Throne of a King or Queen, although there is no scale of precedence of public bodies the Lord Lyon King has expressed the opinion that the proper place should be after the Municipal Authorities and the Sheriff and his officials, and before such bodies as Harbour Commissioners, Naval and Military representatives, &c. This position is accorded to them by the City of Edinburgh on the occasion of the Proclamation of a new Monarch.

APPENDIX XXXV.

STYLES AND FORMS.

1. Questions authorised for First Communicants and for the Baptismal and Marriage Services (1935, xiii, and Reports 1968, pp. 180-183).

A.—Admission to Holy Communion.

1. Do you confess your faith in God as your Heavenly Father, in Jesus Christ as your Saviour and Lord, and in the Holy Spirit as your Sanctifier? **Questions to Applicants for Admission.**

2. Do you promise, in dependence on Divine Grace, to serve the Lord and to walk in His ways all the days of your life?

3. Do you promise to make diligent use of the means of grace, to share dutifully in the worship and service of the Church, and to give of your substance, as the Lord may prosper you, for the advancement of His Kingdom throughout the World?

Or:

1. Do you receive the doctrine of the Christian faith, whereof we make confession, saying: (Apostles' Creed)?

2. Do you promise, in dependance on Divine grace, to serve the Lord and to walk in His ways all the days of your life?

3. Do you promise to make diligent use of the means of grace, to share dutifully in the worship and service of the Church, and to give of your substance, as the Lord may prosper you, for the advancement of His kingdom throughout the world?

Or:

1. Do you believe in one God, Father, Son, and Holy Spirit; and do you confess Jesus Christ as your Saviour and Lord?

2. Do you promise to join regularly with your fellow Christians in worship on the Lord's Day?

3. Do you promise to be faithful in reading the Bible, and in prayer?

4. Do you promise to give a fitting proportion of your time, talents, and money for the Church's work in the World?

5. Do you promise, depending on the grace of God, to confess Christ before men, to serve Him in your daily work, and to walk in His ways all the days of your life?

B.—Baptism of Infants.

1. In presenting this child for Baptism, do you confess your faith in God the Father as your Heavenly Father, in Jesus Christ as your Saviour and Lord, and in the Holy Spirit as your Sanctifier?

2. Do you promise, in dependence on Divine Grace, to teach *him* the truths and duties of the Christian faith; and by prayer, precept, and example to bring *him* up in the nurture and admonition of the Lord, and in the ways of the Church of God?

Or:

1. In presenting this child for Baptism, do you receive the doctrine of the Christian Faith whereof we make confession saying: (Apostles' Creed).

2. Do you promise, in dependance on Divine grace, to teach *him* the truths, and duties of the Christian Faith; and by prayer, precept and example, to bring *him* up in the nurture and admonition of the Lord, and in the ways of the Church of God.

Or:

1. Do you present *this child* to be baptized, earnestly desiring that *he* may be grafted into Christ as a member of His Body the Church?

2. Do you believe in one God, Father, Son, and Holy Spirit; and do you confess Jesus Christ as your Saviour and Lord?

3. Do you promise, depending on the grace of God, to teach *this child* the truths and duties of the Christian Faith; and by prayer and example to bring *him* up in the life and worship of the Church?

C.—Baptism of Adults.

1. Do you confess your faith in God as your Heavenly Father, in Jesus Christ as your Saviour and Lord, and in the Holy Spirit as your Sanctifier?

2. Do you repent of your sins with a humble and contrite heart, and put your trust in the mercy of God which is in Christ Jesus?

3. Do you promise to make diligent use of the means of grace, and to be a faithful member of the Church of God?

Alternatively:

1. Do you receive the doctrine of the Christian faith, whereof we make confession, saying: (Apostles' Creed).

2. Do you repent of your sins with a humble and contrite heart, and put your trust in the mercy of God which is in Christ Jesus?

3. Do you promise to make diligent use of the means of grace, and to be a faithful member of the Church of God?

Note.—A further set of questions has been approved for use (Reports 1969, p. 217) and can be found in the leaflet—Holy Baptism and Confirmation and Admission to the Lord's Supper—issued by the Committee on Public Worship and Aids to Devotion.

D.—Marriage.

(*Minister*) Do you, N., take this woman, N., to be your wedded wife; and do you, in the presence of God and before this congregation (or, these witnesses), promise and covenant to be to her a loving, faithful, and dutiful husband, until God shall separate you by death?

Do you, N., take this man, N., to be your wedded husband; and do you, in the presence of God and before this congregation (or, these witnesses), promise and covenant to be to him a loving, faithful, and dutiful wife, until God shall separate you by death?

Or, alternatively:

(*Man*) I, N., do take thee, N., to be my wedded wife; and do, in the presence of God and before this congregation (or, these witnesses), promise and covenant to be a loving, faithful, and dutiful husband unto thee, until God shall separate us by death.

(*Woman*) I, N., do take thee, N., to be my wedded husband; and do, in the presence of God and before this congregation (or, these witnesses), promise and covenant to be a loving, faithful, and dutiful wife unto thee, until God shall separate us by death.

E.—After an Irregular or Civil Marriage.

Do you acknowledge this woman to be your wedded wife, and do you promise before God to be to her a loving and faithful husband, till death do you part?

Do you acknowledge this man to be your wedded husband, and do you promise before God to be to him a loving and faithful wife, till death do you part?

2. Certificate of Transference.

THE CHURCH OF SCOTLAND.

CERTIFICATE OF TRANSFERENCE.

....19..

It is hereby certified that [1]..
who leaves the congregation of..
and is now resident at..
at this date is in full Communion with the Church of Scotland.

......................*Minister.*

......................*Session Clerk.*[2]

[1] Give in block letters full Christian name and surname. [2] Give address.

This Certificate should be handed as soon as possible to the Minister or Session Clerk of the congregation with which the holder desires to be connected. The holder should write the Names of the Family, if any, on the other side.

Note.—The Kirk Session may authorise *either* the Minister *or* Session Clerk to sign the Certificate of Transference, otherwise it must be signed by both (1961, 1).

THE CHURCH OF SCOTLAND.

RECEIPT OF CERTIFICATE.

....

....19..

It is hereby intimated that [1]..
connected ....self on the above date with the congregation of...

......................*Minister or Session Clerk.*

[1] In block letters.

This Receipt should be issued along with the Certificate, and returned at once by the Minister or Session Clerk receiving the Certificate.

THE CHURCH OF SCOTLAND.

NOTICE OF REMOVAL.

....19..

It is hereby intimated that [1]..

a member of the congregation of..................................
has gone to [2]..
with * Certificate.

........................Minister or Session Clerk.

[1] In block letters. [2] Give residence.

This Notice should be sent *immediately on removal* to the Minister of the congregation with which the member is to be connected, or to the Presbyterial Correspondent (whose name will be found in the Year-Book).

3. Attestation of Communion Roll.

K.S. attestation.

Written at the end of the Roll (or of the Roll Book), the attestation may be—

[*Place and Date.*] The foregoing Roll, having been revised and corrected by the Kirk Session as now containing names, is hereby attested by its appointment and in its presence.

..........*Moderator* or *Clerk*.

4. Commission to Elder to sit in Presbytery and Synod.

At C , the day of 19 , which day and place the Kirk Session of met, and was constituted with prayer by the Rev. A. B., Moderator.

Inter alia,—

The Session appointed a *bona fide* acting Elder of the congregation, to represent it in the Presbytery of , and in the Synod of , during the year ending 30th June 19 .

Extracted from the Records of the Kirk Session by

E. F., *Session Clerk*.

N.B.—The Elder's Address is—

5. (*a*)—Commission to the General Assembly.

Commission to General Assembly.

Ministers.

** Give Christian names or initials.*

Elders.

Give names and Postal Addresses in full.

At the day of One thousand nine hundred and years.—The which day the Presbytery of being convened betwixt the hours of eleven o'clock in the forenoon and eight o'clock in the evening, in order to elect their Representatives to the ensuing General Assembly, pursuant to a resolution entered on their minutes on the day of One thousand nine hundred and did, and hereby do, nominate and appoint * Minister at and Minister at and Minister at with Ruling Elders, their Commissioners to the next General Assembly of the Church of Scotland, indicted to meet at Edinburgh, the day of May next to come, or when and where it shall happen to sit, willing them to repair thereto, and to attend all the diets of the same, and there to consult, vote, and determine in all matters that come before them to the glory of God and the good of His Church, according to the Word of God, the Confession of Faith, and agreeable to the

* State whether with or without Certificate.

constitution of this Church, as they will be answerable; and that they report their diligence therein at their return therefrom. And the said Presbytery do hereby testify and declare, That all the Ministers and Elders above named have signed the Formula.[1]

Attested by

............*Moderator*.
............*Clerk*.

(*b*)—After-Election of a Minister.

At the day of One thousand nine hundred and years.—The which day the Presbytery of being convened betwixt the hours of eleven o'clock in the forenoon and eight o'clock in the evening, and [2]

did, and hereby do, nominate and appoint in place,

their Commissioner to the next General Assembly of the Church of Scotland; and do hereby testify and declare, that signed the Formula; which the Presbytery hereby attest upon proper information.

Attested by

..........*Moderator*.
..........*Clerk*.

(*c*)—After-Election of an Elder.

At the day of One thousand nine hundred and years.—The which day the Presbytery of being convened betwixt the hours of eleven o'clock in the forenoon and eight o'clock in the evening, and [2]

did, and hereby do, nominate and appoint in place,

their Commissioner to the next General Assembly of the Church of Scotland; and do hereby testify and declare, that he is in all respects qualified in the same manner as the Commissioner in whose room he is chosen; which the Presbytery hereby attest upon proper information.

Attested by

..........*Moderator*.
..........*Clerk*.

[1] The clause in the certificate of each representative to the General Assembly "that he has signed the *formula*" shall, in the case of ministers and elders ordained previous to the Union, be understood to mean that he has assented to the formula in use in that Church by which he was ordained.

[2] Here narrate the occasion of the New Election.

(*d*)—CERTIFICATE OF *BONA FIDE* ELDERSHIP.

The Elder hereby certified has been returned to the General Assembly by the Presbytery of

Elder's Certificate.

KIRK SESSION OF

IT is hereby certified this day of *One thousand nine hundred and* *years*, that [1] Ruling Elder, and Member of said Session, is a *bona fide* Acting Elder of [2] Congregation, and that he has signed the Formula.

..........*Moderator.*
..........*Clerk.*

N.B.—This certificate must be signed by the Moderator and Clerk of Kirk Session, but in the absence of *one* of these it may be signed by the other and two elders.

Note.—It is desirable that the Printed Forms of Commissions and of Certificates, which may be obtained from the Clerks of General Assembly, should be always used. Ministers must be designated by the names of their particular charges, and this must be attended to in an after-election, as well as in the original one.

7. CERTIFICATE OF A RULING ELDER AS A MEMBER OF PRESBYTERY AND SYNOD BY A SESSION OF WHICH HE IS NOT A MEMBER, OR ELECTED BY THE PRESBYTERY ITSELF.

This certificate should be in the same form as the *Certificate of a Ruling Elder returned as Commissioner to the General Assembly.*

8. FORM OF COMMISSION FOR CORRESPONDING MEMBERS TO A PROVINCIAL SYNOD.

Commission, cor. members.

.—Which day and place the Synod of , being met and constituted, did and hereby do appoint the Rev. , minister at , and , Ruling Elder, their commissioners to correspond with the reverend Synod of at its ensuing meeting; willing them to repair in due time thereto, attend the several diets thereof, and consult, vote, and determine in all matters that shall come before the said Synod, to the glory of God and for the good of the Church, according to the Word of God, the Confession of Faith, and Acts and constitution of this Church; and that at next meeting of this Synod they report or certify that they have fulfilled this appointment.

Extracted from the records of, &c.,

By , *Synod Clerk.*

9. EXTRACT OF LICENCE.

..........................19..

Extract of Licence.

It is hereby certified, in Name and by Authority of the Presbytery of that Mr , duly certified

[1] Give full name and postal address [2] Give name of the congregation.

as having passed the courses required by the General Assembly of this Church, appeared to be taken on Trials for Licence by this Presbytery; that the Presbytery, having found him duly qualified, did take him upon Public Probationary Trials, and, having declared its satisfaction with the same, agreed that he be Licensed to preach the Gospel.

Whereupon, on the day of 19 , after the usual Questions were put, to which explicit and satisfactory answers were given, and after he had signed the Formula as required by the General Assembly, the said Mr was Licensed to preach the Gospel of the Lord Jesus Christ, and to exercise his gifts as a Probationer for the Holy Ministry; and this Certificate of Licence was granted to him.

.....................*Moderator.*

.....................*Presbytery Clerk.*

10. Presbyterial Certificates.

(*a*) For Probationers.

[*Place and date.*] By order of the Presbytery of of date it is hereby certified that Mr is a probationer of this Church, licensed by [*state Presbytery*], and that his conduct is in every respect becoming his profession.

..........*Presbytery Clerk.*

When an application is received from a person who has received an appointment, and no meeting of Presbytery will occur within seven days, a certificate, signed by the Moderator and Clerk and two, or, in the absence of either official, two other members (1895, viii.), is given in the following or similar form:—

The Clerk of the Presbytery of , having on received an application for a Presbyterial Certificate from Mr in consequence of his appointment to the Church and Parish of , and there being no meeting of Presbytery within seven days thereafter, we hereby certify that [*continue as above*].

(*b*) For Ministers.

[*Place and date.*] The Presbytery of , having this day [*or*, on] accepted Mr 's demission of his charge at , instructed me to give this certificate that he retains his full status as a minister of the Church of Scotland [and that his conduct is in every respect becoming his profession].

..........*Presbytery Clerk.*

(*c*) For Deaconesses.

(See 1964, Reg. 6.).

[*Place and Date.*] By order of the Presbytery of of date it is hereby certified that Miss is a Deaconess of this Church, commissioned by the Presbytery of , and that her conduct is in every respect becoming her profession.

..........*Presbytery Clerk.*

11. Attestation of Rolls and Records by Presbytery or Synod.

Attested in common form.
[*Place and date.*] ....*Presbytery* [*or Synod*] *Clerk.*

Note.—Other forms will be found in Chap. V., pp. 92-94.

12. Brief Narrative to be used at the Induction of a Minister.

This church and parish having become vacant by [*Here narrate cause of vacancy*—i.e., *translation, demission, death of minister*], and the financial arrangements in the vacancy having been approved by the Presbytery and by the General Assembly's Committee on the Maintenance of the Ministry, the congregation elected and appointed Mr to be the minister thereof. The said appointment, with relative papers, having been sustained by the Presbytery [and Mr having been loosed from his present charge by the Presbytery of], the Presbytery appointed this day for his ordination and induction, whereof due notice was given. And no one having appeared to object to the life or doctrine of Mr , the Presbytery now proceed to [ordain him to the holy ministry and] admit him to be minister of this church and parish.

Colleague and successor. In the case of a colleague and successor the first sentence of the "narrative" may be—

The Presbytery having, on the application of Mr , minister of this parish, and after due consideration of all the circumstances, resolved that a colleague and successor to him ought to be appointed, the congregation elected and appointed Mr to be his colleague and successor.

13. Brief Narrative for Admission of Elders.

The Kirk Session, having considered it desirable that the number of the elders of the parish should be increased and having agreed to the election of [*So-and-so,* already ordained an elder of the Church, appointed his admission to take place this day; also of] *So-and-so,* appointed their ordination to take place this day; whereof intimation was duly given, and no objections have been offered. I therefore now proceed to that duty.

Note.—Other forms prescribed by Acts ix. and x., 1932, in connection with the election and admission of ministers and elders will be found in this Appendix, Sections VI. and VII., pp. 813-823.

14. Forms of Petitions in which Kirk Sessions are specially interested.

I. Petition to the Kirk Session with reference to Congregational Matters.

To the Kirk Session of .

Petition to Kirk Session.

The humble Petition of the undersigned showeth,—

That, &c., &c.

Your Petitioners, therefore, crave that you take such steps as you can consistently with the laws of the Church for, &c., &c.

[*Then follow signatures with designations, including Church membership, &c.*]

II. Petition by the Kirk Session or others to the Presbytery with reference to the conduct of the Minister.

To the Reverend the Presbytery of .

Petition by Kirk Session.

The humble Petition of the undersigned showeth,—

That we are painfully constrained by a sense of duty to represent that the Rev. , our minister, has acted in a manner recently which, in our view, calls for your notice and interposition, inasmuch as

1. The
2. &c., &c.
3. &c., &c.

It appears to us that we have no remedy, except in petitioning your Reverend Court. We therefore ask you to take the matter into your consideration, and to make such inquiry as to your wisdom may seem meet, whether by presbyterial visitation or otherwise.

[*Then follow signatures and designations, &c.*]

III. Petition to the Presbytery against arbitrary action of the Kirk Session.

To the Reverend the Presbytery of .

Petition against Kirk Session.

The humble Petition of the undersigned showeth,—

That the Kirk Session of did, and thereby deprived your Petitioners of the usual remedy by appeal. Your Petitioners, therefore, crave the interposition of your Reverend Court to rectify the injustice that has been done.

[*Then follow signatures and designations.*]

IV. Petition to the Presbytery against irregular action of the Deacons' Court or Congregational Board.

To the Reverend the Presbytery of .

Petition against action of Deacons' Court.

The humble Petition of the undersigned showeth,—

That the Deacons' Court [*or* Congregational Board] of the congregation did, by a minute of date , resolve as follows : [*Here take in.*] Your Petitioners regard this resolution as contrary to Act , Assembly , and as *ultra vires* of the Deacons' Court [*or* Congregational Board]. We therefore crave your interposition to rectify what we consider a violation of constitutional order.

[*Then follow signatures and designations.*]

15. Form of Petition to the Presbytery, Provincial Synod, and General Assembly will be found in Chapter V., p. 102.

Form of Overture to the Provincial Synod or General Assembly will also be found in Chapter V., p. 103.

A Form for Returns of Presbyteries to Overtures sent down by the General Assembly is issued in duplicate by the Clerks of Assembly to each Presbytery.

16. Citation of Congregations on Demission of Charge.

Citation. The Presbytery of , having received a letter from Mr demitting his office as minister of this parish, hereby cites the congregation of this parish to attend for their interests at a meeting of the Presbytery, to be held [*place, day and hour*], with certification that if they do not attend they shall be held as consenting to the demission of Mr .

17. Form in Trial by Libel.

(*a*) Form of Libel.

[*Name and designation* (e.g., *A. B., Minister of the Parish of C.*).] You are indicted at the instance of [*The Presbytery of D.—or if the Prosecutors are private persons, name and design them*] and the Charge against you is [*specify clearly and shortly the offence charged*—e.g., *that you were in a state of intoxication on* [*specify date and place*]. *If there be any aggravations, specify them* [e.g., *that you were admonished for drunkenness by the Presbytery of* *on* [*date*] *which is an Aggravation*].

[*List of witnesses*] :—

1.
2.

[Note.—*Numerous other examples will be found in Schedule to Act xix.* 1889, *of the Church of Scotland.*]

(*b*) Order by Presbytery to serve the Libel.

To be written on the Libel.

Service of Libel. At , and on the day of 19 , the Presbytery appoints the foregoing libel (with list of witnesses and documents), and this deliverance, to be served on the said Rev. A. B., and ordain him to compear before the Presbytery, within its usual place of meeting, at on the day of 19 , to answer to said libel: Further, the Presbytery grants warrant for citing witnesses for both parties.

J. G., *Presbytery Clerk.*

(c) Citation.

To be written on the Certified Copy of the Libel issued on the Respondent.

To the Rev. A. B.—Take notice that you will have to compear before the Presbytery of , within its usual place of meeting, at on the day of 19 , to answer to the libel, a copy of which is prefixed. Citation.

Served this day of 19 .

J. K., *Presbytery Officer.*
or, M. N., *Presbytery Clerk.*

[Note.—*The citation shall be signed by the Presbytery Officer when service is made on the respondent personally, or by leaving a copy at his residence, and by the Presbytery Clerk when made by registered letter.*]

(d) Certificate of Service.

To be written on the Libel.

(1) *When served personally, or by being left at Residence.*

A certified copy of the within libel (with list of witnesses and documents), and of the Presbytery's deliverance, dated , as also notice of compearance in terms of said deliverance, was served on the within-designed Rev. A. B., the same being delivered to him personally by me (*or*, the same being left by me within his dwelling-house [*insert address*] with a servant), on the day of 19 , in presence of L. M. [*design him*]. Certificate of Service

J. K., *Presbytery Officer.*

L. M., *Witness.*

(2) *When served by Registered Letter.*

A certified copy of the within libel (with list of witnesses and documents), and of the Presbytery's deliverance, dated , as also notice of compearance in terms of said deliverance, was served on the within-designed Rev. A. B., the same having been sent by registered letter, addressed to him at his ordinary address, as follows [*insert full address as on letter*], the post office receipt for which is here produced, on the day of 19 .

M. N., *Presbytery Clerk.*

18. Forms of Intimation for Congregational Meetings.

1. Annual Business Meeting.

(*For all congregations where such a meeting is held, except when a Model Constitution is in operation.*)

The Annual Business Meeting of this Congregation will be held in

on the day of
19 at o'clock, when statements of the congregational finances will be submitted [and auditors and office-bearers appointed for the ensuing year].

By order of the {Deacons' Court / Committee of Management / Congregational Board (U.F.C.)} *as the case may be.*

................*Clerk.*

2. Stated Annual Meeting.

(*For Congregations where a Model Constitution is in operation.*)

A meeting of the communicants on the Roll of this Church will be held in on the inst., at o'clock for the purpose of electing, if so resolved, certain of their number over eighteen years of age to act along with the minister and elders in administering the financial affairs of the Church, the number so elected not to exceed the number of elders.

At this meeting the Congregational Board will submit a statement of accounts for the preceding year [together with proposals for disposal of the surplus revenue].

By order of the Kirk Session.

................*Session Clerk.*

3. Form of Intimation for a Congregational Meeting for other purposes.

Notice is hereby given that a meeting of this congregation will be held in on the day of
19 for the following purpose :—

[*Here take in purpose of meeting,* e.g., *to consider the erection of church, hall, manse, &c., to consider the question of union, to consider, and, if so resolved, to approve of a Basis of Union.*]
and to take such action thereanent as the congregation may determine.

By order of the Kirk Session.

................*Session Clerk.*

Note (i).—When a special meeting for financial purposes is necessary in a congregation where there is a Committee of Management, the notice will be by order of that Committee and will be signed by its Clerk, but the concurrence of the Kirk Session is required.

(ii) There are special forms for certain congregations in the matter of electing trustees, &c., and also for meetings in connection with the election of ministers, for which see Index of Forms (see p. 455 ff.).

SPECIMENS OF MINUTES.

N.B.—*The following are only specimens of the way in which Minutes may be drafted, and are not binding as forms.*

I.—Specimen Minutes for Congregational Meetings

A.—ANNUAL BUSINESS MEETING.

(*a*) Where there is a Deacons' Court.

At , the day of 19 , the Deacons' Court met with the Congregation, and was constituted, the Moderator in the chair [*or*, in the absence of the Moderator, Mr was called to the chair].

The Clerk read the annual report, with a view to receiving any suggestions from the Congregation. One [*or* two *or* no] suggestion was made.

The Congregation appointed to audit the Congregational accounts for the current year. A draft Minute of the Meeting was submitted and approved.

Closed with prayer.

(*b*) Where there is a Committee of Management.

At , the day of 19 , which place and date the Annual Business Meeting of Congregation was held. Mr , the Chairman, presided, and opened the meeting with prayer.

The Clerk gave in the Report of the actings of the Managers for the year.

The Treasurer submitted the annual Statement of Accounts for the year ended . After questions had been put and answered it was moved, seconded, and unanimously agreed that the Statement be approved.

It was moved, seconded, and agreed that the following instruction be given to the Managers, viz. :—

It was intimated that the following Managers were due to retire by rotation :—

and the following were nominated for election :—

The number nominated not exceeding the number of vacancies, the Chairman declared them to be elected. [*Or*, On a vote being taken, it was found that the following had been elected .] Mr was appointed Chairman ; Mr , Clerk ; and Mr , Treasurer, for the ensuing year. [*Or*, It was remitted to the Managers to elect their own officials.] A draft Minute was submitted and approved.

Closed with prayer.

(*c*) WHERE THERE IS A CONGREGATIONAL BOARD.
(MODEL CONSTITUTION.)

At Church, the day of 19 , which place and date the Stated Annual Meeting of Parish was held. Rev. , Minister of the Church, presided, and opened the meeting with prayer [*or*, in the absence of the Minister, Mr was called to the Chair].

A statement of the accounts for the year ended , showing a balance in hand of £ , together with proposals for the appropriation of the balance as follows:

was submitted, and after discussion the meeting adopted the report.

It was reported that the following members of the Board fell to retire at this time :—

[*Here continue as in previous Minute.*]

A draft Minute was submitted and approved.

Closed with prayer.

(*d*) WHEN THERE IS A CONGREGATIONAL BOARD
(UNITED FREE CHURCH FORM).

The Minute may be the same as for a congregation with a Deacons' Court *mutatis mutandis.*

B.—CONGREGATIONAL MEETING WHEN THE MINISTER THEREOF HAS RECEIVED A CALL.

At Church, the day of 19 , which place and date a meeting of the congregation was held, pursuant to the following intimation made on

[*Here take in Intimation as on p.* 819.]

Rev. , who had been appointed to preside by the Clerk of Presbytery in terms of Act IX., 1932, opened the meeting with prayer.

It was moved, seconded, and unanimously agreed that the congregation acquiesce in the translation of the Minister.

[Messrs were appointed to represent the congregation at the meeting of Presbytery to be held on .]

Closed with prayer.

C.—CONGREGATIONAL MEETING TO APPOINT CONGREGATIONAL COMMITTEE IN A VACANCY.

At Church, the day of 19 , which place and date the congregation of met in terms of intimation made on and on , the terms whereof follow :—

[*Here take in from Act IX.*, 1932, *Sch. C.* 2 ; *p.* 814.]

Rev. , Interim Moderator of the Kirk Session, presided, and opened the meeting with prayer.

It was moved, seconded, and agreed that the number of the Congregational Committee be . Nominations were called for, when the following persons were proposed for the Committee :—

No further nominations having been made, and Messrs having withdrawn their names, a vote was taken on those remaining, when the following were elected members of the Committee, viz. :—

The congregation agreed that the method of voting for the election of a minister be by ballot [*or* open] vote.

The Interim Moderator intimated that the Congregational Committee would meet at the close of this meeting [*or* on at o'clock].

Draft Minute of the Meeting was submitted and approved.

Closed with prayer.

D.—MINUTE OF CONGREGATIONAL MEETING FOR THE ELECTION OF A MINISTER.

At , the day of 19 , there was held a meeting of Congregation. Sederunt, —Rev. , *interim* Moderator of the Kirk Session, Messrs , Elders, and [*number*] members of the Congregation.

The meeting was opened with prayer. The Moderator stated that the intimation calling the meeting had been returned, duly certified as having been made to the Congregation on the two preceding Sundays. He further stated that the business before the meeting was to receive the Report of the Congregational Committee, and, if so resolved, to elect a Minister.

The Report of the Committee was given in, from which it appears that the Committee had agreed to nominate Mr A. B., Mr C. D. and Mr E. F. The names were put to the meeting in the order proposed, when it was found voted for A. B., for C. D. and for E. F. The name of C. D., having the fewest votes, was dropped, and a vote was taken between Mr A. B. and Mr E. F., when Mr A. B. was elected by a considerable majority. The Moderator therefore declared Mr A. B. to be elected, subject to the judgment of the Courts of the Church.

A form of Call was read over and the name of Mr A. B. inserted in it. It was subscribed by all the members present to the number of . A Paper of Concurrence was signed by adherents. The Call and Paper of Concurrence were attested by the Moderator, who intimated that the Call would be left in the hands of the Kirk Session till next, when members might sign in person or by means of mandates. The meeting appointed their commissioners to the meeting of Presbytery.

A draft Minute of the Meeting was submitted and approved.

Closed with prayer.

II.—Forms for a Deacons' Court.

1. Specimen Minute containing Variations from the Forms of Kirk Session Minutes.

At , the day of 19 , the Deacons' Court met.

Deacons' Court Minutes.

Sederunt,— Elders; Deacons.

In the absence of the Moderator, Mr G. was unanimously called to the chair. The meeting was then constituted with prayer.

The minutes of meeting held on were read and approved.

Admission of Elders.

An extract minute of the Session was laid on the table, from which it appeared that Mr and Mr , &c., had been admitted as Elders of this Congregation on the day of .

Of Deacons.

Another extract minute was read, by which it appeared that Mr and Mr , &c., &c., had been admitted as Deacons of this Congregation on the day of .

The Deacons' Court instructed the Clerk to add the names of these persons to their roll in due order.

Person ceased to hold Office.

Another extract minute was read, showing that Mr had ceased to be an Elder and Mr to be a Deacon of this Congregation.

The Court instructed the Clerk to remove the names of these persons from the roll.

Vacant Church Officership.

The Deacons' Court, taking into consideration the vacancy in the Church Officership of this Congregation, resolves that his salary shall be .

Deacons' Districts, &c., Appointment of Treasurers.

It was agreed to collect Seat Rents from present holders on , and to allocate sittings to new applicants the following week.

The Court resolves to divide the Congregation anew into districts to be severally assigned to the Deacons, as follows,—District I., Mr T., &c.

The Court instructed each of the Deacons to take charge of and hold himself responsible for the arrangements for the ingathering of the Fund for the Maintenance of the Ministry in his district, and appointed Mr to be Treasurer for that Fund, Mr remaining Treasurer for the Congregational Funds, Mr for the Foreign Missions Fund, and Mr for the Home Missions Fund.

The Deacons' Court, finding that, after deduction of sums requisite for the claims recognised as primary by the Act of Assembly, there remained a surplus in the Congregational Fund of £ · p, took into consideration the question how far it was reasonable to supplement (or add to the supplement to) the Minister's stipend, and resolved to grant him the sum of £ · p out of the surplus. Supplement to Minister.

The Deacons' Court resolved that a special collection be made on Sunday, the day of , for the relief of poor members of the Congregation at this season. Collection for Poor.

It was moved and seconded—That

It was also moved and seconded—That

The motion was carried by a majority of to .

From this judgment Mr dissented for the following reasons, viz.—1, &c., 2, &c., 3, &c. Mr adhered to the Dissent.

[Note.—*When reasons are produced immediately along with the Dissent in any Church Court, they may be made part of the Minute, if briefly stated.*] Reasons of Dissent

Closed with prayer.

III.—Specimen Minute for a Congregational Board. 1931 Constitution.

At , the day of 19 , which place and date the Congregational Board met in terms of intimation made from the pulpit on

Sederunt,—

Rev. , Minister of the Parish, presided and opened the meeting with prayer. Meeting opened.

The Minute of Meeting held on was read and approved. Minutes.

The order of the Board for the current year was laid on the table and approved.

[The Minister intimated that he did not wish to act as Chairman of the Board, and Mr was appointed Chairman for this year.] Minister declines to be Chairman.

[The Board reappointed Mr to be Clerk and Mr to be Treasurer.]

The Board appointed to be Auditor(s) of the Congregational Accounts for the year. Auditors.

Mr , having intimated his resignation as a member of the Board on account of his removal from the district, the Board appointed Mr in his room. Resignation of member.

Seat Rents.

The Board took into consideration the matter of Seat Rents. It was moved and seconded that—

It was also moved and seconded that—

On a vote being taken, the second motion was carried, and the Board resolved accordingly

Salary of Organist.

The Board took up the question of the Salary of the {Church Officer, / Organist,} when it was unanimously agreed that the salary be £ per annum.

Accounts.

The following accounts were passed for payment, viz. :—

Closed with prayer.

[Note.—*Guidance for Members of the Committee of Management and of the Congregational Board (United Free Church Form) will be found in the Specimen Minutes of Kirk Session, Deacons' Court, and Congregational Board.*]

IV.—Forms for a Kirk Session.

Kirk Session Minutes.

1. Specimen Minute of Kirk Session, in which, for brevity's sake, many particulars are inserted to show how they ought to be dealt with and expressed, though they might never all occur in the same Minute.

At , the day of 19 , the Kirk Session of the Congregation at met, according to intimation from the pulpit, and was constituted with prayer.

Sederunt,—

The Rev. , Moderator ; Messrs and , Ruling Elders.

The Minute of meeting held on was read and approved.

Induction of Minister.

Read certified intimation from the Clerk of Presbytery as follows : [*take it in*]. The Session ordered the intimation to be engrossed in the Minutes of this meeting.

Appointment of Communion.

The Session resolved that the ordinance of the Lord's Supper shall be observed in this Church on Sunday, the day of next.

Elders' Districts.

The Session took into consideration the division of the Congregation into districts for the Elders, and resolved that, in the meantime, it stand as follows : [*take it in*].

Election of Representative Elder.

The Session proceeded to elect a Ruling Elder to represent it in the Presbytery and in the Synod during the ensuing year, in place of , whose term of representation expires at 30th June.

It was moved, seconded and agreed, that be elected. Accordingly the Session appointed of its own number, and *bona fide* an acting Elder in the Congregation to represent it in the Presbytery of , and in the Synod of for the ensuing year.

Elders visiting after Vacancy.

The attention of the Session was called to the importance of the Elders on this occasion visiting their respective districts in good time, previously to the Communion, after the long-protracted vacancy.

The Session found that Mr , Ruling Elder, and Mr , Deacon, had withdrawn from all meetings of Session and Deacons' Court for more than twelve months, without explanation. The Clerk was instructed to write them, inquiring if they had any explanation to make for their absence, and to intimate that, in the event of no satisfactory excuse being given, the Kirk Session would proceed to remove them from office in terms of Act IX., 1933. **Elders and Deacons ceasing to be in Office.**

A letter was read from Mr , Church Officer [*or* Organist], resigning his office. The Kirk Session accepted the resignation, and resolved to intimate same to the Deacons' Court [*or* Committee of Management *or* Congregational Board] in order that the question of salary may be considered in view of a new appointment. It was further agreed to advertise the vacancy. **Resignation of Church Officer or Organist.**

The Kirk Session, considering that its number ought to be increased, *requested the Moderator to communicate with certain persons whom the Kirk Session deemed qualified for the office of the Eldership* [or requested the Moderator to make an intimation on Sunday next, and (should the Session desire it) on the two following Sundays, at the close of public worship, to the effect that the election would take place in the following manner : [*Then let the manner adopted by the Session be stated, whether by the giving in of lists, or by voting at the meeting, or otherwise.*] It was agreed that the number to be elected be , and that the Moderator intimate the number.] **Election of Elders.**

It was also agreed that the Moderator address the people on their duties in this matter, and take occasion to point out the qualifications of Elder. The Kirk Session resolved to meet in the church on the day of , for the purpose [*either of opening lists, or, along with the Congregation, for an election otherwise*].

Thereafter the Session took into consideration the subject of

It was moved and seconded—That

It was also moved and seconded—That **Motion carried on Division.**

After deliberation it was agreed to take the vote. The votes were marked, and it appeared that members had voted for the first motion, and for the second, so that the motion was carried by a majority of . Thereupon the Kirk Session, in terms of that motion, resolved that .

From this judgment Mr dissented, and Mr adhered to the dissent. **Dissent.**

The Moderator reported that the following persons [*or* submitted a list of persons, numbering , who] had applied to be admitted as Communicants for the first time, and that he was satisfied with their knowledge and professions, viz. :— **First Communicants.**

The Kirk Session having no ground for questioning the good character of any of these persons resolved to admit them to Communion with this Congregation, and to add their names to the Communion Roll.

A letter of resignation of his office as an Elder [*or* Deacon] of this Congregation was laid on the table from Mr . **Resignation of Elder or Deacon.**

The Kirk Session appointed Mr and Mr with to confer with Mr as to the reasons for his proposed resignation, and to report.

Closed with prayer.

2. A Second Specimen Minute.

At , the day of 19 , which place and date the Kirk Session of met, through personal citation by the Moderator, and was constituted with prayer.

Sederunt—the Rev. , Moderator; Messrs and , Ruling Elders.

The minute of Meeting held on was read and approved.

Election of Elders (*first method*). Co-option.

The Moderator reported that he had interviewed those persons whom the Kirk Session deemed worthy of the office of the Eldership, and that certain of them were willing to accept office. The Kirk Session then made choice of Messrs to be members of this Kirk Session, appointed their ordination to take place in presence of the congregation on [*date*], and further appointed an edict to this effect to be served on two successive Sundays [*dates*] in common form—objections to be received at a meeting of Session to be held [*time and place*].

Or,

Election of Elders (*second method*). Election by Congregation.

The Moderator intimated that he had complied with the request of the Kirk Session recorded in the minute now read. [*Here let it be stated either that the lists were opened and read and the votes marked, &c., or that the Kirk Session met with the Congregation and proceeded to an election, when motions were made, &c., and the following were elected (either unanimously or by a majority, as the case may be), in the following order, the persons named first having the greatest number of votes.*]

[The Benediction having been pronounced and the Congregation [*or public meeting*] having been dismissed, the Kirk Session continued its meeting alone.]

The Kirk Session being alone, proceeded to judge of the qualifications for the Eldership of the persons named. After deliberation, the Kirk Session found that the following persons had been elected by the Congregation and were duly qualified, viz.:—

It was agreed that the Moderator ascertain the willingness of the above-named to accept office [*or*, It was agreed that the Elders-elect be requested to meet with the Kirk Session on the at o'clock, in order that the Kirk Session might ascertain their willingness to accept office].

Removal of Elder and Deacon from Office.

The Clerk reported that he had communicated with Messrs in regard to their absence from meetings of Kirk Session and Deacons' Court respectively, and that Mr had not replied, and that Mr could give no satisfactory explanation. The Kirk Session therefore declared that Mr had ceased to be a member of Kirk Session and Deacons' Court, and that Mr had likewise ceased to be a member of the Deacons' Court. The Clerk was instructed to intimate accordingly to the persons concerned and to the Clerk of the Deacons' Court.

The applications for the vacant position of Church Officer were considered, when it was resolved to appoint Mr on the following terms and conditions, viz.:—

Mr reported for himself, and that, as instructed by the Kirk Session, they had conferred with Mr as to the reasons of his proposed resignation of his office as an Elder [*or* Deacon], and stated the result of conference. The Kirk Session, being satisfied that there is nothing affecting the character of Mr in the causes of his resignation, resolve to accept it with regret, to remove his name from the Session Roll, and to intimate accordingly to the Deacons' Court [*or*, the Kirk Session find that the reasons for the tender of resignation are not satisfactory, and render it necessary for them to take Mr on discipline. They appoint Mr , Mr , and , to confer again with Mr upon the subject, intimating to him this finding]. Resignation of Elder.

Closed with prayer.

3. A Third Specimen Minute.

At , the day of 19 , which place and date the Kirk Session met and was constituted with prayer.

Sederunt—the Rev. , Moderator ; Messrs and , Ruling Elders.

The minute of Meeting held on was read and approved.

The Moderator reported that he had interviewed the persons elected and found qualified for the Eldership in the Congregation with a view to their acceptance of the office, and that the following persons had agreed to accept—viz., Mr [*or*, Messrs A., B., C., and D., Elders-elect, being present, the Session conferred with them as to their acceptance of office. Messrs A., B. and C. agreed to become Elders in the Congregation, but Mr D. declined]. Election of Elders (*second method*).

The Kirk Session appoints the ordination of Messrs , and the admission of Mr , already ordained to the Eldership in another Congregation, to take place in presence of the Congregation, on Sunday the , after public worship in the , and they direct an edict to this effect to be served in common form on two successive Sundays [*insert dates*], giving notice that if any member of the Congregation have any objections to state to the life or doctrine of any of the foresaid persons, they will have an opportunity of stating the same at a meeting of Session to be held for that purpose in on the day of at o'clock, with certification that, unless such objections be substantiated at said meeting, the ordination and admission will be proceeded with. Appointment of Elders' Ordination (*all methods*).

Closed with prayer.

4. A Fourth Specimen Minute.

At , the day of 19 , which place and date the Kirk Session of met and was constituted with prayer.

Sederunt—the Rev. , Moderator ; Messrs and , Elders.

The minute of Meeting held on was read and approved.

Meeting to receive Objections to Life or Doctrine (*all methods*).

The Moderator reported that he had made edictal intimation of the ordination and admission of Elders according to the request of the Session. The Kirk Session called the Church Officer and instructed him to intimate at the Church door that the Kirk Session had met to give an opportunity for the statement of objections in terms of the edict. Thereafter, the Officer returned from the door and intimated that no objector had appeared. The Kirk Session, accordingly, resolve to proceed with the ordination and admission according to appointment. [N.B.—*If any objections to life or doctrine be brought forward, the Kirk Session considers whether they be substantiated to their satisfaction, or be such as to require it to delay procedure with a view to further investigation. If both these questions be determined in the negative, the Kirk Session finds accordingly, and proceeds with the ordination.*]

Admission to Office (*all methods*).

The Kirk Session proceeded to the Church, when after sermon the Moderator read a narrative of the steps leading up to the admission of Messrs to the office of the Eldership.

The Moderator put to them the prescribed question, to which they gave satisfactory answers, and they thereafter signed the Formula.

The Moderator then, in name of the Kirk Session, did admit Mr , already an ordained Elder of the Church of Scotland, to the said office in this Congregation; and thereafter, with prayer to God, he did solemnly set apart Mr , Mr and Mr , &c., &c., to the office of Eldership, and did admit them to the exercise of the same in this Congregation, and to all the rights and privileges belonging thereto. In token thereof, all the persons now admitted received the right hand of fellowship from the Elders present. The Moderator addressed the newly admitted Elders and the Congregation regarding their respective duties.

Public worship having been concluded, and the Session continuing its meeting, the names of these Elders were added to the Roll of the Kirk Session, and the Session Clerk was instructed to intimate accordingly to the Clerk of the Deacons' Court.

Closed with prayer.

5. A Fifth Specimen Minute.

At , the day of 19 , which place and date the Kirk Session met and was constituted with prayer, &c.

Sederunt, &c.

The minutes of Meetings held on were read and approved

Revisal of Roll.

The Communion Roll was revised, corrected, and attested by the Moderator [*or* Clerk] as now containing names, and to be transmitted to the Presbytery as the Roll as at 31st December last.

Election of Deacons.

The Kirk Session, having taken into consideration the importance of having an addition made to the number of Deacons, resolved to take steps with a view thereto, and accordingly requested the Moderator to make an intimation on Sunday next . . . [*here take in the Form as to Elders—Minute* 1, *p.* 801, *mutatis mutandis*].

Closed with prayer.

6. FURTHER MINUTES, ETC., AS TO ELECTION AND ADMISSION OF DEACONS, ETC., THE SAME AS IN THE CASE OF ELDERS, *mutatis mutandis*, WITH THOSE IN THE CASE OF ELDERS.

[*The only exception is in Minute* 4, *p.* 804, *where, in place of stating that the names were appointed to be added to the Roll, the Minute must be.*] The Kirk Session instruct the Clerk to intimate the admission of Deacons which has this day taken place, to the Clerk of the Deacons' Court, in order that he may communicate it to the Deacons' Court, with a view to its instructing him to add the names of the newly admitted Deacons to its roll of members. **Admission of Deacons.**

7. A SEVENTH SPECIMEN MINUTE (ALTERNATIVE METHOD OF APPOINTING DEACONS).

At , the day of 19 , which place and date the Kirk Session met and was constituted with prayer, &c. **Election of Deacons for a period of years.**

The Kirk Session took into consideration the question of adding to the number of Deacons. The Moderator stated that advantage might be taken of the scheme whereby Deacons are elected for a period of years, the office being open to men or women. After full discussion and explanation it was unanimously agreed that a meeting of the Congregation be held on the day of at o'clock to consider whether the office of Deacon in this Congregation be held as heretofore ; or by members of the Congregation over eighteen years of age who, without ordination, will be set apart to office for three years [*or*, the Kirk Session resolved that voting papers be issued to members on this question].

Closed with prayer.

8. SPECIMEN MINUTE IN REFERRING AN ORDINARY CASE TO THE PRESBYTERY.

The Kirk Session, regarding the question involved in this matter as one of considerable difficulty, hereby refers the whole case to the Presbytery of for advice, and, at the same time, intimates to the parties that they are hereby summoned *apud acta* to the bar of that Presbytery at its next ordinary Meeting. **Reference to Presbytery.**

9. SPECIMEN MINUTE IN CONNECTION WITH THE ELECTORAL REGISTER IN A VACANCY.

At , the day of 19 , which place and date the Kirk Session met and was constituted.

Present, &c.

The Kirk Session having met for the purpose of making up the Electoral Register in terms of Regulation 6, parties were called and none appeared [*or*, and were heard]. The list proposed for the Electoral Roll was then prepared. **Proposed Electoral Register.**

Further, the Session resolved that the place and hours at which the list shall lie for inspection shall be , and that the Kirk Session meet on at o'clock for the purpose of finally adjusting the Electoral Register. It was further agreed to suggest to the Interim Moderator that the time of the meeting of the congregation for the election of a Committee shall be [*day and hour*].

The Kirk Session then adjourned to meet as already appointed on at o'clock, at which place and day the Kirk Session resumed its meeting, [Mr being present in addition to those whose names are already recorded, and Mr being absent].

Electoral Register finally made up.

Parties were called and none appeared [*or*, and were heard]. The list was then revised and finally made up, and ordered to be attested by the Moderator and Clerk as the Electoral Register, in terms of Regulation 7.

The Clerk was instructed to forward the Register as adjusted [*or*, a certified copy thereof] to the Clerk of Presbytery for attestation.

Closed with prayer.

V.—FORMS FOR A PRESBYTERY.

1. SPECIMEN MINUTE OF ORDINARY MEETING OF PRESBYTERY.[1]

Ordinary Meeting.

At , the day of 19 , which place and date the Presbytery of met, and was constituted with prayer.

Sederunt—the Rev. , and Messrs , Ministers; with Messrs , Ruling Elders.

Commissions to Ruling Elders to represent them in the Presbytery were submitted from the Kirk Sessions of and were sustained. The names were added to the Roll.

In order to equalise the number of Ministers and Elders, the Presbytery elected

Election of Moderator.

The Presbytery proceeded to elect a Moderator for the ensuing year when Mr , Minister at , was unanimously elected and took the chair accordingly.

Minutes.

The minute of last ordinary Meeting of date , and of the *in hunc effectum* Meeting of date , and of the *pro re nata* Meeting of date , were read and approved.

Appointment of Presbytery Committees.

The Presbytery resolved to reappoint its Standing Committees with the following changes, viz. :—

Appeal, &c., from Kirk Session.

The Presbytery took up a case of Appeal [*or*, Dissent and Complaint] from the Kirk Session of , against a judgment of that Kirk Session of date , by which the Kirk Session found

The documents in the case were laid on the table. Parties were called, when there appeared for the Appellants Messrs

[1] In this specimen minute many matters are grouped together which might come before a Presbytery, but obviously these would not come before any single meeting.

; [*or*, for the Dissentient and Complainer, Mr]; and for the Kirk Session, Mr and Mr .

The Clerk then read the documents in the case—viz., the Decision appealed against, the Reasons of Appeal and Answers thereto, and the whole record of the proceedings of the Kirk Session.

Mr was heard in support of the Appeal, [*or*, Mr in support of the Complaint] and Mr in support of the judgment of the Kirk Session. Mr was heard in reply.

Parties were removed. It was moved, seconded, and unanimously agreed—

That the Presbytery dismiss the Appeal [*or*, Complaint] and affirm the judgment of the Kirk Session. [*Or*, That the Presbytery sustain the Appeal [*or*, Complaint] and reverse the judgment of the Session, and instruct, &c.]

Parties were recalled and this judgment was intimated, when Mr acquiesced in name of , took instruments, and craved extracts. Against the same judgment Mr , in name of , protested for leave to appeal to the Synod of , took instruments and craved extracts.

Case of Reference from Kirk Session.

The Presbytery took up a case of Reference for Advice from the Kirk Session of .

The minute of Kirk Session making the Reference was read, with relative documents. There appeared in support of the Reference the Rev. and Mr , who were heard.

It was agreed to sustain the Reference.

Thereafter, on the merits of the case, parties were called, when there appeared J. T. and G. D. Parties were heard and removed.

It was moved, seconded, and agreed—

The Presbytery find that , and *quoad ultra* remit to the Kirk Session to deal with the matter in accordance with the law of the Church.

Report on Maintenance of the Ministry Fund.

The Report on the Maintenance of the Ministry Fund was given in by Mr , the Convener. In accordance therewith the Presbytery resolved

Report on Foreign Missions.

Mr reported on Foreign Missions. It was moved, seconded, and agreed that

Report on Examination of Records.

The Committee appointed for the examination of Records reported that the Kirk Session Records, Communion Rolls, Baptismal Registers and Registers of Proclamation of Banns had been produced and examined, as follows :—

The following Records had not been produced :—

On the report of this Committee the Presbytery attested the Records as correctly kept, with the following exceptions :—

The Presbytery ordered up for examination at next Meeting the books not produced at this Meeting.

Examination of Abstracts of Accounts.

There were submitted Abstracts of Accounts of all the Charges within the bounds, with the following exceptions :—

These being found to be in order, were attested, and the Presbytery resolved to call for the Abstracts not produced at next Meeting.

Quoad Sacra **Books.** The Presbytery examined the books and accounts of the following congregations where the 1931 Constitution is in operation, and found the same in order and in accordance with the Constitution of the Church, viz. :—

Application for a Colleague or Successor. There was submitted Schedule of Application for a Colleague and Successor from Rev. , together with relative minutes of the Kirk Session [Deacons' Court, Congregational Board *or* Committee of Management], and the Congregation all concurring in the same, the financial arrangements proposed being—for Senior Minister £ , for Junior Minister £ and Manse.

The Presbytery find that the arrangements for the Senior and Junior Ministers are satisfactory, the Presbytery recommend the application to the General Assembly's Aged and Infirm Ministers' Fund Committee. [*The Presbytery may proceed as in the case of any other vacancy, or defer consideration of this to a subsequent meeting.*]

Demission of Charge. The Clerk laid on the table and read the following letter from the Rev. , demitting his charge. [*Take in.*]

Mr not being present, the Presbytery appointed the following committee to confer with him and report to next Meeting, viz. : [*or*, Mr being present, the Presbytery, being alone, conferred with him].

The Presbytery [being satisfied] resolved to cite the parishioners and congregation of the parish of to attend for their interests [*place and date*].

Translation of Minister. There were laid on the table the following papers : Call signed by members ; and Paper of Concurrence signed by adherents ; extract minutes of the Presbytery of thereanent ; [reasons of translation ;] the citation of the parishioners and congregation of , duly executed. Parties were called, and there compeared, &c. [*or*, no compearance being made, they were held as consenting]. The question was then put, Translate or not translate, and it carried unanimously, Translate. Wherefore the Presbytery did, and hereby do, translate Mr , of the church and parish of , to the church and parish of , in the Presbytery of , declaring that his pastoral relation to [*name his parish*] shall subsist until he is actually admitted to the charge aforesaid ; and they enjoin him to wait for and obey the orders of the Presbytery of as to the time of his admission to ; and they hereby request the Presbytery of to give them intimation of his admission as soon as it takes place. An extract of this minute was then ordered to be sent to the Clerk of the Presbytery of [*or*, was delivered over to Mr , a commissioner, who thereupon took instruments and craved extracts].

Moderator Appointed. The Presbytery appointed Rev. to be Interim Moderator of Kirk Session in view of the impending vacancy. (In terms of 1960, xxiii.)

Question of Union. The Presbytery resolved [not] to raise the question of union or re-adjustment of agencies at ; [they appointed the following Committee to confer with the representatives of the General

Assembly's Committee on Unions and Readjustments, and with the congregations of], and instructed the Clerk to intimate accordingly to the Secretary of the General Assembly's Committee on Unions and Readjustments.

Appointment and Call. There were laid on the table an appointment to the church and parish of in favour of Mr , his letter of acceptance thereof with the required statement that he had used no undue influence to secure the Call, a Call as prescribed [his extract of licence, &c., *as the case may be*].

The Presbytery [having heard parties and] being satisfied with the documents produced, [and that his knowledge of Gaelic is sufficient for the charge], and that there is no cause to decline or delay to sustain the appointments, did and hereby do sustain the appointment and Call of Mr to the church and parish of , and resolve to proceed towards his settlement.

Procedure in case of a Minister. Whereupon the Presbytery ordered the Call and an extract of their procedure thereanent to be sent to the [Moderator or] Clerk of the Presbytery of , along with reasons for the translation.]

The Presbytery [provisionally] appointed [his ordination and] his induction to the church and parish of to take place on [*day*]. The Presbytery further appointed the Rev. [*one of their number*] to preach [*or* to conduct devotional exercises], and the Rev. to address the minister and the congregation.

The Presbytery instructed that the prescribed edict be served in Church on Sundays, .

Vacancy Schedule. A Vacancy Schedule was submitted from Congregation, promising £ per annum for stipend, and a contribution to the Maintenance of the Ministry Fund of £ . The Presbytery resolved to transmit the Schedule, as adequate to the resources of the congregation, to the General Assembly's Committee on the Maintenance of the Ministry.

Application for a Grant. An application for a grant from the General Assembly's Committee on was submitted from . The Presbytery resolved to transmit the application with its recommendation.

Letter from Student. The Clerk submitted a letter from Mr making application to be admitted as a student of theology. It was remitted to the Students' Committee for consideration, and the Clerk was instructed to forward the application with a letter of commendation from his Minister and any information received by the Students' Committee to the Secretary of the Central Board of Selection.

Resolution to elect Assembly's Commissioners. The Presbytery resolved to elect its Commissioners to the ensuing General Assembly at a Meeting to be held in on .

In terms of notice given at last Meeting, Mr moved that the Presbytery transmit an Overture to the ensuing General Assembly on the subject of .

Overture to the General Assembly. The Presbytery then agreed to transmit the following Overture to the General Assembly through the Provincial Synod :—

[*Here take in Overture.* (*For form, see p.* 103.)]

The Presbytery appointed Messrs to support the Overture before the General Assembly.

Overture under Barrier Act. The Presbytery took up consideration of the Overture under the

Barrier Act anent
sent down by last General Assembly. [*Or*, The Presbytery received a Report from the Committee appointed at a previous Meeting to consider the Overture under the Barrier Act anent
sent down by last General Assembly.] It was moved and seconded that the Presbytery approve the Overture. It was also moved and seconded that the Presbytery do not approve the Overture. On a vote being taken, there voted for the first motion , and for the second motion . The Presbytery accordingly approved [*or*, disapproved] the Overture.

The Vote. Overture approved.

Application for Licence.

Mr M. N., having made application to be taken on trials for licence [*Here take in form as given on p.* 787.]

Setting apart of Readers.

The Presbytery then proceeded in terms of its resolution at a former Meeting to set apart Messrs as Readers. The Moderator put to them the questions appointed by 1958, x., and they having returned satisfactory answers to the same and having signed the Formula, the Moderator by prayer set them apart to the office of Lay Reader. The Moderator suitably addressed them. The Clerk was instructed to furnish them with an extract of this minute, and to forward their names to the Secretary of the General Assembly's Committee on Probationers and Transference of Ministers.

Presbytery in private. Report on Visitation.

The Presbytery then met in private. Mr reported on the visitation of congregation. In accordance therewith the Presbytery resolved to express its satisfaction with the state of the congregation and to report to the Synod accordingly [*or*, regretted that it is unable to express satisfaction with the state of the congregation]. The Presbytery again met in open Court.

The Presbytery adjourned to meet *in hunc effectum* in , on the day of , at o'clock; and also in this place on , for ordinary business.

Closed with prayer.

2. Another Specimen Minute.

At , the day of 19 , which place and date the Presbytery of met pursuant to adjournment from [*date*] and was constituted with prayer.

Sederunt—the Rev. , Moderator;
ministers; Messrs
Elders.

Corresponding Members.

Rev. , from the Presbytery of ,
and Rev. , from the Presbytery of ,
being present, were associated with the Presbytery.

The minutes of Meeting held on were read and approved.

Election of Assembly Commissioners.

It being now betwixt the hours of eleven o'clock in the forenoon and eight o'clock in the evening, the Presbytery, pursuant to a resolution entered in the minutes of , did and hereby do nominate and appoint . . . [*take in as on p.* 784].

Nomination of Students.

There was submitted a certificate from the Central Board of Selection approving the application of Mr to be admitted as a student of theology. The Students' Committee of Presbytery having also reported favourably on this application, his minister moved that the applicant be nominated as a student of theology. This was agreed to and the Clerk was instructed to forward the name of Mr to the Joint Secretaries of the Committee on Education for the Ministry.

Compearance of Student.

Compeared Mr , a [second] year student of theology, and a favourable report having been received from the Students' Committee as to his progress, it was agreed to report to the Committee on Education for the Ministry that he had performed his intersessional work to the satisfaction of the Presbytery.

Vacancy Schedule Approved.

There was submitted an extract minute of the General Assembly's Committee on Maintenance of the Ministry approving the financial arrangements in the vacancy at .

Demission of Minister.

The Presbytery resumed consideration of the letter of the Rev. demitting his office of minister of , and there was laid on the table the citation of the congregation duly executed. No appearance was made for the congregation, or by members of the congregation [*or, So-and-so,* members of the congregation, appeared and were heard, &c.]. It was moved, seconded, and agreed that the Presbytery accept, and they hereby do accept, the demission of Mr , and loose him from his charge as from this date [or such subsequent date as the Presbytery may appoint]; and they instruct the Clerk to give to Mr a certificate in terms of Act 1933, xv., that he retains his full status as a minister of the Church of Scotland, and [" *unless they see cause to withhold* " *it*] a Presbyterial certificate that his conduct is in every respect becoming his profession.

And further, the Presbytery appoint Mr to be Interim Moderator of Kirk Session. The Presbytery resolve [not] to raise the question of Union . . . [*see previous minute, p.*]. [*This paragraph to be omitted if there be a Colleague and Successor in office.*]

Induction of Minister.

There was produced and read extract minute of the Presbytery of agreeing to the translation of from to .

The edict was returned duly served. The Officer of Court was instructed to go to the church and make intimation to the assembled congregation that, if any person or persons had any objections to the life and doctrine of Mr , minister of the Gospel, they might now repair to the Presbytery, presently met, and substantiate the same *instanter*. The Officer reported that he had made intimation, as instructed, and that no one had appeared to object.

The Presbytery then proceeded to the church. Mr conducted devotional exercises [and preached from]. Public worship being ended, the Moderator gave a brief narrative of the proceedings in the Call to , and addressed to him the questions appointed to be put to ministers on their ordination and induction to a pastoral charge, and he having returned satisfactory answers to the same, and having signed the Formula, the Moderator, by prayer, *with the imposition of hands in which all the ministers present joined, ordained the said Mr to the office of the Holy Ministry, and* inducted him to the pastoral charge of the congregation. Prayer being ended, the Moderator, addressing Mr in terms of the prescribed form, declared him to be *ordained and* inducted, and gave him the right hand of fellowship—as did also the other members of Presbytery present. Mr was suitably addressed by Rev. , who also in appropriate terms exhorted the congregation.

After praise and prayer the congregation was dismissed, an opportunity being afforded them as they retired of welcoming their minister.

The name of Mr was added to the Roll of the Presbytery, and the Clerk was instructed to send certified intimation of his *Ordination and* Induction to the Kirk Session of .

The Presbytery adjourned, &c.

The Meeting was closed with prayer.

[N.B.—*When the minister-elect is already ordained, omit the portions of the above minute that are in italics.*]

In the case of a University Professor (appointed by a University Court). The following form of minute is suggested in this case: "The Moderator put to the prescribed question, which was satisfactorily answered. Mr having signed the formula, the Moderator admitted him to membership of the Presbytery, consequent on his appointment to the Chair of in the University of , and gave him the right hand of fellowship.

3. Specimen Minutes of *In hunc effectum* and *Pro re nata* Meetings, and Meetings by appointment of Superior Court.

In hunc effectum and *Pro re nata* Meetings.

(1) *Minute of* In hunc effectum *Meeting.*

At, &c.

The Presbytery of met this day *in hunc effectum*, and was constituted with prayer.

Sederunt, &c.—

The part of the minute of last ordinary meeting of date referring to this day's proceedings having been read, the Presbytery [*Here follows the minute of the special business which can alone be transacted*].

Closed with prayer.

(2) *Minute of* Pro re nata *Meeting.*

At, &c.

The Presbytery of met this day *pro re nata*, and was constituted with prayer.

Sederunt, &c.—

The circular addressed by the Moderator to the members was read, the tenor whereof follows: [*Here take in*].

It was moved, seconded, and agreed that the Presbytery approve of the conduct of the Moderator in calling the meeting.

[*Here follows the minute as to the special business.*]

Closed with prayer.

(3) *Meeting by appointment of Superior Court.*

At, &c.

The Presbytery, &c., &c., met by special appointment and authority of the General Assembly [*or*, the Provincial Synod of], and was constituted with prayer.

Sederunt, &c.

Closed with prayer.

(4) *Meeting on the Death of a Minister.*

At, &c.

Which day and place the Presbytery of met

after the funeral of Rev. , in terms of 1931, xx., and was constituted with prayer.

Sederunt, &c.—

The Presbytery appointed a Committee to prepare a minute anent the late Rev. .

It was moved, seconded, and agreed, that the Rev. be appointed Interim Moderator of Kirk Session, with instructions to make the prescribed intimations.

The Presbytery resolved [not] to raise the question of union . . . [*Here proceed as on p.* 807].

Closed with prayer.

VI.—Forms to be used in connection with the Election, Appointment, and Translation of Ministers.

1. Schedules (1932, ix.).

A. *Intimations to be made on Occurrence of Vacancy* (Regs. 1, 5, 6).

1. It is hereby declared, by order of the Presbytery of , that this charge became vacant on by .

Or, Intimation is hereby given that the Presbytery of , on , resolved that a Colleague and Successor shall be appointed in this charge; and it is hereby declared that steps accordingly fall to be taken as if an ordinary vacancy had occurred at that date.

[*When the charge is on the Assembly's list of Gaelic-speaking charges.* Further, it is hereby declared that this being a charge on the Assembly's List of Gaelic-speaking charges, only a Gaelic-speaking person is eligible to be Minister of this charge.]

2. Intimation is hereby given, that the Kirk Session is about to make up an Electoral Register of this congregation; and that all members not already on the Communion Roll, and who claim to be put on the Electoral Register as communicants, shall give in certificates as communicants; and that all parishioners or seat-holders who claim to be put on the Electoral Register as adherents shall give in written claims as adherents, such certificates and claims to be sent to the Session-Clerk, not later than ; and intimation is further given that the Kirk Session will meet in the church (or session-house) on , when it will hear any party having an interest, and decide on said claims. Information as to the form of claim for adherents will be obtained from .

C. D., *Interim Moderator.*

B. *Form of Adherent's Claim* (Reg. 5).

I [*insert name and address*], being not less than 21 years of age, and not being a member of any other congregation in Scotland, claim to have my name placed upon the Electoral Register of the parish of as an adherent.

[*To be signed here.*]

C. *Intimation of Inspection of Register and Election of Committee* (Regs. 7, 8).

1. Intimation is hereby given, that the proposed Electoral Register of the congregation has now been prepared, and that an opportunity of

inspecting it will be given to-day in the session-house [*or*, in the church] between the hours of ; and that it will be open for inspection at on of this week between the hours of each day; and further, that the Kirk Session will meet in the session-house [*or*, in the church] on next at o'clock, when it will hear any party having an interest, and revise and finally make up the Electoral Register.

2. Intimation is also hereby given, that a meeting of this congregation will be held in the church on the day of , at o'clock, for the purpose of appointing a Committee to nominate one or more persons to the Congregation, with a view to the election and appointment of a minister, and to determine the method of election.

C. D., *Interim Moderator.*

D. *Minute of Nomination by Congregational Committee* (Reg. 11).

The Committee chosen by this congregation to nominate one or more persons, with a view to the election and appointment by the congregation of a minister to the vacant church and parish of , at a meeting held at on , resolved [*say as to each name whether unanimously or by a majority*] to name and propose [*give name and designation, or names and designations*], and they accordingly do hereby name and propose the said .

Date......... ....*Convener of Committee.*

E. *Election Notice when One Person is Nominated. Vote by Ballot* (Reg. 13).

Intimation is hereby given, that the Committee chosen by this congregation having, as by minute now read, named and proposed Mr with a view to the election and appointment of a minister by the congregation to the vacant church and parish of , a vote of the congregation will be taken to determine whether or not he shall be elected and appointed. The vote will be taken by voting papers on at between the hours of during the day, and between the hours of in the evening; and the electors shall vote "For" or "Against" electing and appointing the said Mr .

C. D., *Interim Moderator.*

F. *Election Notices when more Persons than One are Nominated. Vote by Ballot* (Reg. 13).

1. Intimation is hereby given, that the Committee chosen by this congregation having, as by minute now read, named and proposed [*here give the names*] with a view to the election and appointment of a Minister to the vacant church and parish of , a vote of the congregation will be taken by voting papers on at between the hours of during the day, and between the hours of in the evening.

C. D., *Interim Moderator.*

2. *When a second or further vote is to be taken.*—A vote of the congregation having been taken, and no one person nominated having received a majority of all the votes recorded, it is hereby intimated that another vote of the congregation falls to be taken. [*Here name the persons between whom the vote will be ; or the person on whom the vote will be " For " or " Against."*] The vote will be taken by voting papers on at , between the hours of during the day, and between the hours of in the evening.

C. D., *Interim Moderator.*

G. *Election Notice. Open Vote* (Reg. 12).

Intimation is hereby given that the Committee chosen by this congregation having as by minute now read named and proposed , a meeting of the congregation will be held on the day of at o'clock in the church to receive the report, and, if so resolved, to elect a minister.

Notice is hereby further given that, if an election takes place, a call to the person elected will be proceeded with.

C. D., *Interim Moderator.*

H. *Voting Paper.*[1]

First Form.—When one person is to be voted on.

No....... Counterfoil.	No.......	
	FOR electing Mr A—— B——	
	AGAINST ,, ,,	

Directions to Voters, to be printed on the Voting Paper.—If you are in favour of electing Mr A—— B——, put a cross opposite his name. If you are against, put a cross opposite " Against." If you put a cross in more than one of the spaces, the paper will not be counted.

Second Form.—When more persons than one are to be voted on.

No....... Counterfoil.	No.......	
	Mr A—— *B*——	
	Mr C—— *D*——	
	AGAINST BOTH the above-named.	

When there are more than two nominees, insert " all " instead of " both," and make the same change in the Directions to Voters.

[1] The voting papers to be used in the election will have to be provided by the Kirk Session in terms of Regulation 14. These may be obtained at a small charge from the Publications Department, 121 George Street, Edinburgh.

Directions to Voters, to be printed on the Voting Paper.—If you are in favour of electing one of the persons named, put a cross opposite his name. If you object to both of the persons, put a cross opposite the words "Against both the above-named." If you put a cross in more than one of the spaces, the paper will not be counted.

I. *Forms of Declaration of Votes in the Election of a Minister.*

1. *When an Election has been made* (Regs. 12, 14).—I hereby declare that the following are the results of the voting for the election and appointment of a minister to the vacant church and parish of [*here give the name of nominee, or names of nominees, and the state of the vote*], and that the said Mr has accordingly been elected and appointed subject to the judgment of the Courts of the Church.

C. D., *Interim Moderator.*

Date..........

2. *When an Election has not been completed* (Reg. 14).—I hereby declare that the following are the results of the voting for the election and appointment of a minister to the vacant church and parish of [*here give the names of the nominees and the state of the vote*], and that no one person having received a majority of all the votes recorded, the election has not been completed.

C. D., *Interim Moderator.*

Date..........

3. *When the Voting has resulted in Failure to Elect* (Regs. 12, 14, 17).—I hereby declare that the following are the results of the voting, &c. [*here give the name of nominee, or names of nominees, and the state of the vote*], and that, in consequence of [*here state the reason*] there has been a failure to elect.

C. D., *Interim Moderator.*

Date..........

J. 1. *Intimation in case of Failure to Nominate* (Reg. 17).

Intimation is hereby given, that a committee having been formerly appointed by this congregation to nominate one or more persons to the congregation with a view to the election and appointment of a minister, and said committee having failed to nominate, a meeting of this congregation will be held in the church on the day of , at o'clock, when they will proceed of new to elect a Committee.

C. D., *Interim Moderator.*

2. *Intimation in case of Failure to Elect followed by the Committee's Declinature to Nominate anew, or their Resignation* (Reg. 17).

Intimation is hereby given, that a Committee having been formerly appointed by this congregation to nominate one or more persons to the congregation, with a view to the election and appointment of a minister, and said Committee having declined to nominate anew [*or having resigned*], a meeting of this congregation will be held in the church on the day of , at o'clock when they will proceed of new to elect a committee.

C. D., *Interim Moderator.*

3. *Intimation on Requisition to the Moderator* (Reg. 17).

Intimation is hereby given, that a requisition to that effect by the required number of qualified electors having been made to the Interim Moderator, a meeting of this congregation will be held in the church on the day of , at o'clock, to determine whether or not the present committee shall be continued in office, and to continue them or to appoint a new committee, as may be resolved.

C. D., *Interim Moderator.*

K. *Intimation with regard to Signing of Call.*

Intimation is hereby given that the congregation, having elected Mr to be their minister [and a call to the said Mr having been signed by those present at the meeting for election], the call will lie in on the day of between the hours of and , and on the day of between the hours of and , when members may sign in person or by means of mandates. Forms of mandates may be obtained from the Session-Clerk.

Notice is hereby further given that the Presbytery will meet to deal with the appointment and call in on the day of at o'clock, and the congregation are hereby cited to attend in their interests.

C. D., *Interim Moderator.*

L. *Attestation of Intimation having been made.*

.... Church, the day of 19 .

The above intimation was duly made by me.

.........., *Minister* (*or Preacher*).

M. *Forms of a Call.*

1. We, the undersigned Elders, Deacons [where there is a Deacons' Court], and members of the Church of Scotland congregation at , desirous of promoting the glory of God and the good of the Church, being destitute of a fixed Pastor, and being assured, by good information and our own experience, of the ministerial abilities, piety, literature, and prudence, as also of the suitableness to our capacities of the gifts of you, Mr S. T., preacher [*or* minister] of the Gospel, have agreed to invite, call, and entreat, like as we by these presents do heartily invite, call, and entreat you, to undertake the office of Pastor among us, and the charge of our souls; and further, upon your accepting this our Call, promise you all dutiful respect, encouragement, and obedience in the Lord, and we promise to contribute heartily, as the Lord shall enable us, towards the maintenance of the Christian Ministry and the furtherance of the Gospel.

In witness whereof, we have subscribed these presents, this day of , One Thousand Nine Hundred and years.

[*Here follow the Signatures.*]

2. We, the Elders, Deacons [where there is a Deacons' Court], and members of the Church of Scotland congregation at , desirous of promoting the glory of God and the good of the Church, considering the importance of a colleague being now appointed to the Rev. A. B., our present minister, in his ministerial Charge; and being satisfied, by good information and our own experience, &c. (*The rest* ut supra.)

3. *Form of Concurrence in a Call by Persons not in Full Communion.*

We, the subscribers, ordinary worshippers in the Church of Scotland congregation of , hereby declare our hearty concurrence in the Call addressed by the members of the said congregation to to be their Pastor.

N. *Form of Mandate to Sign a Call.*

I [*or* We], a member [*or* members] of Church of Scotland congregation, in full communion, hereby authorise the Session-Clerk or any other member of Session to adhibit my name [*or* our names] to the Call to be addressed to to be our minister.

Signature(*s*).
Address(*es*).

Date..........

O. *Forms connected with the Signing of a Call.*

1. *Form of Attestation of Call by Moderator.*

That the above names, to the number of persons, certified to be members of and in full communion with the Church of Scotland congregation of , were subscribed by the parties themselves or their mandatories in my presence, this day of 19 , is attested by .

C. D., *Interim Moderator.*

2. *Form of Attestation of Concurrence.*

That the above names, to the number of persons, regular worshippers in the Church of Scotland congregation of were subscribed by the parties themselves in my presence, this day of 19 , is attested by

C. D., *Interim Moderator.*

3. *Form of Attestation of Call by Elders.*

That the above names, to the number of persons, members of and in full communion with the Church of Scotland congregation of , were subscribed by the parties themselves in our presence, or by one of us at their special request, this day of , is attested by

N. O., *Elder.*
P. Q., *Elder.*

4. *Form of Attestation to Paper of Concurrence.*

That the above names, to the number of persons, regular worshippers in the Church of Scotland congregation of , were subscribed, &c. (*Ut supra.*)

P. *Form of Intimation for Meeting of Congregation in case of a Translating Call.*

Whereas the congregation of has addressed a Call to the Rev. , minister of this congregation, to be its minister, and said Call has been sustained by the Presbytery of as a Call regularly proceeded in :

Notice is hereby given that a meeting of the congregation will be held in this place on the day of , at o'clock, for the purpose of considering the circumstances in which the congregation is placed by the Call given to the minister, and of taking such steps thereanent as may be resolved upon.

Notice is hereby further given that the Presbytery will meet at on the day of , at o'clock, to deal with this Call, and that, if no Commissioners appear to represent this congregation, the congregation will be held to acquiesce in the translation of the minister.

J. G., *Presbytery Clerk.*

2. Exhortation to be Read to Vacant Congregations (1932, ix.)

(*Approved by General Assembly.*)

Dear Brethren,—As a congregation of the Church of Scotland you are entrusted with the responsibility of choosing a Pastor to be over you in the Lord. It is a duty that each one owes to his congregation and his Church, to take his proper part in this matter. Having the best interests of all our congregations at heart, we desire to address to you a few words in connection with this important matter, that may assist in giving your thoughts a right direction in regard to it, and may contribute, under the Divine blessing, to a happy and harmonious settlement.

The first step which you will have to take is to elect a Committee. The office with which the Committee are entrusted is that of selecting one or more persons, whose names are to be submitted to you, with a view to the appointment of a minister. If they can select *one* whom they regard as specially fitted for appointment to the vacant charge, they should arrange that he alone be nominated and heard. If this be not possible, the Committee should, at all events, reduce their selection of persons for hearing to a very small number. The duty, therefore, devolving on the Committee is an extremely important one ; and in choosing those who are to form the Committee, you should act with much deliberation and care. The members of the congregation who are selected for this duty should be such as command your full confidence ; and it is on this account necessary that you should all, as far as possible, take part in the election, and should not leave it to a section only of the congregation. If you show a sincere and general interest in this matter, and appoint a satisfactory Committee—a Committee adequately representing the congregation—it will tend in a pre-eminent degree to the successful issue of the means which fall to be taken for the appointment of a minister. To this very important part of your duty, therefore, it is requisite that you should give your careful attention. The Committee so chosen should receive your co-operation so far as it can be given; and you should offer your earnest prayers for them, that they may be directed to such conclusions as shall result in the highest good of this Church and congregation, and the advancement of the cause of our Lord Jesus Christ.

With these conditions in view, we ask you:—

1. To make the election of a minister a matter of earnest and repeated prayer, not only that you may be guided to the choice of a man who shall come among you as a true messenger of Christ to your souls, but that the election may be conducted in a spirit of brotherly kindness and forbearance, as befits professing followers of Christ.

2. To strive after that love that seeketh not its own—an unselfish spirit, willing that the preferences and judgments, and even the prejudices of others, should have the fullest and kindliest consideration, and resolved that, whatever happens, you will not press your own opinion to the extent of breaking up the outward, or even the inward, unity of the congregation to which you belong.

If all are thoroughly in earnest in these matters, we confidently hope that, by the blessing of God, such a relation will be formed between Pastor and people as shall make them real helpers the one of the other, and shall kindle such a spirit of unity and love in all our congregations, that men shall know that we are true disciples of the Lord Jesus.

3. Edict for the Ordination of a Probationer or Induction of a Minister (1932, ix.).

(To be read to the congregation of   on Sunday the   day of   , and on Sunday the   day of   , and attested on each of these days by the officiating preacher as having been read by him.)

Whereas the Presbytery of   has received a Call from this congregation, addressed to   , preacher [*or* minister] of the Gospel, to be their minister, and the said Call has been sustained as a regular Call, and been accepted by him [and his translation has been agreed to by the Presbytery of   ]:[1]

And whereas the said Presbytery having judged the said   qualified for [the ministry of the Gospel, and][2] this pastoral charge has resolved to proceed to his ordination [*or*, induction] on   the   day of   , unless something occur which may reasonably impede it, Notice is hereby given to all concerned, that if they, or any of them, have anything to object to the life or doctrine of the said   , they may repair to the Presbytery, which is to meet at   on the said   the   day of   , at   o'clock:

With certification that, if no relevant objection be then made, and

[1] To be omitted in the case of an ordination.
[2] To be omitted in the case of an induction.

immediately substantiated, the Presbytery will proceed without further delay.

By order of Presbytery,

J. G., *Presbytery Clerk.*

4. Intimation required when an Appointment has been made by a Presbytery (1932, ix.).

Tanquam jure devoluto.

Intimation is hereby given that the Presbytery of , having appointed to be minister of this Church, the said will conduct public worship on Sunday the day of . [*Add*, if required, both in English and Gaelic.]

Intimation is hereby further given that the Call will lie in the day of between the hours and , and on the day of between the hours of and , when members may sign in person or by means of Mandates. Forms of Mandates may be obtained from the Session-Clerk.

Notice is hereby further given that the Presbytery will meet to deal with the Appointment and Call in on the day of at o'clock, and the congregation are hereby cited to attend in their interests.

J. G., *Presbytery Clerk.*

(The above intimation to be duly attested as having been made to the congregation by the officiating minister.)

VII.—Forms in connection with Admission of Elders and Deacons.

1. Intimation of Election of Elders (1932, x.).

(a) *At a Congregational Meeting.*

Notice is hereby given that the Kirk Session has determined that an addition be made to the number of Elders in this congregation, that the number to be added shall be , and that the method of election shall be by means of nomination at a meeting of the congregation.

Notice is hereby further given that a meeting of this congregation will be held in the Church on the day of at o'clock, for the purpose of nominating persons for the office of the Eldership ; with certification that if the number nominated does not exceed , those nominated will be declared to be elected subject to the judgment of the Kirk Session, and if the number nominated exceeds , a vote of the congregation on those nominated will be taken by standing up or by voting papers as the meeting may determine.

By order of the Kirk Session,

P. Q., *Session-Clerk.*

(b) *By Signed Lists.*

Notice is hereby given that the Kirk Session has determined that an addition be made to the number of Elders in this congregation, that the number to be added shall be , and that the method of election shall be by means of signed lists. Members are therefore requested to hand in lists, which shall be signed by the members giving them in. Such lists should contain the names of members deemed suitable for the office of the Eldership not exceeding in all. Lists may be sent to the Session-Clerk or placed in the box provided for that purpose at the Church door, not later than the day of

By order of the Kirk Session,

P. Q., *Session-Clerk.*

2. Edict for Ordination and Admission of Elders (1932, x.).

Whereas A, B, C, and D, members of this congregation, have lately been elected to be Ruling Elders in the same [and the Kirk Session, having judged them to be duly qualified for the office, has sustained their election [1]]; and the aforesaid A, B, C, and D have intimated their acceptance of the office of the Eldership: Notice is hereby given to all concerned, that if they, or any of them, have objections to state why the said A, B, C, and D, or any of them, should not be ordained (or, *where one of those elected has been already ordained,* why A, B, and C, or any of them, should not be ordained, or D, not admitted) to the Office of Ruling Elder, they repair to the Kirk Session, appointed to meet in the Session-House on the day of at o'clock, to state the same; with certification that if no relevant objection affecting life or doctrine be then made and substantiated, the Kirk Session will proceed to the ordination (or ordination and admission) without delay.

By order of the Kirk Session,

P. Q., *Session-Clerk.*

3. Attestation of Edict being Served (1932, x.).

Church, the day of , 19 .

The above Edict was this day duly served by me, in the face of the congregation.

A. C., *Minister* (or *Preacher*).

4. Forms in connection with Method of Electing Deacons (1932, x.).

(*A*) Life-Appointment. The same forms shall be used, *mutatis mutandis,* as for election of Elders.

(*B*) Appointment for a term of years.

(*a*) Notice is hereby given that a meeting of this congregation will be held in the church on the day of at o'clock for the purpose of considering whether the office of Deacon in this congregation be held as heretofore or by persons, male or female, members of the congregation in full communion over eighteen years

[1] Omit words in brackets when election has been by Resolution of the Kirk Session.

of age, who without ordination will be set apart to office for three years.

(*b*) Notice is hereby given that the Kirk Session has resolved to take a vote of the congregation by means of voting papers on the question as to whether the office of Deacon in this congregation be held as heretofore or by persons, male or female, members of the congregation in full communion over eighteen years of age, who without ordination will be set apart to office for three years. The voting papers will be issued on , and should be returned to the Session-Clerk, or placed in the box provided for the purpose at the Church door, not later than .

By order of the Kirk Session,
P. Q., *Session-Clerk.*

NOTE.—When Deacons are elected after the latter manner, the election may take place either at the Annual Business Meeting or by means of voting papers in accordance with a plan which the congregation shall appoint.

VIII. FORMS IN CONNECTION WITH TRANSLATION OF MINISTER FROM FIRST CHARGE.

SCHEDULES UNDER 1959, XXIV.

FIRST SCHEDULE.

WE, the undersigned, declare that in our opinion there are exceptional circumstances which would justify the translation of .... from his present charge of .... before the expiry of five years from the date of his induction thereto.

................*Moderator of Presbytery.*
................*Clerk of Presbytery.*
................*Member of Presbytery.*
................*Member of Presbytery.*

SECOND SCHEDULE.

At............the............day of............
the Presbytery of............being met and constituted :

Inter alia :

The Presbytery agreed that there were exceptional circumstances which would justify the translation of Mr............from his charge of............before the expiry of five years from the date of his induction thereto. The Presbytery reserved their right to deal with the question of translation if and when it arose.

Extracted from the Records of the Presbytery of............by me,
............*Clerk.*

IX.—BALLOT PAPER.

THE CHURCH OF SCOTLAND.

COMMITTEE ON UNIONS AND READJUSTMENTS.

LOCAL UNION OF CONGREGATIONS.

1. In favour of Union............................
2. Against Union............................

Mark a X opposite the motion preferred.

APPENDIX XXXVI.

NOTE FOR AUDITORS OF CONGREGATIONAL ACCOUNTS, CONGREGATIONAL AGENCIES' ACCOUNTS, AND OTHER CHURCH FUNDS.

It has been suggested that it might be helpful to Auditors who have not had previous practical experience in auditing to have Notes for guidance in the conduct of audits of Congregational Accounts, Congregational Agencies' Accounts, and other Church Funds. Accordingly, the following general lines of procedure are recommended. It will, of course, be recognised that circumstances vary greatly and that the procedure may require adjustment to suit the particular circumstances of any case.

1. *Income.*—All items of income should be instructed by independent evidence as far as possible. For example, weekly offerings should be vouched by the production of Bank Pay-in Slip book, wherein the counterfoil for each 'Pay-in' to Bank should be signed by two officiating office-bearers. The Auditors should also verify that all Investment Income has been received.

2. *Payments.*—For every payment made a voucher should be produced.

3. *General.*—The Bank Passbook should be carefully examined to ensure that Church Collections and other moneys are duly paid into Bank. The total amount of the Collection should be lodged in Bank and all payments should be made by cheque. The Bank balance, as shown by the Treasurer's Books at the end of the accounting period, should be vouched by production of a Certificate of Bank Balance by the Bank and should be reconciled therewith.

4. *Investments.*—Any Investments held for behoof of the congregation or its agencies should be verified by production of Certificates or, in the case of Inscribed Stocks, by verification from the Bank in whose books the Stocks are inscribed.

5. *Auditors' Docquet.*—It is suggested that the Auditors' Docquet should be in the following terms, although it is recognised that it may require amendment to suit particular circumstances :—

> "We have examined the foregoing Accounts for the period from..............................to..............................and we have to report that we have obtained all the information and explanations we have required. The Accounts have been properly vouched and instructed and we have verified the Cash Balances and also the Balances on Bank Accounts as shown by the Treasurer's Books at the close of the period. We have seen Certificates or other evidence of the Investments held for behoof of the Congregation as at the close of the period and we are satisfied that they are in order. In our opinion the Accounts exhibit a true state of affairs as shown by the Treasurer's Books."

APPENDIX XXXVII.

LOOSE-LEAF RECORDS (1964, Reg. 4).

(1) *Communion Rolls.*

That the type of Communion Roll in common use, that is, the permanently bound volume containing details of a member's joining and disjoining together with the record of attendances at Holy Communion, should continue to be available for such Kirk Sessions as wish to use it.

That there be no interference with the various types of loose-leaf Communion Rolls introduced by Kirk Sessions, in accordance with the opinion of the late Sir Randall Phillip; and that Kirk Sessions might continue to use a loose-leaf system of Communion Roll, suitable for their own purposes, if so desired.

The Committee on Publications be authorised to make available for sale to Kirk Sessions the following :—

(*a*) A bound volume to contain the names of Communicants, together with a record of admission to full membership and disjoining ;

(*b*) A loose-leaf volume as in (*a*) the pages of which shall be consecutively numbered, and ultimately bound into permanent book form ;

(*c*) A type of loose-leaf Roll to be used along with (*a*) and (*b*) whereon to record the attendances of members at Holy Communion, with space for recording any other information deemed useful by the Kirk Session ;

(*d*) A loose-leaf Roll combining (*b*) and (*c*).

(2) *Church Records.*

Baptismal and Proclamation Registers.—That no suggestions be made regarding any form of loose-leaf volumes for these Registers.

Minute Books and Finance Books—

(i) That each sheet as it comes into use shall be numbered consecutively from the page it succeeds ;

(ii) That each page as it comes into use shall begin with the last word on the page that it succeeds ;

(iii) That when minutes are approved, each page recording such minutes should be intialled by the Moderator who shall also, with the Clerk, sign at the end of the minutes ;

(iv) That when sufficient pages have been completed to comprise a conveniently sized volume the Court concerned shall have such pages bound into permanent form.

GLOSSARY.

Acquiesce, to give legal assent to a judgment—thereby disqualifying to object.

Act of Sederunt, a resolution of the Court of Session of the nature of a standing order for the regulation of its proceedings.

Acts of Assembly: down to about the middle of the eighteenth century Acts here meant actings—legislative enactments being distinguished as "general acts"; it is now used only of enactments.

Adherents. See p. 19.

Ad vitam aut culpam, for life or until fault. Used of tenure of office.

Alibi, elsewhere.

Ann. in relation to stipend, see p. 294.

Apud acta, in the proceedings, in presence of the court.

Attestation, evidencing or authenticating, by signature of officials or witnesses, with or without relative explanatory words, as the case may be.

Beadle, a parish or church officer. This term is not by itself decisive as to employers or duties.

Bene or *male appellatum*, regularly or irregularly appealed.

Benefice, the provision for the minister of a parish, the living.

Bona fide, in good faith, honestly.

Casus improvisus, something unforeseen and unprovided for.

Causa cognita, a case known, heard, and ripe for judgment.

Certification. See "With," &c., below.

Ceteris paribus, other things being equal.

Charities, in the Parliamentary sense, includes also Church and educational objects.—(Inland Revenue *v.* Pemsel, 1891, A.C. 531.)

Competent, allowed by law.

Contumacy, the ecclesiastical offence of contempt of court, stubbornness.

Coram, in presence.

Corpus delicti, the substance or body of the offence with the specified circumstances of its commission.

Crimen continuum, an offence of several acts, connected and extending over longer or shorter time.

Debitum fructuum, a debt due by (forming a burden on) the produce.

Debitum fundi, a debt due by (forming a burden on) the soil.

Decennalis et triennalis possessor non tenetur docere de titulo, a possessor for thirteen years is not bound to instruct his title. "A clergyman who for thirteen years holds possession of a subject as part of his benefice is presumed to be the rightful possessor without producing any written title to the subject. The thirteen years' possession gives him no actual title, but only raises a presumption in his favour that the possession is legal, and throws the onus of showing that the possession is unwarranted on the challenger."—Lord Trayner.

Decern, to decree, to pass judgment.
De die in diem, from day to day.
De facto, as a matter of fact.
De fideli (*administratione officii*), of the faithful discharge of duty.
De jure, of right.
De novo, anew.
Deposition, (1) statement of a witness on oath; (2) judicial removal from office.
De præsenti, concerning the present. Used of that which is spoken or done to take effect at and from the time of its being so.
Designation: a person's designation includes his address as well as his calling.
Dictum, a saying; *dicta*, sayings.
Edict, a legally authoritative public intimation.
Effeirs, pertains, belongs.
Ewest, an old word meaning near.
Excambion, exchange of equal value of pieces of the same thing.
Ex debito, from duty, from obligation.
Execution of a citation, the certificate that it has been served.
Ex facie, on the face of it.
Ex gratia, from favour—not from right.
Ex officio, from his office—in virtue of the office held.
Ex parte, from and in favour of one party.
Expectant, the old term for a probationer.
Ex proprio motu, of one's own accord.
Extract, a part taken from the minutes of a court by the authorised official (the legal extractor).
Fama, a scandalous report.
Fama clamosa, a clamorous, scandalous report.
Fiars, the average price of the different kinds of grain of one year's crop judicially determined. The origin of the word is unknown.
First instance: the court of first instance is the court before which a matter must first be brought.
Foreshore, the shore between high- and low-water mark.
Formula, a set form of words necessary or prescribed for a certain purpose.
Function, service or duty in the exercise of official capacity and right.
Funditus, from the foundation, utterly.
Habile, competent.
Heresy, opinion at variance with the doctrine of the Church's standards.
Husband-land, 26 acres.
In causa, in the case.
Induciæ, a prescribed interval of time.
Infra, below.
In hoc statu, in the present state of the case.
In hunc effectum, for this purpose only.
In initialibus, in preliminaries. Used of matters affecting the admissibility and credibility of a witness, on which he may be examined before examination in the case (*in causa*).
In mundo, cleanly written out.
In retentis, among things preserved. Used of papers not recorded but kept.
Instanter, immediately.

Instruct: to instruct a fact is to prove it; a fact instructed is a fact proved.

Inter alia, among other things.

Interim, in the meantime.

Interim Act, an Act in force only till next Assembly.

Inter se, among themselves.

In toto, wholly.

Intrant, an old term for a person obtaining, or about to obtain, ordination to the ministry or admission to a parish.

In verbis de præsenti, by sentence operative from that moment thenceforth.

Inter vivos, between living persons. An ordinary deed taking effect during the life of parties is called a deed *inter vivos*, as distinguished from a deed *mortis causa*, which takes effect only on the granter's death.

Ipsis factis et rebus, by the very facts and circumstances.

Ipsissimis verbis, in the very self-same words.

Ipso facto, by the very fact or deed.

Ish and entry, outlet and entry.

Jurisdiction, the authority which a court has to entertain and decide a case. It flows from the supreme power, from which also comes the right, or the freedom, to exercise it; the voluntary consent of persons to accept certain others for their judges does not give jurisdiction to those others.

Jus devolutum, a right devolved on a party because of its not having been exercised within the appointed time by those having priority.

Kirk lands, lands belonging to the clergy before the Reformation.

Lavoir (Mair, p. 490), a flagon or ewer used to bring water for baptism.

Libel, the formal indictment by which a minister or probationer is charged with misconduct or heresy.

Locality, in relation to stipends, see Mair, p. 463.

Locus standi, right to appear before a court.

Members of the Church: this term is not expressly defined, but in the practice of the Church it is used as equivalent to communicants. Strictly speaking, all baptised persons are members of the Church.

Medium filum fluminis, the middle line of the river.

Minister, ministry: these terms are strictly limited to those ordained to discharge all the duties of the ministry.

Ministerially: a court acts ministerially, or administratively, when it merely follows a prescribed course with no duty of judging. Ministerial and judicial functions often accompany and run into each other.

Ministerium vagum, a ministry at large, without a definite sphere of labour.

Mora, delay.

Mortis causa, see *inter vivos*.

Mutatis mutandis, the things being changed that require to be so to suit a new case.

Nec tamen consumebatur, and yet was not consumed (Exod. iii. 2).

Nemine contradicente, no one opposing.

Nobile officium, see p. .

Notour, notorious.

Obiter dictum, an observation in passing—what a judge has taken opportunity to say on some side point when giving judgment.

Onus probandi, the burden of proving.

Ordination, "the solemn setting apart of a person to some public Church office" (Ch. Gov.).

Ox-gate, or ox-gang, 13 acres.

Pari passu, with equal pace.

Parishioner, variously used: in relation to purely ecclesiastical rights, usually any person resident or who has a residence in the parish; in old statute law, one who being on the cess roll was liable to ecclesiastical assessments.

Pars judicis, the function of a judge.

Per se, by itself, by himself.

Pertinents, appendages, or privileges legally accompanying the main property.

Planting a church, the old expression for filling up a vacancy (*e.g.*, F.P., vii. 14). See Mair, p. 429.

Plat (*e.g.*, Commission of Plat), plan.

Plough-gate, 104 acres.

Precognition, statement of what he has to say obtained from a person before citing him as a witness.

Precognosce, to ascertain what one has to say before citing him as a witness.

Prescribe (in law in relation to a claim), to reach the time when it is beyond recovery.

Prima facie, at first sight.

Privilege, protection from penalty for defamatory statements made without malice in discharge of duty. For example, statements in one's duty to a court, or in taking part in its business, or in business ordered by it, are privileged.

Probationer, one who has been licensed to preach is a probationer till called and ordained to a charge—a licentiate, or preacher.

Pro bono ecclesiæ, for the good of the Church.

Promitten de rata, understood to be a common form contraction for the concluding sentence of a commission, guaranteeing that the proceedings of the commissioner shall be ratified, beginning, *Promittentes*, or *Promittens*, &c.

Pro non scripto, as not written.

Pro rata, proportionately.

Pro re nata, for unforeseen business that has arisen.

Pro tanto, for so much, to this extent, so far as it goes.

Pro tempore, for the time.

Protest, the word used to express objection in a legal sense to the decision of a Church court. It protects from being considered a consenting party.

Provisional Order: an Order issued under statutory powers by a Government Department or public authority and having (generally after confirmation by Parliament) the authority of an Act of Parliament. It usually relates to matters which are not of sufficient magnitude to be dealt with by a Private Bill, and the procedure is simpler and cheaper. Applications for a Provisional Order must be lodged with the Secretary of State for Scotland along with a Draft of Proposed Order.

P. t., *pro tempore*.

Qua, in the character of, as such.
Quam primum, as soon as possible, the sooner the better.
Quasi, as if, as it were.
Quoad civilia, in so far as regards civil matters.
Quoad omnia, as regards all matters—civil and sacred.
Quoad sacra, in so far as regards sacred matters.
Quoad ultra, as regards all else than that which has been specified; for the rest.
Quorum, the fixed lowest number that can constitute a valid meeting.
Q. v., *Quod vide*, which see.
Reduction, in civil law the annulling of a sentence or deed.
Register, formerly used in the sense of records.
Res gestæ, the business transacted, the things that have been done.
Res judicata, a matter settled by final judgment.
Res noviter (in full, *res noviter veniens ad notitiam*), matter coming newly to knowledge—that is, unknown at an earlier stage.
Respondent, the party replying in a case.
Rite et solemniter acta, done in due and customary form.
Satisfy production, to produce what is called for by the court.
Sederunt, "they sat," those of whom the meeting consisted. It is the first word of a Latin sentence, *There sat* So-and-so.
Seriatim, one by one in succession.
Serving an edict, proclaiming it in the appointed manner, time, and place.
Simpliciter, simply, neither more nor less.
Sine die, without a time appointed, indefinitely.
Sine mora, without delay.
Singular successor, one who succeeds to property by purchase or otherwise than by descent.
Sist execution of sentence: in any case of trial this is the effect on the sentence pronounced or resolved on (for or against the tried) of an appeal to a higher court—the operation of the sentence is suspended.
Sist parties at the bar, to place and acknowledge each in his proper part there.
Sist procedure, to stop in the meantime.
Slander, a defamatory statement made in malice. It has no privilege.
Socius criminis, one having a share in the commission of a crime.
Soum (sown), grass for a cow, or five (in some places ten) sheep.
Spiritualia, the "spirituality" of a benefice, being the stipend as distinguished from the *temporalia*.
Status (*e.g.*, of a minister) is professional position with its powers and privileges.
Sua sponte, of his own accord, spontaneously.
Sub judice, under the judge, in course of being tried.
Supra, above.
Take instruments, see p. 107.
Tanquam jure devoluto, as by devolved right. See *jus devolutum* above.
Temporalia, the "temporality" of the benefice, being the rest of the benefice as distinguished from stipend.
Teneo, Latin verb to hold, keep, maintain.
το πρεπον, that which is becoming.
Toties quoties, as often as.
Trilapse, a lapse after two restorations in K.S. Discipline Cases.
Ultra vires, beyond the legitimate power of a court.

Ut antea ; ut infra ; ut supra—as before ; as below ; as above.
V., or *vs.*, or *versus*, against.
Visitation by Presbyteries, a visit to a parish by the Presbytery in the exercise of its right of supervision, for judicial or administrative purposes, or even only for the expression of sympathy.
Visitation of Records, examination, inspection, by superior court.
Viva voce, by living voice, " by word of mouth."
" With certification as effeirs " : a phrase forming, when occasion requires, the concluding words of a citation or order, and meaning that the party addressed will have to take the consequences if he does not appear or obey. Instead of " as effeirs " the consequences may be specified.

GENERAL INDEX.